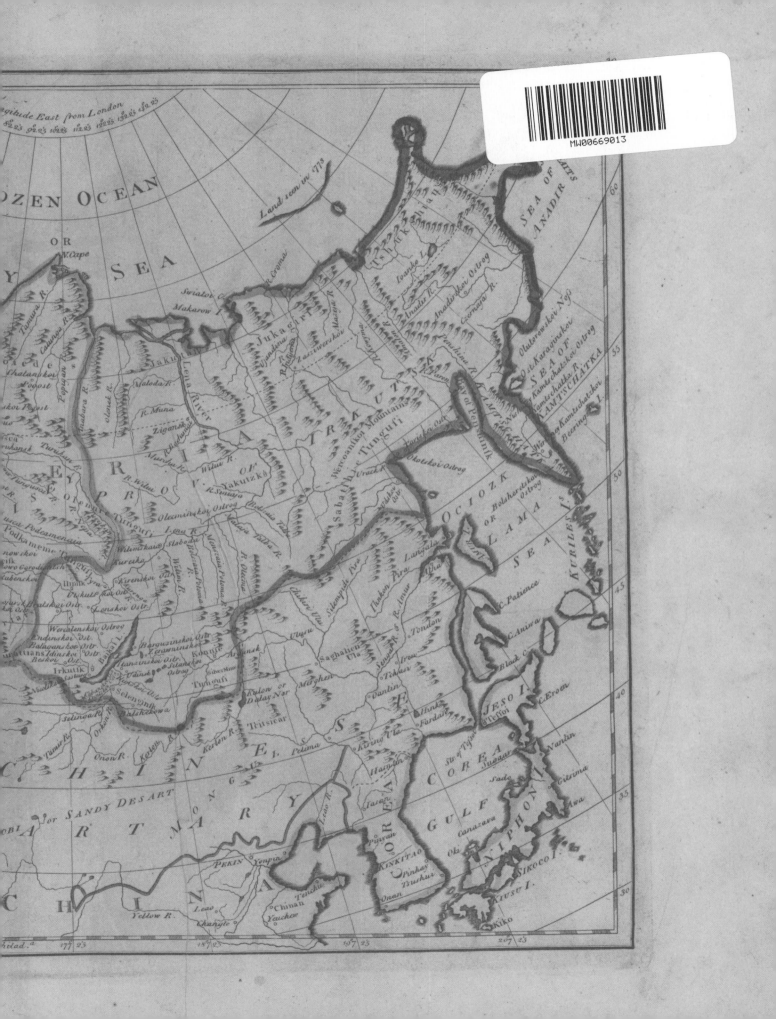

MW00669013

OZEN OCEAN

Longitude East from London

Land seen in 1770

SEA OF STRAITS
ANADIR

OR

N.Cape

SEA

Swiatoi C.

Makarow I.

Tamara R.
Casunga R.

Jukagiri

SEA OF
Kamtschatka
Kamtschatskoi Ostrog
KAMTSCHATKA
Beering's I.

Chatankoi
Pogost

Maloda R.

R.Muna

Zigansk

Jakutskoi

Lena River

Werchnoi Tungusi

Were. sch. Tungusi

IRKUTSK

Weroantkoi Mountains

OF
Yakutzka

Olecminskoi Ostrog

IRERIA

Lenskoi Ostr.

OCIOZK
OR

Okotskoi Ostrog

Bolsheretskoi
Ostrog

LAMA

Werchnoi Tungusi

Kurile

SEA

C.Patience

Kirenskoi Ostr.

Verchnoi Ostr.
Endunskoi Ost.
Balaganskoi Ostr.
Belskoi Ost.
Irkutsk

Baikal L.

Selenginsk

Selinga R.

CHINEY

C.Aniwa

Black C.

JESO I.

C.Eroa

Saghalien
Ula

Tlkasi

Langula

COREA

SANDY DESART

MONGOLY

COREA
GULF

Sado

NIPHON

Awa

PEKIN
Yenpin

Teichu

Chinan

SIKOCO I.

CHI

Yellow R.

Leao
Changte

KIUSU I.

Kiko

ENCYCLOPEDIA OF

# RUSSIAN HISTORY

# EDITORIAL BOARD

**EDITOR IN CHIEF**

James R. Millar
*George Washington University*

**SENIOR ASSOCIATE EDITOR**

Ann E. Robertson
*George Washington University*

**ASSOCIATE EDITORS**

Daniel H. Kaiser
*Grinnell College*

Louise McReynolds
*University of Hawaii*

Donald J. Raleigh
*University of North Carolina*

Nicholas V. Riasanovsky
*University of California, Berkeley*

Ronald Grigor Suny
*University of Chicago*

**ADVISORY BOARD**

Marianna Tax Choldin
*University of Illinois, Urbana–Champaign*

Gregory L. Freeze
*Brandeis University*

Paul R. Gregory
*University of Houston*

Lindsey Hughes
*University College London*

Paul R. Josephson
*Colby College*

Janet L. B. Martin
*University of Miami*

Bruce W. Menning
*U.S. Army Command and Staff College*

Boris N. Mironov
*Russian Academy of Science*

Reginald E. Zelnik
*University of California, Berkeley*

# ENCYCLOPEDIA OF
# RUSSIAN HISTORY

## VOLUME 3: M-R

JAMES R. MILLAR, EDITOR IN CHIEF

Ref
DK
14
.E53
2004
V.4

# Encyclopedia of Russian History
James R. Millar

© 2004 by Macmillan Reference USA.
Macmillan Reference USA is an imprint of
The Gale Group, Inc., a division of
Thomson Learning, Inc.

Macmillan Reference USA™ and
Thomson Learning™ are trademarks used
herein under license.

*For more information, contact*
Macmillan Reference USA
300 Park Avenue South, 9th Floor
New York, NY 10010
Or you can visit our Internet site at
http://www.gale.com

**ALL RIGHTS RESERVED**
No part of this work covered by the copyright
hereon may be reproduced or used in any
form or by any means—graphic, electronic, or
mechanical, including photocopying, recording, taping, Web distribution, or information
storage retrieval systems—without the written
permission of the publisher.

For permission to use material from this
product, submit your request via Web at
http://www.gale-edit.com/permissions, or you
may download our Permissions Request form
and submit your request by fax or mail to:

*Permissions Department*
The Gale Group, Inc.
27500 Drake Rd.
Farmington Hills, MI 48331-3535
Permissions Hotline:
248-699-8006 or 800-877-4253 ext. 8006
Fax: 248-699-8074 or 800-762-4058

While every effort has been made to ensure
the reliability of the information presented in
this publication, The Gale Group, Inc. does
not guarantee the accuracy of the data contained herein. The Gale Group, Inc. accepts to
payment for listing; and inclusion in the publication of any organization, agency, institution, publication, service, or individual does
not imply endorsement of the editors or publisher. Errors brought to the attention of the
publisher and verified to the satisfaction of
the publisher will be corrected in future editions.

**LIBRARY OF CONGRESS CATALOGING-IN-PUBLICATION DATA**

Encyclopedia of Russian history / James R. Millar, editor in chief.
    p. cm.
    Includes bibliographical references and index.
    ISBN 0-02-865693-8 (set hardcover) — ISBN 0-02-865694-6 (v. 1) —
ISBN 0-02-865695-4 (v. 2) — ISBN 0-02-865696-2 (v. 3) — ISBN
0-02-865697-0 (v. 4)
    1. Russia—History—Encyclopedias. 2. Soviet
Union—History—Encyclopedias. 3. Russia
(Federation)—History—Encyclopedias. I. Millar, James R., 1936-

DK14.E53 2003
947'.003—dc21                                                    2003014389

This title is also available as an e-book.
ISBN 0-02-865907-4 (set)
Contact your Gale sales representative for ordering information.

Printed in the United States of America
10 9 8 7 6 5 4 3 2 1

JAN 1 9 2005

**MACARIUS** *See* MAKARY, METROPOLITAN.

## MACHINE TRACTOR STATIONS

The Machine Tractor Stations (MTS) were budget-financed state organizations established in rural areas of the Soviet Union beginning in 1930. Intended mainly as a mechanism to provide machinery and equipment (including repairs and maintenance) to the kolkhozes (collective farms), they also exerted state control over agriculture. Payment for the services of the Machine Tractor Stations was made in kind (product) by the farms. The emergence of the MTS was closely tied to the introduction of the collective farms and especially the continuing debate over organizational arrangements in the countryside, notably the appropriate scale or size of the collective farms. The original model of the Machine Tractor Stations was based upon experimental arrangements of the Shevchenko sovkhoz (state farm) in Ukraine. The Machine Tractor Stations were introduced rapidly. By the end of 1930 there were approximately 150 Machine Tractor Stations controlling approximately 7,000 tractors. By 1933 there were 2,900 stations controlling approximately 123,000 tractors, roughly 50 percent of all tractors in agriculture, the remaining tractors belonging to state farms. Overall, the growth of the tractor park was rapid, from some 27,000 units in 1928 to 531,000 units in 1940.

The Machine Tractor Stations became the dominant mechanism for providing equipment to the kolkhozes. While the stations themselves provided state support to kolkhozes, especially to those producing grain, the political departments of the MTS (the *politotdely*), established in 1933, became an important means for exercising political control over the collective farms. This control extended well beyond the allocation and use of machinery and equipment, and specifically involved the development of production plans after the introduction of compulsory deliveries in 1933. The MTS was, therefore, an integral part of kolkhoz operations, and conflict often arose between the two organizations.

The Machine Tractor Stations were abolished in 1958 during the Khrushchev era. However, their abolition and short-term replacement with the Repair Tractor Stations (RTS) was in fact a part of a much more significant process of continuing agricultural reorganization in the 1950s and thereafter.

**The first tractors coming off the assembly line at the tractor works in Stalingrad.** © HULTON ARCHIVE

In addition to changes within farms during the 1950s, there was continuing emphasis on consolidating farms, converting kolkhozes to sovkhozes, and changing the organizational arrangements above the level of the individual farms. In effect, state control came to be exercised through different organizations, for example, the Territorial Production Associations (TPAs). While the machinery and equipment were dispersed to individual farms, in effect the organizational changes in the agricultural sector during the post-Stalin era consisted largely of agro-industrial integration. The changes introduced during the 1950s were mainly reforms of Nikita Khrushchev, and they became a major factor in Khrushchev's downfall in 1964.

*See also:* COLLECTIVE FARM; COLLECTIVIZATION OF AGRICULTURE

**BIBLIOGRAPHY**

Miller, Robert F. (1970). *One Hundred Thousand Tractors: The MTS and the Development of Controls in Soviet Agriculture.* Cambridge, MA: Harvard University Press.

ROBERT C. STUART

## MAFIA CAPITALISM

Mafia capitalism is a term that emerged to describe Russia's economic system in the 1990s. While the implied parallel goes to the classic protection rackets of the Sicilian mafia, the actual Russian practice was different. In order to reflect this, both scholars and journalists have taken to describing the Russian system of organized crime as "mafiya."

There are obvious similarities between mafia and mafiya, in the form of organized gangs imposing tribute on businesses. This is the world of extortion, hitmen, and violent reprisals against those who fail to pay up. In the case of mafiya, however, it mainly affects the small business sector. Major actors will normally have affiliations with private security providers that operate a "cleaner" business of charging fees for protection against arson and violent assault.

To foreign businesses in particular, the latter offers plausible deniability in claiming that no money is being paid to Russian organized crime.

Money paid to private security providers, or to officials "helping out" with customs or other traditionally "difficult" parts of public administration, may also frequently be offset against lower payments of taxes, customs, and other fees.

The real outcome is one where the Russian state and thus the Russian population at large suffer great damage. Not only is the government's traditional monopoly on violence both privatized and decentralized into hands that are under no effective control by the authorities, but money destined to have been paid to the Russian government ends up instead in the coffers of security firms.

Moreover, businesses in Russia are subjected to demands for tribute not only from organized crime gangs, but also from a broad variety of representatives of the official bureaucracy. This far exceeds the corruption associated with mafia in many other parts of the world, and explains in part why, in the compilation of international indices on corruption, Russia tends to rank amongst the worst cases.

Russian entrepreneurs will typically be subjected to several visits per month, maybe even per week, by representatives of public bodies such as the fire department or the health inspectorate, all of which will expect to receive a little on the side.

The burden on the small business sector in particular should be measured not only in financial terms, as the tribute paid may be offset by tax avoidance. Far more serious is the implied tax on the time of entrepreneurs, which often tends to be the most precious asset of a small business. The number of hours that are spent negotiating with those demanding bribes will have to be taken from productive efforts.

The overall consequences of mafiya for the Russian economy are manifested in the stifling of private initiative and degradation of the moral basis of conducting business.

*See also:* CRONY CAPITALISM; ORGANIZED CRIME

**BIBLIOGRAPHY**

Center for Strategic and International Studies. (1997). *Russian Organized Crime.* Washington, DC: Center for Strategic and International Studies.

Handelman, Stephen. (1995). *Comrade Criminal.* New Haven, CT: Yale University Press.

STEFAN HEDLUND

## MAIN POLITICAL DIRECTORATE

Officials from the Communist Party of the Soviet Union (CPSU) monitored workers in key occupations to ensure their adherence to party doctrine and loyalty to the CPSU and the Soviet Union.

In the Soviet army and navy, the CPSU maintained a shadow system of command parallel with the military chain of command. In the early days of the USSR, Party commanders (*politruks*) ensured the political reliability of regular officers and soldiers. As the Party became more secure in the political allegiance of the military, party commanders became "deputies for political work" (*zampolit*). These officers were directly subordinated to the unit commander, but they had access to higher party officials through a separate chain of command. By and large, the *zampolit* dealt with matters such as morale, discipline, living conditions, training, and political indoctrination. Security issues such as political reliability were the primary concern of the Special Section. The Main Political Directorate also scrutinized the content of military publications, including the official newspaper *Krasnaya zvezda* and military publishing houses.

In the post-Soviet era, military discipline is handled by the Main Directorate for Indoctrination Work. Without the power of the Party behind this institution, problems such as discipline, desertion, crime, and others have become increasingly more serious.

*See also:* COMMUNIST PARTY OF THE SOVIET UNION; MILITARY, SOVIET AND POST-SOVIET

**BIBLIOGRAPHY**

Herspring, Dale R. (1990). *The Soviet High Command, 1967–1989: Personalities and Politics.* Princeton, NJ: Princeton University Press.

Whiting, Kenneth R. (1978). *The Development of the Soviet Armed Forces, 1917–1977.* Maxwell Air Force Base, AL: Air University Press.

ANN E. ROBERTSON

## MAKAROV, STEPAN OSIPOVICH

(1849–1904), naval commander during Russo-Japanese War; prolific writer on naval affairs.

Vice Admiral Stepan Osipovich Makarov, commander of the Pacific Squadron of the Russian navy during the Russo-Japanese War and the author of more than fifty works on naval tactics, technology, and oceanography, was born in Nikolaevsk on the Bug River and graduated from naval school at Nikolaevsk on the Amur in 1865. While still in school he was deployed with the Pacific Squadron in 1863, and after graduation he joined the Baltic Fleet. Serving on the staff of Vice Admiral A.A. Popov from 1871 to 1876, Makarov was involved in naval engineering projects, including studies of problems related to damage control.

During the Russo-Turkish War of 1877–1878, Makarov commanded the *Grand Duke Konstantin* and successfully conducted mine/torpedo warfare against Turkish units in the Black Sea, using steam launches armed with towed mines and self-propelled torpedoes. In 1878 he took part in the unsuccessful effort to construct a mine-artillery position to prevent the British Royal Navy from entering the Turkish Straits and began the development of techniques for underway minelaying. He conducted a major study of the currents in the Turkish Straits during the late 1870s, commanded the riverine flotilla that supported General Mikhail Skobelev's Akhal-Tekke Campaign in Central Asia in 1880-1881, commanded the corvette *Vityaz* on a round-the-world cruise from 1886 to 1889, served with the Baltic Fleet during the early 1890s, and was inspector of naval artillery from 1891 to 1894. During the mid-1890s Makarov completed another round-the-world cruise. In December 1897 he published his essay "Discussions on Questions of Naval Tactics." Makarov wrote extensively on the impact of technology on naval tactics and was one of the foremost authorities on mine warfare at sea. During the late 1890s he directed the construction of the Baltic Fleet's first icebreaker, the *Ermak*. In 1899 he was appointed commander of the naval base at Kronstadt.

After the Japanese surprise attack in January 1904, Makarov assumed command of the Russian squadron at Port Arthur, immediately instituting measures to raise the morale of its crews. On April 13 Makarov ordered a sortie to support Russian destroyers engaged with Japanese vessels. Shortly after getting under way his flagship, the battleship *Petropavlovsk*, struck a mine that detonated the forward magazine. Vice Admiral Makarov died along with most of the ship's crew and the painter Vasily Vereshchagin.

*See also:* ADMIRALTY; BALTIC FLEET; BLACK SEA FLEET; RUSSO-JAPANESE WAR; RUSSO-TURKISH WARS

BIBLIOGRAPHY

Makarov, Stepan Osipovich. (1990). "Discussions of Questions on Naval Tactics." In *Classics of Sea Power*, ed. John B. Hattendorf. Annapolis, MD: Naval Institute Press.

JACOB W. KIPP

## MAKARY, METROPOLITAN

(c. 1482–1563), also known as Macarius; archbishop of Novgorod (1526–1542); metropolitan of Moscow and all Rus (1542–1563); prominent religious and political figure of the sixteenth century.

Makary's parentage is not known, and nothing is known about him before he was tonsured at the Pafnuty-Borovsk Monastery at the end of the fifteenth century. In February 1523, Metropolitan Daniel appointed Makary archimandrite of the Luzhetsk Monastery near Mozhaisk. He became archbishop of Novgorod and Pskov on March 4, 1526, the first archbishop to be appointed to that city since 1508. This appointment may have come about, at least in part, as a result of Makary's support of the divorce of Grand Prince Basil III from his wife Solomonia in 1525 and the subsequent marriage of the grand prince to Elena Glinskaya. As archbishop, Makary undertook reorganization of the monasteries and promoted missionary activity to the Karelo-Finnic population in the northern reaches of his jurisdiction. He also undertook a number of building and restoration projects, including the direction of the unsuccessful construction of the first water mill on the Volkhov River. The greater complexity of Novgorodian church architecture in the 1530s, such as tri-apse constructions and five-cupola designs, has been attributed to Makary's intervention. Makary also undertook a number of literary and mathematical activities, including updating the Novgorod Chronicle, compiling a menology, which became the prototype of the *Great Menology*, and calculating the date of Easter through the year 2072. In 1531 he participated in the council that tried the monks Maxim the Greek, Isaak Sobaka, and Vassian Patrikeyev for holding heretical views.

Makary replaced Ioasaf (Joseph) as metropolitan of Moscow and all Rus on March 16, 1542, and took over responsibility for the education and upbringing of the young Ivan IV. He continued as a close adviser of the tsar until the end of his own life. In 1547 Makary presided over the coronation of Ivan as tsar (January), the marriage of Ivan to Anastasia (February), and (with Ivan) a church council (January–February) that canonized a number of Rus saints. Makary was badly injured in the Moscow fire in June of that year when he was being lowered from the Kremlin wall to escape the flames. Nonetheless, he continued to remain active in religious and political affairs while he recovered. In February 1549, along with Ivan, he presided over another church council that canonized more Rus saints. In June 1550, Makary and Ivan presided over the assembly that compiled the *Sudebnik* of 1550, the first major revision of the law code since 1497. During January and February 1551, Makary presided with Ivan over the *Stoglav* (Hundred-Chapter) church council, which codified the regulations of the Church similar to the way government laws had been codified the previous year in the *Sudebnik*. Also in 1551, Makary released Maxim the Greek from imprisonment and allowed him to move to the Trinity–St. Sergius Monastery in Zagorsk but would not allow him to return to Greece.

While Ivan IV was away on the campaign against Kazan from June through October 1552, Makary, along with Ivan's wife Anastasia and brother Yuri, was left in charge of running the civil affairs of the Muscovite state. By 1553, his first large literary compilation project as metropolitan, the *Great Menology*, was completed. Makary also presided over several significant heresy trials, including those of the archimandrite of the Chudov Monastery Isaak Sobaka (1549), the military servitor Matvei Bashkin, the hegumen of the Trinity–St. Sergius Monastery Artemy (1553–1554), and the monk Feodosy Kosoi (1554–1555). Also in 1555, Makary established the archiepiscopal see of Kazan. In addition, Makary directed the introduction of a new style of icon painting, which combined political and ideological concepts with religious themes. This new style was manifested in the wall and ceiling paintings of the Golden Palace in the Kremlin. The state secretary Ivan Viskovaty criticized a number of the new icons for violating the established standards of Eastern Christian icon painting. As a result, Viskovaty was brought to trial before a Church council in 1553 presided over by Makary. Viskovaty's views were condemned, but he escaped punishment and maintained his position by recanting. During the remainder of his tenure in office, Makary concentrated on a number of construction projects, including the Cathedral of the Intercession of the Virgin on the Moat (1555–1561), popularly known as Basil the Blessed

after one of its chapels, as well as two major literary compilations, the *Book of Degrees* and the *Illuminated Compilation*.

As an ideologist, Makary is credited with formulating the Church-based justification for the Muscovite conquest of Kazan as well as solidifying into a formula the Church's anti-Tatar diatribes. The close relationship between the Church and the State that he fostered was in accord with Eastern Church political theory and received visible articulation in the style of icon painting he helped to introduce. Several important letters and speeches are attributed to Makary, although he cannot be considered a major literary figure. There exist several letters of his from the time he was archbishop of Novgorod and Pskov. In his speech at the coronation of Ivan IV in 1547, Makary, in his role as metropolitan, reminded the new tsar of his duty to protect the Church. His *Reply* (*Otvet*) to Tsar Ivan IV was written around 1550 shortly before the Stoglav Church Council. In it, Makary cites a number of precedents concerning the inalienability of Church and monastic lands, including the Donation of Constantine, the Rule of Vladimir, and the false charter (*yarlyk*) to Metropolitan Peter.

He ends the *Reply* with a plea to the tsar not to take away the "immovable properties" belonging to the Uspensky (Assumption) Cathedral, the seat of the metropolitan. In his speech after the conquest of Kazan, Makary depicted victory as the result of a long-term religious crusade and thereby articulated the Church-based justification for Muscovy's claim to Kazan.

Perhaps Makary's most remarkable achievement was the *Great Menology* (*Velikie minei-chety*), which consisted of twelve volumes, one for each month, and which comprised a total of approximately 13,500 large-format folios. The *Great Menology* included full texts of almost all Church-related writings then known in Russia, including saints' lives, sermons, letters, council decisions, translations, condemnations of heretics, and so forth, all arranged in categories of daily readings. Makary had competed a shorter version of this menology while he was archbishop of Novgorod, and the resources of the Muscovite Church allowed him to expand it to comprehensive proportions.

During his tenure as metropolitan, two other major compendious works were begun that were completed only after his death. One was the *Book of Degrees* (*Stepennaya kniga*), a complete rewriting of the Rus chronicles to provide a direct justification for the ascendancy of the Muscovite ruling dynasty from Vladimir I. The other was the *Illuminated Compilation* (*Litsevoi svod*), based on the Rus chronicles. Twelve volumes were projected, of which eleven volumes are extant with more than ten thousand miniatures.

Makary died on December 31, 1563. He was buried the next day in the Uspensky Cathedral in the Moscow Kremlin. Despite apparent attempts immediately after his death and in the seventeenth century to raise him to miracle worker (*chudotvorets*) status, Makary was not canonized until 1988.

*See also:* BOOK OF DEGREES; IVAN IV; KAZAN; METROPOLITAN; MUSCOVY; SUDEBNIK OF 1550; TRINITY-ST. SERGIUS MONASTERY

**BIBLIOGRAPHY**

Či evskij, Dmitrij. (1960). *History of Russian Literature: From the Eleventh Century to the End of the Baroque.* 's-Gravenhage: Mouton.

Miller, David B. (1967). "The Literary Activities of Metropolitan Macarius: A Study of Muscovite Political Ideology in the Time of Ivan IV." Ph.D. diss., Columbia University, New York.

Pelenski, Jaroslaw. (1974). *Russia and Kazan: Conquest and Imperial Ideology (1438–1560s).* The Hague, Netherlands: Mouton.

DONALD OSTROWSKI

## MAKHNO, NESTOR IVANOVICH

(1889–1934), leader of an insurgent peasant army in the civil war and hero of the libertarian Left.

Born in Ukraine of peasant stock in Hulyai-Pole, Yekaterinoslav guberniya, Nestor Makhno (né Mikhnenko) became an anarchist during the 1905 Revolution. Makhno's father had died when he was an infant, so he worked as a shepherd from the age of seven and as a metalworker in his teens, attending school only briefly. In 1910, following his arrest two years earlier for killing a police officer, Makhno was condemned to death, but the sentence was commuted to life imprisonment because of his youth. Freed in 1917 from a Moscow prison, where he had befriended the anarchist Peter Arshinov, Makhno returned to Hulyai-Pole to chair its soviet and organize revolutionary communes. In 1918, he

established a peasant army in southeastern Ukraine and during the Civil War proved himself to be a brilliant and innovative (if unorthodox) commander. Makhno's forces battled the Central Powers, Ukrainian nationalists, the Whites, and the Reds (although he also periodically collaborated with the latter). Makhno's Revolutionary Insurgent Army played a decisive role in defeating the Whites in South Russia in 1919 and 1920, utilizing techniques of partisan and guerilla warfare to dramatic effect. The Makhnovists also oversaw an enduringly influential anarchist revolution (the *Makhnovshchina*) in southern Ukraine, summoning non-party congresses of workers and peasants and exhorting them to organize and govern themselves. In 1920, having refused to integrate his forces with the Red Army and hostile to Bolshevik authoritarianism, Makhno became an outlaw on Soviet territory. In August 1921, Red forces pursued him into Romania. After suffering imprisonment there and in Poland and Danzig, Makhno settled in Paris in 1924. In 1926, he helped create Arshinov's Organizational Platform of Libertarian Communists, but broke with his former mentor when Arshinov came to terms with Moscow. Thereafter, Makhno devoted himself to writing. In 1934, in poverty and isolation, he died of the tuberculosis he had originally contracted in tsarist prisons, but his name and achievements are revered by anarchists the world over. He is buried in Père La Chaise Cemetery, Paris.

*See also:* ANARCHISM; CIVIL WAR OF 1917–1922

**BIBLIOGRAPHY**

Arshinov, Peter. (1974). *History of the Makhnovist Movement.* Detroit: Black & Red.

JONATHAN D. SMELE

## MALENKOV, GEORGY MAXIMILYANOVICH

(1902–1988), prominent Soviet party official.

Georgy Maximilyanovich Malenkov was born in Orenburg on January 13, 1902. In 1919 he joined the Red Army, where he worked in the political administration at various levels during the Russian civil war. In April 1920, he became a member of the Bolshevik Party, and during the following month he married Valentina Alexeyevna Golubtsova, a worker in the Central Committee (CC) apparatus.

Malenkov's career during the 1920s was typical of many during that period. He was a ruthless party official without any clear political views. He studied at the Moscow Higher Technical Institute between 1921 and 1925, during which time he was a member of a commission investigating "Trotskyism" among fellow students. In 1925 he became a technical secretary of the Organizational Bureau of the Central Committee.

During the early 1930s he worked in the Moscow party committee as the head of the section for mass agitation, conducting a purge of opposition members. Between 1934 and 1939 he ran the party organization for the Central Committee and reviewed party documents in preparation for the Great Purge beginning in 1936. Malenkov took an active role in various aspects of this purge, supervising particularly harsh actions in Belarus and Armenia in 1937.

In 1937 Malenkov was appointed a deputy of the Supreme Soviet of the USSR (he was promoted to the Presidium in 1938), and in this same year became the deputy to Nikolai Yezhov, head of the NKVD. By 1939 Malenkov was also a member of the party Central Committee (CC), and shortly he became the head of the administration of party cadres and a CC secretary.

Before the outbreak of the war with Germany, Malenkov became a candidate member of the Politburo. During the war, he supplied planes to the Red Air Force, and he appears to have undertaken his tasks efficiently. Josef Stalin relied on Malenkov increasingly after 1943. In that year Malenkov headed a committee of the Soviet government for the restoration of farms in liberated areas, and after mid-May 1944, he was the deputy chairman of the Council of Ministers of the USSR (second only to Stalin himself). From March 18, 1946, Malenkov was a member of the ruling Politburo.

During the ascendancy of Andrei Zhdanov after the war, Malenkov's career briefly declined. After the exposure of a scandal in the aviation industry, he lost both his deputy chairmanship of the government and his role as CC secretary controlling party personnel, in March and May 1946, respectively. Thanks to the intervention of Lavrenty Beria, however, he was able to recover both positions by August. In 1948 he took over the position of ideological secretary of the CC and was also given responsibility for Soviet agriculture, at that time the most backward sector of the Soviet economy.

**Georgy Malenkov, Soviet prime minister, 1953–1955.** COURTESY OF THE LIBRARY OF CONGRESS

During the late Stalin period, Malenkov once again played a leading role in new purges, including the Leningrad Affair and the exposure of the "Jewish Anti-Fascist Committee." The aging leader entrusted him to present the main report at the Nineteenth Party Congress (the first party congress in thirteen years). With Stalin's death on March 5, 1953, Malenkov became the chairman of the Council of Ministers (prime minister) and the main party secretary. On March 14, however, the latter position was given to Khrushchev.

Malenkov joined with Khrushchev to overcome a putsch by Beria in 1953, but then a power struggle between the two leaders developed. Malenkov eventually had to make a public confession regarding his failure to revive Soviet agriculture. By

February 1955, he was demoted to a deputy chairman of the government and given responsibility over Soviet electric power stations. Malenkov and former old-guard Stalinists Lazar Kaganovich and Vyacheslav Molotov resented Khrushchev's de-Stalinization speech at the Twentieth Party Congress of February 1956. In 1957 the three engineered a majority vote within the Presidium for Khrushchev's removal. Khrushchev, however, was able to reverse the vote in a CC plenum, which saw the defeat of the so-called Antiparty Group. On June 29, Malenkov lost his positions in the Presidium and the Central Committee.

Though he was still relatively young, Malenkov's career was effectively over. He became the director of a hydroelectric power station in Ust-Kamengorsk, and subsequently of a thermal power station in Ekibastuz. In 1961, the Ekibastuz city party committee expelled him from membership, and Malenkov retired on a pension until his death in Moscow on January 14, 1988. He is remembered mainly as a loyal and unprincipled Stalinist with few notable achievements outside of party politics.

See also: ANTI-PARTY GROUP; KHRUSHCHEV, NIKITA SERGEYEVICH; LENINGRAD AFFAIR; PURGES, THE GREAT; STALIN, JOSEF VISSARIONOVICH

**BIBLIOGRAPHY**

Ebon, Martin. (1953). *Malenkov: A Biographical Study of Stalin's Successor.* London: Weidenfeld and Nicolson.

Radzinsky, Edward. (1996). *Stalin: The First In-Depth Biography Based on Explosive New Documents from Moscow's Secret Archives.* New York: Doubleday.

DAVID R. MARPLES

## MALEVICH, KAZIMIR SEVERINOVICH

(1878–1935), founder of the Suprematist school of abstract painting.

Kazimir Severinovich Malevich was initially a follower of Impressionism. He was influenced by Pablo Picasso and Cubism and became a member of the Jack of Diamonds group, whose members were the leading exponents of avant-garde art in pre–World War I Russia. According to the Suprematists, each economic mode of production generated not only a ruling class but also an official artistic style supported by that dominant social class. Deviations from that official style were the products of subordinate classes. All art, prior to the rule of the proletariat, therefore, manifested the ideology of some class. But the revolution would bring about the destruction not merely of the bourgeoisie, but of all classes as such. Consequently, the art of the proletarian revolution must be the expression of not merely another style but of absolute, eternal, "supreme" values.

Constructivism was brought into Soviet avant-guard architecture primarily by Vladimir Tatlin and Malevich. Malevich's "Arkhitectonica," Tatlin's Monument to the Third International (the "Tatlin Tower"), and El Lissitsky's "Prouns" shaped in large measure the conceptualizations of the modernist architects as they sought a means to combine painting, sculpture, and architecture. Tatlin's stress on utilitarianism was challenged by Malevich's Suprematism, which decried the emphasis of technology in art and argued that artists must search for "supreme" artistic values that would transform the ideology of the people. Malevich thus contrasted the work of engineers, whose creations exhibited simple transitory values, with aesthetic creativity, which he proclaimed produced supreme values. Malevich warned: "If socialism relies on the infallibility of science and technology, a great disappointment is in store for it because it is not granted to scientists to foresee the 'course of events' and to create enduring values" (Malevich, p. 36). His "White on White" carried Suprematist theories to their logical conclusion. With the turn against modern art under Josef Stalin, Malevich lost influence and died in poverty and oblivion.

See also: ARCHITECTURE; CONSTRUCTIVISM; FUTURISM.

**BIBLIOGRAPHY**

Malevich, Kazimir. (1959) *The Non-Objective World*, tr. Howard Dearstyne. Chicago: P. Theobald.

Milner, John. (1996). *Kazimir Malevich and the Art of Geometry.* New Haven, CT: Yale University Press.

HUGH D. HUDSON JR.

## MALTA SUMMIT

A summit meeting of U.S. President George W. Bush and Soviet leader Mikhail Gorbachev took place on December 2–3, 1989, on warships of the two countries anchored at Malta in the Mediterranean. The meeting, the first between the two leaders, followed the collapse of communist bloc governments in East Germany, Poland, Hungary, Bulgaria, and Czechoslovakia (Romania would follow three weeks later). Soviet acceptance of this dramatic change, without intervention or even opposition, dramatically underscored the new outlook in Moscow.

President Bush, who had been reserved and cautious in his assessment of change in the Soviet Union during most of 1989, now sought to extend encouragement to Gorbachev. Most important was the establishment of a confident relationship and dialogue between the two leaders. No treaties or agreements were signed, but Bush did indicate a number of changes in U.S. economic policy toward the Soviet Union to reflect the new developing relationship. Malta thus marked a step in a process of accelerating change.

Two weeks after the Malta summit, Soviet Foreign Minister Eduard Shevardnadze paid an unprecedented courtesy visit to North Atlantic Treaty Organization (NATO) headquarters in Brussels. Clearly the Cold War was coming to an end. Indeed, at Malta, Gorbachev declared that "the world is leaving one epoch, the 'Cold War,' and entering a new one."

Some historians have described the Malta Summit as the last summit of the Cold War; others have seen it as the first summit of the new era. In any case, it occurred at a time of rapid transition and reflected the first time when prospects for future cooperation outweighed continuing competition, although elements of both remained.

*See also:* COLD WAR; UNITED STATES, RELATIONS WITH

## BIBLIOGRAPHY
Beschloss, Michael R., and Talbott, Strobe. (1993). *At the Highest Levels: The Inside Story of the End of the Cold War.* Boston: Little, Brown and Company.

Garthoff, Raymond L. (1994). *The Great Transition: American-Soviet Relations and the End of the Cold War.* Washington, DC: The Brookings Institution.

RAYMOND L. GARTHOFF

# MANDELSHTAM, NADEZHDA YAKOVLEVNA

(1899–1980), memoirist and preserver of her husband Osip Mandelshtam's poetic legacy.

Nadezhda Yakovlevna Mandelshtam (née Khazina) is known primarily for her two books detailing life with her husband, the Modernist poet Osip Mandelshtam, and the years following his death in Stalin's purges. She grew up in Kiev in a tight-knit, intellectually gifted family, fondly recalled in three biographical sketches. With the onset of revolution and civil war, she enjoyed a bohemian existence as a painter in the artist Alexandra Ekster's studio.

In 1922 Nadezhda married Mandelshtam, and the two moved to Moscow and then to Leningrad in 1924. In 1925 her friendship with the poet Anna Akhmatova began. Osip Mandelshtam was arrested in Moscow in 1934 after writing a poem that denounced Josef Stalin. Nadezhda accompanied him into exile in Voronezh until 1937 and in 1938 was present when he was arrested and sent to the gulag where he died. She escaped arrest the same year.

For the next two decades, Nadezhda Mandelshtam survived by teaching English and moved frequently to avoid official attention. In 1951 she completed a dissertation in linguistics. She also began working on her husband's rehabilitation and researching his life and fate. Many of his poems survived because she committed them to memory. Her first book of memoirs, *Vospominaniia* (New York, 1970, translated as *Hope Against Hope*, 1970), was devoted to her final years with Osip Mandelshtam and to a broader indictment of the Stalinist system that had condemned him. The book, which circulated in the Soviet Union in *samizdat*, attracted attention and praise from Soviet and Western readers. Her second book, *Vtoraia kniga* (Paris, 1972, translated as *Hope Abandoned*, 1974), offended some Russian readers with its opinionated descriptions of various literary figures. Treatments of Nadezhda Mandelshtam's work have noted her success in achieving a strong and vibrant literary voice of her own even as she transmitted the cultural legacy of a previous generation.

*See also:* AKHMATOVA, ANNA ANDREYEVNA; GULAG; MANDELSHTAM, OSIP EMILIEVICH; PURGES, THE GREAT; SAMIZDAT

## BIBLIOGRAPHY
Brodsky, Joseph. (1986). "Nadezhda Mandelstam (1899–1980): An Obituary." In *Less Than One: Selected Essays.* New York: Farrar Straus Giroux.

Holmgren, Beth. (1993). *Women's Works in Stalin's Time.* Bloomington: Indiana University Press.

Proffer, Carl R. (1987). *The Widows of Russia and Other Writings.* Ann Arbor, MI: Ardis.

JUDITH E. KALB

## MANDELSHTAM, OSIP EMILIEVICH

(1891–1938), Modernist poet and political martyr.

One of Russia's greatest twentieth-century poets, Osip Mandelshtam died en route to the gulag after writing a poem critical of Josef V. Stalin. Born to a cultured Jewish family in Warsaw, Mandelshtam spent his childhood in St. Petersburg, traveled in Europe, and, in 1909, began to frequent the literary salon of the Symbolist poet Vyacheslav Ivanov. In 1911, while enrolled at St. Petersburg University, he joined the Guild of Poets headed by Nikolai Gumilev and Sergei Gorodetsky and subsequently became a leading figure in a new poetic school called Acmeism. His collections *Kamen* (Stone, 1913), *Tristia* (1922), and *Stikhotvoreniia* (Poems, 1928) show a poet steeped in world culture and focused on themes such as language and time, concepts also addressed in his prose works. In 1922 Mandelshtam married Nadezhda Khazina, who later wrote memoirs of their life together.

Mandelshtam recognized that the Bolshevik takeover in 1917 threatened the cultural values he held dear, and in his poetry and essays of the 1920s he attempted to define the relationship of the poet to the age. Literary prose such as *Shum vremeni* (The Noise of Time, 1925) and *Egipetskaia marka* (The Egyptian Stamp, 1928) included autobiographical themes. By the late 1920s, Mandelshtam's lack of adherence to Soviet norms led to increasing difficulties in getting published. A trip to the Caucasus and Armenia in 1930 provided new inspiration for creativity. But in 1934, after writing a poem critical of Stalin, Mandelshtam was arrested in Moscow and sent to Voronezh for a three-year exile. During this period he wrote *Voronezhskie tetradi* (*Voronezh Notebooks*), preserved by his wife. In May 1938, Mandelshtam was arrested once again, sentenced to a Siberian labor camp, and considered a non-person by the Soviet government. He died the same year. In 1956 his rehabilitation began, and in the 1970s a collection of his poetry was published in the Soviet Union.

*See also:* GULAG; MANDELSHTAM, NADEZHDA YAKOVLEVNA; PURGES, THE GREAT

### BIBLIOGRAPHY

Brown, Clarence. (1973). *Mandelstam.* Cambridge: Cambridge University Press.

Cavanagh, Clare. (1995). *Osip Mandelstam and the Modernist Creation of Tradition.* Princeton, NJ: Princeton University Press.

Freidin, Gregory. (1987). *A Coat of Many Colors: Osip Mandelstam and His Mythologies of Self-Presentation.* Berkeley: University of California Press.

Shentalinskii, Vitalii. (1996). *Arrested Voices: Resurrecting the Disappeared Writers of the Soviet Regime.* New York: Free Press.

JUDITH E. KALB

## MANIFESTO OF 1763

Signed by Empress Catherine II, this lengthy, detailed document that invited foreign settlers to Russia, was published in St. Petersburg by the Senate on August 5, 1763. The official English version appears in Bartlett, *Human Capital* (1979). It evolved from several circumstances. In October 1762 the newly crowned empress ordered the Senate to encourage foreign settlement (except Jews) as a means to reinforce "the well-being of Our Empire." In response, a short manifesto of mid-December 1762 was translated into "all foreign languages" and printed in many foreign newspapers. Both manifestoes crystallized Russian government thinking about immigration in general by considering specific cases and problems amid European populationist discourse over many decades.

Catherine II championed "populationism" even before she gained the throne, probably from reading German cameralist works that postulated increasing population as an index of state power and prestige. Also, Peter the Great had formulated in a famous decree of 1702 the policy of recruiting skilled Europeans, and Catherine endorsed the Petrine precedent. The notion that Russia was underpopulated went back several centuries, an issue that had become acute with the empire's recent expansion, and the Romanov dynasty's rapid Europeanization. Cessation of the European phases of the Seven Years' War (1756–1763) also suggested that the German lands might harbor a reservoir of capable individuals and families eager to settle Russia's huge empty, potentially rich spaces.

The impatient empress felt pressured to demonstrate her governing abilities by pursuing peaceful policies that her immediate predecessors had barely begun. Moreover, she was determined to repair the economic–financial ravages of the war that had just ended. It was one thing to declare a new policy, however, and something else to institute it. In preparing the two manifestoes of 1762–1763 the Senate discovered many partial precedents and several concrete impediments to welcoming masses of immigrants. More than six months elapsed between the issuance of the two manifestoes, during which time governments were consulted and institutions formulated to care for the anticipated newcomers. It was decided that the manifesto should list the specific lands available for settlement and not exclude any groups. Drawing on foreign precedent and the suggestion of Senator Peter Panin, the manifesto of 1763 established a special government office with jurisdiction over new settlers, the Chancery of Guardianship of Foreigners. The first head, Count Grigory Orlov, Catherine's common-law husband and leader of her seizure of the throne, personified the office's high status. The new Russian immigration policy offered generous material incentives, promised freedom of religion and exemption from military recruitment, and guaranteed exemption from enserfment and freedom to leave. These provisions governed immigration policy until at least 1804 and for many decades thereafter. The manifesto of 1763 did not specifically exclude Jews, although Elizabeth's regime banned them as "Killers of Christ," for Catherine highly regarded their entrepreneurship and unofficially encouraged their entry into New Russia (Ukraine) in 1764.

European immigrants responded eagerly to the manifesto, some twenty thousand arriving during Catherine's reign. Germans settling along the Volga were the largest group, especially the Herrnhut (Moravian Brethren) settlement at Sarepta near Saratov and Mennonite settlements in southern Ukraine. Because of the empire's largely agrarian economy, most settlers were farmers. The expense of the program was large, however, so its cost-effectiveness is debatable. A century later many Volga Germans resettled in the United States, some still decrying Catherine's allegedly broken promises.

*See also:* CATHERINE II; JEWS; ORLOV, GRIGORY GRIGORIEVICH; PALE OF SETTLEMENT

**BIBLIOGRAPHY**

Bartlett, Roger P. (1979). *Human Capital: The Settlement of Foreigners in Russia 1762-1804.* Cambridge, UK: Cambridge University Press.

Khodarkovsky, Michael. (2002). *Russia's Steppe Frontier: The Making of a Colonial Empire, 1500-1800.* Bloomington: Indiana University Press.

JOHN T. ALEXANDER

## MANSI

The 8,500 Mansi (1989 census), formerly called Voguls, live predominantly in the Hanti-Mansi Autonomous Region (*Okrug*), in the swampy basin of the Ob river. Their language belongs to the Ugric branch of the Finno-Ugric family. It has little mutual intelligibility with the related Hanti language, farther northeast, and essentially none with Magyar (Hungarian). Most Mansi have Asian features. One of the most distinctive features of Mansi (and Hanti) culture is an elaborate bear funeral ceremony, honoring the slain beast.

The Mansi historical homeland straddled the middle Urals, southwest of their present location on the Konda River. They offered spirited resistance to Russian encroachment during the 1400s, highlighted by prince Asyka's counterattack in 1455. The Russians destroyed the last major Mansi principality, Konda, in 1591. Within one generation, Moscow ignored whatever capitulation treaties had been signed. As settlers poured into the best Mansi agricultural lands, the Mansi were soon reduced to a small hunting and fishing population. By 1750 most were forced to accept the outer trappings of Greek Orthodoxy, while practicing animism in secret. Russian traders reduced people unfamiliar with the notion of money and prices to loan slavery that lasted for generations.

When the Ostiako-Vogul National *Okrug* District—the present Hanti-Mansi Autonomous Oblast—was created in 1930, the indigenous population was already down to 19 percent of the total population. By 1989, the population had dropped to 1.4 percent, due first to a massive influx of deportees and then to free labor, after discovery of oil during the 1950s. The curse of Arctic oil impacted the natives, who were crudely dispossessed, as well as the fragile ecosystem. Gas torching and oil spills became routine.

Post-Soviet liberalization enabled the Hanti and Mansi to organize Spasenie Ugry (Salvation of Yugria, the land of Ugrians) that gave voice to indigenous and ecological concerns. Thirty-seven percent of the Mansi population (and few young people) spoke Mansi in the early 1990s. A weekly newspaper, *Luima Serikos*, had a circulation of 240 in 1995. Novels on Mansi topics by Yuvan Sestalov (b. 1937) have many readers in Russia.

See also: FINNS AND KARELIANS; NATIONALITIES POLICIES, SOVIET; NATIONALITIES POLICIES, TSARIST; NORTHERN PEOPLES

BIBLIOGRAPHY

Forsyth, James. (1992). *A History of the Peoples of Siberia: Russia's North Asian Colony, 1581–1990.* Cambridge, UK: Cambridge University Press.

Taagepera, Rein. (1999). *The Finno-Ugric Republics and the Russian State.* London: Hurst.

REIN TAAGEPERA

## MARI EL AND THE MARI

The Mari, or Cheremis, are an indigenous people of the European Russian interior; their language and that of the Mordvins compose the Volgaic branch of the Finno-Ugric language family.

As subjects of the Volga Bolgars and Kazan Tatars, medieval Mari tribes experienced cultural and linguistic influences mainly from their Turkic neighbors. Later on, Slavic contacts became prominent, and the Russian language became the principal source of lexical and syntactic borrowing. The early twentieth-century initiatives to create a single literary language did not come to fruition. Consequently, there are two written standards of Mari: Hill and Meadow. The speakers of various western, or Hill Mari, dialects constitute hardly more than 10 percent of the Mari as a whole.

In the basin of the Middle Volga, the medieval Mari distribution area stretched from the Volga-Oka confluence to the mouth of the Kazanka River. Under Tatar rule, the Mari were active participants in Kazan's war efforts. Apparently due to their loyalty and peripheral location, Mari tribal communities were granted home rule. However, the final struggle between the Kazan Khanate and Moscow brought an intraethnic cleavage: the Hill Mari sided with the Russians, whereas the Meadow Mari remained with the Tatars until the fall of Kazan in 1552.

The submission to Moscow was painful: The second half of the sixteenth century saw a series of uprisings, known as the Cheremis Wars, which decimated the Meadow Mari in particular. The Russian invasions triggered population movements that also reshaped the Mari settlement area: a part of the Meadow Mari migrated to the Bashkir lands and towards the Urals. For about two hundred years, the resettlement was sustained by land seizures, fugitive peasant migrations, and Christianization policies. The outcome of all this was the formation of the Eastern Mari. In terms of religion, these Mari have largely kept their traditional "paganism," whereas their Middle Volga coethnics are mostly Orthodox, or in a synchretic way combine animism with Christianity.

The Mari ethnic awakening took its first steps with the 1905 and 1917 Revolutions. In 1920 the Bolsheviks established the Mari autonomous province. It was elevated to the status of an autonomous republic in 1936—the year of the Stalinist purges of the entire ethnic intelligentsia. Since 1992, the republic has been known as the Republic of Mari El.

At the time of the 1989 census, 324,000 Mari out of a total of 671,000 were residents of their titular republic. There the Mari constituted 43.2 percent of the inhabitants, whereas Russians made up 47.5 percent. Outside Mari El, the largest Mari populations were found in Bashkortostan (106,000) as well as in Kirov and Sverdlovsk provinces (44,000 and 31,000 respectively). Indicative of linguistic assimilation, 17 percent of the Mari considered Russian their native language during the 1994 microcensus.

In 2000 Mari El was a home for 759,000 people. Within Russia, it is an agricultural region, poor in natural resources and heavily dependent on federal subsides. Within the republic's political elite, the Mari have mainly performed secondary roles, and this situation has deteriorated further since the mid-1990s. Because Russians outnumber the Mari, and because the Mari still lag behind in terms of urbanity, education, and ethnic consciousness, Russians dominate the republic's political life.

See also: FINNS AND KARELIANS; NATIONALITIES POLICIES, SOVIET; NATIONALITIES POLICIES, TSARIST.

BIBLIOGRAPHY

Fryer, Paul, and Lallukka, Seppo. (2002). "The Eastern Mari." <http://www.rusin.fi/eastmari/home.htm>.

Lallukka, Seppo. (1990). *The East Finnic Minorities in the Soviet Union: An Appraisal of the Erosive Trends.* (Annales Academiae Scientiarum Fennicae, Ser. B, vol. 252). Helsinki: Suomalainen Tiedeakatemia.

Taagepera, Rein. (1999). *The Finno-Ugric Republics and the Russian State.* London: Hurst.

SEPPO LALLUKKA

# MARKET SOCIALISM

The economic doctrine of market socialism holds that central planners can make active and efficient use of "the market" as a mechanism for implementing socially desired goals, which are developed and elaborated through central planning of economic activity. Focusing on the elimination of private property and wealth, and on the central determination and control of all investment and development decisions, it posits that the planned determination and adjustment of producers' and asset prices could allow markets to implement the desired allocations in a decentralized manner without sacrificing central or social control over outcomes or incomes. Thus egalitarian social outcomes and dynamic economic growth can be achieved simultaneously, without the disruptions and suffering imposed by poorly coordinated private investment decisions resulting in a wasteful business cycle.

The idea of market socialism arose from the realization that classical socialism, involving the collective provision and distribution of goods and services in natural form, without the social contrivances of property, markets, and prices, was not feasible, since rational collective control of economic activity requires calculations that cannot rely consistently on "natural unit" variables such as energy or labor amounts. It also became clear that the existing computing capabilities were inadequate for deriving a consistent economic plan from a general equilibrium problem. This led, in the Socialist Calculation Debate of the 1930s, to the suggestion (most notably by Oskar Lange) that a Socialist regime, assuming ownership of all means of production, could use markets to find relevant consumers' prices and valuations while maintaining social and state control over production, income determination, investment, and economic development. Managers would be instructed to minimize costs, while the planning board would adjust producers' prices to eliminate disequilibria in the markets for final goods. Thus, at a socialist market equilibrium, the classical marginal conditions of static efficiency would be maintained, while the

State would ensure equitable distribution of incomes through its allocation of the surplus (profit) from efficient production and investment in socially desirable planned development.

Another version of market socialism arose as a result of the reform experiences in east-central Europe, particularly the labor-managed economic system of Yugoslavia that developed following Marshal Tito's break with Josef Stalin in 1950. This gave rise to a large body of literature on the "Illyrian Firm" with decentralized, democratic control of production by workers' collectives in a market economy subject to substantial macroeconomic planning and income redistribution through taxation and subsidies. The economic reforms in Hungary (1968), Poland (1981), China after 1978, and Gorbachev's Russia (1987–1991) involved varying degrees of decentralization of State Socialism and its administrative command economy, providing partial approximations to the classical market socialist model of Oskar Lange. This experience highlighted the difficulties of planning for and controlling decentralized markets, and revealed the failure of market socialism to provide incentives for managers to follow the rules necessary for economic efficiency. Faced with these circumstances, proponents of market socialism moved beyond state ownership and control of property to various forms of economic democracy and collective property, accepting the necessity of real markets and market prices but maintaining the classical socialist rejection of fully private productive property. The early debates on market socialism are best seen in Friedrich A. von Hayek (1935), while the current state of the debate is presented in Pranab Bardhan and John E. Roemer (1993).

*See also:* PERESTROIKA; PLANNERS' PREFERENCE; SOCIALISM; STATE ORDERS

## BIBLIOGRAPHY

Bardhan, Pranab, and Roemer, John E., eds. (1993). *Market Socialism: The Current Debate.* Oxford: Oxford University Press.

Granick, David. (1975). *Enterprise Guidance in Eastern Europe: A Comparison of Four Socialist Economies.* Princeton, NJ: Princeton University Press.

Hayek, Friedrich A. von, ed. (1935). *Collectivist Economic Planning: Critical Studies on the Possibilities of Socialism.* London: Routledge.

Kornai, János. (1992). *The Socialist System: The Political Economy of Communism.* Princeton, NJ: Princeton University Press.

Lange, Oskar, and Taylor, Fred M. (1948). *On the Economic Theory of Socialism.* Minneapolis: University of Minnesota Press.

RICHARD ERICSON

# MARRIAGE AND FAMILY LIFE

As elsewhere in Europe, marriage and family life in Russia have varied across time and by social group, reflecting the complex interplay of competing ideals, changing patterns of social and economic organization, differing forms of political organization and levels of state intrusiveness, and the effects of cataclysmic events. If in the long run the outcome of this interplay of forces has been a family structure and dynamic that conform essentially with those found in modern European societies, the development of marriage and the family in Russia nevertheless has followed a distinctive path. This development can be divided into three broad periods: the centuries preceding the formation of the Russian Empire during the early eighteenth century, the imperial period (1698–1917), and the period following the Bolshevik Revolution and establishment of the Soviet state in October 1917. While the pace of development and change varied significantly between different social groups during each of these periods, each period nonetheless was characterized by a distinctive combination of forces that shaped marital and family life and family structures. In Russia's successive empires, moreover, important differences also often existed between the many ethno-cultural and religious groups included in these empires. The discussion that follows therefore concerns principally the Slavic Christian population.

## PRE-IMPERIAL RUSSIA

Although only limited sources are available for the reconstruction of marital and family life in medieval Russia, especially for nonelite social groups, there appears to have been broad continuity in the structure and functioning of the family throughout the medieval and early modern periods. Family structures and interpersonal relations within marriage and the family were strongly shaped by the forms of social organization and patterns of economic activity evolved to secure survival in a harsh natural as well as political environment. Hence, constituting the primary unit of production and reproduction, and providing the main source of welfare, personal status, and identity, families in most instances were multigenerational and structured hierarchically, with authority and economic and familial roles distributed within the family on the basis of gender and seniority. While scholars disagree over whether already by 1600 the nuclear family had begun to displace the multigenerational family among the urban population, this development did not affect the patriarchal character or the social and economic functions of either marriage or the family. Reflecting and reinforcing these structures and functions, the marriage of children was arranged by senior family members, with the economic, social, and political interests of the family taking precedence over individual preference. Land and other significant assets, too, generally were considered to belong to the family as a whole, with males enjoying preferential treatment in inheritance. Marriage appears to have been universal among all social groups, with children marrying at a young age, and for married women, childbirth was frequent.

After the conversion of Grand Prince Vladimir of Kievan Rus to Christianity in 988, normative rules governing marriage and the family also were shaped and enforced by the Orthodox Church, although the effective influence of the Church spread slowly from urban to rural areas. Granted extensive jurisdiction over marital and family matters first by Kievan and then by Muscovite grand princes, the Church used its authority to establish marriage as a religious institution and to attempt to bring marital and family life into conformity with its doctrines and canons. For example, the Church sought—with varying degrees of success—to limit the formation of marriages through restrictions based on consanguinity and age, to restrict marital dissolution to the instances defined by canon law, to limit the possibility of remarriage, and to confine sexual activity to relations between spouses within marriage for the purpose of procreation. At the same time, through its teachings, canonical rules, and ecclesiastical activities, the Church reinforced the patriarchal order within marriage and the family, thereby providing a religious sanction for established social structures and practices. Hence the extent to which the Church transformed or merely reinforced existing ideals of and relationships within marriage and the family remains disputed.

Although patriarchal attitudes and structures and a gendered division of labor also prevailed within elite households, the role of family and lineage in determining relative status within and between elite groups, access to beneficial appointments and the material rewards that followed from them, and the prospects for forming advantageous marriage alliances between families imparted distinctive characteristics to elite family life, especially after the late fifteenth century. The practice among the Muscovite elite of secluding women in separate quarters (the *terem*), for example, which reached its greatest intensity during the seventeenth century, appears to have been due largely to the desire to protect family honor and ensure the marriage utility of daughters in a context in which the elite was growing in size and complexity. Seclusion itself, however, considerably increased the politically important role of married women in arranging and maintaining family alliances. Similarly, the development of a system of service tenements in land to support the expansion especially of military servitors after the late fifteenth century led initially to a deterioration in the property and inheritance rights of elite women. Yet such women also often had principal responsibility for managing the estates and other affairs of husbands who frequently were away on military campaigns or carrying out other service assignments. Hence within the Muscovite elite, and quite likely among other social groups in pre-Petrine Russia as well, the normative ideal and legal rules supporting the patriarchal family often concealed a more complex reality. This ideal nonetheless provided a powerful metaphor that helped to legitimize and integrate the familial, social, and political orders.

## IMPERIAL RUSSIA

The history of marriage and the family during the imperial period was marked both by a complex pattern of continuity and change and by sharp diversity between social groups, as the exposure of different groups to the forces of change varied significantly. Nonetheless, by the early twentieth century the long-term trend across the social spectrum was toward smaller families, the displacement of the multigenerational family by the nuclear family, a higher age at the time of first marriage for both men and women, declining birth rates, an increased incidence of marital dissolution, and, in urban areas, a decline in the frequency of marriage. Within the family, the structure of patriarchal authority was eroding and the ideal itself was under attack.

The groups that were exposed earliest and most intensively to the combination of forces lying behind these trends were the nobility, state officialdom, the clergy, and a newly emergent intelligentsia and largely urban bourgeoisie. During the eighteenth century, for example, the nobility represented the main target and then chief ally of the state in its efforts to inculcate European cultural forms and modes of behavior and to promote formal education and literacy. Among the effects of such efforts was a new public role for women and the dissemination of ideals of marriage, family, and the self that eventually came to challenge the patriarchal ideal. By helping to produce by the first half of the nineteenth century a more professionalized, predominantly landless, and largely urban civil officialdom, as well as a chiefly urban cultural intelligentsia and professional bourgeoisie, changes in the terms of state service and the expansion of secondary and higher education both provided a receptive audience for new ideals of marriage and the family and eroded dependency on the extended family. By expanding the occupational opportunities not only for men but also for women outside the home, the development of trade, industry, publishing, and the professions had similar effects. Most of these new employment opportunities were concentrated in Russia's rapidly growing cities, where material and physical as well as cultural conditions worked to alter the family's role, structures, and demographic characteristics. For this reason, the marital and demographic behavior and family structures of urban workers also exhibited early change.

At least until after the late 1850s, by contrast, marriage and family life among the peasantry, poorer urban groups, and the merchantry displayed greater continuity with the past. This continuity resulted in large part from the strength of custom and the continued economic, social, and welfare roles of the multigenerational, patriarchal family among these social groups and, at least among the peasantry, from the operation of communal institutions and the coincident interests of family patriarchs (who dominated village assemblies), noble landowners, and the state in preserving existing family structures. Facilitated by the abolition of serfdom in 1861, however, family structures and demographic behavior even among the peasantry began slowly to change, especially outside of the more heavily agricultural central black earth region. In particular, the increased frequency of household division occurring after the emancipation contributed to a noticeable reduction in family size and a decline in the incidence of the multigenerational family by the last third of the

**A young couple exchanges their marriage vows during an Orthodox ceremony in Chelyabinsk.** © Peter Turnley/CORBIS

century, although most families still passed through a cycle of growth and division that included a multigenerational stage. While marriage remained nearly universal, the age at first marriage also rose for both men and women, with the result that birth rates declined somewhat. The growth of income from local and regional wage labor, trade, and craft production and the rapid expansion of migratory labor contributed to all these trends, while also helping to weaken patriarchal structures of authority within the family, a process given further impetus by the exposure of peasants to urban culture through migratory labor, military service, and rising literacy. Although most peasant migrants to cities, especially males, retained ties with their native village and household, and consequently continued to be influenced by peasant culture, a significant number became permanent urban residents, adopting different family forms and cultural attitudes as a result. With the rapid growth of Russian cities and the transformation of the urban environment that took place after the late 1850s, family forms and demographic behavior among the poorer urban social groups and the merchantry also began to change in ways similar to other urban groups.

Normative ideals of marriage and the family likewise exhibited significant diversification and change during the imperial period, a process that accelerated after the late 1850s. If closer integration into European culture exposed Russians to a wider and shifting variety of ideals of marriage, the family, and sexual behavior, the development of a culture of literacy, journalism and a publishing industry, and an ethos of civic activism and professionalism based on faith in the rational use of specialized expertise broadened claims to the authority to define such ideals. These developments culminated in an intense public debate over reform of family law—and of the family and society through law—after the late 1850s. Very broadly, emphasizing a companionate ideal of marriage, the need to balance individual rights with collective responsibilities and limited authority within marriage and the family, and the necessity of adapting state law and religious doctrines to changing social and historical conditions, advocates of reform favored the facilitation of marital dissolution, equality between spouses in marriage, greater rights for children born out of wedlock, the recasting of inheritance rights based on sexual equality and the nuclear family, and the decriminalization of various sexual practices as well as of abortion. Many of these principles in fact were embodied in draft civil and criminal codes prepared by government reform commissions between 1883 and 1906, neither of which was adopted, and proposals to expand the grounds for divorce made by a series of committees formed within the Orthodox Church between 1906 and 1916 proved similarly unsuccessful. Socialist activists adopted an even more radical position on the reconstitution of marriage and the family, in some cases advocating the socialization of the latter. Opponents of reform, by contrast, stressed the social utility, naturalness, and divine basis of strong patriarchal authority within marriage and the family, the congruence of this family structure with Russian cultural traditions, and the role of the family in upholding the autocratic social and political orders. Although significant reforms affecting illegitimate children, inheritance rights, and marital separation were enacted in 1902, 1912, and 1914, respectively, deep divisions within and between the state, the Orthodox Church, and society ensured that reform of marriage and the family remained a contentious issue until the very end of the autocracy, and beyond.

## SOVIET RUSSIA

With respect to marriage and the family, the long-term effect of the Soviet attempt to create a modern socialist society was to accelerate trends already present in the early twentieth century. Hence, by the end of the Soviet period, among all social groups family size had declined sharply and the nuclear family had become nearly universal, the birth rate had dropped significantly, marriage no longer was universal, and the incidence of marital dissolution had risen substantially. But if by the 1980s the structure and demographic characteristics of the Russian family had come essentially to resemble those found in contemporary European societies, the process of development was shaped by the distinctive political and economic structures and policies of Soviet-style socialism.

Soviet policies with respect to marriage and the family were shaped initially by a combination of radical ideological beliefs and political considera-

tions. Hence, in a series of decrees and other enactments promulgated between October 1917 and 1920, the new Soviet government introduced formal sexual equality in marriage, established divorce on demand, secularized marriage, drastically curtailed inheritance and recast inheritance rights on the basis of sexual equality and the nuclear family, and legalized abortion. The party-state leadership also proclaimed the long-term goal of the socialization of the family through the development of an extensive network of social services and communal dining. These measures in part reflected an ideological commitment to both the liberation of women and the creation of a socialist society. But they also were motivated by the political goals of attracting the support of women for the new regime and of undermining the sources of opposition to it believed to lie in patriarchal family structures and attitudes and in marriage as a religious institution. In practice, however, the policies added to the problems of family instability, homelessness, and child abandonment caused mainly by the harsh and disruptive effects of several years of war, revolution, civil war, and famine. For this reason, while welcomed by radical activists and some parts of the population, Soviet policies with respect to marriage and the family also provoked considerable opposition, especially among women and the peasantry, who for overlapping but also somewhat different reasons saw in these policies a threat to their security and self-identity during a period of severe dislocation. In important respects, Soviet propaganda and policies in fact reinforced the self-image that partly underlay the opposition of women to its policies by stressing the ideal and duties of motherhood. Yet the direction of Soviet policies remained consistent through the 1920s, albeit not without controversy and dissent even within the party, with these policies being embodied in the family codes of 1922 and 1926.

The severe social disruptions, strain on resources, and deterioration of already limited social services caused by the collectivization of agriculture, the rapid development of industry, the abolition of private trade, and the reconstruction of the economy between the late 1920s and the outbreak of war in 1941, however, led to a fundamental shift in Soviet policies with respect to marriage and the family. With its priorities now being economic growth and social stabilization, the Soviet state idealized the socialist family (which in essence closely resembled the family ideal of prerevolutionary liberal and feminist reformers), which was proclaimed to be part of the essential foundation of a socialist

Following Soviet tradition, a wedding party walks to Red Square to have pictures taken. © PETER TURNLEY/CORBIS

society. A series of laws and new codes enacted between 1936 and 1944 therefore attempted both to strengthen marriage and the family and to encourage women to give birth more frequently: Divorce was severely restricted, children born out of wedlock were deprived of any rights with respect to their father, thus reestablishing illegitimacy of birth, abortion was outlawed, and a schedule of rewards for mothers who bore additional children was established. Although the goals of women's liberation and sexual equality remained official policy, they were redefined to accommodate a married woman's dual burden of employment outside the home and primary responsibility for domestic work. Economic necessity in fact compelled most women to enter the workforce, regardless of their marital status, with only the wives of the party-state elite being able to choose not to do so. Despite the changes in normative ideals and the law, however, the effects of Soviet social and economic policies in general and of the difficult material conditions resulting from them were a further reduction in average family size and decline in the

birth rate and the disruption especially of peasant households, as family members were arrested, migrated to cities in massive numbers, or died as a result of persecution or famine. The huge losses sustained by the Soviet population during World War II gave further impetus to these trends and, by creating a significant imbalance between men and women in the marriage-age population, considerably reduced the rate of marriage and complicated the formation of families for several decades after the war.

The relaxation of political controls on the discussion of public policy by relevant specialists after the death of Josef Stalin in 1953 contributed to another shift in Soviet policies toward marriage and the family during the mid-1960s. Divorce again became more accessible, fathers could be required to provide financial support for their children born out of wedlock, and abortion was re-legalized and, given the scarcity of reliable alternatives, quickly became the most common form of birth control practiced by Russian women. Partly as a result of these measures, the divorce rate within the Russian population rose steadily after the mid-1960s, with more than 40 percent of all marriages ending in divorce by the 1980s, and the birth rate continued to decline. But these trends also gained impetus from the growth of the percentage of the Russian population, women as well as men, receiving secondary and tertiary education, from the nearly universal participation of women in the workforce, from the continued shift of the population from the countryside to cities (the Russian population became predominantly urban only after the late 1950s), and from the limited availability of adequate housing and social services in a context in which women continued to bear the chief responsibilities for child-rearing and domestic work. These latter problems contributed to the reemergence in the urban population of a modified form of the multigenerational family, as the practices of a young couple living with the parents of one partner while waiting for their own apartment and of a single parent living especially with his or usually her mother appear to have increased. In the countryside, the improvement in the living conditions of the rural population following Stalin's death, their inclusion in the social welfare system, yet the continued out-migration especially of young males seeking a better life in the city also led to a decline in family size, as well as to a disproportionately female and aging population, which affected both the structure of rural families and the rate of their formation. Nonetheless, the ideals of the nuclear family, marriage, and natural motherhood remained firmly in place, both in official policy and among the population.

*See also:* ABORTION POLICY; FAMILY CODE OF 1926; FAMILY CODE ON MARRIAGE, THE FAMILY, AND GUARDIANSHIP; FAMILY EDICT OF 1944; FAMILY LAWS OF 1936; FEMINISM

## BIBLIOGRAPHY

Clements, Barbara Evans; Engel, Barbara Alpern; and Worobec, Christine D., eds. (1991). *Russia's Women: Accommodation, Resistance, Transformation.* Berkeley: University of California Press.

Engel, Barbara Alpern. (1994). *Between the Fields and the City: Women, Work, and Family in Russia, 1861–1914.* New York: Cambridge University Press.

Freeze, ChaeRan Y. (2002). *Jewish Marriage and Divorce in Imperial Russia.* Hanover, NH: Brandeis University Press.

Goldman, Wendy Z. (1993). *Women, the State, and Revolution: Soviet Family Policy and Social Life, 1917–1936.* New York: Cambridge University Press.

Hubbs, Joanna. (1988). *Mother Russia: The Feminine Myth in Russian Culture.* Bloomington: Indiana University Press.

Lapidus, Gail Warshofsky. (1978). *Women in Soviet Society: Equality, Development, and Social Change.* Berkeley: University of California Press.

Levin, Eve. (1989). *Sex and Society in the World of the Orthodox Slavs, 900–1700.* Ithaca, NY: Cornell University Press.

Marrese, Michelle Lamarche. (2002). *A Woman's Kingdom. Noblewomen and the Control of Property in Russia, 1700–1861.* Ithaca, NY: Cornell University Press.

Mironov, Boris N., with Eklof, Ben. (2000). *The Social History of Imperial Russia, 1700-1917.* 2 vols. Boulder, CO: Westview Press.

Pouncy, Carolyn J., ed. and tr. (1994). *The "Domostroi": Rules for Russian Households in the Time of Ivan the Terrible.* Ithaca, NY: Cornell University Press.

Ransel, David L., ed. (1978). *The Family in Imperial Russia: New Lines of Historical Research.* Urbana: University of Illinois Press.

Ransel, David L. (2000). *Village Mothers: Three Generations of Change in Russia and Tataria.* Bloomington: Indiana University Press.

Schlesinger, Rudolf, comp. (1949). *Changing Attitudes in Soviet Russia: The Family in the USSR.* London: Routledge and Paul.

Wagner, William G. (1994). *Marriage, Property, and Law in Late Imperial Russia.* Oxford: Clarendon Press.

Worobec, Christine D. (1991). *Peasant Russia: Family and Community in the Post-Emancipation Period.* Princeton, NJ: Princeton University Press.

WILLIAM G. WAGNER

## MARTOV, YULI OSIPOVICH

(1873–1923), founder of Russian social democracy, later leader of the Menshevik party.

Born Yuli Osipovich Tsederbaum to a middle-class Jewish family in Constantinople, Yuli Martov established the St. Petersburg Union of Struggle for the Liberation of the Working Class with Lenin in 1895. The following year, Martov was sentenced to three years' exile in Siberia. After serving his term, he joined Lenin in Switzerland where they launched the revolutionary Marxist newspaper *Iskra.* Martov broke with Lenin at the Russian Social Democratic Party's Second Congress in Brussels in 1903, when he opposed his erstwhile comrade's bid for leadership of the party and his demand for a narrow, highly centralized party of professional revolutionaries, instead calling for a broad-based party with mass membership. Lenin labelled Martov's supporters the Menshevik (minority) faction; his own followers constituted the Bolsheviks (majority). While Lenin proclaimed that socialists should respond to a successful bourgeois revolution by taking immediate steps to prepare for their own takeover of government, Martov advocated abstention from power and a strategy of militant opposition rooted in democratic institutions such as workers' soviets, trades unions, cooperatives, or town and village councils. These "organs of revolutionary self-government" would impel the bourgeois government to implement political and economic reform, which would, in time, bring about conditions favorable to a successful, peaceful, proletarian revolution. After the outbreak of war, Martov was a founder of the Zimmerwald movement, which stood for internationalism and "peace without victory" against both the "defensism" of some socialist leaders and Lenin's ambition to transform the imperialist war into a revolutionary civil war. Martov returned to Russia in mid-May 1917. His internationalist position and advocacy of militant opposition to bourgeois government brought him into open conflict with Menshevik leaders such as Irakly Tsereteli, who proclaimed "revolutionary defensism" and had days earlier entered a coalition with the Provisional Government's liberal ministers. The collapse of the first coalition ministry in early July prompted Martov to declare that the time was now ripe for the formation of a democratic government of socialist forces. On repeated occasions in subsequent months, however, his new strategy was rejected both by coalitionist Mensheviks and by Bolsheviks intent on seizing power for themselves. After November 1917, Martov remained a courageous and outspoken opponent of Lenin's political leadership and increasingly despotic methods of rule. Although the Bolsheviks repudiated his efforts to secure a role for the socialist opposition, Martov supported the new regime in its struggle against counterrevolution and foreign intervention. Regardless of this, by 1920 the Menshevik party in Russia had been destroyed, and most of its leaders and activists were in prison or exile. In this year Martov finally left Russia and settled in Berlin. There he founded and edited the *Sotsialistichesky vestnik* (Socialist Courier), a widely influential social democratic newspaper committed to mobilizing international radical opinion against the Bolshevik dictatorship and halting the spread of Comintern influence among democratic left-wing movements.

Martov died on April 4, 1923. As his biographer has written, Martov's honesty, strong sense of principle, and deeply humane nature precluded his success as a revolutionary politician, but in opposition and exile he brilliantly personified social democracy's moral conscience (Getzler, 1994).

*See also:* BOLSHEVISM; LENIN, VLADIMIR ILICH; MENSHEVIKS

**BIBLIOGRAPHY**

Getzler, Israel. (1994). "Iulii Martov, the Leader Who Lost His Party in 1917." *Slavonic and East European Review* 72:424-439.

Getzler, Israel. (1967). *Martov: A Political Biography of a Russian Social Democrat.* Cambridge, UK: Cambridge University Press.

NICK BARON

# MARXISM

Karl Marx was born in Trier in Prussia in 1818, and he died in London in 1883. The general approach embodied in Marx's theoretical writings and his analysis of capitalism may be termed historical materialism, or the materialist interpretation of history. Indeed, that approach may well be considered the cornerstone of Marxism. Marx argued that the superstructure of society was conditioned decisively by the productive base of society, so that the superstructure must always be understood in relation to the base. The base consists of the mode of production, in which forces of production (land, raw materials, capital, and labor) are combined, and in which relations among people arise, determined by their relationship to the means of production. As Marx said in the preface to *A Contribution to the Critique of Political Economy* in 1859, "The sum total of these relations of production constitutes the economic structure of society, the real foundation, on which rises a legal and political superstructure and to which correspond definite forms of social consciousness. The mode of production of material life conditions the social, political, and intellectual life process in general." Marx considered the superstructure to include the family, the culture, the state, philosophy, and religion.

In Marx's view, all the elements of the superstructure served the interests of the dominant class in a society. He saw the class division in any society beyond a primitive level of development as reflecting the distinction between those who owned and controlled the means of production, on the one hand, and those who lacked a share of ownership and therefore were compelled to labor in the process of production, on the other hand. That fundamental division had been reproduced in various forms in the stages of European history, from ancient slaveholding society through feudalism to capitalism. In capitalist society (which was the main subject of Marx's writings) the crucial axis of social conflict was between the capitalist class, or bourgeoisie, and the industrial working class, or proletariat. Marx attempted to demonstrate that the antagonism between those classes would continue to intensify, until the workers' revolution would destroy capitalism and usher in communism.

The dialectical mode of interpretation found a new application in Marx's analysis of the development of the capitalist economy. Marx claimed to have detected three "laws of capitalist development": the constant accumulation of capital, the increasing concentration of capital, and the increasing misery of the proletariat. Those laws spelled the progressive polarization of society between an expanding number of impoverished and exploited workers and a decreasing number of wealthy capitalists. As the system became more technologically advanced and productive, the mass of the people in the system would become more destitute and more desperate. The common experience of exploitation would forge powerful solidarity within the ranks of the proletariat, who at the height of the final crisis of capitalism would rise in revolution and expropriate the property of the capitalist class.

Marx wrote far more about capitalism than about the society that would follow the proletarian revolution. He made it clear, however, that he expected the revolution of the working class to socialize the means of production and create a dictatorship of the proletariat. That dictatorship would be the workers' state, but its existence would be temporary, as society moved from the first, transitional phase of communism to the higher phase, in which the full potential of communism would be realized, so that class differences would have disappeared, the state would have died off, and each person would contribute to society according to personal ability and receive material benefits according to need.

Before the end of the nineteenth century Marx's theory and his revolutionary vision had been em-

braced by the leaders of socialist parties in a number of European countries. The spread of Marxism's influence was soon followed by schisms in international socialism, however. By the end of World War I, a fundamental split had taken place between Lenin's version of Marxism in the Soviet Union (which after Lenin's death became known as Marxism-Leninism) and the democratically oriented socialism of major Western socialist parties, which stemmed from the revisionism of Eduard Bernstein. The legacy of that division was a rivalry between socialist and communist parties, which was to hamper the left-wing forces in continental European countries for several decades. Ironically, though Marx's theory suggested that proletarian revolutions would triumph in the most economically advanced capitalist nations, during the twentieth century successful revolutions under the banner of Marxism and in the name of the proletariat were carried off only in countries with mainly agrarian economies, in which industrialization was in its early stages and the working class was relatively small.

*See also:* COMMUNISM; DIALECTICAL MATERIALISM; DICTATORSHIP OF THE PROLETARIAT; SOCIALISM

**BIBLIOGRAPHY**
Avineri, Shlomo. (1971). *Karl Marx: Social and Political Thought.* Cambridge, UK: Cambridge University Press.

Evans, Alfred B., Jr. (1993). *Soviet Marxism-Leninism: The Decline of an Ideology.* Westport, CT: Praeger.

Kolakowski, Leszek. (1978). *Main Currents of Marxism: Its Rise, Growth, and Dissolution.* 3 vols. Oxford, UK: Clarendon.

Leonhard, Wolfgang. (1974). *Three Faces of Marxism: The Political Concepts of Soviet Ideology, Maoism, and Humanist Marxism,* tr. Ewald Osers. New York: Holt, Rinehart and Winston.

ALFRED B. EVANS JR.

## MASLENITSA

Derived from the word *maslo,* or "butter/oil," Maslenitsa was a pagan mythological being personifying death, gloom, and winter as well as a week-long festival that divided winter and spring seasons. The pagan festival was synchronized with Lent and is equivalent to the western European Shrovetide and carnival. Maslenitsa survived among all Eastern Slavs, particularly Russians, who began celebrating it on a Sunday a week prior to Lent, the final day when meat was permitted in the diet according to Church practices. After the last meat meal, for the remainder of the week people consumed milk products and fish, but most commonly butter-covered *bliny*, or pancakes. The festival ended on the following Sunday, the day before Lent, and is known as the day of dispatching Maslenitsa or *Proshcheny Voskresenie* ("Forgiveness Sunday"), as people who had wronged others (alive or deceased) begged for absolution. This day was rounded off with the ritual destruction and burial of Maslenitsa, commonly represented in the form of a female effigy made of straw and dressed in woman's garb, in a bonfire, drowning in a river, or tearing apart. A wooden wheel, symbolizing the sun-disk, was also often burned alongside the effigy, leading to the idea that this festival was celebrated in connection with the spring equinox (usually on March 22) in pre-Christian times.

The annihilation of Maslenitsa symbolized the passing of the winter, spring renewal, and preparation for the new agrarian cycle as well as human and animal procreation. Family-marriage relations were tested among newlywed couples, who were publicly discussed, required to openly show affection, and put through trials testing their love and fidelity. Eligible singles who failed to wed the previous year were publicly ridiculed and punished. Virility of humans, plants, and animals were conjured up by performing magical rites, fist-fighting, dancing, loud singing, and sled-riding contests downhill or on troikas. The continued celebration of this pagan festival cloaked in a Christian holiday into modern times among the Eastern Slavs is a good example of dual faith (*dvoyeverie*) or syncretism.

*See also:* FOLKLORE; RUSSIANS

**BIBLIOGRAPHY**

Ivantis, Linda J. (1989). *Russian Folk Belief*. Armonk, NY: M. E. Sharpe.

ROMAN K. KOVALEV

## MATERIAL BALANCES

Material balance planning substituted for the market as the mechanism for allocating goods in the Soviet economy. Gosplan, the State Planning Committee, was responsible each year for equating supply and demand for the thousands of raw materials and manufactured goods that were used domestically in production processes, allocated to satisfy consumer needs, or earmarked for export. The three-stage process of constructing the annual plan involved identifying the sources and uses for high-priority (funded commodities), medium-priority (planned commodities), and low-priority (decentrally planned) goods, and then establishing a balance between sources and uses. In the first stage, planners sent "control figures" down through the economic hierarchy to the enterprise. Control figures reflected the priorities of top political officials, specified initially as aggregate output targets or percentage growth rates for strategic sectors of the economy, and then disaggregated and matched with projected input requirements by Gosplan. In the second stage, Soviet enterprises provided a detailed listing of the input requirements necessary to fulfill their output targets. In the third stage, planners constructed a material balance that ensured an equilibrium between the planned output target and the material input requirements for all goods involved in the planning process.

In a market economy, prices adjust to eliminate surpluses or shortages; in the Soviet economy, planners adjusted physical quantities to equate supply and demand for each product. A material balance was achieved when the sources of supply (current production, $Q_t$, inventories, $Q_{t-1}$, and imports $M_t$) equaled the sources of demand (interindustry demand, $ID_t$, household demand, $FD_t$, and exports, $X_t$). That is, a material balance existed on paper when, for each of the planned goods: $Q_t + Q_{t-1} + M_t = ID_t + FD_t + X_t$.

The mechanics of establishing a material balance in practice was impeded by several planning policies. First, planners set annual output targets high relative to the productive capacity of the firm. If tire manufacturers failed to meet monthly or quarterly production quotas, for example, this adversely affected downstream firms (producers of cars, trucks, tractors, or bicycles) that relied on tires to fulfill their output targets, and reduced the availability of tires to consumers for replacement purposes. Second, planners constructed a bonus system that allowed additional payments as high as 60 percent of the monthly wage if output targets were fulfilled. Knowing that output targets would be high, managers over-ordered requisite inputs and under-reported their productive capacity during the second stage of the plan-formulation process. Third, when shortages arose, planners refrained from adjusting centrally determined prices of these "deficit" commodities (*defitsitny*). Instead, they used a priority system to restrict the availability of deficit goods to low-priority sectors, typically those sectors most closely involving goods demanded by consumers.

See also: FULL ECONOMIC ACCOUNTING; GOSPLAN; TECH-PROMFINPLAN

**BIBLIOGRAPHY**

Bergson, Abram. (1964). *The Economics of Soviet Planning.* New Haven: Yale University Press.

Montias, John M. (1959). "Planning with Material Balances in Soviet-Type Economies." *American Economic Review* 49: 963–985.

SUSAN J. LINZ

# MATERIAL PRODUCT SYSTEM

For decades the Material Product System (MPS) was used in countries with centrally planned economies as a tool for analyzing economic processes at the macro level and policy making. Essentially, MPS performs the same functions as the System of National Accounts (SNA), but there are important difference between the two.

MPS divides the economy into two parts: material production, where national income (NMP) is created (industry, agriculture, construction, freight transportation, etc.), and the nonmaterial part of the economy. The concept of economic sectors and, hence, sectoral groupings, was entirely omitted in the MPS system. Such an approach toward estimation of macroeconomic indicators met the needs of planners and was instrumental in the process of centralized planning, centralized allocation of material resources, and tracking of plan fulfillment.

Essentially, MPS is a system of tables, of which the most important are the balance of production, consumption, and investment of the social product and national income; the balance of national wealth, the balance of fixed assets, and the balance of labor resources. A significant part of the MPS system was its series of input–output tables, which were compiled in the USSR beginning in 1959. In addition to the main MPS tables, there was a series of supplementary tables that gave a more detailed picture of certain aspects of the economic process.

The MPS as a system of aggregate macro indicators was an important tool for general assessment of the economic situation under the central planning system. Its drawback, however, was that it reflected economic processes in a somewhat inconsistent and partial manner. A large part of the economy, the so-called nonproductive sphere, was neglected in the balance of the national economy. In Soviet statistics, a methodologically sound and systematically integrated system of indicators was available only for the material production and distribution of material product. This significantly reduced the role of macro estimates as an instrument for analysis of economic developments.

Estimates of economic growth and international comparisons were also hindered by the lack of coordination between MPS indicators and financial flows. In the balance of state financial resources and the state budget, the financial resources of enterprises and organizations of both productive and nonproductive spheres are represented as a single entry. The balance of money income and expenditure of households shows the total money income of the population earned from both "productive" and "nonproductive" activities. The method used to derive this indicator is such that it is impossible to separate these two sources of revenue.

As a result, the macroeconomic indicators that reflect material resources are not balanced and comparable with the volume and the structure of financial resources. Also, export and import indicators in MPS are presented in a simplified way and differ from the similar indicators used in the balance of payments (SNA concept). Missing in the MPS approach are such indicators as disposable income, savings, and public debt.

The MPS system, which underwent some changes in the USSR in 1957, remained essentially the same for more than thirty years thereafter until the SNA system was introduced in the statistical practice of the countries in transition following the breakup of the Soviet Union.

See also: COMMAND ADMINISTRATIVE ECONOMY; ECONOMIC GROWTH, SOVIET

**BIBLIOGRAPHY**

Belkindas, Misha V., and Kostinsky, Barry L. (1990). "Official Soviet Gross National Product Accounting." In *Measuring Soviet GNP: Problems and Solutions, A Conference Report.* Washington, D.C.: Central Intelligence Agency, Directorate of Intelligence.

World Bank. (1992). *Statistical Handbook: States of the Former USSR (Studies of Economies in Transformation,* 3). Washington, DC: World Bank.

World Bank. (1993). *Historically Planned Economies, A Guide to the Data,* by Paul Marer, et al. Washington DC: World Bank.

MISHA V. BELKINDAS

## MATRYOSHKA DOLLS

The *matryoshka*, a set of four to eight hollow wooden dolls of graduated size nesting inside each other, is the most familiar item of Russian folk art today and possibly one of the most ancient. Legends abound of similar nesting dolls in Siberia, executed in precious metals, and the rounded female figure was a familiar fertility symbol in pagan Russia. Yet the matryoshka may well be of comparatively recent origin, its form derived from a Japanese prototype that caught the eye of the avant-garde artist Sergei Malyutin during the 1890s. Malyutin's patroness, Princess Tenisheva, was an active promoter of the folk art revival of this period; he sought out items with appeal for the Russian market that could be made at the crafts school on her estate, Talashkino. It was here that Malyutin designed the first known matryoshka.

The most ubiquitous matryoshka is the pink-cheeked peasant woman in native sarafan, her head covered with the traditional scarf. Variations soon appeared, however. Nests of dolls with the faces of famous writers, members of artistic circles, military heroes, or members of a family were created during the early twentieth century. A century later, though the original doll is still being produced, matryoshka painters have adapted to the modern market, creating nesting sets of Soviet political leaders, U.S. presidents, Russian tsars, literary figures, and famous Russian portraits. Modern matryoshkas by skilled artists, who often work in acrylic paint, command correspondingly high prices; though folk art in form, in execution they are works of high art.

**Colorfully painted nesting dolls are essential souvenirs from a trip to Russia.** PHOTOGRAPH BY SUSAN D. ROCK. REPRODUCED BY PERMISSION.

See also: FOLKLORE

**BIBLIOGRAPHY**

Hilton, Alison. (1995). *Russian Folk Art.* Bloomington: Indiana University Press.

PRISCILLA ROOSEVELT

## MATVEYEV, ARTAMON SERGEYEVICH

(1625–1682), military officer, diplomat, courtier, boyar.

The son of a non-noble bureaucrat, Artamon Matveyev began his career at the age of thirteen as a court page and companion to the future Tsar Alexei Mikhailovich. He soon became colonel of a musketeer regiment and traveled much of Russia and its borderlands on military and diplomatic missions. He helped negotiate the union of Ukraine with Russia in 1654, defended the tsar in the Copper Riots of 1662, and guarded many foreign embassies, including the clerics arriving to judge Patriarch Nikon in 1666 and 1667. By 1669, although still a musketeer colonel, he had become a *stolnik* (table attendant, a high court rank), *namestnik* (honorary governor-general) of Serpukhov, and head of the Ukrainian Chancellery (Malorossysky Prikaz).

Soon his fortunes rose even higher. After the death of Tsaritsa Maria Miloslavskaya, the tsar is said to have visited Matveyev's home and met the family's foster daughter Natalia Naryshkina, whom he married. This made Matveyev the tsar's de facto father-in-law, traditionally a very powerful position in Muscovite politics. He quickly added leadership of the Department of Foreign Affairs or Posolsky Prikaz (in effect becoming Russia's prime minister), several other diplomatic or regional departments, and the State Pharmacy to his Ukrainian Chancellery post. He skillfully formulated foreign policy and dealt with governments as diverse as England, Poland, the Vatican, Persia, China, and Bukhara. He also improved Russia's medical facilities, headed publishing, mining, and industrial ventures for the tsar, and organized the creation of a Western-style court theater.

Foreign visitors noted his diverse responsibilities. They often referred to him as "factotum," the man who does everything. They also remarked on his knowledge of and interest in their societies. A patron of education and the arts, he kept musicians

in his home, had his son taught Latin, and collected foreign books, clocks, paintings, and furniture. He remained close to the tsar, although he rose slowly through the higher ranks. At the birth of the future Peter the Great in 1672, he was made *okolnichy* (majordomo), and in 1674 he received the highest Muscovite court rank, boyar.

With the sudden death of Tsar Alexei in 1676, things changed. The succession of sickly fourteen-year-old Tsar Fyodor brought the Miloslavsky family back into power. Matveyev immediately began to lose posts, prominence, and respect. During his journey into "honorable exile"—provincial governorship in Siberia—he was convicted of sorcery. He was stripped of rank and possessions and exiled, first to the prison town of Pustozersk and later to Mezen. Tsar Fyodor's death and Peter's accession in 1682 brought Matveyev back to Moscow in triumph, but only days later he was killed when pro-Miloslavsky rioters surged through the capital.

Because of his decades of service, his prominence, fall, and dramatic death, and a collection of autobiographical letters from exile, Matveyev received frequent and generally favorable attention from Russian writers in the eighteenth and nineteenth centuries. Their works ranged from scholarly biographies and articles to poems, plays, and children's books. He became less visible in the twentieth century, when Soviet historians lost interest in supporters of the old regime. To date there has been only fragmentary treatment of his life in English.

See also: ALEXEI MIKHAILOVICH; BOYAR; COPPER RIOTS; NARYSHKINA, NATALIA KIRILLOVNA; NIKON, PATRIARCH; PETER I

**BIBLIOGRAPHY**

Bushkovitch, Paul. (2001). *Peter the Great: The Struggle for Power, 1671–1725.* Cambridge, UK: Cambridge University Press.

MARTHA LUBY LAHANA

## MAXIM THE GREEK, ST.

(c. 1475–1556), Greek monk canonized in the Orthodox Church.

A learned Greek monk, translator, and writer resident in Muscovy who was imprisoned by Muscovite authorities and never allowed to return home, Maxim had great moral and intellectual authority with contemporaries and posterity and was canonized in 1988. Born Michael Trivolis (Triboles) in the Greek city of Arta some twenty years after the Turkish capture of Constantinople, he went to Italy as a young man, where he was in contact with many prominent Renaissance figures. Under the influence of Savonarola he became a monk in the San Marco Dominican Monastery (1502), but two years later he returned to Greece, entering the Vatopedi monastery on Mount Athos under the monastic name of Maximos, rejecting Roman Catholicism and the humanist world of his youth, and concentrating upon the Eastern Orthodox theological tradition. In 1516 he was sent to Moscow to correct Russian ecclesiastical books. There he fell into disfavor with Grand Prince Vasily and Metropolitan Daniel, the head of the Russian Church, was twice convicted of treason and heresy (1525, 1531), and eventually died in Muscovy without being exonerated or regaining his freedom. During much of this time he translated biblical and Byzantine texts into Russian, and authored original compositions, including critical, historical, liturgical, philological, and exegetical works, demonstrations of his own orthodoxy and innocence, descriptions of the world (he was the first to mention Columbus's discovery of the New World), explication of the ideals and practice of monasticism, and a great deal else. He instructed Russian pupils in Greek, and inspired the study of lexicography and grammar.

Despite his official disgrace, Maxim's voluminous compositions were greatly revered and very influential in Old Russia; his biography and writings have been the subject of thousands of scholarly books and articles.

*See also:* DANIEL, METROPOLITAN; MUSCOVY; MONASTICISM; ORTHODOXY; POSSESSORS AND NON-POSSESSORS

**BIBLIOGRAPHY**

Haney, Jack V. (1973). *From Italy to Muscovy: The Life and Works of Maxim the Greek* Munich: W. Fink.

Obolensky, Dimitri. (1981). "Italy, Mount Athos, and Muscovy: the Three Worlds of Maximos the Greek (c. 1470–1556)." *Proceedings of the British Academy* 67:143–161.

Olmsted, Hugh M. (1987). "A Learned Greek Monk in Muscovite Exile: Maksim Grek and the Old Testament Prophets." *Modern Greek Studies Yearbook* 3:1–73.

Sevcenko, Ihor. (1997). "On the Greek Poetic Output of Maksim Grek [revised version]." *Byzantinoslavica* 78:1–70.

Taube, Moshe, and Olmsted, Hugh M. (1988). "Povest' o Esfiri: The Ostroh Bible and Maksim Grek's Translation of the Book of Esther." *Harvard Ukrainian Studies* 11(1/2):100–117.

HUGH M. OLMSTED

## MAYAKOVSKY, VLADIMIR VLADIMIROVICH

(1893–1930), poet, playwright.

Vladimir Mayakovsky was born in Bagdadi, Georgia (later renamed Mayakovsky in his honor). His father's death of tetanus in 1906 devastated the family emotionally and financially, and the themes of death, abandonment, and infection recurred in many of Mayakovsky's poems. As a student, Mayakovsky became an ardent revolutionary; he was arrested and served eleven months for his Bolshevik activities in 1909. In 1911 he was accepted into the Moscow Institute of Painting, Sculpture, and Architecture, where he met David Burlyuk, who was beginning to gather the Hylaean group of artists and poets: Nikolai and Vladimir Burlyuk, Alexandra Exter, Viktor (Velemir) Khlebnikov, Alexei Kruchenykh, and Benedikt Livshits. In 1912 the group issued its first manifesto, "A Slap in the Face of Public Taste," the highly charged rhetoric that created a scandalous sensation announcing the arrival of Futurism in the artistic culture of Russia. The poets and artists of Hylaea, Mayakovsky in particular, were associated in the popular press with social disruption, hooliganism, and anarchist politics.

Mayakovsky was an enthusiastic supporter of the Bolshevik revolution; much of his artistic effort was devoted to propaganda for the state. He wrote agitational poems and, combining his considerable artistic skill with his ability to write short, didactic poems, constructed large posters that hung in the windows of the Russian Telegraph Agency (ROSTA). He also wrote and staged at the Moscow State Circus a satirical play, *Mystery Bouffe*, which skewered bourgeois culture and the church. His most political poems, "150,000,000" (1919) and "Vladimir Ilich Lenin" (1924), became required reading for every Soviet schoolchild and helped create the image of Mayakovsky as a mythic hero of the Soviet Union, a position that Mayakovsky found increasingly untenable in the later 1920s. Mayakovsky remained a relentless foe of bureaucratism and authoritarianism in Soviet society; this earned him official resentment and led to restrictions on travel and other privileges. On April 14, 1930, the combined pressures of Soviet control and a series of disastrous love affairs, most notably with Lili Brik, led to Mayakovsky's suicide in his apartment in Moscow.

*See also:* BOLSHEVISM; CIRCUS; FUTURISM

**BIBLIOGRAPHY**

Brown, Edward J. (1973). *Mayakovsky: A Poet in the Revolution.* Princeton, NJ: Princeton University Press.

Jangfeldt, Bengt. (1976). *Majakovskij and Futurism, 1917–1921.* Stockholm: Almqvist & Wiksell.

Markov, Vladimir. (1969). *Russian Futurism: A History.* Berkeley: University of California Press.

Woroszylski, Wiktor. (1970). *The Life of Mayakovsky.* New York: Orion Press.

MARK KONECNY

## MAZEPA, HETMAN IVAN STEPANOVICH

(c. 1639–1709), Hetman (Cossack military leader) of Left-Bank Ukraine, 1687 to 1708.

Hetman Ivan Mazepa was raised in Poland and educated in the West, returning to Ukraine in 1663 to enter the service of the Polish-sponsored hetman Peter Doroshenko during the turbulent period of Ukrainian history known as the Ruin. In 1674 he transferred his allegiance to the Moscow-appointed hetman Ivan Samoilovich, whom he replaced when the latter fell from favor during Russia's campaign against the Crimean Tatars in 1687. He owed his promotion partly to the patronage of Prince Vasily Golitsyn.

In the 1680s to 1700s Mazepa remained loyal to Russia. In 1700 he became one of the first recipients of Peter I's new Order of St. Andrew. But he did not regard himself as permanently bound, as he governed in princely style and conducted a semi-independent foreign policy. In 1704, during the Great Northern War against Sweden, he occupied part of right-bank (Polish) Ukraine with Peter I's permission. However, Mazepa was under constant pressure at home to defend Cossack rights and to allay fears about Cossack regiments being reorganized on European lines. The final straw seems to have been Peter's failure to defend Ukraine against a possible attack by the Swedish-sponsored king of Poland, Stanislas Leszczynski. Mazepa

clearly believed that his obligations to the tsar were at an end: "We, having voluntarily acquiesced to the authority of his Tsarist Majesty for the sake of the unified Eastern Faith, now, being a free people, wish to withdraw, with expressions of our gratitude for the tsar's protection and not wishing to raise our hands in the shedding of Christian blood" (Subtelny).

At some point in 1707 or 1708, Mazepa made a secret agreement to help Charles XII of Sweden invade Russia and to establish a Swedish protectorate over Ukraine. In October 1708 he fled to Charles's side. Alexander Menshikov responded by storming and burning the hetman's headquarters at Baturin, a drastic action which deprived both Mazepa and the Swedes of men and supplies. Mazepa brought only 3,000 to 4,000 men to aid the Swedes, who were defeated at Poltava in July 1709. Mazepa fled with Charles to Turkey and died there.

Peter I regarded the defection of his "loyal subject" as a personal insult. Mazepa was "a new Judas," whom he (unjustly) accused of plans to hand over Orthodox monasteries and churches to the Catholics and Uniates. In his absence, Mazepa was excommunicated, and his effigy was stripped of the St. Andrew cross and hanged. He remains a controversial figure in Ukraine, while elsewhere he is best known from romanticized versions of his life in fiction and opera.

*See also:* COSSACKS; MENSHIKOV, ALEXANDER DANILOVICH; PETER I

**BIBLIOGRAPHY**

Babinsky, Hubert. (1974). *The Mazepa Legend in European Romanticism.* New York: Columbia University Press.

Mackiv, Theodore. (1983). *English Reports on Mazepa, 1687–1709.* New York: Ukrainian Historical Association.

Subtelny, Orest. (1978). "Mazepa, Peter I, and the Question of Treason." *Harvard Ukrainian Studies* 2:158–184.

LINDSEY HUGHES

## MEDVEDEV, ROY ALEXANDROVICH

(b. 1925), dissident historian.

Roy Medvedev is renowned as the author of the monumental dissident history of Stalinism, *Let*

*History Judge*, first published in English in 1972. The son of a prominent Soviet Marxist scholar who was murdered by Stalin in the 1930s, Medvedev pursued a teaching career before becoming a researcher in the Soviet Academy of Pedagogical Sciences. Nikita Khrushchev's denunciation of Josef V. Stalin at the Twentieth Party Congress (1956) spurred his interest in the Soviet past. Medvedev joined the Communist Party at this time. The further repudiation of Stalin at the Twenty-Second Congress (1961) impelled him to begin writing his anti-Stalinist tome, which was completed in 1968. Fearful that Stalin would be rehabilitated and repression renewed, Medvedev decided to publish it abroad. *Let History Judge* reflected the dissident thinking that emerged in the 1960s among intellectuals who, like Medvedev, sought a reformed, democratic socialism and a return to Leninism. Meanwhile, his opposition to any rehabilitation of Stalin led to his expulsion from the party. Medvedev was often subject to house arrest and KGB harassment under Leonid Brezhnev, but he managed to publish abroad numerous critical writings on Soviet history and politics. The liberalization under Mikhail Gorbachev allowed publication of a new edition of *Let History Judge* and Medvedev's return to the party and political life. The demise of the Soviet Union and the Communist Party allowed him to found a new socialist party and continue as a prolific, critical writer on Russian political life.

*See also:* DE-STALINIZATION; DISSIDENT MOVEMENT

**BIBLIOGRAPHY**

Medvedev, Roy. (1972). *Let History Judge: The Origins and Consequences of Stalinism*, ed. David Joravsky, tr. Colleen Taylor. London: Macmillan.

Medvedev, Roy. (1989). *Let History Judge: The Origins and Consequences of Stalinism*, rev. and expanded edition, ed. and tr. George Shriver. New York: Oxford University Press.

ROGER D. MARKWICK

## MEDVEDEV, SYLVESTER AGAFONIKOVICH

(1641–1691), author, poet, and polemicist.

Simeon Agafonikovich Medvedev (monastic name: Sylvester) began his career as a secretary (*podyachy*) in one of the Muscovite chancelleries. In that capacity, he participated in diplomatic missions, until in the early 1670s he became a monk. A student of Simeon Polotsky, he acted as his teacher's secretary and editor, and acquired connections in the court of Fyodor Alexeyevich (r. 1676–1682). After Polotsky's death, he assumed the mantle of his teacher as the court poet, first of Fyodor, and then of Sofia Alexeyevna (regent, 1682–1689). After 1678, he also worked as editor (*spravshchik*) in the Printing Office. During the 1680s, he was occupied with three main activities: working in the Printing Office, authoring polemics on the moment of transubstantiation (Eucharist conflict), and teaching in a school in the Zaikonospassky monastery. He repeatedly urged Sophia Alexeyevna to establish an Academy in Moscow, based on a plan (*privilegia*) that Polotsky may well have drawn up. When such an Academy was established in 1685 (the Slavonic-Greek-Latin Academy), it was the Greek Ioannikios and Sophronios Leichoudes, and not Medvedev, who were chosen to head it. This, together with the Eucharist conflict, created enormous animosity between Sylvester and the Greek teachers. Patriarch of Moscow Joakim (in office 1672–1690) gradually but systematically undermined Medvedev, a monk who refused to obey him in the Eucharist conflict. While Sofia was in power, Medvedev felt well protected. After Peter I's coup in August 1689, Medvedev fled Moscow. He was arrested, brought to the Trinity St. Sergius Monastery, tortured, and obliged to sign a confession renouncing his previous errors regarding the Eucharist in 1690. Joakim's victory was complete. After a year of detention, Sylvester was also accused as a collaborator in a conspiracy against Peter the Great, Joakim, and their supporters. He was condemned to death and beheaded in 1691. Author of several polemical works on the transubstantiation moment, he also composed orations, poetry, and panegyrics. To him are also attributed works on Russian bibliography and an account of the musketeer rebellion of 1682.

*See also:* FYODOR ALEXEYEVICH; JOAKIM, PATRIARCH; ORTHODOXY; SLAVO-GRECO-LATIN ACADEMY

**BIBLIOGRAPHY**

Hughes, Lindsey. (1990). *Sophia, Regent of Russia, 1657–1704*. New Haven, CT: Yale University Press.

NIKOLAOS A. CHRISSIDIS

## MEDVEDEV, ZHORES ALEXANDROVICH

(b. 1925), biochemist and author.

Zhores Alexandrovich Medvedev was born in Tbilisi, Georgia. He is the identical twin brother of historian Roy Alexandrovich Medvedev. Zhores Medvedev graduated from the Timiryazev Academy of Agricultural Sciences in 1950 and received a master's degree in biology from the Moscow Institute of Plant Physiology that same year. Between 1951 and 1962 he conducted research at the Timiryazev Academy and soon earned international acclaim for his work on protein biosynthesis and the physiology of the aging process.

In addition to his reputation as a biologist and a gerontologist, Medvedev is known for his criticism of the Lysenko regime in Soviet science. His book *The Rise and Fall of the Lysenko Regime* circulated in samizdat versions in the Soviet Union in the 1960s and was published in the West in 1969. Medvedev was forbidden to travel abroad and was kept under strict KGB surveillance. On May 29, 1970, Medvedev was arrested in his home and put into a mental hospital in the provincial town of Kaluga. He was kept there for two weeks while a psychiatric committee attempted to rationalize his confinement in medical terms.

On his first trip abroad, to London in 1973, Medvedev's Soviet citizenship was revoked, and he settled in London as an émigré. His Soviet citizenship was restored in 1990, and his numerous works have subsequently been published in Russia. Apart from numerous articles and papers on gerontology, genetics, and biochemistry, he has authored books on such important figures as Yuri Andropov and Mikhail Gorbachev and written on Soviet nuclear disasters and Soviet science in general.

*See also:* LYSENKO, TROFIM DENISOVICH; MEDVEDEV, ROY ALEXANDER

**BIBLIOGRAPHY**

Medvedev, Zhores A., and Medvedev, Roy A. (1971). *A Question of Madness.* New York: Knopf.

RÓSA MAGNÚSDÓTTIR

# MELNIKOV, KONSTANTIN STEPANOVICH

(1908–1974), a leading theoretician among modernist architects.

Konstantin Stepanovich Melnikov rose to fame in the West as a result of his design for the Soviet Pavilion at the Paris Exhibition of Decorative Arts in 1925, a building marked by its dramatic formal simplicity and avoidance of decorative rhetoric, bold use of color, windowed front facade, and unusual exterior staircase that cut diagonally across the rectangular two-storied building. But his most impressive work in the Soviet Union was his club architecture, none more striking than the Rusakov Club, designed and built between 1927 and 1929 for the Union of Municipal Workers.

A graduate of the prestigious Moscow school of Painting, Sculpture, and Architecture, Melnikov in 1920 joined the Soviet parallel to the Bauhaus, the Higher State Artistic and Technical Studios (VKhUTEMAS), where the struggle for control over the direction of revolutionary architecture was fought until discussion was terminated by a new Stalinist orthodoxy. Melnikov refused to join either of the two competing architectural organizations, but remained closely associated with the Association of New Architects (ASNOVA), especially in his quest for a new "architectural language" for the age. Despite this association, his work influenced architects in both camps. Melnikov concerned himself with the functional demands of a building and with the rational organization of the composition. But he was most concerned with devising a unique expressive appearance that would unite spatial organization with innovative interior design, employing such forms that would make the buildings appear "as individualists against the general backdrop of urban building." Melnikov's architectural language consisted of elementary geometric forms such as cylinders, cones, and parallelepipeds. It is the cylinder that forms the basis for Melnikov's own home, built between 1927 and 1929 on Krivoarbatsky Lane off Moscow's famed Arbat.

In 1937 Melnikov was accused of practicing the grotesquerie of formalism and of obstructing and perverting the resolution of the problem of the type and form of Soviet architecture. He was driven from architectural practice.

*See also:* ARCHITECTURE

**BIBLIOGRAPHY**

Khan-Magomedov, Selim Omarovich. (1987). *Pioneers of Soviet Architecture: The Search for New Solutions in the 1920s and 1930s.* New York: Rizzoli.

Starr, S. Frederick. (1978). *Melnikov: Solo Architect in a Mass Society.* Princeton, NJ: Princeton University Press.

HUGH D. HUDSON JR.

## MEMORIAL

Memorial, a self-described "international, historical-educational, human rights, and charitable society," was founded in Moscow in 1988. Its original inspiration lay in the work of scattered professional and amateur historians who had quietly and often covertly done independent research on Soviet history, realizing that their works might never see the light of day, at least in their lifetimes. In some cases they had given their work to the young Leningrad historian Arseny Roginsky, who from 1976 to 1981 included them in his anonymously produced *samizdat* (typewritten, self-published) journal *Pamyat*, or *Memory*. He then smuggled the journal abroad, where successive issues were published in Russian as separate volumes.

Memorial emerged in 1987, when individuals started to collect money to erect a monument to the victims of Josef Stalin's "great terror." This goal was achieved when a short tribute to these victims was carved on a boulder from a concentration camp near the Arctic Circle, and, on October 30, 1990, the boulder was installed in a square facing the Moscow headquarters of the KGB. In the meantime, Memorial had chosen the former dissident leader Andrei Sakharov as its honorary chairman and established groups in dozens of towns all over the USSR. However, official resistance to the new organization remained tenacious. Only in 1991 did the authorities give it the legal registration that it needed.

Memorial's mandate for historical research concerns all varieties of official persecution and discrimination conducted against individuals and groups during the Soviet era. Its researchers have sought access to governmental archives, rummaged through the buildings of abandoned concentration camps, and searched for the many unmarked and overgrown burial grounds that hold the remains of millions of prisoners who died in captivity. They have also solicited documents, letters, and oral history from surviving victims and witnesses. Apart from building up Memorial archives in Moscow and elsewhere, the researchers have had their work published by Memorial in Russian and other languages in hundreds of journals, newspapers, and books.

Memorial also researches current violations of human rights in Russia and other former Soviet republics, especially when these occur on a large scale. Examples are atrocities committed during the two Chechnya wars, and continuing official discrimination against the Meskhi Turks, who were deported from southern Georgia in 1944.

Memorial's charitable work consists of helping victims of oppression and their relatives (e.g., materially and with legal problems).

Memorial's activities have been directed from Moscow by a stable core of individuals, including Roginsky, Nikita Okhotin, and Alexander Daniel. Its funding has primarily come from bodies such as the Ford Foundation, the Soros Foundation, and the Heinrich Boll Stiftung in Germany, and a few domestic sources.

Since the early 1990s most of public opinion in Russia has become indifferent or even hostile to the work of Memorial. However, its members derive hope from pockets of societal support and the launching in 1999 of an annual competition for essays on Memorial-type themes by high-school children that attracted 1,651 entries during its first year. Some members recall that, after the fall of Adolf Hitler in Germany, three decades went by before German society began seriously to confront the Nazi era and to create a more reliable national memory. A similar or longer period may be needed in the former USSR, before Russian society, in particular, can face up to myriad grim truths about the seven decades of communism. In the interim, Memorial has unearthed small pieces of truth about hundreds of deportations and millions of deaths.

*See also:* CHECHNYA AND CHECHENS; HUMAN RIGHTS; SAKHAROV, ANDREI

### BIBLIOGRAPHY
Adler, Nanci. (1993). *Victims of Soviet Terror: The Story of the Memorial Movement.* Westport, CT: Praeger.

PETER REDDAWAY

## MENDELEYEV, DMITRY IVANOVICH

(1834–1907), chemist; creator of the periodic table of elements.

Dmitry Mendeleyev was born in Tobolsk, Siberia, where his father was the director of the local gymnasium. In 1853 he enrolled in the Main Pedagogical Institute in St. Petersburg, which trained secondary school teachers. His early interest in chemistry focused on isomorphism—the groups of chemical elements with similar crystalline forms and chemical properties. In 1856 he earned a magisterial degree from St. Petersburg University and was appointed a private docent at the same institution. In 1859 a state stipend took him to the University of Heidelberg for advanced studies in chemistry. In 1861 he returned to St. Petersburg University and wrote *Organic Chemistry*, the first volume of its kind to be published in Russian. He offered courses in analytical, technical, and organic chemistry. In 1865 he defended his doctoral dissertation and was appointed professor of chemistry, a position he held until his retirement in 1890.

In 1868, with solid experience in chemical research , he undertook the writing of *The Principles of Chemistry*, a large study offering a synthesis of contemporary advances in general chemistry. It was during the writing of this book that he discovered the periodic law of elements, one of the greatest achievements of nineteenth-century chemistry. In quality this study surpassed all existing studies of its kind. It was translated into English, French, and German. In 1888 the English journal *Nature* recognized it as "one of the classics of chemistry" whose place "in the history of science is as well-assured as the ever-memorable work of [English chemist John] Dalton."

An international gathering of chemists in Karlsruhe in 1860 had agreed in establishing atomic weights as the essential features of chemical elements. Several leading chemists immediately began work on establishing a full sequence of the sixty-four elements known at the time. Mendeleyev took an additional step: he presented what he labeled the periodic table of elements, in which horizontal lines presented elements in sequences of ascending atomic weights, and vertical lines brought together elements with similar chemical properties. He showed that in addition to the emphasis on the diversity of elements, the time had also come to recognize the patterns of unity.

Beginning in the 1870s, Mendeleyev wrote on a wide variety of themes reaching far beyond chemistry. He was most concerned with the organizational aspects of Russian industry, the critical problems of agriculture, and the dynamics of education. He tackled demographic questions, development of the petroleum industry, exploration of the Arctic Sea, the agricultural value of artificial fertilizers, and the development of a merchant navy in Russia. In chemistry, he elaborated on specific aspects of the periodic law of elements, and wrote a large study on chemical solutions in which he advanced a hydrate theory, critical of Svante Arrhenius's and Jacobus Hendricus van't Hoff's electrolytic dissociation theory. At the end of his life, he was engaged in advancing an integrated view of the chemical unity of nature. Mendeleyev saw the future of Russia in science and in a philosophy avoiding the rigidities of both idealism and materialism.

### BIBLIOGRAPHY

Mendeleev, Dmitry. (1901). *The Principles of Chemistry*, 4 vols. New York: Collier.

Rutherford, Ernest. (1934). "The Periodic Law and its Interpretation: Mendeleev Centenary Lecture," *Journal of the Chemical Society* 1934(1):635–642.

Vucinich, Alexander. (1967). "Mendeleev's Views on Science and Society." *ISIS* 58:342–351.

ALEXANDER VUCINICH

## MENSHEVIKS

The Menshevik Party was a moderate Marxist group within the Russian revolutionary movement. The Mensheviks originated as a faction of the Russian Social Democratic Workers Party (RSDWP). In 1903, at the Second Party Congress, Yuli O. Martov proposed a less restrictive definition of party membership than Vladimir I. Lenin. Based on the voting at the congress, Lenin's faction of the party subsequently took the name Bolshevik, or "majority," and Martov's faction assumed the name Menshevik, or "minority." The party was funded by dues and donations. Its strength can be measured by proportionate representation at party meetings, but membership figures are largely speculative because the party was illegal during most of its existence.

Russian revolutionaries had embraced Marxism in the 1880s, and the Mensheviks retained Georgy Plekhanov's belief that Russia would first experience a bourgeois revolution to establish capitalism before advancing to socialism, as Karl Marx's model implied. They opposed any premature advance to socialism. A leading Menshevik theorist, Pavel Borisovich Akselrod, stressed the necessity of establishing a mass party of workers in order to assure the triumph of social democracy.

During the 1905 Revolution, which established civil liberties in Russia, Akselrod called for a "workers' congress," and many Mensheviks argued for cooperation with liberals to end the autocracy. Their Leninist rivals vested the hope for revolution in a collaboration of peasants and workers. Despite these differences, Bolsheviks and Mensheviks participated in a Unification Congress at Stockholm in 1906. The Menshevik delegates voted to participate in elections to Russia's new legislature, the Duma. Lenin initially opposed cooperation but later changed his mind. Before cooperation could be fully established, the Fifth Party Congress in London (May 1907) presented a Bolshevik majority. Akselrod's call for a workers' congress was condemned. Soon afterward the tsarist government ended civil liberties, repressed the revolutionary parties, and dissolved the Duma.

From 1907 to1914 the two factions continued to grow apart. Arguing that the illegal underground party had ceased to exist, Alexander Potresov called for open legal work in mass organizations rather than a return to illegal activity. Fedor Dan supported a combination of legal and illegal work. Lenin and the Bolsheviks labeled the Mensheviks "liquidationists." In 1912 rival congresses produced a permanent split between the two factions.

During World War I many Mensheviks were active in war industries committees and other organizations that directly affected the workers' movement. Menshevik internationalists, such as Martov, refused to cooperate with the tsarist war effort. The economic and political failure of the Russian government coupled with continued action by revolutionary parties led to the overthrow of the tsar in February (March) 1917. The Mensheviks and another revolutionary party, the Socialist Revolutionaries, had a majority in the workers' movement and ensured the establishment of democratic institutions in the early months of the revolution. Since the Mensheviks opposed an immediate advance to socialism, the party supported the concept of dual power, which established the Provisional Government and the Petrograd Soviet. In response to a political crisis that threatened the collapse of the Provisional Government, Mensheviks who wanted to defend the revolution, labeled defensists, decided to join a coalition government in April 1917. Another crisis in July did not persuade the Menshevik internationalists to join. Thereafter, the Mensheviks were divided on the Revolution. The Provisional Government failed to fulfill the hopes of peasants, workers, and soldiers.

Because the Mensheviks had joined the Provisional Government and the Bolsheviks were not identified with its failure, the seizure of power by the Soviets in November brought the Bolshevik Party to power. Martov's attempts to negotiate the formation of an all-socialist coalition failed. Mensheviks opposed the Bolshevik seizure of power, the dissolution of the Constituent Assembly, and the Treaty of Brest-Litovsk signed by the Bolsheviks, who now called themselves the Communist Party. Marginally legal, the Mensheviks opposed Allied efforts to crush the Soviet state during the civil war and, though repressed by the communists, also feared that counterrevolutionary forces might gain control of the government. Mensheviks established a republic in Georgia from1918 to 1921. At the end of the civil war, some workers adopted Menshevik criticisms of Soviet policy, leading to mass arrests of party leaders. In 1922 ten leaders were allowed to emigrate. Others joined the Communist Party and were active in economic planning and industrial development. Though Mensheviks operated illegally in the 1930s, a trial of Mensheviks in 1931 signaled the end of the possibility of even marginal opposition inside Russia. A Menshevik party abroad operated in Berlin, publishing the journal *Sotsialistichesky Vestnik* under the leadership of Martov. Dan emerged as the leader of this group after Martov's death in 1923. To escape the Nazis the Mensheviks migrated to Paris and then to the United States in 1940, where they continued publication of their journal until 1965.

*See also:* BOLSHEVISM; CONSTITUENT ASSEMBLY; MARTOV, YURI OSIPOVICH; MARXISM; PROVISIONAL GOVERNMENT; SOCIAL DEMOCRATIC PARTY; SOVIET MARXISM

## BIBLIOGRAPHY

Ascher, Abraham, ed. (1976). *The Mensheviks in the Russian Revolution.* Ithaca, NY: Cornell University Press.

Brovkin, Vladimir. (1987). *The Mensheviks After October: Socialist Opposition and the Rise of the Bolshevik Dictatorship.* Ithaca, NY: Cornell University Press.

Galili, Ziva. (1989). *Menshevik Leaders in the Russian Revolution: Social Realities and Political Strategies.* Princeton, NJ: Princeton University Press.

Haimson, Leopold. ed. (1974). *Mensheviks: From the Revolution of 1917 to the Second World War.* Chicago: University of Chicago Press.

ALICE K. PATE

## MENSHIKOV, ALEXANDER DANILOVICH

(c. 1672–1729), soldier and statesman; favorite of Peter I.

Menshikov rose from humble origins to become the most powerful man in Russia after the tsar. Anecdotes suggest that his father was a pastry cook, although in fact he served as a noncommissioned officer in the Semenovsky guards. Alexander served in Peter's own Preobrazhensky guards, and by the time of the Azov campaigns (1695–1696) he and Peter were inseparable. Menshikov accompanied Peter on the Grand Embassy (1697–1698) and served with him in the Great Northern War (1700–1721), rising through the ranks to become general field marshal and vice admiral. His military exploits included the battles of Kalisz (1706) and Poltava (1709), the sacking of Baturin (1708), and campaigns in north Germany in the 1710s. At home he was governor-general of St. Petersburg and president of the College of War.

The upstart Menshikov had to create his own networks, making many enemies among the traditional elite. He acquired a genealogy which traced his ancestry back to the princes of Kievan Rus and a dazzling portfolio of Russian and foreign titles and orders, including Prince of the Holy Roman Empire, Prince of Russia and Izhora, and Knight of the Orders of St. Andrew and St. Alexander Nevsky. Menshikov had no formal education and was only semi-literate, but this did not prevent him from becoming a role model in Peter's cultural reforms. His St. Petersburg palace had a large library and its own resident orchestra and singers, and he also built a grand palace at Oranienbaum on the Gulf of Finland. In 1706 he married Daria Arsenieva (1682–1727), who was also thoroughly Westernized.

Menshikov was versatile and energetic, loyal but capable of acting on his own initiative. He was a devout Orthodox Christian who often visited shrines and monasteries. He was also ambitious and corrupt, amassing a vast personal fortune in lands, serfs, factories, and possessions. On several occasions, only his close ties with Peter saved him from being convicted of embezzlement. In 1725 he promoted Peter's wife Catherine as Peter's successor, heading her government in the newly created Supreme Privy Council and betrothing his own daughter to Tsarevich Peter, her nominated heir. After Peter's accession in 1727, Menshikov's rivals in the Council, among them members of the aristocratic Dolgoruky clan, alienated the emperor

from Menshikov. In September 1727 they had Menshikov arrested and banished to Berezov in Siberia, where he died in wretched circumstances in November 1729.

*See also:* CATHERINE I; GREAT NORTHERN WAR; PETER I; PETER II; PREOBRAZHENSKY GUARDS

**BIBLIOGRAPHY**

Bushkovitch, Paul. (2001). *Peter the Great: The Struggle for Power, 1671–1725.* Cambridge, UK: Cambridge University Press.

Hughes, Lindsey. (1998). *Russia in the Age of Peter the Great.* New Haven, CT: Yale University Press.

LINDSEY HUGHES

## MERCANTILISM

Mercantilism is the doctrine that economic activity, especially foreign trade, should be directed to unifying and strengthening state power. Though some mercantilist writers emphasized the accumulation of gold and silver by artificial trade surpluses, this "bullionist" version was not dominant in Russia.

The greatest of the Russian enlightened despots, Peter the Great, was eager to borrow the best of Western practice in order to modernize his vast country and to expand its power north and south. Toward this end, the tsar emulated successful Swedish reforms by establishing a regular bureaucracy and unifying measures. Peter brought in Western artisans to help design his new capital at St. Petersburg. He granted monopolies for fiscal purposes on salt, vodka, and metals, while developing workshops for luxury products. Skeptical of private entrepreneurs, he set up state-owned shipyards, arsenals, foundries, mines, and factories. Serfs were assigned to some of these. Like the state-sponsored enterprises of Prussia, however, most of these failed within a few decades.

Tsar Peter instituted many new taxes, raising revenues some five times, not counting the servile labor impressed to build the northern capital, canals, and roads. Like Henry VIII of England, he confiscated church lands and treasure for secular purposes. He also tried to unify internal tolls, something accomplished only in 1753.

Foreign trade was a small, and rather late, concern of Peter's. That function remained mostly in the hands of foreigners. To protect the industries in his domains, he forbade the import of woolen textiles and needles. In addition, he forbade the export of gold and insisted that increased import duties be paid in specie (coin).

*See also:* ECONOMY, TSARIST; FOREIGN TRADE; PETER I

**BIBLIOGRAPHY**
Gerschenkron, Alexander. (1970). *Europe in the Russian Mirror.* London: Cambridge University Press.

Spechler, Martin C. (2001). "Nationalism and Economic History." In *Encyclopedia of Nationalism*, vol. 1, ed. Alexander Motyl. New York: Academic Press, pp. 219-235.

Spechler, Martin C. (1990). *Perspectives in Economic Thought.* New York: McGraw-Hill.

MARTIN C. SPECHLER

# MERCHANTS

Kievan Russia supplied raw materials of the forest—furs, honey, wax, and slaves—to the Byzantine Empire. This trade had a primarily military character, as the grand prince and his retinue extorted forest products from Russian and Finnish tribes and transported them through hostile territory via the Dnieper River and the Black Sea. In the self-governing republic of Novgorod, wealthy merchants shared power with the landowning elite. Novgorod exported impressive amounts of furs, fish, and other raw materials with the aid of the German Hansa, which maintained a permanent settlement in Novgorod—the Peterhof—as it did on Wisby Island and in London and Bergen.

Grand Prince Ivan III of Muscovy extinguished Novgorod's autonomy and expelled the Germans. Under the Muscovite autocracy, prominent merchants acted as the tsar's agents in exploiting his monopoly rights over commerce in high-value goods such as vodka and salt. The merchant estate (*soslovie*) emerged as a separate social stratum in the Law Code (*Ulozhenie*) of 1649, with the exclusive right to engage in handicrafts and commerce in cities.

Peter I's campaign to build an industrial complex to supply his army and navy opened up new opportunities for Russian merchants, but his government maintained the merchants' traditional obligations to provide fiscal and administrative services to the state without remuneration. From the early eighteenth century to the end of the imperial period, the merchant estate included not only wholesale and retail traders but also persons whose membership in a merchant guild entitled them to perform other economic functions as well, such as mining, manufacturing, shipping, and banking.

Various liabilities imposed by the state, including a ban on serf ownership by merchants and the abolition of their previous monopoly over trade and industry, kept the merchant estate small and weak during the eighteenth and nineteenth centuries. Elements of a genuine bourgeoisie did not emerge until the early twentieth century.

Ethnic diversity contributed to the lack of unity within the merchant estate. Each major city saw the emergence of a distinctive merchant culture, whether mostly European (German and English) in St. Petersburg; German in the Baltic seaports of Riga and Reval; Polish and Jewish in Warsaw and Kiev; Italian, Greek, and Jewish in Odessa; or Armenian in the Caucasus region, to name a few examples. Moreover, importers in port cities generally favored free trade, while manufacturers in the Central Industrial Region, around Moscow, demanded high import tariffs to protect their factories from European competition. These economic conflicts reinforced hostilities based on ethnic differences. The Moscow merchant elite remained xenophobic and antiliberal until the Revolution of 1905.

The many negative stereotypes of merchants in Russian literature reflected the contemptuous attitudes of the gentry, bureaucracy, intelligentsia, and peasantry toward commercial and industrial activity. The weakness of the Russian middle class constituted an important element in the collapse of the liberal movement and the victory of the Bolshevik party in the Russian Revolution of 1917.

*See also:* CAPITALISM; ECONOMY, TSARIST; FOREIGN TRADE; GUILDS

**BIBLIOGRAPHY**
Freeze, Gregory L. (1986). "The *Soslovie* (Estate) Paradigm and Russian Social History." *American Historical Review* 91:11–36.

Owen, Thomas C. (1981). *Capitalism and Politics in Russia: A Social History of the Moscow Merchants, 1855-1905.* New York: Cambridge University Press.

Owen, Thomas C. (1991). "Impediments to a Bourgeois Consciousness in Russia, 1880–1905: The Estate Structure, Ethnic Diversity, and Economic Regionalism." In *Between Tsar and People: Educated Society and the Quest for Public Identity in Late Imperial Russia*, ed. Edith W. Clowes, Samuel D. Kassow, and James L. West. Princeton, NJ: Princeton University Press.

Rieber, Alfred J. (1982). *Merchants and Entrepreneurs in Imperial Russia*. Chapel Hill: University of North Carolina Press.

THOMAS C. OWEN

# MESKHETIAN TURKS

The Meskhetian Turks are a Muslim people who originally inhabited what is today southwestern Georgia. They speak a Turkic language very similar to Turkish. Deported from their homeland by Josef V. Stalin in 1944, the Meskhetian Turks are scattered in many parts of the former Soviet Union. Estimates of their number range as high as 250,000. Their attempts to return to their homeland in Georgia have been mostly unsuccessful.

While other groups deported from the Caucasus region at roughly the same time were accused of collaborating with the Nazis, Meskhetian Turk survivors report that different reasons were given for their deportation. Some say they were accused of collaborating, others say they were told that the deportation was for their own safety, and still others were given no reason whatsoever. The deportation itself was brutal, with numerous fatalities resulting from both the long journey on crammed railroad cars and the primitive conditions in Central Asia where they were forced to live. Estimates of the number of deaths range from thirty to fifty thousand.

In the late 1950s Premier Nikita Khrushchev allowed the Meskhetian Turks and other deported peoples to leave their camps in Central Asia. Unlike most of the other deported peoples, however, the Meskhetian Turks were not allowed to return to their ancestral homeland. The Georgian SSR was considered a sensitive border region and as such was off limits. The Meskhetian Turks began to disperse throughout the Soviet Union, with many ending up in the Kazakh, Uzbek, and Kyrgyz SSRs and others in Soviet Azerbaijan and southern European Russia. They were further dispersed in 1989 when several thousand Meskhetian Turks fled deadly ethnic riots directed at them in Uzbekistan.

Since the collapse of the Soviet Union, the Meskhetian Turks have tried to return to their ancestral homeland in newly independent Georgia, but they face strong opposition. Georgia already has a severe refugee crisis, with hundreds of thousands of people displaced by conflicts in Abkhazia and South Ossetia. In addition, the substantial Armenian population of the Meskhetian Turks' traditional homeland does not want them back. The Georgians view the Meskhetian Turks as ethnic Georgians who adopted a Turkic language and the Muslim religion. They insist that any Meskhetian Turks who wish to return must officially declare themselves Georgian, adding Georgian suffixes to their names and educating their children in the Georgian language.

The Meskhetian Turks are scattered across the former Soviet Union, with the largest populations in Azerbaijan, Kazakhstan, and Russia. In southern European Russia's Krasnodar Krai, the local population of Meskhetian Turks, most of whom fled the riots in Uzbekistan, have received particularly rough treatment. The Meskhetian Turks of this region are denied citizenship and, according to Russian and international human rights organizations, frequently suffer bureaucratic hassles and physical assaults from local officials intent on driving them away. In 1999, as a condition of membership in the Council of Europe, the Georgian government announced that it would allow for the return of the Meskhetian Turks within twelve years, but despite international pressure it has taken little concrete action in this direction.

*See also:* DEPORTATIONS; GEORGIA AND GEORGIANS; IS-LAM; NATIONALITIES POLICIES, SOVIET; NATIONALI-TIES POLICIES, TSARIST

**BIBLIOGRAPHY**

Blandy, Charles. (1998). *The Meskhetians: Turks or Georgians? A People Without a Homeland*. Camberley, Surrey, UK: Conflict Studies Research Centre, Royal Military Academy.

Open Society Institute. (1998). "Meskhetian Turks: Solutions and Human Security." <http://www.soros.org/fmp2/html/meskpreface.html/>.

Sheehy, Ann, and Nahaylo, Bohdan. (1980). *The Crimean Tatars, Volga Germans and Meskhetians: Soviet Treatment of Some National Minorities*. London: Minority Rights Group.

JUSTIN ODUM

## MESTNICHESTVO

The practice of appointing men from eminent families to high positions in the military or government according to social status and service record.

*Mestnichestvo* or "precedence" refers to a legal practice in Muscovy whereby a military officer sued to avoid serving in a rank, or "place" (*mesto*), below a man whose family he regarded as inferior. The practice was open only to men in the most eminent families and arose in the second quarter of the sixteenth century as a result of rapid social change in the elite. Eminent princely families joining the grand prince's service from the Grand Duchy of Lithuania, the Khanate of Kazan, and Rus principalities challenged the status of the established Muscovite boyar clans. Thus mestnichestvo arose in the process of the definition of a more complex elite and was inextricably connected with the compilation of genealogical and military service records (*rodoslovnye* and *razryadnye knigi*).

Relative place was reckoned on the basis of family heritage and the eminence of one's own and one's ancestors' military service. A complicated formula also assigned ranks to members of large clans so that individuals could be compared across clans. Litigants presented their own clan genealogies and service precedents in comparison with those of their rival and their rival's kinsmen, often using records that differed from official ones. Judges were then called upon to adjudicate cases of immense complexity.

In practice few precedence disputes came to such detailed exposition in court because the state acted in two ways to waylay them. From the late sixteenth century the tsar regularly declared service assignments in a particular campaign "without place," that is, not counting against a person's or his clan's dignity. Secondly, the tsar, or judges acting in his name, peremptorily resolved suits on the spot. Some were dismissed on the basis of evident disparity of clans ("your family has always served below that family"), while other plaintiffs were reassigned or their assignments declared without place. Tsars themselves took an active role in these disputes. Sources cite tsars Ivan IV, Mikhail Fyodorovich, and Alexei Mikhailovich, among others, castigating their men for frivolous suits. Significantly, only a tiny number of mestnichestvo suits were won by plaintiffs. Most resolved cases affirmed the hierarchy established in the initial assignment.

Some scholars have argued that precedence allowed the Muscovite elite to protect its status against the tsars, while others suggest that it benefited the state by keeping the elite preoccupied with petty squabbling. Source evidence, however, suggests that precedence rarely impinged on military preparedness or tsarist authority. If anything, the regularity with which status hierarchy among clans was reaffirmed suggests that precedence exerted a stabilizing affirmation of the status quo.

In the seventeenth century the bases on which precedence functioned were eroded. The elite had expanded immensely to include new families of lesser heritage, lowly families were litigating for place, and many service opportunities were available outside of the system of place. Mestnichestvo as a system of litigation was abolished in 1682, while at the same time the principle of hereditary elite status was affirmed by the creation of new genealogical books for the new elite.

*See also:* LEGAL SYSTEMS; MILITARY, IMPERIAL ERA

### BIBLIOGRAPHY

Kollmann, Nancy Shields. (1999). *By Honor Bound: State and Society in Early Modern Russia*. Ithaca, NY: Cornell University Press.

NANCY SHIELDS KOLLMANN

## METROPOLITAN

A metropolitan is the chief prelate in an ecclesiastical territory that usually coincided with a civil province.

The metropolitan ranks just below a patriarch and just above an archbishop, except in the contemporary Greek Orthodox Church, where since the 1850s the archbishop ranks above the metropolitan. The term derives from the Greek word for the capital of a province where the head of the episcopate resides. The first evidence of its use to designate a Churchman's rank was in the Council of Nicaea (325 C.E.) decision, which declared (canon 4; cf. canon 6) the right of the metropolitan to confirm episcopal appointments within his jurisdiction.

A metropolitan was first appointed to head the Rus Church in 992. Subsequent metropolitans of Kiev and All Rus resided in Kiev until 1299 when

Metropolitan Maxim (1283–1305) moved his residence to Vladimir-on-the-Klyazma. His successor, Peter (1308–1326), began residing unofficially in Moscow. The next metropolitan, Feognost (1328–1353), made the move to Moscow official. A rival metropolitan was proposed by the grand duke of Lithuania, Olgerd, in 1354, and from then until the 1680s there was a metropolitan residing in western Rus with a rival claim to heading the metropoly of Kiev and all Rus.

Until 1441, the metropolitans of Rus were appointed in Constantinople. From 1448 until 1589, the grand prince or tsar appointed the metropolitan of Moscow and all Rus following nomination by the council of bishops. When the metropolitan of Moscow and all Rus was raised to the status of patriarch in 1589, the existing archbishops—those of Novgorod, Rostov, Kazan, and Sarai—were elevated to metropolitans. The Council of 1667 elevated four other archbishops—those of Astrakhan, Ryazan, Tobolsk, and Belgorod—to metropolitan status. After the abolition of the patriarchate in 1721 by Peter I, no metropolitans were appointed until the reign of Elizabeth, when metropolitans were appointed for Kiev (1747) and Moscow (1757). Under Catherine II, a third metropolitan—for St. Petersburg—was appointed (1783). In 1917, the patriarchate of Moscow was reestablished and various new metropolitanates created so that by the 1980s there were twelve metropolitans in the area encompassed by the Soviet Union.

See also: PATRIARCHATE; RUSSIAN ORTHODOX CHURCH

**BIBLIOGRAPHY**

Ellis, Jane. (1986). *The Russian Orthodox Church: A Contemporary History.* London: Croom Helm.

Fennell, John. (1995). *History of the Russian Church to 1448.* London: Longman.

Preobrazhensky, Alexander, ed. (1998). *The Russian Orthodox Church: Tenth to Twentieth Centuries.* Moscow: Progress.

DONALD OSTROWSKI

## MEYERHOLD, VSEVOLOD YEMILIEVICH

(1874–1940), born Karl-Theodor Kazimir Meyerhold, stage director.

Among the most influential twentieth-century stage directors, Vsevolod Meyerhold utilized abstract design and rhythmic performances. His actor training system, "biomechanics," merges acrobatics with industrial studies of motion. Never hesitating to adapt texts to suit directorial concepts, Meyerhold saw theatrical production as an art independent from drama. Born in Penza, Meyerhold studied acting at the Moscow Philharmonic Society (1896–1897) with theatrical reformer Vladimir Nemirovich-Danchenko. When Nemirovich cofounded the Moscow Art Theater with Konstantin Stanislavsky (1897), Meyerhold joined. He excelled as Treplev in Anton Chekhov's *Seagull* (1898). Like Treplev, Meyerhold sought new artistic forms and left the company in 1902. He directed symbolist plays at Stanislavsky's Theater-Studio (1905) and for actress Vera Kommissarzhevskaya (1906–1907).

From 1908 to 1918, Meyerhold led a double life. As director for the imperial theaters, he created sumptuous operas and classic plays. As experimental director, under the pseudonym Dr. Dapertutto, he explored avant-garde directions. Meyerhold greeted 1917 by vowing "to put the October revolution into the theatre." He headed the Narkompros Theater Department from 1920 to 1921 and staged *agitprop* (pro-communist propaganda). His Soviet work developed along two trajectories: He reinterpreted classics to reflect political issues and premiered contemporary satires. His most famous production, Fernand Crommelynck's *Magnificent Cuckold* (1922), used a constructivist set and biomechanics. When Soviet control hardened, Meyerhold was labeled "formalist" and his theater liquidated (1938). The internationally acclaimed Stanislavsky sprang to Meyerhold's defense, but shortly after Stanislavsky's death, Meyerhold was arrested (1939). Following seven months of torture, he confessed to "counterrevolutionary slander" and was executed on February 2, 1940.

See also: AGITPROP; MOSCOW ART THEATER

**BIBLIOGRAPHY**

Braun, Edward. (1995). *Meyerhold: A Revolution in the Theatre.* Iowa City: University of Iowa Press.

Rudnitsky, Konstantin. (1981). *Meyerhold the Director,* tr. George Petrov. Ann Arbor, MI: Ardis.

SHARON MARIE CARNICKE

## MIGHTY HANDFUL

Group of nationally oriented Russian composers during the nineteenth century; the name was coined unintentionally by the music and art critic Vladimir Stasov.

The "Mighty Handful" (*moguchaya kuchka*), also known as the New Russian School, Balakirev Circle, or the Five, is a group of nationalist, nineteenth century composers. At the end of the 1850s the brilliant amateur musician Mily Balakirev (1837–1920) gathered a circle of like-minded followers in St. Petersburg with the intention of continuing the work of Mikhail Glinka. His closest comrades became the engineer Cesar Cui (1835–1918; member of the group beginning in 1856), the officers Modest Mussorgsky (1839–1881, member beginning in 1857), and Nikolai Rimsky-Korsakov (1844–1908, member beginning in 1861), and the chemist Alexander Borodin (1833–1887, member beginning in 1862). The spiritual mentor of the young composers, who shared their lack of professional musical training, was the music and art critic Vladimir Stasov, who publicly and vehemently promoted the cause of a Russian national music separate from Western traditions, in a somewhat polarizing and polemic manner. When Stasov, in an article for the *Sankt-Peterburgskie vedomosti* (St. Petersburg News) about a "Slavic concert of Mr. Balakirev" on the occasion of the Slavic Congress in 1867, praised the "small, but already mighty handful of Russians musicians," he had Glinka and Alexander Dargomyzhsky in mind as well as the group, but the label stuck to Balakirev and his followers. They can be considered a unit not only because of their constant exchange of ideas, but also because of their common aesthetic convictions. Strictly speaking, this unity of composition lasted only until the beginning of the 1870s, when it began to dissolve with the growing individuation of its members.

The enthusiastic music amateurs sought to create an independent national Russian music by taking up Russian themes, literature, and folklore and integrating Middle-Asian and Caucasian influences, thereby distancing it from West European musical language and ending the supremacy of the latter in the musical life of Russian cities. Balakirev, who had known Glinka personally, was the most advanced musically; his authority was undisputed among the five musicians. He rejected classical training in music as being only rigid routine and recommended his own method to his followers instead: composing should not be learned through academic courses, but through the direct analysis of masterpieces (especially those created by Glinka, Hector Berlioz, Robert Schumann, Franz Liszt, or Ludwig van

Beethoven, the composers most venerated by the Five). The St. Petersburg conservatory, founded in 1862 by Anton Rubinstein as a new central music training center with predominantly German staff was heavily criticized, especially by Balakirev and Stasov. Instead, a Free School of Music (*Bezplatnaya muzykalnaya shkola*) was founded in the same year, and differed from the conservatory in its low tuition fees and its decidedly national Russian orientation. Balakirev advised his own disciples of the Mighty Handful to go about composing great works of music without false fear.

In spite of comparatively low productivity and long production periods, due in part to the lack of professional qualifications and the consequent creative crises, in part to Balakirev's willful and meticulous criticisms, and in part to the members' preoccupation with their regular occupations, the composers of the Mighty Handful became after Glinka and beside Peter Tchaikovsky the founders of Russian national art music during the nineteenth century. An exception was Cui, whose compositions, oriented towards Western models and themes, formed a sharp contrast to what he publicly postulated for Russian music. The other members of the Balakirev circle successfully developed specific Russian musical modes of expression. The music dramas *Boris Godunov* (1868–1872) and *Khovanshchina* (1872–1881) by Mussorgsky and *Prince Igor* (1869–1887) by Borodin, in spite of their unfinished quality, are considered among the greatest historical operas of Russian music, whereas Rimsky-Korsakov achieved renown by his masterly accomplishment of the Russian fairy-tale and magic opera. The symphonies, symphonic poems, and overtures of Borodin, Rimsky-Korsakov, and Balakirev stand for the beginnings and first highlights of a Russian orchestral school. Understandably, many of the composers' most important works were created when the Mighty Handful as a community had already dissolved. The personal crises of Balakirev and Mussorgsky contributed to the circle's dissolution, as did the increasing emancipation of the disciples from their master, which was clearly exemplified by Rimsky-Korsakov. He advanced to the status of professional musician, became professor at the St. Petersburg conservatory (1871), and diverged from the others increasingly over time in his creative approaches. In sum, the Mighty Handful played a crucial role in the formation of Russian musical culture at the crossroads of West European influences and strivings for national independence. Through the intentional use of historical and mythical Russian themes, the works of the Mighty Handful have made a lasting contribution to the national culture of recollection in Russia far beyond the nineteenth century.

*See also:* MUSIC; NATIONALISM IN THE ARTS; RIMSKY-KORSAKOV, NIKOLAI ANDREYEVICH; STASOV, VLADIMIR VASILIEVICH

**BIBLIOGRAPHY**

Brown, David; Abraham, Gerald; Lloyd-Jones, David; Garden, Edward. (1986). *Russian Masters, Vol. I: Glinka, Borodin, Balakirev, Musorgsky, Tchaikovsky.* New York, London: W.W. Norton & Company.

Garden, Edward. (1967). *Balakirev: A Critical Study of His Life and Music.* London: Faber & Faber.

MATTHIAS STADELMANN

# MIGRATION

Across time and cultures individuals migrate to improve their lives, seek better opportunities, or flee unbearable conditions. In Russian history, migration highlights social stratification, underscores the importance of social management, and provides insight into post-Soviet population change. Migration motivations in Russia were historically influenced by direct governmental control, providing a unique case for assessing barriers to migration and a window into state and society relations.

The earliest inhabitants of the region now known as Russia were overrun by the in-migration of several conquering populations, with Cimmerians, Scythians (700 B.C.E.), Samartians (300 B.C.E.), Goths (200 C.E.), Huns (370 C.E.), Avars, and Khazars moving into the territory to rule the region. Mongol control (1222) focused on manipulating elites and extracting taxes, but not in-migration. When Moscow later emerged as an urban settlement, eastern Slavs spread across the European plain. Ivan III (1462–1505) pushed expansion south and west, while Ivan IV (1530–1584) pushed east towards Siberia. Restrictions on peasant mobility made migration difficult, yet some risked everything to illegally flee to the southern borderlands and Siberia.

The legal code of 1649 eradicated legal migration. Solidifying serfdom, peasants were now owned by the gentry. Restrictions on mobility could be circumvented. Ambitious peasants could become illegal or seasonal migrants, marginalized socially and economically. By 1787 between 100,000 and 150,000 peasants resided seasonally in Moscow, unable to acquire legal residency, forming an underclass unable to assimilate into city life. Restricted mobility hindered the development of urban labor forces for industrialization in this period, also marked by the use of forced migration and exile by the state.

The emancipation of serfs (1861) increased mobility, but state ability to control migration remained. Urbanization increased rapidly—according to the 1898 census, nearly half of all urbanites were migrants. The Stolypin reforms (1906) further spurred migration to cities and frontiers by enabling withdrawal from rural communes. Over 500,000 peasants moved into Siberia yearly in the early 1900s. Over seven million refugees moved into Russia by 1916, challenging ideas of national identity, highlighting the limitations of state, and crystallizing Russian nationalism. During the Revolution and civil war enforcement of migration restrictions were thwarted, adding to displacement, settlement shifts, and urban growth in the 1920s.

The Soviet passport system reintroduced state control over migration in 1932. Passports contained residency permits, or *propiskas*, required for legal residence. The passport system set the stage for increased social control and ideological emphasis on the scientific management of population. Limiting rural mobility (collective farmers did not receive passports until 1974), restricting urban growth, the exile of specific ethnic groups (Germans, Crimean Tatars, and others), and directing migration through incentives for movements into new territories (the Far East, Far North, and northern Kazakhstan) in the Soviet period echoed previous patterns of state control. As demographers debated scientific population management, by the late Soviet period factors such as housing, wages, and access to goods exerted strong influences on migration decision making. Attempts to control migration in the Soviet period met some success in stemming urbanization, successfully attracting migrants to inhospitable locations, increasing regional mixing of ethnic and linguistic groups across the Soviet Union, and blocking many wishing to immigrate.

With the collapse of the Soviet Union in 1991, migration restrictions were initially minimized, but migration trends and security concerns increased interest in restrictions by the end of the twentieth century. Decreased emigration control led to over

**Nineteenth-century engraving shows a caravan of Russian peasants migrating.** © Bettmann/Corbis

100,000 people leaving Russia yearly between 1991 and 1996, dampened only by restrictions on immigration from Western countries. Russia's population loss has been offset by immigration from the near abroad, where 25 million ethnic Russians resided in 1991. Legal, illegal, and seasonal migrants were attracted from the near abroad by the relative political and economic stability in Russia, in addition to ethnic and linguistic ties. Yet, the flow of immigrants declined in the late 1990s. Refugees registered in Russia numbered nearly one million in 1998. Internally, migration patterns follow wages and employment levels, and people left the far eastern and northern regions. Internal displacement emerged in the south during the 1990s, from Chechnya. By the late 1990s, the challenges of migrant assimilation and integration were key public issues, and interest in restricting migration rose. While market forces had begun to replace direct administrative control over migration in Russia by the end of the 1990s, concerns over migration and increasing calls for administrative interventions drew upon a long history of state management of population migration.

*See also:* DEMOGRAPHY; IMMIGRATION AND EMIGRATION; LAW CODE OF 1649; PASSPORT SYSTEM

**BIBLIOGRAPHY**

Bradley, J. (1985). *Muzhik and Muscovite: Urbanization in Late Imperial Russia.* Los Angeles: University of California Press.

Brubaker, Rodgers. (1995). "Aftermaths of Empire and the Unmixing of Peoples: Historical and Comparative Perspectives" *Ethnic and Racial Studies* 18 (2):189–218.

Buckley, Cynthia J. (1995). "The Myth of Managed Migration." *Slavic Review* 54 (4):896–916.

Gatrell, Peter. (1999). *A Whole Empire Walking: Refugees in Russia During World War I.* Bloomington: Indiana University Press.

Lewis, Robert and Rowlands, Richard. (1979). *Population Redistribution in the USSR: Its Impact on Society 1897–1977.* New York: Praeger Press.

Zaionchkovskaya, Zhanna A. (1996). "Migration Patterns in the Former Soviet Union" In *Cooperation and Conflict in the Former Soviet Union: Implications for Migration,* eds. Jeremy R. Azrael, Emil A. Payin, Kevin

F. McCarthy, and Georges Vernez. Santa Monica, CA: Rand.

CYNTHIA J. BUCKLEY

## MIKHAILOVSKY, NIKOLAI KONSTANTINOVICH

(1842–1904), journalist, sociologist, and a revolutionary democrat; leading theorist of agrarian Populism.

Born in the Kaluga region to an impoverished gentry family, and an early orphan, Nikolai Mikhailovsky studied at the St. Petersburg Mining Institute, which he was forced to quit in 1863 after taking part in activities in support of Polish rebels. From 1860 he published in radical periodicals, held a string of editorial jobs, and experimented at cooperative profit-sharing entrepreneurship. His early thought was influenced by Pierre-Joseph Proudhon, whose work he translated into Russian. In 1868 he joined the team of *Otechestvennye zapiski* (Fatherland Notes), a leading literary journal headed by Nikolai Nekrasov, where he established himself with his essay, "What Is Progress?" attacking Social Darwinism, with his work against the utilitarians, "What Is Happiness?" and other publications, including "Advocacy of the Emancipation of Women." After Nekrasov's death (1877) Mikhailovsky became one of three coeditors, and the de facto head of the journal.

Mikhailovsky was the foremost thinker and author of the mature, or critical stage of populism (*narodnichestvo*). While early populists envisioned Russia bypassing the capitalist stage of development and building a just and equitable economic and societal order on the basis of the peasant commune, Mikhailovsky viewed this scenario as a desirable but increasingly problematic alternative to capitalist or state-led industrialization. The ethical thrust of Russian populism found its utmost expression in his doctrine of binding relationship between factual truth and normative (moral) truth, viewed as justice (in Russian, both ideas are expressed by the word *pravda*), thus essentially tying knowledge to ethics.

Together with Pyotr Lavrov, Mikhailovsky laid the groundwork for Russia's distinct sociological tradition by developing the subjective sociology that was also emphatically normative and ethical in its basis. His most famous statement read that "every sociological theory has to start with some kind of a utopian ideal." In this vein, he developed a systematic critique of the positivist philosophy of knowledge, including the natural science approach to social studies, while working to familiarize the Russian audience with Western social and political thinkers of his age, including John Stuart Mill, Auguste Comte, Herbert Spencer, Emile Durkheim, and Karl Marx. In "What Is Progress?" he argued for the "struggle for individuality" as a central element to social action and the indicator of genuine progress of humanity, as opposed to the Darwinian struggle for survival. According to Mikhailovsky, in society, unlike in biological nature, it is the environment that should be adapted to individuals, not vice versa. On this basis, he attacked the division of labor in capitalist societies as a dehumanizing social pathology leading to unidimensional and regressive rather than harmonious development of humans and, eventually, to the suppression of individuality (in contrast to the animal world, where functional differentiation is a progressive phenomenon). Thus he introduced a strong individualist (and, arguably, a libertarian) element to Russian populist thought, which had traditionally emphasized collectivism. He sought an alternative to the division of labor in the patterns of simple cooperation among peasants. He also worked toward a distinct theory of social change, questioning Eurocentric linear views of progress, and elaborated a dual gradation of types and levels of development (that is, Russia for him represented a higher type but a lower level of development than industrialized capitalist countries, and he thought it necessary to preserve this higher, or communal, type while striving to move to a higher level). In "Heroes and the Crowd" (1882), he provided important insights into mass psychology and the nature of leadership.

Under the impact of growing political repression, Mikhailovsky evolved from liberal critique of the government during the 1860s through short-lived hopes for a pan-Slav liberation movement (1875–1876) to clandestine cooperation with the People's Will Party, thus broadening the purely social goals of the original populism to embrace a political revolution (while at the same time distancing himself from the morally unscrupulous figures connected to populism, such as Sergei Nechayev). He authored articles for underground publications, and after the assassination of Alexander II (1881) took part in compiling the address of the People's Will's Executive Committee to Alexander III, an attempt to position the organization as a negotiating partner of the authorities. In the subsequent crackdown on the movement, Mikhailovsky was banned from St. Petersburg (1882), and *Otechestvennye zapiski* was shut down (1884). Only in 1884 was he able to return to an editorial position by informally taking over the journal *Russkoye bogatstvo* (Russian Wealth). He then emerged as an influential critic of the increasingly popular Marxism, which he saw as converging with top-down industrialization policies of the government in its disdain for and exploitative approach to the peasantry. Simultaneously, he polemicized against Tolstovian anarchism and anti-intellectualism. In spite of the ideological hegemony of Marxists at the turn of the century, Mikhailovsky's writings were highly popular among the democratic intelligentsia and provided the conceptual basis for the neo-populist revival, represented by the Socialist Revolutionary and the People's Socialist parties in the 1905 and 1917 revolutions. Moreover, his work resonates with subsequent Western studies in the peasant-centered "moral economy" of peripheral countries.

See also: INTELLIGENTSIA; JOURNALISM; MARXISM; NEKRASOV, NIKOLAI ALEXEYEVICH; POPULISM

**BIBLIOGRAPHY**

Billington, J.H. (1958). *Mikhailovsky and Russian Populism*. Oxford: Clarendon Press.

Edie, James M.; Scanlan, James P.; and Zeldin, M.B., eds. (1965). *Russian Philosophy*, vol. 2. Chicago, IL: Quadrangle Books.

Ivanov-Razumnik, R.I. (1997). *Istoria russkoi obshchestvennoi mysli*. Vol. 2. Moscow: Respublika, Terra. pp. 228-302.

Ulam, Adam B. (1977). *In the Name of the People: Prophets and Conspirators in Prerevolutionary Russia*. New York: Putnam.

Venturi, Franco. (2001). *Roots of Revolution*, revised ed., tr. Francis Haskell. London: Phoenix Press.

Walicki, A. (1969). *The Controversy Over Capitalism: Studies in the Social Philosophy of the Russian Populists*. Oxford: Clarendon Press.

DMITRI GLINSKI

# MIKHALKOV, NIKITA SERGEYEVICH

(b. 1945), film director, actor.

Nikita Mikhalkov is the best-known Russian director of the late-Soviet and post-Soviet period. Mikhalkov was born in Moscow to a family of accomplished painters, writers, and arts administrators. His father was chief of the Soviet Writers' Union, and his brother, Andrei Mikhalkov-Konchalovsky, is also a successful director. Mikhalkov first came to national and international attention with his film *Slave of Love* (1976), which depicts the last days of prerevolutionary popular filmmaking. He made several more films about late-nineteenth-century elite culture, including *Unfinished Piece for Player Piano* (1977), *Oblomov* (1980), and *Dark Eyes* (1987). *Five Evenings* (1978) is a beautifully photographed, finely etched treatment of love and loss set just after World War II. *Urga* (aka *Close to Eden*, 1992) is a powerful portrait of economic transformation and cultural encounter on the Russian-Mongolian border. *Anna, 6–18* (1993) is a series of interviews with the director's daughter, which highlights the difficulties of growing up in late-communist society. *Burnt by the Sun* (1994), which won a U.S. Academy Award for best foreign language film, treats the complicated personal politics of the Stalinist period. *The Barber of Siberia* (1999) is a sprawling romantic epic with Russians and Americans in Siberia—an expensive multinational production which failed to win an audience. All of Mikhalkov's films are visually rich; he has a deft touch for lightening his dramas with comedy, and his characterizations can be subtle and complex.

Mikhalkov has also had a successful career as an actor. Physically imposing, he often plays characters who combine authority and power with poignancy or sentimentality. During the late 1990s, Mikhalkov became the president of the Russian Culture Fund and the chair of the Union of Russian Filmmakers.

See also: MOTION PICTURES

**BIBLIOGRAPHY**

Beumers, Bergit. (2000). *Burnt By the Sun*. London: I.B. Tauris.

Horton, Andrew, and Brashinsky, Michael. (1992). *The Zero Hour*. Princeton, NJ: Princeton University Press.

Lawton, Anna. (1992). *Kinoglasnost: Soviet Cinema in Our Time*. New York: Cambridge University Press.

Shalin, Dmitri N., ed. *Russian Culture at the Crossroads: Paradoxes of Postcommunist Consciousness*. Boulder, CO: Westview.

JOAN NEUBERGER

# MIKOYAN, ANASTAS IVANOVICH

(1895–1978), Communist Party leader and government official.

Anastas Ivanovich Mikoyan occupied the summits of Soviet political and governmental life for more than five decades. One of Stalin's comrades, he was a political survivor. Armenian by birth, Mikoyan joined the Bolsheviks in 1915, playing a leading role in the Caucasus during the civil war (1918–1920). In 1922 he was elected to the Communist Party's Central Committee, by which time he was already working confidentially for Josef Stalin. After Vladimir Lenin's death (1924) he staunchly supported Stalin's struggle against the Left Opposition. His loyalty was rewarded in 1926 when he became the youngest commissar and Politburo member. Appointed commissar of food production in 1934, he introduced major innovations in this area. By 1935 he was a full member of the Politburo. While not an aggressive advocate of the Great Terror (1937–1938), Mikoyan was responsible for purges in his native Armenia. In 1942, after the German invasion, he was appointed to the State Defense Committee, with responsibility for military supplies. After Stalin's death (1953) he proved a loyal ally of Nikita Khrushchev, the only member of Stalin's original Politburo to support him in his confrontation with the Stalinist Anti-Party Group (1957). Mikoyan went on to play a crucial role in the Cuban missile crisis (1962), mediating between Khrushchev, U.S. president John F. Kennedy, and Cuban leader Fidel Castro, whom he persuaded to accept the withdrawal of Soviet missiles from Cuba. He was appointed head of government in July 1964, three months before signing the decree dismissing Khrushchev as party first secretary. Under Leonid Brezhnev he gradually relinquished his roles in party and government in favor of writing his memoirs, finally retiring in 1975.

*See also:* ANTI-PARTY GROUP; ARMENIA AND ARMENIANS; CUBAN MISSILE CRISIS; LEFT OPPOSITION; PURGES, THE GREAT

### BIBLIOGRAPHY
Medvedev, Roy. (1984). *All Stalin's Men.* (1984). Garden City, NY: Anchor Press.

Taubman, William; Khrushchev, Sergei; and Gleason, Abbott, eds. (2000). *Nikita Khrushchev.* New Haven, CT: Yale University Press.

ROGER D. MARKWICK

# MILITARY ART

Military art is the theory and practice of preparing and conducting military actions on land, at sea, and within the global aerospace envelope.

Historically, Russian military theorists held that the primary function of military art was attainment of victory over an adversary with the least expenditure of forces, resources, and time. This postulation stressed a well-developed sense of intent that would link the logic of strategy with the purposeful design and execution of complex military actions. By the end of the nineteenth century, Russian military theorists accepted the conviction that military art was an expression of military science, which they viewed as a branch of the social sciences with its own laws and disciplinary integrity. Further, they subscribed to the idea, exemplified by Napoleon, that military art consisted of two primary components, strategy and tactics. Strategy described movements of main military forces within a theater of war, while tactics described what occurred on the battlefield. However, following the Russo-Japanese War of 1904–1905, theorists gradually modified their views to accommodate the conduct of operations in themselves, or *operatika*, as a logical third component lying between—and linking—strategy and tactics. This proposition further evolved during the 1920s and 1930s, thanks primarily to Alexander Svechin, who lent currency to the term "operational art" (*operativnoye iskusstvou*) as a replacement for *operatika*, and to Vladimir Triandafillov, who analyzed the nature of modern military operations on the basis of recent historical precedent. Subsequently, the contributions of other theorists, including Mikhail Tukhachevsky, Alexander Yegorov, and Georgy Isserson, along with mechanization of the Red Army and the bitter experience of the Great Patriotic War, contributed further to the Soviet understanding of modern military art. However, the theoretical development of strategy languished under Josef Stalin, while the advent of nuclear weapons at the end of World War II called into question the efficacy of operational art. During much of the Nikita Khrushchev era, a nuclear-dominated version of strategy held near-complete sway in the realm of military art. Only in the mid-1960s did Soviet military commentators begin to resurrect their understanding of operational art to correspond with the theoretical necessity for conducting large-scale conventional operations under conditions of nuclear threat. During the 1970s and

1980s emphasis on new reconnaissance systems and precision-guided weaponry as parts of an on-going revolution in military affairs further challenged long-held convictions about traditional boundaries and linkages among strategy, operational art, and tactics. Further, U.S. combat experience during the Gulf War in 1990–1991 and again in Afghanistan during 2001 clearly challenged conventional notions about the relationships in contemporary war between time and space, mass and firepower, and offense and defense. Some theorists even began to envision a new era of remotely fought or no-contact war (*bezkontaknaya voynau*) that would dominate the future development of all facets of military art.

*See also:* MILITARY, IMPERIAL ERA; MILITARY, SOVIET AND POST-SOVIET

**BIBLIOGRAPHY**

Menning, Bruce W. (1997). "Operational Art's Origins." *Military Review* 76(5):32-47.

Svechin, Aleksandr A. (1992). *Strategy*, ed. Kent D. Lee. Minneapolis: East View Publications.

BRUCE W. MENNING

## MILITARY DOCTRINE

In late Imperial Russia, a common basis for joint military action; in the Soviet Union and the Russian Federation, an assertion of military posture and policy.

The Soviet and Russian understanding of military doctrine is often a source of confusion because other societies usually subscribe to a narrower definition. For most Western military and naval establishments, doctrine typically consists of the distilled wisdom that governs the actual employment of armed forces in combat. At its best, this wisdom constitutes a constantly evolving intellectual construct that owes its origins and development to a balanced understanding of the complex interplay among changing technology, structure, theory, and combat experience.

In contrast, doctrine in its Soviet and Russian variants evolved early to reflect a common understanding of the state's larger defense requirements. The issue first surfaced after 1905, when Russian military intellectuals debated the necessity for a "unified military doctrine" that would impart effective overall structure and direction to war preparations. In a more restrictive perspective, the same doctrine would also define the common intellectual foundations of field service regulations and the terms of cooperation between Imperial Russia's army and navy. In 1912, Tsar Nicholas II himself silenced discussion, proclaiming, "Military doctrine consists of doing everything that I order."

A different version of the debate resurfaced soon after the Bolshevik triumph in the civil war. Discussion ostensibly turned on a doctrinal vision for the future of the Soviet military establishment, but positions hardened and quickly assumed political overtones. War Commissar Leon Trotsky held that any understanding of doctrine must flow from future requirements for world revolution. Others, including Mikhail V. Frunze, held that doctrine must flow from the civil war experience, the nature of the new Soviet state, and the needs and character of the Red Army. Frunze essentially envisioned a concept of preparation for future war shaped by class relations, external threat, and the state's economic development.

Frunze's victory in the debate laid the foundations for a subsequent definition of Soviet and later Russian military doctrine that has remained relatively constant. Military doctrine came to be understood as "a system of views adopted by a given state at a given time on the goals and nature of possible future war and the preparation of the armed forces and the country for it, and also the methods of waging it." Because of explicit linkages between politics and war, this version of military doctrine always retained two aspects, the political (or sociopolitical) and the military-technical. Thanks to rapid advances in military technology, the latter aspect sometimes witnessed abrupt change. However, until the advent of Mikhail S. Gorbachev and perestroika, the political aspect, which defined the threat and relations among states, remained relatively static.

The disintegration of the Soviet Union in 1991 led to a recurring redefinition of the twin doctrinal aspects that emphasized both Russia's diminished great-power status and the changing nature of the threat. Nuclear war became less imminent, military operations more complex, and the threat both internal and external. Whatever the calculus, the terms of expression and discussion continued to reflect the unique legacy that shaped Imperial Russian and Soviet notions of military doctrine.

*See also:* FRUNZE, MIKHAIL VASILIEVICH; MILITARY, IMPE-
RIAL ERA; MILITARY, SOVIET AND POST-SOVIET; TROT-
SKY, LEON DAVIDOVICH

**BIBLIOGRAPHY**
Frank, Willard C., and Gillette, Phillip S., eds. (1992). *Soviet Military Doctrine from Lenin to Gorbachev, 1915–1991.* Westport, CT: Greenwood Press.

Garthoff, Raymond L. (1953). *Soviet Military Doctrine.* Glencoe, IL: Free Press..

BRUCE W. MENNING

# MILITARY-ECONOMIC PLANNING

In the world wars of the twentieth century, it was as important to mobilize the economy to supply soldiers' rations and equipment as it was to enlist the population as soldiers. Military-economic planning took root in the Soviet Union, as elsewhere, after World War I. The scope of the plans that prepared the Soviet economy for war continues to be debated. Some argue that war preparation was a fundamental objective influencing every aspect of Soviet peacetime economic policy; there were no purely civilian plans, and everything was militarized to some degree. Others see military-economic planning more narrowly as the specialized activity of planning and budgeting for rearmament, which had to share priority with civilian economic goals.

The framework for military-economic planning was fixed by a succession of high-level government committees: the Council for Labor and Defense (STO), the Defense Committee, and, in the postwar period, the Military-Industrial Commission (VPK). The armed forces general staff carried on military-economic planning in coordination with the defense sector of the State Planning Commission (Gosplan). Gosplan's defense sector was established on the initiative of the Red Army commander, Mikhail Tukhachevsky, who pioneered the study of future war and offensive operations associated with the concept of deep battle. To support this he advocated ambitious plans for the large-scale production of combat aircraft and motorized armor. Tukhachevsky crossed swords at various times with Josef V. Stalin, Vyacheslav Molotov, and Kliment Voroshilov. The military-economic plans were less ambitious than he hoped, and also less coherent: Industry did not reconcile its production plans beforehand with the army's procurement plan, and their interests often diverged over the terms of plans and contracts to supply equipment. To overcome this Tukhachevsky pressed to bring the management of defense production under military control, but he was frustrated in this too. His efforts ended with his arrest and execution in 1937.

Military-economic plans required every ministry and workplace to adopt a mobilization plan to be implemented in the event of war. How effective this was is difficult to evaluate, and the mobilization plans adopted before World War II appear to have been highly unrealistic by comparison with wartime outcomes. Despite this, the Soviet transition to a war economy was successful; the fact that contingency planning and trial mobilizations were practiced at each level of the prewar command system may have contributed more to this than their detailed faults might suggest.

During World War II the task was no longer to prepare for war but to fight it, and so the distinction between military-economic planning and economic planning in general disappeared for a time. It reemerged after the war when Stalin began bringing his generals back into line, and the security organs, not the military, took the leading role in organizing the acquisition of new atomic and aerospace technologies. Stalin's death and the demotion of the organs allowed a new equilibrium to emerge under Dmitry Ustinov, minister of the armament industry since June 1941; Ustinov went on to coordinate the armed forces and industry from a unique position of influence and privilege under successive Soviet leaders until his own death in 1984. It symbolized his coordinating role that he assumed the military rank of marshal in 1976.

*See also:* GOSPLAN; TUKHACHEVSKY, MIKHAIL NIKOLAYE-
VICH; USTINOV, DMITRY FEDOROVICH; WAR ECON-
OMY

**BIBLIOGRAPHY**
Barber, John, and Harrison, Mark, eds. (2000). *The Soviet Defence-Industry Complex from Stalin to Khrushchev.* Basingstoke, UK: Macmillan.

Harrison, Mark (2001). "Providing for Defense." In *Behind the Façade of Stalin's Command Economy: Evidence from the Soviet State and Party Archives*, ed. Paul R. Gregory. Stanford, CA: Hoover Institution Press.

Samuelson, Lennart. (2000). *Plans for Stalin's War Machine: Tukhachevskii and Military-Economic Planning, 1925–1941.* Basingstoke, UK: Macmillan.

MARK HARRISON

## MILITARY, IMPERIAL ERA

Measured by large outcomes, the Imperial Russian military establishment evolved through two distinct stages. From the era of Peter the Great through the reign of Alexander III, the Russian army and navy fought, borrowed, and innovated their way to more successes than failures. With the major exception of the Crimean War, Russian ground and naval forces largely overcame the challenges and contradictions inherent in diverse circumstances and multiple foes to extend and defend the limits of empire. However, by the time of Nicholas II, significant lapses in leadership and adaptation spawned the kinds of repetitive disaster and fundamental disaffection that exceeded the military's ability to recuperate.

### THE EIGHTEENTH-CENTURY ARMY

The Imperial Russian Army and Navy owed their origins to Peter I, although less so for the army than the navy. The army's deeper roots clearly lay with Muscovite precedent, especially with Tsar Alexei Mikhailovich's European-inspired new regiments of foreign formation. The Great Reformer breathed transforming energy and intensity into these and other precedents to fashion a standing regular army that by 1725 counted 112,000 troops in two guards, two grenadier, forty-two infantry, and thirty-three dragoon regiments, with supporting artillery and auxiliaries. To serve this establishment, he also fashioned administrative, financial, and logistical mechanisms, along with a rational rank structure and systematic officer and soldier recruitment. With an admixture of foreigners, the officer corps came primarily from the Russian nobility, while soldiers came from recruit levies against the peasant population.

Although Peter's standing force owed much to European precedent, his military diverged from conventional patterns to incorporate irregular cavalry levies, especially Cossacks, and to evolve a military art that emphasized flexibility and practicality for combating both conventional northern European foes and less conventional steppe adversaries. After mixed success against the Tatars and Turks at Azov in 1695–1696, and after a severe reverse at Narva (1700) against the Swedes at the outset of the Great Northern War, Peter's army notched important victories at Dorpat (1704), Lesnaya (1708), and Poltava (1709). After an abrupt loss in 1711 to the Turks on the Pruth River, Peter dogged his Swedish adversaries until they came to terms at Nystadt in 1721. Subsequently, Peter took to the Caspian basin, where during the early 1720s his Lower (or Southern) Corps campaigned as far south as Persia.

After Peter's death, the army's fortunes waned and waxed, with much of its development characterized by which aspect of the Petrine legacy seemed most politic and appropriate for time and circumstance. Under Empress Anna Ioannovna, the army came to reflect a strong European, especially Prussian, bias in organization and tactics, a bias that during the 1730s contributed to defeat and indecision against the Tatars and Turks. Under Empress Elizabeth Petrovna, the army reverted partially to Petrine precedent, but retained a sufficiently strong European character to give good account for itself in the Seven Years' War. Although in 1761 the military-organizational pendulum under Peter III again swung briefly and decisively in favor of Prussian-inspired models, a palace coup in favor of his wife, who became Empress Catherine II, ushered in a lengthy period of renewed military development.

During Catherine's reign, the army fought two major wars against Turkey and its steppe allies to emerge as the largest ground force in Europe. Three commanders were especially responsible for bringing Russian military power to bear against elusive southern adversaries. Two, Peter Alexandrovich Rumyantsev and Alexander Vasilievich Suvorov, were veterans of the Seven Years War, while the third, Grigory Alexandrovich Potemkin, was a commander and administrator of great intellect, influence, and organizational talent. During Catherine's First Turkish War (1768–1774), Rumyantsev successfully employed flexible tactics and simplified Russian military organization to win significant victories at Larga and Kagul (both 1770). Suvorov, meanwhile, defeated the Polish Confederation of Bar, then after 1774 campaigned in the Crimea and the Nogai steppe. At the same time, regular army formations played an important role in suppressing the Pugachev rebellion (1773–1775).

During Catherine's Second Turkish War (1787–1792), Potemkin emerged as the impresario of final victory over the Porte for hegemony over the northern Black Sea littoral, while Suvorov emerged as perhaps the most talented Russian field commander of all time. Potemkin inherently understood the value of irregular cavalry forces in the south, and he took measures to regularize Cossack service and bring them more fully under Russian military authority, or failing that, to abolish recalcitrant Cossack hosts. Following Rumyantsev's precedent, he also lightened and multiplied the number of light infantry and light cavalry formations, while emphasizing utility and practicality in drill and items of equipment. In the field, Suvorov further refined Rumyantsev's tactical innovations to emphasize "speed, assessment, attack." Suvorov's battlefield successes, together with the conquest of Ochakov (1788) and Izmail (1790) and important sallies across the Danube, brought Russia favorable terms at Jassy (1792). Even as war raged in the south, the army in the north once again defeated Sweden (1788–1790), then in 1793–1794 overran a rebellious Poland, setting the stage for its third partition.

Under Paul I, the army chaffed under the imposition of direct monarchical authority, the more so because it brought another brief dalliance with Prussian military models. Suvorov was temporarily banished, but was later recalled to lead Russian forces in northern Italy as part of the Second Coalition against revolutionary France. In 1799, despite Austrian interference, Suvorov drove the French from the field, then brilliantly extricated his forces from Italy across the Alps. The eighteenth century closed with the army a strongly entrenched feature of Russian imperial might, a force to be reckoned with on both the plains of Europe and the steppes of Eurasia.

### THE EIGHTEENTH-CENTURY NAVY

In contrast with the army, Muscovite precedent afforded scant inspiration for the Imperial Russian Navy, the origins of which clearly lay with Peter the Great. Enamored with the sea and sailing ships, Peter borrowed from foreign technology and expertise initially to create naval forces on both the Azov and Baltic Seas. Although the Russian navy would always remain "the second arm" for an essentially continental power, sea-going forces figured prominently in Peter's military successes. In both the south and north, his galley fleets supported the army in riverine and coastal operations, then went on to win important Baltic victories over the Swedes, most notably at Gangut/Hanko (1714). Peter also developed an open-water sailing capability, so that by 1724 his Baltic Fleet numbered 34 ships-of-the-line, in addition to numerous galleys and auxiliaries. Smaller flotillas sailed the White and Caspian Seas.

More dependent than the army on rigorous and regular sustenance and maintenance, the Imperial Russian Navy after Peter languished until the era of Catherine II. She appointed her son general admiral, revitalized the Baltic Fleet, and later established Sevastopol as a base for the emerging Black Sea Fleet. In 1770, during the Empress' First Turkish War, a squadron under Admiral Alexei Grigorievich Orlov defeated the Turks decisively at Chesme. During the Second Turkish War, a rudimentary Black Sea Fleet under Admiral Fyedor Fyedorovich Ushakov frequently operated both independently and in direct support of ground forces. The same ground–sea cooperation held true in the Baltic, where Vasily Yakovlevich Chichagov's fleet also ended Swedish naval pretensions. Meanwhile, in 1799 Admiral Ushakov scored a series of Mediterranean victories over the French, before the Russians withdrew from the Second Coalition.

### THE ARMY AND NAVY IN THE FIRST HALF OF THE NINETEENTH CENTURY

At the outset of the century, Alexander I inherited a sizeable and unaffordable army, many of whose commanders were seasoned veterans. After instituting a series of modest administrative reforms for efficiency and economy, including the creation of a true War Ministry, the Tsar in 1805 plunged into the wars of the Third Coalition. For all their experience and flexibility, the Russians with or without the benefit of allies against Napoleon suffered a series of reverses or stalemates, including Austerlitz (1805), Eylau (1807), and Friedland (1807). After the ensuing Tilsit Peace granted five years' respite, Napoleon's Grand Armée invaded Russia in 1812. Following a fighting Russian withdrawal into the interior, Mikhail Illarionovich Kutuzov in September gave indecisive battle at Borodino, followed by another withdrawal to the southeast that uncovered Moscow. When the French quit Moscow in October, Kutuzov pursued, reinforced by swarms of partisans and Cossacks, who, together with starvation and severe cold, harassed the Grand Armée to destruction. In 1813, the Russian army fought in Germany, and in 1814 participated in the coalition victory at Leipzig, followed by a fighting entry into France and the occupation of Paris.

The successful termination of the Napoleonic wars still left Alexander I with an outsized and unaffordable military establishment, but now with the addition of disaffected elements within the officer corps. While some gentry officers formed secret societies to espouse revolutionary causes, the tsar experimented with the establishment of settled troops, or military colonies, to reduce maintenance costs. Although these colonies were in many ways only an extension of the previous century's experience with military settlers on the frontier, their widespread application spawned much discontent. After Alexander I's death, unrest and conspiracy led to an attempted military coup in December 1825.

Tsar Nicholas I energetically suppressed the so-called Decembrist rebellion, then imposed parade-ground order. His standing army grew to number one million troops, but its outdated recruitment system and traditional support infrastructure eventually proved incapable of meeting the challenges of military modernization. Superficially, the army was a model of predictable routine and harsh discipline, but its inherent shortcomings, including outmoded weaponry, incapacity for rapid expansion, and lack of strategic mobility, led inexorably to Crimean defeat. The army was able to subdue Polish military insurrectionists (1830–1831) and Hungarian revolutionaries (1848), and successfully fight Persians and Turks (1826–1828, 1828–1829), but in the field it lagged behind its more modern European counterparts. Fighting from 1854 to 1856 against an allied coalition in the Crimea, the Russians suffered defeat at Alma, heavy losses at Balaklava and Inkerman, and the humiliation of surrender at Sevastopol. Only the experience of extended warfare in the Caucasus (1801–1864) afforded unconventional antidote to the conventional "paradomania" of St. Petersburg that had so thoroughly inspired Crimean defeat. Thus, the mountains replaced the steppe as the southern pole in an updated version of the previous century's north-south dialectic.

During the first half of the nineteenth century, the navy, too, experienced its own version of the same dialectic. For a brief period, the Russian navy under Admiral Dmity Nikolayevich Senyavin harassed Turkish forces in the Aegean, but following Tilsit, the British Royal Navy ruled in both the Baltic and the Mediterranean. In 1827, the Russians joined with the British and French to pound the Turks at Navarino, but in the north, the Baltic Fleet, like the St. Petersburg military establishment, soon degenerated into an imperial parading force. Only on the Black Sea, where units regularly supported Russian ground forces in the Caucasus, did the Navy reveal any sustained tactical and operational acumen. However, this attainment soon proved counterproductive, for Russian naval victory in 1853 over the Turks at Sinope drew the British and French to the Turkish cause, thus setting the stage for allied intervention in the Crimea. During the Crimean War, steam and screw-driven allied vessels attacked at will in both the north and south, thereby revealing the essentially backwardness of Russia's sailing navy.

## THE ARMY AND NAVY DURING THE SECOND HALF OF THE NINETEENTH CENTURY

Alexander II's era of the Great Reforms marked an important watershed for both services. In a series of reforms between 1861 and 1874, War Minister Dmitry Alexeyevich Milyutin created the foundations for a genuine cadre- and reserve-based ground force. He facilitated introduction of a universal service obligation, and he rearmed, reequipped, and redeployed the army to contend with the gradually emerging German and Austro-Hungarian threat along the Empire's western frontier. In 1863–1864 the army once again suppressed a Polish rebellion, while in the 1860s and 1870s small mobile forces figured in extensive military conquests in Central Asia. War also flared with Turkey in 1877–1878, during which the army, despite a ragged beginning, inconsistent field leadership, and inadequacies in logistics and medical support, acquitted itself well, especially in a decisive campaign in the European theater south of the Balkan ridge. Similar circumstances governed in the Transcausus theater, where the army overcame initial setbacks to seize Kars and carry the campaign into Asia Minor.

Following the war of 1877–1878, planning and deployment priorities wedded the army more closely to the western military frontier and especially to peacetime deployments in Russian Poland. With considerable difficulty, Alexander III presided over a limited force modernization that witnessed the adoption of smokeless powder weaponry and changes in size and force structure that kept the army on nearly equal terms with its two more significant potential adversaries, Imperial Germany and Austria-Hungary. At the same time, the end of the century brought extensive new military commitments to the Far East, both to protect expanding imperial interests and to participate in suppression of the Boxer Rebellion (1900).

The same challenges of force modernization and diverse responsibilities bedeviled the navy, perhaps more so than the army. During the 1860s and 1870s, the navy made the difficult transition from sail to steam, but thereafter had to deal with increasingly diverse geostrategic requirements that mandated retention of naval forces in at least four theaters (Baltic, Northern, Black Sea, and Pacific), none of which were mutually supporting. Simultaneously, the Russian Admiralty grappled with issues of role and identity, pondering whether the navy's primary mission in war lay either with coastal defense and commerce raiding or with attainment of true "blue water" supremacy in the tradition of Alfred Thayer Mahan and his Russian navalist disciples. Rationale notwithstanding, by 1898 Russia possessed Europe's third largest navy (nineteen capital ships and more than fifty cruisers), thanks primarily to the ship-building programs of Alexander III.

## THE ARMY AND NAVY OF NICHOLAS II

Under Russia's last tsar, the army went from defeat to disaster and despair. Initially overcommitted and split by a new dichotomy between the Far East and the European military frontier, the army fared poorly in the Russo-Japanese War of 1904–1905. Poor strategic vision and even worse battlefield execution in a Far Eastern littoral war brought defeat because Russia failed to bring its overwhelming resources to bear. While the navy early ceded the initiative and command of the sea to the Japanese, Russian ground force buildups across vast distances were slow. General Adjutant Alexei Nikolayevich Kuropatkin and his subordinates lacked the capacity either to fight expert delaying actions or to master the complexities of meeting engagements that evolved into main battles and operations. Tethered to an 8-thousand-kilometer-long line of communications, the army marched through a series of reverses from the banks of the Yalu (May 1904) to the environs of Mukden (February–March 1905). Although the garrison at Port Arthur retained the capacity to resist, premature surrender of the fortress in early 1905 merely added to Russian humiliation.

The Imperial Russian Navy fared even worse. Except for Stepan Osipovich Makarov, who was killed early, Russian admirals in the Far East presented a picture of indolence and incompetence. The Russian Pacific Squadron at Port Arthur made several half-hearted sorties, then was bottled up at its base by Admiral Togo, until late in 1904 when Japanese siege artillery pounded the Squadron to pieces. When the tsar sent his Baltic Fleet (rechristened the Second Pacific Squadron) to the Far East, it fell prey to the Japanese at Tsushima (May 1905) in a naval battle of annihilation. In all, the tsar lost fifteen capital ships in the Far East, the backbone of two battle fleets.

The years between 1905 and 1914 witnessed renewal and reconstruction, neither of which sufficed to prepare the tsar's army and navy for World

**Nicholas II presents an icon to his troops as they depart for World War I.** © SOVFOTO

War I. Far Eastern defeat fueled the fires of the Revolution of 1905, and both services witnessed mutinies within their ranks. Once the dissidents were weeded out, standing army troops were employed liberally until 1907 to suppress popular disorder. By 1910, stability and improved economic conditions permitted General Adjutant Vladimir Alexandrovich Sukhomlinov's War Ministry to undertake limited reforms in the army's recruitment, organization, deployment, armament, and supply structure. More could have been done, but the navy siphoned off precious funds for ambitious shipbuilding programs to restore the second arm's power and prestige. The overall objective was to prepare Russia for war with the Triple Alliance. Obsession with the threat opposite the western military frontier gradually eliminated earlier dichotomies and subsumed all other strategic priorities.

The outbreak of hostilities in 1914 came too soon for various reform and reconstruction projects to bear full fruit. Again, the Russians suffered from strategic overreach and stretched their military and naval resources too thin. Moreover, military leaders failed to build sound linkages between design and application, between means and objectives, and between troops and their command instances. These and other shortcomings, including an inadequate logistics system and the regime's inability fully to mobilize the home front to support the fighting front, proved disastrous. Thus, the Russians successfully mobilized 3.9 million troops for a short war of military annihilation, but early disasters in East Prussia at Tannenberg and the Masurian Lakes, along with a stalled offensive in Galicia, inexorably led to a protracted war of attrition and exhaustion. In 1915, when German offensive pressure caused the Russian Supreme Command to shorten its front in Russian Poland, withdrawal turned into a costly rout. One of the few positive notes came in 1916, when the Russian Southwest Front under General Alexei Alexeyevich Brusilov launched perhaps the most successful offensive of the entire war on all its fronts. Meanwhile, a navy still not fully recovered from 1904–1905 generally discharged its required supporting functions. In the Baltic, it laid mine fields and protected approaches to Petrograd. In the Black Sea, after initial difficulties with German units serving under Turkish colors, the fleet performed well in a series of support and amphibious operations.

Ultimately, a combination of seemingly endless bloodletting, war-weariness, governmental inefficiency, and the regime's political ineptness facilitated the spread of pacifist and revolutionary sentiment in both the army and navy. By the beginning of 1917, sufficient malaise had set in to render both services incapable either of consistent loyalty or of sustained and effective combat operations. In the end, neither the army nor the navy offered proof against the tsar's internal and external enemies.

See also: ADMINISTRATION, MILITARY; BALKAN WARS; BALTIC FLEET; CAUCASIAN WARS; COSSACKS; CRIMEAN WAR; DECEMBRIST MOVEMENT AND REBELLION; GREAT REFORMS; NAPOLEON I; NORTHERN FLEET; PACIFIC FLEET; RUSSO-TURKISH WARS; SEVEN YEARS' WAR; STRELTSY; WORLD WAR I

**BIBLIOGRAPHY**

Baumann, Robert F. (1993). *Russian-Soviet Unconventional Wars in the Caucasus, Central Asia, and Afghanistan.* Ft. Leavenworth, KS: Combat Studies Institute.

Curtiss, John S. (1965). *The Russian Army of Nicholas I, 1825–1855.* Durham, NC: Duke University Press.

Duffy, Christopher. (1981). *Russia's Military Way to the West: Origins and Nature of Russian Military Power 1700–1800.* London: Routledge & Kegan Paul.

Fuller, William C., Jr. (1992). *Strategy and Power in Russia, 1600–1914.* New York: The Free Press.

Kagan, Frederick W. (1999). *The Military Reforms of Nicholas I: The Origins of the Modern Russian Army.* New York: St. Martin's Press.

Kagan, Frederick W., and Higham, Robin, eds. (2002). *The Military History of Tsarist Russia.* New York: Palgrave.

Keep, John L.H. (1985). *Soldiers of the Tsar: Army and Society in Russia, 1462–1874.* Oxford: Clarendon Press.

LeDonne, John P. (2003). *The Grand Strategy of the Russian Empire, 1650–1831.* New York: Oxford University Press.

Menning, Bruce W. (2000). *Bayonets before Bullets: The Imperial Russian Army, 1861–1914.* Bloomington: Indiana University Press.

Mitchell, Donald W. (1974). *A History of Russian and Soviet Sea Power.* New York: Macmillan.

Reddel, Carl F., ed. (1990). *Transformation in Russian and Soviet Military History.* Washington, DC: U. S. Air Force Academy and Office of Air Force History.

Schimmelpenninck van der Oye, David, and Menning, Bruce W., eds. (2003). *Reforming the Tsar's Army: Military Innovation in Imperial Russia from Peter the Great to the Revolution.* New York: Cambridge University Press.

Stone, Norman. (1975). *The Eastern Front 1914–1917.* New York: Charles Scribner's Sons.

Westwood, J.N. (1986). *Russia against Japan, 1904–1905.* Albany: State University of New York Press.

Woodward, David. (1965). *The Russians at Sea: A History of the Russian Navy.* New York: Frederick A. Praeger.

BRUCE W. MENNING

## MILITARY-INDUSTRIAL COMPLEX

The Russian military industrial complex (*voenno-promyshlennyi kompleks*, or VPK), recently renamed the defense industrial complex (*oboronno-promyshlennyi kompleks*, or OPK), encompasses the panoply of activities overseen by the Genshtab (General Staff), including the Ministry of Defense, uniformed military personnel, FSB (Federal Security Bureau) troops, border and paramilitary troops, the space program, defense research and regulatory agencies, infrastructural support affiliates, defense industrial organizations and production facilities, strategic material reserves, and an array of troop reserve, civil defense, espionage, and paramilitary activities. The complex is not a loose coalition of vested interests like the American military-industrial complex; it has a formal legal status, a well-developed administrative mechanism, and its own Web site. The Genshtab and the VPK have far more power than the American Joint Chiefs of Staff, the secretary of defense, or the patchwork of other defense-related organizations.

The OPK consists of seventeen hundred enterprises and organizations located in seventy-two regions, officially employing more than 2 million workers (more nearly 3.5 million), producing 27 percent of the nation's machinery, and absorbing 25 percent of its imports. Nineteen of these entities are "city building enterprises," defense industrial towns where the OPK is the sole employer. The total number of OPK enterprises and organizations has been constant for a decade, but some liberalization has been achieved in ownership and managerial autonomy. At the start of the post-communist epoch, the VPK was wholly state-owned. As of 2003, 43 percent of its holdings remains government-owned, 29 percent comprises mixed state-private stock companies, and 29 percent is fully privately owned. All serve the market in varying degrees, but retain a collective interest in promoting government patronage and can be quickly commandeered if state procurement orders revive.

Boris Yeltsin's government tried repeatedly to reform the VPK, as has Vladimir Putin's. The most recent proposal, vetted and signed by Prime Minister Mikhail Kasyanov in October 2001, calls for civilianizing some twelve hundred enterprises and institutions, stripping them of their military assets, including intellectual property, and transferring this capital to five hundred amalgamated entities called "system-building integrated structures." This rearrangement will increase the military focus of the OPK by divesting its civilian activities, beneficially reducing structural militarization, but will strengthen the defense lobby and augment state ownership. The program calls for the government to have controlling stock of the lead companies (design bureaus) of the "system-building integrated structures." This will be accomplished by arbitrarily valuing the state's intellectual property at 100 percent of the lead company's stock, a tactic that will terminate the traditional Soviet separation of design from production and create integrated entities capable of designing, producing, marketing (exporting), and servicing OPK products. State shares in non-lead companies will be put in trust with the design bureaus. The Kremlin intends to use ownership as its primary control instrument, keeping

its requisitioning powers in the background, and minimizing budgetary subsidies at a time when state weapons-procurement programs are but a small fraction what they were in the Soviet past. Ilya Klebanov, former deputy prime minister, and now minister for industry, science, and technology, the architect of the OPK reform program, hopes in this way to reestablish state administrative governance over domestic military industrial activities, while creating new entities that can seize a larger share of the global arms market. It is premature to judge the outcome of this initiative, but history suggests that even if the VPK modernizes, it does not intend to fade away.

*See also:* KASYANOV, MIKHAIL MIKHAILOVICH; MILITARY-ECONOMIC PLANNING; MILITARY, SOVIET AND POST-SOVIET

**BIBLIOGRAPHY**

Epstein, David. (1990). "The Economic Cost of Soviet Security and Empire." In *The Impoverished Superpower: Perestroika and the Soviet Military*, ed. Henry Rowen and Charles Wolf, Jr. San Francisco: Institute for Contemporary Studies.

Gaddy, Clifford. (1966). *The Price of the Past: Russia's Struggle with the Legacy of a Militarized Economy.* Washington, DC: Brookings Institution Press.

Hill, Christopher. (2003). "Russia's Defense Spending." In *Russia's Uncertain Future*. Washington, DC: Joint Economic Committee.

Izyumov, Alexei; Kosals, Leonid; and Ryvkina, Rosalina. (2001). "Privatization of the Russian Defense Industry: Ownership and Control Issues." *Post-Communist Economies* 12:485–496.

Rosefielde, Steven. (2004). *Prodigal Superpower: Russia's Re-emerging Future.* Cambridge, UK: Cambridge University Press.

Shlykov, Vitaly. (2002). "Russian Defense Industrial Complex After 9-11." Paper presented at the conference on "Russian Security Policy and the War on Terrorism," U.S. Naval Postgraduate School, Monterey, CA, June 4–5, 2002.

STEVEN ROSEFIELDE

## MILITARY INTELLIGENCE

Although the means have grown more sophisticated, the basic function of military intelligence (*voyennaya razvedka*) has remained unchanged: collecting, analyzing and disseminating information about the enemy's intentions and its ability to carry them out. Since the Soviet era, military intelligence has been classified according to three categories: strategic, operational, and tactical. Strategic intelligence entails an understanding of actual and potential foes at the broadest level, including the organization and capabilities of their armed forces as well as the economy, population, and geography of the national base. Operational intelligence refers to knowledge of military value more directly tied to the theater, and is typically conducted by the staffs of front and army formations, while tactical intelligence is carried out by commanders at all levels to gather battlefield data directly relevant to their current mission.

Before the Great Reforms (1860s–1870s), Russian generals had three basic means of learning about their foes: spies, prisoners of war, and reconnaissance. Thus, at the Battle of Kulikovo (1381) Prince Dmitry Donskoy dispatched a reliable diplomat to the enemy's camp to study the latter's intentions, questioned captives, and personally assessed the terrain, all of which played a role in his famous victory over the Mongols. While capable commanders had always understood the need for good intelligence, until the early eighteenth century the Russian army had neither systematic procedures nor personnel designated to carry them out. Peter I's introduction of a quartermaster service (*kvartirmeisterskaya chast*) in 1711 (renamed the general staff, or *generalny shtab*, by Catherine II in 1763) laid the institutional groundwork. The interception of diplomatic correspondence, a vital element of strategic intelligence, was carried out by the foreign office's *Cabinet Noir* (Black Chamber, also known as the *shifrovalny otdel*), beginning under Empress Elizabeth I (r. 1741–1762). Interministerial rivalry often hampered effective dissemination of such data to the War Ministry.

It would take another century for military intelligence properly to be systematized with the creation of a Main Staff (*glavny shtab*) by the reformist War Minister Dmitry Milyutin in 1865. Roughly analogous to the Prussian Great General Staff, the Main Staff's responsibilities included central administration, training, and intelligence. Two departments of the Main Staff were responsible for strategic intelligence: the Military Scientific Department (*Voyenny ucheny komitet*, which dealt with European powers) and the Asian Department (*Aziatskaya chast*). Milyutin also regularized procedures for operational and combat intelligence in 1868 with new regulations to establish an intelligence section (*razvedivatelnoye otdelenie*) attached to

field commanders' staffs, and he formalized the training and functions of military attachés (*voennye agenty*). The Admiralty's Main Staff established analogous procedural organizations for naval intelligence.

In 1903, the Army's Military Scientific Department was renamed Section Seven of the First Military Statistical Department in the Main Staff. Dismal performance during the Russo–Japanese War inevitably led to another series of reforms, which saw the creation in June 1905 of an independent Main Directorate of the General Staff (*Glavnoye Upravlenie Generalnago Shtaba*, or GUGSh), whose first over quartermaster general was now tasked with intelligence, among other duties. Resubordinated to the war minister in 1909, GUGSh would retain its responsibility for intelligence through World War I.

After the Bolshevik Revolution, Vladimir Lenin established a Registration Directorate (*Registupravlenie*, RU) in October 1918 to coordinate intelligence for his nascent Red Army. At the conclusion of the Civil War, in 1921, the RU was refashioned into the Second Directorate of the Red Army Staff (also known as the Intelligence Directorate, *Razvedupr*, or RU). A reorganization of the Red Army in 1925 saw the entity transformed into the Red Army Staff's Fourth Directorate, and after World War II it would be the Main Intelligence Directorate (*Glavnoye Razvedivatelnoye Upravlenie*, GRU).

Because of the presence of many former Imperial Army officers in the Bolshevik military, the RU bore more than a passing resemblance to its tsarist predecessor. However, it would soon branch out into much more comprehensive collection, especially through human intelligence (i.e., military attachés and illegal spies) and intercepting communications. Despite often intense rivalry with the state security services, beginning with Felix Dzerzhinsky's Cheka, the RU and its successors also became much more active in rooting out political threats, whether real or imagined.

Both tsarist and Soviet military intelligence were respected if not feared by other powers. Like all military intelligence services, its record was nevertheless marred by some serious blunders, including fatally underestimating the capabilities of the Japanese armed forces in 1904 and miscalculating the size of German deployments in East Prussia in 1914. Yet even the best intelligence could not compensate for the shortcomings of the supreme commander, most famously when Josef Stalin refused to heed repeated and often accurate assessments of

Nazi intentions to invade the Soviet Union in June 1941.

See also: ADMINISTRATION, MILITARY; MILITARY, IMPER-IAL ERA; MILITARY, SPECIAL PURPOSE FORCES; SOVIET AND POST-SOVIET; STATE SECURITY, ORGANS OF

## BIBLIOGRAPHY

Fuller, William C. (1984). "The Russian Empire." In *Knowing One's Enemies: Intelligence Assessment before the Two World Wars*, ed. Ernest R. May. Princeton, NJ: Princeton University Press.

Garthoff, Raymond L. (1956). "The Soviet Intelligence Services." In *The Soviet Army*, ed. Basil Liddell Hart. London: Weidenfeld and Nicholson.

Leonard, Raymond W. (1999). *Secret Soldiers of the Revolution: Soviet Military Intelligence, 1918–1933*. Westport, CT: Greenwood Press.

Pozniakov, Vladimir. (2000). "The Enemy at the Gates: Soviet Military Intelligence in the Inter–war Period and its Forecasts of Future War." In *Russia at the Age of Wars*, ed. Silvio Pons and Romano Giangiacomo. Milan: Fetrinellli.

Schimmelpenninck van der Oye, David. (2003). "Reforming Russian Military Intelligence." In *Reforming the Tsar's Army*, ed. David Schimmelpenninck van der Oye and Bruce Menning. New York: Cambridge University Press.

Schimmelpenninck van der Oye, David. (1996). "Russian Military Intelligence on the Manchurian Front." *Intelligence and National Security* 11(1):22–31.

DAVID SCHIMMELPENNINCK VAN DER OYE

# MILITARY REFORMS

Military reform has been one of the central aspects of Russia's drive to modernize and become a leading European military, political, and economic power. Ivan IV (d. 1584) gave away *pomestie* lands to create a permanent military service class, and Tsar Alexei Mikhailovich (d. 1676) enserfed Russia's peasants to guarantee the political support of these military servitors. In the same period, Alexei, seeking to modernize his realm, invited Westerners to Russia to introduce advanced technical capabilities. But as the eighteenth century dawned, Russia found itself surrounded and outmatched by hostile enemies to its north, south, west, and, to a lessor extent, to its east. At the same time, perhaps Russia's most energetic tsar, Peter the Great (d. 1725), adopted a grand strategy based on the goal of conquering adversaries in all directions. Such ambitions required the complete overhaul of the Russian nation. As a result, the reforms of Peter the Great represent the beginning of the modern era of Russian history.

Military reform, designed to create a powerful permanently standing army and navy, was the central goal of all of Peter the Great's monumental reforms. His most notable military reforms included the creation of a navy that he used to great effect against the Ottomans in the sea of Azov and the Swedes in the Baltic during the Great Northern War; the creation of the Guard's Officer Corps that became the basis of the standing professional officer corps until they became superannuated and replaced by officers with General Staff training during the nineteenth century; a twenty-five year service requirement for peasants selected by lot to be soldiers; and his codifying military's existence by personally writing a set of instructions in 1716 for the army and 1720 for the navy. While these reforms transformed the operational capabilities of the Russian military, Peter the Great also sought to create the social and administrative basis for maintaining this newly generated power. In 1720 he created administrative colleges specifically to furnish the army and navy with a higher administrative apparatus to oversee the acquisition of equipment, supplies, and recruits. Peter's final seminal reform, however, was the 1722 creation of the Table of Ranks, which linked social and political mobility to the idea of merit, not only in the military but throughout Russia.

The irony of Peter's culminating reform was that the nobility did not accept the Table of Ranks because it forced them to work to maintain what they viewed as their inherited birthright to power, privilege, and status. While no major military reforms occurred until after the 1853–1856 Crimean War, the work of Catherine II's (d. 1796) "Great Captains," Peter Rumyanstev, Grigory Potemkin, and Alexander Suvorov, combined with the reforming efforts of Paul I (d. 1801), created a system for educating and training officers and defined everything from uniforms to operational doctrine. None of these efforts amounted in scope to the reforms that preceded or followed, but together they provided Russia with a military establishment powerful enough to defeat adversaries ranging from the powerful French to the declining Ottomans. Realizing that the army was too large and too wasteful, Nicholas I (d. 1855) spent the balance of the 1830s and 1840s introducing administrative reforms to streamline and enhance performance but, as events in the Crimea demonstrated, without success.

Alexander II's (d. 1881) 1861 peasant emancipation launched his Great Reforms and set the stage for the enlightened War Minister Dmitry Milyutin to reorganize Russia's military establishment in every aspect imaginable. His most enduring reform was the 1862–1864 establishment of the fifteen military districts that imposed a centralized and manageable administrative and command system over the entire army. Then, to reintroduce the concept of meritocracy into the officer training system, he reorganized the Cadet Corps Academies into Junker schools in 1864 to provide an education to all qualified candidates regardless of social status. In addition, in 1868 he oversaw the recasting of the army's standing wartime orders. The result of these three reforms centralized all power within the army into the war minister's hands. But Milyutin's most important reform was the Universal Conscription Act of 1874 that required all Russian men to serve first in the active army and then in the reserves. Modeled after the system recently implemented by the Prussians in their stunningly successful unification, Russia now had the basis for a modern conscript army that utilized the Empire's superiority in manpower without maintaining a costly standing army.

Milyutin's reforms completely overhauled Russia's military system. But a difficult victory in the 1877–1878 Russo-Turkish War and the debacle of the Russo-Japanese War demonstrated that Russia's military establishment was in need of further and immediate reform in the post-1905 period. In the war's aftermath, the army and the navy were overrun with reforming schemes and undertakings that ranged from the creation of the Supreme Defense Council to unify all military policy, to the emergence of an autonomous General Staff (something Milyutin intentionally avoided), to the 1906 appointment of a Higher Attestation Commission charged with the task of purging the officer corps of dead weight. By 1910, the reaction to military defeat had calmed down, and War Minister Vladimir Sukhomlinov sought to address future concerns with a series of reforms that simplified the organization of army corps and sought to rationalize the deployment of troops throughout the Empire. These reforms demonstrated the future needs of the army well, resulting in the 1914 passage of a bill (The Large Program) through the Duma designed to finance the strengthening of the entire military establishment.

After the imperial army disintegrated in the wake of World War I and the 1917 Revolution, and once the Bolsheviks won the Civil War, the process of creating the permanent Red Army began with the 1924–1925 Frunze Reforms. Mikhail Frunze, largely using the organizational schema of Milyutin's military districts, oversaw a series of reforms designed to provide the Red Army with a sufficiently trained cadre to maintain a militia army. Besides training soldiers as warriors, one of the central goals of these reforms was to provide recruits with Communist Party indoctrination, making military training a vital experience in the education of Soviet citizens. In the meantime, and despite the tragic consequences of the purges of the 1930s, Mikhail Tukhachevsky created a military doctrine that culminated with the Red Army's victorious deep battle combined operations of World War II.

*See also:* FRUNZE, MIKHAIL VASILIEVICH; GREAT REFORMS; MILITARY, IMPERIAL ERA; MILITARY, SOVIET AND POST-SOVIET; MILYUTIN, DMITRY ALEXEYEVICH; PETER I; TABLE OF RANK; TUKHACHEVSKY, MIKHAIL NIKO-LAYEVICH

JOHN W. STEINBERG

## MILITARY, SOVIET AND POST-SOVIET

The Bolshevik Party, led by Vladimir Lenin and Leon Trotsky, seized power in November 1917. It immediately began peace negotiations with the Central Powers and took control of the armed forces. Once peace was concluded in March 1918 by the Treaty of Brest-Litovsk, the demobilization of the old Russian imperial army began.

### THE RED ARMY

Adhering to Marxist doctrine, which viewed standing armies as tools of state and class oppression, the Bolsheviks did not plan to replace the imperial army and intended instead to rely on a citizens' militia of class-conscious workers for defense. The emergence of widespread opposition to the Bolshevik seizure of power convinced Lenin of the need for a regular army after all, and he ordered Trotsky to create a Red Army, the birthday of which was recognized as February 23, 1918. As the number of workers willing to serve on a voluntary basis proved to be insufficient for the needs of the time, conscription of workers and peasants was soon introduced. By 1921 the Red Army had swelled to nearly five million men and women; the majority, however, were engaged full-time in food requisitioning and other economic activities designed to keep the army fed and equipped as Russia's beleaguered economy began to collapse. Because they lacked trained leadership to fight the civil war that erupted in the spring of 1918, the Bolsheviks recruited and impressed former officers of the old army and assigned political commissars to validate their orders and maintain political reliability of the units.

The civil war raged until 1922, when the last elements of anticommunist resistance were wiped out in Siberia. In the meantime Poland attacked Soviet Russia in April 1920 in a bid to establish its borders deep in western Ukraine. The Soviet counteroffensive took the Red Army to the gates of Warsaw before it was repelled and pushed back into Ukraine in August. The Red Army forces combating the Poles virtually disintegrated during their retreat, and the Cossacks of the elite First Cavalry Army, led by Josef Stalin's cronies Kliment Voroshilov and Semen Budenny, staged a bloody anti-Bolshevik mutiny and pogrom in the process. The subsequent peace treaty gave Poland very favorable boundaries eastward into Ukraine.

The onset of peace saw the demobilization of the regular armed forces to a mere half million men. Some party officials wanted to abolish the army totally and replace it with a citizens' militia. As a compromise, a mixed system consisting of a small standing army and a large territorial militia was established. Regular soldiers would serve for two years, but territorial soldiers would serve for five, one weekend per month and several weeks in the summer. Until it was absorbed into the regular army beginning in 1936, the territorial army outnumbered the regular army by about three to one. For the rest of the decade the armed forces were underfunded, undersupplied, and ill-equipped with old, outdated weaponry.

During the 1920s most former tsarist officers were dismissed and a new cadre of Soviet officers began to form. Party membership was strongly encouraged among the officers, and throughout the Soviet period at least eighty percent of the officers were party members. At and above the rank of colonel virtually all officers held party membership.

A unique feature of the Soviet armed forces was the imposition on it of the Political Administration of the Red Army (PURKKA, later renamed GlavPUR). This was the Communist Party organization for which the military commissars worked. Initially every commander from battalion level on up to the

A group of young women Russian soldiers train for military service following the Bolshevik revolution. © HULTON-DEUTSCH COLLECTION/CORBIS

Army High Command had a commissar as a partner. After the civil war, commanders no longer had to have their orders countersigned by the commissar to be valid, and commissars' duties were relegated to discipline, morale, and political education. During the 1930s political officers were added at the company and platoon levels, and during the purges and at the outset of World War II commanders once again had to have commissars countersign their orders. Commissars shared responsibility for the success of the unit and were praised or punished alongside the commanders, but they answered to the political authorities, not to the military chain of command. Commissars were required to evaluate officers' political reliability on their annual attestations and during promotion proceedings, thus giving them some leverage over the officers with whom they served.

### THE 1930S

The First Five-Year Plan, from 1928 to1932, expanded the USSR's industrial base, which then began producing modern equipment, including tanks, fighter aircraft and bombers, and new warships. The size of the armed forces rapidly increased to about 1.5 million between 1932 and 1937. The rapid expansion of the armed forces led to insurmountable difficulties in recruiting officers. As a stopgap measure, party members were required to serve as officers for two- or three-year stints, and privates and sergeants were promoted to officer rank. The training of officer candidates in military schools was abbreviated from four years to two or less to get more officers into newly created units. As a result the competence and cohesion of the leadership suffered.

In the 1930s Soviet strategists such as Vladimir K. Triandifilov and Mikhail Tukhachevsky devised innovative tactics for utilizing tanks and aircraft in offensive operations. The Soviets created the first large tank units, and experimented with paratroops and airborne tactics. During the Spanish Civil War (1936–39) Soviet officers and men advised the Republican forces and engaged in armored and air combat testing the USSR's latest tanks and aircraft against the fascists.

The terror purge of the officer corps instituted by Josef Stalin in 1937–1939 took a heavy toll of the top leadership. Stalin's motives for the purge will never be known for certain, but most plausibly he was concerned about a possible military coup. Although it is very unlikely that the military planned or hoped to seize power, three of its five marshals were executed, as were fifteen of sixteen army commanders of the first and second rank, sixty of sixty-seven corps commanders, and 136 of 199 division commanders. Forty-two of the top forty-six military commissars also were arrested and executed. When the process of denunciation, arrest, investigation, and rehabilitation had run its course in 1940, about 23,000 military and political officers had either been executed or were in prison camps. It was long believed that perhaps as many as fifty percent of the officer corps was purged, but archival evidence subsequently indicated that when the reinstatements of thousands of arrested officers during World War II are taken into account, fewer than ten percent of the officer corps was permanently purged, which does not diminish the loss of talented men. Simultaneous with the purge was the rapid expansion of the armed forces in response to the growth of militarism in Germany and Japan. By June 1941 the Soviet armed forces had grown to 4.5 million men, but were terribly short of officers because of difficulties in recruiting and the time needed for training. Tens of thousands of civilian party members,

sergeants, and enlisted men were forced to serve as officers with little training for their responsibilities. Despite the USSR's rapid industrialization, the army found itself underequipped because men were being conscripted faster than weapons, equipment, and even boots and uniforms could be made for them.

The end of the decade saw the Soviet Union involved in several armed conflicts. From May to September 1939, Soviet forces under General Georgy Zhukov battled the Japanese Kwantung Army and drove it out of Mongolia. In September 1939 the Soviet army and air force invaded eastern Poland after the German army had nearly finished conquering the western half. In November 1939 the Soviet armed forces attacked Finland but failed to conquer it and in the process suffered nearly 400,000 casualties. Stalin's government was forced to accept a negotiated peace in March 1940 in which it gained some territory north of Leningrad and naval bases in the Gulf of Finland. Anticipating war with Nazi Germany, the USSR increased the pace of rearmament in the years 1939–1941, and prodigious numbers of modern tanks, artillery, and aircraft were delivered to the armed forces.

## WORLD WAR II

In violation of the Nazi-Soviet non-aggression pact signed in 1939, Germany invaded the USSR on June 22, 1941. Much of the forward-based Soviet air force was destroyed on the ground on the first day of the onslaught. All along the front the Axis forces rolled up the Soviet defenses, hoping to destroy the entire Red Army in the western regions before marching on Moscow and Leningrad. By December 1941 the Germans had put Leningrad under siege, came within sight of Moscow, and, in great battles of encirclement, had inflicted about 4.5 million casualties on the Soviet armed forces, yet they had been unable to destroy the army and the country's will and ability to resist. Nearly 5.3 million Soviet citizens were mobilized for the armed forces in the first eight days of the war. They were used to create new formations or to fill existing units, which were reconstituted and rearmed and sent back into the fray. To rally the USSR, Stalin declared the struggle to be the Great Patriotic War of the Soviet Union, comparable to the war against Napoleon 130 years earlier.

At the outset of the war, Stalin appointed himself supreme commander and dominated Soviet military operations, ignoring the advice of his generals. Stalin's disastrous decisions culminated in

**Soviet tank regiment passes the Kremlin during the 1988 parade marking the anniversary of the October Revolution.**
© NOVOSTI/SOVFOTO

the debacle at Kiev in September 1941, in which 600,000 Soviet troops were lost because he refused to allow them to retreat. As a result, Stalin promoted Marshal Georgy Zhukov to second in command and from then on usually heeded the advice of his military commanders.

The Soviet Army once again lost ground during the summer of 1942, when a new German offensive completed the conquest of Ukraine and reached the Volga River at Stalingrad. In the fall of 1942 the Soviet Army began a counteroffensive, and by the end of February 1943 it had eliminated the German forces in Stalingrad and pushed the front several hundred miles back from the Volga. July 1943 saw the largest tank battle in history at Kursk, ending in a decisive German defeat. From then on the initiative passed to the Soviet side. The major campaign of 1944 was Operation Bagration, which liberated Belarus and carried the Red Army to the gates of Warsaw by July, in the process destroying German Army Group Center, a Soviet goal since January 1942. The final assault on Berlin began in April 1945 and culminated on May 3. The war in Europe ended that month, but a short campaign in China against Japan followed, beginning in August and ending in September 1945 with the Japanese surrender to the Allies.

### THE COLD WAR

After the war, the armed forces demobilized to their prewar strength of about four million and were assigned to the occupation of Eastern Europe. Conscription remained in force. During the late 1950s, under Nikita Khrushchev, who stressed nuclear rather than conventional military power, the army's strength was cut to around three million. Leonid Brezhnev restored the size of the armed force to more than four million. During the Cold War, pride of place in the Soviet military shifted to the newly created Strategic Rocket Forces (SRF), which controlled the ground-based nuclear missile forces. In addition to the SRF, the air force had bomber-delivered nuclear weapons and the navy had missile-equipped submarines. The army, with the exception of the airborne forces, became an almost exclusively motorized and mechanized force.

The Soviet army's last war was fought in Afghanistan from December 1979 to February 1989. Brought in to save the fledgling Afghan communist government, which had provoked a civil war through its use of coercion and class conflict to create a socialist state, the Soviet army expected to defeat the rebels in a short campaign and then withdraw. Instead, the conflict degenerated into a guerilla war against disparate Afghan tribes that had declared a holy war, or *jihad*, against the Soviet army, which was unable to bring its strength in armor, artillery, or nuclear weapons to bear. The Afghan rebels, or *mujahideen*, with safe havens in neighboring Iran and Pakistan, received arms and ammunition from the United States, enabling them to prolong the struggle indefinitely. The Soviet high command capped the commitment of troops to the war at 150,000, for the most part treating it as a sideshow while keeping its main focus on a possible war with NATO. The conflict was finally brought to a negotiated end after the ascension of Mikhail Gorbachev in 1985, with nearly 15,000 men killed in vain.

Gorbachev's policy of rapprochement with the West had a major impact on the Soviet armed forces. Between 1989 and 1991 their numbers were slashed by one million, with more cuts projected for the coming years. The defense budget was cut, the army and air force were withdrawn from Eastern Europe, naval ship building virtually ceased, and the number of nuclear missiles and warheads was reduced—all over the objections of the military high command. Gorbachev's policy of glasnost, or openness, exposed the horrible conditions of service for soldiers, particularly the extent and severity of hazing, which contributed to a dramatic increase in desertions and avoidance of conscription. The prestige of the military dropped precipitously, leading to serious morale problems in the officer corps. Motivated in part by a desire to restore the power, prestige, and influence of the military in politics and society, the minister of defense, Dmitry Iazov, aided and abetted the coup against Gorbachev in August 1991. The coup failed when the commanders of the armored and airborne divisions ordered into Moscow refused to support it.

### THE POST-SOVIET ARMY

The formal dissolution of the USSR in December 1991 led to the dismemberment of the Soviet armed forces and the creation of numerous national armies and navies. Conventional weapons, aircraft, and surface ships were shared out among the new nations, but the Russian Federation took all of the nuclear weapons. The army of the Russian Federation sees itself as heir to the traditions and heritage of the tsarist and Soviet armies. Although there are advocates of a professional force, the Russian army remains dependent on conscription to fill its ranks. Thousands of officers resigned from the armed forces and thousands of non-Russians transferred their loyalty and services to the emerging armies of the newly independent states. The political administration was promptly abolished after the coup. During the 1990s, the new Russian army fought two small, bloody, and inconclusive wars in Chechnya, a former Soviet republic that sought independence from Moscow.

*See also:* ADMINISTRATION, MILITARY; AFGHANISTAN, RELATIONS WITH; CIVIL WAR OF 1917–1922; COLD WAR; MILITARY DOCTRINE; MILITARY-INDUSTRIAL COMPLEX; OPERATION BARBAROSSA; PURGES, THE GREAT; SOVIET-FINNISH WAR; WORLD WAR II

## BIBLIOGRAPHY

Alexiev, Alexander. (1988). *Inside the Soviet Army in Afghanistan.* Santa Monica, CA: Rand.

Erickson, John. (1975). *The Road to Stalingrad: Stalin's War with Germany.* London: Weidenfeld & Nicolson.

Erickson, John. (1983). *The Road to Berlin: Continuing the History of Stalin's War With Germany.* Boulder, CO: Westview Press.

Erickson, John. (2001). *The Soviet High Command: A Military-Political History, 1918–1941,* 3rd ed. London: Frank Cass.

Jones, Ellen. (1975). *Red Army and Society: A Sociology of the Soviet Military.* Boston: Allen & Unwin.

Reese, Roger R. (2000). *The Soviet Military Experience: A History of the Soviet Army, 1917–1991.* London: Routledge.

Scott, Harriet F., and Scott, William F. (1981). *The Armed Forces of the USSR,* 2nd ed. Boulder, CO: Westview Press.

Von Hagen, Mark.(1990). *Soldier in the Proletarian Dictatorship: The Red Army and the Soviet Socialist State, 1917–1930.* Ithaca, NY: Cornell University Press.

White, D. Fedotoff. (1944). *The Growth of the Red Army.* Princeton, NJ: Princeton University Press.

ROGER R. REESE

# MILYUKOV, PAUL NIKOLAYEVICH

(1859–1943), Russian historian and publicist; Russian liberal leader.

Milyukov was born in Moscow. He studied at the First Gymnasium of Moscow and the department of history and philology at Moscow University (1877-1882). His tutors were Vassily Kliuchevsky and Paul Vinogradov. After graduating from the university, Milyukov remained in the department of Russian history in order to prepare to become a professor. From 1886 to 1895, he held the position of assistant professor in the department of Russian history at Moscow University. In 1892 he defended his master's thesis based on the book *State Economy and the Reform of Peter the Great* (St. Petersburg, 1892). In the area of historical methodology Milyukov shared the views of positivists. The most important of Milyukov's historical works was *Essays on the History of Russian Culture* (St. Petersburg, 1896-1903). Milyukov suggested that Russia is following the same path as Western Europe, but its development is characterized by slowness. In contrast to the West, Russia's social and economic development was generally initiated by the government, going from the top down. Milyukov is the author of o ne of the first courses of Russian historiography: *Main Currents in Russian Historical Thought* (Moscow, 1897). In 1895, he was fired from the Moscow University for his public lectures on the social movement in Russia and sent to Riazan, and then for two years (1897–1899) abroad.

In 1900 he was arrested for attending the meeting honoring the late revolutionary Petr Lavrov in St. Petersburg. He was sentenced to six months of incarceration, but was released early at the petition of Kliuchevsky before emperor Nicholas II. In 1902, Milyukov published a program article "From Russian Constitutionalists in the Osvobozhdenie" ("Liberation"), magazine of Russian liberals, issued abroad. Between 1902 and 1905, Milyukov spent a large amount of time abroad, traveling, and lecturing in the United States at the invitation of Charles Crane. Milyukov's lectures were published as *Russia and Its Crisis* (Chicago, 1905).

In 1905 Milyukov returned to Russia and took part in the liberation movement as one of the organizers and chairman of the Union of Unions. On August, 1905, he was arrested, but after a month-long incarceration was released without having been charged. In October of 1905 Milyukov became one of the organizers of the Constitutional Democratic (Kadet) Party. His reaction towards the October Manifesto was skeptical and he believed it necessary to continue to battle the government. Due to formal issues, he could not run for a place in the First and Second Dumas, but he was basically the head of the Kadet Faction. From 1906, Milyukov was the editor of the *Rech* (*Speech*) newspaper, the central organ of the Cadet Party. From 1907, he was the chairman of the Party's central committee. From 1907 to 1912, he was a member of the third Duma, elected in St. Petersburg. He favored the tactics of "the preservation of the Duma," fearing its dissolution by the tsar. He became a renowned expert in the matters of foreign policy. In the Duma, he gave seventy-three speeches, which total approximately seven hundred large pages. In 1912 Milyukov was reelected to the Duma, once again from St. Petersburg.

After the beginning of World War I, Milyukov assumed a patriotic position and put forth the motto of a "holy union" with the government for the period of the war. He believed it necessary for Russia to acquire, as a result of the war, Bosporus and the Dardanelles. In August of 1915, Milyukov, was one of the organizers and leaders of the oppositionist interparty Progressive Bloc, created with the aim of pressuring the government in the interests of a more effective war strategy. On November 1, 1916, Milyukov made a speech in the Duma that contained direct accusations of the royal family members of treason and harshly criticized the government. Every part of Milyukov's speech ended with "What Is This: Stupidity or Treason?" The speech was denied publication, but became popular through many private copies and later received the name of "The Attacking Sign."

After the February revolution Milyukov served as the foreign minister in the Provisional Government. Milyukov's note of April, 1917, declaring support for fulfilling obligations to the allies provoked antigovernmental demonstrations and caused him to retire. Milyukov attacked the Bolsheviks, demanding Lenin's arrest, and criticized the Provisional Government for its inability to restore order. After the October Revolution, Milyukov left for the Don, and wrote, at the request of general Mikhail Alexeyev, the Declaration of the Volunteer Army. In the summer of 1918, while in Kiev, he tried to contact German command, hoping to receive aid in the struggle against Bolshevism. Milyukov's "German orientation," unsupported by a majority of the Cadet Party, led to the downfall of his authority and caused him to retire as chairman of the party. In November of 1918, Milyukov went abroad, living in London, where he participated in the Russian Liberation Committee. From 1920, he lived in Paris. After the defeat of White armies, he proposed a set of "new tactics," the point of which was to defeat Bolshevism from within. Milyukov's "new tactics" received no support among most emigré Cadets and in 1921 he formed the Paris Democratic Group of the Party, which caused a split within the Cadets. In 1924 the group was modified into a Republican-Democrat Union. From 1921 to 1940 Milyukov

edited the most popular emigré newspaper *The Latest News* (Poslednie Novosti). He became one of the first historians of the revolution and the civil war, publishing *History of the Second Russian Revolution* (Sofia, 1921-1923), and *Russia at the Turning-point* (in two volumes, Paris, 1927).

In 1940, escaping the Nazi invasion, Milyukov fled to the south of France, where he worked on his memoirs, published posthumously. He welcomed the victories of the Soviet army and accepted the accomplishments of the Stalinist regime in fortifying Russian Statehood in his article "The Truth of Bolshevism" (1942). Milyukov died in Aix-les-Bains on March 31, 1943.

*See also:* CONSTITUTIONAL DEMOCRATIC PARTY; FEBRUARY REVOLUTION HISTORIOGRAPHY; LIBERALISM; OCTOBER REVOLUTION

**BIBLIOGRAPHY**

Emmons, Terence. (1999). "On the Problem of Russia's 'Separate Path' in Late Imperial Historiography." In *Historiography of Imperial Russia*, ed Tomas Sanders. Armonk, NY: M. E.Sharpe.

Miliukov, Pavel Nikolaevich. (1942). *Outlines of Russian Culture.* 3 vols., ed. Michael Karpovich; tr. Valentine Ughet and Eleanor Davis. Philadelphia: University of Pennsylvania Press.

Miliukov, Pavel Nikolaevich. (1967). *Political memoirs, 1905–1917,* ed. Arthur P. Mendel, tr. Carl Goldberg. Ann Arbor: University of Michigan Press.

Miliukov, Pavel Nikolaevich. (1978–1987). *The Russian Revolution.* 3 vols., ed. Richard Stites; tr. Tatyana and Richard Stites. Gulf Breeze, FL: Academic International Press.

Miliukov, Pavel Nikolaevich; Seignobos, Charles; and Eisenmann, L. (1968). *History of Russia.* New York: Funk & Wagnalls.

Riha, Thomas. (1969). *A Russian European: Paul Miliukov in Russian Politics.* Notre Dame, IN: University of Notre Dame Press.

Stockdale, Melissa K. (1996). *Paul Miliukov and the Quest for a Liberal Russia, 1880-1918.* Ithaca, NY: Cornell University Press.

OLEG BUDNITSKII

# MILYUTIN, DMITRY ALEXEYEVICH

(1816–1912), count (1878), political and military figure, military historian, and Imperial Russian war minister (1861–1881).

General Adjutant Milyutin was born in Moscow, the scion of a Tver noble family. He completed the gymnasium at Moscow University (1832) and the Nicholas Military Academy (1836). After a brief period with the Guards' General Staff, he served from 1839 to 1840 with the Separate Caucasian Corps. While convalescing from wounds during 1840 and 1841, he traveled widely in Europe, where he decided to devote himself to the cause of reform in Russia. As a professor at the Nicholas Academy from 1845 to 1853, he founded the discipline of military statistics and provided the impulse for compilation of a military-statistical description of the Russian Empire. In 1852 and 1853 he published a prize-winning five-volume history of Generalissimo A. V. Suvorov's Italian campaign of 1799. As a member of the Imperial Russian Geographic Society he associated with a number of future reformers, including Konstantin Kavelin, P. P. Semenov-Tyan-Shansky, Nikolai Bunge, and his brother, Nikolai Milyutin. An opponent of serfdom, the future war minister freed his own peasants and subsequently (in 1856) wrote a tract advocating the liberation of Russian serfs.

As a major general within the War Ministry during the Crimean War, Milyutin concluded that the army required fundamental reform. While serving from 1856 to 1860 as chief of staff for Prince Alexander Baryatinsky's Caucasian Corps, Milyutin directly influenced the successful outcome of the campaign against the rebellious mountaineer Shamil. After becoming War Minister in November 1861, Milyutin almost immediately submitted to Tsar Alexander II a report that outlined a program for comprehensive military reform. The objectives were to modernize the army, to restructure military administration at the center, and to create a territorial system of military districts for peacetime maintenance of the army. Although efficiency remained an important goal, Milyutin's reform legislation also revealed a humanitarian side: abolition of corporal punishment, creation of a modern military justice system, and a complete restructuring of the military-educational system to emphasize spiritual values and the welfare of the rank-and-file. These and related changes consumed the war minister's energies until capstone legislation of 1874 enacted a universal military service obligation. Often in the face of powerful opposition, Milyutin had orchestrated a grand achievement, although the acknowledged price included increased bureaucratic formalism and rigidity within the War Ministry.

Within a larger imperial context, Milyutin consistently advanced Russian geopolitical interests and objectives. He favored suppression of the Polish uprising of 1863–1864, supported the conquest of Central Asia, and advocated an activist policy in the Balkans. On the eve of the Russo-Turkish War of 1877–1878, he endorsed a military resolution of differences with Turkey, holding that the Eastern Question was primarily Russia's to decide. During the war itself, he accompanied the field army into the Balkans, where he counseled persistence at Plevna, asserting that successful resolution of the battle-turned-siege would serve as prelude to further victories. After the war, Milyutin became the *de facto* arbiter of Russian foreign policy.

Within Russia, after the Berlin Congress of 1878, Milyutin pressed for continuation of Alexander II's Great Reforms, supporting the liberal program of the Interior Ministry's Mikhail Loris-Melikov. However, after the accession of Alexander III and publication in May 1881 of an imperial manifesto reasserting autocratic authority, Milyutin retired to his Crimean estate. He continued to maintain an insightful diary and commenced his memoirs. The latter grew to embrace almost the entire history of nineteenth-century Russia, with important perspectives on the Russian Empire and contiguous lands and on its relations with Europe, Asia, and America.

*See also:* MILITARY, IMPERIAL ERA; GREAT REFORMS; MILITARY; SUVOROV, ALEXANDER VASILIEVICH

**BIBLIOGRAPHY**

Brooks, Edwin Willis. (1970). "D. A. Miliutin: Life and Activity to 1856." Ph.D. diss., Stanford University, Stanford, CA.

Menning, Bruce W. (1992, 2000). *Bayonets before Bullets: The Imperial Russian Army, 1861–1914.* Bloomington: Indiana University Press.

Miller, Forrestt A. (1968). *Dmitrii Miliutin and the Reform Era in Russia.* Nashville: Vanderbilt University Press.

LARISSA ZAKHAROVA

## MILYUTIN, NIKOLAI ALEXEYEVICH

(1818–1870), government official and reformer.

Nikolai Milyutin was born into a well-connected noble family of modest means. One of his brothers, Dmitry, would serve as Minister of War from 1861 to 1881. Nikolai entered government service at the age of seventeen and served in the Ministry of Internal Affairs from 1835 until 1861. A succession of ministers, recognizing his industry and talent, had him draft major reports to be issued in their names. He was largely responsible for compiling the Urban Statute of 1846, which, as applied to St. Petersburg and then to other large cities, somewhat expanded the number of persons who could vote in city elections.

Until 1858, Milyutin was a relatively obscure functionary. In the next six years he was the principal author of legislation that fundamentally changed the Russian empire: the Statutes of February 19, 1861, abolishing serfdom; the legislation establishing elective agencies of local self-administration (*zemstva*), enacted in 1864; and legislation intended to end the sway of the Polish nobility after their participation in the insurrection of 1863. He exercised this influence although the highest position he held was Acting Deputy Minister of Internal Affairs from 1859 to 1861—"acting" because Alexander II supposed that he was a radical. He was dismissed as deputy minister as soon as the peasant reform of 1861 was safely enacted.

In the distinctive political culture of autocratic Russia, Milyutin demonstrated consummate skill and cunning as a politician. None of the core concepts of the legislation of 1861 was his handiwork. He was, however, able to persuade influential persons with access to the emperor, such as the Grand Duchess Yelena Pavlovna, to adopt and promote these concepts. He was able, in a series of memoranda written for the Minister of Internal Affairs Sergei Lanskoy, to persuade the emperor to turn away from his confidants who opposed the emerging reform and to exclude the elected representatives of the nobility from the legislative process. And, as chairman of the Economic Section of the Editorial Commission, a body with ostensibly ancillary functions, he was able to mobilize a fractious group of functionaries and "experts" and lead them in compiling the legislation enacted in 1861.

Almost simultaneously he served as chairman of the Commission on Provincial and District Institutions. In that capacity he drafted the legislation establishing the *zemstvo*, an institution which enabled elected representatives to play a role in local affairs, such as education and public health. The reform was also significant because the regime abandoned the principle of *soslovnost*, or status based on membership in one of the hereditary estates of the realm, which had been the lodestone of government policy for centuries. To be sure, the landed nobility, yesterday's serfholders, were guaranteed a predominant role, since there were property qualifications for the bodies that elected *zemstvo* delegates.

Concerning the "western region" (Eastern Poland), Milyutin rewrote the legislation of February 19 so that ex-serfs received their allotments of land gratis and landless peasants were awarded land, often land expropriated from the Catholic Church. He wished to bind the peasants, largely Orthodox Christians, to the regime and detach them from the Roman Catholic nobles, who had risen in arms against it.

Milyutin was well aware of the shortcomings of the reform legislation he produced. He counted on the autocracy to continue its reform course and eliminate these shortcomings. His expectations were not realized. It is the paradox and perhaps the tragedy of Milyutin that, despite his reputation as a "liberal," he saw the autocracy as the essential instrument to produce a prosperous, modern, and law-governed Russia.

*See also:* EMANCIPATION ACT; MILYUTIN, DMITRY ALEXEYEVICH; PEASANTRY; SERFDOM; ZEMSTVO

**BIBLIOGRAPHY**

Field, Daniel. (1976). *The End of Serfdom: Nobility and Bureaucracy in Russia, 1856–1861*. Cambridge, MA: Harvard University Press.

Lincoln, W. Bruce. (1982). *In the Vanguard of Reform: Russia's Enlightened Bureaucrats, 1825–1861*. DeKalb: Northern Illinois University Press.

Zakharova, Larissa. (1994). "Autocracy and the Reforms of 1861–1874 in Russia." In *Russia's Great Reforms, 1855–1881*, eds. B. Eklof, J. Bushnell, and L. G. Zakharova. Bloomington: Indiana University Press.

DANIEL FIELD

# MINGRELIANS

Mingrelians call themselves Margali (plural Margalepi) and are Georgian Orthodox. Mingrelian (like Georgian, Svan, and Laz) is a South Caucasian (Kartvelian) language; only Mingrelian and Laz, jointly known as Zan, are mutually intelligible.

The ancient Zan continuum along the Black Sea's eastern coast from Abkhazia to Rize was broken by Georgian speakers fleeing the Arab emirate (655–1122) in Georgia's modern capital Tiflis, so that Georgian-speaking provinces (Guria and Ajaria) now divide Mingrelia (western Georgian lowlands bounded by Abkhazia, Svanetia, Lechkhumi, Imeretia, Guria, and the Black Sea) from Lazistan (northeastern Turkey). The Dadianis ruled post-Mongol Mingrelia (capital Zugdidi), which came under Russian protection in 1803, although internal affairs remained in local hands until 1857. Traditional home economy resembled that of neighboring Abkhazia.

A late-nineteenth-century attempt to introduce a Mingrelian prayer book and language primer using Cyrillic characters failed; it was interpreted as a move to undermine the Georgian national movement's goal of consolidating all Kartvelian speakers. In the 1926 Soviet census, 242,990 declared Mingrelian nationality, a further 40,000 claiming Mingrelian as their mother tongue. This possibility (and thus these data) subsequently disappeared; since around 1930, all Kartvelian speakers have officially been categorized as "Georgians." Today Mingrelians may number over one million, though fewer speak Mingrelian. Some publishing in Mingrelian (with Georgian characters), especially of regional newspapers and journals, was promoted by the leading local politician, Ishak Zhvania (subsequently denounced as a separatist), from the late 1920s to 1938, after which only Georgian, the language in which most Mingrelians are educated, was allowed (occasional scholarly works apart). While some Mingrelian publishing has restarted since Georgian independence, Mingrelian has never been formally taught. Stalin's police chief, Lavrenti Beria, and Georgia's first post-Soviet president, Zviad Gamsakhurdia, were Mingrelians. The civil war that followed Gamsakhurdia's overthrow (1992) mostly affected Mingrelia, where Zviadist sympathizers were concentrated; even after Gamsakhurdia's death (1993), local discontent with the central authorities fostered at least two attempted coups, reinforcing longstanding Georgian fears of separatism in the area.

See also: ABKHAZIANS; CAUCASUS; GEORGIA AND GEORGIANS; SVANS

**BIBLIOGRAPHY**

Hewitt, George. (1995). "Yet a third consideration of *Völker, Sprachen und Kulturen des südlichen Kaukasus.*" *Central Asian Survey* 14(2):285– 310.

B. GEORGE HEWITT

## MININ, KUZMA

(d. 1616), organizer, fundraiser, and treasurer of the second national liberation army of 1611–1612.

Kuzma Minin was elected as an elder of the townspeople of Nizhny Novgorod in September 1611, when Moscow was still occupied by the Poles. After the disintegration of the first national liberation army, Minin began to raise funds for the organization of a new militia. Its nucleus was provided by the garrison of Nizhny Novgorod and neighboring Volga towns, together with some refugee servicemen from the Smolensk region. At the request of Prince Dmitry Pozharsky, the military commander of the new army, Minin became its official treasurer. When the militia was based at Yaroslavl, in the spring of 1612, Minin was an important member of the provisional government headed by Pozharsky. After the liberation of Moscow in October 1612, Minin, together with Pozharsky and Prince Dmitry Trubetskoy, played a major role in convening the Assembly of the Land, which elected Mikhail Romanov tsar in January 1613. On the day after Mikhail's coronation, Minin was appointed to the rank of *dumny dvoryanin* within the council of boyars; he died shortly afterwards. Along with Pozharsky, Minin became a Russian national hero who served as a patriotic inspiration in later wars. In early Soviet historiography, his merchant status led him to be viewed as a representative of bourgeois reaction against revolutionary democratic elements such as cossacks and peasants. By the late 1930s he was again seen as a patriot, and his relatively humble social origin made him particularly acceptable as a popular hero during World War II.

See also: ASSEMBLY OF LAND; POZHARSKY, DMITRY MIKHAILOVICH; TIME OF TROUBLES; COSSACKS; MERCHANTS; PEASANTRY

**BIBLIOGRAPHY**

Dunning, Chester L. (2001). *Russia's First Civil War: The Time of Troubles and the Founding of the Romanov Dynasty.* University Park, PA: Pennsylvania State University Press.

Perrie, Maureen. (2002). *Pretenders and Popular Monarchism in Early Modern Russia: The False Tsars of the Time of Troubles,* paperback ed. Cambridge, UK: Cambridge University Press.

Skrynnikov, Ruslan G. (1988). *The Time of Troubles: Russia in Crisis, 1604–1618,* ed. and tr. Hugh F. Graham. Gulf Breeze, FL: Academic International Press.

MAUREEN PERRIE

## MINISTRIES, ECONOMIC

The industrial ministries of the Soviet Union were intermediate bodies that dealt directly with production enterprises. They played a key role in resource allocation and were directly responsible for the implementation of state industrial policy as developed and adopted by the Communist Party. In fact, ministers had two lines of responsibilities: one to the Council of Ministers, and the other, more important in the long run, to the Party's Central Committee. The most important ministers were members of Politburo. The ministries negotiated output targets and input limits with Gosplan, which was responsible for fulfilling the directives of the party and the Council of Ministers.

Once output and input targets were set, the ministries organized the activities of their enterprises to achieve output targets and stay within input limits. Normally the ministries petitioned Gosplan to reconsider their output and input target figures if plan fulfillment was threatened. This practice was called corrections (*korrektirovka*). Normally aimed at decreasing planned outputs, it was a common practice, although widely condemned by Party officials. The Council of Ministers had the formal authority to decide on these petitions, but in most cases the actual decision was left to Gosplan. The minister or his deputy and even heads of ministry main administrations (*glavki*) were members of the Council of Ministers and participated in its sessions. Most of the operational work of the ministries was done by the main administrations.

The industrial ministries were the fund holders (*fondoderzhateli*) of the economy. Gosplan and Gossnab (State Committee for Material Technical Supply) allocated the most important industrial raw materials, equipment, and semifabricates to the industrial ministries. Moreover, the ministries had their own supply departments that worked with Gossnab. Centrally allocated materials were called funded (*fondiruyemie*) commodities, which were allocated to the enterprises only by ministries. Enterprises were not legally allowed to exchange funded goods, although they did so.

The ministries existed at three levels. The most important were the All-Union ministries (*Soyuznoe ministerstvo*). Based in Moscow, All-Union ministries managed an entire branch of the economy, such as machine-building, coal, or electrical products. They concentrated enormous power and financial and material resources, and controlled the most important sectors of the economy. Ministries of the military-industrial complex were concentrated in Moscow. They obtained priority funds and limits allocated by Gosplan. Similarly, the significance of corresponding ministers was very high—they were the direct masters of the enterprises located in all republics that constituted the Soviet Union.

At the second level were the ministries of dual subordination—the Union-Republican Ministry (*Soiuzno-respublikanskoe ministerstvo*). As a rule, their headquarters were in Moscow. While the capitals of individual republics were the sites of republic-specific branches that conducted everyday activities, plan approval and resource allocation were subordinated to Moscow. Among the dual subordination ministries were the ministries of the coal industry, food industry, and construction. For example, Ukraine produced a bulk of Soviet coal and food output; therefore Union-ministry branches were located in its capital, Kiev.

The republican ministries occupied the lowest level. They were controlled by the republican Councils of Ministers and the Republican Central Committees of the Communist Party. They produced primarily local and regional products.

There were also committees under the Council of Ministers that enjoyed practically the same rights as the ministries: for example, the State Committee on Radio and Television, or the notorious KGB, which nominally was a committee but probably enjoyed a wide scope of powers.

A typical ministry was run by the minister and by deputy ministers who supervised corresponding *glavki* that, in their turn, controlled all work under their jurisdiction. A special *glavk* was responsible for logistical aspects of the industry's performance; technical glavki were in charge of the planning of the industry's plant operations.

The ministries had authorized territorial representatives in major administrative centers of the Soviet Union who directly supervised the plant's operations. The ministry, however, was dependent on its subordinated enterprises for information. The enterprises possessed better local information and were reluctant to share this information with the ministry.

Ministries had their own scientific and research institutes and higher education establishments that trained professionals for the industry. The industrial ministries were expected to perform a wide variety of tasks: to plan production, manage material and technical supply, arrange transportation, develop scientific policy, and plan capital investment.

The ministers were responsible for the performance of their enterprises as a whole; at the same time, the employees were not motivated and did not have any incentives to work creatively and to their full potential. The bulk of ministerial decision making was devoted to implementing and monitoring the operational plan after the annual plan had been approved. Under constant pressure to meet plan targets, industrial ministries exercised opportunistic behavior: that is, they bargained for lower output targets, demanded extra inputs, and exploited horizontal and vertical integration strategies to achieve more independence from centralized supplies.

During the later period of the Soviet Union, many attempts were made to improve the work of industrial ministries to make them more effective and efficient. However, these attempts were inconsistent, and the number of bureaucrats was hardly reduced. The giant administrative superstructure of the ministries was a heavy burden on the economy and played an increasingly regressive role. It was partially responsible for the economic collapse of Soviet economy. The ministerial bureaucracy continued to play an important role after the collapse of the Soviet Union. In Russia, for example, former ministerial officials gained control of significant chunks of industry during the privatization process.

*See also:* COMMAND ADMINISTRATIVE ECONOMY; GOSPLAN; INDUSTRIALIZATION, SOVIET

**BIBLIOGRAPHY**

Gregory, Paul R., and Stuart, Robert C. (2001). *Russian and Soviet Economic Performance and Structure.* Boston, MA: Addison Wesley.

Hewett, Edward A. (1988). *Reforming the Soviet Economy: Equality Versus Efficiency.* Washington, DC: Brookings Institution.

PAUL R. GREGORY

# MINISTRY OF FOREIGN TRADE

The Ministry of Foreign Trade was a functional ministry subordinate to Gosplan and the Council of Ministers that was responsible for foreign trade in the Soviet economy.

It was a functional ministry in that its jurisdiction cut across the responsibilities of the various branch ministries that managed production and distribution of products. It reported directly to Gosplan and the Council of Ministers. The operating units of the Ministry of Foreign Trade were the Foreign Trade Organizations (FTOs), which controlled exports and imports of specific goods, such as automobiles, aircraft, books, and so forth.

Soviet enterprises generally had no authority or means to export or import to or from abroad. The relevant FTO responded to requests from enterprises under its jurisdiction and, if approved, conducted negotiations, financing, and all other arrangements necessary for the transaction. Imports and exports, and thus the FTOs and the Ministry of Foreign Trade, were subject to the overall annual and quarterly economic plans. In this way, foreign trade was utilized to complement rather than to compete with the plan.

*See also:* COUNCIL OF MINISTERS, SOVIET; FOREIGN TRADE; GOSPLAN

**BIBLIOGRAPHY**

Gregory, Paul R., and Stuart, Robert C. (1990). *Soviet Economic Structure and Performance*, 4th ed. New York: HarperCollins.

Hewett, Ed A. (1988). *Reforming the Soviet Economy: Equality versus Efficiency.* Washington, DC: The Brookings Institution.

JAMES R. MILLAR

# MINISTRY OF INTERNAL AFFAIRS

The extent to which Russian regimes have depended upon the Ministry of Internal Affairs (MVD, *Ministerstvo vnutrennykh del*) is symbolized by its surviving the fall of tsarism and the end of the Soviet Union intact and with almost the same name. The ministry's ancestry runs as far back as the sixteenth century, when Ivan the Terrible established the Brigandage Office to combat banditry. However, a formal Ministry of Internal Affairs was not founded until 1802. From the first, its primary responsibility was to protect the interests of the state, and this was so even before it was made responsible for the Okhranka, or political police, in 1880. The close relationship between regular policing and political control has been a central characteristic of the MVD throughout its existence.

The Bolsheviks came to power with utopian notions of policing by social consent and public voluntarism, but because of the new regime's authoritarian tendencies and the exigencies of the Civil War (1918–1921), it became necessary, by 1918, to transform the "workers' and peasants' militia" into a full-time police force; one year later the militia was militarized. Originally envisaged as locally controlled forces loosely subordinated to the People's Commissariat for Internal Affairs (NKVD), the militia, in practice, were soon closely linked with the Cheka political police force and subject to central control. The NKVD was increasingly identified with political policing; in 1925, the militia and the Cheka's successor, the OGPU (Unified State Political Directorate), were combined, and in 1932 the NKVD was formally subordinated to the OGPU. Two years later, the roles were technically reversed, with the OGPU absorbed into the NKVD, but in practice this actually reflected the colonization of the NKVD by the political police.

The concentration of law enforcement in the hands of the political police well suited the needs of Josef V. Stalin during the era of purges and collectivization, but in 1941 the regular and political police were once again divided. Regular policing again became the responsibility of the NKVD, while the political police became the NKGB, the People's Commissariat of State Security. After the war, the NKVD regained the old title of the Ministry of Internal Affairs, and the NKGB became the MGB, Ministry of State Security. The political police remained very much the senior service, and for a short time (1953–1954) the MVD was reabsorbed into the MGB (which then became the Committee of State Security, KGB), but from this point the regular and political police became increasingly distinct agencies, each with a sense of its own role, history, and identity.

The police and security forces remained a key element of the Communist Party's apparatus of political control and thus the subject of successive reforms, generally intended to strengthen both their subordination to the leadership and their authority over the masses. In 1956, reflecting concerns among the elite about the power of the security forces, the MVD was decentralized. In 1960, the USSR MVD was dissolved, and day-to-day control of the police passed to the MVDs of the constituent Union republics. In practice, though, the law codes of the republics mirrored their Russian counterpart,

and the republican ministries were essentially local agencies for the central government. In 1968 the USSR MVD was reorganized in name as well as practice, after yet one more name change (Ministry for the Defense of Public Order, MOOP, 1962–1968).

The structure of the Ministry for Internal Affairs has not significantly changed, and thus the post-Soviet Russian MVD is similar in essence and organization, if not in scale. In 1991, Boris Yeltsin tried to merge the MVD and the security agencies into a new "super-ministry," but this was blocked by the Constitutional Court and the idea was dropped. Other reforms were relatively minor, such as the transfer of responsibility for prisons to the Justice Ministry.

As guarantor of the Kremlin's authority, the MVD controls a sizeable militarized security force, the Interior Troops (VV). At its peak, in the early 1980s, this force numbered 300,000 officers and men, and its strength of 193,000 in 2003 actually reflected an increase in its size in proportion to the regular army. In the post-Soviet era, most VV units are local garrison forces, largely made up of conscripts, but there are also small commando forces as well as the elite Dzerzhinsky Division, based on the outskirts of Moscow, which has its own armored elements and artillery.

See also: STATE SECURITY, ORGANS OF

**BIBLIOGRAPHY**

Galeotti, Mark. (1993). "Perestroika, Perestrelka, Pereborka: Policing Russia in a Time of Change." *Europe-Asia Studies* 45:769–786.

Orlovsky, Daniel. (1981). *The Limits of Reform.* Cambridge, MA: Harvard University Press.

Shelley, Louise. (1996). *Policing Soviet Society.* London: Routledge.

Weissman, Neil. (1985). "Regular Police in Tsarist Russia, 1990–1914." *Russian Review* 44:45–68.

MARK GALEOTTI

# MIR

The word *mir* in Russian has several meanings. In addition to "community" and "assembly," it also means "world" and "peace." These seemingly diverse meanings had a common historical origin. The village community formed the world for the peasants, where they tried to keep a peaceful society. Thus mir was, in all probability, a peasant-given name for a spontaneously generated peasant organization in early Kievan or pre-Kievan times. It was mentioned in the eleventh century in the first codification of Russian law, *Pravda Russkaya*, as a body of liability in cases of criminal offense.

Over time, the meaning of mir changed, depending on the political structure of the empire, and came to mean different things to different people. For peasants and others, mir presumably was always a generic term for peasant village-type communities with a variety of structures and functions. The term also denoted those members of a peasant community who were eligible to discuss and decide on communal affairs. At the top of a mir stood an elected elder.

Contrary to the belief of the Slavophiles, communal land redistribution had no long tradition as a function of the mir. Until the end of the seventeenth century, individual land ownership was common among Russian peasants, and only special land holdings were used jointly. All modern characteristics, such as egalitarian landholding and land redistribution, developed only as results of changes in taxation, as the poll tax was introduced in 1722 and forced upon the peasants by the landowners, who sought to distribute the allotments more equally and thus get more return from their serfs.

In the nineteenth century, mir referred to any and all of the following: a peasant village group as the cooperative owner of communal land property; the gathering of all peasant households of a village or a *volost* to distribute responsibility for taxes and to redistribute land; a peasant community as the smallest cell of the state's administration; and, most importantly, the entire system of a peasant community with communal property and land tenure subject to repartitioning. The peasant land was referred to as *mirskaya zemlia*.

Only at the end of the 1830s did a second term, *obshchina*, come into use for the village community. Unlike the old folk word mir, the term *obshchina* was invented by the Slavophiles with the special myth of the commune in mind. This term specifically designated the part of the mir's land that was cultivated individually but that was also redistributable. The relation between both terms is that an obshchina thus coincided with some aspects of a mir but did not encompass all of the mir's functions. The land of an obshchina either coincided with that of a mir or comprised a part of mir

holdings. Every obshchina was perforce related to a mir, but not every mir was connected with an obshchina, because some peasants held their land in hereditary household tenure and did not redistribute it. With increasing confusion between both terms, most educated Russians probably equated mir and obshchina from the 1860s onward. Obshchina was also used for peasant groups lacking repartitional land.

Although the mir was an ancient form of peasant self-administration, it was also the lowest link in a chain of authorities extending from the individual peasant to the highest levels of state control. It was responsible to the state and later to the landowners for providing taxes, military recruits, and services. The mir preserved order in the village, regulated the use of communal arable lands and pastures, and until 1903 was collectively responsible for paying government taxes. Physically, the mir usually coincided with one particular settlement or village. However, in some cases it might comprise part of a village or more than one village. As its meaning no longer differed from obshchina, the term mir came out of use at the beginning of the twentieth century.

*See also:* OBSHCHINA; PEASANT ECONOMY; PEASANTRY

**BIBLIOGRAPHY**

Grant, Steven A. (1976). "Obshchina and Mir." *Slavic Review* 35:636–651.

Moon, David. (1999). *The Russian Peasantry 1600–1930: The World the Russian Peasants Made.* London: Longman.

Robinson, Geroid T. (1967). *Rural Russia under the Old Regime.* Berkeley: University of California Press.

STEPHAN MERL

# MIR SPACE STATION

The Mir ("world") space station was a modular space facility providing living and working accommodations for cosmonauts and astronauts during its fifteen-plus years in orbit around the Earth. The core module of Mir was launched on February 20, 1986, and the station complex was commanded to a controlled re-entry into the earth's atmosphere over the Pacific Ocean on March 23, 2001, where its parts either burned up or sank in the ocean.

**The Russian Space Station MIR, photographed from the cargo bay of the U.S. Space Shuttle Atlantis.** © AFP/CORBIS

The core module provided basic services—living quarters, life support, and power—for those staying aboard Mir. In subsequent years, five additional modules were launched and attached to the core to add to the research and crew support capabilities of the space station; the last module was attached in 1996.

More than one hundred cosmonauts and astronauts visited Mir during its fifteen years in orbit. One, Soviet cosmonaut Valery Polyakov, stayed in orbit for 438 days, the longest human space flight in history. Beginning in 1995, the U.S. space shuttle carried out docking missions with Mir, and seven U.S. astronauts stayed on Mir for periods ranging from 115 to 188 days. These Shuttle-Mir missions were carried out in preparation for Russian-U.S. cooperation in the International Space Station program.

Toward the end of its time in orbit, there was an attempt to turn Mir into a facility operated on a commercial basis: for instance, allowing noncosmonauts to purchase a trip to the station. However, Mir was de-orbited before such a trip took place.

The primary legacy of Mir is the extensive experience it provided in the complexities of organizing and managing long-duration human space flights, as well as insights into the effect of long stays in space on the human body. As the Mir station aged, keeping it in operating condition became a full-time task for its crew, and this limited its scientific output.

*See also:* INTERNATIONAL SPACE STATION; SPACE PROGRAM

**BIBLIOGRAPHY**

Burrough, Bryan. (1998). *Dragonfly: NASA and the Crisis aboard Mir.* New York: HarperCollins.

JOHN M. LOGSDON

## MNISZECH, MARINA

(1588–1614), Polish princess and Tsaritsa of Russia (1606).

Marina Mniszech was the daughter of Jerzy Mniszech (Palatine of Sandomierz), a Polish aristocrat who took up the cause of the man claiming to be Dmitry of Uglich in his struggle against Tsar Boris Godunov. The intelligent and ambitious Marina met the Pretender Dmitry in 1604, and they agreed to marry once he became tsar. After invading Russia and toppling the Godunov dynasty, Tsar Dmitry eventually obtained permission from the Russian Orthodox Church to marry the Catholic princess. In May 1606, Marina made a spectacular entry into Moscow, and she and Tsar Dmitry were married in a beautiful ceremony.

On May 17, 1606, Tsar Dmitry was assassinated, and Marina and her father were taken prisoner and incarcerated for two years. Tsar Vasily Shuisky released them in 1608 on the condition that they head straight back to Poland and not join up with an impostor calling himself Tsar Dmitry who was then waging a bitter civil war against Shuisky. In defiance, Marina traveled to Tushino, the second false Dmitry's capital in September 1608, and recognized the impostor as her husband, thereby greatly strengthening his credibility. Tsaritsa Marina even produced an heir, Ivan Dmitrievich. When

Marina's "husband" was killed in 1610, she and her lover, the cossack commander Ivan Zarutsky, continued to struggle for the Russian throne on behalf of the putative son of Tsar Dmitry. Forced to retreat to Astrakhan, Marina, Zarutsky, and Ivan Dmitrievich held out until after the election of Tsar Mikhail Romanov in 1613. Eventually expelled from Astrakhan's citadel, the three were hunted down in the Ural Mountain foothills and executed in 1614.

*See also:* DMITRY, FALSE; DMITRY OF UGLICH; OTREPEV, GRIGORY; SHUISKY, VASILY IVANOVICH; TIME OF TROUBLES

**BIBLIOGRAPHY**

Dunning, Chester. (2001). *Russia's First Civil War: The Time of Troubles and the Founding of The Romanov Dynasty.* University Park: Pennsylvania State University Press.

Perrie, Maureen. (1995). *Pretenders and Popular Monarchism in Early Modern Russia: The False Tsars of the Time of Troubles.* Cambridge, UK: Cambridge University Press.

CHESTER DUNNING

## MOISEYEV, MIKHAIL ALEXEYEVICH

(b. 1939), Army General Chief of the Soviet General Staff from 1988 to 1991.

Mikhail Moiseyev, born January 2, 1939, in Amur Oblast, was raised in the Soviet Far East and attended the Blagoveshchensk Armor School. He joined the Soviet Armed Forces in 1961 and served with tank units. Moiseyev attended the Frunze Military Academy from 1969 to 1972 and rose rapidly to the Rank of General-Major in the late 1970s. He graduated from the Voroshilov Military Academy of the General Staff as a gold medalist in 1982.

Moiseyev enjoyed the patronage of several senior officers in the advancement of his career, including General E. F. Ivanovsky, I. M. Tretyak, and Dmitri Yazov. In the 1980s Moiseyev commanded a combined arms army and then the Far East Military District. With the resignation of Marshal Sergei Akhromeyev in December 1988, Moiseyev was appointed chief of the Soviet General Staff, a post he held until August 22, 1991, when he was removed because of his support for the hardliners' coup. His tenure saw the culmination of intense arms control negotiations, including the

Conventional Forces in Europe (CFE) Treaty; the de-establishment of the Warsaw Treaty Organization; and increased military activism in domestic politics. In 1992 Moiseyev defended his dissertation, "The Armed Forces Command Structure," at the Center for Military-Strategic Studies of the General Staff. He served as a military consultant to the Russian Supreme Soviet in 1992.

Following his retirement, Moiseyev joined the board of the Technological and Intellectual Development of Russia Joint-Stock Company. In December 2000 he founded a new political party, Union, which was supposed to attract the support of active and returned military and security officers under the slogan, "law, order, and the rule of law." President Vladimir Putin appointed Moiseyev to the governmental commission on the social protection of the military. In this capacity he has been involved in programs to provide assistance to retiring military personnel.

*See also:* ARMS CONTROL; AUGUST 1991 PUTSCH; MILITARY, SOVIET AND POST-SOVIET

**BIBLIOGRAPHY**

Borawski, John. (1992). *Security for a New Europe: The Vienna Negotiations on Confidence- and Security-Building Measures, 1989–90 and Beyond.* London: Brassey's.

Golts, Aleksandr. (2002). "Trend Could Hatch Dozens of Pinochets." *The Russian Journal* 40(83).

Green, William C., and Karasik, Theodore, eds. (1990). *Gorbachev and His Generals: The Reform of Soviet Military Doctrine.* Boulder, CO: Westview Press.

Odom, William E. (1998). *The Collapse of the Soviet Military.* New Haven, CT: Yale University Press.

JACOB W. KIPP

# MOLDOVA AND MOLDOVANS

The independent Republic of Moldova has an area of 33,843 square kilometers (13,067 square miles). It is bordered by Romania on the west and by Ukraine on the north, east, and south. The population of as of 2002 was approximately 4,434,000. Moldova's population is ethnically mixed: Moldovans, who share a common culture and history with Romanians, make up 64.5 percent of the total population. Other major groups include Ukrainians (13.8%), Russians (13%), Bulgarians (2.0%), and the Turkic origin Gagauz (3.5%). Approximately 98 percent of the population is Eastern Orthodox.

Historically, the region has been the site of conflict between local rulers and neighboring powers, particularly the Ottoman Empire and Russian Empires. An independent principality including the territory of present-day Moldova was established during the mid-fourteenth century C.E. During the late fifteenth century it came under increasing pressure from the Ottoman Empire and ultimately became a tributary state. The current differentiation between eastern and western Moldova began during the early eighteenth century. Bessarabia, the region between the Prut and Dniester rivers, was annexed by Russia following the Russo-Turkish war of 1806–1812. Most of the remainders of traditional Moldova were united with Walachia in 1858, forming modern Romania.

While under Russian rule, Bessarabia experienced a substantial influx of migrants, primarily Russians, Ukrainians, Bulgarians, and Gagauz. Bessarabia changed hands again once again in 1918, uniting with Romania as a consequence of World War I. Soviet authorities created a new Moldovan political unit, designated the Moldavian Autonomous Soviet Socialist Republic, on Ukrainian territory containing a Romanian-speaking minority to the east of the Dniester River. In June 1940, Romania ceded Bessarabia to the Soviet Union as a consequence of the Ribbentrop-Molotov agreement, allowing formation of the Soviet Socialist Republic of Moldavia.

Independence culminated a process of national mobilization that began in 1988 in the context of widespread Soviet reforms. In the first partly democratic elections for the Republican Supreme Soviet, held in February 1990, candidates aligned with the Moldovan Popular Front won a majority of seats. The Supreme Soviet declared its sovereignty in June 1990. The Republic of Moldova became independent on August 27, 1991. The current constitution was enacted on July 29, 1994.

Moldova's sovereignty was challenged by Russian-speaking inhabitants on the left bank of the Dniester (Trans-Dniestria), and the Gagauz population concentrated in southern Moldova. The Gagauz crisis was successfully ended in December 1994 through a negotiated settlement that established an autonomous region, Gagauz-Yeri, within Moldova. The Trans-Dniestrian secession remains unresolved. Regional authorities declared independence in August 1990, forming the Dniester Moldovan Republic (DMR). Since a brief civil war in 1992, Trans-Dniestrian President Igor Smirnov has led a highly authoritarian government in the region, with the tacit support of the Russian Federation.

Trans-Dniestria has been a central issue in Moldovan foreign affairs. While officially neutral, Russian troops supported the separatists in the 1992 conflict. In August 1994 the Russian and Moldovan governments agreed on the withdrawal of Russian forces from the region within three years; this, however, did not occur. The situation has been complicated by the presence of a substantial Russian weapons depot in Trans-Dniestria. Despite the Trans-Dniestria issue, Moldova entered the Commonwealth of Independent States (CIS) on a limited basis in April 1994 and has maintained positive, if guarded, relations with Russia since then. In 2001, Moldova and the Russian Federation concluded a bilateral treaty that named Russia as guarantor of the Trans-Dniestrian peace settlement.

Moldova's relationship with Romania has become increasingly difficult following independence. Romania was the first state to recognize Moldovan independence. Many Romanians supported unification with Moldova, which they consider an integral part of historic Romania. Romanian nationalists view Moldovan concessions to separatists and the Russian Federation as treason against the Romanian national ideal. This attitude led to a sharp decline in relations, especially following 1994 elections that brought more independence–oriented leaders to power in the capital city of Chişinău. Following the return to power of the Moldovan Communist Party in 2001, hostile rhetoric from official Moldovan sources regarding Romanian interference in Moldovan affairs increased, as did the anger of Romanian nationalists over Moldova's continued relationship with Russia.

The head of state of Moldova is the president of the Republic. The president is charged with guaranteeing the independence and unity, and overseeing the efficient functioning of public authorities. The president may be impeached by vote of two-thirds of the parliamentary deputies. The president can dissolve parliament if it is unable to form a government for a period of sixty days. The president names the prime minister following consultation with the parliamentary majority. Once selected, the prime minister forms a government and establishes a program, which is then submitted to parliament for a vote of confidence. Until 2000 the president was chosen through a direct popular election. In that year, following a long-lasting deadlock between the executive and legislative branches, parliament passed legislation according to which the president is elected by the parliament.

The government of Moldova is made up of a prime minister, two deputy prime ministers, and approximately twenty ministers. Parliament is given the power to dismiss the government or an individual member through a vote of no confidence by a majority vote.

Moldova has a unicameral legislature made up of 101 deputies elected to four-year terms by means of a direct universal vote. Legislators are elected through a proportional representation closed list system, with a six percent threshold for participation. In a move that distinguished it from the vast majority of proportional representation systems, the Moldovans adopted a single national electoral district. The parliament passes laws, may call for referendum, and exercises control over the executive as called for in the constitution.

Moldovan economic conditions deteriorated disastrously in the post-communist period. The collapse of its agricultural exports to Russia badly hurt the rural sector. Simultaneously, the secession of the territory on the left bank of the Dniester dislocated industrial production throughout the republic. Without any significant energy resources, Moldova accrued massive external debts for oil and natural gas imports. Finally, the economic decline was also a consequence of its leaders' failure to provide any clear policy direction. A decade after independence, Moldova was poorer than any other country in Central Europe.

*See also:* COMMONWEALTH OF INDEPENDENT STATES; GAGAUZ; NATIONALITIES POLICIES, SOVIET; NATIONALITIES POLICIES, TSARIST; TRANS-DNIESTER REPUBLIC

**BIBLIOGRAPHY**

Crowther, William. (1997). "The Politics of Democratization in Post–communist Moldova." In *Democratic Changes and Authoritarian Reactions in Russia, Ukraine, Belarus, and Moldova*, eds. Karen Dawisha and Bruce Parrott. London: Cambridge University Press.

Dryer, Donald, ed. (1996). *Studies in Moldavian: The History, Culture, Language, and Contemporary Politics of the People of Moldova.* Boulder, CO: East European Monographs.

King, Charles. (2000). *The Moldovans: Romania, Russia, and the Politics of Culture.* Stanford, CA: Hoover Institution Press.

WILLIAM CROWTHER

## MOLOTOV, VYACHESLAV MIKHAILOVICH

(1880–1986), Russian revolutionary and Soviet politician, often regarded as Stalin's chief lieutenant.

Vyacheslav Molotov was born at Kukarka, Nolinsk district, Vyatka province, on March 9, 1880. His father was the manager of the village store. Molotov's real name was Skryabin; he was the second cousin of the composer and pianist Alexander Skryabin (1872–1915). After attending the village school, he was educated at Kazan Real School from 1902, and became involved in the 1905 Revolution in Nolinsk district, joining the Bolshevik Party in 1906. Engaged in revolutionary agitation in Kazan, particularly among student groups, he was arrested in 1909 and exiled to Vologda province.

In 1911, at the end of his period of exile, he enrolled first in the shipbuilding department but soon transferred to the economics department at St. Petersburg Polytechnic Institute. He continued his revolutionary agitation, again especially among student groups, and from 1912 was involved in the production of the early numbers of *Pravda*, to which he contributed a number of articles. It was at this time he first called himself Molotov (from the word for "hammer") after the hero in Nikolai Pomyalovsky's 1861 novel. In 1915, having been sent by the party to Moscow, he was again arrested and exiled to Irkutsk province, but escaped in 1916. Returning to St. Petersburg to continue his revolutionary activity, he was one of the leading Bolsheviks there in March 1917. He was prominent during the early weeks of the Russian Revolution, again working for *Pravda* and serving on the St. Petersburg Soviet, but retired into the background with the return of Lenin and other senior leaders from exile.

Molotov was involved but did not play a leading part in the Bolshevik revolution in October 1917. In March 1918 Molotov became chairman of the *Sovnarkhoz* (Economic Council) for the northern provinces, thus assuming responsibility for economic affairs in the Petrograd area. In 1919, during the civil war, he was in command of a river steamer charged with spreading Bolshevik propaganda in provinces newly liberated from the White armies. He then spent short spells as a party representative in Nizhny Novgorod and the Donbass.

Molotov now rapidly rose in the Bolshevik party. He was elected to the Central Committee in 1921, was first secretary from 1921 to 1922, preceding Josef Stalin's appointment as General Secretary, and continued to work in the Secretariat until 1930, having become a full member of the Politburo in 1926. During this period he became associated with Stalin, fully supporting him in his struggles against the opposition and becoming Stalin's chief agent in agricultural policy, particularly collectivization.

In December 1930, Molotov became chairman of the Council of People's Commissars (*Sovnarkom*), a post sometimes regarded as equivalent to prime minister, where he was responsible for the implementation of a planned economy and Stalinist industrialization and related economic and social polices. During the later 1930s he was fully identified with the Stalinist repressions, and for a short time in 1936 he was personally in danger for committing Stalin too openly to a pro-German foreign policy.

From May 1939 until 1949 Molotov was foreign minister. In August 1939 he was responsible for negotiating the notorious Nazi-Soviet pact. In May 1941, shortly before the outbreak of war, Stalin replaced him as Sovnarkom chairman. Molotov remained as vice-chairman, and during the war he was also deputy chairman of the State Defence Committee (GKO) with special responsibility for tank production, as well as foreign minister. He was responsible for negotiating the wartime alliance with the United States and Great Britain in 1942; with Stalin he represented the USSR at the major wartime international conferences. He then headed the Soviet delegation to the San Francisco conference of 1945 that established the United Nations organization. Representing the USSR at the United Nations and at postwar foreign ministers' conferences until his dismissal as foreign minister in 1949, he earned a reputation as a blunt, determined, and vociferous opponent of Western policies.

After Stalin's death, Molotov was again foreign minister, from 1953 to 1956, but his relations with Khrushchev were never good, and he was dismissed from his important government offices as a leader of the Antiparty Group in 1957. He then served as Soviet ambassador to Mongolia from 1957 to 1960, and as USSR representative to the International Atomic Energy Commission in 1960 and 1961.

Expelled from the Communist Party in 1962, Molotov lived in retirement until his death in 1986. He was reinstated in the party in 1984. His wife, Polina Semenova (also known as Zhemchuzhina), whom he had married in 1921 and with whom he had two children, also achieved high party and government positions but was incarcerated from 1949 to 1953. Molotov admitted that he had voted in the Politburo for her arrest.

See also: ANTI-PARTY GROUP; BOLSHEVISM; KHRUSHCHEV, NIKITA SERGEYEVICH; NAZI-SOVIET PACT OF 1939; REVOLUTION OF 1917; SOVNARKOM; STALIN, JOSEF VISSARIONOVICH

**BIBLIOGRAPHY**

Chuev, Felix. (1993). *Molotov Remembers: Inside Kremlin Politics*, ed. Albert Resis. Chicago: Ivan R. Dee.

Watson, Derek. (1996). *Molotov and Soviet Government: Sovnarkom, 1930–41*. Basingstoke, UK: CREES-Macmillan.

Watson, Derek. (2002). "Molotov, the Making of the Grand Alliance and the Second Front, 1939–1942." *Europe-Asia Studies* 54(1):51–86.

DEREK WATSON

# MONASTICISM

Monasticism organizes individuals devoted to a life of prayer based upon vows of chastity, poverty, and obedience. It has been an integral part of religious life in Russia since the conversion to Christianity in the late tenth century. Russian monasticism was characterized by the forms that existed in Byzantium, from the anchoritic or eremitical life of hermits to the cenobitic form of communal life; most monasteries, however, organized their life between these ideal types.

The Kievan Caves monastery, founded in the mid-eleventh century by Anthony, was the first important (if not typical) institution. Anthony began as a hermit living in a cave, though his holiness soon attracted others around him. In 1062 Theodosius (d. 1074) became abbot of the growing community and introduced the Studite Rule (the classic Byzantine cenobitic rule, requiring communal eating, labor, property, and worship). Under Theodosius, the monastery upheld high standards

of monastic life and participated in worldly affairs (including charity and politics). Although Theodosius would become a model for Russian monasticism—with his humility, authority, and balance of asceticism and activity—"princely monasticism" dominated Kievan Rus. Princely families founded such monasteries in or near cities, gave the communities their rule and endowments, and appointed abbots. These institutions were influential in ecclesiastical politics and as centers of learning and culture, but were not distinguished by exemplary monastic life. More than fifty monasteries existed in Rus before the Mongol invasion in 1240—though many were destroyed in its wake.

The second half of the fourteenth century witnessed a dramatic expansion of monastic life in Russia, inspired by Sergius of Radonezh (d. 1392). Sergius began as a hermit living in the forest, but, attracting followers, he established the Trinity monastery. Sergius became abbot in 1353 and introduced the Studite rule in 1377. He combined asceticism, humility, charity, and influence in political affairs (like Theodosius), together with contemplative prayer. Inspired by Sergius's example, a pattern emerged in which hermits settled in the forest searching for solitude; followers joined them; they established a monastery, with peasants settling nearby; and again a few monks set off into the uninhabited forest in search of solitude. Much of the Russian north was settled in this manner.

Between 1350 and 1450 some 150 monasteries were founded, and new communities continued to proliferate into the eighteenth century. Monasteries acquired land through purchase or donation, with many becoming major landowners. They played an important role in the economy and political unification of Muscovy in the fifteenth century. By the early sixteenth century their wealth had led to a decline in monastic discipline, giving rise to two differing reform movements. Nil Sorsky (d. 1508) advocated a "skete" style of life, in which monks lived in small hermitages and supported themselves. Nil emphasized contemplative, mystical prayer (based on Byzantine Hesychasm). Joseph of Volotsk (d. 1515) organized his monastery according to the cenobitic rule (demanding strict individual poverty) and emphasized corporate liturgical prayer. Joseph also justified monastery landownership, for this enabled charity and social engagement. Traditional historiography posited an intense political conflict over monastic landownership between two distinct ecclesiastical "parties" (Nil's non-possessors and Joseph's possessors).

Recent research, however, suggests that the conflict has been exaggerated. Small hermitages continued to exist into the seventeenth century, often operating independently of central church control (including resistance to Nikonian liturgical reforms). Ecclesiastical authorities mistrusted and tried to subordinate them to larger monasteries. Thus the tradition inspired by Nil Sorsky gradually died out.

Beginning in the mid-sixteenth century, the state attempted to gain control over monastic landholding due to competition for land and the tax-exempt status of ecclesiastical property. The Law Code of 1649 forbade monasteries from acquiring new estates and established the Monastery Chancellery, which placed the administration of monastic estates under state control (until its abolition in 1677). The eighteenth century witnessed the greatest assertion of state authority over monasticism. Peter the Great initiated measures to restrict the growth of monasticism and make it more socially "useful," and he reestablished the Monastery Chancellery from 1701 to 1720. Peter's successors continued efforts to restrict recruitment, leading to a decline in the number of monks and nuns from 25,000 to 14,000 between 1724 and 1738. The state's assault finally culminated in 1764 when Catherine the Great confiscated all monastic estates. Her secularization reform resulted in the closure of more than half of all monasteries (decreasing from 954 to 387) and a drastic reduction of monastic clergy (leaving fewer than six thousand by the end of the eighteenth century).

Despite the devastating impact of secularization, monasticism experienced a remarkable revival in the nineteenth century and again played a vital role in religious life. By 1914, the number of monasteries rose to 1,025 and the number of monastic clergy reached nearly 95,000. In part, the expansion of monasticism in the nineteenth century was due to the revival of hesychastic contemplative spirituality, inspired by the Ukrainian monk Paisy Velichkovsky (d. 1794). In addition to the repetition of the Jesus prayer and other contemplative practices, placing oneself under the guidance of a spiritual elder (starets) was integral to hesychasm. In the nineteenth century, the role of the starets expanded beyond the walls of the monastery. Famous elders such as Serafim of Sarov (d. 1833) or those of the Optina Hermitage attracted tens of thousands of laypeople, including important intellectual figures (Ivan Kireyevsky, Nikolai Gogol, Fyodor Dostoyevsky, and Leo Tolstoy). A dramatic rise in pilgrimage to monasteries (in combination with renewed permission to acquire land) led to a significant growth in monastic wealth. Though anticlerical intellectuals frequently criticized this wealth, many larger monasteries were actively engaged in charity. In the second half of the century, the number of women joining monastic communities rose dramatically; by the century's end, female monastics far exceeded men. In contrast to male monasticism (which focused on contemplative spirituality), female monasticism was particularly devoted to charitable activity (operating schools, orphanages, hospitals, etc.).

The twentieth century, by contrast, was a succession of crises. Between 1900 and 1917, church and monastic leaders heatedly debated reform measures and the social role of monasticism. After 1917, monasteries were among the Bolshevik's' first targets. While most monasteries were closed by 1921, others transformed themselves into agricultural collectives and survived until collectivization (1928–1929). By 1930 all monasteries in the Soviet Union were officially closed, and former monks and nuns were frequent victims of the purges of 1937 and 1938. In the rapprochement between church and state during World War II, some monasteries were allowed to reopen (or stay open, if located in newly acquired territories). From the early 1960s to the late 1980s, eighteen monasteries and convents existed in the Soviet Union. Today the Moscow Patriarchate reports 480 functioning monasteries.

See also: CAVES MONASTERY; JOSEPH VOLOTZK, ST.; KIRIL-BELOOZERO MONASTERY; MONASTERIES; NIL SORSKY, ST.; ORTHODOXY; PATRIARCHATE; RELIGION; RUSSIAN ORTHODOX CHURCH; SERGIUS, ST.; SIMONOV MONASTERY; SLOVIKI MONASTERY; TRINITY ST. SERGIUS MONASTERY

## BIBLIOGRAPHY

Bolshakoff, Sergius. (1980). *Russian Mystics*. Kalamazoo, MI: Cistercian Publications.

Kenworthy, Scott M. (2002). "The Revival of Monasticism in Modern Russia: The Trinity-Sergius Lavra, 1825-1921." Ph.D. diss., Brandeis University, Waltham, MA.

Meehan, Brenda. (1993). *Holy Women of Russia*. San Francisco: Harper Collins.

Nichols, Robert L. (1985). "The Orthodox Elders (Startsy) of Imperial Russia." *Modern Greek Studies Yearbook* 1:1–30.

Ostrowski, Donald. (1986). "Church Polemics and Monastic Land Acquisition in Sixteenth-Century

Muscovy." *Slavonic and East European Review* 64:355–379.

Spock, Jennifer B. (1999). "The Solovki Monastery, 1460–1645: Piety and Patronage in the Early Modern Russian North." Ph.D. diss., Yale University, New Haven, CT.

Wynot, Jennifer. (2000). "Keeping the Faith: Russian Orthodox Monasticism in the Soviet Union, 1917-1939." Ph.D. diss., Emory University, Atlanta, GA.

SCOTT M. KENWORTHY

# MONETARY OVERHANG

Monetary overhang consists of the liquidity that quantity-constrained consumers may accumulate in excess of the money they would accumulate if commodities were freely available in the market.

Prices in the Soviet-type consumer goods market were in principle supposed to be set so that supply and demand would balance both in the aggregate and for each consumer good. Deficits caused by below-equilibrium prices were not a goal. But in practice many prices—particularly those for basic essentials like food, housing and many services—were set low either as a consumption subsidy or for ideological reasons. Also, because price stability was a goal, prices were not adjusted often enough to respond to changes in producer cost and consumer preferences. While there was excess supply for some goods, typically many goods were in short supply and were not freely available in the market. Consumers faced quantity constraints; they possibly accumulated money in excess of the amount they would have wished to have. This excess money or forced savings is called monetary overhang.

The economics of monetary overhang remain contested. While the existence of short supply for individual goods is generally accepted, whether there was undersupply in the aggregate remains somewhat debatable. The existence of the gray economy and kolkhoz (open collective farm) markets, where prices were freely determined by supply and demand, might be expected to have balanced aggregate demand and supply. But perhaps such consumer goods markets were too limited in size to have the necessary effect. Also, consumers who accumulate monetary overhang might be expected to diminish their labor efforts. Thus, forced savings would lower economic growth. But perhaps that was not institutionally possible.

Empirical research into monetary overhang is hampered both by theoretical problems and by deficient statistics. It is estimated that the share of forced savings in total Russian monetary savings increased from 9 percent in 1965 to 42 percent in 1989. This was largely caused by retail price subsidies, which swelled to 20 percent of state budget expenditure in the late 1980s. Undersupply caused queuing, black markets, bribery, and quality deterioration. Few consumer goods were freely available by 1991.

Monetary overhang can also be seen as repressed inflation: In the absence of price controls, prices would rise to equilibrium levels. In principle, monetary overhang could be abolished before price liberalization by increasing consumer goods supplies, by bringing new commodities and assets to markets (for instance, through privatization), or by a confiscatory monetary reform. In practice, monetary overhang was abolished in transition economies through price liberalization, which turned repressed inflation into open inflation and destroyed the value of savings, both voluntary and forced. This was the case in Russia. The partial price liberalization of January 1992 brought about an annual inflation of 2,400 percent. Many consumers suffered badly, but price liberalization was popular overall, as the consequences of repressed inflation were well known.

*See also:* BLACK MARKET; ECONOMIC GROWTH, SOVIET; REPRESSED INFLATION; WAGES

**BIBLIOGRAPHY**

Easterly, William, and Cunha, Paulo Viera da. (1994). "Financing the Storm." *Economics of Transition* 2:443–466.

Kim, Byung-Yeon. (1999). "The Income, Savings, and Monetary Overhang of Soviet Households." *Journal of Comparative Economics* 4:644-668.

Kornai, János. (1980). *Economics of Shortage.* Amsterdam: North-Holland.

PEKKA SUTELA

# MONETARY SYSTEM, SOVIET

The early Marxists expected that money would die away under socialism, made unnecessary by the

**Soviet kopeks and rubles.** © DALLAS AND JOHN HEATON/CORBIS

abolition of markets, the use of central planning based on nonmonetary units, the replacement of scarcity by abundance, and the worldwide acceptance of socialism. Since none of this came to pass, a monetary system remained, but it was a very peculiar monetary system. In contrast to a market economy, where money-based exchange is fundamental and money plays an active role, under central management money adapts itself to planned production flows and is basically passive.

In a market economy, money has three functions: It is a means of exchange, a measure of value, and a store of value. A whole set of institutions supports these functions. In the Soviet economy, the ruble fulfilled these functions only in a limited way. The set of monetary institutions was similarly restricted.

Money circulation was strictly divided into two spheres. In the state sector, enterprises could legally use only noncash money, in practice transfers through a state-owned banking system. Only transfers sanctioned by a corresponding plan assignment could be legally made, and it was generally impossible to use the banking system for nonsanctioned transactions. The banking system was thus an important control mechanism. Households, on the other hand, lived in a cash economy facing mostly fixed-price markets for labor and consumer goods. There were also legal, more or less free-priced markets such as the kolkhoz markets for foodstuffs as well as illegal, often cash-based markets. To control the economy, Soviet planners put great emphasis on maintaining this duality. By and large, they succeeded. Under perestroika, enterprises found ways to convert noncash to cash money. This contributed to the collapse of the Soviet system.

The ruble was not a means of exchange in the state sector. It was not freely convertible to goods, except for goods allocated in the plan for each enterprise. For households, money was the basic means of exchange, but only goods produced according to plan were legally available (with the relatively small exception of the kolkhoz markets). Because of the frequent shortages, households did not rely on money as the only means of exchange but also used such allocation mechanisms as barter, queuing, and bribery.

As a store of value, money was useless to enterprises, but it was important for households because few other assets were available. In addition to gold and precious stones, one could invest in state bonds, but these were used to mop up excess liquidity. People had little confidence about keeping their wealth in rubles because of the recurring periods of very high inflation—during the civil war, in the early 1930s, during World War II, and afterwards—and also because of the frequent confiscatory money reforms. As foreign currencies were almost unavailable, and possessing them was a serious crime, households used any other store of value, and lacking them, cut down their efforts to earn money. The limited convertibility of the ruble into commodities, together with periods of very high inflation and monetary reform, made money a defective measure of value.

The Soviet Union had a monobank system consisting of a single state bank (Gosbank) that combined the functions of a central bank, a commercial bank, and a savings bank. Gosbank was not autonomous; it was a financial-control agency under the Council of Ministers. Acting as a central bank, it created narrow money (cash in circulation outside the state sector) by authorizing companies to pay wages according to accepted wage plans. Acting as a commercial bank, it issued short-term credit to companies, in accordance with the plan, for working capital. More important, it kept close track of transfers between enterprises to make sure that only transactions sanctioned by an accepted plan took place. Originally, there was a formally separate savings bank, but it was incorporated into Gosbank in 1963. It used the savings of the population to finance budget deficits. A couple of other banks existed for a short time, but like the savings bank were not independent.

The banking system and the budget system were the two pillars of the monetary system. The budget system had three layers—central, regional, and municipal—but, like the Soviet state, it too was unitary. Tax revenue mostly consisted of commodity-specific taxes separating retail and wholesale prices, company-specific profit taxation, usually confiscating any "excessive" revenue companies might have, and foreign trade taxes, used to separate domestic and foreign prices. As state revenue was thus based on fees specifically tailored for commodities, companies, and foreign markets, the system should perhaps not be called taxation at all. Wages were, in principle, set by the state, but there was little use for income taxation.

State revenue was used to pay state-sector wages and for investment, subsidies, and other public expenditure, including the military. To hide the extent of military expenditure and cover up the deficiencies of social services, state finances were always among the best-kept secrets of the Soviet state. This was especially so toward the end of the period, when there was much justified suspicion that the state, unable to cover expenditure by revenue, was actually engaged in the monetization of budget deficits. This created a monetary overhang with several undesired consequences, among them a popular withdrawal of work effort.

During the war communism of 1918 to 1921, Soviet Russia went through a hyperinflation that destroyed the ability of money to fulfill any of its functions. To what degree this came about by design so as to reach full communism immediately, to what degree by default due to inability to control the monetary system during a civil war, is still debated. Along with the partial rehabilitation of markets in the early 1920s, a successful money reform was made by introducing a parallel currency. The establishment of the centrally managed economy again drove the monetary system into turmoil, but in a few years it had found its new contours. World War II intervened before there had been sufficient time for monetary and financial policy to establish themselves. By the mid-1950s the situation had stabilized, but at the same time the need to reform the economic system was increasingly recognized. The reform proposals, based on the idea of indirect centralization, had little room for monetary or other macroeconomic questions. Not unexpectedly, the partial implementation of such thinking during the late 1980s left post-Soviet Russia in a situation of near hyperinflation with a financial system almost in collapse.

*See also:* BANKING SYSTEM, SOVIET; GOSBANK; WAR COMMUNISM

**BIBLIOGRAPHY**
Kornai, Janos. (1992). *The Socialist System.* Oxford: Oxford University Press.

Nove, Alec. (1977). *The Soviet Economic System*, 2nd edition. London: Allen & Unwin.

PEKKA SUTELA

## MONTENEGRO, RELATIONS WITH

Over the course of several centuries, Russia developed what could be termed a "special relationship" with Montenegro (located in the western Balkans) and its largely Serb Orthodox population. Modern Montenegro began to emerge as a result of the collapse of the Serbian empire in the fourteenth century. Occupying land characterized by rugged karst mountains, Montenegrins stubbornly resisted Turkish attempts to subdue their mountain redoubts. Until the secularization of the Montenegrin state in 1852, Montenegro's clans were loosely ruled by *vladike* (prince-bishops)—Orthodox metropolitans who exercised temporal as well as ecclesiastical authority, and who occasionally managed to make the long, difficulty journey to Russia to be formally consecrated in office. After the election of Vladika Danilo I in 1696, succession was restricted to members of his family, the Petrovici, who continued to rule Montenegro until World War I.

Beginning with Peter the Great, Russian rulers bestowed financial awards upon Montenegro and its rulers as an expression of their friendship and as payment for various services rendered in support of Russia's numerous military ventures against the Turks. In the course of the eighteenth century, Russian envoys visited Montenegro, and some Montenegrin youth acquired military training in Russia. The first "modern history" of Montenegro was published by Bishop Vasilije in Russia in 1754. The Russians appealed to the common ethnic and religious heritage of the two peoples and claimed that the war against the Turks was a crusade to rescue the Orthodox Christians of the Balkans from the "Muslim yoke." For their part, Montenegrins responded enthusiastically to these overtures. The nature of the relationship was such that for more than six years during the reign of Vladika Sava (1735–1781), a monk called Šcepan Mali (Stephen the Small) claiming to be Peter III, the murdered husband of Catherine the Great, successfully established himself as the effective ruler of Montenegro. As one British writer later observed, "Russia was a name to conjure with."

Even so, the extent of St. Petersburg's support for Montenegro was necessarily determined by greater Russian geostrategic interests. Accordingly, Montenegro was awarded nothing in the peace treaties ending Russo–Turkish wars in 1711, 1739, 1774, and 1792. The famous bargain struck by Catherine II and Joseph II of Austria in 1781 would have yielded much of the western Balkans to the Habsburg rule, as would have the Austro-Russian Reichstadt Agreement of 1876.

As a result of the 1878 Treaty of Berlin (which replaced the Treaty of San Stefano of the same year), Montenegro secured formal international recognition of its independence as well as territorial aggrandizement. For the next thirty years, Russo-Montenegrin relations were generally cordial, and Nicholas I Petrovic-Njegol (1860–1918), Montenegro's last prince and only king, took steps to keep them that way. Two of his daughters married Russian grand dukes (Peter and Nikolai Nikolayevitch) and served as spokeswomen for Montenegrin interests in the Russian capital. Nicholas carefully followed political trends in St. Petersburg. His introduction of a constitution in 1905 was a partial echo of the tsar's reluctant decision to grant a duma. For its part, Russia contributed large sums of money to Montenegro royal and state coffers, and engaged in a series of projects designed to promote Montenegrin welfare. Russia subsidized not only the Montenegrin army, but also Montenegrin schools, including a famous girls' school founded by the Empress Marie Alexandrovna. Russians also served as nurses in a largely Russian-financed hospital.

On balance, Russia was Montenegro's most generous great-power sponsor in the eighteenth, nineteenth, and early twentieth centuries. Tsar Alexander III once asserted that Nicholas of Montenegro was his only friend, and the Montenegrins reciprocated this affection by shouting their famous slogan "We and the Russians—100 million strong!" Nevertheless, the Montenegrin ruler alienated his Russian benefactors on numerous occasions.

In 1908 Austria-Hungary formally annexed Bosnia–Hercegovina, incurring the wrath of Russia, Serbia, and Montenegro. In 1910 Russia, along with all other European great powers, approved the elevation of Prince Nicholas to the dignity of king. In 1912, Russian diplomats worked behind the scenes to help forge the Balkan League, consisting of Serbia, Greece, Bulgaria, and Montenegro. The First Balkan War ensued, launched by Montenegro in October of the same year. In May 1913 Russia reluctantly joined other European powers in pressuring King Nicholas to withdraw his forces from the Albanian fortress city of Scutari, conquered by Montenegrin troops in April.

In August 1914, Montenegro joined Serbia and Russia in the World War I. One year later, in December 1915, Austro-Hungarian forces occupied Montenegro. Subsequently, official Russian influence was largely limited to Russian representation at the Montenegrin court-in-exile, first in Bordeaux, then in Paris. With the outbreak of the Bolshevik Revolution, official Russo-Montenegrin relations came to an end, and King Nicholas appealed to the Western Allies in a futile attempt to secure the restoration of the Montenegrin kingdom. At war's end, in December 1918, Montenegro was incorporated into the new Kingdom of Serbs, Croats, and Slovenes (Yugoslavia).

After World War I, however, Russian/Soviet influence continued to manifest itself in Montenegro. In initial elections for a Yugoslav constituent assembly, over a third of those Montenegrins voting supported communist candidates. During World War II, many Montenegrins joined the Communist–led Partisan movement headed by Josip Broz Tito. After Tito's split with Stalin in 1948, Montenegro remained a center for limited, underground pro-Cominformist (i.e., pro-Soviet) activity for many years.

See also: BALKAN WARS; CONGRESS OF BERLIN; SERBIA, RELATIONS WITH; YUGOSLAVIA, RELATIONS WITH; WORLD WAR I

**BIBLIOGRAPHY**

Rossos, Andrew. (1981). *Russia and the Balkans: Inter–Balkan Rivalries and Russian Foreign Policy, 1908–1914.* Toronto: University of Toronto Press.

Treadway, John D. (1983). *The Falcon and the Eagle: Montenegro and Austria–Hungary, 1908–1914.* West Lafayette, Indiana: Purdue University Press.

JOHN D. TREADWAY

# MORDVINS

The largest Finno-Ugrian nationality in Russia (over a million), the Mordvins are divided into the Erzia and the Moksha sub-ethnic communities. They are a highly dispersed nationality, with over 70 percent of Mordvins residing outside their republic.

The Mordvins are an ancient people indigenous to the area between the Volga, Oka, and Sura rivers. They are first mentioned as Mordens in the writings of the sixth-century Gothic historian Jordanes. Of the surviving Volga nationalities they were the first to encounter the Russians even before 1103, in the first recorded skirmish in the Russian Chronicles. With the conquest of Kazan in 1552, all Mordvins came under Russian rule.

Their history under the tsars is one of expropriations of lands, harsh exploitation, assault on native animist beliefs, and periodic conversion campaigns that led to rebellion and flight. Native leaders were killed in futile uprisings or enticed to the Russian side, leaving the Mordvins a dispersed nation of illiterate peasants. By the seventeenth century, the Mordvin homeland had become central Russian territory and the Mordvins there a minority; those fleeing eastward were soon overtaken by the Russian advance. By the end of the nineteenth century, all Mordvins were listed as Russian Orthodox and were considered "sufficiently russified" not to require special schools or translations in their language. Yet the language-based 1897 census recorded 1,023,841 Mordvins.

Under the Soviets, despite their dispersion, lack of a common language, and a weak national self-consciousness, the Mordvins achieved significant cultural progress. While attempts to forge a common language failed, both Erzia and Moksha became literary languages widely used in education and publishing. In 1934, the Mordvins acquired their own Autonomous Soviet Socialist Republic (26,200 square kilometers) with its capital in Saransk, albeit the majority were Russians and most Mordvins were left outside. However, by the late 1930s, national revival was halted as the elite was decimated in the purges and Soviet nationality policy shifted to emphasizing the Russian language and culture. The Mordvin population, which had slowly risen to 1,456,300 in 1939, continued to erode, dropping to 1,153,500 in the last Soviet census of 1989.

Since perestroika and the collapse of the Soviet Union, the Mordvins have been trying to stage a national revival. However, despite new freedoms, conditions are unfavorable. Less than 30 percent of the Mordvins live in their republic, where they are a minority and among the poorest. The new national organizations are narrowly based and suffer from separatist demands from militant Erzias. However, hope is still to be found in their relatively large number, the support of fellow Finno-Ugrians abroad, and the world community's concern for endangered cultures and languages.

*See also:* FINNS AND KARELIANS; NATIONALITIES POLICIES, SOVIET; NATIONALITIES POLICIES, TSARIST

**BIBLIOGRAPHY**

Iurchenkov, Valerii. (2001). "The Mordvins: Dilemmas of Mobilization in a Biethnic Community." *Nationalities Papers* 29(1):85–95.

Kreindler, Isabelle. (1985). "The Mordvinian Languages: A Survival Saga." In *Sociolinguistic Perspectives on Soviet National Languages*, ed. Isabelle Kreindler. Berlin: Mouton de Gruyter.

Lallukka, Seppo. (1990). *The East Finnic Minorities in the Soviet Union.* Helsinki: Suomalaisen Tiedeakatemia.

ISABELLE KREINDLER

## MOROZOVA, FEODOSYA PROKOPEVNA

(1632–1675), aristocratic martyr of the Old Believers.

Feodosya Morozova, one of the most remarkable characters of the seventeenth century, was born on May 21, 1632, to Prokopy Sokovnin, a relative of Tsaritsa Maria Miloslavskaya, and his wife Anisya. In 1649 Feodosya was married to Gleb Morozov, brother of the famous Boris Morozov, favorite and tutor of Tsar Alexei Mikhaylovich.

In 1650 Morozova's only child Ivan was born. When her husband died in 1662, one of Muscovy's largest properties came under her control. It is not clear when Morozova first made contact with the Old Believers, who refused Patriarch Nikon's church reforms of the middle of the century. Nikon's most ardent opponent, Archpriest Avvakum, returned in February 1664 from his banishment in Siberia to Moscow and took up residence in Morozova's home. Tsar Alexei ordered the confiscation of her possessions in August 1665, but on the insistence of the tsaritsa they where returned in October 1666.

During the second exile of Avvakum after 1666, Morozova continued her correspondence with the Archpriest and made her house a meeting place for the Old Believers. She prepared writings against the "Nikonian heresy" and missed no opportunity to raise her voice against the official church. Besides the exiled Avvakum, a certain Melanya was of great importance to Morozova. She put herself under the authority of Melanya, whom she regarded as her spiritual "mother," and sought her teaching and advice. At the end of 1670 Morozova took the veil and chose the religious name Feodora.

With the death of Tsaritsa Maria Miloslavskaya in 1669, the Old Believers lost a valuable protectress. When Morozova refused to attend the wedding of the tsar with his second wife Natalya Naryshkina on January 22, 1671, she deeply offended the sovereign. In November 1671 she was arrested along with her sister, Princess Evdokia Urusova. Morozova's estate and landstocks were distributed among the boyars, while all the valuables were sold and proceeds paid into the state treasury. Her tweny-one-year-old son died shortly after her arrest—of grief, as Avvakum noted.

The tsar tried repeatedly to convince Morozova and Urusova to return to the official church, but both refused categorically, even under severe torture. As long as Morozova was imprisoned in or around Moscow, she was able to maintain communication with the Old Believers. A strong, proud, and impressive personality of highest rank, she attracted many noblewomen, who flocked to the monastery to see her. Although she was relocated several times, her numerous admirers persisted in visiting her. Finally, at the end of 1673 or in the beginning of 1674, the alarmed tsar had her transferred to the prison of Borovsk, some 90 kilometers away from Moscow, where she was soon joined by her sister. The two women were held under severe conditions in an earthen hole. In April 1675 the situation worsened, as they were put on starvation rations. Urusova died on September 11 that year, and Morozova on November 1.

Soon after her death, Morozova's life and martyrdom were described by a contemporary, possibly her elder brother. This remarkable literary document is known as the *Tale of Boyarina Morozova.*

*See also:* AVVAKUM; NIKON; OLD BELIEVERS

**BIBLIOGRAPHY**

Michels, Georg. (1995). "Muscovite Elite Women and Old Belief." *Harvard Ukrainian Studies* 19:428–450.

Ziolkowski, Margaret, ed. (2000). *Tale of Boiarynia Morozova: A Seventeenth-Century Religious Life.* Lanham, MD: Lexington Books.

NADA BOSKOVSKA

## MOROZOV, BORIS IVANOVICH

(1590–1661), lord protector and head of five chancelleries under Tsar Alexei Mikhailovich.

Boris Ivanov syn Morozov was an important, thoughtful leader, but he also stands out as an exceptionally greedy figure of the second quarter of the seventeenth century. His cupidity provoked uprisings in early June 1648 in Moscow and then in a dozen other towns, forcing Tsar Alexei to convoke the well-known Assembly of the Land of 1648–1649, the product of which was the famous Law Code of 1649.

Morozov in some ways personified the fact that early modern Russia (Muscovy) was a service state. He was not of princely (royal) origins; his ancestors had been commoners who rose through service to the ruler of Muscovy. Thus his patronymic would have been Ivanov Syn (son of Ivan), rather than Ivanovich, which would have been the proper form were he if noble origin.

By 1633 Morozov was tutor to the heir to the throne, the future Tsar Alexei. He and Alexei married Miloslavskaya sisters. After Alexis came to the throne, Morozov became head of five chancelleries (*prikazy*, the "power ministries": Treasury, Alcohol Revenues, Musketeers, Foreign Mercenaries, and Apothecary) and de facto ruler of the government (Lord Protector). He observed that there were too many taxes and came up with the apparently ingenious solution of canceling a number of them and concentrating the imposts in an increased tax on salt. Regrettably Morozov was not an economist and probably could not comprehend that the demand for salt was elastic. Salt consumption plummeted—and so did state revenues—while popular discontent rose.

As Morozov took over the government, he brought a number of equally corrupt people with him. They abused the populace, provoking a rebellion in June 1648. The mob tore one of his coconspirators to bits and cast his remains on a dung heap. Another was beheaded. Tsar Alexei intervened on behalf of Morozov, whose life was spared on the condition that he would leave the government and Moscow immediately. This arrangement helped to calm the mob. Morozov was exiled on June 12 to the Kirill-Beloozero Monastery, but he returned to Moscow on October 26. He never again played an official role in government, though he was one of Alexis's behind-the-scenes advisers throughout the 1650s.

Morozov's greed led him to appropriate vast estates for himself. They totaled over 80,000 *desiatinas* (216,000 acres) with over 55,000 people in 9,100 households; this made him the second wealthiest Russian of his time. (The wealthiest individual was Nikita Ivanovich Romanov, Tsar Mikhail's uncle, who led the opposition to Morozov's government.) In 1645 the government, in response to a middle service class provincial cavalry petition, promised that the time limit on the recovery of fugitive serfs would be repealed as soon as a census was taken. The census was taken in 1646–1647, but the statute of limitations was not repealed. All the while Morozov's extensive correspondence with his estate stewards reveals that he was recruiting peasants from other lords and moving such peasants about (typically from the center to the Volga region) to conceal them. Morozov was also active in the potash business: he ordered his serfs to cut down trees, burn them, and barrel the ashes for export.

*See also:* ALEXEI MIKHAILOVICH; ASSEMBLY OF THE LAND; BOYAR; CHANCELLERY SYSTEM; ENSERFMENT; LAW CODE OF 1649

**BIBLIOGRAPHY**

Crummey, Robert Owen. (1983). *Aristocrats and Servitors: The Boyar Elite in Russia, 1613–1689.* Princeton, NJ: Princeton University Press.

Hellie, Richard. (1971). *Enserfment and Military Change in Muscovy.* Chicago: The University of Chicago Press.

RICHARD HELLIE

## MOROZOV, PAVEL TROFIMOVICH

(c. 1918–1932), young man murdered in 1932 who became a hero for the Pioneers (members of the Soviet organization for children in the 10 to 14 age group); celebrated in biographies, pamphlets, textbooks, songs, films, paintings, and plays.

Soviet accounts of the life of Pavel Morozov are mythic in tone and often contradictory. All agree that he was born in the western Siberian village of Gerasimovka, about 150 miles from Sverdlovsk (Ekaterinburg), probably in December 1918. He and his younger brother Fyodor were murdered on September 3, 1932. The Morozov murders were taken up by the local press about two weeks after they happened; in late September 1932, the central children's press became aware of the case, and reporters were dispatched to Siberia to investigate and to press for justice against the boys' supposed murderers. In December 1932, the boys' grandparents, their uncle, their cousin, and a neighbor stood trial; four of the five were sentenced to execution.

Like most child murders, the death of the two Morozov brothers provoked outrage; equally typically, press coverage dwelt on the innocence and goodness of the victims. But since the murders also took place in an area that was undergoing collectivization, they acquired a specifically Soviet political resonance. They were understood as an episode in the "class war": A child political activist and fervent Pioneer had been slaughtered by kulaks, wealthy peasants, as a punishment for exposing these kulaks' activities.

Additionally, it was reported that Pavel (or, as he became known, "Pavlik") had displayed such commitment to the cause that he had denounced his own father, the chairman of the local collective farm, for providing dekulakized peasants with false identity papers. His murder by his relations was an act of revenge, and an attempt by them to prevent Pavlik from pushing them into collectivization. All in all, Pavlik came to exemplify virtue so resolute that it preferred death to betrayal of principle. Learning about his life was an important part of the teaching offered the Pioneers; the anniversaries of his death were commemorated with pomp, and statues of Pavlik went up all over the Soviet Union.

But indoctrination did not lead to the emergence of millions of "copycat Pavliks." Memoirs and oral history suggest that most children found the story disturbing, rather than inspiring, even during the 1930s. And during the World War II, attention switched to another type of child hero: the boy or girl who refused to convey information, even under torture. To the postwar generations, Pavlik was a nasty little *stukach*, squealer. Learning about his life was a chore, and he had far less appeal than the Komsomol war heroine Zoya Kosmodemyanskaya. Indeed, surveys indicate that by 2002, the eightieth anniversary of his death, many respondents either could not remember who Pavlik was, or remembered his life inaccurately (e.g., "a hero of the Great Patriotic War"). Statues of him had disappeared (the Moscow statue in 1991), and streets had been renamed. Though the Pavlik Morozov museum in Gerasimovka was still open, few visitors bothered to call there.

See also: CIVIL WAR OF 1917–1922; FOLKLORE; PURGES, THE GREAT

## BIBLIOGRAPHY

Druzhnikov, Iurii. (1997). *Informer 001: the Myth of Pavlik Morozov.* (New Brunswick, NJ: Transaction Publishers.

Kelly, Catriona. (2004). *Comrade Pavlik: The Life and Legend of a Soviet Boy Hero.* London: Granta.

CATRIONA KELLY

## MOSCOW

Moscow is the capital city of Russia and the country's economic and cultural center.

Moscow was founded by Prince Yuri Vladimirovich Dolgoruky in 1147 on the banks of the Moscow River. Its earliest fortifications were raised on the present-day site of the Kremlin. Located in Russia's forest belt, the city was afforded a limited degree of protection from marauders from the south. Its location adjacent several rivers also made it a good trade center. By 1325, following the sacking of Kiev and the imposition of the Mongol Yoke, Moscow's princes obtained the sole right to rule over the Russian territories and collect tribute for the Golden Horde. The head of the Russian Orthodox church relocated to Moscow in recognition of the city's growing authority. A prince of Moscow, Ivan III, ultimately rid Russia of Mongol rule, following which the city became the capital of the expanding Muscovite state, which reunited the Russian lands by diplomacy and military conquest from the fourteenth to the eighteenth centuries.

During the period of expansion, the young state was thrown into chaos when Ivan IV passed away without leaving an heir. His unsuccessful efforts to regain access to the Baltic Sea and Black Sea had left the state further exhausted. In the ensuing power struggle, the country was invaded by several foreign armies before the Russian people were able once again to gain control of Moscow and elect a new tsar, marking the beginning of the Romanov dynasty (1613–1917).

In 1713, Peter the Great moved the Russian capital to St. Petersburg, which he had built on the Baltic Sea as "Russia's window to the West."

Moscow, which Peter loathed for its traditional Russian ways, remained a major center of commerce and culture. Further, all Russian tsars were crowned in the city, providing a link with the past. Recognizing the city's historical importance, Napoleon occupied Moscow in 1812. He was forced from the city and defeated by the Russian Army as foreign invaders before him had been.

The Bolsheviks moved the capital of Russia back to Moscow when German forces threatened Petrograd (previously St. Petersburg) in 1918. When the Germans left Russian land later that year, the capital remained in Moscow and has not been moved since.

During the Soviet era, a metro and many new construction projects were undertaken in Moscow as the city grew in population and importance. At the same time, many cultural sites, particularly churches, were destroyed. As a consequence, Moscow lost much of its architectural integrity and ancient charm. In an effort to recover this, the Russian government has engaged in a number of restoration projects in the wake of the collapse of the Soviet Union. One of the most important has been the rebuilding of the Savior Cathedral, which was meant to mark the city's spiritual revival.

With a population of approximately 8.5 million people (swelling to more than 11 million on workdays), Moscow is the largest city in Russia and its capital. The Kremlin houses the Presidential Administration while both chambers of the national legislature are located just off of Red Square. The prime minister and his most important deputies have their offices in the White House, the building on the banks of the Moscow River that formerly was the location of the Russian Federation's legislature. The various ministries of the government, which report to the prime minister, are located throughout the city.

The city's government historically has occupied a high profile in national politics. This is particularly true of the mayor, who is directly elected by the city's residents for a four-year term. The mayor appoints the Moscow city government and is responsible for the administration of the city. Among the city's administrative responsibilities are managing more than half of the housing occupied by Muscovites, managing a primary health-care delivery system, operating a primary and secondary school system, providing social services and utility subsidies, maintaining roads, operating a public transportation system, and policing the city.

Legislative power lies with the Moscow City Duma, but the mayor has the power to submit bills as well as to veto legislation to which he objects. The city's citizens elect the City Duma in direct elections for a four-year term. It comprises thirty-five members elected from Moscow's electoral districts.

Not only is Moscow the country's political capital, it is also the country's major intellectual and cultural center, boasting numerous theaters and playhouses. Its attractions include the world-renowned Bolshoi Theater, Moscow State University, the Academy of Sciences, the Tretyakov Art Gallery, and the Lenin Library. Only St. Petersburg rivals it architecturally.

Not surprisingly, given its political and cultural importance, Moscow is Russia's economic capital as well, attracting a substantial portion of foreign investment. The city is the country's primary business center, accounting for 5.7 percent of industrial production. More importantly, it serves as the home for most of Russia's export-import industry as well as a major hub for international and national trade routes. As a consequence, the standard of living of Muscovites is well above that of the rest of the country. All of this owes in large part to the substantial degree of economic restructuring that has occurred in the city since 1991 in response to the introduction of a market economy. There has been particularly strong growth in finance and wholesale and retail trade.

The growth of Moscow's economy has not come without problems. Muscovites are increasingly concerned about crime as well as the plight of pensioners and the poor. They are also concerned about the strain being placed on the city's transportation system, increasing environmental pollution caused by the increased use of automobiles, and the degradation of the city's infrastructure, including its schools and health care system.

*See also:* ACADEMY OF SCIENCES; ARCHITECTURE; BOLSHOI THEATER; KREMLIN; LUZHKOV, YURI MIKHAILOVICH; MOSCOW ART THEATER; MUSCOVY; ST. PETERSBURG; YURY VLADIMIROVICH

**BIBLIOGRAPHY**

Colton, Timothy J. (1995). *Moscow: Governing the Socialist Metropolis.* Cambridge, MA: Harvard University Press.

Government of the City of Moscow. (2002). "Information Memorandum: City of Moscow." <http://www.moscowdebt.ru/eng/city/memorandum>.

TERRY D. CLARK

## MOSCOW AGRICULTURAL SOCIETY

A voluntary association chartered in 1819, the Moscow Agricultural Society was a forum for discussing agricultural policy. Its membership came mainly from the serf-owning nobility and included prominent Slavophiles of the 1850s. In the 1830s Finance Minister Egor Kankrin provided a small financial subsidy, but the society's main support came from its members. Its meetings, exhibitions, and publications were devoted to issues of agricultural innovation, such as new crops and species of livestock and new methods of crop rotation. Its earliest activities included a model farm (*khutor*) near Moscow and an agricultural school. After the end of serfdom in 1861, the society's focus turned to economic and administrative questions: taxation, the agricultural role of the new *zemstvo* organs of local government, the provision of agricultural credit, the creation of a Ministry of Agriculture. It cooperated with the Free Economic Society and other organizations in a multivolume study of handicraft trades (1879–1887), advocated expansion of grain exports through the construction of railroad lines and storage facilities, and promoted the mechanization of agriculture. The Moscow Agricultural Society corresponded with agricultural societies in other countries, and with local affiliates in various parts of Russia. At the beginning of the twentieth century some of its members advocated abolition of the peasant commune and the encouragement of private land ownership and a market economy. Others helped create the All-Russian Peasant Union in 1905, and later the moderate League of Agrarian Reform. The organization was dissolved after 1917, but its library was preserved in the Central State Agricultural Library of the All-Union Academy of Agricultural Sciences.

*See also:* AGRICULTURE; FREE ECONOMIC SOCIETY; PEASANTRY; SLAVOPHILES; ZEMSTVO

ROBERT E. JOHNSON

## MOSCOW ART THEATER

Celebrating its centennial anniversary in 1998, The Moscow Art Theater (MAT) represents a twentieth-century bastion of theatrical art. MAT insured the dramatic career of Anton Chekhov, introduced European trends in stage realism to Russia, and solidified the role of the director as the artistic force behind dramatic interpretation and the united efforts of designers. MAT also significantly reformed the procedures by which plays were rehearsed and set new standards for ensemble acting that ultimately influenced theaters around the world. The majority of its productions created realistic illusions, replete with sound effects, architectural details, and archeologically researched costumes and sets.

Following the 1882 repeal of the 1737 Licensing Act, which had made Russian theater an imperial monopoly, playwright Vladimir Nemirovich-Danchenko (head of Moscow's acting school, the Moscow Philharmonic Society) and actor Konstantin Stanislavsky (founder of the renowned theater club, The Society of Art and Literature) founded MAT as a shareholding company. Nemirovich instigated their first legendary meeting in 1897. The enterprise opened in 1898 as The Moscow Publicly Accessible Art Theater, its name embracing the founders' idealistic hopes of providing classic Russian and foreign plays at prices that the working class could afford and fostering drama that educated the community. The first company comprised thirty-nine actors—Nemirovich's most talented students, notably Olga Knipper, later Chekhov's wife; Vsevolod Meyerhold, the future theatricalist director; and Ivan Moskvin, who still performed his popular 1898 role of Tsar Fyodor on his seventieth birthday in 1944—joined with Stanislavsky's most successful amateurs, including his wife Maria Lilina and Maria Andreyeva, the future Bolshevik and wife to Maxim Gorky.

Within a few seasons, financial difficulties and lack of governmental funding forced the founders to raise ticket prices, to drop "Publicly Accessible" from their name, and reluctantly to accept the patronage of the wealthy merchant Savva Morozov. In 1902 Morozov financed the construction of their permanent theater in the art nouveau style and equipped it with the latest lighting technology and a revolving stage.

Following the 1917 revolution, MAT's realistic productions attracted support from the liberal Commissar of Enlightenment, playwright Anatoly Lunacharsky, and Lenin (who was said to have especially admired Stanislavsky's performance as the fussy Famusov in Alexander Griboyedov's *Woe from Wit*). In 1920, MAT became The Moscow Academic Art Theater, its new adjective betokening state support. At this time, Lunacharsky also intervened on behalf of the destitute Stanislavsky in order to secure for him and his family a house with two rooms for rehearsals.

During the 1930s, Stanislavsky strenuously objected to the appointment of Mikhail Geits (1929) as MAT's political watchdog and to governmental pressure to stage productions with insufficient rehearsal. Believing in Stalin's good intentions, Stanislavsky naively appealed to the Soviet leader, winning a pyrrhic victory. Stalin placed MAT under direct governmental supervision in 1931, changing its name to The Gorky Moscow Academic Art Theater one year later, despite the fact that none of Maksim Gorky's plays had been staged since 1905. Under Stalinism, MAT received special privileges denied other artists, in return for public proof of political loyalty. Because of its past dedication to realism, MAT's history could easily be seen as constituting the vanguard of Socialist Realism. Stalin thus turned the company into the single most visible model for Soviet theater, and Stanislavsky's system of actor training, purged of its spiritual and symbolist components, into the sole curriculum for all dramatic schools. Press campaigns ensured this interpretation of MAT's work, even as Stanislavsky's continuing evolution as an artist threatened the view. Given Stanislavsky's international renown, Stalin could not afford the public scandal that would result from his arrest. Instead, Stalin "isolated" Stanislavsky from his public image, maintaining the ailing old man in his house, the site of his internal exile (1934–1938).

Nemirovich and Stanislavsky administered the theater jointly from its inception until 1911 when Stanislavsky's experimental stance toward acting and his growing interest in symbolist plays created unbearable hostility between them. Thereafter, Nemirovich managed the theater until his death in 1943, and Stanislavsky moved his experiments into a series of adjunct studios, some of which later became independent theaters. Stanislavsky continued to act for MAT until a heart attack in 1928, to direct until his death in 1938, and to influence MAT from the sidelines, as he had in 1931. He administered MAT only in Nemirovich's absence, most notably in 1926 and 1927, when Nemirovich toured in the United States. Among the theater's subsequent administrators, actor and director Oleg Yefremov (1927–2000) had the greatest impact on the company. He had studied with Nemirovich at the Moscow Art Theater's school, and founded the prestigious Sovremennik (Contemporary) Theater in 1958, and spoke to the conscience of the country after Stalin's death. He reinvigorated MAT's psychological realism in acting while he relaxed its history of realistic design. When he took charge of MAT in 1970, he found an unwieldy company of more than one hundred actors. In 1987, with perestroika ("reconstruction") occurring in the Soviet Union, Yefremov decided to reconstruct the company by splitting MAT in two. Yefremov retained The Chekhov Art Theater in the 1902 art nouveau building, and actress Tatyana Doronina took charge of The Gorky Art Theater. While Yefremov focused on reviving artistic goals, Doronina made The Gorky a voice for the nationalists of the 1990s. With the fall of the Soviet Union, the Art Theater and all of Russia's theaters struggled to survive. Not only did the loss of governmental subsidies create extraordinary financial instability, but the traditional audiences, who looked to theater for subversive political discussion, deserted theaters for television news. In 2000, Yefremov's student, actor-director Oleg Tabakov, took reluctant charge of the theater's uncertain future.

In its first twenty seasons (1898–1917), MAT revolutionized theatrical art through the production of a repertoire of more than seventy plays. The theater opened in 1898 with two major works: Alexei Tolstoy's *Tsar Fyodor Ionnovich*, which brought mediaeval Russia vividly to life with archeologically accurate designs, and Chekhov's *The Seagull*, which added psychological realism in acting to illusionistic stage environments. MAT premiered all of Chekhov's major plays between 1898 and 1904, with Stanislavsky's staging of *The Three Sisters* (1901) hailed as one of the company's greatest triumphs. Realistic productions, characterized by careful detailing in costumes, properties, sets, and acting choices, predominated. MAT produced more plays by Henrick Ibsen than by any other playwright, with *An Enemy of the People* (1900) providing Stanislavsky with one of his greatest roles. Even Ibsen's abstract play, *When We Dead Awaken*, was directed realistically by Nemirovich (1901). For Gorky's *The Lower Depths* (1902) MAT used representational detail to create a social statement about the underclass. Nemirovich especially furthered the cause of stage realism, often overburdening plays with inappropriate illusion. His unwieldy realistic production of William Shakespeare's *Julius Caesar* (1903) garnered much criticism.

Stanislavsky's growing interest in abstracted styles led to MAT's production of a series of symbolist plays. Notable among these were Stanislavsky's stagings of Leonid Andreyev's *The Life of Man* (1907), which featured stunning stage effects developed by its director, and Maurice Maeterlinck's fantasy, *The Blue Bird* (1908), as well as Gordon Craig's theatricalist production of Shakespeare's

*Hamlet* (1911). 1907 saw the two MAT styles collide uncomfortably when Nemirovich presented his overly naturalistic version of Ibsen's *Brand* alongside Stanislavsky's abstracted production of Knut Hamsun's *The Drama of Life.* When Stanislavsky began to apply his new ideas about acting to Ivan Turgenev's *A Month in the Country* (1909), he utilized abstraction both in the symmetrical set design and in the actors' use of static gestures in order to focus on inner states. This production caused a permanent rift between Stanislavsky and the company.

Although MAT greeted the 1917 revolution optimistically, it lost economic viability. Its first postrevolutionary production was Lord Byron's *Cain* in 1920, interpreted by Stanislavsky as a metaphor of the postrevolutionary civil war. MAT struggled to find the necessary funds and materials to realize the production. In order to survive financially, half of the company toured Europe and the United States from 1924 to 1926 with their most famous realistic productions, among them *Tsar Fyodor Ionnovich* from 1898 and Chekhov's *The Cherry Orchard* from 1904. This tour solidified the international fame of Stanislavsky and MAT. In the late 1920s, MAT participated in the general theatrical trend toward a Soviet repertoire. Stanislavsky staged Mikhail Bulgakov's controversial view of White Russia in *The Days of the Turbins* (1926) and Vsevolod Ivanov's *Armored Train 14-69* (1927). During the 1930s and 1940s, under the yoke of Socialist Realism, MAT's work lost its verve, its productions becoming undistinguished. In the 1970s, Yefremov reinvigorated the company by employing talented actors and revived its repertoire by staging new plays, such as Mikhail Roshchin's portrait of young love in *Valentin and Valentina* (1971) and Alexander Vampilov's *Duck Hunting* (1979), in which Yefremov played the fallen hero.

*See also:* CHEKHOV, ANTON PAVLOVICH; MEYERHOLD, VSEVOLOD YEMILIEVICH; MOSCOW; SILVER AGE; SOCIALIST REALISM; STANISLAVSKY, KONSTANTIN SERGEYEVICH; THEATER

**BIBLIOGRAPHY**

Benedetti, Jean. (1988). *Stanislavsky [sic]: A Biography.* New York: Routledge.

Carnicke, Sharon Marie. (1998). *Stanislavsky in Focus.* London: Harwood/Routledge.

Leach, Robert and Borovsky, Victor. (1999). *A History of Russian Theatre.* Cambridge, UK: Cambridge University Press.

Rich, Elizabeth. (2000). "Oleg Yefremov, 1927–2000: A Final Tribute." *Slavic and East European Performance* 20(3):17–23.

Worrall, Nick. (1996). *The Moscow Art Theatre.* New York: Routledge.

SHARON MARIE CARNICKE

## MOSCOW BAROQUE

Moscow Baroque was the fashionable architectural style of the late seventeenth and early eighteenth centuries, combining Muscovite (Russo-Byzantine) traditions with Western decorative details and proportions; the term also sometimes applied to new trends in late seventeenth-century Muscovite painting, engraving, and literature.

The term *Moscow Baroque* (*moskovskoe barokko*) came into use among Russian art historians in the 1890s and 1900s as a way of categorizing the distinctive style of architecture which flourished in and around Moscow from the late 1670s, and in the provinces into the 1700s. In the 1690s, Peter I's maternal relatives the Naryshkins commissioned many sumptuous churches in the style; hence the supplementary art historical term "Naryshkin Baroque," which is sometimes erroneously applied as a general term for the style. Some of the early examples of Moscow Baroque are reminiscent of mid-seventeenth-century Muscovite churches in their general shape and coloration—cubes constructed in red brick with white stone decorations and topped with one or five domes—but the builders had evidently assimilated a new sense of symmetry and regularity in their ordering of both structural and decorative elements. Old Russian ornamental details were replaced almost entirely by Western ones based on the Classical order system: half-columns with pediments and bases, window surrounds of broken pediments, volutes, carved columns, and shell gable motifs. One of the best concentrations of Moscow Baroque buildings was commissioned by the regent Sophia Alexeyevna in the 1680s in the sixteenth-century Novodevichy Convent in Moscow, which includes the churches of the Transfiguration, Dormition, and Assumption, with a refectory, belltower, nuns' cells, and crenelations on the convent walls in matching materials and style. Similar constructs can be found in the Monastery of St. Peter (Vysokopetrovsky) on Petrovka Street in Moscow. Civic buildings were constructed on the same principles: for example,

Prince Vasily Golitsyn's Moscow mansion (1680s) and the Pharmacy on Red Square (1690s). A number of these projects were carried out by the architectural section of the Foreign Office.

In the 1690s builders regularly incorporated octagonal structures, producing the so-called octagon-on-cube church. One of the finest examples, the Intercession at Fili, built for Peter's uncle Lev Naryshkin in 1690–1693, with its soaring tower of receding octagons, gold cupolas, and intricately carved limestone decoration, bears witness to both the Naryshkins' wealth and their Westernized tastes. Inside, all the icons were painted in a matching "Italianate" style and set in an elaborately carved and gilded iconostasis. This and other churches such as the Trinity at Troitse-Lykovo, Boris and Gleb in Ziuzino, and Savior at Ubory, with their tiers of receding octagons, also owe something to distant prototypes in Russian and Ukrainian architecture (the wooden architecture of the former and the dome configuration of the latter), while the new sense of harmony in their design and planning evokes the Renaissance. The style spread beyond Moscow.

Analogous developments can be seen in allegorical prints of the period, embellished with a characteristic Baroque mix of Christian and Classical imagery, most of which originated in Ukraine. A characteristic example is Ivan Shchirsky's engraving (1683) of Tsars Ivan and Peter hovering above a canopy containing a double eagle, with Christ floating between them and, above Christ, a winged maiden, the Divine Wisdom (Sophia). In icons painted in the Moscow Armory and in workshops in Yaroslavl, Vologda, and other major commercial centers, influences from Western art can be seen in the use of light and shade and decorative details such as scrolls, putti-like angels, ornate swirling cloud and rock motifs, dramatic gestures, and even some borrowings from Catholic iconography: for instance, saints with emblems of their martyrdom; blood dripping from Christ's hands and side. In poetry, syllabic verse and Baroque motifs and devices were imported from Poland and practiced by such writers as Simeon Polotsky, court poet to Tsar Alexis, and Polotsky's pupil Silvester Medvedev.

Art historians have debated whether Moscow Baroque was a direct derivative of Western Baroque, represented a spontaneously generated and original form of baroque, or was the decadent, over-ornate last phase of the "classical" forms of Russo-Byzantine art. It may be best to view it as an example of the belated influence of the Renaissance upon traditional art and architecture, which picked up elements from both contemporary and slightly earlier Western art. No Russian architects are known to have visited the West during this period, and there is scant evidence of Western architects working in Russia. However, Russian craftsmen did have access to foreign books and prints in the Armory, Foreign Office workshops, and other libraries, while contacts with Polish culture, both direct and via Ukraine and Belarus, were influential, especially in literature.

The term *Moscow Baroque* is not generally applied to the architecture of early St. Petersburg, although many buildings constructed in the reigns of Peter I and his immediate successors had much in common with the preceding style: for instance, the use of octagonal structures and the white decorative details against a darker background. In Moscow and the provinces, Moscow Baroque remained popular well into the eighteenth century.

*See also:* ARCHITECTURE; GOLITSYN, VASILY VASILIEVICH; MEDVEDEV, SYLVESTER AGAFONIKOVICH; POLOTSKY, SIMEON; SOPHIA

**BIBLIOGRAPHY**

Cracraft, James. (1990). *The Petrine Revolution in Russian Architecture.* Chicago: University of Chicago Press.

Cracraft, James. (1997). *The Petrine Revolution in Russian Imagery.* Chicago: University of Chicago Press.

Hughes, Lindsey. (1977). "Western European Graphic Material as a Source for Moscow Baroque Architecture." *Slavonic and East European Review* 55:433–443.

Hughes, Lindsey. (1982). "Moscow Baroque: A Controversial Style." *Transactions of the Association of Russian-American Scholars in USA* 15:69–93.

LINDSEY HUGHES

# MOSCOW, BATTLE OF

The Battle of Moscow was a pivotal moment in the early period of the World War II, in which Soviet forces averted a disastrous collapse and demonstrated that the German army was, in fact, vulnerable. The battle can be divided into three general segments: the first German offensive, from September 30 to October 30, 1941; the second German offensive, from November 16 to December 5, 1941;

and the Soviet counteroffensive, from December 5, 1941, to April 5, 1942.

The German attack on Moscow began on September 30, 1941, under the code name "Typhoon." The German High Command hoped to seize the Soviet capital before the onset of winter, surmising that the fall of Moscow would presage the fall of the Soviet Union. With this goal in mind they arrayed a massive force against the Soviet capital, concentrating 1,800,000 troops, 1,700 tanks, 14,000 cannons and mortars, and 1,390 aircraft against Moscow. Led by General Heinz Guderain, this enormous army quickly took advantage of the weakened and retreating Soviet forces to capture several towns on the approaches to the capital in the first week of the campaign. By October 15, the German army, having circumvented the Soviet defensive lines and taken the key towns of Kaluga and Mozhaisk, was within striking distance of the capital.

The lightning speed with which the Germans reached the outskirts of the capital spawned a panic in Moscow as many Muscovites, fearing a German takeover of the city, began to flee to the east. For several days, local authority crumbled completely, and Moscow seemed on the verge of chaos. Even as the capital teetered on the edge of collapse, however, several factors combined to slow the German onslaught. First, the German forces had begun to outpace their supply lines. Second, Josef V. Stalin and the Soviet High Command appointed General Georgy Zhukov as the commander of the Western Front. Fresh from his triumph stabilizing the defensive lines surrounding Leningrad, Zhukov moved to do the same for Moscow, and the Red Army began to stiffen its defense of the capital. Third, the German supply line problems gave the Red Army time to bring reserves from the Far East to Moscow. Until these reserves could be put in place, however, the city's defense leaders ordered ordinary Muscovites organized into *opolchenie*, or home guard units, into the breaches in the capital's defensive lines. These units, often quickly and poorly trained, paid a high price to shore up Moscow's defenses.

Once the German supply had regrouped, German forces mounted another attack in late November. Initially the German forces scored several successes in the areas of Klin and Istra to the northwest and around Tula to the south. The tenacity of the Soviet defense and severity of the Russian winter, however, slowed the German advance and allowed time for Soviet forces to recover and even begin to mount limited counterattacks by early December.

Emboldened by their success in stemming the German onslaught, the Soviet command attempted a more concerted attack against the German invaders on December 5–6, 1941. With the aim of driving the Germans back to Smolensk, Stalin and Zhukov opened a 560-mile front stretching from Kalinin, north of the capital, to Yelets in the south. The ambitious operation quickly met with success as the Red Army, bolstered by units from Central Asia, drove the Germans back twenty to forty miles, liberating Kalinin, Klin, Istra, and Yelets and breaking the German encirclement attempt at Tula. In many places German forces retreated quickly, weakened by their supply problems and their exposure to the Russian winter. Soviet forces, despite their advances, could never capitalize on their initiative. While the Red Army advanced as much as 200 miles into German-held territory on the German flanks to the north and south of Moscow, they had great difficulty dislodging German forces from the Rzhev-Gzhatsk-Viazma salient due west of the capital. By late January their resistance had stiffened to the point that the Red Army's advance began to stall. Although the Soviet offensive continued to grind its way westward, it had lost momentum. This stalemate continued until April 1942 when the Soviet command called a halt to the offensive. It was not until the spring of 1943 that the Red Army finally drove the Germans back from Moscow.

The Battle of Moscow was important for several reasons. It was the first real setback that German forces had absorbed since World War II began in 1939. Despite the fact that Moscow was on the verge of collapse in mid-October 1941, Soviet forces proved that the German army was not invincible. Also, the struggle for the Soviet capital revealed a new breed of Soviet commanders who came to prominence in the defense of the capital. Commanders such as Zhukov, Konstantin Rokossovsky, Ivan Boldin, and Dmitry Lelyshenko demonstrated their competence during this critical period and became the backbone of the Soviet military command for the remainder of the war. Finally, the defense of the capital was an important moral victory for the Soviet command and people alike, and made an indelible impression on the Soviet nation and on the other countries participating in World War II.

*See also:* MOSCOW; WORLD WAR II; ZHUKOV, GEORGY KONSTANTINOVICH

**BIBLIOGRAPHY**

Erickson, John. (1999). *The Road to Stalingrad: Stalin's War with Germany.* New Haven, CT: Yale University Press.

Overy, Richard. (1998). *Russia's War: A History of the Soviet War Effort, 1941–1945.* New York: Penguin.

Werth, Alexander. (1964). *Russia at War, 1941–1945.* New York: Avon Books.

ANTHONY YOUNG

## MOSCOW OLYMPICS OF 1980

The city of Moscow hosted the Summer Olympic Games from July 19 to August 3, 1980. The International Olympic Committee awarded Moscow the games in 1974, in the hopes that international competition might contribute to détente. But superpower politics had a direct impact on these games. Under the leadership of the United States, sixty-two nations boycotted the Moscow Olympics to protest the Soviet invasion of Afghanistan during December of 1979. The Soviet government, along with its allies, retaliated by boycotting the 1984 Los Angeles Summer Olympic Games. Great Britain, France, and Italy supported the condemnation of the Soviet invasion of Afghanistan, but participated in the games.

The Moscow Olympic games were the first held in a socialist country. Soviet leader Leonid Brezhnev, visibly aged, opened the games. The Soviet leadership intended to use the games to showcase the advantages of the socialist system. Toward that end the government ordered that the Moscow streets and parks be cleaned and that petty criminals and prostitutes be rounded up. Government officials also hoped that Soviet athletes would dominate the games. They were not disappointed. The USSR won 195 medals, including 80 gold; the German Democratic Republic (East Germany) won 126 medals, including 47 gold; followed by Bulgaria, Hungary, Poland, and Cuba in that order. Eighty-one nations had participated in the Moscow games, and the USSR and its East European and other socialist allies won the vast majority of the medals. Soviet fans demonstrated poor sportsmanship by constantly jeering Polish and East German competitors. Since 1952, when the USSR first participated in the Olympic games, government officials recognized how gold, silver, and bronze medals

**The Olympic flag is carried out of the Lenin Stadium at the closing ceremony of the 1980 summer Olympic Games.**
© BETTMANN/CORBIS

might be translated into propaganda achievements for the nation.

Some of the notable individual achievements of the games included gymnast Nadia Comaneci of Romania winning two medals; Soviet swimmer Vladimir Salnikov becoming the first to break fifteen minutes in the 1,500 meters; Teofilo Stevenson, a Cuban boxer, becoming the first boxer to win three gold medals in his division; Soviet gymnast Alexander Dityatin winning eight medals; Miruts Yifter of Ethiopia winning the 5,000- and 10,000-meter runs in track; and Britain's Sebastian Coe outkicking countryman Steve Ovett in the 1,500 run. At the closing ceremony, it was said that the mascot of the Moscow Olympics, Misha the Bear, had a tear in his eye.

*See also:* AFGHANISTAN, RELATIONS WITH; SPORTS POLICY; UNITED STATES, RELATIONS WITH

**BIBLIOGRAPHY**

Hulme, Derick L. (1990). *The Political Olympics: Moscow, Afghanistan, and the 1980 U.S. Boycott.* New York: Praeger.

PAUL R. JOSEPHSON

## MOSKVITIN, IVAN YURIEVICH

Seventeenth-century Cossack and explorer of Russia's Pacific coast.

The Cossack adventurer Ivan Yurievich Moskvitin was one of the many explorers and frontiersmen who took part in the great push eastward that transformed Siberia during the reigns of tsars Mikhail (1613–1645) and Alexei (1645–1676).

In 1639 Moskvitin left Yakutsk at the head of a squadron of twenty Cossacks, seeking to confirm the existence of what local natives called the "great sea-ocean." Proceeding east, then southward, Moskvitin encountered the mountains of the Jug-Jur Range, which forms a barrier separating the Siberian interior from the Pacific coastline. Moskvitin threaded his way through the mountains by following the Maya, Yudoma, and Ulya river basins.

Tracing the Ulya to its mouth brought Moskvitin to the shore of the Sea of Okhotsk. He and his men were therefore the first Russians to reach the Pacific Ocean by land. The party also built a fortress at the mouth of the Ulya, Russia's first Pacific outpost. Until 1641, Moskvitin charted much of the Okhotsk shoreline. Mapping an overland route to the eastern coast and establishing a presence there were key moments in Russia's expansion into Siberia and Asia.

*See also:* EXPLORATION; SIBERIA

**BIBLIOGRAPHY**

Bobrick, Benson. (1992). *East of the Sun: The Epic Conquest and Tragic History of Siberia.* New York: Poseidon.

Lincoln, W. Bruce. (1993). *Conquest of a Continent: Siberia and the Russians.* New York: Random House.

JOHN MCCANNON

## MOTION PICTURES

The statement "Cinema is for us the most important of all arts" has been attributed to Vladimir Lenin. This statement, whether apocryphal or not, became the motto of the Soviet motion picture industry. Because of the central part the movies played in Soviet propaganda, the motion picture industry had an enormous impact on culture, society, and politics.

### EARLY RUSSIAN CINEMA, 1896–1918

The moving picture age began in Russia on May 6, 1896, at the Aquarium amusement park in St. Petersburg. By summer of that year, the novelty was a featured attraction at the popular provincial trading fairs. Until 1908, however, the vast majority of movies shown in Russia were French. That year, Alexander Drankov (1880–1945), a portrait photographer and entrepreneur, opened the first Russian owned and operated studio, in St. Petersburg. His inaugural picture, *Stenka Razin*, was a great success and inspired other Russians to open studios.

By 1913, Drankov had been overshadowed by two Russian-owned production companies, Khanzhonkov and Thiemann & Reinhardt. These were located in Moscow, the empire's Hollywood. The outbreak of war in 1914 proved an enormous boon to the fledgling Russian film industry, since distribution paths were cut, making popular French movies hard to come by. (German films were forbidden altogether.) By 1916 Russia boasted more than one hundred studios that produced five hundred pictures. The country's four thousand movie theaters entertained an estimated 2 million spectators daily.

Until 1913 most Russian films were newsreels and travelogues. The few fiction films were mainly adaptations of literary classics, with some historical costume dramas. The turning point in the development of early Russian cinema was *The Keys to Happiness* (1913), directed by Yakov Protazanov (1881–1945) and Vladimir Gardin (1881–1945) for the Thiemann & Reinhardt studio. This full-length melodrama, based on a popular novel, was the legendary blockbuster of the time.

Although adaptations of literary classics remained popular with Russian audiences, the contemporary melodrama was favored during the war years. The master of the genre was Yevgeny Bauer (1865–1917). Bauer's complex psychological portraits, technical innovations, and painterly cinematic style raised Russian cinema to new levels of artistry. Bauer worked particularly well with actresses and made Vera Kholodnaya (1893–1919) a legend. Bauer's surviving films—which include

*Twilight of a Woman's Soul* (1913), *Child of the Big City* (1914), *Silent Witnesses* (1914), *Children of the Age* (1915), *The Dying Swan* (1916), and *To Happiness* (1917)—provide a vivid picture of a lost Russia.

The revolutionary year 1917 brought joy and misgiving to filmmakers. Political, economic, and social instability shuttered most theaters by the beginning of 1918. Studios began packing up and moving south to Yalta, to escape Bolshevik control. By 1920, Russia's filmmakers were on the move again, to Paris, Berlin, and Prague. Russia's great actor Ivan Mozzhukhin (1890–1939, known in France as "Mosjoukine") was one of few who enjoyed as much success abroad as at home.

### SOVIET SILENT CINEMA, 1918–1932

The first revolutionary film committees formed in 1918, and on August 27, 1919, the Bolshevik government nationalized the film industry, placing it under the control of Narkompros, the People's Commissariat for Enlightenment. Nationalization represented wishful thinking at best, since Moscow's movie companies had already decamped, dismantling everything that could be carried.

Filmmaking during the Civil War of 1917–1922 took place under extraordinarily difficult conditions. Lenin was acutely aware of the importance of disseminating the Bolshevik message to a largely illiterate audience as quickly as possible, yet film stock and trained cameramen were in short supply—not to mention projectors and projectionists. Apart from newsreels, the early Bolshevik repertory consisted of "agit-films," short, schematic, but exciting political messages. Films were brought to the provinces on colorfully decorated agit-trains, which carried an electrical generator to enable the agitki to be projected on a sheet. Innovations like these enabled Soviet cinema to rise from the ashes of the former Russian film industry, leading eventually to the formation of Goskino, the state film trust, in 1922 (reorganized as Sovkino in 1924).

Since most established directors, producers, and actors had already fled central Russia for territories controlled by the White armies, young men and women found themselves rapidly rising to positions of prominence in the revolutionary cinema. They were drawn to film as "the art of the future." Many of them had some experience in theater production, but Lev Kuleshov (1899–1970), who had begun his cinematic career with the great prerevolutionary director Bauer, led the way, though he was still a teenager.

Poster advertising the 1925 Soviet film *Strike.* © SWIM INK/ CORBIS

By the end of the civil war, most of Soviet Russia's future filmmakers had converged on Moscow. Many of them (Kuleshov, Sergei Eisenstein, and their "collectives") were connected to the Proletkult theater, where they debated and dreamed.

Because film stock was carefully rationed until the economy recovered in 1924, young would-be directors had to content themselves with rehearsing the experiments they hoped to film and writing combative theoretical essays for the new film journals. The leading director-theorists were Kuleshov, Eisenstein (1898–1948), Vsevolod Pudovkin (1893–1953), Dziga Vertov (1896–1954, born Denis Kaufman), and the "FEKS" team of Grigory Kozintsev (1905–1973) and Leonid Trauberg (1902–1990). Kuleshov wrote most clearly about the art of the cinema as a revolutionary agent, but Eisenstein's and Vertov's theories (and movies) had an impact that extended far beyond the Soviet Union's borders.

The debates between Eisenstein and Vertov symbolized the most extreme positions in the theoretical conflicts among the revolutionary avantgarde of the 1920s. Eisenstein believed in acted cinema but borrowed Kuleshov's idea of the actor as a type; he preferred working with non-professionals. Vertov privileged non-acted cinema and argued that the movie camera was a "cinema eye" (kino-glaz) that would catch "life off-guard" (zhizn vrasplokh)—yet he was an inveterate manipulator of time and space in his pictures. Eisenstein believed in a propulsive narrative driven by a "montage of attractions," with the masses as the protagonists, whereas Vertov was decisively antinarrative, believing that a brilliantly edited kaleidoscope of images best revealed the contours of revolutionary life.

Eisenstein's first two feature films, *Strike* (1925) and *Battleship Potemkin* (1926), enjoyed enormous success with critics and politicians but were much less popular with the workers and soldiers whose interests they were supposed to service. The same was true of Vertov's pictures. The intelligentsia loved *Forward, Soviet!* and *One-Sixth of the World* (both 1926), but proletarians were nonplussed.

Kuleshov, Pudovkin, Kozintsev, and Trauberg (who directed as a team) were more successful translating revolutionary style and content for mass audiences because they retained plot and character at the heart of their films. *The Extraordinary Adventures of Mr. West in the Land of the Bolsheviks* (1924), one of Kuleshov's earliest efforts, appeared as a favorite film in audience surveys through the end of the 1920s. The same was true of Pudovkin's *Mother* (1926), a loose adaptation of Maxim Gorky's famous novel. Kozintsev and Trauberg's *The Overcoat* (1926) is a good example of the extremes to which young directors pushed the classical narrative.

Despite this wealth of talent, Soviet avantgarde films never came close to challenging the popularity of American movies in the 1920s. Douglas Fairbanks's and Charlie Chaplin's pictures drew sell-out audiences. In response to the pressures to make Soviet entertainment films—and the need to show a profit—Goskino and the quasi-private studio Mezhrapbom invested more heavily in popular films than in the avant-garde, to the great dismay of the latter, but to the joy of audiences. The leading popular filmmaker was Protazanov,

who returned to Soviet Russia in 1923 to make a string of hits, starting with the science fiction adventure, *Aelita* (1924).

Also very successful with the spectators were the narrative films of younger directors such as Fridrikh Ermler (1898–1967, born Vladimir Breslav), Boris Barnet (1902–1965), and Abram Room (1894–1976). Ermler earned fame for his trenchant social melodramas (*Katka's Reinette Apples*, 1926 and *The Parisan Cobbler*, 1928). Barnet's intelligent comedies such as *The Girl with the Hatbox* (1927) sparkled, as did his adventure serial *Miss Mend* (1926),. Room was perhaps the most versatile of the three, ranging from a revolutionary adventure, *Death Bay* (1926), to a remarkable melodrama about a ménage à trois, *Third Meshchanskaya Street* (1927, known in the West as *Bed and Sofa*).

It must be emphasized that moviemaking was not a solely Russian enterprise, although distribution politics often made it difficult for films from Ukraine, Armenia, and Georgia to be considered more than exotica. The greatest artist to emerge from the non-Russian cinemas was certainly Ukraine's Alexander Dovzhenko (1894–1956), but Armenia's Amo Bek-Nazarov (1892–1965) and Georgia's Nikolai Shengelaya (1903–1943) made important contributions to early Soviet cinema as well.

In 1927, as the New Economic Policy era was coming to a close, Soviet cinema was flourishing. Cinema had returned to all provincial cities and rural areas were served by cinematic road shows. There was a lively film press that reflected a variety of aesthetic positions. Production was more than respectable, about 140 to 150 titles annually. Six years later, production had plummeted to a mere thirty-five films.

Many factors contributed to the crisis in cinema that was part of the Cultural Revolution. First, in 1927, sound was introduced to cinema, an event with significant artistic and economic implications. Second, proletarianist organizations such as RAPP, the Russian Association of Proletarian Writers, and ARRK, the Association of Workers in Revolutionary Cinematography were infiltrated by extremist elements who supported the government's aims to turn the film industry into a tool for propagandizing the collectivization and industrialization campaigns. This became apparent at the first All-Union Party Conference on Cinema Affairs in 1928. Third, in 1929, Anatoly Lunacharsky, the leading proponent of a diverse cinema, was ousted as commissar of enlightenment, and massive purges of the film industry began that lasted through 1931.

These troubled times saw the production of four great films, the last gasp of Soviet silent cinema: Ermler's *The Fragment of the Empire*, Kozintsev and Trauberg's *New Babylon*, Vertov's *The Man with the Movie Camera* (all 1929), and the following year, Dovzhenko's *Earth*.

## STALINIST CINEMA, 1932–1953

By the end of the Cultural Revolution, it was clear to filmmakers that the era of artistic innovation had ended. Movies and their makers were now "in the service of the state." Although Socialist Realism was not formally established as aesthetic dogma until 1934, (reconfirmed in 1935 at the All-Union Creative Conference on Cinematographic Affairs), politically astute directors had for several years been making movies that were only slightly more sophisticated than the agit-films of the civil war.

In the early 1930s, a few of the great artists of the previous decade attempted to adapt their experimental talents to the sound film. These efforts were either excoriated (Kuleshov's *The Great Consoler* and Pudovkin's *The Deserter*, both 1933) or banned outright (Eisenstein's *Bezhin Meadow*, 1937). Film production plummeted, as directors tried to navigate the ever-changing Party line, and many projects were aborted mid-production. Stalin's intense personal interest and involvement in moviemaking greatly exacerbated tensions.

Some of the early cinema elite avant-garde were eventually able to rebuild their careers. Kozintsev and Trauberg scored a major success with their popular adventure trilogy: *The Youth of Maxim* (1935), *The Return of Maxim* (1937), *The Vyborg Side* (1939). Pudovkin avoided political confrontations by turning to historical films celebrating Russian heroes of old in *Minin and Pozharsky* (1939), followed by *Suvorov* in 1941. Eisenstein likewise found a safe historical subject in the only undisputed masterpiece of the decade, *Alexander Nevsky* (1938). Others, such as Dovzhenko and Ermler, seriously compromised their artistic reputations by making movies that openly curried Stalin's favor. Ermler's *The Great Citizen* (two parts, 1937–1939) is a particularly notorious example.

New directors, most of them not particularly talented, moved to the forefront. Novices such as Nikolai Ekk and the Vasiliev Brothers made two of the enduring classics of Socialist Realism: *The Road to Life* (1931) and *Chapayev* (1934). Another relative newcomer, Ivan Pyrev, churned out Stalin-pleasing conspiracy films such as *The Party Card* (1936), about a woman who discovers her husband is a traitor, before turning to canned socialist comedies, of which *Tractor Drivers* (1939) is the most typical.

Some of the new generation managed to maintain artistic standards. Mikhail Romm's revisionist histories of the revolution, *Lenin in October* (1937) and *Lenin in 1918* (1939), which placed Stalin right at Lenin's side, were the first major hits in his distinguished career. Mark Donskoy's three-picture adaptation of Maxim Gorky's autobiography, beginning with *Gorky's Youth* (1938) also generated popular acclaim. The most beloved of the major directors of the 1930s was, however, Grigory Alexandrov. Alexandrov, who had worked as Eisenstein's assistant until 1932, successfully distanced himself from the maverick director, launching a series of zany musical comedies starring his wife, Lyubov Orlova, in 1934 with *The Jolly Fellows*.

When the German armies invaded the Soviet Union in June 1941, the tightly controlled film industry easily mobilized for the wartime effort. Considered central to the war effort, key filmmakers were evacuated to Kazakhstan, where makeshift studios were quickly constructed in Alma-Ata. With very few exceptions—Eisenstein's *Ivan the Terrible* (1944–1946) being most noteworthy—moviemaking during the war years focused almost exclusively on the war. Newsreels naturally dominated production. The fiction films that were made about the war effort were quite remarkable compared to those of the other combatant nations in that they focused on the active role women played in the partisan movement. One of these, Ermler's *She Defends Her Motherland* (1943), which tells the story of a woman who puts aside grief for vengeance, was shown in the United States during the war as *No Greater Love*.

The postwar years, until Stalin's death in 1953, were a cultural wasteland. Film production nearly ground to a halt; only nine films were made in 1950. The wave of denunciations and arrests known as the anti-cosmopolitan campaign roiled the cultural intelligentsia, particularly those who were Jewish such as Vertov, Trauberg, and Eisenstein. Eisenstein's precarious health was aggravated by the extreme tensions of the time and the disfavor that greeted the second part of *Ivan the Terrible*. He became the most famous casualty among filmmakers, dying of a heart attack in 1948 at the age of only fifty. Cold War conspiracy melodramas

**Movie still of a battle scene from Sergei Eisenstein's classic *Alexander Nevsky* (1938).** © BETTMANN/CORBIS

dominated movie theaters (not unlike McCarthy era films in the United States a few years later), along with ever more extravagant panegyrics to Stalin. Georgian director Mikhail Chiaureli's first ode to Stalin, *The Vow* (1946), was followed by *The Fall of Berlin* (1949), which Richard Taylor has aptly dubbed "the apotheosis of Stalin's cult of Stalin."

### SOVIET CINEMA FROM THE THAW THROUGH STAGNATION, 1953–1985

By the mid-1950s, filmmakers were confident that the Thaw—as Khrushchev's relaxation of censorship was known—would last long enough for them to express long-dormant creativity. The move from public and political toward the private and personal became a hallmark of the period. Thaw pictures were appreciated not only at home, but also abroad, where they received numerous prizes at international film festivals. There was now a human face to the Soviet colossus.

The greatest movies of the period rewrote the history of World War II, the Great Patriotic War. Mikhail Kalatozov's *The Cranes Are Flying* (1957) won the Palme d'Or at Cannes in 1958, signaling that Soviet cinema was once again on the world stage after nearly thirty years. *Cranes* is the story of a woman who betrays her lover, a soldier who is killed at the front, to marry his cousin, a craven opportunist. There is no upbeat ending, no neat resolution. The same can be said of Sergei Bondarchuk's *The Fate of a Man* and Grigory Chukhrai's *The Ballad of a Soldier* (both 1959). In the former, a POW returns home to find his entire family dead; in the latter, a very young soldier's last leave home to help his mother is movingly recorded.

A film that is often considered the last important movie of the Thaw also launched the career of the greatest film artist to emerge in postwar Soviet cinema. This was *Ivan's Childhood* (1962, known in the United States as *My Name Is Ivan*), a stunning antiwar film that won the Golden Lion at the Venice Film Festival. The director was Andrei Tarkovsky (1932–1986). By the time Tarkovsky began work on *Andrei Rublev* in the mid-1960s, Khrushchev had been ousted, and Leonid Brezhnev's era of stagnation had begun. Cultural iconoclasm was no longer tolerated, and Tarkovsky's dystopian epic about medieval Russia's greatest painter was not released in the USSR until 1971, although it won the International Film Critics' prize at Cannes in 1969. Tarkovsky toiled defiantly in the 1970s to produce three more Soviet films, *Solaris* (1972), *The Mirror* (1975), and *Stalker* (1980). He emigrated to Europe in 1984 and died of cancer two years later.

Filmmaking under Brezhnev was generally unremarkable, although two films, Bondarchuk's *War and Peace* (1966) and Vladimir Menshov's *Moscow Does Not Believe in Tears* (1979) each won the Oscar for Best Foreign Film. The most interesting movies (such as Alexander Askoldov's *The Commissar*, 1967) were shelved, not to be released until the late 1980s as part of Mikhail Gorbachev's *glasnost*. Among the exceptions to the mundane fare were Larisa Shepitko's tale of World War II collaboration, *The Ascent* (1976), and Lana Gogoberidze's *Several Interviews on Personal Questions* (1979), which sensitively explored the drab, difficult lives of Soviet women.

The best-known director to have started his career during the Brezhnev era is Nikita Mikhalkov (b. 1945). Son of Sergei Mikhalkov, a Stalinist writer of children's stories, the younger Mikhalkov first made a name for himself as an actor. Mikhalkov achieved his greatest successes in the 1970s and 1980s with his "heritage" films, elegiac recreations of Russian life in the nineteenth and early twentieth centuries, often adapted from literary classics, among them *An Unfinished Piece for Player Piano* (1977), *Oblomov* (1979), and *Dark Eyes* (1983).

## RUSSIAN CINEMA IN TRANSITION, 1985–2000

When Gorbachev announced the advent of perestroika and glasnost in 1986, the Union of Cinematographers stood at the ready. After a sweeping purge of the union's aging and conservative bureaucracy, the maverick director Elem Klimov (b. 1933) took the helm. Although Klimov had made a number of movies under Brezhnev, he did not emerge as a major director until 1985, with the release of his stunning antiwar film *Come and See*. Under Klimov's direction, the union began releasing the banned movies of the preceding twenty years, in effect rewriting the history of late Soviet cinema.

The film that most captured the public's imagination in that tumultuous period was Georgian, not Russian. Tengiz Abuladze's *Repentance* (1984, released nationally in 1986) is a surrealistic black comedy-drama that follows the misdeeds of the Abuladze family, provided a scathing commentary on Stalinism. Although a difficult film designed to provoke rather than entertain, *Repentance* packed movie theaters and sparked a national debate about the legacy of the past and the complicity of the survivors.

Television also became a major venue for filmmakers. Gorbachev's cultural policies encouraged publicistic documentaries that exposed either the evils of Stalin and his henchmen or the decay and degradation of contemporary Soviet life. Fiction films such as *Little Vera* (Vasily Pichul, 1988), *Intergirl* (Pyotr Todorovsky, 1989), and *Taxi Blues* (Pavel Lungin, 1990) followed suit by telling seamy tales about the Soviet underclass.

The movie industry began to fragment even before the end of the Soviet Union in 1991. The Union of Cinematographers decentralized in mid-1990, and Goskino and Sovexportfilm, which provided central oversight over film production and distribution, had completely lost control by the end of 1990. The early 1990s saw the collapse of native film production in all the post-Soviet states. Centralization and censorship had long been the bane of the industry, but filmmakers had no idea how to raise money for their projects—and were even more baffled by being expected to turn a profit. Market demands became known as "commercial censorship." Filmmakers also had to contend for the first time with competition from Hollywood, as second-rate American films flooded the market.

The Russian cinema industry began to rebound in the late 1990s. It now resembled other European cinemas quite closely, meaning that national production was carefully circumscribed, focusing on the art film market. Nikita Mikhalkov emerged the clear winner. By the turn of the century he became the president of the Russian Filmmakers' Union, the president of the Russian Cultural Foundation, and the president of the only commercially successful Russian studio, TriTe. He established a fruitful partnership with the French company Camera One, which coproduced his movies and distributed them abroad. He took enormous pride in the fact that *Burnt by the Sun*, his 1995 exploration of the beginnings of the Great Terror, won the Oscar for Best Foreign Picture that year, only the third Russian-language film to have done so, and certainly the best.

At the beginning of the twenty-first century, therefore, it seems that the glory days of Russian cinema are past. This past, however, has earned Russian and Soviet films and filmmakers an enduring place in the history of global cinema.

*See also:* AGITPROP; ALEXANDROV, GRIGORY ALEXANDROVICH; BAUER, YEVGENY FRANTSEVICH; CHAPAYEV, VASILY IVANOVICH; CULTURAL REVOLUTION; EISENSTEIN, SERGEI MIKHAILOVICH; MIKHALKOV, NIKITA SERGEYEVICH; ORLOVA, LYUBOV PETROVNA; SOCIALIST REALISM; TARKOVSKY, ANDREI ARSENIEVICH; THAW, THE

**BIBLIOGRAPHY**

Horton, Andrew, and Brashinsky, Mikhail. (1992). *The Zero Hour: Glasnost and Soviet Cinema in Transition.* Princeton, NJ: Princeton University Press.

Kenez, Peter. (2001). *Cinema and Soviet Society from the Revolution to the Death of Stalin.* London: I. B. Tauris.

Lawton, Anna. (1992). *Kinoglasnost: Soviet Cinema in Our Time.* New York: Cambridge University Press.

Leyda, Jay. (1960). *Kino: A History of the Russian and Soviet Film.* London: Allen & Unwin.

Taylor, Richard. (1979). *The Politics of the Soviet Cinema, 1917–1929.* Cambridge, UK: Cambridge University Press.

Taylor, Richard. (1998). *Film Propaganda: Soviet Russia and Nazi Germany,* 2nd rev. ed. London: I. B. Tauris.

Taylor, Richard, and Christie, Ian, eds. (1988). *The Film Factory: Russian and Soviet Cinema in Documents, 1896–1939.* Cambridge, MA: Harvard University Press.

Tsivian, Yuri, comp. (1989). *Silent Witnesses: Russian Films, 1908–1919.* Pordenone and London, 1989.

Tsivian, Yuri. (1994). *Early Cinema in Russia and Its Cultural Reception.* Friuli-Venezia: Edizioni Biblioteca dell'immagine; London: British Film Institute.

Woll, Josephine. (2000). *Real Images: Soviet Cinema and the Thaw.* London: I. B. Tauris.

Youngblood, Denise J. (1991). *Soviet Cinema in the Silent Era, 1918-1935.* Austin: University of Texas Press.

Youngblood, Denise J. (1992). *Movies for the Masses: Popular Cinema and Soviet Society in the 1920s.* Cambridge, UK: Cambridge University Press.

Youngblood, Denise J. (1999). *The Magic Mirror: Moviemaking in Russia, 1908-1918.* Madison: University of Wisconsin Press.

DENISE J. YOUNGBLOOD

## MOVEMENT FOR DEMOCRATIC REFORMS

On July 1, 1991, nine well-known close associates of Mikhail Gorbachev, president of the USSR, and Boris Yeltsin, President of the Russian Soviet Federated Socialist Republic (RSFSR), called for the establishment of a Movement for Democratic Reform to unite all those who supported human rights and a democratic future for the USSR. The appeal was signed by Arkady Volsky, Gavril Popov, Alexander Rutskoi, Anatoly Sobchak, Stanislav Shatalin, Eduard Shevardnadze, Alexander Yakovlev, Ivan Silayev, and Nikolai Petrakov. It endorsed the development of a market economy and the maintenance of the USSR in some form, and declared that a founding Congress would be convened in September to decide whether or not to form a political party.

Alexander Yakovlev explained that the movement sought to overcome the Party apparat's resistance to the democratization of the Communist Party of the Soviet Union (CPSU), and he openly appealed to reformist Communists to join the movement. President Gorbachev endorsed its formation (many believed that it had been established to provide him with an alternative political base in the event of a formal split in the CPSU). The Central Committee of the CPSU was skeptical of the movement, and the Communists in the military openly attacked it.

After the abortive coup against President Gorbachev in August 1991, the leaders of the movement were named to important political posts sought to fill the gap created by the dissolution of the CPSU and openly recruited reformist leaders of the Party as well as members of the "military industrial complex."

The founding Congress of the movement was finally convened in December 1991, just days after the collapse of the USSR and the formation of the Commonwealth of Independent States (CIS). The Congress called for the formation of a broad coalition of democratic movements and parties, endorsed market reforms, sought the support of emerging entrepreneurs, and supported the CIS with some misgivings.

In February 1992 the original movement was replaced by the Russian Movement for Democratic Reform (RMDR), and Gavril Popov was chosen as its chairman. In June 1992 he resigned from his position as mayor of Moscow to devote more time to the development of the movement as a "democratic opposition" to the Yeltsin regime.

The RMDR became increasingly critical of the Yeltsin regime's economic policies in 1992 and 1993. It nominated a significant number of candidates for the first elections to the state duma in December 1993. Although it endorsed much of the new Constitution, it was sharply critical of the growth of bureaucracy, the process of privatization, and the continued power of the Communist *nomenklatura*. It advocated sharp reduction of the bureaucracy, the decentralization of economic power, distribution of land to all citizens, local controls over energy, and a clear demarcation of authority between president, parliament, and government. It received almost 9 percent of the vote in St. Petersburg, but failed to gain the 5 percent of the vote needed for representation in the state duma.

After the elections of December 1993 RMDR repeatedly assailed the entire reform model of the Yeltsin regime and sought partners to establish an effective democratic opposition. In September 1994 it formed an alliance with Democratic Russia, and in 1995 it worked with other similar organizations to create a Social Democratic Union (SDU) to contest the 1995 elections. After the SDU's defeat in the elections, the RMDR disappeared from public view.

*See also:* AUGUST 1991 PUTSCH; POPOV, GAVRIL KHARITO- NOVICH; RUTSKOI, ALEXANDER VLADIMIROVICH; SHATALIN, STANISLAV SERGEYEVICH; SHEVARD- NADZE, EDUARD AMVROSIEVICH; SOBCHAK, ANATOLY ALEXANDROVICH; VOLSKY, ARKADY IVANOVICH; YAKOVLEV, ALEXANDER NIKOLAYEVICH

**BIBLIOGRAPHY**

Colton, Timothy J., and Hough, Jerry Hough, eds. (1998). *Growing Pains: Russian Democracy and the Election of 1993*. Washington, DC: Brookings Institution Press.

McFaul, Michael, and Markov, Sergei. (1993). *The Troubled Birth of Russia Democracy Parties, Personalities, and Programs*. Stanford, CA: Hoover Institution Press.

JONATHAN HARRIS

## MOVEMENT IN SUPPORT OF THE ARMY

The movement, In Support of the Army, War Industry, and War Science (DPA) was founded in July 1997 on the initiative and with the guidance of the chair of the Duma defense committee, Lev Rokhlin, a hero of the war in Chechnya. With the degradation of the army, it soon became a significant anti-government force. After the murder of Rokhlin a year later, his successor as chair of the committee, Viktor Ilyukhin, became head of the party. Ilyukhin was famous for having brought a legal action, during his days as prosecutor, against Mikhail Gorbachev. Next in line to Ilyukhin was Colonel General Albert Mashakov, former commander of the Privolga military district, candidate in the 1991 presidential elections, and notorious for his anti-Semitic statements (he once suggested, for instance, that the DPA should be unofficially called the DPZh, or "Movement Against Jews"). Among the strategies considered by the Left on the eve of the 1999 elections, the "three-columns" idea would have had the DPA at the head of one column. Another strategy called for the formation of a bloc of national-patriotic forces consisting of the DPA, the Russian Popular Movement, the Union of Compatriots "Fatherland," and the Union of Christian Rebirth. The second idea had the DPA join a united oppositional bloc with the Communist Party of the Russian Federation (CPRF). A third proposal, the one adopted, had the DPA enter the elections independently. The first three places on the DPA list were taken by Ilyukhin, Makashov, and Yuri Saveliev, rector of the Petersburg Technical University, whose popularity rested on his having fired a professor from the United States because of the NATO bombing of Yugoslavia. The DPA list disappeared, but Ilyukhin and one other candidate were elected to the Duma.

In the early twenty-first century the DPA has little influence and is essentially a satellite of the Communist Party. Ilyukhin, its leader, is a member of the Central Committee of the CPRF. He takes entirely radical positions and plays a certain role in the leadership of the National Patriotic Union of Russia (NPSR).

*See also:* COMMUNIST PARTY OF THE RUSSIAN FEDERATION

**BIBLIOGRAPHY**

McFaul, Michael. (2001). *Russia's Unfinished Revolution: Political Change from Gorbachev to Putin*. Ithaca, NY: Cornell University Press.

McFaul, Michael, and Markov, Sergei. (1993). *The Troubled Birth of Russian Democracy: Parties, Personalities, and Programs.* Stanford, CA: Hoover Institution Press.

McFaul, Michael; Petrov, Nikolai; and Ryabov, Andrei, eds. (1999). *Primer on Russia's 1999 Duma Elections.* Washington, DC: Carnegie Endowment for International Peace.

Reddaway, Peter, and Glinski, Dmitri. *The Tragedy of Russia's Reforms: Market Bolshevism Against Democracy.* Washington, DC: U.S. Institute of Peace Press.

NIKOLAI PETROV

## MSTISLAV

(1076–1132), Vladimir Monomakh's eldest son, grand prince of Kiev, and the progenitor of the dynasties of Vladimir in Volyn and of Smolensk.

In 1088 Mstislav Vladmirovich's grandfather Vsevolod appointed him to Novgorod, but in 1093 his father (Monomakh) sent him to Rostov and Smolensk. In 1095 he returned to Novgorod where he ruled for twenty years. In 1096 his father ordered him to campaign against Oleg Svyatoslavich of Chernigov, who was pillaging his Suzdalian lands. Mstislav's most important victory was defeating Oleg and making him attend a congress of princes in 1097 at Lyubech, where he was reconciled with Monomakh and Svyatopolk of Kiev.

In 1117 Monomakh, now grand prince of Kiev, summoned Mstislav to Belgorod where, it appears, he made Mstislav coruler. He also designated Mstislav his successor in keeping with his agreement with the Kievans, who had promised to accept Mstislav and his descendants as their hereditary dynasty. Monomakh therewith violated the system of lateral succession allegedly introduced by Yaroslav the Wise. When Monomakh died on May 19, 1125, Mstislav succeeded him. Two years later, when Vsevolod Olgovich usurped Chernigov from his uncle Yaroslav, Mstislav violated the lateral order of succession again by confirming Vsevolod's usurpation and thus winning his loyalty. Whereas Monomakh had driven the Polovtsy to the river Don, in 1129 Mstislav drove them even beyond the Volga. In 1130, in keeping with Monomakh's policy of securing his family's control over the other princely families, Mstislav exiled the disloyal princes of Polotsk to Constantinople and replaced them with his own men. Thus, before he died, he controlled, directly or through his brothers or his sons, Kiev, Pereyaslavl, Smolensk, Rostov, Suzdal, Novgorod, Polotsk, Turov, and Vladimir in Volyn. Moreover, Vsevolod of Chernigov was his son-in-law. Mstislav, called "the Great" by some, died on April 15, 1132, and was buried in the Church of St. Theodore, which he had built.

*See also:* KIEVAN RUS; NOVGOROD THE GREAT; ROTA SYSTEM; VLADIMIR MONOMAKH

**BIBLIOGRAPHY**
Dimnik, Martin. (1994). *The Dynasty of Chernigov 1054–1146.* Toronto: Pontifical Institute of Mediaeval Studies.

Franklin, Simon, and Shepard, Jonathan. (1996). *The Emergence of Rus 750–1200.* London: Longman.

MARTIN DIMNIK

## MURAVIEV, NIKITA

(1796–1843), army officer who conspired to overthrow Nicholas I.

Nikita Muraviev was one of the army officers involved in the Decembrist movement to overthrow Tsar Nicholas I. He is best known for the constitution he drafted for a new Russian state. Although he did not actually participate in the uprising on December 14, 1825, he was condemned to death when it failed. His sentence was later commuted to twenty years at hard labor in the Nerchinsk mines. He died in Irkutsk Province.

In 1813, after studying at Moscow University, Muraviev embarked on a military career, and in 1816 he joined with other aristocratic young officers in organizing a secret society called the Union of Salvation. Led by Paul Pestel, it was renamed the Union of Welfare a year later. Stimulated by the French Revolution (1789) and the Napoleonic Wars (1812–1815), the officers had been influenced by the liberal ideas of French and German philosophers while serving in Europe or attending European universities. The new Russian literature, with its moral and social protest against Russia's backwardness, also was an important influence, especially the works of Nikolai Novikov, Alexander Radishchev, and the poets Alexander Pushkin and Alexander Griboyedov. The Arzamas group, an informal literary society founded around 1815, attracted several men who later became Decembrists, including Nikita Muraviev, Nikolai Turgenev, and Mikhail Orlov.

Economic stagnation, high taxation, and the need for major reforms motivated Muraviev and the other Decembrists to take action. They advocated the establishment of representative democracy but disagreed on the form it should take: Muraviev favored a constitutional monarchy; Pestel, a democratic republic. To get rid of tsarist agents and members who were either too dictatorial or too conservative, the organizers dissolved the Union of Welfare in 1821 and set up two new groups: The Northern Society, centered in St. Petersburg, was headed by Muraviev and Nicholas Turgenev, an official in the Ministry of Finance. The more radical Southern Society was dominated by Pestel. During the interregnum between Alexander I and Nicholas I, the two societies plotted the coup.

Muraviev was the ideologist for the Northern Society, drafting propaganda and a constitution that was found among his papers following his arrest. The uncompleted constitutional project reveals the strong impact of the American constitution. Like Pestel, he envisioned a republic: "The Russian nation is free and independent. It cannot be the property of a person or a family. The people are the source of supreme power. And to them belongs the sole right to formulate the fundamental law." Muraviev advocated a constitutional monarchy along the lines of the thirteen original states of North America, separation of powers, civil liberties, and the emancipation of the serfs. Although his constitution guaranteed the equality of all citizens before the law, the landed classes were recognized as having special rights and interests. Thus Muraviev rejected Pestel's idea of universal suffrage; only property-holders would be allowed to vote and to seek elective office.

What distinguishes Muraviev's draft constitution is its advocacy of federalism, an idea not echoed by any major political movement in Russia until the twentieth century. Muraviev argued that "vast territories and a huge standing army are in themselves obstacles to freedom." Too much of a nationalist to call for the breakup of the empire, however, Muraviev urged that Russia adopt a federalist system as a way to reconcile "national greatness with civic freedom."

The Decembrist uprising failed because of the plotters' incompetence and lack of mass support. Some defected, and others, at the last minute, failed to carry out their assignments. Five of their leaders, including the poet Kondraty Ryleyev, were executed. Despite the stricter censorship Nicholas I imposed after the crushed rebellion, the memory of the De-

cembrists inspired many writers and revolutionaries, especially the political refugee Alexander Herzen, who established the journal *The Bell* (*Kolokol*) in London in 1857 to "propagate free ideas within Russia."

*See also:* DECEMBRIST MOVEMENT AND REBELLION; EMPIRE, USSR AS; NICHOLAS I

**BIBLIOGRAPHY**

Mazour, Anatole G. (1937). *The First Russian Revolution, 1825: The Decembrist Movement, Its Origins, Development, and Significance.* Stanford, CA: Stanford University Press.

JOHANNA GRANVILLE

# MUSAVAT

Founded in secrecy in October 1911, Musavat (Equality) ultimately grew into the largest, longest-lived Azerbaijan political party. The founders of the party were former members of Himmat (Endeavor) party, Azerbaijan's first political association, led by Karbali Mikhailzada, Abbas Kazimzada, and Qulan Rza Sharifzada. Formation of Musavat was a response to their disillusionment with the 1905 Russian Revolution. They were also inspired by a common vision of Turkic identity and Azeri nationalism.

Musavat attracted many of its followers from among Azerbaijan's bourgeoisie-intelligentsia, students, entrepreneurs, and other professionals; the party also included workers and peasants among its ranks. In 1917 a new party evolved from the initial merger of these former Himmatists and the Ganja Turkic Party of Federalists, as reflected in the organization's name, the Turkic Party of Federalists-Musavat. At this stage Musavat came under the leadership of Mammad Rasulzade and consisted of two distinct factions, the Left or Baku faction and the Right or Ganja faction. These factions differed on economic and social ideology such as land reform, but closed ranks on two crucial issues, one being secular Turkic nationalism. The other was the vision of Azerbaijan as an autonomous republic and part of a Russian federation of free and equal states. In April 1920, when Azerbaijan came under Soviet domination, the native intelligentsia were afforded some amount of accommodation in accordance with the Soviet nationalist program supervised by Josef Stalin. However, the accommodation only extended to the left wing of the Musavat party.

Members of the right wing were subsequently imprisoned or killed. By 1923 the Musavat came under pressure from communist apparatchiks to dissolve the organization. Musavat members fortunate enough to flee formed exile communities in northern Iran or Turkey and remained abroad for the duration of the Soviet era. The self-proclaimed successor of the Musavat party, Yeni Musavat Partiyasi (New Musavat Party) was reestablished in 1992. Its leadership was drawn from the Azerbaijan Popular Front, an umbrella group representing a broad spectrum of individuals and groups opposed to the communist regime in the waning years of the Soviet Union and active in the post-Soviet transition. In the early twenty-first century Musavat is currently in the forefront of the opposition movement in competition with the Popular Front. Yeni Musavat is characterized as the party of the Azeri intelligensia and is led by Isa Gambar. The key planks of the party platform are the liberation of land captured by Armenian forces in the Karabakh conflict and forcing the resignation of Heidar Aliev's regime, which it views as corrupt and illegitimate.

*See also:* AZERBAIJAN AND AZERIS; CAUCASUS

**BIBLIOGRAPHY**

European Forum. (1999). "Major Political Parties in Azerbaijan." <http://www.europeanforum.bot–consult.se/cup/azerbaijan/parties.htm>.

Suny, Ronald Grigor. (1972). *The Baku Commune, 1917-1918: Class and Nationality in the Russian Revolution.* Princeton, NJ: Princeton University Press.

Swietockhowski, Tadeusz. (1995). *Russia and Azerbaijan: A Borderland in Transition.* New York: Columbia University Press.

GREGORY TWYMAN

# MUSCOVY

The Russian realm that centered around Moscow until approximately 1713 to 1721 is known as Muscovy. Historians differ about when to set its beginning. Moscow is first mentioned in a chronicle under the year 1147 as part of Yuri Dolgoruky's domain. Its first important prince was Alexander Nevsky's son Daniel (d. 1303). Between 1301 and 1304, he and his son Yuri (d. 1325) seized three towns from neighboring Ryazan and Smolensk, thereby making Moscow an important center of power within the grand principality of Vladimir. Yuri's brother Ivan I (d. 1341), who obtained the right to collect tribute for the Mongols from other Rus principalities and persuaded the head of the church to reside in Moscow, established Moscow's preeminent position in northern Rus. Moscow's territory continued to expand under his grandson Dmitry Donskoy (r. 1359–1389) and Dmitry's progeny down to the end of Daniel's sub-dynasty in 1598, with only a few minor setbacks. Highlights of this growth included the incorporation of Nizhny Novgorod and Suzdal under Basil I (r. 1389–1425), Tver, Severia, and Novgorod under Ivan III (r. 1462–1505), Pskov, Smolensk, and Ryazan under Basil III (r. 1505–1533), the Volga khanates Kazan and Astrakhan under Ivan IV (r. 1533–1584), and western Siberia under Fyodor Ivanovich I (1584–1598). Under Alexei (r. 1645–1676), Russia extended its power across Siberia to the Pacific Ocean, recovered territory lost to Poland-Lithuania between 1611 and 1619, added eastern Ukraine, and became in area the world's largest contiguous state. By the time Peter I (r. 1682–1715) moved the capital to St. Petersburg in 1713, he had reacquired eastern Baltic territory lost to Sweden in 1611 to 1617 and added some more. He renamed his realm the Russian Empire in 1721.

Internationally, Moscow developed from a subordinate tributary of the Qipchak khanate (Golden Horde) to a free successor state in the 1480s, and then to ruler of the lands of other khanates, starting in the 1550s. Aiming for semantic equality with other fully sovereign states with imperial pretensions, such as the Ottoman, Persian, and Holy Roman empires, Moscow had to accept parity with Poland-Lithuania and Sweden until the Battle of Poltava in 1709. Refusing a humiliating rank within the overall European state system and its diplomatic hierarchy, Muscovy remained ceremonially if not operationally aloof, but with the Treaty of Nerchinsk in 1689, it became the first European state to make a formal agreement with China.

## CHURCH AND CULTURE

Muscovy's church moved from being the center of an often all-Rus metropolitanate of the patriarchate of Constantinople, to an autocephalous eastern Rus or Russian entity after 1441—the only regional Orthodox church ruled essentially by sovereign Orthodox rulers—to a patriarchate of its own in 1589 with a sense of pan-Orthodox responsibilities, and after 1654 to one actually dominating the Kievan metropolitanate, which had been separate since 1441. Starting in the 1470s, the renovation and enlargement of Moscow's Kremlin and its major churches and palaces gave Muscovy a capital worthy of its pretensions, and in 1547 Ivan IV was crowned officially as tsar as well as grand prince. While remaining under the guise of being devotionally and ritually distinct, Muscovy borrowed elements of material and intellectual culture from western Europe and around 1648 initiated some Western-influenced education.

## ECONOMY

Muscovy's economy was based primarily on agriculture, including flax and cloth made from it; forest products, especially furs, but also wax and honey; fishing; and the production of salt and simple metal goods. The opening of direct English and then Dutch trade with the Russian far north, starting in the 1550s, led to the production of hemp and cordage. Arkhangelsk (founded in 1583) and Astrakhan served as major ports of entry and export, but much of Muscovy's foreign trade went overland. The rise of gun powder technology stimulated both the manufacture of cannon in the 1500s and a native potash industry, especially in the 1600s. In the 1630s Dutch concessionaires opened up Russia's first European-style mining operations. In 1649 Russia ended nearly a century of special trading privileges for the English. Unifying the monetary system in the 1530s, but lacking good sources of specie, Muscovy resorted to restamping or melting down and reminting foreign silver coins and therefore required a trade surplus.

## SOCIETY

From the start, Moscow's princes, boyars, and higher military servitors were at the top of the social hierarchy. As Muscovy expanded, the reliable incorporated princely elites joined the Moscow boyars, while incorporated provincial boyars and elite warriors became regionally based military servitors with some opportunity to advance on the social ladder. Among the major changes over time were the rise of economically active, estate- and enterprise-owning rural monasteries, starting in the late 1300s and continuing through the 1600s; the centralizing of the general obligation to serve via the *pomestie* system, starting in the late 1400s; the rise of cossacks on the southern frontiers of the realm in the 1500s; the binding down of urban and rural plebeians to their communities by the late 1500s; and the conversion of peasants on church, court, boyar, and servitor estates into serfs by 1649. By about 1580, boyars and military servitors had their own special courts and constituted, for Europe, a unique, obligatory-service nobility. The *gosti*, a privileged elite of merchants, undertook commerce on behalf of the state as well as themselves, and sometimes made forced contributions to the central treasury. Cossacks both served the state well and sometimes rebelled, as under Stenka Razin in 1670 to 1671.

## STATE

Muscovy's state polity developed under professional state secretaries (*diak*) from the sovereign's household administration, starting especially in the latter 1400s. Ivan III issued the first national law code (*Sudebnik*) in 1497. By the 1530s Moscow began to assign local fiscal and policing tasks to local elites. By the 1550s there were separate departments (*izba*, later *prikaz*) for foreign affairs, military assignments, military estates, banditry, and taxation, and such offices continued to expand. Ivan IV summoned Muscovy's first ad hoc national assembly (*Zemsky Sobor*) in 1566. During the period of political instability and crises from 1565 to 1619, the governing elites learned the value of managing the central state offices, and in the seventeenth century directly controlled most of them. Provincial bodies, for their part, proved their worth in the national revival of 1611 to 1613 (during the Time of Troubles) in spearheading the expulsion of the Poles and the establishment of a new dynasty. The vastly expanded law code (*Ulozhenie*) of 1649 became the foundation of Russian law down to 1833. How the sovereigns, the boyar council, the major boyar clans and generals, the state secretaries, and the leading prelates and merchants actually made policy remains a mystery, due to want of reliable documentation, but most foreign observers considered Muscovy to be a tyranny or despotism, not a legally limited European-style monarchy.

*See also:* ALEXEI MIKHAILOVICH; ASSEMBLY OF LAND; BASIL I; BASIL III; BOYAR; DANIEL METROPOLITAN; DONSKOY, DMITRY IVANOVICH; FYODOR IVANOVICH; GOSTI; GRAND PRINCE; IVAN I; IVAN IV; LAW CODE OF 1649; PETER I; SUDEBNIK OF 1497; TIME OF TROUBLES; YURI DANILOVICH

## BIBLIOGRAPHY

Crummey, Robert O. (1987). *The Formation of Muscovy, 1304-1613.* London: Longman.

Vernadsky, George. (1969). *A History of Russia*. Vol. 5: *The Tsardom of Moscow, 1547–1682*. New Haven: Yale University Press.

DAVID M. GOLDFRANK

## MUSEUM, HERMITAGE

Sitting on the bank of the Neva River in St. Petersburg, the Hermitage Museum houses one of the world's preeminent collections of artwork. Among its three million treasures are works by Leonardo da Vinci, Rembrandt, Cézanne, and Picasso. The holdings range from Scythian gold to Impressionist paintings. The word *Hermitage* is often used interchangeably with *Winter Palace*, but historically they are distinct facilities. Built during the reign of Empress Elizabeth, between 1754 and 1762, the Winter Palace was the official residence of the tsars. The Palace contains the imperial throne room and grand staterooms such as the Hall of St. George.

During the late eighteenth century Empress Catherine II oversaw the construction of four additional buildings. Between 1765 and 1766 Yuri Velten began the Small Hermitage, a pavilion near Palace Square, as Catherine's intimate retreat from court life. Vallin de la Mothe expanded the Small Hermitage from 1767 until 1769 with a second pavilion connected by Hanging Gardens. Beyond the Small Hermitage to the east lies the New Hermitage (1839–1851) on Palace Square. Along the Neva riverbank is the neoclassical Large Hermitage, designed by Yuri Velten and built between 1771 and 1787 to house Catherine's paintings, library, and copies of the Vatican's Raphael Loggias. The Winter Canal runs along the east side of the Large Hermitage and a gallery spans the canal and connects the Neoclassical Theater (built 1785–1787 and designed by Giacomo Quarenghi) to the rest of the complex.

Nicholas I ordered the New and Large Hermitages to be opened to the public and a new entrance was constructed away from the Palace in

The Hermitage Museum complex includes the magnificent former Winter Palace and its art collection. © YOGI, INC./CORBIS

1852. Following the demise of the Romanov dynasty in 1917, the Bolshevik government combined the Hermitage and Winter Palace into one large complex that was designated as a public museum. The Bolsheviks nationalized the private collections of many wealthy Russians, further enhancing the collection.

During the nine-hundred-day Nazi siege of Leningrad (the city's Soviet-era name), the museum was bombed nineteen times. Many holdings were evacuated to the Urals for safety, while curators moved into the facility to protect the remaining treasures. Twelve air-raid shelters were constructed in the basement, and at one point twelve thousand people were living in the museum complex. They planted vegetables in the Hanging Gardens in order to feed themselves.

The eventual Soviet victory over Germany allowed many priceless works of art to fall into Soviet hands, because Hitler had ordered the seizure of artwork from museums and private collections in occupied lands. Some paintings were immediately placed on display in the USSR, while others were hidden away and only revealed after the fall of the Soviet Union. Restitution of these trophies of war became a contentious issue in Russian politics. While some political leaders thought restitution would be morally and legally correct as well as positive for Russian–European relations, other politicians insisted that they are legitimate reparation for the immense damage and suffering the Soviet people experienced during World War II.

*See also:* CATHERINE II; LENINGRAD, SIEGE OF; NATIONALISM IN THE TSARIST EMPIRE; RASTRELLI, BARTOLOMEO; WINTER PALACE

**BIBLIOGRAPHY**

Eisler, Colin T. (1990). *Paintings in the Hermitage.* New York: Stewart, Tabori, and Chang.

Forbes, Isabella, and Underhill, William. (1990). *Catherine the Great: Treasures of Imperial Russia from the State Hermitage Museum, Leningrad.* London: Booth-Clibborn Editions.

Gosudarstvennyi Ermitazh. (1994). *Treasures of the Hermitage Museum, St. Petersburg.* New York: Harry N. Abrams.

Norman, Geraldine. (1997). *The Hermitage: The Biography of a Great Museum.* London: J. Cape.

Varshavsky, Sergei and Rest, Boris. (1986). *Hermitage: The Siege of Leningrad, 1941–1944.* New York: Harry N. Abrams.

ANN E. ROBERTSON

# MUSIC

The history of music in Russia is closely connected with political and social developments and is characterized by a fruitful tension between reception of and dissociation from the West. As elsewhere, the historical development of music in Russia is densely interwoven with the general history of the country. Political, social, and cultural structures and processes in the imperial and Soviet eras wielded a strong influence on musical forms. Even though aesthetic and creative forces always developed a dynamic of their own, they remained inextricable from the power lines of the political and social system.

The beginning of Russian art music is inseparably linked to a politically induced cultural event in Kievan Rus: the Christianization of the East Slavs under Grand Duke Vladimir I in 988. With religion came sacred music from Byzantium. It was to set the framework for art music in Russia up to the seventeenth century. Condemned by the church as the work of Satan, secular music could hold its own in Old Russia only in certain areas. Whereas the general population mainly cultivated traditional forms of folk music, the tsars, dukes, and nobility were entertained by professional singers and musicians.

The forceful orientation toward Western ways of life under Peter I introduced a new era of Russian history of music following European patterns. After Peter had opened the "window to the West," the sounds of the music of Western Europe, together with its producers, irresistibly found their way into the tsarist court and Russian aristocracy. In the eighteenth century the Italian opera held a key position in Europe. The ambitious court in St. Petersburg brought in the big names of Italian musical culture, including numerous composers and musicians. Since the time of Catherine II the repertory of the newly founded theaters included the first music theater works of Russian composers as well as Italian and French operas. In spite of their native-language librettos, the Russian works were, of course, modelled on the general European style of the Italians. As in many other European countries, the forming of an independent, original, Russian music culture took place in the nineteenth century, which was characterized by "national awakening." Through an intensive integration of European musical forms and contents on the one hand and the adaptation of Russian and partly Oriental folk music on the other, Russian composers created an impressive, specifically Russian art music.

The rich ambivalence of dependence on and distance from Middle and Western Europe can already be found in the operas of Mikhail Glinka, who, regardless of some predecessors, is considered the founder of Russian national music. Among his followers a dispute arose concerning how far a genuine Russian composer should distance himself from Western culture. The circle of the Mighty Handful of Mily Balakirev and his followers—still consisting of highly talented amateurs—decidedly adhered to the creation of Russian national music. Other composers like the cosmopolitan virtuoso Anton Rubinstein or Peter Tchaikovsky, who received his professional training in Russia at the Petersburg conservatory founded in 1862, had fewer reservations about being inspired by the West, though Tchaikovsky, too, wrote genuine Russian music. The work of these pioneers was continued well into the early twentieth century by such composers as Alexander Glazunov, Sergei Rachmaninov, and Alexander Skryabin. The latter, however, in his later compositions made a radical turn from the nineteenth-century mode of musical expression and became a leading figure of multifaceted Russian modernism.

In 1917 a political event again marked a turning point in Russian music life: the Bolshevik October Revolution. Although in the 1920s the Soviet state made considerable room for the most varied aesthetic conceptions, by the mid-1930s the doctrine of "Socialist Realism" silenced the musical avant-garde. Optimistic works easy to understand were the overriding demand of the officials; alleged stylistic departures from the norm could entail sanctions. Nevertheless, composers like Dmitry Shostakovich, Sergei Prokofiev, and others achieved artistic greatness through a synthesis of conformity and self-determination. Although the opportunities for development remained limited until the end of the Soviet Union, Russian musical life always met a high standard, which markedly manifested itself not only in the compositions, but in the outstanding performing artists of the twentieth century (e.g., David Oystrakh, Svyatoslav Richter).

Soviet popular music also succeeded, against ideological constraints, in finding its own, highly appreciated forms of expression. While the 1920s were still dominated by traditional Russian and gypsy romances as well as Western operetta songs, in the 1930s a genuine Soviet style of light music developed. Isaak Dunayevsky created the so-called mass song, which combined cheerful, optimistic music with politically useful texts. His style set the tone of popular music in Stalin's time, even if the sufferings of war furthered the reemergence of more dark and somber romances. Jazz could not establish itself in Soviet musical life until the late 1950s. Russians had welcomed early trends of jazz with great enthusiasm, but the official classification of American-influenced music as capitalist and hostile hindered its development in the Soviet Union until Stalin's death. Later, rock music faced similar problems. Only the years of perestroika allowed Russian rock to emancipate itself from the underground. Until then, the officially promoted hits, widely received by Soviet society, were a blend of mass song, folk music elements, and contemporary pop. In contrast to the unsuspected shallowness of these songs, the so-called bards (e.g., Bulat Okudzhava or Vladimir Vysotsky) did not hesitate to address human problems and difficulties of everyday life in their guitar songs. Probably these poet-singers left behind the most original legacy in Soviet popular music, whereas the other currents of musical entertainment distinguished themselves through their interesting synthesis of Western impulses and Russian characteristics, a central thread in Russian music culture of the modern age.

*See also:* BALALAIKA; DUNAYEVSKY, ISAAKOSIPOVICH; FOLK MUSIC; GLINKA, MIKHAIL IVANOVICH; MIGHTY HANDFUL; NATIONALISM IN ARTS; PROKOFIEV, SERGE SERGEYEVICH; RACHMANINOV, SERGE VASILIEVICH; SHOSTAKOVICH, DMITRI DIMTRIEVICH; STRAVINSKY, IGOR FYODOROVICH; TCHAIKOVSKY, PETER ILYICH

## BIBLIOGRAPHY

Hakobian, Levon. (1998). *Music of the Soviet Age, 1917–1987.* Stockholm: Melos Music Literature.

Maes, Francis. (2002). *A History of Russian Music: From Kamarinskaya to Babi Yar.* Berkeley: University of California Press.

Schwarz, Boris. (1983). *Music and Musical Life in the Soviet Union, 1917–1981.* Bloomington: Indiana University Press.

Starr, S. Frederick. (1994). *Red and Hot: The Fate of Jazz in the Soviet Union, 1917–1991.* New York: Limelight Ed.

Stites, Richard. (1992). *Russian Popular Culture.* Cambridge, UK: Cambridge University Press.

Taruskin, Richard. (1997). *Defining Russia Musically: Historical and Hermeneutical Essays.* Princeton, NJ: Princeton University Press.

MATTHIAS STADELMANN

**MUSKETEERS** *See* STRELTSY.

## MYASOEDOV AFFAIR

On March 20, 1915, the Russian Army Headquarters announced the execution of Sergei A. Myasoedov, a gendarme officer, for espionage only days after his arrest and hasty conviction by military court. The event was a major scandal in the press and is significant for a number of reasons. First, it occurred in the midst of a series of Russian losses on the German section of the front, losses that marked the beginning of what would become known as the Russian Great Retreat that led Russia out of all the Polish provinces and parts of what are now Lithuania, Latvia, Belarus, and Ukraine. Myasoedov, who had plenty of enemies in the army command, security services, and elsewhere, was likely set up as a convenient scapegoat for the extensive Russian losses at the front. After his execution, a wave of arrests targeted anyone who had been associated with him.

If the execution was meant to calm public opinion, it probably had the opposite effect. A series of raids, arrests, and deportations led by the unofficial head of the domestic military counterintelligence service, Mikhail Dmitriyevich Bonch Bruyevich, and especially the hysterical accusations of spying that the Army Chief of Staff Nikolai Yanushkevich leveled against Jews, Germans, and foreigners in the front zones added to what became a wave of popular spy mania that became a constant and important feature of domestic politics for the rest of the war.

Only two months after the arrest of Myasoedov, Moscow erupted into one of the largest riots in Russian history—directed against Germans and foreigners. The scandal also undermined the position of the minister of war, Vladimir A. Sukhomlinov, who had been a close associate of Myasoedov. In fact, the entire episode may also have been part of political intrigues to try to undermine Sukhomlinov, who was forced to resign in June 1915 under a cloud of rumors of his own treasonous acts. Perhaps most importantly, the scandal lent credence to rumors of treason among members of the Russian elite. Such rumors continued to grow through the rest of the war, and came to center on the empress Alexandra, Rasputin, and various individuals with German names in the Russian court, government, and army command. These rumors did a great deal to undermine respect for the monarchy and contributed to the idea that the monarchy stood in the way of an effective war effort—in short, that it would be a patriotic act to overthrow the monarchy.

*See also:* FEBRUARY REVOLUTION; OCTOBER REVOLUTION

### BIBLIOGRAPHY

Katkov, George. (1967). *Russia, 1917: The February Revolution*. London: Longman.

ERIC LOHR

## NAGORNO-KARABAKH

A mountainous region at the eastern end of the Armenian plateau in the south Caucasus and originally part of the Artsakh province of historic Armenia, the Nagorno-Karabakh ("Mountainous Karabakh") region kept its autonomy following the loss of Armenian statehood in the eleventh century. Its right to self-government was formally recognized from 1603 onward by the Persian shahs, giving it a special place in Armenian history.

Nagorno-Karabakh was incorporated into the Russian Empire in 1806, following the first Russo-Persian war. While this meant the dissolution of the region's autonomy, Russia was able to portray itself as the savior of Christians in the region, facilitating Russia's full occupation of the eastern Transcaucasus by 1828.

During the tsarist era, Nagorno-Karabakh was made part of the Elisavetbol province, which included the plains of Karabakh to the east, linking the region to the economy as well as history of the Azeri population and giving it a special place in the development of modern Azerbaijani culture. Following the withdrawal of Russian troops from the southern Caucasus during World War I and the proclamation of independence by Azerbaijan and Armenia in 1918, the two republics fought over the region, which was then considered a disputed territory by the League of Nations. Great Britain, briefly in charge of the region following the defeat of Turkey, facilitated its incorporation in Azerbaijan. Following the Sovietization of the two republics, Nagorno-Karabakh was made part of Azerbaijan as the Autonomous Region of Nagorno-Karabakh (NKAO, 4,800 square kilometers), despite the wishes of its majority Armenian population.

While the NKAO enjoyed relative stability until 1988—the Soviets placed an army base in Stepanakert, the capital of the region—there were intermittent protests by Armenians against Azerbaijani policies of cultural, economic, and ethnic discrimination. Armenians continued to consider the inclusion of the region in Azerbaijan as an unjust concession to Azerbaijan, and Azerbaijanis considered the special status an unfair concession to Armenians.

According to the last Soviet census taken in 1989, NKAO had a population of 182,000, of which 140,000 were Armenian and 40,000 Azeris.

In 1988, following glasnost and perestroika, Soviet Armenians joined NKAO Armenians in demanding the unification of the region with Armenia, leading to pogroms against Armenians in Azerbaijan and the expulsion of about 170,000 Azeris from Armenia and of 300,000 Armenians from Azerbaijan in 1989 and 1990. Following the declaration of independence of Azerbaijan from the USSR in 1991, NKAO declared its own independence from Azerbaijan, while Azerbaijan dissolved the autonomous status of the region. The Azerbaijani decision in 1991 to use military means and blockades to force the region into submission led to a war from 1992 to 1994 that ultimately involved Armenia. Azerbaijan lost the NKAO as well as seven Azeri-populated provinces around the region. The conflict created close to 400,000 Armenian and 700,000 Azeri refugees and internally displaced persons, including those evicted from their homes in both republics.

A cease-fire mediated in 1994 has been maintained since. But negotiations, including those conducted by the Minsk Group of the Organization for Security and Cooperation in Europe, have failed to resolve the problem of the future status of the region. Russia, suspected by Azerbaijanis as the party responsible for the conflict and the lack of progress in its resolution, has been involved in the negotiations both as a major regional actor and as a member and subsequently co-chair of the Minsk Group.

*See also:* ARMENIA AND ARMENIANS; AZERBAIJAN AND AZERIS; NATIONALITIES POLICIES, SOVIET

**BIBLIOGRAPHY**

Coppetiers, Bruno, ed. (1996). *Contested Borders in the Caucasus.* Brussels: VUB Press.

Cornell, Svante. (2001). *Small Nations and Great Powers.* Surrey, UK: Curzon.

Croissant, Michael P. (1998). *The Armenia-Azerbaijan Conflict.* Westport, CT: Praeger.

Hunter, Shireen. (1994). *The Transcaucasus in Transition: Nation-Building and Conflict.* Washington DC: Center for Strategic and International Studies.

GERARD J. LIBARIDIAN

# NAGRODSKAYA, EVDOKIA APOLLONOVNA

(1866–1930), fiction writer.

Evdokia Apollonovna Nagrodskaya was a remarkably candid and avant-garde fiction writer in turn-of-the-century Russia. She was the daughter of Avdotia Yakovlevna Panayeva (1819–1893), a journalist, prominent salon hostess, and mistress of the poet Nikolai Alexeyevich Nekrasov (1821–1877), a coworker of Evdokia's father, Apollon Golovachev, who worked for the "thick journal" *Sovremennik.* Thus raised in an intellectual environment, Nagrodskaya wrote poetry and several novels, including *The White Colonnade* (*Belaya Kolonnada*) in 1900, *The Bronze Door* (*Bronzovaya dver*) in 1911, *Evil Spirits* (*Zlye dukhi*) in 1916, and *The River of Times* (*Reka vremen*) in 1924.

Nagrodskaya is best known, however, for her novel *The Wrath of Dionysus* (*Gnev Dionisa*), which became a bestseller in 1910, although it shocked readers unaccustomed to taboo topics like illicit love, female sexuality, and homosexuality. The novel was published in ten editions and was translated into French, Italian, German, and English. Ultimately the novel became a silent movie in theaters across two continents. The heroine of the story is Tatiana Kuznetsova, a painter who cheats on her supportive but boring fiancé when she meets a dashing, brilliant Englishman named Edgar Stark during a train ride. She begins an affair, but when Stark becomes too possessive, jealous even of her art, she pulls away. Accidentally impregnated by Stark, however, she later decides to stay with him and the baby. Another key character is her homosexual friend Latchinov. The highlight of the story is a dialog between Tatiana and Latchinov, in which the latter confronts Tatiana with her own homosexuality, explaining that she (a masculine woman) and Stark (an effeminate man) are inverted members of their respective genders, and thus complement each other as "normal" men and women do. Suffering from a terminal disease, Latchinov reveals to her his own sexual (but unconsummated) love for Stark, and bids her farewell.

*See also:* NEKRASOV, NIKOLAI ALEXEYEVICH

**BIBLIOGRAPHY**

Barker, Adele Marie. (2002). *A History of Women's Writing in Russia.* New York: Cambridge University Press.

Nagrodskaia, Evdokia, and McReynolds, Louise. (1997). *The Wrath of Dionysus: A Novel.* Bloomington: Indiana University Press.

Von Geldern, James, and McReynolds, Louise. (1998). *Entertaining Tsarist Russia: Tales, Songs, Plays, Movies, Jokes, Ads, and Images from Russian Urban Life, 1779–1917.* Bloomington: Indiana University Press.

JOHANNA GRANVILLE

# NAKHICHEVAN

As part of the Republic of Azerbaijan, the Nakhichevan Republic is located in South Asia, west of Azerbaijan proper and separated from this main territory by the narrow strip of Armenia. The landmass of Nakhichevan is 5,500 square kilometers, occupying the southern slopes of the Darlagez range and the southwestern slopes of the Zangezur Mountains. The Araz river valley extends between these two ranges. Almost 75 percent of the territory is located at an elevation of 1,000 meters. Gapydjik, located in the Zangezur range, is the highest peak in the region at 3,904 meters. The region is also known for its volcanic domes and its frequent, severe earthquakes.

The republic is rich in mineral deposits including marble, gypsum, lime, and sulfur. There are abundant mineral springs including Badamli, Sirab, Nagajir, and Kiziljir.

Nakhichevan's climate is continental, its temperature ranging from 26 degrees Celsius in summer months to -6 degrees Celsius in winter. The pre-Arazian plains region can be described as semiarid. The higher elevations of the mountainous areas are characterized as tundra, typically cold and dry. Precipitation is considerably light throughout the region, with 200 to 300 millimeters annually recorded in the plains region. Periodic flash flooding occurs due to topography and sparse vegetation. Aside from the Araz, there are about forty smaller rivers in the country fed by rain and the mountain runoff of melting snows.

According to legend, Noah's ark is said to have first touched land along the submerged peaks of the Zangezur Mountains before reaching Mount Ararat. The Republic's name is derived from this legend, as "Nakhichevan" is a corruption of *Nukkhtchikhan*, the colony of Noah. Like the surrounding region, Nakhichevan sits at a strategic crossroads and has been subject to military intervention throughout much of its history. In the mid-eighteenth century, after successive battles for supremacy between Iran and Russia, Nakhichevan came under Russian control, in accordance with the treaty of Turkmanchai in 1828. In 1924 Josef Stalin designated Nakhichevan an autonomous republic, a status it maintains today within Azerbaijan.

The economy, based on agriculture, food processing, and mining, has suffered substantially since 1988 with loss of markets and imports due to the Karabakh conflict. While trade corridors are being restored to neighboring Iran and Turkey, economic recovery is slow. Since 2000 almost three-quarters of the state budget has been provided by the central government in Baku.

*See also:* AZERBAIJAN AND AZERIS; CAUCASUS

## BIBLIOGRAPHY

"Azerbaijan and Iran deal in LNG." Alexander's Gas & Oil Connections. July 5, 2002. <http://www.gasandoil.com/goc/news/ntc22239.htm>.

Swietochowski,Tadeusz, and Brian Collins. (1999). *Historical Dictionary of Azerbaijan*. Lanham, MD: Scarecrow Press.

Twyman, Gregory. (2001). "Geography and Climate." In *USACC Investment Guide to Azerbaijan, 2001*. Washington, D.C.: USACC.

GREGORY TWYMAN

# NAKHIMOV, PAVEL STEPANOVICH

(1802–1855), commander of Black Sea Fleet in Crimean war.

Pavel Stepanovich Nakhimov was born into a naval family in Gorodok, Smolensk province. In 1818 he completed his studies in the Naval Cadet Corps and served aboard ships in the Baltic fleet. From 1822 to 1825 Nakhimov participated in a round-the-world cruise abroad the frigate *Kreiser*-36. Nakhimov served aboard Vice-Admiral Geiden's flagship *Azov*-74 at the battle of Navarino on October 21, 1827. During the subsequent 1828–1829 Russo-Turkish War, Nakhimov served in the Russian Mediterranean squadron blockading the Dardanelles, commanding a corvette. Following the end of the war Nakhimov returned to the Baltic fleet base at Kronshtadt. In 1834 Nakhimov was transferred to the Black Sea Fleet, where he was given command of a ship of the line. During the 1840s Nakhimov participated in numerous amphibious landings on the eastern Black Sea Caucasian coast, where the Russian military constructed a chain of coastal forts to interdict arms smuggling to Muslim rebels. Nakhimov was promoted to rear admiral in 1845. Seven years later Nakhimov was promoted to vice admiral and given command of a fleet division. As relations between the Russian and Ottoman empires worsened in the early 1850s, Nakhimov argued for an aggressive naval policy toward the Ottoman Empire. On November 30, 1853,

Nakhimov led a squadron into Sinope harbor on the southern Black Sea coast. Using shell-firing artillery instead of smoothbore cannons, his ships annihilated the Ottoman squadron moored there, producing outrage in Europe. Following the outbreak of the Crimean War in 1854, Nahkimov was appointed commander of the Black Sea Feet and military governor of Sevastopol port in February 1855. Nakhimov supervised the offloading of artillery from the fleet's warships to be integrated in a series of land fortifications under the direction of engineer E. I. Totleben. Nakhimov was mortally wounded by enemy fire on the Malakhov redoubt on July 10, 1855, and interred in the Vladimir church. A monument was raised to Nakhimov in 1898 in Sevastopol on the forty-fifth anniversary of the Sinope battle. The Imperial Navy honored his memory by naming ships in his honor; an *Admiral Nakhimov* cruiser was sunk by her crew after the Tsushima battle on May 27, 1905. Despite the USSR's disavowal of much of its imperial history, the Soviet government on March 3, 1944, established a first- and second-class Nakhimov military order for valor for officers; a Nakhimov medal for lower ranks was also established, and naval cadets attended Nakhimov naval academies. The post-Soviet navy also has a Kirov-class *Admiral Nakhimov* cruiser (formerly *Kalinin*, renamed in 1992).

See also: BLACK SEA FLEET; CRIMEAN WAR; MILITARY, IMPERIAL ERA; SINOPE, BATTLE OF

**BIBLIOGRAPHY**
Daly, Robert Welter. (1958). "Russia's Maritime Past." In *The Soviet Navy*, ed. Colonel M. G. Saunders. New York: Praeger.

JOHN C. K. DALY

# NAPOLEON I

The Russian people first discovered Napoleon as the young and bright general who stood out during the military campaigns of Italy in 1796–1797 and of Egypt in 1798–1799. By that time, he was deeply admired in Russia for his military genius by both civilians and soldiers such as Alexander Suvorov, who saw in him a "new Hannibal." Later on, Napoleon's victories over European armies reinforced the myth of his military invincibility, until the retreat of Berezina in October–November 1812.

Politically, the coup d'état by which Napoleon came to power in October 1799 (Eighteenth Brumaire) at first reassured the tsar Paul and the conservative and liberal elites, who saw in this new authoritarian regime the end of disorders and excesses brought by the French Revolution. But this feeling did not last: Napoleon's proclamation of his First Consulate for life on August 4, 1802, followed by the establishment of the Empire on May 18, 1804, triggered strong negative reactions. For liberals, including the young tsar Alexander I, who acceded to the throne in March 1801, Napoleon became a tyrant who betrayed the Enlightenment ideas through personal interest. For the conservatives, the self-crowned man lacked legitimacy, and his huge political ambitions were dangerous for the European balance.

Alexander first chose to ignore the Napoleonic threat. In 1801 the young tsar decided to maintain Russia outside the European conflict and adopted a pacifist diplomacy: On October 8, 1801, a peace treaty was officially signed with France. But this position became increasingly difficult to maintain when France started to pose a serious threat to Russian interests in the Mediterranean and in the Balkans. So in 1805, Alexander decided to join Austria and Britain in the Third Coalition. The tsar wanted to play a major role in the international theater, lead the fight against Napoleon, and, after the victory, promote a new European order, liberated from the tyrant. However, the military operations were a disaster for Russia, and on December 2, 1805, the battle of Austerlitz was a personal humiliation for Alexander, who, as commander of the Russian forces, ignored General Mikhail Kutuzov's advice not to enter battle before the arrival of more troops.

After the defeat of Friedland on June 14, 1806, judging that his forces were unable to continue fighting, the tsar decided to pursue peace with Napoleon. Napoleon was in favor of an agreement with Russia, as his focus had shifted to political control of Central Europe and the war against Britain. On July 7–9, 1807, several treaties were signed at Tilsit between the two emperors. The terms were difficult for Prussia, which was partitioned. The Polish provinces forming the Duchy of Warsaw under Saxony and the provinces west of the Elbe were combined to make the Kingdom of Westphalia, which had to pay an indemnity. Russia suffered no territorial losses but had to recognise Napoleon's dominant position in Europe and take part in the continental blockade of British trade. In compensation Russia obtained peace, freedom of action in East-

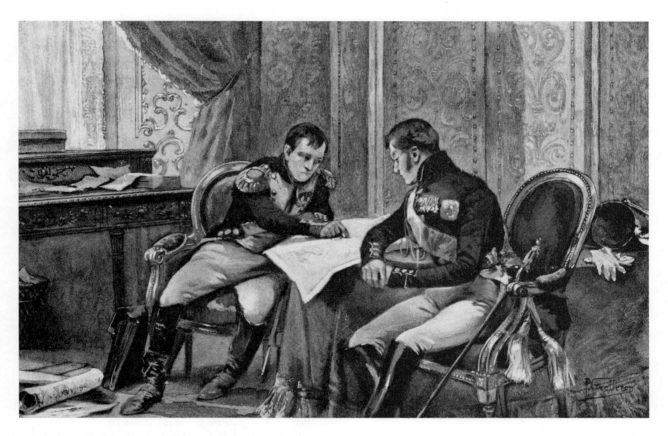

**Napoleon I and Alexander I at Tilsit studying a map of Europe.** © BETTMANN/CORBIS

ern Europe, and the opportunity to gain Finland from Sweden militarily (1808–1809), Bessarabia from the Ottoman Empire (with the Bucharest treaty in 1812), and Georgia from Persia (by the Gulistan treaty in 1813).

Despite these large successes, Russia remained hostile toward Napoleon. In 1805 the Orthodox Church declared Napoleon the Antichrist. And for most of the Russian elite who had been raised with French language and culture, Napoleon was the archetypal expression of Barbary, not a Frenchman but a "damned Corsican."

Despite its renewal on September 27, 1808, at Erfurt, the Russian-French alliance was indeed fragile. The two countries had opposite views on the Polish question and were rivals in the Balkans and in the Mediterranean. The Continental blockade became more and more expensive for that Russian economy and was denounced by Alexander in December 1810.

These tensions led Napoleon to initiate a war that he expected to be short. He invaded the Russ-

ian territory on June 24, 1812, with an army of more than 400,000 men. On June 28, the French were already in Vilna, and on August 18 they entered Smolensk, forcing the Russians to retreat.

For the Russian people, the invasion was a national trauma, not only because of the brutality of the war—in one day, at the battle of Borodino, on September 7, 1812, the Russians lost 50,000 men and the French 40,000—but also because of its blasphemous dimension: Napoleon did not hesitate to use churches as stables. On September 14, when Napoleon entered the sacred capital, Moscow the Mother, he found the city empty and devastated by fires, which went on for five days. The burning of Moscow was a terrible shock, and it generated feelings of resentment from the Russian people toward Alexander. But soon it united all the Russians, whatever their social class, in a patriotic and mystic struggle against the invader. Napoleon's promise to liberate the Russian peasants from serfdom had no effect on the people, who, along with the tsar and his elite, sensed the urgency of a physical, moral, and spiritual danger.

For Napoleon, the situation was impossible: On the one hand the lack of supplies prevented him from going any farther; on the other hand, he was unable to force Alexander to negotiate. On October 16, the retreat of the Grand Army began in difficult conditions. Subject to cold, hunger, and typhus, attacked by the partisan movement and by peasants on their way back, less than 10 percent of the Grand Army was able to leave the Russian territory in December 1812.

The French defeat was a fatal blow to the Napoleonic adventure and made Alexander the conqueror of Napoleon and the "savior of Europe." In February 1815, Napoleon tried to regain his lost power, but the adventure did not last, and the Hundred Days did not harm Alexander's prestige. The tsar personally took part in the Congress of Vienna and engaged in the construction of a new political and geopolitical order in Europe. During the congress, Alexander's Russia took great advantage of the victory over Napoleon from both diplomatic and territorial points of view. But beyond this geopolitical concrete outcome, the collective and messianic triumph over the invader constituted in Russia a major step toward the birth of a modern national identity.

*See also:* ALEXANDER I; AUSTERLITZ, BATTLE OF; BORODINO, BATTLE OF; KUTUZOV, MIKHAIL ILIARONOVICH; FRANCE, RELATIONS WITH; FRENCH WAR OF 1812; TILSIT, TREATY OF; VIENNA, CONGRESS OF; WAR OF THE THIRD COALITION

**BIBLIOGRAPHY**

Cate, Curtis. (1985). *The War of the Two Emperors.* New York: Random House.

Hartley, Janet. (1994). *Alexander I.* London: Longman.

Palmer, Alan. (1967). *Napoleon in Russia.* London: Simon and Schuster.

Tarle, Eugene. (1979). *Napoleon's Invasion of Russia, 1812.* New York: Octagon Books.

Wesling, Molly. (2001). *Napoleon in Russian Cultural Mythology.* New York: Peter Lang.

MARIE-PIERRE REY

## NARIMANOV, NARIMAN

(1870–1925), renowned educator, author, medical doctor, long-time Bolshevik, and head of the first soviet government of Azerbaijan from 1920 to 1922.

In Soviet interpretations, Narimanov loomed large as the key native Bolshevik who supported sovietization of his homeland, Azerbaijan. He chaired the first Soviet of People's Commissars (Sovnarkom), which was established with the Red Army's overthrow of the independent government on April 28, 1920. Narimanov was not in the Azerbaijani capital of Baku at this time, and it is not clear that he supported this means of installing soviet power. Documents released in the late 1980s indicate that Narimanov's vision of soviet rule in Azerbaijan was closer to an anticolonial program leading to native rule than to a means for the dominance of an industrial proletariat that, in Azerbaijan, was largely Russian. During the first years of soviet power, Narimanov found himself increasingly at odds with the nonnative leaders of the Transcaucasian party, especially Stalin's protégé, Sergo Ordzhonikidze. Narimanov's opposition to key policies, among them the merging of the three republics of Azerbaijan, Armenia, and Georgia into a Transcaucasian Federation (Zakfederatsiia, or ZSFSR), led to his removal in 1922 from Baku. His prominence was such that his removal was euphemized as a "promotion" to a post in Moscow.

Narimanov's prerevolutionary record as an educator and writer led him to take a hand in cultural policies in the early soviet period. He supported the Latinization policy for the Azerbaijani Turkish alphabet, which was an indigenous proposal, but which Moscow favored. He backed school reform projects that came from Russia's Commissariat of Enlightenment. His speeches to teachers' conferences, however, revealed that his ultimate goal was wide popular participation in government for Azerbaijani "toilers." His use of that term rather than "proletariat," coupled with his support for rural schools, suggest that he hoped for Azerbaijani villagers to have a genuine partnership in governing with urban workers, both Azerbaijani and other.

Narimanov died in Moscow on March 19, 1925, allegedly of a weak heart. His body was cremated, which has no precedent in Azerbaijani (Muslim) tradition. Some scholars believe he may have been poisoned. His ashes were interred in the Kremlin wall.

*See also:* AZERBAIJAN AND AZERIS; CAUCASUS; SOVNARKOM; TRANSCAUCASIAN FEDERATIONS

BIBLIOGRAPHY

Altstadt, Audrey. (1992). *The Azerbaijani Turks: Power and Identity under Russian Rule.* Stanford, CA: Hoover Institution Press.

AUDREY ALTSTADT

**NARKOMINDEL** *See* PEOPLE'S COMMISSARIAT OF NATIONALITIES.

**NARODNICHESTVO** *See* POPULISM.

## NARVA, BATTLES OF

The first battle of Narva on November 30, 1700, was Peter the Great's first major defeat in the Great Northern War. Immediately after the Russian declaration of war in August 1700, Peter marched his army into Swedish territory to try to capture the port town of Narva in northeastern Estonia, and on September 16 laid siege to the city with some 34,000 men. Meanwhile Charles XII, the King of Sweden, defeated Peter's ally Denmark and brought his army to Estonia to relieve the siege. By November 27 the Russians heard that the Swedes were approaching, and the next day Peter left the army to join the approaching Russian reinforcements. The Russian army deployed in a curved line running from south to northwest of Narva under the command of the recently arrived Belgian officer Duke Eugene de Croy. The traditional Russian gentry cavalry under the boyar Boris Sheremetev held the left (southern) flank near the Narova river. Generals Adam Weyde (a Dutchman) and prince Ivan Trubetskoy held the center, and general Avtomon Golovin the right with the guards regiments, also by the river. After approaching the Russian line in a blinding snowstorm, Charles attacked the Russian center about one o'clock in the afternoon, his right under general Welling smashing Weyde's troops and the Swedish left under General Carl Gustaf Rehnsköld overrunning Trubetskoy. Only some of Golovin's and Sheremetev's men were able to escape, with Russian losses at least eight thousand killed. Peter's army, only recently created along European lines, was smashed. The battle established the eighteen-year-old king of Sweden's military reputation.

Peter returned to Novgorod with the remains of his army, which he rebuilt in the ensuing years while Charles was preoccupied in Poland. In July 1704 the Russian army returned to besiege Narva, held by a small Swedish garrison under general Horn. On August 20, 1704, Narva fell to Peter's generals, Sheremetev, now field marshal, and the Austro-Scottish general Baron Georg Ogilvy. This victory strengthened Russia's hold on the Baltic provinces and further weakened Sweden in its struggle with Peter.

*See also:* GREAT NORTHERN WAR; PETER I; SWEDEN, RELATIONS WITH

PAUL A. BUSHKOVITCH

## NARYSHKINA, NATALIA KIRILLOVNA

(1652–1694), second wife of Tsar Alexei (r. 1645–1676); mother of Peter I.

Natalia was the daughter of a minor nobleman who served for a time in Smolensk, but was related by marriage to the up-and-coming official Artamon Matveyev, later head of the Foreign Office, who may have brought her to the attention of the recently bereaved Tsar Alexei. In 1671 she became the tsar's second wife, giving birth to Peter (1672–1725), Natalia (1673–1716), and Fyodora (1674–1678.) Widowed in 1676, during the early years of the reign of her stepson Theodore Alexeyevich (1676–1682), Natalia and her children were marginalized; however, when Theodore died in 1682, nine-year-old Peter was elected tsar with the patriarch's support, and Natalia prepared to act as regent. She was thwarted by Tsarevna Sofia Alexeyevna and her party, who secured the election of Tsarevich Ivan Alexeyevich as Peter's co-tsar. The fact that Natalia feared for her son's life during the riots of 1682 and felt vulnerable during Sofia's regency may have made her over-protective. After Sofia was ousted in 1689 and the Naryshkins and their clients assumed leading posts, there was a clash of wills between mother and son over such issues as Peter's sailing expeditions and his failure to attend official receptions. The only known portraits show Natalia in nun-like widow's garb with head modestly covered. She exerted the traditional influence of a tsaritsa, raising the fortunes of her clan and their clients, operating her own patronage networks, and undertaking public activities such as alms-giving, visiting shrines, and attending appropriate court ceremonies, but the business of government remained in male hands. Natalia died in January 1694 and was laid to rest in the Ascension Convent in the Kremlin. She remains a shadowy figure.

*See also:* ALEXEI MIKHAILOVICH; PETER I

**BIBLIOGRAPHY**

Longworth, Philip. (1984). *Alexis: Tsar of All the Russias.* London: Secker and Warburg.

Thyret, Isolde. (2000). *Between God and Tsar: Religious Symbolism and Royal Women of Muscovite Russia,* DeKalb: Northern Illinois University Press.

LINDSEY HUGHES

## NATIONAL LIBRARY OF RUSSIA

The oldest state public library in Russia, the National Library of Russia is the second largest library in the Russian Federation, after the Russian State Library, with holdings of more than thirty-three million volumes, and a national center of librarianship, bibliography, and book studies.

Founded in St. Petersburg in 1795 by Empress Catherine II as the Imperial Public Library, the origins of the National Library of Russia lie in Catherine's devotion to the philosophy of the Enlightenment in the early period of her reign. She envisioned a library that would serve as a repository for all books produced in the Russian empire, books published in Russian outside the empire, and books about Russia published in foreign languages, and that would be open to the Russian public for the purpose of general social enlightenment. The library officially opened to the public on January 2, 1814. The nucleus of the original collection was the collection, brought to St. Petersburg from Warsaw in 1795, of Counts Józef Andrzej and Andrzej Stanislaw Zaluski, eminent Polish aristocrats and bibliophiles. In 1810 Tsar Alexander I signed a special statute designating the library as a legal depository entitled to receive two mandatory copies of imprints produced in the Russian empire. Throughout its history, the library has had an enormous influence on the political, cultural, and scientific life of Russia.

From 1845 to 1861 the library administered the Rumyantsev Museum that was later moved to Moscow and eventually became the Russian State Library. In March 1917 the Imperial Public Library was renamed the Russian Public Library. With the consolidation of Soviet power its status was redefined, and in 1925 its name changed to State Public Library in Leningrad, as it was designated the national library of the RSFSR, while the V. I. Lenin State Library of the USSR (later the Russian State Library) assumed the function of all-union state library. In 1932 it was renamed Saltykov-Shchedrin State Public Library, and a Soviet title of honor was added to its name in 1939. The library continued to function during the siege of Leningrad from 1941 to 1944, despite the evacuation of valuable materials. The Zaluski collection was returned to Poland between 1921 and 1927 and destroyed during World War II. In 1992, after the dissolution of the USSR, the facility acquired the name Russian National Library and became one of two national libraries in the Russian Federation.

The library possesses the world's most complete collection of Russian books and periodicals. Among the highlights of the collections are Slavonic incunabula and other early printed works produced within and outside of Russia, including two-thirds of all known sixteenth-century Cyrillic imprints, and all the known publications of Frantsysk Skaryna; the largest collection of books from the Petrine era printed in civil script; and the *Free Russian Press* collection of approximately 15,000 illegal publications dating from 1853 to 1917. The Manuscript Division holds the world's richest collection of Old Russian and Slavonic manuscripts from the eleventh to the seventeenth century. The number of its manuscripts exceeds 400,000, in more than fifty languages. Among the library's other treasures are some 250,000 foreign imprints about Russia produced before 1917, approximately 6,000 incunabula reflecting the growth of printing in western Europe in the fifteenth century, and the personal library of Voltaire, consisting of some 7,000 volumes. It possesses archives of more than 1,300 public figures, writers, scholars, artists, composers, architects, and others, including Peter I, Catherine II, Nicholas II, Mikhail Kutuzov, Alexander Suvorov, Gavriil Derzhavin, Ivan Krylov, Vasily Zhukovsky, Alexander Griboyedov, Nikolai Gogol, Mikhail Lermontov, Fyodor Dostoyevsky, Vissarion Belinsky, Alexander Herzen, Anna Akhmatova, Alexander Blok, Zinaida Gippius, Dmitry Merezhkovsky, Joseph Brodsky, Ivan Kramskoy, Boris Kustodiev, Ilya Repin, Vasily Stasov, Mikhail Glinka, Modest Mussorgsky, Nikolai Rimsky-Korsakov, Peter Tchaikovsky, Fyodor Chaliapin, and Michel Fokine.

The main building, completed in 1801 on the corner of Nevsky Prospect and Sadovaya Street, was designed in the classical style by Yegor Sokolov.

Additions to the building were made over the years, and a large facility was completed in 1998 on Moskovsky Prospect. By virtue of its long-standing role as custodian of Russia's cultural heritage, the library holds a unique place in Russian history and is recognized as one of the foremost cultural institutions of the Russian Federation.

*See also:* ARCHIVES; CATHERINE II; EDUCATION; GOLDEN AGE OF RUSSIAN LITERATURE; RUSSIAN STATE LIBRARY

**BIBLIOGRAPHY**

Kasinec, Edward, and Davis, Robert H., Jr. (2001). "National Library of Russia." In *International Dictionary of Library Histories*, vol. 2, ed. David H. Stam. Chicago: Fitzroy Dearborn.

*The National Library of Russia, 1795–1995.* (1995). Saint Petersburg: Liki Rossii.

Stuart, Mary. (1986). *Aristocrat-Librarian in Service to the Tsar: Aleksei Nikolaevich Olenin and the Imperial Public Library.* Boulder, CO: East European Monographs.

JANICE T. PILCH

# NATIONALISM IN THE ARTS

After the French Revolution and Napoleonic Wars, artists throughout Europe increasingly turned their attention to defining national identities. Although art and culture had performed this task prior to Napoleon, the events of the late eighteenth and early nineteenth centuries provided a focus for a renewed attention to nationalism in the arts. Russia proved no exception to this cultural trend, and particularly after 1812, Russian cultural figures began to articulate ideas about Russianness. These definitions were varied in nature, but all sought to depict what made Russia unique. During the century after Napoleon's defeat, Russian culture came into its own, as literature, art, music, architecture, decorative arts, and popular culture experienced profound changes. The attempt to articulate Russian nationalism provided a dominant theme of these diverse products, and the figures who addressed it include a who's who of Russian artistic giants: Pushkin, Repin, and Mussorgsky are just a few of the names associated with Russian nationalism in the arts.

## SOURCES OF NATIONALISM

Like the other European artists who responded to the Napoleonic era with an outburst of nationalism, Russians defined this identity in terms of Russian uniqueness. Artists looked to Russia's past and its present situation to find inspiration. In particular, several events shaped the way in which Russian nationalism developed in the arts. Peter the Great's "cultural revolution" loomed large in the minds of nineteenth-century Russian cultural figures. At issue was whether or not Peter's attempts to Westernize Russia placed it on the right historical development or destroyed a more organic culture. After the war against Napoleon, this debate heated up, for many Russians came to think that the West, and particularly France, no longer served as a model worth imitating. Russian elites began to look to the period before Peter the Great as a source of inspiration. Old Muscovy represented a more authentic Russia, one idealized by some as a time when the country remained unspoiled by Western influences. This debate crystallized after Peter Chaadayev published his *First Philosophical Letter* in 1836, a momentous year for Russian culture and for the expression of nationalism within it. In the letter, Chaadayev argued that Russia's position between East and West created a state that had contributed nothing to the world. Russia, in Chaadayev's view, had no history. The letter in turn gave birth to the Westernizer-Slavophile debate that dominated Russian philosophy for several decades, and it also added fuel to the search for Russian nationalism expressed in the arts.

A second important theme that helped to give shape to Russian artistic nationalism was the "peasant question." In part this query stemmed from the debate over Petrine reforms, for Russian intellectuals after 1812 began to turn their attention to the peasantry as the repository of authentic Russian culture. Other events and debates that provided inspiration for Russian artists included the role of religion in Russian life; the wars against Turkey throughout the nineteenth century; Russian expansion into the Caucasus and Central Asia; the Crimean War and Great Reforms; and debate over the role of classical versus traditional forms of culture. In short, Russian nationalism in the arts developed at the same time as that of other European countries, but took the forms it did because of Russian events, traditions, and intellectual debates.

## FORMS AND FIGURES OF NATIONALISM: LITERATURE, ART, AND MUSIC

From art to popular culture, Russia's nineteenth-century culture gave expression to ideas of Russianness. Although eighteenth-century writers and intellectuals developed ideas about Russian national consciousness, it took events such as Napoleon's 1812 invasion to fuel a nationwide, century-long explosion of art in the search of nationalism. Literature in many respects took the lead in this quest.

The work of Alexander Pushkin (1799–1837) helped to establish Russian as a literary language and the idea that the writer should play a social role. Pushkin's importance in the expression of Russian national identity rested as much with the myth associated with him as with his verses and writings themselves. Russia's cultural self-definition in many respects centered on the figure of Pushkin, and the cult surrounding him lasted through the Soviet period and beyond. Of his numerous writings, his epic poem "The Bronze Horseman" (1833) dealt the most directly with Russian identity, and it captured many of the ambiguities of Peter's legacies. By the time of his 1837 death, Pushkin had helped to inspire other writers to search for definitions of Russian nationhood.

Important literary figures that featured prominently in the evolving articulation of Russianness include some of the giants of nineteenth-century world literature. Mikhail Lermontov (1814–1841) wrote about Russian expansion in the Caucasus in his novel *A Hero of Our Time* (1840), while his earlier poetry such as "Borodino" (1837) captured the importance of the 1812 battle. Nikolai Gogol (1809–1852) became famous for stories of his native Ukraine, but his tales of St. Petersburg and its bureaucracies helped to establish the "Petersburg myth" central to debates about Peter the Great's legacy. His play *The Inspector General* was hailed as a masterpiece when it appeared in 1836, when even Nicholas I praised it. Ivan Turgenev's (1818–1883) *A Hunter's Sketches* (1847) caused a sensation when it first appeared for its frank portrayal of Russian serfs. These writings in turn inspired the "age of the novel," which was associated above all with Leo Tolstoy (1828–1910) and Fyodor Dostoyevsky (1821–1881). *Tolstoy's War and Peace* (1869) became the defining literary expression of the war against Napoleon, while his *Anna Karenina* (1877) dissected the important society issues of its time. Dostoevsky's *Crime and Punishment* (1866) furthered the "Petersburg myth," while his works such as *The Possessed* (1871–1872) and *The Brothers Karamazov* (1880) described the revolutionary movements in Russia and their impact. These writings motivated the next great wave of literature that explored Russian society after the Great Reforms, particularly in the works of Anton Chekhov (1860–1904), whose plays capture the rural gentry's problems coping in the postemancipation era; and Andrei Bely's symbolist masterpiece, *Petersburg* (1913), which again redefined the Petrine capital as an apocalyptic site struggling with modernization.

Art proved no less important to the articulation of nationalism in nineteenth-century Russia. The driving force behind all artistic production in Russia was the Imperial Academy in St. Petersburg. The Academy stressed classical themes, and as a result, very few paintings with exclusively Russian subjects appeared before the 1850s. The major exception to this trend was Alexei Venetsianov (1780–1847), who first came to prominence through his nationalist caricatures published during the war of 1812. Although not trained in the Academy, Venetsianov was influenced by it in his early artistic life. After the war, however, he painted idealized scenes of Russian rural life, including such works as *The Threshing Floor* (1820). Venetsianov's work and the school he founded, along with the writings of Pushkin, Gogol, and others, helped to inspire future artists who depicted Russia's landscape as a source of its identity. Alexei Savrasov (1830–1897), Ivan Shishkin (1832–1898), and Isaak Levitan (1860–1890) all painted scenes from Russia over the course of the century, and their works defined the landscape on its own terms.

Outside of landscape art, the dictates of the Academy ruled over Russian artistic life. Although classical imagery dominated, works such as Karl Briullov's *The Last Days of Pompei*, which was exhibited in 1836 and much discussed as a symbol of Russian decline, were hailed as harbingers of a new national art. In 1863, however, a group of Academy students refused to follow the rigid demands of the school and broke away from it, revolutionizing Russian art and its articulation of nationalism in the process. The group called themselves the *peredvizhniki*, or "the wanderers," and they dedicated themselves to painting scenes from Russian contemporary and historical life. Ilya Repin (1844–1930), the most famous, was a former serf whose depictions of peasant life such as *Barge Haulers on the Volga* (1870) redefined the "peasant question" in the wake of the 1861 emancipation. Other artists, such as Vasily Surikov (1848–1916), painted scenes from Muscovy and the Petrine era. The work of the peredvizhniki found support from powerful patrons such as Pavel Tretyakov, whose private gallery became the basis for the museum of Russian art in Moscow that bears his name.

Music was the third part of the cultural troika that defined Russian national identity during the nineteenth century. Musical life revitalized itself after 1812 and took off during the 1860s. Romantic and patriotic tunes developed during the first half of the century and found their greatest expression in the works of Mikhail Glinka (1804–1857). Glinka's opera *A Life for the Tsar* debuted in 1836 and told the story of the peasant Ivan Susanin, who sacrificed his life during the Times of Troubles to save the young Mikhail Romanov. The opera was hailed as the beginnings of a national school in Russian music.

Glinka's works paved the way for the foundation of the Russian Musical Society in 1859. The society, founded by the brothers Nikolai and Anton Rubinstein, in turn established conservatories in St. Petersburg and Moscow. The conservatories stressed European musical techniques and training, and their most famous student was Petr Tchaikovsky (1840–1893). Almost immediately after the founding of the conservatories, a group of composers known as the Mighty Handful, or just "the five," rebelled against the stress on European music. Their musical scores instead included folk songs and Russian religious music. The most famous and consistent practitioner of this approach was Modest Mussorgsky (1839–1881), whose best-known works are the historical operas *Boris Godunov* (1869) and *Khovanshchina* (1886), which told the stories of the tragic Muscovite tsar and events early in the reign of Peter the Great, respectively. Mussorgsky used the work of Pushkin as the libretto for the former and claimed that the paintings of Repin inspired the latter. Tchaikovsky, although derided as not Russian enough by the Mighty Handful, also composed works that in turn became associated with the musical expression of Russianness. His ballets *Swan Lake* (1875–1876), *Sleeping Beauty* (1888–1889), and *The Nutcracker* (1891–1892) remain among the most popular and most performed in Russia and abroad, while his "1812 Overture" (1880) is synonymous with patriotic music throughout the world.

Although literature, art, and music served as the most important media through which Russian artists articulated their views on national identity, other cultural forms did the same. By the early twentieth century, the Russian ballet of Sergei Diaghilev, featuring music by Igor Stravinsky and sets designed by artists of the Russian avant garde, became an important tool for expressing ideas of Russianness, particularly abroad. Throughout the century, churches, monuments, and other architectural sites literally built upon ideas of Russian history and culture, from the Alexandrine column dedicated to 1812 in St. Petersburg to the millennium memorial in Novgorod that commemorated the founding of the Russian state. Even decorative arts, including jewelry and porcelain, helped to pioneer the "Russian Style" (*russky stil*) by the late 1800s.

Popular culture also dealt with themes of Russian nationalism and Russia's past. *Lubki*, prints and chapbooks that originated during the seventeenth century, circulated throughout Russia and served as important sources for the expression of national identity and for the dissemination of ideas promoted in other artistic forms. Russian folk art and music was rediscovered by numerous artists over the course of the nineteenth and early twentieth centuries, and helped to inspire works from Mussorgsky's melodies to Wassily Kandinsky's canvases. Moreover, the works of all the artists mentioned above became more widely known through the growth of newspapers, journals, museums, and cultural life throughout Russia.

Russian nationalism expressed in the arts contained a multitude of ideas. For some, "Russia" represented a European state that had developed its own sense of identity since Peter the Great. For others, "Russia" had produced a unique culture that blended East with West. Although no consensus on Russian national identity existed, Russian cultural figures from Pushkin to Tolstoy to Mussorgsky all strove to define it in their own way and all left important manifestations of Russianness in their works.

*See also:* ARCHITECTURE; BALLET; CHAADAYEV, PETER YAKOVLEVICH; MIGHTY HANDFUL; MUSIC; SLAVOPHILES; WESTERNIZERS

**BIBLIOGRAPHY**

Billington, James. (1966). *The Icon and the Axe: An Interpretive History of Russian Culture.* New York: Knopf.

Brumfield, William. (1993). *A History of Russian Architecture.* Cambridge, UK: Cambridge University Press.

Cracraft, James. (2003). *The Revolution of Peter the Great.* Cambridge, MA: Harvard University Press.

Cracraft, James, and Rowland, Daniel, eds. (2003). *Architectures of Russian Identity: 1500 to the Present.* Ithaca, NY: Cornell University Press.

Ely, Christopher. (2002). *This Meager Nature: Landscape and National Identity in Imperial Russia.* DeKalb: Northern Illinois University Press.

Figes, Orlando. (2002). *Natasha's Dance: A Cultural History of Russia.* New York: Metropolitan Books.

Garafola, Lynn, and Baer, Nancy Van Norman, eds. (1999). *The Ballet Russes and Its World.* New Haven, CT: Yale University Press.

Gray, Camilla. (1986). *The Russian Experiment in Art, 1863-1922.* London: Thames and Hudson.

Hilton, Alison. (1995). *Russian Folk Art.* Bloomington: Indiana University Press.

Lincoln, W. Bruce. (1998). *Between Heaven and Hell: The Story of a Thousand Years of Artistic Life in Russia.* New York: Viking.

Marks, Steven. (2002). *How Russia Shaped the Modern World: From Art to Anti-Semitism, Ballet to Bolshevism.* Princeton, NJ: Princeton University Press.

Rogger, Hans. (1960). *National Consciousness in Eighteenth-Century Russia.* Cambridge, MA: Harvard University Press.

Rzhevsky, Nicholas, ed. (1998). *The Cambridge Companion to Modern Russian Culture.* Cambridge, UK: Cambridge University Press.

Stavrou, Theofanis, ed. (1983). *Art and Culture in Nineteenth-Century Russia.* Bloomington: Indiana University Press.

Taruskin, Richard. (1997). *Defining Russia Musically.* Princeton, NJ: Princeton University Press.

Tolz, Vera. (2001). *Russia: Inventing the Nation.* London: Arnold.

Valkenier, Elizabeth Kridl. (1989). *Russian Realist Art: The State and Society; the Peredvizhniki and Their Tradition.* New York: Columbia University Press.

STEPHEN M. NORRIS

# NATIONALISM IN THE SOVIET UNION

The triumph of the October Revolution and collapse of the Russian empire increased national movements among the different nationalities that lived in the country. The Bolshevik government based its nationalities policy on the principles of Marxist-Leninist ideology. According to these principles, all nations should disappear with time, and nationalism was considered a bourgeois ideology. However, the Bolshevik leaders saw that the revolutionary potential inherent in nationalism could advance the revolution, and thus supported the ideas of self-determination of the nations.

The Declaration of the Rights of the People of Russia, proclaimed one month after the October Revolution on November 21, 1917, recognized four major principles:

1. equality and sovereignty of the peoples of the Russian empire;
2. the right of nations to self-determination;
3. abolition of all privileges based on nationality or religion;
4. freedom and cultural development for national minorities (i.e., dispersed nationalities and those living outside their historic territories).

But, after the official declaration of the principles, the Soviet government resisted the realization of these ideals. Even in the cases of Finland and Poland, whose right to independence was acknowledged by Vladimir Lenin before the revolution, acceptance of their independence was given by the Bolsheviks only reluctantly, after several attempts to reverse independence failed. During the Soviet-Polish war of 1920, Bolshevik leaders tried to install a pro-Soviet Polish government, however, they lost the war and thus did not achieve their goal. Of all the different nations which coexisted uneasily in the Russian empire, only Poland, Finland and Baltic countries (Latvia, Lithuania, and Estonia) received independence after the October Revolution. However, the Baltic countries remained independent only until 1940, when the Soviet Army occupied their territory.

After the October Revolution, Soviet leaders had hoped for the sparking of a socialist revolution throughout the world. Bolshevik leader Leon Trotsky proposed the doctrine of "Permanent Revolution" that would spread from country to country. However, this was not to be the reality. By the beginning of the 1920s it became obvious even to the Soviet leaders that autonomous nations would remain.

The final goal of the Soviet national policy was the integration of all national groups into a universal (communist) empire. However, their short and medium-term strategies were completely different, so far as they encouraged the emergence of sub-imperial nationalities, in hopes that such maturation was a necessary historical stage which had to be traversed before proletarian internationalism could become fully effective.

## INTERNATIONAL RESISTANCE TO THE SOVIET REGIME

Different nations of the former Russian empire believed that the collapse of the monarchy gave them a chance for independence. The establishment of Soviet power in the national republics was strongly resisted. The Russian empire had the reputation as the "prison of nations," thus, nationalities that were newly liberated from the one yoke after the February 1917 revolution did not rush into another bondage. But the resistance of the various nations was not strong enough to defend their independence. When the Ukraine National Republic declared independence in 1918, Soviet Russia began its aggression against the newly minted country. The resulting civil war in Ukraine continued for more than three years and ended with the annexation of Ukraine by Russia.

As the Soviet regime was established in Central Asia, native military units called *Basmachi* reclaimed those territories from the communists. During the fall of 1921 most of eastern Bukhara was under control of the Basmachi rebels. The Basmachi movement was divided, and its lack of unified leadership contributed to its defeat. But the resistance of the Central Asian nations against the Soviet regime continued until the middle of the 1920s.

## FORMATION OF THE SOVIET UNION

The Soviet Union was formally established on December 30, 1922. The largest nations of the Soviet Union were allowed their own national republics while the smaller nations had either autonomy or national districts in the territory of national republics and were considered national minorities.

The Soviet Constitution of 1924 established the various levels of national-territorial autonomy and a two-chamber Supreme Soviet (Parliament). The Soviet of the Union was elected from the equally populated electoral districts. The Soviet of Nationalities was formed of delegates elected from the national republics and regions, with each national-territorial unit having equal status and electing the same number of delegates.

## THE POLICY OF KORENIZATSIA

From the 1920s to the first half of the 1930s the main thrust of the national policy in the Soviet Union was of *korenizatsia* (indigenization, from the term *korennoi narod*, meaning "indigenous people"). This policy focused on the promotion of each nation's leadership cadre and support for development of national languages and cultures. The high authorities believed that the policy of korenizatsia would encourage non-Russian nationalities to support the Soviet regime. The plan had some limited success. The Soviet central government received support from the national communists and part of the non-Russian population. After their poor treatment in the Russian empire, national minorities favored the internationalism and national equality in the Soviet Union. The policy of korenizatsia had long-lasting effects and promoted national cultures and national consciousness among the different nations. Thus in the national republics the national languages were made compulsory in schools and offices, national theaters were opened, and books and newspapers were printed in local languages. However, many nations were more or less assimilated into Russian culture and resisted the policy of korenizatsia. Many parents resisted sending their children to the national schools and in the national republics there was considerable resistance to the official use of the national languages. Korenizatsia was especially difficult for the Russian population of the national republics considering that they were used to being the politically dominant population in the Russian empire. Furthermore, Russian nationalists could not tolerate their new status as equals of the other nationalities of the Soviet Union.

## THE RISE OF RUSSIAN NATIONALISM
## IN THE SOVIET UNION

From the second half of the 1930s the national policy of the Soviet Union lost its internationalist coloring. The Soviet leaders enhanced the role of the Russian nation and diminished the relative importance of all others. However, during the Soviet era, all nations became of the victims of sovietization and even Russians were not exempt from this policy. Peasant communities were destroyed, religious institutions devastated, and even the best of the national literatures, music, and art were forbidden for their "anti-socialist contents."

Many Soviet political campaigns affected specific nationalities more than others. For example, the collectivization and mass deportations of rich peasants to Siberia devastated the Ukraine. There the local population had more severely resisted collectivization, and Soviet authorities forcibly took all crops from the peasants. The result of this policy was horrible starvation in Ukraine in 1932–1933 that took the lives of six to seven million people. Another example was the forced settlement of the nomadic population, which decimated the Kazakhs. Also, purges of the national cadres greatly affected the Jews. By the end of the 1930s almost all Jews were dismissed from leading positions in the Communist Party of the Soviet Union and in the government.

During and after World War II, Soviet authorities encouraged the rise of Russian nationalism. In a victory speech, Josef Stalin talked about the special qualities of the Russian people that achieved victory in the war. The new Soviet national anthem emphasized the role of the Great Russia in the creation of the Soviet Union. By the beginning of the 1940s all leaders of the national republics and regions were merely puppets of Moscow and showed complete obedience to the general national policy of the Soviet government.

At the same time there was an increase in chauvinism in the Soviet Union. In the official Soviet ideology there appeared the term "unreliable" nationalities. Accused nationalities were the subject of deportation and collective punishment, based on allegations of collaboration with the Nazis. As the result of this policy, the Volga Germans, Chechens, Crimean Tartars and dozens of smaller nationalities were deported from their homelands to Central Asia and Kazakhstan. Under Stalin, fifty-six nationalities, involving about 3.5 million people, were deported to Siberia and Central Asia.

After World War II the Jewish intelligentsia was persecuted during the political campaign of struggle against "cosmopolitanism." Almost all those who were accused of cosmopolitanism and pro-Western orientation were Jewish. This accusation was followed by loss of employment and by imprisonment. In 1952 the elite of the Jewish intelligentsia, including prominent scientists and Yiddish writers and poets, were secretly tried, convicted, and executed. The anti-Jewish campaign reached its height in the Soviet Union in 1952 with the investigation of the "Jewish doctors' plot." Jewish doctors were accused of intentionally providing incorrect treatments and poisoning the leaders of the Communist Party. These political campaigns provoked mass hysteria and the rise of anti-Semitism among the local population. The growing anti-Semitism was supposed to be a prelude to the planned deportation all Soviet Jews to Birobidzhan in the Far East. Only the death of Stalin on March 5, 1953, saved the Jewish population from deportation.

## NATIONALITIES POLICY IN THE SOVIET UNION: POST-STALIN PERIOD, 1953–1991

First Secretary of the Communist Party Nikita Khrushchev rehabilitated the repressed nationalities and allowed most of them to return to their original homes. The main exceptions were the Crimean Tartars and Volga Germans, because their lands had been taken over by Russians and Ukrainians. However, the national policy of Khrushchev was not consistent. In 1954 he presented the Crimea to Ukraine as "a gift" in spite of the fact that the majority of the population in Crimea was Russian.

During Leonid Brezhnev's leadership the slogan Friendship of Nations became the rule and all national conflicts were explained as hooliganism. Further, all publications about national conflicts were forbidden in the Soviet Union. However, the friendship of nations existed more on paper than in reality. After some liberalization and decreasing repression during the Khrushchev and Brezhnev years, the national intelligentsia attempted to discuss national problems and explore their histories and cultures. However, the Soviet leaders continued to consider nationalism as a bourgeois phenomena and many representatives of the national intelligentsia, who called for national independence, were arrested and exiled in Siberia. Soviet leaders had a double standard toward Russian nationalism versus the nationalism of the other nations of the Soviet Union. Thus the expression of Russian superiority over other nations was permitted. Movies, paintings, and novels were created about the heroic Russian past. The official Soviet ideology called the Russian nation the "older brother" of all nationalities of the Soviet Union.

Meanwhile expressions of national feelings by the non-Russian nations were suppressed. Even demonstrations of respect for some distinguished national figures from the past were forbidden. Thus Soviet authorities forbade gatherings near the monument of the distinguished nineteenth-century Ukrainian poet Taras Shevchenko, nor could flowers be put on his monument on anniversary of his birth. Many members of the Ukrainian national intelligentsia spent years in prison and in exile during Brezhnev's time in power. Ukraine was the second largest republic of the Soviet Union in population after the Russian Federation, and a significant part of the Ukrainian population wanted independence. During World War II Ukrainian nationalists organized military units that fought against both the Nazis and the Soviet Army. Thus Ukrainian nationalism was considered by the Soviet rulers as one of the most serious threats to national unity and was severely suppressed.

The population of the Baltic republics, Latvia, Lithuania, and Estonia, often expressed their anti-Russian and anti-Soviet sentiments during the Khrushchev and Brezhnev times. Soviet authority used a "stick and carrot" policy toward these countries. The active nationalists from these countries were imprisoned and sent to exile. At the same time the Soviet government made larger investments in the economic development of the Baltic countries compared with those of the other national republics. The authorities attempted to maintain higher standards of living in these countries and thus decrease the dissatisfaction of the population. However, the people of Latvia, Lithuania, and Estonia looked at Russians as occupiers and were usually hostile toward the Soviet regime. The Baltic countries were the first to declare their independence during the time of perestroika (1985–1991).

The nationalist-oriented part of the Jewish population participated in the Zionist movement and fought for the right of emigration to Israel. A small percentage of the Jewish population of the Soviet Union emigrated to Israel, the United States, and other countries during the 1970s and early 1980s. However, this emigration was severely restricted by Soviet authorities, who treated the emigrants as traitors to the Motherland.

In the last years of the Soviet Union national conflicts increased in the Caucasus republics. Bloody anti-Armenian pogroms occurred in the Nagorno Karabakh region and in Baku, the capital of Azerbaijan. In Georgia violent conflict occurred between the Georgian and Abkhazian population.

The Soviet nations never harmoniously coexisted. Brezhnev's slogan of Friendship of Nations was an empty propaganda claim. The Union of the Soviet Socialist Republics was cemented by the military power of the communist government, and by fear of repression and persecution of the most active national elements in the Soviet regime. As soon as liberalization appeared with Gorbachev's perestroika policy, the Soviet republics one by one declared their independence. Still the central Soviet government strongly resisted decentralization of the country during the late 1980s. By the order of Soviet leaders, troops were used against civilians in Latvia and Lithuania. But the end of the Soviet empire was fast approaching. The Soviet Union collapsed in December 1991 and many nations of the former union began a new chapter in their history as independent countries.

*See also:* EMPIRE, USSR AS; LANGUAGE LAWS; NATIONALITIES POLICIES, SOVIET; NATION AND NATIONALITIES; RUSSIFICATION

**BIBLIOGRAPHY**

Hosking, Geoffrey, and Service, Robert, eds. (1998). *Russian Nationalism, Past and Present.* New York: St. Martin's Press.

Kostyrchenko, Gennadi. (1995). *Out of the Red Shadows: Anti-Semitism in Stalin's Russia,* tr. from Russian. Amherst, NY: Prometheus Books.

Martin, Terry. (2001). *The Affirmative Action Empire: Nations and Nationalism in the Soviet Union, 1923–1939.* Ithaca, NY: Cornell University Press.

Pipes, Richard. (1980). *The Formation of the Soviet Union; Communism and Nationalism 1917–1923,* 3rd ed. Cambridge, MA: Harvard University Press.

Rancour-Laferriere, Daniel. (2000). *Russian Nationalism From an Interdisciplinary Perspective: Imagining Russia.* Slavic Studies. Vol. 5. Lewiston, NY: Edwin Mellen Press.

Rubenstein, Joshua, and Naumov, Vladimir P., eds. (2001). *Stalin's Secret Pogrom: The Postwar Inquisition of the Jewish Anti-Fascist Committee,* tr. Laura Ester Wolfson. New Haven, CT: Yale University Press.

Service, Robert. (1998). *A History of Twentieth-Century Russia.* Cambridge, MA: Harvard University Press.

Simon, Gerhard. (1991). *Nationalism and Policy toward the Nationalities in the Soviet Union: From Totalitarian Dictatorship to Post-Stalinist Society,* tr. Keren Forster and Oswald Forster. Boulder, CO: Westview Press.

Subtelny, Orest. (2000). *Ukraine: A History,* 3rd ed. Toronto: University of Toronto Press.

Suny, Ronald G. (1998). *The Soviet Experiment: Russia, the USSR, and the Successor States.* New York: Oxford University Press.

VICTORIA KHITERER

# NATIONALISM IN TSARIST EMPIRE

The Russian Empire penetrated Europe as Europe's age of nationalism began. The retreat of Napoleon Bonaparte after his failed invasion brought Russia into the heart of Europe. The Congress of Vienna (1815), which reestablished a European order after Napoleon's defeat, brought Russia's border's farther west than ever before. The ancient Polish capital, Warsaw, was added to the Polish lands taken by Russia in the partitions of the late eighteenth century. The diplomatic settlement established Russia as a great European power, if not as a great European nation. Although Tsar Alexander I was then something of a liberal autocrat, national legitimation would never have entered his mind. The modern idea of the nation as a people inhabiting a territory and deserving of a state ruling in their name was alien at the time, and would long remain so. Between 1815 and 1917, national ideas reached Russia from its western and southern frontiers, providing some with the hope of change, and others with a tool of reaction.

## TENTATIVE CONSTITUTIONALISM, 1815–1830

Nationalism can be a method of rule by those who already hold power. Yet during the early nineteenth century, even the suggestion of popular sovereignty was inimical to the tsars' prerogative of absolute personal power. Any emphasis on the Russian peasantry as a political class would have challenged the right to rule of the Romanov dynasty, as well as the prerogatives of the largely foreign elite that administered the growing imperial state. In any event, as seen from St. Petersburg, nationalism was a force associated with revolution, a challenge to traditional rule rather than a way to bolster it. This was the lesson of the French Revolution and the Napoleonic wars.

As an ideology of change, nationalism was a challenge to the monarchies and empires of *ancien régime* Europe, yet it found few adherents in Russia during the first half of the nineteenth century. The uneducated peasantry was tied to the communal system of land ownership, an isolated world of limited horizons. Few were able to see the peasants as people, let alone as a political nation, before the emancipation decree of 1861. The church, an agent of national revival elsewhere in imperial Europe, was subordinate to the Russian state and aligned with the principles of dynastic and autocratic rule. The nobility, elsewhere in eastern Europe the bearer of historical national consciousness, was in Russia associated with the state, for the Russian state created by Peter I and Catherine I had transformed it into a new cosmopolitan service class.

After 1815, the Russian Empire held the absolute majority of the world's Poles, and about 10 percent of the Polish population was noble. Napoleon, exploiting Polish hopes for statehood, had established a duchy of Warsaw. This quasi-state was revived and enlarged at the Congress of Vienna as the Kingdom of Poland. Although Poland's former eastern lands were absorbed by the Russian Empire, Polish nobles even there held social and economic power. Institutions of the old Polish-Lithuanian Commonwealth, such as the university at Wilno, the Lithuanian Statutes, and the Uniate Church, functioned with little interruption. Alexander ruled these eastern lands as tsar, but the Kingdom of Poland as constitutional monarch.

The Polish gentry, the leading class in the departed Polish–Lithuanian Commonwealth, considered itself a historical nation. Before the commonwealth was dismembered by the partitions, much of the middle gentry had been resolutely conservative, perceiving central power as the greatest threat to their traditional rights. In Russia, the same inclination turned the middle gentry into radicals, attentive to the constitution as the source of the tsar's right to rule Poland as king. The 1830 uprising was premised on social–contract thinking: Since the tsar (Nicholas I) was not fulfilling his obligations as king of Poland, his subjects had the right and duty to rebel. The uprising was national in some sense, since the gentry saw itself as the nation; it was certainly democratic, in that the Polish Diet saw itself as representing a European republic struggling against despotism; but it was not modern nationalism, for its participants neither legitimated their claims on a popular basis nor aroused passions against an enemy nation.

## ROMANTIC AND OFFICIAL NATIONS, 1831–1855

The defeat of the 1830 uprising created the conditions for a sophisticated discussion of the nation by Russian subjects. Poland's ten thousand political emigrés were highly literate, politically engaged, and determined to explain their military and political defeat. Many of the emigrés, and most of the leading figures, were of historical Lithuanian origin. Back in Russia, the 1830s and 1840s saw the end of traditional Lithuanian institutions, such as the university and the Statutes. The Uniate Church was merged with the Russian Orthodox Church in 1839. For the Polish emigration as a whole, the old commonwealth remained the touchstone of political thought. But in time a new generation arose that had no actual memory of the old order and reimagined it in ways that reflected various ideas of nationality.

The nationalist politics of Poles in the Parisian emigration can be divided into two main currents: republican and monarchist. Joachim Lelewel, once a professor at Wilno, propounded a democratic republicanism that drew its optimism from a belief in the pacifism of Slavic peoples. Unlike Russians with similar ideas, Lelewel believed that this pacifism could be destroyed by autocratic rule. The Polish Democratic Society, founded in 1832 on French models, soon fell under Lelewel's influence. The leader of the monarchists was Adam Czartoryski, a great Lithuanian magnate and onetime minister to Alexander I. Czartoryski was a liberal constitutionalist who advocated monarchy on pragmatic grounds. One of his disciples, Józef Bem, led the Hungarian insurrection in Transylvania in 1848. Other Poles justified monarchy in terms of national development. Karel Hoffman argued that a monarch was needed to create cities and middle classes. Janusz Woronicz theorized that a true monarchy mediated between a self–aware nation and the exercise of power. In his view, the partitioning powers were not true monarchies, because they did not represent nations. By the end of the 1830s, the monarchical Party of May 3 had fifteen-hundred members.

The 1830s and 1840s also witnessed intense philosophical discussion of the nation by Russian subjects. The Polish nationalist philosophers of the day generally came from the Polish Kingdom and wrote dissertations at German universities. German philosophy was fashionable in Russia, but the Poles actually completed philosophy doctorates in Germany. Their work was more systematic than that of their Russian contemporaries, and influenced philosophical discussion (especially within Left Hegelianism) rather than simply refracting it through local conditions. Polish philosophy was more open to French ideas than German philosophy, and more open to German ideas than French philosophy. Polish philosophers tended to replace the state with the nation in Hegelian dialectic and supported philosophies in which action was constitutive of the nation. Most of them combined academic philosophy with practical work. The best-known were August Cieszkowski and Karol Libelt.

Polish Romantic poets of the epoch were also concerned with the nation. It should be stressed, however, that many of their preoccupations were unintelligible to later generations of modern nationalists. Adam Mickiewicz's interest in mysticism or Juliusz Słowacki's fascination with spirit are difficult to reconcile with secular ideologies of any kind, even if a simplified form of Mickiewicz's messianism did become a common trope. Pan Tadeusz, the most beautiful and most prosaic of Mickiewicz's major works, became a national poem two generations or so after its completion in 1834. Mickiewicz and Słowacki were regarded as national figures of the first rank during their lives, but their career as national bards was mainly posthumous. As nationalism came to be associated with the language of the folk, poetry came to matter less for

its content than for its form. At the time, the poets (like the philosophers and the politicians) saw the national mission as part of a European or universal regeneration. Polish emigrés were the only group in Europe to remember the Russian Decembrists and recall the predicament of other peoples under imperial rule.

The Decembrists, of course, had opposed the ascendance of Nicholas I in 1825. Nicholas was a man of imposing prejudices against Poles and Jews, and was capable of great hatred against whole nations from time to time, but he was no modern nationalist. His reign (1825–1855) is generally seen in the early twenty-first century as reactionary, as it was by Polish rebels in 1830. Insofar as there was a philosophy of rule during Nicholas's reign, it might be sought in the Official Nationality of his education minister, Sergei Uvarov. Nationality was the third term in Uvarov's famous trio: Autocracy, Orthodoxy, Nationality. Uvarov meant nationality to be subordinate to the first two principles of rule. The Russian nation was the group meant to submit to the tsar according to the teachings of the church. Uvarov's educational program was thus a kind of reverse Enlightenment. Education was not meant to create individuals capable of independent judgment, but rather a collective understanding that the ruled are to be judged by the ruler.

The printing press allowed an emerging group of literate Russians to interpret national ideas according to their own lights. The generation of the 1830s and 1840s, like those that followed, read Nikolai Karamzin's History of the Russian State (published 1816–1826). Two renegade Poles led the way in these years in spreading simple national ideas through the press: Faddei Bulgarin, editor of the Northern Bee, and Osip Senkovsky, editor of the Reader's Library. The mere existence of such periodicals guaranteed that discussions of the nation, even if not at all revolutionary, were unacceptable in Uvarov's limited vision. The press mediated between the dynastic interpretation of official nationality prevalent in St. Petersburg and the rival Romantic conceptions emerging around Moscow University. Slavophiles interpreted Uvarov's trio in their own way: Autocracy left room for the autonomous commune, Orthodoxy was a shield against Catholicism and Protestantism, and Nationality mandated attention to the peasant. This Romantic patriotism, although not meant to undermine Official Nationality, differed on one essential point. Whereas Official Nationality gave priority to the state and sought to consolidate

Peter's achievement, the Slavophiles began to emphasize the people and to critique Peter's cosmopolitan project. Nonetheless, they had little in common with the Polish Romantics of the same generation. Both made reference to the past in the hope of overcoming a crisis of the present. But where the Slavophiles spoke of the unspoiled commune, the Poles imagined a restored commonwealth. The Polish dilemma was statelessness; the Russian dilemma was backwardness.

## STATE AND NATION, 1855–1881

This fact was brought home by the humiliation of the Crimean War. The new tsar, Alexander II, accepted that military defeat justified state reform, and that state reform required the emancipation of the serfs. The twenty years after the emancipation proclamation of 1861 saw the emergence of a new group of prosperous peasants in many parts of the empire, and this group recast the national question, especially on the borderlands. Yet the immediate reaction to reform was rebellion. Reforms initiated in Warsaw led to a revolution of rising expectations, the failure of which accelerated the development of modern ideas of nationality in Poland, Russia, and the lands between. Although there were a few lonely exceptions, such as Alexander Herzen and Mikhail Bakunin, literate Russian society as a whole reacted to the Polish Uprising of 1863 with disgust and antipathy. In this atmosphere, Mikhail Katkov became quite influential. His new journal, *Moscow News*, publicized the idea that the rebellion was a war of nations and compromise would be deadly for Russia. Katkov endorsed the policies of Mikhail N. Muraviev in Lithuania, because Muraviev also cast the struggle in nationalist terms: Russians against Poles and their Jewish allies. Katkov's exposition of the 1863 uprising marked a transition from the Romanticism of his youth to the pessimism of his later years. His writings expressed to his twelve thousand readers the painful disappointment of the Slavophile on learning that others might reject Russia, and the emerging conviction that state power might yet put matters right.

Similar views found a scholarly articulation in the pan-Slavism of Nikolai Danilevsky. He resolved certain apparent tensions in the earlier Slavophile scheme by arguing that the state embodied the ideals of Christianity and the peasant tradition, and peace-loving Slavs needed to use force to unite them. A new civilization founded on these principles would emerge, Danilevsky contended in *Russia and Europe* (1869), when Constantinople fell to Russia. Danilevsky also applied his argument about force to the problem of Slavs who rejected Russian rule. Poland, which he compared to a hideous tarantula, could perhaps be coerced into seeing reason. Pan-Slavism was put to the test by international politics during the second half of the 1870s, when Russia made war against the Ottoman Empire in the name of the Serbs and Bulgarians. The disappointing terms of the Treaty of Berlin brought home the objective limits of Pan-Slavism as an international mission.

Populism was another initiative that failed to pass the test of political reality. Fired by a faith in the essential goodness of the peasant, the *narodniki* went "to the people" in the early 1870s. Had their message been heeded, Russian populism might have followed the path of similar movements toward the ethnic nationalism that many enlighteners embraced farther west. In the event, most of the young people who remained in politics after this failure moved to the hard left, imagining (as in Vera Zasulich's famous correspondence with Karl Marx) that the peasant commune was itself proto-communist. Populist ideas took a different turn where the commune was less established, as in Ukraine, for example. Ukraine had played a crucial role in Russian national history, providing Muscovy's ideologues in the seventeenth century and many of its civil servants in the eighteenth. As Karamzin initiated the new trend toward a Moscow-centric history of the empire during the 1810s and the 1820s, as Romantic ideas reached St. Petersburg during the 1830s and the 1840s, and as the Crimean War brought a sharper Russian nationalism during the 1850s, Ukrainian intellectuals in Kharkiv and Kyiv began to see the Ukrainians and the Russians as separate peoples. The poetry of Taras Shevchenko confirmed not only the distinctive Ukrainian language but the definable place of Ukraine between Russia and Poland. The partitions of Poland had brought right-bank Ukraine into the Russian Empire, and during the 1860s and the 1870s not a few members of the Polish gentry (e.g., the historian Volodymyr Antonovych) chose Ukrainian populism and indeed Ukrainian identity. This Polish influence was cited in the Valuev Decree of 1863, which restricted the use of the Ukrainian language. The 1876 Ems Decree, which prohibited the publication of Ukrainian books, induced many Ukrainian intellectuals to emigrate to Austrian Galicia. The most important example was perhaps Mykhailo Hrushevs'kyi, Antonovych's student, and the greatest historian of Ukraine.

Politicized Ukrainians in Kyiv generally stayed on the left, and anticipated that national questions would be resolved within a reformed Russian state.

Similar patterns soon emerged in other Christian national revivals, such as the Georgian and the Armenian. Georgia boasted an ancient civilization, a solid state tradition, and a mature national literature. Its position as a weak Christian country in the Caucasus had moved its nobles to accept Russian overlordship in 1783. Although some of them had conspired against Russia in 1832, a generation later the Georgian nobility was a model service class. Its traditional position was eroding because there were now many wealthy peasant farmers, Armenian merchants were extending their hold on the better districts of cities, and Russian bureaucrats were arriving in large numbers. A new Georgian intelligentsia, educated in St. Petersburg, tried to protect the endangered Georgian language during the 1870s. Insofar as this tendency was political, it involved no more than vaguely socialist leanings mixed with the hope for national autonomy in the empire. The Armenians were also Christian but had their own church; they too had a historically prominent class, but it was the merchants; and they were even more dispersed among Muslims than the Georgians. The Armenians had good reasons for being loyal to the empire, because they stood to lose much in any conflict with the Georgians or the Muslims. For the Armenians, as for many other established national groups in the borderlands, the use of national questions by the center after 1881 was an unwelcome sign of future trouble.

## NATIONAL OPTIMISM AND PESSIMISM, 1881–1905

Alexander III, who ascended to the throne after his father's assassination in 1881, was more amenable to Russian nationalist ideas than his predecessors. During his reign, national ideas were no longer associated with revolution (as during the early nineteenth century) or with reform (as during the middle of the nineteenth century), but rather with reaction. The 1878 trial of Vera Zasulich for attempting to kill the police chief of St. Petersburg had discredited reform even before another socialist murdered the tsar three years later. During the 1880s, Russian nationalism was an updated and secularized version of the old claim that the Russian nation existed by virtue of its Orthodoxy and its submission to the tsar. Under Alexander III and his successor, Nicholas II, a secular conception of the superiority of the Russians supplemented the traditional divine right to rule. Rule was by now an end in itself, since both external crusades and internal reforms were no longer seriously considered. Cultural Russification was advanced as policy on the grounds that Russians would be better subjects than others, but the tsars ruled in the meantime by turning one group against another. There was a shadow of liberalism here, because the beneficiaries were often peasant nations oppressed for centuries by a traditional gentry elite. In this situation, the peasant nations had, at least for a time, some grounds for optimism: the non-Russian gentry and the Russians themselves had very little.

The most important exponent of this improvisational pessimism was Konstantin Pobedonostsev. As over-procurator of the Holy Synod from 1880 to 1905, Pobedonostsev discriminated against Old Believers, religious minorities, and Jews. He was most influential, however, as tutor to the last two tsars, Alexander III and Nicholas II. He came closest to direct power in the aftermath of Alexander II's assassination, when he drafted the manifesto that delayed reform in the name of the people. For Pobedonostsev, this was no contradiction, since absolutism was Russian and therefore represented the Russian people. Pobedonostsev claimed that Russia was the greatest of nations, and the others were the froth of foreign intrigues. In practice, however, he knew that non-Russians did not share this view and would not wish to become Russian. His policies were grounded in historical temporizing, in the hope that suppressing rival nations now would allow a Russian victory later. Pessimism of this kind was common by the 1880s. One could still find exceptional figures, such as Fyodor Dostoyevsky, who still believed in universal missions. Yet officers and bureaucrats were steeped in a nationalism more like Pobedonostsev's, facing as they did in practice the problems he perceived from on high. Especially in the borderlands, Russian officials had to reconcile their positive view of Russian culture with the essentially negative task of Russification.

At the periphery, Russification involved a triangle consisting of Russia, the traditional local power, and a rising peasant nation. In one pattern, visible in the Baltic region, Russia supported (to a very limited extent) the peasants against the gentry. In Finland, for example, the local hegemony of Swedes was challenged by the introduction of Finnish schools in 1873 and the equal status granted to the Finnish language in 1886. Within a generation, however, the Finnish movement had oriented itself against the Russian state, Finns proving to be as zealous as Swedes in resisting the full incorporation of their kingdom into the Russian Empire. In the lands now known as Estonia and Latvia, Baltic Germans lost much of their traditional authority, some of it to new national movements. During the 1870s, the 1880s, and the 1890s, Estonian and Latvian patriots tended to expect Russian support against local Germans. In both cases, the quick emergence of a propertied farmer class and the rapid creation of a cultural canon signified a new historical self-consciousness. An Estonian daily newspaper began publishing in 1891, and a Latvian in 1877. In Lithuania the gentry had been Polish, and the Lithuanian movement emerged after the defeat of the 1863 uprising. Lithuanians were seen as a passive and loyal element, but some of the children of prosperous peasants (and some Polish nobles) took Russification and university education in St. Petersburg as a prompting to return to the Lithuanian folk. The first modern Lithuanian periodical appeared in 1883.

The failure of the 1863 uprising in Poland inclined many patriots to reject traditional paths such as emigration, speculative philosophy, and Romantic poetry in favor of a sober appreciation of the national predicament. The hope for rescue from abroad, touchingly portrayed by the novelist Boleslaw Prus in The Doll (1887–1889), had now faded as well. In the former Kingdom of Poland, now officially the Vistula Land and nothing more, positivists such as Prus and Alexander Świętochowski urged greater attention to the physical sciences, economics, and pedagogy. They wrote of the possibility of social renewal (a code, under censorship, for national rebirth) through work at society's foundations. Theirs was a national idea designed to create a national society in the absence of a state. Both its limitations in practice and its emphasis on science made it an effective springboard to the Marxism of the next generation. Some of these Marxists, such as Kazimierz Kelles-Krauz, joined the Polish Socialist Party of Józef Piłsudski, founded in 1892. This party treated national independence as a prerequisite of social revolution, and Kelles-Krauz supported its program with the first serious sociological study of nationalism. The positivists' attention to the non-gentry classes of society was a model for the National Democrats, whose movement (founded in 1893) added conspiracy and explicit national content to the earlier program of informal mass education. By 1899 the National Democrats had organized some three thousand educational circles. In 1903 their leader, Roman Dmowski, published a polemical tract entitled *Thoughts of a Modern Pole*, which criticized the traditional leaders of Polish society, the gentry and the post-gentry intelligentsia, and proclaimed a fierce competition between ethnic nations as the wave of the future. Dmowski excluded Jews from the future national community; with time (and later electoral disappointments) anti-Semitism became a central message of National Democracy. Dmowski said little about independence, since he thought the Russian Empire a useful shelter from the powerful German culture; despite this tack he must be considered one of the early modern nationalists of the Russian Empire. Like all Polish activists, Dmowski had to account for the division of Poland lands and people among the three partitioning powers, Germany and Austria as well as Russia.

The problem of division was far deeper in the case of other groups, such as Muslims. There were probably more Muslims in the Russian Empire than in the Ottoman, but the latter was a more logical starting point for any national politics. Beginning in the early 1880s, Muslims in Russia had to respond to the more active program of cultural Russification. An interesting reaction was that of Ismail Bey Gaspirali, who believed that Muslims had to learn Russian to resist Russification and secure their proper place in the empire. In his 1881 work, *Muslims of Russia*, he promoted a national press and a national intelligentsia. Like his Georgian and Armenian contemporaries, Gaspirali was a cosmopolitan who concluded from travel and education that merely cultures were endangered. Himself a Crimean Tatar, he wished to reach Muslims throughout the empire, and his books and newspapers were indeed widely read in Baku and Kazan. The Volga Tatars began a movement of religious and social reform with some limited national content. Shihabeddin Merjani wrote the first history in the Volga Tatar dialect, and, in fact, was the first to call the Muslims of the region Tatars. Like the Muslims, the Armenians found themselves on both sides of the Russian-Ottoman border. Armenian national politics in Russia were initially directed to support for Armenians repressed on the Ottoman side. Penetration by Armenian revolutionaries served as a pretext for massacres of Armenians in the Ottoman Empire in 1894–1896. All of this left Armenians loyal to St. Petersburg. Their immediate Caucasian neighbors, the Georgians, faced internal challenges, and responded with nationally aware socialism.

The Jews were so dispersed that any sort of territorial politics seemed utopian. Since the Congress of Vienna, about half of the world's Jews had been Russian subjects. During the 1880s, at a time when Russian nationalism still left considerable room for certain groups to hope for reform, Jews were immediately touched by its pessimism. Earlier discussions among journalists and liberals about equal status for Jews and Russians were halted by the 1863 uprising, in which Jews were seen (by Ivan Aksakov, for example) as allies of the Poles. The pogroms that followed Alexander II's assassination in 1881 (in Yelizavetgrad, Kiev, Odessa, Warsaw, and elsewhere) convinced many Jews that emigration from Russia was their best hope. The official association of Jews with revolution (by Pobedonostsev, for example) and the expulsion of Jews from Kiev (1886) and Moscow (1891) convinced others. The leaders of the emigrationist movement organized themselves at Katowice in 1884. Yet flight to Palestine was initially an apolitical aspiration, since the emphasis was placed on the practical task of leaving Russia. The emergence of Theodor Herzl's brand of Zionism transformed the personal and the practical into the idealistic and the political, and is usually marked as the beginning of modern Jewish nationalism. Its First Basel Congress (August 1897) called for "a home for the Jewish people in Palestine," a Jewish state. This ideal was influential, but was an imperfect fit with the immediate needs of the world's largest Jewish community. The failure of Herzl's high diplomacy, and then his death in 1904, left room for alternative Zionist ideas: socialist Zionism (Ber Borochov and Po'alei Zion), the revival of Hebrew in Russia (associated with Ahad Ha-'Am), and Zionism aware of neighboring national revivals (exemplified by Yitzhak Gruenbaum and Vladimir Jabotinsky, among many others). That said, the internationalist socialism of the Bund (founded in 1897) was far more attractive to young Jews with Haskalah, or secular, education, and played a more important role in Russian politics. From 1901 the Bund advocated national cultural autonomy within a postrevolutionary Russian state. During the Revolution of 1905, it was one of several socialist and leftist parties working in this direction.

## MASS MOVEMENTS AND RUSSIAN RETRENCHMENT, 1905–1917

The Revolution of 1905 was the baptism of a new Russian nationalism, not entirely dependent upon the state, and modern enough to pay attention to the Russian people. Before 1905 there was nothing like a Russian national movement, and the people were excluded from political discussions on the

right. The revolution prompted monarchists to appeal to the people to support the tsar, and modern nationalists who spoke of a "Russia for the Russians," to cite Alexei Kuropatkin's pamphlet about tasks for the Russian army. Russian liberals believed that reform would create a nation that would strengthen the state within its present borders; national liberals such as Peter Struve spoke of a Russian nation in the making. As a social force Russian nationalism was most important in the west, especially in Ukraine, where Jews, Poles, and Ukrainians were blamed for the instability. Polish socialists did indeed work with the Bund to exploit the revolution: but it had begun, awkwardly, in St. Petersburg, as a result of the war against Japan. Non-socialist Polish parties appealed for the Polonization of schools and for a national assembly. A few Ukrainian parties also requested an assembly, and the Ukrainian Bohdan Kistiakovs'kyi was an interesting proponent of federalism.

National autonomy within existing borders was the typical national demand of minorities in 1905. Lithuanians, Latvians, and Estonians all held national congresses and pressed for reform on these lines. Muslims petitioned for legal nondiscrimination at a congress of 1905. Many Turkish nationalists, such as Yusuf Akchura, soon emigrated to the Ottoman Empire to support the Young Turks project in Istanbul. Muslims in Russia sought a reconciliation of the religious and the secular, but did not yet see the secular as necessarily national. Education in the Arab world or in St. Petersburg still appeared to be a complementary and necessary part of this project. Musa Jarulla Bigi, who was secretary of the Muslim congresses between 1905 and 1917, studied in both places. Armenians had seen their church's lands confiscated by the state in 1903, but internecine violence with Azerbaijani Turks in 1905 left most of them loyal subjects of Russia. The Dashnak movement, founded to support the Armenians in the Ottoman Empire, won temporary popularity in Russia by defending the Armenians in Baku and elsewhere in 1905. Georgian socialists initiated some strike actions in 1905 and mediated between the Armenians and the Azerbaijani Turks, but nothing like a Georgian separatist nationalism emerged at this time. Armenian and Georgian socialists alike generally supported some form of cultural autonomy.

The new parliament (or State Duma), established by Nicholas II in 1905, was the only institution that might have channeled these various national sentiments into a reform of the state. Polish nationalists led by Roman Dmowski made the most concerted effort to profit from this institution; the Polish Circle they organized was national in composition and goals. Yet their only legislative victory was the return of the Polish language to Polish schools, and this was quickly reversed. Only the First and Second Dumas were vaguely representative; from 1907 the goal of the electoral laws was to ensure the election of a Duma "Russian in spirit." Prime Minister Peter Stolypin embodied the great irony of Russian nationalism: on the one hand, he changed the electoral law because he believed that Poles would win wherever they ran; on the other, he claimed that Russian nationality was itself a powerful attractive force. Stolypin famously urged Dmowski to admit that being a Russian subject was the greatest of blessings. The only nationalism represented in the Third and Fourth Dumas was Russian. In 1912 the Duma created a new Chelm district, intending to encourage Uniate converts to Roman Catholicism in the region to convert to Orthodoxy. Here was the use of autocracy to identify nationality with Orthodoxy, or at least the deployment of state power to remove attractive national alternatives. Dmitry Sipiagin had earlier considered Polish-Russian population exchanges as a possible solution to the Chelm problem. Forced population movements became policy during World War I, as Russia removed Germans and Jews from its western territories.

Even in 1914, one would have been hard pressed to find much organized national opposition to the Russian Empire. Opposition to the war was not usually articulated in national terms. Nation-states were created in the aftermath of the Bolshevik Revolution, once imperial power had been discredited and broken. Russian nationalism was the ideology of Anton Denikin and other White officers, but they were defeated by the Bolsheviks. Living in Cracow (in Austria) in 1912, Vladimir Lenin had come to appreciate European national movements and contemplated their exploitation by a socialist revolution. In 1913 he defined "self-determination" to mean either national independence or nothing at all, forcing a choice on nationally aware socialists while making a show of flexibility. Once in power, Lenin collapsed the two alternatives, promoting Soviet republics with national names. In 1913, Lenin had asked Josef Stalin to critique the proposed nationality policy of the Austrian socialists. Stalin's response was important in political if not intellectual terms: He defined nations as stable communities and spoke of national psychologies. These views seemed to gain impor-

tance in his mind as he gained personal power, and can be linked to his national policy during the 1930s. Lenin and Stalin were unusual Russian subjects, but their assimilation of nationalism was determinative of the fate of many of the peoples of the former Russian Empire.

See also: ARMENIA AND ARMENIANS; GEORGIA AND GEORGIANS; JEWS; KARAMZEN, NIKOLAI MIKHAILOVICH; LANGUAGE LAWS; NATIONALITIES POLICY, TSARIST; NATION AND NATIONALITY; OFFICIAL NATIONALITY; PANSLAVISM; POLES; POPULISM; RUSSIFICATION; SLAVOPHILES; UKRAINE AND THE UKRAINIANS

## BIBLIOGRAPHY

Chmielewski, Edward. (1970). *The Polish Question in the Russian State Duma.* Knoxville: University of Tennessee Press.

Frankel, Jonathan. (1981). *Prophecy and Politics: Socialism, Nationalism, and the Russian Jews, 1862–1917.* Cambridge: Cambridge University Press.

Pipes, Richard. (1954). *The Formation of the Soviet Union.* Cambridge, MA: Harvard University Press.

Riasanovsky, Nicholas. (1959). *Nicholas I and Official Nationality in Russia, 1825–1855.* Berkeley: University of California Press.

Rorlich, Azade–Ayse. (1986). *The Volga Tatars.* Stanford: Hoover Institution Press.

Suny, Ronald Grigor. (1988). *The Making of the Georgian Nation.* Bloomington: Indiana University Press.

Thaden, Edward. (1964). *Conservative Nationalism in Nineteenth–Century Russia.* Seattle: University of Washington Press.

Walicki, Andrzej. (1979). *A History of Russian Thought: From the Enlightenment to Marxism.* Stanford: Stanford University Press.

Walicki, Andrzej (1982). *Philosophy and Romantic Nationalism: The Case of Poland.* Notre Dame, IN: University of Notre Dame Press.

Weeks, Theodore. (1996). *Nation and State in Late Imperial Russia: Nationalism and Russification on the Western Frontier, 1863–1914.* Dekalb: Northern Illinois University Press.

TIMOTHY SNYDER

# NATIONALITIES POLICIES, SOVIET

The centerpiece of Bolshevik nationality policy before they came to power in 1917 was the right of nations to self-determination. As outlined by Vladimir I. Lenin in his 1916 work *The Socialist Revolution and the Right of Nations to Self-Determination*, this constituted the "right to free political secession" for all nationalities without qualification. In the same work, Lenin distinguished between different types of national movement, characterizing the Russian Empire as one of the areas where "the twentieth century has especially developed bourgeois-democratic national movements and sharpened the national struggle"(Lenin, 1964, p.151). Therefore national movements could play an important role in the democratic movement to overthrow tsarism, but at the same time Lenin explicitly argued that the right to secede ought in itself to be sufficient to persuade national minorities of the security of their national rights in a democratic state. While supporting the right of nations to self-determination, the Bolsheviks would not necessarily argue in favor of the right of secession being exercised. In any case in a socialist state, the clear economic and political advantages of remaining part of a larger state combined with the guarantees provided by the right to secede and the natural international class unity of the proletariat would ensure that, in most cases, national minorities would choose to remain within the larger state. This argument has led many historians to conclude that the right of nations to self-determination was purely a slogan designed to attract the maximum support from national minorities for Lenin's aim of socialist revolution, and was meaningless when it came to the practicalities of a multinational Soviet state.

## SELF-DETERMINATION TO FEDERALISM, 1917–1923

The principle of self-determination was invoked by the Soviet government in recognizing the independence of Finland at the end of 1917, but was not applied in its literal form thereafter. Nevertheless, it continued to dominate debates on the national question at Bolshevik Party conferences and congresses up until 1921. These arguments were a continuation of long-standing objections to Lenin's policy on the part of a significant group in the party leadership led by Yuri Pyatakov, Nikolai Bukharin, and Karl Radek. They argued that the internationalism of the working class meant that the continued existence of nations in a socialist society was inconceivable, that in the short term they were purely a distraction from the class struggle, and that recognition of national rights simply gave suc-

cor to divisive bourgeois nationalists. A particularly heated debate between this group and Lenin at the Eighth Party Congress in March 1919 led to a compromise resolution that introduced a new qualification to the right to self-determination: The question of who should represent the will of the nation on this matter would depend on the level of historical development of that nation. The implication was that for more developed nations, especially those already within the Soviet system, the national will would be expressed by the proletariat through their representative bodies, the Soviets themselves. Even in this qualified form, no nation was given the opportunity to exercise self-determination, and by 1920 the commissar (equivalent to minister) for nationality affairs, Josef Stalin, had declared self-determination a counterrevolutionary slogan.

Nevertheless, these debates were highly significant. The internationalist arguments of Bukharin and Pyatakov were deployed by substantial numbers of Russian communists working in non-Russian areas and enjoyed widespread support among both leading and rank-and-file Bolsheviks. In fact, it is doubtful whether Lenin ever enjoyed majority support for his policy within his own party. In the non-Russian regions, disputes between Russian and local national administrators and Party officials were frequent. Although these disputes more often than not centered on practical matters such as land distribution or the status of languages, the latter group frequently invoked the spirit of self-determination in support of their demands, while the former were often ready to dismiss their opponents as bourgeois nationalists. Underlying all the arguments about self-determination, then, was disagreement over whether separate national rights should be recognized in any form. Lenin's aversion to Great Russian Chauvinism meant that when the center was called on to intervene in such disputes, as often happened, it was more often than not the local nationals who received the more favorable decision. The predominance of Russians in the regional Bolshevik Party structures, however, ensured that even these interventions could be ignored.

Lack of clarity as to the status of national minorities helped to perpetuate these divisions. Initially the Bolsheviks had no clear blueprint for the organization of their multinational Soviet state. The principles behind Lenin's policy provided some sort of framework: national minorities who had been oppressed under the tsars must be assured that they would not continue to be treated in the same way; they should as far as possible run their own local institutions and be responsible for cultural matters, and they should enjoy the same linguistic and educational rights as Russians, assisted by the center where needed. Lenin also agreed with the need for some kind of national autonomy, various forms of which had been proposed by European Marxists since the beginning of the twentieth century. Within these broad parameters, policy was largely improvised in the key period between the end of the civil war in 1920 and the formation of the Soviet Union in 1924.

Shortly after the October 1917 revolution, a Commissariat for Nationality Affairs (or Narkomnats) was formed under Stalin's leadership. Narkomnats was responsible only for the smaller nationalities located within the Russian Soviet Federative Socialist Republic (RSFSR); until 1924, the larger nationalities of Ukraine, Belorussia and Transcaucasia had formally separate Soviet republics, linked to the RSFSR by treaties but in practice all dominated by the centralized Bolshevik Party. In a 1913 article, "Marxism and the National Question," Stalin had argued for territorial national autonomy, opposing the nonterritorial cultural autonomy espoused by the Austrian Marxists Otto Bauer and Karl Renner. The first autonomous republic, the Bashkir Autonomous Soviet Republic, was created in February 1919 and eventually provided the model for a series of autonomous republics and autonomous regions that proliferated across the RSFSR between 1920 and 1922. Their status was formally defined in separate treaties, but in general the republics and regions were responsible for matters of local government, education, culture, and agriculture, while the center retained authority over industry, the military, and foreign affairs.

In 1922, the unsatisfactory constitutional status of the Ukrainian, Belorussian, and Transcaucasian Soviet Republics was addressed. As Stalin argued, the formal separate status of these republics meant that they could pass their own laws, but if the leadership in Moscow objected, they could have these laws repealed by recourse to the disciplinary procedures of the Bolshevik Party, whose members controlled all the republics. The solution proposed by Stalin was to incorporate these republics into the system of autonomous republics of the RSFSR, which he himself had been instrumental in creating. In September 1922, Lenin objected that it was unacceptable to incorporate such important nationalities on the same basis as the

smaller ones of the RSFSR and to subject them to the authority of a state whose title implied they would become a part of Russia. Instead, he proposed that they should join a new formation on the same footing as the USSR, in a federative union of equals. The title of the new federation was eventually decided on as the Union of Soviet Socialist Republics (USSR), or Soviet Union. Lenin was by this time almost entirely incapacitated by illness, but had time to win this argument and then had to rely on others to carry his policy through. Until recently, most historians have taken this episode as evidence that Lenin stood for a more liberal position in regard to the non-Russians, while Stalin was a ruthless centralizer. More recently it has been argued either that in reality there were no significant differences between the two, or at least that they were not so far apart on this particular point.

The USSR officially came into being on January 1, 1924, consisting of the RSFSR, the Ukrainian Soviet Socialist Republic, the Belorussian SSR, and the Transcaucasian Federation, itself made up of the Georgian, Armenian, and Azerbaijani SSRs (which were later given entirely separate status). In 1925 Central Asia, previously part of the RSFSR as the Turkestan and Kirghiz Autonomous Republics, was divided into separate republics, with further later reorganizations resulting in the five Central Asian SSRs, the Kazakh, Uzbek, Tadzhik, Turkmen, and Kirghiz. Following World War II, newly acquired Soviet territory formed the Estonian, Latvian, Lithuanian, and Moldovan SSRs, making a total of fifteen union republics and dozens of autonomous republics and regions for the remainder of the Soviet period. Federalism between a number of national territories, which had been rejected outright by Lenin and others before 1917, thus became the central organizing principle of the Soviet state by 1924.

Within this constitutional framework, for most of the 1920s the Soviets pursued a range of policies aimed at promoting the national, economic, and cultural advancement of the non-Russians: priority to the local language, a massive increase in native language schools, development of national cultures, and staffing the Soviet administration as far as possible with local nationals. Collectively, these policies were known as *korenizatsiya*, or "rooting." Although widely opposed by local Russian (and some non-Russian) communists, these policies were generally successful in establishing local national leaderships and strengthening national identities associated with particular territories that formed the basis for what later became the post-Soviet independent states.

Economic investment in the non-Russian regions, with the aim of creating or reinforcing a native proletariat and raising the general level of development of the minorities, was one of the key elements of policy emerging from the discussion at the Twelfth Congress of the CPSU (Communist Party of the Soviet Union) in April 1923. During the period of the New Economic Policy (1921–1929), some progress was made in this direction, with the construction of a number of factories and processing plants in Central Asia providing an important impetus to the industrialization of the region. Overall, however, levels of economic investment in the borderlands did not significantly exceed those in central Russia. During the more rapid industrialization of the 1930s, a pattern emerged of concentrating the production of raw materials in the republics, such as cotton in Central Asia and coal in Ukraine, which were then processed in plants and factories in the RSFSR before the final goods were distributed across the Soviet Union. Some commentators have interpreted this as evidence of a deliberate colonial policy, based on comparisons with British practices in India, which served to tie the republics irrevocably into a state of economic dependency on the Soviet Union.

## THE STALIN ERA

Stalin did little to change this system during the early years of his power. However, there were early signs of a change in policy direction. In 1928 and 1929 a series of show trials and purges affected leading intellectuals and politicians in Ukraine, Belorussia, Tatarstan, Crimea, and Kazakhstan. Many of those arrested or demoted had been beneficiaries of the policies of korenizatsiya, and were now charged with fuelling anti-Soviet nationalism directly or indirectly. A more profound shift was evident in 1930 and 1931 when two leading historians, the Marxist Mikhail Pokrovsky and the Ukrainian national historian Mykhailo Hrushevsky, were discredited. Both were associated with an approach to history that had portrayed the Russian Empire as the unremitting oppressor of the non-Russians. As the 1930s progressed, the official version of history shifted to one where the Russian Empire had brought progress and civilization to backward peoples, and where for the first time former Russian tsars and military leaders could be portrayed as national heroes. Whereas previously nationality policy had discriminated against Rus-

sians and frequently denied them national rights allowed to others, now the superiority of the Russian culture and people was increasingly celebrated. This ideological shift was reflected on the ground in the partial abandonment of korenizatsiya policies from 1932 onward and an increasing dominance of Russians in the non-Russian regions. By the end of the decade all of the national leaders of the 1920s had been purged and in many cases replaced by Russians. The semiofficial position of Russian as the lingua franca of the Soviet Union was acknowledged by a law of 1938 that made the study of Russian as a second language compulsory in all non-Russian schools.

These changes have often been interpreted as evidence for a policy of outright Russification. But national cultures continued to be celebrated, albeit in a more "folky" form, the constitutional status of republics remained untouched, and local national politicians and the national language continued to play a major role in the life of the republics. In fact, the historian Terry Martin (2000) has identified a shift to a "primordial" view of nations during the 1930s, which implied that nations were permanent and could therefore never merge or be subsumed by the Russian nation. The emphasis in propaganda was rather on a Brotherhood of Nations in which the Russians would play the leading role. This emphasis gained ground during and immediately after World War II, when Stalin famously proposed a toast to "the health of our Soviet people, and in the first place the Russian people . . . the most outstanding nation of all the nations of the Soviet Union" (Stalin, vol.16, p.54).

The shift in nationality policy of the 1930s has to be seen in the broader context. It was a period of massive upheaval for all the peoples of the USSR. The collectivization of agriculture meant the destruction of traditional peasant cultures, most keenly felt by those such as the Kazakhs who had previously been nomadic and were now forced to settle. Huge numbers of people moved from the countryside to the towns and from one region to another in the course of industrialization, with the consequence that territories where one nationality had earlier been dominant in the overall population now found their numbers diluted by an influx of people from other national backgrounds, particularly Russians and other Slavs. In addition, the threat of a major war raised the fear among the leadership of the Soviet Union splitting along national lines in the event of an invasion, which required a propaganda shift emphasizing the unity rather than the diversity of Soviet nations. A final factor in the change was the clearly expressed disillusionment of Russians living in non-Russian areas, who had felt discriminated against in the allocation of jobs and land.

The new identification of nations as primordial had further implications. If nations were primordial, then all members of a particular nation shared collective traits and characteristics, which could be positive or negative. In the tense international situation of the late 1930s these traits could include a tendency to be unreliable or treacherous in the event of war. Already in Stalin's Great Terror, specific actions had been targeted against Poles, Germans, and Finns. In 1937, as tensions with Japan rose, every single ethnic Korean was deported from a large area of the Far East. Between 1941 and 1944, the Germans of the Volga region and the Karachai, Kalmyks, Chechens, Ingush, Balkars, and Meshketian Turks of Transcaucasia, together with the Tatars of the Crimea, were labeled as treacherous and were deported from their homelands. Every man, woman, and child was loaded into cattle trucks and transported by train to Siberia or Kazakhstan where they were deposited with little provision for their livelihood. Some one and one-half million people in all were treated in this way. Lacking food, water, and sanitation for days or weeks on end, up to half died during the journey, while others perished of disease or hunger soon after arrival at their new destinations. The territories from which they had been deported were simply renamed or disappeared, as if these nations had never existed. But far from eliminating these nations, the experience provided them in many cases with a deeper identity and a myth of survival and hatred of the Soviet system that characterized them later on. Many were rehabilitated by Khrushchev in 1956 and gradually returned to their homelands, while others, like the Crimean Tatars, Meskhetian Turks, and Volga Germans had to wait longer and could only return illegally.

Policy towards other nationalities was more positive during the war years, although Jews, Ukrainians, and Belorussians suffered disproportionately from the Nazi invasion and occupation. The need to mobilize the entire Soviet population for the war effort led to a number of concessions. National units in the Red Army, abolished only in 1938, were restored, and the heroic exploits of some of them were particularly prominent in propaganda. National heroes, especially military ones, who had been discredited in the official histories of the 1930s, were praised. A looser attitude to religion and culture restored the symbols and practices associated with many nationalities. In general Soviet propaganda stressed the unity and brotherhood of all the nations of the Soviet Union, but with the important qualification that the leading role was assigned to the Russians.

The settlement agreed by the Allies at the end of the war brought substantial new territory under Soviet control. The Baltic states of Estonia, Latvia, and Lithuania, which had been independent since the Russian Civil War of 1917–1922, were first occupied by the Red Army and incorporated into the Soviet Union in 1940 under the terms of the 1939 Nazi-Soviet pact. Rapid steps towards the Sovietization of these republics were taken, and were resumed after the interruption of the Nazi occupation of 1941–1945. The nationalization of industry, redistribution of landed estates followed by collectivization, introduction of Soviet school and university curricula, and imposition of the Soviet political system were all carried out with no regard for the independent traditions of the region. The process involved the deportation or execution of more than 300,000 individuals of suspect backgrounds—former members of political parties, army officers, high-ranking civil servants, clergymen, estate owners, or political opponents from the pre-independence period. These deportations were followed up by a deliberate policy of immigration of Russians into Latvia and Estonia in particular, significantly shifting the demographic makeup. In response to Sovietization, national partisan units, some of which were formed to fight against the Nazi occupation, continued to trouble the Soviet authorities until as late as 1952.

During the postwar years, appeals to Russian national sentiment took a further twist in the form of overt anti-Semitism. In 1948 a propaganda campaign against "cosmopolitanism" made little secret of the identity of the real targets. Over the next five years, thousands of Jewish intellectuals, cultural figures, and political leaders were arrested and imprisoned or executed. In 1953 a number of leading doctors, most of them Jewish, were arrested and charged in the so-called Doctors' Plot to kill off Soviet leaders. There is some evidence that at the same time plans were being laid to deport Jews from the western parts of the Soviet Union in an operation similar to, but on a larger scale than, the wartime national deportations. These plans were shelved, and most of the doctors' lives spared, only by the death of Stalin on March 5, 1953. The rapid abatement of anti-Jewish activities and propaganda from this date gives some persuasiveness to the argument that the campaign was based primarily on Stalin's personal anti-Semitism, but Soviet policy in the Middle East and the suspicion that Jewish organizations would gain in influence at home and abroad as a result of the sympathy arising from the Holocaust have also been offered as explanations. In any case anti-Semitism was deeply ingrained in large sections of Russian society, and could easily be mobilized again, as it was during the 1960s and 1970s, though to a lesser extent than during the late Stalin years. During the Brezhnev period, the status of Soviet Jews received international publicity through the fate of the *refuseniks*—those Jews who had been refused permission to emigrate to Israel.

## STALIN SUCCESSION AND THE KHRUSHCHEV AND BREZHNEV ERAS, 1953–1985

The non-Russian nationalities of the USSR played an important role in the competition to succeed Stalin as leader. NKVD (secret police) head Lavrenti Beria, like Stalin a Georgian, gained the ascendancy initially, and one of his first acts was to privately condemn Stalin for departing from Leninist principles in nationalities policy. He replaced the Russian Konstantin Melnikov with the Ukrainian Aleksei Kirichenko as party leader in Ukraine, and made several other personnel changes that established the principle that the first Party secretary in each Union republic should belong to the local nationality, a policy that was generally observed until 1986. "Activating remnants of bourgeois-nationalist elements in the Union republics" was one of the charges laid against Beria on his arrest during the summer of 1953, but nevertheless the republics continued to enjoy a position of relative advantage. Nikita Khrushchev, as general secretary of the CPSU, used his powers of appointment to promote former colleagues from Ukraine, where he had served during the 1930s, into important positions at the center. He also showed favoritism toward Ukraine in granting it control of the Crimean peninsula in 1954, and increased the number of Ukrainians on the Central Committee of the CPSU from sixteen in 1952 to fifty-nine in 1961. Their votes ultimately proved important in defeating Khrushchev's rivals in the Politburo. Khrushchev also gave all of the republics more say over economic matters by decentralizing a number of economic ministries, as well as the Ministry of Justice, to the republic level.

Having beaten off his rivals in 1957, Khrushchev turned many of these reforms on their head. Economic ministries were reorganized once more to the detriment of the republics. A new form of words creeping into the regime's Marxist-Leninist ideology signaled a clear shift in nationalities policy. Instead of describing relations between the nationalities of the USSR as a "Brotherhood of Nations," Khrushchev now began to talk about the "merger of nations" into one Soviet nation. This nation would be based around Slavic culture and the Russian language. Khrushchev took care not to alienate entirely the Ukrainian population, who were easily the second largest nationality, by including them (and to a lesser extent Belorussians) alongside Russians as the more important of the nationalities.

An important policy change was taken in this direction in the context of a general reform of the education system, which Khrushchev introduced in theses announced in November 1958. Article 19 of the theses, while acknowledging the longstanding Leninist principle that each child should be educated in his or her mother tongue, insisted that the question of which languages children should learn or be instructed in was a matter of parental choice. This move was widely opposed in the republics, especially those of Transcaucasia and the Baltics. It meant that Russian immigrants into the republics no longer had to study the local language as a second language, while it also opened the door to Estonians, Azerbaijanis, and others to send their children to Russian schools. Nevertheless, Khrushchev insisted on all the republics introducing legislation to reflect this change. In those republics that failed to do so, Latvia and Azerbaijan, broad purges of the Communist Party leadership were carried out on Moscow's instructions and new legislation forced through.

What the republican leaders feared was that the status of the republic's language would be eroded, provoking an initial popular backlash and opening the door in the long term to the abolition of the national federal system. It is perhaps no coincidence that the republics that displayed most opposition to the reform—Latvia, Estonia, and Azerbaijan—were those where the numerically dominant position of the local nationality in the population as a whole had come under the most pressure. Following the first major period of internal migration in the Soviet Union during the 1930s, several further waves of migration occurred. Immediately after World War II, as thousands of Estonians, Latvians, and Lithuanians were deported from their republics, even greater numbers of Russians moved the other way over a number of years, especially into Latvia and Estonia, where the proportion of Estonians in the total population fell from 88 percent in 1939 to 61.5 percent in 1989. Under Khrushchev, large-scale internal migration was associated with the Virgin Lands campaigns and other policies, while the dominance of republican nationalities was further undermined by later waves of migration.

The changing demographic structure of the USSR might help to explain Khrushchev's new emphasis on the "merger of nations." If particular policies and the demands of modernization entailed a geographically more mobile population, it made sense for everyone to have command of a single language and to owe their primary loyalty to the Soviet state rather than to a particular republic or nationality. The sum total of Khrushchev's policies, then, could be regarded as aiming at a more systematic Russification of the entire population than had ever been attempted by Stalin.

If this was the intention, at least in the short term the actual impact of Khrushchev's policies was minimal in the Union republics. Schools continued to operate much as they had before. For the smaller nationalities of the RSFSR, the impact was more telling. The number of languages used in schools in the RSFSR declined from forty-seven during the early 1960s to seventeen by 1982, most of which were only used in the early grades before instruction switched to Russian. In the longer term, mother-tongue education eventually declined in the larger republics as well, especially Ukraine and Belorussia, and the constitutional status of republican languages was also undermined in a number of cases.

During Leonid Brezhnev's tenure as general secretary of the CPSU (1964–1982), the republics were nonetheless subjected to less drastic policy and personnel changes than under Khrushchev. Typically, republican leaders remained in office for much longer, as illustrated by Uzbek first secretary Sharaf Rashidov, who retained his position from 1959 to 1983. This longevity allowed the republican leaders to build up their own networks of power, which were often associated with endemic corruption, but also meant they could pursue the interests of their republics without interference, so long as they did not cross acceptable boundaries. This happened in Ukraine in 1963, when First Secretary Petr Shelest was dismissed for allegedly pursuing a policy of over-zealous promotion of Ukrainian identity and culture. The regime continued to pursue Russification policies to an extent sufficient to provoke the creation of numerous underground nationalist groupings, which were to emerge at the head of much broader movements at the end of the 1980s.

## GORBACHEV AND THE COLLAPSE OF THE SOVIET UNION

Shortly after assuming the general secretaryship of the CPSU in 1985, Mikhail Gorbachev declared that the Soviet Union had decisively resolved the national question. Events were to disillusion him quickly. When he tried to replace the Kazakh first secretary, Dinmukhamed Kunaev, with a Russian, Gennady Kolbin, in December 1986, the response was widespread rioting on the streets of Alma Ata, the capital of the Kazakh Republic. Gorbachev's reaction was to tread a more cautious line, repealing a number of unpopular language laws, and reforming the Council of Nationalities, which represented the republics at the highest level. Initially, he even gave encouragement to national-minded intellectuals in the Baltic republics, hoping to use them to help force through experimental market reforms in the region. But his failure to instigate an overall consistent policy towards nationalities only served to fuel the explosion of national unrest, which erupted in violent conflict between Azeris and Armenians in Azerbaijan in 1988, and the emergence of national "Popular Fronts," which arose in the Baltic republics during the same year and spread across almost all major nationalities by the end of the decade.

This eruption led to varying responses from Gorbachev, who at times seemed to be making concessions to the national movements, but at other times resorted to repression, leading to bloodshed by government forces in the Georgian capital Tbilisi and the Lithuanian capital Vilnius (although Gorbachev's direct involvement in these events has never been established). The Popular Fronts won spectacular successes in Soviet elections and came to dominate the government in Armenia, Estonia, Latvia, Lithuania, and Georgia. These republics declared first sovereignty, then independence. Other republics followed with declarations of sovereignty (meaning that their own republican laws would take precedence over the laws of the USSR). The decisive blow against the federal USSR came during the summer of 1990 when the RSFSR itself, led by Boris Yeltsin, declared sovereignty. In his rivalry with Gorbachev, Yeltsin was prepared to give every encouragement to national movements, including the Russian one.

Although a referendum organized by Gorbachev early in 1991 showed overwhelming support for maintaining some form of Union among most non-Russians, and Gorbachev himself was working on the terms of a new, much looser, Union Treaty aimed at holding the republics together at the time of the failed coup in August of that year, he was probably already resigned to the independence of the Baltic republics, and it was likely that other republics would follow them. The coup proved the final nail in the coffin as it encouraged other republican leaders to pursue their own paths, and the USSR was formally dissolved at midnight on December 31, 1991.

While the Bolsheviks and their successors were guided by general principles in their treatment of non-Russian nationalities, no single coherent nationalities policy existed for the Soviet period as a whole. Not only did the guiding principles change over time, but they were applied to different degrees to different nationalities, creating a picture far more complex than it is possible to describe here in detail. The size of the nationality, its proportion in the overall population of each republic, the historical strength of national identity, the existence of co-nationals or coreligionists outside the borders of the USSR, and their proximity to Moscow or strategic borderlands were all factors contributing to these differences. Perhaps most important of all, especially in the later Soviet period, was the closeness of individual leaders to the key figures in Moscow and their adeptness at the kind of bargaining that characterized the later years. Ultimately, one of the reasons for the demise of the USSR was the attempt to apply general nationalities policies to the three Baltic republics, which had a quite different historical experience from the other nationalities. But from the earliest days there was an inconsistency in the application of policies that favored national development on the one hand and the demands of a centralized, ideologically and culturally unified state on the other, causing tensions that contributed in no small part to the instability that preceded the downfall of the system.

*See also:* COMMONWEALTH OF INDEPENDENT STATES; EMPIRE, USSR AS; KORENIZATSYA; NATIONALISM IN THE SOVIET UNION; NATIONALITIES POLICIES, TSARIST; OFFICIAL NATIONALITY; RUSSIAN SOVIET FEDERATED SOCIALIST REPUBLIC; RUSSIFICATION; STALIN, JOSEF VISSARIONOVICH

## BIBLIOGRAPHY

Allworth, Edward A., ed. (1998). *The Tatars of Crimea: Return to the Homeland.* Durham, NC: Duke University Press.

Altstadt, Audrey L. (1992). *The Azerbaijani Turks.* Stanford, CA: Hoover Institution Press.

Bennigsen, Alexandre, and Lemercier-Quelquejay, Chantal. (1967). *Islam in the Soviet Union.* London: Pall Mall.

Bilinsky, Yaroslav. (1962). "The Soviet Education Laws of 1958–59 and Soviet Nationality Policy." *Soviet Studies* 14:138–157.

Bremmer, Ian, and Taras, Ray, eds. (1997). *New States, New Politics: Building the Post-Soviet Nations.* Cambridge, UK: Cambridge University Press.

Broxup, Marie Bennigsen, ed. (1992). *The North Caucasus Barrier: The Russian Advance towards the Muslim World.* London: Hurst.

Carrère d'Encausse, Hélène. (1992). *The Great Challenge: Nationalities and the Bolshevik State, 1917–1930.* New York: Holmes and Meier.

Denber, Rachel, ed. (1992). *The Soviet Nationality Reader: The Disintegration in Context.* Boulder, CO: Westview.

Fowkes, Ben. (1997). *The Disintegration of the Soviet Union: A Study in the Rise and Triumph of Nationalism.* London: Macmillan.

Huttenbach, Henry R. (1990). *Soviet Nationaltity Policies: Ruling Ethnic Groups in the USSR.* London: Mansell.

Kaiser, Robert J. (1994). *The Geography of Nationalism in Russia and the USSR.* Princeton, NJ: Princeton University Press.

Kappeler, Andreas. (2001). *The Russian Empire: A Multiethnic History.* London: Longman.

Karklins, Rasma. (1986). *Ethnic Relations in the USSR.* Boston: Allen and Unwin.

Kreindler, Isabelle. (1986). "The Soviet Deportation of Nationalities: A Summary and Update." *Soviet Studies* 38:387–405.

Lenin, Vladimir Ilich. (1964). "The Socialist Revolution and the Right of Nations to Self-Determination." *Collected Works.* London: Lawrence and Wishart.

Levin, Nora. (1990). *The Jews of the Soviet Union since 1917.* London: I. B. Tauris.

Martin, Terry. (2000). "Modernization or Neo-Traditionalism? Ascribed Nationality and Soviet Primordialism". In *Stalinism: New Directions*, ed. Sheila Fitzpatrick. London: Routledge.

Martin, Terry. (2001). *The Affirmative Action Empire: Nations and Nationalism in the Soviet Union, 1923–1939.* Ithaca, NY: Cornell University Press.

Nahaylo, Bohdan, and Swoboda, Victor. (1990). *Soviet Disunion: A History of the Nationalities Problem in the USSR.* London: Hamish Hamilton.

Nekrich, Aleksandr Moiseevich. (1978) *The Punished Peoples: The Deportation and Fate of Soviet Minorities at the End of the Second World War.* New York: Norton.

Pipes, Richard. (1997). *The Formation of the Soviet Union: Communism and Nationalism, 1917–1923,* rev. ed. Cambridge, MA: Harvard University Press.

Simon, Gerhard. (1991). *Nationalism and Policy Toward the Nationalities in the Soviet Union.* Boulder, CO: Westview.

Smith, Graham, ed. (1996). *The Baltic States: The National Self-Determination of Estonia, Latvia, and Lithuania.* London: Macmillan.

Smith, Jeremy. (1997). *The Bolsheviks and the National Question, 1917–1923.* London: Macmillan.

Subtelny, Orest. (1989) *Ukraine: A History.* Toronto: University of Toronto Press.

Suny, Ronald Grigor. (1992). *The Making of the Georgian Nation.* London: I.B. Tauris.

Suny, Ronald Grigor. (1993). *The Revenge of the Past: Nationalism, Revolution, and the Collapse of the Soviet Union.* Stanford, CA: Stanford University Press.

Suny, Ronald Grigor, and Martin, Terry, eds. (2001). *A State of Nations: Empire and Nation-Making in the Age of Lenin and Stalin.* Oxford: Oxford University Press.

Tishkov, Valery. (1997). *Ethnicity, Nationalism, and Conflict in and after the Soviet Union: The Mind Aflame.* London: Sage.

JEREMY SMITH

# NATIONALITIES POLICIES, TSARIST

At the end of the nineteenth century the huge Russian Empire extended from western Poland to the Pacific Ocean, from the Kola peninsula in the Polar Sea to the Caspian Sea and to Central Asia. It comprised regions with different climate, soil, and vegetation and a heterogeneous population with different economies, ways of life, and cultures. Among its inhabitants there were adherents of Christianity (of the Orthodox, Roman Catholic, Protestant, and Armenian variants), Islam, Judaism, Buddhism, and Shamanism. In ethnic terms, Orthodox Eastern Slavs (Russians, 44%; Ukrainians, 18%; and Belorussians, 5%), which officially were considered as three branches of one Russian people, predominated with two-thirds of the total population. Nevertheless Muslims, mostly speaking Turkic languages (11%), Poles (7%), Jews (4%), and dozens of other groups represented strong minorities and (with the exception of the Jews and other diaspora groups) majorities in their core regions.

The tsarist government never formulated a consistent nationalities policy. The policies toward the non-Russians of the empire were of great diversity according to its heterogeneity and the respective time period. Before the beginning of the age of nationalism (i.e., in Russia before the nineteenth century), even the term *nationality* is highly questionable. In the premodern period, national and ethnic categories were not considered important by the tsarist government. Russia was a supranational empire marked by the official term *Rossyskaya imperia,* distinct from the ethnic term *russkaya* (Russian). Its main concerns were the loyalty of all subjects to the ruler and their social/estate status.

In the historiography on tsarist nationalities policies, these distinctions have not always been kept in mind. Historians of the non-Russian nationalities have drawn a rather uniform picture of an oppressive, colonialist, assimilationist, and nationalist policy that from the very beginning consciously aimed at destroying national cultures and identities. On the other hand the imperial Russian and later the Soviet historiography (after 1934) and some of Russian historiography after 1991 usually idealized tsarist rule and its "mission civilisatrice" among non-Russians. In Western historiography there are also controversies about the long-term aims of tsarist nationalities policies. One group advocates a general goal of cultural Russification, at least since the reign of Catherine II; others differentiate between epochs and peoples and usually restrict the term *Russification* to the short period between 1881 and 1905.

Although during the Middle Ages most Rus principalities, especially the city republic of Novgorod, had comprised non-Slavic groups (Karelians, Mordvins, Zyryans/Komi, etc.), it was the conquest of the Kazan Khanate in 1552 by Ivan IV that laid the ground for the polyethnic Russian empire and for a first phase of tsarist nationalities policies. In the war declared to be a crusade against infidels, the Russian troops killed or expelled all Tatars from their capital, and priests began to baptize Muslims by force. Violent protest movements of Tatars and Cheremis (Mari) were suppressed by military campaigns.

The broad resistance, however, caused a fundamental change of policies towards the population of the former Khanate. The tsar's main goals—the maintenance of stability and loyalty and economic profit—were served better by pragmatism than by force. So the missionary efforts among Muslims and animists were stopped for more than a century. Moscow now guaranteed the status quo not only of the religions, but also of the land and duties of the taxable population (together with the Tatar tax, *yasak*) and of the landed property and privileges of the loyal noble Tatars. Many Muslim Tatars were co-opted into the imperial nobility, which already since the fifteenth century had included Tatar aristocrats. Muslim Tatar landowners were even allowed to have Russian peasants as their serfs, whereas Russian nobles were strictly forbidden to have non-Christian serfs. So in opposition to the majority of Russian peasants, enserfed during the sixteenth and seventeenth centuries, the Tatar, Mordvin, Chuvash, Cheremis (Mari), and Votiak (Udmurt) peasants remained personally free "yasak men" (*yasachnye lyudi*) and later state peasants. The lands owned by the Tatar khan and Tatar nobles who were killed or had fled to the East were occupied by the Russian state, Russian nobles, and peasants. They settled in significant numbers in the southern and southeastern parts of the former Kazan Khanate, where, as early as the end of the seventeenth century, Russians outnumbered the native peoples. The towns of the Khanate were also populated by Russians, and the trade and culture of the Muslim Tatars were ruralized.

The two lines of military repression and of pragmatic flexibility following the submission of the non-Russian population served as a model for Russian premodern nationalities policies. Tsarist policies were based on cooperation with loyal non-Russians and a retention of the status quo, regional traditions, and institutions. This facilitated the transfer of power and the establishment of legitimacy. In order for non-Russian aristocrats to be co-opted into the imperial nobility, they needed to have a social position and a way of life that corresponded to that of the Russian nobility. So, among the elites of the Siberian native peoples, who were subjugated by force during the seventeenth and eighteenth centuries, only a small group of western Siberian Tatars became nobles. Nevertheless, Russian officials sought cooperation with the chieftains of Siberian tribes, who became heads of the local administration and had to guarantee the delivery of the yasak. The main aim of Russian policies towards the Siberian native peoples was the exploitation of furs, especially the valuable sable. With a pragmatic policy the government tried to further these economic goals. The shamanist reli-

gion was not persecuted, and missionary efforts of the church were not allowed. However, the regional administrators and the Russian trappers, Cossacks, merchants, and adventurers often did not obey these instructions, and they committed numerous acts of violence against the native peoples.

After the conquest of Kazan and of Astrakhan (1556), Russia gained control over the Volga valley and began to exert pressure on nomadic tribes. Leaders of the Nogai Tatars, the Bashkirs, and (from 1655) the Kalmyks swore oaths of loyalty to the tsar, which were interpreted by Moscow (and by the imperial and Soviet historiographies) as eternal subjugation of their tribes and territories. From the perspective of the steppe nomads, however, these oaths were only temporary and personal unions that did not apply to other clans or tribes. These different interpretations caused diplomatic and military conflicts between the sedentary Russian state and the nomad polities.

Similar problems of interpretation occurred in the case of the Dnieper Cossacks who swore allegiance to Tsar Alexei Mikhailovich in 1654. The Russian government regarded the agreement of Pereyaslav as a voluntary submission and the definitive incorporation of Ukraine into Russia; in the late Soviet Union it was labeled as voluntary reunion of Ukraine with Russia. For Bohdan Khmelnytsky and his Cossacks (and for many Ukrainian historians), however, it was only a temporary military alliance and a temporary Muscovite protectorate. In 1667 Ukraine was divided between Russia and Poland-Lithuania, and its Eastern part on the left bank of the Dnieper (with Kiev on the right bank) became part of the Muscovite state. The so called Hetmanate of the Dnieper Cossacks retained much autonomy within Russia, with its sociopolitical structure under the rule of an elected hetman and its independent army guaranteed. As in the case of the loose protectorates over some of the steppe nomads, military-strategic concerns seem to have been decisive for the cautious policy of the Russian government.

The pattern of pragmatic flexibility that dominated tsarist "nationalities" policies of the sixteenth and seventeenth centuries was fundamentally altered by the Westernization of Russia promoted by Peter the Great (r. 1682–1725). The goal of transforming Russia into a systematized, regulated, and uniform absolutist state based on the Western European model and the adoption of the Western concept of a European "mission civilisatrice" in the East left no room for special rights and traditions of non-Russians. In 1718 cooperation with Tatar Muslim landowners was ended, and they were required to convert to Christianity. The majority of them, remaining faithful to Islam, lost their (Russian) peasants and were degraded to state peasants or merchants. Following the example of Western missions, the majority of animists of the Volga–Ural region and of Siberia were converted to Orthodoxy during the first half of the eighteenth century. Although conversion was enforced with the help of economic pressure and violence, the majority of the Muslims reacted with fierce resistance. In the 1730s and 1740s the Russian army subdued the Muslim Bashkirs in the Southern Ural. However, between 1773 and 1775 Bashkirs and Volga Tatars again were among the most important supporters of the Pugachev uprising. Simultaneously Russian pressure on the Kalmyks increased, and in 1771 more than 100,000 Kalmyks moved eastward, though only a small part of them reached their ancient homeland in western Mongolia.

While during the first half of the eighteenth century tsarist nationalities policies in the East became more repressive, in the Baltic provinces of Livonia and Estonia, conquered in 1710, Peter the Great continued to apply the traditional policy of preservation of the status quo and of cooperation with foreign elites. The privileges and corporate rights of the Baltic German landowners and townsmen were guaranteed, as were the Lutheran Church and the German language in administration and justice. The German Baltic nobles were co-opted into the imperial nobility and served the tsar as military officers, administrators, diplomats, and scholars. The Baltic provinces with their Central European structures and their educated upper class even constituted a model for a Westernized Russia.

Catherine II (r. 1762–1796) furthered the administrative homogeneity of the empire and curtailed the autonomy of the Baltic provinces, but her successors again guaranteed the traditional rights and privileges of the Baltic Germans. Catherine also abolished the autonomy of the Ukrainian Hetmanate and destroyed the host of the formerly independent Zaporozhian Cossacks on the lower Dnieper. Russia had begun to integrate the Hetmanate into the empire after the alliance of Hetman Ivan Mazepa with the Swedish king Charles XII, defeated by the Russians at Poltava in 1709. Nonetheless the tsars continued to cooperate with the loyal Cossack elite, which became a landowning nobility and in 1785 was partially co-opted into the imperial nobility. After a century of Ukrainiza-

tion of Russian culture through graduates of the Kievan Mohyla Academy, Ukrainian culture was Russified from the end of the eighteenth century. After the victory against the Ottoman Empire in 1774, the subjugation of the Khanate of Crimea in 1783, and the annexation of the steppe regions north of the Black Sea, Russia no longer required the military skills of Ukrainian Cossacks. The former Hetmanate was now integrated into the administration, social structure, and culture of Russia. The fertile Southern steppe was first colonized by privileged German and Orthodox South Slav settlers, and in the following decades by Ukrainian and Russian peasants.

The three partitions of Poland (1772–1795) brought large numbers of Poles, Ukrainians, Belorussians, Jews, and Lithuanians under tsarist rule. After having abolished the political structure of the nobles' republic and incorporated the large territory into the imperial administration, Catherine II followed the traditional pattern of cooperation with loyal non-Russian elites. She co-opted many of the numerous loyal Polish nobles into the imperial elite and confirmed their landholdings (with many Ukrainian, Belorussian, and Lithuanian serfs) and their social privileges. She granted self-administration to the towns and recognized the Roman Catholic Church and the Polish language. The tolerance of enlightened absolutism, however, did not apply to the Uniate Church, which was officially dissolved in 1839.

After 1772 Russia had to deal with a great number of Jews for the first time in its history. In the first years the politics of enlightened absolutism proclaimed tolerance and granted equality to the Jews, who were incorporated into the estates of townspeople. But from the 1780s on, and especially from 1804, the Jews of Russia faced discrimination. They were allowed to settle only in the so-called pale of Jewish settlement in the west of the empire and had to pay double taxes. Under Nicholas I (r. 1825–1855) the Jews lost other former rights.

In 1815 the Congress of Vienna established a Kingdom of Poland, often referred to as Congress Poland, which embraced the central provinces of former Poland–Lithuania and was united with the Russian Empire. The new hereditary king of Poland, Tsar Alexander I (r. 1801–1825), granted the kingdom a constitution that was the most liberal in Europe at the time, an almost complete autonomy with a separate army and self-government and a guarantee for the Polish language and the Catholic religion. These were unusual concessions that are explained by the international situation, the striving for independence of many Poles, and a possible role of the kingdom as a model for reforms in Russia. However, conflicts soon arose between the Russian government and Polish nobles who aimed at restoring the old kingdom of Poland-Lithuania. The Polish uprising of November 1830 and the following war with Russia put an end to the Kingdom of Poland. After the defeat of the Poles, Russia gave up cooperation with the "traitorous" Poles and integrated Poland into Russian administration.

In 1809 and 1812, respectively, Finland and Bessarabia were annexed by Russia. The Grand Duchy of Finland was granted a great measure of autonomy through guarantees of the status quo, the Lutheran religion, and the rights and privileges of the population. The Swedish nobility of Finland was co-opted into the imperial nobility, and many of its members served in the Russian army and navy. In contrast to the Polish nobility, they remained loyal to the tsar during the nineteenth century and maintained their social position within the empire. The large autonomy Finland was granted for the first time in 1809 laid the groundwork for the creation of a Finnish nation-state. Bessarabia, the territory between Dniester and Pruth, annexed in 1812 from the Ottoman Empire, was also guaranteed wide autonomy, which, however, was considerably curtailed in 1828. Although St. Petersburg co-opted the Romanian elite into the imperial nobility, the legal and administrative status quo of the former Ottoman province did not fit into the Westernized model of rule in Russia.

In its western peripheries, the tsarist government had to deal with societies that were influenced by the Renaissance, Catholicism, and Protestantism, and by Western legal systems and traditions of estates and urban and regional autonomy—societies that were usually more advanced in terms of education and economic development than the Russians. The empire profited from the special skills of its subjects; for instance, of the Baltic Germans, Poles, and Finns in the army, navy, and bureaucracy; of the Jews and Armenians in trade; and of all of them in education and scholarship.

As pressure on non-Russians in the West became greater under Catherine II, the repressive policy toward non-Christians in the East was lifted, and Russia again looked for cooperation with Muslim elites. Volga Tatar and Crimean Tatar aristocrats were co-opted into the nobility, and Catherine II tried to use Volga Tatar merchants and mullahs

as mediators in the relations with Kazakhstan and Central Asia. She also created special religious administrations for the Muslims of the empire.

The conquest of the Caucasus region in the first two-thirds of the nineteenth century brought new Muslim and Christian groups under Tsarist rule. The Muslim khanates and Georgian kingdoms lost their political self–government and were integrated into the administrative structures of the empire. After the final annexation of southern Caucasia in 1828, Russia began to cooperate with its elites. Many of the very numerous Georgian and Muslim aristocrats were co-opted into the imperial nobility, and the Armenian merchants into the urban estates. So the social and economic status quo was respected. While the autocephaly of the Georgian Orthodox Church was abolished, the privileges of the Armenian Gregorian Church and the (mostly Shiite) Muslims were guaranteed. The mountaineers (gortsy) of the Caucasus rose up against tsarist rule and under Imam Shamil fought a holy war of more than thirty years against Russia. The tsarist armies that fought the Caucasian wars with great brutality succeeded only in 1864 "pacifying" the ethnic groups of Dagestan, the Chechens, and the Circassians. Hundreds of thousands of Caucasians were killed or forced to emigrate to the Ottoman Empire. After the conquest of the North Caucasus, the Russian government respected the religious and social status quo and cooperated with loyal non-Russian Muslim elites. On the other hand the government promoted Russian and Ukrainian colonization in the northern Caucasus, which became a source for new conflicts.

The evolutionist thinking of the European Enlightenment led to a new classification of peoples according to their alleged degree of civilization. Non-sedentary ethnic groups were regarded as inferior subjects, and they were combined in the new legal estate category of inorodtsy (aliens, allogenes) in 1822. During the first half of the nineteenth century most Siberian indigenes and the recently subjugated Kazakh nomads were integrated into the category of inorodtsy. They retained their social organization, their belief systems, and certain rights of local autonomy, but were second-class subjects only. After the military conquest of Central Asia from the 1860s to the 1880s, other Muslim nomads (Kazakhs, Kyrgyz, Turkmen), as well as the sedentary Muslims of its south, were integrated into the estate of inorodtsy (here called tuzemtsy). Here, for the first time, the tsarist government did not accept sedentary foreign aristocrats and merchants as equals. In Central Asia, Russia followed a policy of noninterference, and the Muslim population retained many of its administrative, legal, social, and religious rights. Russia's main interests in Central Asia were strategic (the "Great Game" with Great Britain) and economic (such as the cultivation of cotton). While most of the Central Asian territory was integrated into the imperial administration, the Emirate of Bukhara and the Khanate of Khiva were not annexed to Russia, but formally kept their independence as a Russian protectorate.

The tsarist policy in Central Asia followed a typical colonial pattern. The region was a supplier of raw materials and a market for finished products. The fertile soils of the northern Kazakh steppe in the last decades of tsarist Russia were colonized by millions of European (mostly Russian and Ukrainian) settlers, and the nomads were driven away from their summer pastures. This caused many conflicts, which culminated in an armed uprising in Central Asia in 1916. There was a great cultural gap between the indigenous population of Central Asia and the Russians. The native peoples—not only the nomads, but also the settled Muslims—were segregated from Europeans and regarded as inferiors by Russians. This policy reflected the influence of European colonialism and imperialism. Russia as a European power had to fulfill its "mission civilisatrice" among the "uncivilized" Asians, who in reality were the heirs of a high civilization much older than the Russian.

In the west of the empire, the traditional pattern of rule was altered after the 1860s. First, this change was caused by the Great Reforms aiming at systematization and homogenization of the administrative, juridical, social, and educational structures. The reforms clashed with traditional privileges and rights of autonomy of the regional elites, who often perceived them as measures of Russification. Second, as a result of the growing number of educated Russians, the government was no longer dependent on the special services of non-Russians in the army, bureaucracy, education, and trade. Third, it was nationalism that undermined the foundations of the Russian empire and changed the character of tsarist policy.

The crucial problem from 1830 to 1914 was the Polish question. It heavily influenced tsarist policies in general and especially nationalities policies. Poland was strategically and economically important, and the Poles were the most numerous non-Russian (i.e., non–East Slavic) and non-Orthodox nationality of the empire. The Polish re-

bellions destroyed the traditional bases of tsarist policies. After 1863 Russia renounced cooperation with the Polish nobility and began to rule over Poland without its assistance. The subsequent repressive policy not only against disloyal Polish rebels, but against all signs of Polishness, including the language, the Catholic Church, and even the name Poland, can be interpreted both as punishment and as measures to ensure law and order. Tsarism did not aim at a full assimilation of the Polish nation, but the repressive Russification policy severely hampered the development of Polish culture and society in the Russian Empire.

The change of nationalities policies after 1863 had severe impact on the Ukrainians, Belorussians, and Lithuanians. Their national movements, which had just begun to develop, were thought to be a "Polish intrigue" organized by Polish and Jesuit agitators. In reality they were directed primarily against the social and cultural dominance of the Polish nobility. The printing of publications in Ukrainian, Belorussian, and Lithuanian (in the last case in Latin letters) was prohibited, and the (moderate) activities of the national movements were stopped.

Thus, after 1863 the tsarist government openly pursued the goal of linguistic Russification for the first time. In the case of the Ukrainians and Belorussians, who were regarded as Russians, it aimed at strengthening their genuine Russianness against Polish influences. This policy on the whole was successful, and the Ukrainian and Belorussian national movements were severely hampered. In the case of Poles and Lithuanians, however, the extreme measures, especially against the Catholic Church, led to protest and contributed to the national mobilization of the Lithuanian and Polish peasants.

The Polish uprising of 1863 was also an important catalyst of Russian nationalism. Although the tsarist government regarded Russian nationalism with suspicion, because it called into question traditional legitimacy and the autocratic monopoly on power, nationalism not only mobilized great parts of educated society but made its way into the bureaucracy and had increasing influence on policy making. After 1863, in a spiral of mutual challenge and response, Russian nationalism and tsarist repression escalated.

In the following decades the repressive policy was extended to elites who for a long time had been models of great loyalty to the dynasty. Now their non-Russianness came to be regarded as potential disloyalty. During the reign of Alexander III (1881–1894) a policy of standardization and administrative and cultural Russification was initiated in the Baltic provinces and provoked the resistance of the Baltic Germans. During the 1890s Finland became the object of the policy of forceful integration, which unleashed national mobilization not only of the old Swedish-speaking elite, but of the broad Finnish masses. From 1881 on, the government enforced discriminatory measures against Jews, who were suspected of being revolutionaries and traitors and who were scapegoated. Anti-Semitism became an important part of Russian integral nationalism, although the tsarist government did not organize the anti-Jewish pogroms of 1881 and of 1903 to 1906. In Transcaucasia from the 1870s Russification measures alienated the Georgian noble elite and, after the 1880s, the Armenian Church and middle class.

In the last third of the nineteenth century, the tsarist government renounced cooperation with most of the co-opted loyal nobilities (Poles, Baltic Germans, Finlanders, Georgians) and loyal middle classes (Jews, Armenians). With the rise of ethnic nationalism and growing tensions in foreign policy, loyalty was expected only from members of the Russian nation and not from non-Russian elites, who were regarded with growing suspicion. On the whole the repressive measures against non-Russians in the western and southern periphery had counterproductive results, strengthening national resistance and enlarging national movements.

However, the tsarist policy toward most of the ethnic groups of the East remained basically unchanged. It is true that state and church tried to strengthen Orthodox faith and "Russianness" among the Christianized peoples of the Volga-Ural-Region, but the so-called Ilminsky system, which introduced native languages into missionary work, was above all a defensive measure against the growing appeal of Islam. By creating literary languages and native-language schools for many small ethnic groups, it furthered in the long run their cultural nationalism. In the last fifty years of tsarism, there were only cautious missionary activities and virtually no Russificatory measures among the Muslims of the empire.

In 1905 peasants and workers in the western and southern peripheries were the most active promoters of the revolution. The revolution unleashed a short "spring of nations" that embraced nearly all ethnic groups of the empire. The removal of most political and some cultural restrictions and

the possibility of political participation in the first two State Dumas (1906–1907) caused widespread national mobilization. Although the tsarist government soon afterward restricted individual and collective liberties and rights, it could not return to the former policy of repression and Russification. The violent insurrections of Latvian, Estonian, and Georgian peasants and of Polish, Jewish, Latvian, and Armenian workers made clear that turning away from cooperation with the regional elites had proved to be dangerous for social and political stability. The tsarist government tried to split non-Russians by a policy of divide and rule and partially returned to the coalition with loyal, conservative forces among non-Russians. On the other hand it was influenced by the rising ethnic Russian nationalism, which was used to integrate Russian society and to bridge its deep social and political cleavages. Despite the many unresolved political, social, economic, and ethno-national problems, the government managed to hold together the heterogeneous empire until 1917. The national questions were not among the main causes for the collapse of the tsarist regime in February 1917, but they became crucial for the dissolution of the empire after October 1917.

*See also:* ILMINSKY, NIKOLAI IVANOVICH; NATIONALISM IN THE TSARIST EMPIRE; NATIONALITIES POLICIES, SOVIET; NATION AND NATIONALITY; OFFICIAL NATIONALITY; RUSSIFICATION; SLAVOPHILES

**BIBLIOGRAPHY**

Allworth, Edward, ed. (1998). *Central Asia: 130 Years of Russian Dominance, A Historical Overview.* Durham, NC: Duke University Press.

Brower; Daniel (2003). *Turkestan and the Fate of the Russian Empire.* London, NY: Routledge Curzon.

Brower, Daniel R., and Lazzerini, Edward J., eds. (1997). *Russia's Orient: Imperial Borderlands and Peoples, 1700-1917.* Bloomington: Indiana University Press.

Forsyth, James. (1992). *A History of the Peoples of Siberia: Russia's North Asian Colony, 1581-1990.* Cambridge, UK: Cambridge University Press.

Geraci, Robert P., and Khodarkovsky, Michael, eds. (2001). *Of Religion and Empire: Missions, Conversion, and Tolerance in Tsarist Russia.* Ithaca, NY: Cornell University Press.

Geyer, Dietrich. (1987). *Russian Imperialism.* New Haven, CT: Yale University Press.

Hosking, Geoffrey. (1997). *Russia: People and Empire.* London: HarperCollins.

Kappeler, Andreas. (2001). *The Russian Empire: A Multiethnic History.* Harlow, UK: Longman.

Kappeler, Andreas, Kohut, Zenon E., et al, eds. (2003). *Culture, Nation, and Identity: The Ukrainian–Russian Encounter, 1600–1945.* Toronto: CIUS Press.

Khodarkovsky, Michael (2002). *Russia's Steppe Frontier. The Making of a Colonial Empire, 1500–1800.* Bloomington: Indiana University Press.

Klier, John Doyle. (1986). *Russia Gathers Her Jews: The Origins of the "Jewish Question" in Russia, 1772–1825.* Dekalb: Northern Illinois Press.

Kohut, Zenon E. (1988). *Russian Centralism and Ukrainian Autonomy: Imperial Absoprtion of the Hetmanate, 1760s–1830s.* Cambridge, MA: Harvard University Press.

Lantzeff, George V., and Pierce, Richard A. (1973). *Eastward to Empire: Exploration and Conquest on the Russian Open Frontier, to 1750.* Montreal: McGill–Queens University Press.

Lieven, Dominic. (2000). *Empire: The Russian Empire and Its Rivals.* London: John Murray.

Loewe, Heinz–Dietrich. (1993). *The Tsars and the Jews: Reform, Realism, and Anti–Semitism in Imperial Russia, 1772–1917.* Chur, Switzerland: Harwood Academic Publications.

Raeff, Marc. (1971). "Patterns of Russian Imperial Policy Toward the Nationalities." In *Soviet Nationality Problems*, ed. Edward Allworth. New York: Columbia University Press.

Riasanovsky, Nicholas V. (1959). *Nicholas I and Official Nationality in Russia, 1825–1855.* Berkeley: University of California Press.

Rogger, Hans. (1986). *Jewish Policies and Right–Wing Politics in Imperial Russia.* Berkeley: University of California Press.

Rywkin, Michael, ed. (1988). *Russian Colonial Expansion to 1917.* London: Mansell Publishing Ltd.

Saunders, David. (2000). "Regional Diversity in the Later Russian Empire." *Transactions of the Royal Historical Society* 6(10):143–163.

Starr, S. Frederick. (1978). "Tsarist Government: The Imperial Dimension." In *Soviet Nationality Policies and Practices*, ed. Jeremy R. Azrael. New York: Praeger.

Suny, Ronald Grigor, ed. (1983). *Transcaucasia. Nationalism and Social Change: Essays in the History of Armenia, Azerbaijan, and Georgia.* Ann Arbor: University of Michigan Press.

Thaden, Edward C., ed. (1981). *Russification in the Baltic Provinces and Finland, 1855–1914.* Princeton, NJ: Princeton University Press.

Thaden, Edward C., with the collaboration of Marianna Forster Thaden. (1984). *Russia's Western Borderlands, 1710–1870.* Princeton, NJ: Princeton University Press.

Tillett, Lowell. (1969). *The Great Friendship: Soviet Historians on the Non-Russian Nationalities.* Chapel Hill: University of North Carolina Press.

Vucinich, Wayne S., ed. (1972). *Russia and Asia: Essays on the Influence of Russia on the Asian Peoples.* Stanford, CA: Stanford University Press.

Weeks, Theodore R. (1996). *Nation and State in Late Imperial Russia: Nationalism and Russification on the Western Frontier, 1863–1914.* De Kalb: Northern Illinois University Press.

ANDREAS KAPPELER

# NATION AND NATIONALITY

The concepts of nation and nationality are extremely difficult to define. According to one important view, a nation is a sovereign people—a voluntary civic community of equal citizens; according to another, a nation is an ethnic community bound by common language, culture, and ancestry. Civic nations and ethnic nations as defined here are ideals that do not exist in reality, for most nations combine civic and ethnic characteristics, and either civic or ethnic features may predominate in any given community. In national communities where citizenship is seen as a major unifying force, the term *nationality* usually denotes citizenship; in nations whose unity rests largely on common culture and ancestry, *nationality* generally refers to ethnic origin.

There is little agreement about the balance between ethnic and civic components within nations, or between subjective characteristics, such as memory and will, and objective elements, such as common language or territory. Most scholars hold that nations are modern sociopolitical constructs, by-products of an industrializing society. But the nature of the links between modern nations and earlier types of communities (e.g., premodern ethnic groups) is hotly contested.

Several definitions of *nation* have existed in Russia since the late eighteenth century, and there was no serious effort to regularize the terminology for discussing the issue of nationality until the 1920s and 1930s. Although the concept of nation was developed in Western Europe and was not applicable to Russia for much of the nineteenth century, the question of what constituted a nation and nationality were debated passionately.

## PREREVOLUTIONARY PERIOD

In the prerevolutionary period, several different words were used in intellectual and political discussions of what constituted a nation in the context of the Russian Empire: *narod*, *narodnost*, *natsionalnost*, *natsiya*, and *plemya*. Despite some efforts to differentiate these terms, they were generally used interchangeably.

In the 1780s and the 1790s, under the impact of the Enlightenment and the French Revolution, a few liberal Russian intellectuals began to use the word *narod* (people) in the meaning most closely approximating the French definition of a nation as a sovereign people. For literary figures like Nikolai Novikov and Alexander Radishchev, nobility and peasantry were united in the narod. They recognized, of course, that such a community was not a reality in Russia but an ideal to be achieved someday. Liberal periodicals of the time proudly printed the word with a capital *N*. The understanding of narod as referring only to the peasantry was a later invention of the so-called Slavophiles of the 1830s and the 1840s, whose ideas were strongly influenced by German Romanticism, which held that folk tradition was the embodiment of the spirit of the nation. The Slavophiles also explicitly separated and juxtaposed the narod and the upper classes, whom they termed "society" (*obshchestvennost*), arguing that society, because Europeanized, was cut off from the indigenous national tradition.

In 1819, the poet Peter Vyazemsky coined the term *narodnost* in reference to national character. A search for manifestations of narodnost in literature, art, and music began. In 1832, the government responded to this growing interest in the national question by formulating its own view of Russia's essential characteristics. The future minister of enlightenment, Count Sergei Uvarov, stated that the three pillars of Russia's existence were Orthodoxy, Autocracy, and Nationality (narodnost, i.e., national character manifested in the folk tradition).

Whereas the Slavophiles looked for manifestations of narodnost in Orthodox Christianity and peasant culture, the Westernizer and literary critic Vissarion Belinsky insisted, in the 1840s, that the educated classes—the product of Peter the Great's Europeanizing policies—were the bearers of a modern national tradition. Belinsky was thus arguing against the Slavophiles as well as Uvarov. He also offered a more precise definition of the words used to describe nation and nationality. For him, narodnost referred to a premodern stage in people's de-velopment, whereas nationalnost and natsiya described superior developmental stages. Belinsky concluded that "Russia before Peter the Great had only been a narod [people] and became a natsiya [nation] as a result of the impetus which the reformer had given her" (Kara-Murza and Poliakov 1994, p. 25).

Other authors adopted Belinsky's distinction between narod and natsiya, but the interchangeable usage prevailed. Even the word *plemya* (tribe), which in the twentieth century was applied to primitive communities, often meant a nation in the nineteenth. Thus, in the 1870s and the 1880s, politicians and intellectuals justified government policies of linguistic Russification in the imperial borderlands by referring to the national consolidation of "the French and German tribes." Nor did Belinsky's search for Russian national tradition in the Europeanized culture of the educated classes have a significant following. Instead, the exclusion of the upper classes from the narod by the early Slavophiles was further developed by the writer and socialist thinker Alexander Herzen in the late 1840s and the early 1850s and by members of the populist movement in the 1870s. After the February Revolution of 1917, in the discourse of elites as well as in popular usage, the upper classes, termed *burzhui* (the bourgeoisie), were excluded from the nation.

The concepts of nation and nationality began to influence tsarist government policies around the time of Alexander II's reforms in the 1860s. At the turn of the twentieth century, the government began to use the language-based idea of nationality (narodnost), rather than religion, as a criterion to distinguish Russians from non-Russians and to differentiate different groups of non-Russians. Narodnost based on language was one of the categories in the all-Russian census of 1897.

The question of how to define the boundaries and membership of a nation or nationality was as much debated by intellectuals, scholars, and government officials in the late nineteenth and the early twentieth centuries as it is in the early twenty-first century. The bibliographer Nikolai Rubakin's survey of the debate on the national question in Russia and Europe (1915) divided the definitions of a nation into three categories: psychological—nations are defined by a subjective criterion, such as the will to belong voluntarily to the same community, as exemplified by the French tradition; empirical—nations are defined by objective characteristics, such as language, customs, common history, sometimes common religion and laws, as exemplified by the German tradition; and economic materialist—nations are a modern construct typical of capitalism, as maintained by Marxists. Rubakin also separately mentioned two other definitions, one equating nation and state, and the other defining nation racially as a community of individuals related by blood. In his view, all of the definitions, except for the psychological one, were expounded in the writings of Russian thinkers. The most influential of them were the concept of nationality based on language and the view that the Europeanized upper classes did not rightfully belong to the national community.

### SOVIET PERIOD

How nation and nationality were defined became exceedingly important in the Soviet period, because, from the earliest days of the communist regime, nationality became a central category of policy-making for the new government. The founders of the Soviet state, Vladimir Lenin and Josef Stalin, followed Karl Marx's perception of nations as historically contingent and modern rather than primordial communities. In 1913, Stalin affirmed that "a nation is not racial or tribal, but a historically constituted community of people" (Hutchinson and Smith 1994, p. 18). Yet the Soviet leaders admitted the reality of nations and recognized their aspiration for self-determination. Although Lenin and Stalin followed Marx's belief in the eventual disappearance of nations in the post-capitalist world, they accepted that nations would continue to exist for some time and that their aspirations would need to be satisfied during the construction of socialism. In an unprecedented experiment, the Bolshevik government institutionalized ethnoterritorial federalism, classified people according to their ethnic origins, and distributed privileges as well as punishments to different ethnically defined groups.

These policies required criteria for defining nations and nationalities more specific than those in effect before the October Revolution. The new criteria were developed in the 1920s and 1930s in preparation for the all-union censuses of 1926, 1937, and 1939. In 1913, Stalin had described a nation (natsiya) as "a stable community of people, formed on the basis of a common language, territory, economic life, and psychological make-up manifested in a common culture" (Hutchinson and Smith 1994, p. 20). In the 1920s, it became apparent that the application of this definition would exclude certain distinct groups from being recog-

nized and recorded in the census. Therefore, in 1926 the less precise category of narodnost was accepted for the census. Given that various groups were seen as denationalized (i.e., they used Russian rather than the original native language of their community), a narodnost could also be defined by customs, religious practices, and physical type. At the same time, people's self-definitions in relation to nationality were taken into account. By 1927, 172 nationalities had received official status in the USSR. Policies aimed at satisfying their "national aspirations" were central to the communist reconstruction of society.

In the 1930s, the number of officially recognized nationalities was drastically reduced, on the grounds that the adoption of the narodnost category had allowed too many groups to receive official recognition. The 1937 and 1939 censuses used a different category, nationality (nationalnost); in order to qualify for the status of natsionalnost, communities had not only to possess a distinct culture and customs but also to be linked to a territory and demonstrate "economic viability." In turn, narodnost began to refer only to smaller and less developed communities. By 1939, a list of fifty-nine major nationalities (glavnye natsionalnosti) was produced.

In an another important development, the 1930s were marked by a departure in official discourse from the view of nations as modern constructs toward an emphasis on their primordial ethnic roots. This development was a result of the government's "extreme statism." By using sociological categories as the basis for organizing, classifying, and rewarding people, the communists were obliged to treat as concrete realities factors that, as they themselves recognized, were actually artificial constructs. This approach, in which nationality was not a voluntary self-definition but a "given" determined by birth, culminated in the introduction of the category of "nationality" (meaning not citizenship but ethnic origin inherited from parents) in Soviet passports in 1932.

The view of nations as primordial ethnic communities was reinforced in the 1960s and 1970s by the new theory of the "ethnos," defined by the Soviet ethnographer Yuly Bromlei as "a historically stable entity of people developed on a certain territory and possessing common, relatively stable features of culture . . . and psyche as well as a consciousness of their unity and of their difference from other similar entities" (Tishkov 1997, p. 3). For Bromlei, the ethnos attains its highest form in the nation. Only communities with their own union or autonomous republics were considered socialist nations.

The same period was marked by a debate about the "Soviet narod," whose existence as a fully formed community was postulated by Leonid Brezhnev in 1974. The Soviet narod was defined as the historical social unity of the diverse Soviet nationalities rather than a single nation. Some ethnographers claimed, however, that a united nation with one language was being created in the USSR.

In the post-communist period, the view of nations as primordial ethnosocial communities continued to be strong. Also widespread was the perception that only one nation can have a legitimate claim on any given territory. Views of this kind are at the root of the ethnic conflicts in the post-Soviet space. At the same time, a competing definition of the nation as a voluntary civic community of equal citizens, regardless of ethnic origin, is gathering strength. Constitutions and citizenship laws in the newly independent states of the former USSR reflect the tensions between these conflicting perceptions of nationhood.

*See also:* ENLIGHTENMENT, IMPACT OF; ETHNOGRAPHY, RUSSIAN AND SOVIET; LANGUAGE LAWS; NATIONALITIES POLICIES, SOVIET; NATIONALITIES POLICIES, TSARIST; SLAVOPHILES

## BIBLIOGRAPHY

Hirsch, Francine. (1997). "The Soviet Union as a Work-in-Progress: Ethnographers and the Category Nationality in the 1926, 1937, and 1939 Censuses." *Slavic Review* 56 (2):251–278.

Hutchinson, John, and Smith, Anthony D., eds. (1994). *Nationalism.* Oxford: Oxford University Press.

Kara-Murza, A., and Poliakov, L., eds. (1994). *Russkie o Petre I.* Moscow: Fora.

Martin, Terry. (2000). "Modernization or Neo-Traditionalism? Ascribed Nationality and Soviet Primordialism" In *Stalinism: New Directions,* ed. Sheila Fitzpatrick. London: Routledge.

Suny, Ronald, and Martin, Terry, eds. (2001). *A State of Nations: Empire and Nation-Making in the Age of Lenin and Stalin.* New York: Oxford University Press.

Tishkov, Valery. (1997). *Ethnicity, Nationalism and Conflict in and After the Soviet Union.* London: Sage.

Tolz, Vera. (2001). *Russia.* New York: Oxford University Press.

VERA TOLZ

**NATO** *See* NORTH ATLANTIC TREATY ORGANIZATION.

## NAVARINO, BATTLE OF

The Battle of Navarino on October 20, 1827, resulted from a joint Anglo-French-Russian effort to mediate the Greek–Ottoman civil war. The three countries decided to intervene in the increasingly brutal conflict, which had been raging since 1821, and on October 1, 1827, British vice admiral Edward Codrington took command of a combined naval force. Codrington ordered his squadron to proceed to Navarino Bay on the southwestern coast of the Peloponnese, where an Ottoman-Egyptian fleet of three ships of the line, twenty-three frigates, forty-two corvettes, fifteen brigs, and fifty transports under the overall command of Ibrahim Pasha was moored.

Before entering the bay, the allied commanders sent Ibrahim an ultimatum demanding that he cease all operations against the Greeks. Ibrahim was absent, but his officers refused, and they opened fire when the allies sailed into the bay on the morning of October 20. In the intense fighting that ensued, the *Azov,* the Russian flagship, was at one point engaged simultaneously by five enemy vessels. Commanded by Mikhail Petrovich Lazarev, the *Azov* sank two frigates and damaged a corvette. The battle was over within four hours. The Ottoman-Egyptian fleet lost all three ships of the line along with twenty-two frigates and seven thousand sailors. Only one battered frigate and fifteen small cruisers survived. The Russian squadron left fifty-nine dead and 139 wounded.

In the aftermath, the recriminations began almost immediately. The duke of Wellington, Britain's prime minister, denounced Codrington's decision to take action as an "untoward event." From the British standpoint, the annihilation of the Turkish-Egyptian fleet was problematic, because it strengthened Russia's position in the Mediterranean. Shortly after the battle Codrington was recalled to London. Tsar Nicholas I awarded the Cross of St. George to Vice Admiral L. P. Geiden, the commander of the Russian squadron, and promoted Lazarev to rear admiral. The *Azov* was granted the Ensign of St. George, which in accordance with tradition would be handed down, over the generations, to other vessels bearing the same name. The Russian squadron recovered from the battle and repaired its ships at Malta. During the Russo-Turkish War of

1828 to 1829, Geiden took command of Rear Admiral Peter Rikord's squadron from Kronstadt. The Russian fleet now numbered eight ships of the line, seven frigates, one corvette, and six brigs. Geiden and Rikord blockaded the Dardanelles and impeded Ottoman-Egyptian operations against the Greeks. After the war's end, Geiden's squadron returned to the Baltic.

*See also:* GREECE, RELATIONS WITH; RUSSO-TURKISH WARS

**BIBLIOGRAPHY**

Anderson, Roger Charles (1952). *Naval Wars in the Levant, 1559–1853.* Princeton, NJ: Princeton University Press.

Daly, John C. K. (1991). *Russian Seapower and the "Eastern Question," 1827–1841.* London: Macmillan.

Daly, Robert Welter. (1959). "Russia's Maritime Past." In *The Soviet Navy*, ed. Malcolm G. Saunders. London: Weidenfeld & Nicolson.

Woodhouse, Christopher Montague. (1965). *The Battle of Navarino.* London: Hoddler & Stoughton.

JOHN C. K. DALY

**NAVY** *See* BALTIC FLEET; BLACK SEA FLEET; MILITARY, IMPERIAL ERA; MILITARY, SOVIET AND POST-SOVIET; NORTHERN FLEET; PACIFIC FLEET.

**Nursultan Nazarbayev, president of independent Kazakhstan.**
HULTON/ARCHIVE. REPRODUCED BY PERMISSION.

## NAZARBAYEV, NURSULTAN ABISHEVICH

(b. 1940), Communist Party, Soviet, and Kazakh government official.

Born into a rural family of the Kazakh Large Horde in the Alma-Ata region, Nursultan Abishevich Nazarbaev finished technical school in 1960, attended a higher technical school from 1964 to 1967, and married Sara Alpysovna, an agronomist-economist. He joined the Communist Party (CPSU) in 1962, began working in both the Temirtau City Soviet and Party Committee in 1969, and advanced rapidly thereafter. In 1976 he graduated from the external program of the CPSU Central Committee's Higher Party School, and from 1977 to 1979 he led the Party's Karaganda Committee. Nazabayev's abilities as a "pragmatic technocrat," and the support of such patrons as the Kazakh Party's powerful first secretary Dinmukhammed Kunayev and Mikhail Andreyevich Suslov and Yuri Vladimirovich Andropov in Moscow ensured his election as a secretary of the Kazakh Central Committee in 1979,

to the Soviet Party's Central Auditing Commission from 1981 to 1986, to chairmanship of the Kazakh SSR's Council of Ministers in 1984, and to the CPSU Central Committee in March 1986.

In the riots following Kunaev's ouster in December 1986, Nazarbayev sought to control student demonstrators. Rather than harming his career, his stance won him considerable support among Kazakh nationalists, and loyalty to Mikhail Gorbachev ensured his place on the Soviet Central Committee. Elected to the new Congress of People's Deputies, he quickly became the Kazakh Party's first secretary when ethnic riots again broke out in June 1989. From February 1990 he also was chairman of the Kazakh Supreme Soviet, which elected him the Kazakh SSR's president in April. He joined the Soviet Politburo in that July but, after briefly temporizing during the August 1991 putsch, left the Soviet Party the following September. He presided over the Kazakh Party's dissolution in October, and then won a massive electoral victory on December 1, 1991. As president, Nazarbaev oversaw formation of an independent Republic of Kazakhstan and its entry into the Commonwealth of Independent States (CIS). Despite deep ethnic, religious, and linguistic divisions; continuing economic crisis; Russian neglect; and bitter political disputes within the elite, he maintained Kazakhstan's unity and position within the CIS. To this end he replaced the parliament with a People's Assembly in 1995, and a referendum extended his term until 2000. Surprising the opposition by calling new elections, Nazarbaev became virtual president-for-life in January 1999 and, with his family dynasty, dominates a powerful cabinet regime that often constrains, but has not abolished, Kazakh civil liberties.

*See also:* COMMUNIST PARTY OF THE SOVIET UNION; KAZAKHSTAN AND KAZAKHS; NATIONALITIES POLICIES, SOVIET

**BIBLIOGRAPHY**

Bremmer, Ian, and Taras, Ray. (1997). *New Politics: Building the Post-Soviet Nations.* Cambridge, UK: Cambridge University Press.

Olcott, Martha Brill. (1995). *The Kazakhs*, 2nd ed. Stanford, CA: Hoover Institution.

Olcott, Martha Brill. (2000). *Kazakhstan: Unfilled Promise.* Washington, DC: Carnegie Endowment for International Peace.

Morozov, Vladimir, ed. (1995). *Who's Who in Russia and the CIS Republics.* New York: Henry Holt.

DAVID R. JONES

## NAZI-SOVIET PACT OF 1939

The Nazi-Soviet Pact is the name given to the Treaty of Non-Aggression signed by Ribbentrop for Germany and Molotov for the USSR on August 23, 1939.

In August 1939, following the failure of attempts to negotiate a treaty with Great Britain and France for mutual assistance and military support to protect the USSR from an invasion by Adolf Hitler, the Soviet Union abandoned its attempts to achieve collective security agreements, which was the basis of Maxim Maximovich Litvinov's foreign policy during the 1930s. Instead, Soviet leaders sought an accommodation with Germany. For German politicians, the dismissal of Litvinov and the appointment of Vyacheslav Mikhailovich Molotov

as commissar for foreign affairs on May 3, 1939, was a signal that the USSR was seeking a rapprochement. The traditional interpretation that Molotov was pro-German, and that his appointment was a direct preparation for the pact, has been called into question. It seems more likely that in appointing Molotov, Joseph Vissarionovich Stalin was prepared to seize any opportunity that presented itself to improve Soviet security.

Diplomatic contact with Germany on economic matters had been maintained during the negotiations with Great Britain and France, and in June and July of 1939, Molotov was not indifferent to initial German approaches for an improvement in political relations. On August 15, the German ambassador proposed that Joachim von Ribbentrop, the German foreign minister, should visit Moscow for direct negotiations with Stalin and Molotov, who in response suggested a nonaggression pact.

Ribbentrop flew to Moscow on August 23, and the Treaty of Nonaggression was signed in a few hours. By its terms the Soviet Union and Germany undertook not to attack each other either alone or in conjunction with other powers and to remain neutral if the other power became involved in a war with a third party. They further agreed not to participate in alliances aimed at the other state and to resolve disputes and conflicts by consultation and arbitration. With Hitler about to attack Poland, the usual provision in treaties of this nature, allowing one signatory to opt out if the other committed aggression against a third party, was missing. The agreement was for a ten-year period, and became active as soon as signed, rather than on ratification.

As significant as the treaty, and more notorious, was the Secret Additional Protocol that was attached to it, in which the signatories established their respective spheres of influence in Eastern Europe. It was agreed that "in the event of a territorial and political rearrangement" in the Baltic states, Finland, Estonia, and Latvia were in the USSR's sphere of influence and Lithuania in Germany's. Poland was divided along the rivers Narew, Vistula, and San, placing Ukrainian and Belorussian territories in the Soviet sphere of influence, together with a part of ethnic Poland in Warsaw and Lublin provinces. The question of the maintenance of an independent Poland and its frontiers was left open. In addition, Germany declared itself "disinterested" in Bessarabia.

**USSR foreign minister Vyacheslav Molotov (right), German foreign minister Joachim von Ribbentrop (left), and Josef Stalin (center) at the signing of the Nazi-Soviet Non-Aggression Pact, August 23, 1939.** © CORBIS

The treaty denoted the USSR's retreat into neutrality when Hitler invaded Poland on September 1, 1939, and Great Britain and France declared war. Poland collapsed rapidly, but the USSR delayed until September 17 before invading eastern Poland, although victory was achieved within a week. From November 1939, the territory was incorporated in the USSR. Estonia and Latvia were forced to sign mutual assistance treaties with the USSR and to accept the establishment of Soviet military bases in September and October of 1939. Finnish resistance to Soviet proposals to improve the security of Leningrad through a mutual assistance treaty led to the Soviet–Finnish War (1939–1940). Lithuania was assigned to the Soviet sphere of influence in a supplementary agreement signed on September 28, 1939, and signed a treaty of mutual assistance with the USSR in October. Romania ceded Bessarabia following a Soviet ultimatum in June 1940.

It is often argued that, in signing the treaty, Stalin, who always believed that Hitler would attack the USSR for *lebensraum*, was seeking time to prepare the Soviet Union for war, and hoped for a considerably longer period than he received, for Germany invaded during June of 1941. Considerable efforts were made to maintain friendly relations with Germany between 1939 and 1941, including a November 1940 visit by Molotov to Berlin for talks with Hitler and Ribbentrop.

The Secret Protocol undermined the socialist foundations of Soviet foreign policy. It called for the USSR to embark upon territorial expansion, even if this was to meet the threat to its security presented by Germany's conquest of Poland. This may explain why, for a long period, the Secret Protocol was known only from the German copy of the document: The Soviet Union denied its existence, a position that Molotov maintained until his death in 1986. The Soviet originals were published for the first time in 1993.

In all Estonia, Latvia, and Lithuania, during August 1987, during the *glastnost* era, demonstrations on the anniversary of the pact were evidence of resurgent nationalism. In early 1990 the states declared their independence, the first real challenge to the continued existence of the USSR.

*See also:* GERMANY, RELATIONS WITH; MOLOTOV, VYACHESLAV MIKHAILOVICH; WORLD WAR II

**BIBLIOGRAPHY**

Read, Anthony, and Fisher, David. (1988) *The Deadly Embrace: Hitler, Stalin, and the Nazi–Soviet Pact, 1939–1941.* New York: Norton.

Roberts, Geoffrey. (1989) *The Unholy Alliance: Stalin's Pact with Hitler.* London: I.B. Tauris.

DEREK WATSON

# NEAR ABROAD

The term *near abroad* is used by the Russian Federation to refer to the fourteen Soviet successor states other than Russia. During the Yeltsin era Russia had to cope with the collapse of Communism and the transition to a market economy, and the end of the Cold War and the loss of superpower status. This caused a national identity crisis that engendered key shifts in Russian foreign policy toward what it designates the near abroad. (The fourteen republics do not call themselves "near abroad.") Should Russia assert itself as the dominant power throughout the territories of the ex-USSR in its desire to protect Russians living abroad? Or alternatively, now that the Cold War was over, should Russia adopt a position enabling reduced prospects of nuclear war and the possibility of the expansion of NATO to include the near abroad countries? This uncertainty, compounded by widespread economic, social, and political instability, affected Russian objectives toward the near abroad. Three different approaches emerged. First, the integrationalists and reformers (such as Andrei Kozyrev) argued that Russia's expansionist days were over and that it must therefore identify more closely with the West, promote Russia's integration into world economy, and ensure that the European security system includes Russia. This means taking a soft, noninterventionist stance on the near

abroad. Second, Centrists and Eurasianists (including Victor Chernomyrdin and Yevgeny Primakov) stressed the need to take into account Russia's history, culture, and geography and to ensure that Russia's national interest is protected. They sought to gain access to the military resources of the successor states, seal unprotected borders, and contain external threats, namely Islamic fundamentalism in Central Asia. For these reasons Centrists and Eurasianists wanted to forge links or build bridges between Russia and Asia (namely Turkey, Iran, Afghanistan, and China). Finally, the traditionalists and nationalists (such as Vladimir Zhirinovsky and Gennady Zyuganov) are anti-Western and pro-Russian/Slavophile. They advocate a neo-imperialist Russian policy that seeks to restore the old USSR (Zyuganov) or at least build stronger links between Russia and other Slavic nations (Zhirinovsky). Such politicians have frequently made reference to alleged abuses of the rights of ethnic Russian or Russian-speaking populations in near abroad countries to justify such a stance.

Throughout the 1990s, reactions to key issues relating to the near abroad varied considerably. Thus nationalists tended to oppose NATO enlargement, criticize Western policy toward the Balkans and Iraq, and be concerned about the fate of Russians abroad, whereas liberals favored growing Western involvement in the ex-USSR and a moderate stance on the near abroad. Russians in general were concerned about the nuclear weapons left in successor states (i.e., Ukraine), with the role of ex-USSR armed forces, and with the possibility that conflicts in successor states (including Tajikistan, Georgia, Moldova, and Azerbaijan) may spread to Russia. Despite the West's initial fears and Russian criticism of NATO's Eastern enlargement, it still went ahead, because Yeltsin preferred to mend fences with Ukraine and improve relations with China and Japan. Also some of his government colleagues (e.g., Primakov) preferred closer relations with Belarus, while others such as Anatoly Chubais wanted closer relations with the West (via IMF, etc.). Furthermore, Yeltsin wanted to retain Western support for Russia's drive toward market and liberal democracy, so he was willing to sacrifice old "spheres of influence" and adopt a less aggressive stance on the near abroad. Yeltsin realized that Russia, weakened by the loss of its superpower status, was no longer able to police the ex-USSR. As a consequence, Yeltsin largely ignored the near abroad in favor of alliances with other powers resentful of American supremacy (e.g., China, India). Throughout the 1990s, Yeltsin pursued a Gorbachev-style policy concerning the West and continued to cut ties with the East while maintaining a watchful eye over the near abroad, a new area of concern, given the presence of up to 30 million ethnic Russians in these countries. Wherever possible Yeltsin sought to maximize Russian influence over the other former Soviet republics. Vladimir Putin has continued to walk the tightrope between assertiveness and integration, taking into account the nature of the new world order of the twenty-first century.

*See also:* CHERNOMYRDIN, VIKTOR STEPANOVICH; KOZYREV, ANDREI VLADIMIROVICH; PRIMAKOV, YEVGENY MAXIMOVICH; YELTSIN, BORIS NIKOLAYEVICH

**BIBLIOGRAPHY**

Kolsto, Pal. (1995). *Russians in the Former Soviet Republics.* Bloomington: Indiana University Press.

Trofimenko, Henry. (1999). *Russian National Interests and the Current Crisis in Russia.* Aldershot, UK: Ashgate.

Williams, Christopher. (2000). "The New Russia: From Cold War Strength to Post-Communist Weakness and Beyond." In *New Europe in Transition*, ed. Peter J. Anderson, Georg Wiessala, and Christopher Williams. London: Continuum.

Williams, Christopher, and Sfikas, Thanasis D. (1999). *Ethnicity and Nationalism in Russia, the CIS, and the Baltic States.* Aldershot, UK: Ashgate.

CHRISTOPHER WILLIAMS

# NECHAYEV, SERGEI GERADIEVICH

(1847–1882), Russian revolutionary terrorist.

Sergei Nechayev epitomizes the notion of using any means, however ruthless, to further revolution. He is perhaps best known for his coauthorship of what is commonly known as the *Catechism of a Revolutionary* (1869). From its initial sentence, "The revolutionary is a doomed man," to its twenty-sixth clause, calling for an "invincible, all-shattering force" for revolution, the *Catechism* has inspired generations of revolutionary terrorists. A public reading of the brief tract and the investigation of the murder of a member of his own organization at the trial of his followers in 1871 gave Nechayev instant notoriety. The notion that the end justified any means repelled most Russian revolutionaries, but others, then and later, admired Nechayev's total commitment to revolution. One of his admirers was Vladimir Lenin. Fyodor Dostoyevsky demonized Nechayev in the guise of Peter Verkhovensky in *The Possessed* (1873), but Rodion Raskolnikov in *Crime and Punishment* (1866) has more psychological features in common with the real person.

Born in Ivanovo, a Russian textile center, the gifted Nechayev had little hope of realizing his ambitions there. In 1866 he moved to St. Petersburg, where he obtained a teaching certificate. He quickly involved himself in the lively student movement in the city's institutions of higher education, and he joined radical circles. The regime's policies had driven the most committed revolutionaries underground, where they formed conspiracies to assassinate Alexander II and to incite the peasants to revolt. In 1868 and 1869 Nechayev began to show his ruthlessness in his methods of recruitment. When a police crackdown occurred in March 1869, he fled to Switzerland to make contact with Russian emigrés, who published the journal *The Bell* in Geneva. Nechayev falsified the extent of the movement and his role in it in order to gain the collaboration of Mikhail Bakunin and Nikolai Ogarev, who, with Alexander Herzen, published the journal. The romantic Bakunin especially admired ruthless men of action, and his connection with Nechayev foreshadowed future relationships between the theorists of revolution and unsavory figures. Before Nechayev's return to Russia in September 1869, he and Bakunin wrote the *Catechism of a Revolutionary* and several other proclamations heralding the birth of a revolutionary conspiracy, the People's Revenge. Bakunin's tie with Nechayev figured in the former's expulsion from the First International in 1872.

With vast energy and unscrupulous methods, Nechayev involved more than one hundred people in his conspiracy. Its only notable achievement, however, was the murder of Ivan Ivanov, who had tried to opt out. Nechayev and four others lured Ivanov to a grotto on the grounds of the Petrov Agricultural Academy in Moscow, where they murdered him on November 21, 1869. Nechayev escaped to Switzerland and remained at large until arrested by Swiss authorities in August 1872. They extradited him to Russia, where he was tried for Ivanov's murder and imprisoned in 1873. Nechayev died in the Peter and Paul Fortress in 1882.

Some historians have presented Nechayev as an extremist who harmed his cause, while others have studied him as a clinical case. Early Soviet historians admired him as a Bolshevik type. In the period of glasnost and after, Russian writers saw in Nechayev a forerunner of Stalin and other pathologically destructive dictators.

See also: BAKUNIN, MIKHAIL ALEXANDROVICH; DOSTOYEVSKY, FYODOR MIKHAILOVICH; HERZEN, ALEXANDER IVANOVICH; TERRORISM

## BIBLIOGRAPHY

Avrich, Paul. (1974). *Bakunin and Nechaev*. London: Freedom Press.

Pomper, Philip. (1979). *Sergei Nechaev*. New Brunswick, NJ: Rutgers University Press.

Prawdin, Michael [Charol, M.]. (1961). *The Unmentionable Nechaev*. New York: Roy Publishers.

Venturi, Franco. (1960). *Roots of Revolution*. New York: Knopf.

PHILIP POMPER

## NEKRASOV, NIKOLAI ALEXEYEVICH

(1821–1878), one of Russia's most famous poets.

Painfully aware of the injustice of serfdom, Nikolai Nekrasov (the "master poet of the peasant masses") was the first poet to make the "People" (*narod*) the focal point of his poetry—especially the downtrodden, who became the symbol of national suffering and exploitation. In one of his masterpieces, the satiric folk epic *Who Can Be Happy and Free in Russia?* (written between 1873 and 1877), seven peasants try endlessly to guess the answer to the question in the title. Nekrasov also served for thirty years as editor of *Sovremenik* (*The Contemporary*), a journal he bought in 1847. Ivan Turgenev, Alexander Herzen, Vissarion Belinsky, and Fyodor Dostoevsky gladly sent their writings to him, and soon Nekrasov became a leading intellectual figure of the time. Censorship was at its height at the beginning of his career, intensified by the French Revolution of 1848 and later the Crimean War (1854–1856), and Nekrasov was only able to write freely after the death of Nicholas I and the accession of the liberal Alexander II.

The decade from 1855 to 1865 was one of the bright periods in Russian literature. Serfdom was abolished (1861), *Sovremenik*'s readership steadily increased, and Nekrasov published some of his finest poems, including "The Peasant Children," "Orina, the Mother of a Soldier," "The Gossips,"

"The Peddlers," and "The Railway." Some contemporaries criticized Nekrasov for his didacticism and prosiness. The enthusiastic response of radical revolutionaries to his poetry confirmed their suspicion that he was primarily a propagandist. But Nekrasov, as he wrote to Leo Tolstoy, believed that the role of a writer was to be a "teacher" and a "representative for the humble and voiceless."

Nekrasov's empathy for the poor and oppressed stemmed from his life experiences. He was the son of a noble family that had lost its wealth and land. His father, an officer in the army, had eloped with the daughter of a Polish aristocrat, inducing her to give up her wealth. The couple settled in Yaroslav Province on the Volga River, where the young Nekrasov could hear and see convicts pass on their way to Siberia. His father, who had become the local police chief, often took Nekrasov with him on his rounds, during which the boy heard the condescending way he spoke to peasants and witnessed the cruel corporal punishments he inflicted on them. When Nekrasov was seventeen, his father sent him to St. Petersburg to join the army, cutting off his funds when he disobeyed and tried to enter the university instead. It took the poet three years of near-starvation before he could make enough money from his writing to survive.

See also: GOLDEN AGE OF RUSSIAN LITERATURE; POPULISM

## BIBLIOGRAPHY

Birkenmayer, Sigmund S. (1968). *Nikolaj Nekrasov: His Life and Poetic Art*. Paris: Mouton.

Kates, J. (1999). *In the Grip of Strange Thoughts: Russian Poetry in a New Era*. Brookline, MA: Zephyr Press.

Peppard, Murray B. (1967). *Nikolai Nekrasov*. New York: Twayne.

Smith, Vassar W. (1996). *Lermontov's Legacy: Selected Poems of Eight Great Russian Poets, with Parallel Texts in English Verse Translation*. Palo Alto, CA: Zapad Press.

JOHANNA GRANVILLE

## NEMCHINOV, VASILY SERGEYEVICH

(1894-1964), Soviet statistician, mathematical economist, and reformer.

Though originally trained as a statistician, Nemchinov became one of the most versatile and productive members of the Soviet economics establishment. During the early period of his career, his specialty was agricultural economics and statistics, on which he published a number of important theoretical works. He developed methods for measuring livestock herds and grain harvests from aerial observations, which were intended to remove human error but led ironically to the scandalous exaggeration of Soviet grain harvests. In 1940 he became director of the Timiryazev Agricultural Academy in Moscow. He was elected academician of the Belorussian Academy of Sciences in 1940, and of the USSR Academy of Sciences in 1946.

Nemchinov was often in political trouble. In 1948, in the struggle with Trofim Lysenko over genetics, he harbored a number of modern geneticists in the Timiryazev Academy and defended them against the Lysenko forces. As a result, he was forced out as Academy director and was even removed from his position in the statistics department. He went home to await arrest, but the Soviet Academy of Sciences stood by him, and he was appointed chairman of a new Council on Productive Forces. He remained an important figure in the Academy, holding, for example, the position of academician-secretary of the department of economic, philosophical, and legal sciences from 1954 to 1958.

The final phase of his career centered on the introduction of mathematical methods into Soviet economics. In 1958, he organized in the Academy of Sciences the first laboratory devoted to the application of mathematical methods in economics, which later became the Central Economic-Mathematical Institute. He was the driving force in setting up the first conference on mathematical methods in economic research and planning in 1960. He headed the scientific council on the use of mathematical methods and computer technology in economic research and planning in the Academy and organized the faculty of mathematical methods of analysis of the economy at Moscow State University. His role in developing linear programming methods and economic models was rewarded posthumously in 1965 by the conferral of the Lenin Prize.

See also: ACADEMY OF SCIENCES; LYSENKO, TROFIM DENISOVICH

BIBLIOGRAPHY

Nemchinov, Vasilii. (1964). *Use of Mathematics in Economics*. Edinburgh: Oliver and Boyd.

ROBERT W. CAMPBELL

## NEMTSOV, BORIS IVANOVICH

(b. 1959), prominent liberal politician and leader of the Union of Right Forces.

Born in Sochi, Boris Ivanovich Nemtsov received a doctorate in physics in 1990. From 1990 to 1993 he was a member of the Congress of People's Deputies, serving on the Council for Legislative Affairs. In 1991 President Boris Yeltsin made him the governor of Nizhny Novgorod.

Nemtsov quickly moved to transform the province into a cutting-edge experiment in free-market economics. Obtaining a license to open a business in post-communist Russia plunged would-be entrepreneurs into a nightmare of bureaucratic corruption. Nemtsov made it possible to register new businesses by mail, and allowed the project to go forward if the petitioner received no answer within a reasonable amount of time. Equally innovative in agricultural affairs, Nemtsov enabled members of collective farms to acquire individual plots, and he introduced tax breaks for struggling businesses. To deal with the inefficient Soviet practice whereby industrial enterprises had to provide housing and other social services for employees, the new governor encouraged companies to raise wages instead so that their workers could afford to pay for rent and utilities. These policies and Nemtsov himself proved immensely popular, and he was elected governor outright in 1995, receiving 60 percent of the vote. Nemtsov was so popular, in fact, that the Yeltsin camp of reformers briefly considered running him for president in 1996 against the communist Gennady Zyuganov. Nothing came of this, but in 1997, after Yeltsin's reelection, Nemtsov reluctantly accepted the office of first deputy prime minister.

In Moscow Nemtsov and his colleagues launched a program of economic "shock therapy." The new deputy minister was charged with making bidding for government contracts more open and competitive, forcing railroads and electricity suppliers to cut their prices, reducing household utility rates by 30 percent, and overhauling the Pension and Securities Insurance Fund. Little wonder Nemtsov called his job "politically suicidal" (Aron, 2000, p. 367).

Nemtsov began by making all government contracts valued at more than 900 million rubles, including military contracts, subject to competitive bidding. He then plunged into the state's sale of 25 percent of Svyazinvest, the national telecommunications enterprise. Nemtsov publicly declared that the sale would be a national test of the government's ability to take on the notorious "oligarchs" who had looted many of Russia's assets in the years after communism.

The losers in the bidding for Svyazinvest used their media outlets to open a blistering campaign against the government, but more serious was a sharp drop in global oil prices, a vital source of government income. Simultaneously a financial crisis that had begun in Asia spread to Russia, causing investors to flee from emerging market economies. By the spring of 1998 Russia was on the verge of economic collapse, and in March Yeltsin dismissed his entire cabinet, including Nemtsov. The following year Nemtsov was elected to the Duma of the Russian Federation.

*See also:* BUREAUCRACY, ECONOMIC; KIRIYENKO, SERGEI VLADILENOVICH; PRIVATIZATION; SHOCK THERAPY; YELTSIN, BORIS NIKOLAYEVICH

**BIBLIOGRAPHY**

Aron, Leon. (2000). *Yeltsin: A Revolutionary Life.* London: HarperCollins.

Talbott, Strobe. (2002). *The Russia Hand: A Memoir of Presidential Diplomacy.* New York: Random House.

HUGH PHILLIPS

**A Nenets woman and her two children from Antipayuta settlement, northern Russia.** © JACQUES LANGEVIN/CORBIS SYGMA

# NENETS

The Nenets are the most numerous of Russia's northern peoples, numbering about 35,000, and one of the most northerly. Their homelands stretch along the Arctic coast, from northeastern Europe to the Taymyr Peninsula. Most Nenets are concentrated in the Nenets Autonomous District and the Yamalo-Nenets Autonomous District. Much of their territory is tundra; and their economy, based on large-scale reindeer pastoralism, has been the main adaptation to this harsh environment. The Nenets language belongs to the Samoyedic branch of the Uralic languages. Language retention among Nenets is higher than among most other northern peoples, due to the remoteness of their settlements and their continuing nomadism.

Western Nenets have a long history of contact with Russians, some paying tribute to Novgorod by the thirteenth century, and to the Tatars shortly thereafter. As Russians began to colonize Siberia in the mid-seventeenth century they met occasional fierce resistance from Nenets groups. They also incorporated Nenets into state-building projects, resettling some to Novaya Zemlya in the nineteenth century, in an effort to ensure sovereignty over those islands.

The Soviets began to establish reindeer-herding collective farms in Nenets territory in 1929. Repression of wealthy herders followed, as did the confiscation of their reindeer and the general sedentarization of children, elderly, and some women. Nenets opposed such moves in several uprisings, which the Soviets quelled, then covered up. However, given the minimal prospects for developing this part of the Arctic, the Soviets generally encouraged the continuation of traditional Nenets activities.

Nenets homelands are particularly rich in oil and gas deposits. As technology improved by the latter twentieth century, making exploitation of these resources viable even given the harsh Arctic clime, development ensued. The greatest challenges for the Nenets became the construction of gas wells and pipelines across their reindeer pastures. Reindeer herds at the beginning of the twenty-first century exceeded pasture carrying capacity, and pasture destruction due to hydrocarbon development has exacerbated this problem. Development also encouraged massive in-migration into Nenets homelands by non-Nenets peoples. In post-Soviet years, these gas-rich areas experienced less out-migration than other northern areas.

Since the demise of the Soviet Union, Nenets have actively pursued their rights, creating regional Nenets organizations for this purpose. Reindeer-herding leaders have established ties with herders in Finland, Sweden, and Norway to pursue complementary agendas of economic development and environmental protection.

*See also:* NATIONALITIES POLICIES, SOVIET; NATIONALITIES POLICIES, TSARIST; NORTHERN PEOPLES; SIBERIA

**BIBLIOGRAPHY**

Golovnev, Andrei V., and Osherenko, Gail. (1999). *Siberian Survival: The Nenets and Their Story.* Ithaca, NY: Cornell University Press.

Krupnik, Igor. (1993). *Arctic Adaptations: Native Whalers and Reindeer Herders of Northern Eurasia.* Hanover, NH: University Press of New England.

GAIL A. FONDAHL

# NEOCLASSICISM

Neoclassicism is often termed simply classicism in Russia as, unlike those European countries which had experienced the Renaissance, Russia was exploring the classical vocabulary of ancient Greece and Rome for the first time. Classical motifs had appeared in Russia in the seventeenth and early eighteenth centuries but it was not until the 1760s that a coherent classical revival emerged, fueled by the work of scholars such as Johann Joachim Winckelmann, whose publications were generating a more comprehensive understanding of the forms and functions of classical art. The effect of this growing veneration for the noble grandeur of classical forms is evident in the Marble Palace (1768–1785) in St. Petersburg by Antonio Rinaldi, in which the flamboyant exuberance of the Baroque is partially displaced by a more dignified restraint. Jean-Baptiste Vallin de la Mothe also applied neoclassical principles in his design for the Academy of Arts (1765–1789), itself a prime conduit of European artistic debates. The low dome, rusticated basement, and giant order of columns and pilasters serve as a visual reminder of the classical ideal to which the Academy's students were expected to aspire.

During Catherine II's reign, neoclassicism flourished in the private sphere, notably in the work that the Scottish architect Charles Cameron undertook at Tsarskoye Selo after his arrival in Russia in 1779. Cameron, who greatly admired the studies of the antique by Andrea Palladio and Charles-Louis Clérisseau and had himself published drawings of Roman baths, decorated his interiors at Tsarskoye Selo with glass or ceramic columns and molded plaster reliefs inspired by recently-discovered classical sites. Cameron went on to work for Catherine's son Paul at Pavlovsk, where his Temple of Friendship (1780–1782) in the park correctly deployed the Greek Doric order for the first time in Russia. The classical revival was also gathering momentum in the work of the Italian architects Vincenzo Brenna and Giacomo Quarenghi, who had worked with the great neoclassical artist Anton Raphael Mengs in Rome. The Hermitage Theater (1783–1787), one of Quarenghi's masterpieces, is articulated with giant engaged Corinthian columns, niches, and statuary, while the great curved form of the auditorium is visible from the outside.

Russian as well as foreign architects were working in the neoclassical style. Vasily Bazhenov, who had studied abroad as one of the first two recipients of a travel scholorship from the Academy of Arts, designed an enormous new palace complex for the Moscow Kremlin in 1768. While never realized for financial reasons, it would have applied the language of classicism on a monumental scale. His contemporary Matvei Kazakov never studied abroad, as Bazhenov had done, but brought Moscow neoclassicism to its apogee in the Senate in the Kremlin (1776–1787). Like its near contemporary in London, William Chambers's Somerset House, the Senate building uses the authority of classical forms to signify power and public purpose.

Under Alexander I, neoclassicism, also known in this period as the Alexandrian or Empire style, became increasingly prominent in the public domain. Designed by the serf-architect Andrei Voronikhin, the Mining Institute (1806–1811) in St. Petersburg included a twelve-column Doric portico and pediment based on the Temple of Poseidon at Paestum, while Thomas de Thomon reconstructed the Stock Exchange (1805–1810) as a Greek temple. The most ambitious project was Adrian Zakharov's new Admiralty (1806–1823), in which strong geometric masses and classical ornamentation coexist with specifically Russian references. The great central pavilion is decorated with free-standing and low-relief sculptures and an open colonnade, and yet is topped by a golden spire which recalls that of the old Admiralty, while the frieze over the portal depicts Neptune presenting a trident to Peter the Great. These allegorical and structural references to the Russian past result in a distinctly national interpretation of the neoclassical style.

Not that the language of classicism was always suitable for Russian aims. The awkward proportions of the Cathedral of St. Isaac (1819–1859) by Auguste Montferrand is testimony to how disastrous some attempts to design an Orthodox church in a classical style could be. Far more successful during Nicholas I's reign is the work of Carlo Rossi, whose concern with entire architectural ensembles in St. Petersburg underlines his flair for the classical organization of space, for example in the streets, squares, and buildings that he designed to complement his Alexandrinsky Theatre (1828–1832), or in the General Staff Building (1819–1829), which completed Palace Square. This interest in town planning reverberated in provincial towns such as Odessa, where boulevards parallel to the cliff-top benefit from the dramatic views over the Black Sea.

Painting and sculpture made a less distinguished contribution to neoclassicism in Russia than architecture, but certain artists stand out. During the last quarter of the eighteenth century, Mikhail Kozlovsky produced some notable sculpture on classical themes, and his monument to General Suvorov portrayed the military leader rather improbably as an athletic young Mars. Ivan Martos, who had studied with Mengs in Rome, also attempted to invest his work with both Russian meanings and references to antiquity in his statue of Minin and Pozharsky (1804–1818) on Red Square, in which seventeenth-century heroes are clothed in a hybrid of classical tunics and the traditional Russian garb of long, belted shirts worn over trousers. Martos deployed the extravagant rhetorical gestures typical of much ancient sculpture, a device continued in Boris Orlovsky's statues of Marshal Kutuzov and Barclay de Tolly in front of the Cathedral of the Virgin of Kazan in St. Petersburg. On a more intimate note, Fyodor Tolstoy designed bas-relief sculptures reminiscent of the work of the English neoclassical sculptor John Flaxman, while his acclaimed portrait medallions commemorating the Napoleonic War filtered patriotic sensibilities through the classical tradition of coin and medal design.

In painting, Anton Losenko's Vladimir and Rogneda of 1770 initiated a tradition of depicting Russian historical subjects in the so-called Grand Manner, the approved Academic approach which drew heavily on the classical practice of idealization, by the nineteenth century academic history painters were expected to work in the neoclassical style. In Fyodor Bruni's painting *Death of Camilla, the Sister of Horatio* (1824), the classical hero, who has placed civic virtue above familial sentiment, strikes a suitably grandiloquent pose in the center of a composition arranged like a bas-relief. But the pictorial devices of neoclassicism were already being tempered by Romantic sensibilities, as is evident in Orest Kiprensky's *Portrait of Alexander Pushkin* (1827) and Karl Bryullov's *The Last Day of Pompeii* (1830–1833). Kiprensky may include a classical statuette in his portrait, and Bryullov may have chosen a classical subject, but the emphasis is now on the Romantic values of subjectivity and personal emotion, as opposed to the harmonic proportion and physical perfection of classical art.

*See also:* ACADEMY OF ARTS; ARCHITECTURE; CATHERINE II; KREMLIN; MOSCOW BAROQUE

**BIBLIOGRAPHY**

Auty, Robert, and Obolensky, Dmitri, eds. (1980). *An Introduction to Russian Art and Architecture.* Cambridge, UK: Cambridge University Press.

Brumfield, William C. (1993). *A History of Russian Architecture.* Cambridge, UK: Cambridge University Press.

Kennedy, J. (1983). "The Neoclassical in Russian Sculpture." In *Art and Culture in Nineteenth-Century Russia,* ed. T. G. Stavrou. Bloomington: Indiana University Press.

Sarabianov, Dmitry. (1990). *Russian Art from Neoclassicism to the Avant-Garde.* London: Thames and Hudson.

Shvidkovsky, Dmitry. (1996). *The Empress and the Architect: British Architecture and Gardens at the Court of Catherine the Great.* New Haven, CT: Yale University Press.

ROSALIND P. GRAY

# NERCHINSK, TREATY OF

The Treaty of Nerchinsk was a Sino-Russian peace treaty negotiated and signed at the Siberian border point of Nerchinsk in August and September 1689.

Armed conflict in the Far East of Russia rose out of the advance of Russian colonists to Dahuria during the middle of the seventeenth century, since the Manchus claimed the Amur basin. The growing tension came to a head in the sieges of the fortress of Albazin in 1685 and 1686, when the Manchus ultimately forced the Russians to surrender. In a bid to settle the problem, in 1685 the Russian government appointed Fyodor Alexeyevich Golovin as its first ambassador plenipotentiary to China. His brief was to delineate a border on the Amur and gain the Russians a secure right to trade in the river valley.

After two weeks of negotiations with Songgotu and T'ung Kuo-kang, a peace treaty was signed in September 1689 and the preconditions created for a stable trading relationship. The Russians ended up ceding all rights to the Amur valley, as well as to Albazin, but gained a regularized and potentially lucrative commercial relationship. The Chinese, having secured the areas near the Ch'ing dynasty's ancestral home, permitted the Russians to keep Nerchinsk, recognizing its potential for trade. Merchants from either side were to be permitted to visit the other with proper passports. The arrival of the Manchu delegation for the negotiations also marked the beginning of large-scale border trade: At least 14,160 rubles' worth of goods were imported that year from China through the new frontier trading post.

The treaty envisaged Russian caravans traveling to Beijing once every three years, but during the decade following Nerchinsk, such trips were made more or less annually. In 1696 alone, 50,000 rubles' worth of furs were exported via Nerchinsk.

The treaty put an end to Sino-Russian armed conflict for 165 years.

See also: CHINA, RELATIONS WITH; FOREIGN TRADE

**BIBLIOGRAPHY**

Foust, Clifford M. (1969). *Muscovite and Mandarin: Russia's Trade with China and its Setting, 1725–1805.* Chapel Hill: University of North Carolina Press.

Mancall, Mark. (1971). *Russia and China: Their Diplomatic Relations to 1728* (Harvard East Asian Series 61). Cambridge, MA: Harvard University Press.

Miasnikov, Vladimir Stepanovich. (1985). *The Ch'ing Empire and the Russian State in the Seventeenth Century,* tr. Vic Schneierson. Moscow: Progress.

JARMO T. KOTILAINE

# NERONOV, IVAN

(1591–1670), ardent worker for church reform, first in the provinces and later in Moscow. He opposed Nikon and church reforms he implemented and suffered for his opposition.

Neronov was of humble birth, but learned to read. He entered a church near Ustiug as a reader and chanter. Appalled by the lax manners and morals of the local clergy, Neronov complained to Patriarch Filaret, manifesting his zeal for religious reform. By the mid-1620s, Neronov had relocated to a village in the Nizhny Novgorod region. Many of those who would be energetic supporters of church reform in the second half of the seventeenth century were connected with this region. During the Smolensk War (1632–1633), Neronov moved to Moscow. In the mid-1640s he was associated with the Zealots of Piety, a circle of church reformers centered on the court and led by Tsar Alexis Mikhailovich's confessor, Stefan Vonifatiev. In 1649 he was named archpriest of the Kazan Cathedral in Moscow. Early in 1653 Neronov was among the first to challenge the revised liturgical books printed under Patriarch Nikon. Retribution was swift: By the end of 1653 Neronov had been defrocked and exiled in chains to a monastery near Vologda. There he took monastic vows and assumed the name Grigory. Called before the Church Council of 1666, Neronov renounced his opposition to the new liturgies. Subsequently he was made archimandrite of a monastery near Moscow, where he lived out his days seeking reform within his monastery.

See also: CHURCH COUNCIL; MONASTICISM; PATRIARCHATE; RELIGION; RUSSIAN ORTHODOX CHURCH

**BIBLIOGRAPHY**

Michels, Georg B. (1999). *At War with the Church: Religious Dissent in Seventeenth-Century Russia.* Stanford, CA: Stanford University Press.

CATHY J. POTTER

# NESSELRODE, KARL ROBERT

(1770–1862), Russian foreign minister equivalent, 1814–1856; chancellor, 1845–1856.

A baptized Anglican son of a Catholic Westphalian in Russia's diplomatic service, a Berlin gymnasium graduate, and briefly in the Russian navy and army, Karl Nesselrode began his diplomatic career in 1801. Posted in Stuttgart, Berlin, and the Hague and attracted to the conservative equilibrium ideas of Friedrich von Gentz even more than Metternich was, Nesselrode became an advocate of the Third Coalition, yet assisted in the drawing up the Treaty of Tilsit (1807) and served in Paris. He played a major role in the forging of the 1813–1814 coalitions and the first Treaty of Paris (1814) and became Alexander I's chief plenipotentiary at Vienna (1814–1815). Sharing the direction of Russia's foreign affairs from 1814 to 1822 with the more liberal state secretary for foreign affairs, Ioannes Capodistrias, Nesselrode participated in the Congresses of Aix-la-Chapelle (1818), Laibach (1821), and Verona (1822). His European approach to the Eastern Question won over Alexander and led to the compromises after the Greek Rebellion of 1821.

Nesselrode's wide knowledge, clarity, complete loyalty to the crown, and earlier briefings of Nicholas I before 1825 led to retention by the latter in 1826. Though Nicholas often directed policy himself, Nesselrode remained the single most influential Russian in external affairs. He shepherded the London Protocol (with Britain, 1826) and the Convention of Akkerman (with Turkey, 1827), convinced Nicholas I to accept the moderate Treaty of Adrianople (with Turkey, 1829), and helped dissuade Nicholas from trying to depose Louis-Philippe of France (1830). Partially behind the defensive Russo-Turkish Treaty of Unkiar-Skelessi (1833), he promoted the Conventions of Münchengrätz and Berlin (1833), which associated Austria and Prussia with a status quo policy regarding the Ottoman Empire.

Nesselrode subsequently helped prevent rising tensions with Britain from turning violent in 1838 by blocking a scheme to send warships into the Black Sea and removing Russia's belligerently anti-British envoy to Tehran. Promoting compromises with Britain during the entire Eastern crisis of 1838–1841, Nesselrode blocked support of Serbian independence in 1842–1843 and limited the damage from Nicholas's indescretions during his 1844 visit to England. Fearful of liberalization in Central Europe, Nesselrode supported the full restoration of monarchial power and the status quo there in 1848 and 1850 against both popular and Prussian expansionist aspirations.

During the Eastern Crisis of 1852–1853, Russia's nationalists achieved the upper hand. Nessel-

rode alerted the emperor about the dangers of undue pressure on the Ottomans but abetted the deceptions perpetrated by Russian's mission in Istanbul and his own ministry's Asiatic Department. Although he was one of the best "spin doctors" of his era, his eighteenth-century logic, devotion to the 1815 settlement, and impeccable French prose could not prevail over the determination of Nicholas and the nationalists to risk war with Britain and France and have their way with Turkey regarding the Holy Places and Russia's claimed protectorate over the Ottoman Orthodox. Nor could he convince Austria to back Russia, but in the course of the Crimean War he continuously promoted a compromise and helped convince Alexander II to end hostilities in 1856.

*See also:* ALEXANDER I; CRIMEAN WAR; NICHOLAS I; VIENNA, CONGRESS OF

## BIBLIOGRAPHY

Grimsted, Patricia Kennedy. (1969). *The Foreign Ministers of Alexander I.* Berkeley: University of California Press.

Ingle, Harold N. (1976). *Nesselrode and the Russian Rapprochement with Britain, 1836–1844.* Berkeley: University of California Press.

Walker, Charles E. (1973). "The Role of Karl Nesselrode in the Formulation and Implementation of Russian Foreign Policy, 1850–1956." Ph.D. diss., University of West Virginia, Morgantown.

DAVID M. GOLDFRANK

# NET MATERIAL PRODUCT

Net material product (NMP), the approach to national accounts based on Material Product System (MPS), was introduced in the USSR in the 1920s. Harmonized in 1969 by the Statistical Commission of the Council for Mutual Economic Assistance (CMEA), it was adopted by all centrally planned economies.

The central indicator of the (Western) System of National Accounts (SNA) is gross domestic product (GDP), which is a basic measure of a country's overall economic performance. For planned economies, the role of the main indicator in the MPS is assigned to the net material product.

NMP covers material production (industry, agriculture, construction) and also includes material services that bring material consumer goods from producers to consumers (transport and trade) and maintain the capital stock (maintenance and repairs). Nonmaterial services, such as health, education, administration, business, and personal services, are not included in productive activities; therefore, the central indicator NMP encompasses only the total income generated in the material branches, and the distinction is kept between "intermediate" and "final" products and between consumption and accumulation.

The division of services into "material" and "nonmaterial" originates from a theoretical proposition of Karl Marx's writings. Marx , in the classical tradition of Adam Smith, considered as productive only activities that yield tangible, material goods.

Numerous incidental differences exist between GDP and NMP, including the treatment of business travel expenses, which are intermediate consumption in the SNA but labor compensation, and therefore part of the sectoral NMP, in the MPS. Cultural and welfare services provided by enterprises to employees are also intermediate consumption in the SNA but final consumption in the MPS. Some losses on fixed capital, the borderline between current and capital repair, and other relatively small items are treated differently. SNA has displaced MPS in all transition economies.

*See also:* ECONOMIC GROWTH, SOVIET; MARXISM

**BIBLIOGRAPHY**

World Bank. (1992). *Statistical Handbook: States of the Former USSR.* Studies of Economies in Transformation, 3. Washington, DC: World Bank.

World Bank. (1993). *Historically Planned Economies: A Guide to the Data.* Washington, DC: World Bank.

MISHA V. BELKINDAS

## NEVSKY, ALEXANDER YAROSLAVICH *See* ALEXANDER YAROSLAVICH.

## NEW ECONOMIC POLICY

As the civil war wound down in late 1920 and famine caused millions of deaths, peasant rebellions broke out against the compulsory grain procurements (*prodrazverstka*), which had been extracted by force and had led to reduced plantings. Strikes occurred in Petrograd and elsewhere. Late that winter an uprising occurred at Kronstadt, the naval base near the northern capital. Fearing counterrevolution from within, Vladimir Ilich Lenin accepted a "retreat" at the Tenth Party Congress in March, 1921. Under the New Economic Policy (NEP), Russia would have a mixed economy "seriously and for a long time," as Lenin said. It would be based on an alliance (*smychka*) between the workers and the peasants.

Requisitions from the peasantry would be replaced by a tax in kind (*prodnalog*) based on the rural household's level of income and its number of dependents. (By 1923–1924, by which time the inflation was halted, this tax was converted to cash.) Peasants would be free to market any surplus left after mandatory deliveries, which were reduced from the quotas imposed in 1920–1921. Some effort was made to establish scientific farms and to persuade peasants to enter cooperatives, but few did until the forced collectivization of 1928–1929. Rural, interregional, and retail trade was freed, somewhat reluctantly, and taken up by privateers, known universally as "nepmen." Prices were effectively free, despite the government's efforts to fix them for such monopolized commodities as tobacco, salt, kerosene, and matches. Trade unions became voluntary, and workers were free to seek whatever employment they could find.

In 1921 the Soviet government decided to lease back or sell back most medium- and small-sized enterprises to private owners or cooperatives. The largest 8.5 percent of them, called the "commanding heights," were retained. They employed six-sevenths of all the industrial workers and produced more than nine-tenths of all industrial output even at the peak of NEP in 1925–1926. These larger factories were coordinated by the Supreme Council of National Economy (*Vesenkha*) and its "trusts." Banks, railroads, and foreign trade also remained in the hands of the state. But the state had insufficient fuel and materials to keep the larger plants open. Unemployment grew. Efforts to attract foreign concessionaires to provide timber, oil, and other materials were mostly unavailing. The sixty-eight foreign concessions that existed by 1928 provided less than 1 percent of industrial output. Foreign capitalists were rather reluctant to invest in a hostile and chaotic environment with a Bolshevik state that had defaulted on all tsarist debts, confiscated foreign property, and declared its intentions to overthrow the capitalist order worldwide.

To achieve some measure of efficiency the state now required industrial enterprises to operate on commercial principles (*khozraschet*), paying wages and other bills and to sell, even at distressed prices relative to the rising relative price of foodstuffs. By 1923–1924, the government balanced its budget by levying excise taxes, enterprise and personal taxes on income and property, and a forced bond issue. The tsarist vodka monopoly was reintroduced, to the dismay of many. Centralized expenditures, especially on education, were cut, and school fees introduced. All this allowed stabilization of the new currency (*chervonets*), which had replaced the ruined ruble or *sovznak* notes used before.

The NEP period was also the golden era of Soviet economics, with many different points of view, mathematical and sociological, permitted to publish and debate. Nikolai Kondratiev, Alexander Chayanov, Yevgeny Preobrazhensky, Grigory Feldman, Stanislav Strumilin, and the young Vasily Leontiev, inventor of input–output analysis, were active at this time. In addition to theoretical matters, the industrialization debate centered on whether Russia's peasant economy could produce enough voluntary savings to permit industrialization beyond the recovery phase. That debate, and most free inquiry, would end in 1928. Political freedom had already been closely limited to the Bolsheviks alone; by 1922 publications had to pass prior censorship.

In practice, planning was still rudimentary. There was no operational program for command allocations, as there would be during the 1930s, but the "balance of national economy," patterned on German wartime experience, served as a kind of forecast for key sectors and basis for discussion of investment priorities.

These policies were strikingly successful in allowing the Soviet economy to regain its prewar levels of agricultural and industrial production by 1926–1927. School enrollment exceeded the prewar numbers. But food marketings, both domestic and export, were down significantly, probably owing to the higher cost and relative unavailability of manufactured goods the peasants wanted to buy and also the breakup of larger commercial farms during the Revolution and civil war. Yet by 1927 reduced grain marketings convinced many in the Party (particularly the so-called left opposition) that administrative methods would be needed in addition to market incentives. Even though this was largely due to a mistaken price and tax policy by the government—comparable to the earlier Scissors Crisis—the authorities now began to use "extraordinary measures" to seize grain early in 1928. This policy and its consequences effectively ended the NEP, for once it was decided that industrialization and military preparedness required more investments than could be financed from voluntary savings in this largely peasant country, the way was open for Josef Stalin to pursue a radical course of action, once advanced by his enemies Leon Trotsky and his allies on the left.

*See also:* COMMANDING HEIGHTS OF THE ECONOMY; GOODS FAMINE; GRAIN CRISIS OF 1928; SCISSORS CRISIS; TRUSTS, SOVIET; WAR COMMUNISM

**BIBLIOGRAPHY**

Carr, Edward Hallett. (1958). *Socialism in One Country, 1924–1926*, vol. 1. London: Macmillan.

Davies, R. W. (1989). "Economic and Social Policy in the USSR, 1917–41." In *The Cambridge Economic History of Europe from the Decline of the Roman Empire, Vol. 8: The Industrial Economies: The Development of Economic and Social Policies*, ed. Peter Mathias and Sidney Pollard. Cambridge, UK: Cambridge University Press.

Erlich, Alexander. (1960). *The Soviet Industrialization Debate, 1924–1928*. Cambridge, MA: Harvard University Press.

Nove, Alec. (1969). *An Economic History of the USSR*. London: Allen Lane.

MARTIN C. SPECHLER

# NEW-FORMATION REGIMENTS

The term *new-formation* ("western-model," "foreign-model," or "western-formation") regiment refers to military units organized in linear formations, utilizing gunpowder weapons and tactics developed in the West. These regiments consisted of eight to ten companies, each ideally numbering 100 (infantry) to 120 (cavalry and dragoons) soldiers, though few regiments were at full strength. The colonel and lieutenant colonel commanded the first and second companies of the regiment, though de facto command of the colonel's company was given to a first (lieutenant) captain. Captains or lieutenants (either Russian or European) commanded the remaining companies. Other personnel included ensigns, sergeants, and corporals, at the company level, and administrative officers, such as captains of arms, quartermasters, camp masters, clerks, priests, drummers, and buglers. The regiments featured combined arms: muskets, pikes, artillery, grenadiers, and engineers (sappers, miners). The predominant organizational features of the new-formation regiment were its hierarchical command structure and its relative tactical flexibility.

New-formation regiments participated in the major campaigns of the seventeenth century. The first regiments were formed prior to the Smolensk War (1632–1634). The state employed European officers to train and arm Russians to fight in the Western manner, which represented a significant departure from the former practice of hiring entire regiments of foreign troops. The impact of these officers is reflected in the fact that the Treaty of Polyanovka (1634) ordered Russia's foreign mercenary commanders to leave Muscovy after the war, though Alexander Leslie, Adam Gell-Seitz, and others returned to help reorganize Muscovy's regiments again during the 1640s.

Between 1630 and 1634 ten regiments were formed, comprising seventeen thousand men, nearly half of the Russian army at Smolensk. During the Thirteen Years' War, new-formation regiments constituted a significant portion of Russia's armed forces: fifty-five infantry and twenty cavalry regiments. The cost of these regiments was greater than traditional forces because the state supported their supply and salary needs.

The regiments in the 1630s were formed from marginal groups, such as landless gentry, Cossacks, Tatars, and free people (*volnye liudi*, unattached to towns, estates, or communes). Increased income and status associated with state service motivated these groups to assimilate into the new-formation regiments. During the 1650s and 1660s the new-formation regiments included more and more peasants and townsmen, whom the Russians conscripted to offset heavy wartime losses. The nature of the soldiers serving in the new-formation regiments changed over time, though they continued to include marginal groups. Later in the century (1680s–1690s), the new-formation regiments continued to be a stage for retraining traditional forces.

The state continued to hire European officers to command new-formation regiments throughout the seventeenth century. Russians also held command positions in the regiments, most predominantly in ranks below colonel. Tensions existed among the foreign and Russian officers, especially regarding administration and implementation of the regiments. The foreign officers brought with them their military experience and technical literature to train their regiments. Since few printed military manuals were available in Russian, the foreign officers' contribution to military reform is immeasurable. Nonetheless the state distributed a translation of Johann Jacobi von Wallhausen's *Kriegskunst zu Fuss* (*Military Art of Infantry*) to the colonels for use in training, and the state also received input from European officers—in the form of reports and letters—about the training and equipment needs of the regiments.

*See also:* SMOLENSK WAR; THIRTEEN YEARS' WAR

**BIBLIOGRAPHY**

Hellie, Richard. (1971). *Enserfment and Military Change in Muscovy.* Chicago: Chicago University Press.

Reger, W. M., IV. (1997). "In the Service of the Tsars: European Mercenary Officers and the Reception of Military Reform in Russia, 1654–1667." Ph.D. diss., University of Illinois, Urbana–Champaign.

Stevens, Carol. (1995). *Soldiers on the Steppe: Army Reform and Social Change in Early Modern Russia.* DeKalb: Northern Illinois University Press.

W. M. REGER IV

# NEW POLITICAL THINKING

The phrase "New Political Thinking" (or, simply, "New Thinking") was introduced in the Soviet Union early in the Gorbachev era. While to some observers it seemed no more than a new twist to Soviet propaganda, in fact it represented an increasingly radical break with fundamentals of Soviet ideology.

The New Thinking linked Soviet domestic political reform with innovation in foreign policy. Gorbachev was in a minority within the Soviet leadership in espousing ideas that were radically new in the Soviet context. However, he was able to draw on intellectual support from research institutes in which fresh ideas had surfaced but had hitherto lacked political support where it mattered-at the top of the Communist Party hierarchy. With the institutional resources of the general secretaryship at his disposal, Gorbachev was able to give decisive support to innovative thinkers and to legitimize new concepts. Initially, as in Gorbachev's 1987 book, *Perestroika: New Thinking for Our Country and the World*, the new ideas were already revising previous Soviet ideology in significant ways; but a year or two later they had gone much further, amounting to a conceptual revolution that shook the Soviet system to its foundations.

It was in 1987 that Gorbachev first used the term "pluralism" in a positive sense, albeit in a qualified form as "socialist pluralism" or a "pluralism of opinion." Hitherto, "pluralism" had always been a pejorative term in the Soviet lexicon, condemned as an alien and bourgeois notion. Once the taboo on praising pluralism had been broken, articles on the need to develop pluralism within the Soviet Union began to appear, often without the "socialist" qualifier. By 1990 Gorbachev himself was advocating "political pluralism." Another concept on which an anathema had been pronounced for many years was "market," but again—for example, in his 1987 book—Gorbachev embraced the idea of a "socialist market." Before long other contributors to the growing debates in the Soviet Union were advocating a market economy, some of them explicitly differentiating this from socialism as they understood it.

The New Political Thinking could, in its earliest manifestations, be seen as a new Soviet ideology, a codified, albeit genuinely innovative, body of correct thinking. It gave way, however, to a growing freedom of speech and of debate both within the Communist Party and in the broader society—a new political reality that partly resulted from the boldness of the intellectual breakthrough.

Among the new concepts that were given Gorbachev's official imprimatur between 1985 and 1988 were the principle of a state based on the rule of law, the idea of checks and balances, glasnost (openness or transparency), perestroika (literally reconstruction, but a term that became a synonym for the radical reform of the Soviet system), democratization (which initially meant freer discussion within the Communist Party but by 1988—at the Nineteenth Party Conference—had come to embrace the principle of contested elections for a new legislature), and civil society.

The New Political Thinking represented no less of a break with the Soviet past in its foreign policy dimension. A class approach to international relations was explicitly discarded in favor of the idea of all-human interests and universal values. The idea of global interdependence superseded the zero-sum-game philosophy of *kto kogo* (who will crush whom). Whereas in the past the "struggle for peace" had often been a thin disguise for the pursuit of Soviet great-power interests, the new thinking endorsed by Gorbachev stressed that in the

nuclear age peace was the only rational option if humankind was to survive. This provided justification for a new and genuinely cooperative approach to international relations.

*See also:* DEMOCRATIZATION; GLASNOST; GORBACHEV, MIKHAIL SERGEYEVICH; PERESTROIKA

**BIBLIOGRAPHY**

Brown, Archie (ed.). (2004). *The Demise of Marxism-Leninism in Russia.* London: Palgrave.

Chernyaev, Anatoly. (2000). *My Six Years with Gorbachev.* Philadelphia: Pennsylvania State University Press.

Gorbachev, Mikhail. (1987). *Perestroika: New Thinking for our Country and the World.* London: Collins.

Nove, Alec. (1989). *Glasnost in Action.* London: Unwin Hyman.

Palazchenko, Pavel. (1997). *My Years with Gorbachev and Shevardnadze: The Memoir of a Soviet Interpreter.* Philadelphia: Pennsylvania State University Press.

Yakovlev, Alexander. (1993). *The Fate of Marxism in Russia.* New Haven, CT: Yale University Press.

ARCHIE BROWN

# NEWSPAPERS

The first news sheet issued with some regularity in Russia was *Sankt Peterburgskie vedemosti* (*St. Petersburg Herald*), a biweekly published by the Imperial Academy of Sciences, beginning in 1727. Until the Great Reforms of 1861–1874, nearly all newspapers in Russia were official bulletins issued by various government institutions. To the extent that there was a print-based public sphere in pre-Reform Russia, it was dominated by the "thick journals" that published literary criticism and philosophical speculation.

The relaxing of censorship and limits on private publications during the Great Reforms, advances in printing technology, and the spread of literacy in Russian cities led to the development of a mass-market, commercial press by the 1880s. Daily papers targeting various markets covered stock-market news and foreign affairs, as well as the more sensational topics of crime, sex scandals, and natural disasters. As Louise McReynolds has demonstrated, Russian commercial mass newspapers resembled their counterparts in North America and Western Europe in appealing to and fostering nationalist sentiment.

By World War I "copeck" (penny) newspapers in Moscow and St. Petersburg achieved circulations comparable to those of mass circulation organs in the United States and Western Europe. The most popular newspaper in the Russian Empire in 1914 was *Russkoe slovo* (*Russian Word*), with a circulation of 619,500.

After the Bolsheviks seized power in October 1917, they created an entirely new kind of mass press. By the summer of 1918 the Soviet government had shut down all non-Bolshevik newspapers on their territory. Bolshevik newspapers during the years of revolution and civil war (1917–1921) aimed to mobilize the populace in general and Party members in particular for war. Resources were scarce, and typical civil war newspaper editions were only two pages long. The state funded the press throughout the Soviet era.

The Bolsheviks shared with most Russian intellectuals of the revolutionary era a profound contempt for the sensationalistic urban copeck newspapers that aimed to entertain a mass audience. They created a mass press that was supposed to educate, guide, and mobilize readers, not entertain them. Other important functions of Soviet newspapers were the gathering of intelligence on popular moods and the monitoring of corruption in the Party or state apparatus. To fulfill these tasks, the newspapers solicited and received literally millions of readers' letters, some of which were published. The editorial staff also forwarded letters denouncing crime and corruption to the appropriate police or prosecutorial organs. They used letters to compose reports on popular attitudes that were sent to all levels of party officialdom.

The role of direct censorship in Soviet newspaper production has been overemphasized. Agenda-setting by party and state organs was more important. The role of official censors in controlling press content was negligible. Soviet journalists were generally self-censoring, and they followed agendas set by the Communist Party's Central Committee and other official institutions.

Illegal newspapers were central to Bolshevik Party organization in the prerevolutionary years. This heritage of underground political culture contributed to a Soviet fetishization of newspapers as the mass medium *par excellance*. As a result of this fetishization, Communist propaganda officials and journalists were slow to understand and effectively use the media of radio and television. By the 1970s, Soviet means and methods of mass persuasion and mobilization were far inferior to those developed by advertising agencies and governments in the wealthy liberal democracies.

*See also:* CENSORSHIP; IZVESTIYA; JOURNALISM; PRAVDA; THICK JOURNALS

**BIBLIOGRAPHY**

Brooks, Jeffrey. (2000). *Thank You, Comrade Stalin!* Princeton, NJ: Princeton University Press.

Hopkins, Mark. (1970). *Mass Media in the Soviet Union.* New York: Pegasus Books.

Kenez, Peter. (1985). *The Birth of the Propaganda State: Soviet Methods of Mass Mobilization, 1917–1929.* Cambridge, UK: Cambridge University Press.

McReynolds, Louise. (1991). *The News Under Russia's Old Regime.* Princeton, NJ: Princeton University Press.

MATTHEW E. LENOE

## NEW STATUTE OF COMMERCE

The New Commerce Statute (a translation of the Russian *Novotorgovy ustav* of April 22, 1667; *ustav* might also be translated as "regulations") was the Russian expression of Western mercantilism and was sponsored by boyarin Afanasy Lavrentievich Ordin-Nashchokin (1605–1680), a former governor of Pskov, the westernmost of Russia's major cities, who in 1667 was head of the Chancellery of Foreign Affairs. The 1667 document was an expansion of the Commerce Statute (or Regulations) of 1653, which introduced a unified tariff schedule while repealing petty transit duties and increasing protectionist duties against foreigners. The 1667 regulations remained in force until replaced by the Customs Statute of 1755.

The 1667 document regulated both internal trade and trade relations with foreigners. In a 1649 petition to the government, the Russian merchants lamented that they could not compete with the foreign merchants, who were forbidden to engage in internal Russian trade (where they had been giving favorable credit terms to local, smaller Russian merchants) and were restricted to the port cities at times when fairs were being held. The foreigners were accused of selling shoddy goods, which was forbidden. Foreigners were forbidden to sell any goods retail in the provinces or in Moscow, or any Russian goods among themselves upon pain of confiscation of the merchandise. Internal customs duties of 5 percent were to be collected from Russians on sales of weighed goods (ad valorem sales) and 4 percent from unweighed goods. A duty of 10 percent was to be collected on salt and 15 percent on liquor. Excepting liquor, foreigners had to pay a 6 percent duty on their foreign goods sold to authorized Russian wholesalers. A foreigner had to pay a 10 percent export duty, except when he paid for the goods with gold and silver currency. The export of gold and silver from Muscovy was forbidden. Local officials (acknowledged by Moscow as likely to be corrupt) were ordered repeatedly in the statute not to interfere with commerce. Much paperwork was required to ensure compliance with the 1667 regulations.

*See also:* FOREIGN TRADE; MERCHANTS; ORDIN-NASH-CHOKIN, AFANASY LAVRENTIEVICH.

**BIBLIOGRAPHY**

Hellie, Richard, ed. and tr. (1967). *Readings for Introduction to Russian Civilization.* Chicago: Syllabus Division, The College, University of Chicago.

RICHARD HELLIE

## NICARAGUA, RELATIONS WITH

The Soviet Union had no diplomatic or economic relations with Nicaragua before the Somozas' fall in 1979. Contacts were through Communist Party organizations such as the Nicaraguan Socialist Party (PSN), founded in 1937 and illegal until 1979. While not opposing revolutionary violence in principle, the Communists believed that conditions in Nicaragua were not ripe for armed revolt. A member of the Party who had visited the USSR in 1957, Carlos Fonseca Amador, broke with the PSN on this issue. He called for insurrection and founded the Sandinista Front of National Liberation (FSLN) in 1961.

The Sandinistas led the revolutionary upheaval that overthrew the Somozas in 1979. They took full control of Nicaragua and ignored the communists (PSN). Unlike other Soviet satellites, the Sandinistas left about half of the economy in private hands, and agriculture was not collectivized. The FSLN leader, Daniel Ortega, lacked the authority in the Council of State that Leonid Brezhnev and Mikhail Gorbachev had in the Soviet Politburo.

In spite of the fact that the Sandinistas' success meant defeat for the local Communists, Moscow

quickly established good relations with the Sandinista government. Soviet economic and military aid approached billions of rubles, far less than to Cuba. While offering political, economic, and military support, Moscow sought to limit Nicaragua as an economic and strategic burden. Cuba actively supported the Sandinistas in Nicaragua and abroad.

Meanwhile, the Reagan administration was backing an armed paramilitary force, the contras, which sought to overthrow the Sandinistas. The United States also aided a right-wing regime in El Salvador besieged by revolutionary forces supposedly encouraged by the Sandinistas. Both U.S. efforts were inconclusive.

Early in 1990 President George Bush and General Secretary Gorbachev began cooperating in the region, as they were in Eastern Europe, to end these conflicts. Central American countries, the United Nations, and the two great powers negotiated a regional settlement. The United States stopped supporting the contras, the Sandinistas agreed to free elections, and the USSR mollified Cuba. Later Ortega was defeated in the elections for the Nicaraguan presidency, and Moscow was no longer an actor on the Central American scene.

*See also:* CUBA, RELATIONS WITH; UNITED STATES, RELATIONS WITH

**BIBLIOGRAPHY**

Blachman, Morris J.; Leogrande, William; and Sharpe, Kenneth. (1986). *Confronting Revolution: Security through Diplomacy in Central America.* New York: Pantheon.

Blasier, Cole. (1987). *The Giant's Rival: The USSR and Latin America.* Pittsburgh, PA: University of Pittsburgh Press.

COLE BLASIER

## NICHOLAS I

(1796–1855), tsar and emperor of Russia from 1825 to 1855.

Nicholas Pavlovich Romanov came to power amid the Decembrist Revolt of 1825 and died during the Crimean War. Between these two events, Nicholas became known throughout his empire and the world as the quintessential autocrat, and his Nicholaevan system as the most oppressive in Europe.

When Nicholas I was on his deathbed, he spoke his last words to his son, soon to become Alexander II: "I wanted to take everything difficult, everything serious, upon my shoulders and to leave you a peaceful, well-ordered, and happy realm. Providence decreed otherwise. Now I go to pray for Russia and for you all." Earlier in the day, Nicholas ordered all the Guards regiments to be brought to the Winter Palace to swear allegiance to the new tsar. These words and actions reveal a great deal about Nicholas's personality and his reign. Nicholas was a tsar obsessed with order and with the military, and his thirty years on the throne earned him a reputation as the Gendarme of Europe. His fear of rebellion and disorder, particularly after the events of his ascension to the throne, would affect him for the remainder of his reign.

### EDUCATION, DECEMBER 1825, AND RULE

Nicholas I was not intended to be tsar, nor was he educated to be one. Born in 1796, Nicholas was the third of Paul I's four sons. His two elder brothers, Alexander and Constantine, received upbringings worthy of future rulers. In 1800, by contrast, Paul appointed General Matthew I. Lamsdorf to take charge of the education of Nicholas and his younger brother, Mikhail. Lamsdorf believed that education consisted of discipline and military training, and he imposed a strict regimen on his two charges that included regular beatings. Nicholas thus learned to respect the military image his father cultivated and the necessity of order and discipline.

Although Nicholas received schooling in more traditional subjects, he responded only to military science and to military training. In 1814, during the war against Napoleon, he gave up wearing civilian dress and only appeared in his military uniform, a habit he kept. Nicholas also longed during the War of 1812 to see action in the defense of Russia. His brother, Alexander I, wanted him to remain in Russia until the hostilities ended. Nicholas only joined the Russian army for the victory celebrations held in 1814 and 1815. The young Nicholas debuted as a commander and was impressed with the spectacles and their demonstration of Russian political power. For Nicholas, as Richard Wortman has noted, these parades provided a lifelong model for demonstrating political power.

After the war, Nicholas settled into the life of a Russian grand duke. He toured his country and Europe between 1816 and 1817. In 1817 Nicholas married Princess Charlotte of Prussia, who was baptized as Grand Duchess Alexandra Fyodorovna. The following year, in April 1818, Nicholas became the first of his brothers to father a son, Alexander, the future Alexander II. For the next seven years, the family lived a quiet life in St. Petersburg's Anichkov Palace; Nicholas later claimed this period was the happiest of his life. The idyll was only broken once, in 1819, when Alexander I surprised his brother with the news that he, and not Constantine, might be the successor to the Russian throne. Alexander and Constantine did not have sons, and the latter had decided to give up his rights to the throne. This agreement was not made public, and its ambiguities would later come back to haunt Nicholas.

Alexander I died in the south of Russia in November 1825. The news of the tsar's death took several days to reach the capital, where it caused confusion. Equally stunning was the revelation that Nicholas would succeed Alexander. Because of the secret agreement, disorder reigned briefly in St. Petersburg, and Nicholas even swore allegiance to his older brother. Only after Constantine again renounced his throne did Nicholas announce that he would become the new emperor on December 14.

This decision and the confusion surrounding it gave a group of conspirators the chance they had sought for several years. A number of Russian officers who desired political change that would transform Russian from an autocracy rebelled at the idea of Nicholas becoming tsar. His love for the military and barracks mentality did not promise reform, and so three thousand officers refused to swear allegiance to Nicholas on December 14. Instead, they marched to the Senate Square where they called for a constitution and for Constantine to become tsar. Nicholas acted swiftly and ruthlessly. He ordered an attack of the Horse Guards on the rebels and then cannon fire, killing around one hundred. The rest of the rebels were rounded up and arrested, while other conspirators throughout Russia were incarcerated in the next few months.

Although the Decembrist revolt proved ineffective, its specter continued to haunt Nicholas. His first day in power had brought confusion, disorder, and rebellion. During the next year, Nicholas pursued policies and exhibited characteristics that would define his rule. He personally oversaw the interrogations and punishments of the Decembrists, and informed his advisors that they should be dealt with mercilessly because they had violated the law. Five of the leaders were executed; dozens went into permanent Siberian exile. At the same time he pursued justice against the Decembrists, Nicholas established a new concept of imperial rule in Russia, one that relied upon the parade ground and the court as a means of demonstrating power and order. Within the first few months of his rule, he initiated ceremonies and reviews of military and dynastic might that became hallmarks of his reign. Above all, the Decembrist revolt convinced Nicholas that Russia needed order and firmness and that only the autocrat could provide them.

The Nicholaevan system of government built upon these ideas and upon the tsar's mistrust for the Russian gentry in the wake of the Decembrist Revolt. Nicholas placed a circle of ministers in important positions and relied on them almost exclusively to govern. He also used His Majesty's Own Chancery, the private bureau for the tsar's personal needs, to rule. Nicholas divided the Chancery into sections to exert personal control over the functions of governing—the First Section continued to be responsible for the personal needs of the tsar, the Second Section was established to enact legislation and codify Russian laws, and the Fourth was responsible for welfare and charity. The Third Section, established in 1826, gained the most notoriety. It had the task of enforcing laws and policing the country, but in practice the Third Section did much more. Headed by Count Alexander Beckendorff, the Third Section set up spies, investigators, and gendarmes throughout the country. In effect, Nicholas established a police state in Russia, even if it did not function efficiently.

It was through the Second Section that Nicholas achieved the most notable reform of his reign. Established in 1826 to rectify the disorder and confusion within Russia's legal system that had manifested itself in the Decembrist revolt, the Second Section compiled a new Code of Law, which was promulgated in 1833. Nicholas appointed Mikhail Speransky, Alexander I's former advisor, to head the committee. The new code did not so much make new laws as collect all those that had been passed since the last codification in 1648 and categorize them. Published in forty-eight volumes with a digest, Russia had a uniform and ordered set of laws.

Nicholas came to epitomize autocracy in his own lifetime, largely through the creation of an official ideology that one of his advisers formulated in 1832. Traumatized by the events of 1825 and the calls for constitutional reform, Nicholas believed fervently in the necessity of Russian autocratic rule. Because he had triumphed over his

**Equestrian portrait of Nicholas I by Alexander Petrovich Schwabe.** © Archivo Iconografico, S.A./CORBIS

opponents, he searched for a concrete expression of the superiority of monarchy as the institution best suited for order and stability. He found a partner in this quest in Count Sergei Uvarov (1786–1855), later the minister of education. Uvarov articulated the concept of Official Nationality, which in turn became the official ideology of Nicholas's Russia. It had three components: Orthodoxy, Autocracy, and Nationality.

Uvarov's formula gave voice to trends within the Nicholaevan system that had developed since 1825. For Nicholas and his minister, an ordered system could function only with religious principles as a guide. By invoking Orthodoxy, Uvarov also stressed the Russian Church as a means to instill these principles. The concept of Autocracy was the clearest of the principles—only it could guarantee the political existence of Russia. The third concept was the most ambiguous. Although usually translated as "nationality," the Russian term used was *narodnost*, which stressed the spirit of the Russian people. Broadly speaking, Nicholas wanted to emphasize the national characteristics of his people, as well as their spirit, as a principle that made Russia superior to the West.

Nicholas attempted to rule Russia according to these principles. He oversaw the construction of two major Orthodox cathedrals that symbolized Russia and its religion—St. Isaac's in St. Petersburg (begun in 1768 and finished under Nicholas) and Christ the Savior in Moscow (Nicholas laid the cornerstone in 1837 but it was not finished until 1883). He dedicated the Alexander column on Palace Square to his brother in 1834 and a statue to his father, Paul I, in 1851. Nicholas also held countless parades and drills in the capital that included his sons, another demonstration of the might and timelessness of the Russian autocracy. Finally, Nicholas cultivated national themes in performances and festivals held throughout his empire. Most prominently, Mikhail Glinka's *A Life for the Tsar* (1836) became the national opera, while General Alexander Lvov and Vasily Zhukovsky's "God Save the Tsar" became Russia's first national anthem in 1833.

Nicholas also dealt with two other areas of Russian society. The first involved local government and ruling over such a vast country, long a problem for Russian monarchs. Nicholas oversaw a reform in the local government in 1837 that granted more power to the governors. More importantly, Nicholas expanded the Russian bureaucracies and training for the civil service. The Nicholaevan system thus became synonymous with bureaucrats, as the writings of Nikolai Gogol brilliantly depict.

The second pressing concern was serfdom. Nicholas appointed a secret committee in 1835 that tackled the question of reform, and even abolition, of serfdom. Led by Paul Kiselev (1788–1872), the committee recommended abolition, but its conclusions were not implemented. Instead, Nicholas declared serfdom an evil but emancipation even more problematic. He had Kiselev head a Fifth Section of the Chancery in 1836 and charged him with improving farming methods and local conditions. Finally, Nicholas passed a law in 1842 that allowed serf owners to transform their serfs into "obligated peasants." Few did so, and while continued committees recommended abolition, Nicholas halted short of freeing Russia's serfs. By 1848, therefore, Nicholas had established a system of government associated with Official Nationality, order, and might.

## WAR, 1848, AND THE CRIMEAN DEBACLE

Nicholas defined himself and his system as a militaristic one, and the first few years of his rule also witnessed his consolidation of power through force. He continued the wars in the Caucasus begun by Alexander I, and consolidated Russian power in Transcaucasia by defeating the Persians in 1828. Russia also fought the Ottoman Empire in 1828–1829 over the rights of Christian subjects in Turkey and disagreements over territories between the two empires. Although the fighting produced mixed results, Russia considered itself a victor and gained concessions. One year later, in 1830, a revolt broke out in Poland, an autonomous part of the Russian Empire. The revolt spread from Warsaw to the western provinces of Russia, and Nicholas sent in troops to crush it in 1831. With the rebellion over, Nicholas announced the Organic Statute of 1832, which increased Russian control over Polish affairs. The Polish revolt brought back memories of 1825 for Nicholas, who responded by pushing further Russification programs throughout his empire. Order reigned, but nationalist reactions in Poland, Ukraine, and elsewhere would ensure problems for future Russian rulers.

Nicholas also presided over increasingly oppressive measures directed at any forms of perceived opposition to his rule. Russian culture began to flourish in the decade between 1838 and 1848, as writers from Mikhail Lermontov to Nikolai Gogol and critics such as Vissarion Belinsky and Alexander Herzen burst onto the Russian cultural scene. Eventually, as their writings increasingly criticized the Nicholaevan system, the tsar cracked down, and his Third Section arrested numerous intellectuals. Nicholas's reputation as the quintessential autocrat developed from these policies, which reached an apex in 1848. When revolutions broke out across Europe, Nicholas was convinced that they were a threat to the existence of his system. He sent Russian troops to crush rebellions in Moldavia and Wallachia in 1848 and to support Austrian rights in Lombardy and Hungary in 1849. At home, Nicholas oversaw further censorship and repressions of universities. By 1850, he had earned his reputation as the Gendarme of Europe.

In 1853, Nicholas's belief in the might of his army set off a disaster for his country. He provoked a war with the Ottoman Empire over continued disputes in the Holy Land that brought an unexpected response. Alarmed by Russia's aggressive policies, England and France joined the Ottoman Empire in declaring war. The resulting Crimean War led to a humiliating defeat and the exposure of Russian military weakness. The war also exposed the myths and ideas that guided Nicholaevan Russia. Nicholas did not live to see the final humiliation. He caught a cold in 1855 that grew serious, and he died on February 18. His dream of creating an ordered state for his son to inherit died with him.

Alexander Nikitenko, a former serf who worked as a censor in Nicholas's Russia, concluded: "The main shortcoming of the reign of Nicholas consisted in the fact that it was all a mistake." Contemporaries and historians have judged Nicholas just as harshly. From Alexander Herzen to the Marquis de Custine, the image of the tsar as tyrant circulated widely in Europe during Nicholas's rule. Russian and Western historians ever since have largely seen Nicholas as the most reactionary ruler of his era, and one Russian historian in the 1990s argued "it would be difficult to find a more odious figure in Russian history than Nicholas I." W. Bruce Lincoln, Nicholas's most recent American biographer (1978), argued that Nicholas in many ways helped to pave the way for more significant reforms by expanding the bureaucracies. Still, his conclusion serves as an ideal epitaph for Nicholas: He was the last absolute monarch to hold undivided power in Russia. His death brought the end of an era.

*See also:* ALEXANDER I; ALEXANDRA FEDOROVNA; AUTOCRACY; CRIMEAN WAR; DECEMBRIST MOVEMENT AND REBELLION; NATIONAL POLICIES, TSARIST; UVAROV, SERGEI SEMENOVICH

**BIBLIOGRAPHY**

Curtiss, J. H. (1965). *The Russian Army under Nicholas I, 1825–1855.* Durham, NC: Duke University Press.

Custine, Astolphe, Marquis de. (2002). *Letters From Russia.* New York: New York Review of Books.

Gogol, Nikolai. (1995). *Plays and Petersburg Tales.* Oxford: Oxford University Press.

Herzen, Alexander. (1982). *My Past and Thoughts.* Berkeley: University of California Press.

Kasputina, Tatiana. (1996). "Emperor Nicholas I, 1825–1855." In *The Emperors and Empresses of Russia: Rediscovering the Romanovs,* ed. Donald Raleigh. Armonk, NY: M.E. Sharpe.

Lincoln, W. Bruce. (1978). *Nicholas I: Emperor and Autocrat of All the Russias.* Bloomington: Indiana University Press.

Lincoln, W. Bruce. (1982). *In the Vanguard of Reform: Russia's Enlightened Bureaucrats, 1825–1861.* DeKalb: Northern Illinois University Press.

Riasanovsky, Nicholas. (1959). *Nicholas I and Official Nationality in Russia, 1825–1855.* Berkeley: University of California Press.

Whittaker, Cynthia. *The Origins of Modern Russian Education: An Intellectual Biography of Count Sergei Uvarov, 1786–1855.* DeKalb: Northern Illinois University Press.

Wortman, Richard. (1995). *Scenarios of Power: Myth and Ceremony in Russian Monarchy, Vol. 1: From Peter the Great to the Death of Nicholas I.* Princeton, NJ: Princeton University Press.

STEPHEN M. NORRIS

# NICHOLAS II

(1868–1918), last emperor of Russia.

The future Nicholas II was born at Tsarskoe Selo in May 1868, the first child of the heir to the Russian throne, Alexander Alexandrovich, and his Danish-born wife, Maria Fedorovna. Nicholas was brought up in a warm and loving family environment and was educated by a succession of private tutors. He particularly enjoyed the study of history and proved adept at mastering foreign languages, but found it much more difficult to grasp the complexities of economics and politics. Greatly influenced by his father, who became emperor in 1881 as Alexander III, and by Konstantin Pobedonostsev, one of his teachers and a senior government official, Nicholas was deeply conservative, a strong believer in autocracy, and very religious. At the age of nineteen, he entered the army, and the military was to remain a passion throughout his life. After three years service in the army, Nicholas was sent on a ten-month tour of Europe and Asia to widen his experience of the world.

In 1894 Alexander III died and Nicholas became emperor. Despite his broad education, Nicholas felt profoundly unprepared for the responsibility that was thrust upon him and contemporaries remarked that he looked lost and bewildered. Within a month of his father's death, Nicholas married; he had become engaged to Princess Alix of Hesse in the spring of 1894 and his accession to the throne made marriage urgent. The new empress, known in Russia as Alexandra, played a crucial role in Nicholas's life. A serious and devoutly religious woman who believed fervently in the autocratic power of the

**Coronation of Nicholas II, Russian engraving.** THE ART ARCHIVE/BIBLIOTHÈQUE DES ARTS DÉCORATIFS PARIS/DAGLI ORTI

Russian monarchy, she stiffened her husband's resolve at moments of indecision.

The couple had five children, Olga (b. 1895), Tatiana (b. 1897), Maria (b. 1899), Anastasia (b. 1901), and Alexei (b. 1904). The birth of a son and heir in 1904 was the occasion for great rejoicing, but this was soon marred as it became clear that Alexei suffered from hemophilia. Their son's illness drew Nicholas and Alexandra closer together. The empress had an instinctive aversion to high society, and the imperial family spent most of their time at Tsarskoe Selo, only venturing into St. Petersburg on formal occasions.

While Nicholas's reign began with marriage and personal happiness, his coronation in 1896 was marked by disaster. Public celebrations were held at Khodynka on the outskirts of Moscow, but the huge crowds that had gathered there got out of

hand and several thousand people were crushed to death. That night the newly crowned emperor and empress appeared at a ball, apparently oblivious to the catastrophe. The image of Nicholas II enjoying himself while many of his subjects lay dead gave his reign a sour start.

### THE RUSSO-JAPANESE WAR

Nicholas followed his father's policies for much of his first decade as monarch, relying on the men who had advised Alexander III, especially Sergei Witte, the minister of finance and the architect of Russia's economic growth during the 1890s. Russian industry grew rapidly during the decade, aided by investment from abroad and particularly from France, assisted by a political alliance between the two countries signed during the last months of Alexander III's reign. Russia was also expanding in the Far East. The construction of the Trans-Siberian Railroad, linking European Russia with the empire's Pacific coast, had begun in 1891, and this resurgence of Russian interest in the region worried Japan. The twin developments of industrialization and Far Eastern expansion both came to a head early in the twentieth century. In 1904, Japan launched an attack on Russia. Nicholas II believed this was no more than "a bite from a flea," but his confidence in Russia's armed forces was misplaced. The Japanese inflicted a crushing and humiliating defeat on them, forcing the army to surrender Port Arthur in December 1904 and destroying the Russian fleet in the Battle of Tsushima in May 1905.

## THE REVOLUTION OF 1905

The emperor was stoical about Russia's military failure, but by the time peace negotiations began in the summer of 1905, the war with Japan was no longer the central problem. On January 9, 1905, a huge demonstration took place in St. Petersburg, calling for better working conditions, political changes, and a popular representative assembly. Although the demonstrators were peaceful, troops opened fire on them, killing more than a thousand people on what came to be known as "Bloody Sunday." This opened the floodgates of discontent. Workers throughout the Russian Empire went out on strike to show sympathy with their 1905 slain compatriots. As spring arrived, peasants across Russia voiced their discontent. There were more than three thousand instances of peasant unrest where troops were required to subdue villagers.

Nicholas II's reaction was confused. Believing that he had a God-given right to rule Russia and must pass his patrimony on unchanged to his heir, he tried to put down the revolts by force and resisted any attempt to erode his authority. But this tactic did not stem the surge of urban and rural discontent, and the fragility of the regime's position was brought home to him by the assassination of his uncle, the governor-general of Moscow, Grand Duke Sergei Alexandrovich, in February. Against his natural instincts, the emperor agreed to a series of concessions, culminating in October with the establishment of an elected legislature, the Duma. Nicholas resented this encroachment on his autocratic prerogatives and resentfully blamed it on Witte, the chief author of the October Manifesto. "There was no other way out," Nicholas wrote to his mother immediately afterwards "than to cross oneself and give what everyone was asking for." The emperor's character is shown in sharp focus

**Nicholas II leads Russian soldiers marching off to World War I.**
© BETTMANN/CORBIS

by the events of 1905. Nicholas was a determined man who knew his own mind and had a clear sense of where his duty lay. But he was stubborn and very slow to recognize the need for change.

Nicholas found it difficult to accept that his powers had been limited, and he tried to act as though he were still an autocrat. He was encouraged in this by the government's ability to put down the rebellions across Russia. The appointment in April 1906 of a new minister of the interior, Peter Stolypin, marked the beginning of a policy of repression combined with reform. Elevated to prime minister in the summer of 1906 because of his success in quelling discontent, Stolypin recommended a wide range of reforms. Nicholas II, however, did not agree on the need for reform. Once an uneasy calm had been reestablished across the empire, he concluded that further change was unnecessary. Nicholas wanted to return to the pre-1905 situation and to continue to rule as an autocrat. The 1913 celebration of the tercentenary of the Ro-

Nicholas II in full military dress. © BETTMANN/CORBIS

manov dynasty gave ample illustration of his view of the situation—he and the empress posed for photographs dressed in costumes styled to reflect their ancestors in the seventeenth century. Nicholas wanted to hark back to an earlier age and reclaim the power held by his forebears.

### WORLD WAR I

The test of World War I exposed Nicholas's weaknesses. The dismal performance of the Russian armies in the early stages of the war brought his sense of duty to the fore and he took direct charge of the army as commander-in-chief, although his ministers tried to dissuade him, arguing that he would now be personally blamed for any further military failures. Nicholas was, however, convinced that he should lead his troops at this critical moment, and after August 1915 he spent most of his time at headquarters away from Petrograd (as St. Petersburg had been renamed when

the war began). This had important consequences for the government of the empire. The empress was one of the main conduits by which Nicholas learned what was happening in the capital, and in his absence she became increasingly reliant on Rasputin, a "holy man" who had gained the trust of the imperial family through the comfort he was able to offer the hemophiliac Alexei. The empress, already isolated from Petrograd society, grew even more distant during the war and was highly susceptible to Rasputin's influence. She wrote to Nicholas frequently at headquarters, giving him the views of "Our friend" (as she termed Rasputin) on ministerial appointments and other political matters. The emperor too was a lonely figure as the war progressed. He had alienated much of Russia's moderate political opinion even before 1914, and the regime's refusal to countenance any participation in government by these parties, even as the military situation worsened, had caused attitudes to harden on both sides. Wider popular opinion also turned against the emperor. Alexandra's German background gave rise to a widespread belief that she wanted a Russian defeat, and this, allied with increasingly extravagant rumors about Rasputin, served to discredit the imperial family.

### ABDICATION AND DEATH

When demonstrations and riots broke out in Petrograd at the end of February 1917, there was no segment of society that would support the monarchy. Nicholas was at headquarters at Mogilev, four hundred miles south of the capital, and his attempt to return to Petrograd by train was thwarted. Military commanders and politicians urged him to allow parliamentary rule, but even at this critical moment, Nicholas clung to his belief in his own autocracy. "I am responsible before God and Russia for everything that has happened and is happening," he told his generals. His failure to make immediate concessions cost Nicholas his throne. By the time he was willing to compromise, the situation in Petrograd had so deteriorated that abdication was the only acceptable solution. On March 2 he gave up the throne, in favor of his son. After medical advice that Alexei was unfit, he offered the throne to his brother, Mikhail. When he refused, the Romanov dynasty came to an end.

In the aftermath of the revolution, negotiations took place to enable Nicholas and his family to seek exile in Britain. These came to nothing because the British government feared a popular reaction if it offered shelter to the Russian emperor. Nicholas was placed under arrest by the new Provisional Government at Tsarskoe Selo, but in August 1917, he and his family were moved to the town of Tobolsk in the Urals, 1,200 miles east of Moscow. After the Bolshevik Revolution in October 1917, the position of the imperial family became much more precarious. The outbreak of the civil war raised the possibility that the emperor might be rescued by opponents of the Bolshevik government. At the end of April 1918, Nicholas II and his family were moved to Yekaterinburg, the center of Bolshevik power in the Ural region, and in mid-July orders came from Moscow to kill them. Early in the morning of July 17, they were all shot. Their bodies were thrown into a disused mine-shaft and remained there until after the collapse of the Soviet Union. In 1998, their remains were brought back to St. Petersburg and interred in the Peter-Paul fortress, the traditional burial place of Russia's imperial family.

See also: FEBRUARY REVOLUTION; OCTOBER REVOLUTION; PROVISIONAL GOVERNMENT; REVOLUTION OF 1905; RUSSO-JAPANESE WAR

## BIBLIOGRAPHY

Ananich, Boris Vasilevich, and Ganelin, R. S. (1996). "Emperor Nicholas II, 1894–1917." In *The Emperors and Empresses of Russia: Rediscovering the Romanovs*, ed. Donald J. Raleigh. Armonk, NY: M. E. Sharpe.

Lieven, Dominic D. (1993). *Nicholas II: Emperor of All the Russias*. London: John Murray.

Verner, Andrew M. (1995). *The Crisis of Russian Autocracy: Nicholas II and the 1905 Revolution*. Princeton, NJ: Princeton University Press.

PETER WALDRON

## NIHILISM AND NIHILISTS

Nihilism was a tendency of thought among the Russian intelligentsia around the 1850s and 1860s; nihilists, a label that was applied loosely to radicals in the intelligentsia from the 1860s to the 1880s.

Although the term *intelligentsia* came into widespread use only in the 1860s, the numbers of educated young Russians of upper- or middle-class origins had been growing for some decades before that time, and under the influence of the latest Western philosophical and social theories, the Russian intelligentsia had included members with increasingly radical ideas in each new generation after the 1840s. "Nihilism" was a term that was first popularized by the novelist Ivan Turgenev in 1862 (though it had been used in Russia and abroad for several decades before that time) to characterize the rebellious and highly unconventional youths who had appeared in Russia by the late 1850s. The nihilists rejected the idealism and relative optimism of the heroes of a previous generation of the Russian intelligentsia, who had been led by the essayist Alexander Herzen and the literary critic Vissarion Belinsky. Nihilism, with its "critical realism," gave intellectual respectability to a rebellion against the established values and conventions of polite society that defended the institutions of family, nobility, church, and state. Many of the young nihilists belonged to the growing numbers of the *raznochintsy*, or the people of various ranks in society, such as the sons and daughters of priests, lower officials, and others of strata below the aristocracy.

One of the models for the nihilists was Dmitry Pisarev, a literary critic who attacked the world's most famous products of art and literature and took an extreme position in favor of naturalistic realism and scientific utiltarianism. The most famous prototype of the nihilist was the character of Bazarov in Turgenev's novel *Fathers and Sons* (*Otsy i deti*), who repudiated all conventional values and standards. That novel aroused a storm of controversy with its depiction of a schism between the idealistic Russian liberals of the preceding generation and the apparently amoral nihilists of the younger generation. While leading figures of the previous generation who had endorsed liberal principles and socialist ideals had held out the hope of gradual reform in society and improvements in the moral consciousness of individuals, the nihilists called for revolutionary changes, with the complete destruction of established institutions. It is often said that the rise of nihilism in the intelligentsia reflected the weakness of social roots and affiliation with the traditions of the past among many young members of the intelligentsia. Turgenev himself continued to be sympathetic toward gradual reforms, but Pisarev welcomed the label of nihilist as a form of praise.

The nihilists flaunted their unconventionality and supposedly hardheaded realism. As Adam Yarmolinsky describes in *Road to Revolution: A Century of Russian Radicalism* (1962), "to the conservatives frightened by the threatening effects of the new freedom, nihilism connoted atheism, free love, sedition, the outraging of every decency and accepted belief by men, and as often, by the unwomanly 'emancipated' woman." And yet the term "nihilism" was a misnomer from the start. Though the nihilists were often described as people who no longer believed in anything, in actuality they believed in their own ideas with passionate and indeed fanatical intensity. The nihilists believed that "the emancipation of the person," or the emergence of independent, critically thinking individuals, whose outlook had replaced sentimental idealism with scientific rigor and realism, was the means of leading the way to a new society, since it was possible for only an exceptional minority to achieve enlightenment. The nihilists were influenced by theories that had come from Western Europe, including German philosophy and French socialist thought, but they were most impressed by new discoveries and theories in the realm of the natural sciences, so that they virtually worshiped science, which they saw as guiding individuals of the new type who would usher in a new society.

Nihilism was soon succeeded by populism among the radical intelligentsia. The distinction between nihilism and populism is blurred in many accounts, as indeed it was in the writings of many observers from the 1860s to the 1880s, who referred to Nikolai Chernyshevsky, the great hero of the populists, as a nihilist. In reality, although the populists were deeply influenced by the nihilists, there were sharp differences between the two schools of thought. While the nihilists had glorified the minority of supposedly brilliant, bold, and unconventional intellectuals, and felt disdain for the unenlightened majority in society, the populists idealized the Russian peasants as morally superior, and were theoretically committed to learning from the peasants, who for a new generation of radicals constituted the *narod* (the people). While the populists agreed that revolutionary change was necessary, they believed that the peasant commune could be the basis for a uniquely Russian form of socialism. The nihilists had never developed any coherent program for political change. This may explain in part why they were succeeded by the populists, even though the populist strategy for transformation had some gaps of its own.

*See also:* BAZAROV, VLADIMIR ALEKSANDROVICH; INTELLI-GENTSIA; PISAREV, DMITRY IVANOVICH; POPULISM; TURGENEV, IVAN SERGEYEVICH

**BIBLIOGRAPHY**

Kelly, Aileen M. (1998). *Toward Another Shore: Russian Thinkers Between Necessity and Chance.* New Haven, CT: Yale University Press.

Tompkins, Stuart Ramsay. (1957). *The Russian Intelligentsia: Makers of the Revolutionary State.* Norman: University of Oklahoma Press.

Venturi, Franco. (1960). *Roots of Revolution: A History of the Populist and Socialist Movements in Nineteenth-Century Russia,* tr. Francis Haskell. New York: Weidenfeld and Nicolson.

ALFRED B. EVANS JR.

# NIJINSKY, VASLAV FOMICH

(1889–1950), Russian dancer and choreographer.

The most famous Russian male dancer, Vaslav Fomich Nijinsky was also a choreographer, though madness cut short his career. Nijinsky, like his colleague Anna Pavlova, achieved international fame through his appearances with Sergei Diagilev's Ballets Russes in Paris, beginning in 1909. Trained at the Imperial Theater School in St. Petersburg, Nijinsky joined the Imperial Ballet in 1907, but left the troupe in 1911, his international career already well established. Onstage, Nijinsky's somewhat sturdy frame became a lithe instrument of unprecedented lightness and elevation. Noted for seemingly effortless leaps, Nijinsky's photographs also reveal the dancer's uncanny ability to transform himself from role to role. Nijinsky's first choreography, for *L'Après-midi d'un Faune* (1912), to Debussy's music, scandalized Paris with its eroticism, though the ballet's true innovation lay in its turn from the virtuosity for which Nijinsky had become famous. Niji nsky's choreography for Igor Stravinsky's *Le Sacre du printemps* (1913) went even farther in demonstrating the choreographer's disdain for the niceties of ballet convention and his embrace of primitivism. Asymmetrical and unlovely, the work was dropped from the Ballets Russes repertory after some nine performances.

Nijinsky, once the lover of Diagilev, married in 1913 and was dismissed from Diagilev's company. After itinerant and often unsuccessful performances during World War I, Nijinsky was diagnosed a schizophrenic in 1919. The remaining years of the great dancer's life were spent mostly in sanitoriums.

*See also:* BALLET; BOLSHOI THEATER; DIAGILEV, SERGEI: PAVLOVICH; PAVLOVA, ANNA MATVEYEVNA

**BIBLIOGRAPHY**

Buckle, Richard. (1971). *Nijinsky*. New York: Simon and Schuster.

Nijinsky, Vaslav. (1999). *The Diary of Vaslav Nijinsky*, tr. Kyril FitzLyon; ed. Joan Acocella. New York: Farrar, Strauss and Giroux.

Ostwald, Peter. (1991). *Vaslav Nijinsky: A Leap into Madness*. New York: Carol.

TIM SCHOLL

## NIKITIN, AFANASY

Famed Russian merchant and autobiographer; exact dates of birth and death unknown.

Afanasy Nikitin was a Russian merchant from Tver who left a diary of his travels to Iran and India during a four-year period between 1466 and 1475. The traveler's own account remains the primary source of information on his personal history and the purpose of his long journey. Under the title *The Journey Beyond Three Seas*, Afanasy's travel record is a document of great interest, both to historians studying the interactions of medieval Russians with the Muslim East, and in general as one of the first autobiographical accounts in the literature. It has been repeatedly published in the original Russian with annotations and translated into many languages.

Afanasy's notes describe how he left Tver, intending to join a trade expedition headed for the Caucasian principality of Shirvan. On the way, his party was robbed of their goods. He was rescued by the Shah of Shirvan, but, despite the high risk, decided to continue his journey to Derbent, a market familiar to him, and then to Baku, rather than return to Tver empty-handed. He went on to cross the Caspian Sea, continued his travels across Iran, and then crossed the Indian Ocean to the Deccan. After surveying the markets, customs, and courts of the Bahmani and Vijayanagar empires, he made his way back to Russia, crossing the Black Sea. Somewhere in the region of Smolensk, he met an untimely death. Merchants brought his notes to Vasily Mamyrev, secretary to Grand Prince Ivan III of Moscow. The L'vov chronicler reports that he received Afanasy's notes in 1475 and incorporated them into his annalistic record, but was unable to locate any further information on the traveler.

The first historians to study his notes saw Afanasy as a daring explorer and patriot. Looking at the journey in commercial perspective, however, historian Janet Martin concludes that although Afanasy did travel farther than other Russian travelers of his era, and visitied places they did not, his notes reveal him as a cautious, even conservative merchant who made a series of discrete, limited decisions to continue his journey on the basis of information about markets conveyed by merchants that he met. He initially planned to take advantage of a lull in hostilities between Muscovy and the Great Horde to bring furs to the Caucasus and the lower Volga, a venture which had good prospects for high profits. His journey to Iran followed a well-established trade route, with extended stops at towns known for their bazaars. Afanasy indicates that his decision to continue to India was based on information from Muslim merchants whom he met in Iran. His notes on India, a market unfamiliar to Russian merchants, contain the most detailed information on goods and markets, as well as advice on finding shelter and warnings about the high customs fees exacted against Christians and the pressures to convert to Islam. This information would have been of great value to merchants considering such a venture. Only when he concluded that further travel would not bring new opportunities for commerce did he decide to return to Russia.

Long passages in creolized Arabic containing prayers and expression of fears about the traveler's inability to practice Christianity in India have inspired a variety of hypotheses. Nikolai Trubetskoy characterized Afanasy's notes as a lyrical tale of a committed Orthodox Christian who suffered from his religious isolation, but kept the faith of his homeland; the foreign terms and phrases added local color to the narrative, shaping its unique artistic structure, while concealing the traveler's most intimate thoughts from all but a handful of readers. Others questioned Afanasy's faith. Yuri Zavadovsky noted Afanasy's extensive knowledge of Muslim prayers and of the requirements for conversion to Islam. Afanasy's reports of his own behavior suggested to historian Gail Lenhoff that he was a social convert to Islam. This decision to convert appears to have been initially dictated by commercial interests, since Muslims did not have to pay taxes or customs duties and could trade more freely in the Deccan markets. His conversion obligated him to pray in Arabic and to observe Muslim customs in public. The increasing proportion of Arabic prayers in the autobiography and the existence of a final prayer of thanks to Allah for surviving a storm, uttered as he approached Christian soil and duly recorded in his diary, could indicate that by the end of his journey Afanasy had assimilated the Muslim faith.

*See also:* FOREIGN TRADE; ISLAM; MERCHANTS

**BIBLIOGRAPHY**

Lenhoff, Gail and Martin, Janet. (1989). "The Commercial and Cultural Context of Afanasij Nikitin's Journey Beyond Three Seas." *Jahrbücher für Geschichte Osteuropas* 37 (3):321–344.

Major, Richard H., ed. (1857). "The Travels of Athanasius Nikitin," tr. Mikhail M. Wielhorsky. In *India in the Fifteenth Century*. Hakluyt Society, ser. 1. volume 22. London: Hakluyt Society.

Martin, Janet. (1985). "Muscovite Travelling Merchants: The Trade with the Muslim East (Fifteenth and Sixteenth Centuries)." *Central Asian Studies* 4 (3):21–38.

Trubetskoy, Nikolay S. (1978). "Afanasij Nikitin's Journey Beyond Three Seas as a Work of Literature." In *Readings in Russian Poetics: Formalist and Structuralist Views*, ed. Ladislav Matejka and Krystyna Pomorska. Ann Arbor: University of Michigan Slavic Publications.

GAIL LENHOFF

## NIKON, PATRIARCH

(1605–1681), patriarch of Moscow and all Russia; implemented a program of church reform that inspired vociferous opposition, ultimately culminating in the schism and the emergence of Old Belief.

Nikita Minich or Minov (as a monk, Nikon) was born to a peasant couple in the village of Veldemanov near Nizhny Novgorod. His mother died shortly after his birth, and the child was sent to a local tutor who taught him to read. As a youth, he continued his studies at the Makariev Zheltovodsky monastery, not far from Nizhny Novgorod. The author of Nikon's *Life* reports that the young man was an avid student and attracted to the monastic life. Nonetheless, in 1625 he obeyed his dying father's request to return home. He married a year later and obtained a position as a deacon at a nearby village church. Soon he was ordained a priest, and he and his wife moved to Moscow.

In 1636 Minich persuaded his wife to enter a convent. He himself departed for the Anzersky *skete* in the far north. Upon arrival he took monastic vows and the name Nikon. In 1649 a disagreement with the elder Eliazar prompted Nikon to transfer to the Kozheozersky monastery. Within three years he was made abbot. In 1646 Nikon traveled to Moscow on monastery business. There he attracted the attention of the young Tsar Alexei Mikhailovich. The tsar ordered him to remain in Moscow and made him abbot of the New Savior monastery. Energetic and talented, Nikon soon became a confidant and spiritual advisor of the tsar. He also became an important figure in the Zealots of Piety, the circle of reformers gathered around the tsar's confessor, Stefan Vonifatiev.

In March 1649, Nikon was named metropolitan of the important of see of Novgorod. He maintained contact with the reformers in Moscow and sought to implement their program in Novgorod. *Mnogoglasie*, the practice of simultaneously performing different parts of the liturgy in order to complete it more quickly, was abolished. Greek and Kievan chants replaced the traditional style of singing. Metropolitan Nikon's sermons at the episcopal cathedral attracted great crowds. In 1650 severe grain shortages caused famine and inflation in Novgorod. The people responded with violence, and Nikon played an important role in bringing the situation under control without bloodshed.

In the spring of 1652, Metropolitan Nikon was entrusted with the task of traveling to the Solovetsky monastery, collecting the relics of St. Philip, and returning with them to Moscow. The translation of St. Philip's relics exemplified the views of the Zealots of Piety. As metropolitan of Moscow, St. Philip had died a martyr's death for publicly rebuking the cruel and unchristian acts of Tsar Ivan IV ("the Terrible"). St. Philip's example highlighted the duty of the clergy to remind the laity, including tsars, of their Christian duties. The translation of his relics emphasized the dignity and importance of the church. Nikon was on the return path to Moscow when he received a letter from Tsar Alexei Mikhailovich, informing him that Patriarch Joasif had died and assuring him that he would be selected as the next patriarch. A church council convened and duly elected Nikon. On July 25, 1652, Nikon was consecrated patriarch of Moscow and all Russia.

Nikon was chosen patriarch to direct a reform program advocated by the Zealots of Piety and supported by the tsar. If all reformers concurred on the need to elevate popular piety and reform popular religious practices, the revision of the liturgical books to bring them into conformity with contemporary Greek practice and the exercise of power within the church were more sensitive issues. Consecrated patriarch, Nikon moved decisively to advance the liturgical reform with all possible speed. In February 1653 a revised edition of the *Psalter* was printed, minus two articles present in earlier editions. An instruction calling for sixteen full prostrations during a Lenten prayer was modified, and a section teaching that the sign of the cross should be made with two fingers was removed. Correctors (*spravshchiki*) at the government Printing Office, men long associated with the work of the Zealots of Piety, protested the changes. They promptly were removed from their posts and replaced by supporters of Nikon. By the end of the year, Patriarch Nikon assumed direct control of the Printing Office.

In addition, according to later accounts of Nikon's opponents, shortly after the appearance of the new *Psalter*, the patriarch sent a communication to Ivan Neronov, archpriest of the Kazan Cathedral, calling attention to the revisions and ordering that they be introduced into the liturgy. Confronted with what he perceived to be an error, Neronov prayed for guidance and then discussed the order with his associates, including Archbishop Paul of Kolomna and the archpriests Avvakum, Daniil, and Login. Avvakum and Daniil gathered evidence against the revisions in the newly printed *Psalter* and presented a petition to the tsar. The tsar ignored it. By the end of 1653 the archpriests Login and Neronov had been defrocked and exiled. Avvakum escaped defrocking through the personal intervention of the tsar but was transferred to the distant post of Tobolsk.

Patriarch Nikon's reform activities were not limited to liturgical reform. During the six years of his active patriarchate, he worked to bring the church under episcopal control, freeing the clergy and church affairs from the interference of secular authorities and creating a hierarchy of authority flowing from the patriarch to the laity. As contemporaries noted, however, Nikon freed the prelates and other clergy from secular powers only to subordinate them to his own. Too often he neglected to consult a church council before he acted, provoking resentment and resistance where he needed support. Nikon also was energetic in the area of monastic reform, sternly punishing those who flouted the monastic rule. Perhaps Nikon's more important contributions in this area were the three monasteries he founded: the Monastery of the Cross, the Monstery of the Iveron Mother of God,

and the Monastery of the Resurrection (or New Jerusalem). Richly endowed, both materially and spiritually, the latter two were centers of learning as well as piety. All were subordinated directly to Nikon. Finally, Nikon did not ignore the shortcomings in the popular practice and celebration of religion. He initiated campaigns against the wandering minstrels and jesters, with their profane music and ribald jokes, and also against icons he deemed painted in an improper manner. Such campaigns manifested his zeal to dignify popular piety and reform popular religious practices, but they often offended the powerful as well as the humble.

Scholars have disagreed as to whether Nikon's goal was to assert the superiority of church over state, or simply to achieve the symphony between church and state that is the Byzantine ideal. In reality, Nikon's power depended on the tsar's favor. As long as Nikon enjoyed the confidence and support of the tsar, those whom he offended in his zeal were powerless against him. By 1658, however, the tsar's attitude towards Nikon had cooled. On July 10, 1658, feeling snubbed by the tsar's failure to invite him to an important state reception, Nikon celebrated the liturgy in the Cathedral of the Dormition, donned simple monastic garb, announced to those assembled that he would no longer be patriarch, and walked away.

Nikon's action was without precedent. After two years, Tsar Alexei Mikhailovich convened a church council to address the situation. All agreed that a new patriarch should be chosen, but no consensus could be achieved on what to do with Nikon. Nikon complicated the matter by asserting that he had renounced the patriarchal throne but not his calling, and that he alone had the power to establish a new patriarch.

In 1666, after lengthy exchanges, the patriarchs of Alexandria and Antioch agreed to travel to Moscow to participate in a church council to resolve the affair. Before the eastern patriarchs arrived, delegates assembled and reaffirmed the correctness of the reform program itself. Those who opposed the reform were condemned as heretics. Thus officially began the church schism. The eastern patriarchs arrived, and on November 7 another church council convened for the purpose of deciding the case of Nikon. On December 12, 1666, Nikon was found guilty of abandoning the patriarchal throne; of slandering the tsar, the Russian Church, and all the Russian people as heretics; of insulting the eastern patriarchs; and of deposing and exiling bishops without a church council. He was removed officially as patriarch, stripped of his priestly functions, demoted to the rank of a simple monk, and exiled to the Ferapontov monastery in the far north. In 1676 he was transferred to the Kirillov monastery, also in the north. In 1681, as a result of the intercession of Tsar Fyodor Alexeyevich, Nikon was given permission to return to Moscow. He died on the return journey, on August 17, 1681, and was buried in the Monastery of the Resurrection.

*See also:* ALEXEI MIKHAILOVICH; AVVAKUM PETROVICH; OLD BELIEVERS; RUSSIAN ORTHODOX CHURCH; ZEALOTS OF PIETY

**BIBLIOGRAPHY**

Lobachev, S.V. (2001). "Patriarch Nikon's Rise to Power." *Slavonic and East European Review* 79(2):290–307.

Lupinin, Nickolas. (1984). *Religious Revolt in the Eighteenth Century: The Schism of the Russian Church.* Princeton, NJ: Kingston Press.

Meyendorff, Paul. (1991). *Russia, Ritual, and Reform: The Liturgical Reforms of Nikon in the Seventeenth Century.* Crestwood, NY: St. Vladimir's Press..

Michels, Georg B. (1999). *At War with the Church: Religious Dissent in Seventeenth-Century Russia.* Stanford, CA: Stanford University Press.

Palmer, William. (1871). *The Patriarch and the Tsar.* 6 vols. London: Trübner.

Soloviev, Sergei M. (2000). *History of Russia*, Vol. 21: *The Tsar and the Patriarch: Stenka Razin Revolts on the Don, 1662–1675*, tr. and ed. T. Allan Smith. Gulf Breeze, FL: Academic International Press.

CATHY J. POTTER

# NIL SORSKY, ST.

(c. 1433–1508), ascetic master and editor-copyist.

Brother of the state secretary Andrei Maykov (active 1450s–1490s), Nil entered the Kirillov-Belozersk monastery in the 1440s or 1450s, went to Mt. Athos at some time for special training, and in 1470 was a leading Kirillov elder. Dissatisfied with materialism and secular interests there, he founded the Sorsky Hermitage on a Kirillov property, where he enforced a strict, self-supporting regimen and taught the Athonite, hesychastic mode of prayer. By favoring monastic dispensation of only spiritual alms, he avoided the amassing of goods and dependent labor required for material charity. In 1489, Archbishop Gennady of Novgorod sought out Nil, who helped produce Joseph of Volok's anti-heretical, theological polemics.

Nil's disciples included his traveling companion Innokenty Okhlyabinin, founder of another hermitage based on Nil's precepts; the Kirillov elders Gury Tushin and German Podolny, one a bibliophile, the other an opponent of condemning heretics; the disgraced prince-boyar Vassian Patrikeyev, the most strident "Non-possessor" during 1511–1531; and two of Joseph's leading acolytes.

Nil's expert book-copying, most notably an authoritative collection of saints lives, was distinguished by use of Greek originals to make corrections. His polished corpus of well-respected writings include the regulatory *Tradition* (*Predanie*) for his hermitage; an eleven-discourse, patristic-based *Rule* (*Ustav*) for "spiritual activity"; and didactic epistles to German, Gury, and Vassian. The leitmotifs are nonattachment, stillness with mytical prayer, and combating the eight pernicious "thoughts" (the Catholic seven deadly sins plus despondency). Contemporary writings do not show that Nil himself opposed and protested the execution of heretics or advocated confiscation of monastic villages, as later claimed and still widely believed.

Locally venerated, Nil has been seen as Russia's great elder and as relatively liberal for his day. He was added as a saint to official church calendars only in modern times.

*See also:* CHURCH COUNCIL; KIRILL-BELOOZERO MONASTERY; POSSESSORS AND NON-POSSESSORS; MONASTICISM; ORTHODOXY; SAINTS

**BIBLIOGRAPHY**

Maloney, George A. (2000). *Nil Sorsky.* Costa Mesa, CA: Paulist Press.

Ostrowski, Donald. (1988). "Toward Establishing the Canon of Nil Sorsky's Works." *Oxford Slavonic Papers* 31:35–50.

Ostrowski, Donald. (1995). "Loving Silence and Avoiding Pleasant Conversations. The Political Views of Nil Sorskii." *Harvard Ukrainian Studies* 19: 476-96.

DAVID M. GOLDFRANK

**NKVD** *See* STATE SECURITY, ORGANS OF.

## NOGAI

The Nogai, known as *Mangit ulus* in contemporary sources, was a loosely forged tribal union of nomadic Turkic (Kipchak–Uzbek) pastoralists claiming descent from Nogai (d. 1299), the founder of the Golden Horde. Sunni Muslim, Nogai khanate was formed in 1391, when the Tatar general Edigü, the leader of the Mangit Mongol tribe, seceded from the political orbit of the Golden Horde. Initially, Nogai lands stretched from the left bank of the lower Volga to the Ural River. The capital Saraichik, the only town in the khanate, was situated on the lower Ural in Central Asia. With Muscovite incorporation of the khanates of Kazan (1552) and Astrakhan (1556), the Nogai Horde divided into three parts: the Great Nogai Horde, occupying the original core of the khanate's lands, apparently became Muscovite vassals; the Lesser Nogai Horde, located along the right bank of the Volga-Kuban-Azov region, submitted to the Crimean Khanate; and the Altiul Horde, which occupied the Emba basin. Due to famine and pressures from nomadic Kalmyks to the east in the 1570s through the early 1600s, the Great and Lesser Nogai Hoards reunited and joined the Ottoman-Crimean alliance. During Catherine II's (r. 1762–1796) wars with the Ottomans, most of the remnants of the Nogai were incorporated into the Russian Empire.

Because of its decentralized government, diverse trading partners, and conflicting allegiances with the other Mongol khanates, Muscovy, and the Ottomans, the Nogai had contradictory foreign policies that complicated their relations with other states in the region. However, since they wielded great military power, good diplomatic relations with the Nogai were sought after by the rival powers in the area. Aside from being occasional allies of the Muscovites, they were also key suppliers of horses, forwarding up to fifty thousand per delivery. In exchange, the Muscovites provided the Nogai with weapons, grain, textiles, and other goods that nomadic economies could not produce themselves. From the 1550s, the Nogai also acted as Muscovy's intermediaries in relations with Central Asia.

*See also:* ASTRAKHAN, KHANATE OF; CATHERINE II; GOLDEN HORDE; KALMYKS; NATIONALITIES POLICIES, TSARIST; RUSSO-TURKISH WARS

**BIBLIOGRAPHY**
Golden, Peter B. (1992). *An Introduction to the History of the Turkic Peoples.* Wiesbaden: Harrassowitz Verlag.

Lantzeff, George A., and Pierce, Richard A. (1973). *Eastward to Empire: Exploration and Conquest on the Russian Open Frontier to 1750.* Montreal: McGill-Queen's University Press.

ROMAN K. KOVALEV

## NOMENKLATURA

The term *nomenklatura* was often used in the USSR throughout the Stalin and post-Stalin periods to designate members of Soviet officialdom. The term was not generally known in the West until the 1960s. Members of the nomenklatura included Communist Party officials (particularly Party secretaries at any level of the Party organization), government officials, and senior officers in the Soviet armed forces who were Party members. Almost all members were, in fact, Communist Party members. At a minimum, the Party controlled access to nomenklatura jobs. Most often the term was used to describe full-time professional Party officials, also known as apparatchiki, since mere rank-and-file Party members did not hold important executive posts.

No definite tally of the number of the nomenklatura was ever published officially. But Russian and Western scholars generally agree that their numbers exceeded 500,000. Yet the entire membership of the Communist Party amounted on average to only about 7 percent of the Soviet population.

Wherever they served throughout the multinational Soviet Union, most of the nomenklatura were Russians, Ukrainians, or Belorussians. Almost always, native nomenklatura members posted in any of the non-Slavic Republics among the fifteen constituent republics of the USSR were supervised ultimately by ethnic Russians, Ukrainians, or Belorussians.

*See also:* COMMUNIST PARTY OF THE SOVIET UNION

**BIBLIOGRAPHY**
Weeks, Albert L., ed. (1991). *Soviet Nomenklatura: A Comprehensive Roster of Soviet Civilian and Military Officials,* 3rd ed. Washington, DC: Washington Institute Press.

Voslensky, Michael. (1984). *Nomenklatura: The Soviet Ruling Class,* tr. Eric Mosbacher. New York: Doubleday.

ALBERT L. WEEKS

## NORMANIST CONTROVERSY

The Normanist Controversy is the most tendentious issue in early Russian history. It centers on the degree of influence Scandinavians had on the foundation of Kievan Rus and early Rus law, government, language, paganism, and trade. Normanist scholars argue for varying degrees of Scandinavian influence, and their opponents are anti-Normanists.

The controversy's origins date to the mid-eighteenth century, when historians, many of ethnic German background, began to publish the medieval Russian sources. It initially focused on the ethnic attribution of the Rus tribe (Greek *Ros*, Arabic *ar-Rus*), the name for Rurik and his clan, who were allegedly invited by a confederation of Slavic and Finnic tribes to rule over them in 862. The first Normanist scholars (Bayer, Müller, Schlötzer) argued that the Rus were a tribe deriving their name either from their homeland, Roslagen in central Sweden, or from the Finnic word for Swedes, *Ruotsi*. Further, they noted the Norse personal names in the 911 and 940 treaties between the Rus and Byzantium, Constantine Porphyrogenitus's listing of both Slavic and Norse names for the Dnieper cataracts, and more than fifty Norse words in the Russian language. Norse origins were also ascribed to early Rus law and the pagan Slavic pantheon. Mikhail Lomonosov and other early anti-Normanists argued that the Rus were Slavs who were named after a right-bank tributary of the Dnieper, the Ros River.

Nineteenth-century debates were shaped by German and Russian nationalism and the publication of more sources on the Rus, such as the medieval Arab and Persian geographical accounts (Ibn Khurdadbheh, Ibn Rusta, Ibn Fadlan), which mention a people called the ar-Rus who traded along the Russian river systems. The ar-Rus differed from other fair-skinned peoples of the north, including the Slavs (Saqalib). Although this theory is compelling, the medieval Islamic authors appeared to use ar-Rus as an occupational descriptive rather than an ethnic indicator, since they had not been to Rus themselves and could therefore not distinguish a Scandinavian from other peoples of the north. Nineteenth-century research also showed no more than sixteen Norse words in Russian, the independent development of Rus law and Scandinavian law, and a common Indo-European origin of both the Scandinavian and Slavic gods and languages.

Having exhausted the written texts, the Normanist and anti-Normanist schools stood firmly entrenched in the early twentieth century. The new scientific archaeology and innovations in the methodology of historical numismatics, however, revealed fresh source material, and henceforth the Normanist Controversy became an archaeological and numismatic question. In 1914, Swedish archaeologist T. J. Arne argued for a mass Viking-age Scandinavian colonization of Eastern Europe. Arne's theories remained largely unchallenged until the 1940s, when anti-Normanism, in part a reaction to the Nazi invasion of the Soviet Union, was proclaimed official Soviet state dogma. Postwar USSR witnessed a golden age for Soviet archaeology, with the state sponsorship of thousands of archaeological excavations. Key to the anti-Normanist position were the excavations at Gnezdovo and Staraya Ladoga, near Smolensk and Novgorod respectively. Normanists considered both to be Scandinavian settlements, but Soviet archaeologists (Artsikhovsky, Avdusin, Ravdonikas) claimed minimal evidence for Scandinavian residence at these sites. Soviet scholars did not deny the passage of Scandinavians through Russia for purposes of international trade between northern Europe and the Islamic caliphate; they simply rejected that a mass Scandinavian colonization took place or that the colonists founded the Kievan state.

The 1970s onward has witnessed a convergence between the extremes of the Normanist and anti-Normanist positions. More recent excavations at sites with Scandinavian material and long-distance trade goods (Islamic silver dirhams, Eastern beads), indicate that Scandinavians maintained an active exchange network in the late eighth and ninth centuries with the Near East and, in the tenth century, mainly with Central Asia. Based on the current state of research, therefore, it is possible to reconstruct the following chronology of Scandinavian activity in eastern Europe. From the 760s, Scandinavians lived part of the year at Staraya Ladoga on the lower Volkhov River, where goods were reloaded from large seagoing vessels to smaller craft more appropriate for the journey along eastern Europe's often-treacherous rivers. By the early ninth century, when trade with the Near East was fully underway, other settlements formed to the south of Ladoga along the entire Volkhov River, which serviced the north-south trade. In the 860s, *Rurikovo gorodishche*, the Volkhov's largest settlement, with strong Scandinavian and West Slavic elements and precursor to Novgorod, was founded.

To the west, a second albeit less archaeologically discernible trade route with a few Scandinavian finds begins to the south of Lake Peipus at Izborsk, Kamno, and Pskov, possibly from the beginning of the ninth century. Both routes connect to the south and east, to the watersheds of the Western Dvina, Dnieper, and Volga rivers.

Archaeological and numismatic evidence implies that the 860s and 870s were a turbulent period: the burning down of Staraya Ladoga and Pskov, a smaller fire at Rurikovo gorodishche, and a marked increase in the deposition of coin hoards, suggesting times of danger. At the same time, the written sources speak of the invitation to Rurik and the unsuccessful Viking attack on Constantinople in 860. Finally, in the 880s and 890s there occurred a major decline in the import of silver and beads from the Near East. However, in around 900 new routes were opened with Central Asia, which provided an unprecedented new source of silver and other goods. Additionally, at this time Staraya Ladoga and Rurikovo underwent expansion, Scandinavian-style graves appeared to the southeast of Lake Ladoga, and the Lake Peipus trade was concentrated at a reconstructed Pskov.

A strong Scandinavian presence has become evident to the south, with the beginning of settlement and the cemeteries at Gnezdovo, and further south at Shestovitsa on the middle Dnieper River. Such phenomena are contemporary with the Russian Primary Chronicle's account of the Rus expansion to Kiev beginning in the late ninth century and Rus attacks on Byzantine territories including Constantinople in 907/911 and 940. The revival of the Rus trade with the Islamic East is seen also in the hundreds of hoards of mostly Central Asian dirhams deposited in eastern Europe's soil during the tenth century. Thomas Noonan estimates that during the tenth century more than 125 million dirhams from Central Asia alone were exported to northern Europe, which were exchanged for products of the northern forests, such as furs, honey, wax, sword blades, walrus ivory, and slaves. From the 950s, however, a silver crisis in Central Asia and the subsequent decline in the export of silver initiated a reorientation in Rus trade, with silver thenceforward coming to Kievan Rus from western and central Europe. By the late tenth century, archaeological signs of Scandinavian activity diminish, even though the Russian Primary Chronicle and Icelandic sagas speak of Scandinavians enlisting as mercenaries in the courts of Kievan Rus and Byzantium throughout the eleventh century. One must bear in mind,

however, that there were never many Scandinavians on the territory of eastern Europe at any given time, with no more than two hundred Scandinavian graves found there for a more than two-hundred year period.

Taken as a whole, the archaeological, numismatic, and textual evidence clearly shows Scandinavian influence during the pre-Kievan and Kievan periods. The main question, however, remains: What role did the Scandinavians actually play in the Kievan state-building process? Prior to the arrival of Scandinavians and Slavs to northwestern Russia in the eighth and ninth centuries, the region was sparsely populated by small groups of Finno-Ugric hunters and gatherers. There were simply no wealthy peoples to colonize or raid, in contrast with the burgeoning Anglo-Saxon or Carolingian states. In this light, it is more prudent to place Scandinavian activity in an inclusive model of inter-ethnic economic cooperation, such as one of regional survival strategies developed by Noonan. Early medieval European Russia was home to many ethnic groups, all practicing different survival strategies, all of which were essential to the development of the Kievan Rus economy and state. The Finno-Ugrian tribes of the northern Russian forests were consummate hunters who supplied the furs sought after by foreign and domestic markets. The Slavic agriculturalists, migrating from the fertile lands of southwestern Ukraine, brought advanced farming techniques and tribal administrative experience. Nomadic Turkic pastoralists residing in the Rus steppe zone introduced mounted-fighting tactics to the Slavic population. Finally, the Scandinavians contributed the long-distance shipping, commercial practices, and a military organization (including weapons) that facilitated the Islamic and Byzantine trade. Using older, more localized routes, the Scandinavians helped to create a commercial system that united all of European Russia for the first time in its history. Thus, the joining of these diverse economic strategies created conditions for the emergence of a powerful state in a territory that was both geographically and climatically daunting to maintain given the rudimentary communication and transportation systems of the early Middle Ages.

The Scandinavians, therefore, played an important role in the creation of the Kievan state, but they were only part of a complex ethno-cultural process. Normanists and anti-Normanists have benefited progressively from nineteenth-century advances in Indo-European linguistics, studies in comparative religion, and modern archaeological and numismatic research. The Normanist Controversy is placed into proper perspective by moving away from the emphasis placed on this one group by the medieval chroniclers and, instead, viewing it in the light of modern research that examines the development of eastern Europe as a whole.

*See also:* GNEZDOVO; KIEVAN RUS; NOVGOROD THE GREAT; PRIMARY CHRONICLE; VIKINGS

**BIBLIOGRAPHY**

Brisbane, Mark A., ed. (1992). *The Archaeology of Novgorod, Russia: Recent Results from the Town and its Hinterland.* Lincoln, UK: Society for Medieval Archaeology.

Cross, Samuel H., and Sherbowitz-Wetzor, Olgerd P. eds. (1953). *The Russian Primary Chronicle: Laurentian Text.* Cambridge, MA: Mediaeval Academy of America.

Franklin, Simon, and Shepared, Jonathan. (1996). *The Emergence of Rus, 750–1200.* London: Longman.

Noonan, Thomas S. (1991). "The Vikings in Russia: Some New Directions and Approaches to an Old Problem." In *Social Approaches to Viking Studies*, ed. Ross Samson. Glasgow: Cruithne Press.

Noonan, Thomas S. (1994). "The Vikings in the East: Coins and Commerce." In *Developments around the Baltic and the North Sea in the Viking Age*, ed. Björn Ambrosiani and Helen Clarke. Stockholm: Birka Project.

Noonan, Thomas S. (1998). *The Islamic World, Russia, and the Vikings, 750–900: The Numismatic Evidence.* Aldershot, UK: Ashgate Variorum.

Riasanovsky, Nicholas V. (1947). "The Norman Theory of the Origin of the Russian State." *Russian Review* 7(1):96–110.

HEIDI M. SHERMAN

# NORTH ATLANTIC TREATY ORGANIZATION

The North Atlantic Treaty Organization (NATO) is a collective defense/collective security organization based on security guarantees and mutual commitments between North America and Europe. It was created in response to the growing Soviet threat in Europe after World War II, including the communist takeovers in eastern and central Europe, pressure on Norway, Greece, and Turkey, and the 1948 blockade of Berlin. The Washington Treaty establishing NATO was signed on April 4, 1949, by Belgium, Canada, Denmark, France, Iceland, Italy, Luxembourg, the Netherlands, Norway, Portugal, the United Kingdom, and the United States. NATO's membership was subsequently enlarged, bringing in Greece and Turkey in 1952, the Federal Republic of Germany (West Germany) in 1955, Spain in 1982, and Poland, Hungary, and the Czech Republic in 1999. In 2002 NATO invited Bulgaria, Estonia, Latvia, Lithuania, Romania, Slovakia, and Slovenia to join the alliance in 2004.

At the core of NATO's mutual defense commitment is Article 5 of the Washington Treaty, which states that an attack on one or more members of the alliance will be considered an attack on all. Also central are Article 2, which speaks of the members' commitment to their shared values and free institutions; Article 4, which provides for consultations if a member's security is threatened; and Article 10, which gives the members the option to invite additional states to join the alliance.

Headquartered in Brussels, NATO is an intergovernmental organization. Its decisions require consensus. The permanent ambassadors of the member-states meet in the North Atlantic Council (NAC), chaired by the secretary general. The NAC and other senior policy committees, such as the Defense Planning Committee (DPC) and the Nuclear Planning Group (NPG), meet at regular intervals. At least twice per year NATO holds foreign ministers' meetings. Meetings also occur at the level of defense ministers, and when key decisions are to be taken NATO holds summits of the heads of state.

The military structures of NATO are headed by the Military Committee, which meets regularly at the level of the chiefs of defense of the member-states. The committee's daily work is conducted by their permanent military representatives. NATO's two principal strategic commands are the Supreme Allied Commander Europe (SACEUR) with headquarters (SHAPE) in Mons, Belgium, and the Supreme Allied Commander Atlantic (SACLANT) with headquarters in Norfolk, Virginia. These key commands are supported by a number of regional commands. Allies who are members of the military structures contribute forces to NATO's integrated military structures, but some of the members do not participate in them. France withdrew from NATO's military structures in 1966 (it remains a full member of its political structures); Spain joined NATO in 1982 but remained outside its military component until 1997; Iceland has no armed forces and is represented at the military level by a civilian.

When NATO was established, the first secretary general, Lord Ismay, allegedly quipped that its mission in Europe was "to keep the Americans in, the Russians out, and the Germans down." During the Cold War, the principal function of NATO was to provide common defense against the Soviet bloc. NATO also ensured that American and European security remained interconnected, and provided a formula for the reintegration of postwar Germany into the Western security system. Finally, NATO provided a platform for consultations on issues outside the alliance, both formal and informal.

After the collapse of the Soviet Union, some argued that NATO had completed its mission and ought to be dissolved. However, the alliance has endured and undergone considerable transformation. It assumed "out-of-area" responsibilities by intervening in the Balkans, providing stabilization forces in Bosnia (IFOR/SFOR), and intervening and providing stabilization forces there (KFOR) in Kosovo. It also offered assistance to the United States during the 2001 campaign in Afghanistan and contributed to peacekeeping afterwards.

The new 1999 Strategic Concept, which outlines NATO's broad goals and means, has made conflict prevention and crisis management the fundamental security tasks of the alliance. Another NATO task since 1990 has been to stabilize postcommunist central and eastern Europe. Through the Partnership for Peace program (PfP), which allows NATO to cooperate with nonmembers; the Membership Action Plan (MAP), which assisted applicants preparing for the 2002 round of enlargement; and greater cooperation with Russia in the new institutional setting of the NATO-Russia Council, the alliance has contributed to the postcommunist transition. The landmark in this process was the 1999 enlargement that brought Poland, Hungary, and the Czech Republic into the alliance. Three years later, at a summit in Prague, NATO invited an additional seven members to join in 2004.

The future of NATO is unclear. Critics argue that NATO has outlived its usefulness as a defense organization and has become merely a political forum with residual military structures. They point to the fact that in the fifty-plus years of NATO's history, the core Article 5 has been invoked only once, in the aftermath of the September 11, 2001, terrorist attack on the United States; yet U.S. military operations against Islamic terrorists have not been conducted as NATO operations. A contribut-

ing factor in the progressive downgrading of NATO's military value has been the widening capability gap between the United States and its European allies. In addition, the allies have found it difficult at times to reach consensus on the area of operations, with the Americans arguing for a global role, while the Europeans take a more traditional regional view. Fissures within NATO surfaced publicly during the 2003 war with Iraq, with France and Germany openly opposing the U.S. position. The American decision to rely on the "coalition of the willing" raised questions about the long-term viability of the alliance.

The proponents of NATO argue that it is too early to proclaim its end as the premier Euro-Atlantic security organization. They point out that NATO has responded to change by undertaking fundamental reforms, seeking to adjust its structures and its military capabilities. At the Prague summit on November 21 and 22, 2002, the alliance established the NATO Response Force (NRF) of twenty thousand for deployment into crisis areas, becoming fully operational in 2006. The nations at the summit set goals for reorganizing their armed forces in order to increase their mobility and allow sustained operations outside their territory. The next important step in reforming NATO was taken at the defense ministers' meeting in Brussels on June 12 and 13, 2003: NATO approved a new military command structure to reflect its new missions and its transition to smaller forces. The new command structure envisions the creation of a new Allied Command Operations, based at SHAPE in Mons. SACLANT will cease to exist, replaced by the Allied Command Transformation to oversee the restructuring of NATO's military. The number of commands will be reduced from twenty to eleven, and their responsibilities redefined.

These structural changes, combined with the development of "niche capabilities" by the member-states, suggest that, given political consensus, NATO may yet reinvent itself with a new division of tasks and specializations in place. The long-term viability of the alliance will also be affected by whether the emerging defense capabilities of the European Union complement or duplicate NATO's. Most important, the future of NATO will be determined by the future state of transatlantic relations.

*See also:* COLD WAR; WARSAW TREATY ORGANIZATION

## BIBLIOGRAPHY

Goldgeier, James M. (1999). *Not Whether But When: The U.S. Decision to Enlarge NATO.* Washington, DC: Brookings Institution Press.

Kaplan, Lawrence S. (1999). *The Long Entanglement: NATO's First Fifty Years.* Westport, CT: Praeger.

Kay, Sean. (1998). *NATO and the Future of European Security.* Lanham, MD: Rowman & Littlefield.

Michta, Andrew A., ed. (1999). *America's New Allies: Poland, Hungary and the Czech Republic in NATO.* Seattle: University of Washington Press.

*NATO Handbook.* (2001). Brussels: NATO Office of Information and Press.

North Atlantic Organization. Available from <http://www.nato.int>.

Osgood, Robert E. (1962). *NATO: The Entangling Alliance.* Chicago: University of Chicago Press.

Szayna, Thomas S. (2001). *NATO Enlargement, 2000–2015: Determinants and Implications for Defense Planning and Shaping.* Santa Monica, CA: RAND Corp.

ANDREW A. MICHTA

# NORTHERN CONVOYS

"Northern Convoys" is the widely used name of one of the shortest and most dangerous routes of transportation of lend-lease cargoes to the USSR by its allies in the anti-Hitler coalition from 1941 to 1945. Running from Scottish and Icelandic ports to Murmansk and Arkhangelsk, they extended for 2,000 miles (3,219 kilometers) and took ten to twelve days to cross. Until the end of 1942, Northern Convoys that went to the USSR had "PO" index; those returning from the USSR, "OP"; the subsequent Northern Convoys carried indices "JW" and "RA." The defense of cargo transports was carried out by the Allied, mainly British, Navy. In 1941 the route was passed by seven convoys to the USSR (from trial "P" or "Derwish" in August 1941 up to PO-6), and four convoys to Great Britain.

During the spring of 1942, in order to cut the Allies' northern sea route, the Nazi German headquarters sent large fleets and aircraft forces to occupied Norway. As a result, in July 1942, almost the entire convoy PO-17 was defeated (twenty-three of thirty-six transports were sunk). Thirteen of forty cargo ships were lost in September 1942 in PO-18. In total, from 1941 to 1945, forty-one Northern Convoys, which consisted of 839 transports, were sent to the northern Soviet ports, of

which 741 arrived safely. Sixty-one were lost, and thirty-seven returned to their own ports. Thirty-six Northern Convoys of 738 transports were sent from Soviet ports; of these, 699 reached their ports of destination, thirty were lost, and eight turned back. In addition, thirteen transports were lost during single passages and on berths in ports. While covering Northern Convoy 22, Allied fighting ships, including two cruisers and seven destroyers, were sunk.

In total, four million tons of cargo were delivered to the Soviet northern ports of the USSR, including 4,909 aircraft, 7,764 tanks, and 1,357 guns. Northern Convoys have added one more heroic page to a history of World War II and fighting cooperation of the USSR with the countries of the anti-Hitler coalition.

*See also:* NORTHERN FLEET; WORLD WAR II

## BIBLIOGRAPHY

Ruegg, Bob, and Hague, Arnold. (1992). *Convoys to Russia: Allied Convoys and Naval Surface Operations in Arctic Waters, 1941–1945.* Kendal, UK: World Ship Society.

Woodman, R. (1994). *The Arctic Convoys, 1941–1945.* London: John Murray.

MIKHAIL SUPRUN

# NORTHERN FLEET

The Northern Fleet is the largest of the four Russian naval fleets. It differs from the Baltic and Black Sea Fleets in that it (like the Pacific Fleet) has operated nuclear-powered vessels for more than forty years. In fact, two-thirds of Russia's nuclear-powered vessels are assigned to the Northern Fleet at the Kola Peninsula. The others are based at Pacific Fleet bases near Vladivostok. The Northern Fleet is organized into departments with separate spheres of responsibility. Other duties are divided among government committees and ministries. While the navy is responsible for the nuclear submarines and the three shipyards that service and maintain them, the State Committee for the Defense Industry (Goskomoboronprom) maintains the other shipyards. The Ministry for Atomic Energy (Minatom) is responsible for the nuclear fuel used in naval reactors, and the Ministry of Transport is in charge of shipments of new and spent nuclear fuel by railroad.

Before the Soviet collapse in 1991, nuclear submarines from the Northern and Pacific Fleets regularly patrolled the east and west coasts of the United States, the South China Sea, and outside the Persian Gulf. During the early twenty-first century, however, Russian nuclear submarines are rarely seen in these waters. The number of nuclear-powered submarines in operation in the Northern Fleet decreased from 120 during the late 1980s to less than forty in 2001. The Northern Fleet has six naval bases and shipyards on the Kola Peninsula to serve its nuclear vessels: Severomorsk, Gadzhievo, Gremikha, Vidyaevo, Sayda Bay, and Zapadnaya Litsa. Its main base and administrative center is Severomorsk, a city with a population of 70,000 situated 25 kilometers (15.5 miles) north of Murmansk on the eastern side of the Murmansk Fjord. Three nuclear-powered *Kirov*-class battle cruisers are based in Severomorsk: *Admiral Ushakov*, *Admiral Nakhimov*, and *Peter the Great*. However, no nuclear submarines are permanently stationed there. Safonovo, a rural town in the Severomorsk area, is the repair center for nuclear submarines and surface vessels, including the largest Northern Fleet submarines, such as the *Typhoon* class.

The strategic importance of the Kola Peninsula became apparent to Russian military planners with the rise of German naval power in the Baltic Sea and the outbreak of World War I. Recognizing the need for access to ice-free harbors in the north, Russia built a modern port in Alexandrovsk (today called Polyarny) at the mouth of the Murmansk Fjord in 1899. A naval force dedicated to the northern region was established shortly after the outbreak of World War I. In 1917, a railroad line was built to Murmansk, connecting the rest of Russia to an ice-free port open year round. Not until Josef Stalin's visit to Polyarny during the summer of 1933 was the Soviet Fleet of the Northern Seas actually established, however. Renamed the Northern Fleet in 1937, it consisted (before World War II) of just eight destroyers, fifteen diesel-powered submarines, patrol boats, minesweepers, and some smaller vessels. During World War II, supplies from the Western Allies were transported by convoy to Murmansk and then taken by railroad to military fronts in the south. A major naval buildup began after World War II in an effort to catch up with the United States. The first Soviet nuclear submarine (the *K-3 Leninsky Komsomol*) was commissioned to the Northern Fleet on July 1, 1958, just four years after the commissioning of the first American nuclear submarine, the *Nautilus*. During the period from 1950 to 1970, the Northern Fleet

grew from the smallest to the largest and most important of the four Soviet fleets.

*See also:* BALTIC FLEET; BLACK SEA FLEET; PACIFIC FLEET

### BIBLIOGRAPHY

Burns, Thomas S. (1978). *The Secret War for the Ocean Depths: Soviet-American Rivalry for Mastery of the Seas.* New York: Rawson Associates.

Jordan, John. (1982). *An Illustrated Guide to the Modern Soviet Navy.* New York: Arco.

Nilsen, Thomas; Kudrik, Igor; and Nikitin, Alexandr. (1996). *The Russian Northern Fleet: Sources of Radioactive Contamination.* Oslo: Bellona Foundation.

Nitze, Paul H., and Sullivan, Leonard. (1979). *Securing the Seas: The Soviet Naval Challenge and Western Alliance Options: An Atlantic Council Policy Study.* Boulder, CO: Westview Press.

JOHANNA GRANVILLE

## NORTHERN PEOPLES

Russia's Northern Peoples (*Malochislennye narody severa*, literally, "numerically small peoples of the north") constitute a distinct legal category of native peoples who live in the north, number less than fifty thousand each, and pursue traditional ways of life. During the early Soviet period, such a category was created as the focus for a special set of policies, informed by the state's belief that, due to the "backwardness" of these peoples, they needed special protection and help to reach the stage of communism. The number of peoples belonging to this group varied over time, but at the end of the Soviet period it included twenty-six peoples: Sami, Khanty, Mansi, Nenets, Enets, Nganasan, Selkup, Tofalar, Evenki, Even, Yukagir, Chukchi, Chuvans, Eskimos, Aleut, Koryak, Itelmen, Dolgan, Ket, Negidal, Nanai, Ulchi, Oroki, Orochi, Udege, and Nivkhi. Together, these peoples numbered slightly under 182,000 in 1989.

The Northern Peoples inhabit an immense swath of Russia, from the Kola Peninsula to the Bering Sea, the Chinese border, and Sakhalin Island. They belong to numerous language groups, and have distinctive cultures, traditions, and adaptations to diverse ecosystems. At the outset of the Soviet era, most pursued traditional activities that included reindeer herding, hunting, fishing, and marine mammal hunting. Most were nomadic and

A group of Dolgans stand together at their camp near the village of Syndassko, Russia, in 1993. © JACQUES LANGEVIN/CORBIS SYGMA

lived in small kin-based groups. Most were organized into clans, although these had been disrupted by the twentieth century. During the tsarist period, most had been subjugated, and were required to pay a tribute of furs (*yasak*) to the state. Some missionary activity had occurred, but most groups remained largely animistic.

The Soviets brought sweeping changes to the Northern Peoples, introducing compulsory schooling (first in their own languages, but soon afterward in Russian) and health care; imposing collective farms, confiscating reindeer and hunting equipment; and repressing leaders, wealthier individuals, and shamans. The Soviets also settled as much of the population as possible in newly created villages. These policies radically disturbed the local family structures and the transmission of knowledge from elder to younger generations. Alcohol abuse and violent death became rampant, and by the end of the Soviet period, life expectancy of the Northern Peoples averaged a generation less than the (already low) Russian level. At the same time, the state nurtured a small indigenous intelligentsia, including doctors, teachers, writers, artists,

and political leaders. Within these leaders the state engendered the larger, composite identity of "Northern Peoples," laying the foundation of a common, pan-native response, once the political climate allowed for such.

The late Soviet policy of glasnost enabled the Northern Peoples to publicly address their horrific situation for the first time. A strong nativist movement ensued, with the organization of the Russian Association of the Indigenous Peoples of the North (RAIPON) in 1990. Native leaders lobbied for laws that would protect native rights, with special focus on the issue of native lands, which had been subject to extensive resource extraction and environmental degradation. Key federal legislation outlining native rights and mechanisms for land claims was finally adopted in 1999–2001. One outcome of the legislation has been the increase in the number of peoples included in the designation; several groups who were not considered distinct peoples during the Soviet period, among them the Shors, Teluets, and Kereks, have achieved recognition as Northern Peoples since 1991. The number of native persons claiming membership in the overall group has also increased, largely due to revitalized pride in native identity. While political reforms have encouraged native political development, economic reforms, including reduced northern subsidies, have severely challenged Northern Peoples' livelihoods.

*See also:* EVENKI; CHUKCHI; DOLGANS; KHANTY; KORYAKS; MANSI; NATIONALITIES POLICIES, SOVIET; NATIONALITIES POLICIES, TSARIST; NENETS; SAMI

**BIBLIOGRAPHY**

Fondahl, Gail; Lazebnik, Olga; Poelzer, Greg; and Robbek, Vassily. (2001). "Native 'land claims,' Russian style." *The Canadian Geographer* 45(4):545–561.

Pika, Aleksandr, ed. (1999). *Neotraditionalism in the Russian North: Indigenous Peoples and the Legacy of Perestroika.* Edmonton: Canadian Circumpolar Institute Press.

Russian Association of Indigenous Peoples of the North website. Available at <http://www.raipon.org/>.

Slezkine, Yuri (1994). *Arctic Mirrors: Russia and the Small Peoples of the North.* Ithaca, NY: Cornell University Press.

Wessendorf, Kathrin, and Køhler, Thomas, trs. (2002). *Towards a New Millenium. Ten Years of the Indigenous Movement in Russia.* IWGIA Document No. 107. Copenhagen: International Working Group on Indigenous Affairs.

GAIL A. FONDAHL

# NORWAY, RELATIONS WITH

Geographically driven relations between northern Norway and the Russian Arctic coast predate the Slavic and Scandinavian colonization of the northern periphery of Europe starting in the twelfth century. Norwegian Vikings referred to the White Sea region as Bjarmeland, and had at least sporadic contacts with the local inhabitants by 900 C.E. Norwegian trading expeditions to the northern Dvina estuary took place regularly until the early thirteenth century, and there were at least occasional journeys into the Russian interior. A 1276 law code refers to Norwegian commercial expeditions via the Baltic to Novgorod.

Interest in the northern fisheries attracted a growing number of settlers to the Arctic coast in the Middle Ages. Commercial and military interaction in the area included raids that sometimes esca-

lated to open warfare. The Norwegian–Novgorodian peace treaty of 1326 reaffirmed the status quo and ensured free shipping and trade. No formal border was demarcated and many regions were *de jure* placed under joint administration in the fourteenth century. Some Norwegian settlers may have lived on the Kola Peninsula early on, and the Norwegians claimed control over the peninsula for centuries, notwithstanding its steady Russification. The Russian word *murmasky*, referring to the northern Kola coast, is derived from *nordmann* ("Norwegian").

The Norwegian fortress of Vardøhus near the present-day border was built around 1300, whereas the main economic center on the Russian side came to be the Orthodox Solovki Island monastery in the White Sea. The first Russian town in the region, Kola (near the present-day Murmansk), was not founded until 1583, but soon had a Norwegian guesthouse. Perhaps during the fifteenth century, but definitely by the 1550s, another Orthodox monastery was founded in the ill-defined border region of the Pechenga Valley. The monks regularly traded with Vardøhus. Norwegian merchants, often from the ports of Bergen (with historic monopoly rights over the northern waters) and Trondheim, regularly attended the Russian border market of Kegor, as well as Kola. However, trade with the Murman coast appears to have stagnated during the seventeenth century and been limited to local products. Merchants from Bergen and Trondheim periodically also visited the Russian port of Arkhangelsk, especially to ship sporadic Russian grain subsidies to Denmark-Norway. Conflicting territorial claims made border disputes quite common during the sixteenth century and the early seventeenth century, and the Norwegian castellan of eastern Finnmark made symbolic visits to Kola to demand tribute from the local population until 1813.

Regular commercial contacts between the neighboring coastal regions, with Vardøhus as the main center, were well established by the late seventeenth century, driven primarily by Russians. Russian flour, cloth, hides, and tallow became important products for the northern Norwegian economy. By the 1760s, Russian vessels made annual trips to the Finnmark and Troms coasts, and Russian fishing in northern Norwegian waters was common. This was countenanced with some limitations by the Danish government because of its good relations with Russia. Norwegians are known to have settled in northern Russia starting in the eighteenth century. The interaction between Norwegians and Russians produced a unique local pidgin language known as *russenorsk*, "Russian Norwegian." The regime of open borders continued until an 1826 treaty delineated the frontier and granted two-thirds of the shared territory to Russia.

Trade in northern Norway was gradually liberalized in 1789 as part of a plan to stimulate the region's economic development. New port towns were built and direct Russian trade with Norwegian fishermen was formally authorized. Most remaining restrictions were eliminated in 1839, and regular steamship traffic between northern Russia and Finnmark began during the 1870s. Up to 350 Russian ships visited northern Norway each year during the course of the eighteenth century. Attempts to control Russian trade and fishing in Norway became more serious during the period when Norway was under Swedish rule. All foreign fishing was formally banned in 1913.

Political relations became more tense during the nineteenth century because of Russian concern about perceived Norwegian expansionism in the Arctic. In contrast, the Norwegian administration in the United Kingdom of Sweden-Norway often found itself moderating the growing Swedish Russophobia. However, its pragmatism was repeatedly tempered by fears that Russia might be eyeing some of the ice-free harbors of Finnmark. The accelerating Russian settlement on the Kola Peninsula and the steady stream of immigrants to northern Norway from Russian-controlled Finland heightened the sense of alarm during the second half of the nineteenth century. The Norwegian popular mood began to favor a more nationalistic policy in the north. Systematic Norwegianization was seen as a way to effectively control the ethnically mixed territory. Russia was perceived negatively because of its authoritarianism even though it was the only great power lending active support to Norwegian independence in 1905, albeit clearly with a view to weakening Sweden. Newly independent Norway unsuccessfully sought to regain control of the Russian borderlands at the Versailles Conference.

The October Revolution led to a freeze in Russian-Norwegian relations, with devastating consequence to some northern Norweigian communities, as well as a geographic separation when Finland gained control of the Pechenga-Petsamo region. Although the Finnish threat in some ways replaced the weakened Bolshevik regime as a source of concern, diplomatic relations between Norway and the Soviet state were not established until 1924. The Norwegian government actively sought to curb the activities of leftist pro-Soviet organizations and reinforced the garrisons in northern Norway. During World War II the Norwegian government-in-exile was very worried about Soviet territorial ambitions in northern Norway. Its fears seemed confirmed when the Red Army temporarily occupied eastern Finnmark in 1944. The Soviets also claimed some of the Norwegian-controlled northern Atlantic islands (Bear Isle, Spitsbergen).

Norwegian Russophobia and a sense of vulnerability after the German occupation led to a strong cross-party consensus in favor of NATO membership in 1949. Although it continued to distrust the Soviets, the Oslo government adopted a pragmatic stance, de-emphasizing the defense of Finnmark and prohibiting the stationing of foreign troops and nuclear weapons in the country. Intergovernmental relations remained formal, and most Norwegian-Russian interaction was localized to the northern border regions. Perestroika and the collapse of the Soviet Union did a great deal to restore the historically close ties between northern Russia and Finnmark, and during the early twenty-first century there are many lively economic, political, and cultural ties.

*See also:* COLD WAR; FINLAND; SWEDEN, RELATIONS WITH; VIKINGS

**BIBLIOGRAPHY**

Kirby, David. (1990). *Northern Europe in the Early Modern Period: The Baltic World, 1492–1772*. London: Longman.

Kirby, David. (1995). *The Baltic World, 1772–1993: Europe's Northern Periphery in an Age of Change*. London: Longman.

Larsen, Karen. (1948). *A History of Norway*. Princeton, NJ: Princeton University Press.

Libaek, Ivar. (1991). *History of Norway: From the Ice Age to the Oil Age*. Oslo: Grondahl and Son.

JARMO T. KOTILAINE

# NOVGOROD, ARCHBISHOP OF

The archbishop was the highest ecclesiastical office and symbolic head of the city—Lord Novgorod the Great. The chronicles refer to him as *vladyka*, a term meaning "lord," or "ruler," reflecting his duties as the representative of the city. He resided within the city's fortress (*detinets*), met with Western ambassadors and Russian princes, mediated disputes in the city, and officiated in the city's main Cathedral of St. Sophia.

The Novgorodian office of bishop traditionally dates to the reign of Vladimir, who brought in Ioakim of Cherson in 989, but there is little firm evidence of its existence until the mid-1030s, when Luka Zhidyata served. The bishop received tithes from fines and wergild payments, but from the late 1130s onward a fixed income from the prince's treasury was set. Landholding, however, constituted the basis of the church's wealth, and by the fourteenth and fifteenth centuries the Novgorodian Church was the largest landholder, employing religious and secular workers and even hiring soldiers.

Following Novgorod's independence from Kiev in 1136, the first election of the bishop occurred in 1156 when the "people of the entire town," perhaps in a meeting of an assembly (*veche*), chose Arkady. However, the ability of Novgorod to select its own archbishop did not make the Church independent of the metropolitan, who still confirmed candidates. After Arkady's death in 1163, Ilya was appointed (not elected) first archbishop of Novgorod in 1165. The next election of an archbishop occurred in 1186 when townsmen, prince, hegumens, and priests selected Gavriil, Ilya's brother. After 1186 it became customary for the townspeople, prince, and clergy to elect their archbishops in a veche, but it is not clear whether all free Novgorodians participated. When there was no clear candidate the city utilized lots (for example, in 1229 and 1359): Three names were placed on the altar of St. Sophia and one would be chosen.

Sometime during the thirteenth century the archbishop came to preside over the Council of Lords (*Sovet gospod*), the highest executive and judicial body. It consisted of some fifty to sixty members, including the sitting lord mayor and chiliarch (commander of troops), former lord mayors, and current mayors of the five boroughs. The meetings took place within the archbishop's quarters, and later in the archbishop's Palace of Facets, constructed in 1433. The Novgorodian Judicial Charter notes that referral hearings convened in the archbishop's quarters.

The archbishop did not directly control the city's monasteries, which fell under the jurisdiction of one of the five district hegumens (heads of monasteries). The monasteries were ultimately under the jurisdiction of the archimandrite, who also was chosen by the veche.

Moscow conquered Novgorod in 1478, and two years later Grand Prince Ivan III arrested and imprisoned Archbishop Theophilus. Ivan forced Theophilus to resign and replaced him with Gennadius in 1484, bringing the archbishopric more firmly under the metropolitan of Moscow. In 1489 Ivan confiscated most of the archbishop's estates and half the lands of the six wealthiest monasteries. These lands became the basis of Moscow's system of military service landholdings (*pomeste*).

*See also:* BIRCHBARK CHARTERS; CATHEDRAL OF ST. SOPHIA, NOVGOROD; NOVGOROD JUDICIAL CHARTER; NOVGOROD THE GREAT; POSADNIK; PRIMARY CHRONICLE; RUSSIAN ORTHODOX CHURCH; VECHE.

**BIBLIOGRAPHY**

Birnbaum, Henrik. (1981). *Lord Novgorod the Great.* Columbus, OH: Slavica.

LAWRENCE N. LANGER

## NOVGOROD JUDICIAL CHARTER

The Novgorod Judicial Charter exists in a sixteenth-century fragment but was likely first compiled around 1471. By then Novgorod faced a growing military threat from Moscow. In 1456 Moscow imposed the Treaty of Yazhelbitsy, which limited Novgorod's independence in foreign policy, forced the city to cede important territories, and imposed a heavy indemnity payment. Novgorod retained its internal administrative structure, but the city became torn politically between pro-Lithuanian and pro-Muscovite factions. Moscow decisively defeated Novgorod at the Shelon River and imposed a huge indemnity of sixteen thousand rubles. Grand Prince Ivan III received Novgorodian delegations at the mouth of the Shelon and concluded a peace based on the earlier Yazhelbitsy Treaty. The Charter was probably drawn up at this time or soon thereafter, as it reflects Novgorod's administrative structure and liberties before Ivan's arrests of some leading Novgorodians in late 1475 and 1476, and his annexation of the city in 1478.

The Charter records that the archbishop, leading political officers, and urban free population (mayors [*posadniki*], chiliarchs [*tysyatski*], boyars, well-to-do or ranking men [*zhiti lyudi*], merchants, and taxable population) from all five boroughs, who, having met in Yaroslav's court in an assembly (*veche*), and having conferred with Grand Prince Ivan III and his son, agreed to the provisions of the Charter. The incomplete Charter abruptly ends in the midst of Article 42. Much of the Charter concerns the prerogatives of the city's judicial system. Significantly, the first four articles asserted the rights of the courts of the archbishop, mayor, and chiliarch. The archbishop conducts his court according to the canons of the Church, and the chiliarch retains the independence of his court. The mayor, however, must conduct his judicial proceedings with that of the grand prince's lieutenant (*namestnik*). Although this appears as a limitation of the mayor's prerogatives, it likely reflects longstanding practice, as the text notes that they are to direct the court jointly in accordance with traditional custom. On the other hand, Article 5 affirmed the prohibition against removing the mayor, chiliarch, lieutenant of the archbishop, and all their judges from their courts. The grand prince's lieutenants and judges (*tyuny*, who were probably slaves) retained a customary right of review.

Heavy fines were exacted according to status for slandering or intimidating the mayor, chiliarch, any of the other judges, or the decisions of trial by combat (the latter a common feature of the Pskov Judicial Charter). Boyars paid fifty rubles, the well-to-do (non-aristocratic wealthy merchants and landowners) twenty rubles, and the remaining free urban population (*molodshi*, or young ones) ten rubles to the grand prince and Novgorod. These were all prohibitive fines designed to preserve the integrity of the courts. Cases were to be tried and completed within a month, but land disputes could take up to two months; the Charter also stipulated the fees the courts and their officials received.

Court procedures required the two litigants (or their representatives) and no others to confront one another and conduct their cases. Participants including all judges had to kiss the cross, attesting to their truthfulness and Christian faith. Failure to kiss the cross resulted in the loss of the case. Sons could kiss the cross on behalf of their widowed mothers; if a son refused, then the widow could kiss the cross in her home in the presence of the bailiffs. Character witnesses could be called, but the Pskov populace and slaves could not serve as character witness, although a slave could testify against another slave. Litigants were normally given two weeks to rebut witnesses. Boyars and the wealthy

conducted referral hearings within the archbishop's residence, which meant that they were probably under the jurisdiction of the Council of Lords. The Charter carefully regulated procedures concerning postponements.

Of particular interest are the Charter's references to the administrative subdivisions of the city. Each borough, street, hundred, or row could send two people to a court or investigation. Unfortunately, the Charter does not clarify the social composition or administrative responsibilities of the urban divisions, which have been the subject of much historical debate. Novgorod consisted of five boroughs, which were divided into hundreds, streets, and rows. The boroughs were under the jurisdiction of boyars, and the hundreds were originally administered by a complex arrangement of princely and urban officials that, by the late twelfth century, was dominated by the city's boyars. The streets and rows may have reflected the interests or administration of the general population of lesser merchants and craftsmen.

*See also:* NOVGOROD THE GREAT; PSKOV JUDICIAL CHARTER; SUDEBNIK OF 1497

**BIBLIOGRAPHY**

Kaiser, Daniel, tr. and ed. (1992). *The Laws of Russia,* Series 1, Vol. 1: *The Laws of Rus', Tenth to Fifteenth Centuries.* Salt Lake City, UT: Charles Schlacks, Jr.

Vernadsky, George. (1969). *Medieval Russian Laws.* New York: Norton.

LAWRENCE N. LANGER

## NOVGOROD THE GREAT

Novgorod the Great was a city-state located in northwestern Russia, existing from the mid-tenth century to its annexation by Muscovy in 1478.

Although Novgorod was named in the Laurentian redaction of the *Primary Chronicle* as the political seat occupied by Ryurik in 862, archaeological evidence indicates that the city was founded in the mid-tenth century. Located on the Volkhov River near its origins at Lake Ilmen, the city quickly emerged as a leading commercial center. Shortly after Prince Vladimir adopted Christianity for Kievan Rus, Novgorod became the seat of a bishopric and became a major ecclesiastic and cultural center. Its political institutions represented an alternative to the strong princely regime developing in north-eastern Russia. At the peak of its power, Novgorod controlled lands stretching from the Baltic Sea to the White Sea and the northern Urals Mountains, but it was subjugated by Muscovy in 1478.

## POLITICAL ORGANIZATION AND HISTORY

As Kievan Rus formed, Novgorod emerged as the second most important city of that state. Kiev's princes appointed their sons or other close associates to govern Novgorod. Thus, when Svyatoslav died in 972, his son Vladimir was serving as prince in Novgorod. Similarly, when Vladimir died in 1015, his son Yaroslav was ruling Novgorod. Both Svyatoslav and Vladimir were able to use troops from Novgorod and Scandinavia to secure their own positions as princes of Kiev. Although it has been argued that Prince Yaroslav of Kiev intended Novgorod to become the hereditary seat of his son Vladimir, most scholars concur that Novgorod continued to be ruled by appointees of the Kievan princes. This arrangement distinguished Novgorod from the other major towns of Kievan Rus, towns which, during the eleventh century, became patrimonies of different branches of the Rurikid dynasty.

In 1136 the Novgorodians asserted their right to name their own prince. For the next century they selected princes from the Rurikid dynastic lines that ruled in Chernigov, Smolensk, and Vladimir-Suzdal and that competed for power in Kievan Rus. Novgorod's affiliation with a particular dynastic branch frequently gave its princes advantages over their competitors. Novgorod consequently also became an object of contention among the rival dynastic branches, which sought to influence Novgorod's choice of prince through political, economic, and military pressure. In 1148–1149 and again in 1169 Novgorod clashed violently with Suzdalia, which was able to block supplies, including food, to the city. By the second quarter of the thirteenth century, princes from Vladimir-Suzdal had gained dominance in Novgorod.

In the absence of a single branch of the dynasty permanently ruling the city and its associated lands, Novgorod developed a political system that was unique within the lands of Rus. Princes exercised considerable authority and were responsible for defending the city. But they were obliged to reside outside the city and to govern in conjunction with the city's administrators, its mayor (posadnik) and militia commander (tysyatsky), who were elected from Novgorod's wealthy, landowning elite, known as the Novgorodian boyars. In addition, the city irregularly convened a town assembly, or veche. The bishops of Novgorod, elevated to archbishops in 1165 and regarded as significant unifying influences in the city, also participated in the city's administration, its diplomatic affairs, its economic activities, and its judicial system. The functions of these offices and institutions and division of authority among them remain imperfectly understood; scholars have therefore characterized Novgorod variously as a republic with its popular town assembly and as an oligarchy politically dominated by a few boyar families.

The Mongol invasion of Kievan Rus in the period from 1238 to 1240 did not reach Novgorod. But in 1259, the Mongols accompanied by Prince Alexander Nevsky (r. 1252–1263), who had led the defense of Novgorod from the Swedes at the Neva River in 1240 and from the Teutonic Knights at Lake Peipus in 1242, forced Novgorod to submit to a census and pay tribute. Novgorod continued to recognize the grand princes of Vladimir, all of whom were also princes of Moscow after the mid-fourteenth century, as its own.

During the fourteenth century local officials played a greater role in the city's governance and administration. Tensions between them and their princes developed as disputes arose over the princes' demands for tribute payments and control of territories in Novgorod's northern empire, including the North Dvina land, which Grand Prince Vasily I (r. 1389–1425) unsuccessfully tried to seize in 1397. The conflicts between Novgorod and Moscow reached critical proportions in the fifteenth century. Novgorod occasionally, in the late fourteenth and fifteenth centuries, turned to Lithuania for a prince and resisted making tribute payments to Moscow. In 1456 Grand Prince Vasily II (r. 1425–1462) defeated Novgorod militarily. The ensuing Treaty of Yazhelbitsy curtailed Novgorod's autonomy, particularly in foreign affairs. When Novgorod nevertheless sought closer relations with Lithuania in 1470–1471, Grand Prince Ivan III defeated Novgorod at the Battle of Shelon (1471). In 1478 he removed the symbolic veche bell, replaced Novgorod's local officials with his own governors, and effectively annexed Novgorod to Muscovy.

## COMMERCE

Novgorod's political importance derived from its commercial strength. Its location on the Volkhov River, which flowed northward into Lake Ladoga, gave it access through the Baltic Sea to Scandinavia and northern Europe. It thus became the northern Rus terminus of the route "from the Varangians to the Greeks," which followed the Dnieper River to Kiev and beyond to the Black Sea and Byzantium. Novgorod was also linked by waterways and portages to the Volga River, the route to Bulgar on the Volga, Khazaria, the Caspian Sea, and the Muslim East.

Novgorod's commerce was the main source of silver for the Russian lands. In the tenth century, silver dirhams were imported from the Muslim East. Some were reexported to the Baltic region; others circulated in the lands of Rus. From the eleventh century, when the Islamic silver coins were no longer available, Novgorod imported silver from its European trading partners. In addition, Novgorod imported European woolen cloth, weapons, metals, pottery, alcoholic beverages, and salt. From the east and Byzantium it imported silks and spices, gems and jewelry, and glassware and ceramic pottery.

Novgorod not only functioned as a transit center, reexporting imported goods; it also traded its own goods, chiefly wax, honey, and fur. By the end of the twelfth century Novgorod extended its authority over a vast northern empire stretching to the White Sea and to the Ural Mountains. It collected tribute in fur from the region's Finno-Ugric populations; its merchants traded with them as well. By these means it secured a supply of luxury fur pelts for export. In the fourteenth and fifteenth centuries it also exported large quantities of squirrel pelts.

During the tenth and eleventh centuries Novgorod's main European trading partners were Scandinavians. By the twelfth century they had established their own trading complex around the Church of St. Olaf on the market side of the city. From the twelfth century, German merchants, who established their own trading depot at Peterhof, were successfully competing with the Scandinavians for Novgorod's trade. In the 1130s Prince Vsevolod transferred control over weights and measures—the fees collected for weighing and measuring goods that were sold in the marketplace—and judicial authority over trade disputes to Novgorod's bishop, the wax merchants' association, which was associated with the Church of St. John, and the *tysyatsky*.

Novgorod's commerce survived the invasion of the Mongols, who encouraged the transport of imported and domestic goods as tribute and as commercial commodities down the Volga River to their

capital at Sarai. Although disputes led to occasional interruptions in Novgorod's trade with the Hansa, as in 1388 to 1392 and in 1443 to 1448, it persisted until 1494, when Grand Prince Ivan III closed Peterhof.

**SOCIETY AND CULTURE**

Novgorod was one of the largest cities in the lands of Rus. In the twelfth century it covered an area of over one thousand acres. With the exception of the area containing the Cathedral of St. Sophia, which was set within a citadel from the mid-eleventh century, Novgorod was an open city until the late fourteenth century or early fifteenth century, when a town wall was built. The Volkhov River divided the city into two halves, the Sophia side on the west bank and the market side on the east. It was further subdivided into five boroughs (*kontsy*) and streets.

Novgorod's population in the early eleventh century is estimated to have been between ten and fifteen thousand and to have doubled by the early thirteenth century. Estimates for the fifteenth century range from twenty-five to fifty thousand. The wealthiest and most politically active and influential strata in Novgorod's society were the boyars and great merchants. Lower strata included merchants of more moderate means, a diverse range of artisans and craftsmen, unskilled workers, and slaves. Clergy also dwelled in and near the city. Peasants occupied rural villages in the countryside subject to Novgorod.

Civil strife repeatedly occurred within the city. In the extreme, riots broke out, and victims were thrown off the bridge into the Volkhov River. But more commonly, order was maintained by the combined princely-local administration that regulated business and adjudicated legal disputes. The populace relied on formal documentation issued by city officials for business transactions, property sales and donations, wills, and other legal actions. Birchbark charters, unearthed in archaeological excavations, attest that it was common for Novgorodians to communicate about daily personal, household, and business activities in writing. The bishops' court also was a center of chronicle writing.

The urban population dwelled in a wooden city. Roads and walkways were constructed from split logs. Urban estates owned by boyars and wealthy merchants lined the roads. While they dwelled in the central residential buildings on the estates, shopkeepers, craftsmen, and other dependents lived and worked in smaller houses in the courts, which also included nonresidential buildings and were surrounded by wooden fences. Although the city boasted a drainage system, the accumulation of refuse required repeated repaving of the roads; frequent fires similarly required the reconstruction of buildings. Many of the town's craftsmen were correspondingly engaged in logging, carpentry, and other trades involving wood.

Some buildings, especially churches, were of masonry construction. The Cathedral of St. Sophia, built in 1045–1050 from undressed stone set in pink-colored mortar and adorned with five domes, was the first such structure built in Novgorod. Sponsored by Prince Vladimir Yaroslavich, it became the bishop's cathedral, the centerpiece of the Sophia side of the city. From the beginning of the twelfth century, princes, bishops, and wealthy boyars and merchants were patrons of dozens of masonry churches. Generally smaller than the Cathedral of St. Sophia, they were located on both sides of the river and also in monasteries outside the city. Novgorodian and visiting artists and artisans designed and built these churches and also painted icons and frescoes that decorated their interiors. By the fourteenth and fifteenth centuries they had developed distinctive Novgorodian schools of architecture and icon painting.

The boyars and wealthy merchants of the city also owned landed estates outside the city. Although women generally did not participate in public and political affairs, they did own and manage property, including real estate. Among the best known of them was Marfa Boretskaya, who was one of the wealthiest individuals in Novgorod on the eve of its loss of independence. On those provincial estates, peasants and nonagricultural workers engaged in farming, animal husbandry, fishing, hunting, iron and salt manufacture, beekeeping, and related activities. Although it was not uncommon for the region's unfavorable agricultural conditions to produce poor harvests, which occasionally caused famine conditions, the produce from these estates was usually not only sufficient to feed and supply the population of the city and its hinterlands, but was cycled into the city's commercial network. After Ivan III subjugated Novgorod, he confiscated the landed estates and arrested or exiled the boyars and merchants who had owned them. He seized landed properties belonging to the archbishop and monasteries as well.

*See also:* BIRCHBARK CHARTERS; KIEVAN RUS; NOVGOROD, ARCHBISHIOP OF; NOVGOROD JUDICIAL CHARTER; POSADNIK; ROUTE TO GREEKS; RURIKID DYNASTY; VIKINGS

**BIBLIOGRAPHY**
Birnbaum, Henrik. (1981). *Lord Novgorod the Great: Essays in the History and Culture of a Medieval City-State*, Part I: *Historical Background.* Columbus, OH: Slavica.

Dejevsky, N. J. (1977). "Novgorod: The Origins of a Russian Town." In *European Towns: Their Archaeology and Early History*, ed. M. W. Barley. London: Council for British Archaeology by Academic Press.

Karger, Mikhail K. (1975). *Novgorod: Architectural Monuments, 11th–17th Centuries.* Leningrad: Aurora Art Publishers.

Langer, Lawrence N. (1976). "The Medieval Russian Town." In *The City in Russian History*, ed. Michael Hamm. Lexington: University of Kentucky Press.

Michell, Robert and Forbes, Nevill, trs. (1914). *The Chronicle of Novgorod 1016–1471.* London: Royal Historical Society.

Raba, Joel. (1967). "Novgorod in the Fifteenth Century: A Re-examination." *Canadian Slavic Studies* 1:348–364.

Thompson, Michael W. (1967). *Novgorod the Great.* New York: Praeger.

JANET MARTIN

# NOVIKOV, NIKOLAI IVANOVICH

(1744–1818), writer, journalist, satirist, publisher, and social worker.

Nikolai Ivanovich Novikov was a prominent writer, journalist, publisher, and social worker who began the vogue of the satirical magazine. Catherine II's efforts to proliferate ideas of the Enlightenment had injected new vigor in Russian writers in the early 1760s. Hoping to demonstrate to the West that Russia was not a despotic state, she established a "commission for the compilation of a new code of laws" in 1767 and published "instructions" for the commission in major European languages—a treatise entitled *Nakaz dlya komissii po sochineniyu novogo ulozheniya.* She also began the publication in early 1769 of a satirical weekly modeled on the English *Spectator* entitled *All Sorts and Sundries (Vsyakaya vsyachina)* and urged intellectuals to follow her example. For a brief period, all editors were freed from preliminary censorship.

An enthusiastic believer in the Enlightenment, Nikolai Novikov accepted the challenge and published a succession of successful journals—*Truten* (*The Drone*, 1769–1770), *Pustomelya* (*The Tattler*) in 1770, *Zhivopisets* (*The Painter*) in 1772, and others. Novikov became a pioneer in the journalistic movement in the 1770s and 1780s, and the works of prose appearing in his journals amounted to both a new literary phenomenon for Russian culture and a new form for the expression of public opinion. He took Catherine's "instructions" seriously and cultivated works that delved deeply into questions of political life and social phenomena that formerly lay within the sole jurisdiction of the tsarist bureaucracy—topics that could be considered before only in secret and with official approval. In addition to editing and publishing four periodicals and a historical dictionary, *The Library of Old Russian Authors* (1772–1775) in thirty volumes, Novikov also took over the Moscow University Press in 1778. His publishing houses operated first in St. Petersburg and then in Moscow, offering a prodigious quantity of books designed to spread Enlightenment ideas at a modest price. Novikov dedicated himself and his fortune to the advancement of elementary education as well, publishing textbooks and even the first Russian magazine for children.

Novikov can be viewed as a tragic figure in Russian history. Abruptly in 1774 Catherine II blocked publication of his journals because of their sharp attacks on serious social injustice. By imperial order she stopped further books from being produced. In 1791 she closed his printing presses. Regarding education as her own bailiwick, she was probably irked by Novikov's successful activities. Novikov's association with the Freemasons also alienated her. A middle-of-the-road theorist rather than a purist, Novikov was sometimes caught in a paradox between his keen appreciation of European Enlightenment and his high regard for the ancient Russian virtues. Freemasonry seemed to offer a way out of the paradox to a firm moral standpoint.

Catherine II, however, had always opposed secret societies, which had been outlawed in 1782 (although Freemasonry had been exempted). Her predecessor Peter III, whom she had skillfully dethroned, had been favorably disposed towards Freemasonry. Equally, her political rival and personal enemy, the Grand Duke Paul, was a prominent Freemason. Further, since the break with England, Russian Freemasonry had come under the influence of German Freemasonry, of which Frederick the Great, the archenemy of Catherine, was a dominant figure. To Catherine, it must have seemed that everyone she disliked intensely was a Freemason.

Novikov was arrested but never tried and was sentenced by imperial decree to detention in the fortress of Schlüsselburg for fifteen years. He was released when Paul became emperor in 1796, but retired from public life in disillusionment to study mysticism. He never could engage fully in Moscow's literary world again.

*See also:* CATHERINE II; ENLIGHTENMENT, IMPACT OF; JOURNALISM

**BIBLIOGRAPHY**

Jones, W. Gareth. (1984). *Nikolay Novikov, Enlightener of Russia*. New York: Cambridge University Press.

Levitt, Marcus C. (1995). *Early Modern Russian Writers: Late Seventeenth and Eighteenth Centuries*. Detroit: Gale Research.

JOHANNA GRANVILLE

## NOVOCHERKASSK UPRISING

On June 1, 1962, in response to a sharp increase in the price of butter and meat, a strike erupted at the Novocherkassk Electric-Locomotive Works, which employed 13,000 workers. The stoppage immediately spread to neighboring industrial enterprises. Efforts of the local authorities to halt the strike proved fruitless. So alarmed was the central government headed by Nikita Khrushchev that six of the top party leaders were sent to deal with the situation. Although a negotiated settlement was not ruled out, several thousand troops, as well as tank units, were deployed.

The following day, thousands of workers marched into town to present their demands for price rollbacks and wage increases. During the confrontation between the strikers and the government forces, shooting broke out that resulted in twenty-four deaths and several score serious injuries. Hundreds were arrested, and a series of trials followed. Seven strikers were condemned to death, and many more were imprisoned for long terms. The regime effectively covered up what had occurred. Outside the USSR, little was known about the events until

Alexander Solzhenitsyn devoted several pages to them in *The Gulag Archipelago*. In the last years of the Gorbachev era, information was published in Soviet media for the first time.

The Novocherkassk events, which became known as "Bloody Saturday," contributed to the demise of the USSR. Never daring to raise food prices again, the leadership was compelled to subsidize agriculture even more heavily, thus severely unbalancing the economy. Moreover, as information about the massacre of strikers became known, the legitimacy of what has long been proclaimed "the workers' state" was decidedly undermined.

*See also:* KHRUSHCHEV, NIKITA SERGEYEVICH; SOLZHENITSYN, ALEXANDER ISAYEVICH

**BIBLIOGRAPHY**

Baron, Samuel H. (2001). *Bloody Saturday in the Soviet Union: Novocherkassk, 1962*. Stanford, CA: Stanford University Press.

Kozlov, Vladimir A. (2002). *Mass Uprisings in the USSR*. Armonk, NY: M. E. Sharpe.

SAMUEL H. BARON

# NOVOSIBIRSK REPORT

The Novosibirsk Report was a document that helped provide the technical background for Gorbachev's perestroika policy.

The document that became known as the "Novosibirsk report" was written by Tatiana Zaslavskaya for a conference that was held in the western Siberian city of Novosibirsk in 1985. The organizers of that conference had a limited number of copies of her report made for participants in the conference. Within a short time, however, copies of the report were handed over to Western journalists in Moscow, ensuring that the document would become widely known and hotly debated. Communist Party officials sharply reprimanded Zaslavskaya and Abel Aganbegian, the chief organizer of the conference, for the unorthodox conclusions that she had offered. After Mikhail Gorbachev came to power, the kind of thinking found in Zaslavkaya's writings was endorsed by the highest leadership of the Party–state regime. Zaslavskaya became one of Gorbachev's advisers, the head of the Soviet Sociological Association, and a member of the Congress of People's Deputies of the USSR. She has become a legendary figure among Russian sociologists.

Zaslavskaya's report for the conference in Novosibirsk in 1983 was of great significance in Soviet intellectual history because it challenged principles that had been fundamental to the social sciences since they were imposed by Josef Stalin in the 1930s. Stalin had asserted that in a socialist society, in contrast to capitalist society, there was a basic consistency between the forces of production (including natural resources, labor, and technology) and the relations of production (the mechanisms of managing the economy). Zaslavskaya argued that in the Soviet Union, the level of technology and the skills and attitudes of the workforce had undergone enormous change since the 1930s, while the centralized institutions that managed the economy had changed very little, setting the system up for crisis unless basic changes were made. Stalin had also authored the doctrine of the moral and political unity of Soviet society, based on the assumption that there were no fundamental conflicts among classes or groups in the USSR. Zaslavskaya pointed out that there were groups with a vested interest in resisting changes in the system of management of the economy, and that reform would arouse conflicts among groups with mutually opposed interests. She also repudiated the habit of regarding workers as "labor resources" analagous to machines, and called for greater attention to the "human factor" in production, which would require consideration of the values and attitudes of workers, including their desire for a form of management that would give them greater independence. Zaslavskaya's reasoning provided the background for the drive for radical restructuring of the Soviet system, though she assumed that reform would take place within the framework of a socialist economy.

*See also:* PERESTROIKA; ZASLAVSKAYA, TATIANA IVANOVNA

**BIBLIOGRAPHY**

Zaslavskaia, Tat'iana I. (1984). "The Novosibirsk Report." *Survey* 28(1):88–108.

Zaslavskaia, Tat'iana I. (1989). *A Voice of Reform: Essays by Tat'iana I. Zaslavskaia*, ed. and intro. Murray Yanowitch. Armonk, NY: M. E. Sharpe.

Zaslavskaia, Tat'iana I. (1990). *The Second Socialist Revolution: An Alternative Soviet Strategy*, tr. Susan M. Davies and Jenny Warren. Bloomington: Indiana University Press.

ALFRED B. EVANS JR.

## NOVOSILTSEV, NIKOLAI NIKOLAYEVICH

(1761–1836), friend and adviser to Emperor Alexander I.

Nikolai Nikolayevich Novosiltsev was the illegitimate son of a woman whose brother, Alexander Sergeyevich Stroganov, was an important government official. Stroganov took the boy in and raised him in a household known for its hospitality and refinement, although, according to a contemporary, he was "brought up by his generous uncle like a poor relation" (Saunders, p. 5).

Novosiltsev served in the army from 1783 to 1795, and during this time apparently made the acquaintance of the future emperor Alexander I. In 1796, when Alexander's father, Paul I, ascended to the throne, Alexander asked Novosiltsev to draw up a "programmatic introduction" to the constitutional reforms Alexander was then considering. The document has been lost, but it appears to have focused on the education of those who would someday represent the empire's vast population. In 1798 Novosiltsev helped Alexander found the *St. Petersburg Journal* and became a frequent contributor. Paul, meanwhile, was becoming suspicious of Novosiltsev's liberalism and his influence on Alexander, so in 1797 the young man left Russia for Britain. He spent four years there attending university lectures and meeting such notables as Jeremy Bentham.

In 1801, when Paul was murdered and Alexander became emperor, Novosiltsev returned to Russia, where he became a member of Alexander's Unofficial or Secret Committee, which regularly met with the emperor over the next two years to discuss plans for reform. Novosiltsev persuaded the committee to review the domestic situation and various departmental reforms and then draft a constitution. Within a matter of weeks Alexander began to voice doubts about the project. In an August 1801 memorandum to Alexander, Novosiltsev revealed the limits to his proposed reform program, stating that the Senate, an appointed body established by Peter the Great to govern the empire while the tsar was away, would be unable to implement and manage reform. Only the ruler could bring about the "Natural Rights, the Lawful Freedom and the security of each member of society." In a similar vein Novosiltsev urged Alexander to reject a proposal to introduce the right of habeas corpus, arguing that since a future situation may require it to be suspended, it would be best to not enact it at all.

In 1801 Novosiltsev was appointed chairman of a new commission on laws, and from 1802 to 1808, as assistant to the minister of justice, he helped draw up the Statute on Free Cultivators, a singularly ineffective effort to emancipate some of the serfs. From 1803 to 1810 he was president of the Imperial Academy of Sciences. In 1804 he undertook a diplomatic mission to Britain to obtain an alliance against Napoleon. The British were offended by his vanity and arrogance and viewed with bewilderment or hostility his proposals dealing with the Ottoman Empire and a German Confederation. The talks failed to produce a treaty until Napoleon's annexation of Genoa in 1805 forced Russia and Britain into an alliance.

After the defeat of Napoleon, Novosiltsev served as Russia's imperial-royal commissioner for Poland, which was then a constitutional monarchy under Alexander. In 1820, at the emperor's request, Novosiltsev prepared a constitutional charter for Russia. Its key feature was decentralization and a genuinely federal structure. The empire was to be divided into twelve "vice-regencies" with elected assemblies at the local and national levels. The document, which also emphasized personal and civil liberties, was never implemented, and its effect on Alexander, if any, is unclear. His successor, Nicholas I, found the charter "most objectionable" and ordered all copies destroyed.

Novosiltsev has been described as an aggressively ambitious but poorly educated man. He was covetous of a place in Russian society, but he felt excluded from it. He was without doubt a talented and intelligent person, but he was unable to bridle his arrogance and cynicism, especially as administrator of Poland and as a diplomat.

*See also:* ALEXANDER I; NAPOLEON I; PAUL I; POLAND

### BIBLIOGRAPHY
Grimstead, Patricia Kennedy. (1969). *The Foreign Ministers of Alexander I.* Berkeley: University of California Press.

Hartley, Janet M. (1994). *Alexander I.* New York: Longman.

Saunders, David. (1992). *Russia in the Age of Reaction and Reform, 1801–1881.* London: Longman.

HUGH PHILLIPS

# NOVOZHILOV, VIKTOR VALENTINOVICH

(1892–1970), Soviet economist who made important contributions to the revival of modern economics in the Soviet Union, especially via the concept of opportunity cost.

Novozhilov was educated at Kiev University, finishing in 1915. While still a student, he wrote two serious economic works, one of which was awarded a gold medal in 1913. Among his teachers were two famous economists, Yevgeny Yevgenievich Slutsky and Mikhail Ivanovich Tugan-Baranovsky. He taught at universities in Ukraine until 1922, when he went to Leningrad. There he taught and worked for the rest of his life. He was often in political trouble for his economic views, and had a very difficult time getting his work published. In the post-Stalin years, however, he gained authority and influence, and in 1965 he received the Lenin Prize (along with Vasily Sergeyevich Nemchinov and Leonid Vitaliyevich Kantorovich). In November 1965, he moved to the Leningrad branch of the Central Economic-Mathematical Institute. He was elected a full member of the Academy of Sciences of the USSR.

Novozhilov was one of the most creatively significant of the Soviet economists. His most notable scientific contribution concerned the capital intensity issue, which grew out of his participation over many years in the work of institutes designing new plants and technologies. It was on the basis of this experience that he wrote his doctoral dissertation, titled *Methods of Measuring the National Economic Effectiveness of Project Variants*, a theme which ultimately led him to a general opportunity-cost theory of value and allocation.

Novozhilov was a rarity in Soviet economics, a representative of the prerevolutionary intelligentsia who managed to preserve its values in the Soviet environment. He was a man of sterling character and attractive personality, an erudite scholar with a cosmopolitan view of the world, and an accomplished violinist and painter. He understood English, though he did not feel comfortable speaking it.

*See also:* SLUTSKY, YEVGENY YEVGENIEVICH; TUGAN-BARANOVSKY, MIKHAIL IVANOVICH

## BIBLIOGRAPHY

Robert Campbell. (1961). "Marx, Kantorovich, and Novozhilov: Stoimost Versus Reality," *Slavic Review* 20: 402–418.

Novozhilov, Valentin. (1970). *Problems of Cost-Benefit Analysis in Optimal Planning*. White Plains, NY: International Arts and Sciences Press.

ROBERT W. CAMPBELL

# NOVY MIR

*Novy Mir* (*New World*), a literary, critical, and political journal based in Moscow, was founded in 1925 as part of an official initiative to revivify the Russian tradition of the thick journal in the wake of the Bolshevik Revolution. True to that tradition, *Novy Mir* published political and social commentaries along with its staple of fiction, poetry, and literary criticism. Having come into being during the mid–1920s, during the last few years of relative cultural openness in the young Soviet Union, the journal published works by the most prominent writers of the day. The major works of literature published in the journal during this period were Maxim Gorky's novel *The Life of Klim Samgin* (*Zhizn Klima Samgina*) and Alexei Tolstoy's *Road to Calvary* (*Khozhdenie po mukam*).

Like Soviet culture as a whole, from the early 1930s until Stalin's death in 1953, what *Novy Mir* could publish was severely limited by the strictures of the official doctrine of Socialist Realism, which dictated that all publications must actively support the building of socialism in the Soviet Union. Following the death of Stalin in 1953, however, *Novy Mir* soon established itself as the most prestigious literary journal of the post-Stalin period. Under the editorship of the poet Alexander Tvardovsky, the journal ushered in the ensuing period of cultural liberalism with the publication of the groundbreaking article by the critic Vladimir Pomerantsev, "On Sincerity in Literature" (Ob iskrennosti v literature), which called for the "unvarnished" portrayal of reality in Soviet literary works. Tvardovsky's first tenure as editor of the journal ended when, in reprisal for his publication of politically questionable works, he was replaced by the prose writer Konstantin Simonov in 1954. Simonov himself, however, fell victim to the uncertain cultural "thaw" of the times and was deposed as editor in the wake of his 1956 publication of Vladimir Dudintsev's controversial novel, *Not by Bread Alone* (*Ne khlebom edinym*). Tvardovsky was reappointed editor in 1958 and led the journal through its most illustrious period.

The journal, with its distinctive pale blue cover, became the leading literary periodical of the cultural relaxation under Khrushchev. Its most historically resonant publication of this period was Alexander Solzhenitsyn's novella, *One Day in the Life of Ivan Denisovich* (*Odin den Ivana Denisovicha*), in 1962. During the years of cultural stagnation under Brezhnev, the limits of the allowable in Soviet literature and culture again tightened. Tvardovsky struggled to maintain *Novy Mir*'s liberal profile until he was forced by increasing political pressure to resign from the editorship in 1970. The journal came into its own again during the glasnost period. The prose writer Sergei Zalygin assumed the editorship of the journal in 1986 and, like Tvardovsky before him, steered the journal to a leading role in the liberalization of Soviet culture under Gorbachev. The landmark *Novy Mir* publications of the glasnost period included the appearance in 1988 of Pasternak's novel *Doctor Zhivago*, which had been rejected for publication in the journal in 1950s. *Novy Mir* also served as the primary outlet for Sozhenitsyn's previously banned publications during this period. Since the collapse of the Soviet Union and the emergence of a market economy in Russia, *Novy Mir*, like other major Soviet publications, has struggled to adjust to the changing economic and cultural situation.

*See also:* GLASNOST; GORKY, MAXIM; INTELLIGENTSIA; PASTERNAK, BORIS LEONIDOVICH; SIMONOV, KONSTANTIN MIKHAILOVICH; SOCIALIST REALISM; THAW, THE; THICK JOURNALS; TOLSTOY, LEO NIKOLAYEVICH; SOLZHENITSYN, ALEXANDER ISAYEVICH

**BIBLIOGRAPHY**

Glenny, Michael, ed. (1967). *Novy Mir: A Selection, 1925–1967.* London: Jonathan Cape Ltd.

Spechler, Dina R. (1982). *Permitted Dissent in the USSR: Novy Mir and the Soviet Regime.* New York: Praeger.

CATHARINE NEPOMNYASHCHY

## NYSTADT, TREATY OF

The Treaty of Nystadt was signed on August 30 (September 10, O.S.), 1721, in the Finnish town of Nystadt. It ended the twenty-one year Great Northern War between Russia and Sweden. The treaty was the result of several years of negotiations between the warring parties. The clauses were:

1. "Eternal peace" was established on land and sea
2. All hostilities were committed to oblivion, except for the crimes of the Russian Cossacks who had aided the Swedes
3. All military action ceased
4. Sweden agreed to cede to Russia Livonia (Lifliandia), Estonia (Estliandia), Ingermanland (Ingria), part of Karelia with Vyborg district, with the towns of Riga, Dünamünde, Pernau, Reval (Tallinn), Dorpat, Narva, Vyborg, Kexholm, and the islands of Oesel, Dago, and Meno
5. Russia agreed to evacuate Finland (invaded in 1713–1714) and to pay Sweden two million thalers compensation
6. Sweden was granted entitlement to trade in Riga, Reval, and Arensburg, and to purchase grain duty-free
7. Russia agreed not to interfere in Swedish domestic affairs
8. The border was defined in detail
9. The former Swedish provinces annexed to Russia were to retain all their privileges and rights unwaveringly
10. The Protestant faith was to enjoy the same freedoms as Orthodoxy
11. Claims to landed estates in Livonia and Estonia were to be settled, and
12. Swedish citizens with claims to land could retain their estates only if they swore allegiance to the Russian crown
13. Russian troops still in Livonia were to be provisioned, but they were required to take all their weapons and supplies when they left, and to return archives and documents
14. Prisoners of war were to be returned (unless they wished to stay)
15. The kingdom of Poland, as an ally of both signatories, was included in the treaty, but Sweden was free to conclude a separate treaty with Poland
16. There was to be free trade between Sweden and Russia
17. Swedish merchants were allowed to maintain warehouses in Russian towns and ports
18. The parties agreed to help each other in case of shipwrecks and
19. To greet ships of both nations with the usual friendly shots
20. Ambassadors and envoys were to pay their own expenses, but the host power would provide escorts
21. Other European powers were given the option to enter the treaty within three months

22. Quarrels and disputes were to be settled equitably, without breaching the peace
23. Traitors, murderers, and criminals would be extradited
24. The treaty was to be ratified in three weeks in Nystadt

The treaty was published in Russian in large print runs of five thousand copies in 1721 and twenty thousand copies in 1723, following the authorization of the map showing the new borders. It sealed both Russia's rising status as a leading player in European politics and Sweden's decline as a major military power, marking its disappearance from the southern shores of the Baltic, to the advantage of Denmark, Prussia, and Russia. It also underlined Poland's status as a client state. At the official celebrations in St. Petersburg in October 1721, Peter accepted the titles Great, Emperor, and Father of the Fatherland from the Senate, further arousing the belief in some European countries that Russian influence was to be feared "more than the Turks." Except for the changes related to Finland, the treaty defined Russia's Baltic presence for the rest of the imperial era. The acquisition of ports brought Russia both economic and strategic advantages as well as an influx of highly educated Baltic German personnel to work in the imperial civil service.

*See also:* GREAT NORTHERN WAR; PETER I; SWEDEN, RELATIONS WITH

**BIBLIOGRAPHY**

Bagger, H. (1993). "The Role of the Baltic in Russian Foreign Policy 1721–1773." In *Imperial Russian Foreign Policy*, ed. Hugh Ragsdale. Cambridge, UK: Cambridge University Press.

Hughes, Lindsey. (1990). *Russia in the Age of Peter the Great.* New Haven, CT: Yale University Press.

LINDSEY HUGHES

# OBROK

Rent in kind or money (quitrent).

*Obrok* was land rent paid by a peasant to his lord either in kind or in money. Although there is disagreement about its status prior to the Mongol conquest, scholars agree that from the mid 1200s to the end of the 1400s, rents in kind dominated the economy after the Mongol invasion destroyed the urban market and caused a precipitous population decline.

As a market reemerged in the late 1400s and 1500s, dues paid in money increased significantly. But by the end of the fifteenth century, the new money dues were forcibly converted into more profitable labor dues (*barshchina*). The latter became predominant on seigniorial estates into the early eighteenth century.

By the last third of the 1700s, market development and major agricultural expansion into the black soil region produced regional economic specialization. Rent in cash and in kind came to predominate in the non-black soil region, which extended north from Moscow. Fifty-five percent of the serfs in the region were on obrok. Increasingly the payments were in cash, which was earned largely from nonagricultural wages. This overall proportion remained relatively stable down to the emancipation, even though there was a strong shift from labor dues to cash payments near the capital as wages rose.

There has been a major controversy over what happened to the level of cash payments in the last hundred years of serfdom. Clearly, the nominal value of the payments increased rather sharply. But when adjustments are made for inflation and price increases, Western, Soviet, and post-Soviet scholars agree the increase was fairly moderate.

*See also:* BARSHCHINA; SERFDOM

## BIBLIOGRAPHY

Blum, Jerome. (1961). *Lord and Peasant in Russia from the Ninth to the Nineteenth Century.* Princeton, NJ: Princeton University Press.

Moon, David. (1999). *The Russian Peasantry, 1600–1930: The World the Peasants Made.* London: Longman.

ELVIRA M. WILBUR

## OBRUCHEV, NIKOLAI NIKOLAYEVICH

(1830–1904), imperial Russian general staff officer, military statistician, planner and chief of the Main Staff.

General-Adjutant Nikolai Obruchev was born in Warsaw, the son of an officer of modest means. He completed the First Cadet Corps in 1848 and the Nicholas Military Academy in 1854. Subsequently, as professor at the Academy, he was a founder of Russian military statistics. In 1858 he became the first editor of the military professional monthly *Voyenny sbornik* (*Military Collection*), but was soon removed for the printing of articles critical of Russian logistics in the Crimean War. In 1863, under War Minister Dmitry Milyutin's tutelage, he became the secretary of the Military Academic Committee within the Main Staff. From this position he supported creation of an independent general staff and actively advanced Milyutin's military reforms. Obruchev played a major role in planning for the Russo-Turkish War of 1877–1878. His subsequent plans for the military preparation of Russian Poland in the event of war against the Dual Alliance were influential until 1914.

Although Obruchev's scheme for a lightning war against Turkey was never realized, he was posted to the Caucasus theater in July 1877, where he successfully planned the rout of the Turkish army. Several months later in the Balkan theater, he devised a plan for winter operations across the Balkan divide that led to Turkish capitulation in early 1878. After Alexander II's assassination in 1881, Obruchev became War Minister Peter Semenovich Vannovsky's chief of the Main Staff. In this capacity Obruchev oversaw the rearmament of the Russian Army, the fortification of the western military frontier, and preparations for a possible amphibious operation against the Bosporus. He assumed an especially important role in working out the Franco-Russian Military Convention of 1892. Despite Nicholas II's inclinations, he opposed Russian military intervention in the Far East during the Sino-Japanese War of 1894–1895. Obruchev retired from active service in 1897 and died in his wife's native France in June 1904. An outstanding planner and an adroit soldier-diplomat, Obruchev left his stamp during the last quarter of the nineteenth century on virtually every important facet of Russian preparation for future war.

*See also:* MILITARY, IMPERIAL ERA; MILYUTIN, DMITRY ALEXEYEVICH; RUSSO-TURKISH WARS

### BIBLIOGRAPHY

Kennan, George F. (1984). *The Fateful Alliance.* New York: Pantheon.

Rich, David Alan. (1998). *The Tsar's Colonels: Professionalism, Strategy, and Subversion in Late Imperial Russia.* Cambridge, MA: Harvard University Press.

OLEG R. AIRAPETOV

## OBSHCHINA

Usually translated as "community," this term refers primarily to a landholding group of peasants in pre-1917 Russia.

Pre-emancipation serfs, in common with state and other nonbound peasants, still had a large degree of freedom to organize their own affairs within the limits of the village itself. The obshchina represents the village as it looked inward—an economic unit based on the land it worked. It differed from what might be called the peasant mir (literally, "world" or "society"), representing the village as it looked outward. The mir assembly carried out the administrative, legal, and fiscal affairs of the village.

While not modern in its outlook, for many, if not most peasants, the obshchina was fairly well suited to carry out the necessary, limited functions of distributing land (and thus taxes and other dues) among people whose society was based largely, though implicitly, on a labor theory of value. The common but not universal obshchina practice of periodic redistribution of land, based on manpower and thus taxpaying ability, gave rise to much discussion among Russian intellectuals. The subject of widespread Romantic, philosophical, religious, economic, and political theorizing throughout the nineteenth and early twentieth centuries, the real-life obshchina was never the idealized, optimally Christian body of the Slavophiles nor the proto-communist organization of the peasant-oriented revolutionaries known as *narodniki* (populists). It was often guilty (from majority self-interest) of stymieing rational agrarian practices, but not always the culprit that Marxists blamed for peasant immiserization, socioeconomic inequality, and the obstructed development of a progressive class mentality. Living in an institution with social strengths and some economic weaknesses, most obshchina peasants sought not to maximize earnings or profits—as liberal economists would have them—nor to escape Marx's "idiocy of rural life," but to "satisfise" their lives (in H. Simon's concept), that is, to achieve and maintain a satisfactory standard of living.

See also: MIR; PEASANT ECONOMY

**BIBLIOGRAPHY**

Bartlett, R., ed. (1990). *Land Commune and Peasant Community in Russia.* New York: St. Martin's Press.

Mironov, Boris, and Eklof, Ben. (2000). *A Social History of Imperial Russia, 1700–1917.* Boulder, CO: Westview.

STEVEN A. GRANT

# OCCULTISM

Occult books of fortune-telling, dreams, spells, astrology, and speculative mysticism entered medieval Russia as translations of Greek, Byzantine, European, Arabic, and Persian "secret books." Their prohibition by the Council of a Hundred Chapters (*Stoglav*) in 1551 enhanced rather than diminished their popularity, and many have circulated into our own day.

The Age of Reason did not extirpate Russia's occult interests. During the eighteenth century more than 100 occult books were printed, mostly translations of European alchemical, mystical, Masonic, Rosicrucian, and oriental wisdom texts. Many were published by the author and Freemason Nikolai Novikov.

As the nineteenth century began, Tsar Alexander I encouraged Swedenborgians, Freemasons, mystical sectarians, and the questionable "Bible Society," before suddenly banning occult books and secret societies in 1822. The autocracy and the church countered the occultism and supernaturalism of German Romanticism with an increasingly restrictive system of church censorship, viewing the occult as "spiritual sedition."

Nevertheless, Spiritualism managed to penetrate Russia in the late 1850s, introduced by Count Grigory Kushelev-Bezborodko, a friend of Daniel Dunglas Home (1833–1886), the famous medium who gave seances for the court of Alexander II. Their coterie included the writers and philosophers Alexei Tolstoy, Vladimir Soloviev, Vladimir Dal,

Alexander Aksakov, and faculty from Moscow and St. Petersburg Universities.

By the end of the nineteenth century, Russia, like Europe, experienced the French "Occult Revival," a reaction against prevailing scientific positivism. Spiritualism, theosophy, hermeticism, mystery cults, and Freemasonry attracted the interest of upper- and middle-class Russian society and configured decadence and symbolism in the arts.

Theosophy, founded in New York in 1875 by Russian expatriate Elena Blavatsky (1831–1891), was a pseudo-religious, neo-Buddhist movement that claimed to be a "synthesis of Science, Religion, and Philosophy." It appealed to the god-seeking Russian intelligentsia (including, at various times, Vladimir Soloviev, Max Voloshin, Konstantin Balmont, Alexander Skryabin, Maxim Gorky). A Christianized, Western form of theosophy, Rudolf Steiner's anthroposophy, attracted the intellectuals Andrey Bely, Nikolai Berdyayev, and Vyacheslav Ivanov.

Russian Freemasonry revived at the end of the nineteenth century. Masons, Martinists, and Rosicrucians preceded the mystical sectarian Grigory Rasputin (1872–1916) as "friends" to the court of Tsar Nicholas II. After the Revolution of 1905–1906, Russian Freemasonry became increasingly politicized, eventually playing a role in the events of 1916-1917.

The least documented of Russia's occult movements was the elitist hermeticism (loosely including philosophical alchemy, gnosticism, kabbalism, mystical Freemasonry, and magic), heir of the Occult Revival. Finally, sensational (or "boulevard") mysticism was popular among all classes: magic, astrology, Tarot, fortune-telling, dream interpretation, chiromancy, phrenology, witchcraft, hypnotism.

More than forty occult journals and papers and eight hundred books on occultism appeared in Russia between 1881 and 1922, most of them after the censorship-easing Manifesto of October 17, 1905. After the Bolshevik coup, occult societies were proscribed. All were closed by official decree in 1922; in the 1930s those members who had not emigrated or ceased activity were arrested.

In the Soviet Union, occultists and *ekstra-sensy* existed underground (and occasionally within in the Kremlin walls). The post-1991 period saw the return of theosophy and anthroposophy, shamanism, Buddhism, Hare Krishnas, Roerich cults, neo-paganism, the White Brotherhood, UFOlogy, and other occult trends.

*See also:* FREEMASONRY; PAGANSIM; RELIGION

**BIBLIOGRAPHY**

Carlson, Maria. (1993). *"No Religion Higher Than Truth": A History of the Theosophical Movement in Russia, 1875–1922.* Princeton, NJ: Princeton University Press.

Rosenthal, Bernice Glatzer, ed. (1997). *The Occult in Russian and Soviet Culture.* Ithaca, NY: Cornell University Press.

MARIA CARLSON

## OCTOBER 1993 EVENTS

During the October 1993 events, Boris Yeltsin's forcible dissolution of parliament took Russia to the edge of civil war. Seen as decisive and essential by his supporters, the dissolution was a radically divisive action, the consequences of which continued to reverberate through Russian society in the early twenty-first century.

In 1992 and 1993 a deep divide developed between the executive and legislative branches of government. The root cause of this was President Yeltsin's decision to adopt a radical economic reform strategy, urged on him by the West, for which he and his government were not able to generate sustained parliamentary support. Faced with resistance from the legislators, Yeltsin made only minimal concessions and on most issues chose to confront them. This subjected Russia's new political and judicial institutions to strains that they could not adequately handle. In addition, the confrontation became highly personalized, with the principal figures forcefully manipulating institutions to benefit themselves and their causes.

Apart from Yeltsin, key individuals on the executive side of the confrontation were Yegor Gaidar and Anatoly Chubais. They were the ministers most responsible for launching and implementing the radical economic reforms known as shock therapy. Leading the majority in parliament was its speaker Ruslan Khasbulatov, a former ally of Yeltsin and an inexperienced and manipulative politician of high ambition. Over time, he was increasingly joined by Yeltsin's similarly ambitious and inexperienced vice-president, former air force general Alexander Rutskoi.

On March 20, 1993, Yeltsin made a first attempt to rid himself of parliament's opposition. Declaring the imposition of emergency rule, he said that henceforth no decisions of the legislature that negated decrees from the executive branch would have juridical force. However, the Constitutional Court ruled his action unconstitutional, some of his ministers declined to back him, and the parliament came close to impeaching him. Yeltsin backed off.

At this time, Khasbulatov and the Constitutional Court's chairman, Valery Zorkin, separately sought to engage Yeltsin in a compromise resolution of the "dual power" conflict. The proposed basis was the so-called zero option. The centerpiece of this approach was simultaneous early elections to both the presidency and the parliament. However, Yeltsin had no desire to share power substantively, even with a newly elected parliament.

In taking this stance, he sought and obtained the support of Western governments by repeatedly inflating the negligible threat of a communist revanche. He also got some qualified backing from the Russian public, when an April 1993 referendum showed that a small majority of the population trusted him, and an even smaller majority approved of his socioeconomic policies.

On September 21, Yeltsin announced that to resolve the grave political crisis he had signed decree 1400, which annulled the powers of the legislature. Elections would be held on December 12 for a parliament of a new type. And the same day a referendum would be held on a completely new constitution.

In response, the Supreme Soviet immediately voted to impeach Yeltsin and, in accordance with the constitution, to install Vice President Alexander Rutskoi as acting president. Rutskoi proceeded to annul decree 1400 (whereupon Yeltsin annulled Rutskoi's decree) and precipitously appointed senior ministers of nationalist and communist views to his own government, thus alienating many centrists. On September 23, with pro-government deputies boycotting the proceedings, the congress confirmed Yeltsin's impeachment by a vote of 636 to 2.

The next ten days were occupied by a war of words between the rival governments, as they

**Pro-Yeltsin soldiers watch the Soviet parliament building as it burns.** © PETER TURNLEY/CORBIS

sought to build support around Russia, and by official acts of harassment, like switching off the electricity in the parliament's building, known as "the White House." Although most Russians remained passive, adopting the attitude "a plague on both your houses," small groups demonstrated for one or the other camp, or sent messages. According to Yeltsin's government, 70 percent of the regional soviets supported the parliament. From five locations around Moscow, Kremlin representatives solicited visits from wavering deputies and offered them—if they would change sides—good jobs, cash payments equal to nearly $1,000, and immunity from future prosecution.

On September 27, Yeltsin explicitly rejected the zero option. Three days later the Orthodox patriarch suggested that the church should mediate. The two sides agreed and began talks the next day. However, on October 3, events moved rapidly to their denouement. The exact sequence of events remains murky. A march organized by purported supporters of parliament was mysteriously allowed through a cordon around the White House. Then, apparently,

hidden Kremlin snipers fired on it. Then Rutskoi, instead of calling on the crowd to defend the White House, urged it to storm the city hall, the Kremlin, and the Ostankino television center. Thereafter, acts of violence on both sides, and an unexplained episode of the Kremlin not at first defending Ostankino, ensured that events got out of control and many people were killed. Throughout, the Yeltsin team appeared to use cunning methods to create a situation in which it would appear that parliament's side, not its own, had used violence first.

That night, the Kremlin team, not wanting to order the army in writing to open fire, had great difficulty persuading key military leaders to go take action. However, the next day a light tank bombardment of the White House softened up the by now depleted body of parliamentarians, who soon surrendered. Twenty-seven leaders were arrested, only to be amnestied four months later. According to the Kremlin, a total of 143 people were killed during the confrontation. However, an impartial investigation by the human rights group Memorial gave an estimate of several hundred.

Over the next three months Yeltsin exercised virtually dictatorial powers. He shut down the Constitutional Court; abolished the entire structure of regional, city, and district legislatures; and banned certain nationalist and communist parties and publications. With minimal public debate, he pushed through a new constitution that was officially approved by referendum on December 12, although widespread charges of falsified results were not answered and the relevant evidence was destroyed. He also broke the promise he gave in September to hold a new presidential election in June 1994, and postponed the event by two years.

Although in September 1993 most of the parliament's leaders were no less unpopular than Yeltsin and his government, and although Russia would probably have been ruled no better—more likely worse—if they had won, Yeltsin's resort in October to violence instead of compromise seriously undermined Russia's infant democracy and the legitimacy of his government.

*See also:* CHUBAIS, ANATOLY BORISOVICH; GAIDAR, YEGOR TIMUROVICH; MILITARY, SOVIET AND POST-SOVIET; RUTSKOI, ALEXANDER VLADIMIROVICH; YELTSIN, BORIS NIKOLAYEVICH

**BIBLIOGRAPHY**

McFaul, Michael. (2001). *Russia's Unfinished Revolution: Political Change from Gorbachev to Putin.* Ithaca, NY: Cornell University Press.

Reddaway, Peter, and Glinski, Dmitri. (2001). *The Tragedy of Russia's Reforms: Market Bolshevism Against Democracy.* Washington, DC: U.S. Institute of Peace Press.

Shevtsova, Lilia. (1999). *Yeltsin's Russia: Myths and Realities.* Washington, DC: Carnegie Endowment for International Peace.

PETER REDDAWAY

## OCTOBER GENERAL STRIKE OF 1905

The general strike of October was the culminating event of the 1905 Revolution and the most inclusive and consequential of several general strikes that took place in 1905, resulting in the announcement of the Manifesto of October 17. It was initiated first and foremost by workers in larger industrial enterprises, many of whom nursed unsatisfied demands from strikes earlier in the year. Although the ripeness of workers to strike in many diverse working situations across the empire was paramount, the call of the All–Russian Union of Railroad Workers for a national rail strike on October 4 provided a timely impetus. The railroaders' strike gave them control of Russia's means of communication, allowing them to spread word of the strike throughout the empire, while their immobilization of rail traffic forcibly idled many trades and industries.

Although workers and the urban public generally found themselves at different stages of organizational and political development in October, a unique synergy arose that stirred them all to greater effort. The spread of the strikes from the generally more unified and mobilized factory workers to artisans, small businesses, and white–collar workers of the city centers lent the October strike its general character and explained its success. In St. Petersburg, the strike's most important site in terms of its political outcome, the participation of tram drivers, shop clerks, pharmacists, printers, and even insurance, zemstvo, and bank employees, meant that the center of the capital closed down, bringing the strike directly into the lives of most citizens by encompassing the broadest array of occupations and the broadest social spectrum of all the strikes in 1905.

Many of the worker strikes supplemented their factory demands with demands for political rights and liberties, so that the labor strikes blended seamlessly with the broader, ongoing political protests of the democratic opposition. University students in particular, but also secondary schoolers and educated professionals, promoted the strike with gusto and imagination, especially in Moscow, St. Petersburg, and other university towns. Students opened their lecture halls to public meetings, where workers met the wider urban public for the first time and where much support for the strike was generated. The volume of this protest gave pause to the police and the government, providing an even greater margin of de facto freedom of speech and assembly. Many craft and service workers took the opportunity to organize their first trade unions. Several political parties, including the Kadet or Constitutional Democratic Party, were organized in this interval. Slower moving populations, such as peasants, soldiers, and policemen, drew inspiration from the widespread protests and began to demand their rights.

The revolutionary organizations prospered from the upsurge of labor militancy in October, recruiting new members and becoming better known among rank–and–file workers. Revolutionary organizers, especially Mensheviks, were indispensable in the creation and leadership of the Soviets of Workers' Deputies, informal bodies of elected factory delegates organized in about fifty locales during 1905, especially in October, to lead and assist strikers over entire urban and industrial areas. The Soviet of St. Petersburg, the most celebrated of these organs of direct democracy, went beyond strike leadership to pursue a revolutionary agenda in the capital. Its arrest on December 3 cut short its political promise, but its brief career and its flamboyant second president, Leon Trotsky, inspired similar organs in later revolutions around the world.

In response to the January strikes, the tsarist government had granted an elected assembly to discuss, but not implement, legislation (the "Bulygin Duma"). To maintain the integrity of autocratic rule, several of Emperor Nicholas's ministers began to advocate a unified government, headed by a prime minister. Sensing the country's mood in early October and led by the respected Count Sergei Yu. Witte, they advised Nicholas to grant political and civil rights, legislative authority, and an expanded electorate. Nicholas hesitated between liberalization and forceful repression of the strikers; after deliberating several days, he reluctantly agreed to the former. The Manifesto of October 17 was the most significant political act of the 1905 Revolution. It provoked powerful, euphoric expectations of a total transformation of Russian life. These expectations remained over the long run, themselves transforming Russian politics and culture, though in the short run the promise of a constitutional state divided the opposition and enabled the government to restore the authority of the autocracy by early 1906 through a bloody repression not possible in October.

*See also:* BLOODY SUNDAY; DUMA; NICHOLAS II; REVOLUTION OF 1905; WORKERS

**BIBLIOGRAPHY**

Ascher, Abraham. (1988). *The Revolution of 1905*, Vol. 1: *Russia in Disarray*. Stanford, CA: Stanford University Press.

Engelstein, Laura. (1982). *Moscow, 1905: Working Class Organization and Political Conflict*. Stanford, CA: Stanford University Press.

Harcave, Sidney. (1964). *First Blood: The Russian Revolution of 1905*. New York: Macmillan.

Reichman, Henry. (1987). *Railwaymen and Revolution: Russia, 1905*. Berkeley: University of California Press.

Surh, Gerald D. (1989). *1905 in St. Petersburg: Labor, Society, and Revolution*. Stanford, CA: Stanford University Press.

Trotsky, Leon. (1971). *1905*, tr. Anya Bostock. New York: Random House.

Verner, Andrew M. (1990). *The Crisis of Russian Autocracy: Nicholas II and the 1905 Revolution*. Princeton, NJ: Princeton University Press.

GERALD D. SURH

## OCTOBER MANIFESTO

The October Manifesto was published at the peak of Revolution of 1905, following the general strike of October of 1905 in which 2 million people took to the streets and railroads were blocked. The government considered two possible solutions to the crisis: a military dictatorship and liberal reforms to win popular support. Those who supported reforms were led by Sergei Witte, who wrote a report urging Tsar Nicholas II to grant a constitution, a representative assembly, and civil freedoms. On October 27 (October 14 O.S.) Nicholas ordered that the main points of the report were to be listed in the form of a manifesto. The draft was written overnight by Prince Alexei Obolensky. Nicholas signed it on October 30 (October 17 O.S.), and the next day it was published in the newspaper *Pravitelstvennyi Vestnik* (*Governmental Courier*).

The October Manifesto gave the ruling body permission to use every means to end disorders, disobedience, and abuse, and gave the "highest government" the responsibility to act, in accordance with the tsar's "unbendable" will, to "Grant the population the undisputable foundation for civil freedom on the basis of protection of identity, freedom of conscience, speech, assemblies and unions." Voting rights were promised, "to some extent, to those classes of the population that, at present, do not have the right to vote," and it was proclaimed as an "undisputable rule that no law can be passed without the approval of the Duma and for the possibility of supervision of the lawfulness of the actions of the administration to be given to the national representatives." The manifesto concluded by calling upon "all true sons of Russia to end . . . the unimaginable revolt" and, along with the emperor, "to concentrate all forces on restoring peace and quiet on the homeland."

The October Manifesto was highly controversial. There were mass meetings and demonstrations welcoming its promise of freedom in the regional capitals and many other cities. Similarly, there were mass meetings and demonstrations, often violent, calling for an autocracy of "patriots" and condemning the manifesto as perpetrated by revolutionaries and Jews. In the three weeks after the manifesto was issued, there were outbreaks of violence in 108 cities, 70 small towns, and 108 villages, leaving at least 1,622 dead, and 3,544 crippled and wounded.

The liberal reaction to the manifesto was mixed. Right-wing liberals saw it as a realization of their political hopes and united as the Union of October 17. Left-wing liberals, joining together to organize the Constitutional Democratic Party, believed that further reforms were needed, and their leader, Paul Milyukov, stated that nothing changed and the struggle would continue. Left-wing parties and leaders saw the manifesto as a sign of the government's weakness; its capitulation under revolutionary pressure showed that the pressure on the government had to be intensified.

The political program embodied in the manifesto began to take effect on October 19, 1905, with the appointment of a government headed by Witte. Between October 1905 and March 1906 the government published a series of orders regarding political amnesties, censorship, modification of the State Council, and other matters. All of these were incorporated in the second edition of the *Fundamental Laws*, passed on April 23, 1906.

The most important outcome of the October Manifesto was the creation of a bicameral representative institution and the legalization of political parties, trade unions and other social organizations, and a legal oppositionist press.

*See also:* CONSTITUTIONAL DEMOCRATIC PARTY; DUMA; FUNDAMENTAL LAWS OF 1906; OCTOBER GENERAL STRIKE OF 1905; REVOLUTION OF 1905; WITTE, SERGEI YULIEVICH

**BIBLIOGRAPHY**

Ascher, Abraham. (1988, 1992). *The Revolution of 1905.* Vol.1: *Russia in Disarray*; Vol. 2: *Authority Restored.* Stanford, CA: Stanford University Press.

Harcave, Sidney. (1970). *First Blood: The Russian Revolution of 1905.* New York: Macmillan.

Harcave, Sidney, trans. and ed. (1990). *The Memoirs of Count Witte.* Armonk, NY: M. E. Sharpe.

Mehlinger, Howard D., and Tompson, John M. (1972). *Count Witte and the Tsarist Government in the 1905 Revolution.* Bloomington: Indiana University Press.

Szeftel, Marc. (1976). *The Russian Constitution of April 23, 1906: Political Institutions of the Duma Monarchy.* Brussels: Editions de la Libraire encyclopédique.

OLEG BUDNITSKII

## OCTOBER REVOLUTION

During the October 1917 Russian Revolution, the liberal, western-oriented Provisional Government headed by Alexander Kerensky, which was established following the February 1917 Russian Revolution that overthrew Tsar Nicholas II, was removed and replaced by the first Soviet government headed by Vladimir Lenin. The October Revolution began in Petrograd (now St. Petersburg), then the capital of Russia, and quickly spread to the rest of the country. One of the seminal events of the twentieth century in terms of its worldwide historical impact, the October Revolution is also one of the most controversial and hotly debated historical events in modern times.

Most western historians, especially at the height of the Cold War, viewed the October Revolution as a brilliantly organized military coup d'état without significant popular support, carried out by a tightly knit band of professional revolutionaries brilliantly led by the fanatical Lenin. This interpretation, severely undermined by western "revisionist" social history in the 1970s and 1980s, was rejuvenated after the dissolution of the Soviet Union at the end of the Gorbachev era, even though information from newly declassified Soviet archives reinforced the revisionist view. At the other end of the political spectrum, for nearly eighty years Soviet historians, bound by strict historical canons designed to legitimate the Soviet state and its leadership, depicted the October Revolution as a broadly popular uprising of the revolutionary Russian masses. According to them, this social upheaval was deeply rooted in Imperial Russia's historical development and shaped by universal laws of history as formulated by Karl Marx and Lenin. There are kernels of truth and considerable distortion in both of these interpretations.

### WAR AND REVOLUTION
The outbreak of World War I in August 1914 found Russian politics and society in great flux. To be

Leaders of the Bolshevik party are pictured around their leader, Vladimir Lenin. Top row (from left): Rykov, Radek, Pokrovsky, Kamenev; middle row: Trotsky, Lenin, Sverdlov; bottom row: Bukharin, Zinoviev, Krylenko, Kollontai, Lunacharsky. Stalin is not included in this 1920 collage. © HULTON-DEUTSCH COLLECTION/CORBIS

sure, the autocratic tsarist political system had somehow managed to remain intact throughout the revolutions of the late eighteenth and early nineteenth centuries. Even the Revolution of 1905, which resulted in the creation of a constitutional monarchy with an elected parliament (the Duma), had left predominant political authority in the hands of Tsar Nicholas II. The abolition of serfdom by Alexander II in 1861 had freed the Russian peasantry, the vast bulk of the empire's population, from personal bondage. However, the terms of the emancipation were such that most peasants remained impoverished. Moreover, a fundamental land reform program initiated by Peter Stolypin in 1906 was so complex that, irrespective of the long-term prospects, when it was interrupted by the war in 1914, the Russian countryside was in particularly great turmoil.

In the late nineteenth century, enlightened officials such as Sergei Witte had reversed govern-ment opposition to industrialization and spear-headed a program of rapid economic development. However, the pace of this development was too slow to meet Russia's needs, and the industrial revolution resulted in the crowding of vast numbers of immiserated workers into squalid, rat-infested factory ghettos in St. Petersburg, Moscow, and other major Russian cities. It is small wonder, then, that in the opening years of the twentieth century, the major Russian liberal and socialist political parties that were destined to play key roles in 1917 took shape and began to attract popular follow-ings. Likewise, it is no surprise that the Russian government was suddenly faced with a growing, increasingly ambitious and assertive professional middle class, waves of peasant rebellions, and bur-geoning labor unrest.

Framed against these political and social reali-ties, the significant degree of popular support en-joyed by the Russian government at the start of the war, in so far as it was visible, must have been heartening to Nicholas II. The Constitutional Democratic or Kadet Party, Russia's main liberal party, officially proclaimed a moratorium on opposition to the monarchy and pledged its unqualified support for the war effort. Beginning in early 1915, when the government's extraordinary incompetence became fully apparent, the Kadets, despite their anguish, made use of the Duma only to call for the appointment of qualified ministers (rather than demand fundamental structural change). With good reason, they calculated that a political upheaval in the existing circumstances would be equally damaging to the war effort and prospects for the eventual creation of a liberal, democratic government. Members of the populist Socialist Revolutionary (SR) Party and the moderate social democratic Menshevik Party were split between "defensists," who supported the war effort, and "internationalists," who sought an immediate cessation of hostilities and a compromise peace without victors or vanquished. Only Lenin advocated the fomenting of immediate social revolution in all of the warring countries; however, for the time being, efforts by underground Bolshevik committees in Russia to kindle popular opposition to the war failed.

The February 1917 Revolution, which grew out of prewar instabilities and technological backwardness, along with gross mismanagement of the war effort, continuing military defeats, domestic economic dislocation, and outrageous scandals surrounding the monarchy, resulted in the creation of two potential Russian national governments. One was the Provisional Government formed by members of the Duma to restore order and to provide leadership pending convocation of a popularly elected Constituent Assembly based on the French model. The Constituent Assembly was to design Russia's future political system and take responsibility for the promulgation of other fundamental reforms. The second potential national government was the Petrograd Soviet of Workers' and Soldiers' Deputies and its moderate socialist-led Executive Committee. Patterned after similar "worker parliaments" formed during the Revolution of 1905, in succeeding weeks similar institutions of popular self-government were established throughout urban and rural Russia. In early summer 1917, the First All-Russian Congress of Soviets of Workers' and Soldiers' Deputies and the First All-Russian Congress of Peasants' Deputies formed leadership bodies, the All-Russian Central Executive Committee of Workers' and Soldiers' Deputies and the

All-Russian Executive Committee of Peasants' Deputies, to represent soviets around the country between national congresses. Until the fall of 1917, when it was taken over by the Bolsheviks, the Executive Committee of the Petrograd Soviet strived to maintain order and protect the revolution until the convocation of the Constituent Assembly. This was also true of the All-Russian Central Executive Committee of Workers' and Soldiers' Deputies and the All-Russian Executive Committee of Peasants' Deputies. The Soviet, led by the moderate socialists, made no effort to take formal power into its own hands, although it was potentially stronger than the Provisional Government because of its vastly greater support among workers, peasants, and lower–level military personnel. This support skyrocketed in tandem with popular disenchantment with the economic results of the February Revolution, the effort of the Provisional Government to continue the war effort, and its procrastination in convening the Constituent Assembly.

## "ALL POWER TO THE SOVIETS!"

At the time of the February Revolution, Lenin was in Switzerland. He returned to Petrograd in early April 1917, demanding an immediate second, "socialist" revolution in Russia. Although he backed off this goal after he acquainted himself with the realities of the prevailing situation (including little support for precipitous, radical revolutionary action even among Bolsheviks), his great achievement at this time was to orient the thinking of the Bolshevik Party toward preparation for the replacement of the Provisional Government by a leftist "Soviet" government as soon as the time was ripe. Nonetheless, in assessing Lenin's role in the October Revolution, it is important to keep in mind that he was either away from the country or in hiding and out of regular touch with his colleagues in Russia for much of the time between February and October 1917. In any case, top Bolshevik leaders tended to be divided into three distinct groups: Lenin and Leon Trotsky, among others, for whom the establishment of revolutionary soviet power in Russia was less an end in itself than the trigger for immediate worldwide socialist revolution; a highly influential group of more moderate national party leaders led by Lev Kamenev for whom transfer of power to the soviets was primarily a vehicle for building a strong alliance of left socialist groups which would form a socialist coalition government to prepare for fundamental social reform and peace negotiations by a socialist-friendly Constituent Assembly; and a middle group of independent-minded leaders whose views on the development of the revolution fluctuated in response to their reading of existing conditions.

Then too, events often moved so rapidly that the Bolshevik Central Committee had to develop policies without consulting Lenin. Beyond this, circumstances were frequently such that structurally subordinate party bodies had perforce to develop responses to evolving realities without guidance or contrary to directives from the center. Also, in 1917 the doors to membership were opened wide, and the Bolshevik organization became a genuine mass political party. In part as a result of such factors, Bolshevik programs and policies in 1917 tended to be developed democratically, with strong inputs from rank-and-file members, and therefore reflected popular aspirations.

Meanwhile, the revolution among factory workers, soldiers, sailors, and peasants had a dynamic of its own. At times, the Bolsheviks followed the masses rather than vice versa. For example, on July 14 (July 1 O.S.) the Bolshevik Central Committee, influenced by party moderates, began preparing for a left–socialist congress aimed at unifying all internationalist elements of the "Social Democracy" (e.g., Menshevik-Internationalists and Left SRs) in support of common revolutionary goals. Yet only two days later, radical elements of the Bolshevik Petersburg Committee and Party Military Organization (responsive to their ultra-militant constituencies) helped organize the abortive July uprising, against the wishes of Lenin and the Central Committee, who considered such action premature.

The July uprising ended in an apparent defeat for the Bolsheviks. Lenin was forced into hiding, numerous Bolshevik leaders were jailed, and efforts to form a united left-socialist front were temporarily ended. Still, in light of the success of the Bolsheviks in the October Revolution, perhaps the main significance of the July uprising was that it reflected the great popular attraction for the Bolshevik revolutionary program, as well as the party's strong links to Petrograd's lower classes, links that would prove valuable over the long term.

What was the Bolsheviks' program? Contrary to conventional wisdom, in 1917 the Bolsheviks did not stand for a one-party dictatorship (neither in July nor at any time before the October Revolution). Rather, they stood for democratic "people's power," exercised through an exclusively socialist, soviet, multiparty government, pending convoca-

tion of the Constituent Assembly. The Bolsheviks also stood for more land to individual peasants, "workers' control" in factories, prompt improvement of food supply, and, most important, an early end to the war. All of these goals were neatly packaged in the slogans "Peace, Land, and Bread!" "All Power to the Soviets!" and "Immediate Convocation of the Constituent Assembly!" The interplay and political value of these two key factors—the attractiveness of the Bolshevik platform and the party's carefully nurtured links to revolutionary workers, soldiers, and sailors—were evident in the fall of 1917, after the left's quick defeat of an unsuccessful rightist putsch led by the commander-in-chief of the Russian army, General Lavr Kornilov (the so-called Kornilov affair).

### THE BOLSHEVIKS COME TO POWER

Following the ill–fated July uprising, Lenin, alienated by moderate socialist attacks on the Bolsheviks and by their support of the Provisional Government and dismissive of the soviets' revolutionary potential, tried unsuccessfully to persuade the party leadership to abandon its emphasis on transfer of power to the soviets and shift its strategy to a unilateral seizure of power. Subsequently, in the aftermath of the Kornilov affair, during which Lenin remained in hiding, he briefly reconsidered this position and allowed for a peaceful transition to soviet power. However, this moderation was fleeting. Isolated from day-to-day developments and decision making in the Russian capital, and evidently influenced primarily by clear signs of deepening social unrest at home and abroad, at the end of September (mid-September O.S.) Lenin decided that the time had come for another revolution in Russia: a socialist revolution that would serve as the catalyst for popular rebellions in other European countries. In two emphatic letters to Bolshevik committees in Petrograd written from a hideout in Finland, he now demanded that the party organize an armed uprising "without losing a single moment."

These letters were received in Petrograd at a time when prospects for peaceful creation of an exclusively socialist government suddenly brightened. After passage by the Petrograd Soviet of a momentous Bolshevik resolution to this effect proposed by Kamenev, the Bolsheviks won majority control of that key body. Trotsky became its chairman. Around the same time, the Bolsheviks also gained control of the Moscow Soviet. Moreover, the Bolshevik leadership was just then focused on trying to persuade the Democratic State Conference, a national conference of "democratic" organizations convened to reconsider the government question, to abjure further coalition with the Cadets and to establish exclusively socialist rule. A hastily convened secret emergency meeting of the party Central Committee unceremoniously rejected Lenin's directives within hours of their receipt. For the Bolsheviks, this was just as well. Not long after the October Revolution, Lenin himself acknowledged this. The party was saved from likely disaster by the stubborn resistance of national and lower-level Bolsheviks on the spot who, like Kamenev, were primarily concerned with building the broadest possible support for the formation of an exclusively socialist government or were skeptical of Lenin's strategy of mobilizing the masses behind an "immediate bayonet charge" independent of the soviets.

In part as a consequence of their continuing interaction with workers, soldiers, and sailors, these leaders on the scene possessed a more realistic appreciation than Lenin of the limits of the party's influence and authority among the Petrograd lower classes, as well as of their allegiance to soviets as legitimate democratic organs in which all genuinely revolutionary groups would work to fulfill the revolution. They were forced to recognize that by appearing to usurp the prerogatives of the soviets they risked losing a good deal of their hard–won popular support and suffering a defeat as great as, if not greater than, the one they had suffered in July. Therefore, after hopes that the Democratic State Council would initiate fundamental political change were dashed, they reoriented their tactics toward the formation of an exclusively socialist government at another All-Russian Congress of Soviets of Workers' and Soldiers' Deputies, which at the insistence of leftist delegates to the Democratic State Conference was scheduled for early November (late October O.S.). At the same time, the Bolshevik Central Committee initiated steps to convene an emergency party congress just prior to the start of the soviet congress. This was to be the forum in which the party's revolutionary tactics, and the closely related question of the nature and makeup of a future government, were to be decided.

Meanwhile, Lenin had moved to the Petrograd suburbs and intensified pressure for immediate revolutionary action. As a result, on October 23 (October 10 O.S.), the Bolshevik Central Committee, with Lenin in attendance, resolved to make the seizure of power "the order of the day." However, in the days immediately following, it became clear

that most Petrograd workers and soldiers would not participate in a unilateral call to arms against the Provisional Government by the Bolsheviks prior to the start of the national Congress of Soviets, scheduled to open on November 7 (October 25 O.S.). Kamenev, the leader of party moderates, was so alarmed by the possibility that the party would act precipitously that he virtually disclosed the Central Committee's decision in *Novaia zhizn (New Life)*, the Left Menshevik newspaper edited by the writer Maxim Gorky.

Consequently, with considerable wavering caused largely by pressure for bolder direct action from Lenin, the Bolshevik leadership in Petrograd pursued a strategy based on the following general principles: (1) that the soviets (because of their stature in the eyes of workers and soldiers), and not party groups, should be employed for the overthrow of the Provisional Government; (2) that for the broadest support, any attack on the government should be masked as a defensive operation on behalf of the soviet; (3) that action should therefore be delayed until a suitable excuse for giving battle presented itself; (4) that to undercut potential resistance and to maximize the possibility of success, every opportunity should be utilized to subvert the authority of the Provisional Government peacefully; and (5) that the formal removal of the existing government should be linked with and legitimized by the decisions of the Second Congress of Soviets. At the time, Lenin mocked this approach. However, considering the development of the revolution to that point, as well as the views of a majority of leading Bolsheviks around the country, it appeared as a natural, realistic response to the prevailing correlation of forces and popular mood.

Between November 3 and 6 (October 21–24 O.S.), a majority of Bolshevik leaders staunchly resisted immediate revolutionary action in favor of preparing for a decisive struggle against the Provisional Government at the congress. Among other things, in the party's press and at huge public rallies they attacked the policies of the Provisional Government and reinforced popular support for the removal of the Provisional Government by the Congress of Soviets. Moreover, they reached out to the Menshevik-Internationalists and Left SRs. Simultaneously, using as an excuse the Provisional Government's announced intention of transferring the bulk of the Petrograd garrison to the front, and cloaking every move as a defensive measure against the counterrevolution, they utilized the Bolshevik-

**Red Guards marching through the streets of Moscow in 1917.** © CORBIS

dominated Military Revolutionary Committee of the Petrograd Soviet (MRC), established to monitor the government's troop dispositions, to take control of most Petrograd-based military units. Weapons and ammunition from the city's main arsenals were distributed to supporters. Although the MRC did not cross the boundary between moves that could be justified as defensive and moves that might infringe on the prerogatives of the congress, for practical purposes the Provisional Government was disarmed without a shot being fired.

In response, early on the morning of November 6 (October 24 O.S.), only hours before the scheduled opening of the Second All-Russian Congress of Soviets, a majority of which was poised to vote in favor of forming an exclusively socialist, Soviet government, Kerensky took steps to suppress the left. Orders were issued for the rearrest of leading Bolsheviks who had been detained after the July uprising and released at the time of the Kornilov Affair. Loyalist military school cadets and

shock battalions from the suburbs were called to the Winter Palace, the seat of the government, and the main Bolshevik newspaper, *Rabochii put (Workers' Path)*, was shut down. Not until these steps had been taken, and even then only after Lenin's personal direct intervention in the party's headquarters at Smolny, did the military action against the Provisional Government begin, action that Lenin had been demanding for a month. This occurred before dawn on November 7 (October 25 O.S.). At that time, all pretense that the MRC was simply defending the revolution and attempting primarily to maintain the status quo pending expression of the congress's will was abruptly dropped. Rather, an open, all-out effort was launched to confront congress delegates with the overthrow of the Provisional Government prior to the start of their deliberations.

During the morning of November 7, military detachments supporting the MRC seized strategically important bridges, key government buildings,

**Soldiers fire rifles in Palace Square outside the Winter Palace.** © BETTMANN/CORBIS

rail and power stations, communication facilities, and the State bank without bloodshed. They also laid siege to the Winter Palace, defended by only meager, demoralized, and constantly dwindling forces. Kerensky managed to flee to the front in search of troops before the ring was closed. The "storming of the Winter Palace," dramatically depicted in an Eisenstein film, was a Soviet myth. After nightfall, the historic building was briefly bombarded by cannon from the Fortress of Peter and Paul and occupied with little difficulty, after which remaining members of the government were arrested.

The Soviet Congress was faced with a fait accompli. Lenin proclaimed the demise of the Provisional Government even before the congress opened that night. The thunder of cannon punctuated its first sessions. The effect was precisely what Lenin hoped for and what Bolshevik moderates, Menshevik-Internationalists, and Left SRs feared.

The Mensheviks, SRs, and even the Menshevik-Internationalists responded to Bolshevik violence by walking out of the congress. Lenin now superintended passage of the revolutionary Bolshevik program by the rump congress and the appointment of an interim Soviet national government (the Soviet of People's Commissars or *Sovnarkom*) made up exclusively of Bolsheviks.

Still, as delegates departed Smolny at the close of the Second Congress on the morning of November 9 (October 27 O.S.), the vast majority of them, most Bolsheviks included, expected that all genuine revolutionary groups would unite behind the interim government they had created and that it would quickly be reconstructed according to the Bolshevik pre-October platform: that is, as an exclusively socialist, Soviet coalition government reflecting the relative strength of the various socialist parties originally in the congress and supportive of its revolutionary decrees. Important exceptions to

**Revolutionaries unfurl the red flag in Moscow in 1918.** © BETTMANN/CORBIS

Bolshevik leaders holding this views included Lenin and Trotsky who, having successfully engineered the overthrow of the Provisional Government before the start of the Congress of Soviets, were now most concerned to retain complete freedom of action at virtually any price. Most departing delegates also believed that the new government would in any case yield its authority to the Constituent Assembly, scheduled to be elected at the end of November.

Among political parties seeking to restore a broad socialist alliance and to restructure the Sovnarkom in the immediate aftermath of the Second Congress, most prominent were the Menshevik-Internationalists and the Left SRs; the latter were especially important to the success of the revolution because of their growing strength among peasants in the countryside, where Bolshevik influence was critically weak. Among labor organizations seeking to play a similar role was the All-Russian Executive Committee of the Union of Railway Workers (Vikzhel). Vikzhel announced that it would declare an immediate nationwide rail stoppage if the Bolsheviks did not participate in negotiations to create a homogeneous socialist government responsible to the soviets and including all socialist groups.

Under Vikzhel's aegis, intensive talks were held in Petrograd November 11–18 (October 29–November 5 O.S.). With Kamenev in charge of negotiations for the Bolsheviks, they began auspiciously. Indeed, on November 2 even the Bolshevik press reported that the discussions were on the verge of success. However, they ultimately foundered, primarily because of such factors as the impossibly high demands made by the moderate socialists (essentially requiring repudiation of Soviet power and most of the accomplishments of the Second Congress, as well as the exclusion of Lenin and Trotsky from any future government), the defeat by Soviet forces of an internal insurrection and of loyalist Cossack units outside Petrograd, and the consolidation of Soviet power in Moscow. These factors immeasurably strengthened Lenin's and Trotsky's hands, enabling them to torpedo the Vikzhel talks. During the run–up to the Constituent Assembly in December, Bolshevik moderates made a valiant bid to steer the party's delegation toward support of its right to define Russia's future political system. However, by then the moderates had been squeezed out of the party leadership, and this effort also failed. All of this made a long and bitter civil war inevitable.

## THE SIGNIFICANCE OF THE
## OCTOBER REVOLUTION

The October Revolution cannot be adequately characterized as either a military coup d'état or a popular uprising (although it contained elements of both). Its roots are to be found in the peculiarities of prerevolutionary Russia's political, social, and economic development, as well as in Russia's wartime crisis. At one level, it was the culminating event in a drawn-out battle between leftists and moderates: on the one hand, an expanding spectrum of left socialist groups supported by the vast majority of Petrograd workers, soldiers, and sailors dissatisfied by the results of the February revolution; and on the other, the increasingly isolated liberal–moderate socialist alliance that had taken control of the Provisional Government and national Soviet leadership during the February days. By the time the Second All-Russian Congress of Soviets convened on November 7 (October 25 O.S.), the relatively peaceful victory of the former was all but assured. At another level, the October Revolution was a struggle, initially primarily within the Bolshevik leadership, between proponents of a multiparty, exclusively socialist government that would lead Russia to a Constituent Assembly in which socialists would have a dominating voice, and Leninists, who ultimately favored violent revolutionary action as the best means of striking out on an ultra-radical, independent revolutionary course in Russia and triggering decisive socialist revolutions abroad.

Muted for much of 1917, this conflict erupted with greatest force in the wake of the February Revolution, in the immediate aftermath of the July uprising, and during the periods immediately preceding and following the October Revolution. Such factors as the walkout of Mensheviks and SRs from the Second All–Russian Congress of Soviets, prompted by the belated military operations pressed by Lenin and precipitated by Kerensky; the adoption of the Bolshevik program at the Second All-Russian Congress of Soviets; the intransigence of the moderate socialists at the Vikzhel talks; and the Bolsheviks' first military victories over loyalist forces decisively undermined the efforts of moderate Bolsheviks to achieve a multiparty, socialist

democracy and facilitated the rapid ascendancy of Leninist authoritarianism. In this sense, the October Revolution extinguished prospects for the development of a Western-style democracy in Russia for the better part of a century. Also, in the immediate post-revolutionary years, it led to the catastrophic Russian civil war. Finally, it laid the foundation for Stalinism and the Cold War. However, despite these outcomes, the October revolution was in large measure a valid expression of popular aspirations.

*See also:* BOLSHEVISM; CIVIL WAR OF 1917–1922; FEBRUARY REVOLUTION; JULY DAYS; LENIN, VLADIMIR ILICH; REVOLUTION OF 1905; TROTSKY, LEON DAVIDOVICH

## BIBLIOGRAPHY

Acton, Edward. (1990). *Rethinking the Russian Revolution.* London: Edward Arnold.

Acton, Edward; Cherniaev,Vladimir Iu.; and Rosenberg, William G., eds. (1997). *Critical Companion to the Russian Revolution, 1914–1921.* Bloomington: Indiana University Press.

Figes, Orlando. (1989). *A People's Tragedy: The Russian Revolution.* Oxford: Oxford University Press.

Melgunov, S. P. (1972). *Bolshevik Seizure of Power*, tr. James S. Beaver. Santa Barbara, CA: Clio.

Pipes, Richard. (1990). *The Russian Revolution.* New York: Knopf.

Rabinowitch, Alexander. (1976). *The Bolsheviks Come to Power: The Revolution of 1917 in Petrograd.* New York: Norton.

Raleigh, Donald J. (1986). *Revolution on the Volga: 1917 in Saratov.* Ithaca, NY: Cornell University Press.

Bone, Ann, tr. (1974). *The Bolsheviks and the October Revolution: Minutes of the Central Committee of the Russian Social-Democratic Labour Party (Bolsheviks) August 1917–February 1918.* London: Pluto Press.

Sukhanov, N. N. (1962). *The Russian Revolution, 1917,* tr. and ed. Joel Carmichael. New York: Harper.

Wildman, Allan. (1987). *The End of the Russian Imperial Army,* Vol. 2: *The Road to Soviet Power and Peace.* Princeton, NJ: Princeton University Press.

ALEXANDER RABINOWITCH

## OCTOBRIST PARTY

The Octobrist Party was founded in 1906 by Russian moderate liberals, taking its name from the October Manifesto. Unequivocal support for the new constitutional system and rejection of compulsory land expropriation except in extreme state need distinguished it from the major left party, the Constitutional Democratic Party (Cadets), which represented more radical liberal opinion.

In the elections to the First and Second Dumas (1906–1907), the Octobrist Party fared relatively poorly while parties to its left had strong showings. The government, finding itself unable to work with the first two Dumas, dissolved them. Alexander Guchkov, the Octobrists' first leader, during the Second Duma softened some of the party's positions, thus enabling cooperation with the government. Loyalty to the new constitutional system and willingness to work with the government to achieve its full implementation and accompanying social reform were now the broad guiding principles of the party. Dissolving the Second Duma, Peter Stolypin, chairman of the Council of Ministers (1906–1911), restricted the voting franchise which lessened the voting power of the peasants and working classes. His goal was to limit the number of radical left deputies and increase Octobrist Party representation so that it could provide a solid base of support for the government in the Duma. Stolypin found himself in a difficult position in the Duma, stuck between the right with its hatred for the new system and the radical left. In the 1907 elections to the Third Duma the Octobrist Party more than tripled its representation, receiving 153 seats.

The party's unity and its relationship with the government depended on the latter's dedication to the spirit of the constitutional system and policy of reform. The great increase in the party's numbers made maintenance of unity between its left and right wings problematic.

Initially the Stolypin-Octobrist alliance worked relatively well, especially in regard to peasant reform. However, by 1909 conservatives fearful of the institutionalization of the new system by the Stolypin–Octobrist partnership worked to break it. The Naval General Staff crisis was the first step in this direction. The Octobrists regarded Nicholas II's rejection, with the urging of conservatives, of a bill concerning the Naval General Staff that had already been passed by both houses of parliament, as a violation of the spirit of the October Manifesto. Conservative attacks on Stolypin and increased fragmentation within the party forced Stolypin to turn increasingly to the right, thereby placing his relationship with the Octobrists and their unity under additional strain.

In 1911 the conservatives in the State Council, with the help of Nicholas II, rejected the Western Zemstvo Bill already passed by the Duma. Stolypin, infuriated by constant conservative attempts to block his policies, forced Nicholas II to disband the parliament provisionally, as allowed by Article 87 of the Fundamental Laws, and make the bill law by decree. The Octobrists, although they had supported this bill, considered Stolypin's step to be a betrayal and undermining of the constitutional system. They went into opposition.

In elections to the Fourth Duma (1912), the Octobrists, while remaining the largest party, saw their share of the vote collapse to ninety-five. Morale in the party was at an all-time low, reflecting the overall disappointment with the gradual but successful emasculation of the constitutional system by conservatives and Nicholas II.

Octobrist unity cracked in 1913 when Guchkov, admitting that attempts to cooperate with the government to achieve needed reform had failed, urged adoption of a more aggressive stance toward the government, which since the assassination of Stolypin in 1911 had showed few signs of continuing reform. While the Central Committee supported this step, the larger body of deputies split on this issue. Disappointed with lack of party backing for such a move, some twenty-two deputies formed the Left Octobrists. The majority formed the Zemtsvo Octobrists under the leadership of M.V. Rodzyanko, the party's leader. Some ten to fifteen remained uncommitted to either side. The party ceased to have any real power.

The weakening and fragmentation of the Octobrist Party mirrored the collapse of Russia's experiment with constitutional monarchy.

*See also:* CONSTITUTIONAL DEMOCRATIC PARTY; NICHOLAS II; OCTOBER MANIFESTO; STOLYPIN, PETER ARKADIEVICH

**BIBLIOGRAPHY**

Hosking, Geoffrey. (1973). *The Russian Constitutional Experiment: Government and Duma, 1907–1914.* London: Cambridge University Press.

Seton-Watson, Hugh. (1991). *The Russian Empire, 1801–1917.* Oxford: Oxford University Press.

Waldron, Peter. (1998). *Between Two Revolutions: Stolypin and the Politics of Renewal in Russia.* London: UCL Press.

ZHAND P. SHAKIBI

## ODOYEVSKY, VLADIMIR FYODOROVICH

(1804–1869), romantic and gothic fiction writer, pedagogue, musicologist, amateur scientist, and public servant.

A Russian thinker with encyclopedic knowledge whom contemporaries dubbed "the Russian Faust" (a character in one of his novels), Vladimir Odoyevsky was mentioned in his day in the same breath as Alexander Pushkin and Nikolai Gogol. He is perhaps best known for the philosophical fantasy *Russian Nights* (*Russkie nochi*), published in 1844. In 1824–1825 he edited, with Wilhelm Küchelbecker, four issues of the influential periodical *Mnemosyne*. Its purpose was to champion Russian literature and German philosophy at a time when everyone else seemed fascinated with French ideas. Odoyevsky contributed works such as "The City Without a Name" (1839) to Nekrasov's influential magazine *Sovremennik (Contemporary)*. In 1823 he founded a group called "Lovers of Wisdom" (*Lyubomudry*, a literal translation of the Greek word "philosophy"). Propounding ideas of philosophic realism, the group was dissolved soon after the Decembrist uprising in 1825, even though the group's pursuits truly were only philosophical, not political. The failed rebellion deeply affected Odoyevsky, because—like the poet Pushkin—he had many friends among the Decembrists, including his cousin, the poet and guards' officer, Alexander Odoyevsky (1802–1839), and the writer Wilhelm Küchelbecker (1797–1846), both of whom were imprisoned and exiled after the uprising.

A Slavophile of sorts, Odoyevsky believed in the decline of the West and the future greatness of Russia. He met regularly with other Slavophile thinkers, such as Ivan Kireyevsky, Alexander Koshelev, Melgunov, Stepan Shevyrev, Mikhail Pogodin (the last two were professors at Moscow State University), and the young poet Dmitry Venevitinov.

In the 1830s Odoyevsky was preoccupied with political questions, antislavery, anti-Americanism, Russian messianism, the innate superiority of Russia over the West, and criticisms of Malthus, Bentham, and the Utilitarians. The novel *Russian Nights* contains a mixture of these ideas. Odoyevsky proposed a revealing subtitle, which his editor later rejected: "Russian Nights, or the Indispensability of a New Science and a New Art." Throughout the novel the main characters grapple with topics such as the meaning of science and art, logic, the sense of human existence, atheism and belief, education, government rule, the function of individual sciences, madness and sanity, poetic creation, Slavophilism, Europe and Russia, and mercantilism.

Odoyevsky also cherished music and musicians, composing chamber music as early as his teens and writing critical appraisals of composers such as Mikhail Glinka. He was devoted to the history and structure of church singing and collected notational manuscripts to preserve them for future generations. As he wrote in one of his letters: "I discovered the definite theory of our melodies and harmony, which is similar to the theory of medieval Western tunes, but has its own peculiarities."

Odoyevsky excelled the most in the genre of the short story, particularly ones geared toward children. Two stories rank among the best in children's fare: "Johnny Frost" and "The Town in a Snuff Box." Generally, Odoyevsky's fiction reflects two main tendencies. First, he expresses his philosophical convictions imaginatively and often fantastically. His stories typically move from a recognizable setting to a mystical realm. Secondly, he injects commentary on the shortcomings of social life in Russia, usually in a satiric mode.

*See also:* GOLDEN AGE OF RUSSIAN LITERATURE; LOVERS OF WISDOM, THE; SLAVOPHILES

### BIBLIOGRAPHY

Cornwell, Neil. (1998). *Vladimir Odoevsky and Romantic Poetics: Collected Essays*. Providence, RI: Berghahn Books.

Minto, Marilyn. (1994). *Russian Tales of the Fantastic*. London: Bristol Classical Press.

Rydel, Christine. (1999). *Russian Literature in the Age of Pushkin and Gogol*. Detroit: Gale Group.

Smith, Andrew. (2003). *Empire and the Gothic: the Politics of Genre*. New York: Palgrave Macmillan.

JOHANNA GRANVILLE

## OFFICIAL NATIONALITY

In 1833, Sergei Uvarov, in his first published circular as the new minister of education, coined the tripartite formula "Orthodoxy, Autocracy, Nationality" as the motto for the development of the Russian Empire. The three terms also became the main ingredients of the doctrine that dominated the era of Emperor Nicholas I, who reigned from 1825 to 1855, and that came to be called "official nationality." About two dozen periodicals, scores of books, and the entire school system propagated the ideas and made them the foundation for guiding Russia to modernity without succumbing to materialism, revolutionary movements, and blind imitation of foreign concepts.

The meaning of Orthodoxy and autocracy were clear. The Orthodox faith had formed the foundation of Russian spiritual, ethical, and cultural life since the tenth century, and had always acted as a unifying factor in the nation. It also proved useful in preaching obedience to authority. Autocracy, or absolute monarchy, involved the conviction that Russia would avoid revolution through the enlightened leadership of a tsar, who would provide political stability but put forth timely and enlightened reforms so that Russia could make constant progress in all spheres of national life. Political theory had long argued, and Russia's historical lessons seemed to demonstrate, that a single ruler was needed to maintain unity in a vast territory with varied populations.

The third term in the tripartite formula was the most original and the most mysterious. The broad idea of nationality (narodnost) had just become fashionable among the educated public, but there was no set definition for the concept. In 1834, Peter Pletnev, a literary critic and professor of Russian literature at St. Petersburg University, noted: "The idea of nationality is the major characteristic that contemporaries demand from literary works . . . ," but, he went on, "one does not know exactly what it means." A variety of schools of thought on the subject arose in the 1830s and 1840s.

The romantic nationalists, led by Michael Pogodin and Stephen Shevyrev of Moscow University and the journal The Muscovite, celebrated Russia's absolutist form of government, its uniqueness, its poetic richness, the peace-loving virtues of its denizens, and the notion of the Slavs as a chosen people, all of which supposedly bestowed upon Russia a glorious mission to save humanity and made it superior to a "decaying" West. The Slavophiles, led by Moscow-based landowners including the Aksakov and Kireyevsky brothers, opposed such western concepts as individualism, legalism, and majority rule, in favor of the notion of sobornost: a community, much like a church council (sobor), should engage in discussion, with the aim of achieving a "chorus" of unanimous decision and thus preserving a spirit of harmony, and

brotherhood. The people then would advise the tsar, through some type of land council (zemsky sobor), a system, the Slavophiles believed, that was the "true" Russian way in all things. The Westernizers, in contrast, sympathized with the values of other Europeans and assumed that Russian development, while traveling by a different path, would occur in the context of the liberal tradition that valued the individual over the state. All three groups, however, agreed on the necessity for emancipation, legal reform, and freedom of speech and press.

The doctrine of official nationality represented the government's response to these intellectual currents, as well as to the wave of revolutions that had spread through much of the rest of Europe beyond Russia's borders. The proponents of this doctrine, however, did not speak with one voice. For instance, because of their support for the existing state, the romantic nationalists are often defined as proponents of official nationality. However, the most influential group, sometimes called dynastic nationalists, included Emperor Nicholas I and the court, and their views were propagandized in the far-flung journalistic enterprises of Fadei Bulgarin, Nicholas Grech, and Osip Senkovsky. Their understanding of narodnost was based on patriotism, a defensive doctrine used to support the status quo and Russia's great-power status. For them, "Russianness," even for Baltic Germans or Poles, revolved around a subject's loyalty to the autocrat. In other words, they equated the nation with the state as governed by the dynasty, which was seen as both the repository and the emblem of the national culture.

Sergei Semenovich Uvarov's own views of nationality straddled the many schools of thought. He shared the bulk of the opinions of the dynastic nationalists, patronized the romantic nationalists and their journal, praised the Slavophiles for their Orthodox spirit, and accepted some Westernizing tendencies in Russia's historical development. But this architect of official nationality espoused a doctrine that lacked appeal and vitality. Instead of regarding the people as actively informing the content of nationality, Uvarov believed that the state should define, guide, and impose "true" national values upon a passive population. In a word, his concept of narodnost excluded the creative activity of the narod and made it synonymous with loyalty to throne and altar. The doctrine, while it achieved the stability which was its aim, proved anachronistic and did not survive Nicholas I and Uvarov, both of whom died in 1855.

See also: NATIONALISM IN TSARIST EMPIRE; NATIONALITIES POLICIES, TSARIST; NATION AND NATIONALITY NICHOLAS I; SLAVOPHILES; UVAROV, SERGEI SEMENOVICH; WESTERNIZERS

## BIBLIOGRAPHY

Lincoln, W. Bruce. (1978). *Nicholas I: Emperor and Autocrat of All the Russias*. Bloomington: Indiana University Press.

Riasanovsky, Nicholas. (1967). *Nicholas I and Official Nationality in Russia, 1825–1855*. Berkeley: University of California Press.

Whittaker, Cynthia H. (1984). *The Origins of Modern Russian Education: An Intellectual Biography of Count Sergei Uvarov, 1786–1855*. DeKalb: Northern Illinois University Press.

CYNTHIA HYLA WHITTAKER

## OGARKOV, NIKOLAI VASILEVICH

(1917–1994), marshal, chief of the Soviet General Staff, Hero of the Soviet Union, (1917–1944).

Nikolai Ogarkov was one of the outstanding military leaders of the Soviet General Staff, who combined technical knowledge with a mastery of combined arms operations. He was born on October 30, 1917, in the village of Molokovo in Tver oblast and graduated from an engineering night school in 1937. In 1938 he joined the Red Army and graduated from the Kuybyshev Military Engineering Academy in 1941. Ogarkov served as combat engineer with a wide range of units on various fronts throughout World War II. After the war he completed the advanced military engineering course at the Kuybyshev Military Engineering Academy. Ogarkov advanced rapidly in command and staff assignments and graduated in 1959 from the Voroshilov Academy of the General Staff. Thereafter he commanded a motorized rifle division in East Germany and held command and staff postings in various military districts. In 1968 he assumed the post of deputy chief of the General Staff and head of the Operations Directorate, where he was involved in planning the military intervention in Czechoslovakia. In 1974 he assumed the post of first deputy chief of the General Staff, and then chief of the General Staff in 1977. Ogarkov held that post until 1984. During his tenure he oversaw the Soviet intervention in Afghanistan and was the voice of the Soviet government in the aftermath of the shooting down of the Korean airliner, KAL

007. He was an articulate advocate of the Revolution in Military Affairs, which he believed was about to transform military art. He stressed the impact of new technologies associated with automated command and control, electronic warfare, precision strike, and weapons based on new physical principles upon the conduct of war. His advocacy of increased defense spending contributed to his removal from office in 1984. Ogarkov died on January 23, 1994.

See also: AFGHANISTAN, RELATIONS WITH; MILITARY, SOVIET AND POST-SOVIET

## BIBLIOGRAPHY

Kokoshin, Andrei A. (1998). *Soviet Strategic Thought, 1917–91*. Cambridge, MA: MIT Press.

Odom, William E. (1998). *The Collapse of the Soviet Military*. New Haven, CT: Yale University Press.

Zisk, Kimberly Marten. (1993). *Engaging the Enemy: Organization Theory and Soviet Military Innovation, 1955–1991*. Princeton, NJ: Princeton University Press.

JACOB W. KIPP

## OGHUZ *See* TORKY.

## OKOLNICHY

Court rank used in pre-Petrine Russia.

The term *okolnichy* (pl. *okolnichie*) meaning "someone close to the ruler," is derived from the word *okolo* (near, by). The sources first mention an okolnichy at the court of the prince of Smolensk in 1284. In the fourteenth and fifteenth centuries, okolnichie acted as administrators, judges, and military commanders, and as witnesses during compilation of a prince's legal documents. When a prince was on campaign, okolnichie prepared bridges, fords, and lodging for him. Okolnichie usually came from local elite families. By the end of the fifteenth century, the rank of okolnichy became part of the hierarchy of the Gosudarev Dvor (Sovereign's Court), second after the rank of boyar. Unlike boyars, who usually performed military service, okolnichie carried out various administrative assignments in the first half of the sixteenth century. Later, the okolnichie conceded their administrative functions to the secretaries.

Under Ivan IV, the majority of okolnichie belonged to the boyar families who had long connections with Moscow. For most elite courtiers, with the exception of the most distinguished princely families, service as okolnichie was a prerequisite for receiving the rank of boyar. The rank of okolnichy also served as a means of integrating families of lesser status into the elite. By the end of the sixteenth century, the distinction between boyars and okolnichie was based largely on genealogical origin and seniority in service. From the middle of the seventeenth century, the number of okolnichie increased because of the growing size of the court. Many historians believe that all okolnichie were admitted to the royal council, the Boyar Duma, though in fact only a few of them attended meetings with the tsar.

*See also:* BOYAR; BOYAR DUMA

**BIBLIOGRAPHY**

Kleimola, Ann M. (1985). "Patterns of Duma Recruitment, 1505–1550." In *Essays in Honor of A. A. Zimin*, ed. Daniel Clarke Waugh. Columbus, OH: Slavica.

Poe, Marshall T. (2003). *The Russian Elite in the Seventeenth Century*. 2 vols. Helsinki: The Finnish Academy of Science and Letters.

SERGEI BOGATYREV

# OKUDZHAVA, BULAT SHALOVICH

(1924–1997), Russian poet, singer, and novelist.

Bulat Okudhava's parents were both professional Party workers. In 1937 they were arrested; the father was executed and the mother imprisoned in the Gulag until 1955. At age seventeen Okudzhava volunteered for the army, saw active service, and was wounded. After the war he graduated from Tbilisi University, then became a schoolteacher in Kaluga. In 1956 he joined the Communist Party of the Soviet Union (CPSU) and moved to Moscow. He worked as a literary journalist, and joined the Union of Writers in 1961. He made his name as a prose writer with the controversially unheroic war story "Goodbye, Schoolboy," and followed this with a series of historical novels depicting various episodes from nineteenth-century gentry life.

In the late 1950s Okudzhava pioneered "guitar poetry" songs performed by the author to his own guitar accompaniment. This genre drew on long-established traditions of Russian drawing-room art song ("romance"), student song, and gypsy song, as well as that of the French chansonniers, who became well known in Russian intellectual circles in the late 1950s (Okudzhava's favorite was Georges Brassens). Okudzhava cultivated an amateur-sounding performance manner. In actual fact, he was an extremely gifted natural melodist, creating dozens of original and unforgettable tunes. Okudzhava's songs are suffused with nostalgic, agnostic sadness. They deal with three principal themes: love, war, and the streets of Moscow. In his treatment of love he is an unrepentant romantic, idealizing women and portraying men as subordinate and flawed. In his treatment of war he is anti-heroic, emphasizing fear, loss, and mankind's seeming inability to find a more humane way of settling disputes. In his treatment of Moscow he looks back to a time before the city became a Soviet metropolis, when it offered refuge for the vulnerable and sensitive in its courtyards and neighborhoods, especially the Arbat district. His treatment of war and Moscow were particularly at odds with official notions about these matters. At about the time that Okudzhava created his basic corpus of songs, the tape recorder became available to private citizens in the USSR, and the songs were duplicated in immense numbers, completely bypassing official controls.

By the mid-1960s Okudzhava had become, after Vladimir Vysotsky, the most genuinely popular figure in the literary arts in Russia. He was unique in that, while he remained a member of the Party and the Union of Writers, his work was published abroad (without permission) and circulated unofficially in Russia, while continuing to be published officially in the USSR. Shielded by his popularity and his fundamental patriotism, he was never subjected to severe repression. From the mid-1980s until his death he was something of a Grand Old Man of Russian literature, the doyen of the "men of the 1960s." In 1994, his novel *The Closed Theatre*, a barely fictionalized account of his parents' life and fate through the eyes of their son, won the Russian Booker Prize.

*See also:* JOURNALISM; MUSIC; UNION OF SOVIET WRITERS

**BIBLIOGRAPHY**

Smith, Gerald Stanton. (1984). *Songs to Seven Strings: Russian Guitar Poetry and Soviet "Mass Song."* Bloomington: Indiana University Press.

Makarov, Dmitriy; Vardenga, Maria; and Zubtsova, Yana. (2003). "Boulat Shalvovich Okoudjava." <http://www.russia-in-us.com/Music/Artists/Okoudjava>.

GERALD SMITH

## OLD BELIEVER COMMITTEE

In 1820, Emperor Alexander I convened a secret committee to guide him in policies regarding the Old Believers (also known as Old Ritualists or *raskolniki*—schismatics). The secret committee included some of the most important churchmen and ministers in Russia, including the minister of religion and education (Prince Vasily Golitsyn) and Archbishop Filaret Drozdov, later to become metropolitan of Moscow and the preeminent prelate of mid–nineteenth–century Russia. Originally given the task of finding an appropriate form of toleration within the Russian legal system, the committee quickly broke into liberal and conservative factions. Internal politics of the committee, added to the emperor's own vacillating desire for a "spiritual revolution" in Russia, weakened its ability to make significant changes. Ascendance of conservative members pushed the committee's views from tolerance of the Old Belief to more stringent enforcement of punitive laws against them. After the death of Emperor Alexander, the secret committee became mostly a forum for discussion of anti-Old Believer policies in the Russian government. It continued to exist into the reign of Alexander III, whose landmark law of 1883 finally revised the legal status of Old Believers in the Russian empire.

*See also:* ALEXANDER I; FILARET DROZDOV, METROPOLITAN; OLD BELIEVERS; ORTHODOXY

### BIBLIOGRAPHY

Nichols, Robert L. (2004). "The Old Belief under Surveillance during the Reign of Alexander I." In *Russia's Dissenting Old Believers*, ed. Georg Michels and Robert L. Nichols. Minneapolis: Minnesota Mediterranenean and East European Monographs.

ROY R. ROBSON

## OLD BELIEVERS

The term Old Believers (or Old Ritualists) includes a number of groups that arose as a result of Russian church reforms initiated between 1654 and 1666. Old Believers desired to maintain the traditions, rites, and prerogatives of Russian Orthodoxy, whereas Nikon, patriarch of the Russian Orthodox Church, wanted to make Russian practices conform to those of the contemporary Greek Orthodox Church. Nikon's opponents, conscious of both a departure from tradition and an encroachment of central control over local autonomy, refused to change practices.

### ORIGINS OF THE MOVEMENT

The reforms took two general forms—textual and ritual. In the first, a group of editors changed all Russian liturgical books to conform with their contemporary Greek counterparts, rather than old Russian or old Greek versions. The most famous of these was the change in spelling of "Jesus" from "Isus" to "Iisus." While the Old Believers rejected all innovation, the symbolic centerpiece of resistance was the sign of the cross. Traditionally, Russians put together their thumb, fourth, and fifth fingers in a symbol of the Trinity. The second finger was held upright, to confirm Jesus' form as perfect man; the middle finger was bent to the level of the second, symbolizing Jesus' Godly form that bent down to become human. These two fingers touched the body during the sign of the cross, showing that both natures of Jesus (human and divine) existed on the cross. In Greek practice, the fingers were reversed—thumb, second, and third fingers were held together and touched the body, while the fourth and fifth fingers were held down toward the palm. When Nikon obliged his flock to change their hands, it seemed that he wanted them to discount the icons in their churches and the instructions in their psalm books, which explicitly showed the old Russian style of the sign. In fact, the Stoglav Council, convened exactly a century earlier, had condemned anything but the "two–fingered sign."

The implementation of reforms were draconian. Ivan Neronov and Avvakum Petrovich, who had been part of Nikon's circle, challenged the patriarch. Sometimes left alone, at other times persecuted, Nikon's opponents included some of the most respected churchmen in Muscovy. In an unusual move, Neronov was finally allowed to continue using the old books for his services, but Avvakum was exiled to Siberia and finally burned at the stake for his extreme anti–reform posture. Even women were not spared—the boyarina Feodosia Morozova was carried out of Moscow to the Borovsk Monastery, where she perished in jail.

For each of the famous anti–reformists, thousands more pious Russians simply paid no heed to the calls for reform and continued to pray according to the old style. Their existence underlined the limit of Nikon's other goal, which was to limit the expansion of central control of religious affairs to the patriarch alone, taking away local prerogatives. The vast majority of Old Believers simply refused to accept either the reforms or the centralization that Nikon imposed on his flock. The traditionalists, of course, perceived themselves as true Orthodox, and called followers of the reformed ritual "new believers" or "Nikonians." Much of this early history, however, is still poorly understood. Recent scholarship has shown that the Old Belief did not coalesce into a movement until perhaps a generation after the schism. Because local concerns tended to override any broader organization of Old Believers, the leadership of the Old Belief probably had only limited authority over a small core of supporters.

## ORGANIZATIONAL STRUCTURE

For the Old Believers, the possible loss of sacramental life splintered the movement shortly after the 1666 schism. Since no bishops consecrated new hierarchs according to the old ritual, Old Believers quickly found themselves bereft of canonical clergy. Old Believer communities solidified into a number of *soglasiya*, translatable as "concords." The differences among the concords lay not so much in doctrinal issues as in sacramental procedures and interaction with the state.

Old Believers developed a spectrum of views on the sacraments. Half–Old Believers, for example, accepted some Russian Orthodox sacramental life but prayed regularly only with other half–Old Believers. Many such half–Old Believers never openly aligned themselves with any specific concord but instead maintained a secret allegiance to the Old Belief. Although scores of small, locally formed groups sprang up, they tended to wither and die, leaving few traces of their history.

The priestly Old Believers (*popovtsy*), on the other hand, at some point in their history came to accept clergy from new-rite sources. These priestly Old Believers included the Belokrinitsy and the *beglopopovtsy* (fugitive-priestly), the latter accepting clergy consecrated in the state-sponsored church. Furthest from the church were the priestless Old Ritualists—the Pomortsy, Fedoseyevtsy, Filippovtsy, and Spasovtsy—all of whom firmly believed that the sacramental life had been taken up into heaven,

just as Elijah had ridden his fiery chariot away from a sinful world, only to return in the last days. Priestless Old Believers were more likely to reject accommodation with the state than their priestly coreligionists, sometimes even eschewing the use of money or building permanent homes. While some Old Believers lived openly in their communities, others traveled from place to place, preaching and living off alms.

In broad terms, Old Believer communities on the local level were organized according to similar patterns, regardless of concord. Clergy (priests, preceptors, and abbots) usually came from within the community or from one nearby, and all members of the concord elected the group's clerical leadership. Democratic management of religious affairs found precedent in both the autonomous organization of pre-Nikon parishes and in the monastic rule maintained at the Solovki Monastery in Russia's extreme north. This monastery, a dramatic holdout against the Russian Orthodox church, saw its continued expression in the Vyg and Leksa monastic settlements that, in turn, established the Pomortsy concord.

## LEGAL AND SOCIAL STATUS IN IMPERIAL RUSSIA

Reaction against Old Believers emanated from both the Russian Orthodox Church and the secular state. In pushing through his ritual and textual changes, Patriarch Nikon relied heavily on his relationship with Tsar Alexei Mikhailovich to suppress popular opposition. The history of the Old Belief's early years tells of numerous confrontations between agents of the state and Old Believers. At times, they were subjected to corporal punishment such as having a tongue cut out, being burnt at the stake, or even being smoked alive "like bacon." Sometimes, however, death came at the hands of Old Believers themselves. On some occasions, Old Believers burned themselves alive in their churches rather than accept the ritual changes of the revised Russian Orthodox Church. Although this was the most extreme form of resistance and did not happen often, it did provide an effective and surprisingly frequent deterrent to state seizure of Old Believer groups. Self-immolation continued even into the period of Peter I, a whole generation after the first reforms.

Peter I's position regarding the Old Believers was mixed. Old Believers were not tolerated as political opponents of the state, especially of Peter's

**Woodcut ordered by Peter I to encourage men to shave their beards and to ridicule Old Believers who refuse to shave.**

© HULTON ARCHIVE

Western-looking reforms. He implemented a double poll tax on Old Believers and even imposed a tax on the beards that Old Believers refused to shave, as well as the traditional clothing that they would not exchange for Western European dress. In matters advantageous to the state, however, Peter I allowed Old Believers to live as they wished. For example, he refused to persecute Old Believers in the Vyg community while they were producing ore.

Even when allowed to exist, Old Believers often suffered under separate laws and governmental decrees, some of which were secret and therefore not published. The situation of the Old Believers improved dramatically, however, during the reign of Peter III, who tolerated them. During the rule of Catherine II, the great Old Believer centers of Preobrazhenskoe and Rogozhskoe were founded. In these centers, curiously known only as "cemeteries," Old Believers created large complexes of chapels, churches, bell towers, and charitable institutions, such as hospitals and almshouses. Pre-

obrazhenskoe and Rogozhskoe became the focus of Old Believer merchant and industrial development for succeeding generations.

Meanwhile, the church itself had softened its attitude about the Old Ritual. In 1800, it created the *edinoverie*, an arm of the official church that continued to use the old rite. Although initially successful, the edinoverie never swayed the majority of priestly Old Believers, and even fewer of the priestless Old Believers, who had become convinced that priesthood would be lost until the Second Coming of Christ.

With the succession of Nicholas I to the throne, Old Believers once more found their legal status eroded. Even by the end of Alexander's reign, the state had already begun again to refer to Old Believers as *raskolniki* (schismatics). This name had earlier been dropped as too judgmental. As Nicholas worked out a new relationship between church and state, he began to close the Old Believers' places of worship, seize their property, and harrass the faithful. By 1834, the gains made by Old Believers before 1822 had been completely lost.

The policy of the next tsar, Alexander II, toward Old Believers proved much more liberal than that of his father. Although laws from Tsar Nicholas's period curtailing Old Believer freedom stayed on the books, the state generally stopped enforcing them. Old Believers again flourished both in Moscow and in the far reaches of the empire. The Russian Orthodox Church remained an adamant opponent of the schism but began to pursue expanded missionary activity to the Old Believers, rather than engage in direct persecution.

The succession of Alexander III further revised the Old Believers legal status. Study of the Old Ritualist question increased during the early years of Alexander III's administration and culminated in the law on Old Believers of May 1883. This new law served as the capstone to imperial policy on the Old Belief until the revolutionary changes of 1905. At that time, against the wishes of the Russian Orthodox Church, the emperor granted full toleration of all religious groups through his edict of April 17, 1905. In the late imperial period, this date would be celebrated by Old Believers as the beginning of a silver age of growth and wide public acceptance.

No one knows how many Old Believers lived in Russia. The first census of the empire had convinced Old Believers that to be counted was tantamount to being enrolled in the books of Antichrist.

Moreover, Old Believers realized that being counted made them more easily subject to the double poll tax. Thus, Old Believers rarely cooperated with imperial authorities during enumerations. The Old Believers could hide from the authorities simply by calling themselves members of the Russian Orthodox Church, especially if they had bribed the local priest to enroll them on parish registers. The question of numerical strength in relation to gender remains sketchy at best. The figure of ten percent of the total population, however, has been regarded as authoritative for the imperial period.

Old Believers tended to live either in Moscow or on the outskirts of European Russia. Often far from imperial power, Old Believer communities tended to include active roles for women and devised self-help programs to insure economic survival. The wealth of Old Believer merchants and industrialists has been noted many times, but even the most modest Old Believer communities usually made provisions for mutual aid, rendering their settlements more prosperous-looking than other Russian villages. Old Believer industrialists were also widely reported to give preferential treatment, good benefits, and high pay for co–religionists working at their factories. Russian Orthodox authorities even claimed that the Old Believers lured poor adherents of the established church, including impoverished pastors, into the arms of the schism.

## OLD BELIEVERS IN THE SOVIET AND POST–SOVIET PERIOD

The situation for Old Believers in post-1917 Russia has not been thoroughly studied, though some generalizations can be made. In many cases, churches were closed and their believers persecuted, especially in the period of the cultural revolution. Activists were jailed or sent to the Gulag camps, as were many other religious believers. In other cases, Old Believers followed a path of partial accommodation with the state, much like the practices of some Russian Orthodox. Taking advantage of Soviet laws, some Old Believer communities used their previous history of persecution and tradition of communal organization to appeal for churches to stay open. This strategy had mixed results. A few major centers were allowed to exist in Moscow, for example, and, after World War II, in Riga, but others were closed or destroyed.

Old Belief was weakened significantly during the communist period. Ritual life regularly became covert, rather than public. After having been baptized as children, Old Believers often ceased to take part in church rituals as they grew older. Some, especially in the urban centers, became Communist Party members, perhaps to revive their religious life in retirement. Older women, with little to lose politically or economically, attended churches more openly and frequently than working men and women.

Many Old Believers, however, retreated into their old practices of secrecy in worship, use of homes instead of officially sanctioned churches, and even flight into the wilderness. Rural Old Believers continued to be skeptical of outsiders, especially communists, and tried to retain ritual distance between the faithful and the unbelievers. Sometimes, illegal or informal conferences debated the problems of secular education, military service, and intermarriage. In the most extreme cases, Old Believer families moved ever farther into Siberia, sometimes even crossing into China. Notably, Old Believers also emigrated to Australia, Turkey, the United States, and elsewhere, continuing a trend that that had begun in the late nineteenth century.

The period of glasnost and perestroika created significant international scholarly and popular interest in the Old Believers, though that has waned during the years of economic difficulty following the breakup of the USSR. In post-communist Russia, Old Believers have become bolder and more public, reviving publications, building churches, and reconstituting community life. They have fought to have the Old Belief recognized by the government as one of Russia's historical faiths, hoping to put the Old Belief on par with the Russian Orthodox Church as a pillar of traditional (i.e., noncommunist) values. Old Believers have continued to struggle with the demands of tradition in a rapidly changing political, social, cultural, and economic environment.

*See also:* ALEXANDER MIKHAILOVICH; AVVAKUM PETROVICH; CHURCH COUNCIL, HUNDRED CHAPTERS; NIKON, PATRIARCH; OLD BELIEVER COMMITTEE; ORTHODOXY; RUSSIAN ORTHODOX CHURCH

## BIBLIOGRAPHY

Cherniavsky, Michael. (1996). "The Old Believers and the New Religion." *Slavic Review* 25:1–39.

Crummey, Robert O. (1970). *The Old Believers and the World of Antichrist: The Vyg Community and the Russian State, 1694–1855.* Madison: University of Wisconsin Press.

Michels, Georg Bernhard. (1999). *At War with the Church: Religious Dissent in Seventeenth–Century Russia.* Stanford, CA: Stanford University Press.

Peskov, Vasily. (1994). *Lost in the Taiga: One Russian Family's Fifty-Year Struggle for Survival and Religious Freedom in the Siberian Wilderness*, tr. Marian Schwartz. New York: Doubleday.

Robson, Roy R. (1995). *Old Believers in Modern Russia.* DeKalb: Northern Illinois University Press.

Scheffel, David Z. (1991). *In the Shadow of Antichrist: The Old Believers of Alberta.* Lewiston, NY: Broadview Press.

ROY R. ROBSON

# OLD STYLE

Until January 31, 1918, Russia used the Julian calendar, while Western Europe had gradually changed to the Gregorian calendar after its introduction by Pope Gregory XIII in 1582. Orthodox Russia, associating the Gregorian calendar with Catholicism, had resisted the change. As a result, Russian dates lagged behind contemporary events. In the nineteenth century, Russia was twelve days behind the West; in the twentieth century it was thirteen days behind. Because of the difference in calendars, the revolution of October 25, 1917, was commemorated on November 7. To minimize confusion, Russian writers would indicate their dating system by adding the abbreviation "O.S." (Old Style) or "N.S." (New Style) to their letters, documents, and diary entries. The Russian Orthodox Church continues to use the Julian system, making Russian Christmas fall on January 7.

*See also:* CALENDAR

**BIBLIOGRAPHY**

Gerhart, Genevra. (1974). *The Russian's World: Life and Language.* New York: Harcourt Brace Jovanovich.

Hughes, Lindsey. (1998). *Russia in the Age of Peter the Great.* New Haven, CT: Yale University Press.

ANN E. ROBERTSON

# OLEG

(died c. 912), first grand prince of Kiev, asserted his rule over the East Slavic tribes in the middle Dnieper region and concluded treaties with Constantinople.

When Rurik was on his deathbed in 879 he gave his kinsman Oleg "the Sage" control over his domains in northern Russia and placed his young son Igor into Oleg's care. It is not known whether Oleg succeeded Rurik in his own right or as the regent for Igor. In 882 he assembled an army of Varangians and East Slavs and traveled south from Novgorod, capturing Smolensk and Lyubech. At Kiev, he tricked the boyars Askold and Dir into coming out to greet him. Accusing them of having no right to rule the town because they were not of princely stock as he and Igor were, he had them killed. Oleg became the prince of Kiev and proclaimed that it would be "the mother of all Rus towns." He waged war against the neighbouring East Slavic tribes, made them Kiev's tributaries, and deprived the Khazars of their jurisdiction over the middle Dnieper. Oleg thus became the founder of Rus, the state centered on Kiev.

In 907 Oleg attacked Constantinople. Although some scholars question the authenticity of this information, most accept it as true. His army, constituting Varangians and Slavs, failed to breach the city walls but forced the Greeks to negotiate a treaty. One of Oleg's main objectives was to obtain the best possible terms for Rus merchants trading in Constantinople. He was thus the first prince to formalize trade relations between the Rus and the Greeks. In 911 (or 912) he sent envoys to Constantinople to conclude another more juridical treaty. The two agreements were among Oleg's greatest achievements. According to folk tradition, he died in 912 after a viper bit him when he kicked his dead horse's skull. Another account says he died in 922 at Staraya Ladoga.

*See also:* KIEVAN RUS; RURIKID DYNASTY; VIKINGS

**BIBLIOGRAPHY**

Franklin, Simon, and Shepard, Jonathan. (1996). *The Emergence of Rus, 750–1200.* London: Longman.

Vernadsky, George. (1948). *Kievan Russia.* New Haven, CT: Yale University Press.

MARTIN DIMNIK

# OLGA

(d. 969), Kievan grand princess and regent for her son Svyatoslav.

Under the year 903, the *Primary Chronicle* reports that Oleg, Rurik's kinsman and guardian to his son Igor, obtained a wife for Igor from Pskov by the name of Olga. It is unclear whether Igor was actually the son of Rurik, the semi-legendary founder of the Kievan state, but, as Igor and Olga's son Svyatoslav was born in 942, it is very likely that the chronology in the text is faulty and that the marriage did not take place in 903. Legend has it that Olga was of Slavic origin, but evidence is again lacking.

On a trip to collect tribute from an East Slavic tribe called the Derevlians (forest dwellers) in 945, Igor was killed, and the Derevlians decided that Mal, their prince, should marry Olga, who was serving as regent for her minor son. Olga pretended to go along with the plan, but then violently put down their uprising by means of three well-planned acts of revenge, after which she destroyed the Derevlian capital Iskoresten. The chronicle account of Olga's revenge is formulaic, based on folklore-like riddles that the opponent must comprehend in order to escape death. The tales are clearly intended to demonstrate Olga's wisdom. From 945 to 947, after her defeat of the Derevlians, Olga established administrative centers for taxation, which eliminated the need for collecting tribute. During her regency she significantly expanded the land holdings of the Kievan grand princely house.

Olga was the first member of the Rus ruling dynasty to accept Christianity. Scholars have debated when and where she was converted, as the sources give conflicting accounts, but there is some evidence that she became a Christian in Constantinople in 954 or 955 and was hosted by Constantine Porphyrogenitus as a Christian ruler during a subsequent visit in 957. According to the *Primary Chronicle* account, which is likely intended to mirror her rejection of Mal, Olga eludes a marriage proposal from Constantine by resorting once again to cunning, although this time her actions are nonviolent and motivated by Christian chastity rather than revenge.

Despite considerable effort, Olga was unable to establish Christianity in Rus, and failed to secure help to that end either from Byzantium or the West. In 959 after her Byzantine efforts had yielded no results, she requested a bishop and priest from the German king, Otto I. Although a mission under Bishop Adalbert was sent after much delay, it was not well received and departed soon afterwards. When her regency ended, Olga continued to play an influential role, as Svyatoslav was frequently away on military campaigns.

Olga died in 969 and was eventually canonized by the Orthodox Church. The *Primary Chronicle* does not report where she was buried, but Jakov the Monk writes in his *Memorial and Encomium to Vladimir* that her remains later lay in the Church of the Holy Theotokos (built in 996) and that their uncorrupted state indicated that God glorified her body because she glorified Him. One of the most enduring images associated with Olga is first encountered in the *Sermon on Law and Grace* (mid-eleventh century) by Metropolitan Hilarion, but repeated often in later works. In praising Olga and Vladimir, Hilarion compares them to the first Christian Roman emperor, Constantine, and his mother Helen, who discovered the Holy Cross.

*See also:* KIEVAN RUS; PRIMARY CHRONICLE; RURIKID DYNASTY; SVYATOSLAV I; VLADIMIR, ST.

**BIBLIOGRAPHY**

Franklin, Simon, and Shepard, Jonathan. (1996). *The Emergence of Rus, 750–1200*. London: Longman.

Hollingsworth, Paul. (1992). *The Hagiography of Kievan Rus'*. Cambridge, MA: Ukrainian Research Institute of Harvard University.

Poppe, Andrzej. (1997). "The Christianization and Ecclesiatical Structure of Kyivan Rus' to 1300." *Harvard Ukrainian Studies* 21:311–392.

Cross, Samuel Hazzard, and Sherbowitz-Wetzor, Olgerd P., ed and tr. (1953). *The Russian Primary Chronicle: Laurentian Text*. Cambridge, MA: The Mediaeval Academy of America.

DAVID K. PRESTEL

# OPERA

Opera reached Russia in 1731, when an Italian troupe from Dresden visited Moscow. In 1736 it was established at the tsarist court in St. Petersburg. Early Russian opera was mostly in Italian and French. Works in Russian were usually set in Russia, but representations of Russian history on the operatic stage began only in 1790 with *The Early Reign of Oleg*, a collaboration of the court composers Vasily Pashkevich (a Russian), Carlo Canobbio, and Giuseppe Sarti (both Italians) on a Russian libretto written by Catherine II.

The popularity of the court theaters in the early nineteenth century made their stages a possible venue of propaganda. This potential was fully realized in Mikhail Glinka's first opera (1836), with a libretto written by Baron Rosen, secretary of the

**Soviet opera singers perform *Rock Flower* in 1950.** © YEVGENY KHALDEI/CORBIS

successor to the throne. Initially named for its protagonist, Ivan Susanin, the opera was renamed *A Life for the Tsar* when Glinka dedicated it to Nicholas I (Soviet legend had it that the new title was imposed against Glinka's will). In its wholesale affirmation of the doctrine of "official nationality" as proclaimed by Nicholas, the opera became a symbol of Russian autocracy.

Opera was now the most popular form of entertainment in Russia, but apart from Glinka there were no notable domestic composers. To satisfy the demand, a new Italian troupe was established in St. Petersburg in 1843. Its repertory was the same as that of other Italian enterprises abroad; except for censorial changes to libretti, there was nothing Russian about it. This artistic showcase, cherished not only by the aristocracy but also by the radical intelligentsia, slowed down the development of Russian opera (and Russian music in general). Russian musicians, then mostly amateurs (composers and performers alike), even suffered from legal discrimination: Until 1860, "musician" was not a recognized profession; moreover, for a long time a limit was imposed on the yearly income of Russians (but not of foreigners) in the performing arts, and Russian composers were expressly forbidden to write for the Italian company. Only after the establishment of conservatories in the 1860s did Russian opera become really competitive; performance standards rose, and gradually a Russian repertory accumulated.

The first successful Russian opera after Glinka was Alexander Serov's *Rogneda* (1865). Its fictional plot unfolds against the background of the "baptism of Russia" in 988. As affirmative of the official view on Russian history as *A Life for the Tsar*, it earned its creator a lifelong pension from Alexander II. Soon after, three composers from the "Mighty Handful" embarked on operas based on Russian history: Nikolai Rimsky-Korsakov's *The Maid of Pskov* (based on Ivan IV, after Lev Mey, 1873), Modest Musorgsky's *Boris Godunov* (after Alexander Pushkin's play, 1874), and Alexander Borodin's *Prince Igor* (premiered posthumously, 1890). While *Prince Igor* affirmed autocracy, the other two works did not; furthermore, their protagonists were Russian tsars, whose representation on the operatic stage was forbidden. The ban was partly lifted, which made the production of the two operas possible. It remained in force for members of the House of Romanov, however, and that is why, in Musorgsky's second historical opera, *Khovanshchina* (unfinished; produced posthumously in 1886), the curtain falls before an announced appearance of Peter I; the same happens with Catherine II in Peter Tchaikovsky's *The Queen of Spades* (1891). The representation of Orthodox clergy was also forbidden; while the Jesuits in *Boris Godunov* presented no problem, the Orthodox monks had to be recast as "hermits," and a scene set in a monastery was omitted. But before 1917 no Russian composer ever withdrew an opera instead of complying with the censor's demands, nor did anyone try to circumvent the censorship by having a banned Russian opera performed abroad.

After the accession of Alexander III, the crown's monopoly of theaters was revoked (1882), and private opera companies emerged; Savva Mamontov's in Moscow became the most famous. In 1885 the Italian troupe was disbanded. Russian opera took over its representative and social functions as well as its repertory. While opera continued to be a favorite of the public, leading Russian composers gradually lost interest in it, turning to ballet and instrumental genres instead. Fairy-tale operas were favored over depictions of Russian history, but Rimsky-Korsakov's last opera, *The Golden Cockerel* (after Pushkin, Moscow 1909), is often seen as a satire on Russian autocracy.

Censorship was restored after the 1917 revolution, although it took a different turn. *A Life for the Tsar* was banned until revised as *Ivan Susanin* with a new libretto by Sergei Gorodetsky (Moscow 1939). Other pre-1917 operas underwent minor modifications. There were also new operas interpreting history in Soviet terms and even "topical" operas intended to educate the public. Ivan Dzerzhinsky's "song opera" *Quiet Flows the Don* (Moscow 1934, after Mikhail Sholokhov's novel) was held up as a model against Dmitry Shostakovich's anarchic *Lady Macbeth of the Mtsensk District* (1934; not based on history, but in a realistic historical setting), which was banned in 1936. Josef Stalin's megalomania shows through Sergei Prokofiev's *War and Peace* (after Leo Tolstoy's novel). Composed in response to the German invasion of 1941, this most ambitious of Soviet operas was revised several times and was staged uncut only after the deaths of Stalin and Prokofiev (Moscow 1959).

During the Stalinist era an effort was made to establish national operatic traditions in the various Soviet republics. Russian composers were sent to the republics to collaborate with local composers on operas based on local folklore (and sometimes on local history) that generally sound like Rimsky-Korsakov.

In the post-Stalinist decades, major composers rarely tried their hand at opera. In the late 1980s Alfred Schnittke wrote *Life with an Idiot*, a surrealist lampoon on Vladimir Lenin after a story by Viktor Yerofeyev. It was premiered abroad (Amsterdam 1992), but in Russian and with a cast including "People's Artists of the USSR." Since the fall of the Soviet Union the musical has superseded opera as the leading theatrical genre. It even serves as a medium for patriotic representations of Russian history, such as *Nord-Ost*, the show staged in Moscow whose performers and audience were taken hostage by Chechen terrorists in 2002.

Outside Russia, Russian history has rarely served as the subject matter for opera. The earliest example is Johann Mattheson's *Boris Goudenow* (sic, Hamburg 1710), while the best-known is Albert Lortzing's *Tsar and Carpenter* (Leipzig 1837). Lortzing's comic opera exploits the sojourn of Peter I in the Netherlands disguised as a carpenter's apprentice. Because of its depiction of a tsar from the Romanov dynasty, it did not reach the Russian stage until 1908.

See also: GLINKA, MIKHAIL IVANOVICH; MIGHTY HANDFUL; MUSIC; NATIONALISM IN THE ARTS; RIMSKY-KORSAKOV, NIKOLAI ANDREYEVICH; TCHAIKOVSKY, PETER ILYICH; THEATER

**BIBLIOGRAPHY**

Buckler, Julie A. (2000). *The Literary Lorgnette: Attending Opera in Imperial Russia.* Stanford, CA: Stanford University Press.

Campbell, Stuart, ed. (1994). *Russians on Russian Music, 1830–1880: An Anthology.* Cambridge, UK: Cambridge University Press.

Campbell, Stuart, ed. (2003). *Russians on Russian Music, 1880–1917: An Anthology.* Cambridge, UK: Cambridge University Press.

Morrison, Simon Alexander. (2002). *Russian Opera and the Symbolist Movement.* Berkeley: University of California Press.

Sadie, Stanley, ed. (1992). *The New Grove Dictionary of Opera.* London: Macmillan.

Taruskin, Richard. (1993). *Opera and Drama in Russia: As Preached and Practiced in the 1860s,* 2nd ed. Rochester, NY: University of Rochester Press.

Taruskin, Richard. (1997). *Defining Russia Musically.* Princeton, NJ: Princeton University Press.

ALBRECHT GAUB

## OPERATION BARBAROSSA

"Operation Barbarossa" was the name given by the Germans to their invasion of the Soviet Union, starting June 22, 1941. The operation was named after the medieval Holy Roman emperor Frederick Barbarossa, whom legend claimed would return to restore Germany's greatness.

In the last half of 1941 Germany and its allies conquered the Baltic states, Belarus, almost all of Ukraine, and western Russia. They surrounded Leningrad and advanced to the gates of Moscow. The Red Army lost millions of soldiers and thousands of tanks and aircraft as it reeled back from the German onslaught. Nevertheless the Soviet government was able to evacuate entire factories from threatened areas to Siberia and Central Asia. It was able to raise and arm new armies to face the Germans and finally halt their advance. Helped by Germany's ruthless policy in conquered Slavic areas, the Soviet government was able to rally the population against the invader. By December 1941 the Red Army was able to mount a successful counteroffensive against the overextended Germans.

The initial German attack in 1941 involved three million troops and three thousand tanks but nevertheless achieved strategic surprise, catching the Soviet air force on the ground and most troops far from their operational areas. In spite of the unmistakable signs of a military build-up along the border, German reconnaissance flights over the western Soviet Union, and warnings from sources as diverse as communist spies and the British government, the Soviet government refused to mobilize for war. It preferred to avoid any action that might spark an accidental conflict, and this inaction proved disastrous once the war began.

In the first months of the war German armored spearheads sliced through the unprepared, disorganized Red Army, encircling entire armies near Minsk, Kiev, and Viazma. The German success came at a great price, though. Casualties mounted, and supply lines became more tenuous as they lengthened. Soviet resistance stiffened as the Red Army deployed new tanks (T-34 and KV-1) and artillery (Katyusha rockets) that were technically much better than their German counterparts. Soviet reinforcements also poured in from the Far East after the Soviet spy Richard Sorge reported that Japan planned to move south against the United States and Great Britain rather than attack Siberia. A final factor in the USSR's survival was the weather. Optimistic German planners expected to complete the conquest of Russia before the onset of the autumn rains. The delay in the start of the invasion due to the Balkans campaign, the unknown depth of the Red Army's reserves, and its unexpectedly strong resistance meant that the German army faced winter in the field without suitable clothing or equipment.

It also faced a Soviet population mobilized for resistance. Soviet propaganda publicized German atrocities against the civil population and lauded the suicidal bravery of pilots who crashed their planes into German bombers and of foot soldiers who died blowing up enemy tanks. Restrictions against the Orthodox Church were loosened, and church leaders joined party leaders in defiantly calling for a Holy War (the name of a popular song) against the foe. While the Soviet Union suffered enormous damage in 1941, it was not defeated.

See also: GERMANY, RELATIONS WITH; SORGE, RICHARD; WORLD WAR II

**BIBLIOGRAPHY**

Erickson, John. (1999). *The Road to Stalingrad*. New Haven, CT: Yale University Press.

Glantz, David, and House, Jonathan. (1995). *When Titans Clashed: How the Red Army Stopped Hitler*. Lawrence: University Press of Kansas.

A. DELANO DUGARM

# OPRICHNINA

Tsar Ivan IV's personal domain between 1565 and 1572, and by extension the domestic policy of that period.

The term *oprichnina* (from *oprich*, "separate") denoted a part of something, usually specific landholdings of a prince or a prince's widow. Ivan IV (the Terrible, or Grozny) established his Oprichnina after he unexpectedly left Moscow in December 1564. He settled at Alexandrovskaya sloboda, a hunting lodge northeast of Moscow, which became the Oprichnina's capital. Ivan IV accused his old court of treason and demanded the right to punish his enemies. He divided the territory of his realm, his court, and the administration into two: the Oprichnina under the tsar's personal control; and the *Zemshchina* (from *zemlya*, "land"), officially under the rule of those boyars who stayed in Moscow.

The servitors were divided between the Zemshchina and the Oprichnina courts on the basis of personal loyalty to the tsar, but the courts were largely drawn from the same elite clans. The Oprichnina court was headed by Alexei and Fyodor Basmanov-Pleshcheev, Prince Afanasy Vyazemsky, and the Caucasian Prince Mikhail Cherkassky, brother-in-law of Ivan IV. They were succeeded in around 1570 by the high-ranking cavalrymen Malyuta Skuratov-Belsky and Vasily Gryaznoy. The Oprichnina army initially consisted of one thousand men; later its numbers increased five- to sixfold. Most of them came from the central part of the country, although there were also many non-Muscovites (Western mercenaries, Tatar and Caucasian servitors) in the Oprichnina. Both the leading Muscovite merchants (the Stroganovs) and the English Muscovy Company also sought admission to the Oprichnina.

To maintain the Oprichnina army, the tsar included in his domain prosperous peasant and urban communities in the north, household lands in various parts of the country (mostly in its central districts), mid-sized and small districts with numerous conditional landholdings, and some quarters of Moscow. The northern lands produced revenues and marketable commodities (furs, salt), the household lands provided the Oprichnina with various supplies, and the regions with conditional landholdings supplied servitors for the Oprichnina army. The territory of the Oprichnina was never stable, and eventually included sections of Novgorod. The authorities deported non-Oprichnina servitors from the Oprichnina lands and granted their estates to the *oprichniki* (members of the Oprichnina), but the extent of these forced resettlements remains unclear.

The Oprichnina affected various local communities in different ways. The Zemshchina territories bore the heavy financial burden of funding the organization and actions of the Oprichnina; some Zemshchina communities were pillaged and devastated. In early 1570, the tsar and his oprichniki sacked Novgorod, where they slaughtered from three thousand to fifteen thousand people. At the same time, the lower-ranking inhabitants of Moscow escaped Ivan's disgrace and forced resettlements. For taxpayers in the remote north, the establishment of the Oprichnina mostly meant a change of payee.

The tsar sought to maintain a close relationship with the clergy by expanding the tax privileges of important dioceses and monasteries and including some of them in the Oprichnina. In exchange, he demanded that the metropolitan not intervene in the Oprichnina and abolished the metropolitan's traditional right to intercede on behalf of the disgraced. The Oprichnina's victims included Metropolitan Philip Kolychev, who openly criticized the Oprichnina (deposed 1568, killed 1569) and Archbishop Pimen of Novgorod, the tsar's former close ally (deposed and exiled 1570).

The Oprichnina policy was a peculiar combination of bloody terror and acts of public reconciliation. The social background of its victims ranged from members of the royal family and prominent courtiers, including some leaders of the Oprichnina court, to rank-and-file servitors, townsmen, and clergy. Indictments and repressions, however, were often followed by amnesties. The mass exile of around 180 princes and cavalrymen to Kazan and the confiscation of their lands (1565) were counterbalanced when they were pardoned and their property partially restored. As a gesture of spiritual reconciliation with the executed, the tsar ordered memorial services in monasteries for more than three thousand victims. The Oprichnina involved the ritualization of executions and peculiar symbolism that alluded to the tsar and his *oprichniki* as punitive instruments of divine wrath. The *oprichniki* dressed in black, acted like a pseudo-monastic order, and carried dog's heads and brooms to show they were the "dogs" of the tsar who would sweep treason from the land.

The tsar abolished the Oprichnina in 1572 after its troops proved ineffective during a raid of Tatars on Moscow. Together with the Livonian War, famines, and epidemics, the Oprichnina led to the country's economic decline. During the Oprichnina, Ivan IV thought to strengthen his personal security by taking to extremes such Muscovite political traditions as disgraces, persecution of suspects, and forced resettlements. The Oprichnina revealed the vulnerability of the social and legal mechanisms for personal protection when confronted by authorities exceeding the political system's normal level of violence. Transgressions and sudden changes in policy contributed to the image of the tsar as an autocratic ruler accountable only to God. The court system, however, survived the turmoil of the Oprichnina. Despite the division of the realm and purges, members of established clans maintained their positions in the court hierarchy and participated in running the polity throughout the period of the Oprichnina.

Some historians believe that the main force behind the Oprichnina was Ivan IV's personality, including a possible mental disorder. Such interpretations prevailed in the Romantic historical writings of Nikolai Karamzin (early nineteenth century) and in the works of Vasily Klyuchevsky, foremost Russian historian of the early twentieth century. The American historians Richard Hellie and Robert Crummey offered psychoanalytical explanations for the Oprichnina, surmising that Ivan IV suffered from paranoia. Priscilla Hunt and Andrei Yurganov saw the Oprichnina as an actualization of the cultural myth of the divine nature of the tsar's power and eschatological expectations in Muscovy. According to other historians, the Oprichnina was a conscious struggle among certain social groups. In his classic nineteenth-century Hegelian history of Russia, Sergei Solovyov interpreted the Oprichnina as a political conflict between the tsar acting in the name of the state and the boyars, who guarded their hereditary privileges. In

the late nineteenth century, Sergei Platonov took those views further by arguing that the Oprichnina promoted service people of lower origin and eliminated the hereditary landowning of the aristocracy. In the mid-twentieth century, Platonov's conception was questioned by Stepan Veselovsky and Vladimir Kobrin, who reexamined the genealogical background of the Oprichnina court and the redistribution of land during the Oprichnina. According to Alexander Zimin, the Oprichnina was aimed at the main separatist forces in Muscovy: the church, the appanage princes, and Novgorod. Ruslan Skrynnikov accepted a modified multiphase version of Platonov's views.

*See also:* AUTOCRACY; IVAN IV

**BIBLIOGRAPHY**

Hellie, Richard. (1987). "What Happened? How Did He Get Away with It? Ivan Groznyi's Paranoia and the Problem of Institutional Restraints." *Russian History* 14(1–4):199–224.

Hunt, Priscilla. (1993). "Ivan IV's Personal Mythology of Kingship." *Slavic Review* 52:769–809.

Platonov, Sergei F. (1986). *Ivan the Terrible*, ed. and tr. Joseph L. Wieczynski, with "In Search of Ivan the Terrible," by Richard Hellie. Gulf Breeze, FL: Academic International Press.

Skrynnikov, Ruslan G. (1981). *Ivan the Terrible*, ed. and tr. Hugh F. Graham. Gulf Breeze, FL: Academic International Press.

Zimin, A. A. (2001). *Oprichnina*, 2nd ed. Moscow: Territorriya.

SERGEI BOGATYREV

# ORDIN-NASHCHOKIN, AFANASY LAVRENTIEVICH

(c. 1605–1680), military officer, governor, diplomat, boyar.

Afanasy Lavrentievich Ordin-Nashchokin was born to a gentry family near Pskov in the first quarter of the seventeenth century, probably around 1605. He received an unusually good education for a Russian of the time, learning mathematics and several languages, and entered military service at fifteen. Exposed at a young age to foreign customs, he put his insights and ideas to good use throughout his life. In 1642 he helped settle a border dispute with Sweden, honing his talents for careful preparation, thorough investigation, and skillful negotiation. Next he led a mission to Moldavia, gaining experience and valuable information on the Poles, Turks, Cossacks, and Crimeans who populated the tsar's southern borders. For most of the 1650s he served as a military officer and governor of several regions in western Russia. While working to draw the local population to Moscow's side and achieving diplomatic agreements with Courland and Brandenburg, he also pondered ways to improve Russia's military, economic, and political standing. In 1658 he was able to achieve some of his greater goals in negotiating the three-year Valiesar truce with Sweden, gaining Russia peace, free trade, Baltic access, and all the territories it had conquered in the region. For this coup Ordin-Nashchokin received the rank of *dumny dvoryanin* (consiliar noble).

In 1660 his son Voin, likewise educated in foreign languages and customs, fled to Western Europe. A grieving and humiliated Ordin-Nashchokin requested retirement, but the tsar was reluctant to lose his able statesman and refused to hold the father accountable for his son's actions. Ordin-Nashchokin continued to negotiate for peace with Poland and to govern Pskov, becoming *okolnichy* (a high court rank) in 1665.

The peak of his career came in 1667 when he signed the Andrusovo treaty, ending a long war with Poland and establishing guidelines for a productive peace. For this achievement he was made boyar (the highest Muscovite court rank) and head of the Department of Foreign Affairs (Posolsky Prikaz). The same year he dispatched envoys to nearly a dozen countries to announce the peace and offer diplomatic and commercial ties with Russia. He also drew up the New Commercial Statute, aimed at stimulating and centralizing trade and industry and protecting Russian merchants. Over the next four years as head of Russia's government he enacted administrative reforms; supervised the construction of ships; established regular postal routes between Moscow, Vilna, and Riga; expanded Russia's diplomatic representation abroad; and began the compilation of translated foreign newspapers (*kuranty*). The number and character of his innovations have sometimes led to his description as a precursor of Peter the Great.

By 1671, however, his day was passing. Always outspoken and demanding, he began to irritate the tsar with his contentiousness. Worse, his views of international politics—he perceived Poland as Russia's natural ally, Sweden as its natural foe—

no longer fit Moscow's immediate interests. Artamon Matveyev, the more flexible new favorite, was ready to step in. In 1672 Ordin-Nashchokin retired to a monastery near Pskov to be tonsured under the name Antony. In 1679 he briefly returned to service to negotiate with Poland, but soon retreated to his monastery and died the next year.

*See also:* ANDRUSOVO, PEACE OF; BOYAR; MATVEYEV, ARTAMON SERGEYEVICH; OKOLNICHY; TRADE STATUTES OF 1653 AND 1667

**BIBLIOGRAPHY**

Kliuchevsky, V. O. (1968). "A Muscovite Statesman. Ordin-Nashchokin." In *A Course in Russian History: The Seventeenth Century*, tr. Natalie Duddington. Chicago: Quadrangle Books.

O'Brien, C. Bickford. (1974). "Makers of Foreign Policy: Ordin-Nashchokin." *East European Quarterly* 8: 155–165.

MARTHA LUBY LAHANA

# ORDZHONIKIDZE, GRIGORY KONSTANTINOVICH

(1886–1937), leading Bolshevik who participated in bringing Ukraine and the Caucasus under Soviet rule and directed industry during the early five-year plans.

Grigory Konstantinovich ("Sergo") Ordzhonikidze was born in Goresha, Georgia, to an impoverished gentry family. In 1903, while training as a medical assistant, he joined the Bolshevik faction of the Russian Social Democratic Workers' Party, and in 1906 met Josef Stalin, with whom he formed a close, lifelong association. After a time in prison and exile, Ordzhonikidze traveled to Paris where in 1911 he met Vladimir Lenin and studied in the party school. In January the following year, Ordzhonikidze became a member of the Bolshevik Central Committee and organizer of its Russian Bureau. Returning to Russia, he was again arrested in April 1912 and spent the next five years in prison and then Siberian exile. During 1917 Ordzhonikidze was a member of the Executive Committee of the Petrograd Soviet. After the Bolshevik takeover, he participated in the civil war in Ukraine and southern Russia and played a leading role in extending Soviet power over Azerbaijan, Armenia, and Georgia. A close ally of Stalin, Ordzhonikidze was promoted to the Central Committee of the Communist Party in 1921. He remained in charge of the Transcaucasian regional Party organization until 1926, when he became a Politburo candidate member, chairman of the Party's Central Control Commission and commissar of the Workers' and Peasants' Inspectorate (Rabkrin). During the First Five-Year Plan, Ordzhonikidze organized the drive for mass industrialization. In 1930 he was promoted to full Politburo membership and in 1932 was appointed commissar for heavy industry. During the mid-1930s, Ordzhonikidze sought to use his proximity to Stalin to temper the Soviet leader's increasing use of repression against party and economic officials. Although Ordzhonikidze's sudden death in early 1937 was officially attributed to a heart attack, it is more likely that, in an act of desperate protest at the impending terror, he committed suicide.

*See also:* BOLSHEVISM; INDUSTRIALIZATION, SOVIET; STALIN, JOSEF VISSARIONOVICH

**BIBLIOGRAPHY**

Haupt, Georges, and Marie, Jean–Jacques, eds. (1974). *Makers of the Russian Revolution.* London: Allen and Unwin.

Khlevniuk, Oleg V. (1995). *In Stalin's Shadow: The Career of "Sergo" Ordzhonikidze.* Armonk, NY: M.E. Sharpe.

NICK BARON

## ORGANIZED CRIME

The term *Russian mafia* is widely used, but Russian-speaking organized crime is not all Russian, nor is it organized in the same ways as the Italian mafia. Russian-speaking organized crime emerged in the former Soviet Union, and during the decade after the collapse it became a major force in transnational crime.

Because Russia's immense territorial mass spans Europe and Asia, it is easy for organized crime groups to have contacts both with European and Asian crime groups. Russia's crime groups have a truly international reach and operate in North and South America as well as in Africa. Thus they have been among the major beneficiaries of globalization. Russia's technologically advanced economy has given Russian organized crime a technological edge in a world dominated by high tech-

nology. Moreover, the collapse of the social control system and the state control apparatus have made it possible for major criminals to operate with impunity both at home and internationally.

During the 1990s, Russian law enforcement declared that the number of organized crime groups was escalating. Between 1990 and 1996, it rose from 785 to more than 8,000, and membership was variously estimated at from 100,000 to as high as three million. These identified crime groups were mostly small, amorphous, impermanent organizations that engaged in extortion, drug dealing, bank fraud, arms trafficking, and armed banditry. The most serious forms of organized crime were often committed by individuals who were not identified with specific crime groups but engaged in the large-scale organized theft of state resources through the privatization of valuable state assets to themselves. Hundreds of billions of Russian assets were sent abroad in the first post-Soviet decade; a significant share of this capital flight was money laundering connected with large-scale post-Soviet organized crime involving people who were not traditional underworld figures. In this respect, organized crime in Russia differs significantly from the Italian mafia or the Japanese Yakuza—it is an amalgam of former Communist Party and Komsomol officials, active and demobilized military personnel, law enforcement and security structures, participants in the Soviet second economy, and criminals of the traditional kind. Chechen and other ethnic crime groups are highly visible, but most organized crime involves a broad range of actors working together to promote their financial interests by using violence or threats of violence.

In most of the world, organized crime is primarily associated with the illicit sectors of the economy. Although post-Soviet organized crime groups have moved into the drug trade, especially since the fall of the Taliban, the vast wealth of Russian organized crime derives from its involvement in the legitimate economy, including important sectors like banking, real estate, transport, shipping, and heavy industry, especially aluminum production. Involvement in the legitimate economy does not mean that the crime groups have been legitimized, for they continue to operate with illegitimate tactics even in the legitimate economy. For example, organized criminals are known to intimidate minority shareholders of companies in which they own large blocks of shares and to use violence against business competitors.

**Russian anti-Mafia investigators perform a routine ID check at a Moscow market.** © PETER BLAKELY/CORBIS SABA

Crime groups also engage in automobile, drug, and arms smuggling. The involvement of former military personnel has given particular significance to sales of military technology to foreign crime groups. Weapons obtained from Russian crime groups have been used in armed conflicts in many parts of the world, including Africa and the Balkans. Foreign crime groups, especially in Asia, see Russia as a new source of supply for weapons.

There is, in addition, a significant trade in stolen automobiles between Western Europe and the European parts of Russia. From Irkutsk west to Vladivostok, the cars on the road are predominantly Japanese, some of them stolen from their owners.

Tens of thousands of women have been trafficked abroad, often sold to foreign crime groups that in turn traffic them to more distant locales. Women are trafficked from all over Russia by small-scale criminal businesses and much larger entrepreneurs via an elaborate system of recruitment, transport facilitators, and protectors of the trafficking networks. Despite prevention campaigns, human trafficking is a significant revenue source for Russian organized crime.

Russia's vast natural resources are much exploited by crime groups. Many of the commodities handled by criminals are not traded in the legitimate economy. These include endangered species, timber not authorized for harvest, and radioactive minerals subject to international regulation.

Despite the government's repeated pledges to fight organized crime, the leaders of the criminal organizations and the government officials who facilitate their activities operate with almost total impunity. Pervasive corruption in the criminal justice system has impeded the prosecution of Russian organized criminals both domestically and internationally. Thus organized crime will continue to be a serious problem for the Russian state and the international community.

*See also:* MAFIA CAPITALISM; PRIVATIZATION

**BIBLIOGRAPHY**

Handelman, Stephen. (1987). *Comrade Criminal: Russia's New Mafiya.* New Haven, CT: Yale University Press, 1995.

Satter, David. (2003). *Darkness at Dawn: The Rise of the Russian Criminal State.* New Haven, CT: Yale University Press.

Shelley, Louise. (1996). "Post-Soviet Organized Crime: A New Form of Authoritarianism." *Transnational Organized Crime* 2 (2/3):122–138.

Volkov, Vadim. (2002). *Violent Entrepreneurs: The Use of Force in the Making of Russian Capitalism.* Ithaca, NY: Cornell University Press, 2002.

Williams, Phil, ed. (1997). *Russian Organized Crime: The New Threat.* Portland, OR: Frank Cass.

LOUISE SHELLEY

## ORGBURO

The organizational bureau (or Orgburo) was one of the most important organs in the CPSU after the Politburo. The Orgburo was created in 1919 and had the power to make key decisions about the organizational work of the Party. The key role of the Orgburo was to make all the important decisions of an administrative and personnel nature by supervising the work of local Party committees and organizations and overseeing personnel appointments. For instance, the Orgburo had the power to select and allocate Party cadres. The Orgburo was elected at plenary meetings of the Central Committee. There was a great degree of overlap between the Politburo and the Orgburo with many key Party figures being members of both organs. In its early days Josef V. Stalin, Vyacheslav Molotov, and Lazar Kaganovich were all Orgburo members. The Politburo often confirmed Orgburo decisions, but it also had the power to veto or rescind them. Nevertheless, the Orgburo was extremely powerful in the 1920s and retained significant scope for autonomous action until its functions, responsibilities, and powers were transferred to the Secretariat in 1952.

Since the declassification of Soviet archives, scholars can now access the protocols of the Communist Party's Orgburo, the transcripts of many of its meetings, and all of the preparatory documentation. The latter are crucial insofar as they give scholars insight into Party life from the New Economic Policy period until the end of the Stalin era.

*See also:* COMMUNIST PARTY OF THE SOVIET UNION; POLITBURO

**BIBLIOGRAPHY**

Gill, Graham. (1990). *The Origins of the Stalinist Political System.* Cambridge, UK: Cambridge University Press.

Howlett, Jana; Khlevniuk, Oleg; Kosheleva, Ludmila; and Rogavia, Larisa. (1996). "The CPSU's Top Bodies under Stalin: Their Operational Records and Structures of Command." Stalin-Era Research and Archives Project, Working paper No.1. Toronto: Centre for Russian and East European Studies, University of Toronto.

CHRISTOPHER WILLIAMS

**ORGNABOR** *See* ADMINISTRATION FOR ORGANIZED RECRUITMENT.

## ORLOVA, LYUBOV PETROVNA

(1902–1975), film actress.

The most beloved movie actress of the 1930s, Lyubov Petrovna Orlova trained as a singer and dancer in Moscow. She began her career in musical theater in 1926 and made her film debut in 1934. Although she worked with other Soviet directors, Orlova's personal and professional partnership with Grigory Alexandrov led to her greatest successes on screen. As the star of Alexandrov's four wildly successful musical comedies—*The Jolly Fellows* (1934), *The Circus* (1936), *Volga-Volga* (1938), and *The Shining Path* (1940)—Orlova became a household name in the USSR.

Although in her early thirties when she began her movie career, Orlova nonetheless specialized in ingenue parts. She was the role model for a generation of Soviet women. They admired her wholesome good looks, her energy, her cheeriness, her zest for life, and her spunkiness in the face of adversity. She was also said to be Stalin's favorite actress, not surprising given his love for movie musicals. Interestingly, given Orlova's importance as the cinematic exemplar of Soviet womanhood, she also played Americans several times in her career. The most famous example was her portrayal in *The Circus* of Marion Dixon, the entertainer who fled the United States with her mixed-race child, but also worth noting is her role as "Janet Sherwood" in Alexandrov's *Meeting on the Elba* (1949).

In 1950 Orlova was honored as a People's Artist of the USSR, her nation's top prize for artistic achievement, but she acted in only a few pictures after that, and died in 1975. In 1983 Orlova's husband, Grigory Alexandrov, produced a documentary about her life entitled *Liubov Orlova*.

*See also:* ALEXANDROV, GRIGORY ALEXANDROVICH; MOTION PICTURES

**BIBLIOGRAPHY**

Kenez, Peter. (2001). *Cinema and Soviet Society from the Revolution to the Death of Stalin*. London: I. B. Tauris.

DENISE J. YOUNGBLOOD

# ORLOV, GRIGORY GRIGORIEVICH

(1734–1783), count, prince of the Holy Roman Empire, soldier, statesman, imperial favorite.

Second eldest of five brothers born to a Petrine officer and official, Grigory Orlov had looks, size, and strength. His early years are little known before he won distinction at the battle of Zorndorf in 1758, where he fought the Prussians despite three wounds. He accompanied Count Schwerin and captured Prussian adjutant to St. Petersburg, where both met the "Young Court" of Grand Princess Catherine and Crown Prince Peter Fyodorovich. In the capital Orlov gained repute by an affair with the beautiful mistress of Count Pyotr Shuvalov. By 1760 intimacy with Catherine facilitated promotion to captain of the Izmailovsky Guards and paymaster of the artillery, crucial posts in Catherine's coup of July 11, 1762. Two months earlier she had secretly delivered their son, Alexei Grigorievich Bobrinskoi (1762–1813).

The Orlov brothers were liberally rewarded by the new regime. All became counts of the Russian Empire. Grigory became major general, chamberlain, and adjutant general with the Order of Alexander Nevsky, a sword with diamonds, and oversight of the coronation. He figured prominently in the reign as master of ordnance, director general of engineers, chief of cavalry forces, and president of the Office of Trusteeship for Foreign Colonists. Such political connections with Catherine did not bring marriage, however, because of opposition at court and her reluctance. He patronized many individuals and institutions, such as the scientist polymath Lomonosov, the Imperial Free Economic Society,

the Legislative Commission of 1767–1768, and projects to reform serfdom. He publicly (and unsuccessfully) invited Jean-Jacques Rousseau to take refuge in Russia. He sat on the new seven-member imperial council established in 1768 to coordinate foreign and military policy in the Russo-Turkish war, where he favored a forward policy, volunteering his brother Alexei to command the Baltic fleet in Mediterranean operations.

This conflict spawned an incursion of bubonic plague culminating in the collapse of Moscow amid riots in late September 1771. Orlov volunteered to head relief efforts, restored order, reinforced antiplague efforts, and punished the rioters. Projecting composure in public, Orlov privately doubted success until freezing weather finally arrived. He was triumphantly received by Catherine at Tsarskoye Selo in mid-December with a gold medal and a triumphal arch hailing his bravery.

In 1772 Orlov headed the Russian delegation to negotiate with the Turks at Focsani, but he broke off the talks when his terms were rejected and, learning of his replacement in Catherine's favor, rushed back to Russia only to be barred from court. From his Gatchina estate he negotiated a settlement: a pension of 150,000 rubles, 100,000 for a house, 10,000 serfs, and the title of prince of the Holy Roman Empire. He kept away from court until May 1773, maintaining cordial relations with Catherine, on whom he bestowed an enormous diamond that she placed in the imperial scepter (and actually paid for). He supported her amid the crisis of Paul's majority and the Pugachev Revolt. With Potemkin's emergence as favorite in early 1774, however, Orlov and Catherine had a stormy falling out; he withdrew from public life and traveled abroad.

Upon return to Russia Orlov married his young cousin, Ekaterina Nikolayevna Zinovieva (1758–1781), whom the empress appointed lady-in-waiting and awarded the Order of Saint Catherine. She died of consumption in Lausanne, hastening Orlov's slide into insanity before death. Orlov's career advertised the rewards of imperial favor and consolidated the family's aristocratic eminence.

*See also:* CATHERINE II; MILITARY, IMPERIAL ERA; RUSSO-TURKISH WARS

**BIBLIOGRAPHY**

Alexander, John T. (1989). *Catherine the Great: Life and Legend*. New York: Oxford University Press.

Alexander, John T. (2003). *Bubonic Plague in Early Modern Russia: Public Health and Urban Disaster*, rev. ed. New York: Oxford University Press.

Baran, Thomas. (2002). *Russia Reads Rousseau, 1762–1825.* Evanston, IL: Northwestern University Press.

Montefiore, Simon Sebag. (2000). *Prince of Princes: The Life of Potemkin.* London: Weidenfeld and Nicolson.

JOHN T. ALEXANDER

# ORTHODOXY

Orthodoxy has been an integral part of Russian civilization from the tenth century to the present.

The word *Orthodox* means right belief, right practice, or right worship. Also referred to as Russian Orthodoxy or Eastern Orthodoxy, all three terms are synonymous in Orthodox self-understanding. Orthodoxy uses the vernacular language of its adherents, but its beliefs and liturgy are independent of the language used. The Russian Church is Eastern Orthodox because it maintains sacramental ties (intercommunion) with the Ecumenical Patriarch in Constantinople. This differentiates it from Oriental Orthodox groups such as the Nestorians, Monophysites, and Jacobites who broke with Byzantium over doctrinal and cultural differences between the fifth and eighth centuries. The distinctive characteristics of Orthodoxy in comparison with other expressions of Christianity explain some unique features of Russian historical development.

## THEOLOGY

Orthodox theology is generally characterized by a strong emphasis on incarnation. It upholds Christian dogma related to the life, teachings, crucifixion, and resurrection of Jesus Christ, as expressed through Christian tradition shaped by the Bible (both Old and New Testaments), the earliest teachings of the Christian leaders in the second to fourth centuries (the Church Fathers), and the decisions of seven ecumenical or all-church councils held between the fourth and eighth centuries. God is understood to be creator of the universe and a single being who finds expression in the Trinity or three persons—Father, Son, and Holy Spirit. Although the essence of God is unknowable to human beings, they can gain knowledge of God through nature, the revelation of Christ, and Christian tradition. God is described as eternal, perfectly good, omniscient, perfectly righteous, almighty, and omnipresent.

Human beings are described as possessing both body and soul and having been originally made in the image and likeness of God. The image of God remains, although the divine likeness is seen as corrupted by original sin, a spiritual disease inherited from Adam and Eve, the first humans. Thus, Orthodox doctrine does not support the idea of total human depravity as defined by the fourth-century western theologian St. Augustine of Hippo. The goal of human existence in Orthodox theology is deification, often described using the Greek term *theosis*. Humans are understood to be striving for the restoration of the divine likeness, becoming fully human and divine following the example of Christ.

Incarnational theology is expressed in popular practice as well as in dogma. Holy images or icons express incarnation through religious paintings that provide a window into the redeemed creation. The subjects of icons are God, Jesus, biblical scenes, the lives of saints, and the Virgin Mary, who is referred to as *Theotokos* (God bearer). Icons are holy objects that are always venerated for the images they represent. Some icons also are believed to have divine power to protect or heal. Miracle-working icons are sites of divine immanence, where the energies of God are physically accessible to the Orthodox believer. Immanence is also seen in holy relics, graves, and even natural objects such as rocks, fountains, lakes, and streams.

### LITURGY AND WORSHIP

The Orthodox faith is expressed through the *Divine Liturgy*—a term synonymous with Eucharist, Mass, or Holy Communion in Western Christianity—and other services. All Orthodox services center around the prayers of the faithful; for Orthodox believers, worship is communal prayer. Monasticism had a particularly strong influence on the Russian liturgical tradition. From the sixteenth century, worship in parish churches imitated the long, complex forms found in monasteries. The structure of the Orthodox liturgy has unbroken continuity with the earliest forms of Christian worship and has remained basically unchanged since the ninth century, just before the conversion of Russia. Russian as a written language traces its origins to the work of two brothers, Cyril and Methodius, who were missionaries to the Slavs in the ninth century. The Russian Orthodox Church has maintained the lan-

# THE PEOPLE

Two Kyrgyz women weave cloth on a portable loom outside their yurt. The Kyrgyz are a nomadic people of Turkic descent living in the northern Tien Shan mountain range in Central Asia. In the early 1900s, the Kyrgyz staged massive uprisings against the threat of drafting ethnic Kyrgyz into the Russian Army during World War I, as well as during the Russian Revolution. © JANET WISHNETSKY/CORBIS

*Top right:* **A herder tries to lasso reindeer during the annual antler harvest in Madagan Oblast, a region in far eastern Russia. The far eastern region's vast mineral resources, especially gold and diamonds, have attracted large-scale foreign investment.** © PAUL A. SOUDERS/CORBIS

*Below:* **Two Nentsy children lie in a sledge in the Antipayuta settlement in Russia's far north, at the mouth of the Taz River. As Russians began to colonize Siberia in the mid-seventeenth century they met fierce resistance from Nenets groups, which now comprise the largest ethnic group among Russia's Northern Peoples.** © JACQUES LANGEVIN/CORBIS

*Top left:* **Belarusian women harvest wheat near the village of Timiryazev, 140 kilometers south of Minsk, July 20, 2001.** © AFP/CORBIS

*Below:* **A Tajik woman sells vegetables at a street market in Tajikistan's capital, Dushanbe, October 2001. After gaining its independence after the Soviet collapse in 1991, Tajikistan has been embroiled in civil war and clan rivalries.** © AFP/CORBIS

*Top:* **A member of the Karelian folk music ensemble Kizh plays the balalaika. The traditional Russian instrument was first mentioned in written records in 1688, Moscow.** © Dave G. Houser/CORBIS

*Middle:* **Dressed in a peasant blouse decorated with traditional red embroidery, a babushka joins the dancing at a local festival. Russian folk music includes songs marking seasonal and ritual events, and music for figure or circle dances (*korovody*) and the faster *chastye* or *plyasovye* dances.** © David Turnley/CORBIS

*Bottom:* **A Tatar Dance Group in traditional dress, Tatarstan. Tatars are the second largest nationality in Russia.** © Gregor Schmid/CORBIS

*Below:* **A woman lights candles during a Russian Orthodox ceremony in Mikaduke, north of Kazakhstan, September 21, 2001. In 988 C.E., Grand Prince Vladimir of Kiev adopted Eastern Orthodoxy from Byzantium and inaugurated a gradual Christianization of Russia, establishing Russian Orthodoxy as Russia's primary religion for over 1,000 years.** © AFP/CORBIS

*Top right:* **A Soviet policeman stands by a queue of people waiting to enter a newly opened McDonald's on Gorky Street in Moscow in 1990. Gorbachev's perestroika, a policy of political and economic restructuring, welcomed the establishment of western-style capitalism.** © PETER TURNLEY/CORBIS

*Below:* **Children of cosmonauts-in-training line up for a singing and marching competition at the Komarov School in Star City, 1987.** © ROGER RESSMEYER/CORBIS

**Top left:** Children wearing protective glasses undergo light deprivation treatment at their school in Stavropol. Strong full-spectrum fluorescent light is intended to lessen the effects of the long, dark Russian winter. © WALLY MCNAMEE/CORBIS

**Below:** Anna Kournikova of Russia serves during her match during the French Open at Roland Garros stadium May 31, 2000. Born in Moscow in 1981, her movie-star looks and savvy marketing have made Kournikova one of Russia's top international sports icons. © REUTERS NEWMEDIA INC./CORBIS

*Below:* **Buryat girls in traditional Mongolian-style dress. Buryatia, in southern Siberia, was part of the Mongols' khanate of the Golden Horde from the tenth to the mid-fifteenth century.** © WOLFGANG KAEHLER/CORBIS

guage and forms of worship that it received from Byzantium during the tenth century, including the use of Old Church Slavic as a liturgical language. As a result, the Russian Orthodox liturgy sounds archaic and at times even incomprehensible to modern Russians.

Orthodox worship includes the seven sacraments defined by the Roman Catholic Church (baptism, chrismation, Eucharist, repentance, ordination, marriage, and anointing of the sick). Orthodox theologians frequently note, however, that their church's sacramental life is not limited to those seven rites. Many other acts, such as monastic tonsure, are understood to have a sacramental quality. Baptism is the rite of initiation, performed on infants and adults by immersion. Chrismation, also known as confirmation in the West, involves being anointed with holy oil and signifies reception of the gift of the Holy Spirit. The Eucharist lacks any theological interpretation of transubstantiation or consubstantiation. Instead, the transformation of bread and wine into the body and blood of Christ is explained as a mystery beyond human understanding. Communicants receive both bread and wine, which are mixed together in the chalice and served to them by the priest on a spoon. Repentance involves confession of sin to a priest followed by an act of penance (in Russian, *epitimia*). Ordination is the sacrament for inducting men into clerical orders. The Orthodox ceremony of marriage is distinctive in its use of crowns placed on the heads of the bride and groom. Anointing of the sick, as known as unction, is not reserved for those who are dying but can be used for anyone who is suffering and seeks divine healing.

## CLERGY

Orthodox believers are served by three types of clergy: bishops, priests, and deacons. All clergy are male and are differentiated by the color of their liturgical vestments, which are in turn related to their form of ecclesiastical service. Married priests and deacons who serve in parishes are called the white clergy (*beloye dukhovenstvo*), while those who take monastic vows are known as the black clergy (*chernoye dukhovenstvo*). Men who wish to marry must do so before being ordained. They cannot remarry, either before or after ordination, and their wives cannot have been married previously.

Marital status decides clergy rank. Married clergymen can be either priests or deacons who are ordained by a single bishop and can serve in either monasteries or parish churches. Priests assist bish-

ops by administering the sacraments and leading liturgical services in places assigned by their bishop. Deacons serve priests in those services. As long as his wife is alive, a member of the white clergy cannot rise to the episcopacy. Should his wife die, he must take monastic vows and, with very rare exceptions, enter a monastery. Bishops are chosen exclusively from the monastic clergy and must be celibate (either never married or widowed). A new bishop is consecrated when two or three bishops lay hands upon him. He then becomes part of the apostolic succession, which is the unbroken line of episcopal ordinations that began with the apostles chosen by Jesus. Bishops can rise in the hierarchy to archbishop, metropolitan, and patriarch, but every bishop in the Russian Orthodox Church is understood to be equal to every other bishop regardless of title.

## HISTORY

The rise of Kiev in the ninth century as the center of Eastern Slavic civilization was accompanied by political centralization that promoted the adoption of Orthodox Christianity. The process of Christianization began with the conversion of individual members of the nobility, most notably Princess Olga, the widow of Grand Prince Igor of Kiev. Her grandson, Prince Vladimir, officially adopted Orthodoxy in 988 and enforced mass baptisms into the new faith. Vladimir's motives for this decision to abandon the animistic faith of his ancestors remain unclear. He was probably influenced both by a desire to strengthen ties with Byzantium and by a need to unify his territory under a common religious culture. The story of Vladimir's purposefully choosing Orthodox Christianity over other faiths— a story that is difficult to substantiate despite its inclusion in the Russian Primary Chronicle—plays an important role in Russian Orthodoxy's sense of divine election. Christianity spread steadily throughout the Russian lands from the tenth to thirteenth centuries, aided by state support and clergy imported from Byzantium. Close cooperation between political and ecclesiastical structures thus formed an integral part of the foundations of a unified Russian civilization. Slavic animistic traditions merged with Orthodox Christianity to form *dvoyeverie* ("dual faith") that served as the basis for popular religion in Russia.

The years of Tatar rule (the Mongol Yoke, 1240–1480) gave an unexpected boost to the spread of Orthodox Christianity among the Russian peoples. The collapse of the political structure that accompanied the fall of Kiev forced the church to become guardian of both spiritual and national values. Church leaders accepted the dual task of converting the populace in the countryside, where Orthodoxy had only slowly spread, and promoting a new political order that would avoid the internecine political squabbles among princes that had led to the Mongol defeat of Russia. The church accomplished its political goals by backing leaders such as Prince Alexander Nevsky for his defense of Russia against western invaders (he was canonized for his efforts). Conversion of the masses took place largely through the efforts of monastic communities that spread throughout Russia during the period of Mongol domination. Hesychastic or quietist spirituality based on meditative repetition of the Jesus Prayer fed the proliferation of monasteries under the influence of St. Sergius of Radonezh (1314–1392), founder of the Holy Trinity Monastery outside Moscow. Monastic leaders gained significant political influence, as evidenced by St. Sergius's blessing of Prince Dmitry Donskoy as he marched his army to victory over the Mongols at Kulikovo Pole in 1380.

Moscow emerged as the true political and religious center of Russia by the middle of the fifteenth century. The senior bishop of Russia acknowledged his support for the Muscovite princes and their drive to reunify the Russian state by moving to Moscow in 1326. The Russian Orthodox hierarchy declared independence from Byzantium after the Council of Florence-Ferrara (1439–1443) where Constantinople tried in vain to solicit western military aid in return for acceptance of Roman Catholic policies and dogma. Church leaders promoted a messianic vision for Muscovite Russia after the fall of Constantinople in 1453. Having broken Mongol domination, Muscovy understood its role as the only independent Orthodox state to mean that it must defend the true faith. The description of Moscow as "the Third Rome" captured this messianic mission when it came into use at the beginning of the sixteenth century.

Russian political power grew increasingly independent from Orthodoxy in the Muscovite state, however, and church leaders struggled with the consequences. During the early 1500s, a national church council sided with abbots who argued for the rights of their monasteries to accumulate wealth ("possessors") and against monastic leaders who advocated strict poverty for monks ("nonpossessors"). The possessor position promised greater political influence for the church. Tensions

between secular and ecclesiastical power increased under Tsar Ivan IV ("the Terrible," 1530–1584), although the Stoglav Council held in 1551 issued strict rules for everyday Orthodox life. The struggle for succession to the throne following Ivan's death also brought religious instability by the end of the century. Success in elevating the Moscow metropolitan to the rank of patriarch in 1589 added to the church's influence in defending Russia from foreign invaders and internal chaos during the Time of Troubles (1598–1613). Rivalry developed between secular and ecclesiastical powers by the middle of the seventeenth century when Tsar Alexei Mikhailovich disagreed with the prerogatives claimed by Patriarch Nikon. Nikon's position was undermined by the Old Believer schism (raskol) that resulted from his attempts to reform Russian Orthodoxy following contemporary Greek practice. Nikon was exiled and eventually deposed on orders from the tsar, who with other Russian nobles of the time became fascinated with Western lifestyles and religion. Limitations on the power of institutional Orthodoxy increased through the second half of the seventeenth century.

Orthodoxy in the imperial period (1703–1917) was heavily regulated by the state. The authoritarian, Westernized system of government implemented by Peter I ("the Great") and his successors meant that secular Russian society lived side-by-side with traditional Orthodox culture. The Moscow patriarchate was replaced with a Holy Synod in 1721. Church authority was limited to matters of family and morality, although the church itself was never made subservient to the state bureaucracy. Western ideas had a striking influence on the clergy, who became a closed caste within Russian society due to new requirements for education. Church schools and seminaries were only open to the sons of clergy, and these in turn tended to marry the daughters of clergy. The curriculum for educating clergy drew heavily on Catholic and Protestant models, and clergy often found themselves at odds with both parishioners and state authorities. Monastic power declined due to government-imposed limitations on the numbers of monks at each monastery and the secularization of most church lands in 1763. Monastic influence recovered in the nineteenth century with the emergence of saints embraced by Russian believers who saw them as models for piety and social involvement. An intellectual revival in Orthodoxy took place at this time, when writers including Alexei Khomyakov, Fyodor Dostoyevsky, and Vladimir Soloviev sought to combine Orthodox traditions and Western culture. Various leaders in church and state also embraced pan–Slavism with an eye toward Russian leadership of the whole Orthodox world.

Twentieth-century developments shook Russian Orthodoxy to its core. The revolutions of 1905 and 1917 weakened and then destroyed the governing structures upon which the institutional church depended. The emergence of a radically atheistic government under Lenin and the Bolsheviks promised to undermine popular Orthodoxy. Nationalization of all church property was quickly followed by the separation of church from state and religion from public education. Orthodox responses included the restoration of the Moscow patriarchate by the national church council (*sobor*) of 1917–1918 as well as an attempt by some parish priests to combine Orthodoxy and Bolshevism in a new Renovationist or Living Church. In reality, the institutional church was unable to find any defense against the ideologically motivated repression of religion during the first quarter century of the Soviet regime. Neither confrontation nor accommodation proved effective within emerging Soviet Russian culture that emphasized the creation of a new, scientific, atheistic worldview. The Stalin Revolution of the 1930s accompanied by the Great Terror led to mass closures of churches and arrests of clergy.

Orthodoxy remained embedded in Russian culture, however, as seen by its revival during the crisis that accompanied Nazi Germany's invasion of the Soviet Union in 1941. Soviet policy toward the Russian Orthodox Church softened for nearly two decades during and after World War II, tightened again during Nikita Khrushchev's de-Stalinization campaign (1959–1964), and then loosened to a limited extent under the leadership of Leonid Brezhnev (1964–1982). Mikhail Gorbachev turned to the church for help in the moral regeneration of the Soviet Union in the late 1980s. This started a process of reopening Orthodox churches, chapels, monasteries, and schools throughout the country. The collapse of the Soviet Union accelerated that process even as it opened Russia to a flood of religious movements from the rest of the world. Orthodoxy in post-communist Russia struggles to maintain its institutional independence while striving to establish a position as the primary religious confession of the Russian state and the majority of its population. It faces the dilemma of accepting or rejecting various aspects of modern, secular culture in light of Orthodox tradition.

*See also:* ARCHITECTURE; BYZANTIUM, INFLUENCE OF; DVOEVERIE; HAGIOGRAPHY; METROPOLITAN; MONASTICISM; PATRIARCHATE; RELIGION; RUSSIAN ORTHODOX CHURCH

## BIBLIOGRAPHY

Belliustin, I. S. (1985). *Description of the Parish Clergy in Rural Russia: The Memoir of a Nineteenth-Century Parish Priest*, tr. and intro. Gregory L. Freeze. Ithaca, NY: Cornell University Press.

Cracraft, James. (1971). *The Church Reform of Peter the Great.* London: Macmillan.

Cunningham, James W. (1981). *A Vanquished Hope: The Movement for Church Renewal in Russia, 1905-1906.* Crestwood, NY: St. Vladimir's Seminary Press.

Curtiss, John S. (1952). *The Russian Church and the Soviet State, 1917–1950.* Boston: Little, Brown.

Davis, Nathaniel. (1995). *A Long Walk to Church: A Contemporary History of Russian Orthodoxy.* Boulder, CO: Westview Press.

Fedotov, G. P. (1946). *The Russian Religious Mind.* 2 vols. Cambridge, MA: Harvard University Press.

Fennell, John L. I. (1995). *A History of the Russian Church to 1448.* New York: Addison-Wesley.

Florovsky, Georges. (1979). *Collected Works:* Vols. 5–6, *Ways of Russian Theology*, ed. Richard S. Haugh; tr. Robert L. Nichols. Belmont, MA: Nordland.

Freeze, Gregory L. (1977). *The Russian Levites: Parish Clergy in the Eighteenth Century.* Cambridge, MA: Harvard University Press.

Freeze, Gregory L. (1983). *The Parish Clergy in Nineteenth–Century Russia: Crisis, Reform, Counter-Reform.* Princeton, NJ: Princeton University Press.

Husband, William B. (2000). *"Godless Communists": Atheism and Society in Soviet Russia, 1971–1932.* DeKalb: Northern Illinois University Press.

Levin, Eve. (1989). *Sex and Society in the World of the Orthodox Slavs, 900–1700.* Ithaca, NY: Cornell University Press.

Meehan, Brenda. (1993). *Holy Women of Russia.* New York: Harper San Francisco.

Michels, Georg B. (2000). *At War With the Church: Religious Dissent in Seventeenth-Century Russia.* Stanford, CA: Stanford University Press.

Ouspensky, Leonid. (1992). *Theology of the Icon*, 2 vols. Crestwood, NY: St. Vladimir's Seminary Press.

Ware, Timothy. (1993). *The Orthodox Church*, new ed. New York: Penguin.

EDWARD E. ROSLOF

**ORUZHEINAYA PALATA** *See* ARMORY.

## OSETINS

The Osetins are an Iranian nationality of the central Caucasus. They speak a language from the Eastern Iranian group of the Indo-European language family. The three major ethnic and linguistic subdivisions of the Osetins are the Taullag, Iron, and Digor groups. The territories they inhabit straddle the primary land routes across the central Great Caucasus mountain range.

Their remote origins can be traced to Iranian-speaking warrior and pastoralist groups such as the Scythians and Alans. Byzantine, Armenian, and Georgian sources from the seventh through thirteenth centuries suggest that the Alans became a major power in the central Caucasus, and linguistic and ethnographic evidence links the modern Osetins to the Alans. In the tenth century the Alans often allied with the Byzantine Empire. Over the next two centuries Christian missionaries gained wide influence among the Alans. In the upper Kuban, Teberda, Urup, and Zelenchuk river valleys many churches and monasteries were constructed. By the twelfth century Kypchaks became the main power in the region, and the Alans were eclipsed by their Turkic neighbors. During the Mongol invasions of the thirteenth century Alans took refuge high in the mountains and abandoned their centers in the territory of modern-day Karachaevo-Cherkessia. At some point before the mid-sixteenth century, the Osetins came under the domination of princes in Kabarda.

As Russian influence in the central Caucasus began to grow in the mid-eighteenth century, Osetin elders sought political alliances and trade ties with the imperial government. In 1774 negotiations between an Osetian delegation and the imperial government recognized the incorporation of Osetia into the Russian empire. In subsequent decades imperial authorities facilitated the relocation of loyal Osetins from the mountains to settlements and forts in the plains between Vladikavkaz and Mozdok. Beginning in the second half of the eighteenth century Russian Orthodox missionaries worked to revitalize Christianity among the Osetins, who had remained nominally Christian but practiced a combination of pagan and Christian rituals. The construction of military road networks through Osetia in the nineteenth century facilitated the economic development of the central Caucasus and the extension of Russian rule to Georgia and Chechnya. During the Russian Revolution and civil war, both Red and White armies vied for control of Vladikavkaz, the main political and economic center of the region. A South Osetian autonomous region was established in 1922 within the Georgian Soviet Republic, and a North Osetian autonomous region was established in 1924 within the boundaries of the Russian Soviet Federated Socialist Republic (RSFSR). Although their territories were occupied by German forces during the World War II, the Osetins were considered reliable by the Soviet regime and, with the exception of some Muslim Digors, they avoided deportation to Central Asia. During the Gorbachev period Osetins began to pressure for unification of the two autonomous republics into a single entity. In 1991 attempts by Georgian authorities to suppress local autonomy led to a war between Georgian and South Osetian militias. In 1992 conflicts also broke out in the suburbs of Vladikavkaz between Osetin and Ingush groups. While Northern Osetia became a republic of the Russian Federation and renamed itself Alania in the 1990s, the precise juridical status of Southern Osetia within Georgia remained unresolved.

Traditionally Osetins residing in the mountains subsisted on stock-raising, and Osetins inhabiting the plains pursued agriculture. In the late nineteenth century many Osetins began to migrate to cities in search of employment, and by the last decades of the twentieth century the majority of Osetins lived in urban areas. In the twentieth century the Osetin population grew from 250,000 to more than 600,000. An Osetin literary language based upon the Iron dialect was developed during the imperial period, and Osetins were one of the few groups in the North Caucasus to possess a standardized literary language and to have developed literature in their native tongue before the revolution.

*See also:* CAUCASUS; GEORGIA AND GEORGIANS; NATIONALITIES POLICIES, SOVIET; NATIONALITIES POLICIES, TSARIST

**BIBLIOGRAPHY**

Wixman, Ronald. (1980). *Language Aspects of Ethnic Patterns and Processes in the North Caucasus.* Chicago: University of Chicago Press.

BRIAN BOECK

## OSORINA, YULIANYA USTINOVNA

(d. 1604), noblewoman, local saint of Murom.

Yulianya Osorina is known through the *Life [or Tale] of Yulianya Lazarevskaya*, a remarkable document of the seventeenth century. Written by the saint's son Druzhina Osorin in the 1620s or 1630s, it stands out among *vitae* (lives of saints) in that it is tied to precise historical time and events. Most striking is its subject: an ordinary laywoman, the only Russian saint who was not a martyr, ruler, or nun.

Yulianya was born into a family of the upper ranks of the service nobility. Her father, Ustin Nedyurev, was a cellarer of Ivan IV; her mother was Stefanida Lukina from Murom. Orphaned at the age of six, Yulianya was brought up by female relatives and proved to be a serious, obedient, and God-loving child. At the age of sixteen she was married to the wealthy servitor Georgy Osorin. The *Life* throws some light on the wide scope of duties expected of a noblewoman of that time. Osorina's parents-in-law passed on to her the supervision of all household affairs; in the frequent absence of her husband she ran the estate and managed family affairs: for instance, giving an adequate burial and commemoration to her mother- and father-in-law. The *Life* shows no trace of the alleged seclusion that has been usually postulated for Muscovite women of some status.

Yulianya began helping widows and orphans in her youth and continued the commitment after marriage. During her widowhood she intensified the charity work, giving away all but the most basic material necessities. Having donated all her belongings in the years of the terrible famine (1601–1603), she died in poverty on January 2, 1604.

The genre of the *Life* has been disputed widely. In 1871 Vasily Osipovich Klyuchevsky was the first to describe it as a secular biography. The Soviet scholar Mikhail Osipovich Skripil shared this view and chose for his 1948 edition the title *Tale of Ulianya Osorina*, abolishing traditional headings such as *Life of Yulianya Lazarevskaya*. On the other hand, Western scholars T. A. Greenan and Julia Alissandratos, as well as the Russian philolologist T. R. Rudi, insist on the hagiographic character of the work. Different signs of saintliness can be found in the *Life*: For instance, when Yulianya died, "everyone saw around her head a golden circle just like the one that is painted around the heads of saints on icons." When in 1615 her son was buried and her coffin opened, "they saw it was full of sweet-smelling myrrh," which turned out to be healing. According to Greenan, the *Life* is firmly rooted in Russian religious tradition, especially in the popular fourteenth-century collection *Izmaragd*, which emphasizes the possibility of salvation in the world, a central theme in the *Life*.

The *Life* was meant both to edify and to advance the cause of Yulianya. Though there is no indication of an official sanctification, she has been worshipped as a saint since the latter half of the seventeenth century in and around the village of Lazarevo, near Yulianya's burial site in Murom. She is commemorated on October 15 and January 2. Her relics are preserved in the Murom City Museum.

*See also:* HAGIOGRAPHY; RELIGION; SAINTS

### BIBLIOGRAPHY

Greenan, T. A. (1982). "Iulianiya Lazarevskaya." *Oxford Slavonic Papers* 15:28–45.

Howlett, Jana, tr. (2002). "The Tale of Uliania Osor'ina." Available at <http://www.cus.cam.ac.uk/~jrh11/uliania.html>.

NADA BOSKOVSKA

## OSTARBEITER PROGRAM *See* WORLD WAR II.

## OSTROMIR GOSPEL

The Ostromil Gospel is an eleventh-century Gospel book, and the earliest dated Slavic manuscript.

According to its postscript, the Ostromir Gospel was copied by the scribe Gregory for the governor (*posadnik*) of Novgorod, Ostromir, in 1056 and 1057. The manuscript contains 294 folios, and each folio is divided into two columns. Gospels or evangeliaries were books of Gospel readings arranged for use in specific church services. In the Slavic tradition they were called *aprakos* Gospel, which derives from the Greek for "holy day." Because of their important function in the celebration of the liturgy, they were very frequently copied. There are two types of evangeliaries. Short evangeliaries contain readings for all days of the cycle from Palm Sunday until Pentecost and for Saturday and Sunday for the remainder of the year. Full evangeliaries have Saturday and Sunday readings for Lent as well as for all days of the week for the rest of the year. The Ostromir Gospel is the oldest of the short evangeliaries. It is notable for its East Slavic dialect features, its remarkable miniatures depicting three of the Gospel writers, and its dignified uncial writing, which was often used in copying biblical texts. Some scholars have maintained that the Ostromir Gospel goes back to an East Bulgarian reworking of an earlier Macedonian Glagolitic text, while others deny a Glagolitic connection. The pioneering Russian philologist Alexander. Vostokov produced an influential edition of the Ostromir Gospel in 1843 (reprint 1964). Facsimile editions were published in St. Petersburg/Leningrad in 1883 and 1988. First preserved in the St. Sophia cathedral in Novgorod and then in one of the Kremlin churches in Moscow, the Ostromir Gospel is now located in the Russian National Library in St. Petersburg (formerly the State Public Library).

*See also:* KIEVAN RUS; RELIGION

**BIBLIOGRAPHY**
Schenker, Alexander, M. (1995). *The Dawn of Slavic: An Introduction to Slavic Philology.* New Haven, CT: Yale University Press.

DAVID K. PRESTEL

## OSTROVSKY, ALEXANDER NIKOLAYEVICH

(1823–1886), playwright and advocate of dramatists' rights.

Alexander Nikolayevich Ostrovsky wrote and coauthored some fifty plays, translated foreign plays into Russian, and worked tirelessly to improve conditions for actors, dramatists, and composers. Half a dozen of his works form the core repertory for the popular theater movement, a series of initiatives to advance enlightenment and acculturation that steadily expanded theater production and attendance in Russia from the 1860s to World War I.

Young Ostrovsky studied languages, ancient and modern, with tutors and his stepmother, a Swedish baroness. While a student at Moscow University, he regularly attended performances at the Maly Theater. A civil service position, as clerk in the Commercial Court, acquainted him with the subculture of the Russian merchantry in the "Over-the-River" district south of the Kremlin in the 1840s. Merchants then seemed exotic to educated Russians because, like the peasants, they had resisted Westernization, maintained the patriarchal family life and customs prevalent from the sixteenth century, and held a strictly formal attitude toward legality. Ostrovsky's first published work, revised as *It's a Family Affair—We'll Settle It Ourselves* (1849) brought him to the attention of the publisher of the journal *The Muscovite,* and he became its editor in 1850. In his "Slavophile period" Ostrovsky set out to explore with a circle of friends what was good and unique about Russians. They studied and sang folk songs and frequented taverns, especially at festival times, to savor the witty repartee between factory hands and performers.

Ostrovsky would go on to write historical plays that let him exploit the pithy Russian of the sixteenth and seventeenth centuries that predated the language's syntactical remodeling and massive borrowing of foreign words. In this way, and by focusing on cultural enclaves that had survived into the modern period, Ostrovsky mined the equivalent of an Elizabethan linguistic vein for dramatic purposes. A new regime in politics brought him an unparalleled opportunity to steep himself in the living residue of Old Russian. After the Crimean War, Alexander II's Naval Ministry commissioned professional writers to go to various river ports and describe the local people and manners. Ostrovsky, assigned a section of the Volga, traveled there in 1856 and 1857. He noted on index cards hundreds of unfamiliar words and expressions with examples of usage. As he traveled, he observed how the steamship and other innovations were undercutting ancient patterns of courtship and family organization and overturning assumptions about the world.

His best-known play, *The Storm* (1859), which drew on this experience, won the prestigious Uvarov prize for literature. It shows the old ways—at their harmonious best and despotic worst—compromised by a transportation revolution that was shrinking space and accelerating time, and urbanization that promoted civic life as a value while redefining public and private space. Commercial prosperity and a scientific outlook increasingly sanctioned individual autonomy and rights.

From the beginning, Ostrovsky wrote in a realist style, freely depicting the rude manners and behavior observable in actual life. For a time this caused censors to deny permission to perform his plays. But as cultural nationalism advanced, his

**Playwright Alexander Ostrovsky.**

portrayal of strengths set in relief by flaws and crudeness became irresistible. His true-to-life situations made his plays enormously accessible. He seemed to define "Russianness" by showing individuals confronting concrete social and ethical dilemmas as they moved beyond the traditional culture, where custom dictated behavior.

In 1881 he drafted a proposal for a Russian national theater, which appealed to Alexander III's Great Russian chauvinism by arguing that the existence of a Russian school of painting and Russian music gave reason to hope for a Russian school of dramatic art. He claimed that an already extant body of Russian plays demonstrated the ability to teach the "powerful but coarse peasant multitude that there is good in the Russian person, that one must look after and nurture it in oneself."

When Ostrovsky died at Shchelykova, his country estate located between the Volga towns of Kostroma and Kineshma, he was at his desk translating one of Shakespeare's plays into Russian. In the Soviet period a community for retired actors would be built on the property. His plays continue to be performed in Russia to enthusiastic audiences. The richness of their language and the deft incorporation of folk songs and dances in the works of his Slavophile period ensure their survival, even as the historical nuances of authority and status that motivate much of the action recede from living memory.

*See also:* SLAVOPHILES; THEATER

**BIBLIOGRAPHY**

Hoover, Marjorie L. (1981). *Alexander Ostrovsky.* Boston: Twayne Publishers.

Thurston, Gary. (1998). *The Popular Theatre Movement in Russia, 1862–1919.* Evanston, IL: Northwestern University Press.

Wettlin, Margaret. (1974). "Alexander Ostrovsky and the Russian Theatre before Stanislavsky." In *Alexander Ostrovsky: Plays.* Moscow: Progress Publishers.

GARY THURSTON

## OTREPEV, GRIGORY

(c. 1580–1606), Russian monk who supposedly became the false Tsar Dmitry.

Yuri Bogdanovich Otrepev, the son of an infantry officer, became the monk Grigory as a teenager and eventually entered the prestigious Miracles Monastery in the Moscow Kremlin. There he became a deacon, and his intelligence and good handwriting soon brought him to the attention of Patriarch Job (head of the Russian Orthodox Church), who employed Grigory as a secretary.

In 1602 a group of monks, including Grigory and the future Tsar Dmitry, fled to Poland-Lithuania. Their departure greatly upset Tsar Boris Godunov and Patriarch Job. When one of the runaways identified himself as Dmitry of Uglich (the youngest son of Tsar Ivan IV who supposedly died as a child), the Godunov regime launched a propaganda campaign identifying "False Dmitry" as Grigory Otrepev. Stories were fabricated that Grigory had become a sorcerer and tool of Satan or that he had committed crimes while in the service of the Romanov family (opponents of Tsar Boris). Although no credible witnesses ever came forward to verify that Grigory and "False Dmitry" were the same person, Tsar Dmitry's enemies never tired of claiming that he was really Otrepev.

The sensational image of the evil, debauched, and bloodthirsty monk Grigory pretending to be Tsar Dmitry continues to haunt modern scholarship. Many historians have accepted at face value the most lurid propaganda manufactured by Dmitry's enemies, but careful study of the evidence reveals that it is impossible to merge the biographies of Grigory and "False Dmitry." Grigory Otrepev was last seen by an English merchant shortly after the assassination of Tsar Dmitry in 1606; then he disappeared.

*See also:* DMITRY, FALSE; GODUNOV, BORIS FYODOROVICH; TIME OF TROUBLES

**BIBLIOGRAPHY**

Dunning, Chester. (2001). *Russia's First Civil War: The Time of Troubles and the Founding of the Romanov Dynasty.* University Park: Pennsylvania State University Press.

Perrie, Maureen. (1995). *Pretenders and Popular Monarchism in Early Modern Russia: The False Tsars of the Time of Troubles.* Cambridge, UK: Cambridge University Press.

CHESTER DUNNING

## OUR HOME IS RUSSIA PARTY

Our Home Is Russia (*Nash Dom—Rossiya*, or NDR) was a sociopolitical movement and a ruling party from 1996 to 1998. Formed in the spring of 1995 according to a plan of the president's administration as one of two ruling parties—the party of the "right hand," with the prime minister at the head—it immediately launched forward. The NDR movement's council, founded in May 1995 with Victor Chernomyrdin at the head, included thirty-seven heads of regions, a few ministers, and heads of large industrial enterprises and banks. The federal NDR list for the Duma elections was headed by Chernomyrdin, the famous film director Nikita Mikhalkov, and General Lev Rokhlin, a Chechnya war hero. Subsequently both the prime minister and the film director renounced the mandates, and Rokhlin, entering the Duma, soon came into opposition against

Boris Yeltsin and he then left the NDR fraction; and founded the Movement in Support of the Army. The NDR list received seven million votes (10.1%, third place) and forty-five Duma seats; this was taken as defeat of the ruling party. In the single-mandate districts, out of 108 proposed candidates, ten were elected. In the 1996 presidential elections, NDR backed Yeltsin.

With Chernomyrdin leaving the prime ministership in the spring of 1998, NDR entered a period of crisis. The effort on the part of the young ambitious leader of the NDR fraction in the Duma, Vladimir Ryzhkov, to turn NDR from a party of heads into a neoconservative political party of "values" proved unsuccessful. Discussions of merging with the blocs *A Just Cause* and *Voice of Russia* and the movement *New Force* were fruitless as well. Allies of NDR in the elections amounted to the weak *Forward, Russia* of Boris Fyodorov and the Muslim movement *Medzhlis*. The programmatic positions of NDR amount to moderate-reformist ideas and a declaration of conservative-liberal values. The federal list was headed by Chernomyrdin and the Saratov governor Dmitry Ayatskov. NDR did not make it into the Duma, as it received 0.8 million votes (1.2 percent). Nine NDR candidates from single-mandate districts, including Chernomyrdin and Ryzhkov, entered the pro-government fraction *Unity* and the group *People's Deputy*. In May 2000, the eighth and last congress of NDR, which at the time had 125,000 members, decided to form part of the party *Unity*, created on the foundation of the movements Unity, All Russia, and NDR.

*See also:* CHERNOMYRDIN, VIKTOR STEPANOVICH; MOVEMENT IN SUPPORT OF THE ARMY; UNITY (MEDVED) PARTY

**BIBLIOGRAPHY**

McFaul, Michael. (2001). *Russia's Unfinished Revolution: Political Change from Gorbachev to Putin.* Ithaca, NY: Cornell University Press.

McFaul, Michael, and Markov, Sergei. (1993). *The Troubled Birth of Russian Democracy: Parties, Personalities, and Programs.* Stanford, CA: Hoover Institution Press.

Reddaway, Peter, and Glinski, Dmitri. (2001). *The Tragedy of Russia's Reforms: Market Bolshevism against Democracracy.* Washington, DC: U.S. Institute of Peace Press.

NIKOLAI PETROV

## PACIFIC FLEET

The Pacific Fleet is headquartered in Vladivostok, capital of the Maritime (Primorsky) Territory. Not surprisingly, given Russia's status as a Pacific nation with vital interests in the Asia-Pacific region, the Pacific Fleet is one of Russia's most powerful naval forces. The city of Vladivostok, established in 1860, occupies most of Muraviev-Amursky Peninsula, named after the governor general of Eastern Russia during the mid-nineteenth century. Two bays, Amursky and Ussurysky, wrap the peninsula, mirroring with their names two great rivers of the Russian Far East, the Amur, and the Ussury, its tributary.

Beginning in the 1600s, Russian explorers first reached Siberia's eastern coastline and founded the city of Okhotsk (1647). Until the mid-1800s, however, China's dominance of the southern regions of eastern Siberia restricted Russian naval activities. The construction of the port city of Vladivostok intensified Russia's need for adequate transportation links. Tsar Alexander III drew up plans for the Trans-Siberian Railway and began building it in 1891. Despite the enormity of the project, a continuous route was completed in 1905, stimulated by the outbreak of the Russo-Japanese War a year earlier. Vladivostok became Russia's main naval base in the east after Port Arthur (located in Chinese territory and ceded to Russia in 1898) fell in January 1905 during the war. After World War I, Japan seized Vladivostok and held the key port for four years, initially as a member of the Allied interventionist forces that occupied parts of Russia after the new Bolshevik government proclaimed neutrality and withdrew from the war. At the end of World War II, Stalin broke the neutrality pact that had existed throughout the war in order to occupy vast areas of East Asia formerly held by Japan. It was through Vladivostok, moreover, that some of the Lend-Lease aid, the most visible sign of U.S.-Soviet cooperation during World War II, passed on its way to Murmansk.

The Pacific Fleet includes eighteen nuclear submarines that are operationally subordinate to the Ministry of Defense and based at Pavlovsk and Rybachy. The blue-water striking power of the Pacific Fleet lies in thirty-four nonnuclear submarines and forty-nine principal surface combatants. The Zvezda Far Eastern Shipyard in Bolshoi Kamen, a couple of hours north of Vladivostok, serves as the chief recycling facility for the Fleet, although it is in disrepair. The Pacific Fleet's additional home ports include Petropavlovsk-Kamchatsky, Magadan, and Sovetskaya Gavan. As far as air power is concerned, the Pacific Fleet consisted during the mid-1990s of 250 land-based combat aircraft and helicopters. Two bomber regiments stationed at Alekseyevka constituted its most powerful strike force. Each regiment consisted of thirty supersonic Tu-22M Backfire aircraft. The land power of the Pacific Fleet consisted of one naval infantry division and a coastal defense division. The naval infantry division included more than half of the total manpower in the Russian naval infantry. During the mid-1990s, the Pacific Fleet infantry was reorganized into brigades.

During the late 1990s, a joint headquarters was established commanding the land, naval, and air units stationed on the Kamchatka Peninsula. Despite funding shortfalls during the early twenty-first century, the Russian Pacific Fleet continues to demonstrate its resolve to increase combat readiness. Russian Pacific Fleet submarines carry out missions of regional security, strategic deterrence, protection of strategic assets, and training for anti-surface warfare.

*See also:* BALTIC FLEET; BLACK SEA FLEET; MILITARY, IM-PERIAL ERA; MILITARY, SOVIET AND POST-SOVIET; NORTHERN FLEET; TRANS-SIBERIAN RAILWAY

**BIBLIOGRAPHY**

Busmann, Gerd, and Meier, Oliver. (1997). *The Nuclear Legacy of the Former Soviet Union: Implications for Security and Ecology.* Berlin: Berliner Information-szentrum für Transatlantische Sicherheit (BITS) in cooperation with Heinrich-Böll-Stiftung.

Da Cunha, Derek. (1990). *Soviet Naval Power in the Pacific.* Boulder, CO: Lynne Rienner.

Morris, Eric. (1977). *The Russian Navy: Myth and Reality.* New York: Stein and Day.

Stephan, John J. (1994). *The Russian Far East: A History.* Stanford, CA: Stanford University Press.

JOHANNA GRANVILLE

# PAGANISM

Due to the concerted efforts of both the eastern and western churches, Christianity largely replaced Slavic paganism during the course of the ninth and tenth centuries. There are primarily three sources for information about Slavic paganism: written accounts, archaeological discoveries, and ethnographic evidence. As literacy was introduced to the East Slavs only with their conversion to Christianity in 988 C.E., and the written sources were most often compiled by Christian monks or missionaries, much of what is known about East Slavic paganism from written accounts is of questionable accuracy. The sources begin with the Byzantine historian Procopius (sixth century) and include Arab travel accounts, reports of Christian missionary activity, and references in the *Primary Chronicle* and the *First Novgorod Chronicle.* Archaeological evidence has provided some information on pagan temples, particularly among the West Slavs on the island of Rügen in the Baltic Sea. In addition, what may have been a temple to Perun, god of thunder, was excavated near Peryn, south of Novgorod in 1951, and several sites that were likely associated with cult practices have been found at Pskov, in the Smolensk region, and Belarus. Generally, however, archaeological sites are able to provide more information about material culture than about the spiritual life of a preliterate people. Ethnographic material was not systematically collected until the nineteenth century, which makes it difficult to separate genuine information from later accretions. One can summarize, based on evidence from all these sources, however, that early Slavic religion was animistic, in that it personified natural elements. It also deified heavenly bodies and recognized the existence of various spirits of the forest, water, and household. Ritual sacrifice was likely used to appease the pagan deities, and amulets were used to ward off evil. In accordance with widespread Indo-European practice, the early Slavs likely cremated their dead, but even before the Christian era burial was also practiced. Chernaya Mogila, a burial site in Chernigov that dates from the tenth century provides strong evidence for a belief in the afterlife, as three members of a princely family were interred with the horses, weapons, and utensils that they would need for existence in the next world.

Procopius makes reference to a Slavic god who is the ruler of everything, but evidence for a larger pantheon comes much later. The twelfth-century *Primary Chronicle* relates how Prince Vladimir set up idols in the hills of Kiev to Perun, "made of wood with a head of silver and a mustache of gold," as well as to Khors, Dazhbog, Stribog, Simargl, and Mokosh. In the entries for 907 and 971 C.E., the chronicle reports that the Rus swore by their gods Perun and Volos, the god of the flocks. Perun is associated with thunder and the oak tree, thought to be a favorite target of the lightning bolts unleashed by the thunder god. Much less is known about the other gods mentioned in the chronicle. Khors seems to refer to the sun and, as Jakobson points out, is closely connected with Dazhbog, the "giver of wealth," and Stribog, "the apportioner of wealth." Simargl appears to be a form of Simorg, the Iranian winged monster, who is at times depicted as a winged dog. The only female in the pantheon is Mokosh, whose name is probably derived from moist, and who is likely a personification of Moist Mother Earth. Some scholars view Mokosh as a remnant of the Great Goddess cult, which struggled against the patriarchal religion of the Varangians (Vikings). The god Volos, identified in the peace treaties as the god of cattle, may be connected with death and the underworld. The association with cattle possibly comes from the efforts of Christian writers to connect him with St. Blasius, a martyred Cappadocian bishop who became the protector of flocks. Although not listed in Vladimir's pantheon, the god Rod, with his consort Rozhanitsa, is mentioned in other East Slavic sources as a type of primordial progenitor.

After the conversion of Rus, elements of paganism continued in combination with Christian beliefs, a phenomenon that has been called "dvoeverie" or "dual belief" in the Slavic tradition. References to pagan deities occasionally occur in Christian era texts, most notably as rhetorical ornamentation in such works as the *Slovo o polku Igoreve*. Syncretism is also apparent in the transformation of Perun into the Old Testament Elijah, who was taken to heaven in a fiery chariot.

*See also:* DVOEVERIE; KIEVAN RUS; OCCULTISM; VIKINGS

**BIBLIOGRAPHY**

Barford, Paul M. (2001). *The Early Slavs: Culture and Society in Early Medieval Eastern Europe.* Ithaca, NY: Cornell University Press.

Gimbutas, Marija. (1971). *The Slavs.* London: Thames and Hudson.

Hubbs, Joanna. (1989). *Mother Russia: The Feminine Myth in Russian Culture.* Bloomington: Indiana University Press.

Jakobson, Roman. (1950) "Slavic Mythology." *Funk and Wagnalls Standard Dictionary of Folklore, Mythology and Legend.* Vol. 2. New York: Funk and Wagnalls.

*The Russian Primary Chronicle: Laurentian Text.* (1953). Ed. and tr. Samuel Hazzard Cross and Olgerd P. Sherbowitz-Wetzor. Cambridge, MA: The Mediaeval Academy of America.

DAVID K. PRESTEL

# PAKISTAN, RELATIONS WITH

An affinity between Pakistan and the Soviet Union would have seemed natural, given the Pakistan's status as a British colony (until 1947) and the Soviet Union's role as supporter of nations oppressed by capitalist imperialists. However, in 1959 Pakistan—along with Turkey and Iran—joined the Central Treaty Organization (CENTO), which was engineered by President Dwight Eisenhower's energetic secretary of state, John Foster Dulles. The security treaty replaced the Baghdad Pact and was intended to provide a southern bulwark to Soviet expansion toward the Indian Ocean and the oil fields of the Persian Gulf. CENTO also enabled the United States to aid Pakistan and cement a close security relationship with the country that has thus become the cornerstone of U.S. policy in South Asia for more than three decades. This relationship reinforced Moscow's efforts to maintain close relations with Pakistan's rival, India. Beginning in June 1955 with Indian prime minister Jawaharlal Nehru's visit to Moscow, and First Secretary Nikita Khrushchev's return trip to India during the fall of 1955, the foundations were laid for cordial Soviet-Indian relations. While in India, Khrushchev announced Moscow's support for Indian sovereignty over the Kashmir region. Leading to the eventual partition of British India in 1947, contention between Hindus and Muslims has focused on Kashmir for centuries. Pakistan asserts Kashmiris' right to self-determination through a plebiscite in accordance with an earlier Indian pledge and a United Nations resolution. This dispute triggered wars between the two countries, not only in 1947 but also in 1965 (Moscow maintained neutrality in 1965). In December 1971, Pakistan and India again went to war, following a political crisis in what was then East Pakistan and the flight of millions of Bengali refugees to India. The two armies reached an impasse, but a decisive Indian victory in the east resulted in the creation of Bangladesh.

New strains appeared both in Soviet-Pakistani relations after the 1979 Soviet invasion of Afghanistan. Pakistan supported the Afghan resistance, while India implicitly supported Soviet occupation. Pakistan accommodated an influx of refugees (more than 3.2 million people) resulting from the Soviet occupation (December 1979–February 1989). In the following eight years, the USSR and India voiced increasing concern over Pakistani arms purchases, U.S. military aid to Pakistan, and Pakistan's nuclear weapons program. In May 1998 India, and then Pakistan, conducted nuclear tests.

After the September 11, 2001, terrorist attacks, Pakistan's relations with Washington grew strained, while its relations with Moscow improved. Although Pakistan's military ruler, General Pervez Musharraf, agreed to provide the United States with bases in Pakistan for launching military operations against Pakistan's erstwhile ally—the Taliban—in Afghanistan, his actions fueled electoral successes of Islamic fundamentalists in Pakistan who opposed his pro-U.S. stance. Meanwhile, Russian President Vladimir Putin played a key mediation role in the Indo-Pakistani conflict. In February 2003, Musharraf met with Putin in Moscow to discuss trade and defense ties. This was the first official state visit by a Pakistani leader to Moscow since Zulfiqar Ali Bhutto in the 1970s. Pakistan and India massed about a million troops along the UN-drawn Line of Control that divides their sectors of the state officially called Jammu and Kashmir—raising international fears of a possible nuclear war.

*See also:* AFGHANISTAN, RELATIONS WITH

**BIBLIOGRAPHY**

Hershberg, Eric, and Moore, Kevin W. (2002). *Critical Views of September 11: Analyses from Around the World.* New York: New Press.

Jones, Owen Bennett. (2002). *Pakistan: Eye of the Storm.* New Haven, CT: Yale University Press.

Weaver, Mary Anne. (2002). *Pakistan: in the Shadow of Jihad and Afghanistan.* New York: Farrar, Straus and Giroux.

Wirsing, Robert. (1994). *India, Pakistan, and the Kashmir Dispute: On Regional Conflict and Its Resolution.* New York: St. Martin's Press.

JOHANNA GRANVILLE

## PALEKH PAINTING

Palekh painted lacquer boxes, popularly thought to be a traditional Russian folk art, were actually a product of the Soviet period. Palekh painting, a delicate and elegant miniature style, is done on the lids of lacquered, *papier-mâché* black boxes with crimson interiors. The subjects depict Russian fairy tales, legends, and folk heroes, and during the Soviet period also included scenes of rural life, industrialization, and Soviet leaders and heroes. Palekh boxes, originally created for Soviet citizens, developed a worldwide reputation after being sold at international arts and crafts fairs.

The term *palekh* comes from the most famous of the three villages (Kholui, Mstera, and Palekh) in which Palekh painting originated. Ivan Golikov, a Palekh icon painter, derived the inspiration for this style from lacquered boxes he saw at the Kustar Museum in 1921. Golikov and others applied egg tempera, rather than oil, to papier-mâché boxes and, employing techniques used in icon painting, created objects that resembled traditional folk art. The Artel of Early Painting, a craft collective for Palekh painters founded by Golikov and his colleagues, was established in Palekh in 1924 (artels also existed in Khuloi and Mstera). Palekh painting became an integral part of Soviet applied arts with the establishment of a four-year training program. Exhibitions dedicated to Palekh boxes were held throughout the 1930s. Academic articles on this medium, and artistic debates discussing the appropriate style and content of Palekh painting, continued from the 1930s to the 1960s. Since the 1970s, Palekh painted boxes and brooches have been viewed as the quintessential tourist souvenir from Russia.

*See also:* FOLKLORE

**BIBLIOGRAPHY**

Hilton, Alison. (1995). *Russian Folk Art.* Bloomington: Indiana University Press.

K. ANDREA RUSNOCK

## PALE OF SETTLEMENT

As a result of the Napoleonic Wars and the acquisition of the central and eastern provinces of Poland by the Russian Empire during the late eighteenth century, the area extending from the Baltic to the Black Sea became known as the Russian "Pale of Settlement." Originally established by Catherine the Great in 1791, the Pale (meaning "border") eventually covered roughly 286,000 square miles (740,700 square kilometers) of territory and grew to include twenty-five provinces (fifteen Russian and ten Polish), including Kiev, Grodno, Minsk, Lublin, Bessarabia, and Mogilev. Along with the favorable acquisition of Polish land, the Russian government was faced with a population of ethnic groups that came with the various territories. Although the territories consisted of various groups, including Byzantine Catholics, Germans, Armenians, Tartars, Scots, and Dutchmen, it was the large number of Jews (10% of the Polish population) that was most troubling to the tsars.

In 1804, intending to protect the Russian population from the Jewish people, Alexander I issued a decree that prevented Jews from living outside the territories of the Pale, the first of many statutes designed to limit the freedoms of Russia's new Jewry. With more than five million Jews eventually living and working within its borders, Russian lawmakers used the confines of the Pale as an opportunity to limit Jewish participation in most facets of social, economic, and political life. With few exceptions, Jews were forced to reside within the Pale's overcrowded cities and small towns called shtetls, restricted from traveling, prevented from entering various professions (including agriculture), levied with extra taxation, forbidden to receive higher education, and kept from engaging in various forms of trade to subsidize their livelihood. Although Jews in the Pale were destined to a endure a life of poverty and restriction, most managed to make their way into the local economies by working as tailors, cobblers, peddlers, and small shopkeepers. Others, who were less fortunate, survived only by committed mutual aid efforts and strong local networks of support.

As the Russian Empire started experiencing the early stages of industrialization during the 1880s, the Pale began to witness a steady decline in its agricultural, artisanal, and petty entrepreneurial economies. Because of this transition, many independent producers of goods and services could no longer subsist and were forced to find jobs in factories. Very few, especially the Jewish artisans and tailors, were able to continue producing independently or as middlemen to larger manufacturing plants. By the start of the twentieth century, the manufacturing sector was increasingly becoming the primary source of employment in the Pale, with wage laborers producing cigarettes, cigars, knit goods, gloves, textiles, artificial flowers, buttons, glass, bricks, soap, candy, and various other goods. It was ultimately the deteriorating economy within the Pale, coupled with years of anti-Semitism, that

served as catalyst for more than two million Jews to emigrate to America between 1881 and 1914. Not long after this exodus, the Pale of Settlement was abolished with the overthrow of the tsarist regime in 1917.

*See also:* ALEXANDER I; BESSARABIA; CATHERINE II; JEWS; NATIONALITIES POLICIES, TSARIST

**BIBLIOGRAPHY**
Klier, John. (1986). *Russia Gathers Her Jews: The Origins of the "Jewish Question" in Russia, 1772–1825.* DeKalb: Northern Illinois University Press.

Ro'i, Yaacov, ed. (1995). *Jews and Jewish Life in Russia and the Soviet Union.* Portland, OR: Frank Cass.

DIANA FISHER

# PALEOLOGUE, SOPHIA

(d. 1503) niece of the last two Byzantine emperors and the second wife of Grand Prince Ivan III of Moscow.

Sophia Paleologue (Zoe) improved the Russian Grand Prince's international standing through her dynastic status and promoted Byzantine symbolism and ceremony at the Russian court.

Zoe Paleologue was the daughter of Despot Thomas of Morea, the younger brother of the Byzantine emperors John VIII and Constantine IX, and Catherine, daughter of Prince Centurione Zaccaria of Achaea. After the conquest of Morea by the Ottoman Turks in 1460 and her parents' subsequent death, Paleologue became a ward of the Uniate cardinal Bessarion, who gave her a Catholic education in Rome as a dependent of Pope Sixtus IV.

After protracted negotiations with the Russian Grand Prince, who saw an opportunity to increase his prestige in a marital union with a Byzantine princess, the Vatican offered Paleologue in a betrothal ceremony to one of Ivan III's representatives on June 1, 1472. During Paleologue's trip to Russia, the Byzantine princess assured the Russian populace in Pskov of her Orthodox disposition by abjuring Latin religious ritual and dress and by venerating icons. Paleologue married Ivan III on November 12, 1472, in an Orthodox wedding ceremony in the Moscow Kremlin and took the name Sophia.

Paleologue gave birth to ten children, one of which was the future heir to the Russian throne,

Basil III. The existence of Ivan Molodoy, the surviving son of Ivan III's union with his first wife, Maria of Tver, and natural successor to the throne, caused friction between the grand prince and Paleologue. According to contemporary Russian chronicles, Paleologue intrigued against Ivan Molodoy and his wife, Elena Voloshanka. Paleologue's situation at court deteriorated even more after Voloshanka gave birth to a son, Dmitry Ivanovich. The untimely death of Ivan Molodoy in 1490 inspired rumors that Paleologue had poisoned him. The focus of Paleologue's and Voloshanka's dynastic struggle shifted to Dmitry Ivanovich. Ivan III's decision to make Dmitry his heir in 1497 caused Paleologue and her son Basil to revolt. Although Ivan III disgraced Sophia and crowned Dmitry as his successor in the following year, the Byzantine princess emerged victorious in 1499, when Basil was made Grand Prince of Novgorod and Pskov. Conspiring with the Lithuanians, Paleologue put pressure on her husband to imprison Voloshanka and her son Dmitry and to proclaim Basil Grand Prince of Vladimir and Moscow in 1502.

In pursuing her political and dynastic goals, Paleologue exploited traditional Byzantine methods to advertise her claims. In a liturgical tapestry she donated to the Monastery of Saint Sergius of Radonezh in 1498, she proclaimed her superior heritage by juxtaposing her position as Tsarevna of Constantinople with the grand princely title of her husband. By exploiting Byzantine religious symbolism, in the same embroidery she expressed her claim that Basil III was the divinely chosen heir to the Russian throne. While there has been no substantiation for the claim of some scholars that Paleologue was responsible for the introduction of wide-ranging Byzantine ideas and practices at the Russian court, the Byzantine princess's knack for political messages draped in religious language and imagery undoubtedly left a lasting mark on medieval Russian culture.

See also: BASIL III; IVAN III

**BIBLIOGRAPHY**
Fennell, J. L. I. (1961). *Ivan the Great of Moscow*. London: Macmillan.

Fine, John V. A., Jr. (1966). "The Muscovite Dynastic Crisis of 1497–1502." *Canadian Slavonic Papers* 8:198–215.

Kollmann, Nancy Shields. (1986). "Consensus Politics: the Dynastic Crisis of the 1490s Reconsidered." *Russian Review* 45(3):235–267.

Miller, David. (1993). "The Cult of Saint Sergius of Radonezh and Its Political Uses." *Slavic Review* 52(4): 680–699.

Thyrêt, Isolde. (2001). *Between God and Tsar: Religious Symbolism and the Royal Women of Muscovite Russia*. DeKalb: Northern Illinois University Press.

ISOLDE THYRÊT

# PALLAS, PETER-SIMON

(1741–1811), explorer, geologist, botanist.

Peter-Simon Pallas was born in Berlin, where he received his formal education. He also spent some time in Holland and England working in museums with rich collections in natural history. One of his early studies dealing with polyps and sponges was published in the Hague in 1761 and immediately attracted wide professional attention, not only because of the richness and originality of the presented empirical data, but also with its precisely stated general theoretical propositions. In 1763 Pallas became a member of the St. Petersburg Academy of Sciences, and a year later he led an exploratory expedition to the Caspian and Baikal areas, concentrating on both natural history and ethnography. Published in three volumes between 1771 and 1778, under the title *Travels through Various Provinces in the Russian Empire*, and written in German, the study was immediately translated into Russian, and then into French, Italian, and English. Pallas guided several other exploratory expeditions; the trip to Southern Russia, with a heavy concentration on Crimea, proved especially enlightening. All these studies manifested not only Pallas's observational talents but also his profound familiarity with contemporary geology, botany, zoology, mineralogy and linguistics. His *Flora Rossica* provided a systematic botanical survey of the country's trees.

Pallas's studies extended beyond the limits of traditional natural history. He pondered the general processes and laws related to geology: For example, he presented a theory of the origin of mountains in intraterrestrial explosions. He also made a technically advanced study of regional variations in the Mongolian language, articulated a transformist view of the living forms, which he later abandoned, and, responding to a suggestion made by Catherine II, worked on a comparative dictionary. He also made a historical survey of land tracts discovered by the Russians in the stretches of ocean between Siberia and Alaska. In the journal of the *Free Economic Society*, established in the age of Catherine II, he published a series of articles on relations of geography to agriculture.

Most of Pallas's studies offered no broad scientific formulations; their strength was in the richness and novelty of descriptive information. Charles Darwin referred to Pallas in four of his major works, always with the intent of adding substance to his generalizations. Georges Cuvier, by contrast, credited Pallas with the creation of "a completely new geology." Pallas's writings appealed to a wide audience not only because, at the time of the Enlightenment, there was a growing interest in the geographies and cultures of the world previously unexplored, but also because they were masterworks of lucid and spirited prose.

Together with the great mathematician Leonhard Euler, Pallas was a major contributor to the elevation of the St. Petersburg Academy of Sciences to the level of the leading European scientific institutions.

*See also:* ACADEMY OF SCIENCES

**BIBLIOGRAPHY**

Pallas, Peter-Simon. (1802–1803). *Travels through the Southern Provinces of the Russian Empire.* 2 vols. London: Longman and Kees.

Vucinich, Alexander. (1963). *Science in Russian Culture.* Stanford, CA: Stanford University Press.

ALEXANDER VUCINICH

# PAMYAT

The Pamyat (Memory) society was established in 1978 to defend Russian cultural heritage. Pamyat came to adopt extreme rightist platforms, particularly under the direction of Dmitry Vasilyev from late 1985. It rose to prominence as the most visible and controversial Russian nationalist organization of the *neformaly* (informal) movement in the USSR during the late 1980s. Although not representative of all strains of Russian nationalist thought, Pamyat was representative of a broad xenophobic ideology that gained strength in the perestroika years.

At the heart of Pamyat's platform was the defense of Russian traditions. Pamyat ideologues deplored both Soviet-style socialism and western democracy and capitalism. They held tsarist autocracy as the ideal model of statehood. Much of their ideology drew on the ideas of the Black Hundreds, which organized pogroms against Jews in Tsarist Russia. This reactionary ideology contained a strong Orthodox Christian element. Alongside provisions for the recognition of the place of Orthodoxy in Russian history, Pamyat made demands for the priority of Russian citizens in all fields of life.

In 1988 Pamyat had an estimated twenty thousand members and forty branches in cities throughout the Soviet Union. It later splintered into a number of anti-Semitic and xenophobic groups. Competing factions emerged, the two most prominent being the Moscow-based National-Patriotic Front Pamyat and the National-Patriotic Movement Pamyat. This factional conflict belied an ideological symmetry; both groups emphasized the importance of Russian Orthodoxy and blamed a Jewish-Masonic conspiracy for everything from killing the tsar to "alcoholizing" the Russian population. The success of Pamyat's xenophobic platforms sparked debates about the negative consequences of glasnost and perestroika.

Factional disputes, crude national chauvinism and contradictory political platforms led many Russian nationalists to distance themselves from Pamyat. Pamyat and its many splinter groups were largely discredited and their influence much reduced by the time the USSR collapsed in 1991. Nevertheless, it is widely recognized that Pamyat was a forerunner of post-Soviet Russian national chauvinist and neo-fascist groups.

*See also:* NATIONALISM IN THE SOVIET UNION

**BIBLIOGRAPHY**

Garrard, John. (1991). "A Pamyat Manifesto: Introductory Note and Translation." *Nationalities Papers* 19 (2):135–145.

Laqueur, Walter. (1993). *Black Hundred: The Rise of the Extreme Right in Russia.* New York: HarperCollins.

ZOE KNOX

# PANSLAVISM

*Panslavism* in a general sense refers to the belief in a collective destiny for the various Slavic peoples—

generally, but far from always, under the leadership of Russia, the largest Slavic group or nation. Thus the seventeenth-century author of *Politika* (*Politics*), Juraj Krizanic (1618–1683) is often regarded as a precursor of Panslavism because he urged the unification of all Slavs under the leadership of Russia and the Vatican. His writings were largely unknown until the nineteenth century. The Czech philologist Pavel Jozef Safarik (1795–1861) and his friend, poet Jan Kollar, regarded the Slavs historically as one nation. Safarik believed that they had once had a common language. However, despite his belief in Slavic unity, he turned against Russia following the suppression of the Polish rebellion in 1830 and 1831. The Ukrainian national bard, Taras Shevchenko (1814–1861), also hoped for a federation of the Slavic peoples.

In a narrower and more common usage, however, *Panslavicism* refers to a political movement in nineteenth-century Russia. Politically, Panslavism would not have taken the shape it did without the Russian claims of tutelage over the Slavic populations of the declining Ottoman Empire. Intellectually, however, Panslavism drew on the nationalist ideas of people such as Mikhail Pogodin (1800–1875), the most important representative of "Official Nationality" and especially of the Slavophiles. Slavophilism focused critically on Russia's internal civilization and its need to return to first principles, but it bequeathed to Panslavism the idea that Russia's civilization was superior to that of all of its European competitors. Of the early Slavophiles, Alexei Khomyakov (1804–1860) wrote a number of poems ("The Eagle"; "To Russia"), which can be considered broadly Panslav, as well as a "Letter to the Serbs" in the last year of his life, in which he demanded that religious faith be "raised to a social principle." Ivan Aksakov (1823–1886) actually evolved from his early Slavophilism to full-blown Panslavism over the course of his journalistic career.

The advent of Alexander II and the implementation of the so-called Great Reforms began the long and complex process of opening up a public arena and eventually a public opinion in Russia. Ideas stopped being the privilege of a small number of cultivated aristocrats, and the 1870s saw a reorientation from philosophical to more practical matters, if not precisely to politics, a shift that affected both Slavophiles and Westernizers. It is against this background that one needs to view the eclipse of classical Slavophilism and the rise of Panslavism.

It is plausible to date the beginning of Panslavism as a movement—albeit a very loose and undisciplined one—to the winter of 1857–1858, when the Moscow Slavic Benevolent Committee was created to support the South Slavs against the Ottoman Empire. A number of Slavophiles were involved, and the Emperor formally recognized the organization, upon the active recommendation of Alexander Gorchakov, Minister of Foreign Affairs. In 1861 Pogodin became president and Ivan Aksakov secretary and treasurer, and for the next fifteen years the Committee was active in education, philanthropy, and a sometimes strident advocacy journalism.

In 1867 the committee organized a remarkable Panslav Congress, which went on for months. It involved a series of lectures, an ethnographic exhibition, and a number of banquets, speeches, and other demonstrations of welcome to the eighty-one foreign visitors from the Slavic world—teachers, politicians, professors, priests, and even a few bishops. But the discussions clearly demonstrated the suspicions that many non-Russians entertained of their somewhat overbearing big brother. No Poles attended, nor did any Ukrainians from the Russian Empire. Even to the friendly Serbs the Russian demands for hegemony seemed excessive.

Panslav agitation was growing at the turn of the decade, partly due to the bellicose *Opinion on the Eastern Question* (1869) by General Rostislav Andreyevich Fadeev (1826–1884). In that same year appeared a more interesting Panslav product, *Russia and Europe*, by Nikolai Yakovlevich Danilevsky (1822–1885). It charted the maturation and decay of civilizations and foresaw Russia's Panslav Empire triumphing over the declining West. The aims of the Slavic Benevolent Committee seemed closest to fulfillment during the victorious climax to the Russo-Turkish War of 1877–1878, when Constantinople appeared within the grasp of Russian arms. Yet, despite the imperial patronage that the Committee had enjoyed for over a decade, the government drew back from the seizure of Constantinople, and then was forced by the European powers at the Congress of Berlin (1878) to minimize Russian gains. Aksakov's subsequent tirade about lost Russian honor resulted in the permanent adjournment of the Committee. Panslav perspectives lingered, but the movement declined into political insignificance during the course of the 1880s.

*See also:* NATIONALISM IN TSARIST EMPIRE; OFFICIAL NATIONALITY; SLAVOPHILES

## BIBLIOGRAPHY

Fadner, Frank J. (1962). *Seventy Years of Pan-Slavism in Russia: Karazin to Danilevskii, 1800–1870.* Washington, DC: Georgetown University Press.

Geyer, Dietrich. (1987). *Russian Imperialism: The Interaction of Domestic and Foreign Policy in Russia, 1860–1914.* New Haven: Yale University Press.

Greenfeld, Liah. (1992). *Nationalism: Five Roads to Modernity.* Cambridge, MA: Harvard University Press.

Kohn, Hans. (1953). *Pan-Slavism: Its History and Ideology.* Notre Dame, IN: University of Notre Dame.

Petrovich, Michael Boro. (1956). *The Emergence of Russian Panslavism 1865–1870.* New York: Columbia University Press.

Tuminez, Astrid. (2000). *Russian Nationalism Since 1856.* Lanham, MD: Rowman and Littlefield.

Walicki, Andrzej. (1975). *The Slavophile Controversy: History of a Conservative Utopia in Nineteenth-Century Russian Thought.* Oxford: Clarendon.

ABBOTT GLEASON

# PARIS, CONGRESS AND TREATY OF 1856

Facing an empty treasury, a new French naval ordnance that might pierce the Kronstadt walls, and possible Swedish and Prussian hostilities, Alexander II and a special Imperial Council accepted an Austrian ultimatum and agreed on January 16, 1856, to make peace on coalition terms and conclude the Crimean War. Even before Sevastopol fell (September 12, 1855), Russia had accepted three of the Anglo-French-Austrian Four Points of August 1854: guarantee of Ottoman sovereignty and territorial integrity; general European (not exclusively Russian) protection of the Ottoman Christians; and freeing of the mouth of the Danube. The details of the third point, as well as reduction of Russian Black Sea preponderance and additional British particular conditions, completed the agreement. The incipient entente with Napoleon III, who all along had hoped to check Russian prestige without fighting for British imperial interests, was a boon to Russia.

Russia was ably represented in the Paris congress (February 25–April 14) by the experienced extraordinary ambassador and privy councillor Count Alexei F. Orlov and the career diplomat and envoy to London, Filip Brunov. They were joined at the table by some of the key statesmen in the diplomatic preliminaries of the war from Turkey,

England, France, and Austria, as well as Camilio Cavour of Piedmont-Sardinia. Russia's chief concession was to remove its naval presence from the Black Sea, but they worked out the details of its neutralization directly with the Turks, not their British allies. The affirmation of the 1841 Convention, which closed the Turkish Straits to warships in peacetime, was actually more advantageous to Russia, which lacked a fleet on one side, than to Britain, which had one on the other. Russia's sole territorial loss was the retrocession of the southern part of Bessarabia to Ottoman Moldavia, the purpose of which was to secure the Russian withdrawal from the Danubian Delta.

In addition, the Russians agreed to the demilitarization of the land Islands in the Baltic, a provision that held until World War I. The Holy Places dispute, the diplomatic scrape which had led directly to the war preliminaries, was settled on the basis of the compromise effected in Istanbul in April 1853 by the three extraordinary ambassadors, Alexander Menshikov, Edmond de la Cour, and Stratford (Canning) de Redcliffe, before Russia's diplomatic rupture with Turkey. The Peace Treaty was signed on March 20, 1856.

The British at first did not treat the Russians as complying and kept some forces in the Black Sea. However, the 1857 India Mutiny, due in part to Russian-supported Persian pressure on Afghanistan, led to British withdrawal and facilitated the unimpeded success of Russia's long-standing campaign to gain full control of the Caucasus.

As some contemporary observers noted, adherence to the naval and strategic provisions of the treaty depended upon Russian weakness and coalition resolve. During the Franco-German war of 1870–1871, Alexander Gorchakov announced that Russia would no longer adhere to the "Black Sea Clauses" mandating demilitarization, and a London conference accepted this change. During the Turkish War of 1877–1878, Russia re-annexed Southern Bessarabia to the chagrin of its Romanian allies.

*See also:* CRIMEAN WAR; NICHOLAS I; SEVASTOPOL

## BIBLIOGRAPHY

Baumgart, Winfried. (1981). *The Peace of Paris, 1856: Studies in War, Diplomacy, and Peacemaking.* Santa Barbara, CA: ABC-CLIO.

Mosse, Werner. (1963). *The Rise and Fall of the Crimean System, 1855-71: The Story of a Peace Settlement.* London: The English Universities Press.

DAVID M. GOLDFRANK

## PARIS, FIRST AND SECOND TREATIES OF

After the disastrous military campaigns of 1813 marked in particular by the severe defeat of Leipzig, Napoleon's political and military power was on the decline. The emperor was unable to avoid the entry of the Allied powers in Paris on March 31, 1814, and was forced to abdicate in April 1814. On May 30, 1814, following the restoration of Louis XVIII, Charles Maurice de Talleyrand, the plenipotentiary of the new king, signed the first Treaty of Paris with representatives of King George III of England; of François I, emperor of Austria; of King Frederic-William III of Prussia; and of Tsar Alexander I. This treaty, which put an end to the war between France and the Fourth Coalition and to the French hegemony in Europe, covered both territorial and geopolitical matters.

France retained its boundaries of January 1, 1792. Thus it was allowed to keep Avignon and the Comtat-Venaissin, a large part of Savoy, Montbeliard, and Mulhouse, but had to surrender Belgium and the left bank of Rhine as well as territories annexed in Italy, Germany, Holland, and Switzerland. No indemnity was requested, and England gave back all the French colonies except for Malta, Tobago, St. Lucia in the Antilles, and the Isle of France in the Indian Ocean. In addition, the Allied powers had to withdraw from French territory. Last, the treaty included secret clauses that ceded the territory of Venetia to Austria and the port of Genoa to the Kingdom of Sardinia.

On the political level, the treaty called for a general congress to be held at Vienna to settle all questions about boundaries and sovereignty and to confirm the decisions taken by the Allied powers: Switzerland was to be independent, Holland was to be united under the House of Orange, Germany was to become a federation of independent states, and Italy was to be composed of sovereign states.

The relative leniency of the treaty was largely due to the diplomatic ability of Talleyrand; yet, despite its moderation, the document was badly received by the French public opinion and it contributed to the discredit of the Bourbons.

At the time the treaty was signed, Napoleon I was prisoner on the island of Elba and separated from his family. He escaped from the island and landed on March 1, 1815, at Golfe Juan with nine hundred faithful soldiers. He tried to take advantage of his strong popularity to drive Louis XVIII off the throne and restore his own personal power.

But that attempt lasted only one hundred days and collapsed with the catastrophic defeat at Waterloo on June 18, 1815. Napoleon had to abdicate again and was sent to the island of Sainte-Hélène, where he died on May 5, 1821.

Following this final abdication, a new treaty was signed in Paris on November 20, 1815. It was much tougher than the previous one; the cost of the one hundred days was high. France was confined to its former boundaries of 1790. It was authorized to keep Avignon and the Comtat-Venaissin, Montbéliard and Mulhouse, but lost the duchy of Bouillon and the German fortresses of Philippeville and Marienbourg given to the Netherlands, Sarrelouis and Sarrebruck attributed to Prussia, Landau given to Bavaria, the area of Gex attached to Switzerland, and a large part of Savoy given to the king of Piedmont. Regarding the colonies, the loss of Malta, St. Lucia, Tobago, and of the Isle of France was confirmed. A financial cost was added to this territorial cost: the French state had to pay an indemnity of 700 million francs and to undergo in its northeast frontier areas a military occupation. This occupation was limited to five years and 150,000 men but had to be paid by the French budget.

Despite its severity, the second Treaty of Paris was faithfully respected by King Louis XVIII; this respect allowed France to get rid of the foreign occupation as early as 1818—two years earlier than expected—and to play again at that date a significant role in the international relations.

*See also:* ALEXANDER I; FRANCE, RELATIONS WITH; NAPOLEAN I

MARIE-PIERRE REY

## PARTY CONGRESSES AND CONFERENCES

Party congresses, the nominal policy-setting conclaves of the Communist Party of the Soviet Union, were held at intervals ranging from one to five years, and extended from the First, in 1898, to the last, the Twenty-Eighth, in 1990. Made up since the 1920s of two- to five thousand delegates from the party's local organizations, party congresses were formally empowered to elect the Central Committee, to determine party rules, and to enact resolutions that laid down the party's basic programmatic guidelines. Party conferences, from the

**Table 1.**

## Communist Party Congresses and Conferences

| Number | | Date | Locale | Delegates (Voting) | (Non-voting) |
|---|---|---|---|---|---|
| 1st | Congress | March 1898 | Minsk | 9 | |
| 2nd | Congress | July 1903 | Brussels and London | 43 | 14 |
| 3rd | Congress | April 1905 | London | 24 | 14 |
| 1st | Conference | December 1905 | Tammerfors | 41 | |
| 4th | Congress | April 1906 | Stockholm | 112 | 22 |
| 2nd | Conference | November 1906 | Tammerfors | 32 | ca. 15 |
| 5th | Congress | May–June 1907 | London | 336 | |
| 3rd | Conference | July (August) 1907 | Kotka (Finland) | 26 | |
| 4th | Conference | November 1907 | Helsingfors | 27 | |
| 5th | Conference | January 1909 | Paris | 16 | 2 |
| 6th | Conference | January 1912 | Prague | 12 | 4 |
| "March Conference" | | March 1917 | Petrograd | ca. 120 | |
| 7th | Conference | April 1917 | Petrograd | 133 | 18 |
| 6th | Congress | August 1917 | Petrograd | 157 | 110 |
| 7th | Congress | March 1918 | Moscow | 47 | 59 |
| 8th | Congress | March 1919 | Moscow | ca. 300 | ? |
| 8th | Conference | December 1919 | Moscow | 45 | 73 |
| 9th | Congress | March 1920 | Moscow | 554 | 162 |
| 9th | Conference | September 1920 | Moscow | 116 | 125 |
| 10th | Congress | March 1921 | Moscow | ca. 700 | ca. 300 |
| 10th | Conference | May 1921 | Moscow | ? | |
| 11th | Conference | December 1921 | Moscow | 125 | 116 |
| 11th | Congress | March–April 1922 | Moscow | 520 | 154 |
| 12th | Conference | August 1922 | Moscow | 129 | 92 |
| 12th | Congress | April 1923 | Moscow | 408 | 417 |
| 13th | Conference | January 1924 | Moscow | 128 | 222 |
| 13th | Congress | May 1924 | Moscow | 748 | 416 |
| 14th | Conference | April 1925 | Moscow | 178 | 392 |
| 14th | Congress | December 1925 | Moscow | 665 | 641 |
| 15th | Conference | October–November 1925 | Moscow | 194 | 640 |
| 15th | Congress | December 1927 | Moscow | 898 | 771 |
| 16th | Conference | April 1929 | Moscow | 254 | 679 |
| 16th | Congress | June–July 1930 | Moscow | 1268 | 891 |
| 17th | Conference | January–February 1932 | Moscow | 386 | 525 |
| 17th | Congress | January–February 1934 | Moscow | 1225 | 736 |
| 18th | Congress | March 1939 | Moscow | 1569 | 466 |
| 18th | Conference | February 1941 | Moscow | 456 | 138 |
| 19th | Congress | October 1952 | Moscow | 1192 | 167 |
| 20th | Congress | February 1956 | Moscow | 1349 | 81 |
| 21st | "Extraordinary" Congress | January–February 1959 | Moscow | 1269 | 106 |
| 22nd | Congress | October 1961 | Moscow | 4408 | 405 |
| 23rd | Congress | March–April 1966 | Moscow | 4620 | 323 |
| 24th | Congress | March–April 1971 | Moscow | 4740 | 223 |
| 25th | Congress | February–March 1976 | Moscow | 4998 | non-voting |
| 26th | Congress | February–March 1981 | Moscow | 4994 | non-voting |
| 27th | Congress | February–March 1986 | Moscow | ca. 5000 | non-voting |
| 19th | Conference | June 1988 | Moscow | 4976 | non-voting |
| 28th | Congress | July 1990 | Moscow | 4863 | non-voting |

SOURCE: Courtesy of the author.

first in 1905 to the nineteenth in 1988, were smaller and less authoritative gatherings, usually held midway in the interval between congresses. Like the congresses, they issued policy declarations in the form of resolutions, but did not conduct elections to the top party leadership.

Before the Revolution of 1917 and for the first few years thereafter, party congresses and con-ferences were marked by lively debate. The tran-scripts of those proceedings, published at the time and republished during the 1930s, are important sources concerning the problems the country faced and the viewpoints of the various party leaders and factions. With the ascendancy of Josef Stalin, however, party congresses and conferences became creatures of the central party leadership. As described by the concept of the circular flow of power, local officials who were de facto appointed by the center handpicked their delegations to the national congress, which in turn endorsed the makeup of the Central Committee and the central leadership itself, thus closing the circle.

## PREREVOLUTIONARY PARTY CONGRESSES AND CONFERENCES

The meeting that is traditionally considered the First Party Congress was an ephemeral gathering in Minsk in March 1898 of nine Marxist undergrounders who managed to proclaim the establishment of the Russian Social Democratic Workers Party (RSDWP) before they were arrested by the tsarist police. Before the Revolution, there were four more congresses and numerous conferences, distinguished by struggles between the Bolshevik and Menshevik wings of the party that led up to their ultimate split. The Second Party Congress, convened in Brussels in July 1903 with fifty-seven participants but forced to move its proceedings to London under threat of arrest, was the first true congress of the RSDWP. It saw the outbreak of the Bolshevik-Menshevik schism when Vladimir Lenin tried to impose his definition of party membership as a core of professional revolutionaries rather than the broad democratic constituency favored by the Menshevik leader Yuly Martov.

The next congress, later counted by the Communists as the Third, was an all-Bolshevik meeting in London in April 1905, with just twenty-four voting delegates plus invited guests. The First Party Conference (as counted by the communists) was a gathering in December 1905 of forty Bolsheviks and a lone Menshevik in the city of Tammerfors (Tampere) in Russian-ruled Finland. They endorsed reunification with the Mensheviks and supported boycotting the tsar's new Duma (over Lenin's objections). At this meeting, Stalin made his initial appearance at the national level and first met Lenin face-to-face.

Following the abortive revolutionary events of 1905, the Bolsheviks and Mensheviks came together in Stockholm in April 1906 for the Fourth Party Congress (by the Bolshevik enumeration), styled the Unification Congress, with a Menshevik majority among the 112 voting delegates. The two factions met together again in London in April and May 1907; this Fifth Party Congress was the last embracing both wings, and the last before the Revolution.

Small meetings later considered by the Bolsheviks as their Second through Fifth Party Conferences were held between 1906 and 1909, mostly in Finland, with Bolshevik, Menshevik, and other Social-Democratic groups represented. These gatherings continued to revolve around the questions of party unity and parliamentary tactics.

In 1912, going their separate ways, the Bolsheviks and Mensheviks held separate party conferences. Twelve Bolsheviks plus four nonvoting delegates (including Lenin) met in Prague in January of that year for what they counted as the Sixth Party Conference. Excluding not only the Mensheviks but also the Left Bolsheviks denounced by Lenin after the Fifth Party Conference in 1909, this gathering established an organizational structure of Lenin's loyalists (including Grigory Zinoviev), to whom Stalin was added soon afterwards as a co-opted member of the Central Committee. The Sixth Party Conference was the real beginning of the Bolshevik Party as an independent entity under Lenin's strict control.

## FROM THE REVOLUTION TO WORLD WAR II

Shortly after the fall of the tsarist regime in the February Revolution of 1917 (March, New Style), but before Lenin's return to Russia, the Bolsheviks convened an All-Russian Meeting of Party Workers of some 120 delegates. Contrary to the stand Lenin was shortly to take, this March Conference, of which Stalin was one of the leaders, leaned toward cooperation with the new Provisional Government and reunification with the Mensheviks. For this reason, the March Conference was expunged from official communist history and was never counted in the numbering.

A few weeks later the Bolsheviks met more formally in Petrograd, with 133 voting delegates and eighteen nonvoting, for what was officially recorded as the Seventh or April Party Conference. On this occasion, by a bare majority, Lenin persuaded the party to reject the Provisional Government and to oppose continued Russian participation in World War I. Unlike postrevolutionary party conferences, the Seventh elected a new Central Committee, with nine members, including Lev Kamenev and Yakov Sverdlov along with Lenin, Zinoviev, and Stalin.

The Sixth Party Congress, all-Bolshevik, with 157 voting delegates and 110 nonvoting, was held in the Vyborg working-class district of Petrograd in August 1917 under semi-clandestine conditions, after the Provisional Government tried to suppress the Bolsheviks following the abortive uprising of the July Days. Lenin and other leaders were in hiding or in jail at the time, and Stalin and Sverdlov were in charge. The congress welcomed Leon Trotsky and other left-wing Mensheviks into the Bolshevik Party, and Trotsky was included in the expanded Central Committee of twenty-one. However, the gathering could hardly keep up with events; it made no plans directed toward the Bolshevik seizure of power that came soon afterwards.

Four congresses followed the Bolshevik takeover in quick succession, all facing emergency circumstances of civil war and economic collapse. The Seventh, dubbed "special," was convened in Moscow in March 1918, with only forty-seven voting delegates, to approve the Treaty of Brest-Litovsk ending hostilities with Germany and its allies. Lenin delivered a political report of the Central Committee, a function thereafter distinguishing the party's chief, while Nikolai Bukharin submitted a minority report for the Left Communists against the treaty (a gesture last allowed in 1925). After bitter debate between the Leninists and the Left, the treaty was approved, and Russia left the war. However, Bukharin was included in the new Central Committee of fifteen members. The Seventh Party Congress also formally changed the party's name from Russian Social-Democratic Party (of Bolsheviks) to Russian Communist Party (of Bolsheviks). All subsequent party congresses continued to be held in Moscow.

The Eighth Party Congress met in March 1919 at the height of the civil war, with around three hundred voting delegates. It adopted a new revolutionary party program, approved the creation of the Politburo, Orgburo, and Secretariat, and saw its Leninist majority beat down opposition from the Left, who opposed the trend toward top-down authority in both military and political matters. The first postrevolutionary party conference, the Eighth, was held in Moscow (like all subsequent ones) in December 1919. It updated the party's rules and heard continued complaints about centralism in government.

Three months later, at the Ninth Party Congress in March 1920, Lenin and Trotsky and their supporters again had to fight off the anti-centralizers of the Left on both political and economic issues. Such protest was carried much farther at the Ninth Party Conference, which met in September 1920.

The "Group of Democratic Centralists" denounced bureaucratic centralism and won a sweeping endorsement of democracy and decentralism, unfortunately undercut by their acquiescence with respect to organizational efficiency and a new control commission.

This spirit of reform was soon smothered at the Tenth Party Congress, meeting in March 1921 with approximately seven hundred voting delegates. After some three hundred of its participants were dispatched to Petrograd to help suppress the Kronstadt Revolt, the congress voted in several crucial resolutions over the futile opposition of the small left-wing minority. It condemned the "syndicalist and anarchist deviation" of the Workers' Opposition, banned organized factions within the party in the name of unity, and supported the tax in kind, Lenin's first step in introducing the New Economic Policy. The Central Committee was expanded to twenty-five, but Trotsky's key supporters were dropped from this body as well as from the Politburo, Orgburo, and Secretariat.

Party congresses and conferences during the 1920s marked the transformation from a contentious, policy-setting gathering to an orchestrated phalanx of disciplined yes-men. This progression took place as Stalin perfected the circular flow of power through the party apparatus, guaranteeing his control of congress and conference proceedings. The Eleventh Party Congress, which met in March and April 1922, was the last with Lenin's participation. It focused on consolidating party discipline and strengthening the new Central Control Commission to keep deviators in line. Immediately after the Eleventh Party Congress, the Central Committee designated Stalin to fill the new office of General Secretary.

The Twelfth Party Congress took place in April 1923 during the interregnum between Lenin's incapacitation in December 1922 and his death in January 1924. Trotsky, Stalin, and Zinoviev were all jockeying for advantage in the anticipated struggle to succeed the party's ailing leader. Debate revolved particularly around questions of industrial development and policy toward the minority nationalities, while Stalin maneuvered to cover up Lenin's break with him and pack the Central Committee (expanded from twenty-seven to forty) with his own supporters.

The Tenth and Eleventh Party Conferences in 1921 and the Twelfth in 1922 were routine affairs, but the Thirteenth proved to be a decisive milestone.

At this gathering just before Lenin's death, the left opposition faction supporting Trotsky was condemned as a petty-bourgeois deviation. Stalin demonstrated his mastery of the circular flow of power by allowing only three oppositionists among the voting delegates.

By the time of the Thirteenth Party Congress in May 1924, the Soviet political atmosphere had changed even more. Lenin was dead; the triumvirate of Stalin, Zinoviev, and Kamenev was trumpeting the need for discipline and unity; and opposition had been virtually outlawed. Stalin's party apparatus had ensured that among the 748 voting delegates there was not a single voice to represent the opposition, and Trotsky, merely one of the 416 nonvoting delegates, temporarily recanted his criticisms of the party. The Central Committee was expanded again, to fifty-two, to make room for even more Stalin loyalists, especially from the regional apparatus.

The Fourteenth Party Conference, held in April 1925, endorsed Stalin's theory of socialism in one country and condemned Trotsky's theory of permanent revolution. It marked the high point of the New Economic Policy (NEP) by way of liberalizing policy toward the peasants. However, this emphasis contributed to growing tension between the Stalin-Bukharin group of party leaders and the Zinoviev-Kamenev group.

At the Fourteenth Party Congress in December 1925 these two groups split openly. The so-called Leningrad Opposition, led by Zinoviev and Kamenev and backed by Lenin's widow Nadezhda Krupskaya, rebelled against Stalin's domination of the party and took with them the sixty-two Leningrad delegates. Kamenev openly challenged Stalin's suitability as party leader, but the opposition was soundly defeated by the well-disciplined majority. The NEP, especially as articulated by Bukharin, was for the time being reaffirmed, although subsequent Stalinist history represented the Fourteenth Congress as the beginning of the new industrialization drive. The Central Committee was expanded again, to sixty-three.

Acrimony between the majority and the newly allied Zinovievists and Trotskyists was even sharper at the Fifteenth Party Conference of October–November 1926. Kamenev now denounced Stalin's theory of socialism in one country as a falsification of Lenin's views. Nevertheless, the opposition was unanimously condemned as a "Social-Democratic" (i.e., Menshevik) deviation.

When the Fifteenth Party Congress met in December 1927, the left opposition leaders Trotsky, Zinoviev, and Kamenev had been dropped from the party's leadership bodies, and Trotsky had been expelled from the party altogether. At the congress itself, the opposition was condemned and its followers were expelled from the party as well. At the same time, the congress adopted resolutions on a five-year plan and on the peasantry that subsequently served as legitimation for Stalin's industrialization and collectivization drives. Eight more members were added to the Central Committee, not counting replacements for the condemned oppositionists, bringing the total to seventy-one (a figure that held until 1952).

By the time of the Sixteenth Party Conference in April 1929, the Soviet political scene had changed sharply again. Stalin had defeated the Right Opposition led by Bukharin, government chairman Alexei Rykov, and trade-union chief Mikhail Tomsky, and was initiating his five-year plans and forced collectivization. The main task of the conference was to legitimize the First Five-Year Plan (already approved by the Central Committee), backdating its inception to the beginning of the annual economic plan that had already been in force since October 1928. A new party purge, in the older sense of weeding out undesirables from the membership, was also authorized by the conference.

The Sixteenth Party Congress, held in June and July 1930, could hardly keep up with events. Bukharin, Rykov, and Tomsky had been condemned and had recanted, although the congress allowed them to keep their Central Committee seats for the time being. The congress unanimously acclaimed the program of the Stalin Revolution in industry and agriculture. The industrialization theme was echoed by the Seventeenth Party Conference of January–February 1932; it approved the formulation of the Second Five-Year Plan, to commence in January 1933 (even though by that time the First Five-Year Plan would have been formally in effect for only three years and eight months).

When the Seventeenth Party Congress convened in January–February 1934, collectivization had been substantially accomplished despite the catastrophic though unacknowledged famine in the Ukraine and the southern regions of the Russian Republic. Following the accelerated termination of the First Five-Year Plan, the Second had begun. The congress was dubbed "the Congress of Victors," while Stalin addressed the body to reject the philosophy of egalitarianism and emphasize the authority of individual managers and party leaders. Yet there was surreptitious opposition over the harshness of Stalin's program, and behind-the-scenes talk of replacing him with Leningrad party secretary Sergei Kirov. In the end, nearly three hundred delegates out of 1,225 voted against Stalin in the slate of candidates for the Central Committee. Stalin got his revenge in the purges of 1936 through 1938, when the party apparatus was decimated and more than half of the people who had been congress delegates in 1934 were arrested and executed.

The Eighteenth Party Congress came only after a lapse of over five years, in March 1939. An almost entirely new Central Committee was installed, Nikita Khrushchev achieved membership in the Politburo, and the Third Five-Year Plan was belatedly approved. Stalin further revised Marxist ideology by emphasizing the historical role of the state and the new intelligentsia. A follow-up party conference, the Eighteenth, was held in February 1941; it endorsed measures of industrial discipline, but was mainly significant for the emergence of Georgy Malenkov into the top leadership. The institution of the party conference then fell into abeyance, until Mikhail Gorbachev revived it in 1988.

### FROM WORLD WAR II TO THE
### COLLAPSE OF COMMUNIST PARTY RULE

After the Eighteenth Party Congress, none was held for thirteen years, during the time of war and postwar recovery. When the Nineteenth Party Congress finally convened in October 1952, the question of succession to the aging Stalin was already impending. Stalin implicitly anointed Malenkov as his replacement by designating him to deliver the political report of the Central Committee. At the same time, the party's leading organs were overhauled: the Politburo was renamed the Party Presidium, with an expanded membership of twenty-five (including Leonid Brezhnev), and the Orgburo was dissolved. The congress also officially changed the party's name from All-Union Communist Party (of Bolsheviks) to Communist Party of the Soviet Union.

By the time of the Twentieth Party Congress, convened in February 1956, Stalin was dead, Khrushchev had prevailed in the contest to succeed him, and the Thaw, the abatement of Stalinist terror, was underway. Nevertheless, Khrushchev proceeded to astound the party and ultimately the world with his Secret Speech to the congress, de-

nouncing Stalin's purges and the cult of personality. To this, he added a call, in his open report to the congress, for peaceful coexistence with the noncommunist world. The congress also established a special bureau of the Central Committee to superintend the business of the party in the Russian Republic, which, unlike the other union republics, had no distinct Communist Party organization of its own.

In January–February 1959 Khrushchev convened the Extraordinary Twenty-First Party Congress, mainly for the purpose of endorsing his new seven-year economic plan in lieu of the suspended Sixth Five-Year Plan. As an extraordinary assembly, the congress did not conduct any elections to renew the leadership.

At the Twenty-Second Party Congress of October 1961, with its numbers vastly increased to 4,408 voting and 405 nonvoting delegates, Khrushchev introduced more sensations. Along with renewed denunciation of the Anti-Party Group that had tried to depose Khrushchev in 1957, and condemnation of the ideological errors of communist China, the congress approved the removal of Stalin's body from the Lenin mausoleum on Red Square. The congress also issued a new party program, the first to be formally adopted since 1919, with emphasis on Khrushchev's notions of egalitarianism and of overtaking capitalism economically.

Four party congresses were held under Leonid Brezhnev's leadership, all routine affairs with little change in the aging party leadership. The Twenty-Third Party Congress in March–April 1966 emphasized political stabilization. It reversed Khrushchev's innovations by changing the name of the party presidium back to Politburo and by abolishing the party bureau for the Russian Republic, but took no new initiatives regarding either Stalinism or the economy. The Twenty-Fourth Party Congress convened in March–April 1971, a year later than originally planned; further economic growth was stressed, but the issue of decentralist reforms was straddled. The Twenty-Fifth Party Congress in February–March 1976 was distinguished only by more blatant glorification of General Secretary Brezhnev, as the 4,998 delegates (no nonvoting delegates from this time on) heard him stress tighter administrative and ideological controls in the service of further economic growth. Continuity still marked the Twenty-Sixth Party Congress in February–March 1981: Brezhnev was in his dotage and his entourage was dying off, and economic inefficiency and inertia, especially in agriculture, remained at the center of attention. The years spanned by the Twenty-Third through the Twenty-Sixth Congresses were aptly known afterwards as the era of stagnation.

With the Twenty-Seventh Party Congress, attended by approximately five thousand delegates in February–March 1986, the dissolution of the Communist Party dictatorship in the Soviet Union had begun. Gorbachev had taken over as General Secretary after Brezhnev's death and the brief administrations of Yury Andropov and Konstantin Chernenko, and had undertaken a sweeping renovation of the aging leadership. At the congress itself, more than three-fourths of the delegates were participating for the first time, and the new Central Committee elected by the congress had more new members than any since 1961. Gorbachev's main themes of socialist self-government and acceleration in the economy were dutifully echoed by the congress, without intimating the extent of changes soon to come.

An even more significant meeting was Gorbachev's convocation in June 1988 of the Nineteenth Party Conference, the first one since 1941, and a far larger gathering than under the old practice, with 4,976 delegates. Faced with growing opposition by conservatives in the party organization, Gorbachev could not rely on the circular flow of power, but had to campaign for the election of pro-reform delegates—without much success. He had hoped to give the conference the authority of a party congress to shake up the Central Committee, but had to defer this step. Nevertheless, as Gorbachev himself noted, debate at the conference was more frank than anything heard since the 1920s. The outcome was endorsement of sweeping constitutional changes that shifted real power from the party organization to the government, with a strong president (Gorbachev himself) and the elected Congress of People's Deputies.

In July 1990, as Gorbachev's reform program was peaking, the Twenty-Eighth Party Congress convened with 4,863 delegates. It proved to be the last party congress before the collapse of Communist rule and the breakup of the Soviet Union. In the freer political space allowed by Gorbachev's steps toward democratization, including surrender of the party's political monopoly, the party had broken into factions: the conservatives led by Party Second Secretary Yegor Ligachev, the radical re-

formers led by the deposed Moscow Party Secretary Boris Yeltsin, and the center around Gorbachev. At the congress, the conservatives submitted to Gorbachev in the spirit of party discipline, but Yeltsin demonstratively walked out and quit the party. Nonetheless, calling for a new civil society in place of Stalinism, Gorbachev presided over the most open, no-holds-barred debate since the communists took power in 1917. He radically shook up the Communist Party leadership, restaffed the Politburo as a group of union republic leaders, and terminated party control of governmental and managerial appointments maintained under the old "nomenklatura" system. For the first time, congress resolutions were confined to the internal organizational business of the party, and steered clear of national political issues. Barely more than a year later, in August 1991, the conservatives' attempted *coup d'état* against Gorbachev discredited what was left of Communist Party authority and set the stage for the demise of the Soviet Union.

*See also:* BOLSHEVISM; BREZHNEV, LEONID ILICH; COMMUNIST PARTY OF THE SOVIET UNION; FIVE-YEAR PLANS; GORBACHEV, MIKHAIL SERGEYEVICH; KAMENEV, LEV BORISOVICH; KHRUSHCHEV, NIKITA SERGEYEVICH; LENIN, VLADIMIR ILICH; MENSHEVIKS; STALIN, JOSEF VISSARIONOVICH; TROTSKY, LEON; ZINOVIEV, GRIGORY YEVSEYEVICH

**BIBLIOGRAPHY**

Armstrong, John A. (1961). *The Politics of Totalitarianism: The Communist Party of the Soviet Union from 1934 to the Present.* New York: Random House.

Brown, Archie. (1996). *The Gorbachev Factor.* Oxford: Oxford University Press.

*Current Soviet Policies: The Documentary Record of the Communist Party,* eds. Leo Gruliow et al. 11 vols. Columbus, OH: Current Digest of the Soviet Press.

Dan, Fyodor. (1964). *The Origins of Bolshevism.* New York: Harper and Row.

Daniels, Robert V. (1960, 1988). *The Conscience of the Revolution: Communist Opposition in Soviet Russia.* Cambridge, MA: Harvard University Press, and Boulder, CO: Westview.

Daniels, Robert V. (1966). "Stalin's Rise to Dictatorship." In *Politics in the Soviet Union: Seven Cases,* eds. Alexander Dallin and Alan F. Westin. New York: Harcourt, Brace, and World.

Daniels, Robert V. (1993). *The End of the Communist Revolution.* London: Routledge.

Keep, John H. L. (1963). *The Rise of Social Democracy in Russia.* Oxford: Clarendon.

Mawdsley, Evan, and White, Stephan. (2000). *The Soviet Elite from Lenin to Gorbachev: The Central Committee and its Members, 1917–1991.* Oxford: Oxford University Press.

McNeal, Robert H., ed. (1974). *Resolutions and Decisions of the Communist Party of the Soviet Union.* 4 vols. Toronto: University of Toronto Press.

Meissner, Boris. (1975). *The Communist Party of the Soviet Union: Party Leadership, Organization, and Ideology.* Westport, CT: Greenwood.

Ponomaryov, Boris N., et al. (1960). *History of the Communist Party of the Soviet Union.* Moscow: Foreign Languages Publishing House.

Rigby, T. H. (1990). *The Changing Soviet System: Mono-Organizational Society from Its Origins to Gorbachev's Restructuring.* Aldershot, UK: E. Elgar.

Schapiro, Leonard B. (1960). *The Communist Party of the Soviet Union.* New York: Random House.

Schapiro, Leonard B. (1977). *Origin of the Communist Autocracy: Political Opposition in the Soviet State, First Phase, 1917–1922,* 2nd ed. Cambridge, MA: Harvard University Press.

Stalin, Joseph V. (1947). *Problems of Leninism.* Moscow: Foreign Languages Publishing House.

ROBERT V. DANIELS

# PARTY OF RUSSIAN UNITY AND ACCORD

The Party of Russian Unity and Accord (Partiya Rossiyskogo Yedinstva i Soglasiya, or PRES) was founded for the 1993 elections as a regional variant of the ruling party. Its founder, a visible politician of the early Boris Yeltsin period, deputy prime minister Sergei Shakhrai, was at the time the head of the State Committee on Federal and Nationalist Issues, whose apparatus was used in the provinces as a base for party construction. Even the constituent assembly of the PRES in October 1993 took place not in Moscow but in Novgorod. The party proclaimed as its goal the preservation of Russia's unity through securing equal rights of the subjects of the Russian Federation. The PRES list at the 1993 elections was headed by Shakhrai; Alexander Shokhin, deputy prime minister and an economist; and Konstantin Zatulin, chair of the association Entrepreneurs for a New Russia. Two federal ministers were included on it as well: Yuri Kalmykov and Gennady Melikian, and also the future public figures Valery Kirpichnikov (minister of regional politics in 1998–1999), Vladimir Tumanov (chair of the Constitutional Court in 1995–1996), and

others. The list received 3.6 million votes (6.7%, seventh place), mainly in the national republics, and eighteen mandates; four PRES candidates in single-mandate districts were elected. The PRES fraction started out with thirty Duma delegates and ended with twelve, due to disagreement over the Chechnya question as well as interfractional maneuvering. During the 1995 campaign, PRES first joined with Our Home Is Russia (NDR), but then made its own list with Shakhrai at the head and registered twenty-three candidates in the districts. However, Shakhrai's political stardom was already on the decline, and when he left the State Committee on Federal and Nationalist Issues, he lost his base in the provinces. The list received 246,000 votes (0.4%), and in the majority districts only Shakhrai won, joining with the group Russian Regions. In the 1999 elections, the PRES did not participate independently. Shakhrai, joining with Yuri Luzhkov, was included in the original version of the Fatherland—All Russia (OVR) list, but excluded at the bloc's congress. In May 2000 the PRES merged into Unity when the latter was restructured from a movement into a party.

*See also:* SHAKHRAI, SERGEI MIKHAILOVICH; UNITY (MEDVED) PARTY

**BIBLIOGRAPHY**

McFaul, Michael. (2001). *Russia's Unfinished Revolution: Political Change from Gorbachev to Putin.* Ithaca, NY: Cornell University.

McFaul, Michael, and Markov, Sergei. (1993). *The Troubled Birth of Russian Democracy: Parties, Personalities, and Programs.* Stanford, CA: Hoover Institution Press.

Reddaway, Peter, and Glinski, Dmitri. (2001). *The Tragedy of Russia's Reforms: Market Bolshevism Against Democracy.* Washington, DC: U.S. Institute of Peace Press.

NIKOLAI PETROV

# PASSPORT SYSTEM

For the first time since the revolution, the Soviet regime introduced an internal passport system in December 1932. Most rural residents were not given passports, and peasants acquired the automatic right to a passport only during the 1970s. The OGPU/NKVD (Soviet military intelligence service and secret police), which administered the passport system, initially issued these documents to persons over sixteen years of age who lived in towns, workers' settlements, state farms, and construction sites. They were required to obtain and register their passport with the police, who would then issue the necessary residence permit.

People who did not qualify for a passport were evicted from their apartments and denied the right to live and work within city limits. The categories of people who were denied a passport and urban residence permit included: the disenfranchised, kulaks or the dekulakized, all persons with a criminal record, persons not engaged in socially useful work, and family members of the aforementioned categories. The stated purpose of the new passport system was to relieve the urban population of persons not engaged in socially useful labor, as well as hidden kulak, criminal, and other antisocietal elements.

Some scholars note that the passport law emerged in response to the massive urban migration that followed the 1932 famine. The resulting movement of peasants from the countryside into the cities strained the urban rationing and supply systems. The selective distribution of passports offered a solution to this crisis by restricting urban residency and limiting access to city services and goods. Other scholars emphasize that the passport system was established to manage the urban population. Passports emerged as an instrument of repression and police control. By issuing passports, the state could more precisely identify, order, and purge the urban population. Nonetheless, scholars agree that the system of internal passports and urban residence permits sought to remove unreliable elements from strategic cities, limit the flow of people into these cities, and relieve the pressure on the urban rationing and supply systems.

Passports categorized the Soviet population into distinct groups with varying rights and privileges. The internal passport recorded citizens' social position or class, occupation, nationality, age, sex, and place of residence. The identity fixed on a person's passport determined where that individual could work, travel, and live. Only those with certain social, ethnic, and occupational identities were allowed residency in privileged cities, industrial sites, and strategic border and military areas. The passport also tied individuals to geographic areas and restricted their movements.

In the process of assigning passports, Soviet police removed dangerous, marginal, and anti-Soviet elements from the major cities. Many people fled the cities as passports were being introduced, fearful that they would arrested by the police as socially harmful elements. Passportization operations were also used to purge the western borderlands of Polish, German, Finnish, and other anti-Soviet groups.

In the initial phases, the internal passport and urban registration system often functioned in an irregular and erratic manner. Many people circumvented the system by forging passports, and others lived in towns without a valid passport.

*See also:* FAMINE OF 1932-1933; KULAKS; MIGRATION; STATE SECURITY, ORGANS OF

## BIBLIOGRAPHY

Alexopoulos, Golfo. (1998). "Portrait of a Con Artist as a Soviet Man." *Slavic Review* 57:774–790.

Fitzpatrick, Sheila. (1994). *Stalin's Peasants*. New York: Oxford University Press.

Fitzpatrick, Sheila. (1999). *Everyday Stalinism*. New York: Oxford University Press.

Kessler, Gijs. (2001). "The Passport System and State Control over Population Flows in the Soviet Union, 1932–1940." *Cahiers du monde Russe* 42:477–504.

GOLFO ALEXOPOULOS

## PASTERNAK, BORIS LEONIDOVICH

(1890–1960), poet, writer, translator.

Boris Leonidovich Pasternak was the most prominent figure of his literary generation, a great poet deeply connected with his age. His work unfolded during a period of fundamental changes in Russian cultural, social, and political history. It is therefore no wonder that many of his works, and most notably his novel, *Doctor Zhivago*, are imbued with the spirit of history and relate its effect on the lives, thoughts, and preoccupations of his contemporaries. In 1958 he was awarded the Nobel Prize for his achievements in lyrical poetry and the great Russian epic tradition.

Pasternak was born in Moscow into a highly cultured Jewish family. His father, Leonid Pasternak, was a well-known impressionist painter and professor at the Moscow School of Painting; his mother was an accomplished pianist. During his formative years, Pasternak studied music and philosophy but abandoned them for literature. At the beginning of his literary career, he was associated with the artistic avant-garde, and his modern sensibility was strongly expressed in his first two volumes of poetry, *Twin in the Clouds* (1914) and *Above the Barriers* (1916), and in his early experiments in fiction (1911–1913). Most of Pasternak's works written between 1911 and 1931 explore possibilities far beyond realism and are characterized by dazzling metaphorical imagery and complex syntax reminiscent of Cubo-Futurist poetry, associated especially with Vladimir Mayakovsky. Pasternak's cycle, *My Sister-Life*, published in 1922, is recognized as his most outstanding poetic achievement.

Pasternak's initial support of the Bolshevik Revolution of 1917 vanished when the new regime revealed its authoritarian and ruthless features. Like many other Soviet writers during the 1920s, Pasternak felt pressured by the authorities, who were in the process of establishing control over literature, to portray the revolutionary age in epic form. Despite his contempt for the party's promotion of the epic, and his disappointment over the decline of lyrical poetry, Pasternak realized that, in order to survive as a poet, he had to adjust to the new cultural-political climate and try the epic genre. During the course of the 1920s, therefore, Pasternak wrote four epics: *Sublime Malady* (1924), *The Year Nineteen Five* (1927), *Lieutenant Schmidt* (1926), and *Spektorsky* (published in installments between 1924 and 1930). There is a perceptible stylistic and thematic difference between Pasternak's previous works and his epic poems.

During the early 1930s, Pasternak was lifted into the first rank of Soviet writers. He was the only poet of his generation who was allowed to publish. Osip Mandelstam was out of favor with the government, Anna Akhmatova was not publishing, Mayakovsky and Sergei Yesenin committed suicide, and Marina Tsvetaeva was living abroad. Pasternak was the sole poet whom the government was initially willing to tolerate. During this period, he completed only one cycle of poetry, *Second Birth* (1932), a book whose optimistic title and tone Pasternak himself soon came to dislike as a collection for which he had compromised his poetic standards, and in which he had simplified the language for the sake of a mass readership.

Starting in 1932, the Central Committee of the Communist Party abolished all literary schools and associations and moved decisively toward consolidating its control over all writers' activities and their artistic production. In 1934 the Party established the Union of Soviet Writers and implemented

**Author and poet Boris Pasternak.** © JERRY COOKE/CORBIS

the official new artistic method of "socialist realism" that demanded from the artist "truthfulness" and "an historically concrete portrayal of reality in its revolutionary development." Writers were now treated as builders of a new life and "engineers of human souls." Pasternak's modernist autobiography *Safe Conduct* was banned in 1933 and not published again until the 1980s.

The most oppressive period in Soviet history began in 1936, and a reign of terror marked the next few years. Many of Pasternak's friends became victims of the Great Terror. The poet himself fell from grace and survived by mere chance. He nearly abandoned creative writing, devoting himself almost exclusively to translations. While this relieved him from the pressure of having to write pro-Stalinist poetry during the worst years of the Great Terror, it also pushed him into an increasingly peripheral position. Translating became a means of material survival for him during the darkest years of Soviet history, and his translations from this period alone would assure Pasternak a notable place in the history of Russian literature.

During World War II Pasternak published only two collections of poetry, *On Early Trains* (1943), and *Earth's Vastness* (1945). Both collections were written in the vein of socialist realism, with all traces of Pasternak's early avant-garde poetics obliterated. The official critical reception of *On Early Trains* was warm, but Pasternak himself found it embarrassing and repeatedly apologized for the small number and eclectic selection of poems.

After the war, Stalin launched a campaign against antipatriotic and cosmopolitan elements in Soviet society. This campaign came to be known as *zhdanovshchina*, after Andrei Zhdanov, the secretary of the Central Committee, who obligingly unleashed a slanderous campaign against some major cultural figures. Zhdanov's scapegoats in literature became the satirist Mikhail Zoshchenko and the poet Akhmatova. Pasternak's work came under attack too, and he ended up writing almost nothing during zhdanovshchina. Translations provided his major creative outlet.

After Stalin's death in 1953, Soviet culture experienced a period of liberalization known as the Thaw. It was precipitated by the so-called Secret Speech delivered by the new first secretary of the Communist Party, Nikita Khrushchev, at the Twentieth Party Congress in 1956. In this speech, Khrushchev exposed Stalin's crimes and denounced his personality cult. It was at that time that Pasternak attempted to publish his novel *Doctor Zhivago* (written between 1945 and 1955). No Soviet publisher, however, was willing to publish this work, because of its controversial portrayal of the Revolution. Pasternak sent the manuscript to an Italian publisher, Giangiacomo Feltrinelli, who offered to publish it. *Doctor Zhivago* thus first appeared in Italian, without official Soviet approval, in November 1957 and became an overwhelming success. Over the next two years the novel was translated into twenty-four languages.

In 1958 Pasternak was awarded the Nobel Prize in literature. This honor played a double role in Pasternak's literary career: on the one hand, it established his international literary stature, while on the other it made him the target of a vicious ideological campaign unleashed against him by the Soviet authorities. The fact that the poet had been nominated previously for the Nobel Prize for his poetry—specifically in 1947 and again in 1953—did not seem to bear any significance for the cultural bureaucrats. Pasternak was expelled from the Union of Soviet Writers and accused of betraying his country and negatively portraying the Social-

ist revolution and Soviet society—by people who, for the most part, never even read *Doctor Zhivago*. Under enormous psychological pressure and the threat of deportation to the West, Pasternak was forced to decline the Nobel Prize. But the attacks against him never stopped. *Doctor Zhivago* was published in the Soviet Union only posthumously, in 1988. During the last decade of his life, Pasternak's most distinct poetic achievement was *When the Weather Clears*, a collection of poetry from 1959. It shows him moving toward an increasingly contemplative mood and linguistic simplicity. Pasternak died in his dacha in Peredelkino in 1960.

Pasternak was the only great literary figure of his generation whose works continued to be published throughout his career. Although he had to pay a price, both artistic and personal, for his poetic freedom, he generally managed to preserve his moral and artistic integrity. Pasternak's work continues the best traditions of Russian literature and is permeated with devotion to individual freedom, moral and spiritual values, intolerance of oppressive governments, and a concern with the present and future of Russia. What distinguishes Pasternak's contribution to Russian literature is the life-affirming and resilient nature of his work and its remarkable power to present everyday reality in a unique and vibrant vision.

*See also:* CENSORSHIP; UNION OF SOVIET WRITERS

**BIBLIOGRAPHY**

Barnes, Christopher. (1989). *Boris Pasternak: A Literary Biography*, Vol. 1, 1860–1928. Cambridge, MA: Cambridge University Press.

Barnes, Christopher. (1998). *Boris Pasternak: A Literary Biography*, Vol. 2, 1928–1960. Cambridge, MA: Cambridge University Press.

Conquest, Robert. (1966). *Courage of Genius: The Pasternak Affair*. London: Collins and Harvill.

Fleishman, Lazar. (1990). *Boris Pasternak: The Poet and His Politics*. Cambridge, MA: Harvard University Press.

Gifford, Henry. (1977). *Pasternak: A Critical Study*. London: Cambridge University Press.

Livingstone, Angela. (1989). *Boris Pasternak: Doctor Zhivago*. New York: Cambridge University Press.

Mallac, Guy de. (1981). *Boris Pasternak: His Life and Art*. Norman: University of Oklahoma Press.

Rudova, Larissa. (1997). *Understanding Boris Pasternak*. Columbia: University of South Carolina Press.

LARISSA RUDOVA

# PATRIARCHATE

In 1589 the metropolitan of Moscow, head of the Orthodox Church in Russia, received the new and higher title of patriarch. This title made him equal in rank to the four other patriarchs of the Eastern Church: those of Jerusalem, Antioch, Alexandria, and Constantinople. Patriarch Jeremias II of Constantinople bestowed the new title on Metropolitan Job, who had been metropolitan since 1586.

The establishment of the Moscow patriarchate was the result of a complex arrangement between Boris Godunov, de facto regent of Russia in the time of Tsar Fyodor (r. 1584–1598), and the Greeks. The new title implied the acceptance by the Greek church of the autocephaly (autonomy) of the Russian church and considerably reinforced the prestige of the Russian church and state. In return the Greeks found a protector for the Orthodox peoples of the Ottoman Empire and a strong source of financial support for their church. Building on the powers and position of the earlier metropolitans, the patriarchs of Moscow were the leading figures in the church in Russia until the abolition of the office after the death of the last patriarch in 1700. The power of the patriarch came not only from his authority over the church, but also from his great wealth in land and serfs in central Russia. As the Russian church, like the other Orthodox churches, was a conciliar church, the power of the patriarchs was limited by the power of the tsar as well as by the requirement that, when making important decisions, a patriarch call a council of the bishops and most influential abbots.

Job, the first patriarch, supported Boris Godunov as regent and later as tsar. The defeat of Boris by the first False Dmitry at the beginning of the Time of Troubles led to the ouster of Job in 1605. The Greek bishop Ignaty replaced him that year, only to be expelled in turn after the Moscow populace turned against the False Dmitry. The new patriarch Germogen (1606–1612) was one of the leaders of Russian resistance to Polish occupation during the later years of the Troubles. Only after the final end of the Troubles and the election of Mikhail Romanov as tsar was the situation calm enough to permit the choosing of a new patriarch. This was tsar Mikhail's father, Patriarch Filaret (1619–1633). An important boyar during the 1590s, he had been exiled by Boris Godunov and forced to enter a monastery. Imprisoned in Poland during the Troubles, in 1619 he was allowed to return home, where the Greek patriarch of Jerusalem, Theo-

phanes; the Russian clergy; and tsar Mikhail chose him to lead the church. Filaret quickly settled several disputed points of liturgy and began to rebuild the Russian church after the desolation of the Time of Troubles. Much of the time during his patriarchate was occupied with matters having to do with relations with the Orthodox of the Ukraine and Belorussia under Polish Catholic rule. Filaret also played a major role in Russian politics.

Under patriarchs Joseph I (1634–1640) and Joseph (1640–1652) the church was quiet. Only in the last years of Joseph's patriarchate did new currents arise, the Zealots of Piety under the leadership of Stefan Vonifatev, spiritual father to Tsar Alexei (r. 1645–1676). The Zealots wanted reform of the liturgy and more preaching, with the aim of bringing the Christian message closer to the laity. Iosif was skeptical of their efforts, and their triumph came only after his death under the new patriarch Nikon (1652–1666, d. 1681). Nikon accepted the Zealots' program, but his liturgical reforms led to a schism in the church and the formation of groups known as Old Ritualists or Old Believers. Conflict with tsar Alexei led Nikon to abdicate in 1658, and he was formally deposed at a church council in 1666, which also condemned the Old Ritualists. The short patriarchates of Joseph II (1667–1672) and Pitirim (1672–1673) were largely devoted to efforts to defeat the Old Ritualists and restore order after the eight-year gap in church authority. Their successor Patriarch Joakim (1674–1690) was a powerful figure reminiscent in some ways of Nikon. He attempted to reorganize the diocesan system of the church, found schools, and suppress the Old Ritualists, an increasingly fruitless effort. Russia's first European-type school, the Slavo-Greco-Latin Academy, was set up with his patronage in 1685. He supported the young Peter the Great in overthrowing his half-sister, the regent Sophia, in 1689. The last patriarch, Adrian (1690–1700), usually considered a cultural conservative, was actually a complex figure who supported some of the new currents in Russian culture coming from Poland and the Ukraine. His relations with Peter the Great were never warm, and, when he died, Peter did not permit the church to replace him, and placed the Ukrainian Metropolitan of Ryazan, Stefan Yavorsky, as administrator of the church without the patriarchal title. Ultimately, Peter abolished the position and organized the Holy Synod in 1719, a committee of clergy and laymen and under a layman, to take the place of the patriarch. The Synod headed the Orthodox church in Russia until 1917.

Beginning at the end of the nineteenth century, voices within the Orthodox Church called for the reestablishment of the patriarchate. Such a move would mean the lessening of state control over the church and the beginning of separation of church and state, so both the government and many conservative churchmen opposed it. The collapse of the tsarist regime in March 1917 made such a radical change not only possible but necessary. Consequently, the Synod organized a council of the Russian church, which opened in August 1917. Its work continued after the Bolshevik seizure of power, and elected Tikhon, the metropolitan of Moscow, to the dignity of patriarch on November 21, 1917. Patriarch Tikhon's fate was to head the church during the Russian Civil War and the early years of Soviet power. Tikhon was sympathetic to the White anti-Bolshevik cause and was faced with a radically anticlerical and explicitly atheist revolutionary regime. He suffered imprisonment and harassment from the state, as well as internal dissent in the church. Upon his death in 1925, the church was in no position to replace him. The ensuing decades saw fierce antireligious propaganda by the Soviet authorities and massive persecution. Most churches in the USSR were closed, and thousands of priests and monks were imprisoned and executed.

In 1943 Josef Stalin suddenly decided to once again legalize the existence of the Orthodox church. He met with the few remaining members of the hierarchy to explain the new policy and permitted a council of the church to choose a new patriarch. The choice was Sergei, metropolitan of Moscow, senior living bishop and erstwhile prerevolutionary rector of the St. Petersburg Spiritual Academy. The elderly Patriarch Sergei died early in 1944, and in 1945 Alexei, metropolitan of Leningrad, replaced him, continuing to lead the church until his death in 1970. In these years the Soviet state permitted a modest revival of worship and religious life, but also placed the church under the watchful eye of the state Council on the Russian Orthodox Church, headed in 1943–1957 by Major General Georgy Karpov of the KGB. Patriarch Alexei endured the last major attack on the church under Nikita Khrushchev as well as the modus vivendi of the later Soviet years. His successors were patriarchs Pimen (1970–1990) and Alexei II (beginning in 1990).

See also: ALEXEI I, PATRIARCH; ALEXEI II, PATRIARCH; FILARET ROMANOV, PATRIARCH; HOLY SYNOD; JOAKIM, PATRIARCH; JOB, PATRIARCH; METROPOLITAN; NIKON, PATRIARCH; PIMEN, PATRIARCH; RUSSIAN ORTHODOX CHURCH; SERGEI, PATRIARCH; TIKHON, PATRIARCH

**BIBLIOGRAPHY**

Bushkovitch, Paul. (1992). *Religion and Society in Russia: the Sixteenth and Seventeenth Centuries.* New York: Oxford University Press.

Pospielovsky, Dmitry. (1984). *The Russian Church under the Soviet Regime, 1917–1982.* 2 vols. Crestwood, NY: St. Vladimir's Seminary Press.

PAUL A. BUSHKOVITCH

# PAUL I

(1754–1801), tsar of Russia 1796–1801.

Tsar Paul I (Paul Petrovitch) was born on September 20, 1754. He was officially the son of Tsarevitch Peter and his wife Catherine, but more probably the son of Sergei Saltykov—chamberlain at the court and lover of Catherine since 1752. At his birth, the child was taken away from his parents by his great-aunt, ruling Empress Elizabeth, who brought him to her court, supervised his education, and surrounded him with several tutors such as the old count Nikita Panin. He was eight in July 1762 when, six months after Elizabeth's death and his father's coronation as Peter III, his mother acceded to the throne as Catherine II by a coup that first led to the deposition of the tsar and then to his assassination, intended or not, by Alexei Orlov, one of the main leaders of the conspiracy. From that time on Catherine II, who feared his popularity, kept the child far away from power; Paul Petrovitch grew up in relative loneliness that contributed to make him distrustful. In September 1773, he married Princess Wilhelmine of Hesse-Darmstadt who died in April 1776 while delivering her first baby. In September of that same year, pushed by his mother who wanted an heir, he married Princess Sophia Dorothea of Württemberg (Maria Fiodorovna), who would give birth to ten children. Empress Catherine took away the first two boys, Alexander (born in December 1777) and Constantin (born in April 1779); she personally took care of their education and later intended to appoint Alexander as her heir, instead of Paul.

From September 1781 to August 1782, Paul and his wife made an eleven-month tour that brought them to all the European courts and allowed the future tsar to discover European political models and ways of life.

After returning to Russia, still deprived of their older sons and of any power, Paul and Maria Fiodorovna lived at Gatchina, a large estate given to them by Catherine. At Gatchina, the tsarevitch had his own court and a personal small army, composed of 2,400 soldiers and 140 officers. Isolated, fascinated by the Prussian model, Paul began to show an abnormal obsession for military parades and processions and started to tyrannize his soldiers. But at the same time, he established a hospital where peasants could receive free medical care, founded a school for the children of his serfs, and was tolerant of the Lutheran faith of his Finnish serfs.

On November 5, 1796, the death of Catherine made him tsar at the age of forty-two. He made many decisions—more than two thousand ukases in five years—that revealed the rejection of his mother's heritage, but they were not always consistent. In domestic policy, he first issued on April 1797 a decree establishing the principle of male primogeniture for succession to the throne, so as to eliminate any political turmoil. He proclaimed a general amnesty, freed all of Catherine's political prisoners, including the thinker Nikolai Novikov, and liberated the twelve thousand Poles kept in Russian jails since the last Polish war of independence led by Tadeusz Kociuszko. His hate for Catherine's immoral behavior and way of governing brought him to exile his mother's lovers and to cut down court expenses. His piety led him to forbid landowners from forcing serfs to work on Sundays and on religious feasts, while his mistrust of the nobility led him to impose a new tax on nobles' estates. All these measures, as well as the reorganization of the Russian military service according to the Prussian model and the reintroduction of corporal punishment for nobles, made him very unpopular quickly among the aristocracy.

At the same time, deeply hostile to the French Revolution and anxious about its potential impact on the Russian Empire, he heavily censored intellectual and political productions, rejecting the symbols of a French liberal influence in all spheres, even in the more superficial ones such as fashion. Relying on a growing bureaucracy, he reinforced the autocratic regime, condemning random innocents to Siberia or jail to show his unlimited power. He also systematically repressed peasant riots and extended serfdom to the Southern colonies. His domestic policy was therefore a mixture of generous and tyrannical measures.

In foreign policy, his choices were much more consistent. He pursued his mother's policy of ex-

**Emperor Paul I by Vladimir Lukic Borovikovsky.** © THE STATE RUSSIAN MUSEUM/CORBIS

pansionism in the Far East and Caucasus: in 1799, he chartered a Russian-American Company to favor Russian economic and commercial expansion in the North Pacific; and in December 1800 he annexed the kingdom of Georgia. As to war in Europe, he first chose to abstain but finally decided in 1798–1799 to join the Second Coalition against Napoleon I, together with Great Britain, Naples, Portugal, Austria, and the Ottoman Empire. Russian troops obtained brilliant successes: in winter 1798–1799, Admiral Fyodor Ushakov took the Ionian Islands from the French armies and established a republic occupied by the Russians. Meanwhile, General Alexander Suvarov won impressive battles in Italy (Cassano and Novi) and Switzerland in 1798–1800. And in November 1798, opposing Napoleon's claim to the Island of Malta, Paul agreed to become the protector and Great-Master of the Order of Malta. But in 1800, irritated by the suspicious behavior of his Austrian and British allies and convinced that an alliance with Napoleon could favor the Russian national interests, Paul abruptly changed his mind. He led Russia into a rapproche-ment with France and a war against Britain; to this end, in January 1801 he launched a military ex-pedition toward India. These last decisions were perceived as dangerous and even foolish by a fac-tion of the court. Encouraged by Charles Whit-worth, the British ambassador in St. Petersburg, and with the passive complicity of Tsarevitch Alexander, several figures close to the tsar, such as Nikita Panin the young, Count Peter von Pahlen, general governor of St. Petersburg, and Leontii Ben-nigsen, led a conspiracy that culminated with Paul's brutal assassination in March 1801.

*See also:* CATHERINE II; NOVIKOV, NIKOLAI IVANOVICH

**BIBLIOGRAPHY**

McGrew, Roderick Erle. (1992). *Paul I of Russia, 1754–1801.* Oxford: Clarendon Press; New York: Oxford Uni-versity Press.

Ragsdale, Hugh. (1998). *Tsar Paul and the Question of Madness: An Essay in History and Psychology.* New York: Greenwood Press.

MARIE-PIERRE REY

## PAVLIUCHENKO, LYUDMILA MIKHAILOVNA

(1916–1974), soldier, historian, and journalist.

A World War II heroine who a became cham-pion sniper with 309 kills to her credit, including thirty-six enemy snipers, Pavlyuchenko was the first Soviet citizen received at the White House. She retired at the rank of major after serving in the No. 2 Company, Second Battalion, 54th Razin Reg-iment, 25th "V.I. Chapayev" Division of the Inde-pendent Maritime Army, and was awarded the status of Hero of the Soviet Union on 25 October 1943.

Born in Belaya Tserkov, Pavliuchenko com-pleted high school while working in the Arsenal factory in Kiev, where she mastered small arms in a military club. She also trained as a sniper at the paramilitary Osoaviakhim (loosely translated as "Society for the Promotion of Aviation and Chem-ical Defense") and took up hang-gliding and para-chuting. After enrolling at the State University of Kiev, she successfully defended her master's thesis on Bohdan Khmelnitsky.

Pavliuchenko volunteered for military service during the summer of 1941 and became an expert sniper for the Independent Maritime Army in Odessa and Sevastopol. Invited by Eleanor Roo-sevelt, she toured North America in August 1942 and was presented with a Winchester rifle in Toronto. In 1943 she completed the Vystrel Courses for Officers. On graduating from Kiev Uni-versity in 1945, she became a military historian and journalist. Affected with a concussion and wounded four times, Pavliuchenko died prema-turely and was buried at the prestigious Novode-vichye Cemetery in Moscow.

*See also:* AVIATION; WORLD WAR II

**BIBLIOGRAPHY**

Cottam, Kazimiera J. (1998). *Women in War and Resis-tance: Selected Biographies.* Nepean, Canada: New Mil-itary Publishing.

Pavlichenko, Liudmila Mikhailovna. (1977). "I was a sniper." In *The Road of Battle and Glory,* ed. I.M. Dan-ishevsky, tr. David Skvirsky. Moscow: Politizdat.

KAZIMIERA J. COTTAM

## PAVLOVA, ANNA MATVEYEVNA

(1881–1931), the most famous of Russian balleri-nas.

Anna Matveyevna Pavlova (patronymic later changed to Pavlovna) began her career in the St. Petersburg Imperial Theaters in 1898, which ended amidst her usual flurry of performing in 1930, only weeks before her death. Pavlova's rise to the rank of ballerina in the Imperial Theaters (by 1906) was rapid, though her artistic breakthrough came the following year, when she appeared in several short works choreographed by Michel Fokine. Two of these works (*Les Sylphides* and *Le Pavillon d'Armide*) would join the roster of Serge Diagilev's Ballets Russes (as would their star performers, Pavlova and Vaslav Nijinsky). Both the ballets and dancers achieved unprecedented fame in that com-pany's Paris season of 1909. Pavlova debuted an-other Fokine composition in St. Petersburg in 1908, a solo that would become her signature work and that remains strongly identified with her: *The Swan,* to music of Camille Saint-Saëns. Popularly known as the dying swan, this evanescent figure suited Pavlova's physical type and stage temperament. Pavlova excelled in ethereal, romantic roles such as

**Prima ballerina Anna Pavlova is considered one of the premier dancers of the twentieth century.** © CORBIS. REPRODUCED BY PERMISSION.

"Giselle," and would later create for herself a multitude of roles in which she portrayed butterflies, roses, snowflakes, dragonflies, poppies, leaves, and various other delicate creatures. After achieving international stardom with Diagilev's Ballets Russes, Pavlova struck out on her own, first negotiating an enviable contract with the Imperial Theaters, and subsequently abandoning the Russian stage to settle in London. In twenty years of touring the globe, Pavlova came to personify the peripatetic Russian ballerina, the touring star whose only home was the stage.

*See also:* BALLET; NIJINKSY, VASLAV FOMICH

**BIBLIOGRAPHY**

Money, Keith. (1982). *Pavlova: Her Art and Life.* New York: Knopf.

TIM SCHOLL

## PAVLOV, IVAN PETROVICH

(1849–1936), Russian physiologist and Nobel Prize winner.

Ivan Pavlov was born in Ryazan. His father, a local priest, wanted him to attend the theological seminary, but Pavlov's interest in natural sciences led him to enroll in St. Petersburg University in 1870. In 1883 he completed his doctoral dissertation and in 1890 became professor and head of the physiology division of the St. Petersburg Institute of Experimental Medicine, where he remained until 1925. Pavlov's work on the functioning of the digestive system earned him the Nobel Prize in 1904. His originality lay in his approach to physiology, which considered the coordinated functioning of the organism as a whole, as well as his innovative surgical technique, which allowed him to observe digestion in live animals.

Pavlov's most well known research involved the study of conditioned reflexes. In his famous experiment, he placed a dog in a room free of all distractions. He found that the dog, accustomed to hearing a bell ring when being fed, would eventually salivate at the sound of the bell alone. Pavlov also applied his findings to the human nervous system. His work advanced the understanding of physiology and influenced international developments in medicine, psychology, and pedagogy.

Pavlov did not support the Bolshevik Revolution and in 1920 asked for permission to leave with his family. Vladimir Lenin, aware of the international prestige Pavlov brought to science in the Soviet Union, personally intervened to guarantee the resources for Pavlov to continue his research. In 1935, the International Congress of Physiologists awarded Pavlov the distinction of world senior physiologist. He died of pneumonia in Leningrad at the age of eighty-seven.

*See also:* EDUCATION

**BIBLIOGRAPHY**

Joravsky, David. (1989). *Russian Psychology: A Critical History.* Cambridge, MA: Blackwell Publishers.

Porter, Roy, ed. (1994). *The Biographical Dictionary of Scientists*, 2nd ed. New York: Oxford University Press.

SHARON A. KOWALSKY

## PAVLOV, VALENTIN SERGEYEVICH

(1937–2003), prime minister.

Valentin Sergeyevich Pavlov was Soviet leader Mikhail Gorbachev's minister of finance when perestroika was in full swing during the 1980s and the last prime minister of the Union of Soviet Socialist Republics before its collapse. Discharged on August 22, 1991 by President Gorbachev's decree for his role in the coup attempt that month, Pavlov was arrested a week later, imprisoned for sixteen months, and finally amnestied in May 1994. He died on March 30, 2003, at the age of sixty-five.

For most of his career, Pavlov occupied positions in the Russian SFSR and USSR related to finance. Having joined the Communist Party in 1962, he headed the Finance Department in the State Planning Committee (Gosplan) in 1979. After working briefly as first deputy finance minister in Nikolai Ryzhkov's government in 1986, Pavlov became chairman of the State Committee for Prices from August 1986 to June 1989. With approval of the party leadership, Pavlov reformed prices, withdrawing high-denomination notes from circulation overnight. This act caused a financial crisis and a great measure of unpopularity for him. Frustrated by his inability to maintain a grip on the ruble's value, while allowing the Soviet economy some small exposure to the free market, Pavlov blamed a plot by western banks for his decision to withdraw the bank notes. As the Soviet economy grew increasingly unstable and inflation skyrocketed, Pavlov tried other unpopular economic measures, but soon realized that the political and economic crisis was out of his control. The contradictions between Gorbachev's desire to reform the Soviet Union and keep it intact came to a head in August 1991. While the president was resting on the Black Sea, KGB chief Vladimir Kryuchkov formed the "State Committee for the State of Emergency" and placed Gorbachev under house arrest.

Along with eleven other men, Pavlov joined the emergency committee on August 19, 1991. This was no doubt Pavlov's least distinguished moment. Rather than conducting himself as a viable substitute for the supposedly ill president, Pavlov stayed in bed, claiming that he was too sick. His co-conspirators later said that he spent much of the three days of the attempted coup drunk.

See also: AUGUST 1991 PUTSCH; PERESTROIKA

BIBLIOGRAPHY

Copson, Raymond W. (1991). *Soviet Coup Attempt: Background and Implications.* Washington, DC: Congressional Research Service.

Goldman, Marshall I. (1987). *Gorbachev's Challenge: Economic Reform in the Age of High Technology.* New York: Norton.

Matlock, Jack F. (1995). *Autopsy on an Empire: the American Ambassador's Account of the Collapse of the Soviet Union.* New York: Random House.

JOHANNA GRANVILLE

## PEASANT ECONOMY

The term *peasant economy* refers to modes of rural economic activity with certain defined characteristics. The first characteristic is that the basic unit of production is the household; therefore, the demographic composition of the household was of paramount importance in determining the volume of output, the percentage of output consumed by the household, and, thus, the net remainder to be used for investment or savings. Second, the majority of household income is derived from agricultural production, that is, the household is dependent upon its own labor. Third, because the household depended upon agricultural production for survival, peasant households were assumed to be conservative and resistant to changes that would threaten their survival. In particular, a school of thought called the "moral economy" arose, which argued that peasant households would resist the commercialization of agriculture because it violated their values and beliefs—their moral economy—and attempted to replace the patterns of interaction among personal networks in the villages with impersonal transactions based on market principles.

Perhaps the greatest theorist of the peasant economy was a Russian economist named Alexander Chayanov, who lived from 1888 to 1939. Chayanov published a book entitled *Peasant Farm Organization*, which postulated a theory of peasant economy with application for peasant economies beyond Russia. He argued that the laws of classical economics do not fit the peasant economy; in other words, production in a household was not based upon the profit motive or the ownership of the means of production, but rather by calculations made by households as consumers and workers. In modern terminology, the family satisfied rather than maximized profit.

According to Chayanov, the basic principle for understanding the peasant economy was the balance between the household member as a laborer and as a consumer. Peasant households and their members could either increase the number of hours they worked, or work more intensively, or sometimes both. The calculation made by households whether to work more or not was subjective, based upon an estimate of how much production was needed for survival (consumption) and how much was desired for investment to increase the family's productive potential. Those estimates were balanced against the unattractiveness of agricultural labor. Households sought to reach an equilibrium between production increases and the disutility of increased labor. In short, households increased their production as long as production gains outweighed the negative aspects of increased labor. This principle of labor production in the peasant economy led Chayanov to argue that the optimal size of the agricultural production unit varied according to the sector of production at a time the official policy of the Communist Party of the Soviet Union was pushing for large collective farms. As a result of this disagreement with Marxist economists and the Party line, Chayanov was arrested in 1930 and executed in 1939.

Josef Stalin's collectivization, begun in 1929, fundamentally changed the basis of the Russian peasant economy by forcibly incorporating households into large farms, the latter becoming the basic production unit of Soviet agriculture. Moreover, production decisions were removed from the household and were no longer based upon the demographic composition of the household.

Even during the Stalin period, however, peasant resistance to mass collectivization and food shortages forced a compromise that allowed continued small-scale agricultural production by households in kitchen gardens or so-called private plots, and the sale of a portion of their produce at farm markets, which were free from state control. Consequently, peasant agriculture did not disappear with collectivization and continues to survive in Russia during the early twenty-first century, but on a much reduced scale.

*See also:* CHAYANOV, ALEXANDER VASILIEVICH; COLLECTIVIZATION OF AGRICULTURE; PEASANTRY; STALIN, JOSEF VISSARIONOVICH

**BIBLIOGRAPHY**

Chayanov, A. V. (1966). *The Theory of Peasant Economy,* ed. Daniel Thorner, Basile Kerblay, and R. E. F. Smith. Homewood, IL: Irwin.

Danilov, Viktor P. (1988). *Rural Russia under the New Regime.* Bloomington: Indiana University Press.

Scott, James C. (1976). *The Moral Economy of the Peasant: Rebellion and Subsistence in Southeast Asia.* New Haven, CT: Yale University Press.

STEPHEN K. WEGREN

# PEASANTRY

The original agriculturists of the northern Eurasian plain lived a communal, seminomadic existence, based on slash-and-burn cultivation. By the time of Kievan Rus, the defining characteristics of a peasantry were in already in evidence: an agricultural population bound by trade and tribute to a wider world, but in an incomplete and dependent way. Princes imposed taxes and compulsory services, but only with the rise of Muscovy (from the fifteenth to seventeenth centuries) were peasants enserfed—permanently bound to their lords or lands. Despite periodic revolts, this condition continued until 1861.

Peter I inaugurated a campaign of Westernization that imitated European modes of life and government. Perhaps ironically, in an age when Western Europe was abandoning serfdom, these initiatives increased the exploitation, as well as the traditionalism, of Russian peasants. St. Petersburg's Italianate palaces were built with conscripted peasant labor, and Russia's new Western-style army and bureaucracy were supported by a range of new taxes, among them the "soul tax" that was now demanded of peasants on top of the dues they paid their lords. Exploitation, however, was often indirect. The village commune (*obshchina*) distributed lands and obligations among its members, serving as a buffer between peasants and the outside world.

Although peasants generally regarded the cities and the Europeanized elite with suspicion, they were not totally isolated from urban society. Permanently bound to the soil, they could still depart temporarily to earn money in crafts, trade, or wage employment. In some provinces more than half the adult males engaged in work away from villages. A few even became millionaires.

Peasant agriculture flourished among the Slavic (and mainly Orthodox Christian) population of the Russian Empire. During the eighteenth century arable cultivation expanded into the steppe grass-

**Russian peasant women in the 1930s show their support for efforts to strengthen the collective farm system.** © AUSTRIAN ARCHIVES/CORBIS

lands of the south and southeast, and some serf-owners tried to introduce new crops and systems of cultivation into these regions. Most, however, left peasants to organize and cultivate the land according to traditional norms. Under communal tenure, which flourished among Russian peasants but not among Ukrainians and other non-Russians, each household received strips of land in many different fields. The number of these could be increased or decreased to match a family's ability to work. Grains were planted in a fixed rotation, and crop yields were often disappointing, even in areas of higher fertility.

Russia's defeat in the Crimean War (1855) convinced its leaders to modernize, and the result was a vast array of reforms, foremost among them emancipation of the serfs in 1861. For the sake of social stability, former serf owners were generously compensated, retaining a substantial share of the

land. Freed peasants had to reimburse the state for their land. The commune kept the job of distributing lands and tax obligations. This arrangement produced little innovation and less prosperity, though migration to Western Siberia during the later nineteenth century did offer some hopeful signs of change. At the end of the nineteenth century crop yields grew more rapidly than the population, and the Russian Empire became a major exporter of grain and other agricultural products.

In the general census of 1897, the empire had a population of 125,000,000, of whom roughly three-fourths were legally classified as peasants, and an even greater proportion resided in rural areas. Peasant unrest was endemic, and in the revolution of 1905–1907 peasants rose up to confiscate private lands and drive off their former lords. Harsh punishment was followed by a new ("Stolypin") land reform promoted by Prime Minister Peter

Stolypin, designed to replace communal tenure with private ownership, but the outbreak of World War I prevented its full implementation. In 1917, unrest returned. Private lands were seized and redistributed and manor houses destroyed. The village commune took on a new life.

At this time peasants were roughly eighty percent of Russia's population, impoverished, tradition-minded, and suspicious of outsiders. Vladimir Lenin's Bolshevik (Communist) Party tried to enlist them in its revolution, but needed their grain and labor power more than their goodwill. During the Civil War of 1917–1922 and later during the industrialization drive of the 1930s the Party resorted to confiscation and coercion. Poor and landless peasants were thought to be natural allies of the urban proletariat, but efforts to promote class warfare in the villages produced instability and food shortages. Under Josef Stalin's leadership collective agriculture was forcibly introduced, but instead of producing efficiency it caused disruption and starvation, with the loss of millions of lives. After several years of turmoil peasants were assured the right to cultivate small private plots alongside their duties to the collective farm (kolkhoz). Throughout the following decades these plots produced a vastly disproportionate share of the country's food.

The Soviet Union became an urban industrial society, but its rural roots were poorly nourished. At the time the USSR ceased to exist, some twenty-five percent of Russia's population continued to lived on the land, resistant (for the most part) to privatization or economic reform.

*See also:* AGRICULTURE; COLLECTIVIZATION OF AGRICULTURE; ENSERFMENT; PEASANT ECONOMY; SERFDOM

**BIBLIOGRAPHY**

Blum, Jerome. (1961). *Lord and Peasant in Russia.* Princeton, NJ: Princeton University Press.

Moon, David. (1999). *The Russian Peasantry, 1600–1930: The World the Peasants Made.* New York: Addison-Wesley.

Robinson, Geroid T. (1932). *Rural Russia Under the Old Regime: A History of the Landlord-Peasant World and a Prologue to the Peasant Revolution of 1917.* London and New York: Longmans, Green and Company.

Shanin, Teodor. (1985). *The Roots of Otherness: Russia's Turn of Century.* New Haven, CT: Yale University Press.

ROBERT E. JOHNSON

# PEASANT UPRISINGS

Also known as "Peasant wars"; peasant uprisings in broad usage, were a number of rural-based rebellions from the seventeenth to the twentieth centuries, a typical form of protest in Russia against socioeconomic, religious, and cultural oppression and, occasionally, against political power holders.

Peasant uprisings in the narrow sense belong to the period of serfdom. Most of them followed a significant worsening of the conditions of the peasantry. The four major rebellions of this period were led by: 1) Ivan Bolotnikov, 1606–1607; 2) Stepan ("Stenka") Razin, 1667–1671; 3) Kondrat Bulavin, 1707–1708; and 4) the largest of all, by Yemelyan ("Yemelka") Pugachev, 1773–1775. The leadership in each case was largely symbolic, as an inherent feature of peasant wars was anarchic spontaneity with little organization, subordination, and planning.

The geographic center of the uprisings was in Southern Russia, between the Don and the Volga rivers and between the Black and the Caspian seas. However, they spread over wider territories and, in the case of the Bolotnikov rebellion, involved a battle in the vicinity of Moscow (which the rebels lost, in December 1606). The key initiative was played by Cossacks (Razin and Bulavin were Cossack atamans, and Pugachev a prominent Cossack as well). The rank and file included serfs and free peasants, as well as ethnic and religious minorities (e.g., Tatars in the Razin rebellion and Bashkirs in the Pugachev rebellion; ethnically Russian Old Believers in the Razin, Bulavin, and Pugachev rebellions). The Bolotnikov uprising, as part of the Time of Troubles, also involved impoverished or discontented gentry, some of whom, however, parted company with the rebels at a crucial stage. The religious and cultural aspect of the uprisings reflected discontent with top-down autocratic reforms along foreign patterns. Some also view the uprisings as a cultural response of the Cossack frontier to excess regulation by the imperial center.

Rebel demands are known from their own documents (e.g., "Seductive Letters" issued by Razin) and government reports. These demands involved land redistribution, the change of peasants' status from serfs to Cossacks, and often the elimination of the privileged classes. None of the uprisings was directed against the institution of monarchy; some rebels allied themselves with contenders to the throne (e.g., Bolotnikov with one of the Pseudo-

Dmitrys and then with another self-styled tsarevich, Peter), while Bulavin and Pugachev claimed their own rights to the tsar's scepter. On the territories occupied by rebels, peasants were declared free of servitude and debt, and Cossack-style self-rule was decreed. The uprisings were characterized by mass casualties and brutality on both sides. All of them were violently suppressed and their leaders executed; in the longer run, they may have spurred policy changes and reform efforts emanating from the top.

The most famous Pugachev rebellion was distinguished by the fact that its leader claimed to be Tsar Peter III (the actual tsar was murdered a decade earlier, in 1762, in a coup that brought his wife, Catherine II, to power). He issued his first manifesto in this capacity in September 1773. Pugachev promised to give peasants "back" their freedom "stolen" from them by the gentry, making them into Cossacks. The army of his followers counted about twenty-five thousand people. This rebellion was the first one of the manufacturing era, and was joined by serfs laboring at the manufactures in the Urals. Its suppression was followed in the short run by the strengthening and further spread of the institution of serfdom, as well as the incorporation of Cossacks into the state bureaucracy. During the nineteenth century, peasant uprisings never rose to the scale of wars. A major uprising in 1861 in the Kazan region reflected discontent with the conditions attached to the emancipation of the serfs.

Peasant guerrilla culture in Russia (as in some other countries) involved the operation of a parallel, or shadow community beyond the reach of the state, abruptly revealing itself in mass action. Guerrilla tactics followed by peasant rebels played a role in the twentieth-century revolutions (both on the Bolshevik and anti-Bolshevik side), due to the numerical and cultural influence of peasantry (or recent peasants among urban workers and the intelligentsia). These tactics were also employed in defense against foreign invasions (the 1812 Patriotic War and World War II).

Scholars emphasizing the continuity of peasant resistance over centuries view the revolutions of 1905–1907 and 1917 as a resumption of peasant wars, in a different socioeconomic environment. Some of them consider the 1917–1933 period as "the Great Peasant War" suppressed by Josef Stalin through artificially organized famine and collectivization of the peasantry.

Peasant wars figured prominently in Russian folklore and modern arts. Alexander Pushkin, in characterizing a "Russian rebellion" as "senseless and merciless," perpetuated the view of peasant wars as destructive explosions, characterized by savage brutality on both sides, after seemingly endless patience of the oppressed. Revolutionary democrats of the Populist tradition cultivated a heroic image of peasant rebels, while orthodox Marxists dismissed them as anarchists and enemies of the modernizing state.

*See also:* BOLOTNIKOV, IVAN ISAYEVICH; COSSACKS; DMITRY, FALSE; PEASANTRY; PUGACHEV, EMELIAN IVANOVICH

## BIBLIOGRAPHY

Avrich, Paul (1976). *Russian Rebels, 1600–1800.* New York: Norton.

Graziosi, Andrea. (1997). *The Great Soviet Peasant War: Bolsheviks and Peasants, 1917–1933.* Cambridge, MA: Harvard University Press.

Longworth, P. (1973). "The Last Great Cossack Peasant Rising." *Journal of European Studies* 3.

Pushkin, Alexander. (1987). *Captain's Daughter.* New York: Hyperion.

Pushkin, Alexander. (2001). *The History of Pugachev.* London: Phoenix.

Raeff, Marc. (1970) "Pugachev's Rebellion." In *Preconditions of Revolution in Early Modern Europe*, eds. Robert Forster and Jack P. Greene. Baltimore: John Hopkins Press.

Wolf, Eric (1969). *Peasant Wars of the Twentieth Century.* New York: Harper & Row.

DMITRI GLINSKI

# PECHENEGS

During the late ninth century, under the pressure from the Torky and Khazars, the Pechenegs, a nomadic Turkic-speaking tribal confederation, migrated from the Volga-Ural region and occupied the area stretching from the Don-Donets to the Danube. Like other nomads inhabiting the southern Russian steppe from around 965 to around 1240, the Pechenegs did not create a true state. Politically, they were united into eight tribal unions, each occupying one of the four provinces (running in strips from north to south) on each side of the Dnieper. Disunited, the Pechenegs never threatened the existence of the Rus state. The Pechenegs raided

Rus territories and traded such items as livestock for goods unavailable in nomadic economies (grain and luxury goods). At other times, they acted as Rus allies in military campaigns, as in the 944 Rus war against Byzantium. From 980 onward, they likewise served as mercenaries in the conflicts between Rus princes. The Byzantines also used the Pechenegs to counter the Rus. Thus, in 972, while returning to Kiev from his Byzantine campaign, the Pechenegs killed Prince Svyatoslav, probably on the request of the Byzantines. The Pechenegs' one major attack on Kiev was decisively repulsed by Yaroslav the Wise in 1036. Defeated and under pressure from the Torky, most Pechenegs migrated toward the Balkans, where they were massacred by Byzantine-Cuman forces in 1091. The few who remained joined the Rus border guards known as Chernye klobuky or Black Hoods. Until around 1010, the Pechenegs probably practiced shamanist-Täri religion, but thereafter began to convert to Islam.

*See also:* KHAZARS; YAROSLAV VLADIMIROVICH

**BIBLIOGRAPHY**

Golden, Peter B. (1990). "The Peoples of the South Russian Steppe." In *The Cambridge History of Early Inner Asia*, ed. Denis Sinor. Cambridge, UK: Cambridge University Press.

Golden, Peter B. (1992). *An Introduction to the History of the Turkic Peoples.* Wiesbaden, Germany: Harrassowitz Verlag.

Pritsak, Omeljan. (1975). "The Pečenegs, A Case of Social and Economic Transformation." *Archivum Eurasiae Medii Aevi* 1:211–236.

ROMAN K. KOVALEV

## PEKING, TREATY OF

The Treaty of Peking (November 14, 1860) confirmed and extended the territorial gains Russia had wrested from China in the Treaty of Aigun (1858). By its terms, the eastern boundary between the two empires was set along the Amur and Ussuri Rivers. The Ussuri boundary gave Russia possession of what became the Maritime Province (Primorskii Krai). Vladivostok, the major city of the Russian Far East, was established in this territory, providing direct access to the Sea of Japan and through the Pacific Ocean. Therefore, the Treaty of Peking was the foundation of Russia's attempts to become a Pacific power. The treaty also established, for the

first time, a Russo-Chinese boundary line in the west (Central Asia) according to Russian demands, and provided for the opening of Russian consulates in Urga (Mongolia) and Kashgar (Xinjiang). The entire border was opened to free trade between the two empires.

General Nikolai Ignatiev, appointed Russia's minister to China in 1859, took advantage of the Second Opium War, an Anglo-French conflict with China, to advance Russia's imperial interests. At a moment of supreme danger to the Qing court, whose capital Beijing the Anglo-French forces had already occupied and ransacked, Ignatiev offered his services as mediator to the beleaguered Chinese. He urged them to accede to the demands of the Anglo-French expeditionary force while promising to intercede with his fellow Westerners on behalf of the Chinese. In exchange for his services, which were actually superfluous, he demanded and received China's acceptance of Russia's own territorial, diplomatic, and commercial demands.

By the Treaty of Peking, Russia became a full-fledged player in the Western imperialist assault upon China's sovereignty and territorial integrity, and sowed the seeds of Chinese anger that matured during the twentieth century.

*See also:* AIGUN, TREATY OF; CHINA, RELATIONS WITH

**BIBLIOGRAPHY**

Clubb, O. Edmund. (1971). *China and Russia : The "Great Game."* New York: Columbia University Press .

Mancall, Mark. (1971). *Russia and China: Their Diplomatic Relations to 1728.* Cambridge, MA: Harvard University Press.

Paine, S. C. M. (1997). *Imperial Rivals: Russia, China, and Their Disputed Frontier.* Armonk, NY: M. E. Sharpe.

Quested, Rosemary. (1984). *Sino-Russian Relations: A Short History.* Sydney: George Allen and Unwin.

Tien-fong Cheng. (1973). *A History of Sino-Russian Relations.* Westport, CT: Greenwood Press (reprint of Public Affairs Press, 1957).

STEVEN I. LEVINE

## PELEVIN, VIKTOR OLEGOVICH

(b. 1962), novelist and short-story writer.

Born in Moscow to a military family, Viktor Olegovich Pelevin received his education at the

Moscow Energy Institute and the Gorky Institute of World Literature (Moscow). Praised and panned by critics ever since his work first gained public recognition during the early 1990s, Pelevin has been a controversial figure in the Russian literary establishment. Nonetheless, he is one of the most important figures in the world of post-Soviet letters. Pelevin is virtually the only serious writer in contemporary Russia to gain a wide readership, appealing in particular to the burgeoning youth counterculture.

Pelevin's works can be classified broadly as satire, but the author's concerns are more cultural and metaphysical than political. His first short novel, *Omon Ra* (1992), tells the story of a young man who dreams of being a cosmonaut, only to discover that the entire Soviet space program is a government-perpetrated fraud masking the country's inability to launch a single rocket. Pelevin's second novel, *The Life of Insects* (1993), reveals the preoccupation with Eastern mysticism and hallucinogenic drugs that characterize both his subsequent novels and many of the short stories collected in *The Blue Lantern* (1991) and *The Yellow Arrow* (1998). His 1996 novel *Buddha's Little Finger* combines an absurdist approach to Soviet cultural heroes with an equally ironic satire of Western popular culture (Arnold Schwarzenegger makes a brief appearance). In 1999 he published *Babylon*, which reflects his ongoing fascination with computer culture and virtual reality. *Babylon* is populated both by real human beings and digitally constructed simulacra, and the resemblance between the two is enhanced by Pelevin's longstanding rejection of the traditions of Russian psychological realism.

*See also:* SCIENCE FICTION; SOCIALIST REALISM

**BIBLIOGRAPHY**

Dalton-Brown, Sally. (1997). "Ludic Nonchalance or Ludicrous Despair? Viktor Pelevin and Russian Postmodernist Prose." *Slavonic and East European Review* 75(2):216–233.

Genis, Alexander. (1999). "Borders and Metamorphoses: Viktor Pelevin in the Context of Post-Soviet Literature." In *Russian Postmodernism: New Perspectives on Post-Soviet Culture*, eds. Mikhail Epstein, Alexander Genis, and Slobodanka Vladiv-Glover. New York: Berghan.

ELIOT BORENSTEIN

## PEOPLE'S COMMISSARIAT OF NATIONALITIES

While the tsarist empire had no specific ministry to deal with the non-Russian peoples, upon coming to power the Bolsheviks established a People's Commissariat of Nationalities, with Josef Stalin at its head, in its first government. Soviet policy toward the nationalities was based on both ideology and pragmatism. Both Vladimir Lenin and Stalin upheld the Marxist (and liberal) principle of the right of nationalities to self-determination, even in the face of opposition from many of their comrades. Lenin and Stalin believed that nationalism arose from non-Russians' distrust (*nedoverie*) of an oppressive nationality, such as the Russians. Secure in their faith that "national differences and antagonisms between peoples are vanishing gradually from day to day" and that "the supremacy of the proletariat will cause them to vanish still faster," the Bolshevik leaders were prepared to grant autonomy, cultural and language rights, and even territory to non-Russian peoples in order to stave off separatism and chauvinist nationalism. Even as national Communist leaders in Ukraine, Transcaucasia, and elsewhere took over the development of their national populations, the Commissariat of Nationalities (abbreviated as Narkomnats) managed the affairs of dozens of peoples in the Russian Soviet Socialist Federation and beyond.

Immediately after taking power, the Bolsheviks issued a series of declarations on "the rights of the toiling and exploited peoples," "to all Muslim toilers of Russia and the East," and on the disposition of Turkish Armenia. Most importantly, with little real ability to effect its will in the peripheries, the Soviet government made a strategic shift in response to the growing number of autonomies and accepted by January 1918 the principle of federalism. In each national area the government promoted programs to favor the local indigenous peoples, a kind of cultural affirmative action. Not only were native languages supported, but indigenous leaders, if they were loyal to the Communist enterprise, were also supported. Within the Commissariat there were separate sub-commissariats for Jewish, Armenian, and other nationalities' affairs—even a Polar Subcommittee for the "small peoples of the north." The newspaper *Zhizn' natsional'nostei* was the official house organ of the Commissariat.

As commissar, Stalin was often absent from the affairs of his Commissariat. Yet on important occasions he settled decisive issues, as in 1921 when he supported the inclusion of the Armenian region of Mountainous Karabakh in the neighboring state of Azerbaijan. Stalin favored the formation of a Transcaucasian Federation of Armenia, Azerbaijan, and Georgia, against the desires of many local Bolsheviks, particularly among the Georgians. On this issue, and the even more important question of how centralized the new Union of Soviet Socialist Republics would be, Stalin came into conflict with Lenin, who was far more suspicious of the "Great Power chauvinism" of the Russians and favored more rights for the non-Russians. Both men, however, supported the general line known as *korenizatsya*, which sought to indigenize the areas in which non-Russian peoples lived by developing local cultures, political elites, and national languages.

Activists from Narkomnats were involved in setting up autonomous regions for non-Russian peoples, establishing newspapers, publishing pamphlets, and fostering literacy. Many of them saw themselves as protectors of the weak, a bulwark against the potential destruction of native cultures. But at the same time the government's policies betrayed a kind of paternalism directed toward "backward" or "primitive" peoples who were, in many cases, not considered able to run their own affairs. Officials in Moscow acknowledged at times that they knew little about the peoples in more remote reaches of their vast country. Much linguistic and ethnographic work had still to be done to evaluate just which group belonged to which nationality, and Narkomnats assisted in developing Soviet anthropology and ethnography. In a real sense government intervention and the work of intellectuals helped draw the lines of distinction that later took a reality of their own between various peoples.

With the formation of the Soviet Union in early 1924, the Commissariat of Nationalities was dissolved, and its activities shifted to the new Soviet parliament. But by that time the broad and lasting contours of Soviet nationality policy had been worked out. Only during the 1930s, with the growing autocratic power of Stalin, the radical social transformations of his "revolution from above," and the fear of approaching war in Europe was the policy of korenizatsya moderated in favor of a more Russophilic and nationalist policy.

*See also:* KORENIZATSYA; NATIONALITIES POLICIES, SOVIET

## BIBLIOGRAPHY

Blank, Stephen. (1994). *The Sorcerer as Apprentice: Stalin as Commissar of Nationalities, 1917–1924.* Westport, CT: Greenwood Press.

Martin, Terry. (2001). *The Affirmative Action Empire: Nations and Nationalism in the Soviet Union, 1923–1939.* Ithaca, NY, and London: Cornell University Press.

Slezkine, Yuri. (1994). *Arctic Mirrors: Russia and the Small Peoples of the North.* Ithaca, NY, and London: Cornell University Press.

Smith, Jeremy. (1999). *The Bolsheviks and the National Question, 1917–23.* New York: St. Martin's Press.

Suny, Ronald Grigor. (1993). *The Revenge of the Past: Nationalism, Revolution, and the Collapse of the Soviet Union.* Stanford, CA: Stanford University Press.

RONALD GRIGOR SUNY

# PEOPLE'S CONTROL COMMITTEE

The Soviet leadership used several organizations to ensure popular compliance with its policies, ideology, and morality. During the 1920s and 1930s, the Central Party Control Committee ensured Party discipline by verifying the thoughts and actions of Party members and candidates. Simultaneously, Rabkrin (the Workers' and Peasants' Inspectorate) used workers and peasants to supervise local administrators.

Josef Stalin gradually subordinated the Central Control Commission to the Party's Central Committee and ultimately himself. In 1923 he merged it with the Workers and Peasant's Inspectorate. From the beginning, the Central Control Commission was given a broad and vague mandate, allowing excesses and abuse of power. Not only did it investigate cases of poor work performance, failure to meet production quotas, corruption, or even drunkenness, but it found violations as needed when Stalin's purges began during the 1930s.

As part of his de-Stalinization campaign following Stalin's death in 1953, Nikita Khrushchev announced he was going back to the party's Leninist roots. While maintaining a tamer Party disciplinary structure, Khrushchev also recreated the Workers' and Peasants' Inspectorate, now known as the Party-State Control Committee (PSCC). Using thousands of volunteers to supplement its small permanent staff, the PSCC was designed as more of a grassroots organization working to ensure fulfillment of the five-year plans. Instead of top-down surveillance, Khrushchev saw the Committees as a way of channeling factory-level information to top planners, such as hidden stockpiles of goods or resources.

Following Khrushchev's ouster in 1964, the committee was renamed in December 1965, becoming the People's Control Committee. It continued to rely on volunteers—about ten million in 1980—to monitor government and economic activities. In addition, the Committee's chair, Alexander Shelepin, was removed, as Party leaders feared he held too many powerful posts at once. He was succeeded by Pavel Kovanov, who was replaced by Gennadiy Ivanovich Voronov in 1971. Voronov was replaced in 1974 by Alexei Shkolnikov.

Following his election as general secretary in 1985, Mikhail Gorbachev began to restructure the PCC in accordance with his overall reform program. He appointed Sergei Manykin to chair the PCC in March 1987. Among the changes ordered was to reduce the number of inspections, because they were disruptive and actually contributed to inefficiency. In 1989 the organization was reconfigured as the USSR People's Control Committee under the newly constituted USSR Supreme Soviet. Professional staff replaced the volunteers. In June 1989, Manyakin was replaced by Gennady Kolbin, who launched an ambitious program to link inspection reports to proposed legislation in the Supreme Soviet. Kolbin also sought to ensure that punishments were actually implemented, not overturned by appeals to a party patron.

*See also:* COMMUNIST PARTY OF THE SOVIET UNION; DE-STALINIZATION; PERESTROIKA; PURGES, THE GREAT; RABKRIN.

**BIBLIOGRAPHY**

Adams, Jan S. (1978). "Institutional Change in the 1970s: The Case of the USSR People's Control Committee." *Slavic Review* 37(3):457–472.

Adams, Jan S. (1989). "USSR People's Control Committee and Perestroika." *Radio Liberty Report on the USSR* 1(4):1–3.

ANN E. ROBERTSON

## PEOPLE'S HOUSES

(*Narodnye doma*), cultural-educational centers for the working classes that usually contained a reading room, lecture hall, tea room, and theater.

The movement to construct people's houses or people's palaces with cultural and educational facilities for the working classes began in Britain during the second half of the nineteenth century and soon spread to Germany, Belgium, the Netherlands, France, Austria, and other countries.

In Russia the first people's houses were built by the semiofficial Guardianships of Popular Temperance, which operated under the auspices of the Finance Ministry. During the 1890s the Russian Finance Ministry began introducing a state liquor monopoly to regulate liquor sales and increase state revenues. The Ministry set up local Guardianships of Popular Temperance to monitor adherence to the liquor laws. The Guardianships were also instructed to encourage moderate drinking habits among the population by disseminating information on the dangers of excessive drinking, providing facilities for the treatment of alcoholism, and organizing "rational recreations" as an alternative to the tavern.

By the early 1900s the Guardianships of Popular Temperance were running people's houses in St. Petersburg, Moscow, Kiev, and other cities. St. Petersburg's imposing Emperor Nicholas II People's House was the largest recreational facility in the Russian Empire. It contained a dining hall, tea room, lending library, reading rooms, an observatory, a clinic for the treatment of alcoholics, a museum devoted to alcoholism, a cinema, a 1,500-seat theater, and an opera house. Besides performances of drama and opera, the Nicholas II People's House organized scientific and religious lectures, evening adult classes, gymnastic exercises, classes in choral singing and folk music, and activities for children. From 1900 to 1913 almost two million people annually attended the entertainments at the Nicholas II People's House, which was famed for its spectacular productions of historical plays and fantasy extravaganzas. Leading actors and artists sometimes appeared on the stage of the Nicholas II People's House, where Fyodor Shalyapin, Russia's greatest opera singer, gave a free concert for workers in 1915.

Zemstvos, dumas, and literacy societies also constructed people's houses throughout Russia. The Kharkov Literacy Society built a people's house in 1903; the Moscow duma opened a municipal people's house with a theater in 1904. The liberal philanthropist Countess Sofia Panina opened her Ligovsky People's House in 1903 in a poor district of St. Petersburg; there workers could attend evening courses, and Pavel Gaideburov and Nadezhda

Skarskaya ran a very successful theater. By 1913 there were at least 222 people's houses in the Russian Empire. During World War I, when prohibition against alcohol was enacted, interest in people's houses increased, but the Petrograd and Moscow dumas' ambitious plans for extensive networks of people's houses were never realized due to the financial strains of the war.

The Russian people's houses primary aim was to promote sobriety among the lower classes by offering them "rational recreations" in the form of theater performances, lectures, reading rooms, excursions, and other sober pursuits. Although their impact on popular alcohol consumption is doubtful, the people's houses did offer the common people modest educational opportunities and a diverse variety of affordable theatrical entertainments. After the October Revolution the people's houses were reorganized under the Soviet regime as "palaces of culture" and workers' clubs but continued many of the same activities as before.

*See also:* ALCOHOLISM; ALCOHOL MONOPOLY

**BIBLIOGRAPHY**

Swift, E. Anthony. (2002). *Popular Theater and Society in Tsarist Russia.* Berkeley: University of California Press.

Thurston, Gary. (1998). *The Popular Theatre Movement in Russia, 1862–1919.* Evanston, IL: Northwestern University Press.

E. ANTHONY SWIFT

# PEOPLE'S PARTY OF FREE RUSSIA

The People's Party of "Free Russia" (Narodnaya Partiya "Svobodnaya Rossiya," or NPSR) has its origins in the democratic wing of the Communist Party, which formed in July 1991 into the Democratic Party of Communists of Russia (DPKR) as part of the Communist Party of the Soviet Union (CPSU). Serving as its base was the group Communists for Democracy in the Congress of People's Deputies of the Russian Soviet Federative Socialist Republic (RSFSR) (the leader was Alexander Rutskoi, elected Russia's vice president in June 1991), and the Democratic Movement of Communists (Vasily Lipitsky's group). After the August 1991 putsch and the dissolution of the CPSU, the DPKR in its first congress was renamed the People's Party of

"Free Russia," and was headed by Rutskoi and Lipitsky. It flourished from 1991 to 1993, when it was considered a potential ruling party. Moving in March 1992 into constructive opposition to the course of the Boris Yeltsin-Yegor Gaidar administration, the NPSR reached an agreement with the Democratic Party of Russia, on the basis of which the bloc Civic Union was formed.

In the 1993 conflict between Yeltsin and the delegates, Rutskoi sided with the latter and landed in prison after the attack on the White House. After his amnesty in May 1994, the party changed its name again, this time to the Russian Social-Democratic People's Party (RSDNP). Its main goals were the creation of conditions for free and thorough development of the citizens of Russia; elevation of their welfare; guarantee of citizens' rights and freedoms; and establishment of a civic society, a social-market economy, and a lawful government. Leaders had different ideas for the party's development: Rutskoi called upon the delegates to participate in the creation of the social-patriotic movement Power, whereas Lipitsky supported the idea of transforming the RSDNP into a social-democratic party of the Western European variety. In March 1995, the split became fact in congress, after which both sides essentially ceased existing. Rutskoi's group began working in the social-patriotic movement Power, and Lipitsky's in the Russian Social-Democratic Union.

In the 1995 elections, Lipitsky's supporters participated in the bloc Social-Democrats (0.13% of the vote), and Power pushed forward its federal list, on account of which a new split occurred in the leadership of the movement, and a number of politicians left it. The new list of Power with Rutskoi at the head received 1.8 million votes (2.6%), while in Rutskoi's homeland, Kursk, it received more than 30 percent. In 1996, Power was unable to collect the required number of signatures for its presidential candidate Rutskoi, and it joined with the bloc of popular-patriotic forces headed by Gennady Zyuganov. Soon afterward, Rutskoi was elected first as cochair of the Popular-Patriotic Union of Russia, and then, with its support, governor of Kursk Oblast. He resigned as chair of Power and fell into conflict with the NPSR and Communist Party of the Russian Federation (KPRF). In 1998, Power, under the chairmanship of Konstantin Zatulin, entered the movement Fatherland of Moscow mayor Yuri Luzhkov, and on the very eve of elections it split yet again and disappeared from the political scene.

See also: COMMUNIST PARTY OF THE SOVIET UNION; DE-MOCRATIC PARTY; RUTSKOI, ALEXANDER VLADIMIRO-VICH; ZYUGANOV, GENNADY ANDREYEVICH.

**BIBLIOGRAPHY**

McFaul, Michael. (2001). *Russia's Unfinished Revolution: Political Change from Gorbachev to Putin.* Ithaca, NY: Cornell University.

McFaul, Michael, and Markov, Sergei. (1993). *The Troubled Birth of Russian Democracy: Parties, Personalities, and Programs.* Stanford, CA: Hoover Institution Press.

Reddaway, Peter, and Glinski, Dmitri. (2001). *The Tragedy of Russia's Reforms: Market Bolshevism Against Democracy.* Washington, DC: U.S. Institute of Peace Press.

NIKOLAI PETROV

# PEOPLE'S WILL, THE

The People's Will was the most famous illegal revolutionary organization in late nineteenth-century Russia. This "party," as it was termed, represented the culmination of the rapidly evolving revolutionary movement of the 1870s, the decade when radical members of the intelligentsia first made contact on a significant scale with Russian peasants and workers, the *narod*, or common people. The ideology of this movement was a peasant-oriented socialism known as *narodnichestvo* (populism). The umbrella group Land and Freedom (*Zemlya i Volya*), which linked most of the radical circles at the time, split in 1879 over frustration at government repression and the lack of effective peasant response to the group's propaganda initiatives. Those radicals who were determined to incorporate the new tactic of terrorism into their activity formed a party called the People's Will (Narodnaya Volya). By terrorism they meant primarily the targeting of hated government officials for assassination. This extreme measure was variously justified as a means of exerting pressure on the government for reform, as the spark that would ignite a vast peasant uprising, and as the inevitable response to the regime's use of violence against the revolutionaries.

The People's Will was headed by an Executive Committee, including such famous figures as Andrei Zhelyabov and Sofia Perovskaya. Day-to-day activities were supervised by special subgroups in charge of propaganda and organization of three critical groups—workers, students, and military officers—and included underground printing operations; keeping an eye on police infiltration efforts; and planning and carrying out assassinations. In addition to well-organized groups in St. Petersburg and Moscow, there was a growing number of provincial organizations, mostly circles of students and workers. The participation of a small number of women represented a noteworthy development. While historians have tended to identify the People's Will with its small but well-defined Executive Committee, the organization in fact encompassed a broad range of members and supporters, numbering in the thousands, as well as many sympathizers. More peaceful activities, however, were overshadowed by the aura of drama and violence surrounding the party's daring struggle against the tsarist regime, culminating in the assassination of the tsar, Alexander II, on March 1, 1881. In the predictable aftermath, five members of the People's Will were hanged and many more imprisoned.

Contrary to the standard historiographical treatment, the People's Will did not disappear from the scene following March 1, but rather continued to exist in a more widespread and decentralized form. Radicals calling themselves *narodovoltsy* (supporters of the People's Will) continued to engage in propaganda and organizing activities among students and workers in provincial towns and industrial centers, as well as in St. Petersburg and Moscow, throughout the 1880s and into the 1890s. By this time, narodovoltsy were taking second place in the revolutionary movement to radicals who identified themselves as social democrats (Marxists). The populist tradition experienced a revival with the formation of the Socialist Revolutionary Party during the early twentieth century. In a sense, however, both revolutionary parties of the period leading up to the 1917 revolution, the Social Democrats as well as the Socialist Revolutionaries, can be considered the heirs of the People's Will, whose banner, at a crucial stage, symbolized the revolutionary movement in Russia.

*See also:* LAND AND FREEDOM PARTY; POPULISM

**BIBLIOGRAPHY**

Naimark, Norman M. (1983). *Terrorists and Social Democrats: The Russian Revolutionary Movement Under Alexander III.* Cambridge, MA: Harvard University Press.

Offord, Derek. (1986). *The Russian Revolutionary Movement in the 1880s.* Cambridge, UK: Cambridge University Press.

Pearl, Deborah. (1996). "From Worker to Revolutionary: The Making of Worker Narodovol'tsy." *Russian History* 23(1–4):11–26.

Venturi, Franco. (1966). *Roots of Revolution: A History of the Populist and Socialist Movements in Nineteenth Century Russia*, tr. Francis Haskell. New York: Universal Library.

DEBORAH PEARL

# PERESTROIKA

*Perestroika* was the term given to the reform process launched in the Soviet Union under the leadership of Mikhail Gorbachev in 1985. Meaning "reconstruction" or "restructuring," perestroika was a concept that was both ambiguous and malleable. Its ambiguity lay in the fact that it might convey no more than a reorganization of existing Soviet institutions and thus be a synonym for reform of a modest kind or, alternatively, it could signify reconstruction of the system from the foundations up, thus amounting to transformative change. The vagueness and ambiguity were initially an advantage, for even the term *reform* had become taboo during the conservative Leonid Brezhnev years after the Soviet leadership had been frightened by the Prague Spring reforms of 1968.

Perestroika had the advantage of coming without political and ideological baggage. Everyone could—in the first two years, at least, of the Mikhail Gorbachev era—be in favor of it. Its malleability meant that under this rubric some urged modest change that in their view was enough to get the economy moving again while others who wished to transform the way the entire system worked were able to advance more daring arguments, taking cover under the umbrella of perestroika. Within Gorbachev's own top leadership team, both Yegor Ligachev and Alexander Yakovlev expressed their commitment to perestroika, but for the latter this meant much more far-reaching political reform than for the former. Once political pluralism had by 1989 become an accepted norm, perestroika as a concept had largely outlived its political utility.

For Gorbachev himself the term "perestroika" meant different things at different times. Initially, it was a euphemism for "reform," but later it came to signify systemic change. Gorbachev's views underwent a major evolution during the period he held the post of General Secretary of the Central Committee of the CPSU and that included the meaning he imparted to perestroika. In an important December 1984 speech before he became Soviet leader, Gorbachev had said that one of the important things on the agenda was a "perestroika of the forms and methods of running the economy." By 1987 the concept for Gorbachev was much broader and clearly embraced radical political reform and the transformation of Soviet foreign policy. Gorbachev's thinking at that time was set out in a book, *Perestroika: New Thinking for our Country and the World*. While the ideas contained were far removed from traditional Soviet dogma, they by no means yet reflected the full evolution of Gorbachev's own position (and, with it, his understanding of perestroika). In 1987 Gorbachev was talking about radical reform of the existing system. During the run-up to the Nineteenth Conference of the Communist Party, held in the summer of 1988, he came to the conclusion that the system had to be transformed so comprehensively as to become something different in kind. In 1987 he still spoke about "communism," although he had redefined it to make freedom and the rule of law among its unfamiliar values; by the end of the 1980s, Gorbachev had given up speaking about "communism." The "socialism," of which he continued to speak, had become socialism of a social democratic type.

Perestroika became an overarching conception, under which a great many new concepts were introduced into Soviet political discourse after 1985. These included such departures from the Marxist-Leninist lexicon as *glasnost* (openness, transparency), *pravovoe gosudarstvo* (a state based on the rule of law), checks and balances, and pluralism. One of the most remarkable innovations was Gorbachev's breaking of the taboo on speaking positively about pluralism. Initially (in 1987) this was a "socialist pluralism" or a "pluralism of opinion." That, however, opened the way for others in the Soviet Union to talk positively about "pluralism" without the socialist qualifier. By early 1990 Gorbachev himself had embraced the notion of "political pluralism," doing so at the point at which he proposed to the Central Committee removing from the Soviet Constitution the guaranteed "leading role" of the Communist Party.

Even perestroika as understood in the earliest years of Gorbachev's leadership—not least because of its embrace of glasnost—opened the way for real political debate and political movement in a system which had undergone little fundamental political change for decades. In his 1987 book, *Perestroika*,

**Mikhail Gorbachev reacts to the announcement of foreign minister Eduard Shevardnadze' planned resignation at a Congress of the People's Deputies meeting held December 20, 1990.** BORIS YURCHENKO/ASSOCIATED PRESS. REPRODUCED BY PERMISSION.

Gorbachev wrote: "Glasnost, criticism and self-criticism are not just a new campaign. They have been proclaimed and must become a norm in the Soviet way of life . . . . There is no democracy, nor can there be, without glasnost. And there is no present-day socialism, nor can there be, without democracy." Such exhortation was alarming to those who wished to preserve the Soviet status quo or to revert to the status quo ante. It was, though, music to the ears of people who wished to promote the more rapid democratization of the Soviet system, even to advocate moving further and faster than Gorbachev at the time was prepared to endorse.

If perestroika is considered as an epoch in Soviet and Russian history, rather than a concept (though conceptual change in a hitherto ideocratic system was crucially important), it can be seen as one in which a Pandora's box was opened. The system, whatever its failings, had been highly effective in controlling and suppressing dissent, and it

was far from being on the point of collapse in 1985. Perestroika produced both intended and unintended consequences. From the outset Gorbachev's aims included a liberalization of the Soviet system and the ending of the Cold War. Liberalization, in fact, developed into democratization (the latter term being one that Gorbachev used from the beginning, although its meaning, too, developed within the course of the next several years) and the Cold War was over by the end of the 1980s. A major aspect of perestroika in its initial conception was, however, to inject a new dynamism into the Soviet economy. In that respect it failed. Indeed, Gorbachev came to believe that the Soviet economic system, just like the political system, needed not reform but dismantling and to be rebuilt on different foundations.

The ultimate unintended consequence of perestroika was the disintegration of the Soviet Union. Liberalization and democratization turned what Gorbachev had called "pre-crisis phenomena" (most notably, economic stagnation) during the early 1980s into a full-blown crisis of survival of the state by 1990–1991. Measuring such an outcome against the initial aims of perestroika suggests its failure. But the goals of the foremost proponents of perestroika, and of Mikhail Gorbachev personally, rapidly evolved, and democratization came to be given a higher priority than economic reform. At the end of this experiment in the peaceful transformation of a highly authoritarian system, there were fifteen newly independent states and Russia itself had become a freer country than at any point in its previous history. Taken in conjunction with the benign transformation of East-West relations, these results constitute major achievements that more than counterbalance the failures. They point also to the fact that there could be no blueprint for the democratization of a state that had been at worst totalitarian and at best highly authoritarian for some seven decades. Perestroika became a process of trial and error, but one that was underpinned by ideas and values radically different from those which constituted the ideological foundations of the unreformed Soviet system.

*See also:* DEMOCRATIZATION; GLASNOST; GORBACHEV, MIKHAIL SERGEYEVICH; NEW POLITICAL THINKING

**BIBLIOGRAPHY**

Brown, Archie. (1996). *The Gorbachev Factor.* New York: Oxford University Press.

English, Robert D. (2000). *Russia and the Idea of the West: Gorbachev, Intellectuals, and the End of the Cold War.* New York: Columbia University Press.

Gorbachev, Mikhail. (1987). *Perestroika: New Thinking for Our Country and the World.* London: Collins.

Gorbachev, Mikhail, and Mlynar, Zdenek. (2002). *Conversations with Gorbachev: On Perestroika, the Prague Spring, and the Crossroads of Socialism.* New York: Columbia University Press.

Hough, Jerry F. (1997). *Democratization and Revolution in the USSR.* Washington, DC: Brookings Institution.

Matlock, Jack F., Jr. (1995). *Autopsy of an Empire: The American Ambassador's Account of the Collapse of the Soviet Union.* New York: Random House.

ARCHIE BROWN

# PERMANENT REVOLUTION

"Permanent Revolution" was Leon Trotsky's explanation of how a communist revolution could occur in an industrially backward Russia. According to classical Marxism, only a society of advanced capitalism with a large working class was ripe for communist revolution. Russia met neither prerequisite. Further, Karl Marx conceived of a two-stage revolution: first the bourgeois revolution, then in sequence the proletarian revolution establishing a dictatorship for transition to communism. Trotsky argued that the two-stage theory did not apply. Rather, he said, Russia was in a stage of uneven development where both bourgeois and proletarian revolutions were developing together under the impact of the advanced West.

Trotsky predicted that once revolution broke out in Russia it would be in permanence as the result of an East–West dynamic. The bourgeois majority revolution would be overthrown by a conscious proletarian minority that would carry forward the torch of revolution. However, a second phase was necessary: namely, the proletarian revolution in Western Europe ignited by the Russian proletariat's initiative; the West European proletariat now in power rescues the beleaguered proletarian minority in Russia; and the path is opened to the international communist revolution.

Trotsky's theory seemed corroborated in the 1917 Russian revolution. Tsarism was overthrown by a bourgeois Provisional Government in February which the Bolsheviks then overthrew in October. However, the second phase posited by Trotsky's theory, the West European revolution, did not materialize. The Bolsheviks faced the dilemma of how to sustain power where an advanced industrial economy did not exist. Was not Bolshevik rule doomed to failure without Western aid?

Usurping power, Josef Stalin answered Trotsky's theory with his "socialism in one country." Curiously, his recipe was similar to a strategy Trotsky earlier proposed, namely, command economy, forced industrialization, and collectivization. With the communist collapse in Russia in 1991 both Trotsky's and Stalin's theories became moot.

*See also:* BOLSHEVISM; MARXISM; SOCIALISM IN ONE COUNTRY; TROTSKY, LEON DAVIDOVICH

**BIBLIOGRAPHY**

Trotsky, Leon. (1969). *The Permanent Revolution.* New York: Pathfinder Press.

CARL A. LINDEN

## PEROVSKAYA, SOFIA LVOVNA

(1853–1881), Russian revolutionary populist, a member of the Executive committee of "Narodnaya Volya" ("People's Will"), and a direct supervisor of the murder of emperor Alexander II.

Sofia Perovskaya was born in St. Petersburg to a noble family; her father was the governor of St. Petersburg. In 1869 she attended the Alarchin Women's Courses in St. Petersburg, where she founded the self-education study group. At age seventeen, she left home. From 1871 to 1872 she was one of the organizers of the Tchaikovsky circle. Her remarkable organizational skills and willpower never failed to gain her leading positions in various revolutionary societies. To prepare for "going to the people," she passed a public teacher's exam and completed her studies as a doctor's assistant. In January 1874 she was arrested and detained for several months in the Peter and Paul Fortress and faced the Trial of 193 (1877–1878), but was proven innocent. She joined the populist organization *Zemlya i Volya* (Land and Freedom) and took part in an unsuccessful armed attempt to free Ippolit Myshkin, who was proven guilty at the Trial of 193. During the summer of 1878 she was once again arrested, and exiled to Olonetskaya province, but on the way there she fled and assumed an illegal status. In June 1879 Perovskaya took part in the Voronezh assembly of Zemlya i Volya, soon after which the organization split into Narodnaya Volya (People's Will) and *Cherny Peredel* (The Black Repartition). From the autumn of 1879, she was a member of the executive committee of Narodnaya Volya. In November 1879 she took part in the organization of the attempt to blow up the tsar's train near Moscow. She played the role of the wife of railroad inspector Sukhorukov (Narodnaya Volya member Lev Gartman): The underground tunnel that led to the railroad tracks where the bomb was planted came from his house. By mistake, however, it was the train of the tsar's entourage that got blown up. During the spring of 1880, Perovskaya took part in another attempt to kill the tsar in Odessa. In the preparation of the successful attempt on March 13, 1881, on the Yekaterininsky channel in St. Petersburg, she headed a watching squad, and after the party leader Andrei Zhelyabov (Perovskaya's lover) was arrested, she headed the operation until it was completed, having personally drawn the plan of the positions of the grenade throwers and given the signal to attack. Hoping to free her arrested comrades, after the murder Perovskaya did not leave St. Petersburg and was herself arrested. At the trial of *pervomartovtsy* (participants of the murder of the tsar), Perovskaya was sentenced to death and hanged on April 15, 1881, on the Semenovsky parade ground in St. Petersburg, becoming the first woman in Russia to be executed for a political crime.

*See also:* ALEXANDER II; LAND AND FREEDOM PARTY; PEOPLE'S WILL, THE

### BIBLIOGRAPHY

Figner, Vera. (1927). *Memoirs of a Revolutionist.* New York: International Publishers.

Footman, David. (1968). *Red Prelude: A Life of A.I. Zhelyabov.* London: Barrie & Rockliff .

Venturi, Franco. (1983). *Roots of revolution: A History of the Populist and Socialist Movements in Nineteenth-Century Russia.* Chicago: University of Chicago Press.

OLEG BUDNITSKII

## PERSIAN GULF WAR

The Persian Gulf War of 1990 and 1991 began as the high point of Soviet-American cooperation in the postwar period. However, by late December 1990, a chilling of Soviet-American relations had set in as Soviet leader Mikhail Gorbachev sought to play both sides of the conflict, only to have the USSR suffer a major political defeat once the war came to an end.

Following the Iraqi invasion of Kuwait in August 1990, Soviet foreign minister Eduard Shevardnadze joined U.S. secretary of state James Baker in severely condemning the Iraqi action, and the United States and USSR jointly supported numerous U.N. Security Council Resolutions demanding an Iraqi withdrawal and imposing sanctions on Iraq for its behavior.

Nonetheless, while supporting the United States (although not committing Soviet forces to battle), Gorbachev also sought to play a mediating role between Iraq and the United States, in part to salvage Moscow's important economic interests in that country (oil drilling, oil exploration, hydroelectric projects, and grain elevator construction, as well as lucrative arms sales), and in part to bolster his political flank against those on the right of the Soviet political spectrum (many of whom were later to stage an abortive coup against him in August 1991), who were complaining that Moscow had "sold out" Iraq, a traditional ally of the USSR and one with which Moscow had been linked by a Treaty of Friendship and Cooperation since 1972.

Responding to these pressures, Gorbachev twice sent a senior Soviet Middle East Expert, Yevgeny Primakov, to Iraq to try to mediate on Iraqi withdrawal from Kuwait, albeit to no avail. Instead, the Soviet specialists working in Iraq were swiftly taken hostage in advance of the January 15, 1991, United Nations deadline for an Iraqi withdrawal.

In late December 1990, as it became more and more apparent that the U.S.-led coalition would begin its attack against Iraq on January 15, Shevardnadze suddenly resigned as Soviet foreign minister in the face of mounting pressure from Soviet right-wing forces. His replacement, Alexander Bessmertnykh, was far less pro-U.S., and his remarks utilized the old Soviet jargon of "balance of power" rather than Gorbachev's "balance of interests" terminology. Nonetheless, this did not inhibit the coalition attack on Iraq that took place on January 15 and that thoroughly defeated Saddam Hussein's forces and drove them out of Kuwait by the end of February 1991. Gorbachev's behavior during the fighting, as he sought the best possible deal for Hussein from the United States, resembled that of a trial lawyer seeking to plea bargain for his client under increasingly negative conditions. This was particularly evident in his peace plan of February 21, which provided for a lifting of sanctions against Iraq before it had fully withdrawn its troops from Kuwait. The United States, however, neither accepted Gorbachev's entreaties nor paid much attention to the increasingly hostile warnings of Soviet generals as U.S. troops advanced.

By the time the war ended, Washington had emerged as the dominant power in the Middle East, while the USSR lost much of its influence both in the Middle East and in the world. After the war, the United States consolidated its military position in the Persian Gulf and reinforced its relations with Saudi Arabia, Kuwait, and the other members of the Gulf Cooperation Council, while Moscow sat on the diplomatic sidelines.

Given Moscow's diminished position in the region and in the world as a whole after the Gulf War, Gorbachev tried to salvage the USSR's prestige to the greatest degree possible. Thus, besides trying to reinforce relations with Iran, he sought to retain a modicum of influence in Iraq by opposing U.N. intervention following the postwar massacres of Iraqi Shiites and Kurds by Hussein's forces. Primakov, whose influence in the Russian government was rising, stated that he believed Hussein "has sufficient potential to give us hope for a positive development of relations with him."

Nonetheless, Gorbachev's attempts to protect Hussein availed him little. Less than a year after the end of the Gulf War, the USSR collapsed, and Gorbachev fell from power.

See also: IRAQ, RELATIONS WITH; UNITED STATES, RELATIONS WITH

**BIBLIOGRAPHY**

Beschloss, Michael R., and Talbott, Strobe. (1993). *At the Highest Levels: The Inside Story of the End of the Cold War*. Boston: Little, Brown.

Freedman, Robert O. (2001). *Russian Policy Toward the Middle East Since the Collapse of the Soviet Union: The Yeltsin Legacy and the Challenge for Putin (Donald W. Treadgold Papers in Russian, East European, and Central Asian Studies*, no. 33). Seattle: University of Washington: Henry M. Jackson School of International Studies.

Nizamedden, Talal. (1999). *Russia and the Middle East*. New York: St. Martins.

Rumer, Eugene. (2000). *Dangerous Drift: Russia's Middle East Policy*. Washington, DC: Washington Institute for Near East Policy.

Shaffer, Brenda. (2001). *Partners in Need: The Strategic Relationship of Russia and Iran*. Washington, DC: Washington Institute for Near East Policy.

Vassiliev, Alexei. (1993). *Russian Policy in the Middle East: From Messianism to Pragmatism*. Reading, UK: Ithaca Press.

ROBERT O. FREEDMAN

# PESTEL, PAVEL IVANOVICH

(1793–1826), a leader of the Decembrist movement.

Pavel Ivanovich Pestel, the son of Ivan Borisovich Pestel and Elisaveta Ivanovna von Krok, was born in Moscow into a family of German and Lutheran background. He was sent to Dresden at the age of twelve to be educated, and on his return four years later he joined the Corps of Pages in St. Petersburg, where he began to study political science. On graduating Pestel entered the army and in time joined several secret societies. The most important of these was the Society of Salvation, founded in 1817 and later renamed the Society of Welfare. Several of Pestel's fellow officers had been in Paris and Western Europe during the war against Napoleon, and from them he became familiar with the ideas of the French Revolution. Transferred to the southern Russia in 1818, Pestel organized a local branch of the Society of Welfare, where he and his friends discussed such ideas as constitutional monarchy and republican government, as well as the means by which the imperial family might be coerced into accepting the former or made to abdicate in favor of the latter.

Pestel left two unfinished works, *Russkaia Pravda* (*Russian Truth*) and *Prakticheskie nachala politicheskoy ekonomy* (*Practical Principles of Political Economy*). The first outlines a program for political reform in Russia; the second, a rambling essay on economics, expresses admiration for the prosperity made possible by political freedom in the United States. Pestel's ideas, especially in their tendency to favor radical solutions to the problem of Russia's political backwardness, relied heavily on the ideas of the French writer Antoine Louis Claude Destutt de Tracy, but they had other French and German sources as well.

When Alexander I died in December 1825 there was some confusion about the succession. There was also confusion among those who were plotting a revolt. The more radical revolutionaries were in the south under Pestel's leadership. Betrayed by informants in the Southern Society, Pestel was arrested on December 13, the same day that three thousand soldiers demonstrated in Senate Square in St. Petersburg on behalf of Alexander I's brother, Constantine, who had already given up his claim to the throne in favor of his brother, Nicholas. Pestel's colleague Sergei Muraviev-Apostol attempted to lead a revolt, but it was crushed by imperial troops. Pestel was found guilty of treason and executed in 1826 with four of his fellow revolutionaries, Muraviev-Apostol, Peter Kakhovsky, Mikhail Bestuzhev-Ryumin, and Kondraty Ryleyev.

*See also:* DECEMBRIST MOVEMENT AND REBELLION; RYLEYEV, KONDRATY FYODOROVICH

### BIBLIOGRAPHY

Mazour, Anatole G. (1937). *The First Russian Revolution, 1825: The Decembrist Movement: Its Origins, Development, and Significance.* Stanford, CA: Stanford University Press.

Walsh, Warren B. (1968). *Russia and the Soviet Union: A Modern History.* Ann Arbor: University of Michigan Press.

PAUL CREGO

## PETER I

(1672–1725), known as Peter the Great, tsar and emperor of Russia, 1682–1725.

The reign of Peter I is generally regarded as a watershed in Russian history, during which Russia expanded westward, became a leading player in European affairs, and underwent major reforms of its government, economy, religious affairs, and culture. Peter is regarded as a "modernizer" or "westernizer," who forced changes upon his often reluctant subjects. In 1846 the Russian historian Nikolai Pogodin wrote: "The Russia of today, that is to say, European Russia, diplomatic, political, military, commercial, industrial, scholastic, literary—is the creation of Peter the Great. Everywhere we look, we encounter this colossal figure, who casts a long shadow over our entire past." Writers before and after agreed that Peter made a mark on the course of Russian history, although there has always been disagreement about whether his influence was positive or negative.

### CHILDHOOD AND YOUTH

The only son of the second marriage of Tsar Alexei Mikhailovich of Russia (r. 1645–1676) to Nathalie Kirillovna Naryshkina, Peter succeeded his half-brother Tsar Fyodor Alexeyevich (1676–1682) in May 1682. In June, following the bloody rebellion of the Moscow musketeers, in which members of his mother's family and government officials were massacred, he was crowned second tsar jointly with his elder, but severely handicapped, half-brother Ivan V. Kept out of government during the regency of his half-sister Sophia Alexeyevna (r. 1682–1689), Peter pursued personal interests that later fed into his public activities; these included meeting foreigners, learning to sail, and forming "play" troops under the command of foreign officers, which became the Preobrazhensky and Semenovsky guards. On Tsar Ivan's death in 1696, Peter found himself sole ruler and enjoyed his first military victory, the capture of the Turkish fortress at Azov, a success which was facilitated by a newly created fleet on the Don river. From 1697 to 1698 he made an unprecedented tour of Western Europe with the Grand Embassy, the official aim of which was to revive the Holy League against the Ottomans, which Russia had entered in 1686. Peter traveled incognito, devoting much of his time to visiting major sites and institutions in his search for knowledge. He was particularly impressed with the Dutch Republic and England, where he studied shipbuilding. On his return, he forced his boyars to shave off their beards and adopt Western dress. In 1700 he discarded the old Byzantine creation calendar in favor of dating years in the Western manner from the birth of Christ. These symbolic acts set the agenda for cultural change.

## THE GREAT NORTHERN
### WAR, 1700–1721

After making peace with the Ottoman Empire in 1700, Peter declared war on Sweden with the aim of regaining a foothold on the Baltic, in alliance with Denmark and King Augustus II of Poland. After some early defeats, notably at Narva in 1700, and the loss of its allies, Russia eventually gained the upper hand over the Swedes. After Narva, King Charles XII abandoned his Russian campaign to pursue Augustus into Poland and Saxony, allowing Russia to advance in Ingria and Livonia. When he eventually invaded Russia via Ukraine in 1707–1708, Charles found his troops overextended, under-provisioned, and confronted by a much improved Russian army. Victory at Poltava in Ukraine in 1709 allowed Peter to stage a successful assault on Sweden's eastern Baltic ports, including Viborg, Riga, and Reval (Tallinn) in 1710. Defeat by the Turks on the river Pruth in 1711 forced him to return Azov (ratified in the 1713 Treaty of Adrianople), but did not prevent him pursuing the Swedish war both at the negotiating table and on campaign, for instance, in Finland in 1713–1714 and against Sweden's remaining possessions in northern Germany and the Swedish mainland. The Treaty of Nystadt (1721) ratified Russian possession of Livonia, Estonia, and Ingria. During the celebrations the Senate awarded Peter the titles Emperor, the Great, and Father of the Fatherland. In 1722–1723 Peter conducted a campaign against Persia on the Caspian, capturing the ports of Baku and Derbent. Russia's military successes were achieved chiefly by intensive recruitment, which allowed Peter to keep armies in the field over several decades; training by foreign officers; home production of weapons, especially artillery; and well-organized provisioning. The task was made easier by the availability of a servile peasant population and the obstacles which the Russian terrain and cli-

**Peter I in battle at Poltava.** © THE STATE RUSSIAN MUSEUM/CORBIS

mate posed for the invading Swedes. The navy, staffed mainly by foreign officers on both home-built and purchased ships, provided an auxiliary force in the latter stages of the Northern War, although Peter's personal involvement in naval affairs has led some historians to exaggerate the fleet's importance. The galley fleet was particularly effective, as exemplified at Hango in 1714.

## DOMESTIC REFORMS

Many historians have argued that the demands of war were the driving force behind all Peter's reforms. He created the Senate in 1711, for example, to rule in his absence during the Turkish campaign. Among the ten new Swedish-inspired government departments, created between 1717 and 1720 and known as Colleges or collegiate boards, the Colleges of War, Admiralty, and Foreign Affairs consumed the bulk of state revenues, while the Colleges of

Mines and Manufacturing concentrated on production for the war effort, operating iron works and manufacture of weapons, rope, canvas, uniforms, powder, and other products. The state remained the chief producer and customer, but Peter attempted to encourage individual enterprise by offering subsidies and exemptions. Free manpower was short, however, and in 1721 industrialists were allowed to purchase serfs for their factories. New provincial institutions, based on Swedish models and created in several restructuring programs, notably in 1708–1709 and 1718–1719, were intended to rationalize recruitment and tax collection, but were among the least successful of Peter's projects. As he said, money was the "artery of war." A number of piecemeal fiscal measures culminated in 1724 with the introduction of the poll tax (initially 74 kopecks per annum), which replaced direct taxation based on households with assessment of individual males. Peter also encouraged foreign trade and diversified indirect taxes, which were attached to such items and services as official paper for contracts, private bathhouses, oak coffins, and beards (the 1705 beard tax). Duties from liquor, customs, and salt were profitable.

The Table of Ranks (1722) consolidated earlier legislation by dividing the service elite—army and navy officers, government and court officials—into three columns of fourteen ranks, each containing a variable number of posts. No post was supposed to be allocated to any candidate who was unqualified for the duties involved, but birth and marriage continued to confer privilege at court. The Table was intended to encourage the existing nobility to perform more efficiently, while endorsing the concept of nobles as natural leaders of society: Any commoner who attained the lowest military rank— grade 14—or civil grade 8 was granted noble status, including the right to pass it to his children.

Peter's educational reforms, too, were utilitarian in focus, as was his publishing program, which focused on such topics as shipbuilding, navigation, architecture, warfare, geography, and history. He introduced a new simplified alphabet, the so-called civil script, for printing secular works. The best-known and most successful of Peter's technical schools was the Moscow School of Mathematics and Navigation (1701; from 1715, the St. Petersburg Naval Academy), which was run by British teachers. Its graduates were sent to teach in the so-called cipher or arithmetic schools (1714), but these failed to attract pupils. Priests and church schools continued to be the main suppliers of primary education, and religious books continued to sell better than secular ones. The Academy of Sciences is generally regarded as the major achievement, although it did not open until 1726 and was initially staffed entirely by foreigners. In Russia, as elsewhere, children in rural communities, where child labor was vital to the economy, remained uneducated.

## THE CHURCH

The desire to deploy scarce resources as rationally as possible guided Peter's treatment of the Orthodox Church. He abolished the patriarchate, which was left vacant when the last Patriarch died in 1700, and in 1721 replaced it with the Holy Synod, which was based on the collegiate principle and later overseen by a secular official, the Over-Procurator. The Synod's rationale and program were set out in the *Spiritual Regulation* (1721). Peter siphoned off church funds as required, but he stopped short of secularizing church lands. He slimmed down the priesthood by redeploying superfluous clergymen into state service and restricting entry into monasteries, which he regarded as refuges for shirkers. Remaining churchmen accumulated various civic duties, such as keeping registers of births and deaths, running schools and hospitals, and publicizing government decrees. These measures continued seventeenth-century trends in reducing the church's independent power, but Peter went farther by reducing its role in cultural life. Himself a dutiful Orthodox Christian who attended church regularly, he was happy for the Church to take responsibility for the saving of men's souls, but not for it to rule their lives. His reforms were supported by educated churchmen imported from Ukraine.

## ST. PETERSBURG AND
## THE NEW CULTURE

The city of St. Petersburg began as an island fort at the mouth of the Neva river on land captured from the Swedes in 1703. From about 1712 it came to be regarded as the capital. In Russia's battle for international recognition, St. Petersburg was much more than a useful naval base and port. It was a clean sheet on which Peter could construct a microcosm of his New Russia. The Western designs and decoration of palaces, government buildings, and churches, built in stone by hired foreign architects according to a rational plan, and the European fashions that all Russian townspeople were forced to wear, were calculated to make foreigners feel that they were in Europe rather than in Asia. The city became a "great window recently opened in the north through which Russia looks on Europe" (Francesco Algarotti, 1739). Peter often referred to it as his "paradise," playing on the associations with St. Peter as well as expressing his personal delight in a city built on water. The central public spaces enjoyed amenities such as street lighting and paving and public welfare was supervised by the Chief of Police, although conditions were less salubrious in the backstreets. Nobles resented being uprooted from Moscow to this glorified building site. Noblewomen were not exempt. They were wrenched from their previously sheltered lives in the semi-secluded women's quarters or terem and ordered to abandon their modest, loose robes and veils in favor of Western low cut gowns and corsets and to socialize and drink with men. Some historians have referred to the "emancipation" of women under Peter, but it is doubtful whether this was the view of those involved.

## PETER'S VISION AND METHODS

Peter was an absolute ruler, whose great height (six foot seven inches) and explosive temper must have intimidated those close to him. His portraits, the first thoroughly Westernized Russian images painted or sculpted from life, were embellished with Imperial Roman, allegorical, military, and naval motifs to underline his power. Yet he sought to deflect his subjects' loyalty from himself to the state, exhorting them to work for the common good. A doer rather than a thinker, he lacked formal education and the patience for theorizing. Soviet historians favored the image of the Tsar-Carpenter, emphasizing the fourteen trades that Peter mastered, of which his favorites were shipbuilding and wood turning. He also occasionally practiced dentistry and surgery. Ironically, Peter often behaved in a manner that confirmed foreign prejudices that Russia was a barbaric country. Abroad he frequently offended his hosts with his appalling manners, while Western visitors to Russia were perplexed by his court, which featured dwarfs, giants, and human "monsters" (from his Cabinet of Curiosities), compulsory drinking sessions, which armed guards prevented guests prevented from leaving, and weird ceremonies staged by the "All-Mad, All-Jesting, All-Drunken Assembly," which, headed by the Prince-Pope, parodied religious rituals. Throughout his life Peter maintained a mock court headed by a mock tsar known as Prince Caesar, who conferred promotions on "Peter Mikhailov" or "Peter Alexeyev," as Peter liked to be known as he worked his way through the ranks of the army and navy.

One of the functions of Peter's mock institutions was to ridicule the old ways. Peter constantly lamented his subjects' reluctance to improve themselves on their own initiative. As he wrote in an edict of 1721 to replace sickles with more efficient scythes: "Even though something may be good, if it is new our people will not do it." He therefore resorted to force. In Russia, where serfdom was made law as recently as 1649, the idea of a servile population was not new, but under Peter servitude was extended and intensified. The army and navy swallowed up tens of thousands of men. State peasants were increasingly requisitioned to work on major projects. Previously free persons were transferred to the status of serfs during the introduction of the poll tax. Peter also believed in the power of rules, regulations, and statutes, devised "in order that everyone knows his duties and no one excuses himself on the grounds of ignorance." In 1720, for example, he issued the General Regulation, a "regulation of regulations" for the new government apparatus. Not only the peasants, but also the nobles, found life burdensome. They were forced to serve for life and to educate their sons for service.

## ASSOCIATES AND OPPONENTS

Despite his harsh methods, Peter was supported by a number of men, drawn from both the old Muscovite elite and from outside it. The most prominent of the newcomers were his favorite, the talented and corrupt Alexander Menshikov (1673–1729), whom he made a prince, and Paul Yaguzhinsky, who became the first Procurator-General. Top men from the traditional elite included General Boris Sheremetev, Chancellor Gavrila Golovkin, Admiral Fyodor Apraksin and Prince Fyodor Romodanovsky. The chief publicist was the Ukrainian churchman Feofan Prokopovich. It is a misconception that Peter relied on foreigners and commoners.

Religious traditionalists abhorred Peter, identifying him as the Antichrist. The several revolts of his reign all included some elements of antagonism toward foreigners and foreign innovations such as shaving and Western dress, along with more standard and substantive complaints about the encroachment of central authority, high taxes, poor conditions of service, and remuneration. The most serious were the musketeer revolt of 1698, the Astrakhan revolt of 1705, and the rebellion led by the

Don Cossack Ivan Bulavin in 1707–1708. The disruption that worried Peter most, however, affected his inner circle. Peter was married twice: in 1689 to the noblewoman Yevdokia Lopukhina, whom he banished to a convent in 1699, and in 1712 to Catherine, a former servant girl from Livonia whom he met around 1703. He groomed the surviving son of his first marriage, Alexei Petrovich (1690–1718), as his successor, but they had a troubled relationship. In 1716 Alexei fled abroad. Lured back to Russia in 1718, he was tried and condemned to death for treason, based on unfounded charges of a plot to assassinate his father. Many of Alexei's associates were executed, and people in leading circles were suspected of sympathy for him. Peter and Catherine had at least ten children (the precise number is unknown), but only two girls reached maturity: Anna and Elizabeth (who reigned as empress from 1741 to 1761). In 1722 Peter issued a new Law of Succession by which the reigning monarch nominated his own successor, but he failed to record his choice before his death (from a bladder infection) in February (January O.S.) 1725. Immediately after Peter's death, Menshikov and some leading courtiers with guards' support backed Peter's widow, who reigned as Catherine I (1725–1727).

### VIEWS OF PETER AND HIS REFORMS

The official view in the eighteenth century and much of the nineteenth was that Peter had "given birth" to Russia, transforming it from "nonexistence" into "being." Poets represented him as Godlike. The man and his methods were easily accommodated in later eighteenth-century discourses of Enlightened Absolutism. Even during Peter's lifetime, however, questions were raised about the heavy cost of his schemes and the dangers of abandoning native culture and institutions. As the Russian historian Nikolai Karamzin commented in 1810: "Truly, St. Petersburg is founded on tears and corpses." He believed that Peter had made Russians citizens of the world, but prevented them from being Russians. Hatred of St. Petersburg as a symbol of alien traditions was an important element in the attitude of nineteenth-century Slavophiles, who believed that only the peasants had retained Russian cultural values. To their Westernizer opponents, however, Peter's reforms, stopping short of Western freedoms, had not gone far enough. In the later nineteenth century, serious studies of seventeenth-century Muscovy questioned the revolutionary nature of Peter's reign, underlining that many of Peter's reforms and poli-

cies, such as hiring foreigners, reforming the army, and borrowing Western culture, originated with his predecessors. The last tsars, especially Nicholas II, took a nostalgic view of pre-Petrine Russia, but Petrine values were revered by the imperial court until its demise.

Soviet historians generally took a bipolar view of Peter's reign. On the one hand, they believed that Russia had to catch up with the West, whatever the cost; hence they regarded institutional and cultural reforms, the new army, navy, factories, and so on as "progressive." Territorial expansion was approved. On the other hand, Soviet historians were bound to denounce Peter's exploitation of the peasantry and to praise popular rebels such as Bulavin; moreover, under Stalin, Peter's cosmopolitanism was treated with suspicion. Cultural historians in particular stressed native achievements over foreign borrowings. In the 1980s–1990s some began to take a more negative view still, characterizing Peter as "the creator of the administrative-command system and the true ancestor of Stalin" (Anisimov, 1993). After the collapse of the USSR, the secession of parts of the former Empire and Union, and the decline of the armed forces and navy, many people looked back to Peter's reign as a time when Russia was strong and to Peter as an ideal example of a strong leader. The debate continues.

*See also:* ALEXEI PETROVICH; CATHERINE I; ELIZABETH; FYODOR ALEXEYEVICH; MENSHIKOV, ALEXANDER DANILOVICH; PATRIARCHATE; PEASANTRY; SERFDOM; ST. PETERSBURG; TABLE OF RANKS

### BIBLIOGRAPHY

Anderson, M. S. (1995). *Peter the Great.* London: Longman.

Anisimov, E. V. (1993). *Progress through Coercion: The Reforms of Peter the Great.* New York: M. E. Sharpe.

Bushkovitch, Paul. (2001). *Peter the Great: The Struggle for Power, 1671–1725.* Cambridge, UK: Cambridge University Press.

*Canadian American Slavic Studies.* 8 (1974). Issue devoted to Peter's reign.

Cracraft, James. (1971). *The Church Reform of Peter the Great.* Oxford: Oxford University Press.

Cracraft, James. (1990). *The Petrine Revolution in Russian Architecture.* Chicago: University of Chicago Press.

Cracraft, James. (1997). *The Petrine Revolution in Russian Imagery.* Chicago: University of Chicago Press.

Hughes, Lindsey. (1998). *Russia in the Age of Peter the Great.* New Haven, CT: Yale University Press.

Hughes, Lindsey, ed. (2000). *Peter the Great and the West: New Perspectives.* Basingstoke, UK: Palgrave.

Hughes, Lindsey. (2002). *Peter the Great: A Biography.* New Haven, CT: Yale University Press.

Kliuchevsky, Vasily. (1958). *Peter the Great,* tr. L. Archibald. New York: St. Martin's Press.

Pososhkov, Ivan. (1987). *The Book of Poverty and Wealth,* ed., tr. A. P. Vlasto, L. R. Lewitter. London: The Athlone Press.

Raeff, Marc. ed. (1972). *Peter the Great Changes Russia.* Lexington, MA: Heath.

Riasanovsky, Nicholas. (1984). *The Image of Peter the Great in Russian History and Thought.* Oxford: Oxford University Press.

LINDSEY HUGHES

## PETER II

(1715–1730), emperor of Russia, May 1727 to January 1730.

Son of Tsarevich Alexis Petrovich and Princess Charlotte of Wolfenbüttel, and grandson of Peter I, the future Peter II had an unfortunate start in life. His German mother died soon after his birth, and in 1718 his father died in prison after being tortured and condemned to death for treason. Peter I did not mistreat his grandson, but feared him as a possible rallying point for conservatives. He did not groom him as his heir, and a new Law on Succession (1722) rejected primogeniture and made it possible for the ruler to nominate his successor. During the reign of his step-grandmother, Catherine I (1725–1727), young Peter found himself under the protection of Prince Alexander Menshikov, who betrothed him to his daughter Maria and persuaded Catherine to name him as her successor, in the hope of stealing ground from the old nobility and gaining popularity by restoring the male line. On the day of Catherine's death, Peter was proclaimed emperor.

For the rest of Peter's short life it was a question of who could manipulate him before he developed a mind of his own. At first Menshikov kept the emperor under his wing, but, following a bout of illness in the summer of 1727, Menshikov was marginalized then banished by members of the powerful Dolgoruky clan, backed by the emperor's grandmother, Peter I's ex-wife Yevdokia. Peter II was crowned in Moscow on March 8 (February 25 O.S.), 1728. His chief adviser was now Prince Alexis

Grigorevich Dolgoruky, but the power behind the government was Heinrich Osterman. Both men were members of the Supreme Privy Council. After his coronation Peter stayed in Moscow, where he devoted much of his time to hunting. Portraits show a handsome boy dressed in the latest Western fashion. His short reign has sometimes been associated with a move to reject many of Peter's reforms, but there is no evidence that Peter II or his circle planned to return to the old ways, even if magnates welcomed the opportunity to spend more time on their Moscow estates. According to one source, young Peter wished to "follow in the steps of his grandfather." He did not get the chance. In fall 1729 he was betrothed to Prince Dolgoruky's daughter Catherine, but the wedding never took place. On January 29 (January 18 O.S.), 1730, he died from smallpox, without nominating a successor. The last of the Romanov male line, he was buried in the Archangel Cathedral in Moscow.

*See also:* CATHERINE I; MENSHIKOV, ALEXANDER DANILOVICH; ROMANOV DYNASTY

**BIBLIOGRAPHY**
Raleigh, D. J. (1996). *The Emperors and Empresses of Russia: Rediscovering the Romanovs.* Armonk, NY: M. E. Sharpe.

LINDSEY HUGHES

## PETER III

(1728–1762), emperor of Russia, January 5, 1762, to July 9, 1762.

The future Peter III was born Karl Peter Ulrich in Kiel, Germany, in February 1728, the son of the duke of Holstein and Peter I's daughter Anna Petrovna, who died shortly after his birth. His paternal grandmother was a sister of Charles XII of Sweden; this relation gave him a claim to the Swedish throne. In 1742 his aunt, the Empress Elizabeth (reigned 1741–1762 [1761 O.S.]), brought him to Russia to be groomed as her heir. Raised a Lutheran with German as his first language, he received instruction in Russian and the Orthodox religion, to which he converted. In 1745 he was married to the fifteen-year-old German Princess Sophia of Anhalt Zerbst, the future Catherine II ("the Great"). On Christmas Day 1761 (O.S.), Elizabeth died, and Peter succeeded her.

**Emperor Peter III, husband of Catherine the Great.** © ARCHIVO
ICONOGRAFICO, S.A./CORBIS

Catherine II's *Memoirs* drew a bleak picture of her marriage, recording bizarre details of Peter court-martialing rats, bringing hunting dogs to bed, and spying on Empress Elizabeth through a hole in the wall. Moreover, she hinted strongly that the marriage was never consummated and that her first child, the future Emperor Paul (born 1754), was in fact the son of her lover. Peter was an "absurd husband," in fact, not a husband at all. Contemporary accounts corroborate the essence, if not all the details, of Catherine's portrait of her husband. Peter seems to have been immature, impulsive, and unpredictable. He had a keen interest in military affairs, particularly drill and fortification, and played the violin quite well, but he also loved dolls and puppets and enjoyed crude practical jokes and drinking. Surviving portraits indicate an unprepossessing appearance.

But a ruler has never been denied his rightful throne merely on account of being "absurd," childlike, and plain. On the contrary, powerful courtiers could easily accommodate and even welcomed such monarchs. Although Peter brought a number of Ger-

mans from Holstein into his council, influential figures from Elizabeth's regime such as D. V. Volkov, A. I. Glebov, and members of the Vorontsov clan remained powerful. There was even some support for Peter's controversial personal decision to make peace with Prussia, "out of compassion for suffering humanity and personal friendship toward the King of Prussia." The treaty of May 5 (April 24 O.S.) 1762 restored all the territories taken by Russia during the Seven Years War. Peace triggered Peter's most famous edict, the manifesto releasing the Russian nobility from compulsory state service, issued on February 29 (February 8 O.S.), 1762, which Peter himself probably played little part in drafting. With the prospect of many officers returning from active service, it suited the government to save salaries and re-deploy personnel. The manifesto declared that compulsory service was no longed needed, because "useful knowledge and assiduity in service have increased the number of skillful and brave generals in military affairs, and have put informed and suitable people in civil and political affairs." But this was not an invitation to wholesale desertion. There were restrictions on immediate release: Nobles must educate their sons and, on receipt of the monarch's personal decree, rally to service. Those who had never served were to be "despised and scorned" at court.

Other measures issued during Peter's short reign included a reduction in the salt tax, a temporary ban on the purchase of serfs for factories, and some easing of restrictions on peasants entering and trading in towns. Sanctions were lifted on Old Believers who had fled into Poland. The Secret Chancery was abolished and some of its functions transferred to the Senate. In fulfillment of a decision already made under Elizabeth, the two million peasants on church estates were transferred to the jurisdiction of the state College of Economy, a measure that did not constitute liberation but was regarded as an improvement in the peasants' status. In conjunction with the emancipation of the nobility, this measure increased speculation that Peter might have been planning to liberate the serfs.

None of these measures saved Peter III. He demoted the Senate, thereby alienating some top officials. Confiscating its peasants alienated the church. The decision to end the war with Prussia suited some influential men, but most opposed Peter's further plans to win back Schleswig, formerly the possession of his Holstein ancestors, with Prussian support. He disbanded the imperial bodyguard, and there were rumors that he intended to replace the existing guards, now required to wear Prussian uniforms, with men from Holstein. His fate was further sealed by his alleged contempt for Orthodoxy. It was rumored that he did not observe fasts and that he intended to convert Russia to Lutheranism. Such accusations were exaggerated by Peter's opponents, who now focused on replacing him with his more popular wife, who was beginning to fear for her own safety. On July 5 (June 28 O.S.), 1762, Catherine seized power with the support of guards regiments led by her lover Grigory Orlov. "All unanimously agree that Grand Duke Peter Fyodorovich is incompetent and Russia has nothing to expect but calamity," she declared. After vain efforts to rally support, Peter abdicated and was taken to a residence not far from Peterhof palace. On July 16 (July 5 O.S.) he died, officially of colic brought on by hemorrhoids, although rumors hinted at murder by poison, strangulation, suffocation, beating, or shooting. His escort later admitted that an "unfortunate scuffle" had occurred, but nothing was proven and no one charged. Even if Peter was not killed on Catherine's explicit orders, his death, while not arousing her regret, often came back to haunt her.

The somewhat mysterious circumstances of Peter III's death and the promising nature of some of his edicts later made his a popular identity for a series of pretenders to the throne, culminating in the Pugachev revolt in 1773 and 1774. Following Catherine II's death in 1796, Emperor Paul I, who never doubted that Peter was his father, had his parents buried side by side in the Peter and Paul Cathedral.

*See also:* CATHERINE II; ELIZABETH

**BIBLIOGRAPHY**

Hughes, Lindsey. (1982). "Peter III." *Modern Encyclopedia of Russian and Soviet History* 27:238–244. Gulf Breeze, FL: Academic International Press.

Jones, Robert, E. (1973). *The Emancipation of the Russian Nobility, 1782–1785.* Princeton: Princeton University Press.

Leonard, Carol. (1993). *Reform and Regicide: The Reign of Peter III of Russia.* Bloomington: University of Indiana Press.

Madariaga, Isabel de. (1981). *Russia in the Age of Catherine the Great.* London: Weidenfeld and Nicolson.

Raeff, Marc. (1970). "The Domestic Policies of Peter III and His Overthrow." *American Historical Review* 75:1289–1310.

LINDSEY HUGHES

## PETER AND PAUL FORTRESS

The Peter and Paul Fortress was established in May 1703, the third year of the Great Northern War with Sweden, which would last until 1721. Having reduced Swedish positions along the Neva River from Lake Ladoga, Peter I needed a fortified point in the Neva estuary to protect Russia's position on the Gulf of Finland. Some twenty thousand men were conscripted to surround the island with earthen walls and bastions, and by November the fortress of Sankt Piter Burkh—"Saint Peter's Burg"—was essentially completed. It was named in honor of the Russian Orthodox feast day of Saints Peter and Paul (June 29).

Peter intended the fortress at the center of his city to serve not only a military function, but also as a symbol of his union of state and religious institutions within a new political order in Russia. To implement this reformation in the architecture of Saint Petersburg and its fortress, Dominico Trezzini, the most productive of the Petrine architects, capably served Peter. After the completion of the earthen fortress, Peter ordered a phased rebuilding with masonry walls. In May 1706, the tsar assisted with laying the foundation stone of the Menshikov Bastion, and for the rest of Trezzini's life (until 1734) the design and building of the Peter-Paul fortress, with its six bastions, would remain one of his primary duties. The major sections of the fortress, including the six bastions—were named either for a leading participant in Peter's reign, such as Alexander Menshikov, or for a member of the imperial house, not excluding Peter himself.

Within the fortress the dominant feature is the Cathedral of Saints Peter and Paul, designed by Trezzini in a radical departure from traditional Russian church architecture. Trezzini created an elongated structure, whose baroque dome on the eastern end is subordinate to the tower and spire over the west entrance. The tower was the focus of Peter's interest and had priority over the rest of the structure, which was not completed until 1732. By 1723, the spire, gilded and surmounted with an angel holding a cross, reached a height of 367 feet (112 meters), which exceeded the bell tower of Ivan the Great by 105 feet (32 meters).

On the interior, the large windows that mark the length of the building provide ample illumination for the banners and other imperial regalia. It is not clear whether this great hall was originally intended to serve as a burial place for the Romanov tsars; but with the death of Peter the Great, this function was assumed from the Archangel Cathedral in the Kremlin. The centerpiece of the interior is the gilded icon screen, designed by Ivan Zarudnyi and resembling the triumphal arches erected to celebrate Peter's victories. The frame was carved between 1722 and 1726 by craftsmen in Moscow and assembled in the cathedral in 1727. Some of the cathedral's ornamentation was lost after a lightning strike and fire in 1756, although prompt response by the garrison preserved the icon screen and much of the interior work.

The eighteenth century witnessed the construction of many other administrative and garrison buildings within the fortress, including an enclosed pavilion for Peter's small boat and the state Mint. At the turn of the nineteenth century the fortress became the main political prison of Russia. Famous cultural and political figures detained there include Alexander Radishchev, Fyodor Dostoevsky, and Nikolai Chernyshevsky. In 1917, the garrison sided with the Bolsheviks and played a role in the shelling of the Winter Palace. During the early twenty-first century the fortress serves primarily as a museum.

*See also:* MENSHIKOV, ALEXANDER DANILOVICH; PETER I

### BIBLIOGRAPHY

Brumfield, William Craft. (1993). *A History of Russian Architecture.* New York: Cambridge University Press.

Hamilton, George Heard. (1975). *The Art and Architecture of Russia.* Harmondsworth, UK: Penguin Books.

WILLIAM CRAFT BRUMFIELD

## PETER THE GREAT *See* PETER I.

## PETRASHEVSKY, MIKHAIL *See* BUTASHEVICH-PETRASHEVSKY, MIKHAIL VASILIEVICH.

## PETRASHEVTSY

Given the oppressive power of the state under Nicholas I and the weakness of civil society in Russia, the political ferment that rocked Europe during the 1840s took the relatively subdued form of discussion groups meeting secretly in private homes. The most important of such groups met on Friday evenings in the St. Petersburg home of a young official of the Ministry of Foreign Affairs, Mikhail Butashevich-Petrashevsky, from late 1845 until the group was disbanded by the police in a wave of repression following the revolutions that erupted in Western Europe in 1848. More than one hundred members of the group were arrested and interrogated, and twenty-one of the leading figures were condemned to death. In an infamous instance of psychological torture, on December 22, 1849, the condemned men were led to the scaffold and hooded, and the firing squad ordered to shoulder arms, before an imperial adjutant rode up with a last-minute reprieve commuting the sentences to imprisonment or banishment. Among those sent to Siberia was the novelist Fyodor Dostoyevsky, who later depicted the members of the group in his novel *The Possessed.*

The meetings of the Petrashevtsy, as the police labeled the men who met in Petrashevsky's home, were open to invited guests as well as regular members. Thus, over the course of the group's existence, several hundred men took part in the discussions. Some attendees were wealthy landowners or eminent writers or professors, such as the poets Alexei Pleshcheyev and Apollon Maikov and the economist V. A. Milyutin. The majority, however, were of modest means and held middle- or low-ranking positions in state service or were students or small-scale merchants. Serious about political ideas, they amassed a large collection of works in several languages on political philosophy and economics. While Petrashevsky himself was committed to the utopian socialism of Charles Fourier, and socialist thought was the dominant theme of the discussions, members of the group held a range of ideological and tactical approaches to the problem of transforming Russian society. Their most important project was the publication in 1845 and 1846 of *A Pocket Dictionary of Foreign Terms,* an effort to propagate their ideas through political articles disguised as dictionary entries. The censors eventually realized the subversive nature of the dictionary and ordered it confiscated, but not in time to prevent the sale of part of the second, more radical, edition.

The Petrashevtsy were not opposed in principle to a violent overthrow of the tsar's government, but in practice most saw little hope of a successful revolution in Russia and therefore advocated partial reforms such as freedom of speech, freedom of press, and reform of the judicial system. The more radical members, led by Nikolai Speshnev, hoped to transform the group into a revolutionary organization that would prepare the ground for an armed revolt. Through subsidiary discussion circles that branched off from the original group, such as the one to which the novelist Nikolai Chernyshevsky belonged while a university student, the Petrashevtsy played an important role in propagating socialist ideas in Russia.

See also: CHERNYSHEVSKY, NIKOLAI GAVRILOVICH; DOSTOYEVSKY, FYODOR MIKHAILOVICH; NICHOLAS I

**BIBLIOGRAPHY**

Seddon, J. H. (1985). *The Petrashevtsy: A Study of the Russian Revolutionaries of 1848*. Manchester, UK: Manchester University Press.

Walicki, Andrzej. (1979). *A History of Russian Thought: From the Enlightenment to Marxism*. Stanford, CA: Stanford University Press.

KATHRYN WEATHERSBY

## PETROV, GRIGORY SPIRIDONOVICH

(1868–1925), Orthodox priest and a leading proponent of Christian social activism.

Grigory Petrov was born in Iamburg, St. Petersburg province. He was educated at the diocesan seminary and the St. Petersburg Ecclesiastical Academy (1887–1891), and on graduating became a priest in a St. Petersburg church.

Petrov was also active as a writer. In his most successful work, *The Gospel as the Foundation of Life* (1898), he argued that Christian believers were required to apply the literal teachings of Jesus to every aspect of their lives in order to begin building the Kingdom of God here on earth. Petrov knew of the American Social Gospel movement, but his ideas were shaped by his encounters with new conceptions of pastorship and Christian activism then developing among the clergy of St. Petersburg.

Petrov's writings found a ready audience and made him famous. In 1903, however, conservatives began to attack his ideas in the ecclesiastical press, and as a result in 1904 the church dismissed Petrov from his pulpit and banned him from public speaking. Nevertheless, Petrov continued to write.

He became interested in Christian politics and was an activist during the Revolution of 1905. He established the newspaper *God's Truth* in Moscow in 1906 and was elected to the first Duma as a Constitutional Democrat.

Petrov never served in the Duma, however, because he was charged before an ecclesiastical court with false teaching. Although exonerated, he was confined to a monastery under church discipline. Despite popular sympathy for Petrov, the church defrocked him in 1908 and banned him from the capital and from public employment. He then became a journalist for a liberal newspaper, *The Word*. After the revolutions of 1917 he emigrated to Serbia, and then in 1922 to France. He died in Paris in 1925.

Petrov's main importance was in his contribution to the development of a modern, liberal understanding of Christianity in the Russian Orthodox context.

See also: ORTHODOXY

**BIBLIOGRAPHY**

Valliere, Paul. (1977). "Modes of Social Action in Russian Orthodoxy: The Case of Father Petrov's *Zateinik*." *Russian History* 4(2):142–158.

JENNIFER HEDDA

## PETRUSHKA

Petrushka was a Russian puppet theater spectacle and also the name of its main character (cf. the English Punch).

The play *Petrushka* seems to derive from a native older Russian buffoon and minstrel tradition and the Western European puppet theater tradition with its roots in the Italian commedia dell'arte. Possible evidence of the Petrushka play in Russia is found as early as 1637 in an engraving and description by a Dutch traveler, Adam Olearius. From around the 1840s to the 1930s, the Petrushka show was one of the most popular kinds of improvisational theater in Russia, often performed at fairs and carnivals and on the streets on a temporary wooden stage (*balagan*). The show was presented by two performers, one of whom manipulated the puppets, while the other played a barrel-organ. Recorded textual variants from the nineteenth and twentieth centuries depict the adventures of Petrushka, a dauntless prankster and joker, who uses his wit as well as a vigorously wielded club to get the better of his adversaries, who often represent established authority. The themes tend to be sexist and violent. Petrushka is usually dressed in a red caftan and pointed red cap, and has a hunchback, a large hooked nose, and a prominent chin. The most popular scenes involve Petrushka and a handful of characters, among them his fiancée or wife, a gypsy horse trader, a doctor or apothecary, an army corporal, a policeman, the devil, and a large fluffy dog. Igor Stravinsky's ballet *Petrushka* (1911) is probably the most famous adaptation of this puppet theater show.

*See also:* FOLKLORE; FOLK MUSIC; STRAVINSKY, IGOR FYO-DOROVICH.

**BIBLIOGRAPHY**

Kelly, Catriona. (1990). *Petrushka: The Russian Carnival Puppet Theatre.* Cambridge, UK: Cambridge University Press.

Zguta, Russell. (1978). *Russian Minstrels: A History of the Skomorokhi.* Philadelphia: University of Pennsylvania Press.

PATRICIA ARANT

# PETTY TUTELAGE

Petty tutelage in the Soviet economy meant that the day-to-day operations of enterprises could be (and frequently were) directly influenced or controlled by decisions or actions of the industrial ministry to which the enterprise was subordinate. While Soviet enterprise managers ultimately were responsible for producing the goods identified by planners, industrial ministry officials exercised control over the firm in a number of ways. First, the industrial ministry annually allocated the plan targets among the enterprises subordinate to it, thereby defining changes in output requirements by firm over time. That is, ministry officials were responsible for disaggregating the targets they received from Gosplan, the State Planning Committee, and preparing the annual enterprise plan, the *techpromfinplan.* Second, industrial ministry officials distributed the financial resources provided to them by state committees to individual firms. Financial resources included funds for wages and in-

vestment purposes. Third, each industrial ministry redistributed profits earned by firms subordinate to them among these same firms. Finally, ministry officials responded to requests from enterprise managers to change or "correct" output plan targets or input allocations over the course of the planning period if circumstances precluded successful plan fulfillment.

During perestroika, numerous policies were adopted to reduce petty tutelage by industrial ministry officials over Soviet enterprise operations. Some view the reduction of ministerial tutelage and the corresponding increase in decision-making authority by enterprises as a cornerstone of perestroika. Ministry officials were to cease exercising routine daily control over enterprises and focus instead on long-term issues such as promoting investment and technological advance. However, performance measures applied to the industrial ministry remained linked to the performance of their firms, and the ministry retained control over funds and resources to be allocated to Soviet enterprises. Consequently, in practice, it is unlikely that petty tutelage declined.

*See also:* GOSPLAN; TECHPROMFINPLAN

**BIBLIOGRAPHY**

Berliner, Joseph S. (1957). *Factory and Manager in the USSR.* Cambridge, MA: Harvard University Press.

Gregory, Paul R. (1990). *Restructuring the Soviet Economic Bureaucracy.* New York: Cambridge University Press.

SUSAN J. LINZ

# PHOTOGRAPHY

The development of photography in Russia during the nineteenth century followed a history similar to that of other European countries. After Louis-Jacques-Mandé Daguerre and William Henry Fox Talbot made public their methods for capturing images on light-sensitized surfaces in 1839, I. Kh. Gammel, corresponding member to the Russian Academy of Sciences, visited both inventors to learn more about their work and collected samples of daguerreotypes and calotypes for study by Russian scientists. The Academy subsequently commissioned Russian scientists to further investigate both processes. As elsewhere, Russian experimenters quickly introduced a variety of refinements to the initial processes.

Photography found immediate popular success in Russia with the establishment of daguerreotype portrait studios in the 1840s. The similarity of the photograph to the Orthodox icon (an image that is believed to be a direct and truthful record of a physical being) heightened the early reception of photography and resulted in the persistence of portraiture as a major genre in Russia. While the first generation of photographers was largely foreign, native practitioners soon appeared. Some, such as Sergei Levitsky, achieved international recognition for their role in the development of photography. A personal acquaintance of Daguerre, Levitsky established studios in both France and Russia, serving as court photographer for the Romanovs and Napoleon III. During the later nineteenth century, Russian photography became institutionalized with the establishment of journals, professional societies, and exhibitions.

While photography was initially largely rejected as an art, it became widely accepted with the emergence of Realism. Russian photographers used the camera to capture the changing social landscape that accompanied the liberation of the serfs and growing urbanization. Simultaneously, ethnographic photography became an important genre with the expansion of the Russian Empire and the opening of Central Asia. Numerous photographic albums and research projects documented the peoples, customs, landscape, and buildings of diverse parts of the Russian Empire. With the rise of Symbolism, a younger generation of pictorialist photographers rejected the photograph as document in pursuit of more aestheticizing manipulated images.

At the turn of the century, technological developments led to the appearance of popular illustrated publications and the emergence of modern press photography. The Bulla family established the first Russian photo agency; they documented such events as the Russo-Japanese War, World War I, and the 1917 Revolutions. The growing commercial availability of inexpensive cameras and products rendered photography more pervasive in Russia. However, with the commercialization of photography, Russian practitioners became increasingly dependent upon foreign equipment and materials. With the outbreak of World War I, photographers were largely cut off from their supplies, and the ensuing crisis severely limited photographic activity until the mid-1920s.

After the October Revolution, Russian photography followed a unique path due to the ideological imperatives of the Soviet regime. The Bolsheviks quickly recognized the propaganda potential of photography and nationalized the photographic industry. During the civil war, special committees collected historical photographs, documented contemporary events, and produced photopropaganda. In the early 1920s, Russian modernist artists, such as Alexander Rodchenko, experimented with the technique of photomontage, the assembly of photographic fragments into larger compositions. With the growing politicization of art, photomontage and photography soon became important media for the creation of ideological images. The 1920s also witnessed the foundation of the Soviet illustrated mass press. Despite a shortage of experienced photojournalists, the development of the illustrated press cultivated a new generation of Soviet photographers. Mikhail Koltsov, editor of the popular magazine *Ogonek*, laid the groundwork for modern photojournalism in the Soviet Union by establishing national and international mechanisms for the production, distribution, and preservation of photographic material. Koltsov actively promoted photographic education and the further development of both amateur and professional Soviet photography through the magazine *Sovetskoye foto*.

During the First Five-Year Plan, creative debates emerged between modernist photographers and professional Soviet photojournalists. While both groups shunned aestheticizing pictorialist approaches and were ideologically committed to the development of uniquely Soviet photography, differences arose concerning creative methods, especially the relative priority to be given to the form versus content of the Soviet photograph. These debates stimulated the further development of Soviet documentary photography. The illustrated magazine *USSR in Construction* (*SSSR na stroike*; 1930–1941, 1949) was an important venue for Soviet documentary photography. Published in Russian, English, French, and German editions, it featured the work of top photographers and photomontage artists. Like the nineteenth-century ethnographic albums, *USSR in Construction* presented the impact of Soviet industrialization and modernization in diverse parts of the USSR in film-like photographic essays. As the 1930s progressed, official Soviet photography became increasingly lackluster and formulaic. Published photographs were subjected to extensive retouching and manipulation—not for creative ends, but for the falsification of reality and history. An abrupt change took place during World War II, when Soviet photojournalists equipped with 35-millimeter cameras produced spontaneous images that captured the terrors and triumphs of war.

Soviet amateur photography flourished in the late 1920s with numerous worker photography circles. Amateur activity was stimulated by the development of the Soviet photography industry and the introduction of the first domestic camera in 1930. Later that decade, however, government regulations increasingly restricted the activity of amateur photographers, and the number of circles quickly diminished. The material hardships of the war years further compounded this situation, practically bringing amateur photographic activity to a standstill. With independent activity severely circumscribed, Soviet photography was essentially limited to the carefully controlled area of professional photojournalism.

During the Thaw of the late 1950s, the appearance of new amateur groups led to the cultivation of a new generation of photographers engaged in social photography that captured everyday life. Their activity, however, was largely underground. By the 1970s, photography played an important role in Soviet nonconformist and conceptual art. Artists such as Boris Mikhailov appropriated and manipulated photographic imagery in a radical critique of photography's claims to truth. After the collapse of the Soviet Union, many photographic publications and industrial enterprises gradually disappeared. While professional practitioners quickly adapted to the new market system and creative photographers achieved international renown, the main area of activity was consumer snapshot photography, which flourished in Russia with the return of foreign photographic firms.

*See also:* CENSORSHIP; NATIONALISM IN THE ARTS

### BIBLIOGRAPHY

Elliott, David, ed. (1992). *Photography in Russia, 1840–1940*. London: Thames and Hudson.

King, David. (1997). *The Commissar Vanishes: The Falsification of Photographs and Art in Stalin's Russia*. New York: Metropolitan Books.

Sartori, Rosalind. (1987). "The Soviet Union." In *A History of Photography: Social and Cultural Perspectives,* ed. Jean-Claude Lemagny and André Rouillé. Cambridge, UK: Cambridge University Press.

Shudakov, Grigory (1983). *Pioneers of Soviet Photography.* New York: Thames and Hudson.

*USSR in Construction.* (1930–1941, 1949). Moscow: Gosizdat.

Walker, Joseph, et al. (1991). *Photo Manifesto: Contemporary Photography in the USSR.* New York: Stewart, Tabori & Chang.

ERIKA WOLF

# PIMEN, PATRIARCH

(1910–1990), patriarch of the Russian Orthodox Church from June 2, 1971, to May 3, 1990.

Sergei Mikhailovich Izvekov took monastic vows in 1927 and worked with church choirs in Moscow. Later, as Patriarch Pimen, his excellent musical sense led him to forbid singers to embellish the liturgy with operatic flourishes.

During World War II Pimen allegedly concealed his monastic vows and served as an army officer in communications or intelligence. When discovered, he was incarcerated, and his political vulnerability was said to have figured in the Soviet authorities' decision that he could be controlled as patriarch. More friendly sources recount his heroism in protecting his men with his own body under bombardment. His official biography omits his military service.

Judgments of Pimen as patriarch are mixed. He was accused of being withdrawn, passive, and increasingly infirm. On the other hand, he was a gifted poet, radiated spirituality, and was said to have defended the integrity of the Church against corrupting modernism and reckless innovation. Pimen's moment came when Communist General Secretary Mikhail Gorbachev decided to greet the millennium of Russia's conversion to Christianity by improving relations with the Church. Gorbachev received Pimen on April 29, 1988, and more than eight hundred new parishes were permitted to open that year. Sunday schools, charitable works, new seminaries and convents, and other concessions to church needs followed. Whether these tangible benefits justified Pimen's political collaboration with the Soviet regime is a controversial question.

*See also:* RUSSIAN ORTHODOX CHURCH; RUSSIFICATION

**BIBLIOGRAPHY**

Pospielovsky, Dimitry. (1984). *The Russian Church Under the Soviet Regime 1917–1982.* 2 vols. Crestwood, NY: St. Vladimir's Seminary Press.

NATHANIEL DAVIS

## PIROGOV, NIKOLAI IVANOVICH

(1810–1881), scientist, physician, proponent of educational reform.

Nikolai Pirogov was born in Moscow where his father managed a military commissary. After graduating from the medical school of Moscow University, he enrolled at the Professors' Institute at Dorpat University to prepare for teaching in institutions of higher education. In Dorpat he specialized in surgical techniques and in pathological anatomy and physiology. After five years at Dorpat, he went to Berlin University in search of the latest knowledge in anatomy and surgical techniques. While in Berlin he was appointed a professor at Dorpat, where he quickly acquired a reputation as a successful contributor to anatomy and an innovator in surgery. In 1837–1839 he published *Surgical Anatomy of Arterial Trunks and Fasciae* in Latin and German.

In 1841 Pirogov accepted a teaching position at the Medical and Surgical Academy in St. Petersburg, the most advanced school of its kind in Russia. He lectured on clinical service in hospitals and pathological and surgical anatomy. His major work published under the auspices of the Medical and Surgical Academy was the four-volume *Anatomia Topographica* (1851–1854) describing the spatial relations of organs and tissues in various planes. He was also the author of *General Military Field Surgery* (1864), relying heavily on his experience in the Crimean War (1853–1855). In recognition of his scholarly achievement, the St. Petersburg Academy of Sciences elected him a corresponding member.

Tired of petty academic quarrels and intrigues, Pirogov resigned from his professorial position in 1856. In the same year he published "The Questions of Life," an essay emphasizing the need for a reorientation of the country's educational system. The article touched on many pedagogical problems of broader social significance, but the emphasis was on an educational philosophy that placed equal emphasis on the transmission of specialized knowledge and the acquisition of general education fortified by increased command of foreign languages. He also pointed out that, because of the low salaries, Russian teachers were compelled to look for additional employment, which limited their active involvement in the educational process. In his opinion, one of the most pressing tasks of the Russian government was to make the entire school system accessible to all social strata and ethnic groups.

The government not only listened to Pirogov's plea for a broader humanistic base of the educational system, but in the same year appointed him superintendent of the Odessa school district. Two years later, he became the superintendent of the Kiev school district. In his numerous circulars and published reports he advocated a greater participation of teachers' councils in decisions on all aspects of the educational process.

Apprehensive of the long list of his liberal reforms, the Ministry of Public Education decided in 1861 to ask Pirogov to resign from his high post in education administration. His dismissal provoked a series of rebellious demonstrations by Kiev University students.

Pirogov's government service, however, did not come to an end. In 1862 he was assigned the challenging task of organizing and supervising the education of Russian students enrolled in Western universities. In 1866 the government again retired him; the current minister of public education thought that the supervision of foreign education could be done more effectively by a "philologist" than by a "surgeon."

In 1881 a large group of scholars gathered in Moscow to celebrate the fiftieth anniversary of Pirogov's engagement in science. Four years later, an even larger group founded the Pirogov Society of Russian Physicians with a strong interest in social medicine. It was not unusual for the periodic conventions of the Society to be attended by close to two thousand persons.

*See also:* EDUCATION

**BIBLIOGRAPHY**

Frieden, Nancy M. (1981). *Russian Physicians in an Era of Reform and Revolution, 1856–1905.* Princeton, NJ: Princeton University Press.

Vucinich, Alexander. (1963–1970). *Science in Russian Culture*, vols. 1–2. Stanford, CA: Stanford University Press.

ALEXANDER VUCINICH

## PISAREV, DMITRY IVANOVICH

(1840–1868), noted literary critic, radical social thinker, and proponent of "rational egoism" and nihilism.

Born into the landed aristocracy, Dmitry Ivanovich Pisarev studied at both Moscow University and St. Petersburg University, concentrating on philology and history. From 1862 to 1866, Pisarev served as the chief voice of the journal *The Russian Word* (*Russkoye slovo*), a journal somewhat akin to *The Contemporary* (*Sovremennik*), which was published and edited by the poet Nikolai Nekrasov (1821–1878). In 1862 Pisarev was imprisoned in the Petropavlovsk Fortress for writing an article criticizing the tsarist government and defending the social critic Alexander Herzen, editor of the London-based émigré journal *The Bell* (*Kolokol*). Ironically, Pisarev's arrest marked his own rise to prominence, coinciding with the death of Nikolai Dobrolyubov in 1861 and arrest of Nikolai Chernyshevsky in 1862. During his incarceration for the next four and one-half years, Pisarev continued to write for the *The Russian Word*, including several influential articles exhibiting his literary panache: "Notes on the History of Labor" (1863), "Realists" (1864), "The Historical Ideas of Auguste Comte" (1865), and "Pushkin and Belinsky" (1865). His articles on Plato and Prince Metternich, and especially the article "Scholasticism of the Nineteenth Century" brought him fame as a literary critic.

Pisarev differed from other, more liberal, social reformers of the first half of the decade, since he stressed individual-ethical aspects of socioeconomic reforms, such as family problems and the difficult position of women in society. When Chernyshevsky's novel *What is to Be Done* (*Chto delat?*) came out in 1863, Pisarev praised it as a utilitarian tract focusing on the positive aspects of nihilism (generally, the view that no absolute values exist). At the same time, Pisarev criticized Chernyshevsky for his intellectual timidity and failure to develop his ideas far enough. According to Pisarev, a functional society did not need literature ("art for art's sake"), and literature, therefore, should simply merge with journalism and scholarly investigation as descriptions of reality. He even assaulted the reputation of Alexander Pushkin, claiming that the poet's work hindered social progress and should be consigned to the dustbin of history.

Rather than scorn Ivan Turgenev's novel *Fathers and Sons* (*Otsy i deti*), written in 1862, as Chernyshevsky did, claiming it castigated the radical youth, Pisarev strongly identified with the novel's hero Bazarov—a nihilist who believes in reason and has a scientific understanding of society's needs, but rejects traditional religious beliefs and moral values. "Bazarov," Pisarev wrote, "is a representative of our younger generation; in his person are gathered together all those traits scattered among the mass to a lesser degree." To Pisarev, Bazarov's "realism" and "empiricism" reduced all matters of principle to individual preference. Turgenev's hero is governed only by personal caprice or calculation. Neither over him, nor outside him, nor inside him does he recognize any regulator, any moral law. Far above feeling any moral compunction against committing crimes, the new hero of the younger generation would hardly subordinate his will to any such antiquated prejudice.

Pisarev's readers gleaned in the author himself some of these same extremist, nihilist tendencies. However, while Pisarev was an extremist intellectual, he was an honest one. He eloquently advocated such practical social types as Bazarov—activists for the intelligentsia, that is, people who could play the role of a "thinking proletariat." Yet Pisarev himself did not advocate a political revolution. He believed society, and above all the mass of the people, could be transformed through socioeconomic change. He simply denounced whatever stood in the way of such peaceful change more trenchantly than any of his predecessors had. Thus this urging to attack anything that seemed socially useless sounded more revolutionary than it really was.

Upon his release from prison, Pisarev contributed articles to the journals *The Task* (*Delo*) and *Notes of the Fatherland* (*Otechestvennye zapiski*). Although he drowned in the Gulf of Riga in 1868, at the age of twenty-eight, his ideas continued to influence other writers, notably Fyodor Dostoyevsky. In *Crime and Punishment* (*Prestuplenie i nakazanie*) Dostoyevsky's hero Raskolnikov (from the word *raskol* or "split") shows what occurs when one flaunts moral principles and takes a human life. In *The Possessed* (*Besy*) Dostoyevsky shows his reader the worst ways in which human beings can abuse their freedom. Several characters in this novel act on horrifying beliefs, leaving numerous dead bodies in their wake. Raskolnikov's views pale next to the shocking behavior of the "demons" whom Dostoyevsky feared most: human beings who lose their perspective and let the worst side of their natures predominate.

*See also:* DOSTOYEVSKY, FYODOR MIKHAILOVICH; GOLDEN AGE OF RUSSIAN LITERATURE; INTELLIGENTSIA; NIHILISM AND NIHILISTS; TURGENEV, IVAN SERGEYEVICH

**BIBLIOGRAPHY**

Berdiaev, Nikolai, and Shatz, Marshall. (1994). *Vekhi: A Collection of Articles About the Russian Intelligentsia.* Armonk, NY: M.E. Sharpe.

Freeborn, Richard. (1982). *The Russian Revolutionary Novel: Turgenev to Pasternak.* New York: Cambridge University Press.

Glicksberg, Charles Irving. (1975). *The Literature of Nihilism.* Lewisburg, PA: Bucknell University Press.

Hingley, Ronald. (1969). *Nihilists: Russian Radicals and Revolutionaries in the Reign of Alexander II, 1855–81.* New York: Delacorte Press.

Pozefsky, Peter C. (2003). *The Nihilist Imagination: Dmitrii Pisarev and the Cultural Origins of Russian Radicalism (1860–1868).* New York: Peter Lang.

JOHANNA GRANVILLE

## PLANNERS' PREFERENCES

The term "planners' preferences" was introduced by Abram Bergson, in his study (1961) of Soviet national income, to capture the idea that the Soviet economy was ultimately directed by the top leadership of the Communist Party, rather than by consumer sovereignty as in market economies. The preferences of said leadership provide the determining orientation and socially desired objectives of a socialist economic plan designed to govern all economic activity over a defined period. As such, the term refers to the objective function used in economic analyses to "rationalize" the decisions and actions of producers and distributors of economic goods and services in a planned or Soviet-type economy. These objectives are to replace the objectives implicit in the market aggregation of consumers' and users' preferences in a properly functioning market economic system. Such preferences (tastes, needs, and desires), together with income constraints, determine the demands for goods and services. These demands, together with technological possibilities for supply, then determine the market prices offered for these goods and services, and hence underlie the market prices (key coordinating and incentive signals) in a market economy. Similarly, planners' preferences are supposed to underlie planned prices and production and distribution

commands in a centrally planned economy, capturing the rationale of, and rationality behind, the comprehensive economic plan. In principle they can reflect social and collective objectives beyond any individual or organizational preference ordering, and hence capture and optimally respond to "externalities" of a social, political, or environmental nature. As such, they are sometimes used to describe the objective function in a formal welfare economic analysis of policy issues or problems. In the practice of centrally planned economies, however, they appear largely to reflect the interests and objectives of the dictator or (later) ruling elite (*nomenklatura*), when not merely serving as an ex post facto rationalization for observed planning decisions.

*See also:* BUREAUCRACY, ECONOMIC; MARKET SOCIALISM

**BIBLIOGRAPHY**

Bergson, Abram. (1961). *The Real National Income of Soviet Russia since 1928.* Cambridge, MA: Harvard University Press.

Bergson, Abram. (1964). *The Economics of Soviet Planning.* Cambridge, MA: Harvard University Press.

RICHARD ERICSON

## PLATON (LEVSHIN)

(1737–1812), Orthodox metropolitan of Moscow.

Born the son of a church sexton in the village of Chasnikovo near Moscow, Peter Levshin (the future Metropolitan Platon) attended the Slavonic-Greek-Latin Academy in Moscow before taking monastic vows at the St. Sergius–Holy Trinity Lavra in 1758. He adopted the name Platon and within three years had become rector of the Lavra seminary.

Platon's eloquence and learning attracted Empress Catherine II (r. 1762–1796), who in 1763 appointed him tutor to her son and heir, Paul. Platon's lectures for the tsarevich were published in 1765 under the title *Orthodox Teaching; or, a Short Course in Christian Theology.* Translated into German and English, this work earned Platon an international reputation as an Orthodox thinker.

In 1766 Platon became a member of the Holy Synod, the ruling council of the Russian Orthodox Church. Consecrated archbishop of Tver in 1770, he was appointed archbishop of Moscow in 1775, a post he retained for the rest of his life. Platon proved to be an effective administrator. Immediately upon taking office, he revamped the ecclesiastical bureaucracy by issuing new rules for clerical superintendents. He also worked to improve the education and material living standards of the secular clergy. In his effort to create an enlightened clergy, Platon added modern foreign languages, medicine, history, and geography to the seminary curriculum. In recognition of his achievements, Catherine promoted him to the rank of metropolitan in 1787.

By then, however, Platon's relationship to the empress had begun to deteriorate. In 1785 Catherine II had ordered him to investigate Nikolai Novikov (1744–1816), a Freemason and prominent publisher. To her dismay, Platon declared Novikov an exemplary Christian. Despite Platon's finding, Catherine had Novikov arrested a few years later in 1792. That same year, she granted Platon permission to enter a partial retirement by moving to Bethany, his monastic retreat on the grounds of the Holy Trinity Lavra.

During the reign of Emperor Paul (r. 1796–1801), Platon negotiated the return to the state church of some Old Believers (religious dissenters who had broken with the Orthodox Church because they rejected the liturgical innovations of Patriarch Nikon [r. 1652–1658]). The Old Believers accepting this compromise, known as the *yedinoverie*, or union, agreed to recognize the legitimacy and authority of the state church in exchange for the right to follow pre-Nikonian rituals and practices. As an ecumenical effort by the Russian Orthodox Church, the union failed to win over many adherents.

Platon died in 1812, shortly after hearing of Napoleon Bonaparte's retreat from Moscow. An excellent administrator and inspired preacher, he did not use his position to voice social criticism. Instead, he sought to make the church more effective in a limited ecclesiastical sphere through education and regulation. Platon's collected works, which include his autobiography and a short history of the Russian Orthodox Church, fill twenty volumes.

*See also:* NIKON, PATRIARCH; OLD BELIEVERS; ORTHODOXY

**BIBLIOGRAPHY**

Papmehl, K. A. (1983). *Metropolitan Platon of Moscow (Petr Levshin, 1737–1812): The Enlightened Prelate, Scholar, and Educator.* Newtonville, MA: Oriental Research Partners.

J. EUGENE CLAY

## PLATONOV, SERGEI FYODOROVICH

(1860–1933), Russian historian.

Born in Chernigov, Sergei Platonov graduated from a private gymnasium in St. Petersburg (1878) and the Department of History and Philology of St. Petersburg University (1882). His tutor was Konstantin Bestuzhev-Ryumin, who recommended that he be allowed to remain at the university in order to "prepare to be a professor." Platonov was influenced also by the works of Vasily Klyuchevsky. He belonged to the "St. Petersburg school" of Russian historiography, which paid special attention to the study and publication of historical sources. In 1888 Platonov defended his master's thesis on the topic of *Old Russian Legends and Tales About the Seventeenth-Century Time of Troubles as a Historical Source* (published in the same year and honored with the Uvarov Award of the Academy of Sciences).

Despite not yet having earned a doctorate, in 1889 Platonov headed the Department of Russian History of St. Petersburg University. In 1899 Platonov defended his doctorate thesis by presenting a monograph, *Studies in the History of the Troubles in the Muscovite State in the Sixteenth and Seventeenth Centuries.* This work was Platonov's masterpiece, based on a scrupulous analysis of sources. Platonov sought to "show, with facts, how . . . a modern state was being formed." The main purpose of the "political mishaps and social tension" of the early seventeenth century was, according to Platonov, the replacement of the boyar aristocracy with the nobility. He defined the *Oprichnina* of Ivan the Terrible, which became one of the initial causes of the Time of Troubles, not as the "whim of a timid tyrant," but as a thought-out system of actions aimed at destroying the "appanage aristocracy." Platonov was also one of the first to show that one of the aspects of the Time of Troubles was the tension between the nobility and the serfs over land and freedom.

Platonov earned wide acclaim through the repeatedly republished *Lectures on Russian History* (1899) and the *Russian History Textbook For Middle School* (in two parts, 1909–1910). From 1900 to

1905, Platonov was the dean of the History and Philology Department of St. Petersburg University, and from 1903 to 1916 he served as the director of the Women's Pedagogical Institute.

Despite his negative opinions of the October Revolution, Platonov continued to work actively in several scholarly institutions. From 1918 to 1923, he was the head of the Petrograd branch of the Main Directorate of Archival Affairs. From 1918 he served as the chairman of the Archaeographical Commission of the Academy of Sciences. In 1920 Platonov was elected as a member of the Academy of Sciences. Platonov worked in the Academy of Sciences as the director of the Pushkin House (1925–1928) and the Library of the Academy of Sciences (1925–1929). The peak of his academic career was his election as the head (academic secretary) of the Department of Humanities and a member of the presidium of the Academy of Sciences in March 1929.

During the 1920s Platonov published biographies of Boris Godunov (1921), Ivan the Terrible (1923), and Peter the Great (1926) and the monographs *The Past of the Russian North* (1923) and *Muscovy and the West in the Sixteenth and Seventeenth Centuries* (1925). Platonov opposed the nihilist views on history before the Russian revolution and the purely negative depiction of the actions of Russian tsars.

From 1929 to 1931 Platonov was the central figure of the so-called Academic Affair. The formal explanation for the persecution of scholars was the presence of political documents, including the act of resignation of Nicholas II, in the Library of the Academy of Science. The real motive of the Soviet regime in the Academic Affair was to bring the Academy under its control. In November 1929 the Politburo decided to release Platonov from all positions that he held. On January 12, 1930, Platonov was arrested. He was accused of being a member of the International Union of Struggle Toward the Rebirth of Free Russia, a monarchist organization fabricated by the prosecutors. According to the OGPU (secret police), the purpose of this fictional organization was to overthrow the Soviet regime and establish a constitutional monarchy; Platonov was the supposed future prime minister.

While in custody Platonov was expelled from the Academy of Sciences. In August 1931 he was sentenced by the OGPU to five years of exile and deported, with his two daughters, to Samara. He died in Samara.

*See also:* ACADEMY OF SCIENCES; PUSHKIN HOUSE

**BIBLIOGRAPHY**

Platonov, Sergei F. (1925). *History of Russia.* New York: Macmillan.

Platonov, Sergei F. (1970). *The Time of Troubles: A Historical Study of the Internal Crises and Social Struggle in Sixteenth- and Seventeenth-Century Muscovy.* Lawrence: University Press of Kansas.

Platonov, Sergei F. (1972). *Moscow and the West.* Hattiesburg, MS: Academic International.

Platonov, Sergei F. (1973). *Boris Godunov, Tsar of Russia,* with an introductory essay, "S.F. Platonov: Eminence and Obscurity," by John T. Alexander. Gulf Breeze, FL: Academic International Press.

Platonov, Sergei F. (1974). *Ivan the Terrible.* Gulf Breeze, FL: Academic International Press.

Tsamutali, Aleksei Nikolaevich. (1999). "Sergei Fedorovich Platonov (1860–1933): A Life for Russia." In *Historiography of Imperial Russia,* ed. Tomas Sanders. Armonk, NY: M.E. Sharpe.

OLEG BUDNITSKII

# PLEHVE, VYACHESLAV KONSTANTINOVICH

(1846–1904), leader of imperial police then minister in governments of Tsar Alexander III and Tsar Nicholas II.

As a conservative statesman in late imperial Russia, Vyacheslav Plehve (von Plehwe) was a key figure in the tsarist regime's struggle against revolution. An experienced prosecutor, he was tapped in 1881 to head the imperial police following the assassination of Tsar Alexander II. His success in arresting the perpetrators and destroying the People's Will terrorist organization, combined with his remarkable energy and talent, led to appointments as Assistant Minister of the Interior (1885–1894), Minister State-Secretary for Finland (1894–1902), and Minister of the Interior (1902–1904).

Assuming the post of minister in the wake of widespread peasant disorders and his predecessor's murder by revolutionaries, Plehve sought above all to reimpose order and control. With the help of former Moscow police chief Sergei Zubatov, he extended throughout Russia a network of "security sections" (*okhrany*), which used covert agents to penetrate revolutionary and labor groups. He fired

Zubatov when his police-sponsored worker organizations triggered widespread strikes in 1903. He repressed the liberal press and the *zemstvo* organs of local self-government, leading to bitter clashes with leading public figures. His heavy-handed tactics alienated both the Russian public and his government colleagues, especially arch-rival Sergei Witte, the talented Finance Minister whose efforts to modernize Russia were seen by Plehve as contributing to unrest. But he won the support of Tsar Nicholas II, who relieved Witte of his ministry in August 1903, and he backed aggressive ventures that helped provoke the Russo-Japanese War of 1904–1905. He also cracked down on subject nationalities such as Finns, Armenians and Jews; his alleged efforts to divert public anger from the government toward the Jews may have contributed to the Kishinev anti-Jewish pogrom of 1903. Ironically, this so incensed the Jewish police agent Evno Azef, who had managed to infiltrate the terrorists, that he helped them arrange Plehve's murder in July 1904. Plehve thus died a failure, disparaged by both contemporaries and later historians.

*See also:* NATIONALITIES POLICIES, TSARIST; NICHOLAS II; ZUBATOV, SERGEI VASILIEVICH

**BIBLIOGRAPHY**

Gurko, Vladimir I. (1939). *Features and Figures of the Past.* Stanford, CA: Stanford University Press.

Judge, Edward H. (1983). *Plehve: Repression and Reform in Imperial Russia, 1902–1904.* Syracuse, NY: Syracuse University Press.

Witte, Sergei I. (1990). *Memoirs of Count Witte.* Armonk, NY: M. E. Sharpe.

Zuckerman, Fredric S. (1996). *The Tsarist Secret Police and Russian Society, 1880–1917.* New York: New York University Press.

EDWARD H. JUDGE

# PLEKHANOV, GEORGY VALENTINOVICH

(1856–1918), the "Father of Russian Marxism."

Georgi Valentinovich Plekhanov was born into a minor gentry family, in Tambov Province. In 1876 he abandoned his formal education to devote himself entirely to the underground populist movement. It sought to instigate a peasant revolution that would overthrow the tsarist regime and create an agrarian socialist society. After years of in-

tensive revolutionary activity, he fled abroad in 1880 and spent most of the rest of his life in Switzerland. Becoming disillusioned with populist ideology, and drawn instead to Marxian thought, in 1883, together with a few friends, he formed the first Russian Marxist organization, the Emancipation of Labor Group. In two major works, *Socialism and Political Struggle* and *Our Differences* Plekhanov endeavored to adapt Marxian ideas to Russian circumstances. Rather than the peasants, the nascent proletariat would constitute the principal revolutionary force. But a socialist revolution was out of the question for his backward homeland, he believed. Accordingly, Russia was destined to experience two revolutions: the first to establish a "bourgeois-democratic" political system; the second, after industrial capitalism and the proletariat had become well developed, to create a socialist society.

During the 1890s, numbers of able individuals, including Vladimir Lenin, rallied to Plekhanov's banner. In 1903, they convened a congress to establish a Russian Social-Democratic Workers' Party. At its birth, the party split into two factions, the Bolsheviks (led by Lenin) and the Mensheviks. Initially Plekhanov sided with Lenin, but soon broke with him and thereafter usually sided with the Mensheviks.

During the Revolution of 1905, Plekhanov's theory was tested and found wanting. When world war broke out in 1914, unlike most Russian socialists Plekhanov supported Russia and its allies against Germany. He returned to Russia after the overthrow of tsarism in 1917. He vigorously attacked Lenin and the Bolsheviks, who were pressing for a second, socialist revolution. Because his views conflicted with those of the radicalized antiwar masses, he gained little support. With a broken heart, Plekhanov died in May 1918.

*See also:* BOLSHEVISM; LENIN, VLADIMIR ILICH; MARXISM; MENSHEVIKS; REVOLUTION OF 1905

SAMUEL H. BARON

# PLENUM

A plenum, or plenary session, is a meeting of any organization, group, association, etc., which all members are expected to attend. During the Soviet period, the term *plenum* referred specifically to a meeting of all members of a Communist Party committee at a national, regional, or local level. According to the Rules of the Communist Party of the Soviet Union, the Central Committee was required to hold a plenum at least once every six months, attended by both full and candidate members. At the first plenum after a Party Congress, the Central Committee elected the Politburo, Secretariat, and General Secretary. Other plenums usually coincided with important party or state events, such as a meeting of the Supreme Soviet or a significant international incident. During the three- to five-day session, members heard reports on party matters and approved prepared resolutions. Though originally intended by Vladimir Lenin to serve as the party's supreme decision-making body between Party Congresses—proof of the party's collective leadership—the Central Committee plenum became a more ceremonial than deliberative body by the mid-twentieth century. The plenum's main function was to endorse Politburo decisions. Infrequently, the Central Committee plenum was called on to resolve Politburo conflict; for example, a 1964 plenum removed Nikita Khrushchev from power. Proceedings remained secret, but a formal statement was issued at the end of a plenum. All decisions approved at the plenum became formal party policy. Party plenums at lower levels (e.g., regional or local) convened more often than the Central Committee, endorsing party directives and deciding how best to implement them.

See also: COMMUNIST PARTY OF THE SOVIET UNION

**BIBLIOGRAPHY**

Hill, Ronald J., and Frank, Peter. (1986). *The Soviet Communist Party*, 3rd ed. London: George Allen & Unwin.

Smith, Gordon B. (1992). *Soviet Politics: Struggling With Change*, 2nd ed. New York: St. Martin's Press.

JULIE K. DEGRAFFENRIED

## POBEDONOSTSEV, KONSTANTIN

(1827–1907), conservative statesman, professor and chair of civil law at Moscow University (1860–1865), senator, chief procurator of the Holy Synod (1880–1905).

Konstantin Petrovich Pobedonostsev has often been seen as one of the primary conservative influences on Alexander III and Nicholas II. Although the "grey eminence" undoubtedly exerted influence upon domestic policy and was influential in bringing about a new version of "Orthodoxy, Autocracy, and Nationality," historians have disputed the degree of his direct influence on policy formation.

Pobedonostsev, son of a Moscow University professor, grew up in Moscow in an atmosphere of scholarship, discipline, and close family ties. He was the youngest of eleven children, and his father closely supervised his early education before sending him off to the School of Jurisprudence from 1841 to 1846. Pobedonostsev graduated second in his class and upon graduation was assigned a position in the eighth department of the Senate in Moscow. He worked diligently in his position while also pursuing scholarly research and writing. Throughout his life Pobedonostsev remained a prolific writer, publishing articles on law, education, philosophy, and religion in book form and in journals such as *Grazhdanin* (*The Citizen*), *Moskovskie Vedomosti* (*Moscow News*) and *Russky Vestnik* (*Russian Newsletter*). In 1853 he became secretary of the seventh department of the Senate, and in 1855 he served as secretary to two Moscow departments. By 1859 he had received a lectureship in Russian civil law at Moscow University.

His scholarship, publications, translations, and reputation as an interesting and respected professor brought him to the attention of the court in 1861, and he was asked to tutor Grand Duke Nicholas Alexandrovich, heir to the throne. In that capacity he went on a tour of Russia with the heir and his entourage in 1863. According to several scholars, this journey profoundly influenced Pobedonostsev's view of Russia and his ideas about its future. When Nicholas died in 1865, Pobedonostsev was asked to tutor Grand Duke Alexander and became executive secretary to the first department of the Senate. Although Pobedonostsev was honored by his appointments and felt bound by duty to accept them, he apparently missed Moscow and felt uncomfortable in court life. According to Pobedonostsev's biographer, Robert Byrnes, this appointment "removed him from the library, the study, and the classroom and placed him in a position in which he was to develop a most inflexible political and social philosophy and to exert profound influence upon the course of Russian history" (p. 35). Pobedonostsev served in the senate from 1868 and in the State Council from 1872. He received his most important post, Ober Procurator of the Holy Synod, in 1880 and was to remain in it until his retirement in 1905.

Pobedonostsev worked closely with education ministers as well and was instrumental in developing policies he hoped would prevent radicalism in the universities. Contemporaries and historians have usually felt that Pobedonostsev worked for the appointment of Ivan Delyanov (Minister of Education, 1882–1898) and that together they worked toward establishing a quota system in order to restrict the numbers of non-Russian and non-Orthodox students admitted to Russian universities. He also reestablished a separate network of primary schools, which came under the jurisdiction of the Holy Synod rather than the Ministry of Education. Despite concerns about the level of education that could be delivered in church schools, Pobedonostsev believed that the moral benefits of church schools would outweigh any intellectual deficiencies.

Pobedonostsev has been considered one of the "most baleful influences on the reign" of Nicholas II and the ultra-conservative and reactionary force behind many of Alexander III's and Nicholas II's manifestos. Peter Banks, minister of finance from 1914 to 1917, noted that Pobedonostsev was the teacher who had the most influence on the tsar. Despite Pobedonostsev's reputation as an arch-conservative, he was actively involved in work on preparing the liberal judicial statute of 1861. He also read widely, communicated with Boris Chicherin, Fyodor Dostoyevsky, and Slavophile thinkers, and was aware of the intellectual debates of his day.

The year 1881 was a significant one for Pobedonostsev and for Russia. After the assassination of Alexander II, Pobedonostsev became one of the strongest forces arguing against the Mikhail Loris-Melikov constitution and Western-style reforms. He was responsible for drafting the manifesto that Alexander III read in April 1881 pledging to "preserve the power and justice of autocratic authority . . . from any pretensions to it." Pobedonostsev is usually assumed to be the writer responsible for Nicholas II's "senseless dreams" speech in 1895 when he proclaimed "it is known to me that voices have been heard of late in some zemstvo assemblies of persons carried away by senseless dreams of the participation of zemstvo representatives in the affairs of internal government."

If the height of Pobedonostsev's influence was after the assassination of Alexander II, his influence had significantly waned by 1896. His last years were quiet ones. He had never enjoyed court life, and in his later years he went out even less frequently. He did not officially retire until 1905, but

by then younger men had been appointed, Nicholas II had ascended to the throne, and many of Pobedonostsev's policies were once again being disputed. Pobedonostsev died of pneumonia in 1907. By the time of his death, other statesmen had assumed power, and his funeral was little noticed, with only a few in attendance.

*See also:* ALEXANDER III; HOLY SYNOD; NICHOLAS II; SLAVOPHILES

**BIBLIOGRAPHY**
Byrnes, Robert F. (1968). *Pobedonostsev: His Life and Thought.* Bloomington: Indiana University Press.

MICHELLE DENBESTE

# PODGORNY, NIKOLAI VIKTOROVICH

(1903–1983), party and government leader.

Nikolai Podgorny rose to political prominence under Nikita Khrushchev in the 1950s, only to play a key role in his ousting in October 1964. Ukrainian by birth and an engineer by vocation, Podgorny started his career in the Ukrainian sugar industry in the 1930s. Throughout the war he held a number of posts responsible for food production, particularly in the Ukraine, where he developed close links with Khrushchev. After the war, his career path shifted to the party. By 1953, the year Josef Stalin died, he was Second Secretary of the Ukrainian Communist Party. Podgorny's star rose as Khrushchev rose to power. In 1956, the year Khrushchev denounced Stalin, Podgorny was elected to the Communist Party of the Soviet Union (CPSU) Central Committee. Khrushchev personally nominated him for Ukrainian Communist Party First Secretary in 1957 and for the powerful post of CPSU Central Committee Secretary in 1963, by which time he was also a full member of the CPSU's leading body, the Presidium. While somewhat conservative, Podgorny was an enthusiastic supporter of some of Khrushchev's more "hare-brained schemes" (the accusation used to justify his dismissal in October 1964), such as the division of the party into industrial and agricultural sections. Nevertheless, Podgorny, like almost all Khrushchev's Ukrainian appointees, turned against his patron, colluding with Leonid Brezhnev in seeking Central Committee support to remove Khrushchev as party First Secretary. Podgorny went on to become Soviet head of state, but rivalry with party secretary Brezhnev saw his demise in 1977.

*See also:* BREZHNEV, LEONID ILICH; CHANCELLERY SYSTEM; KHRUSHCHEV, NIKITA SERGEYEVICH

**BIBLIOGRAPHY**

Taubman, William; Khrushchev, Sergei; and Gleason, Abbott, eds. (2000). *Nikita Khrushchev.* New Haven, CT: Yale University Press.

Tompson, William J. (1995). *Khrushchev: A Political Life.* Houndmills, Basingstoke, UK: Macmillan with St Antony's College, Oxford.

ROGER D. MARKWICK

# PODYACHY

The clerk (*podyachy*), who wrote, filed, and handled government documents of the seventeenth-century Russian central and provincial administration.

Little-known during the 1500s, chancellery clerks expanded: 575 in 1626, but 2,762 in 1698. After 1700, their numbers plunged. Divided in three salary groups (senior, middle, junior) by service record and seniority, clerks' pay varied from 0.5 to fifty rubles; the mean decreased from 11.5 to 9.5 rubles. Most earned from one to ten rubles. Pay was also in service land and kind. Clerks could receive supplements for special assignments, holidays, and other needs, and resort to bribery. Signatory (*podyachy so pripisyuu*) and document (*podyachy so spravoy*) clerks were elite senior clerks. Clerk novitiates between ages ten and fifteen learned skoropis (cursive longhand) and documentary formulae, and acquired office sense; many were washed out. During the 1600s, the number of clerks working without regular pay, thanks to budgetary constraints, increased significantly.

Numbers varied from 446 in the Service Land Chancellery to one in several smaller chancelleries; median and mean figures per chancellery were ten and nine (1620s) and twenty-three and fifty-two (1680s). Between three percent and ten percent were promoted to *dyak*. Not part of the Moscow service group, they were nonetheless respected for their expertise. Central clerks were dispatched into the field (land surveys, military headquarters duty, diplomatic service, etc.); mortality was high.

The number of provincial clerks varied from 750 (1640s) to nearly 1,900 (1690s). They worked under the town military governor (*voyevoda*), subordinated to the chancelleries. Working in Moscow and the provinces, the private scribe (*ploshchadnoy podyachy*) read and wrote private documents for a fee.

*See also:* CHANCELLERY SYSTEM; DYAK

**BIBLIOGRAPHY**

Brown, Peter B. (1978). "Early Modern Russian Bureaucracy: the Evolution of the Chancellery System from Ivan III to Peter the Great, 1478–1717." Ph.D. diss., University of Chicago.

Plavsic, Borovoi. (1980). "Seventeenth-Century Chanceries and Their Staffs." In *Russian Officialdom: The Bureaucratization of Russian Society from the Seventeenth Century to the Twentieth Century,* eds. Walter McKenzie Pintner and Don Karl Rowney. Chapel Hill: University of North Carolina Press.

PETER B. BROWN

# PODZOL

Podzols are subarctic soils of the cold, humid northern coniferous forest (*taiga*), found between the mixed forests of the temperate zone and the tundras of the arctic zone. Known as spodosol in the Seventh Approximation Soil Classification system, podzol derives from the Russian terms *pod*, or "under," and *zol*, or "ash." Very infertile because of the leaching of basic soil nutrients (calcium, sodium, potassium, magnesium, and so on), podzols are composed of layers known as horizons. The A-horizon comprises a shallow needleleaf litter zone, a narrow strongly acidic humus zone, and a broader ash-grey to chalky leached (A-2) horizon made up of silica, or sand. Beneath this infertile horizon is the zone of illuviation, or B-horizon, in which the leached nutrients of the A-horizon accumulate. Beyond the B-horizon is a totally inorganic C-horizon composed of weathered bedrock. Without substantial fertilization, podzols are suitable only for the growing of berries and root crops.

*See also:* CLIMATE; GEOGRAPHY

**BIBLIOGRAPHY**

Strahler, Arthur N. (1969). *Physical Geography*, 3rd ed. New York: Wiley.

VICTOR L. MOTE

## POGODIN, MIKHAIL PETROVICH

(1800–1875), prominent Russian historian, journalist, and publisher.

A Slavophile and professor of Russian history at Moscow University (1835–1844), Mikhail Pogodin wrote a seven-volume history of Russia (1846–1857) and a three-volume study entitled *The Early History of Russia* (1871). His conservative journal *The Muscovite* (1841–1856) defended the policies of Tsar Nicholas I.

Pogodin began life in humble circumstances, as the son of a serf, but his ultranationalist views helped to boost him to prominence. His association with the secret society Lovers of Wisdom (*Lyubomudry*) at Moscow University also helped his career. Founded in 1823 toward the end of the reign of Alexander I by Prince Vladimir Odoyevsky (1803–1869) and others, this society was, to some extent, a continuation of the Masonic Astrea Lodge. The circle—consisting of a dozen members who met in secret—tended to disregard politics and propound the philosophic ideas of Friedrich von Schelling and other Romantic thinkers. The society published the journal *Mnemosyne* until it was dissolved soon after the Decembrist uprising in 1825.

Pogodin believed that the natal gentry-style aristocracy had compromised and outlived itself. He wrote that Nicholas I, who died in 1855, had imposed upon Russia "the quiet of a graveyard, rotting and stinking, both physically and morally." As a Pan-Slavist, he often suggested that God's hand was at work in Russian history, preparing the nation for a great mission of peace and order. He compared the conquest of Siberia by Yermak in 1581 with that of South America by Hernando Cortéz. "We have discovered one third of Asia," he wrote in 1837. "Is that not worthy of celebration like America's discovery by Christopher Columbus?"

During the 1850s, Pogodin got into a debate with Ukrainian historian Mykhailo Maksymovych (1804–1873) over the legacy of Kievan Rus. Pogodin developed the untenable thesis that the Great Russians originally inhabited the Kiev region and that only after the Mongols forced them to flee to the northeast during the eleventh and twelfth centuries did the Ukrainians ("Little Russians") migrate into the area. According to Pogodin, the Ukrainians arrived much later from somewhere in the Carpathian Mountains. Pogodin's views were expanded on by the philologist Alexei Sobolevsky.

The oldest school of thought about the legacy of Kievan Rus claims that the first leaders and organizers of the state were the Varangians, a group of Scandinavians who raided the eastern shores of the Baltic Sea during the ninth century and penetrated into Eastern Europe toward Byzantium along the Dnieper River. This Norman (Normanist) theory rests mainly on a literal interpretation of the Primary Chronicle (*Tale of Bygone Years*, or *Povest vremennykh let*), a document written by monks of the Kievan Monastery that covers the period up to 1118.

Throughout the nineteenth century, Ukrainian historians challenged the Normanist theory, downplaying the Varangian influence on the formation of Rus. They argued that Ukrainians were autochthonous (indigenous) in their territories and that the principality of Galicia-Volhynia was the successor to the Kievan state.

However, the tsarist autocracy constantly censored these revisionists, which, besides Maksymovych, included Mykola Kostomarov, Volodymyr Antonovych, Mykhailo Hrushevsky, Dmytro Bahalii, Dmytro Doroshenko, and Mykola Chubaty. Nonetheless, the Normanist theory, with certain modifications, remains the basis of Western historiography of Russia and Ukraine.

Despite Pogodin's humble beginnings, his portrait was painted by the famous artist Vasily Perov (1834–1882), and he was buried with other luminaries in the Novodevichy Cemetery.

*See also:* NORMANIST CONTROVERSY; SLAVOPHILES

### BIBLIOGRAPHY

Wilson, Andrew. (2000). *The Ukrainians: Unexpected Nation.* New Haven, CT: Yale University Press.

JOHANNA GRANVILLE

## POGROMS

*Pogrom*, a Russian word that originally had several meanings, such as "beating," "defeat," "smashing," or "destruction," has come to be identified with violent attacks on the persons and property of one ethnicity by large crowds of other ethnicities, in particular, attacks on Jews by ethnic Russians. The first occurrence that historians generally agree was a pogrom took place in Odessa in 1821, and pogroms against Armenians took place in Azerbaijan in 1988 and 1990. Most pogroms in Russian history, however, took place in three major waves: 1881–1884, following the assassination of Alexander II; 1903–1906, following the announcement of the October Manifesto; and 1919–1921, during the Russian Civil War. In the first wave, more than 250 pogroms were recorded, mostly within the Pale of Settlement in present-day Ukraine. Beginning in April 1881, the largest and most violent were in the large cities, but then radiated out through the countryside, often along the railroad lines. Most pogroms occurred in the spring and summer of 1881, with ever smaller numbers in the next three years. These were less violent than later waves, with probably only forty deaths in 1881. The next wave began in 1903 with the infamous Kishinev pogrom, accelerated through the dislocations of war and revolution, and reached a great crescendo at the end of 1905. In the two weeks after the October Manifesto, it is estimated that seven hundred pogroms occurred throughout Russia, leaving nine hundred dead and eight thousand wounded. Unlike other waves, pogroms occurred at this time in many places outside of the Pale of Settlement, including small cities with an insignificant or nonexistent Jewish population; in the latter cases, students and political activists were often the major targets.

The classic explanation of these pogroms was that either the tsarist regime, or forces close to and supportive of the regime, encouraged these pogroms as a way of directing popular discontent away from the government and onto a visible minority group. While still widely held today, this explanation has been convincingly challenged in recent years by historians who have pointed out the complex and varied reactions the regime had to pogroms, the lack of archival evidence for such a conspiracy, the regime's deep fear of any sort of popular violence, and a general belief that the Russian government was incapable of organizing such widespread and, in the case of October 1905, simultaneous disturbances. However, if the old conspiracy theory is breaking down, no consensus explanation has emerged to replace it. The last great wave of pogroms, in 1919–1921, was the bloodiest and the most atypical, occurring after the fall of the imperial regime and during conditions of bitter strife in which violence of every kind was unrestrained. Concentrated in Ukraine, all parties to the conflict carried out pogroms at one point or another, but the most organized and bloodiest were perpetrated by the White Volunteer Army. Condoned by officers and carried out by Cossacks, with some looting by peasants, these pogroms may account for 150,000 deaths.

*See also:* CIVIL WAR OF 1917-1922; JEWS; NATIONALITIES POLICIES, TSARIST; OCTOBER MANIFESTO; PALE OF SETTLEMENT

**BIBLIOGRAPHY**

Aron, I. Michael. (1990). *Troubled Waters: The Origins of the 1881 Anti-Jewish Pogroms in Russia.* Pittsburgh, PA: University of Pittsburgh Press.

Judge, Edward H. (1992). *Easter in Kishinev: Anatomy of a Pogrom.* New York: New York University Press.

Klier, John D. (1993). "Unravelling of the Conspiracy Theory: A New Look at the Pogroms." *East European Jewish Affairs* 23:79–89.

Klier, John D., and Lambroza, Shlomo, eds. (1992). *Pogroms: Anti-Jewish Violence in Modern Russian History.* Cambridge, UK: Cambridge University Press.

DAVID PRETTY

# POKROVSKY, MIKHAIL NIKOLAYEVICH

(1868–1932), leading Soviet historian of the 1920s and early 1930s, chief administrator of the social sciences, and a principal enforcer of Marxist orthodoxy.

Mikhail Pokrovsky served as Vice-Commissar of Education; Chairman of the Presidium of the Communist Academy and Chairman of its Society of Marxist Historians; Full Member of the Soviet Academy of Sciences (briefly before his death); and was also a member of the Presidium of the Central Control Commission and held numerous other positions.

Pokrovsky studied history at the Imperial Moscow University under the supervision of Vasily Klyuchevsky and Pavel Vinogradov. In 1905 he embraced Marxism as a creed and methodology. As a result of revolutionary activities, he spent the years from 1907 to 1917 in exile, mostly in France. There he produced his most important scholarly works, notably his five-volume *History of Russia since Ancient Times.* In it he stated his major thesis: Russian history manifested the same pattern of development as did other European societies in that capitalism was a natural outcome of class conflict and not a foreign implant. Russian autocracy, a mere variant of European absolutism, was created by and served the interests of merchant capitalism. The latter was an ill-defined category that Pokrovsky borrowed from Karl Marx. This thesis placed Pokrovsky at odds with most other Russian historians, who asserted that Russian autocracy, unlike European absolutism, had the power to fashion social relationships; it was, in a certain sense, "supraclass." Most of Pokrovsky's numerous subsequent writings reiterated this thesis and attacked the non-Marxist historians who did not share it.

Pokrovsky returned to Russia in August 1917 and held prominent positions in the Moscow Soviet. After the Bolsheviks took power he largely confined his activities to the pedagogical, scholarly and propaganda institutions of the Soviet government and the Communist Party. He was the party-designated leader of what was called the historical front, an array of institutions designed to establish the hegemony of Marxist doctrine and to circumscribe and finally eliminate all non-Marxist doctrines and convert or silence their adherents.

Pokrovsky elaborated a theory of cultural revolution that justified the provisional pluralism implied by the policies mentioned above: the building of communism with the hands of non-communists, at least in the short term. The policy and his theory began to flounder during the late 1920s. His concept of merchant capitalism and his leadership of the historical front came under attack from a faction of rival historians. Hastening to get in step with Josef Stalin, Pokrovsky aggressively attacked non-Marxist scholars as class enemies, but his theory of merchant capitalism clashed with Stalin's theory of socialism in one country. In 1931 Stalin upheld the authority of Pokrovsky. His "school" (i.e., associates and former students) dominated the scholarly and propaganda apparatus until 1936. In that year Stalin signaled a vituperative campaign against the ideas of Pokrovsky: he was branded as anti-Marxist and petty bourgeois, largely because his works were devoid of nationalist sentiment. Pokrovsky had helped to devise the repressive instruments that were used against him posthumously. Almost his entire school was physically annihilated. Because Pokrovsky was an anti-Stalin symbol, he received a partial rehabilitation in the years of Nikita Khrushchev's predominance. During the early twenty-first century his name has almost entirely lost its symbolic weight.

*See also:* MARXISM; STALIN, JOSEF VISSARIONOVICH

### BIBLIOGRAPHY
Barber, John. (1981). *Soviet Historians in Crisis, 1928–1932.* London: Macmillan Press in association with the Centre for Russian and East European Studies, University of Birmingham.

Enteen, George M. (1978). *The Soviet Scholar-Bureaucrat: M.N. Pokrovsky and the Society of Marxist Historians.* University Park: Pennsylvania State University Press.

Pokrovsky, M. N. (1966). *History of Russia from the Earliest Times to the Rise of Commercial Capitalism,* tr. J. D. Clarkson and M. R. M. Griffiths. 2nd ed. Bloomington, IN: University Prints and Reprints.

Pokrovsky, M. N. (1993). *Brief History of Russia,* tr. D. S. Mirsky. 2 vols. London: Martin Lawrence Limited.

GEORGE ENTEEN

# POLAND

Relations between Poles and Russians have never been easy. Despite their close linguistic and ethnic ties, differences rather than similarities characterize the relationship between them. In religious denomination, political tradition, worldview, even the alphabets in which they write their related languages, Poles and Russians are clearly distinct. Russia took its form of Christianity during the late ninth century from Byzantium while Poland was christened by emissaries from the pope almost a century later. Russia came to be the very essence of autocratic rule under Ivan IV and the Romanovs, while Poland developed in an opposite direction, toward a highly decentralized polity linked with Lithuania and dominated by the nobility. Throughout history, Poland has tended to see itself as the easternmost outpost of Western values and traditions: unlike Russia, Poland participated in the Renaissance and Reformation. Defining themselves as Europeans, Poles have often depicted their Eastern neighbors as barbarians and schismatics. Russians returned the favor, describing Poles as flighty, hysterical, and treacherous.

### MUSCOVY AND POLAND-LITHUANIA
The first significant clashes between the Polish state and Muscovy occurred after the Union of Lublin (1569). During the 1550s and 1560s Muscovy had pursued an aggressive westward policy, seizing some Lithuanian lands. When Muscovite political authority dissolved into anarchy during the Time of Troubles during the early seventeenth century, Poland was ready to fish in troubled Russian waters. Polish nobles and Jesuits supported the first

"False Dmitry," who claimed to be Ivan IV's son and triumphantly entered Moscow in 1605. In great part because of the large Polish retinue and openly Catholic sympathies of "Dmitry," he was soon deposed and murdered. But Polish interference in confused Muscovite politics continued. Most spectacularly, King Sigismund III of Poland succeeded in having his son Wladyslaw proclaimed tsar in 1610. The Polish presence in Moscow was not to last; by 1613 the Poles had been slaughtered or forced to flee, and Mikhail Romanov was elected tsar.

As Russia recovered and expanded under the Romanovs, Poland grew weaker. Poland's highly decentralized government and elected king meant that the central government could not impose its will on the provinces. Increasingly, power devolved to the local magnates, further weakening the center. The anti-Polish rebellion of Bohdan Khmelnitsky in 1648 allowed Muscovy to extend its power into the Ukraine with the Treaty of Pereiaslavl (1654). Additional Polish territory, including the cities of Smolensk and Kiev, was lost to the Russians during the following decade.

### THE EIGHTEENTH CENTURY

The eighteenth century witnessed further Polish descent into anarchy. Already during the 1690s Polish king Jan Sobieski had complained of his inability to force the Polish magnates to obey him. Worse was to come. The fact that Polish kings were elected allowed Poland's neighbors to put up their own candidates in the hope of influencing future policy. Poland also had the misfortune to be placed geographically between three rising absolutist states—Prussia, Russia, and Habsburg Austria. In 1764, St. Petersburg succeeded in placing its candidate on the Polish throne. Stanisław-August Poniatowski, a former lover of Catherine the Great, was to be the last Polish king.

### PARTITIONS AND RUSSIAN RULE

The impetus toward partition came not from Russia, but from Poland's western neighbor, Prussia. That state's ambitious ruler, Frederick II ("the Great") suggested a dividing up of Polish territory to prevent destabilizing "anarchy." In the first Partition of Poland (1772), Russia absorbed some thirteen percent of the commonwealth's territory. The shock of the partition fueled a push for serious political reforms, including a strengthening of the central government and the king. The partitioning powers, including Russia, feared a strong Poland.

A 1772 drawing shows Polish King Stanislav trying to hold onto his crown while Poland is split between Catherine II and Frederick II. © BETTMANN/CORBIS

They were particularly disturbed by the fruitful efforts of the Four-Years-Sejm, including the Polish constitution of May 3, 1791. Once again using the excuse of Polish anarchy, Prussia and Russia seized more Polish territory in the Second Partition of 1793, calling forth a Polish national uprising. However, the heroic efforts of insurrectionist Tadeusz Kosciuszko could not prevent the Third Partition of 1795, after which Poland disappeared from the European map for more than a century.

After the Napoleonic wars, borders between the partitioning powers were altered significantly, bringing a large portion of ethnic Poland under Russian rule. The majority of Poles thus became subjects of the Russian tsar. Tsar Alexander I afforded the Kingdom of Poland considerable rights and autonomy. The Poles enjoyed their own coinage, legal system, army, legislature, and constitution. Disagreements between Warsaw and St. Petersburg over the limits of Polish autonomy exploded into the open during the November Upris-

**Russian troops in Warsaw after the January insurrection of 1863–1864.** © HULTON-DEUTSCH COLLECTION/CORBIS

ing of 1830, which lasted well into the following year. After Nicholas I put down this insurrection, he abolished the Kingdom of Poland's legislature, constitution, and army. Still, legal and administrative differences existed between Russian and Polish provinces—though these differences would be considerably narrowed after the crushing of the subsequent January 1863 uprising.

The final half century of Romanov rule over much of historic Poland has generally been characterized as a period of Russification. Certainly, St. Petersburg viewed Poles en masse as at least potentially disloyal subjects, and Polish culture was kept on a very tight leash. Poles in the Russian Empire could not use their native tongue in education at any level except the most elementary—and even here Russian was often introduced. In the so-called Western Provinces (present-day western Ukraine, Lithuania, Belarus) even speaking Polish in public could lead to fines or worse. Still, there was no systematic attempt to Russify the Polish nation in the sense of total cultural (or religious) assimilation.

Rather, Russification amounted to a severe limiting of Polish civil and cultural rights in this period.

### WORLD WAR I AND INDEPENDENCE

The outbreak of World War I transformed relations between the partitioning powers and Poles. Now securing the loyalty of Poles became a paramount consideration for both Russia and the Central Powers. The Russian commander-in-chief, Grand Duke Nikolai Nikolayevich, issued a manifesto in mid-August 1914, holding out the postwar promise of a unified Polish state under the Romanov scepter. In the end, force of arms decided the issue: By autumn 1915 Russian armies had for the most part been pushed out of ethnic Poland. With the Bolsheviks' coming to power in October 1917 and the subsequent Treaty of Brest-Litovsk (March 1918), all hopes of continued Russian—or Soviet—domination over Poland came to an end. In late 1918 Poland regained its independence.

Relations between Poland and the fledgling Soviet state got off to a very bad start. Moscow was vitally interested in exporting revolution to Western Europe, most likely by way of Poland. Further, the unclear borders between Poland and its neighbors to the east presented a serious potential for conflict. Historically, Poles had been very prominent as landowners and townspeople in these border regions between ethnic Poland and ethnic Russia. Thus Poles figure in early Soviet propaganda as portly mustachioed noblemen bent on enslaving Ukrainian or Belarusian peasants. Between 1919 and 1921 Soviet Russia and newly independent Poland clashed on the battlefield, the Poles occupying Kiev and, at the opposite extreme, the Red Army getting all the way to the Vistula River in central Poland. In March 1921, both sides, exhausted for the moment, signed the Peace of Riga.

The USSR was not satisfied with the treaty's terms. In particular, hundreds of thousands of ethnic Belarusians and Ukrainians ended up on the Polish side of the frontier, providing the USSR with a would-be constituency for extending the border westward. Nor did relations between Poland and the USSR improve in the interwar period. The two primary politicians of interwar Poland, Józef Piłsudski and Roman Dmowski, both despised and feared the Soviet state. The Communist Party was outlawed in Poland, and many Polish communists fled to the USSR, often straight into the Gulag. Even Adolf Hitler's coming to power in 1933 did not bring the USSR and Poland closer. Rather, the later 1930s witnessed the Great Purges in the USSR and a downward spiral in Polish politics toward an increasingly vicious form of Polish chauvinism and official anti-Semitism.

Poland was stunned by the Molotov-Ribbentrop Pact of August 1939. This agreement between Josef Stalin's USSR and Hitler's Germany demonstrated that their mutual enmity toward the Polish state outweighed ideological differences. The pact allowed Hitler to invade on September 1, 1939, and the Red Army, following a secret protocol, occupied eastern Poland later that month. Once again Poland disappeared from the map. When the Polish state was resurrected in 1945, it was devastated. The large and vibrant Polish Jewish community had been all but wiped out during the Holocaust, some three million non-Jewish Poles had lost their lives, and the capital city Warsaw was a wasteland, systematically destroyed by the Germans in retaliation for the Warsaw Uprising of August 1944. Polish nationalists and some Western writers contend that the Red Army, by that time nearing the eastern outskirts of the city, could have

prevented the Nazi devastation of the city. Others argue that the Red Army had been successfully repulsed by the Germans. In any case, the failure of the Soviets to move into Warsaw allowed the Nazis to massacre Polish fighters who might very well have opposed the imposition of communist rule.

## PEOPLE'S POLAND

Having liberated Poland from the Nazis, Stalin was determined to see a pro-Soviet government installed there. Despite the tiny number of native Polish communists and little support for communist or pro-Soviet candidates, intimidation and rigged voting placed a Stalinist Polish government, led by Bolesław Bierut, in power in 1948. Bierut launched a crash industrialization drive, attempted to collectivize Polish agriculture, and jailed many Catholic clergymen. After Bierut's death in 1956, leadership passed to the more flexible Wladyslaw Gomulka who allowed Poles a considerable amount of cultural and economic leeway while reassuring Moscow of People's Poland's stability.

Unfortunately for Gomulka, Poles compared their economic and cultural situation not with that in the USSR, but with conditions in the West. As the 1960s progressed, the relative backwardness of Poland compared with Germany or the United States only increased. Domestically, internal party tensions led to an ugly state-sponsored anti-Semitic episode in 1968, during which Poland's few remaining Jews—most highly assimilated—were hounded out of the country. Thus, Gomulka's position was already weak before the notorious price hikes on basic foodstuffs of December 1970 that led to rioting and his replacement by Edward Gierek. Gierek promised prosperity, but was never able to deliver. In 1980, price increases caused civil disturbances and his resignation.

The discontent of 1980 also spawned something quite new: the Polish trade union Solidarity. This first independent trade union in a communist bloc country appeared in late 1980, was banned just more than one year later, and was resurrected—more properly, relegalized—during the late 1980s. Solidarity represented a novel phenomenon for a People's Democracy: a popular and independent trade union that brought together intellectuals and workers. The outlawing of Solidarity by General Wojciech Jaruzelski in December 1981 was a desperate measure taken, according to Jaruzelski himself, to forestall an actual Soviet invasion of the country. One may doubt Jaruzelski's account, but tensions between the USSR and Poland certainly ran high, and the threat of invasion cannot be entirely discounted. Ultimately, however, Jaruzelski's attempt to save People's Poland failed. Early in 1989 Solidarity was relegalized and in summer of that year the communists handed over power to Tadeusz Mazowiecki, the first noncommunist prime minister since the 1940s. The refusal of Soviet leader Mikhail Gorbachev to intervene in Polish affairs made possible this peaceful transfer of power.

Relations between Poland and Russia during the 1990s have been remarkably positive, considering the amazing changes brought by that decade. Despite grumbling and even saber rattling from Moscow over Poland's plans to join the North Atlantic Treaty Organization (NATO), in the end NATO expansion took place in 1999 without a hitch. At the same time, economic and cultural links between Moscow and Warsaw have weakened considerably as Poland has turned toward the West both institutionally (NATO, European Union) and culturally (learning English instead of Russian). Still, the correct if not always cordial relations between the two countries during the 1990s give reason for hope that the two largest Slavic nations will finally be able to both live together and prosper.

*See also:* CATHOLICISM; LITHUANIA AND LITHUANIANS; NATIONALISM IN THE SOVIET UNION; NATIONALISM IN TSARIST EMPIRE; ORGANIC STATUTE OF 1832; POLES; POLISH REBELLION OF 1863; POLISH-SOVIET WAR; SARMATIANS; TIME OF TROUBLES

**BIBLIOGRAPHY**

Davies, Norman. *Heart of Europe: A Short History of Poland.* (1984). Oxford, UK: Oxford University Press.

Gross, Jan. (1988). *Revolution from Abroad: The Soviet Conquest of Poland's Western Ukraine and Western Belorussia.* Princeton, NJ: Princeton University Press.

Jedlicki, Jerzy. (1999). *A Suburb of Europe: Nineteenth-Century Polish Approaches to Western Civilization.* Budapest: Central European University Press.

Polonsky, Antony. (1972). *Politics in Independent Poland 1921–1939: The Crisis of Constitutional Government.* Oxford, UK: Clarendon Press.

Snyder, Timothy. (2003). *The Reconstruction of Nations: Poland, Ukraine, Lithuania, Belarus, 1569–1999.* New Haven, CT: Yale University Press.

Walicki, Andrzej. (1991). *Russia, Poland, and Universal Regeneration: Studies on Russian and Polish Thought of the Romantic Epoch.* Notre Dame, IN: University of Notre Dame Press.

Wandycz, Piotr. (1974). *The Lands of Partitioned Poland, 1795–1918.* Seattle: University of Washington Press.

THEODORE R. WEEKS

## POLAR EXPLORERS

From its earliest days, Russia was concerned with Arctic settlement and development. Actual exploration began during the eighteenth century and continued, although Russia took little part in the classic race for the North and South poles. Interest heightened after 1920, as the USSR transformed itself into a key player in North polar exploration. After 1956, the USSR became an important force in Antarctic research.

Russian migration to the Arctic coast began during the eleventh century. Further settlement was tied to the foundation of religious communities (such as the Solovetsky Monastery, built in 1435); demand for furs and precious metals; the search for the Northeast Passage (in Russian, the Northern Sea Route); the establishment of ports such as Arkhangelsk (1584); and Russia's eastward expansion into Siberia during the sixteenth and seventeenth centuries.

Scientific and exploratory work got underway during the 1700s and 1800s. On behalf of the Russian government, Danish captain Vitus Bering, with Alexei Chirikov as his second-in-command, launched his Kamchatka (1728–1730) and Great Northern (1733–1749) expeditions. Afterward, the Admiralty and Academy of Sciences sponsored many voyages and expeditions, surveying or exploring Spitsbergen, Novaya Zemlya, the New Siberian Islands, Wrangel Island, and Franz Josef Land. The colonization of Alaska and incorporation of the Russian-American Company (1799) necessitated greater familiarity with the Arctic. Key figures from this period include Fyodor Rozmyslov (d. 1771), Vasily Chichagov (1726–1809), Matvei Gedenshtrom (1780–1843), Academy of Sciences president Fyodor Litke (1797–1882), and Alexander Sibiryakov (1844–1893). The latter sponsored the first successful crossing of the Northeast Passage: Adolf Erik Nordenskjold's 1878–1879 voyage in the *Vega.*

During the late 1800s and early 1900s, as international audiences thrilled to the daring exploits of explorers like Peary and Scott, Russian polar work focused on scientific, commercial, and military concerns. Admiral Stepan Makarov formed a Russian icebreaker fleet, while naval officer Alexander Kolchak, later famous as a White commander during the Russian civil war, explored the Arctic. Early twentieth-century expeditions under Ernst Toll, Vladimir Rusanov, Georgy Brusilov, and Georgy Sedov ended in tragedy. By contrast, in 1914, Yan Nagursky became the first pilot successfully to fly an airplane above the Arctic Circle. In 1914–1915, Boris Vilkitsky completed the second traversal of the Northeast Passage.

Under the Soviet regime, polar exploration and development fell to agencies such as the All-Union Arctic Institute (VAI) and, after 1932, the Main Administration of the Northern Sea Route (GUSMP). Prominent Arctic scientists included Vladimir Vize, Georgy Ushakov, and Rudolf Samoilovich of the VAI, as well as Otto Shmidt, head of GUSMP. The USSR made impressive headway during the 1920s and 1930s in building an economic and transportational infrastructure in the polar regions. This was also an era of spectacular public triumphs, including the rescue of Umberto Nobile and the crew of the dirigible *Italia* (1928); participation in the Arctic flight of the airship *Graf Zeppelin* (1931); the *Sibiryakov*'s first single-season crossing of the Northeast Passage (1932); the airlift of the *Chelyuskin*'s crew and passengers, who survived two months on the Arctic ice after their ship sank (1933–1934); the flights of Valery Chkalov and Mikhail Gromov over the North Pole on their way to the United States (1937); the first airplane landing at the North Pole (1937); and the establishment of the first research outpost at the North Pole, the SP-1, under the leadership of Ivan Papanin (1937–1938). In 1941 the Soviets also accomplished the first airplane landing at the Pole of Relative Inaccessibility. There was, of course, an ugly underside to Soviet achievement in the Arctic: Not only was much Soviet polar work characterized by inefficiency and periodic mishaps, both major and minor, but it was closely linked to the steady expansion of forced labor in the GULAG system.

Soviet polar exploration resumed after World War II. A new generation of researchers, including A.A. Afanasyev, Vasily Burkhanov, Mikhail Somov, Alexei Treshnikov, Boris Koshechkin, and others, came to the forefront. A second North Pole outpost (SP-2) was established in 1950, and until the late 1980s, the USSR operated at least two SP stations at any given time. In 1977, the atomic icebreaker *Arktika* became the first surface vessel to reach the North Pole.

As for the Antarctic, Russian mariners Fabian Bellingshausen (1770–1852) became, in 1820, one of the first three explorers knowingly to sight the Antarctic continent (the first person to sight Antarctica remains a matter of debate). The USSR did not engage in serious exploration of the Antarctic until 1956. During the International Geophysical Year of 1957–1958, the USSR was one of twelve nations to establish stations in Antarctica. In 1959, the USSR signed the Antarctic Treaty, which went into effect in 1961. As with the Arctic, the collapse of the USSR in 1991 made it difficult for the Russians to continue Antarctic research, although Russia still maintains stations there year-round.

*See also:* BERING, VITUS JONASSEN; CHIRIKOV, ALEXEI ILICH

**BIBLIOGRAPHY**

Armstrong, Terence. (1958). *The Russians in the Arctic.* London: Methuen.

Armstrong, Terence. (1965). *Russian Settlement in the North.* Cambridge, UK: Cambridge University Press.

McCannon, John. (1998). *Red Arctic: Polar Exploration and the Myth of the North in the Soviet Union, 1932–1939.* New York: Oxford University Press.

Taracouzio, T. A. (1938). *Soviets in the Arctic.* New York: Macmillan.

JOHN MCCANNON

# POLES

The Poles represent the northwestern branch of the Slavonic race. They speak Polish, a member of the Western Slavic branch of the Indo-European language family. It is most closely related to Belorussian, Czech, Slovak, and Ukrainian. From the very earliest times the Poles have resided on the territory between the Carpathians, Oder River, and North Sea. Bolesław I "Chrobny" or the Brave (967–1025) united all the Slavonic tribes in this region into a Polish kingdom, which reached its zenith at the close of the Middle Ages and slowly declined during the mid to late eighteenth century. Hostility to Polish nationalism formed a common bond between the Russian, Prussian, and Austrian governments. Thus, Poland was partitioned four times. The first partition (August 1772) divided one-third of Poland between the three above-named countries. The second partition (January 1793) was mostly to the advantage of Russia; Austria did not acquire land. In the third partition (October 1795), the rest of Poland was divided up between the three autocracies. After the defeat of Napoleon and collapse of his puppet state, the Grand Duchy of Warsaw (1807–1814), a fourth partition occurred (1815), by which the Russians pushed westward and incorporated Warsaw. Until then Warsaw had been situated in Prussian Poland from 1795 to 1807. Potent anti-Russian sentiment has long prevailed among the Poles who are predominantly Catholic, especially during the eighteenth and nineteenth centuries, as evidenced by four popular uprisings against the Slavic colossus to the east: 1768, 1794, 1830–1831, and 1863. According to the 1890 census about 8,400,000 Poles resided in the Russian Empire.

Finally in 1918, an independent Poland was reconstituted. Later in August 1939 a pact was signed between Adolf Hitler's Germany and Josef Stalin's Soviet Union, which contained a secret protocol authorizing yet a fifth partition of Poland: "In the event of a territorial and political rearrangement of the areas belonging to the Polish state the spheres of influence of Germany and the USSR shall be bounded approximately by the line of the rivers Narew, Vistula, and San." The next month Hitler's Germany invaded Poland; the Red Army did not interfere.

After more than four decades of the Cold War, during which Poland was a Soviet "satellite" and belonged to the Soviet-led Warsaw Pact, partially free elections were held in 1989. The Solidarity movement won sweeping victories; Lech Wałęsa became Poland's first popularly elected post-Communist president in December 1990. In 1999 Poland joined the North Atlantic Treaty Organization, along with Hungary and the Czech Republic. It is scheduled to enter the European Union in 2004.

See also: NATIONALITIES POLICIES, SOVIET; NATIONALITIES POLICIES, TSARIST; POLAND

**BIBLIOGRAPHY**

Connor, Walter D., and Ploszajski, Piotr. (1992). *The Polish Road from Socialism: The Economics, Sociology, and Politics of Transition.* Armonk, NY: M. E. Sharpe.

Hunter, Richard J., and Ryan, Leo. (1998). *From Autarchy to Market: Polish Economics and Politics, 1945–1995.* Westport, CT: Praeger.

Lukowski, Jerzy, and Zawadzki, Hubert. (2002). *A Concise History of Poland.* New York: Cambridge University Press.

Michta, Andrew A. (1990). *Red Eagle: The Army in Polish Politics, 1944–1988.* Stanford, CA: Hoover Institution Press.

Snyder, Timothy. (2003). *The Reconstruction of Nations: Poland, Ukraine, Lithuania, Belarus, 1569–1999.* New Haven, CT: Yale University Press.

JOHANNA GRANVILLE

**POLICE** *See* STATE SECURITY, ORGANS OF.

## POLISH REBELLION OF 1863

After decades of harsh limits on Polish autonomy, many Poles were hopeful that the situation would improve after the 1855 coronation of Alexander II. There were indeed concessions: Martial law was lifted, an amnesty was declared for all political prisoners, a new Archbishop of Warsaw was named (the position had been vacant since 1830), and censorship was made somewhat less restrictive. In 1862 a Pole named Aleksander Wielopolski was made governor of the Polish Kingdom, in an attempt to cooperate with the aristocratic elite and marginalize more radical national separatists and democratic revolutionaries. All these attempts at conciliation failed, as patriotic demonstrations broke out in late 1861 and intensified throughout 1862. The Russians tried to suppress these protests with deadly force, but that only generated more anger among the Poles, and the unrest spread.

Wielopolski tried to quash the disturbances on the night of January 23 by organizing an emergency draft into the army targeted at the young men who had been leading the demonstrations. This, too, failed, as it prompted the national movement leaders to proclaim an uprising (which was being planned in any case). The rebels proclaimed the existence of the "Temporary National Government," which would lead the revolt and (they hoped) pave the way for a true independent Polish government afterwards.

The "January Uprising" (as it is known in Poland) was fought primarily as a guerrilla war, with small-scale assaults against individual Russian units rather than large pitched battles (which the Poles lacked the forces to win). Over the next one and one-half years, 200,000 Poles took part in the fighting, with about 30,000 in the field at any one moment.

After the revolt was crushed, thousands of Poles were sent to Siberia, hundreds were executed, and towns and villages throughout Poland were devastated by the violence. All traces of Polish autonomy were lost, and the most oppressive period of Russification began.

*See also:* POLAND

**BIBLIOGRAPHY**

Leslie, R. F. (1963). *Reform and Insurrection in Russian Poland, 1856–1865*. London: University of London, Athlone Press.

Wandycz, Piotr. (1974). *The Lands of Partitioned Poland, 1795–1918*. Seattle: University of Washington Press.

BRIAN PORTER

# POLITBURO

The Politburo, or Political Bureau, was the most important decision-making and leadership organ in the Communist Party, and has commonly been seen as equivalent to the cabinet in Western political systems. For most of the life of the Soviet system, the Politburo (called the Presidium between 1952 and 1966) was the major focus of elite political life and the arena within which all important issues of policy were decided. It was the heart of the political system.

The Politburo was formally established at the Eighth Congress of the Party in March 1919 and held its first session on April 16. Formed by the Central Committee (CC), the Politburo was to make decisions that could not await the next meeting of the CC, but over time its smaller size and more frequent meeting schedule meant that effective power drained into it and away from the CC. There had been smaller groupings of leaders before, but these had never become formalized nor had they taken an institutional form. The establishment of the Politburo was part of the regularization of the leading levels of the Party that saw the simultaneous creation of the Orgburo and Secretariat, with these latter two bodies meant to ensure the implementation of the decisions of leading Party organs, in practice mostly the Politburo.

From its formation until late 1930, the Politburo was one arena within which the conflict between Josef Stalin and his supporters on the one side and successive groups of oppositionists among the Party leadership was fought out, but with the removal of Mikhail Tomsky in 1930, the last open oppositionist disappeared from the Politburo. Henceforth the body remained largely controlled by Stalin. Its lack of institutional integrity and power is illustrated by the fact that various of its members were arrested and executed during the terror of the mid- to late 1930s. After World War II, the Politburo ceased even to meet regularly, being effectively replaced by ad hoc groupings of leaders that Stalin mobilized on particular issues and when it suited him.

Following Stalin's death in 1953, the leading Party organs resumed a more regular existence, although Nikita Khrushchev's style was not one well suited to the demands of collective leadership; he often sought to bypass the Presidium. Under Leonid Brezhnev, the Politburo became more regularized, and the overwhelming majority of national issues seem to have been discussed in that body, although an important exception was the decision to send troops into Afghanistan in 1979. For much of the Mikhail Gorbachev period, too, the Politburo was at the heart of Soviet national decision making, although the shift of the Soviet system to a presidential one and the restructuring of the Politburo at the Twenty-Eighth Congress in 1990 effectively sidelined this body as an important institution.

The Politburo was always a small body. The first Politburo consisted of five full and three candidate (or nonvoting) members; at its largest, when it was elected at the Nineteenth Congress in 1952 and was probably artificially large because Stalin was planning a further purge of the leadership (it was also envisaged that there would be a small, inner body), it comprised twenty-five full and eleven candidate members. Generally in the post-Stalin period it had between ten and fifteen full and five to nine candidates. Membership has tended to include a number of CC secretaries, leading representatives from state institutions (although the foreign and defense ministers did not become automatic members until 1973) and sometimes one or two republican party leaders. Gorbachev changed this pattern completely in 1990 by making all republican party leaders members of the Politburo along with the general secretary and his deputy, and eliminating candidate membership. It was overwhelmingly a male institution, with only two women (Ekaterina Furtseva and Alexandra Biriukova) gaining membership, and it was always dominated by ethnic Slavs, especially Russians.

While the frequency of Politburo meetings is somewhat uncertain for much of its life, it seems to have met on average about once per week in the Brezhnev period and after, with provision for a further meeting if required. Meetings were attended by all members plus a range of other people who might be called in to address specific items on the agenda. In addition, some issues were handled by circulation among the members, thereby not requiring explicit discussion at a meeting. No public differences of opinion between Politburo members were aired before the breakdown of many of the rules of Party life under Gorbachev, and public unanimity prevailed. It is not clear that votes were actually taken; issues seem to have been resolved through discussion and consensus. Whatever the process, the Politburo was the central leadership site of the Party and the Soviet system as a whole.

*See also:* BREZHNEV, LEONID ILICH; CENTRAL COMMITTEE; COMMUNIST PARTY OF THE SOVIET UNION; GORBACHEV, MIKHAIL SERGEYEVICH; PRESIDIUM OF SUPREME SOVIET; STALIN, JOSEF VISSARIONOVICH

### BIBLIOGRAPHY

Laird, Roy D. (1986). *The Politburo: Demographic Trends, Gorbachev and the Future.* Boulder, CO: Westview Press.

Lowenhardt, John; Ozinga, James R.; and van Ree, Erik. (1992). *The Rise and Fall of the Soviet Politburo.* London: UCL Press.

GRAEME GILL

## POLITICAL PARTY SYSTEM

Following years of one-party politics in the Soviet Union, post-communist Russia experienced a burst of party development during the 1990s. Still, Russia's party system remains underdeveloped. Although political parties run candidates in national parliamentary elections, Russia's first two presidents, Boris Yeltsin and Vladimir Putin, chose not to affiliate themselves with political parties. Russia's constitution gives the president the power to form the government without reference to the balance of party strength in the parliament. Politicians in the State Duma usually affiliate themselves with parties or party-like factions, but almost no parties have well-developed organizational bases among the electorate. Most voters have only dim conceptions of the policy positions of the major political parties. New parties constantly form and dissolve. The function often ascribed to political parties in developed democracies—that of linking voters' interests with the policy decisions of government—is scarcely visible in Russia. Nonetheless, a rudimentary party system was in place by the late 1990s.

Russia's parties may be characterized as falling into five major types. On the left are Marxist-Leninist parties. The most prominent example is the Communist Party of the Russian Federation, headed by Gennady Zyuganov. The CPRF is characterized by a militantly anti-capitalist stance, which it combines with appeals to Russian statist, nationalist, and religious traditions. It is the strongest political party in Russia both in its membership and in the number of votes it attracts in elections (it can count on the support of about 20 to 25 percent of the electorate). It also enjoys a distinct ideological identity in voters' minds. Despite its large following, however, it has been unable to exercise much influence in policy making at the national level. Other parties on the left are still more radical in their ideologies and call for a return to Soviet-era political and economic institutions; some expressly advocate a return to Stalinism.

A second group of parties can be called "social democratic." They accept the principle of private ownership of property. At the same time, they call for a more interventionist social policy by the government to protect social groups made vulnerable by the transition from communism. The party headed by Grigory Yavlinsky, called Yabloko, is an example. Yabloko attracts 7 to 10 percent of the vote in national elections. Other parties that identify themselves as social democratic—including a party organized by former president Mikhail Gorbachev—have fared poorly in elections.

A third group of parties strongly advocate market-oriented policies. They press for further privatization of state assets, including land and industrial enterprises. They also seek closer integration of Russia with the West and the spread of values such as respect for individual civil, political, and economic liberties. The most prominent example of such a party is the Union of Rightist Forces, which drew around 8 percent of the vote in the 2000 parliamentary election.

A fourth group of parties appeal to voters on nationalist grounds. Some call for giving ethnic Russians priority treatment in Russia over ethnic minorities. Others demand the restoration of a

Russian empire. They denounce Western influences such as individualism, materialism, and competitiveness. Some believe that Russia's destiny lies with a Eurasian identity that straddles East and West; others take a more straightforwardly statist bent and call for restoring Russian military might and centralized state power. Nationalist groups are numerous and skillful at attracting attention, but tend to be small. However, Vladimir Zhirinovsky's Liberal Democratic Party of Russia gained some successes in elections during the 1990s (22% in 1993, 12% in 1995).

The fifth group may be called "parties of power." These are parties that actively avoid taking explicit programmatic stances. They depend instead on their access to state power and the provision of patronage benefits to elite supporters. Their public stance tends to be centrist, pragmatic, and reassuring. The major party of power in the 2000 election was "Unity," which benefited from an arms-length association with Vladimir Putin. The problem for parties of power is that they have little to offer voters except their proximity to the Kremlin; if their patrons reject them or lose power, they quickly fade from view.

Many voters can identify a party that they prefer over others, but Russian voters on the whole mistrust parties and feel little sense of attachment to them. Likewise most politicians, apart from Communists, feel little loyalty or obligation to parties. The conditions favoring the development of a party system—a network of civic and social associations able to mobilize support behind one or another party, and a political system in which the government is based on a party majority in parliament—remain weak in Russia. It is likely that the development of a strong, competitive party system will be a protracted process.

See also: COMMUNIST PARTY OF THE RUSSIAN FEDERATION; LIBERAL DEMOCRATIC PARTY; UNION OF RIGHT FORCES; YABLOKO.

**BIBLIOGRAPHY**

Colton, Timothy J. (2000). *Transitional Citizens: Voters and What Influences Them in the New Russia.* Cambridge, MA: Harvard University Press.

Fish, M. Stephen. (1996). *Democracy from Scratch: Opposition and Regime in the New Russian Revolution.* Princeton, NJ: Princeton University Press.

McFaul, Michael. (2001). *Russia's Unfinished Revolution: Political Change from Gorbachev to Putin.* Ithaca, NY: Cornell University Press.

White, Stephen; Rose, Richard; and McAllister, Ian. (1996). *How Russia Votes.* Chatham, NJ: Chatham House Publishers.

—THOMAS F. REMINGTON

## POLL TAX *See* SOUL TAX.

## POLOTSKY, SIMEON

(1629–1680), major religious and cultural figure at the Russian court from 1664 until his death in 1680.

Simeon Polotsky, born Samuil Petrovsky-Sitnianovich, was a Belorussian monk from Polotsk. He introduced new forms of religious literature derived from Western models, and created the first substantial body of poetry in Russian.

Native to a largely Orthodox area of the Polish-Lithuanian state during a period of intense Catholic-Orthodox rivalry, Samuil Sitnyanovich entered the Kiev Academy around 1650, where he received a typical Western education from Ukrainian Orthodox teachers. He mastered Polish and Latin as well as the neo-Aristotelian curriculum dominant in Polish and Ukrainian schools. He continued his education at the Jesuit academy in Wilno. The Russo-Polish War of 1653–1667 that followed on the Ukrainian Cossack revolt of 1648 restored Orthodoxy to power in Polotsk, and Samuil returned to his native town. In 1656 he became a monk with the name Simeon in the local Bogoyavlenie Monastery; he also became a teacher in a school for Orthodox boys. During these early years he wrote both verse and declamations in Polish and Latin as well as Slavonic. On his first trip to Moscow in 1660 with a delegation of Polotsk clergy he presented Tsar Alexei Mikhaylovich with a series of verse greetings and other compositions for court occasions. Long commonplace in Poland and the West, such court poetry was unknown in Russia. With the revival of Polish military fortunes toward the end of the war, Polotsk returned to Catholic rule and Simeon left for Moscow in 1664, never to return.

In Moscow Simeon played a major role in the cultural and religious life of the court. After the Church Council of 1666–1667, he prepared the official reply to the claims of the Old Ritualists that that liturgical reforms of Patriarch Nikon were heretical (*Zhezl pravleniia/The Staff of Governance*, Moscow, 1668). In 1667 and 1670 he was tutor to the heirs to the throne, Tsarevich Alexei (d. 1670) and the future tsar, Fyodor (1672–1682), and also kept a school in the Zaikonospassky Monastery on Red Square. Simeon continued to write occasional verse for the court and church, celebrating important events and people. Many of these poems seem to have been declaimed in public, though they remained unpublished at his death. He was also a prolific writer of sermons, two large volumes of which appeared after his death, one of sermons at church festivals (*Obed dushevny/The Soul's Dinner*, Moscow 1681) and the other of sermons for particular occasions, such as funerals of prominent boyars (*Vecheria dushevnaya/The Soul's Supper*, Moscow, 1683). The sermons, delivered in churches in and around the Kremlin to the Russian elite, encouraged a shift in religious experience away from the central preoccupation with liturgy toward the inner experience of Christianity and its moral teachings.

Simeon's work introduced new genres to literature, poetry to court life, and a new style to Orthodox spirituality in Russia. His most important pupil was Silvester Medvedev (1641–1691), and he was popular both at court and in the church. Patriarch Ioakim (1674–1690), however, was less favorable, apparently distrusting the religious implications of his Western orientation. Simeon was a major influence for a generation after his death, but his baroque forms and Slavonic style soon rendered him too old-fashioned for later Russian poets and preachers. Nineteenth-century literary scholars, who looked askance at baroque style and genres such as court poetry, paid little attention to Simeon. Twentieth-century appreciation of the Baroque allowed him recognition as a major cultural figure, and the broader publications of his poetry have given him a greater audience. Historians of religion have recognized his pivotal role in the reorientation of Orthodoxy in the years preceding the great cultural changes of the time of Peter the Great.

*See also:* ORTHODOXY

**BIBLIOGRAPHY**

Bushkovitch, Paul. (1992). *Religion and Society in Russia: The Sixteenth and Seventeenth Centuries.* New York: Oxford University Press.

Vroon, Ronald. (1995). "Simeon Polotsky." In *Early Modern Russian Writers: Late Seventeenth and Eighteenth Centuries*, ed. Marcus C. Levitt (*Dictionary of Literary Biography*, vol. 150). Detroit: Gale Research.

PAUL A. BUSHKOVITCH

# POLOVTSY

Polovtsy, a nomadic Turkic-speaking tribal confederation (Polovtsy in Rus sources, Cumans in Western, Kipchaks in Eastern) began migrating in about 1017 or 1018 from eastern Mongolia and occupied the area stretching from Kazakhstan to the Danube by 1055. Politically disorganized and lacking a unified policy in their relations with Rus, various Polovtsian tribes became involved in Rus inter-princely conflicts and, at times, fought as Rus allies against other Polovtsy. Dynastic intermarriages often solidified Polovtsy-Rus political unions. Rus sources note two distinct Polovtsy: "Wild" (Rus enemies) and "Non-Wild" (Rus allies). Most Rus-Polovtsy confrontations resulted from their differing economies. As agriculturalists, the Rus desired to convert the steppe into cultivated lands, while the nomadic Polovtsy required the steppe for grazing animals. Consequently, conflict was inevitable: Rus sources often speak of Polovtsian raids on lands settled by Rus and subsequent Rus counterattacks. However, because of the political disunity of both sides, no permanent peace was ever reached, and by the 1230s and 1240s, both were conquered and absorbed into the Mongol Empire.

Polovtsy had settlements, probably occupied by impoverished Polovtsy and Rus migrants who practiced agriculture. Located between Rus and the Black Sea, Polovtsy controlled trade between the two regions and directly participated in commercial activities. For their livestock, they received agricultural products and luxury items from Rus. Controlling much of the Crimea (particularly Sudak), the Polovtsy engaged in the sale of slaves and furs to Byzantium and the Islamic East. While some Polovtsy may have converted to Christianity and Islam, the overwhelming majority retained their shamanist-Täri religion.

*See also:* CRIMEA; KAZAKHSTAN AND KAZAKHS; KHAZARS; KIEVAN RUS; POLYANE; VIKINGS.

**BIBLIOGRAPHY**

Golden, Peter B. (1990). "The Peoples of the South Russian Steppe." In *The Cambridge History of Early Inner Asia*, ed. Denis Sinor. Cambridge, UK: Cambridge University Press.

Golden, Peter B. (1991). "Aspects of the Nomadic Factor in the Economic Development of Kievan Rus'." In *Ukrainian Economic History: Interpretive Essays*, ed. I.S. Koropeckyj. Cambridge, MA: Harvard Ukrainian Research Institute.

Golden, Peter B. (1992). *An Introduction to the History of the Turkic Peoples.* Wiesbaden, Germany: Harrassowitz Verlag.

Noonan, Thomas S. (1992). "Rus', Pechenegs, and Polovtsy: Economic Interaction Along the Steppe Frontier in the Pre-Mongol Era." *Russian History/ Histoire Russe* 19:301–326.

Pritsak, Omeljan. (1982). "The Polovcians and Rus'." *Archivum Eurasiae Medii Aevi* 2:321–280.

ROMAN K. KOVALEV

## POLTAVA, BATTLE OF

The Battle of Poltava was the defining battle of the Great Northern War (1700–1721), fought on June 27, 1709, between the Swedish and Russian armies along the River Vorskla to the north of the Ukrainian city of Poltava.

After the rejection of a Russian peace offer in 1707, the Swedish King Karl (Charles) XII spent much of the summer of 1708 in Lithuania waiting for supplies for an assault on Russia. However, in September he decided to move down to the Ukraine where he expected to gain the support of the Cossack Hetman Ivan Mazepa. In the meantime, Tsar Peter I managed to defeat the Swedish forces Charles had been waiting for (the battle of Lesnaia, September 28, 1708) and seized the supplies. The Swedish forces suffered a great deal during the cold winter of 1709 and were regularly attacked by Russian units. Even though the Swedish forces had been besieging Poltava since April 1709, they were severely weakened by the time Peter was ready to attack.

Three days before the battle Charles XII was immobilized by a leg wound caused by a stray bullet and was thus unable to personally lead the Swedish forces into battle. It had, moreover, become apparent that no help would be arriving in time from either the Polish-Lithuanian forces of Stanislaw Leszczyński or other Swedish units. In spite of this, a Swedish victory presented the prospect of easing supply problems, of helping Leszczyński, and—possibly—of inducing Ottomans and Tatars to commit to the Swedish side. Moreover, a Swedish withdrawal would have presented serious risks.

The Swedish force of 22,000–28,000 responded to a Russian challenge with a major assault, although Peter—at the helm of a much larger force

of some 45,000 men—appears to have viewed Poltava as primarily a defensive encounter. However, confusing orders left part of the Swedish force attacking Russian T-shaped redoubts rather than the main camp. These Swedish units, led by Carl Gustav Roos, lost contact with the main force as well as two-fifths of their men. They eventually retreated and were forced to surrender. The other two-thirds of the Swedish force successfully regrouped for an attack on the camp awaiting Roos. The Swedes, however, lost their momentum during the two-hour wait, whereas the Russians were revitalized by news of the surrender. A Russian force of 22,000 men and sixty-eight field guns now attacked the remaining four thousand Swedes led by Adam Ludvig Lewenhaupt. Disorganization and inferior numbers ultimately led to a chaotic Swedish retreat. The Swedes lost 6,901 dead or wounded and 2,760 captured. The Russian losses were 1,345 dead and 3,290 wounded.

Three days after the battle, Charles went into exile in the Ottoman Empire and the Swedish force of 14,000–17,000 surrendered at Perevolochna. Even though the Treaty of Nystad was only concluded twelve years later, the defeat suffered at Poltava marks the end of Sweden as a great power.

*See also:* GREAT NORTHERN WAR

**BIBLIOGRAPHY**

Frost, Robert I. (2000). *The Northern Wars: War, State and Society in Northeastern Europe, 1558–1721.* Harlow, UK, and New York: Longman.

Hughes, Lindsey. (1998). *Russia in the Age of Peter the Great.* New Haven: Yale University Press.

JARMO T. KOTILAINE

## POLYANE

Polyane is one of the Eastern Slavic tribes that inhabited the Kievan Rus state, as noted in the *Russian Primary Chronicle*.

According to the *Russian Primary Chronicle*, the Polyane occupied the middle Dnieper River region: Kiev, the capital of the Rus state, as well as Vyshgorod, Vasilev, and Belgorod. The Polyane received their name (meaning "people of the field") on account of their settlement in the open terrain of the middle Dnieper. With its *chernozem* soils, the middle Dnieper was ideal for agriculture, the primary economy of the Polyane. Archaeologists believe that the Polyane belonged to a larger group of Slavs, known as Duledy, who migrated east from southeastern Europe sometime during the sixth to seventh centuries. By the eighth to ninth centuries, the Polyane settled both sides of the middle Dnieper and came to form their own ethnic identity. During the ninth century, the middle Dnieper was under the control of the Khazar state, to which the Polyane paid tribute in furs. Kiev itself functioned as the western-most military outpost and a commercial center for the Khazars. During the late ninth century, the Rus prince Oleg (legendary reign 880–913) allegedly incorporated the middle Dnieper and the Polyane into the expanding Rus state, although evidence suggests that it was Grand Prince Igor (r. 924–945) who brought the two under Rus control around 930. While predominantly Slavic, the Polyane appear to have had Iranian, Turkic, and Finno-Baltic ethnic elements. Evidence for this is found through archaeological and linguistic studies of the Polyane and from *Chronicle* descriptions of their pre-Christian religious practices.

*See also:* IGOR; KHAZARS; KIEVAN RUS; OLEG; PRIMARY CHRONICLE; VIKINGS

**BIBLIOGRAPHY**

Golb, Norman, and Pritsak, Omeljan. (1982). *Khazarian Hebrew Document of the Tenth Century*. Ithaca, NY: Cornell University Press.

*The Russian Primary Chronicle.* (1973). Tr. and ed. Samuel Hazzard Cross and Olgerd P. Sherbowitz-Wetzor. Cambridge, MA: Mediaeval Academy of America.

ROMAN K. KOVALEV

# POMESTIE

*Pomestie*, "service landholding," was a parcel of land (hopefully inhabited by rent-paying peasants, later serfs [see Serfdom]) in exchange for which the holder (not owner) had to render lifelong service to the state, typically military service, but occasionally service in the government bureaucracy. Ideally, when the service ended, the landholder had to surrender the pomestie to another serviceman. The pomestie was granted for use only to support the serviceman and his family (including slaves) by peasant rent payments to him in lieu of cash. It has been calculated that this was far more efficient than paying servicemen entirely in cash: the trans-

action costs of collecting taxes, taking them to Moscow, and then paying them to the servicemen were likely to result in a fifty percent loss, whereas there was no such shrinkage when the rent and taxes did not go through Moscow. Occasionally pomestie is translated a "military fief," but this is totally misleading. There was no feudalism in Russia. The pomestie was granted directly by the government's Service Land Chancellery (*Pomestny prikaz*) to a specific serviceman for his support in lieu of support of other kinds (such as cash, or feeding in barracks). There were no reciprocal rights and obligations between the Service Land Chancellery and the serviceman, and there was no subinfeudation.

The pomestie bears at least superficial resemblance to forms of land tenure elsewhere, especially the Byzantine *pronoia* and the Persian *ikhta*. It is dubious, however, that the Russian pomestie was borrowed from either, and it seems likely that it was an autonomous creation by the Russians themselves.

The origins of the pomestie are shrouded in the mists of the early Muscovite Middle Ages. The first recorded use of the term was in 1499, but the phenomenon definitely existed before then. During the fourteenth and fifteenth centuries, servitors (probably military) at the Muscovite court may occasionally have been given temporary grants of land in exchange for service, but that was an extraordinarily uncertain form of compensation and therefore cannot have been used often. Until the 1450s all peasants were free and could not be compelled to pay rent to anyone [see Enserfment], and they could move at a moment's notice. Thus no system of compensating servicemen by conditional grants of land developed at that time.

The origins of the pomestie system (and also the service state) can be traced to Moscow's annexation of Novgorod in 1478. Some elite Novgorodian laymen and churchmen preferred either to remain independent or to have Lithuania as a suzerain rather than Moscow. Those people were purged after 1478 and either executed or forcibly resettled elsewhere. Their vast landholdings were confiscated by Moscow and parceled out to loyal cavalry servicemen (*pomeshchiki*) for their support. The census books compiled subsequently by Moscow indicate that each serviceman was probably assigned land occupied by roughly thirty peasant households. It is fairly certain that the servicemen did not live directly on their land grants, but in groups nearby. A third party collected the traditional rent and gave it to the servicemen. Thus the servicemen had no direct connection with "their" peasants and no control over them. Moscow soon discovered that this was an efficient way to assure control over newly annexed territory while simultaneously maximizing the size of the army. As Moscow annexed other lands, it handed them out to servicemen as pomestie estates. The pomestie came to embody the essence of the service state. Each eligible serviceman had an entitlement (*oklad*) based on his service. If he could locate land up to the limit of his entitlement, it was his. This was an effective incentive system, and servicemen strove mightily to increase their entitlements.

Two or three generations later, during the reign of Ivan IV ("the Terrible"), several important events occurred concerning the pomestie. For one, the government advanced the service state significantly in 1556 by decreeing that all holders of service estates (pomestie) and hereditary estates (*votchiny*) had to render the same quantity of military service (i.e., provide one mounted cavalryman per one hundred *cheti* of land actually possessed). Second, it is probable that during Ivan's reign sons began to succeed to their fathers' service landholdings when their fathers died or could no longer render the required lifetime service. Third, during Ivan's *Oprichnina*, service landholders were given control over their peasants, including the right to set the level of rent payments (a change that caused massive peasant flight from the center to the expanding frontiers [see Colonial Expansion]). And fourth, the Oprichnina exterminated so many owners of hereditary estates that it appeared as though outright ownership of land was on the verge of extinction.

The holders of pomestie estates were primarily members of the provincial middle service class cavalry who began to live directly on their service landholdings somewhere during the middle of the sixteenth century. This experience, combined with the developments of the reign of Ivan IV, convinced them that they had the right to consider the pomestie as their personal property, which not only could be left to their male heirs, but also could be alienated like *votchina* property: sold, donated to monasteries, given to anyone, used as a dowry, and so forth. This project became the goal of a middle service class "political campaign," somewhat akin to the political campaign to enserf the peasantry. Such aspirations totally violated the initial purpose of the pomestie and undermined the basic principles of the service state. The Law Code of 1649 carefully retained the distinction between the pomestie (chapter 16, nearly all of whose sixty-nine articles are postdated 1619) and the votchina (chapter 17), but the distinctions were fading in reality. During the first half of the seventeenth century, the pomestie essentially became hereditary property, but service still was compulsory and holders could not freely alienate it. During the Thirteen Years War (1654–1667), new formation military units began to replace the obsolescent middle service class cavalry, and after 1667 the service state nearly disintegrated. With it went the principle that service was compulsory from pomestie land.

Peter the Great restored the service state in 1700, and all landholders and landowners had to render military service again. But the uniqueness of the pomestie was lost in 1714 when it and the votchina were juridically merged into a single form of land ownership.

*See also:* DVORIANSTVO; ENSERFMENT; LAW CODE OF 1649; SERFDOM; SYN BOYARSKY; VOTCHINA

**BIBLIOGRAPHY**

Hellie, Richard. (1971). *Enserfment and Military Change in Muscovy*. Chicago: University of Chicago Press.

Hellie, Richard, ed. and tr. (1988). *The Muscovite Law Code (Ulozhenie) of 1649*. Irvine, CA: Charles Schlacks.

RICHARD HELLIE

## PONOMAREV, BORIS KHARITONOVICH

(1905–1995), party official and historian.

Boris Ponomarev was a leading Communist Party of the Soviet Union (CPSU) ideologue who for three decades (1954–1986) headed the International Department of the CPSU Central Committee, the body responsible for relations with foreign communist parties. Ponomarev joined the Bolsheviks in 1919. A civil war veteran (serving from 1918 to 1920), he graduated from Moscow State University in 1926. From 1933 to 1936, at a time when historiography was coming under party control, he was deputy director of the CPSU's Institute of Red Professors. He was on the executive committee of the Comintern, the Soviet-dominated organization of international communist parties, in its last years (1936–1943), and later head of the Comintern's successor, the Cominform (1946–1949).

In 1954 he became head of the International Department. He was elected to the Central Committee in 1956. A party historian, he was elected a candidate member of the Academy of Sciences in 1959, becoming a full Academician in 1962. After Nikita Khrushchev's denunciation of Josef Stalin at the Twentieth CPSU Congress in 1956, Ponomarev led the team of historians who wrote the new, official *History of the Communist Party of the Soviet Union* (1959), which replaced Stalin's notorious *Short Course* history (1938). But Stalin's portrait continued to hang on Ponomarev's office wall. Appointed a secretary of the Central Committee in 1961, he eventually rose to the rank of candidate member of the Politburo in 1972. Never comfortable with reform, Ponomarev, in 1986, was removed as head of the International Department by Mikhail Gorbachev, who retired him from the Central Committee in April 1989.

*See also:* CENTRAL COMMITTEE; COMMUNIST PARTY OF THE SOVIET UNION

**BIBLIOGRAPHY**

Brown, Archie, ed. (1989). *Political Leadership in the Soviet Union*. Houndmills, Basingstoke, UK: Macmillan with St Antony's College, Oxford.

Nekrich, Aleksandr. (1991). *Forsake Fear: Memoirs of an Historian*, tr. Donald Lineburgh. Boston: Unwin Hyman.

ROGER D. MARKWICK

# POPOV, ALEXANDER STEPANOVICH

(1859–1905), prominent mathematician and physicist.

Russia claims that Alexander Stepanovich Popov invented the radio before the Italian scientist Guglielmo Marconi. Determining who was the official inventor of the radio is complicated by nationalistic pride, inadequate documentation of events, and differing interpretations of what constitutes inventing the radio. By what most persons in the West consider objective analysis of the facts known, however, Marconi's work invariably is recognized as having priority over Popov's. However, Popov's numerous achievements do merit both recognition and respect. Popov was the chair of the Department of Physics at St. Petersburg University in 1901 and director of the St. Petersburg Institute of Electrical Engineering in 1905. On May 7, 1895,

Popov demonstrated that a receiver could detect the electromagnetic waves produced by lightning discharges in the atmosphere many miles away. Popov's receiver consisted of a "coherer" made of metal filings, together with an antenna, a relay, and a bell. The relay was used to activate the bell that both signaled the occurrence of lightning and served as a "decoherer" (tapper) to ready the coherer to detect the next lightning discharge. The value this instrument could have in weather forecasting was obvious. In 1865 the Scottish physicist James Clerk Maxwell had predicted that electromagnetic waves existed. In 1888 a German scientist Heinrich Hertz had proven that electromagnetic waves definitely did exist. Still, no one had yet found any practical use for these electromagnetic or "Hertzian" waves.

Almost a year after his first experiment, Popov conducted another public experiment on March 24, 1896 that demonstrated the transmission and reception of information by wireless telegraphy. On that day the Russian Physical and Chemical Society convened at St. Petersburg University. Wireless telegraph signals, transmitted a distance of more than 800 feet (243 meters) from another building on the campus, were audible to all in the meeting room. One professor stood at the blackboard and recorded the alphabetical letters represented by the Morse code signals. The letters spelled out the name "Heinrich Hertz."

Unfortunately this experiment was never officially recorded. Meanwhile Guglielmo Marconi filed an application for the patent on wireless telegraphy on June 2, 1896, and his first public demonstration occurred in July of that year. Although both of Popov's experiments took place before Marconi filed the patent, it is widely known that Marconi had already made considerable breakthroughs prior to Popov's March 24, 1896, experiment, including the transmission and reception of simple messages. Nevertheless, Popov's achievements were recognized. In 1900 he was awarded a Gold Metal at the Fourth World Congress of Electrical Engineering.

*See also:* TELEVISION AND RADIO

**BIBLIOGRAPHY**

Birch, Beverley. (2001). *Guglielmo Marconi: Radio Pioneer*. Woodbridge, CT: Blackbirch Press.

Kraeuter, David W. (1992). *Radio and Television Pioneers: A Patent Bibliography*. Metuchen, NJ: Scarecrow Press.

Radovskii, M. I. (1957). *Alexander Popov, Inventor of Radio.* Moscow: Foreign Language Pub. House.

JOHANNA GRANVILLE

## POPOV, GAVRIIL KHARITONOVICH

(b. 1936), economist and democratic reformer; mayor of Moscow.

Gavriil Popov was born and educated in Moscow. While studying at Moscow State University (MGU), he headed the Komsomol organization. He joined the economics faculty at MGU in 1959, eventually becoming dean in 1977. In his academic career, Popov authored numerous articles and books focusing on economic management and was editor of the Academy journal *Voprosi Ekonomiki* (*Economic Questions*) from 1988 to 1991.

Popov moved from economic research and advising to political activism, consulting with government on management reforms starting in the mid-1960s. The apex of his political career occurred during the late 1980s and early 1990s. After joining the Congress of People's Deputies in 1989, Popov founded and co-chaired the Inter-Regional Deputies' Group (MDG) with Boris Yeltsin, Yury Afanasiev, and Andrei Sakharov. The MDG advocated democratic reforms; Popov adopted a pragmatic stance relative to other leaders in the group. In March 1990, reformers won control of the Moscow City Council, and Popov was elected chairman. He resigned from the Communist Party of the Soviet Union in July 1990.

In June 1991, Popov became the first popularly elected mayor of Moscow, with Yuri Luzhkov as his vice-mayor. After opposing the August coup attempt, he pursued reforms such as privatization of housing and retail establishments. He resigned from the post of mayor in June 1992, and subsequently formed electorally unsuccessful organizations. His Russian Movement for Democratic Reforms (RDDR) did not win enough votes to gain party-list seats in the 1993 Duma elections. He later joined with other politicians to form the Social Democrats, a party that participated in the 1995 and 1999 elections and likewise failed to gain seats. Popov founded Moscow International University and became its president. He continues to publish commentaries on public policy issues.

*See also:* INTER-REGIONAL DEPUTIES' GROUP; MOSCOW

**BIBLIOGRAPHY**
Colton, Timothy J. (1996). *Moscow: Governing the Socialist Metropolis.* Cambridge, MA: Belknap Press.

ERIK S. HERRON

## POPOV, PAVEL ILICH

(1872–1950), author of the first "balance of the national economy," the forerunner of the tool of economic analysis now known as input-output.

Pavel Popov went to St. Petersburg in 1895 to enter the university, but once there he was diverted to participation in the revolutionary movement. He was arrested and spent the years 1896 to 1897 in prison. Exiled to Ufa gubernia, he began to study statistics and in 1909–1917 worked in the Tula zemstvo as a statistician. After the February Revolution he became head of the department of the agricultural census in the Ministry of Agriculture in the provisional government. After the Bolsheviks came to power in 1918, he became the first chairman of the Central Statistical Administration. He was an able organizer and, among other things, oversaw development of the first "balance" of inputs and outputs. He continued as chairman of the Central Statistical Administration until 1926, and then had a long, apparently untroubled, career in the Russian Soviet Federative Socialist Republic Gosplan until his death. During the early, statistical, stage of his career, he published some books and reports but apparently nothing after he became associated with Gosplan. Thus, apart from the input-output work, his contribution to Soviet economics was as an organizer rather than as an economic thinker or theorist.

*See also:* CENTRAL STATISTICAL AGENCY; GOSPLAN

**BIBLIOGRAPHY**
Spulber, Nicolas. (1964). *Foundations of Soviet Strategy for Economic Growth: Selected Soviet Essays, 1924–1930.* Bloomington: Indiana University Press

ROBERT W. CAMPBELL

## POPULAR FRONT POLICY

Comintern policy during the mid-1930s that encouraged cooperation between communist and non-communist parties in order to stop the spread of fascism.

During the 1930s, Soviet foreign policy changed several times in response to the evolving political situation in Europe. At the beginning of the decade, Josef Stalin would not allow cooperation between communist and noncommunist parties. This policy had particularly tragic results in Germany, where enmity between communists and socialists divided the opposition to the Nazis. After Adolf Hitler's rise to power and his adoption of an aggressive anti-Soviet foreign policy, Stalin began to fear the spread of fascism to other European countries and the possible creation of an anti-Soviet bloc. In response to this potential threat, the Soviet Union changed policy and promoted collective security among non-fascist states. In 1934 the USSR joined the League of Nations and the following year signed a mutual defense treaty with France and Czechoslovakia. Stalin realized that the program of the Communist International had to be brought into line with the new Soviet foreign policy, and a Comintern congress was called for the summer of 1935 in order to accomplish this transformation.

The Seventh Comintern Congress met in Moscow in July–August 1935. Five hundred delegates representing sixty-five communist parties participated and elected Georgi Dimitrov, a Bulgarian communist, as general secretary of the Comintern. In this capacity, Dimitrov delivered the keynote address and outlined the new policy. Declaring that "fascism has embarked upon a wide offensive," Dimitrov called for the creation of a united anti-fascist front that included support for anti-fascist government coalitions. While maintaining that capitalism remained the ultimate enemy, Dimitrov argued that the immediate threat to the workers came from the fascists and that all communists should participate in the campaign to stop the spread of this dangerous movement. Whereas communists and communist parties previously had opposed all bourgeois and capitalist governments, and considered fascism simply a variant of capitalism, members of the Comintern were now being told to support bourgeois governments and to postpone the struggle against capitalism.

The Popular Front concept had its greatest impact in Spain, France, and China. In Spain, the election of a Popular Front coalition in February 1936 led to civil war. After three years the forces of the fascist General Francisco Franco took power. In France, where the prospect of a fascist victory frightened the Soviet Union, a Popular Front government came to power in June 1936. Like all French governments of the time, it remained weak, and it fell after only one year. In China, the prospect of cooperation between the Nationalist government of Chiang Kai-shek and the communist forces of Mao Zedong led the Japanese military to launch a preemptive strike during the summer of 1937.

In the end the Popular Front concept was not about an ideological shift in communist perceptions of the world, but a tactical Stalinist response to the specific threat of fascism as perceived during the mid-1930s. The defense of the Soviet Union took precedence over all other considerations, and in 1939 the Popular Front was abandoned with the signing of the Nazi-Soviet Non-Aggression Pact.

*See also:* LEAGUE OF NATIONS; NAZI-SOVIET PACT OF 1939

**BIBLIOGRAPHY**

Dimitrov, Georgi. (1935). *United Front against Fascism and War; The Fascist Offensive and the Tasks of the Communist International in the Fight for the Unity of the Working Class Against Fascism.* New York: Workers Library Publishers.

Haslam, Jonathan. (1984). *The Soviet Union and the Struggle for Collective Security in Europe, 1933–39.* New York: St. Martin's Press.

Tucker, Robert C. (1990). *Stalin in Power: The Revolution from Above, 1928–1941.* New York: Norton.

Ulam, Adam B. (1968). *Expansion and Coexistence: The History of Soviet Foreign Policy, 1917–1967.* New York: Praeger.

HAROLD J. GOLDBERG

# POPULISM

Scholars differ on the question of when the tendency known as populism (*narodnichestvo*) was most significant in Russian social and political thought. Some suggest that populism was prominent from 1848 to 1881; others, that it was a revolutionary movement in the period between 1860 and 1895. Soviet scholars primarily focused on the 1870s and 1880s. There is also disagreement about what populism represented as an ideology. There are three ways of looking at it: as a reaction against Western capitalism and socialism, as agrarian socialism, and as a theory advocating the hegemony of the masses over the educated elite.

As this should make evident, populism meant different things to different people; it was not a single coherent doctrine but a widespread movement in nineteenth-century Russia favoring such goals as social justice and equality. Populism in Russia is generally believed to have been strongly influenced by the thinking of Alexander Herzen and Nikolai Chernyshevsky, who during the 1850s and 1860s argued that the peasant commune (*mir*) was crucial to Russia's transition from capitalism to socialism via a peasant revolution.

There were three strands in the Russian populist movement. The first, classical populism, was associated with Peter Lavrovich Lavrov (1823–1900), a nobleman by birth who had received a military education and later became a professor of mathematics. Lavrov was an activist in the student and intellectual movement of the 1860s, and a consequence was forced to emigrate from Russia in 1870. His experience in the Paris Commune during the 1870s convinced him of the need for change, especially in the aftermath of the Great Reforms of the 1860s. In his *Historical Letters* (1868–1869), Lavrov stated that human progress required a revolution that would totally destroy the existing order. Again in his *Historical Letters* (1870) and in his revolutionary journal *Vpered* (*Forward*) from 1870 to 1872, Lavrov argued that intellectuals had a moral obligation to fight for socialism, and in order to achieve this goal they would have to work with the masses. As he saw it, preparation for revolution was the key. In *The State in Future Society*, Lavrov outlined the establishment of universal suffrage, the emergence of a society in which the masses would run the government, and above all, the introduction of the notion of popular justice.

The second type of Russian populism was more conspiratorial, for it grew out of the failure of the classical variant to convert the majority of the Russian people to socialism via preparation and self-education. The major thinkers here were Peter G. Zaichnevsky (1842–1896), Sergei G. Nechaev (1847–1883), and Peter Nikitich Tkachev (1844–1885). Zaichnevsky, in his pamphlet *Young Russia*, called for direct action and rejected the possibility of a compromise between the ruling class (including liberals) and the rest of society. He argued that revolution had to be carried out by the majority, using force if necessary, in order to transform Russia's political, economic, and social system along socialist lines. Not surprisingly, Zaichnevsky's ideas are often seen as a blueprint for the Bolshevik Revolution of 1917. Nechaev pointed to two lessons that

could be learned from the failure of classical populism: first, the need for tighter organization, stricter discipline, and better planning, and second, the effort to go to the people had proved that the intelligentsia were very remote from the masses. In his *Catechism of a Revolutionary*, Nechaev argued that individual actions must be controlled by the party and advocated a code for revolutionaries in which members were dedicated, committed to action not words, adhered to party discipline, and above all, were willing to use every possible means to achieve revolution. Finally, Tkachev, who is probably the most significant of the three chief conspiratorial populists, advocated a closely knit secret organization that would carry out a revolution in the name of the people. For obvious reasons, he is often described as the forerunner of Vladimir Lenin or as the first Bolshevik. All three of these thinkers envisioned a revolution by a minority on behalf of the majority, followed by agitation and propaganda to protect its gains. The similarity to the events around the 1917 October Revolution is evident.

Populists of the classical and conspiratorial varieties rejected terrorism as a method, and Tkachev maintained that it would divert energy away from the revolution. The terrorist wing of Russian populism, however, insisted that agitprop and repeated calls for revolution would accomplish nothing, and therefore direct action was essential. This position was associated with the two main groups that grew out of the Land and Freedom (*Zemlya i Volya*) organization, People's Will (*Narodnaia Volya*), and Black Partition (*Cherny Peredel*). The failure of the earlier populist movements and the situation in late nineteenth-century Russia (i.e., no political parties or real trade unions, government intervention in every area of life) led to a direct attack on the state, culminating in the assassination of Alexander II in March 1881. Although the clamp-down and greater censorship that followed this event reduced the degree of terrorism, they did not eliminate it altogether, as shown by the emergence of a workers' section and young People's Will after 1881.

The populists did not accept the idea that the Russian people had a unique character or destiny. Instead they emphasized Russia's backwardness, but in their view it was not necessarily a disadvantage, because backwardness would enable Russia to avoid the capitalist path and embark upon agrarian socialism based on a federal structure of self-governing units of producers and consumers. When this did not come to pass, some populists turned to more extreme measures, such as terrorism. All in all, the lessons learned from the failure of populism paved the way for a gradual move toward the emergence of social democracy in Russia during the 1890s.

*See also:* GREAT REFORMS; LAND AND FREEDOM PARTY; PEOPLE'S WILL, THE; SOCIAL DEMOCRATIC WORKERS PARTY

**BIBLIOGRAPHY**

Geifman, Anna. (1993). *Thou Shalt Kill: Revolutionary Terrorism in Russia, 1894–1917.* Princeton, NJ: Princeton University Press.

Offord, Derek. (1987). *The Russian Revolutionary Movement in the 1880s.* Cambridge, UK: Cambridge University Press.

Pipes, Richard. (1964). "*Narodnichestvo*: A Semantic Inquiry." *Slavic Review* 23(3):441–458.

Venturi, Franco. (1983). *Roots of Revolution: A History of the Populist and Socialist Movements in 19th Century Russia.* Chicago: University of Chicago Press.

Wortman, Richard. (1967). *The Crisis of Russian Populism.* New York: Cambridge University Press.

CHRISTOPHER WILLIAMS

## PORT ARTHUR, SIEGE OF

Originally constructed by the Chinese as a fortress in 1892, Port Arthur (modern Lushun) protected an important naval base and roadstead at the foot of the Liaotung Peninsula. In the great-power race for Chinese bases and influence that followed the Sino-Japanese War of 1894 to 1895, Russia in 1898 obtained a twenty-five-year lease on Port Arthur's naval facilities and the surrounding territory. In an age of coal-burning vessels, Port Arthur was an important fueling station that would enable the growing Russian Pacific Squadron to interdict Japanese naval communications in the Yellow Sea and beyond.

Short of resources, the Russians only began seriously improving Port Arthur in 1901. The Japanese surprise attack that opened the Russo-Japanese War on the night of February 8–9, 1904, caught Russian naval units and Port Arthur unprepared. Admiral Heihachiro Togo's fleet soon bottled up the Russian squadron, while a Japanese army advanced overland from Dairen (Ta-lien) to lay siege to the Russian ground defenses. Although poorly led, the Russian defenders withstood four major assaults

before the Japanese seizure of 203 Meter Hill enabled artillery observers to subject the warships in the port to accurate siege mortar fire. They were soon pounded to pieces. The garrison capitulated on January 2, 1905, thus freeing the besieging army to reinforce the four Japanese field armies already operating against Adjutant General Alexei N. Kuropatkin's army group near Mukden.

Port Arthur was both a symbol of heroic Russian resistance and a distraction that goaded Kuropatkin to decisive field action earlier and farther south than he had originally planned. On the Russian home front, the fall of Port Arthur added fuel to the fire of popular disturbances that culminated in the Revolution of 1905.

*See also:* CHINA, RELATIONS WITH; JAPAN, RELATIONS WITH; KUROPATKIN, ALEXEI NIKOLAYEVICH; RUSSO-JAPANESE WAR

**BIBLIOGRAPHY**

Menning, Bruce W. (2000). *Bayonets before Bullets: The Imperial Russian Army, 1861–1914.* Bloomington: Indiana University Press.

Westwood, J. N. (1986). *Russia against Japan, 1904–05: A New Look at the Russo-Japanese War.* Albany: State University of New York Press.

BRUCE W. MENNING

## PORTSMOUTH, TREATY OF

Signed September 5 (August 23 O.S.), 1905, in Portsmouth, Maine, this treaty terminated the Russo-Japanese war. U.S. president Theodore Roosevelt had offered to mediate between the warring parties, fearing that continued fighting would destabilize the Far East and jeopardize U.S. commercial interests in China. (Roosevelt went on to win the Nobel Prize for Peace for his efforts.)

Russia recognized Japan's interests in Korea, and ceded its lease over the Liaotung Peninsula to Japan, as well as the southern half of Sakhalin island and control of the Southern Manchurian railroad to Chang-chun. Russia also pledged that Manchuria would remain a part of China.

The treaty ended any Russian hope of establishing protectorates over Manchuria and Korea. In addition, it represented the first defeat of a European Great Power by an Asian state during the modern age.

The fall of Port Arthur, the defeat of the Russian Army at Mukden, the destruction of the Russian Baltic Fleet at Tsushima, and the outbreak of the 1905 Revolution convinced the government of Tsar Nicholas II that the war had to end. Count Sergei Witte was sent as plenipotentiary with orders to secure the best possible deal for Russia. A cunning negotiator, Witte skillfully used the U.S. press to swing international opinion against Japan. He also realized that Japan lacked the resources to follow up on its initial military victories and that he could afford to prolong the talks. In the end, Japan dropped its demands for a sizable indemnity and the complete evisceration of Russia's position in the Far East. Witte's diplomacy helped to compensate for Russia's military weakness.

Nevertheless, the Treaty of Portsmouth was perceived as a defeat for Russia and diminished its international stature, notably in the 1908 Bosnia crisis. Josef Stalin was to justify the Soviet entry into the war against Japan in 1945 in part on the grounds of reversing the 1905 "defeat."

*See also:* RUSSO-JAPANESE WAR; WITTE, SERGEI YULIEVICH

**BIBLIOGRAPHY**
Fuller, William C., Jr. (1992). *Strategy and Power in Russia, 1600–1914.* New York: Free Press.

Riasanovsky, Nicholas V. (1984). *A History of Russia.* Oxford: Oxford University Press.

NIKOLAS GVOSDEV

**PORUKA** *See* COLLECTIVE RESPONSIBILITY.

## POSADNIK

A term meaning "mayor," the leading political figure of Novgorod and Pskov.

In Novgorod the *posadnik* was second only to the archbishop, the symbolic ruler of the city. The term derives from the verb *posaditi*, to sit, and reflects the practice of Kievan princes who "sat" their representatives, often family members, as princes of Novgorod.

Toward the end of the tenth century the Novgorodian posadnik was separated from the governing prince, and after 1088 was chosen by a *veche* (assembly or gathering). Following Novgorod's independence from Kiev in 1136, princely power slowly declined as princes had to share their authority with the mayor. The boyar elite of Novgorod and Pskov dominated the office of mayor.

At first only one mayor in Novgorod was chosen for life. In the fourteenth century a collective mayoralty developed (*posadnichestvo*) consisting of six mayors, one for each of the five districts (two from Prussian Street), and one who served as Lord Mayor (*stepenny posadnik*). In 1354 the term of Lord Mayor was shortened to one year, and after 1387 the office rotated among Novgorodian borough mayors. In 1416 and 1417 the term was reduced to six months, while the number of borough mayors increased to eighteen. In 1423 the borough mayors grew to twenty-four, and in the second half of the fifteenth century to thirty-four. Current and former Lord Mayors, together with the chiliarch (the leader of a thousand men or troops) and sitting borough mayors, comprised Novgorod's Council of Lords. The mayoralty disappeared with the fall of Novgorod to Moscow in 1478.

*See also:* BOYAR; NOVGOROD JUDICIAL CHARTER; NOVGOROD THE GREAT; VECHE

**BIBLIOGRAPHY**
Langer, Lawrence. (1974). "V. L. Ianin and the History of Novgorod." *Slavic Review* 33:114–119.

Langer, Lawrence. (1984). "The *Posadnichestvo* of Pskov: Some Aspects of Urban Administration in Medieval Russia." *Slavic Review* 43:46–62.

LAWRENCE N. LANGER

## POSSESSORS AND NON-POSSESSORS

Possessors and non-possessors were purported rival monastic and church factions, c. 1480–1584.

The binary opposition *stiazhatel/nestiazhatel* (literally, acquirer/non-acquirer; translated as "Possessor"/"Non-possessor" in the literature) is misleading. The possessions of cenobites theoretically belonged to their cloister, while hermitages were dependent upon the wealthy monasteries.

The real justification for the movable and landed wealth of the church lay in its economic, political, cultural, ceremonial, and charitable functions. The practical politics of ecclesiastical wealth involved several confiscations of Novgorodian church lands under Ivan III, the concrete provisions of new or revised immunity charters, and the state, church, and combined legislation of 1550–1551, 1562, 1572, 1580, and 1584, which both protected and limited monastic land. By the early 1500s a new juncture of developments favored state confiscation of lands: the state needed military service lands, and a faction of monks condemned monastic opulence, with some advocating state management of church lands.

The leading "Possessors" were well-placed figures who mobilized coworkers, disciples, employees, and consultants: Archbishop Gennady of Novgorod (r. 1484–1504); the founder-abbot Joseph of Volotsk (d. 1515); the latter's successor and then Metropolitan of Moscow, Daniel (r. 1515–1522–1539); Archbishop of Novgorod and then Metropolitan of Moscow, Macarius (r. 1526–1542–1563); and several other prelates, mostly trained in the Iosifov-Volokolamsk Monastery. They defended church lands and Orthodoxy and created an inquisition of sorts. They also promoted commemorations, reformed and rationalized monasteries, strengthened episcopal administration and missionary activity, nationalized regional saints, patronized religious art, allowed allegorical innovations, commissioned a few scientific translations, attempted to introduce printing, contributed original compilations of history, hagiography, and canon law, and aided the state and court with ceremonies, ideology, military chaplains, colonizing clergy, and canon-legal decisions.

The "Non-possessors" are harder to pin down. Vassian Patrikeyev (active from 1505 to 1531 and personally influential from 1511 to 1522) and those in charge of his literary legacy also expressed heated opposition to execution of even relapsed and obdurate heretics, while Artemy of Pskov (active 1540s–1550s) disputed that the people on trial were genuine heretics. Other erudite critics of monastic wealth, Maxim the Greek (active in Russia, 1517–1555) and Yermolai-Yerazm (active 1540s–1560s), did not take a stand on these two issues. Furthermore, the roles of Vassian and his "Trans-Volgan" mentor Nil Sorsky (d. 1508) in politicizing the latter's stringent hesychastic spiritual principles are not clear. Recent textual analysis questions the traditional assumption, in place by 1550, that Nil had counseled Ivan III at a synod in 1503 to confiscate monastic villages, and shows that Nil, like Maxim, Ermolai-Erazm, and Artemy, staunchly defended Orthodoxy. As individuals, some "Non-possessors" made outstanding contributions to Russian spiritual, literary, and legal culture and

political thought, but as a group they carried little weight.

"Possessors" more or less dominated the Russian Church during 1502–1511, 1522–1539, and 1542–1566. The Josephites—Iosifov monastery elders and alumni prelates—were a formidable and often disliked "Possessor" faction, and not only by Kirillov-Belozersk Monastery elders, who patronized the northern Trans-Volgan hermitages. If Nil and Joseph collaborated against dissidence, Vassian and the Josephites were at loggerheads. Daniel had both Maxim and Vassian condemned and imprisoned for heresy. Later Macarius did the same to Artemy and maybe sponsored a purge of hermitages suspected of harboring dissidents.

*See also:* DANIEL, METROPOLITAN; IVAN III; JOSEPH OF VOLOTSK, ST; MAKARY METROPOLITAN; MAXIM THE GREEK, ST.; RUSSIAN ORTHODOX CHURCH

### BIBLIOGRAPHY

Ostrowski, Donald. (1986). "Church Polemics and Monastic Land acquisition in Sixteenth-Century Muscovy." *Slavonic and East European Review* 64:355–79.

Treadgold, Donald W. (1973). *The West in Russia and China: Religious and Secular Thought in Modern Times.* Vol. I, Russia, 1472–1917. Cambridge, UK: Cambridge University Press.

DAVID M. GOLDFRANK

## POSTAL SYSTEM

The first regular postal routes in Russia (Moscow–Voronezh and later Moscow–St. Petersburg) were established at the start of the eighteenth century. In 1741 the service was expanded and intended to encompass all provinces of the empire. In reality, postal services were largely concentrated in European Russia, and mail was only delivered to one central location in a town, often a tavern. Beginning in the mid-eighteenth century, it became possible to send parcels through the mail as well as letters. Between 1830 and 1840, larger urban centers began to create systems for mail delivery within their confines, and this development spurred an increase not only in the number of mail distribution points within a given city but also in the number of letters being sent. In 1848 the first prestamped envelopes appeared, and periodicals began to be distributed by mail. Postal services were gradually extended to some larger villages in Russia starting in the 1870s.

During the eighteenth century, postal affairs were in the hands of the Senate, but in 1809 they were transferred to the jurisdiction of the Ministry of Internal Affairs. In 1830 a Main Postal Administration was established as a separate government organ, and it was superseded from 1865 to 1868 by a new Ministry of Post and Telegraph. After 1868 the postal system again became part of the Ministry of Internal Affairs.

The turmoil of the Russian Revolutions and Civil War greatly affected the postal system. Services had to be reestablished gradually as outlying areas were subdued by the Bolsheviks. At the center, a new ministry, The People's Commissariat of Post and Telegraph (Narkompochtel) was established, but it was not until the mid-1920s that services were restored across the country. In 1924 the "circular-post" was set up, whereby horse-drawn carts were used to distribute mail and sell postal supplies along regular routes. Within a year, the network had 4,279 routes with more than 43,000 stopping points, and it covered 275,000 kilometers (170,900 miles). Permanent village postmen emerged in larger settlements as well in 1925, and they became responsible for home delivery when that aspect of the postal service was created in 1930.

In 2002 the postal system was divided administratively into ninety-three regional postal departments with 40,000 offices and 300,000 employees. However, since the collapse of the Soviet Union, the postal system has declined dramatically. Letters routinely take weeks to arrive, and a sizeable number of customers are beginning to bypass the postal system in favor of private courier services. In order to remain profitable, many post offices have had to branch out into a wide array of services, including offering Internet access or renting some of their space to other retail outlets. The Russian government has also begun to consider the idea of merging the regional departments into a single joint-stock company to be called "Russian Post."

See also: MINISTRY OF INTERNAL AFFAIRS

BIBLIOGRAPHY

Rowley, Alison. (2002). "Miniature Propaganda: Self-Definition and Soviet Postage Stamps, 1917–1941." *Slavonica* 8:135–157.

Skipton, David, and Michalove, Peter. (1989). *Postal Censorship in Imperial Russia*. Urbana, IL: J. H. Otten.

ALISON ROWLEY

## POTEMKIN, GRIGORY ALEXANDROVICH

(1739–1791), prince, secret husband of Catherine II, statesman, commander, imperial viceroy, eccentric.

Grigory Potemkin's life contains many mysteries. His year of birth and paternity are both disputed. His father, Alexander Vasilievich Potemkin (c. 1690–1746), an irascible retired army officer from the Smolensk region, courted young Daria Skuratova (1704–1780) while she was still married. Grigory was the fifth born and sole male of seven children. A Moscow cousin provided care for the family after the father's death. At school in Moscow, Potemkin displayed remarkable aptitude in classical and modern languages and Orthodox theology. Clerical friends led him to consider a church career. Potemkin entered the Horse Guards while continuing school at age sixteen. In 1757 he was one of a dozen students presented at court by Ivan Shuvalov, curator of Moscow University. Despite a gold medal, his academic career ceased with expulsion for laziness and truancy. He began active service with the Guards in Petersburg, participating in Catherine's coup of July 1762, for which he was promoted to chamber-gentleman and granted six hundred serfs. Accidental loss of an eye—mistakenly blamed on his patrons, the Orlov brothers—lent mystique to his robust physique and ebullient personality. He became assistant procurator of the Holy Synod in 1763 and spokesman for the non-Russian peoples at the Legislative Commission of 1767–1768. On leave from court for active army service in the Russo-Turkish War of 1768–1774, he fought with distinction under Field Marshal Peter Rumyantsev from 1769 to December 1773. At Petersburg he dined at court in autumn 1770, enhancing a reputation for devilish intelligence and wit, hilarious impersonations, and military exploits.

After Catherine's break from Grigory Orlov in 1772–1773, she sought a fresh perspective amid multiple crises. In December 1773 she invited Potemkin to Petersburg to win her favor. Installation as official favorite swiftly followed. He sat beside her at dinner and received infatuated notes several times per day. He was made honorary sub-colonel of the Preobrazhensky Guards, member of the Imperial Council, vice-president (later president) of the War Department, commander of all light cavalry and irregular forces, and governor-general of New Russia, and given many decorations capped by Catherine's miniature portrait in diamonds—only Grigory Orlov had another. Potemkin helped to conclude the war on victorious terms, to oversee the end of the Pugachev Revolt, and to craft legislation strengthening provincial government against renewed disorders.

Apparently the lovers arranged a secret wedding in Petersburg on June 19, 1774. They spent most of 1775 in Moscow to celebrate victories over the Turks and Pugachev, ceremonies that Potemkin choreographed. Catherine supposedly gave birth to Potemkin's daughter, Elizaveta Grigorevna Temkina (a tale debunked in Simon Montefiore's biography). From early 1776, despite elevation to Prince of the Holy Roman Empire, Potemkin drifted away as a result of persistent quarrels over power and rivals. In New Russia he supervised settlement and arranged annexation of the Crimea, finally accomplished with minimal bloodshed in 1783 and renamed the Tauride region. This was part of the Greek Project that Potemkin and Catherine jointly pursued in alliance with Austria and that foresaw expulsion of the Turks from Europe and reconstitution of the Byzantine Empire under Russian tutelage. The couple constantly corresponded about all matters of policy and personal concerns, especially hypochondria. She regretted his ailments however petty, but when she fell into depression from favorite Alexander Lanskoi's death in 1784, Potemkin rushed back to direct her recovery. He planned the flamboyant Tauride Tour of 1787 that took her to Kiev, then by galley and ship to the Crimea, and then back via Moscow. This inspired the myth of "Potemkin villages," a term synonymous with phony display. He was awarded the surtitle of Tavrichesky ("Tauride") during the tour.

The Turks declared war in August 1787, Potemkin taking supreme command of all Russian forces in the south. He panicked for some weeks when the new Black Sea fleet was scattered by storms and Ottoman invasion threatened, but Catherine kept faith in his military abilities, and Potemkin led Russia to land and sea victories that eventually won the war in 1792. He missed the final victory, however, dying theatrically in the steppe outside Jassy on October 16, 1791.

See also: CATHERINE II; PUGACHEV, EMELIAN IVANOVICH; RUSSO-TURKISH WARS

**BIBLIOGRAPHY**

Alexander, John T. (1989). *Catherine the Great: Life and Legend.* New York: Oxford University Press.

Madariaga, Isabel de. (1981). *Russia in the Age of Catherine the Great.* New Haven: Yale University Press.

Montefiore, Simon Sebag. (2000). *Prince of Princes: The Life of Potemkin.* London: Weidenfeld and Nicolson.

Raeff, Marc. (1972). "In the Imperial Manner." In *Catherine the Great: A Profile,* ed. Marc Raeff. New York: Hill and Wang.

JOHN T. ALEXANDER

## POTEMKIN MUTINY

The Potemkin Mutiny that took place during the 1905 Russian Revolution on board of battleship *Knyaz Potemkin Tavricheskiy* of the Russian Black Sea Fleet on June 14–25, 1905.

The *Potemkin*, commissioned in 1902, was commanded by Captain Golikov. On June 14, while at sea on artillery maneuvers, its sailors protested over the quality of meat that was brought on board that day for their supper. The ship's doctor inspected the meat and declared it fit for human consumption.

The sailors, dissatisfied with this verdict, sent a deputation, headed by Grigory Vakulenchuk, a sailor and a member of the ship's Social Democrat organization, to Golikov. There was a confrontation between the delegation and Commander Gilyarovsky, the executive officer, who killed Vakulenchuk. This sparked a revolt, during which Golikov, Gilyarovsky, and other senior officers were killed or thrown overboard. Afanasy Matushenko, a torpedo quartermaster and one of leaders of the ship's Social Democrats, took command.

On June 15, the *Potemkin* arrived at Odessa, where the crew hoped to get support from striking workers. At 6 A.M., the body of Vakulenchuk was brought to the Odessa Steps, a staircase that connected the port and the city. By 10 A.M., some five thousand Odessans gathered there in support of the sailors. The gathering was peaceful throughout the day, but toward evening there was rioting, looting, and arson throughout the harbor front. By 9:30 P.M., loyal troops occupied strategic posts in the port and started firing into the crowd.

On June 16, authorities allowed the burial of Vakulenchuk, but refused sailors' demand for amnesty. That day, the *Potemkin* shelled Odessa with its six-inch guns. On June 17, mutiny broke out on the battleship *Georgi Pobedonosets* and other ships of the Black Sea Fleet. However, by June 19 this mutiny was put down.

On June 18 the *Potemkin* set out from Odessa to the Romanian port of Constanza, where sailors' request for supplies was refused. The ship left the port the following day, but returned on June 25, after failing to secure supplies in Feodosia. The sailors surrendered the ship to Romanian authorities and were granted safe passage to the country's western borders.

The Potemkin mutiny was a spontaneous event, which broke the plans by socialist organizations in the Black Sea Fleet for a more organized rebellion. However, it tapped into widespread disaffection on the part of the Russian people over their conditions during the reign of Nicholas II. The mutineers found sympathy among the people of Odessa. While the mutiny was crushed, it, together with other events in the 1905 Russian Revolution, provided an important impetus to constitutional reforms that marked the last years of the Russian Empire.

*See also:* BLACK SEA FLEET; REVOLUTION OF 1905

**BIBLIOGRAPHY**

Ascher, Abraham. (1988). *The Revolution of 1905.* Stanford, CA: Stanford University Press.

Hough, Richard. (1961). *The Potemkin Mutiny.* New York: Pantheon Books.

Matushenko, Afansky. (2002). "The Revolt on the Armoured Cruiser *Potemkin.*" <http://www.marxist .com/History/potemkin.html>.

IGOR YEYKELIS

# POTSDAM CONFERENCE

The Potsdam Conference was the last of the wartime summits among the Big Three allied leaders. It met from July 17 through August 2, 1945, in Potsdam, a historic suburb of Berlin. Representing the United States, the Soviet Union and Great Britain respectively were Harry Truman, Josef Stalin and Winston Churchill (who was replaced midway by Clement Atlee as a result of elections that brought Labor to power). Germany had surrendered in May; the war with Japan continued. The purpose of the Potsdam meeting was the implementation of the agreements reached at Yalta. The atmosphere at Potsdam was often acrimo-

nious, presaging the imminent Cold War between the Soviet Union and the West. In the months leading up to Potsdam, Stalin took an increasingly hard line on issues regarding Soviet control in Eastern Europe, provoking the new American president and the British prime minister to harden their own stance toward the Soviet leader.

Two issues were particularly contentious: Poland's western boundaries with Germany and German reparations. When Soviet forces liberated Polish territory, Stalin, without consulting his allies, transferred to Polish administration all of the German territories east of the Oder-Neisse (western branch) Rivers. While Britain and the United States were prepared to compensate Poland for its territorial losses in the east, they were unwilling to agree to such a substantial land transfer made unilaterally. They would have preferred the Oder-Neisse (eastern branch) River boundary. The larger territory gave Poland the historic city of Breslau and the rich industrial area of Silesia. Reluctantly, the British and Americans accepted Stalin's *fait accompli*, but with the proviso that the final boundary demarcation would be determined by a German peace treaty.

Reparations was another unresolved problem. The Soviet Union demanded a sum viewed by the Western powers as economically impossible. Abandoning the effort to agree on a specific sum, the conferees agreed to take reparations from each power's zone of occupation. Stalin sought, with only limited success, additional German resources from the British and American zones. Agreements reached at Potsdam provided for:

Transference of authority in Germany to the military commanders in their respective zones of occupation and to a four-power Allied Control Council for matters affecting Germany as a whole.

Creation of a Council of Foreign Ministers to prepare peace treaties for Italy, Bulgaria, Finland, Hungary, and Romania and ultimately Germany.

Denazification, demilitarization, democratization, and decentralization of Germany.

Transference of Koenigsberg and adjacent area to the Soviet Union.

Just prior to the conference, Truman was informed of the successful test of the atomic bomb in New Mexico. On July 24 he gave a brief account of the weapon to Stalin. Stalin reaffirmed his commitment to declare war on Japan in mid-August.

While the conference was in session, the leaders of Britain, China, and the United States issued a proclamation offering Japan the choice between immediate unconditional surrender or destruction.

Though the facade of allied unity was affirmed in the final communiqué, the Potsdam Conference marked the end of Europe's wartime alliance.

*See also:* TEHERAN CONFERENCE; WORLD WAR II; YALTA CONFERENCE

### BIBLIOGRAPHY
Feis, Herbert. (1960). *Between War and Peace: The Potsdam Conference.* Princeton, NJ: Princeton University Press.

Gormly, James L. (1990). *From Potsdam to the Cold War: Big Three Diplomacy, 1945–1947.* Wilmington, DE: SR Books.

McNeil, William H. (1953). *America, Britain and Russia: Their Cooperation and Conflict, 1941–1946.* London: Oxford University Press.

Wheeler-Bennett, John W., and Nicholls, Anthony. (1972). *The Semblance of Peace: The Political Settlement after the Second World War.* London: Macmillan.

JOSEPH L. NOGEE

## POZHARSKY, DMITRY MIKHAILOVICH

(1578–1642), military leader of the second national liberation army of 1611–1612.

Prince Dmitry Mikhailovich Pozharsky belonged to the Starodub princes, a relatively minor clan. He came to prominence as a military commander during the reign of Vasily Shuisky. While recovering from wounds sustained during service in the first national liberation army of 1611, Pozharsky was invited to lead the new militia, which was being organized by Kuzma Minin at Nizhny Novgorod. In March 1612 he led an army from Nizhny to Yaroslavl, where he remained for four months as head of a provisional government that made military and political preparations for the liberation of Moscow from the Poles. The capital was still besieged by Cossacks under Ivan Zarutsky, who supported the claim to the throne of tsarevich Ivan, the infant son of the Second False Dmitry and Marina Mniszech; others, including Prince Dmitry Trubetskoy, swore allegiance to a Third False Dmitry who had appeared in Pskov. Pozharsky himself, perhaps to neutralize the threat

from the Swedes who had occupied Novgorod, seemed to favor the Swedish prince Charles Philip. Pozharsky left Yaroslavl only after Zarutsky and Trubetskoy had renounced their candidates for the throne. Following Zarutsky's flight from the encampments surrounding Moscow, Pozharsky and Trubetskoy liberated the capital in October 1612 and headed the provisional government, which convened the Assembly of the Land that elected Michael Romanov as tsar in January 1613. Pozharsky was made a boyar on the day of Michael's coronation, and he performed a number of relatively minor military and administrative roles during Michael's reign. Along with Minin, Pozharsky was subsequently regarded as a national hero and served as a patriotic inspiration in later wars.

*See also:* ASSEMBLY OF THE LAND; COSSACKS; MININ, KUZMA; ROMANOV, MIKHAIL FYODOROVICH; TIME OF TROUBLES

### BIBLIOGRAPHY
Dunning, Chester L. (2001). *Russia's First Civil War: The Time of Troubles and the Founding of the Romanov Dynasty.* University Park: Pennsylvania State University Press.

Perrie, Maureen. (2002). *Pretenders and Popular Monarchism in Early Modern Russia: The False Tsars of the Time of Troubles,* paperback ed. Cambridge, UK: Cambridge University Press.

Skrynnikov, Ruslan G. (1988). *The Time of Troubles: Russia in Crisis, 1604–1618,* ed. and tr. Hugh F. Graham. Gulf Breeze, FL: Academic International Press.

MAUREEN PERRIE

## PRAVDA

*Pravda* (the name means "truth" in Russian) was first issued on May 5, 1912, in St. Petersburg by the Bolshevik faction of the Russian Social Democratic Party. Its aim was to publicize labor activism and expose working conditions in Russian factories. The editors published many letters and articles from ordinary workers, their primary target audience at the time.

*Pravda* was a legal daily newspaper subject to postpublication censorship by the tsarist authorities. These authorities had the power to fine the paper, withdraw its publication license, confiscate a specific issue, or jail the editor. They closed the

**Nikolai Bukharin and Maria Ulyanova, sister of Lenin, at work at the Communist Party newspaper,** *Pravda.* © HULTON-DEUTSCH COLLECTION/CORBIS

paper eight times in the first two years of its existence, and each time the Bolsheviks reopened it under another name ("Worker's Truth," etc.). In spite of police harassment the newspaper maintained an average circulation of about forty thousand in the period 1912 to 1914, probably a higher number than other socialist papers (but small compared to the commercial "penny newspapers"). About one-half of *Pravda*'s circulation was distributed in St. Petersburg. After the authorities closed the paper on July 21, 1914, it did not appear again until after the February Revolution of 1917.

*Pravda* reopened on March 5, 1917, and published continuously until closed down by Russian Republic president Boris Yeltsin on August 22, 1991. From December 1917 until the summer of 1928 the newspaper was run by editor in chief Nikolai Bukarin and Maria Ilichna Ulyanova, Lenin's sister. When Bukharin broke with Josef

Stalin over collectivization, Stalin used the *Pravda* party organization to undermine his authority. Bukharin and his supporters, including Ulyanova, were formally removed from the editorial staff in 1929. By 1933 the newspaper, now headed by Lev Mekhlis, was Stalin's mouthpiece.

Throughout the Soviet era access to *Pravda* was a necessity for party members. The paper's primary role was not to entertain, inform, or instruct the Soviet population as a whole, but to deliver Central Committee instructions and messages to Soviet communist cadres, foreign governments, and foreign communist parties. Thus, as party membership shifted, so did *Pravda*'s presentation. In response to the influx of young working-class men into the Party in the 1920s, for example, editors simplified the paper's language and resorted to the sort of journalism that they believed would appeal to this audience—militant slogans, tales of heroic feats of production, and denunciation of class enemies.

*Pravda* also produced reports on popular moods. This practice began in the early 1920s as Bukharin and Ulianova played a leading role in organizing the worker and peasant correspondents' movement in the Soviet republics. Workers and peasants (many of them Party activists) wrote into the newspaper with reports on daily life, often shaped by the editors' instructions. Newspapers, including *Pravda*, received and processed millions of such letters throughout Soviet history. Editors published a few of these, forwarded some to prosecutorial organs, and used others to produce the summaries of popular moods, which were sent to Party leaders.

After the collapse of the USSR nationalist and communist journalists intermittently published a print newspaper and an online newspaper under the name *Pravda*. However, the new publications were not official organs of the revived Communist Party.

*See also:* JOURNALISM; NEWSPAPERS

### BIBLIOGRAPHY

Brooks, Jeffrey (2000). *Thank You, Comrade Stalin! Soviet Culture from Revolution to Cold War.* Princeton, NJ: Princeton University Press.

Kenez, Peter (1985). *The Birth of the Propaganda State: Soviet Methods of Mass Mobilization, 1917–1929.* New York: Cambridge University Press.

Lenoe, Matthew. (1998). "Agitation, Propaganda, and the 'Stalinization' of the Soviet Press, 1922–1930." Pittsburgh, PA: Carl Beck Papers in Russian and East European Studies, no. 1305.

Roxburgh, Angus (1987). *Pravda: Inside the Soviet News Machine.* New York: George Brazillier.

MATTHEW E. LENOE

# PREOBRAZHENSKY GUARDS

The Preobrazhensky Regiment and its slightly junior counterpart, the Semenovsky Life Guard Regiment, trace their histories to 1683, when Peter the Great as tsarevich created two "play regiments." Named after villages near Moscow, the regiments initially consisted of Peter's boyhood cronies and miscellaneous recruits who engaged in war games in and around the mock fortress of Pressburg. The regiments attained formal status in 1687, followed in 1700 by official appellation as Guards. More than guarantors of the tsar's physical security, these regiments served as models for the emergence of a standing regular Russian army. With adjustments, Peter structured them on the pattern of European-style units that Tsar Alexis Mikhailovich had first introduced into Russian service. As they evolved, the guards became officer training schools for an assortment of gentry youths and foreigners who remained reliably close to the throne. In setting the example, the tsar himself advanced through the ranks of the Preobrazhensky Regiment, serving notably in 1709 as a battalion commander at Poltava. Non-military missions for guards officers and non-commissioned officers often extended to service as a kind of political police for the sovereign. By 1722, Peter's guards (with cavalry) numbered about three thousand troops, and his Table of Ranks recognized their elite status by according their complement two-rank seniority over comparable grades in the regular army.

During the half-century after Peter's death, a mixture of tradition, proximity to the throne, elite status, and gentry recruitment propelled the Preobrazhensky Regiment into court politics. Every sovereign after Peter automatically became chief of the regiment; therefore, appearance of the ruler in its uniform symbolized authority, continuity, and mutual acceptance. Meanwhile, because Peter had made gentry service mandatory, noble families often registered their male children at birth on the regimental list, thus assuring early ascent through the junior grades before actual duty. In effect, the Guards became a bastion of gentry interests and sentiment, and various parties at court eventually drew the Preobrazhensky Regiment into a series of palace intrigues and coups. Officers of the regiment played conspicuous roles in the palace coups of 1740 and 1741 that overthrew successive regents for the infant Ivan VI in final favor of Empress Elizabeth Petrovna. Members of the regiment displayed an even higher profile during the coup of July 1762 that deposed Peter III in favor of his German-born wife, who became Empress Catherine II. She counted prominent supporters within the regiment, and she pointedly dressed as a Preobrazhensky colonel during the campaign on the outskirts of the capital to arrest her husband. On re-entry into St. Petersburg, Catherine personally rode at the head of the regiment. Yet, whatever the level of guards' participation in this and previous coups, there was never any genuine impulse to create an alternative military government; solicitous attention from the traditional monarchy seemed adequate recompense for guards' conspiratorial complicity.

The onset of Catherine II's reign marked the zenith of the Preobrazhensky's role as power broker, although association with the regiment continued to retain symbolic significance. To forestall repetition of events, a new generation of military administrators increasingly recruited non-noble subjects with outstanding physical characteristics as rank-and-file guards, while Tsar Paul I subsequently diluted the guards with recruits from his Gatchina corps. Moreover, other sources of officer recruitment, including the cadet corps, soon supplanted the guards. Only in 1825, during the Decembrist revolt, when a Preobrazhensky company was the first unit to side with Tsar Nicholas I, was there more than brief allusion to a political past. Subsequently, the Preobrazhensky Regiment remained the bearer of a proud combat tradition that included distinguished service in nearly all of imperial Russia's wars. The sons of illustrious families vied for appointment to its officer cadre, while the tsars continued to wear its distinctive dark green tunic on ceremonial occasions.

See also: CATHERINE II; MILITARY, IMPERIAL ERA; PETER I

### BIBLIOGRAPHY

Alexander, John T. (1989). *Catherine the Great: Life and Legend.* New York: Oxford University Press.

Keep, John. L. H. (1985). *Soldiers of the Tsar: Army and Society in Russia, 1462–1874.* Oxford: Clarendon Press.

BRUCE W. MENNING

## PREOBRAZHENSKY, YEVGENY ALEXEYEVICH

(1886–1937), Russian revolutionary, oppositionist, and Marxist theorist.

Born in Bolkhov, Orel province, Yevgeny Preobrazhensky began his political activism at age fifteen as a Social Democrat and later became a Bolshevik and a regional leader. Together with Nikolai Bukharin, Preobrazhensky led the Left Communist opposition to the Brest-Litovsk Treaty with Germany (1918). In 1920 he became one of three secretaries of the Bolshevik Party, together with Nikolai Krestinsky and Leonid Serebryakov,

all later active in the Trotskyist Opposition. The three were removed from these posts in 1922, when Josef Stalin was made General Secretary of the Party Central Committee.

In 1923 Preobrazhensky authored the "Platform of the Forty-Six," which attacked the growing bureaucratization and authoritarianism of the Party apparatus. Also in 1923 he published *On Morality and Class Norms*, in which he attacked the apparatus's growing privileges. From this point Preobrazhensky became a close ally of Leon Trotsky and a leader of the various Trotskyist oppositions. Following the suppression of the 1927 Joint Opposition, he was expelled from the Party in 1928, but in 1929 became one of the first Trotskyists to recant his views and return to the Party fold. He was arrested in 1935 and testified against Grigory Zinoviev and Lev Kamenev at the first Moscow show trial in 1936. He was scheduled to be a defendant in the second trial in 1937, but refused to confess and was shot in secret in that same year. He was rehabilitated during Gorbachev's *perestroika*.

Preobrazhensky was a major theorist and one of the Soviet Union's leading economists of the 1920s. He opposed Stalin's and Bukharin's policy of "Socialism in One Country" and the slow pace of industrialization. In his major work, *The New Economics*, he put forward the theory of primary socialist accumulation, in which he argued that successful industrial development had to extract resources from the peasant economy. However, he resolutely opposed the use of force to achieve this, and by 1927 had concluded that only a revolution in the advanced countries of Western Europe could save the Soviet Union from a political and economic impasse. While he purported to welcome Stalin's solution to this dilemma (forced collectivization and industrialization), in 1932 he published his second theoretical masterpiece, *The Decline of Capitalism*. This was a serious analysis in its own right of the Great Depression, but it contained a less-than-veiled attack on Stalin's five-year plans and the policy of developing heavy industry at the expense of consumption.

See also: BUKHARIN, NIKOLAI IVANOVICH; STALIN, JOSEF VISSARIONOVICH; TROTSKY, LEON DAVIDOVICH

### BIBLIOGRAPHY

Day, Richard B. (1981). *The "Crisis" and the "Crash": Soviet Studies of the West (1917–1939).* London: NLB.

Erlich, Alexander. (1960). *The Soviet Industrialization Debate.* Cambridge, MA: Harvard University Press.

Preobrazhensky, E. A. (1965). *The New Economics.* Oxford: Clarendon.

Preobrazhensky, E. A. (1973). *From NEP to Socialism.* London: New Park.

Preobrazhensky, E. A. (1980). *The Crisis of Soviet Industrialization,* ed. Donald A. Filtzer. London: Macmillan.

Preobrazhensky, E. A. (1985). *The Decline of Capitalism,* ed. Richard B. Day. Armonk, NY: M. E. Sharpe.

DONALD FILTZER

# PRESIDENCY

The presidency is the most powerful formal political institution in post-communist Russia. Except for the ceremonial title given to the head of the USSR Supreme Soviet, the Soviet Union did not have a presidency until its waning years, although the adoption of one was discussed under Josef Stalin and again under Nikita Khrushchev. New proposals resurfaced in the late 1980s, prompting intense debate among Communist Party elites about the efficacy of introducing an institution that could challenge the party's authority. Despite concerns about the concentration of power in the hands of a single individual, the Supreme Soviet and the Congress of People's Deputies approved the Soviet presidency in 1990. The first presidential election was to be held by the legislature, with subsequent popular elections. Mikhail Gorbachev became president in March 1990, receiving 71 percent of the votes in the Congress of People's Deputies.

The union republics began electing presidents before the dissolution of the USSR. In June 1991, Boris Yeltsin was chosen as Russia's first president in an election that pitted him against five competitors. In his first term, following the breakup of the USSR, Yeltsin faced a recalcitrant parliament that opposed many of his initiatives. The conflict between the executive and legislative branches culminated in Yeltsin's issuing a decree that dissolved parliament on September 21, 1993. Parliament rejected the decree and declared Vice President Alexander Rutskoi to be acting president. The forces opposing Yeltsin assembled armed supporters, occupied the Russian White House, and attempted to take control of the main television network. Pro-Yeltsin forces attacked the White House and crushed the parliamentary rebellion in early October 1993.

The constitutional crisis led to the formal strengthening of the presidency, codified in the 1993 constitution. Rather than a pure presidential system, the Russian Federation adopted a semi-presidential system in which the president is the popularly elected head of state, and the prime minister, nominated by the president, is the head of government. The president is elected to a four-year term using a majority-runoff system that requires a majority vote to win in the first round of competition. If no candidate gains a majority, a runoff is held between the top two candidates from the first round. The president wields substantial formal powers and thus has more authority than the leaders in parliamentary and many other semipresidential systems. Among other things, the president can veto laws, make decrees, initiate legislation, call for referenda, and suspend local laws that contravene the constitution. The president is limited to two consecutive terms in office.

Yeltsin was reelected president in July 1996, after defeating the candidate of the Communist Party of the Russian Federation, Gennady Zyuganov, in the second round of competition. Yeltsin resigned from the presidency on December 31, 1999. Vladimir Putin served briefly as acting president and then was elected in March 2000. Putin reasserted presidential authority, strengthening central control over the regions, challenging powerful business interests, and extending control over the press.

*See also:* CONSTITUTION OF 1993; GORBACHEV, MIKHAIL SERGEYEVICH; PUTIN, VLADIMIR VLADIMIROVICH; YELTSIN, BORIS NIKOLAYEVICH

**BIBLIOGRAPHY**

Huskey, Eugene. (1999). *Presidential Power in Russia.* Armonk, NY: M. E. Sharpe.

Nichols, Thomas M. (2001). *The Russian Presidency.* New York: St. Martin's.

ERIK S. HERRON

# PRESIDENTIAL COUNCIL

In March 1990, when the Communist Party of the Soviet Union lost its political monopoly and Mikhail Gorbachev was elected president of the

USSR, he created a new Presidential Council to replace the Politburo as the major policy-making body in the Soviet Union. The council's task, according to the newly revised Soviet constitution, was to determine the USSR's foreign and domestic policy. This was a major institutional innovation. The Presidential Council was to be independent of the Communist Party, which at this stage was viewed as incapable of reform, and was intended to challenge the power of the Defense Council (subsequently abolished) and to increase and reinforce Gorbachev's new presidential power. Gorbachev's choice of members to compose the Council was very controversial. The sixteen members, only five of whom were Politburo members, included Chingiz Aitmatov, a Kyrghiz writer; Vadim Bakatin, minister of the interior; Valery Boldin, head of the Central Committee General Department; KGB chief Vladimir Kryuchkov; Anatoly Lukyanov, chair of the Supreme Soviet; Yuri Maslyukov, chairman of the state planning commission; Yevgeny Primakov, chairman of the Soviet of the Union; Valentin Rasputin, the nationalist writer and only non-communist; Prime Minister Nikolay Ryzhkov; Stanislav Shatalin, economist; Eduard Shevardnadze, the foreign minister; Alexander Yakovlev, a senior secretary of the Central Committee and minister without portfolio; Venyamin Yarin, leader of the United Workers Front; and Marshal Dmitry Yazov, minister of defense. Depending upon which source one consults, the council also included two of the following: Yuri Osipian, physicist; Georgy Revenkov, chair of the Council of the Union of the Supreme Soviet; and Vadim Medvedev. The council experiment did not work because the members could not act collectively and the council's policies were rarely put into practice. As a result, making the necessary changes in the Soviet constitution, Gorbachev abolished the Presidential Council in November 1990. The council was resurrected several times during the presidency of Boris Yeltsin but had no clearly defined functions and little political clout.

*See also:* GORBACHEV, MIKHAIL SERGEYEVICH; POLITBURO; PRESIDENCY

**BIBLIOGRAPHY**

Brown, Archie. (1996). *The Gorbachev Factor.* Oxford: Oxford University Press.

Gill, Graeme. (1994). *The Collapse of a Single-Party System: The Disintegration of the Communist Party of the Soviet Union.* Cambridge, UK: Cambridge University Press.

Sakwa, Richard. (1990). *Gorbachev and His Reforms, 1985–1990.* New York: Philip Allan.

CHRISTOPHER WILLIAMS

## PRESIDIUM OF SUPREME SOVIET

The Russian word *soviet* means "council." The Supreme Soviet beginning in 1936 was the pre-1991 equivalent of the Parliament or Congress in democratic countries. It consisted of two chambers. The upper chamber (the Council of Nationalities) consisted of representatives ("people's deputies") of the hundred-plus nationalities of the USSR; the lower chamber (the Council of the Union) represented the population at large on a per-capita representative basis. Initially they were elected for four-year terms, then, beginning in 1977, for five-year terms. There were eleven convocations (following eleven elections) of the Supreme Soviet between December 12, 1937, and March 26, 1989, which met in eighty-nine sessions. The Supreme Soviet met for only a few days semiannually to vote unanimously for the government's (in reality, the Communist Party's) program. It elected the Presidium, which was a standing body that had more functions; as well as nominally formed the government, including the Council of Ministers of the USSR; chose the procurator general (chief prosecutor, equals attorney general) of the USSR; and appointed the Supreme Court of the USSR.

The Brezhnev Constitution of 1977 converted the Supreme Soviet into a fuller legislative and control organ elected by the Congress of the Council of Nationalities and Council of the Union. The Supreme Soviet itself appointed the Council of Ministers, the Control Commission, the chief prosecutor, and chose the Presidium from among its members.

In 1989 the old Supreme Soviet was converted into the Congress of People's Deputies of the USSR, a standing body with 2,250 deputies, one-third elected from equal territories, one-third from nationality regions, and one-third from social organizations. Five such congresses met between 1989 and 1991. From its members it chose by secret ballot a new Supreme Soviet, in accord with a law of December 1, 1988, which was subordinate to it. The new Supreme Soviet had the same two chambers as before with 266 deputies in each.

**Table 1.**

### Presidium of the Supreme Soviet

| Individual | Dates in Office |
|---|---|
| Mikhail I. Kalinin | 1938-1946 |
| Nikolai M. Shvernik | 1946-1953 |
| Klimentii E. Voroshilov | 1953-1960 |
| Leonid I. Brezhnev | 1960-1964 |
| Anastas I. Mikoian | 1964-1965 |
| Nikolai V. Podgornyi | 1965-1977 |
| Leonid I. Brezhnev | 1977-1982 |
| Iurii V. Andropov | 1983-1984 |
| Konstantin U. Chernenko | 1984-1985 |
| Andrei A. Gromyko | 1985-1988 |
| Mikhail S. Gorbachev | 1988-1989 |

SOURCE: Courtesy of the author.

The heads of the Presidium were the nominal heads of state of the Soviet Union: Mikhail Ivanovich Kalinin (1938–1946), Nikolai Mikhailovich Shvernik (1946–1953), Kliment Efremovich Voroshilov (1953–1960), Leonid Ilich Brezhnev (1960–1964 and 1977–1982), Anastas Ivanovich Mikoyan (1964–1965), Nikolai Viktorovich Podgorny (1965–1977), Yuri Vladimirovich Andropov (1983–1984), Konstantin Ustinovich Chernenko (1984–1985), Andrei Andreyevich Gromyko (1985–1988), and Mikhail Sergeyevich Gorbachev (1988–1989). Most of them were figureheads, for power actually lay in the Communist Party, and the state authorities were its rubber stamps. However, when Brezhnev in 1977 decided to combine the jobs of head of the Communist Party of the Soviet Union (CPSU) and of the USSR (followed in this by Andropov, Chernenko, and Gorbachev), the heads of the Presidium were the most important figures in the Soviet Union. The Presidium also had the office of first assistant to the head, but this office was so insignificant that it was not created until 1944, and then was not appointed from 1946 to 1977.

The men who made the Presidium work were its secretaries: A. F. Gorkin (1938–1953 and 1956–1957), N. M. Pegov (1953–1956), M. P. Georgadze (1957–1982), and T. N. Menteshashvili (1982–1989).

To the extent that the Soviet service state (q.v.) functioned efficiently or not, the Presidium secretaries deserve much of the credit or blame. They embodied the meritocratic principles of the service state and the last two, as Georgians, personified the multinational nature of the Soviet empire.

Occasionally the plenum of the Central Committee of the CPSU, the Council of Ministers of the USSR, and the Presidium of the Supreme Soviet of the USSR met together, as happened on March 5, 1953, from 10 to 10:40 P.M., when they adopted resolutions on governmental organization after Stalin's death.

The Supreme Soviets met only a few days annually, and its Presidium carried on its business in the intervals. (The two organs paralleled the Communist Party's All-Union Congresses and the Politburo. In theory, the CPSU made policy; the government carried it out.) According to Article 119 of the 1977 Constitution, the Presidium had thirty-seven members. The chairman was nominally in charge; then there were fifteen vice-chairs, one for each republic, who were present more for decoration than for work. Then there was the secretary, the workhorse of the Presidium, and twenty others who had area responsibilities corresponding to the ministries that ran the USSR. The presidium had a long list of functions, only some of which can be mentioned here. It set the dates for the election of the Supreme Soviet and convened its sessions. It was responsible for the government observing the Constitution and that all laws were constitutional. It had the task of interpreting the laws when dispute arose. The Presidium instituted and awarded orders and medals, including military ones. It ruled on matters of citizenship. It formed the Council of Defense and appointed and dismissed the leaders of the armed forces. It was the body that could proclaim martial law, declare war and peace, and order the mobilization of the armed forces. It ratified foreign treaties and dealt with diplomatic matters. Article 121 of the Constitution authorized the Presidium to create and disband governmental ministries and to appoint and fire ministers.

*See also:* CONGRESS OF PEOPLE'S DEPUTIES; CONSTITUTION OF 1977; COUNCIL OF MINISTERS, SOVIET; SUPREME SOVIET

**BIBLIOGRAPHY**

Kudriavtsev, V. N., et al., eds. (1986). *The Soviet Constitution. A Dictionary.* Moscow: Progress.

RICHARD HELLIE

**PRIKAZY** *See* CHANCELLERY SYSTEM.

## PRIMAKOV, YEVGENY MAXIMOVICH

(b. 1929), orientalist, intelligence chief, foreign minister, and prime minister under Boris Yeltsin.

Born in Kiev, Yevgeny Maximovich Primakov grew up in Tbilisi; his father disappeared in the purges. Trained as an Arabist, Primakov worked in broadcasting in the 1950s and then became a Middle East correspondent for *Pravda* (and perhaps a covert foreign intelligence operative). In the 1970s he assumed academic posts as deputy director of the Institute of World Economics and International Relations (IMEMO), then as director of the Institute of Oriental Studies, and in 1985 as director of IMEMO.

In 1986 Primakov became a candidate member of the Central Committee of the Communist Party of the Soviet Union, and a foreign policy advisor to Mikhail Gorbachev. He was chosen in June 1989 to chair the Congress of People's Deputies, the lower house of the Supreme Soviet formed pursuant to Gorbachev's new constitution. His party status rose accordingly: full Central Committee member in April 1989 and candidate member of the Politburo in September. He was a leading contributor to the "New Thinking" regarding international cooperation that was identified with Gorbachev.

Primakov condemned the attempted coup by hard-line communists in August 1991; Gorbachev then made him First Deputy Chairman of the KGB and head of foreign intelligence. He was one of the few Gorbachev appointees to be retained in office by Russian President Boris Yeltsin after the Soviet Union was dissolved in December 1991.

Appointed foreign minister in January 1996, Primakov was a realistic and cool professional. He was a strong defender of Russian national interests, as opposed to the pro-Western stance of his predecessor Andrei Kozyrev, and often manifested pro-Arab sympathies. Espousing a "multipolar" world, he nonetheless avoided direct confrontation with the West and bargained for a Russian presence at NATO as it was expanding eastward. Later he criticized the 1999 NATO bombing campaign against Yugoslavia but kept open a Russian role in the Kosovo settlement.

Following the August 1998 economic and political crisis, Primakov emerged as a compromise candidate for prime minister. Overwhelmingly confirmed by the Duma in September, he was the most popular politician in Russia. His model for eco-

Russian statesman Yevgeny Primakov served Boris Yeltsin as foreign minister, prime minister, and spy master. PHOTOGRAPH BY ALEXANDER ZEMLIANICHENKO. AP/WIDE WORLD PHOTOS. REPRODUCED BY PERMISSION.

nomic stabilization was President Franklin Roosevelt's New Deal in the United States.

As prime minister, Primakov soon aroused the jealousy of the ailing Yeltsin and alarmed the president's family and cronies by investigating corruption. Yeltsin emerged from a long period of torpor and dismissed Primakov in May 1999 in favor of Interior Minister Sergei Stepashin. In reply, Primakov accepted the leadership of the "Fatherland-All Russia" bloc to oppose Yeltsin's forces in the Duma elections of December 1999, and was a strong contender for the presidency in the elections due the following year. But in August Yeltsin replaced Prime Minister Stepashin with Vladimir Putin, who set up his own party, Unity, and capitalized on the war in Chechnya to forge ahead of Primakov's people. Primakov withdrew as a presidential contender in order to run for speaker of the new Duma; however, Putin made a deal with the communists to keep Gennady Seleznyov as speaker and marginalize Primakov. Those maneuvers not-withstanding, in the March 2000 election Primakov endorsed Putin, who subsequently tapped him for occasional diplomatic missions. In 2001 Primakov retired from the presidency of Fatherland-All Russia as it was preparing to merge with Unity.

*See also:* FATHERLAND-ALL RUSSIA; GORBACHEV, MIKHAIL SERGEYEVICH; YELTSIN, BORIS NIKOLAYEVICH

**BIBLIOGRAPHY**

Daniels, Robert V. (1999). "Evgenii Primakov: Contender by Chance." *Problems of Post-Communism* 46(5): 27–36.

Shevtsova, Lilia F. (1999). *Yeltsin's Russia: Myths and Reality.* Washington, DC: Carnegie Endowment for International Peace.

Simes, Dmitri K. (1999). *After the Collapse: Russia Seeks Its Place as a Great Power.* New York: Simon & Schuster.

ROBERT V. DANIELS

## PRIMARY CHRONICLE

The compilation of chronicle entries known as the *Povst' vremennykh lt* (*PVL*) is a fundamental source for the historical study of the vast eastern European and Eurasian lands that include major parts of Ukraine and Belarus, as well as extensive parts of the Russian Federation and Poland. As the single most important source for the study of the early Rus principalities, it contains the bulk of existing written information about the area inhabited by the East Slavs from the ninth to the twelfth century, and has been the subject of many historical, literary, and linguistic analyses. The *PVL* in various versions appears at the beginning of most extant chronicles compiled from the fourteenth through seventeenth centuries

The *PVL* may have been compiled initially by Silvestr, the hegumen of St. Michael's Monastery in Vydobichi, a village near Kiev, in 1116. The attribution to Silvestr is based on a colophon in copies of the so-called Laurentian branch where he declares, "I wrote down this chronicle," and asks to be remembered in his readers' prayers (286,1–286,7). It is possible that Silvestr merely copied or edited an already existing complete work by the Kiev Caves Monastery monk mentioned in the heading (i.e., "The Tale of Bygone Years of a monk of the Feodosy Pechersky Monastery [regarding] from

where the Rus lands comes and who first in it began to rule and from where the Rus land became to be"), but it is also possible that this monk merely began the work that Silvestr finished. An interpolation in the title of the sixteenth-century Khlebnikov copy has led to a popular notion that Nestor was the name of this monk and that he had completed a now-lost first redaction of the complete text. But that interpolation is not reliable evidence, since it may have been the result of a guess by the interpolator, in which case the name of the monk referred to in the title or when he compiled his text is not known. So the simplest explanation is that Silvestr used an earlier (perhaps unfinished) chronicle by an unknown monk of the Caves Monastery along with other sources to compile what is now known as the *PVL*. Silvestr's holograph does not exist; the earliest copy dates to more than 260 years later. Therefore, researches have to try to reconstruct what Silvestr wrote on the basis of extant copies that are hundreds of years distant from its presumed date of composition.

There are five main witnesses to the original version of the *PVL*. The term "main witness," refers only to those copies that have independent authority to testify about what was in the archetype. Since most copies of the *PVL* (e.g., those found in the Nikon Chronicle, Voskresenskii Chronicle, etc.) are secondary (i.e., derivative) from the main witnesses, they provide no primary readings in relation to the archetype. The five main witnesses are:

1. Laurentian (RNB, F.IV.2), dated to 1377;
2. Radziwill (BAN, 34. 5. 30), datable to the 1490s;
3. Academy (RGB, MDA 5/182), dated to the 15th century;
4. Hypatian (BAN, 16. 4. 4), dated to c. 1425;
5. Khlebnikov (RNB, F.IV.230), dated to 16th century.

In addition, in a few places, the Pogodin Chronicle fills in lacunae in the Khlebnikov copy:

6. Pogodin (RNB, Pogodin 1401), dated to early 17th century.

One can also draw textual evidence from the corresponding passages in the later version of the Novgorod I Chronicle. To date, there are no lithographs or photographic facsimilies of any manuscript of the Novgorod I Chronicle. The three copies of the published version of Novg. I are:

1. Commission (SPb IRI, Arkh. kom. 240), dated to 1450s;
2. Academy (BAN 17.8.36), dated to 1450s;

**Figure 1.**

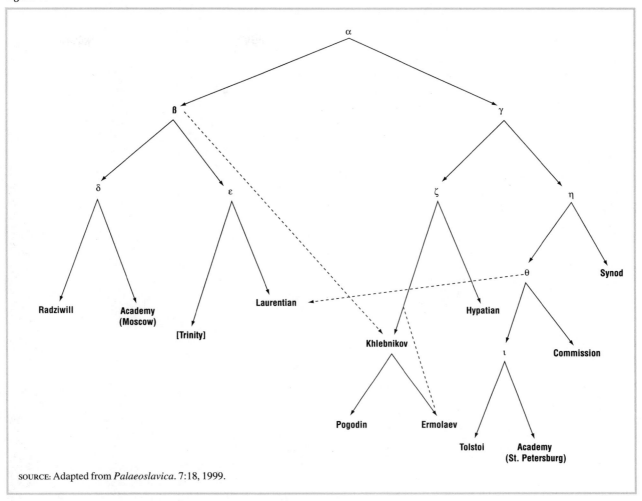

SOURCE: Adapted from *Palaeoslavica*. 7:18, 1999.

3. Tolstoi (RNB, Tolstovoi F.IV.223), dated to 1820s.

One can also utilize certain textual readings from the corresponding passages of Priselkov's reconstruction of the non-extant Trinity Chronicle.

The *stemma*, or family tree, shows the genealogical relationship of the manuscript copies.

Although various theories have been proposed for the stages of compilation of the *PVL*, little agreement has been reached. The sources that the compiler(s) utilized, however, are generally recognized. The main source to 842 is the *Chronicle of Georgius Hamartolu* and to 948 the *Continuation of Symeon the Logothete*. Accounts of the ecumenical councils could have been drawn from at least three possible sources: (1) a Bulgarian collection, which served as the basis for the *Izbornik of 1073*; (2) the *Chronicle of Hamartolus*; and (3) the *Letter of Patriarch Photius to Boris, Prince of Bulgaria*. Copies of treaties between Byzantium and Rus appear under entries for 907, 912, 945, and 971. The *Creed of Michael Syncellus* was the source of the Cree d taught to Volodimir I in 988. Metropolitan Hilarion's *Sermon on Law and Grace* is drawn upon for Biblical quotations regarding the conversion of Volodimir I. There are also excerpts from the *Memoir and Eulogy of Volodimir* that are attributed to the monk James. *The Life of Boris and Gleb* appears in the *PVL* but in a redaction different from the independent work written by Nestor. Quotations in the *PVL* attributed to John Chrysostom seem to be drawn from the *Zlatoustruiu* (anthology of his writings). Subsequently two references are made in the *PVL* to the *Revelations of Pseudo-Methodius of Patara*. Various parts of the *PVL* draw on the *Paleia* (a synopsis of Old Testament history with interpretations).

In the entries for 1097 to 1100, there is a narrative of a certain Vasily who claims to have been an eyewitness and participant in the events being described. Volodimir Monomakh's *Testament* and *Letter to Oleg* appear toward the end of the text of the chronicle. Finally, oral traditions and legends seem to be the basis for a number of other accounts, including the coming of the Rus'.

Although the text of the *PVL* has been published a number of times including as part of the publication of later chronicles, only recently has a critical edition based on a *stemma codicum* been completed.

*See also:* BOOK OF DEGREES; CHRONICLES; KIEVAN RUS; RURIKID DYNASTY

**BIBLIOGRAPHY**

Cross, Samuel H., and Sherbowitz-Wetzor, Olgerd P. (1953). *The Russian Primary Chronicle: Laurentian Text.* Cambridge, MA: Mediaeval Academy of Sciences.

Ostrowski, Donald. (2003). *The Povest' vremennykh let: An Interlinear Collation and Paradosis*, 3 vols., assoc. ed. David J. Birnbaum (Harvard Library of Early Ukrainian Literature, vol. 10, parts 1–3). Cambridge, MA: Harvard University Press.

DONALD OSTROWSKI

# PRIMARY PARTY ORGANIZATION

Primary Party Organization (PPO) was the official name for the lowest-level organization in the structure of the Communist Party of the Soviet Union. PPOs were set up wherever there were at least three Party members, and every member of the Party was required to belong to one. PPOs existed in urban and rural areas, usually at Party members' places of work, such as factories, state and collective farms, army units, offices, schools, and universities. The highest organ of a PPO was the Party meeting, which was convened at least once per month and elected delegates to the Party conference at the raion or city level. In the larger PPOs, a bureau was elected for a term of up to one year to conduct day-to-day Party business. But if a PPO had fewer than fifteen members, they elected a secretary and deputy secretary rather than a bureau. Occupants of the post of PPO secretary or PPO bureau head had to have been Party members for at least a year. PPO secretaries were usually paid or released from their regular work if their cell included more than 150 Party members. Although the PPO may seem insignificant in comparison to the higher organs of the CPSU, it performed crucial political and economic functions, such as admitting new members; carrying out agitation and propaganda work (e.g., educating Party members in the principles of Marxism-Leninism), and ensuring that Party discipline was maintained. Finally, PPOs were vital to the fulfillment of Party objectives (e.g., meeting planned quotas and production targets).

*See also:* COMMUNIST PARTY OF THE SOVIET UNION

**BIBLIOGRAPHY**

Hill, Ronald J., and Frank, Peter. (1981). *The Soviet Communist Party.* London: George Allen & Unwin.

CHRISTOPHER WILLIAMS

# PRIME MINISTER

The prime minister (or premier) was the chief executive officer of the Soviet government. The position was formally known as the chairman of the Council of Ministers (also known as the Sovnarkom, 1917–1946, and the Cabinet of Ministers, 1990–1991). The prime minister led sessions of the Council of Ministers and the more exclusive and secretive Presidium of the Council of Ministers. The prime minister was charged with overall responsibility for managing the centrally planned command economy and overseeing the extensive public administration apparatus.

Representing one of the most powerful positions in the Soviet leadership hierarchy, the post of prime minister carried automatic full membership in the Politburo, the top executive body in the political system. The prime minister's seat was frequently the object of intense intra-party factional conflicts to control the economic policy agenda.

The Soviet Union's first prime minister was Bolshevik Party leader Vladimir Lenin, who chaired the Sovnarkom, the principal executive governing body at that time. Lenin, who was not fond of extended debates, began the practice of policy making through an inner circle of ministers. Following Lenin's death in 1924, the positions of government head and Party leader were formally separated from one another.

Alexei Rykov, an intellectual with economic expertise, was appointed prime minister, overseeing the administration of the mixed-market New Economic Policy (NEP). In the late 1920s, as party sentiment turned against the NEP, leadership contender Josef Stalin maneuvered to dislodge Rykov from this post. Next, Prime Minister Vyacheslav Molotov, a staunch ally of Stalin, presided over and spurred on the ambitious and tumultuous state-led industrialization and collectivization campaigns of the 1930s. In 1939, with war looming, Molotov was dispatched to the foreign ministry, and Stalin claimed the position, accumulating even greater personal power.

When Stalin died in 1953, it was deemed necessary once again to separate the posts of Party and government leadership. Georgy Malenkov, who had managed the wartime economy as de facto premier, was officially promoted to prime minister. Malenkov attempted the diversion of resources away from military industry to the consumer sector, but was forced to resign by political rivals. The prime minister's post was occupied next by Nikolai Bulganin, whose expertise lay in military matters. In 1958 Communist Party leader Nikita Khrushchev appointed himself prime minister, in violation of Party rules.

Following Khrushchev's removal in 1964, the prime minister's position became more routinized within the leadership hierarchy, though the Politburo had the last say on economic policy. As industry developed and the economy grew more complex, the responsibilities of the prime minister became increasingly technocratic, requiring greater command of economic issues and firsthand managerial experience. Prime ministers in the late Soviet period struggled unsuccessfully with the challenge of devising economic strategies to regenerate growth from the declining command economy.

Individuals holding the post of prime minister included: Vladimir Lenin (1917–1924), Alexei Rykov (1924–1929), Vyacheslav Molotov (1930–1939), Josef Stalin (1939–1953), Georgy Malenkov (1953–1955), Nikolai Bulganin (1955–1958), Nikita Khrushchev (1958–1964), Alexei Kosygin (1964–1980), Nikolai Tikhonov (1980–1985), Nikolai Ryzhkov (1985–1990), and Valentin Pavlov (1990–1991).

*See also:* COMMUNIST PARTY OF THE SOVIET UNION; COUNCIL OF MINISTERS, SOVIET; POLITBURO; SOVNARKOM

**BIBLIOGRAPHY**

Hough, Jerry, and Fainsod, Merle. (1979). *How the Soviet Union is Governed*, rev. ed. Cambridge, MA: Harvard University Press.

Rigby, T. H. *Lenin's Government: Sovnarkom, 1917–1922.* Cambridge, UK: Cambridge University Press.

GERALD M. EASTER

# PRIMITIVE SOCIALIST ACCUMULATION

Primitive Socialist Accumulation was a concept developed by the Soviet economist Yevgeny Preobrazhensky to analyze the New Economic Policy (NEP) of the 1920s.

Adam Smith and other classical economists referred to "previous" or "primitive" accumulation of capital to explain the rise of specialization of production and the division of labor. Specialized production required the prior accumulation of capital to support specialized workers until their products were ready for sale. Previous accumulation occurred though saving, and the return to capital represented the reward for saving. Karl Marx parodied this self-congratulatory thesis, arguing instead that primitive capitalist accumulation represented no more than "divorcing the producer [i.e., labor] from the means of production." It was the process of creating the necessary capitalist institutions: private monopoly ownership of the means of production and wage labor.

Preobrazhensky sought to develop a comparable concept for capital accumulation in the Soviet Union of the 1920s. The NEP meant that private small-scale capitalist enterprises, including peasant farms, coexisted with the state's control of the "commanding heights" of the economy. To attain socialism the socialized sector had to grow more rapidly than the private sector. Preobrazhensky therefore set about to determine what institutional relations were necessary to attain this end. Primitive socialist accumulation was his answer.

As for capitalist accumulation, force would need to be the agent of primitive socialist accumulation, and it was to be applied by the. revolutionary socialist state in the form of tax, price, and financial policies to expropriate the surplus value created in the private sector and transfer it to the socialist sector, thereby guaranteeing its differential growth. Under what he called "premature socialist conditions" that characterized the USSR,

Preobrazhensky recommended nonequivalent exchange, that is, the turning of the terms of trade against the peasantry and other private enterprises, as the main means to collect and transfer the surplus. During the transition, workers in socialist enterprises would experience "self-exploitation." Over time, therefore, primitive socialist accumulation would eliminate the private sector.

Although the concept appears to be consistent with Marx's use of it in the analysis of capitalism, Preobrazhensky's theory was roundly criticized by Nikolai Bukharin and other Bolshevik theorists, probably because he used the term "exploitation" in prescribing a socialist economic policy.

*See also:* MARXISM; NEW ECONOMIC POLICY; PREO-BRAZHENSKY, YEVGENY ALEXEYEVICH; SOCIALISM

**BIBLIOGRAPHY**

Erlich, Alexander. (1960). *The Soviet Industrialization Debate, 1921–1928.* Cambridge, MA: Harvard University Press.

Millar, James R. (1978). "A Note on Primitive Accumulation in Marx and Preobrazhensky." *Soviet Studies* 30(3):384–393.

Preobrazhensky, E. (1965). *The New Economics,* tr. Brian Pearce. Oxford: Oxford University Press.

JAMES R. MILLAR

## PRISONS

Up to the beginning of the nineteenth century monasteries and fortresses often served as prisons (*tyurma* from German turm = tower). The Russian prisons in about 1850 were mostly overcrowded wood buildings that had not been built for the purpose of the accommodation of prisoners, many of whom left the prisons with destroyed health. Russian authorities were more likely to use other forms of punishment, such as whipping and other corporal punishment for small offences and hard labor and exile to Siberia for serious crimes. As early as the eighteenth century there were fruitless attempts at prison reform. In 1845 the tsar compiled a new Code of Punishments that featured a hierarchy of incarcerations including preliminerary prisons, strait houses, correctional prisons, and punitive prisons. According to the model of the Pentonville Prison in England, the isolation of the prisoner was viewed as a condition for his improvement.

There was no uniform prison management. Supervision was exercised by the ministry of the interior (MVD), the Department of Justice, and the respective governors. The public prosecutor's office was responsible for the well being of the prisoners. The prison question became topical by the penal reform of April 17, 1863: Corporal punishment was deemed antiquated and prison sentences became more typical. Now for smaller offenses the punishment was up to seven days of custody. This reform led, therefore, to a quick increase of the prison population and chaos in management. In the 1860s and 1870s various committees dealt with reform of the prison system. In 1877 a newly formed committee called Grot petitioned for a new hierarchy of punishment with seven steps, from fines up to the death penalty. The prisoners were to be separated except for work details. It was suggested a Main Prison Administration (GTU) should be established within the Ministry of the Interior, to be

**The towers of a makeshift mosque and Russian Orthodox chapel are visible behind inmates at a prison colony in Udarny, Russia, 2001.** PHOTOGRAPH BY MAXIM MARMUR/ASSOCIATED PRESS. REPRODUCED BY PERMISSION.

**Prisoners eating in a cafeteria, Norilsk, Russia, July 1991.** © DAVID TURNLEY/CORBIS

responsible for all questions of the Russian prison system. The suggestions of the Grot committee became law on February 27, 1879. At this time there were about seven hundred prisons with a capacity of 54,253 inmates, but actually 70,488 persons were housed there. In the next few decades, significant efforts were undertaken in the repair of old prisons and the construction of new ones. Between 1879 and 1905, the GTU succeeded in improving the conditions in the Russian prisons, during which time, in 1895, the GTU was transferred from the MVD to the Department of Justice. As a result of the waves of arrests after the revolution of 1905, the number of prisoners doubled from 1906 to 1908. After the February 1917 revolution the GTU was renamed the Main Administration of Places of Incarceration (GUMZ), and many prisoners who had been granted amnesty were re-arrested.

In April 1918 the new People's Commissioner's Office for Justice (NKYu) dissolved the GUMZ and formed the Central Penal Department (TsKO). Soon there developed in parallel to the activity of the

NKYu a system of places of incarceration of the VChK (All-Russian Extraordinary Commission on Struggle against Counterrevolution, Sabotage and Speculation). In the prisons of the TsKO were housed the usual criminals; the VChK was responsible for putative and real opponents of the revolution. A principal purpose of prisons was the re-education of the delinquent; accordingly the TsKO was renamed the Central Working Improvement Department (TsITO) in October 1921. Hunger was common in TsITO facilities.

In early 1922 the VChK was integrated into the People's Commissioner's Office for Internal Affairs (NKVD). On July 1, 1922, the handing over of all places of incarceration from the NKYu to the NKVD was effected and the prison management was reorganized in the Main administration of Places of Incarceration (GUMZ NKVD). Additionally, the secret police (United State Political Administration, OGPU) had prisons under its jurisdiction. In the time of the Big Terror many prisoners were in the gulag. Under the new people's commissioner,

Beriya, all prisoners able to work were removed from the prisons; in the Soviet Union after Stalin relatively few were incarcerated.

On May 7, 1956, the MVD of the USSR issued regulations for inmates, distinguishing between a "general" and an "austere" regime, the latter for prison who systematically violated regulations. On October 8, 1997, the penal enforcement system was subordinated by an Ukas of the president of the Russian Federation, moving again to the Department of Justice, where a State Administration for the Penal Enforcement (GUIN) was founded. Regardless of jurisdiction, however, the prisons continue to receive inadequate funding and, as they were in 1850, continue to be overcrowded, with inmates often afflicted with communicable diseases.

*See also:* GULAG; LEFORTOVO; LUBYANKA; STATE SECURITY, ORGANS OF

**BIBLIOGRAPHY**

Adams, Bruce F. (1996). *The Politics of Punishment: Prison Reform in Russia 1863–1917.* DeKalb: Northern Illinois University Press.

GEORG WURZER

# PRISON SONGS

Given Russia's vast prison population, prison songs always constituted a considerable part of popular culture. Interestingly enough, in contemporary Russian prisons themselves, prison songs are not as popular as is commonly thought. As experienced prisoners explain, if the person likes to sing, he or she may receive the nickname "Tape recorder" and may be "turned on" at any moment, meaning that anyone may ask him or her to sing at any moment for someone's pleasure. This subordinate position brings down the status of the convict who thus cannot be very popular or prestigious. But in normal life outside of prison, these songs acquired tremendous popularity starting from the second half of the twentieth century.

Contemporary prison songs originate from the older traditions of the sixteenth through nineteenth centuries, such as brigand songs of those in active opposition to the state and social authorities,

drawling songs of hard–labor convicts, and thieves' cant as a creature of urban environment closely related to the genre of city romance. The latter became widespread at the turn of the twentieth century due to rapid social changes and marginalization of Russian society in the years of the Revolution. The most popular song of the period, *Murka*, tells a dramatic story of an undercover policewoman killed by her criminal lover for her betrayal.

From the second half of the twentieth century, prison songs occupied a leading position in Soviet underground culture. In the 1960s the most popular bards, such as Vladimir Vysotsky, Alexander Galich, and others, attracted intelligentsia by singing prison songs, thus giving a form of expression of hidden protest against the regime. In their songs prison is associated with the state as a whole; it is implied that under this regime everone is a convict, whether past, present, or future. Rich metaphorical content, antistate motivation, and strong heroic poetics made these songs the sign of the time when the truth about the regime became known with gulag prisoners first being rehabilitated after Stalin's death. This tradition stems from the political, not the criminal, environment and was closely connected to the dissident movement of the time.

In contrast to the dissident content of prison songs of the 1960s and 1970s, contemporary prison songs emphasize the criminal element more and are targeted at a specific audience with a clear criminal past and present. Recently these songs successfully entered the popular music industry. These songs are based on the most popular genre of contemporary prison folklore such as ballads. Most of them are "humble" songs: They aim at compassion for the lot of any marginal personality, such as thieves, prostitute, and social outcasts. Their subject is misery, tragic accident, or cruel destiny. Several verses of the ballad cover the entire life of the hero with its happiness, tears, love and betrayal, crime, and custody. Another type of song, by contrast, aims to unite people who share asocial values as a group claiming brotherhood and heroism of a few against conventional authorities.

*See also:* DISSIDENT MOVEMENT; GULAG; PRISONS

**BIBLIOGRAPHY**

Stites, Richard. (1992). *Russian Popular Culture: Entertainment and Society since 1900.* New York: Cambridge University Press.

JULIA ULYANNIKOVA

# PRIVATIZATION

Privatization may be pursued with different aims in mind. The *political* aim is to break away from the past and create a new class of capitalists as quickly as possible. The *efficiency* aim is to create a better management system for the enterprises, and to set up a market environment. If this aim is dominant, it requires complex institution-building and thus precludes rapid completion of the process. Privatization may have a *financial* aim: in this case the state-owned enterprises (SOEs) should be sold at their highest value so as to bring revenues to the state. Finally, an *equity* aim may involve returning property to those who had been deprived of it by the nationalization process (an aim pursued in some Central European countries), giving priority to employees for buying shares in their enterprises, or even giving away state assets to the citizens.

In Russia, privatization began in January 1992, together with the implementation of the stabilization program, and assumed the form of liberalization of small-scale trade (street vending). This "small privatization" was conducted at a quick pace in the services sector, which consisted of trade, catering, services to households, construction, individual transportation activities, and housing. It was often marred by racketeering and crime. The small-scale state enterprises (which had already been transferred to the local authorities in 1991) were sold to citizens, local entrepreneurs, and/or employees, basically through auctions. At the same time, as prices and individual activities were liberalized, it became immediately possible to create new, small-scale businesses, especially in fields where human capital was the main requirement, such as consulting, engineering, private teaching, and computer services. Actually, such activities were already privately conducted in the Soviet era within the shadow economy.

The main challenge lay in the privatization of the big SOEs, or *large-scale privatization*. The Russian government was clearly privileging the political objective, and hence opted for a quick mass privatization scheme. It also favored equity considerations, so that the people would benefit from the divestment of the state. In June 1992, the mass privatization program was adopted, and in October the voucher system was launched. All Russian citizens received 10,000 rubles' worth of privatization vouchers (equivalent then to 50 U.S. dollars), immediately redeemable in cash, or exchangeable against shares in the enterprises selected for privatization that had been transformed into joint stock companies. These enterprises were sold at direct public auctions. The staff (employees and management) could opt for three variants, of which the most popular was the allocation of 51 percent of the shares to the employees at a discounted price. Seventy percent of the enterprises were thus privatized by the end of June 1994; past this deadline the vouchers were no longer valid. The second wave of large-scale privatization proceeded much more slowly and was far from complete in 2002. It had to be based upon sales to foreigners or domestic buyers. It was slowed by several factors: the Russian financial crisis of 1998, which led to a collapse of the banking sector; the scandals linked with the outcomes of the first wave, when several notorious deals evidenced the dominant role of insiders who managed to acquire large assets with very little cash; and, finally, the enormous stakes of the second wave, which involved privatization of the energy sector (oil, gas, and electricity) and the telecommunications sector.

Who owned the Russian enterprises? The most prominent owners were the oligarchs, who controlled the largest firms of the energy and raw materials sector, but who became less powerful after Boris Yeltsin's resignation in 1999. More generally, the former *nomenklatura* of the Soviet system, along with a small number of newcomers, took advantage of a privatization process lacking transparency and clear legal rules. Restructuring of enterprises and improving of corporate governance did not proceed along with the change in ownership. Privatization was close to completion in Russia as of 2002, when 75 percent of the GDP was created by the private sector. However, the private sector had yet to function according to the rules of a transparent market.

*See also:* ECONOMY, POST-SOVIET; LIBERALISM; SHOCK THERAPY; TRANSITION ECONOMIES.

## BIBLIOGRAPHY

Boycko, Maxim; Shlejfer, Andrei; and Vishny, Robert. (1995). *Privatizing Russia*. Cambridge, MA: MIT Press.

European Bank for Reconstruction and Development (EBRD). (1999). *Transition Report 1999: Ten Years of Transition*. London: EBRD.

Hedlund, Stefan. (2001). "Property Without Rights: Dimensions of Russian Privatisation." *Europe-Asia Studies* 53(2):213–237.

MARIE LAVIGNE

# PROCURACY

The prosecutor's office in the Russian Federation plays a pivotal role in law enforcement, including criminal investigations and prosecution, representation of the state's interests in civil disputes, supervision of the functioning of prisons and places of detention, and investigation of citizens' grievances.

The Procuracy was introduced in 1722 by Peter the Great in an effort to create a public law system similar to those in Western Europe. However, in practice, the Procuracy focused primarily on supervising the prompt and full execution of the tsar's edicts. Catherine II extended procuratorial supervision to regional and local levels, where procurators served as the "eyes of the tsar" in monitoring the activity of provincial governors and other officials. This function was widely resented by provincial governors and was eliminated by the legal reforms of 1864.

A decree of November 24, 1917, of the Council of People's Commissars abolished the Procuracy and all other tsarist legal institutions in favor of more informal control mechanisms. In 1922 the Bolshevik government reestablished the Procuracy to serve as the "eyes of the state," insuring full and complete cooperation in executing the policies of the state and the Communist Party.

During the Stalin era the Procuracy, under the leadership of Procurator-General Andrei Vyshinsky, aggressively pursued suspected opponents of Stalin's regime and secured their speedy imprisonment or execution. The Procuracy's jurisdiction was also extended to non-legal matters, such as overseeing the successful implementation of industrialization and collectivization.

After Stalin's death in 1953, the Procuracy shifted its emphasis from coercion and repression to prosecuting ordinary criminals and supervising legality in the operations of various governmental agencies. The Procuracy grew in power and prestige during the post-Stalin period. By the 1980s it employed more than 18,000 lawyers and supervised an additional 18,000 criminal investigators; together they comprised more than one-quarter of the Soviet Union's legal profession.

Prosecutors were slow in responding to Gorbachev's reforms, viewing them as a threat to their wide-ranging authority. The Procuracy managed to defend its privileged position in the Russian legal system even after the demise of the USSR. A

new "Law on the Procuracy of the Russian Federation" was enacted in 1995. The law enshrined the Procuracy as a single, unified, and centralized institution charged with "supervising the implementation of laws by local legislative and executive bodies, administrative control organs, legal entities, public organizations, and officials, as well as the lawfulness of their acts." While the Procuracy's jurisdiction remained broad, it lost power to supervise the operation of the courts, which was transferred to the Ministry of Justice.

The powers of the Procuracy have been further restricted by the new criminal procedure code, which was enacted in July 2002. According to the code, prosecutors may no longer issue search warrants or order suspects to be detained. In addition, prosecutors must appear in court to present the state's case, rather than rely on an extensive dossier compiled during the preliminary investigation. These and other restrictions were undertaken to limit the Procuracy's privileged status in criminal prosecutions, engender a more adversarial process, and elevate the status and independence of the courts.

*See also:* LEGAL SYSTEMS

**BIBLIOGRAPHY**

Mikhailovskaya, Inga. (1999). "The Procuracy and Its Problems." *East European Constitutional Review* 11:1–2.

Smith, Gordon B. (1978). *The Soviet Procuracy and the Supervision of Administration.* Alphen aan den Rijn, Netherlands: Sijthoff & Noordhoff.

Smith, Gordon B. (1996). *Reforming the Russian Legal System.* New York: Cambridge University Press.

GORDON B. SMITH

# PRODNALOG

"Food Tax."

The word *prodnalog* comes from the nouns "food" (*prodovolstvie*) and "tax" (*nalog*). It is translated as "food tax," or "tax in kind." The food tax was an instrument of state policy to collect food and was used twice during the Soviet period. The first introduction of the food tax was in 1921, during the period of the New Economic Policy (NEP). During the period of war communism (1918–1921), the Soviet state used forced requisitions to confiscate food from peasant households. As a result of forced requisitions, peasants reduced the acreage they cultivated and the volume of food they produced. The food they produced was often hidden from the state, so the net result was national famine and starvation in the cities, which in turn led to massive de-urbanization from 1918 to 1920.

In March 1921, with the introduction of the New Economic Plan (NEP), the Communist Party changed its strategy toward the peasantry and adopted a food tax, replacing food requisitions. The food tax specified target quotas of food that were to be delivered to the state. After the delivery quota was met, any food grown by the peasantry could be used as desired—for sale through legalized private channels, for livestock, or for consumption. Delivery quotas for the food tax were established well below the levels of forced confiscation, thereby lessening the burden on peasants, providing them stability in their calculations, and giving them incentives to produce as much as they could. The result was a rebound in agricultural production by the mid-1920s. In 1924 the food tax was replaced by a monetary tax on peasant households.

The second usage of the food tax occurred in 1991. Once again, the stimulus was the state's inability to obtain sufficient food for the urban population. In 1991 the government of the Russian Republic adopted a food tax that was to be fulfilled in addition to the state order (goszakaz). The size of the state order averaged around 30 percent of production, and the food tax added another 40 percent. The tax was assessed on state and collective farms and other agricultural enterprises. Newly created peasant farms were exempt from the food tax. In order to enforce this tax, penalties for noncompliance consisted of monetary fines, or the withholding of fuel, machinery, and other needed inputs. However, as Communist Party strength diminished in the countryside and throughout society in 1991, penalties for noncompliance were often absent, and the food tax was not successful. It was abolished in 1992.

See also: AGRICULTURE; NEW ECONOMIC POLICY; PRODRAZVERSTKA

**BIBLIOGRAPHY**

Carr, Edward Hallet. (1952). *A History of Soviet Russia: The Bolshevik Revolution, 1917–1923,* vol. 2. New York: Macmillan.

Medvedev, Zhores A. (1987). *Soviet Agriculture.* New York: W. W. Norton.

Nove, Alec. (1982). *An Economic History of the USSR.* New York: Penguin.

STEPHEN K. WEGREN

## PRODRAZVERSTKA

Grain requisitions from peasant households by the Soviet state during the period of war communism (1918–1921). These grain requisitions were compulsory, although official policy stated that food deliveries were to come from peasant surpluses of food. In reality, state policy took two main forms: very low prices paid to peasants for their grain, so that the requisition essentially amounted to confiscation; or outright confiscation of all the grain possessed by the peasantry, with no payment. The policy of grain requisition was used as an instrument of class warfare in the countryside, setting poor and middle peasants against rich peasants, the so-called kulaks. The policy of prodrazverstka was bitterly opposed by the vast majority of peasants and led to widespread violence in the countryside against the committees of poor peasants (kombedy) that worked for the Soviet state to seize grain that was being hoarded by peasant households. In response to the confiscation of their grain, peasant households drastically reduced the acreage cultivated and the amount of grain produced, which led to mass starvation and famine throughout the nation.

Grain requisitions were replaced with a food tax during the period of the New Economic Policy (1921–1928). However, prodrazverstka was reintroduced during the collectivization drive of the 1930s and expanded to include not only grains but other food commodities as well. The policy of food requisitions became an integral part of the planned economy, evolving into a system of state orders (goszakazy) in which state and collective farms were required to sell defined volumes of their production to state procurement agents, such as state-owned food processors, at state-regulated prices. State orders remained in effect until the end of the Soviet Union.

See also: AGRICULTURE; PEASANTRY; PRODNALOG

**BIBLIOGRAPHY**

Carr, Edward Hallet. (1952). *A History of Soviet Russia: The Bolshevik Revolution, 1917–1923,* vol. 2. New York: Macmillan.

Medvedev, Zhores A. (1987). *Soviet Agriculture*. New York: Norton.

Nove, Alec. (1982). *An Economic History of the USSR*. New York: Penguin.

STEPHEN K. WEGREN

## PRODUCTION SHARING AGREEMENT

A Production Sharing Agreement is made between two or more independent enterprises and/or government agencies that specifies the way in which and for what period of time the signatories will share in the output of a particular commodity.

The production sharing agreement (PSA) offers an alternative to the joint venture as a way for two or more economic entities to collaborate on the development and production of a commodity. Russian officials and business entrepreneurs have been reluctant to allow foreign firms to acquire direct ownership and managerial control over domestic resources and firms. The Russian government has also been reluctant to privatize valuable domestic resources completely, especially with respect to oil and gas reserves and companies. The PSA is the principal way for foreign firms to invest in Russia and for the Russian government to maintain a degree of control over valuable resources. Under a standard form of PSA, the entity that invests in a development project is the first to capture the investment from revenues generated by the forthcoming output.

The Russian Duma has been reluctant to condone foreign ownership, or, in some cases, even foreign participation in the economy. Legislation governing PSAs was not passed in the Duma until late 1998 under the government of Yevgeny Primakov. In certain fields PSAs must be approved by the Duma. In the oil and gas industries, the PSA is the single most important form of collaboration between the government and the oil companies and with foreign oil and gas companies as well.

*See also:* FOREIGN TRADE; PRIMAKOV, YEVGENY MAXIMOVICH

### BIBLIOGRAPHY
Gregory, Paul R., and Stuart, Robert C. (2001). *Russian and Soviet Economic Performance and Structure*. New York: Addison-Wesley.

JAMES R. MILLAR

## PROKOFIEV, SERGEI SERGEYEVICH

(1891–1953), composer and pianist, one of the most important figures of the early Russian modernism, later of Socialist Realism.

Sergei Sergeyevich Prokofiev studied at the Petersburg conservatory from 1904 to 1914. By 1915 he was already one of the outstanding figures of modern Russian music. In his early works, Prokofiev employed new modes of expression while audibly referring to the musical language of the late nineteenth century. Prokofiev followed various stylistic courses. He was known as a radical exponent of provocative new music and also distinguished himself through his neoclassical experiments. Later he would be known precisely for his synthesis of the unusual and the familiar, of complexity and simplicity, of constructive rationality and melodious emotionalism.

In 1918, hoping for greater artistic perspectives, Prokofiev left Russia for the United States. After mixed experiences there, he left in 1922 to settle in Paris. Prokofiev was not a "classical" emigrant: He assumed Soviet citizenship in 1924 and often travelled to the Soviet Union to give concerts. Finally, in 1936, the artist returned to Russia with his family. His decision can be attributed to a deep longing for his home country, a diffuse sympathy for the political developments there, a marked interest in the privileged position of an exceptional artist in the Soviet state, and a sense of invulnerability. It was not difficult for Prokofiev to fulfil the ideological standards of "Socialist Realism," given the melodious simplicity of his work. He had long ago given up his futuristic inclinations and instead tried to realize a new rhythmic-motoric, tonally tense, poignant style. Yet in 1948 even Prokofiev was severely criticized by the Soviet government, which perceived "formalistic distortions and anti-democratic tendencies" in the works of leading Soviet composers. Prokofiev criticized himself, and until his death (on the same day as Stalin's) he attempted to reconcile his own stylistic conceptions with the party line.

*See also:* MUSIC; SOCIALIST REALISM

### BIBLIOGRAPHY
Jaffé, Daniel. (1998). *Sergey Prokofiev*. London: Phaidon.

Robinson, Harlow L. (1987). *Sergei Prokofiev: A Biography*. New York: Viking.

MATTHIAS STADELMANN

## PROKOPOVICH, FEOFAN

(1681–1736), prelate, philosopher, writer, and liaison between the Russian Orthodox Church and Protestantism.

Born to a merchant family in Kiev but orphaned early, Feofan received an education at the Kiev Academy, one of the few institutions for ecclesiastical education at the time. Like other gifted students of the time, he nominally converted to the Uniate (Eastern Catholic) faith in order to qualify for studies in Rome—in his case, at a Jesuit institution, the College of St. Athanasius. In 1701 he left Rome, imbued with a profound animosity toward Catholicism and, his critics would later charge, uncritical fondness for Protestantism. In any case, in 1702 he returned to Kiev with an exceptionally strong training in philosophy and theology. After repudiating his Catholic faith of convenience, he embarked on a brilliant career in the Russian Orthodox Church. He first made his mark at the Kiev Academy, where he became not only its rector but also a prolific writer, his works including a five-act "tragicomedy" *Vladimir* that ridiculed paganism and superstition. In 1709, in the presence of Peter, he delivered a sermon celebrating the Russian victory at Poltava; such perorations caught the emperor's eye, earned him a summons to St. Petersburg, and led to his elevation to the episcopate (first in 1718 as the bishop of Pskov, and then in 1720 as archbishop of Novgorod).

During these years Feofan became one of Peter's more erudite ideologists and propagandists. Drawing upon European political theory and exalting the just and creative power of the ruler, Feofan was a principal architect of Peter's new conception of dynamic autocracy. Feofan played a key role in composing a number of state documents, from the "Preface" to the *Naval Charter* (1719) to the famous *Truth about the Monarch's Will* (1722), defending Peter's right—and duty—to override custom and designate the most qualified person as his successor. Feofan also served as a key liaison with the Protestant world, reinforcing the suspicions of contemporaries and impelling Orthodox historians to dismiss him as a mere "Protestant." By far his most important work was the *Ecclesiastical Regulation* (1721), drafted at Peter's behest. Significantly, this critical document—which served as the institutional charter of the Russian Church until 1917—contained much more than a mere justification of Peter's decision to replace the patriarchate with a collegial board (first called the

Spiritual College but renamed the Holy Synod). Namely, the *Ecclesiastical Regulation* adumbrated an ambitious program to bring enlightenment and extinguish superstition in the Church, chiefly by improving ecclesiastical administration, establishing seminaries to educate parish clergy, and extirpating superstition among the laity. Feofan played a key role in the new Synodal administration and, simultaneously, authored several important works, including a treatise on the patriarchate, a catechism, and a tract critical of monasticism.

Peter's death in 1725 initially left Feofan vulnerable to a concerted attack by conservatives, but in 1730 the astute prelate once again gained favor by siding with the new monarch, Anna, against a coterie of magnates seeking to limit her authority. He thus enjoyed considerable influence in church affairs until his death on September 8, 1736.

*See also:* HOLY SYNOD; PETER I; PROTESTANTISM

**BIBLIOGRAPHY**

Cracraft, James. (1973). "Feofan Prokopovichy." In *The Eighteenth Century in Russia*, ed. J. G. Garrard. Oxford: Clarendon.

Cracraft, James. (1975). "Feofan Prokopovich: A Bibliography of His Works." *Oxford Slavonic Papers* 8:1–36.

Della Cava, Olha. (1971). "Feofan Prokopovich: His Life and His Sermons, 1681–1736." Ph.D. diss. Columbia University, New York.

GREGORY L. FREEZE

## PROLETKULT

An acronym for "proletarian cultural-educational organizations," Proletkult was a loosely structured cultural organization that first took shape in Petrograd (now St. Petersburg) a few days before the Bolshevik Revolution in 1917. It began as a loose coalition of clubs, factory committees, workers' theaters, and educational societies devoted to the cultural needs of the working class. By 1918, when the organization held its first organizational conference under Soviet power, it had expanded into a national movement with a much more ambitious purpose: to define a unique proletarian culture that would inform and inspire revolutionary Russian society.

The Proletkult's most important theorist was a left-wing Bolshevik intellectual named Alexander

Bogdanov. Before the Bolshevik Revolution, Bogdanov emerged as an articulate critic of Vladimir Lenin. Bogdanov contended that in order for a proletarian revolution to succeed, the working class had to develop its own ideology and proletarian intelligentsia to take and wield power. His insistence on working-class autonomy put him at odds with Lenin's interpretation of revolutionary change. Bogdanov's influence was clearly evident in the Proletkult's political stance; its leaders insisted that the organization remain separate from government cultural agencies and the Communist Party.

At its peak in the fall of 1920, the Proletkult claimed a mass following of almost half a million people spread over three hundred local groups. These figures must be viewed with caution because they cannot be verified by existing records. Moreover, they imply a kind of cohesion that the organization did not possess during the chaotic years of the Russian civil war (1917–1922), when the Bolshevik regime was fought for its survival. Certainly, not all participants understood that they were supposed to be creating original forms of proletarian culture. Probably even fewer were aware of the national leadership's demand for independence from the Soviet state and Communist Party.

Much of the organization's work during the Civil War continued the activities of prerevolutionary adult education schools called People's Homes (narodnye doma) and people's universities. Proletkult participants took part in literacy and foreign language classes, as well as lectures on current events and recent scientific achievements. They also attended musical concerts, plays, and readings offered by professional artists. In addition, the organization sponsored classes in music, literature, and the visual arts. A number of important artists from middle- and upper-class backgrounds took part in the Proletkult's many workshops, including the symbolist writer Andrew Bely, and the avant-garde painter Olga Rozanova. Some came for the salary and rations that teaching positions provided. Others found a sympathetic environment for artistic experimentation. The future film director Sergei Eisenstein, for example, transformed the First Workers' Theater in Moscow into one of the nation's most inventive stages.

Proletkult studios nurtured new talent, such as the actress Judith Glizer, who went on to a very successful theatrical and film career. However, the best-known proletarian artists associated with the Proletkult had already begun their creative work before the Revolution. Writers were particularly prevalent. The poetry, plays, and stories of authors such as Vladimir Kirillov, Michael Gerasimov, and Paul Bessalko formed the creative center of Proletkult publications. Eventually they left the organization to form an influential writers' circle called The Smithy (Kuznitsy), which was an important contributor to debates on the place of art in Soviet society during the 1920s.

Although much of the Proletkult's work was on a rudimentary educational level, its demands for autonomy put it on a collision course with the Communist Party. In December 1920, Lenin issued a devastating critique of the organization, attacking not only its independence but also the very idea of a unique proletarian culture. In short order, the Proletkult was made into a subsection of the governmental cultural agency, the Commissariat of Enlightenment. In an attempt to stabilize the economy after the conclusion of the Civil War, the government slashed funds for all cultural projects. These steps drastically reduced the organization's size and influence.

During the 1920s, the Proletkult continued to operate on a small scale in Moscow, Leningrad, and a few provincial cities. In the creative arts, it was overshadowed by newer professional organizations, such as the Proletarian Writers' Union, which claimed to represent workers' cultural interests. Instead, the organization invested most of its energy in providing services to trade union clubs. During the First Five-Year Plan (1928–1932), it saw a brief period of growth. However, in April 1932, the Communist Party summarily closed down the Proletkult along with all other cultural associations that assumed special ties to workers. From now on, the Communist Party decreed, Soviet artistic works had to appeal to all social classes, not just the proletariat. The Proletkult's final demise marked an important step on the path to socialist realism.

See also: CULTURAL REVOLUTION; LENIN, VLADIMIR ILLICH

## BIBLIOGRAPHY

Fitzpatrick, Sheila. (1970). The Commissariat of Enlightenment: Soviet Organization of Education and the Arts Under Lunacharsky, October 1917–1921. Cambridge, UK: Cambridge University Press.

Mally, Lynn. (1990). Culture of the Future: The Proletkult Movement in Revolutionary Russia. Berkeley: University of California Press.

Sochor, Zenovia A. (1988). *Revolution and Culture: The Bogdanov-Lenin Controversy*. Ithaca, NY: Cornell University Press.

Steinberg, Mark D. (2002). *Proletarian Imagination: Self, Modernity, and the Sacred in Russia, 1910–1925*. Ithaca, NY: Cornell University Press.

LYNN MALLY

## PROPP, VLADIMIR IAKOVLEVICH

(1895–1970), folklorist, best known for *Morphology of the Folktale*, a structuralist analysis and fundamental work on the theory of narrative.

Vladimir Iakovlevich Propp was born and educated in St. Petersburg, where he received a degree in philology. After teaching Russian and German for a short time, he concentrated exclusively on folklore, chairing the Folklore Department of Leningrad State University from 1863 to 1964.

*Morphology of the Folktale* (1928) was an attempt to reduce all folktales to one structure. Dissatisfied with the classification system in the *Aarne-Thompson Tale Type Index*, Propp proposed a different tale unit, a plot element he called the function. He found that all the tales in Alexander N. Afanasev's *Russkie narodnye skazki* (Russian fairy tales) had the same thirty-one functions appearing in the same order, and that the actors in the tales could be reduced to a dramatis personae of seven. *Morphology of the Folktale* became known in the West through Claude Lévi-Strauss, who criticized Propp's construct and favored a different approach, and Alan Dundes, who showed that it applied beyond European tales.

Propp's next book, *The Historical Roots of the Magic Tale* (1946), sought to show that folktales originated in ritual, especially initiation and funeral rites. In 1948, along with other Soviet scholars, Propp came under official attack. His *Morphology* was criticized for being too formalist, and his *Historical Roots* was said to be too dependent on Western scholarship and too willing to place Russian narrative in a global context. While he was never arrested and retained his university position, Propp shifted his focus, and his *Russian Heroic Epic* (1958) is a more Marxist interpretation, linking epic to stages of socioeconomic development. In his final major work, *Russian Agrarian Holidays* (1963), Propp returned to his earlier methodology and elucidated common elements in calendrical ritual.

*See also:* FOLKLORE

**BIBLIOGRAPHY**
Propp, Vladimir. (1975). *Morphology of the Folktale*, 2nd ed., tr. Laurence Scott, ed. Louis A. Wagner. Austin: University of Texas Press.

Propp, Vladimir. (1984). *Theory and History of Folklore*, tr. Ariadna Y. Martin and Richard P. Martin, ed. Anatoly Liberman. Minneapolis: University of Minnesota Press.

NATALIE O. KONONENKO

## PROSTITUTION

Until the mid-eighteenth century, Russian authorities treated prostitution as a crime against morality and public decorum, and enacted laws and decrees to keep prostitutes invisible and isolated. Nevertheless, contemporary observers often remarked the presence of prostitutes in Moscow and, by the early eighteenth century, in the new capital of St. Petersburg. In the late 1700s prostitutes became regarded more as sources of venereal disease, and policies changed accordingly. The first attempts to reduce the medical danger associated with prostitutes took place during the reign of Catherine the Great, with the designation of a hospital in St. Petersburg for their confinement.

The nineteenth century brought the rise of a system of medical and police regulation to control prostitutes in terms of both their public behavior and the threat they represented to public health. In 1843 Tsar Nicholas I's minister of internal affairs subjected prostitution to surveillance based on a European model of inscription, inspection, and incarceration. Ministry guidelines called for licensing brothels, registering streetwalkers, regular medical examinations for women identified as prostitutes, and compulsory hospitalization for those apparently suffering from venereal disease. Prostitution remained officially illegal, but the ministry's regulations superseded the law so long as prostitutes registered their trade and brothels were under police supervision. Thus, medical-police regulation was in place even before Russia's serfs had been emancipated and before Russia's cities grew in response to policies promoting industrialization in the late nineteenth century.

At the turn of the twentieth century, Russia's burgeoning civil society considered both prostitution and its regulation major social and political problems. Physicians, jurists, feminists, socialists, temperance advocates, philanthropists, and elected local authorities seized on this issue to advance their political agendas and to aid working-class women. Nonetheless, despite charges that regulation fostered police corruption, oppressed women from the lower classes, and made little sense in light the lack of an effective cure for venereal diseases and the lack of controls over prostitutes' clients, medical-police surveillance remained official policy until the Provisional Government that emerged in February 1917 declared its abolition. The Bolsheviks also rejected regulation, heeding its critics and, like other socialist theorists, considering prostitution a transient symptom of industrial capitalism.

Prostitution, however, did not disappear during the Soviet era; it remained a viable source of income and favors. During the Civil War of 1917–1922, authorities were known to treat prostitutes as "labor deserters," but a more laissez-faire attitude emerged during the New Economic Policy (NEP, 1921–1928), with its toleration of private trade. Under the presumption that prostitutes could be rehabilitated through manual labor, the Soviet government dispatched former prostitutes to sanitariums and made a distinction between prostitutes, who were regarded as victims, and other individuals who profited from the sex trade. Yet authorities still associated prostitutes with disease and disorder; repression became the practice once NEP ended. Soviet officials claimed that prostitution disappeared, but it simply went underground, prosecuted under categories pertaining to labor desertion and illegal income.

Not until the 1980s, during the relative openness of Mikhail Gorbachev's tenure, was prostitution again acknowledged as a social problem. Economic instability, persistent gender inequality, and prostitution's attraction as a source of income all combined to increase the numbers of prostitutes in late- and post-Soviet Russia. Correspondingly, some municipal authorities resurrected regulation, presuming that it would prevent the spread of AIDS and other sexually transmitted diseases.

*See also:* FEMINISM; GLASNOST

**BIBLIOGRAPHY**
Bernstein, Laurie. (1995). *Sonia's Daughters: Prostitutes and Their Regulation in Imperial Russia.* Berkeley: University of California Press.

Engel, Barbara Alpern. (1989). "St. Petersburg Prostitutes in the Late Nineteenth Century: A Personal and Social Profile." *Russian Review* 48:21–44.

Engelstein, Laura. (1988). "Gender and the Juridical Subject: Prostitution and Rape in Nineteenth-Century Russian Criminal Codes." *Journal of Modern History* 60:458–495.

Healey, Dan. (2001). "Masculine Purity and 'Gentlemen's Mischief': Sexual Exchange and Prostitution between Russian Men, 1861–1941." *Slavic Review* 60:233–265.

Stites, Richard. (1983). "Prostitute and Society in Pre-Revolutionary Russia." *Jahrbücher für Geschichte Osteuropas* 31:348–364.

LAURIE BERNSTEIN

## PROTAZANOV, YAKOV ALEXANDROVIC

(1881–1945), film director.

A highly successful moviemaker both before and after the revolutions of 1917, Yakov Alexandrovich Protazanov began his career in 1907 as an actor and scriptwriter, becoming a director in 1911. In 1913 he and Vladimir Gardin co-directed the biggest box-office sensation of early Russian cinema, *The Keys to Happiness,* based on Anastasia Verbitskaya's best-selling novel.

Protazanov was the master of the cinematic melodrama. While he preferred to adapt his screenplays from popular literature, he also scored major hits with classics like *War and Peace* (1915), *The Queen of Spades* (1916), and *Father Sergius* (1918). His last Russian "sensation" before he emigrated to France in 1920 was *Satan Triumphant* (1917), which Soviet critics considered the epitome of bourgeois decadence.

Protazanov quickly established himself in the West and made six pictures before he returned to Soviet Russia in 1923. He worked for Mezhrabpom-Rus, a quasi-independent company that focused on profits as well as politics. Protazanov's skillfully made, highly entertaining, and superficially politicized blockbusters gave the studio the profits it needed to support the more revolutionary (but less profitable) work of young Soviet filmmakers like Vsevolod Pudovkin.

Protazanov's most important Soviet movies were *Aelita* (1924), *His Call* (1925), *The Tailor from Torzhok* (1925), *The Case of the Three Million* (1926), *The Forty-First* (1927), and *Don Diego and Pelageia*

(1928). Throughout the 1920s, Protazanov displayed a finely tuned talent for social satire. He also introduced talented actors such as Nikolai Batalov, Igor Ilinsky, Anatoly Ktorov, and Yulia Solntseva to the Soviet screen.

Satire was definitely out of favor in the political climate of the 1930s. In the final decade of his long career in the movies, Protazanov marshalled his skills as an actor's director to make "realist" movies, returning to the classics for his most notable success, *Without a Dowry* (1937). Protazanov's history is one of the more remarkable survival tales in Soviet cinema.

*See also:* MOTION PICTURES; VERBITSKAYA, ANASTASIA ALEXEYEVNA

**BIBLIOGRAPHY**

Youngblood, Denise J. (1992). *Movies for the Masses: Popular Cinema and Soviet Society in the 1920s.* Cambridge, UK: Cambridge University Press.

Youngblood, Denise J. (1999). *The Magic Mirror: Moviemaking in Russia, 1908–1918.* Madison: University of Wisconsin Press.

DENISE J. YOUNGBLOOD

# PROTESTANTISM

Protestantism originally derived from the sixteenth-century Reformation movement begun in western Europe by Martin Luther and John Calvin.

The Reformation, the movement that gave rise to Protestantism, was particular to western Christendom. Russia, as a part of eastern Orthodox Christendom, never experienced an analogous development. Consequently Protestantism in Russia was an imported phenomenon rather than an indigenous product.

Two forms of Protestantism in Russia can be identified. The older form was introduced to Russia by European non-Russian ethnic groups. A later form emerged in the nineteenth century when ethnically Slavic people embraced teachings of European Protestants. Converts to the older form comprised people who moved at various times from Europe to Russia or who were conquered by Russian western expansion. Converts to the later form derived from missionary activity among Russians in the aftermath of the Alexandrine reforms of the mid-nineteenth century that produced groups who were variously called Shtundists, Baptists, Evangelical Christians, Adventists, and, in the twentieth century, Pentecostals.

Protestantism entered Muscovy during the reign of Ivan IV. Initially viewing Protestants favorably, the tsar permitted building two Protestant churches, one Lutheran and one Calvinist, in Moscow. But he came to view Protestantism as heretical and in 1579 ordered both churches destroyed. Protestantism was relegated to an enclave outside the city that came to be known as the "German suburb."

Russia's Protestant population grew in the eighteenth century when Russia conquered Estonia and Latvia, where many Lutherans lived, and when German colonists of Lutheran and Mennonite persuasions settled in south Russia at the invitation of Catherine II. In the first quarter of the nineteenth century, Protestant notions received some high-level support from Emperor Alexander I, who was fascinated with German pietism.

Only in the aftermath of the abolition of serfdom did Protestantism win substantial adherents within the Slavic population of Russia. This was the result of preaching activity—in St. Petersburg by the English Lord Radstock and in the Caucasus by Baltic Baptists—and of the influence of German colonists in the Ukraine. Russian Protestantism was institutionalized in the Russian Baptist Union in 1884. The official response to this development was expressed in harsh persecution predicated on Chief Procurator Konstantin Pobedonostev's declaration, "there are not, and there cannot be, any Russian Baptists."

Protestants benefited from the tsarist declaration of religious tolerance of 1905 and even more from the Bolshevik declaration of separation of church and state of 1917. By 1929 there were up to one million Protestants in the Soviet Union, less than 1 percent of the population.

Communist antireligious policy limited legal protestant activity between 1929 and 1989 to one formally recognized structure, the All-Union Council of Evangelical Christians-Baptists (AUCECB), and scattered autonomous congregations of such denominations as Lutherans and Methodists, primarily in the Baltic republics, and German Baptists in Siberia. AUCECB claimed to comprise five thousand protestant congregations.

After 1991, Protestants expanded their activity within Russian society. At the end of 2000 the Russian Ministry of Justice reported that there were about 3,800 officially registered Protestant congregations in Russia, out of more than 20,000 religious organizations in the Russian Federation. These included 1,500 congregations of Baptists, 1,300 Pentecostals, 560 Adventists, and 200 Lutherans. Sociological surveys estimated that Protestants, at approximately one million, constituted about two-thirds of one percent of the total population of the Russian Federation.

*See also:* CATHOLICISM; RELIGION; RUSSIAN ORTHODOX CHURCH

**BIBLIOGRAPHY**

Billington, James. (1966). *Icon and the Axe.* New York: Random House.

Heard, Albert F. (1887). *Russian Church and Russian Dissent.* New York: Harper Brothers.

Heier, Edmund. (1970). *Religious Schism in the Russian Aristocracy, 1860–1900: Radstockism and Pashkovism.* The Hague, Netherlands: Nijhoff.

Sawatsky, Walter. (1981). *Soviet Evangelicals since World War II.* Scottdale, PA: Herald Press.

PAUL D. STEEVES

# PROTOPOPOV, ALEXANDER DMITRIEVICH

(1866–1918), minister of the interior, 1916–1918.

A member of an upper-class family, mentioned in Russian historical records from mid-sixteenth century, Alexander Dmitrievich Protopopov had an honorable, if not distinguished, career in the zemstvo (local self-government), and he also served in the third and fourth Duma, indeed as vice president from 1914. A left-wing Octobrist by party affiliation, Protopopov was active in the formation of the Progressive Bloc of deputies. His appointment as minister of the interior in September 1916 was not inappropriate, and it could even be considered as an effort by Nicholas II to go beyond narrow court circle and extreme rightist ideologies. Yet it proved to be a total disaster for two reasons: It foregrounded Protopopov's connection with the notorious Rasputin, and it coincided with the onset of mental illness. The emperor wanted to dismiss his new minister, but he was blocked by the empress,

the chief protectress of all connected with Rasputin. And so, in the words of one historian, "a man verging on insanity remained at the head of the Ministry of Interior until the Revolution. This case gives the measure of the decadence of the bureaucratic system."

*See also:* NICHOLAS II; RASPUTIN, GRIGORY YEFIMOVICH

**BIBLIOGRAPHY**

Ferro, Marc. (1993). *Nicholas II: The Last of the Tsars.* New York: Oxford University Press.

Florinsky, Michael T. (1931). *The End of the Russian Empire.* New Haven, CT: Yale University Press.

NICHOLAS V. RIASANOVSKY

# PROVISIONAL GOVERNMENT

The Provisional Government is most often remembered for its weakness and its inability to prevent the Bolshevik seizure of power in October 1917 or to manage the mass movements that ensured the victory of Vladimir Lenin. The experience and meaning of the Provisional Government are not well understood, however, and indeed the same might be said for the February Revolution as a whole. Certain basic facts about the Provisional Government should be stated at the outset. It was the product of a long and intricate process of prerevolutionary party and parliamentary politics that came to a head during World War I just prior to the outbreak of the revolution. It was a government that went through several transformations, from a largely liberal cabinet to a coalition of liberals, socialists, and populists, and finally to a crisis-driven statist cabinet led by Alexander Kerensky that barely could express its moderately socialist ideological underpinnings.

The Provisional Government was formed during the February days as a result of negotiations between the Temporary Duma Committee and the Petrograd Soviet. The Provisional Government was in fact an executive authority, or cabinet, headed by a minister president, that governed through the inherited ministerial apparatus of the old regime. It had legislative authority as well. Although the Provisional Government claimed power and the mantle of legitimacy, it was never clear during its brief eight-month existence whether this legitimacy derived from the Revolution or from inherited continuities of power or a mixture of the two. The first Provisional Government was clearly a product of the old regime Duma and its factional politics. But the new government chose not to base its authority on a Duma elected under prerevolutionary laws (its leadership, in any case, did not want to share power with certain Duma eminences and parties), and in official terms, at least, the Duma was pushed to the sidelines with no official status in the new governing structures (though it did continue to operate during 1917).

The First Provisional Government cabinet consisted largely of Cadets (Andrei Shingarev, Paul Miliukov), but it included Progressists (Mikhail Tereshchenko), Octobrists (Alexander Guchkov), and one nominal Socialist Revolutionary, Alexander Kerensky. The minister president was Prince Georgy Lvov, a romantic activist who had made his mark during the war as head of the All-Russian Union of Zemstvos and Towns and the Red Cross. As minister of foreign affairs, Miliukov stood firmly on the side of the Allies in their demand for Russia's continued participation in the war. Miliukov believed in the war aims of the tsar's government because he championed the state above all (albeit a rule-of-law state) and detested German authoritarianism and imperialism, so it was no leap to continue fighting alongside the democratic Western powers. Guchkov, as minister of war, shared this view and attempted to stave off what turned out to be a mass army mutiny during the course of 1917.

The first Provisional Government enunciated its revolutionary program in a declaration on March 8. The primary goal was to establish the rule of law and representative government based upon universal suffrage, self-government, and breaking the traditional power of the bureaucracy and police. The declaration also called for freedom of conscience and religion, reform of the judiciary and education, and lifting of the onerous restrictions upon the empire's nationalities. The final form of Russia's statehood was to be determined at a Constituent Assembly. The Provisional Government, in its various cabinets, tried to attain these goals. However, the revolution was unforgiving and the range of problems was so great that the government found itself adopting statist positions as it tried to maintain authority, prepare for the late spring offensive promised to the Allies, and adjudicate the multitude of social and political demands unleashed by the revolution.

Continuation of the war brought on the first government power crisis in April, and this led to the formation of the first of a series of coalition cabinets that included socialist ministers from the Menshevik and Socialist Revolutionary parties. Effective Bolshevik propaganda and use of symbolic fields of discourse for revolutionary ends made these more moderate socialists, now co-opted within the boundaries of power, look responsible for the deepening crisis in every sphere of public life. The Provisional Government implemented reforms in self-government, labor relations, and the judiciary. It established a grain monopoly and set the stage for many subsequent Bolshevik administrative and economic policies. Thus it was hardly a "bourgeois" government, but it was made to look so. Perhaps its greatest domestic failures were its inability to solve the land question on short notice and in the midst of revolution and, of course, its weak and perhaps idealistic approach to modern nationalism and the explosive new desires of the empire's non-Russians for self-determination. Its efforts in these and other areas were inadequate to stem the revolutionary tide.

The government finally collapsed under the strange leadership of Alexander Kerensky. A Socialist Revolutionary, he came to power in July in the midst of what turned out to be a failed military offensive. His leadership was marked by ill-conceived adventurism (the Kornilov Affair) and a clear desire to act as and represent himself as an executive strong man.

*See also:* FEBRUARY REVOLUTION; KERENSKY, ALEXANDER FYODOROVICH; KORNILOV AFFAIR; OCTOBER REVOLUTION

**BIBLIOGRAPHY**

Abraham, Richard. (1987). *Alexander Kerensky: The First Love of the Revolution.* New York: Columbia University Press.

Rabinowitch, Alexander. (1976). *The Bolsheviks Come to Power: The Revolution of 1917 in Petrograd.* New York: Norton.

Rosenberg, William G. (1975). *Liberals in the Russian Revolution: The Constitutional Democratic Party, 1917–1921.* Princeton, NJ: Princeton University Press.

Wade, Rex A. (1969). *The Russian Search for Peace, February–October 1917.* Stanford, CA: Stanford University Press.

DANIEL ORLOVSKY

## PRUSSIA, RELATIONS WITH

Tracing Russia's relations with Prussia is complicated by the fact that Prussia only slowly took shape as a nation. A reasonable starting point is during the reign of Peter the Great and the Great Northern War fought with Sweden for supremacy in northern Europe. King Frederick I sympathized with the Russians but could not afford financially to open hostilities; he moreover was distracted by the wars to his west involving most of Europe against Louis XIV of France. In 1714, Prussia felt compelled to enter the Northern War when Charles XII of Sweden attacked the fortress of Stralsund on Prussia's border. At the end of the war, Prussia, with Russia's blessings, acquired both banks of the lower Oder River and the first-class port city of Stettin.

In the latter half of the eighteenth century, however, relations deteriorated considerably. Frederick II embarked on a major war with Austria for Silesia. The Russian Empress, Elizabeth, sided with Austria and her armies inflicted severe defeats on Prussia in 1758–1759. Upon her death in 1762, Peter III ascended to the throne and as a great admirer of Frederick, withdrew Russia from the war. Partly as a result of this move, Peter was soon assassinated and replaced by Catherine the Great. Catherine and Frederick, with the collusion of Empress Maria Theresa of Austria, were able to agree on taking territory from the extraordinarily weak state of Poland. The result was that by 1795, Poland ceased to exist to the aggrandizement of the three powers. Henceforth, Russia and Prussia would have a mutual interest in the suppression of the Poles.

The Napoleonic wars drew Russia and Prussia closer, both being the victims of Bonaparte's ambitions. When Prussia signed an alliance with Napoleon in 1812, King Frederick William III assured Emperor Alexander I, that, if war came, Prussia's participation would be purely nominal. The next year, Russia, Prussia, Austria, and Britain pledged not to conclude a separate peace with France. At the Congress of Vienna, Russia and Prussia supported their respective claims to Poland and Saxony, something that provoked an alliance of Britain, Austria, and France. The crisis passed when Russia accepted about half of Poland and Prussia took two-fifths of Saxony. One of the most important consequences of the Napoleonic wars was a conviction on the part of the Prussians that they owed their national survival to Russia.

The Polish issue flared again in 1830, this time in revolution. After some negotiations, Emperor Nicholas I launched a full-scale invasion. The Poles appealed without success for Austrian aid but they knew there was no point looking to Prussia. As Russian arms triumphed, Poles who fled into Prussia were disarmed and returned to Russian forces.

At the same time the "eastern question," that is, the fate of the Ottoman Empire in Europe, became central to Russian foreign policy. This led eventually to the Crimean War but Prussia played little role in the initial stages of the affair. Nicholas went so far in 1833 as to inform the Prussians that they need not concern themselves with Near Eastern matters.

However, the revolutions of 1848 strained the relations between Berlin and St. Petersburg. Nicholas was the ultimate supporter of legitimacy and he was irritated when King Frederick William IV retained the constitution he had accepted, Nicholas believed, under duress. Nicholas also disliked his brother-in-law's sympathy for the national aspirations of German liberals. The animosity came to a head in 1848 over the duchies of Schleswig and Holstein. These two states rebelled against Danish rule and sought admission into the German confederation. Prussia sent its army to drive out the Danes and Nicholas saw this as an affront to the order established by the Congress of Vienna. He threatened war if Prussia did not speedily withdraw its troops. By 1850, the matter was settled and the Danes enjoyed a complete victory. Even worse, Nicholas and Emperor Franz Joseph of Austria forced Prussia to drop its proposal for a Prussian-led union of the German peoples.

The Crimean War did much to ease this antagonism. Of all the powers, Prussia was the only one who did not actively fight or criticize the Russians. On the other hand, all but Austria went to war with Russia. If conflict should flare between Prussia and Austria, the former could reasonably assume Russia's position would not be a repeat of 1850. Such was the thinking of Prussia's new minister president, Otto von Bismarck. While serving as Prussia's ambassador to St. Petersburg, Bismarck went out of his way to ingratiate himself with his hosts. In 1863, the year after Bismarck came to power in Berlin, he actively cooperated with the Russians in repressing yet another Polish uprising.

When he provoked war with Austria in 1866, he did not even need to consult the Russians beforehand so certain he was of their support.

In 1868, two years before Bismarck completed the unification of Germany through a war with France, he ensured himself of Russian support. Specifically, Alexander II promised that if Prussia and France went to war, he would mobilize 100,000 men on the Austrian border to ensure that Vienna could not intervene on the side of France. Thus Russia played an important role in the Prussian-led unification of Germany. And Russia would pay a high price for this in 1914–1918.

See also: GERMANY, RELATIONS WITH; GREAT NORTHERN WAR; POLAND; SEVEN YEARS' WAR; VIENNA, CONGRESS OF; WORLD WAR I

**BIBLIOGRAPHY**

Albrecht-Carrie, Rene. (1958). *A Diplomatic History of Europe since the Congress of Vienna.* New York: Harper.

Bridge, F. R., and Bullen, Roger. (1980). *The Great Powers and the European States System: 1815–1914.* New York: Longman.

Fay, Sidney. (1937). *The Rise of Brandenburg-Prussia to 1786.* New York: Holt.

Florinsky, Michael. (1953–55). *Russia: A History and an Interpretation.* 2 Vols. New York: Macmillan.

Pflanze, Otto. (1990). *Bismarck and the Development of Germany,* Vol. 1: *The Period of Unification, 1815–1871.* Princeton, NJ: Princeton University Press.

Schroeder, Paul. (1994). *The Transformation of European Politics, 1763–1848.* New York: Oxford University Press.

Taylor, A. J. P. (1971). *The Struggle for Mastery in Europe, 1848–1918.* New York: Oxford University Press.

HUGH PHILLIPS

heavily on an uprising of the Balkan Christians in Wallachia and Moldavia to redress the numerical imbalance. However, Wallachian support did not materialize, leaving the Russian armies without crucial supplies and reinforcements.

The fighting raged from July 9–11. The Russian situation quickly became critical because Peter had earlier sent the Russian cavalry to the Ottoman rear for the purpose of capturing or destroying Ottoman supplies. The outnumbered Russian infantry made a stand at Stanelishte on the banks of the Pruth without cavalry support. The Russians were completely surrounded by the larger Turkish force. Short of food and water, and with no possibility of breaking through the encircling Ottoman forces, the Russians opened negotiations.

The Treaty of Pruth was signed July 12, 1711, between Russia and the Ottoman Empire. The treaty dictated that Russia give up the fortresses of Azov and Tagonrog, lose its permanent ambassador in the Ottoman Empire, and dismantle both its forts on the lower Dnieper and its Black Sea fleet. In addition, Russian troops were to leave Poland and King Charles XII of Sweden would be permitted to return to Sweden without Russian interference. In return, the defeated Russian army received the right to retreat unhindered to Russian territory. The effect of this treaty was to nullify the military gains Peter had accrued against the Ottoman Empire throughout his reign.

See also: PETER I; TURKEY, RELATIONS WITH

**BIBLIOGRAPHY**

Massie, Robert K. (1980). *Peter the Great His Life and World.* New York: Ballantine.

JEAN K. BERGER

# PRUTH RIVER, CAMPAIGN AND TREATY OF

The Campaign of Pruth River was the Russian response to a declaration of war by the Ottoman Empire in November 1710. By June 1711, the Russian army under the command of Field Marshal Count Boris Sheremetev and Tsar Peter the Great arrived at the Pruth River in Ottoman territory. The Russians had about 38,000 infantry and 14,000 cavalry. The Ottoman forces, led by Grand Vizier Baltadji Mehmed Pasha, numbered about 120,000 infantry and 80,000 cavalry. Peter was counting

# PSKOV JUDICIAL CHARTER

The Pskov Judicial Charter consists of 120 articles. The preamble states that the Charter was copied from charters of Grand Prince Alexander and Prince Constantine. Most scholars believe the Charter dates back to Alexander Mikhailovich of Tver' (prince of Pskov between 1327 and 1337). Later additions were made by Alexander of Rostov (governed sporadically between 1410 and 1434) and Constantine Dmitrievich (served three times as prince between 1407 and 1414) with further redactions made in 1462 and 1474–1475. The Charter notes that the provisions were blessed by the priests of the five cathedrals in a meeting of the assembly (*veche*) in 1397, but the fifth cathedral was not founded until 1462. In 1397 Novgorod and Pskov concluded an "eternal peace," and it is possible that a redaction was made to formalize Pskov's independence, which existed de facto since 1348. Article 108 stipulates that only the *veche* may make changes in the Charter.

Princes played important roles in judicial proceedings, particularly for theft, and received judicial fines for such crimes as murder. The prince, mayor (*posadnik*), and Novgorodian archbishop all had independent courts. The prince and the mayor had to hold joint courts in the prince's quarters and not in the *veche*. The Charter consistently admonishes the courts to kiss the cross, judge justly, protect the innocent, and condemn the guilty. Mayors, before leaving office, must conclude all litigation on their docket.

The Charter provides for the death penalty for robbery within the central fortress, stealing horses, treason, or arson. Execution is also mandated for the third offense of theft within the *posad*, the area outside the fortress. The Council of Lords (*gospoda*), the highest administrative and judicial body, decided conflicts over land and forests, and could direct litigants to settle their dispute by duel (trial by combat). Duels were utilized for a wide variety of cases and could end in the death of one of the parties. The old and the weak, the clergy, and women could hire substitutes to fight a man, but duels were permitted between women. Duels were also common in later Muscovite law, despite the opposition of the Church to such practice.

Written and physical evidence and eyewitness testimony were important, as was the kissing of the cross and the giving of oaths, which carried great weight in judicial proceedings. In property disputes, four or five witnesses might be called to testify, but absent such corroborating witnesses, the taking of an oath was sufficient to exonerate a defendant.

The Charter offered certain protections to craftsmen, the poor, and women. A master craftsman had the right to sue for unpaid wages. Even indentured laborers (singular, *zakupen*) and herdsmen could sue for their property or grain before the Council of Lords. A widow whose husband died without leaving a last will had the usufruct of the property, unless she remarried. Women could inherit property and leave behind their own wills. The Charter enjoined children to feed their parents, or forfeit their rights to an inheritance.

The Charter gives particular attention to tenant farmers (*izorniki*), who could contest the claims of their lords over loans. Lords were required to produce as many as four or five witnesses to support their claims. Tenant farmers, gardeners, and fishermen could not leave their villages except on St. Philip's Fast (November 14), a provision that anticipated the limitations imposed on peasant movement in the Muscovite Law Code (*sudebnik*) of 1497. Conflicts over tenant farmers who left their villages legally, or lords who terminated their contracts with a farmer, were resolved by each receiving one-half of the harvest. Lords could recover their loans by seizing the property of tenant farmers who fled illegally. The Charter also provided for inheritance rights of tenant farmers, while it protected a lord's right to recover his loans.

The Charter outlines the duties of bailiffs and their fee schedules. Court procedure required only the two litigants to appear in court to speak for themselves. Women and children, along with monks, nuns, the elderly, and the deaf could have spokesmen. Mayors in particular were forbidden from supporting claimants in court.

The Charter also carefully delineates procedures concerning suits over loans, collateral guarantees, and interest payments, all of which reflect the commercial character of the city. It allowed master craftsmen to sue their apprentices over the cost of their training. Creditors and debtors retained their rights to sue one another over their agreements. Many of these cases would appear before the Council of Lords. There are also provisions regulating brawls that broke out at feasts. Each fraternity (*bratchina*), an association perhaps of craftsmen, had jurisdiction over its own members.

*See also:* NOVGOROD JUDICIAL CHARTER; NOVGOROD THE GREAT; POSADNIK

**BIBLIOGRAPHY**

Kaiser, Daniel, tr. and ed. (1992). *The Laws of Russia, Series 1, Vol. 1: The Laws of Rus', Tenth to Fifteenth Centuries.* Salt Lake City, UT: Charles Schlacks, Jr.

Vernadsky, George. (1969). *Medieval Russian Laws.* New York: Norton.

LAWRENCE N. LANGER

## PUBLIC OPINION STUDIES

Public opinion research had a long and checkered career in Soviet times, alternately encouraged then frowned upon from the 1950s through the 1980s. After the fall of the Communist Party and dissolution of the Soviet Union, attitudinal research began to play a much more important role in public life in Russia (as elsewhere in the former USSR). The Moscow-based All-Union Center for the Study of Public Opinion (VTsIOM)—renamed the All-Russian Center under the same acronym—continued its existence, now as a quasi-state body. But the monopoly held mostly by VTsIOM and sociologists working at the Academy of Sciences (AN) had already been broken in the late 1980s with the establishment of new, private polling firms.

Among the first of these independent companies was Vox Populi (headed by Boris Grushin, formerly at VTsIOM); ROMIR (directed by Yelena Bashkirova, formerly a researcher at the AN's Institute of Sociology [ISAN]); and CESSI (directed by Vladimir Andreyenkov, former chief of methodology at ISAN). The Center for Human Values—also staffed by former ISAN researchers—and Moscow State University also conduct public opinion research.

As public opinion studies became more important in the political and social life of the country, these companies had to evolve as well. Their practices changed to meet world standards. Sampling methodology, interviewing techniques, and data workup all rose in quality to satisfy the demands of both domestic and, increasingly, foreign clients. The number of primary and secondary sampling units, and sampling points, often tripled or quadrupled in order to provide greater variance. Interviewing through self-administered questionnaires—standard in Soviet times—gave way to face-to-face interviews in the homes or workplaces of respondents. Data entry and weighting improved substantially also.

Other offshoots of ISAN or VTsIOM, such as INDEM, headed by Georgy Satarov, and the Public Opinion Foundation (FOM), with Alexander Oslon in charge, played a second role. As Russian presidents Boris Yeltsin and especially Vladimir Putin increasingly took public opinion into account in deciding domestic policy, they turned to experts like Satarov, Grushin, and Oslon for counsel.

Public opinion research in Russia today takes many forms. Most common is the nationwide survey of adult Russians chosen by random sampling. A typical sample size is 1,500 to 2,000 adults, but some samples are larger. Other polls are of elites only, with much smaller samples drawn from political leaders (in the government or in parties) at the central and local level; state economic managers and private entrepreneurs; military officers; media figures; and members of the cultural and scientific intelligentsia. A third form of research involves (typically) 8 to 10 focus groups, in 3 to 5 cities; these small groups (usually of 8 to 12 people) of predetermined composition discuss in depth one or two important issues in an agenda set by the research firm and its client.

Many research firms disseminate their poll results widely—in newspapers or their own publications, through news agencies, and on television. Even more important, several have their own Web sites and put up current (and archived) poll results. Unfortunately, much information about sample sizes, dates of interviewing, and margins of sampling error are not usually given in popular citations of the research, severely limiting the usefulness of the findings.

*See also:* DEMOCRATIZATION; ECONOMY, POST-SOVIET; GLASNOST

STEVEN A. GRANT

## PUGACHEV, EMELIAN IVANOVICH

(c. 1742–1775), Russian cossack rebel and imperial impostor, leader of the Pugachevshchina.

Emelian Pugachev headed the mass uprising of 1773–1774 known as *Pugachevshchina* (loosely translated as "Pugachev's Dark Deeds"). The bloodiest rebellion against central state authority and serfdom between 1618 and the Revolutions of 1905 and 1917, it disrupted an immense territory and momentarily threatened the Muscovite heartland. Thousands of individuals from disparate social groups and ethnicities challenged Catherine II's legitimacy and aggravated international tension from prolonged Russo-Turkish hostilities. Many suspected upper-class, religious, or foreign inspiration behind the upheaval, widely reported by the European press. Particularly provocative was Pugachev's impersonation of Peter III (1728–1762), which recalled Catherine's usurpation of power.

The revolt originated among the Yaik (Ural) cossacks, a frontier "warrior democracy" that resisted pressure from state expansion. Disputes over the elected leadership led to government suppression of a cossack mutiny in January 1772, which left the community divided and resentful. Pugachev, a Don cossack fugitive, visited the area in late 1772. A typical primitive rebel, Pugachev was illiterate and his biography obscure. His imposture was not original; he was one of some seven pretenders since 1764. Shrewd, energetic, and experienced in military affairs, he was also charismatic. It is unclear whether he initiated renewed revolt or was persuaded to lead it by the cossacks.

About sixty rebels issued a first manifesto in late September 1773, presumably dictated by Pugachev or cossack scribes, calling on cossacks, Kalmyks, and Tatars to serve Peter III in pursuit of glory, land, and material reward. The rebels focused on frontier freedom or autonomy, but Peter III's name lent national stature to the burgeoning movement. Within weeks their forces exceeded two thousand besieging the fortress of Orenburg and spreading the revolt into the Ural Mountains with specific appeals to diverse social and ethnic groups. Turkic Bashkirs joined in force as the regional rebellion evolved into three chronological-territorial phases.

The Orenburg-Yaitsk phase lasted from October 1773 until April 1774, when the rebel sieges of Orenburg, Yaitsk, and Ufa were broken, Pugachev barely escaping. Shielded by spring roadlessness, the rebels replenished ranks while fleeing northward through the Urals. This second phase culminated in the plunder of Kazan on July 23 before the horde was defeated and scattered. With rebel whereabouts unknown, panic seized Moscow, but news of peace with the Turks soon allayed fears.

Pugachev fled southward down the Volga, exterminating the nobility and government officials—the third and final phase. This rampage sparked many local outbreaks sometimes called "Pugachevshchina without Pugachev." The main rebel force was decisively defeated south of Tsaritsyn on September 5. To save themselves, some cossacks turned Pugachev over to tsarist authorities at Yaitsk on September 26, 1774. After lengthy interrogation he was beheaded and then quartered in Moscow on January 21, 1775. To erase reminders of the revolt, Yaitsk, the river, the cossacks, and Pugachev's birthplace were all renamed, his wife and children exiled. Late in life Alexander Pushkin (1799–1837) popularized Pugachev in history and fiction. "The Captain's Daughter" became an instant classic, famously declaiming "God save us

from seeing a Russian revolt, senseless and merciless." But agrarian anarchist dissidents found inspiration in Pugachev for grassroots rebellion. After 1917 the Soviet regime endorsed Pugachev's fame, recasting the revolt as a peasant war against feudal society and autocratic government.

*See also:* CATHERINE II; PEASANTRY; PETER III; PUSHKIN, ALEXANDER SERGEYEVICH

**BIBLIOGRAPHY**

Alexander, John T. (1969). *Autocratic Politics in a National Crisis: The Imperial Russian Government and Pugachev's Revolt, 1773–1775.* Bloomington: Indiana University Press.

Alexander, John T. (1973). *Emperor of the Cossacks: Pugachev and the Frontier Jacquerie of 1773–1775.* Lawrence, KS: Coronado Press.

Pushkin, Alexander. (1983). "The Captain's Daughter" and "A History of Pugachev." In *Alexander Pushkin: Complete Prose Fiction*, ed. Paul Debreczeny. Stanford, CA: Stanford University Press.

Raeff, Marc. (1970). "Pugachev's Rebellion." In *Preconditions for Revolution in Early Modern Europe*, eds. Robert Forster and Jack P. Greene. Baltimore: Johns Hopkins University Press.

JOHN T. ALEXANDER

# PUGO, BORIS KARLOVICH

(1937–1991), Party official involved in the 1991 coup attempt against Boris Yeltsin.

Born in Latvia, Boris Karlovich Pugo was a Communist Party and state functionary whose career was shaped by Leonid Brezhnev's "mature socialism." This was a time of ossification in the leadership and mounting economic crisis that gave way to attempts to reform the system from within under the direction of Yuri Andropov, former head of the KGB, and then, after a brief interval, to more systemic reforms under Mikhail Gorbachev. Like many leaders of the Brezhnev era, Pugo began his career as an official in the Komsomol. His career was closely connected with Soviet power in his native Latvia, where he served as head of the local KGB and later as first secretary of the Latvian Communist Party.

Pugo came to prominence with the advent of glasnost and perestroika. In 1988 he was appointed chairman of the powerful CPSU Control Commis-

In August 1991 Pugo joined in the desperate attempt by the State Committee for the State of Emergency to remove Gorbachev and prevent the approval of a new union treaty that would bring about a radical shift in power from all-union institutions to the constituent republics, especially the Russian Federation under its popularly elected president, Boris Yeltsin. The so-called putsch in which the committee attempted to seize power was poorly organized and badly prepared. Within a matter of days it collapsed. Boris Pugo committed suicide on August 22, together with his wife, Valentina. His suicide note contained a brief explanation of his actions: "I put too much trust in people. I have lived my life honestly."

*See also:* AUGUST 1991 PUTSCH; SOYUZ FACTION

**BIBLIOGRAPHY**

Albats, Yevgeniia. (1994). *The State Within a State: The KGB and Its Hold on Russia—Past, Present, and Future.* New York: Farrar, Straus, Giroux.

Aron, Leon. (2000). *Yeltsin: A Revolutionary Life.* New York: St. Martin's Press.

Lieven, Anatol. (1993). *The Baltic Revolution: Estonia, Latvia, Lithuania, and the Path to Independence.* New Haven, CT: Yale University Press.

Medevev, Roy. (2002). "Yesteryear: Three Suicides." *Moscow News* No. 023 (August 21).

JACOB W. KIPP

**Interior Minister Boris Pugo bows his head during the press conference held by the leaders of the August 1991 coup. He committed suicide days later.** © SHEPARD SHERBELL/CORBIS SABA

sion in Moscow, a post he held for two years. This was a time of struggle within the Communist Party, for Gorbachev's effort to use it as a vehicle for reform had failed and only managed to split the Party along pro- and anti-reform lines. In the Baltic republics even the local Communist parties were joining in the call for independence by the summer of 1990. In December, Gorbachev appointed Pugo minister of internal affairs.

The appointment came at a time of crisis for perestroika. There were increasing calls for independence in the Baltic republics. Opponents of reform in Moscow, such as the "Black Colonel" Viktor Alksnis, were calling for a crackdown against anti-Soviet elements, especially in the Baltic republics. Hardliners argued that the impending war between the United States and Iraq would distract international opinion from a Soviet crackdown. As one of his first acts as minister of internal affairs, Pugo took a leading role in the attempt to reassert Soviet power in the Baltic republics. The crackdown in Vilnius, poorly organized and indecisive, collapsed in the face of popular resistance in the republics and Gorbachev's failure to support it publicly.

# PURGES, THE GREAT

The term *Great Purges* does not accurately designate the chaotic chain of events to which it is applied and was never used by the Soviet authorities. The regime tried to cover up the large-scale violence it had deployed between the summer of 1936 and the end of 1938. Although scholars apply the term *purges* to this period, many of them agree that the appellation is misleading. It implies that the Bolshevik attempts to eliminate the system's presumed enemies were a carefully planned, faithfully executed series of punitive operations, and this was far from being the case. The terror of 1936 to 1938 emerged without clear design—it targeted ill-defined categories of people and it proceeded haphazardly. Although purges victimized around 1.5 million individuals, they did not succeed in ridding the country of the problems they were supposed to stamp out.

**Workers in a Leningrad turbine shop listen to a report on the trial and execution of Grigory Zinoviev, Lev Kamenev, and fourteen others convicted of plotting against Stalin.** © HULTON-DEUTSCH COLLECTION/CORBIS

**FEAR OF OPPOSITION**

The Bolsheviks were convinced that the USSR was threatened by internal adversaries. They never hesitated to attribute discontent among the people to instigation by irreconcilably hostile elements, and they frequently did not even trust fellow militants. In the course of the 1930s, failure was increasingly imputed to deliberate sabotage.

There was barely a sector of life where the regime's initiatives succeeded. Collectivized agriculture did not feed the country properly, industry did not work according to plans, the Communist Party and the state administration did not carry out important directives. Peasants on collective farms did their best to avoid work, officeholders in the countryside vacillated between compromising with rural ways and taking brutal measures, workers were hard to discipline, managers invented ways to seem to be doing their jobs, officials in all institutions eagerly covered up for incompetent colleagues and the true state of affairs. The Bolsheviks were unwilling to acknowledge that the masses were only reacting to the outcome of the regime's policies, and top decision-makers were unable to grasp that subordinates were following their own example of not speaking out about inextricable issues, leaving problems unsolved, blaming whipping boys for their own miscalculations, and lavishing praise on achievements that were more than dubious. The elite never came close to recognizing

that the monopoly of the Party-state in nearly every domain left no room for checks and balances, and that attempts to improve the situation could not bring results as long as they were entrusted to the very establishment whose practices had to be corrected. The leaders could not see that the regime's difficulties were part-and-parcel of the system and could not be overcome without changing it completely.

Unwilling to accept responsibility for the system's failures, the Bolsheviks intensified the search for hidden enemies. Even top leaders were convinced that intractable problems were due to subversion. They projected the secretive character of their own dealings onto controlled aspects of the Party and state apparatus, and imagined conspiratorial intrigues behind the USSR's accumulating troubles. For Bolsheviks, there was no question but that the remnants of the prerevolutionary elite, adherents of defunct parties, and former kulaks represented a threat. They also suspected erstwhile oppositionists of disloyalty. Many of the Trotskyites and other deviationists of the 1920s had the same revolutionary credentials as their persecutors and thus were seen as dangerous rivals for legitimate authority. Josef V. Stalin feared that they might try to claim power if the situation worsened.

Although thousands of deviationists remained in the Communist Party until 1937, many others were expelled during membership screenings in 1935 and 1936. Starting in 1935, secret directives instructed the NKVD to detect their terrorist intentions, even if they were in exile and detention. A show trial highlighted the terrorist designs of the deviationist leaders Lev B. Kamenev and Grigory E. Zinoviev in August 1936, and this date is seen as the starting point of the Great Purges.

### THE PURGES BEGIN

The trial of Lev B. Kamenev and Grigory Y. Zinoviev and subsequent directives from the Central Committee triggered a vigilance campaign within the Party. The campaign targeted not only the opposition, but also Party members who had criticized the Party or whose work and lifestyle brought discredit to the Bolsheviks. The failures of agriculture, construction, industry, and other branches of the economy provided a legion of opportunities to denounce workers and managers. Poor results, errors, and accidents were reclassified as intentional sabotage. There were plenty of motives to level accusations of poor discipline, since the campaign came during a severe crop failure and in the wake of a Stakhanovist drive that had disorganized production and undermined workplace safety. Leading cadres were reluctant to dig too deeply into conditions in their workplaces, and it was safer to single out alleged Trotskyites as scapegoats, for the Party already had a tendency to blame them for nearly every shortcoming.

Sabotage is more accurately described as the regime's daily routine. Inefficiency, abuses, and heavy-handed handling of subordinates and the population disrupted the proper functioning of the Party, the state, and the national economy. The charge of oppositionist schemes was more problematic. It was used to justify the elimination of imprisoned Party members who had been dissidents in the 1920s. It was also used to stigmatize anyone who could be blamed for the regime's shortcomings without having to indicate any fault other than alleged sympathy, association, or even simple acquaintance with Trotskyites. Insinuations of this sort obscured Party efforts to correct official misconduct, facilitated scapegoating, and deflected blame onto the most vulnerable cadres. But there was hardly any other feasible way to dissociate the regime from its misdeeds and to suggest that the culprits were foreign or hostile to the Soviet ideal.

The scapegoats singled out in this way were made to answer for the defects of the Soviet system. Since many officeholders were at least partly responsible for the difficult living and working conditions imposed on them, the masses were not impervious to the argument that their superiors were enemies of the people. Quite a few citizens were ready to take up this argument against unpopular bosses as a way of venting their discontent and avenging past mistreatment and humiliations.

The leaders of the purges often emphasized that the alleged enemies were Party members in order to exploit tensions within the Party, in government agencies, and in other administrations. A show trial in January 1937 abundantly featured charges of wrecking and treason against Yuri L. Piatakov, deputy commissar of heavy industry and former member of the Central Committee, and other prominent figures in economic management and foreign affairs. Those who engineered this attack on leading Communists also tried to mobilize support in the lower ranks of the Party. The plenum of the Central Committee in February and March 1939 decided to reelect officeholders by secret ballot. It also decided to use the secret ballot at forthcoming elections for the Supreme Soviet, where, for the first time since the Revolution, all citizens were supposed to vote and have the right to be run for office. High officials at the plenum warned that subversive elements were likely to take advantage of the election campaign. They were aware of the discontent among the masses that had surfaced in public discussions about the recently adopted constitution, and especially that some people were attempting to invoke their constitutionally guaranteed rights to reclaim confiscated property and to freely practice religion.

The Party elections were expected to eliminate disruptive practices and boost the regime's reputation by replacing unruly and unpopular cadres. The targeted members did everything possible to ensure their reelection, because fallen communists risked jail—or worse. Networks of mutual aid were set in motion to rescue colleagues whose defeat would have endangered the position of everyone connected to them. While many targeted communists were saved, others were irreparably damaged when the police stepped in. By the summer of 1937, the winners of the intra-Party elections increasingly faced charges of having deceived the Party faithful. By that time, Party members alarmed by the increasing popular unrest had convinced the top leadership that it was necessary to launch an extensive purge. The crackdown came suddenly. No arrangements had been made to prepare concentration camps for the arrival of several hundred thousands of prisoners.

Seen as a preventive strike before the elections to the Supreme Soviet, the massive operation targeted a wide spectrum of so-called class enemies: kulaks, members of dissolved parties, ecclesiastics, sectarians, recidivist criminals. Moscow ordered the regional administrations to shoot, imprison, or deport specific quotas of enemies. Three-member boards (troikas) handed down summary sentences. This operation had hardly begun when another terror campaign was initiated. The new campaign was ostensibly aimed at ethnic Poles accused of being agents of the Polish government, but it was soon extended to other minorities, most of whom were not even mentioned in the central directives. No limits were set on the number of victims of this cleansing. Both operations were expected to end in December 1937, on the eve of the elections.

At first glance, it was easy to identify people on the basis of their past activities or political affiliations, especially former oppositionists. Nonetheless, it was impossible to know what constituted *deviation* because the term applied to attitudes as well as behaviors. In the same way, there was no guarantee that only declassed people and believers were dissatisfied with the regime. Moreover, there was no guarantee that potential subversion by foreign governments could be countered by massacring their ethnic kin.

## OUTCOME

The Great Purges resulted in chaos. About 100,000 Party members were arrested, often tortured to confess to concocted charges, and sent before the firing squad or to camps. But it soon became evident that many of them were victims of overzealous officials, some of whom were themselves later purged. The mass terror took almost a year more than projected. This was partly because zealous cadres sought to demonstrate their vigilance by requesting new quotas from Moscow for additional arrests and shootings. The names of purported accomplices were frequently obtained by cruelly mistreating the detainees. People were sometimes punished because of a foreign-sounding name or simply because anyone could be accused of being a German, Japanese, Latvian, or Greek spy. The campaign took on a life of its own. Even when it was halted in November 1938, scheduled executions continued in some regions.

More than 680,000 people were killed in 1937 and 1938, and about 630,000 were deported to

Siberia. Nevertheless, two years after the purge the number of persons listed as politically suspect by the secret police exceeded 1,200,000. But official misconduct, incompetence, and networks of solidarity did not change, despite the massive change in the leading personnel. The national economy and the administration suffered from the loss of valuable specialists, and the hunt for enemies in the army decapitated the high command and decimated the officer corps. Many of the victims were sincerely devoted to the principles of Bolshevism.

The Great Purges are usually associated with Joseph V. Stalin and his police chiefs, Nikolai I. Yezhov and Lavrenty P. Beria. But their true origin lay in the Soviet regime's inability to utilize modern techniques for managing institutions, political processes, and social relations. The purges showed that indiscriminate campaigns, police operations, and violence would play an important role as policy instruments and take priority over economic and administrative incentives to enlist popular support. They also showed the disastrous consequences of the system's lack of independent watchdog agencies that could, if necessary, restrain the Party-state's actions. The intent behind the purges bore some resemblance to social engineering, but the sociopolitical framework led to an outcome that had little in common with the original aims.

*See also:* BERIA, LAVRENTI PAVLOVICH; GULAG; KOMANEV, LEV BORISOVICH; SHOW TRIALS; STALIN, JOSEF VISSARIONOVICH; STATE SECURITY, ORGANS OF; YEZHOV, NIKOLAI IVANOVICH; ZINOVIEV, GRIGORY YEVSEYEVICH

## BIBLIOGRAPHY

Chase, William J. (2001). *Enemies Within the Gates? The Comintern and the Stalinist Repression, 1934–1939.* New Haven, CT: Yale University Press.

Conquest, Robert. (1990). *The Great Terror: A Reassessment.* New York: Oxford University Press.

Getty, J. Arch. (1985). *Origins of the Great Purges: The Soviet Communist Party Reconsidered, 1933–1938.* Cambridge, UK: Cambridge University Press.

Getty, J. Arch. (1999). *The Road to Terror: Stalin and the Self-Destruction of the Bolsheviks, 1932–1939.* New Haven, CT: Yale University Press.

Getty, J. Arch. (2002). "'Excesses Are Not Permitted': Mass Terror and Stalinist Governance in the Late 1930s." *Russian Review* 2:113–138.

Getty, J. Arch, and Manning, Roberta T., eds. (1993). *Stalinist Terror: New Perspectives.* Cambridge, UK: Cambridge University Press.

Siegelbaum, Lewis, and Sokolov, Andrei. (2000). *Stalinism as a Way of Life: A Narrative in Documents*. New Haven, CT: Yale University Press.

GABOR T. RITTERSPORN

## PUSHKIN, ALEXANDER SERGEYEVICH

(1799–1837), considered Russia's greatest poet, author of lyrics, plays, prose, and the novel in verse *Eugene Onegin*.

Of the Russian poets, none is mentioned by Russians with more reverence than Alexander Sergeyevich Pushkin. His work has been set to opera by Mikhail Glinka, Modest Mussorgsky, Nikolai Rimsky-Korsakov, and Peter Tchaikovsky; his lyrics have been memorized by young schoolchildren throughout the former Soviet Union; and leading poets of the twentieth century, such as Anna Akhmatova, Marina Tsvetaeva, and Alexander Blok, emphasized his impact on their work and lives. Pushkin may indeed have opened the door for the later part of the so-called Golden Age of Russian literature. At the 1880 ceremony following the unveiling of the Pushkin statue in Moscow, Ivan Turgenev credited Pushkin with giving birth to the Russian literary language; Fyodor Dostoyevsky, in an impassioned, near-hysterical speech, declared Pushkin superior to Shakespeare.

Such reverence is certainly merited, but reverence has its dangers. The author of the novel in verse *Eugene Onegin*, the historical play in verse *Boris Godunov*, the cryptic yet fluid "Belkin Tales," the brilliant "Little Tragedies" (four plays in blank verse, three of which deal with crimes of passion) the stylized folktale "Ruslan and Lyudmila," the tense, fatalistic story "Queen of Spades," and hundreds of lyrics, a master of style who absorbed and transformed European literary traditions and gave Russian folklore an unprecedented poetic expression, Pushkin attained quasi-mythological status in the twentieth century, becoming a hero figure for the Soviet establishment and dissidents alike. Yet Pushkin was a complex figure: profoundly solitary yet immersed in the social life of the aristocracy; devoted to his friends but easily incited to violence. His female characters, such as Tatiana in *Eugene Onegin*, have remarkable depth and soul, but he himself was primarily attracted to physical beauty in women, and brought about his own early death partly on account of this. These contradictions in his character, while perhaps limiting his literary offering, account in part for its richness; his work is both immediate and layered, both sincere and wry.

Pushkin was born in Moscow in 1799. His father Sergei descended from boyars, one of whom, mentioned in Pushkin's *Boris Godunov*, had been a supporter of the False Dmitry during the Time of Troubles. Pushkin's mother Nadezhda was the granddaughter of Abram Gannibal, an African slave. Abram had been brought from Africa as a gift for Peter I, who favored him and sent him to Paris for military education. With the accession of Elizabeth to the throne, Abram rose through the ranks to the status of general, but was retired following Elizabeth's death. Pushkin took pride in his African heritage, referring to it often in his lyrics. Abram's daughter Mariya, Pushkin's grandmother, not only played the role of surrogate parent to Pushkin, whose own parents gave him little attention or affection, but also recounted family history, to be reflected later in Pushkin's unfinished novel *The Blackamoor of Peter the Great*.

Pushkin's parents embraced the lifestyle of the aristocracy, though they could not afford it. Sergei, an adept conversationalist with a vast knowledge of French literature, invited some of Russia's leading literary figures to the household, including the historian Nikolai Karamzin and poets Konstantin Batyushkov and Vasily Zhukovsky. Pushkin and his sister and brother grew up surrounded by literati. However, Pushkin's childhood was unhappy. Pushkin was the least favored child, perhaps in part because of his African features and awkward manner. Only his grandmother and his nanny Arina Rodionova nurtured him emotionally; the latter told him folk tales and entertained him with gossip, and served later as the model for Tatiana's nanny in *Eugene Onegin*.

In 1811 Pushkin's parents sent him to boarding school, the Lyceum, newly established by Alexander I in a wing of his palace in Tsarskoye Selo. There Pushkin received a first-rate education (though he was not a stellar student) in a relaxed and nurturing environment, and formed friendships that would prove lifelong, with classmates Ivan Pushchin, Anton Delvig, Wilhelm Kyukhelbecker, and others. While at the Lyceum, Pushkin enjoyed a social life filled with pranks and light romantic encounters, and he amazed his teachers and classmates with his verse. The aged poet Gavryl Derzhavin, upon hearing Pushkin recite his "Recollections in Tsarskoye Selo" during an examina-

**Portrait of Alexander Pushkin.** THE BETTMAN ARCHIVE

tion in 1815, recognized sixteen-year-old Pushkin as his poetic successor.

Pushkin graduated from the Lyceum in 1817. From there he moved to Petersburg, where he spent his days sleeping late, taking walks, and attending parties in the evenings. Erratic and excitable, he made public scenes at the theater on several occasions. He frequented houses of prostitutes and had a number of romantic affairs. He was a member of the literary circle "The Green Lamp," whose members, including Pushchin and Delvig, were also involved in secret political activities aimed at reform. Pushkin was not invited to join in the secret meetings, but he did write lyrics challenging the tsarist autocracy, including his ode "Freedom" (1817), "Noelles" (1818), and "The Village" (1819). The lyrics caused a stir; Pushkin was ordered to appear before Count Miloradovich, governor-general of St. Petersburg. Following that meeting in 1820, the tsar sent Pushkin into exile in the form of military service in South Russia under Lieutenant General Inzov.

Pushkin's exile was in many ways pleasant. He befriended General Rayevsky and his family and traveled with them around Caucasus and Crimea.

He then spent nearly three years in Kishinev, where he wrote the verse tales "The Prisoner of the Caucasus" (1820–1821), "The Bandit Brothers" (1821–1822), and "The Fountain of Bakchisaray" (1821–1823). In addition, he wrote the scathing, mock-religious "Gavriiliada" (1821) and began his novel in verse *Eugene Onegin* (1823–1831). During this time Pushkin was captivated by Lord George Gordon Byron, particularly his *Childe Harolde.*

In July 1823 he was transferred to Odessa, where he had a lively social life, attended theater, and had affairs with two married women. He finished "The Fountain of Bakchisaray" and chapter one of *Eugene Onegin,* and began "The Gypsies."

From 1824 to 1826 he was exiled to his mother's estate of Mikhailovskoye in North Russia. There he finished "The Gypsies" and wrote the historical play in verse *Boris Godunov,* "Graf Nulin," and chapter two of *Eugene Onegin.*

In November 1825, while Pushkin was still in Mikhailovskoye, Alexander I died. The confusion over the successor provided the opportunity for secret political societies (called the Decembrists after the event) to rise up in armed rebellion against the aristocracy before Nicholas was proclaimed emperor. The uprising took place in Petersburg in December 1825 and involved poet Kondraty Ryleev, Colonel Pavel Pestel, Pushchin, Kyukhelbecker, and others. Pushkin, while not present or involved, was implicated, as some Decembrists quoted his poetry in support of their movement. Ryleev and Pestel were sentenced to death, Pushchin and Kyukhelbecker to hard labor.

In the spring of 1826 Pushkin petitioned Tsar Nicholas I for a release from exile. He met with the tsar and was granted release, but restrictions continued as before. He was under constant scrutiny, and his most minute activities were reported to the tsar.

In 1829 Pushkin met and proposed to Natalia Goncharova, a society beauty. They were formally engaged on May 18, 1830. Pushkin was given permission to publish *Boris Godunov.* In September 1830 Pushkin went to Boldino in east-central Russia to make wedding arrangements. Because of the outbreak of asiatic cholera, he was forced to stay three months there. This time was the most productive of his life. As part of an overall transition from poetry to prose, he wrote the magnificent *Tales of Belkin,* a collection of stories in taut, swift-moving prose, revolving around mistaken identity and, according to Andrej Kodjak (1979), containing an encoded message concerning the Decembrist uprising. Other works during this period include his "Little Tragedies" ("The Avaricious Knight," "Mozart and Salieri," "The Stone Guest," and "Feast in the Time of the Plague"), as well as "The Little House in Kolomna," "The Tale of the Priest and his Workman Balda," the last chapter of *Eugene Onegin*, and some of his finest lyrics, including "The Devils." He married Goncharova in February 1831, shortly after the unexpected death of Delvig, his closest friend after Pushchin.

Pushkin's marriage to Goncharova proved unhappy. She had little appreciation for his work, and he was unable to finance her extravagant lifestyle. Pushkin was beset with financial worries, and wrote little (including "Tale of the Golden Cockerel" (1834), the cycle of poems "Stone Island" (*Kamenny ostrov*, 1836) and his novel *The Captain's Daughter* (1836). He published a quarterly journal *The Contemporary*, which added to his troubles and did not fare well.

Natalia Goncharova loved mingling with the high aristocracy and playing society coquette; her many admirers included the tsar. The flirtation took on more serious tones when Baron Georges Charles d'Anthès, a French exile living in St. Petersburg under the protection of the Dutch ambassador, began to pursue her in earnest. A duel between d'Anthès and Pushkin took place on February 10, 1837. Pushkin, severely wounded, died two days later.

Of Pushkin's works, *Eugene Onegin* is the best known in the West, though by no means his sole masterpiece. Written over the course of eight years, it consists of eight chapters, each chapter broken into numbered stanzas in iambic tetrameter. Narrated by a stylized version of Pushkin himself, it portrays a Byronic antihero, Eugene Onegin, a bored society dandy who rejects the sincere and somber Tatiana. Onegin then flirts casually with Tatiana's sister Olga, provokes a duel with his friend Vladimir Lensky, a second-rate poet infatuated with Olga, and kills Lensky in the duel. After some travels, Onegin returns to Petersburg to find out that Tatiana has married a wealthy general. He falls in love with her, but she rejects him out of loyalty to her husband. The work holds immense popular and scholarly appeal thanks to the playfulness and perfection of the verse, the layers of confession and commentary, the appeal of the heroine, and the complex element of prophecy of Pushkin's own death.

*See also:* DECEMBRIST MOVEMENT AND REBELLION; DERZHAVIN, GAVRYL ROMANOVICH; GOLDEN AGE OF RUSSIAN LITERATURE; PUSHKIN HOUSE

## BIBLIOGRAPHY

Bethea, David M. (1998). *Realizing Metaphors: Alexander Pushkin and the Life of the Poet.* Madison: University of Wisconsin Press.

Binyon, T. J. (2002). *Pushkin: A Biography.* London: HarperCollins.

Evdokimova, Svetlana. *Pushkin's Historical Imagination.* New Haven, CT: Yale University Press.

Greenleaf, Monika. (1994). *Pushkin and Romantic Fashion: Fragment, Elegy, Orient, Irony.* Stanford, CA: Stanford University Press.

Pushkin, Alexander Sergeyevich. (1983). *Complete Prose Fiction,* tr. Walter W. Arndt and Paul Debreczeny. Stanford, CA: Stanford University Press.

Pushkin, Alexander Sergeyevich. (1991). *Eugene Onegin,* reprint ed., tr. Vladimir Nabokov. Princeton, NJ: Princeton University Press.

Vitale, Serena. (1999). *Pushkin's Button,* tr. Ann Goldstein and Jon Rothschild. New York: Farrar, Straus and Giroux.

DIANA SENECHAL

# PUSHKIN HOUSE

Pushkin House (*Pushkinsky Dom*), the Institute of Russian Literature of the Russian Academy of Sciences (abbreviated in Russian *IRLI RAN*), was founded in St. Petersburg, in 1905 and named after Alexander Sergeyevich Pushkin (1799–1837).

The idea of creating a new monument to Russia's premiere poet came about during the celebration of his centenary in 1899 and the Pushkin Exhibit organized by the Academy in May of that year. By 1907 the task of this monument supported by literary societies, theaters, and other groups from around Russia had evolved into gathering manuscripts, artifacts, and collections of works of prominent Russian authors. The acquisition of Pushkin's personal library in 1906 with government funds laid the foundation for the institute's library. At this time Pushkin House occupied temporary space at the Academy's main building while the search for a permanent location continued. World War I and the February and October Revolutions delayed the process but also increased the institute's holdings, especially those of the manuscript department. Among important additions were the archives, saved from the burning building of the gendarmes' headquarters in February 1917, of the tsar's secret police, documenting police surveillance of Pushkin and other nineteenth-century writers; Pushkin and Lermontov museum collections transferred in 1917 from the Lyceum in Tsarskoye Selo for safekeeping; and the Paris museum collection of A. F. Onegin contracted for in 1909 and transferred to Pushkin House in 1927, after the owner's death. Pushkin House became a member institute of the Academy in 1918 and eventually received its own building in 1927, the old customs house at 2 Tuchkov Embankment (now Makarov Embankment). Thanks in part to the protection of Soviet writer Maxim Gorky, Pushkin House was able to continue acquiring manuscripts and literary memorabilia in the 1920s and 1930s. Publishing of scholarly works on Russian literature, source texts, textology, bibliography and the study of literary history, catalogs, and periodicals got underway in the 1920s. Since then, the academic editions of complete works by authors such as Pushkin, Dostoevsky, Tolstoy, Gogol, and Lermontov produced by the institute have been considered authoritative and are used and cited by scholars around the world.

Pushkin House continued to operate during the siege of Leningrad during World War II, although most of the manuscripts and staff were evacuated to cities in the country's interior. The institute returned to the job of preparing specialists after the war and continues to train graduate and post-graduate students in Russian literature, awarding degrees in Russian literature (Ph.D. equivalent and professorship). The structure of the institute is divided into ten departments, including medieval Russian literature, oral poetry and audio archive, modern Russian literature (eighteenth and nineteenth centuries), Pushkin department, new Russian literature (twentieth century), Russian and foreign literary ties, manuscript department and medieval manuscript repository, library, and literary museum. After the fall of the Soviet Union in 1991, Pushkin House, like most government institutions, experienced serious funding deficits but rapid expansion of cooperation with foreign scholars and universities that led to foreign grants, joint publishing projects, exchanges, and international conferences.

*See also:* ACADEMY OF SCIENCES; EDUCATION; PUSHKIN, ALEXANDER SERGEYEVICH; UNIVERSITIES

VANESSA BITTNER

# PUTIN, VLADIMIR VLADIMIROVICH

(b. 1952), second president of the Russian Federation.

Vladimir Putin was appointed acting president of the Russian Federation on December 31, 1999, and on March 26, 2000, he was elected to the presidency. Putin was born in Leningrad (now St. Petersburg). He attended school there and practiced judo, eventually becoming the city champion. As a boy, Putin dreamed of joining the secret police (KGB). When he was seventeen he went to KGB headquarters and asked a startled officer what he should do to "join up." He was told to attend the university and major in law. Putin took his advice and attended Leningrad State University. In his second semester one of his teachers was Anatoly Sobchak, a man who would play a major role in his life. In 1974 Putin was offered a job in the KGB but told he had to wait a full year before entering the organization. In 1976 Putin was assigned to the First Directorate, the section engaged in spying outside of the USSR. In 1983 he married Ludmila Schkrebneva, a former airline hostess. Putin had hoped to be stationed in West Germany, but instead, in 1985, he was assigned to Dresden, in East Germany. While it is unclear what he did there, all indications are that he focused on recruiting visiting West German businessmen to spy for the USSR. In any case, he left as a lieutenant colonel, suggesting that his spying career was less than spectacular.

In May 1990 Putin's former professor Anatoly Sobchak was elected mayor of St. Petersburg, and he asked Putin, who was well aware that both the USSR and the KGB were falling apart, to come work for him. Putin agreed, left the KGB, and by all accounts impressed everyone he met with his ability to "get things done." He was efficient, effective, honest, and decent to the people he interacted with, characteristics that were in short supply at that time. When Sobchak lost the mayoralty in the election of July 1996, Putin quit, but unknown to him he had been noticed by Anatoly Chubais, who helped him obtain a job with Paul Borodin, who ran the presidential staff in the Kremlin. As a result, he moved to Moscow.

Few people would have given the rather faceless and bland Putin much chance of being noticed by President Boris Yeltsin. Yet he did stand out, perhaps because he was so efficient. Equally important, he did not appear to be seeking higher office.

Yeltsin took note of Putin and in 1998 appointed him head of the Federal Security Service, formerly the KGB. Then, on August 16, 1999, Yeltsin surprised the world by making Putin prime minister and designating him as his successor. If that was not enough, Yeltsin once again surprised the world on December 31, 1999 by resigning and making Putin acting president. On March 26, 2000, Putin stood for election and won a majority in the first round.

Putin was a new kind of president. While Boris Yeltsin had presided over the collapse of communism and in that sense was a revolutionary leader, Putin saw the job differently. Russia had been through enough turmoil and conflict since the collapse of the USSR. Besides, the country was in a mess. The economy had come close to collapse, corruption and social problems were rampant, cynicism toward the central government was at an all-time high, and on the international level, Russia was almost irrelevant with U.S.-Russian relations at an all-time low. It is not an exaggeration to suggest that Russia was considered by many to be "the sick man of Europe."

Putin's approach to these many problems contrasted markedly with Yeltsin's. He was very organized and structured, and as his Millennium Speech (January 1, 2000) made clear, he stood in stark contrast to his Soviet predecessors. He told the Russian people the truth about the depth and seriousness of the country's problem. In addition to taking this straightforward approach, Putin believed that the only way Russia could survive as a viable nation was to rebuild the Russian state. So he immediately began to reestablish Moscow's control over the country's governors, many of whom were paying little attention to the central government. First, he took on the Federation Council, the parliament's upper house, where the regional governors held considerable power. By the time Putin was through, considerable power had been shifted to Moscow. Then he set up seven "super" districts, headed by personally selected "super" governors, to oversee the regional officials. He even succeeded in firing one of the country's most corrupt and strongest governors, Yegeny Nazdratenko of Primorski Krai.

The Putin style of governance avoided spectacular, high-profile actions. Instead, he preferred to work behind the scenes whenever possible. In his view, there had already been too much of the kind of high-profile activity associated with Yeltsin.

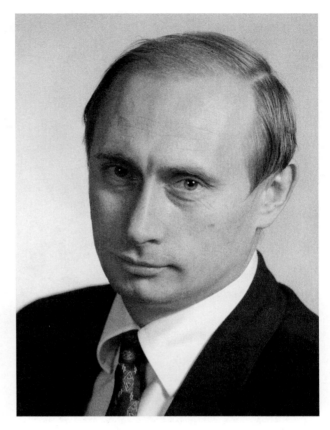

**Ex-KGB agent Vladimir Putin became Russia's second president.**
© R.P.G./CORBIS SYGMA. REPRODUCED BY PERMISSION.

Russia was tired of that sort of thing, which in the end generally made very little difference in the life of the average citizen. Military reform provides an example of Putin's approach. How to restructure Russia's armed forces had been a subject of discussion ever since the collapse of the Soviet Union— and even before then. When Putin appointed Sergei Ivanov, one of his closest associates, as defense minister, there was some expectation that he would immediately try to institute major changes. In fact, that did not happen. Instead, Putin pushed the Defense Ministry to make changes, and it has gradually responded.

Putin's style of governance was not repressive, but neither was it democratic in the way the term was understood in the West. Instead, he followed a course of what might be called "managed democracy." He set the parameters of what was permitted and what was prohibited. As long as citizens remained within the parameters, they would have all the freedom they wanted. But if they went beyond the parameters, they would be in trouble. For

**President Vladimir Putin speaks during a 2002 meeting with Kyrgyzstan president Askar Akayev.** PHOTOGRAPH BY ALEXANDER ZEMLIANICHENKO/ASSOCIATED PRESS. REPRODUCED BY PERMISSION.

example, when Putin took on the media, he made it clear that the "chaotic" press and television of the Yeltsin period was unacceptable. While the media remained free in comparison to the Soviet era, the situation was a far cry from the independent news coverage of the 1990s.

Putin did not have a grand plan for the restructuring of society. He was a problem-solver. Rather than instituting a full-scale reform of the judicial system, for instance, he raised the salaries of judges and increased the money available to the police. The same was true of an even more serious problem, the tax system. The government was bankrupt because no one was paying taxes. Putin dealt with the problem by introducing a 13 percent flat tax to be paid by everyone, and the system seemed to work relatively well. There were still major problems in both areas, but as was typical of Putin, important if partial changes had been implemented.

Putin was also an effective diplomat. When George W. Bush became president of the United States, it looked as if U.S.-Russian relations were going nowhere. Putin showed he had patience. When the terrorist attack on the World Trade Center in New York occurred on September 11, 2001, he was the first foreign leader to call President Bush and express his condolences. He also stood by the United States during the subsequent war in Afghanistan. Most surprising, however, was his ability to remain a close friend and ally of the United States even though he opposed the American invasion of Iraq. In contrast to the Washington–Paris relationship, Washington and Moscow remained close allies despite their differences over Iraq.

Putin also demonstrated that he knew how to make use of events. For example, he used the September 11 attacks to force Russia's anti-American general staff to change its approach to dealing with the United States. On September 24, 2001, just prior to his visit to the United States, he met with the country's generals and admirals, and made it clear that cooperation was the order of the day. The military quickly fell into line and cooperation between the two sides was as close as it had ever been.

Many observers wondered whether Putin's partial but determined approach would provide the political, military, social, and economic stability Russia needed to reenter the ranks of the world's major powers. When his presidency began, Putin was unknown, and few believed he could do anything other than be a KGB thug. Within a short time, without taking the repressive actions that many expected, he had begun to reestablish the Russian state and to restore its status as an important player in the international arena. The economy had begun to turn around, even if it continued to be too heavily based on oil.

*See also:* SOBCHAK, ANATOLY ALEXANDROVICH; STATE SECURITY, ORGANS OF; YELTSIN, BORIS NIKOLAYEVICH

**BIBLIOGRAPHY**

Herspring, Dale R., ed. (2003). *Putin's Russia: Past Imperfect, Future Uncertain.* Boulder, CO: Rowman & Littlefield.

Putin, Vladimir. (2000). *First Person: An Astonishingly Frank Self-Portrait of Russia's President, Vladimir Putin,* tr. Catherine A. Fitzpatrick. New York: Public Affairs.

Shevtsova, Lilia. (2003). *Putin's Russia.* Washington, DC: Carnegie Endowment for International Peace.

DALE HERSPRING

# PYTATAKOV, GEORGY LEONIDOVICH

(1890–1937), a leading Bolshevik in Ukraine who opposed Vladimir Lenin's policy on a nation's right to self-determination.

An extraordinary economic administrator, Georgy Pytatakov held numerous important political positions including deputy chairman of Gosplan (1922); deputy chairman of the Supreme Council of the National Economy (VSNKh) (1923); chairman of the State Bank (1929); deputy chairman of the Commissariat of Heavy Industry (1930); and member of the Supreme Economic Council (1930).

In the 1920s Pytatakov allied with Leon Trotsky and ultimately became a leading figure in the Left Opposition (the so-called Trotskyite opposition). From 1922 to 1926 Pytatakov advocated rapid industrialization and supported Yevgeny Preobrazhensky's theory of "primitive socialist accumulation." In a public bid for rank-and-file support for the Left's position, Pytatakov took part in a demonstration at a Moscow factory Party meeting in 1926. He was subsequently removed from his position at VSNKh for being an oppositionist and sent abroad. The following year he was expelled from the Party.

In 1928 Pytatkov recanted his position and applied for readmission into the Party. It was granted the following year, along with an appointment to head the State Bank. Beginning in 1929 he published articles hailing Josef Stalin's genius and condemning oppositionists. However, this could not erase the stigma of his association with the Left Opposition. In 1936 he was arrested as a Trotskyite and, along with Karl Radek, was a central figure in the second Moscow Show Trial in 1937. Under torture and drugs, he confessed, was found guilty, and shot immediately after the trial.

*See also:* LEFT OPPOSITION; TROTSKY, LEON DAVIDOVICH

## BIBLIOGRAPHY

Conquest, Robert. (1990). *The Great Terror: A Reassessment*. New York: Oxford University Press.

Khlevniuk, Oleg. (1995). *In Stalin's Shadow: The Career of "Sergo" Ordzhonikidze*. New York: M. E. Sharpe.

KATE TRANSCHEL

## QUADRUPLE ALLIANCE AND QUINTUPLE ALLIANCE

The Quadruple Alliance was signed in November 1815 by Russia, Britain, Austria, and Prussia, following the long series of wars that began in the aftermath of the French Revolution and concluded with the defeat of Napoleon. It was essentially a continuation of the Treaty of Chaumont of 1814, in which the four powers vowed to defeat France and remain allied for twenty years to keep France in check. At the time Russia was the preeminent military power in Europe. From 1813 to 1814, Europeans had watched with a mixture of amazement and horror as Russian soldiers drove Napoleon's Grand Army out of their country and, joined by Prussia, Britain, and finally Austria, all the way to Paris. Britain ruled the seas, but no army rivaled Russia's, and fear of this new power was keen in Austria and Britain until its disastrous defeat in the Crimean War.

The individual most responsible for the complete destruction of Napoleon's power was Emperor Alexander I (r. 1801–1825). The other continental powers had been willing to negotiate a settlement with Napoleon, but Alexander had insisted on total victory. Since at least 1805 he had been convinced that only Russia and Britain had the resources to vanquish Napoleon and reestablish order in Europe based on a new treaty system.

With the final defeat of Napoleon in 1815, the victorious powers faced two related problems: how to contain France, and how to prevent revolution. In November, the British foreign secretary, Viscount Castlereagh, proposed a continuation of the alliance system, bolstered by a system of great-power congresses to deal with crises as they arose. Alexander's vague response was a "Holy Alliance" of Christian monarchs who would treat one another with Christian brotherhood and charity. This proposal had no practical effect.

Castlereagh had his way, and in the Quadruple Alliance the victorious powers pledged to maintain the political system established at the Congress of Vienna for the next twenty years, by force if necessary, and to meet periodically to consult on the maintenance of order and stability. The foreign secretary declared that Britain would never intervene militarily in the internal affairs of another state. When Alexander pressed him to promise support for the restored Bourbon monarchy in France,

Castlereagh refused. This did much to fuel Alexander's suspicions of British policy.

As Alexander's anti-British feelings grew, he came to regard France in a more favorable light. Prodded by his advisers, particularly Corfiote Capodistrias, he concluded that if France were admitted into the Quadruple Alliance, it could become a counterweight to Britain and, to a lesser extent, Austria, especially if Prussia continued to follow Russia's diplomatic lead.

The result was the Congress of Aix-la-Chapelle in 1818. Ostensibly convened to end the military occupation of France, it really had the goal of restoring France into the great-power system. Its outcome was twofold: France joined the alliance, which became the Quintuple Alliance, but the Quadruple Alliance was reconfirmed because the victors, despite their mutual distrust, were still fearful of a resurgent France. Over the next few decades, however, fear of Russian power and expansionism would seize all the great powers except Prussia, until they united to defeat Russia in the Crimean War.

*See also:* CRIMEAN WAR; HOLY ALLIANCE; NAPOLEON I; VIENNA, CONGRESS OF

**BIBLIOGRAPHY**

Albrecht-Carrie, Rene. (1958). *A Diplomatic History of Europe Since the Congress of Vienna.* New York: Harper.

Bridge, F.R., and Bullen, Roger. (1980). *The Great Powers and the European States System: 1815–1914.* New York: Longman.

Jelavich, Barbara. (1974). *St. Petersburg and Moscow: Tsarist and Soviet Foreign Policy: 1814–1974.* Bloomington: Indiana University Press.

HUGH PHILLIPS

## RABBINICAL COMMISSION

The Rabbinic Commission (1848–1910) was a consultative body under the Ministry of Internal Affairs (specifically the Department of Spiritual Affairs for Foreign Faiths), organized to deal with matters of the Jewish faith. Its creation conformed to the general state policy of centralizing the religious administration of foreign confessions in a single department. Its primary duties were to answer inquiries from the state about Jewish laws and customs, to supervise the activities of rabbis, and to examine controversial Jewish divorce suits. While the state had created this institution to gather information about internal Jewish life, the Commission gradually transformed into a higher court of appeals for private divorce cases (which remained under rabbinical jurisdiction until 1917) and a vehicle for preserving traditional religious and family values.

The changing profile of the Commission's members reflected the transformation in its mission and identity. The first session (1852) included obscure individuals who were well versed neither in the Russian language nor Jewish law: the merchant Bernshtein (Odessa), D. Orshansky (Poltava), Shimel Merkel (Kovno province), and Dr. Cherolzon (Oszeisky province). They examined queries about the censorship of Jewish books, Hasidic sects, the Jewish oath, registration, and marriage of Jewish soldiers. The second meeting (1857) involved more prominent Jews: Dr. Abraham Neumann (Riga), the merchant Yekutiel-Zisl Rapoport (Minsk), the merchant Chlenov, (Kremenchug), and Rabbi Yakov Barit (Vilna). Among other topics, they discussed the establishment of state schools for Jewish girls.

In addition to the previous members, the third session (1861–1862) included Itskhok Eliiagu (Eliyahu) Landau (Kiev), German Barats (Vilna), and A. Maidevsky (Poltava), Iosef Evzel Gintsburg, and two learned Jews from the Ministry of the People's Education—Iosif Zeiberling (St. Petersburg) and Samuel Iosif Fin (Vilna). The Commission examined ten cases on Jewish religious life and its first divorce case.

The fourth session (1879) was an "assembly of rabbis without rabbis." Apart from state rabbi German Faddeyevich Blyumenfeld (Odessa) and Dr. Avraham Harkavy (an Orientalist), the others were secular professionals: Hirsh Shapiro (Kovno), Zelman Lyubich (Minsk), Meier Levin (Pinsk), Baron Goratsy Gintsburg (Kiev), and I. I. Kaufman (Odessa). They examined eight cases of divorce and bigamy.

The fifth session (1893–1894) reflected the aggressive campaign of the Jewish Orthodox leadership to reassert their authority and preserve tradition. It involved four enlightened Jews (German Barats, Iakov Gottesman, Samuil Simkhovich, Avraam Katlovker) and three prominent Orthodox leaders: rabbis Tsvi Rabinovich (Vilna), Samuel Mogilever (Grodno), and theologian Yuriya Mileikovsky (Mogilev). They examined twenty-seven cases on marriage, divorce, and religious rituals.

The final sixth session (1910) was a victory for the Orthodox camp, which promised to wean Jews from revolutionary activities. Save for one jurist, Moisie Mazor (Kiev), the others were rabbis: Yehuda Leib Tsirelson (Kishinev), Khaim Soloveichik (Brest-Litovsk), Oizer Grodzensky (Vilna), Sholom Shneerson (Liubavich), Shmuel Polinkovsky (Odessa), and Mendel Khein (Nezhin). They examined twenty-three cases on marriage and divorce, as well as questions about burials, cemeteries, spelling of Jewish names, oaths, and censorship of books.

Although the Rabbinic Commission only met six times, it addressed key religious and family issues that plagued Russian Jewry. The shift in influence from the enlightened to Orthodox camp brought a reassertion of traditional values, including the refusal to modify Jewish law to suit modern expectations. The state ceased to convene the Rabbinic Commission as the empire descended into war and revolution.

*See also:* JEWS

**BIBLIOGRAPHY**
Freeze, ChaeRan Y. (2002). *Jewish Marriage and Divorce in Imperial Russia.* Hanover, NH: University Press of New England.

CHAERAN Y. FREEZE

## RABKRIN

Rabkrin is the contracted name of Narodnyi Kommissariat Raboche–Krest'ianskoi Inspektsii (The People's Commissariat of the Workers' and Peasants' Inspection), the Soviet governmental institution responsible between 1920 and 1934 for overseeing state administration.

On February 7, 1920, the Soviet Central Executive Committee established Rabkrin to succeed the People's Commissariat for State Control (estab-

lished December 3, 1917). It was charged with ensuring the effectiveness of government administration and monitoring the implementation of state decrees. The former commisar of state control, Josef Stalin, remained in charge of Rabkrin until he was replaced in April 1922 by A. D. Tsyurupa.

The Soviet leadership soon became concerned that Rabkrin was failing to halt the growth of bureaucraticism, mismanagement, and corruption in the government apparatus. In April 1923, Rabkrin was merged with the Communist Party's Central Control Commission under Valerian Vladimirovich Kuibyshev. The new body was given the broad task of supervising and rationalizing the administration of all party, state, and economic functions. From November 1926 to November 1930, Stalin's close ally, Sergo Ordzhonikidze, headed the joint control agency, which became a powerful political weapon for the consolidation of Stalin's power. In 1928, it was charged with overseeing implementation of the First Five-Year Plan, and played a major role in promoting unrealistically ambitious industrial planning and militaristic campaign methods of economic administration. In November 1930, Andrei Andreyevich Andreyev succeeded as head of the joint control agency until October 1931, when he was replaced by Yan Ernestovich Rudzutak. To strengthen the power of the economic commissariats, the Seventeenth Party Congress (1934) dissolved Rabkrin and transferred its functions to an emasculated Commission for State Control, attached to Sovnarkom and separate from the new Commission for Party Control subordinated to the Central Committee.

*See also:* CENTRAL CONTROL COMMISSION; SOVNARKOM; STALIN, JOSEF VISSARIONOVICH

**BIBLIOGRAPHY**
Rees, E. A. (1987). *State Control in Soviet Russia. The Rise and Fall of the Workers' and Peasants' Inspectorate, 1920-1934.* Basingstoke: Macmillan.

NICK BARON

## RACHMANINOV, SERGEI VASILIEVICH

(1873–1943), one of the most famous of Russian composers.

Sergei Vasilievich Rachmaninov was born in Oneg, Russia. He first established himself with his much-performed *Prelude in C Sharp Minor*, presented with Rachmaninov at the piano in the Moscow Conservatory auditorium in 1892. A few years later he composed his famous *Piano Concerto No. 2 in C Minor*. Soon after these successes he was appointed conductor at the Bolshoi Theater. Among his other works were an opera (*Aleko*, 1892), *The Bells* (a dramatic choral symphony composed in 1910), three instrumental symphonies, three other piano concertos, the *Vocalise* (two versions, 1916 and 1919) and other songs, the *Rhapsody on a Theme by Paganini* (1934), and the *Symphonic Dances* (1940).

With the coming of the Bolshevik seizure of power in Russia in 1917, Rachmaninov exiled himself first to Germany, then to the United States. In the United States he had conducted his first (in 1909) but by no means only concert tour. His several succeeding appearances in New York City's Carnegie Hall won him early fame. Critics remarked at the unusual span of his hands as his fingers raced through the rich chords and arpeggios.

After his departure from Russia, Rachmaninov's writing remained outstanding. Found in the repertoires of orchestras worldwide, the *Symphony No. 3 in A Minor* (1936) is a stunning work whose structure is studied in music school composition classes. Some of Rachmaninov's music was included in film scores. Among these was the eerie music of "Isle of the Dead" in a 1945 film with Boris Karloff. Various parts of his other works turn up in many films.

Rachmaninov's music is considered Romantic while bearing traces of typically Russian themes and style of composition. Although banned in Soviet Russia for more than seventy years, Rachmaninov's music is as much admired in his homeland as the music of Tchaikovsky, Mussorgsky, Rimsky-Korsakov, or Stravinsky. Beginning just before the demise of Communist rule in the early 1980s, Rachmaninov's music again adorned the repertoires of Russian orchestras.

*See also:* BOLSHOI THEATER; MIGHTY HANDFUL; MUSIC

ALBERT L. WEEKS

# RADEK, KARL BERNARDOVICH

(1885–1939), revolutionary internationalist and publicist.

Born Karl Sobelsohn to Jewish parents in Lvov, Karl Radek dedicated his life to international revolution and political writing. He was active in socialist circles from age sixteen and in 1904 joined the Social Democratic Party of the Kingdom of Poland and Lithuania. Before World War I, Radek moved comfortably among Europe's Marxist revolutionaries. He became a member of the German Social Democratic Party's left wing in 1908, and wrote on party tactics and international affairs for the party's press.

Radek opposed World War I and was active in the Zimmerwald movement, an international socialist antiwar movement organized in 1915. He joined the Bolsheviks after the 1917 Revolution and was a delegate to the Brest-Litovsk peace talks, although he opposed the treaty and supported the Left Communist opposition. Nonetheless, in 1918, he became the head of the Central European Section of the Commissariat of Foreign Affairs and helped to organize the founding congress of the German Communist Party. In 1919, he was elected to the Bolshevik Party's Central Committee and became the Comintern secretary. He was removed from this post in 1920, but remained a member of the Comintern's executive committee and the Central Committee, and was active in German communist affairs until 1924.

In 1924, Radek sided with Trotsky's Left Opposition and in consequence was removed from the Central Committee. That same year he also opposed changes in Comintern policy and thus was removed from its executive committee. He was expelled from the Party in 1927 and exiled. After recanting his errors in 1929, he was readmitted to the Party and became the director of the Central Committee's information bureau and an adviser to Joseph Stalin on foreign affairs. Radek helped to craft the 1936 Soviet constitution, but later that year he was arrested and again expelled from the Party. At his January 1937 Moscow show trial, he was convicted of being a Trotskyist agent and sentenced to ten years in prison. He died in 1939.

Radek published routinely in the Soviet press and authored several books on Comintern and international affairs.

*See also:* CENTRAL COMMITTEE; COMMUNIST INFORMATION BUREAU; COMMUNIST INTERNATIONAL; COMMUNIST PARTY OF THE SOVIET UNION; LEFT OPPOSITION; PURGES, THE GREAT; TROTSKY, LEON DAVIDOVICH

## BIBLIOGRAPHY
Lerner, Warren. (1970). *Karl Radek: The Last Internationalist.* Stanford, CA: Stanford University Press.

Radek, Karl B., with Haupt, Georges (1974). "Karl Bern-hardovich Radek." In *Makers of the Russian Revolution*, ed. Georges Haupt and Jean-Jacques Marie, tr. C.I.P. Ferdinand and D.M. Bellos. Ithaca, NY: Cornell University Press.

WILLIAM J. CHASE

## RADISHCHEV, ALEXANDER NIKOLAYEVICH

(1749–1802), poet, thinker, and radical critic of Russian society.

Alexander Nikolayevich Radishchev was arrested for sedition by Catherine II in 1790 for the publication of a fictional travelogue. Newly promoted from assistant director to director of the St. Petersburg Customs and Excise Department, he had benefited from Catherine's earlier enthusiasm for the European Enlightenment. Following service as a page at the Imperial Court from 1762 to 1767, he had been selected as one of an elite group of students sent to study law at Leipzig University, where he had absorbed the progressive thinking of the leading French *philosophes*. After completing his studies in 1771 he returned to Russia, where he responded to Catherine's encouragement for translating the works of the European thinkers of the Enlightenment. His first literary venture, in 1773, was a translation of Gabriel Bonnot de Mably's *Observations sur l'histoire de la Grèce*, which idealized republican Sparta. Radishchev's first significant original work, published in 1789, was his memoir, *Zhitie Fedora Vasilevicha Ushakova* (*The Life of Fedor Vasilevich Ushakov*), recalling idealistic conversations with a fellow student in Leipzig on oppression, injustice, and the possibilities for reform. This was a prelude for *Puteshestvie iz Peterburga v Moskvu* (*A Journey from St. Petersburg to Moscow*), in which an observant, sentimental traveler discovers the various deficiencies in contemporary Russian society.

At each staging post, an aspect of the state of Russian society is revealed. For example, at Tosna, the traveler observes feudalism; at Liubani, it is forced peasant labor. Chudovo brings unchecked bureaucratic power to his attention; he learns of autocracy at Spasskaya Polest; and at Vydropusk his attention is taken by the imperial court and courtiers. Other stops along the road illuminate issues such as religion, education, health, prostitu-

tion, poverty, and censorship in an encyclopedic panorama of a sick society. No single cure is proposed for Russia's ills, but the underlying message is that wrongs must be righted by whatever means prove to be effective.

Deeply affected by the French Revolution of 1789, Catherine now read the work as an outrageous attempt to undermine her imperial authority. An example was made of Radishchev in a show trial that exacted a death sentence, later commuted to Siberian exile. He was permitted to return to European Russia in 1797, but he remained in exile until 1801. Crushed by his experiences, he committed suicide the following year. His *Journey* remained officially proscribed until 1905. Its author's fate, however, as much as the boldness of its criticism, had won Radishchev the reputation of being the precursor of the radical nineteenth-century intelligensia.

*See also:* CATHERINE II; ENLIGHTENMENT, IMPACT OF; INTELLIGENTSIA

### BIBLIOGRAPHY
Clardy, Jesse V. (1964). *The Philosophical Ideas of Alexander Radishchev*. New York: Astra Books.

Lang, David M. (1959). *The First Russian Radical: Alexander Radishchev (1749–1802)*. London: Allen and Unwin.

McConnell, Allen. (1964). *A Russian Philosophe: Alexander Radishchev 1749–1802*. The Hague: Nijhoff.

W. GARETH JONES

## RADZINSKY, EDVARD STANISLAVICH

(b. 1936), playwright, author, popular historian, and television personality.

A man of the 1960s, Edvard Radzinsky was born in Moscow to the family of an intellectual. He trained to be an archivist but began writing plays during the late 1950s. During the 1960s and the 1970s Radzinsky dominated the theatrical scene in Moscow and gained international recognition. His early plays explored the themes of love, commitment, and estrangement (*101 Pages About Love; Monologue About a Marriage; "Does Love Really Exist?," Asked the Firemen*). In the final decades of stagnation under mature socialism, Radzinsky wrote a cycle of historical–philosophical plays exploring the themes of personal responsibility, the struggle between ideas and power, and the roles of victim and executioner (*Conversations with Socrates*; *I, Lunin*; and *Theater in the Time of Nero and Seneca*). In the same period he also wrote several grotesques that drew their inspirations from great literary themes and myths: *The Seducer Kolobashkin* (the Faust legend) and *Don Juan Continued* (Don Juan in modern Moscow).

Radzinsky refused to define his dramatic imagination by the political events of 1917 and looked to a larger intellectual world. With the collapse of the Soviet Union, he shifted his creative efforts to literature, writing *Our Decameron* on the deconstruction of the Soviet intellectual life and history, as well as writing unconventional biographies of Nicholas II (*The Last Tsar*), Stalin, and Rasputin. In each work Radzinsky enjoyed access to new archival sources and wrote for a popular audience. His works became international bestsellers. Some historians criticized the special archival access he obtained through his close ties with the government of Boris Yeltsin. Others noted his invocation of mystical and spiritual themes in his treatment of the murder of the tsar and his family. Radzinsky has shown a profound interest in the impact of personalities on history but is much opposed to either a rationalizing historicism or an ideology-derived historical inevitability. Radzinsky became a media celebrity thanks to his programs on national television about riddles of history. In 1995 he was elected to the Academy of Russian Television and was awarded state honors by President Yeltsin. Appointed to the Government Commission for the Funeral of the Royal Family, Radzinsky worked diligently to have the remains of Nicholas II and his family buried in the cathedral at the Peter and Paul Fortress in St. Petersburg.

*See also:* NICHOLAS II; RASPUTIN, GRIGORY YEFIMOVICH; STALIN, JOSEF VISSARIONOVICH; THEATER

**BIBLIOGRAPHY**

Kipp, Maia A. (1985). "The Dramaturgy of Edvard Radzinskii." Ph.D. diss. University of Kansas, Lawrence.

Kipp, Maia A. (1985). "Monologue About Love: The Plays of Edvard Radzinsky." *Soviet Union/Union Soviétique* 12(3):305–329.

Kipp, Maia A. (1989). "In Search of a Synthesis: Reflections on Two Interpretations of E. Radzinsky's 'Lunin, or, the Death of Jacques, Recorded in the Presence of the Master.'" *Studies in Twentieth Century Literature* 3(2):259–277.

Kipp, Maia A. (1993). "Edvard Radzinsky." In *Contemporary World Writers* ed. Tracy Chevalier. London: Saint James Press.

Radzinsky, Edvard. (1992). *The Last Tsar: The Life and Death of Nicholas II*. New York: Doubleday.

Radzinsky, Edvard. (1996). *Stalin*. New York: Doubleday.

Radzinsky, Edvard. (2000). *The Rasputin File*. New York: Nan A. Telese.

JACOB W. KIPP

## RAIKIN, ARKADY ISAAKOVICH

(1911–1987), stage entertainer, director, film actor.

Arkady Raikin ranks as one of the most popular and acclaimed stage entertainers of the Soviet era. He was particularly well known for his uncanny ability to alter his appearance through the use of makeup, and his witty, satirical monologues and one-man sketches endeared him to several generations of fans. As a young man Raikin worked for a short time as a lab assistant in a chemical factory, but his real passion was acting. He enrolled in the Leningrad Theater Institute, and upon his graduation in 1935 he found employment with the Leningrad Theater of Working-Class Youth (TRAM). He also found his way into the movies, and in 1938 he starred in *The Fiery Years* and *Doctor Kaliuzhnyi*. He also appeared in films later in his life and wrote and directed the 1974 television film *People and Mannequins*.

But Raikin devoted the bulk of his creative energies to entertaining on the stage. In 1939 he joined the prestigious Leningrad Theater of Stage Entertainment and Short Plays (Leningradsky teatr estrady i miniatyur), and in 1942 he became artistic director of the theater. He remained affiliated with this theater for the remainder of his career, even after it moved to Moscow in 1982, where it was renamed the State Theater of Short Plays. Raikin also found success as master of ceremonies for stage shows that allowed him to entertain audiences.

His many awards included People's Artist of the USSR (1968), Lenin Prize (1980), and Hero of Socialist Labor (1981). In 1991 the Russian government honored him by issuing a postage stamp in his name, and the Satyricon Theater (formerly the State Theater of Short Plays) was named in Raikin's honor in 1991.

See also: MOTION PICTURES; THEATER

**BIBLIOGRAPHY**

Beilin, Adolf Moiseevich. (1960). *Arkadii Raikin.* Leningrad: Iskusstvo.

Uvarova, E. (1986). *Arkadii Raikin.* Moscow: Iskusstvo.

ROBERT WEINBERG

# RAILWAYS

The first Russian railways, built as early as 1838, were tsarist whimsies that ran from St. Petersburg to the summer palaces of Tsarskoye Selo and Pavlovsk. Emperor Nicholas I (r. 1825–1855) ordered the construction of these and the Moscow–St. Petersburg line, which, according to legend, the tsar designed by drawing a line on a map between the two cities using a straight-edge and pencil. One hundred fifty years later, the railway system had expanded to almost 150,000 kilometers (90,000 miles), or almost two-thirds the length of the network serving the United States. With 2.3 times the territory of the United States, however, the net density of the Soviet Union's rail system was only about one-fourth as concentrated. It was, and is, a system of trunk lines with very few branches, which supplied only minimum service to major sources of tonnage.

Naturally, this spartan system was severely strained at any given time. Soviet freight turnover was more than 2.5 times as great as that of the United States, making it the most densely used rail network in the world. At the time of the collapse of the USSR, Soviet railways carried 55 percent of the globe's railway freight (in tons per kilometer) and more than 25 percent of its railway passenger-kilometers. Compared to other domestic transportation alternatives, Soviet railways had no comparison: They hauled 31 percent of the tonnage, accounted for 47 percent of the freight turnover (in billions of ton-kilometers), and circulated almost 40 percent of the inter-city passenger-kilometers.

## REGIONAL RAIL SYSTEMS AND COMMODITIES

In the Russian Federation of the early twenty–first century, the leading rail cargoes, ranked according to tonnage, comprise coal, oil and oil products, ferrous metals, timber, iron ore and manganese, grain, fertilizers, cement, nonferrous metals and sulfurous raw materials, coke, perishable foods, and mixed animal feedstocks. The most conspicuous Russian carrier is the Kemerovo Railway, which hauls more than 200 million tons of freight per year, two-thirds of which is coal from the mines of the Kuznetsk Basin (Kuzbas), Russia's greatest coal producer. When the West Siberian and Kuznetsk steel mills operate at full capacity, the Kemerovo Line also carries iron and manganese, iron and steel metals, fluxing agents, and coke. Rounding out the freight structure are cement and timber.

The only other railway that ships more than 200 million tons of freight is the Sverdlovsk, or Yekaterinburg, Railway in the Central Urals. The system's most important cargoes include timber from the nearby forests; ferrous metals from iron and steel mills at Nizhniy Tagil, Serov, Chusovoy and others; and petroleum products from the refineries at Perm and Omsk. Other heavily used railways comprise the October (St. Petersburg), Moscow, North Caucasus, South Ural, and Northern lines, each shipping more than 140 million tons per year. The much-heralded Baikal-Amur Mainline (BAM) Railway, which became fully operational in December 1989, remains Russia's most lightly used network. Three-fifths of the freight it transports is coal from the South Yakutian Basin.

## REGIONAL BOTTLENECKS

In terms of combined freight and passenger turnover (ton- and passenger-kilometers), the world's most heavily used segment of railroad track stretches between Novokuznetsk in the Kuzbas and Chelyabinsk in the southern Urals. Parts of the Kemerovo, West Siberian, and South Urals railways each maintain a share of this traffic. While touring the Soviet Union in 1977, geographer Paul Lydolph observed train frequencies on this segment as often as one every three minutes in different locations and at various times during the day. By the 1990s, operating at 95 percent of its capacity, the West Siberian arm of the Trans-Siberian Railway was critically overloaded. Ironically, 40 percent of the freight cars were usually empty: Had these cars not been on the track, the West Siberian line would have been running at only 48 percent of capacity! Such was the waste inherent in the Soviet centrally planned command economy.

Since 1991, because of the alterations in the freight-rate structure—the Soviet system was heavily subsidized to keep the rates artificially low—and the post-Soviet depressed economy throughout Russia, particularly in coal mining, iron and steel, and other bulk sectors, both the Kemerovo and West Siberian railway networks have witnessed sharp declines in usage. They continue to represent bottlenecks, but these were much less severe than the ones they became in the Soviet period. The worst bottlenecks in the post-Soviet era occur in ports—both river and sea—and at junctions. The absolute worst are found in Siberia and the Russian Far East, where traffic is heavy, there are few lines, and management traditionally has been lax.

## POST–SOVIET PROBLEMS

Since 1991, railway headaches have been less associated with capacity and more with costs. In the early 1990s, the Yeltsin government introduced free–market principles and eliminated the artificial constraints on prices and freight rates that had prevailed in the USSR. The de-emphasis on the military sector, which controlled at least one-fourth of the Soviet economy, proved to be a devastating blow to heavy industry and rail transport. The multiplier effect diffused throughout the economy of the Russian Federation, and soon fewer goods and less output required circulation, and those needing it had to be sent it at burdensome rates. Spiraling inflation and underemployment brought many industries to the edge of bankruptcy. Those industries that survived often were deep in debt to the railroads, which carried the output simply because they had nothing else to carry. Soon the railroads, which were themselves in debt to their energy suppliers, began to demand payment from the indebted industries. This engendered a vicious cycle wherein everyone was living on IOUs: industries owed the railways, which owed the energy suppliers, who in turn owed the mining companies that owed the miners, who could not buy the products of industry.

By 1991, the Soviet rail network was 35 to 40 percent electrified, and much of this electricity came from coal-fired power plants. When the railways could not pay their energy bill, coal miners did not get paid. Since 1989, miners' strikes over wages and perquisites have often crippled the electrified railways. At times the miners have blocked the track to protest their privations. Since the year 2000, this vicious cycle has been alleviated because of high international prices on petroleum and natural gas. The resultant increase in foreign exchange income

**Vladivostok is the eastern terminus of the Trans-Siberian Railway.** © WOLFGANG KAEHLER/CORBIS

has brought some relief to the Russian economy. Wage arrears have been eliminated at least temporarily, and the economy, including the Russian railways, appears to have turned the corner.

*See also:* BAIKAL-AMUR MAGISTRAL RAILWAY; INDUSTRIALIZATION; TRANS-SIBERIAN RAILWAY

## BIBLIOGRAPHY

Ambler, John, et al. (1985). *Soviet and East European Transport Problems.* New York: St. Martin's Press.

Hunter, Holland. (1957). *Soviet Transportation Policy.* Cambridge, MA: Harvard University Press.

Lydolph, Paul E. (1990). *Geography of the USSR.* Elkhart Lake, WI: Misty Valley Publishing.

Mote, Victor L. (1994). *An Industrial Atlas of the Soviet Successor States.* Houston, TX: Industrial Information Resources, Inc.

Westwood, John N. (1964). *A History of the Russian Railways*. London: George Allen & Unwin Ltd.

VICTOR L. MOTE

## RAIONIROVANIE

Having inherited from the tsarist government a large number of territorial divisions and subdivisions, the Soviet leadership attempted to reduce their numbers and simplify their bureaucracies. Undertaken in the 1920s, this project to reorganize the internal administrative map of Soviet Russia was called *raionirovanie*, which can be translated as regionalization. Soviet planners implemented raionirovanie not only as a way of rationalizing administrative structures, but as an essential tool for the centralized planning of economic activity.

Before the reforms, Soviet central officials regarded the territorial divisions they inherited as cumbersome and archaic obstacles to economic growth. The basic divisions in tsarist administration were the province (*guberniya*), county (*uezd*), rural district (*volost*), and village (*selo*). Their number expanded quickly in the first five years of the new regime, fueling Bolshevik concerns about bureaucratism—the perils of an expanding, unruly, and unresponsive state administration. Specialists in Gosplan (the State Planning Commission) desired to reshape territorial administration to conform to their vision of the economic needs of the country. Its planners designed new territorial units that sought to follow the contours of regional agricultural and industrial economies, based on natural resources, culture, and patterns of production.

As a result of raionirovanie, the country's provinces were replaced by regions (*oblast* or *krai*), which were divided into departments (*okrugs* replaced the counties), which were themselves divided into districts (*raions*, which replaced the old rural counties.) In light of a scarcity of trained administrators, each of these new units was larger than the old, and therefore had less contact with the population. The first areas subject to regionalization were the Urals, the Northern Caucasus, and Siberia, between 1924 and 1926. Raionirovanie continued in other areas of the country throughout the decade, and was largely complete by 1929. The process of creating regional economic planning agencies under the direct, centralized leadership of Moscow became a part of the essential infrastructure of the Five-Year plans, first adopted in 1928.

Objections to regionalization were raised by the Commissariat of Nationalities and local leaders in the autonomous and national republics, especially in Ukraine, on the grounds that the centrally designed plans overlooked diversity in local culture and tradition as they sought to rationalize and centralize administration while maximizing economic growth. Indeed, regionalization sought to eliminate much of what remained of the tsarist administration in the countryside and the provinces. Beyond the reorganization of territorial subdivisions, names of cities, towns, and capitals were changed, as were traditional borders, and, so planners hoped, loyalties to the old ways. Similar to Napoleonic-era bureaucratic reforms in France, the ultimate aim was not only to rationalize administration and economy, but to reshape popular mentalities in line with conditions in a new, post–revolutionary era.

*See also:* LOCAL GOVERNMENT AND ADMINISTRATION; NATIONALITIES POLICIES, SOVIET

**BIBLIOGRAPHY**

Carr, Edward Hallett. (1964). *Socialism in One Country, 1924–1926*. London: Macmillan.

JAMES HEINZEN

## RAPALLO, TREATY OF

The Treaty of Rapallo was signed by Germany and the Russian Socialist Federated Soviet Republic on April 16, 1922.

As part of a plan to encourage economic recovery after World War I, the Allies invited Germany and Soviet Russia to a European conference in Genoa, Italy, in April 1922. Lenin accepted the invitation and designated Foreign Minister Georgy Chicherin to lead the Soviet delegation. Accompanied by Maxim Litvinov, Leonid Krasin, and others, Chicherin stopped in Berlin on his way to Italy and worked out a draft treaty. The German government, still hopeful for a favorable settlement at Genoa, refused to formalize the treaty immediately. In Genoa, the Allied delegations insisted that the Soviet government recognize the debts of the prerevolutionary governments. The Soviets countered with an offer to repay the debts and compensate property owners if the Allies paid for the destruction caused by Allied intervention. While these negotiations remained deadlocked, the German delegation worried that an Allied-Soviet treaty would leave Germany further isolated. When the Soviet delegation proposed a private meeting, the Germans accepted, and the Russian-German treaty was signed by Chicherin and German foreign minister Walter Rathenau.

The two sides agreed to drop all wartime claims against each other, to cooperate economically, and to establish diplomatic relations. The Treaty of Rapallo surprised the Western powers. Germany ended its isolation with an apparent shift to an Eastern policy, while Soviet Russia found a trading partner and won normalization of relations without resolving the debt issue. This special relationship between Soviet Russia and Germany, including some military cooperation, lasted for ten years.

*See also:* GERMANY, RELATIONS WITH; WORLD WAR I

**BIBLIOGRAPHY**

*League of Nations Treaty Series*, Vol. 19. (1923). London: Harrison and Sons.

HAROLD J. GOLDBERG

**RAPP** *See* RUSSIAN ASSOCIATION OF PROLETARIAN WRITERS.

**Grigory Rasputin, photographed in 1916.** THE ART ARCHIVE/MUSÉE DES 2 GUERRES MONDIALES PARIS/DAGLI ORTI

# RASPUTIN, GRIGORY YEFIMOVICH

(1869–1916), mystic and holy man who befriended Nicholas II and attained considerable power in late Imperial Russia.

Born at Pokrovskoye, Siberia, January 10, 1869, Rasputin was the son of Yefim, a prosperous, literate peasant. Young Grigory was alternately moody and mystical, drunken and rakish. Marriage did not settle him, but a pilgrimage to Verkhoture Monastery, as punishment for vandalism (1885), was decisive. The hermit Makary persuaded Grigory to become a *strannik* (wanderer, religious pilgrim). Rasputin also met the *khlysty* (flagellants, Pentecostalists); though not a member (as often charged), he embraced some of their ideas.

Rasputin's captivating personality, his eyes, and a memory for biblical passages made him a local religious authority. Grigory never held a formal position in the Church, but people recognized him as a *starets* (elder, wise counselor). His spiritual gifts apparently included healing. Although of medium height and build, and not handsome, Rasputin's sensitive, discerning manner attracted women and brought him followers and sexual conquests. His pilgrimages included Kiev, Jerusalem, and Mt. Athos. Charges of being a khlyst forced Rasputin to leave Pokrovskoye for Kazan in 1902. By then, his common-law wife Praskovya had borne him three children.

Rasputin impressed important clergy and laypeople in Kazan, and they made possible his first trip to St. Petersburg in 1903. He captivated church and social leaders, and on a second visit, he met Nicholas II. For a year, his friendship with the royal family was based upon their interest in peasants with religious interests and messages. Rasputin first alleviated the sufferings of their hemophiliac son Alexei in late 1906. For the next ten years, Rasputin served the tsarevich unfailingly in this capacity. Joseph Fuhrmann's biography reviews the theories offered to explain this success, concluding that Rasputin exercised healing gifts through prayer. Robert Massie explores hypnosis, rejecting the suggestion that hypnosis alone could suddenly stop severe hemorrhages.

Rasputin exercised some influence over church-state appointments before World War I. The high point of his power came when Nicholas assumed command at headquarters away from St. Petersburg, in August 1915. This elevated his wife's importance in government. Alexandra, in turn, relied upon Rasputin's advice in appointments, though neither controlled policies. As difficulties and defeats mounted, Russians became convinced that Rasputin and Alexandra were German agents, and that Nicholas was their puppet. Fearing this would topple the dynasty, Felix Yusupov organized a conspiracy resulting in Rasputin's murder in Petrograd on December 17, 1916. Rasputin was poisoned, severely beaten, and shot three times, and yet autopsy reports disclosed that he died by drowning in the Neva River. Rasputin was buried at Tsarskoye Selo until revolutionary soldiers dug up the body to desecrate and burn it on March 9, 1917.

Rasputin favored Jews, prostitutes, homosexuals, and the poor and disadvantaged, including and, in particular, members of religious sects. He understood the danger of war, and did what he could to preserve peace. But Rasputin was selfish and shortsighted. He took bribes and was party to corruption and profiteering during the war. Rasputin ended as a womanizer and hopeless drunk, who undermined the regime of Nicholas II and hastened its collapse.

See also: ALEXANDRA FEDOROVNA; FEBRUARY REVOLUTION; NICHOLAS II

**BIBLIOGRAPHY**

Fuhrmann, Joseph T. (1990). *Rasputin: A Life*. New York: Praeger.

King, Greg. (1995). *The Man Who Killed Rasputin: Prince Felix Youssoupov and the Murder That Helped Bring Down the Russian Empire*. Secaucus, NJ: Carol Publishing Group.

Massie, Robert K. (1967). *Nicholas and Alexandra*. New York: Atheneum.

Radzinsky, Edvard. (2000). *The Rasputin File*. New York: Nan A. Talese/Doubleday.

JOSEPH T. FUHRMANN

## RASTRELLI, BARTOLOMEO

(1700–1771), Italian architect who defined the high baroque style in Russia under the reigns of Anne and Elizabeth Petrovna.

Bartolomeo Francesco Rastrelli spent his youth in France, where his father, the Florentine sculptor and architect Carlo Bartolomeo Rastrelli, served at the court of Louis XIV. After the death of the Sun King in 1715, the elder Rastrelli left Paris with his son

and arrived the following year in St. Petersburg. Recent research suggests that the young architect did not return to Italy for study but remained in Petersburg, where he worked on a number of palaces during the years between the death of Peter (1725) and the accession of Anne (1730). Rastrelli's rise in importance occurred during the reign of Anne, who commissioned him to build a number of palaces in both Moscow and St. Petersburg.

Despite the treacherous court politics of the period, Rastrelli not only remained in favor after the death of Anne (1740), but gained still greater power during the reign of Elizabeth Petrovna (1741–1761), for whom he built some of the most lavish palaces in Europe. Rastrelli's major projects for Elizabeth included a new Summer Palace (1741–1743; not extant), the Stroganov Palace (1752–1754), the final version of the Winter Palace (1754–1764), and the Smolny Convent with its Resurrection Cathedral (1748–1764). In addition, Rastrelli greatly enlarged the existing imperial palaces at Peterhof (1746–1752) and Tsarskoe Selo (1748–1756).

With the accession of Catherine II, who disliked the baroque style, Rastrelli's career suffered an irreversible decline. He had received the Order of St. Anne from Peter III and promotion to major general at the beginning of 1762, but after the death of Peter in July, Ivan Betskoi replaced Rastrelli as director of imperial construction and granted him extended leave to visit Italy with his family. Although Rastrelli returned the following year, he had in effect been given a polite dismissal with the grant of a generous pension. He died in 1771 in St. Petersburg.

See also: ANNA IVANOVNA; ARCHITECTURE; CATHERINE II; ELIZABETH; WINTER PALACE

**BIBLIOGRAPHY**

Brumfield, William Craft. (1993). *A History of Russian Architecture*. New York: Cambridge University Press.

Orloff, Alexander, and Shvidkovsky, Dmitri. (1996). *St. Petersburg: Architecture of the Tsars*. New York: Abbeville Press.

WILLIAM CRAFT BRUMFIELD

## RATCHET EFFECT

The ratchet effect in the Soviet economy meant that planners based current year enterprise output plan targets on last year's plan overfulfillment. Fulfilling output targets specified in the annual enterprise plan, the *techpromfinplan*, was required for Soviet enterprise managers to receive their bonus, a monetary payment equaling from 40 to 60 percent of their monthly salary. Typically, output plan targets were high relative to the resources allocated to the enterprise, as well as to the productive capacity of the firm. If managers directed the operations of the enterprise so that the output targets were overfulfilled in any given plan period (monthly or quarterly), the bonus payment was even larger. However, planners practiced a policy of "planning from the achieved level," the ratchet effect, so that in subsequent annual plans, output targets would be higher. Higher plan targets for output were not matched by a corresponding increase in the allocation of materials to the firm. Consequently, overfulfilling output plan targets in one period reduced the likelihood of fulfilling output targets and receiving the bonus in subsequent periods.

Planners estimated enterprise capacity as a direct function of past performance plus an allowance for productivity increases specified in the plan. Knowing that output targets would be increased, that is, knowing that the ratchet effect would take effect, Soviet enterprise managers responded by over-ordering inputs during the planning process and by continually demanding additional investment resources to expand productive capacity. For Soviet enterprises, cost conditions were not constrained by the need to cover expenses from sales revenues. In other words, Soviet managers faced a "soft budget constraint." The primary risk associated with excess demand for investment was the increase in output targets when the investment project was completed. However, the new capacity could not be included as part of the firm until it was officially certified by a state committee. By the time this occurred, the manager typically had another investment project underway.

In response to the ratchet effect, Soviet enterprise managers also tended to avoid overfulfilling output targets even if it were possible to produce more than the planned quantity. Several options were pursued instead. Managers would save the materials for future use in fulfilling output targets, or unofficially trade the materials for cash or favors to other firms. Managers would produce additional output, but not report it to planning authorities, and then either hold or unofficially sell the output. Due to persistent and pervasive shortages in the Soviet economy, and the uncertainty

associated with timely delivery of both the quantity and quality of requisite material and technical supplies, the incentive to unofficially exchange materials or goods between firms was very high, and the risk of detection and punishment was very low. Despite the comprehensive nature of the annual enterprise plan, Soviet managers exhibited a substantial degree of autonomy in fulfilling output targets.

During perestroika, policy makers lengthened the plan period to five years in order to eliminate the pressures of the ratchet. However, in an environment without a wholesale market, enterprise managers were dependent upon their supplier enterprises to meet their plan obligations, and fulfilling annual output plan targets remained the most important determinant of the bonus payments. In practice, lengthening the plan period did not eliminate the ratchet effect.

*See also:* ENTERPRISE, SOVIET; HARD BUDGET CONSTRAINTS

**BIBLIOGRAPHY**

Birman, Igor. (1978). "From the Achieved Level," *Soviet Studies* 31(2):153–172.

Gregory, Paul R. (1990). *Restructuring the Soviet Economic Bureaucracy.* New York: Cambridge University Press.

SUSAN J. LINZ

## RAZIN REBELLION

Of the four great rebellions that Russia experienced between 1600 and 1800, the rebellion led by the Don Cossack Stepan (Stenka) Razin has evoked the most popular feeling. It did not involve the most territory nor the widest diversity of population, but it lasted the longest, and the name of Stenka Razin has come to signify the very essence of Russian folk spirit.

Stepan Razin's life as a rebel began abruptly at the age of thirty-seven, in April of 1667, when he led a group of fellow Cossacks from their Don River settlements to the Volga River for the purpose of brigandage. The rebellion on the Lower Volga started as a Cossack attack on a fleet of tsarist ships sailing to Astrakhan. This success whetted the appetite of the experienced frontier warriors for further conquest. The state offered no resistance, despite the brigands' obvious intentions. In fact, government troops at garrisons in Tsaritsyn,

Chernyi Yar, and in Astrakhan occasionally joined the rebels in looting and pillaging the rich commerce of the Lower Volga. In the spring of 1668, after wintering at Yaitsk, Razin ventured into the Caspian Sea, lured by the bountiful traffic of the Shah of Persia. As many as one thousand Cossacks took part in this campaign, which struck not only at the shipping on the Caspian, but also attacked commercial settlements and towns of the Caucasus along the western shore, from Derbent south to Baku. After wintering along the southern shore in Persia, Razin's band resumed the campaign in 1669 along the eastern shore among the settlements of the Turkmen population of Central Asia. They then decided to return to the Don in the fall of 1669, with the riches and memories of their long and exhilarating adventure that provided the material for songs and legends that would be handed down for generations.

In March of 1670, Razin announced to the Cossack assembly (krug) that he intended to return to the Volga, but instead of sailing against the Turks or the Persians to the south, this time he pledged to go "into Rus against the traitorous boyars and advisers of the Tsar." After once again securing Tsaritsyn, Chernyi Yar, and Astrakhan by leaving comrades in charge of these fortress towns at the mouth of the Volga, Razin's band moved quickly up the river. In June and July, the townsfolk of Saratov and Samara opened their gates to the Cossacks, and the garrisons surrendered and joined the rebel army. Razin again left Cossacks in charge to supervise the looting and pillaging, while he set out for the next fortified town, Simbirsk. (This town was called Ulianovsk for six decades in the twentieth century, commemorating it as the birthplace of Lenin.)

Razin was forced to lay siege to Simbirsk. After four unsuccessful assaults in September 1670, and threatened by the approach of a major tsarist force, Razin retreated down the Volga in early October. In the meantime, a massive uprising, involving tens of thousands of Russians and native non-Russians (Mordvinians, Chuvash, Cheremiss, and Tatars) erupted in a forty thousand square mile expanse of land called the Middle Volga region. For two months, local rebels controlled virtually all of the territory within a rectangle bordered roughly on four corners by the major towns of Nizhny Novgorod, Kazan, Simbirsk, and Tambov. The type of protest, the levels of violence, the character of leadership, and the extent of popular interaction reflected the socioeconomic realities of the vast region as they appeared on the eve of Razin's arrival. Local issues determined the pattern and ensured the stunning success of the Middle Volga rebellion in the first two months. At the same time, these regional particulars eventually determined the failure of the complex and uncoordinated insurgency in the ensuing two or three months. The uprising was finally crushed in January of 1671 by the combined efforts of five Tsarist armies coordinated by Prince Yuri Dolgorukov from a command post in the midst of the region at Arzamas. In the spring of 1671, a group of Cossacks betrayed the location of Razin's camp on the Don to the Cossack chieftain (ataman), Kornilo Yakovlev. Yakovlev's forces captured Stenka Razin in May and brought him in an iron cage to Moscow, where he was tried and condemned for leading the rebellion, was anathematized by the Russian Orthodox Church, and on June 6 was hanged not far from Red Square and the Kremlin just across the Moscow River.

Thus the state succeeded eventually in destroying Stepan Razin and in imposing its will upon the townsfolk, peasantry, the military, and the rambunctious Russian and non-Russian Volga frontier population. The rebellion solved nothing in the long run, and very little in the short run. Nonetheless, the name of Stenka Razin would live forever as a reminder of this exciting time, and as an enduring promise of relief to the oppressed. The Razin Rebellion expresses a profound truth about the meaning of Russia and its history. That truth is exhilarating and romantic, but at the same time it is violent, bloody, and hopelessly tragic.

See also: ALEXEI MIKHAILOVICH; COSSACKS; ENSERFMENT; PEASANT UPRISINGS

**BIBLIOGRAPHY**

Avrich, Paul. (1972). *Russian Rebels: 1600–1800.* New York: Norton & Company.

Chapygin, Alexei Pavlovich. (1946). *Stepan Razin,* tr. Paul Cedar. London: Hyperion Press.

Field, Cecil. (1947). *The Great Cossack.* London: Herbert Jenkins.

Longworth, Philip. (1969). *The Cossacks.* New York: Holt, Rinehart, and Winston.

Mousnier, Roland. (1970). *Peasant Uprisings in Seventeenth-Century France, Russia, and China.* New York: Harper Torchbooks.

Ure, John. (2003). *The Cossacks: An Illustrated History.* New York: Overlook Press.

JAMES G. HART

## RAZNOCHINTSY

Raznochintsy were people of various ranks, a judicial category of population consisting of educated individuals from classes and estates in Russia in the eighteenth and nineteenth centuries. This included members of the clergy, merchants, petty townspeople, peasantry, minor officials, and impoverished nobility who had received an education and left their former estates.

From the 1840s the raznochintsy had a significant influence on the development of Russian society and culture, and became the main social stratum for the formation of the Russian intelligentsia in the 1860s.

The development of capitalism in Russia after the abolition of serfdom in 1861 demanded more educated people. After the opening of university education for the middle class, the number of educated people in the Russian empire rapidly increased. Thus increased the number of raznochintsy. Raznochintsy worshiped education and had a cult of science, believing that the main principles of life should be materialism, utilitarianism, and scientism. They thought that art should serve utilitarian purposes. The hero of the novel *Fathers and Sons* (1862), by Ivan Turgenev, Evgeny Bazarov was a typical raznochinets and nihilist. He believed only in the value of science and denied the worth of art and poetry.

Among the raznochintsy at that time was widespread nihilism (from the Latin nihil meaning nothing). They denied the traditional values of the society, such as marriage and private property, and derided sentimentalism. They created their own morality and style of life. They called themselves "developed individuals," "thinking realists," "new people" and "critically thinking individuals." The women nihilists had short haircuts and smoked cigarettes. They often live in communes and participated in various groups and societies, where they discussed political and social problems. Raznochintsy usually chose independent liberal professions such as writers, journalists, teachers, scientists, and scholars rather than toiling in government service.

The Russian writers and literary critics Vissarion Belinsky, Nikolai Chernyshevsky and Nickolai Dobrolubov were raznochintsy. The "Letter to Gogol" by Belinsky became the ". . . testament and gospel" of (the Russian) radicals.

Intolerance and unwillingness to accept compromise was very typical for nihilists, the generation of raznochintsy of the 1850s and 1860s. Denying traditional values of the hypocritical society, they were very intolerant of the contrary opinions and created their own system of restrictions and limitations. Some historians explain the radicalism of raznochintsy by their social origins: many of them were the sons of provincial priests and former seminarians, and they were idealists and dreamt about creation of an ideal and fair state. Due to their radicalism, raznochintsy played a central role at the crucial moment in the formation of the revolutionary intelligentsia. By the 1870s nihilism as a social phenomenon almost disappeared and gradually raznochintsy transformed into part of the Russian intelligentsia.

*See also:* INTELLIGENTSIA; NIHILISM AND NIHILISTS

### BIBLIOGRAPHY

Becker, Christopher. (1959). "Raznochintsy: The Development of the Word and the Concept," *American Slavic and E. European Review*, 18: 63–74.

Pomper, Philip. (1970). *The Russian Revolutionary Intelligentsia.* New York: Thomas Y. Crowell Company, Inc.

Wirtschafter, Elise K. (1994). *Structures of Society: Imperial Russia's "Peoples of Various Ranks."* DeKalb: Northern University Press.

VICTORIA KHITERER

## REDEMPTION PAYMENTS

One of Alexander II's reforms was the emancipation of twenty million serfs in 1861. The Russian government paid former serf-holders for land that was then issued in allotments to the newly freed serfs. The peasants, however, were obligated to pay the government back for this land (plus interest) through what were called redemption payments. Each peasant household generally got less land (and less desirable land) in the emancipation settlement than it had tilled before emancipation, and the redemption payments were often in excess of the rental cost of the allotment.

The traditional peasant commune (mir or obshchina) was given the responsibility of assuring that its members would pay their redemption debt. The communes accomplished this by limiting the rights of peasants to leave the commune prior to paying off their debt, and by redistributing land between households in the commune. This method of periodic redistribution ensured that each household had the resources to make its redemption payments, but continued a pattern of a peasants holding many small strips of land rather than one contiguous field. It further required that all peasants retain the primitive three-field system of crop rotation, and discouraged individual peasants from improving their holdings.

Peasants never accepted the redemption debt as legitimate, and many communes accumulated large arrears, which periodically were written off and then accumulated again. By 1905 the government realized that the payments were more of an irritation to the peasantry than they were worth as a source of income, and on November 3 of that year an imperial decree abolished them, partly as a vain attempt to forestall growing peasant unrest that led to the 1905 revolution.

*See also:* ENSERFMENT; EMANCIPATION ACT; GREAT REFORMS; MIR; OBSHCHINA; PEASANTRY; SERFDOM

**BIBLIOGRAPHY**

Lincoln, W. Bruce. (1990). *The Great Reforms.* DeKalb: Northern Illinois University Press.

Robinson, Geroid T. (1967). *Rural Russia under the Old Regime.* Berkeley: University of California Press.

A. DELANO DUGARM

# RED GUARDS

Red Guards (also called Workers' Militia) were volunteer armed bands formed by industrial workers in the cities during the Russian Revolution of 1917. They played an important role in the turmoil of 1917, in the Bolshevik seizure of power, and in securing the new Soviet government. The term *Red Guard* originated in Finland during the Revolution of 1905 and reemerged in 1917, especially after April, to signify the more politically militant armed workers.

Volunteer armed workers' bands were formed during and after the February Revolution by industrial workers at factories to protect and advance the interests of the industrial workers during the revolution, to maintain public safety, and to guard against counterrevolution. They were loosely organized (mostly self-organized), chose their own leaders, and were independent of all political parties and the new Provisional Government. They attracted the more militant members of the working class and gravitated politically toward the radical end of the spectrum (thus the tendency in later writing to associate them with the Bolsheviks, even though Socialist Revolutionaries [SRs], anarchists, and even Mensheviks participated, along with nonparty elements). Indeed, they were a symbol of the most emphatic worker self-organization and self-assertion. Their organizational base was the factory, and their loyalty was to it and to the factory committees and the soviets of workers' and soldiers' deputies, in Petrograd (the capital) and other cities. The government and more moderate socialists were suspicious of them but unable to suppress them.

The Red Guard grew in size and militancy during the summer and early fall as political tensions increased, the economic situation worsened, and workers sensed that the gains they had made after February were slipping away. Industrial workers increasingly saw the Red Guards as essential to protecting their economic and political interests. By the October Revolution, Red Guard detachments totaled about 150,000 to 175,000 men across the country, about 25,000 to 30,000 of them in Petrograd. The Red Guards and the Bolsheviks found common ground in the slogan "All Power to the Soviets" and the call for radical social reforms and an end to the war. As a result, a close working relationship developed between them.

The Red Guards played an important role in the October Revolution and the first few months of the new Bolshevik regime. In Petrograd they joined with soldiers to secure the overthrow of the Provisional Government and the proclamation of "Soviet power"—the new Bolshevik government. Red Guard bands played a similar role in the transfer of power in Moscow and provincial cities. They fought the initial armed efforts to overthrow the Bolsheviks and provided the new government with much-needed armed coercion. The Red Guards were an important part of expeditionary forces sent from Petrograd and Moscow in late 1917 and early 1918 to secure control over outlying regions. Some Red Guard detachments were incorporated into the new Red Army in 1918, others withered away, and the Soviet government formally abolished the Red Guard in April 1918. The essential features of the Red Guard and workers' militias—self-organization, local orientation, and elected leaders—were not suited to the demands of civil war or the new Communist era.

*See also:* BOLSHEVISM; FEBRUARY REVOLUTION; OCTOBER REVOLUTION; WORKERS

**BIBLIOGRAPHY**

Wade, Rex A. (1984). *Red Guards and Workers' Militias in the Russian Revolution.* Stanford, CA: Stanford University Press.

REX A. WADE

# RED SQUARE

Red Square, like the Moscow Kremlin on which it borders, is one of the best known locales of modern world culture. Associated with military parades, aggressive rhetoric, and the Lenin mausoleum, Red Square came to symbolize Soviet power from 1918 until the demise of the Soviet Union. The term "red" in fact derives not from political sources but from a former meaning of the Russian word *krasnaia:* "beautiful."

From the earliest days of Moscow's existence in the twelfth century, some form of trading area probably existed to the east of the fortified center (kremlin) of the settlement. By the second half of the fourteenth century, evidence suggests that there was a more clearly defined area devoted to trade and located near the main, east towers of the Kremlin, whose log walls were at that time being rebuilt in limestone by Prince Dmitry Ivanovich. This space was enlarged for defensive purposes by the decree of Ivan III after the great fire of 1493, which destroyed many ramshackle trading booths.

The sixteenth century witnessed dramatic changes in the form and meaning of Red Square. Between 1508 and 1516, Basil III ordered that a large moat be dug along the east wall of the Kremlin, which had been rebuilt of strong brick under the supervision of Italian engineers. The highest sections of the wall faced Red Square, which had no natural defensive barrier, whereas the Moscow and Neglinnaia Rivers flowed along the other two sides of the Kremlin triangle. Between 1535 and 1538, the construction of brick walls around the larger trading district of Kitai gorod (Chinatown, lying to the east of the Kremlin) gave Red Square its own defensive system, and the moat was soon drained. Within a few years of the conquest of Kazan by Ivan IV in 1552, work began on the most renowned of Moscow's architectural monuments, the Cathedral of the Intercession on the Moat, pop-

ularly called Saint Basil's (1555–1561). With the consecration of this complex structure, Red Square gained a focal point that has remained to this day.

The first ruler to attempt to bring order into the chaotic trading zone of Red Square was Boris Godunov, who in 1595 ordered the construction of brick trading rows on the east side of the square. These rows, designated Upper, Middle, and Lower, faced the east wall of the Kremlin and descended almost to the bank of the Moscow River. Tsar Boris also commanded the rebuilding of Lobnoe mesto, the site from which state proclamations were read. First mentioned in 1547, this wooden platform was rebuilt as a circular limestone form with a low parapet. From the sixteenth through the eighteenth centuries, the area near Lobnoe mesto became notorious as a place of state executions.

The deliverance of Moscow from the Time of Troubles (1598–1613, an interregnum that included the occupation of the city by Polish forces) in the early seventeenth century was commemorated by the construction of the Church of the Kazan Mother of God (consecrated in 1636, razed in 1936, rebuilt in 1990–1993). In the same period, Red Square was repaved with flat logs, and during the reign of Alexei Mikhailovich, its north boundary was given a more imposing form with the construction of the brick Resurrection Gate (1680; razed in 1931 and rebuilt between 1994 and 1996). By the latter part of the eighteenth century, Catherine the Great embarked on another campaign to rid the square of wooden structures. As part of this process, the trading rows were expanded and Lobnoe mesto was shifted eastward to its present position.

In 1804 the square was repaved with cobblestones, but not until the rebuilding of Moscow after the 1812 fire was the dry moat filled and planted with trees. With the surge in Moscow's economic and cultural significance in the latter half of the nineteenth century, Red Square underwent a fundamental change that included the building of the Historical Museum (1874–1883) and the expansion of the Upper and Middle Trading Rows (1888–1893 and 1889–1891, respectively).

After the shift of the Soviet capital to Moscow in 1918, Red Square became the site of the country's major demonstrations and its cobblestones were replaced with flat, granite paving blocks. The Lenin Mausoleum, first built of wood (1924) and then in its current form (1930), became the most visible symbol of the regime. On November 7,

1941, ranks of soldiers marched past the mausoleum tribune directly to the front during the deciding phase of the Battle of Moscow. During the postwar period the world's attention continued to be riveted by the Red Square parades, but perhaps the most startling event occurred on May 28, 1987, when Mathias Rust, a teen-aged German pilot, landed a small plane in the center of Red Square. The repercussions of this act, which Rust proclaimed a gesture of peace, extended not only to the Defense Ministry but to the entire Soviet governing apparatus.

In the post-Soviet area, Red Square continued to be a place of public demonstrations and tours. Although debates have continued about the role of certain features, such as the Lenin Mausoleum, Red Square seems to be one of the few areas of Moscow that will retain its present form into the twenty-first century.

*See also:* ARCHITECTURE; CATHEDRAL OF ST. BASIL; KREMLIN; MOSCOW

**BIBLIOGRAPHY**

Brumfield, William Craft. (1993). *A History of Russian Architecture.* New York: Cambridge University Press.

Murrell, Kathleen Berton. (1990). *Moscow: An Architectural History.* New York: St. Martin's Press.

WILLIAM CRAFT BRUMFIELD

# RED TERROR

Initiated in 1918, Red Terror was a state policy of the Bolshevik government to suppress, intimidate, or liquidate real or potential adversaries of the regime. It started on September 5, when the survival of the Bolshevik regime was threatened by foreign and domestic foes. Individual guilt did not matter; belonging to a suspect social class did. It was, in other words, a class-based approach not to justice but to settling accounts with potential enemies. Its first victims were former tsarist officers, policemen, aristocracy, opposition parties' leaders, and property owners who had enjoyed privileges under the old regime. In 1918 about fifteen thousand were executed. In 1919, other social groups were targeted: former landlords, entrepreneurs, and Cossacks, attacked for their suspected anti-Bolshevik attitudes. In 1920 the policy was extended to peasants in rebellious provinces, along with thousands of captured White Russian officers and their families. White Russians were the counterrevolutionaries; the color white was a symbol of the old order and the color red was a symbol of revolution and communism.

Red Terror was carried out by a new institution, called the Cheka (an abbreviation of the Russian for "extraordinary commission"). The Cheka was a state institution, subordinate only to the Communist Party Central Committee. It was a political police force that did not enforce the law but instead administered systematic terror arbitrarily. Local Chekas, especially in the Ukraine, were notorious for their cruelty, and for mass executions carried out in the summer of 1919. It was a party instrument for the conduct of legalized lawlessness. Settling of accounts and personal gain were often motives for denunciation. New concepts entered the lexicon, among them "enemies of the people," "hidden enemies," and "suspect social origin." The long term consequence of Red Terror was a disregard for individual guilt or innocence, the institutionalization of a class-based approach to justice, the designation of "suspect social groups," fear and intimidation of entire population and, subsequently, an even greater wave of state-sponsored terror under Josef Vissarionovich Stalin.

*See also:* BOLSHEVISM; DZERZHINSKY, FELIX EDMUNDOVICH; STATE SECURITY, ORGANS OF; TERRORISM

**BIBLIOGRAPHY**

Brovkin, Vladimir. (1994). *Behind the Front Lines of the Civil War: Political Parties and Social Movements in Russia.* Princeton, NJ: Princeton University Press.

Courtois, Stéphane et al. (1999). *The Black Book of Communism: Crimes, Terror, Repression,* tr. Jonathan Murphy and Mark Kramer, consulting ed., Mark Kramer. Cambridge, MA: Harvard University Press.

Figes, Orlando. (1989). *Peasant Russia, Civil War: The Volga Countryside in Revolution.* London: Oxford University Press.

Leggett, George. (1981). *The Cheka: Lenin's Political Police.* New York: Oxford University Press.

Maximoff, G.P. (1979). *The Guillotine at Work: The Leninist Counterrevolution.* Orkney, UK: Cienfigos Press.

Melgunov, Sergey. (1974). *The Red Terror in Russia.* Westport, CT: Hyperion.

Pipes, Richard. (1995). *Russia under the Bolshevik Regime.* New York: Vintage Books.

Swain, Geoffrey. (1996). *The Origins of the Russian Civil War*. London: Longman.

VLADIMIR BROVKIN

## REFERENDUM OF APRIL 1993

The Referendum of April 1993 was the first and second-to-last referendum in new Russia, if one counts the national vote on the constitution in December 1993. It was held as a result of opposition between President Boris Yeltsin and the Congress of People's Deputies. Yeltsin, who was highly popular at the time, relied on direct mandate, which he received two years earlier in the elections, and the Congress made active efforts at limiting his power, changing the constitution in its favor. Not one of the referendum questions provided for direct action; thus they were only significant as cards in a political game.

There were four referendum questions:

1. Do you have confidence in Boris Yeltsin, president of the Russian Federation? ("yes": 58.7%; "no": 39.3%);
2. Do you approve of the socioeconomic political policy conducted by the president of the RF (Russian Federation) and by the RF government since 1992? ("yes": 53%; "no": 44.5%);
3. Do you consider it necessary to hold early elections for the president of the RF? ("yes": 49.5%, or 31.7% of all voters, "no": 47%, or 30.1% of voters);
4. Do you consider it necessary to hold early elections for RF delegates? ("yes": 67.2%, or 43% of voters; "no": 30.1%, or 19.3% of voters).

With 64 percent participation, all questions but the third (concerning early presidential elections) had a majority of "yes" votes; however, less than half the voters responded to the questions concerning early presidential and RF delegate elections. The last point is significant in that, according to a decision of the Constitutional Court, the third and fourth questions, affecting the Constitution, required a constitutional majority. For this reason the referendum had a purely psychological impact, though a great one at that. It showed that with increasing conflict, neither the executive nor the representative branches of power enjoyed the support of the absolute majority of the population. Despite all the burdens of economic reform, the president and the government he formed still had a signifi-

cant store of popular confidence. Taking into account Chechnya, where the referendum did not take place, and Tatarstan, where participation was little over 20 percent, voters in 28 out of 89 regions, including 14 national formations, did not express confidence in the president.

Appealing to popular support that he received in the referendum, Yeltsin first accelerated the process of revising of the new, "presidential" constitution, and in the fall he resolved the conflict with the representative branch by means of force. The congress was dismissed, and a vote was scheduled for the new constitution, as well as elections to parliament on the basis of this new constitution.

*See also:* CONGRESS OF PEOPLE'S DEPUTIES; CONSTITUTION OF 1993; OCTOBER 1993 EVENTS; YELTSIN, BORIS NIKOLAYEVICH

**BIBLIOGRAPHY**

McFaul, Michael. (2001). *Russia's Unfinished Revolution: Political Change from Gorbachev to Putin*. Ithaca, NY: Cornell University Press.

McFaul, Michael, and Markov, Sergei. (1993). *The Troubled Birth of Russian Democracy: Parties, Personalities, and Programs*. Stanford, CA: Hoover Institution Press.

Reddaway, Peter, and Glinski, Dmitri. (2001). *The Tragedy of Russia's Reforms: Market Bolshevism against Democracy*. Washington, DC: U.S. Institute of Peace Press.

White, Stephen; Rose, Richard; and McAllister, Ian. (1997). *How Russia Votes*. Chatham, NJ: Chatham House.

NIKOLAI PETROV

## REFERENDUM OF DECEMBER 1993

A referendum of December 12, 1993, ratified a new constitution for the Russian Federation, which had long been sought by President Boris Yeltsin. The collapse of the USSR in late 1991 made the ratification of a new constitution most urgent. As the USSR no longer existed as a legal entity, its laws technically no longer had legal force. To fill this void, President Yeltsin and the parliament concurred that the constitution and laws of the former RSFSR would continue to be observed until a new constitution could be adopted. This was a necessary but unsatisfactory situation, since the 1978 Constitution of the Russian Federation was the product of the Brezhnev era and reflected the values of the now repudiated communist system.

Throughout the period from 1991 to 1993, Yeltsin quarreled with the parliament over the outlines of a new constitution. In particular, progress toward approving a new constitution was delayed by heated disputes over three major issues: the allocation of powers between the executive branch and the legislative branch, the allocation of powers between central and subnational institutions, and the process for ratifying a new constitution. The deadlock was finally broken on September 21, 1993, when Yeltsin issued a decree dissolving the parliament. Anti-Yeltsin members of parliament refused to disband but were evicted by force on October 4, as Yeltsin ordered troops to fire on the Russian White House.

The violent events of October 1993 cleared the way for new elections to be held on December 12, in which voters were asked to approve a draft constitution favorable to the president and also to elect a new lower house of parliament (Duma), called for in the draft.

President Yeltsin issued a degree on October 15 calling for a plebiscite on his draft constitution. The document was made public on November 9, leaving only one month for debate and discussion. Yeltsin's choice of terminology "plebiscite" rather than "referendum" was not accidental. According to the 1990 Law on Referenda, issues affecting the constitution required the support of a majority of all registered voters, rather than a majority of all those voting.

Voter turnout for the December 12 referendum was low compared to previous elections. Only 54.8 percent of eligible voters turned out, and of those, only 58.4 percent supported the new constitution. Had ratification of the new constitution depended on the referendum, it would have lost, since only about 31 percent of all eligible voters supported the new constitution. However, Yeltsin declared a victory for the new constitution in the plebiscite, and the document became generally regarded as the legitimate Constitution of the Russian Federation.

*See also:* CONSTITUTION OF 1993; OCTOBER 1993 EVENTS; YELTSIN, BORIS NIKOLAYEVICH

## BIBLIOGRAPHY

Marsh, Christopher. (2002). *Russia at the Polls: Voters, Elections and Democratization.* Washington, DC: CQ Press.

White, Stephen; Rose, Richard; and McAllister, Ian. (1997). *How Russia Votes.* Chatham, NJ: Chathan House.

GORDON B. SMITH

# REFERENDUM OF MARCH 1991

On March 17, 1991, a referendum was held in the Soviet Union in which voters were asked the following question: "Do you consider necessary the preservation of the Union of Soviet Socialist Republics as a renewed federation of equal sovereign republics, in which the rights and freedoms of an individual of any nationality will be fully guaranteed?" The referendum was sponsored by the Soviet president, Mikhail S. Gorbachev, who hoped it would make clear that despite rising separatist sentiments in many parts of the USSR, a majority of Soviet citizens wanted the country to remain unified. The six union republics where separatist aspirations were strongest—Armenia, Estonia, Georgia, Latvia, Lithuania, Moldavia (Moldova)—boycotted the referendum. However, their populations made up only approximately 7 percent of the total USSR population. Overall turnout was 80.0 percent, and 76.4 percent of those participating voted "yes." In Russia, turnout was 75.4 percent, with 71.3 percent voting "yes," while in Ukraine turnout was 83.5 percent, with 70.2 percent voting "yes" (the lowest percentage among all union republics). In all six republics with traditionally Muslim majorities, well over 90 percent voted "yes."

The results were initially interpreted as a victory for Gorbachev and other defenders of the union. However, the significance of the referendum was undermined by the ambiguity of the question. It was unclear, for example, what was meant by "a renewed federation of equal sovereign republics." In addition, some of the participating republics added supplemental questions to the ballot. In Russia, for example, voters were asked to endorse the establishment of a directly elected Russian Soviet Federated Socialist Republic (RSFSR) president, which was understood as an opportunity to support the leader of the Russian government and Gorbachev's principal rival at the time, Boris Yeltsin. In Ukraine, Kyrgyzstan, and Uzbekistan, voters were asked whether they supported their republic's sovereignty as part of a new union, while in Kazakhstan the wording of the referendum was changed by substituting "equal sovereign states" for "equal sovereign republics." In each case, the electorate approved the supplemental questions. Thus the referendum failed to resolve the Soviet Union's crisis of territorial integrity. Nine months later, the USSR passed into history as a legal entity. Nevertheless, in the long term the referendum left a legacy of post-independence resentment in those areas where the electorate had voted in favor of a preserved union; many people felt that the USSR's dissolution had been opposed by the great majority of Soviet voters.

*See also:* GORBACHEV, MIKHAIL SERGEYEVICH; NATIONALITIES POLICIES, SOVIET; YELTSIN, BORIS NIKOLAYEVICH

**BIBLIOGRAPHY**

Brady, Henry E., and Kaplan, Cynthia S. (1994). "Eastern Europe and the Former Soviet Union." In *Referendums around the World: The Growing Use of Direct Democracy,* ed. David Butler and Austin Ranney. Washington, DC: AEI Press.

Walker, Edward W. (2003). *Dissolution: Sovereignty and the Breakup of the USSR.* Boulder, CO: Rowman & Littlefield.

EDWARD W. WALKER

# REFUSENIKS

Beginning in the mid-1960s, a movement began among Soviet Jews seeking permission to emigrate to Israel. Despite an agreement to allow emigrations, Soviet authorities subjected most of those who sought to leave to a campaign of intimidation: Soviet citizenship might be revoked; many were fired from their jobs; they were harrassed, their phones were bugged, and they faced hostile interrogations. The most vocal activists, such as Anatoly (later Natan) Sharansky and Vladimir Slepak, were arrested on charges of treason and espionage and sent to psychiatric hospitals or labor camps. Although eventually, in the 1970s and again in the Gorbachev era, tens of thousands of Jews were allowed to leave, many were denied exit visas for months, years, and even decades on grounds of national security or political animosity. These unfortunates became known as "refuseniks," and their plight, both in itself and as shorthand for the plight of Soviet Jewry in general was a *cause célèbre* in the West and a sticking point in U.S.-Soviet relations.

Jews had always faced pervasive discrimination in the USSR, but several factors coincided in the 1960s to crystallize Jewish national consciousness and stimulate a drive to emigrate. Some were the same factors that spurred the dissident movement. The Khrushchev-era Thaw produced new interest in Jewish culture. The trial of Andrei Sinyavsky and Yuly Daniel in 1966 signaled a crackdown on the intelligentsia, a disproportionate number of whom were Jews. The 1968 invasion of Czechoslovakia convinced many that their hopes for reform were pipe dreams.

Other factors were specific to the Jewish question. Jewish groups in the West began to organize around the issue of Soviet antisemitism and to make contact with Soviet Jews. Most importantly, Israel's stunning victory in the Six-Day War (1967) stirred the imagination of Soviet Jews and made them listen more attentively to Israel's call, while the vicious and scurrilous anti-Zionist campaign that followed made Jews feel that there was no place for them in the USSR.

Large-scale Jewish emigration began in earnest in 1971. Nearly 13,000 left that year, followed by 32,000 in 1972. Most of the early immigrants went to Israel. The flow of émigrés ebbed in the mid-1970s, then soared to a high of 50,000 in 1979, with more than half going to the United States before slowing to a trickle following the U.S. boycott of the 1980 Olympics in Moscow under the repressive hands of Yuri Andropov and Konstantin Chernenko. Why did the Soviet government allow Jews to emigrate at all? One theory cites external factors, including intense pressure from Jewish and human-rights organizations in the West, Soviet attempts to win concessions in the era of détente, and legal measures such as the Jackson-Vanik Amendment in the United States, which tied most-favored-nation trading status to a country's emigration policies. Another theory gives primary credit to internal factors: the pressure of Jewish nationalism itself, a desire to rid the country of troublemakers, the hope of using emigration to plant spies in capitalist countries. Both theories presume that Soviet emigration policy was coherent and followed a set of clear goals articulated at the top. Archival documents reveal the contrary; the central authorities had little expertise on the issue and reacted on the spur of the moment to biased reports from self-interested bureaucracies.

In 1987, after initial hesitation, Mikhail Gorbachev allowed the majority of refuseniks to leave as perestroika and glasnost gathered steam. With the fall of the Soviet Union, most restrictions on emigration were rescinded, and the Jewish exodus became a flood.

*See also:* ISRAEL, RELATIONS WITH; JEWS; SINYAVSKY-DANIEL TRIAL; THAW, THE

**BIBLIOGRAPHY**

Lewin-Epstein, Noah; Ro'i, Yaacov; and Ritterband, Paul, eds. (1997). *Russian Jews on Three Continents: Migration and Resettlement.* London: Frank Cass.

Morozov, Boris, ed. (1999). *Documents on Soviet Jewish Emigration.* Portland, OR: Frank Cass.

JONATHAN D. WALLACE

# REGIONALISM

Regionalism is the idea or practice of dividing a country into smaller units for political, economic, social, and cultural purposes. Politically, regionalism is linked to decentralized or federalist governments. Regionalism is both cultural and political, as its political success is linked to the development of a regional culture. From 1759 to the 1860s, Russian regionalism was primarily cultural. After 1861, Siberian regionalism combined cultural with political demands. Under the Soviets, regionalism retreated to a mainly cultural sphere of action. After 1991, regionalism became a major political force.

In the eighteenth century, regional studies arose from the center's interest in geography and from the periphery's traditions of chronicle writing and regional pride. In the Petrine era, Vasily Tatishchev established regional geography in theory and practice by organizing expeditions to explore the regions. During the eighteenth century, medieval chronicles evolved into more secular histories of a town or region. In 1759 Vasily Krestinin founded the first Russian local historical society, the Society for Historical Investigations, in Arkhangelsk. Krestinin's work on Arkhangelsk history merged the statist genre of descriptive geography with the chronicle traditions of the Russian north. Regional journals, such as *The Solitary Bumpkin* (*Uyedinenny Poshekhonets*) (Yaroslavl, 1786–1787) and *Irtysh* (Tobolsk, 1789–1791), also helped to foster a regional identity. The establishment of provincial newspapers in all European provinces in 1837 furthered the process.

In the 1850s and 1860s, Siberian regionalism (*oblastnichestvo*) combined the scholarship of federalist historian Afanasy Shchapov and the political activity of Nikolai Yadrintsev, for which the latter and his group were arrested for separatism and exiled to Arkhangelsk until 1874. Siberian regionalists argued that Siberia was a colony of Moscow and demanded political rights. After 1905, Siberian regionalists were elected to the Duma and discussed the idea of a Siberian regional duma. The provincial statistical committees, established in 1834, the zemstvo (1864), and the provincial scholarly archival commissions (1884) all published widely on regional issues.

After the October Revolution in 1917, the Bolsheviks set out to centralize the country. During the civil war, regions such as Siberia and Kaluga proclaimed their independence. By the end of the civil war, however, political regionalism was under attack. The most viable regionalist institution was the *sovnarkhozy*, or the regional economic councils. In 1932 they were eliminated. Until Gorbachev, there was little room for political regionalism. Moscow appointed regional leaders and, apart from some passive resistance, they were obedient. Culturally, the 1920s were the golden age of regional studies (*krayevedenie*), but that ended in 1929 and 1930, when the Academy of Sciences and the Central Bureau of Regional Studies and their regional affiliates were purged. In 1966, the Society for Preservation of Monuments of History and Culture was established, with the right to open provincial branches, which helped to create an institutional base for regional studies.

In 1985, when Mikhail Gorbachev came to power, the regions began to rise in political power. Legally, there were eighty-nine regions within the Russian Soviet Federated Socialist Republic (RSFSR). The RSFSR was unusual in that it was a federation within the larger federation of the Soviet Union. Its administrative divisions can be grouped into two main categories: the mainly non-Russian ethnically-based republics and the ethnically Russian territorially based regions. In 1990 the "parade of sovereignties" began, as the Union Republics (republics of the Soviet Union) became independent states. The RSFSR declared its sovereignty on June 12, 1990. Boris Yeltsin, who had just been elected chair of the RSFSR's Supreme Soviet, hoped to make Gorbachev's leadership of the Soviet Union redundant by ending the Soviet Union. In August 1990, Yeltsin told the heads of two of the RSFSR's autonomous republics to "take as much sovereignty as you can swallow." In 1991 the Soviet Union collapsed, despite Gorbachev's efforts to save it with the Union Treaty. The RSFSR's autonomous republics had been about to sign the Union Treaty both as members of the RSFSR and as Union Republics. Later, several of the autonomous republics argued for their sovereignty as independent states. After 1991 there were two rounds of treaties to bind the eighty-nine "subjects" (as all the administrative divisions were termed) together as the Russian Federation. The first was the Federation Treaties, which divided powers between the center and the republics and regions in an often ambiguous manner. The 1993 Russian Constitution superseded the Federation Treaties, setting off the second round of treaties, which often allowed conflicting laws to coexist. Yeltsin's administration was marked by an increase in regionalism, as regional elites gained power while the central state collapsed. Yeltsin signed a series of bilateral treaties with the subjects, ceding central power and producing an ad hoc system of asymmetrical freedom.

Vladimir Putin has made curbing regionalism a main priority of his presidency. One of his primary interests has been to create a single legal space in the Russian Federation by ensuring that the law of the subjects can no longer contradict federal law. To this end, he has created seven super regions superimposed over the other eighty-nine and staffed by presidential appointees. In general, Putin's desire for a strong central state is not easily reconciled with regionalist demands for a more decentralized government.

*See also:* FEDERATION TREATIES; GEOGRAPHY; GORBACHEV, MIKHAIL SERGEYEVICH; SOVNARKHOZY; UNION TREATY; YELTSIN, BORIS NIKOLAYEVICH

**BIBLIOGRAPHY**

Evtuhov, Catherine. (1998). "Voices from the Provinces: Living and Writing in Nizhnii Novgorod, 1870–1905." *Journal of Popular Culture* 34(4):33–48.

Gel'man, Vladimir. (1999). "Regime Transition, Uncertainty, and Prospects for Democratisation: The Politics of Russia's Regions in a Comparative Perspective." *Europe-Asia Studies* 51:939–956.

Herd, Graeme P., and Aldis, Anne, eds. (2003). *Russian Regions and Regionalism: Strength through Weakness.* London: RoutledgeCurzon.

Nikitin, N. P. (1966). "A History of Economic Geography in Pre-Revolutionary Russia." *Soviet Geography: Review and Translation* 7(9):3–37.

Von Mohrenschildt, Dimitri. (1981). *Toward a United States of Russia: Plans and Projects of Federal Reconstruction of Russia in the Nineteenth Century.* Rutherford, NJ: Fairleigh Dickinson University Press.

SUSAN SMITH-PETER

# REITERN, MIKHAIL KHRISTOFOROVICH

(1820–1890), financial official during the reign of Alexander II.

As minister of finances, state secretary, member of the State Council, and chairman of the Council of Ministers, Count Mikhail Khristoforovich Reitern oversaw Russia's finances during the epoch of the Great Reforms. Reitern was born in the city of Poreche in Smolensk guberniya. His father, a Livonian-German nobleman who distinguished himself in Russian military service, died when the boy was thirteen, leaving his widow to raise fourteen children. Mikhail attended the prestigious Imperial Lyceum at Tsarskoe Selo on a scholarship and graduated in 1839. Like most of his classmates, he embarked upon a career in state service, joining the Ministry of Finance in 1840. Three years later he transferred to the Ministry of Justice, where he remained until 1854, when he joined the staff of the chief of the Main Naval Staff, Grand Duke Konstantin Nikolayevich (the second son of Emperor Nicholas I).

As one of the so-called Konstantinovtsy, the circle of reform-minded officials around the grand duke, Reitern carried out a variety of special commissions and inspections, and championed a series of innovations that included cutting the number of state-owned enterprises, abolishing obligated labor, and contracting with private firms. He was largely responsible for the Naval Ministry's establishing a pension fund for naval officers. In 1855 Reitern went abroad to study finance and administrative practices in Prussia, the United States, France, and England. His reports stressed the utility of private capital in the development of the national economy. On his return in 1854, he was appointed to the special committees on railroad development and the banking system. The latter led to the founding in 1860 of Russia's first central bank, the State Bank. Reitern subsequently returned to the Ministry of Finances as a senior official and in 1861 was named to the Commission on Financing Peasant Affairs, which worked out the financial arrangements for the emancipation of the serfs.

In 1862 Alexander II appointed Reitern minister of finances, a post he held until 1878. During his tenure he fostered greater glasnost in Russian state finances (including the first published budget in 1862) and reformed the tax system to include more indirect taxation, such as excise taxes on spirits and salt. He sought unsuccessfully to restore the convertibility of Russia's paper rubles into gold and silver, and in addition worked to balance the budget but did not succeed until in the sixth year of his tenure. Reitern was keen to sustain the empire's credit rating on international financial markets, but his efforts were frustrated by the economic consequences of the Polish Rebellion of 1863. Reitern promoted private railroad construction, shaped the policies of the State Bank to enhance private investment, and drafted legislation for joint stock companies. His tenure witnessed a great expansion of Russian railroads from a little more than a thousand miles in 1862 to close to fourteen thousand by 1878. He favored both the integration of the national economy into the world economy and the development of Russian industry as necessary to ensure the empire's welfare and security. In 1876, as war loomed with Turkey, Reitern warned Alexander II that the conflict would threaten Russia's credit and finances, offering to resign when Alexander II nonetheless decided upon war. At the emperor's request, he remained in office until the conflict was over and resigned in June 1878.

Reitern remained a member of the State Council, and in 1881 Alexander III appointed him chairman of the Council of Ministers, a post he held until 1886, when he retired because of poor health.

*See also:* ECONOMY, TSARIST; GREAT REFORMS; RAILWAYS

**BIBLIOGRAPHY**

Kipp, Jacob W. (1975). "M. Kh. Reutern on the Russian State and Economy: A Liberal Bureaucrat during the Crimean Era." *Journal of Modern History* 47 (3): 437–459.

JACOB W. KIPP

# RELIGION

Russia has been multireligious from its very inception. When Kiev Rus adopted Eastern Orthodoxy in 988, a gradual Christianization began, advancing slowly from urban elites to the lower classes and countryside. Pagan belief and practice persisted, however, and was sometimes incorporated into Orthodox ritual. Prerevolutionary historians termed the resulting syncretism "dual faith" (*dvoyeveriye*), emphasizing the survival of paganism and superficiality of the Orthodox veneer. While simplistic, that reductionist view of popular religion suggests the complexity of religious cultures, the institutional backwardness of the church, and the daunting geographic scale of the task it faced. Not until the eighteenth century did the church, in any real sense, construct the administrative tools needed to standardize and regulate popular Orthodoxy.

By that time the empire was exploding in size and religious diversity. Although medieval Russia had absorbed peoples of other faiths (such as the Muslim Tatars), religious pluralism became a predominant feature in the modern period. The state annexed vast new territories of Siberia and eastern Ukraine (in the seventeenth century) and then added an array of new lands and peoples in the eighteenth (Baltics, western Ukraine, Belarus) and nineteenth centuries (the Caucasus, Poland, Finland, and Central Asia). That expansion increased the size and complexity of the non-Orthodox population exponentially. Although, according to the census of 1897, the population remained predominantly Eastern Orthodox (69.3%), the empire had substantial numbers of non-Orthodox believers (often concentrated in geographic areas): Muslims (11.1%), Catholics (9.1%), Jews (4.2%), Lutherans (2.7%), Old Believers (1.8%), and various other Christian and non-Christian groups. Indeed, the figures on the non-Orthodox side are understated: the census failed to record adherents of persecuted movements seeking to evade legal trouble.

This waxing religious pluralism posed a serious problem for a regime once imbued with a messianic identity as the Third Rome. Although the process of accommodation commenced in the seventeenth century, it sharply accelerated in the eighteenth, as the regime sought to recruit foreign mercenaries, specialists, and colonists. To reaffirm the precedence of the Russian Orthodox Church, the government adopted the principle of static religious identity: each subject was to retain the original faith (the sole permissible form of conversion being to Orthodoxy, with conversion from Orthodoxy criminalized as apotasy). For state officials devoted to *raison d'état* what mattered most was stability, not salvation—much to the chagrin of Orthodox zealots. Indeed, that secularity prevailed in the imperial manifesto of April 17, 1905, which, in a futile attempt to quell the revolution of 1905, granted freedom of religious belief. After an interlude of broken promises and rising tensions, the February Revolution finally brought full religious freedom (including freedom of official religious affiliation and practice).

That freedom was short-lived: Once the Bolshevik regime came to power in October 1917, it persecuted religious groups, with the assumption that such superstition would promptly wither away. Dismayed by signs of a religious revival, in 1929 the party unleashed a massive assault on all religions, systematically closing houses of worship

**Procession of clergy outside Moscow's city walls, 1867.** © AUSTRIAN ARCHIVES/CORBIS

and subjecting not only clergy but also believers to repression. To no avail: The January 1937 census revealed that 55.3 percent of those over age 14 declared themselves believers. That impelled the regime to redouble its efforts. In 1937–1941, hundreds of thousands were arrested and large numbers executed.

Although World War II forced the Stalinist regime to tolerate the reestablishment of many religious organizations, these encountered growing pressure that continued past Stalin's death in 1953. The post-Stalinist regimes proved indefatigable in efforts to efface the remnants of superstition. They did achieve a reduction in organized religion: the number of religious organizations in the USSR declined by a third (from 22,698 in 1961 to 15,202 in 1985).

Even if religious organizations had dwindled, the government proved far less effective in com-

bating religious observance. Indeed, data from the latter period of Soviet rule showed clear signs of religious revival. In the case of baptism, for example, even if the aggregate figures between 1979 and 1984 decreased (by 6.7%), authorities could not fail to notice increases in some non-Russian republics (19.9% in Georgia, for example) and even in the RSFSR (1.5%). Baptism rates, moreover, skyrocketed among non-Orthodox Christians, with increases of 43.6 percent among Lutherans, 33.3 percent among Methodists, and 52.1 percent among Mennonites. Data about monetary contributions—an increase of 17.8 percent between 1979 and 1984—gave the regime further cause for worry. These funds allowed established religions to bolster their central administrations (45.9% of funds), expand support for clergy (14.3%), and spend more on religious artifacts and literature (17.4%).

Mikhail Gorbachev's perestroika in the mid-1980s brought a significant improvement in the status and activism of religion. That, doubtless, was a key factor behind the stunning 36.6 percent increase in religious groups in the Soviet Union (from 12,438 in 1985 to 16,990 in 1990); in the RSFSR, the rate of growth was only slightly slower—32.6 percent (from 3,003 in 1985 to 3,983 in 1990). The expansion of organized religion hardly abated after the fall of the Soviet Union in 1991: In the Russian Federation, the number of registered religious organizations rose fivefold (to 20,200 on December 31, 2000).

That growth has been somewhat troubling for the Russian Orthodox Church. Although a majority of the citizens in the Russian Federation profess some vague allegiance to Orthodoxy, observants are relatively few (4.5%), and still fewer attend services on a regular basis. Still more alarming has been the exponential growth of non-Orthodox religious groups, especially Christian evangelical and Pentecostal movements. In an effort to contain cult movements, the law on religious organizations (October 1997) posed barriers to the registration of new religious groups, that is, those that had emerged within the last fifteen years, chiefly from foreign missions. Nevertheless, by the closing deadline for registration on December 31, 2000, Russian Orthodoxy claimed only a slight majority (10,913) of the 20,200 religious organizations in the Russian Federation; the rest consisted of Muslim (3,048), Evangelicals (1,323), Baptists (975), Evangelical Christians (612), Seventh-Day Adventists (563), Jehovah's Witnesses (330), Old Believers (278), Catholics (258), Lutherans (213), Jews (197), and various smaller groups.

*See also:* CATHOLICISM; HAGIOGRAPHY; ISLAM; JEWS; MONASTICISM; ORTHODOXY; PAGANISM; PROTESTANTISM; RUSSIAN ORTHODOX CHURCH; SAINTS

**BIBLIOGRAPHY**

Anderson, John. (1994). *Religion, State, and Politics in the Soviet Union and Successor States.* New York: St. Martin's Press.

Corley, Felix. (1996). *Religion in the Soviet Union: An Archival Reader.* New York: New York University Press.

Geraci, Robert P., and Khodarkovsky, Michael. (2001). *Of Religion and Empire: Missions, Conversion, and Tolerance in Tsarist Russia.* Ithaca, NY: Cornell University Press.

Hosking, Geoffrey A. (1991). *Church, Nation, and State in Russia and Ukraine.* New York: St. Martin's Press.

Lewis, David C. (1999). *After Atheism: Religion and Ethnicity in Russia and Central Asia.* New York: St. Martin's Press.

GREGORY L. FREEZE

## RENOVATIONISM *See* LIVING CHURCH MOVEMENT.

## REPIN, ILYA YEFIMOVICH

(1844–1930), Russia's most celebrated realist painter.

The future master of realism, whose genius with the canvas put him on par with the literary and musical luminaries of Russia's nineteenth century, Ilya Yefimovich Repin arose from truly inauspicious surroundings. His father, a peasant, was a military colonist in the Ukrainian (then, "Little Russia") town of Chuguev. His talent manifested itself early, and at age twenty, he entered St. Petersburg's Academy of Arts. His first major piece, *The Raising of Jarius's Daughter,* won him the gold medal in academic competition, and with it, a scholarship to study in France and Italy. Although the Impressionists at that time were beginning their critical reappraisal of representation, Repin remained a realist, although his use of light shows that he did not escape the influence of the new style. Upon his return to Russia, he developed a nationalist strain in his paintings that reflected the political mood of his era. In this work, he connected the realism of style with that of politics, bringing his viewers' attentions to the arduous circumstances under which so many of their fellow citizens labored, reflected in his first major work beyond the Academy, *Barge Haulers on the Volga.*

Although Repin was never specifically a political activist, he was nonetheless involved with other artists in challenging the conservative, autocratic status quo. For example, he joined with other painters who, calling themselves the *peredvizhniki,* or "itinerants," revolted against the system of patronage in the arts and circulated their works throughout the provinces, bringing art to the emergent middle classes. Moreover, they chose compositions that depicted their surroundings, as opposed to the staid classicism of mythology; Repin shifted from *Jarius's Daughter* to Russian legends, exemplified by several versions of Sadko, a popular figure from medieval, merchant Novgorod. More impressive, though, were those among his works that evoked the reality of all aspects of contemporary life, from the revolutionary movement to Russia's colonial enterprise, from *The Student-Nihilist* to *The Zaporozhian Cossacks*.

Repin also excelled as a portrait painter because he was able to communicate the psychology of his subjects. For example, his portrait of the tortured Modest Mussorgsky stuns with its ability to bring out varied aspects of the composer's personality. Repin's oeuvre includes portraits of most prominent liberals of his era, from Leo Tolstoy to Savva Mamantov, as well as the archconservative Konstantin Pobedonostsev. His paintings of historical figures, *Ivan the Terrible and His Son Ivan* and *Tsarevna Sophia Alexeevna in the Novodevichy Convent*, likewise stand out for their capacity to evoke the emotional.

Repin returned to the Academy of Arts in 1894, directing a studio there until 1907 and serving briefly as director (1898–1899). In 1900 he moved to an estate in the Finnish village of Kuokalla, outside of St. Petersburg, where a constant stream of visitors engendered a famously stimulating atmosphere. When Finland received its independence from the Russian Empire in 1918, Repin chose to remain there. The reacquisition of Kuokalla by the Soviet army in 1939 resulted in the renaming of the village to "Repino," a museum to the artist.

*See also:* ACADEMY OF ARTS; NATIONALISM IN THE ARTS

**BIBLIOGRAPHY**

Parker, Fan and Parker, Stephen Jan. (1980). *Russia on Canvas: Ilya Repin*. University Park: Pennsylvania State University Press.

Sternin, Grigorii Iurevich, comp. (1987). *Ilya Repin*. Leningrad: Aurora Publishers, 1987.

Valkenier, Elizabeth Kridl. (1990). *Ilya Repin and the World of Russian Art*. New York: Columbia University Press.

LOUISE MCREYNOLDS

# REPRESSED INFLATION

The Soviet State Price Committee (Goskomtsen) set prices for 27 million products during the post World War II era. It compiled data on the unit labor and capital cost of each good, and added a profit mark up. The resulting prime cost–based prices were supposed to be permanently fixed, but many were revised every decade or so to reflect changes in labor and non-labor input costs. These adjustments should have been small, because the state raised wages gradually, and improved technologies reduced material input costs. Some sectors like machine building, where productivity growth was especially rapid, even reported falling unit input costs, creating a condition called "repressed deflation" during the interval between the establishment of the initial price and its revision. Had the Soviet Union been a competitive market economy, characterized by rapid technological progress and state wage fixing, strong deflationary pressures would have caused prices to fall continuously.

However, many prominent Soviet economists such as Grigoriy Khanin contend that it was inflation, not deflation that was repressed by the Soviet brand of price fixing. They argue that while prices were supposed to be fixed, enterprise managers driven by a desire to maximize bonuses tied to profits, circumvented the authorities, causing intermediate input prices and therefore unit costs to rise. Had the Soviet Union been a competitive market economy, strong cost-push inflationary pressures would have forced prices to steadily rise.

Some Soviet economists, such as Igor Birman, have claimed that repressed inflation was exacerbated by weak monetary discipline and soft budgetary constraints, which allowed firms to spend more than they were authorized. The purchasing power of these offending enterprises, and of the public, therefore exceeded the cost of goods supplied. This created inflationary excess demand that was easily observed in empty shop shelves, rapidly increasing savings deposits, and the public conviction that money was worthless because there weren't enough things to buy.

The evidence for this position is inconclusive, because goods were often distributed in worker canteens instead of shops, and there could have been many alternative reasons why bank savings rose. Nonetheless, the consensus holds that the USSR was, in some important sense, an economy of shortage, in a state of monetary disequilibrium that subverted effective planning and contributed to the system's undoing. Although repressed inflation may have seemed innocuous because Soviet growth between 1950 and 1989 was always positive, most specialists consider it to have been an insidious source of destabilization.

Repressed inflation was specific to the Soviet period, and has not carried over into the post-communist epoch, because prices are no longer fixed or controlled. Price liberalization produced a bout of hyper-inflation in 1992, only partly explained by the so-called Soviet "ruble overhang," but the problem subsequently subsided.

*See also:* ECONOMIC GROWTH, SOVIET; HARD BUDGET CONSTRAINTS; MONETARY OVERHANG; RATCHET EFFECT

**BIBLIOGRAPHY**

Bornstein, Morris. (October 1978). "The Administration of the Soviet Price System," *Soviet Studies* 30(4): 466–490.

Grossman, Gregory. (1977). "Price Controls, Incentives and Innovation in the Soviet Economy." In *The Socialist Price Mechanism*, ed. Alan Abouchar. Durham, NC: Duke University Press.

STEVEN ROSEFIELDE

# REVOLUTION OF 1905

The immediate background to the first Russian revolution, which, despite its designation as the "Revolution of 1905," actually began in 1904 and ended in 1907, was the unexpected and humiliating defeat of Russia by the Japanese. The defeat emboldened the liberals, who in the fall and winter of 1904–1905 unleashed the so-called banquet campaign for constitutional change. Meeting in twenty-six cities, the liberals called for civil liberties, amnesty for political prisoners, and a democratically elected constituent assembly. The banquets were a prelude to the dramatic events of Bloody Sunday (January 9, 1905), when government troops fired on peaceful marchers (organized by Father Gapon, founder of the Assembly of the Russian Factory and Mill Workers of the City of St. Petersburg) who wished to present Tsar Nicholas II (r. 1894–1917) with a petition for political and social reforms similar to those advocated by liberals (significantly, without any demand for abolition of the monarchy or introduction of socialism).

In light of the peaceful tactics and reformist platform of the marchers, it is not surprising that the massacre of 130 people and the wounding of some three hundred provoked widespread outrage. Within a few weeks, many industrial workers throughout the empire went on strike to protest the government's conduct, assuming the role of a viable political force for the first time. Students at universities and high schools followed suit soon afterward, disorders broke out among minorities seeking cultural autonomy and political rights, peasants attacked landlords' estates, members of the middle class defied governmental restrictions on public meetings and the press, and on several occasions soldiers and sailors mutinied. The entire structure of society appeared on the verge of collapse.

Incapable of coping with the growing unrest, the government alternated between strident assertions of the autocratic principle and vague promises of reform, satisfying no one. The revolution peaked in October, when a general strike, spontaneous and unorganized, brought the government to its knees. Once workers in Moscow walked off their jobs, the strike spread quickly throughout the country, even drawing support from various middle-class groups. Numerous cities came to a standstill. After about ten days, in mid-October, Tsar Nicholas, fearing total collapse of his regime, reluctantly issued the October Manifesto, which promised civil liberties and the establishment of a legislature (duma) with substantial powers. Most significantly, the tsar agreed not to enact any law without the approval of the legislature. In conceding that he was no longer the sole repository of political power, Nicholas did what he had vowed never to do: He abandoned the principle of autocracy.

During the Days of Liberty, the period immediately succeeding the issuance of the October Manifesto, the press could publish whatever it pleased, workers could form trade unions, and political parties could operate freely. It was a great victory for the opposition, but in a matter of days it became evident that the revolutionary crisis had not been overcome. The tsar made every effort to undo his concessions. Large numbers of supporters of the monarchy, enraged at the government's concessions, violently and indiscriminately attacked Jews and anyone else deemed hostile to the old regime. In the opposition, the St. Petersburg Soviet (council of workers' deputies) grew increasingly militant. The upshot was that the Days of Liberty came to an end within two months in a torrent of government repression provoked by the uprising of Moscow workers. Led by Bolsheviks and other revolutionaries, this uprising was brutally quashed by the authorities within ten days.

Nevertheless, the elections to the duma took place. On the whole they proceeded fairly, with some twenty to twenty-five million participant voters. To the government's surprise, the over-

**Massacre at Tiflis Municipal Council, October 1905.** THE ART ARCHIVE/DOMENICA DEL CORRIERE/DAGLI ORTI (A)

whelming majority of the elected deputies belonged to opposition parties. The newly formed Octobrist Party, satisfied with the political changes introduced by the October Manifesto, held only thirteen seats; the extreme pro-tsarist right held none. On the other hand, the Kadets, or Constitutional Democrats, who favored a parliamentary system of government, held 185 seats, more than any other party, and dominated the proceedings of the legislature. Predictably, relations between the Duma and the government quickly soured because of the legislature's demands for a constitutional order and for agrarian measures involving compulsory distribution of privately owned land to land-hungry peasants. On July 1906 the government dissolved the Duma. The deputies protested the action at a meeting in Vyborg, Finland, and called for passive resistance, but to no avail. The Second Duma, which met on February 20, 1907, and was more radical than the first, met a similar fate on June 3 of that year. This marked the end of the Revolution of 1905. At this point the authorities changed the electoral law by depriving many peasants and minorities of the vote, ensuring the election of a conservative Duma.

Never before had any European revolution been spearheaded by four popular movements: the middle class, the industrial proletariat, the peasantry, and national minorities (who demanded autonomy or, in a few cases, independence). But because of the disagreements and lack of coordination among the various sectors of the opposition, and because the government could still rely on the military and on financial support from abroad, the tsarist regime survived. Nevertheless, Russia had changed significantly between 1904 and 1907. The very existence of an elected Duma, whose approval was necessary for the enactment of most laws, diminished the power of the tsar and the bureaucracy. The landed gentry, the business class, and the upper stratum of the peasantry, all of whom continued to participate in the elections of the Duma, now exercised some influence in public affairs. Moreover, trade unions and various associations of cooperatives that had been allowed to form during the revolutionary turbulence remained active, and censorship over the press and other publications was much less stringent. In short, Russia had taken a modest step away from autocracy and toward the creation of a civil society.

*See also:* AUTOCRACY; BLOODY SUNDAY; BOLSHEVISM; CONSTITUTIONAL DEMOCRATIC PARTY; DUMA; LIBERALISM; NICHOLAS II; OCTOBER GENERAL STRIKE OF 1905; OCTOBER MANIFESTO; OCTOBRIST PARTY; WORKERS

**BIBLIOGRAPHY**
Ascher, Abraham. (1988–92). *The Revolution of 1905*. 2 vols. Stanford, CA: Stanford University Press.

Bushnell, John S. (1985). *Mutineers and Repression: Soldiers in the Revolution of 1905–1906*. Bloomington: Indiana University Press.

Emmons, Terence. (1983). *The Formation of Political Parties and the First National Elections in Russia*. Cambridge, MA: Harvard University Press.

Engelstein, Laura. (1982). *Moscow, 1905: Working-Class Organization and Political Conflict*. Stanford, CA: Stanford University Press.

Harcave, Sidney. (1964). *First Blood: The Russian Revolution of 1905*. New York: Macmillan.

Mehlinger, Howard D. and Thompson, John M. (1972). *Count Witte and the Tsarist Government in the 1905 Revolution*. Bloomington: Indiana University Press.

Sablinsky, Walter. (1976). *The Road to Bloody Sunday: Father Gapon and the St. Petersburg Massacre of 1905*. Princeton, NJ: Princeton University Press.

Surh, Gerald D. (1989). *1905 in St. Petersburg: Labor, Society and Revolution*. Stanford, CA: Stanford University Press.

Verner, Andrew M. (1990). *The Crisis of Russian Autocracy: Nicholas II and the 1905 Revolution*. Princeton, NJ: Princeton University Press.

ABRAHAM ASCHER

# REYKJAVIK SUMMIT

A summit meeting of U.S. president Ronald Reagan and Soviet leader Mikhail Gorbachev took place in Reykjavik, Iceland, on October 11–12, 1986. This second meeting of the two leaders was billed as an "interim summit" and was not carefully prepared and scripted in advance as was customary.

The Reykjavik summit unexpectedly became a remarkable far-reaching exploration of possibilities for drastic reduction or even elimination of nuclear weapons. Gorbachev took the initiative, advancing comprehensive proposals dealing with strategic offensive and defensive weapons. Agreement seemed at hand for reductions of at least 50 percent in strategic offensive arms. When Reagan proposed a subsequent elimination of all strategic ballistic missiles, Gorbachev counterproposed eliminating all strategic nuclear weapons. Reagan then said he would be prepared to eliminate all nuclear weapons—and Gorbachev promptly agreed.

This breathtaking prospect was stymied by disagreement over the issue of strategic defenses. As a condition of his agreement on strategic offensive arms, Gorbachev asked that research on ballistic missile defenses be limited to laboratory testing. Reagan was adamant that nothing be done that would prevent pursuit of his Strategic Defense Initiative (SDI). The meeting ended abruptly, with no agreement reached.

Many saw the failure to reach accord as a spectacular missed opportunity, while others were relieved that what they saw as a near disaster had been averted. Subsequent negotiations built on the tentative areas of agreement explored at Reykjavik and led to agreements eliminating all intermediate-range missiles (the INF Treaty in 1987) and reducing intercontinental missiles (the START I Treaty in 1991). Thus, although the Reykjavik summit ended in disarray, in retrospect the exchanges there constituted a breakthrough in strategic arms control.

*See also:* ARMS CONTROL; STRATEGIC ARMS LIMITATION TREATIES; STRATEGIC DEFENSE INITIATIVE; UNITED STATES, RELATIONS WITH

**BIBLIOGRAPHY**

Garthoff, Raymond L. (1994). *The Great Transition: American-Soviet Relations and the End of the Cold War.* Washington, DC: The Brookings Institution.

Shultz, George P. (1993). *Turmoil and Triumph: My Years as Secretary of State.* New York: Charles Scribner's Sons.

RAYMOND L. GARTHOFF

**RIGA, TREATY OF (1921)** *See* SOVIET-POLISH WAR.

# RIGHT OPPOSITION

The Right Opposition, sometimes called Right Deviation, represents a moderate strand of Bolshevism that evolved from the New Economic Policy (NEP). Headed by Nikolai Bukharin, the party's leading theoretician after Vladimir Ilich Lenin's death, the Right Opposition also included Alexei Rykov, Mikhail Tomsky, Felix Dzerzhinsky, and A. P. Smirnov. In part reacting against the harsh policies of War Communism, the right urged moderation and cooperation with the peasantry to achieve socialism gradually. It favored industrialization, but at a pace determined by the peasantry, and prioritized the development of light industry over heavy industry.

Until early 1928 the platform of the right coincided with the policies of the Soviet government and the Politburo. This is not surprising given that Rykov was chairman of the Council of People's Commissars (Sovnarkom) from 1924 to 1930, and Bukharin, Rykov, Tomsky, and their then ally Josef Stalin held a majority in the Politburo until 1926. Participating in the struggles for power following Lenin's death, the right opposed Leon Trotsky and his policies, as well as Grigory Zinoviev, Lev Kamenev, and eventually the United Opposition. Toward the end of the 1920s, as Stalin increasingly secured control over the party apparatus, Trotsky, Zinoviev, and Kamenev were expelled from the Politburo and replaced by Stalin's handpicked successors, thereby enhancing the position of the right.

Their good fortune changed, however, following the decisive defeat of the Left Opposition at the Fifteenth Party Congress in December 1927. Having supported Bukharin and the right's position on the cautious implementation of the NEP, Stalin, in 1928, abruptly reversed his position and adopted the rapid industrialization program of the left. He and his new majority in the Politburo then attacked the Right Opposition over various issues including forced grain requisitions, the anti–specialist campaign, and industrial production targets for the First Five–Year Plan. Outnumbered and unable to launch a strong challenge against Stalin, the Right Opposition sought an alliance with Kamenev and Zinoviev, for which the Right Opposition was subsequently denounced at the Central Committee plenum in January 1929.

Under attack politically, Bukharin, Rykov, and Tomsky signed a statement acknowledging their "errors" that was published in *Pravda* in November 1929. Nonetheless, Bukharin was removed from the Politburo that same month. The following year Rykov and Tomsky were also expelled from the Politburo. By the end of 1930 the trio was removed from all positions of leadership, and moderates throughout the party were purged; this officially marked the defeat of the Right Opposition. Having already destroyed the Left Opposition, Stalin was now the uncontested leader of the Soviet Union.

The Great Purges of the late 1930s brought further tragedy to the leaders of the defunct Right Opposition. With his arrest imminent, Tomsky committed suicide in 1936. Two years later Bukharin and Rykov were arrested and tried in the infamous show trials of 1938. Despite the fact that they could not possibly have committed the crimes that they were accused of, and that their confessions were clearly secured under torture, both were found guilty and executed.

See also: BUKHARIN, NIKOLAI IVANOVICH; LEFT OPPOSITION; RYKOV, ALEXEI IVANOVICH; TOMSKY, MIKHAIL PAVLOVICH; UNITED OPPOSITION

BIBLIOGRAPHY

Cohen, Stephen, F. (1973). *Bukharin and the Bolshevik Revolution: A Political Biography, 1888–1938*. New York: Oxford University Press.

Erlich, Alexander. (1960). *The Soviet Industrialization Debate, 1924–1928*. Cambridge, MA: Harvard University Press.

Merridale, Catherine. (1990). *Moscow Politics and the Rise of Stalin: The Communist Party in The Capital, 1925–32*. New York: St. Martin's Press.

KATE TRANSCHEL

# RIMSKY-KORSAKOV, NIKOLAI ANDREYEVICH

(1844–1908), prominent Russian composer who contributed to the formation of a Russian national music in the nineteenth century.

Nikolai Andreyevich Rimsky-Korsakov, a naval officer by training, came to study professionally as a member of Mily Balakirev's amateur circle of composers ("Mighty Handful"). An active composer under Balakirev's guidance since 1861, he became a professor of composition and instrumentation at the St. Petersburg conservatory ten years later. Rimsky-Korsakov is regarded as one of the most significant composers and musicians of Russia in the nineteenth century.

Together with Balakirev and Alexander Borodin, who numbered among his closest creative partners in the 1860s, Rimsky-Korsakov developed a specific Russian idiom in orchestral music. As an opera composer, although he wrote a few historical operas, Rimsky-Korsakov especially stands for the Russian fairy and magic opera, the genre of which he brought to a culmination. Of high though not undisputed merit were the completions, revisions, and instrumentations of opera torsos of Borodin and Musorgsky, even if Rimsky-Korsakov partly neglected the composers' original intentions. Finally, he made significant contributions to musical education. Not only did his textbook of harmony become the widely acknowledged standard in Russia, but he also acted as a teacher and example for outstanding Russian composers. His support of students in the Revolution of 1905 (leading to his dismissal as professor) and his opera "The Golden Cockerel" (1907), which was condemned by censorship, because it could be interpreted as criticism of tsarist rule, conributed to his renown and reputation as an artist with political revolutionary leanings. Furthermore, as one of the masters of Russian national music in the nineteenth century, he achieved enormous importance and influence in the cultural history of the Soviet Union, particularly since the cultural changes toward Great Russian patriotism under Stalin.

See also: MIGHTY HANDFUL; MUSIC; NATIONALISM IN THE ARTS

BIBLIOGRAPHY

Seaman, Gerald R. (1988). *Nikolai Andreevich Rimsky-Korsakov: A Guide to Research*. New York: Garland.

MATTHIAS STADELMANN

# RODZIANKO, MIKHAIL VLADIMIROVICH

(1859–1924), an anti-Bolshevik who led the conservative faction of the Octobrist Party in the pre-revolutionary legislative Duma and served as president of that body from 1911 to 1917, then emigrated in 1920 to Yugoslavia, where he completed a memoir, *The Reign of Rasputin*.

Devoutly Orthodox, conservative, nationalist, and loyal to the tsar, Mikhail Rodzianko also believed in the semiconstitutional system established in 1906 and strove to make it work. He never grasped that Nicholas II at heart rejected the new order. The Duma leader was therefore always puzzled when the tsar ignored Rodzianko's pleas to rid the court of Rasputin's pernicious influence and to form a competent ministry.

An archetype of the old order, he came from a prosperous landed family, received an elite education, served in the army, and then became a district marshal of nobility and zemstvo executive. Chosen for the State Council in 1906 and elected to the Third Duma in 1907, Rodzianko became Duma president in 1911. He actively promoted the war effort after 1914, and in 1916 warned the tsar that incompetent ministers were undermining the struggle against the Central Powers and endangering the survival of the monarchy itself.

During the Revolution of 1917, Rodzianko urged the tsar to appoint a government in which the people would have confidence and which he hoped to head. As the revolution deepened he reluctantly agreed to help persuade Nicholas to abdicate. Because of his political conservatism, he was not asked, however, to serve in the new Provisional Government.

As a believer in both the tsardom and constitutionalism, he could only watch in dismay as Russia sank into radical revolution and civil war. In emigration he found himself reviled by monarchists as having betrayed the tsar, and rejected by liberals as having failed to be reformist enough.

*See also:* DUMA; NICHOLAS II; OCTOBRIST PARTY; REVOLUTION OF 1905

**BIBLIOGRAPHY**

Hasegawa, Tsuyoshi. (1981). *The February Revolution, Petrograd, 1917.* Seattle: University of Washington Press.

Hosking, Geoffrey. (1973). *The Russian Constitutional Experiment: Government and Duma, 1907-14.* Cambridge, UK: Cambridge University Press.

Rodzianko, Mikhail V. (1973). *The Reign of Rasputin: An Empire's Collapse.* Gulf Breeze, FL: Academic International Press.

JOHN M. THOMPSON

# ROERICH, NICHOLAS KONSTANTINOVICH

(1874–1947), artist, explorer, and mystic.

Born in St. Petersburg and educated at the Academy of Arts, Roerich established himself as a painter of scenes from Slavic prehistory. Works such as *The Messenger* (1897), *Visitors from Overseas* (1901–1902), and *Slavs on the Dnieper* (1905) combined a bold use of color with Roerich's expertise as a semi-professional archaeologist. Roerich joined the World of Art Group and designed sets and costumes for Sergei Diaghilev's Ballets Russes. His greatest fame resulted from his designs for *Prince Igor* (1909) and *The Rite of Spring* (1913), the libretto of which he cowrote with Igor Stravinsky.

In 1918, Roerich and his family left Soviet Russia for Scandinavia, England, then the United States. In New York, Roerich and his wife, Helena, founded a spiritual movement: Agni Yoga, an offshoot of Theosophy. Roerich's followers included Henry Wallace, Franklin Roosevelt's secretary of

agriculture (and later vice-president). His backers built a museum for him in Manhattan and sponsored him on two expeditions to Asia. From 1920 onward, Roerich's painting took on an Asiatic, mystical character, featuring gods, gurus, and Himalayan mountainscapes.

Roerich visited India in 1923. From 1925 to 1928, he and his family completed a mammoth trek through Ladakh, Chinese Turkestan, the Altai Mountains, the Gobi Desert, and Tibet. Ostensibly leading an American archaeological, ethnographic, and artistic expedition, the Roerichs also secretly visited Moscow, and the true purpose of their journey remains a matter of debate. Roerich established a research facility in the Himalayan village of Naggar, India, and lobbied for the passage of an international treaty to protect art in times of war. This effort gained him two nominations for the Nobel Peace Prize. In 1934–1935, Roerich, bankrolled by Wallace and the U.S. government, traveled to Manchuria and Mongolia. The expedition stirred up great scandal, leading Wallace and most of Roerich's supporters to break with him by 1936. Roerich's U.S. assets were seized. The Roerichs remained in India, supporting the freedom movement there and befriending its leaders, such as poet Rabindranath Tagore and Jawaharlal Nehru. Roerich died in 1947. Nehru, the new leader of independent India, gave his eulogy.

Roerich's occultism and the mysteries surrounding his expeditions have shaped both popular and academic understanding of his life. Western scholars acknowledge the importance of his early art, but have criticized his later works; they have tended to be suspicious about the political and mystical motives underlying his expeditions. After the late 1950s, Soviet scholars reinstated Roerich as an important figure in the Russian artistic canon, but downplayed his occultism and controversial actions. Non-academic writing on Roerich is either hagiographic—Agni Yoga has a worldwide following, and the Russian movement has enjoyed tremendous popularity since 1987—or lurid and sensationalistic, accusing Roerich of espionage and collaboration with the Soviet secret police. Since the early 1990s, emerging evidence indicates that the Roerichs believed a new age was imminent and that one of its necessary preconditions was the establishment of a pan-Buddhist state linking Siberia, Mongolia, Central Asia, and Tibet. The Roerichs also sought to involve themselves in the struggle between Tibet's key political figures, the Panchen (Tashi) Lama and Dalai Lama. Rather than straightforward espionage, the purpose of Roerich's expeditions seems to have been the fulfillment of these grandiose, but ultimately quixotic, ambitions.

*See also:* BALLET; OCCULTISM

**BIBLIOGRAPHY**

Decter, Jacqueline. (1997). *Messenger of Beauty: The Life and Visionary Art of Nicholas Roerich.* Rochester, VT: Park Street Press.

McCannon, John. (2001). "Searching for Shambhala: The Mystical Art and Epic Journeys of Nikolai Roerich." *Russian Life* 44(1):48–56.

Meyer, Karl, and Brysac, Shareen Blair. (1999). *Tournament of Shadows: The Great Game and the Race for Empire in Central Asia.* Washington, DC: Counterpoint.

Williams, Robert C. (1980). *Russian Art and American Money: 1900–1940.* Cambridge, MA: Harvard University Press.

JOHN MCCANNON

# ROMANIA, RELATIONS WITH

Founded in the thirteenth and fourteenth centuries, the principalities of Moldavia and Wallachia gained their autonomy from the Hungarian kings with the election of native princes. The status of these principalities was comparable to that of the Grand Duchy of Moscow, and they shared allegiance to the patriarch of Constantinople. During the fifteenth century, the chief threat they faced was Turkish expansionism in the Balkans. Their earliest contact with Moscow occurred when Ivan III negotiated a marriage alliance with Steven the Great of Moldavia (1457–1604). His daughter, Elena, became the bride of Ivan the Young, whose son Dmitry became heir to the throne.

### THE LIBERATION OF ROMANIAN
### LANDS FROM THE TURKS

As the power of the Romanian princes declined and those of the grand dukes increased, the former tried to switch their allegiance from Constantinople to Moscow. Such contacts encouraged Nicholas Milescu, a Moldavian boyar, to serve Tsar Alexei as ambassador to China. The earliest attempt at signing a treaty of alliance with Russia was made by Prince Dmitry Cantemir of Moldavia, who invited Peter the Great (r. 1682–1725) to deliver the country from the Turks. The liberation failed with Peter's defeat on the River Pruth in 1711, but it opened a career for Dmitry at St. Petersburg as a

Westernizer, and for his daughter, Maria, who dedicated herself to emancipating the Russian women.

The true liberator of Romanian lands was Catherine the Great (r. 1762–1796) who, in three campaigns against the Turks, reached the Dniester River. The Treaty of Kutchuk Kainardji (1774) gave Russia formal influence in the principalities, with two consuls at Bucharest and Jassy. French interference with these provisions occasioned the Russo-Turkish War of 1802–1812, which gave Russia the Bessarabian half of Moldavia. Although the Greek revolution of 1821 began in Moldavia, Tsar Alexander I (r. 1801–1825) denounced it because of the anti-revolutionary stance of the Holy Alliance (an informal agreement among Christian monarchs to preserve European peace). Russia's greatest gain occurred following the Treaty of Adrianople, when Tsar Nicholas I (r. 1825–1855) established a protectorate over both Romanian provinces, thus taking over the nominal Turkish suzerainty. Although native Romanian princes continued to be elected, power now resided with the two Russian proconsuls who were headquartered in Bucharest and Jassy.

Russia demanded that the new generations be schooled at St. Petersburg, but Romanians preferred the schools in Paris, where many of their young people participated in the 1848 revolution against the July monarchy. When they returned home and attempted to continue that revolution in the Romanian capitals, Russia suppressed the movement and reoccupied the provinces under more stringent conditions. The Congress of Paris, which followed the Crimean War (1853–1856), suppressed the Russian protectorate, internationalized Danubian navigation, reunited Bessarabia with Romania, and attempted to revise the constitution of both states. The Romanians took the initiative of electing Alexander Ion Cuza in 1859 as prince of the United Principalities, as Moldavia and Wallachia were now called, but this arrangement disturbed Austria and Turkey more than it did Russia.

The overthrow of Cuza in a military coup, and the advent of Prince Charles of Hohenzollern Sigmaringen in 1866, was greeted positively by Austria after he visited Tsar Alexander II (r. 1855–1881) at Livadia in 1869. The Bosnian crisis that led to the Balkans war of independence (1877–1878) gave Russia the opportunity to avenge its defeat in 1856. Initially neutral during this war, Romania nonetheless gave Russia a right of passage to Bulgaria, albeit with misgivings. However, when Grand Duke Nicholas ran into difficulties at Plevna, in Bulgaria, he appealed to Prince Charles for military assistance, and placed him in command of the Russo-Romanian forces, which were ultimately victorious. At the Congress of Berlin (1878), where postwar negotiations took place, Russia demanded retrocession of southern Bessarabia in exchange for recognition of Romania's independence.

Relations between Romania and Russia improved when the heir to the Romanian throne, Ferdinand of Hohenzollern-Sigmaringen, married Princess Marie, a forceful personality and the granddaughter of Tsar Alexander and Queen Victoria. In February 1914 Prince Ferdinand visited St. Petersburg to arrange another political marriage, this time between his son Prince Carol with one of Tsar Nicholas' daughters. During the summer the entire imperial family sailed to Constanta to further the marital alliance, but it came to naught because it incurred protests from Vienna.

With the outbreak of World War I, King Charles felt bound by treaty to join the Central Powers (Prussian and Austria) against Russia, but politicians of all the parties that had been affected by Hungary's repression of the Romanias in Transylvania forced a declaration of neutrality. Wooed both by Russia, which supported Romania's claim to Transylvania, and by the Central Powers who offered the return to Romania of Bessarabia, Romania's prime minister Ion Bratianu ultimately declared war on Germany and Austria Hungary, largely because he was impressed by Russian general Alexei Brusilov's victories in Poland. In 1916, the joint German-Bulgarian offensive forced the Romanian army to withdraw to Moldavia, where Russian troops helped them to stabilize the front. However, the fall of Russia's Provisional Government under Alexander Kerensky in November 1917 and the advent of the Bolsheviks to power in Russia undermined resistance and led to the Russo-German Treaty of Brest-Litovsk (December 1917), which the Romanians refused to attend.

Plans to evacuate the Romanian royal family to Russia were scrapped, although the Romanian gold reserves that had been sent ahead to Moscow for this purpose were never returned. When the pro-German government of Marghiloman finally surrendered in the Treaty of Bucharest, Southern Dobrogea was ceded to Germany's ally, Bulgaria, and southern Bessarabia was returned to Romania. Within the province there raged civil war between the Red army, Ukrainian partisans, and Romanian nationalists who had convened a council and proclaimed independence from Russia.

Great Romania of the interwar years formally came into existence as a result of the Conference of Paris in 1918. The cession of Bessarabia and Northern Bukovina was signed at the Treaty of Sevres, but was never recognized by the newly reconstituted Soviet Union. Romania initially had no contact with the Soviets, and a *cordon sanitaire* was maintained by a network of alliances (known as the "little entente"), with French backing (1921). Diplomatic relations were finally reopened in 1934 due to the efforts of Romania's long-serving foreign secretary, Nicolae Titulescu, who worked against the wishes of the newly crowned King Carol II. Conscious of Hitler's increasing threat to European security at this time, Titulescu worked out a pact of mutual assistance with the Soviet Union on the eve of the Munich crisis of 1938. This pact allowed the Soviet airforce to cross Romanian territory in defense of Czechoslovakia, but Stalin never took advantage of this offer, having secretly allied himself with Hitler at that time.

When Hitler and Russia attacked and then divided Poland, neutral Romania gave refuge to the remnants of the Polish opposition forces, most of whom had come from the Russian zone and later fought alongside the French and British, much to Stalin's annoyance. With the fall of France, Romania also fell within the German orbit, leading to the dictatorship of Marshall Ion Antonescu. The dismantling of Romania began with the Molotov-Ribentrop Pact, which ceded Bessarabia and northern Bucovina to the Soviet Union (August 2, 1940). It therefore was inevitable that Antonescu would join the Wehrmacht in its attack on the Soviet Union (June 1941). The Romanian army occupied Odessa, which became the capital of "Transnistria," a newly created territory that was administrated but never formally annexed by the Romanian authorities. The siege of Stalingrad, in which 300,000 Romanians were killed or wounded, provided a decisive turning point for Romania's participation in the war, and persuaded Marshall Antonescu and King Michael to withdraw from the fighting. Though Molotov preferred negotiating with Antonescu, it was King Michael who, on August 23, 1944, did a political "about-face" and ordered the Romanian army to attack the Germans. The breakdown of the Romanian front greatly facilitated the liberation of Hungary and Czechoslovakia, hastened the Allied push to Berlin, and ultimately shortened the war in Europe.

In spite of Allied promises not to change the country's social structure, Romania's fate was sealed by an agreement between Winston Churchill and Josef Stalin, in which 90 percent of Romania's territory was ceded to the Soviets. A Stalinist regime was established in the annexed territory, with Stalin's protégé, Ana Pauker, placed in charge. The Treaty of Paris (1947) confirmed the cession of Bessarabia and northern Bukovina to Russia and northern Dobrogea to Bulgaria. Northern Transylvania, which had been taken by Hitler and given to the Hungarians, was returned to Romania at the insistence of Vyacheslav Mikhailovich Molotov. Romania faced severe economic and financial conditions as a result of war reparations claims made by the Soviets, and the country was never formally recognized for their ultimate support of the Allied cause during the final years of the war.

With the forced abdication of King Michael in December 1947, the People's Republic of Romania was initially organized upon the Soviet model. Agriculture was collectivized, industry nationalized, the language Slavicized, and the former ruling class exterminated in Soviet-run labor camps. In 1952, even before Stalin's death, the secretary general of the Communist Party in Romania, Gheorghe Gheorghiu Dej, began purging those who were deemed to have been Stalinist supporters, and he attempted to construct a Romanian socialist state. The Polish and Hungarian crisis of 1956 and Nikita Krushchev's denunciation of Stalin triggered Romania's further disengagement from the Soviet bloc. Although cofounders of the Warsaw Pact and member of the Council for Mutual Economic Assistance, Dej also sought admission to the United Nations and UNESCO; refused to be involved in the Soviet conflicts with the Chinese, Yugoslavs, or Albanians; retained good relations with Israel; vetoed Khruschev's plans to make Romania an agricultural state; and, in 1958, eliminated the Soviet army of occupation.

Dej's successor, Nicolae Ceausescu, who came to office in 1965, created the Romanian Socialist Republic and added to the Presidency of the Council the title of President of the Republic, becoming the leading political official in the state. Although obligated to resume Romania's alliance with the USSR, Ceausescu also established diplomatic relations with West Germany and strengthened contact with France and the United States by hosting Charles de Gaulle in 1968 and Richard Nixon in 1969. He also visited the Queen of England and reestablished trade relations with the West.

During the Czech crisis of 1968, Ceausescu joined Tito in repealing Leonid Brezhnev's doctrine of the right of intervention and refused to allow Romania's participation in military exercises with members of the Warsaw Pact. He went so far as to question Russia's right to occupy Bessarabia. Ceausescu also ignored Mikhail Gorbachev's attempt to soften his dictatorial rule over Romania, despite the fall of the Berlin Wall and that event's implications for the fate of the now crumbling Soviet Union. This precipitated a bloody revolution and, ultimately, Ceausescu's death. Post-communist Romania has made considerable progress with democratization and, with Moscow's consent, joined NATO in 2002.

*See also:* CRIMEAN WAR; PARIS, CONGRESS AND TREATY OF 1856; WORLD WAR I; WORLD WAR II

## BIBLIOGRAPHY

Florescu, Radu R. (1997). *The Struggle against Russia in the Romanian Principalities.* IASI: Center for Romanian Studies.

Moseley, M. P. E. (1934). *Russian Diplomacy and the Opening of the Eastern Question in 1838 and 1839.* Cambridge, UK: Cambridge University Press.

RADU R. FLORESCU

## ROMANOVA, ANASTASIA

(d. 1560), first wife of Russia's first official tsar, Ivan IV, and dynastic link between the Rurikid and the Romanov dynasties.

Anastasia Romanova, daughter of a lesser boyar, Roman Yuriev-Zakharin-Koshkin, and his wife, Yuliania Fyodorovna, became Ivan IV's bride after an officially proclaimed bride-show. After her wedding in November 1547, Romanova had difficulty producing royal offspring. Her three daughters died in infancy, and her eldest son, Dmitry Ivanovich, died as a baby in a mysterious accident during a pilgrimage by his parents in 1553. Her second son, Ivan Ivanovich (born in 1554), suffered an untimely end in 1581 at the hands of his own father. The incident caused the transfer of power after Ivan IV's death to Romanova's last son, the sickly Fyodor Ivanovich (1557–1598), whose childlessness set the stage for the Time of Troubles and the emergence of the Romanov dynasty. After a prolonged illness, Romanova passed away in August 1560 and was buried in the Monastery of the Ascension in the Kremlin, much mourned by the common people of Moscow.

Scholars generally emphasize Romanova's positive influence on Ivan IV's disposition, her pious and charitable nature, and her dynastic significance as the great-aunt of Tsar Mikhail Fyodorovich Romanov. This view, however, is largely based on later sources and thus reflects more the tsarina's image than her actual person. Recent research on Romanova's pilgrimages to holy sites and embroideries from her workshop suggests that Romanova actively shaped her role as royal mother by promoting the cults of Russian saints who were credited with the ability to promote royal fertility and to protect royal children from harm.

*See also:* IVAN IV; ROMANOV DYNASTY; RURIKID DYNASTY

**BIBLIOGRAPHY**

Kaiser, Daniel. (1987). "Symbol and Ritual in the Marriages of Ivan IV." *Russian History* 14(1–4):247–262.

Thyrêt, Isolde. (2001). *Between God and Tsar: Religious Symbolism and the Royal Women of Muscovite Russia.* DeKalb: Northern Illinois University Press.

ISOLDE THYRÊT

## ROMANOVA, ANASTASIA NIKOLAYEVNA

(1901–c. 1918), youngest daughter of Tsar Nicholas II and Tsarina Alexandra Fedorovna.

Anastasia Nikolayevna's place in history derives less from her life than from the legend that she somehow survived her family's execution. The mythology surrounding her and the imperial family remains popular in twentieth-century folklore.

Following the fall of the Romanov dynasty in 1917, members of the royal family were imprisoned, first at the Alexander Palace outside Petrograd and later in the Siberian city of Tobolsk. Finally Nicholas and his immediate family were confined to the Ipatiev House in the Urals city of Yekaterinburg (Sverdlovsk). According to official accounts, local communist forces executed Nicholas, Alexandra, their five children, and four retainers during the night of July 16, 1918. Because no corpses were immediately located, numerous individuals emerged claiming to be this or that Romanov who had miraculously survived the massacre. Most claimants were quickly dismissed as frauds, but one "Anastasia" seemed to have better credentials than the others.

The first reports of this "Anastasia" came in 1920 from an insane asylum in Berlin, where a young woman was taken following an attempt to drown herself in a canal. Anna Anderson, as she came to be known, was far from the beautiful lost princess reunited with her grandmother, as Hollywood retold the story. Instead, she was badly scarred, both mentally and physically, and spent the remainder of her life rotating among a small group of patrons, eventually marrying historian John Mahanan and settling in Charlottesville, VA, where she remained until her death on February 12, 1984.

No senior surviving member of the Romanov family ever formally recognized Anderson as being Anastasia. Instead, her supporters came largely from surviving members of the royal court, many of whom were suspected of using Anderson for financial gain. Anderson did file a claim against tsarist bank accounts held in a German bank. Extensive evidence was offered on her behalf, from eyewitness testimony to photographic comparisons. The case lasted from 1938 to 1970, and eventually the German Supreme Court ruled that her claim could neither be proved nor disproved.

Interest in Anderson's case revived in 1991, following the discovery of the Romanov remains outside Yekaterinburg. Two skeletons were unaccounted for, one daughter and the son. Anderson's body had been cremated, but hospital pathology specimens were later discovered and submitted for DNA testing in 1994. Although the results indicated that Anderson was Franziska Schanzkowska, a Polish factory worker, Anderson's most die-hard supporters still refused to accept the results. The Yekaterinburg remains were interned in the Cathedral of the Peter and Paul Fortress in St. Petersburg on July 17, 1998, eighty years after the execution.

*See also:* NICHOLAS II; ROMANOV DYNASTY

**BIBLIOGRAPHY**

Kurth, Peter. (1983). *Anastasia: The Riddle of Anna Anderson.* Boston: Little, Brown.

Massie, Robert K. (1995). *The Romanovs: The Final Chapter.* New York: Random House.

ANN E. ROBERTSON

## ROMANOV DYNASTY

Ruling family of Russia from 1613 to 1917; before that, a prominent clan of boyars in the fourteenth through sixteenth centuries.

The origins of the Romanovs are obscured by later (post-1613) foundation myths, though it appears certain enough that the founder of the clan was Andrei Ivanovich Kobyla, who was already a boyar in the middle of the fourteenth century when he appears for the first time in historical sources. Because of the way the line of descent from Andrei Kobyla divided and subdivided over time, there has often been confusion and misidentification of the last names of this clan before it became the ruling dynasty in 1613 under the name Romanov. Andrei Kobyla's five known sons were the progenitors of numerous boyar and lesser servitor clans, including the Zherebtsovs, Lodygins, Boborykins, and others. The Romanovs—as well as the Bezzubtsevs and the Sheremetev boyar clan—descend from the youngest known son of Andrei Kobyla, Fyodor, who had the nickname "Koshka." The Koshkin line, as it would become known, would itself subdivide into several separate clans, including the Kolychevs and the Lyatskys. The Romanovs, however, derive from Fyodor Koshka's grandson Zakhary, a boyar (appointed no later than 1433) who died sometime between 1453 and 1460. Zakhary lent his name to his branch of the clan, which became known as Zakharins. Zakhary's two sons, Yakov and Yuri, were both prominent boyars in the last quarter of the fifteenth century (and for Yakov, into the first decade of the sixteenth). Yuri's branch of the family took the name Yuriev. Yuri's son, Roman, from whom the later Russian dynasty derives its name, was not a boyar, but he is mentioned prominently in service registers for the second quarter of the sixteenth century. Roman's son Nikita was one of the most important boyars of his time—serving as an okolnichy (from 1559) and later as a boyar (from 1565) for Ivan the Terrible. Nikita served in the Livonian War, occupied prominent ceremonial roles in various court functions including royal weddings and embassies, and, on the death of Ivan the Terrible in 1584, took a leading part in a kind of regency council convened in the early days of Ivan's successor, Tsar Fyodor Ivanovich. Nikita retired to a monastery in 1585 as the monk Nifont. Roman Yuriev's daughter Anastasia married Tsar Ivan the Terrible in 1547, a union that propelled the Yuriev clan to a central place of power and privilege in the court and probably accounts for the numerous and rapid promotions to boyar rank of many of Nikita's and Anastasia's relatives in the Yuriev clan and other related clans. It was also during this time that the Yurievs established marriage ties with many of the other boyar clans at court, solidifying their political position through kinship-based alliances. With the marriage of Anastasia to Ivan, the Yuriev branch of the line of descent from Andrei Kobyla came firmly and finally to be known as the Romanovs.

The transformation of the Romanovs from a boyar clan to a ruling dynasty occurred only after no fewer than fifteen years of civil war and interregnum popularly called the Time of Troubles. During the reign of Tsar Fyodor Ivanovich (1584–1598), Nikita's son Fyodor became a powerful boyar; and inasmuch as he was Tsar Fyodor's first cousin (Tsar Fyodor's mother was Anastasia Yurieva, Fyodor Nikitich's aunt), he had been considered by some to be a good candidate to succeed to the throne of the childless tsar. The election to the throne fell in 1598 on Boris Godunov, however, and by 1600, the new tsar began systematically to exile or forcibly tonsure members of the Romanov clan. Scattered to distant locations in the north and east, far from Moscow, the disgrace of the Romanovs took its toll. In 1600 Fyodor Nikitich was tonsured a monk under the name Filaret and was exiled to the remote Antoniev-Siidkii monastery on the Dvina River. His brothers suffered exile and imprisonment as well: Alexander was sent to Usolye-Luda, where he died shortly thereafter; Mikhail was sent to Nyrob, where he likewise died in confinement; Vasily was sent first to Yarensk then to Pelym, dying in 1602; Ivan was also sent to Pelym, but would be released after Tsar Boris's death in 1605. Fyodor Nikitich's (now Filaret's) sisters and their husbands also suffered exile, imprisonment, and forced tonsurings. Romanov fortunes turned only in 1605 when Tsar Boris died suddenly and the first False Dmitry assumed the throne. The status of the clan fluctuated over the next few years as the throne was occupied first by Vasily Shuisky, the "Boyar Tsar," then by the second False Dmitry, who elevated Filaret to the rank of patriarch.

When finally an Assembly of the Land (Zemsky sobor) was summoned in 1613 to decide the question of the succession, numerous candidates were considered. Foreigners (like the son of the king of Poland or the younger brother of the king of Sweden) were quickly ruled out, though they had their advocates in the Assembly. Focus then turned to domestic candidates, and then in turn to Mikhail Romanov, the sixteen-year-old son of Filaret, who was elected tsar. Debate among historians has since ensued about the reasons for this seemingly unlikely choice. Some point to the kinship ties of the Romanovs with the old dynasty through Anastasia's marriage to Ivan the Terrible, or to the gen-

A 1914 portrait of Nicholas II, his wife, and children. Clockwise from left: Olga, Maria, Empress Alexandra Fedorovna, Anastasia, Tsarevich Alexei, and Tatiana. POPPERFOTO/ARCHIVE PHOTOS/HULTON/ARCHIVE. REPRODUCED BY PERMISSION.

eral popularity of the Yuriev clan during Ivan's violent reign. Others point to the fact that Mikhail Romanov was only sixteen and, according to some, of limited intelligence, indecisive, and sickly, and therefore presumably easily manipulated. Still others point to the Cossacks who surged into the Assembly of the Land during their deliberations and all but demanded that Mikhail be made tsar, evidently because of the close ties between the boy's father (Filaret) and the Cossack supporters of the second False Dmitry. A final and persuasive argument for the selection of Mikhail Romanov in 1613 may well be the fact that, in the previous generation, the Yuriev-Romanov clan had forged numerous marriage ties with many of the other boyar clans at court and therefore may have been seen by the largest number of boyars attending the Assembly of the Land as a candidate "of their own."

At the time of Mikhail Romanov's election, his father Filaret was a prisoner in Poland and was released only in 1619. On his return, father and son ruled together—Filaret being confirmed as patriarch

of Moscow and All Rus and given the title "Great Sovereign." Mikhail married twice, in 1624 to Maria Dolgorukova (who promptly died) and to Yevdokia Streshneva in 1626. Their son Alexei succeeded his father in 1645 and presided over a particularly turbulent and eventful time—the writing of the Great Law Code (Ulozhenie), the Church Old Believer Schism, the Polish Wars, and the slow insinuation of Western culture into court life inside the Kremlin. Alexei married twice, to Maria Miloslavskaya (in 1648) and to Natalia Naryshkina (in 1671). His first marriage produced no fewer than thirteen known children, including a daughter, Sophia, who reigned as regent from 1682 to 1689, and Tsar Ivan V (r. 1682–1696). His second marriage gave Tsar Alexei a son, Peter I ("the Great"), who ruled as co-tsar with his half brother Ivan V until the latter's death in 1696, then as sole tsar until his own death in 1725.

Succession by right of male primogeniture had been a long-established if never a legally formulated custom in Muscovy from no later than the fifteenth century onward. The first law of succession ever formally promulgated was on February 5, 1722, when Peter the Great decreed that it was the right of the ruler to pick his successor from among the members of the ruling family without regard for primogeniture or even the custom of exclusive male succession. By this point, the dynasty had few members. Peter's son by his first marriage (to Yevdokia Lopukhina), Alexei, was executed by Peter in 1718 for treason, leaving only a grandson, Peter (the future Peter II). Peter the Great also had two daughters (Anna and the future Empress Elizabeth) by his second wife, Marfa Skavronska, better known as Catherine I. Peter had half sisters—the daughters of Ivan V, his co-tsar, including the future Empress Anna—but even so, the dynasty consisted of no more than a handful of people. Perhaps ironically, Peter failed to pick a successor before his death, but his entourage selected his widow Catherine as the new ruler over the obvious rights of Peter's grandson. This grandson, Peter II, took the throne next, on Catherine's death in 1727, but he died in 1730; and with his passing, the male line of the Romanov dynasty expired. Succession continued through Ivan V's daughter, Anna, who had married Karl-Friedrich of Holstein-Gottorp. Their son, Karl-Peter, succeeded to the throne in 1762 as Peter III. Except for the brief titular reign of the infant Ivan VI (1740–1741)—the great grandson of Ivan V who was deposed by the Empress Elizabeth Petrovna (ruled 1741–1762)—all Romanov rulers from 1762 onward are properly speaking of the family of Holstein-Gottorp, though the convention in Russia always was to use the style "House of Romanov."

The law on dynastic succession was revised by the Emperor Paul I (ruled 1796–1801) after he was denied his rightful succession by his mother, Catherine II ("the Great," ruled 1762–1796). Catherine, born Sophia of Anhalt-Zerbst, had married Karl-Peter (the future Peter III) in 1745. After instigating a palace coup that ousted Peter (and later consenting to his murder), Catherine assumed the throne herself. When Paul ascended the throne on her death, he promulgated a law of succession in 1796 that established succession by male primogeniture and female succession only by substitution (that is, only in the absence of male Romanovs). This law endured until the end of the empire and continues today as the regulating statute for expatriate members of the Romanov family living abroad.

Romanov rulers in the nineteenth century were best known for their defense of the autocratic system and resistance to liberal constitutionalism and other social reforms. Paul's sons Alexander I (ruled 1801–1825), the principal victor over Napoleon Bonaparte, and Nicholas I (ruled 1825–1855) each resisted substantive reform and established censorship and other limitations on Russian society aimed at stemming the rise of the radical intelligentsia. Nicholas I's son, Alexander II (the "Tsar-Liberator," ruled 1855–1881) inherited the consequences of the Russian defeat in the Crimean War and instituted the Great Reforms, the centerpiece of which was the emancipation of Russia's serfs. Alexander II was assassinated in March 1881, and his successors on the throne, Alexander III (ruled 1881–1894) and Nicholas II (ruled 1894–1917), adopted many reactionary policies against revolutionaries and sought to defend and extend the autocratic form of monarchy unique to Russia at the time.

The anachronism of autocracy, the mystical-religious leanings of Nicholas II and his wife, Alexandra Feodorovna, and, perhaps most important, the string of defeats in World War I, forced Nicholas II to abdicate in February 1917. Having first abdicated in favor of his son Alexei, Nicholas II edited his abdication decree so as to pass the throne instead on to his younger brother, Mikhail—an action that in point of fact lay beyond a tsar's power according to the Pauline Law of Succession of 1796. In any event, Mikhail turned down the throne, ending more than three hundred years of Romanov rule in Russia. Nicholas and his family were immediately placed under house arrest in their palace at Tsarskoye Selo, near St. Petersburg, but in July they were sent into exile to Tobolsk. With the seizure of power by the Bolsheviks, Nicholas and his family were sent to Ekaterinburg, where Bolshevik control was firmer and where, under the threat of a White Army advance, they were executed on the night of July 17, 1918. On days surrounding this, executions of other Romanovs and their relatives (including morganatic spouses) were carried out. In 1981, Nicholas II, his wife and children, and all the other Romanovs who were executed by the Bolsheviks were glorified as saints (or more properly, royal martyrs) by the Russian Orthodox Church Abroad.

After the abdication of Nicholas and the Bolshevik coup, many Romanovs fled Russia and established themselves in Western Europe and America. Kirill Vladimirovich, Nicholas II's first cousin, proclaimed himself to be "Emperor of All the Russias" in 1924; nearly all surviving grand dukes recognized his claim to the succession, as did that part of the Russian Orthodox Church that had fled revolutionary Russia and had set itself up first in Yugoslavia, then in Germany, and finally in the United States. Kirill's son Vladimir assumed the headship of the dynasty (but not the title "emperor") on his father's death in 1938, though his claim was less universally accepted. Today the Romanov dynasty properly consists only of Leonida Georgievna, Vladimir's widow; his daughter Maria; and her son Georgy, and Princess Ekaterina Ioannovna. The question of the identity of Anna Anderson, who claimed to be Anastasia Nikolayevna, the youngest daughter of Nicholas II, was finally and definitively put to rest with the results of a DNA comparison of Anderson with surviving Romanov relatives. Other lines of descent in the Romanov family exist as well, but are disqualified from the succession due to the prevalence of morganatic marriages in these lines, something that is prohibited by the Pauline Law of Succession. The question of who the rightful tsar would be in the event of a restoration remains hotly contested in monarchist circles in emigration and in Russia.

*See also:* ALEXANDER I; ALEXANDER II; ALEXANDER III; ALEXEI MIKHAILOVICH; ANNA IVANOVNA; CATHERINE I; CATHERINE II; ELIZABETH; FILARET ROMANOV, PATRIARCH; IVAN V; IVAN VI; NICHOLAS I; NICHOLAS II; PAUL I; PETER I; PETER II; PETER III; ROMANOV, MIKHAIL FYODOROVICH; SOPHIA; TIME OF TROUBLES

**BIBLIOGRAPHY**

Dunning, Chester S. L. (2001). *Russia's First Civil War: The Time of Troubles and the Founding of the Romanov Dynasty.* University Park: Pennsylvania State University Press.

Klyuchevsky, Vasilii O. (1970). *The Rise of the Romanovs,* tr. Liliana Archibald. London: Macmillan.

Lincoln, W. Bruce. (1981). *The Romanovs: Autocrats of All the Russias.* New York: The Dial Press.

Nazarov, V. D. (1993). "The Genealogy of the Koshkins-Zakharyns-Romanovs and the Legend about the Foundation of the Georgievskiy Monastery." *Historical Genealogy* 1:22–31.

Orchard, G. Edward. (1989). "The Election of Michael Romanov." *The Slavonic and East European Review* 67:378–402.

RUSSELL E. MARTIN

# ROMANOV, GRIGORY VASILIEVICH

(b. 1923), first secretary of the Leningrad Oblast Party Committee during the Brezhnev years.

Grigory Romanov was born on February 9, 1923, to Russian working-class parents. He served in the Red Army during World War II. He joined the Communist Party of the Soviet Union (CPSU) in 1944, and received a night-school diploma in ship building in 1953. Romanov almost immediately went to work within the Leningrad party apparatus, climbing through the ranks from factory, to ward, to city, and ultimately to oblast-level positions. He served as first secretary of the Leningrad Oblast Party Committee from 1970 to 1983, and was known for encouraging production and scientific associations, as well as the forging of links between such groups to implement new technologies. As a result, Leningrad achieved enviable production levels under Romanov. He was named a candidate member of the Politburo in 1973, and was promoted to full membership in 1976. Romanov advanced to the CPSU Central Committee Secretariat in June 1983, with responsibility for the defense industry. Though mentioned as a candidate for the office of general secretary, his many years spent outside the Moscow left Romanov unable to build allies in the Politburo.

Once Gorbachev had claimed the general secretary post in March 1985, he began purging his rivals from the top leadership, and Romanov was among them. Despite his innovations in Leningrad, Romanov was a conservative, not inclined to alter the complacency—and corruption—of the Brezhnev era. Romanov was formally relieved of his duties on July 1, 1986.

*See also:* COMMUNIST PARTY OF THE SOVIET UNION; POLITBURO

**BIBLIOGRAPHY**

Medish, Vadim. (1983). "A Romanov in the Kremlin?" *Problems of Communism* 32(6): 65–66.

Mitchell, R. Judson. (1990). *Getting to the Top in the USSR.* Stanford, CA: Hoover Institution Press.

Ruble, Blair A. (1983). "Romanov's Leningrad." *Problems of Communism* 32(6): 36–48.

ANN E. ROBERTSON

# ROMANOV, MIKHAIL FYODOROVICH

(1596–1645), tsar of Russia from 1613 to 1645 and first ruler of the Romanov Dynasty.

Born in 1596, Mikhail Fedorovich Romanov was the son of Fyodor Nikitich Romanov and his wife

**Mikhail Fyodorovich Romanov, the first Romanov tsar.**
© HULTON ARCHIVE

Ksenia Ivanovna Shestova. His family had long served as boyars in the court of the Muscovite rulers. The Romanovs, while still known as the Yurievs, were thrust into the center of power and politics in 1547, when Anastasia Romanovna Yurieva, Mikhail's great aunt, married Tsar Ivan IV ("the Terrible"). This union produced Tsar Fyodor Ivanovich, the last of the old Riurikovich rulers of Russia, who died in 1598 without heirs. The extinction of the tsarist line left the succession in question, but the throne finally went to Boris Godunov, a prominent figure in Tsar Fyodor Ivanovich's court.

## FROM GODUNOV TO THE ROMANOV DYNASTY

The reign of Boris Godunov was a difficult time for the Romanov clan. Many members were exiled and forcibly tonsured (required to become monks or nuns) by the new tsar, including Mikhail's father

and mother, who took the monastic names Filaret and Marfa, respectively. The young Mikhail, then only nine years old, similarly was exiled, at first in rather harsh conditions at Beloozero, then in somewhat better circumstances on the family's own estates, in both cases living with relatives.

Fortunes changed definitively for the better for Mikhail only after 1605, with the unexpected death of Tsar Boris and the brief reign of the First False Dmitry. Mikhail was reunited with his mother, and took up residence in Moscow before moving in 1612 to the Ipatev Monastery near Kostroma, where his mother's family had estates. In the next year, an Assembly of the Land (Zemsky Sobor) was summoned to elect a new tsar for the throne that, by then, had lain vacant for three years. After having ruled out any foreign candidates (the younger brother of the Swedish king, Karl Phillipp, had enjoyed some support among segments of the boyar elite), the assembly began to discuss native candidates. At length, the assembly elected Mikhail to be tsar, and with this election the three hundred year reign of the House of Romanov began.

## WHY MIKHAIL ROMANOV?

Historians have long speculated on the reasons the election might have fallen on Mikhail in 1613. Some have pointed to his youth (he was only sixteen years old at the time); or to his inexperience in political matters; or to his supposed weak will and poor health. These rationales suggest that perhaps the electors in the Assembly of the Land saw in him someone who could easily be manipulated to suit their own clan interests. Others have pointed to the role of the Cossacks, who, according to contemporary sources, rushed into the assembly and demanded, at the point of a pike, that Mikhail be recognized as the "God-annointed tsar." The fact that the Romanovs appear in some later accounts to have maintained their good name and enjoyed some popularity even through the darkest and most violent phases of Ivan the Terrible's reign, may also have worked to their advantage in 1613. It must be acknowledged, however, that some of these sources were compiled after 1613, and thus may reflect Romanov self-interest.

Some sources have claimed that Tsar Fyodor Ivanovich, as death approached in 1598, nominated Fyodor Nikitich, Mikhail's father, to succeed him on the throne—a nomination that was, evidently, ignored after the tsar's death. One fact, often overlooked in treatments of Mikhail's life and reign, is that the Romanov boyar clan—Mikhail's ancestors—

were remarkably successful during the decades after the 1547 marriage of Anastasia Yurieva and Ivan the Terrible at forging numerous marriage alliances between their kin and members of most of the other important boyar clans at court. These marriages linked the Romanovs directly with a sizeable portion of the boyar elite. This web of kinship to which the Romanovs belonged, plus the other factors mentioned, may have made the young Mikhail a viable and highly desirable candidate for the throne, since electing him would tend to secure the high ranks and privileged positions of the boyars, most of whom were already Mikhail's relatives.

## EARLY CHALLENGES

For whatever reason he was elected, Mikhail's early years on the throne were nonetheless rocky. Novgorod and Pskov still lay under Swedish occupation until a final peace was concluded and a military withdrawal obtained by the Treaty of Stolbovo (1617). Mikhail's father still languished in a Polish prison, released only in 1619, after peace with Poland was finally concluded at the Treaty of Deulino (1618). Rivals for the throne still roamed the countryside, particularly in the south—some proclaiming themselves to be yet another Tsarevich Dmitry. Zarutsky's band of Cossacks proved to be still a menace, supporting the widow of the First False Dmitry.

The security and legitimacy of the new dynasty were hardly fixed by the election in 1613. Matters improved with the return of Mikhail's father in 1619. Having been forcibly tonsured a monk earlier, he had been proclaimed patriarch by the Second False Dmitry; and on his return to Moscow he was formally and officially installed in that office. From then to his death in 1633, Filaret ruled in all respects jointly with his son, and had even been given the unique title of Great Sovereign. The competent governance of Filaret and, after his death, of other Romanov relatives, plus the absence of successional squabbles, gradually produced the stability that, by the end of Mikhail's reign, helped to firmly establish Romanov dynasticism in Russia and the peaceful succession of Mikhail's son, Alexei, to the throne.

## ENSURING THE DYNASTIC SUCCESSION

Mikhail Romanov's family life was full of intrigue and failures. In 1616, Mikhail picked Maria Ivanovna Khlopova from several prospective brides, and he seems genuinely to have felt fondness for her. His mother, however, was dead set against the match,

as were his mother's relatives, Mikhail and Boris Saltykov, the former of whom was among the chief figures of the court. The Saltykov brothers appear to have had another candidate in mind for Mikhail, and so they conspired to ruin the match by poisoning Maria, causing her to have a fit of vomiting. Maria and her family were immediately dispatched to Tobolsk, in Siberia, as punishment for their presumed conspiracy to conceal a serious illness from the tsar (one that, it was believed, might have implications for the reproductive capacity of the new bride).

Further efforts to marry Mikhail off to a foreign bride ensued and matches were proposed (with the daughter of the grand duke of Lithuania, the daughter of the duke of Holstein-Gottorp, and with the sister of the elector of Brandenburg), but all failed. An investigation of the Khlopov affair was opened up in 1623, and shortly thereafter the truth of the Saltykov conspiracy was discovered and the two brothers were disgraced and sent into exile. Even so, no serious reconsideration of the Khlopov match ever materialized, for Mikhail's mother remained adamantly opposed to the match.

In 1624 Mikhail married Maria Dolgorukova, possibly the young girl that had been the original choice of the Saltykovs, but she died within a few months of the wedding. Mikhail next married (in 1626) Evdokya Streshneva, with whom he had six daughters and three sons, including his heir, Alexei. In the last year of his life he attempted to marry off one of his daughters, Irina, to Prince Waldemar, the natural son of the king of Denmark, Christian IV. Waldemar's refusal to convert to Orthodoxy doomed the marriage project, but the controversy stimulated a fertile theological and political debate about baptism and the confessional lines between Orthodoxy and Heterodoxy. Mikhail died on July 12, 1645, on his name-day (St. Mikhail Malein, not, as is often assumed and asserted, St. Mikhail the Archangel).

*See also:* ASSEMBLY OF THE LAND; COSSACKS; DMITRY, FALSE; FILARET ROMANOV, PATRIARCH; GODUNOV, BORIS FYODOROVICH; IVAN IV; ROMANOV DYNASTY; SIBERIA; STOLBOVO, TREATY OF; TIME OF TROUBLES

## BIBLIOGRAPHY

Bain, R. Nisbet. (1905). *The First Romanovs, 1613–1725: A History of Muscovite Civilization and the Rise of Modern Russia Under Peter the Great and His Forerunners.* New York: E. P. Dutton.

Dunning, Chester S. L. (2001). *Russia's First Civil War: The Time of Troubles and the Founding of the Romanov*

*Dynasty.* University Park: Pennsylvania State University Press.

Klyuchevsky, Vasilii O. (1970). *The Rise of the Romanovs*, tr. Liliana Archibald. London: Macmillan St. Martin's.

Orchard, G. Edward. (1989). "The Election of Michael Romanov." *Slavonic and East European Review* 67: 378–402.

Platonov, S. F. (1985). *The Time of Troubles*, tr. John T. Alexander. Lawrence: University of Kansas Press.

RUSSELL E. MARTIN

# ROMANTICISM

Unlike the Enlightenment, a cultural movement that was imported into Russia from the West and thus, in the words of the poet Alexander Pushkin, "moored on the banks of the conquered Neva" (referring to the river that flows through St. Petersburg), Romanticism had a more indigenous quality, building on the earlier cultural tradition of sentimentalism. The awakening of the heart experienced by Russian society in the second half of the eighteenth century resulted in an oversensitive, reflective personality—a type that persisted in the next generation and evolved into the superfluous man epitomized by Pushkin in the character of Eugene Onegin in the poem of the same name, and by Mikhail Lermontov in Pechorin, the protagonist of *A Hero of Our Time*. The full-fledged Romantic type was born in Russia during the reign of Alexander I (1801–1825), which witnessed Napoleon's invasion and subsequent fall and the Russian army's triumphant entry into Paris. These cataclysmic events powerfully enhanced, in the conscience of a sensitive generation, a fatalistic conception of change to which both kingdoms and persons are subject—a conception shared by Alexander. At the same time, an idea of freedom and happiness "within ourselves"—notwithstanding the doom of external reality—was put forward with unprecedented strength. The Alexandrine age saw an extraordinary burst of creativity, especially in literature.

## WESTERN INFLUENCES

Russian Romanticism was strongly influenced by cultural developments in the West. Vasily Zhukovsky's masterly translations and adaptations from German poetry are representative of the transitional 1800s and early 1810s. Later, British literary influence became dominant. "It seems that, in the present age, a poet cannot but echo Byron, as well as a novelist cannot but echo W. Scott, notwithstanding the magnitude and even originality of talent," wrote the poet and critic Peter Vyazemsky in 1827. More philosophical authors such as Vladimir F. Odoyevsky persistently looked to German thought for inspiration; Schelling was particularly important. The evolution of French literature was also keenly followed: Victor Hugo (but hardly the dreamy Lamartine) aroused much sympathy in the Russian Romantics. A seminal event was the sojourn in St. Petersburg and Moscow of the exiled Polish poet Adam Mickiewicz. However, the study of European models only convinced Russian authors and critics that Romanticism necessarily implied originality. "Conditioned by the desire to realize the creative originality of the human soul," Romanticism owes its formation "not just to every individual nation, but, what is more, to every individual author," wrote Nikolai Polevoy, a leading figure in the Russian Romantic movement. Characteristically, Pushkin struggled to dispel the image of Russian Byron, while Lermontov explicitly declared his non-Byronism.

## CONTROVERSIES

The Russian Romantic movement consolidated. In the late 1810s, the Classic–Romantic controversy broke out, continuing throughout the 1820s and 1830s. Russian literary journals took sides. Academic circles, too, were engaged in the controversy: Nikolai Nadezhdin's Latin dissertation on Romantic poetry is a case in point. The Classicists claimed that Romanticism sought anarchy in literature and in the fine arts, whereas "Art, generally, is obedience to rules." Indeed, the Romantics, especially in their poetic declarations, blissfully proclaimed the lawlessness of artistic creation. In theoretical discussions, however, they did not simply reject the classical rigidities, but undertook to formulate alternative laws, loosely, those of nature, beauty, and truth. A more specific agreement was difficult to reach, not just on specific issues such as the principles of Romantic drama, but also on the very meaning of Romanticism. Vladimir Nabokov has identified at least eleven various interpretations of "Romantic" current in Pushkin's time. As might be expected, the internal controversy emerged in the Romantic camp. The polemics, piercing other than purely theoretical issues, often involved angry exchanges. Literary alliances were vulnerable, as in the case of Pushkin and Nikolai Polevoy. Yet, the early nineteenth century witnessed a remarkable tendency, on the part of the authors, artists, and musicians, to form circles, attend salons, and group around enlightened patrons.

## CROSSING BORDERS

In this kind of atmosphere, crossing of borders between different arts was common. Vasily Zhukovsky produced brilliant drawings; Lermontov nearly abandoned writing for the sake of painting; Vladimir Odoyevsky was a musicologist as well as a poet and novelist; the playwright Alexander Griboyedov, a talented composer. As art historian Valery Turchin points out, it was the musician rather than the poet who was eventually promoted, in the view of the Romantics, to the role of the supreme type of artistic genius. This precisely reflected the Romantics' quest for the spiritual, for music, of all the arts, was considered the least bound by materiality. Arguably, Romanticism was a later phenomenon in Russian music than in literature and art. Anyway, a contemporary of Pushkin, the composer Mikhail Glinka, renowned for his use of Russian folk tradition, was a major contributor to the Romantic movement. The painter Orestes Kiprensky commenced his series of Romantic portraits during the very dawn of literary Romanticism. Somewhat later emerged the Romantic schools of landscape and historical painting. Even in architecture, the art most strongly bound by matter, new trends showed up against the neoclassical background: neogothicism, exotic orientalism, and, finally, the national current exemplified in Konstantin Ton's churches. During the reign of Nicholas I (1825–1855) Romanticism began to be diffused in the more general quest for history and nationality.

## SLAVOPHILISM

The important offshoot of this development was Slavophilism. Nicholas I typified the new epoch in the same way as Alexander I had typified the previous age. In his youth, Nicholas had received a largely Romantic education. He was an admirer of Walter Scott and was inclined to imitate the kings of Scott's novels. Characteristically, Pushkin, during the reign of Nicholas, persistently returns to the twin themes of nobility and ancestry, lamenting (in a manner closely resembling Edmund Burke) the passing of the age of chivalry. The dominant mood of the period, however, was nationalistic and messianic, and here again the Romantics largely shared the inclinations of the tsar. Notably, it was Peter Vyazemsky who coined the word *narodnost* (the Russian equivalent of "nationality"), which became part of the official ideological formula ("Or-

thodoxy, Autocracy, Nationality"). Odoevsky argued that because of their "poetic organization," the Russian people would attain superiority over the West even in scientific matters. Pushkin welcomed the suppression of the Polish uprising of 1831, interpreting it in Panslavic terms. Nonetheless, there was an unbridgeable psychological rift between the tsar and the Romantic camp, which had its origin in the catastrophe of December 1825. Several of the Decembrists (most importantly, Kondraty Ryleyev, one of the five executed) were men of letters and members of the Romantic movement. Throughout the reign, a creative personality faced fierce censorship and remained under the threat of persecution. Many could say with Polevoy (whose ambitious Romantic enterprise embraced, beside literature, history and even economics, but whose *Moscow Telegraph*, Russia's most successful literary journal, was closed by the government): "My dreams remained unfulfilled, my ideals, unexpressed." The split between ideal and reality was the central problem for Romanticism universally, but in Russia this problem acquired a specifically bleak character.

*See also:* GOLDEN AGE OF RUSSIAN LITERATURE; LERMONTOV, MIKHAIL YURIEVICH; ODOYEVSKY, VLADIMIR FYODOROVICH; PUSHKIN, ALEXANDER SERGEYEVICH; SLAVOPHILES; ZHUKOVSKY; VASILY ANDREYEVICH

## BIBLIOGRAPHY

McLaughlin, Sigrid (1972). "Russia: Romaničeskij-Romantičeskij-Romantizm." In *"Romantic" and Its Cognates: The European History of a Word*, ed. Hans Eichner. Toronto: University of Toronto Press.

Peer, Larry H. (1998). "Pushkin and Romantizm," In *Comparative Romanticisms: Power, Gender, Subjectivity*, ed. Larry H. Peer and Diane Long Hoeveler. Columbia, SC: Camden House.

Riasanovsky, Nicholas V. (1992). *The Emergence of Romanticism*. New York: Oxford University Press.

Rydel, Christine, ed. (1984). *The Ardis Anthology of Russian Romanticism*. Ann Arbor, MI: Ardis.

YURI TULUPENKO

## ROSTISLAV

(d. 1167), grand prince of Kiev and the progenitor of the Rostislavichi, the dynasty of Smolensk.

After Rostislav's father Mstislav Vladimirovich gave him Smolensk around 1125, he freed it from its subordination to southern Pereyaslavl, fortified it with new defensive walls, founded churches, and patronized culture. Around 1150, despite opposition from Metropolitan Kliment (Klim) Smolyatich and the bishop of Pereyaslavl, he also freed the Church of Smolensk from its dependence on Pereyaslavl by making it an autonomous eparchy. Manuel, a Greek, was its first bishop, and the Church of the Assumption, built by Rostislav's grandfather Vladimir Vsevolodovich "Monomakh," became his cathedral. Rostislav also issued a charter (*gramota*) enumerating the privileges of the bishop and the church in Smolensk. The document is valuable as a source of ecclesiastical, social, commercial, and geographic information.

Rostislav had political dealings with neighbouring Polotsk and Novgorod, but his most important involvement was in Kiev. After 1146 he helped his elder brother Izyaslav win control of the capital of Rus. Following the latter's death in 1154, the citizens invited Rostislav to rule Kiev with his uncle Vyacheslav Vladimirovich, but his uncle Yury Vladimirovich "Dolgoruky" replaced him in the same year. Although Rostislav regained Kiev in 1159, his rule was not secured until 1161, when his rival Izyaslav Davidovich of Chernigov died. As prince of Kiev, he asserted his authority over the so-called kernel of Rus and placated many of the princes. He failed, however, to stop the incursions of the Polovtsy. He died on March 14, 1167, and was buried in Kiev.

*See also:* IZYASLAV MSTISLAVICH; KIEVAN RUS; VLADIMIR MONOMAKH

**BIBLIOGRAPHY**

Dimnik, Martin. (1983). "Rostislav Mstislavich." In *The Modern Encyclopedia of Russian and Soviet History*, ed. Joseph L. Wieczynski, 31:162–165. Gulf Breeze, FL: Academic International Press.

MARTIN DIMNIK

# ROSTOVTSEV, MIKHAIL IVANOVICH

(1870–1952), Russian-American historian and archeologist of Greek and Roman antiquity.

Mikhail Ivanovich Rostovtsev was born in Kiev and educated at the Universities of Kiev and St. Petersburg. He taught at St. Petersburg University, and in the Higher Women's Courses until 1918, rising to become a professor in 1912. His career before the revolution shows the international nature of academic life: He published widely in English, French, and German as well as Russian.

Rostovtsev refused to serve either in the Provisional Government or in the Communist government, and in emigration published extensive polemics against the Communists. In 1918 Rostovstev fled Russia, first to Oxford (1918–1920), and then to the United States where he was professor first at the University of Wisconsin (1920–1925) and then Yale University (1925–1944).

Rostovtsev's academic interests were extensive. Trained as a philologist, he wrote monographs on Roman tax farming and land tenure. As an art historian he also published important works on the art and history of south Russia that traced cultural influences in Scythian art from Greece to the borders of China. From 1928 to 1936 he lead Yale's excavations at Dura-Europos in Syria.

His greatest fame, however, rests on two large monographs: *Economic and Social History of the Roman Empire* (Oxford, 1926) and *The Social and Economic History of the Hellenistic World* (Oxford, 1941). In both these works he emphasizes the role of the urban bourgeoisie in the development of the two related cultures, and their decline due to state intervention and outside attacks.

*See also:* EDUCATION; UNIVERSITIES

**BIBLIOGRAPHY**

Momigliano, Arnaldo. (1966). *Studies in Historiography*. London: Weidenfeld and Nicolson.

Vernadsky, George. (1931). "M. I. Rostovtsev." *Seminarium Kondakovianum* 4:239–252.

A. DELANO DUGARM

# ROTA SYSTEM

Also known as the "ladder system," the rota system describes a collateral pattern of succession, according to which princes of the Rurikid dynasty ascended the throne of Kiev, the main seat of Kievan Rus. The system prevailed from the mid-eleventh century until the disintegration of Kievan Rus in the thirteenth century. It also determined succession for the main seats in secondary principalities within Kievan Rus and survived in the northern Rus principalities into the fourteenth and fifteenth centuries.

The design for the rota system has been attributed to Prince Yaroslav the Wise (d. 1054), who in his "Testament" or will divided his realm among his sons. He left Kiev to his eldest son. He assigned secondary towns, which became centers of principalities that comprised Kievan Rus, to his younger sons and admonished them to obey their eldest brother as they had their father. Although the Testament did not provide a detailed order for succession, the nineteenth- and early twentieth-century historians Sergei Soloviev and Vasily Klyuchevsky concluded that it set up an arrangement for the entire Rurikid dynasty to possess and rule the realm of Kievan Rus. It created a hierarchy among the princely brothers and, in later generations, cousins that was paralleled by a hierarchy among their territorial domains. It anticipated that when the prince of Kiev died, he would be succeeded by the most senior surviving member of his generation, who would move from his seat to Kiev. The next prince in the generational hierarchy would replace him, with each younger prince moving up a step on the ladder of succession. When all members of the eldest generation of the dynasty had died, succession would pass to their sons. For a prince to become eligible for the Kievan throne, however, his father must have held that position.

The rota system was revised by a princely agreement concluded at Lyubech in 1097. The agreement ended the practice of rotation of the princes through the secondary seats in conjunction with succession to Kiev. Instead, a designated branch of the dynasty would permanently rule each principality within Kievan Rus. The princes of each dynastic branch continued to use the rota system to determine succession to their primary seat. The exceptions were Kiev itself, where rotation among the eligible members of the entire dynasty resumed after 1113, and Novgorod, which selected its own prince after 1136.

Succession to the Kievan throne was, nevertheless, frequently contested. Scholars have interpreted the repeated internecine conflicts and their meaning for the existence and functionality of the rota system in a variety of ways. Some regard the rota system to have been intended to apply only to Yaroslav's three eldest sons and the three central principalities assigned to them. Others have argued that the system was not fully formulated by Yaroslav, but evolved as the dynasty grew, took possession of a greater expanse of territory, and had to confront, by diplomacy and by war, unforeseen complications in determining "seniority." Others

contend that the Rurikid princes had no succession system, but threatened or used force to determine which prince would sit on the Kievan throne.

Despite the conflicts over succession, which have been cited as an indicator of a weak political system and a lack of unity within the ruling dynasty, the rota system has also been interpreted as a constructive means of accommodating competing interests and tensions among members of a large dynasty. It enabled the dynasty to provide a successor to the Kievan throne in an age when high mortality rates tended to reduce the number of eligible princes. It also emphasized the symbolic centrality of Kiev even as the increasing political and economic strength of component principalities of Kievan Rus undermined the unity of the dynastic realm.

After the Mongol invasions of 1237 through 1240 and the disintegration of Kievan Rus, the rota system continued to prevail in the northeastern Rus principalities until Yuri (ruled 1317–1322) and Ivan I Kalita (ruled 1328–1341) of Moscow, whose father had not held the position, became grand princes of Vladimir. Their descendants monopolized the position and replaced the rota system with a vertical succession system, according to which the eldest surviving son of a reigning prince was heir to the throne.

*See also:* KIEVAN RUS; YAROSLAV VLADIMIROVICH

**BIBLIOGRAPHY**
Dimnik, Martin. (1987). "The 'Testament' of Iaroslav 'The Wise': A Re-examination." *Canadian Slavonic Papers* 29(4):369–386.

Kollmann, Nancy Shields. (1990). "Collateral Succession in Kievan Rus'." *Harvard Ukrainian Studies* 14(3/4): 377–387.

Stokes, A. D. (1970). "The System of Succession to the Thrones of Russia, 1054–1113." In *Gorski Vijenac: A Garland of Essays offered to Professor Elizabeth Mary Hill*, ed. R. Auty, L. R. Lewitter, A. P. Vlasto. Cambridge, UK: The Modern Humanities Research Association.

JANET MARTIN

# ROUTE TO GREEKS

The key commercial and communication route between Kievan Rus and Byzantium, and called "The Way From the Varangians [Vikings] to the Greeks" in the Russian *Primary Chronicle*, this riverine route began in the southeastern Baltic at the mouth of the Western Dvina, connecting to the upper Dnieper at portage areas near Smolensk, and continued through Kiev to the lower Dnieper, where it entered the Black Sea, finally terminating in Constantinople. An alternative route in the north passed from Smolensk portages to the Lovat, which led to Lake Ilmen and, via the Volkhov and Novgorod, on to Lake Ladoga and thence, by way of the Neva, to the Gulf of Finland and the eastern Baltic. While segments of this route were used from the Stone Age onward, it did not achieve its fullest extent until the late ninth and early tenth centuries when Rus princes unified the waterways and adjoining lands under the Rus state.

In the mid-tenth century, the Byzantine emperor Constantine Porphyrogenitus described (*De administrando imperio*) the southern part of the route, noting the existence of seven cataracts in the lower Dnieper, passable only by portage, and the attendant dangers of Pecheneg attacks. According to Constantine, the Slavs—from as far north as Novgorod—cut *monoxyla* (dugouts) during the winter and floated them downstream to Kiev in spring. There, these boats were rebuilt and equipped with oars, rowlocks, and "other tackle." In early summer, the Rus filled these boats with goods to sell in Constantinople and rowed downstream to the island of St. Aitherios (Berezan) in the mouth of the Dnieper, where they again re-equipped their boats with "tackle as is needed, sails and masts and rudders which they bring with them." Thereafter, they sailed out into the Black Sea, following its western coast to Constantinople. With the Rus-Byzantine commercial treaties of 907, 911, 944, and 971, Rus traders were common visitors in Constantinople, where they stayed for as long as six months annually, from spring through the summer months, at the quarters of St. Mamas.

The Rus traded furs, wax, and honey for Byzantine wine, olive oil, silks, glass jewelry and dishware, church paraphernalia, and other luxuries. During the tenth century and perhaps a bit later, the Rus also sold slaves to the Byzantines. Rus and Scandinavian pilgrims and mercenaries also traveled to the eastern Mediterranean via this route. On several occasions in the tenth century and in 1043, the Rus used this route to invade Byzantium.

During inter-princely Rus disputes, the route was sometimes closed, as at the turn of the twelfth century when Kiev blockaded trade with Novgorod. On occasion, nomadic peoples south of Kiev also blocked the route or impeded trade, and Rus princes responded with military expeditions. With the occupation of Constantinople by Latin Crusaders in 1204, Rus merchants shifted their trade to the Crimean port of Sudak. The route was abandoned following the Mongol conquest of Rus in about 1240. However, up to that time, Kiev's trade via the route flourished, particularly from the eleventh to the mid-thirteenth centuries.

*See also:* BYZANTIUM, INFLUENCE OF; FOREIGN TRADE; KIEVAN RUS; NORMANIST CONTROVERSY; PRIMARY CHRONICLE; VIKINGS

**BIBLIOGRAPHY**

Cross, Samuel Hazzard and Sherbowitz-Wetzor, Olgerd P., tr. and ed. (1973). *The Russian Primary Chronicle.* Cambridge, MA: Mediaeval Academy of America.

Kaiser, Daniel, tr. and ed. (1992). *The Laws of Russia,* Series 1, Vol. 1: *The Laws of Rus', Tenth to Fifteenth Centuries.* Salt Lake City, UT: Charles Schlacks, Jr.

Noonan, Thomas S. (1967). "The Dnieper Trade Route." Ph.D. diss., University of Michigan, Ann Arbor.

Noonan, Thomas S. (1991). "The Flourishing of Kiev's International and Domestic Trade, ca. 1100–ca. 1240." In *Ukrainian Economic History: Interpretive Essays,* ed. I. S. Koropeckyj. Cambridge, MA: Ukrainian Research Institute.

ROMAN K. KOVALEV

**RSFSR** *See* RUSSIAN SOVIET FEDERATED SOCIALIST REPUBLIC.

# RUBLE

The basic unit of Russian currency.

The term *ruble* (*rubl'*) emerged in thirteenth-century Novgorod, where it referred to half of a grivna. The term derives from the verb *rubit* (to cut), since the original rubles were silver bars notched at intervals to facilitate cutting. The ruble was initially a measure of both value and weight, but not a minted currency. Under the monetary reform of 1534, the ruble was defined as equal to 100 kopecks or 200 dengi. Other subdivisions of the ruble were the altyn (3 kopecks), the grivennik (10 kopecks), the polupoltina (25 kopecks), and the

**A five-ruble Russian banknote.** TNA Associates.

poltina (50 kopecks). A highly inflationary copper ruble circulated during Alexei Mikhailovich's currency reform (1654–1663), the first instance of minted ruble coins.

In 1704 the government began the regular minting of silver rubles, defined initially as equal to 28 grams of silver but declining steadily to 18 grams by the 1760s. Gold coins were minted in 1756 and 1779, copper rubles in 1770 and 1771. From 1769 to 1849, irredeemable paper promissory notes called *assignatsii* (sing. *assignatsiya*) circulated alongside the metal currency.

Nicholas I reestablished the silver ruble as the basic unit of account. In 1843 he introduced a new paper ruble that remained convertible only until 1853. In 1885 and 1886, the silver ruble, linked to the French franc, was reinstated as the official currency. Sergei Witte's reforms in 1897 introduced a gold ruble, and Russia remained on the gold standard until 1914. Fully convertible paper currency circulated at the same time. A worthless paper ruble (kerenka) was used at the close of World War I.

The first Soviet ruble—a paper currency—was issued in 1919, and the first Soviet silver ruble appeared in 1921. Ruble banknotes were introduced in 1934. A 1937 reform set the value of the ruble in relation to the U.S. dollar, a practice that ended in 1950 with the adoption of a gold standard. Monetary reforms were implemented in 1947, 1961, and 1997.

*See also:* ALTYN; DENGA; GRIVNA; KOPECK; MONETARY SYSTEM, SOVIET

**BIBLIOGRAPHY**

Spassky, Ivan Georgievich. (1968). *The Russian Monetary System: A Historico-Numismatic Survey*, tr Z. I. Gorishina and rev. L. S. Forrer. Amsterdam: J. Schulman.

JARMO T. KOTILAINE

## RUBLE CONTROL

The Soviet economy was predominantly centrally controlled, with production and supply targets set using physical indicators or quasi-physical units, and with prices fixed according to criteria that were far removed from any consideration of the demand and supply equilibrium. Given the dual monetary circulation in the economy, only physical or quasi-physical units were to be used inside the state sector. Households, on the other hand, participated in a mostly fixed-price cash economy. Central control of monetary units was called ruble control. It aimed both at the quasi-physical monetary units used for decision-making within the state sector and the mostly fixed-price monetary units that the household sector faced.

In the broad sense of the phrase, ruble control thus included central control over any activities that used monetary units. This primarily encompassed prices, wages, costs, profits, investment, and finance, as well as credits. Because the use of monetary units is broadly pervasive in a multiresource and multiproduct economy, the field of ruble control was extensive, even in a centrally managed economy. In addition to being another general control tool, ruble control was supposed to focus on improving efficiency and equilibrium in the economy. The more the economy moved from direct central control of entrepreneurial and other behaviors to the more indirect control based on prices and other monetary units, the more the importance of ruble control tended to grow. However, the monetary units used were administratively determined, and enterprises had soft budget constraints with little real decision-making independence, so that ruble control remained just one more way of implementing central management, and did not become an element of market relations.

Because the centrally managed economy had a wide variety of monetary units, ruble control also had a large number of subjects, from business enterprises to governmental ministries to the State Bank. The variety of controlling agencies and their always badly defined prerogatives, as well as the inevitable divergence of interests among these disparate groups, meant that ruble control was far from an optimal management tool. Different controllers sent different or even contradictory commands, giving subordinated units at least some decision-making room. Businesses had an impact at the planning stage on the directives and parameters that would ultimately be given to them. In addition, since these enterprises had soft budget constraints, the availability of finance was not a binding constraint if a priority target threatened to go unfulfilled. This is because, although costs were theoretically under ruble control, they could be exceeded if necessary in order to meet output targets. Soviet leaders thought they could well accept inefficiency if that helped them to reach goals with a higher priority, because they believed that resources were in almost unlimited supply. In other words, central management was based on priority thinking, and ruble control had to accommodate the established priorities.

The negative consequences of this logic were visible from the very beginning of central management. Already by 1931, many proposals were circulated for enhancing ruble control. Among these were more rational pricing, fuller cost-accounting, and better coordination of different

controls, as well as increased decentralization, at least in plan fulfillment. It is revealing about the priority-planning logic that very similar, even identical proposals for rationalizing central management were put forward during all the waves of Soviet reform discussion until the 1980s. Still, in the early 1980s the system functioned very much as it had fifty years earlier, with one crucial difference: Mass terror had been abolished and increased consumption had become a priority. On one hand, this had made ruble control more important. On the other, by weakening other controls and by increasing the autonomy both of managers and households, these developments had made ruble control more difficult. There were markets and quasi-markets, but market-based policy instruments remained absent.

*See also:* HARD BUDGET CONSTRAINTS; MONETARY SYSTEM, SOVIET; REPRESSED INFLATION

**BIBLIOGRAPHY**

Kornai, Janos. (1992). *The Socialist System.* Oxford: Oxford University Press.

Nove, Alec. (1977). *The Soviet Economic System,* 2nd edition. London: Allen & Unwin.

PEKKA SUTELA

# RUBLEV, ANDREI

(c. 1360–1430), fifteenth century Russian artist.

Among all the known icon painters in Russian history, Andrei Rublev stands out as most prominent. Early in his life he joined the Trinity-Sergius Lavra Monastery, becoming a monk and a pupil of the artist Prokhor of Gorodets. Later he moved near Moscow, to the Spaso Andronikov Monastery, where he died on January 29, 1430, after painting frescoes in that monastery's Church of the Savior. He was buried in the altar crypt beside the artist, Daniel Chorni.

Rublev is considered the founder of the Moscow School of painting. The earliest reference to Rublev's work is to paintings in the Annunciation Cathedral of the Moscow Kremlin. Here in 1405 he worked with the eminent Theophanes the Greek (who strongly influenced his style) and the monk Prokhov of Gorodets. On the iconostasis (the screen separating the church nave from the altar area) Rublev is credited with the scenes of the annunciation to the Virgin Mary and scenes from the life of Christ that show his nativity, baptism, transfiguration, the resurrection of Lazarus, entry into Jerusalem, and the presentation in the Temple.

Rublev worked extensively outside of Moscow as well. In about 1400, in the Dormition Cathedral on Gorodok in Zvenigorod, Rublev, assisted by Daniel Chroni, painted a number of wall frescoes, including those of St. Laurus and St. Florus, and several panel icons, including Archangel Michael, Apostle Paul, and the Christ. In the Cathedral of the Dormition in Vladimir, assisted again by Daniel Chorni, he painted frescoes of the Last Judgment in 1408. He is also credited with five surviving icons.

The last reference to Rublev's work refers to his work on the iconostasis in the Cathedral of the Trinity at Zagorsk (Trinity-Sergius Monastery), where he was assisted once again by Daniel Chorni. It was here that he produced his most famous icon, the Old Testament Trinity (1411; now in the Tretyakov Gallery, Moscow). Ordered by Nikon and painted in honor of Father Sergius of Radonezh (d. 1392), it was originally displayed at the latter's grave. The ethereal and beautifully-integrated group of three angels has never been surpassed. Of the other icons on this iconostasis, Rublev was credited with those depicting the Archangel Gabriel, St. Paul, and the Baptism of Christ. Rublev is believed to have painted two more icons for other venues: a Christ in Majesty (c. 1411, now at the Tretyakov Gallery) and a version of the Vladimir Mother of God (c. 1409, Vladimir Museum).

Rublev's fame continued to increase after his death. The Church Council held in Moscow in 1551 prescribed the official canon for the correct representation of the Trinity: ". . . to paint from ancient models, as painted by the Greek painters and as painted by Andrei Rublev." It is the other-worldly, spiritual, and contemplative quality of Rublev's painting that sets him apart from his contemporaries. His Old Testament Trinity has had by far had the strongest impact on subsequent icon painting up through the twentieth century, not only in the Russian Orthodox Church, but in Catholic and Protestant circles as well. In Soviet Russia, gifted filmmaker Andrei Tarkovsky produced an epic-length, classic film titled *Andrei Rublev* in 1966. It was widely acclaimed, and continues to be shown in art theaters and at Russian conferences.

See also: DIONISY; ICONS; THEOPHANES THE GREEK

BIBLIOGRAPHY

Lazarev, Viktor Nikitich. (1966). *Old Russian Murals & Mosaics from the XI to the XVI Century.* London: Phaidon.

Lazarev, Viktor Nikitich. (1980). *Moscow School of Icon Painting.* Moscow: Iskusstvo.

A. DEAN McKENZIE

# RUBLE ZONE

"Ruble zone" refers to the accidental currency union that emerged when the Soviet Union broke up in December 1991, after which several independent states (former republics) each used the ruble as their primary currency. This sparked an intense debate among the Central Bank of Russia (CBR), the Russian government, the other post-Soviet governments, and the international financial institutions over the pros and cons of retaining the ruble zone. The ruble zone at first encompassed all fifteen former Soviet republics, grew progressively smaller through 1992 and 1993 as the new states introduced their own currencies, and disappeared completely in 1995 when Tajikistan adopted the Tajik ruble as its sole legal tender. The three Baltic states, having no intention of staying in the ruble zone, introduced their own currencies in mid-1992, but the other post-Soviet states initially chose to remain.

The ruble zone's existence presented a significant dilemma for the CBR, because it prevented the CBR from controlling the Russian money supply. Only the CBR could print cash rubles, because all of the printing presses were on Russian territory. However, a legacy of the Soviet-style currency system (called the dual monetary circuit) allowed any central bank in the ruble zone to freely issue ruble credits to its domestic banks. These banks then loaned the credits to domestic enterprises, which could in turn use them to purchase goods from other ruble zone states (primarily Russia). In effect, the ruble zone states self-financed their trade deficits with Russia through these credit emissions. In addition, several ruble zone states issued so-called "coupons" or parallel currencies to circulate alongside the ruble in 1992 and 1993, thereby increasing the cash money supply in the ruble zone as well.

In an attempt to mitigate the impact of this credit expansion on the Russian economy, as of

July 1992 the CBR began keeping separate ruble credit accounts for each state. In August 1992 it announced that Russian goods could be purchased only with CBR-issued credits, and it suspended the other banks' credit-granting privileges entirely in May 1993. During this process, Ukraine and Kyrgyzstan left the ruble zone. The CBR then fatally undermined the ruble zone through a currency reform in July 1993. It began to print new Russian ruble notes (circulating at equivalency with the old Soviet ones) in early 1993, but did not send these new rubles to the other states; they received their cash shipments solely in Soviet rubles. On July 24, the CBR announced that all pre-1993 ruble notes would become invalid in Russia, forcing the other ruble zone members either to leave or to cede all monetary sovereignty to the CBR. Azerbaijan and Georgia left the ruble zone immediately, while Armenia, Belarus, Kazakhstan, Moldova, Turkmenistan, and Uzbekistan left in November 1993 after talks on creating a ruble zone of a new type broke down. Although this effectively destroyed the ruble zone, its formal end came in May 1995 when war-torn Tajikistan finally introduced its own currency.

*See also:* MONETARY SYSTEM, SOVIET; RUBLE

**BIBLIOGRAPHY**

Abdelal, Rawi. (2001). *National Purpose in the World Economy: Post-Soviet States in Comparative Perspective.* Ithaca, NY: Cornell University Press.

Chavin, James. (1995). "The Disintegration of the Soviet Ruble Zone, 1991–1995." Ph.D. diss. Berkeley, CA: University of California, Berkeley.

Goldberg, Linda; Ickes, Barry; and Ryterman, Randi. (1994). "Departures from the Ruble Zone: The Implications of Adopting Independent Currencies." *World Economy* 17 (3):239–322.

Johnson, Juliet. (2000). *A Fistful of Rubles: The Rise and Fall of the Russian Banking System.* Ithaca, NY: Cornell University Press.

JULIET JOHNSON

## RUMYANTSEV, PETER ALEXANDROVICH

(1725–1796), military commander, from 1774 known as Rumiantsev-Zadunaisky for his military victories "across the Danube."

Peter Alexandrovich Rumyantsev was the son of Alexander Ivanovich Rumyantsev, who rose to prominence in the circle of Peter I, and Maria Andreyevna Matveyeva, whose father was an ambassador and senator. Early in the reign of Empress Anna (1730–1740), the Rumyantsevs fell from favor, but Alexander resumed service in 1735 and was rewarded with the hereditary title of count. In 1748 Peter Rumyantsev married Princess Ekaterina Mikhailovna Golitsyna, with whom he had three sons, Mikhail, Nikolai, and Sergei. He was estranged from his wife early in the marriage.

Despite earning a reputation for dissolute behavior, young Peter Rumyantsev received several commissions in the army. He served with distinction in the Seven Years' War (1756-1762), commanding a cavalry regiment during several successful Russian actions. Having been promoted by Emperor Peter III, he expected to be exiled when Catherine II (r. 1762-1796) seized power, but in 1764 she made him governor–general of Ukraine, with the task of integrating that territory into the Russian administrative and fiscal system. He carried out a major survey and census, introduced a new postal system and courts, and revised laws on peasants. In 1767 he was summoned to participate in the Legislative Commission and was required to investigate Ukrainian delegates to minimize claims for independent privileges and institutions for the region.

At the outbreak of the Russo–Turkish war in 1768, Rumyantsev was first given command of Russia's Second Army and charged with the responsibility of guarding the southern borders. He then took over the First Army from Prince Alexander Mikhailovich Golitsyn. He won victories in July 1770 at Larga and Kagul against great odds and went on to capture towns in Ottoman-held Moldavia and Wallachia. In 1771 he moved west to the Danube, and in 1773 he laid siege to towns in the region but was forced to retreat by supply difficulties. In 1774 Rumyantsev's forces outmaneuvered the Turkish vizier and forced him to accept peace terms at Kuchuk Kainardji.

Rumyantsev was made a field marshal and received the orders of St. George and St. Andrew, as well as lavish rewards that included landed estates. He returned to Ukraine to implement Catherine's Provincial Reform (1775). In the second Russo–Turkish War (1787–1792) Rumyantsev commanded the Ukrainian army, but was in the shadow of Grigory Potemkin. His last major campaign was in Poland in 1794 against Tadeusz Kosciusko. When he died, Emperor Paul ordered three days mourning in the army in his honor.

*See also:* MILITARY, IMPERIAL ERA; RUSSO-TURKISH WARS; SEVEN YEARS' WAR

**BIBLIOGRAPHY**

Alexander, John T. (1983). "Rumiantsev, Petr Aleksandrovich." In *Modern Encyclopedia of Russian and Soviet History,* edited by Joseph L. Wieczynski, vol. 31, 15-19. Gulf Breeze, FL: Academic International Press.

LINDSEY HUGHES

## RURIK

(d. 879), Varangian (Viking) leader who established his rule over the Eastern Slavs in the Novgorod region and became the progenitor of the line of princes, the Rurikid dynasty (Rurikovichi), that ruled Kiev and Muscovy.

The *Primary Chronicle* reports that a number of Eastern Slavic tribes quarreled but agreed to invite a prince to come and rule them and to establish peace. They sent their petition overseas to the Varangians called the Rus. In 862 three brothers came with their kin. Sineus occupied Beloozero and Truvor took Izborsk, but they died within two years. Consequently Rurik, who initially may have ruled Staraya Ladoga, made Novgorod his capital and asserted his control over the entire region. He sent men to Polotsk, Rostov, Beloozero, and Murom. In doing so, he controlled the mayor river routes carrying trade between the Baltic to the Caspian Seas. Rurik allowed two boyars, Askold and Dir, to go to Constantinople; on the way they captured Kiev. In 879, while on his deathbed, Rurik handed over authority to his kinsman Oleg and placed his young son Igor into Oleg's custody.

The chronicle information about the semilegendary Rurik has been interpreted in various ways. For example, the so-called Normanists accept the reliability of the chronicle information showing that the Varangians, or Normans, founded the first Russian state, but the so-called Anti-Normanists look upon the chronicle reports as unreliable if not fictitious. Some identify Rurik with Rorik of Jutland, who was based in Frisia. Significantly, other written sources and archaeological evidence neither prove nor disprove the chronicle information.

*See also:* KIEVAN RUS; NOVGOROD THE GREAT; RURIKID DYNASTY; VIKINGS

**BIBLIOGRAPHY**

Franklin, Simon, and Shepard, Jonathan. (1996). *The Emergence of Rus 750–1200.* London: Longman.

MARTIN DIMNIK

## RURIKID DYNASTY

Ruling family of Kievan Rus, the northern Rus principalities, and Muscovy from the ninth century to 1598.

The Rurikid dynasty ruled the lands of Rus from the ninth century until 1598. The dynasty was allegedly founded by Rurik. According to an account in the *Primary Chronicle* he and his brothers, called Varangian Rus, were invited in 862 by East Slav and Finn tribes of northwestern Russia to rule them. Rurik survived his brothers to rule alone a region stretching from his base in Novgorod northward to Beloozero, eastward along the upper Volga and lower Oka Rivers and southward to the West Dvina River. Although it has been postulated that Rurik was actually Rorik of Jutland, there is no scholarly consensus on his identity, and the account of his arrival is often considered semi–legendary. Varangians or Vikings, however, had been operating in the region as adventurers and merchants. The tale of Rurik represents the stabilization and formalization of the relationship between these groups of adventurers and the indigenous populations.

After Rurik died (879), his kinsman Oleg (r. 882–912), acting as regent for Igor, identified as Rurik's young son, seized control of Kiev (c. 882), located on the Dnieper River. From Kiev, which became the primary seat of the Rurikid princes until the Mongol invasions between 1237 and 1240, Igor (r. 913–945), his widow Olga (r. 945–c. 964), their son Svyatoslav (r. c. 964–972), and his son Vladimir (r. 980–1015), replacing other Varangian and Khazar overlords, subordinated and exacted regular tribute payments from the East Slav tribes on both sides of the Dnieper River and along the upper Volga River. Their strong ties to Byzantium resulted in Prince Vladimir's conversion of his people to Christianity in 988. The dynasty and the church combined to provide a common identity to the disparate lands and peoples of the emerging state of Kievan Rus.

The Rurikids enlarged Kievan Rus territory and through diplomacy, war, and marriage established ties with other countries and royal houses from Scandinavia to France to Byzantium. But the Rurikids themselves were not always unified. Vladimir as well as his son Yaroslav the Wise gained the Kievan throne through fraticidal wars. To avoid further succession struggles, Yaroslav wrote a testament for his sons before he died in 1054. In it he assigned the central princely seat at Kiev to his eldest, surviving son Izyaslav. He gave other towns, which became centers of principalities within Kievan Rus, to his other sons while admonishing them to respect the seniority of their eldest brother.

Although Yaroslav's testament did not prevent internecine warfare, it established a dynastic realm shared by the princes of the dynasty. Members of each generation succeeded one another by seniority through a hierarchy of princely seats until each in his turn ruled at Kiev. This system, known as the rota or ladder system of succession, functioned imperfectly. Ongoing discord combined with attacks from the Polovtsy (nomads of the steppe, also known as Kipchaks or Cumans) motivated the princes to meet at Lyubech in 1097; they agreed that each branch of the dynasty would rule one of the principalities within Kievan Rus as its patrimonial domain. Kiev alone remained a dynastic possession.

Under this revised method of succession Svyatopolk Izyaslavich ruled Kiev to 1113. He was succeeded by his cousin, Vladimir Vsevolodich, also known as Vladimir Monomakh (r. 1113–1125), and subsequently by Monomakh's sons. Although the system brought order to dynastic relations, it also reinforced division among the dynastic branches, which was paralleled by a weakening in the cohesion among the component principalities of Kievan Rus.

By the end of the twelfth century the dynasty had divided into approximately a dozen branches, each ruling its own principality. The princes of four dynastic lines, Vladimir–Suzdal, Volynia, Smolensk, and Chernigov, remained in the Kievan rotational cycle and engaged in fierce competition particularly when the norms of succession were challenged. One campaign, launched by Andrei Bogolyubsky of Vladimir, resulted in the sack of Kiev in 1169. Although fought to defend the traditional succession system, this campaign is often cited as evidence of the fragmentation of the dynasty and Kievan Rus.

When the Mongols invaded and destroyed Kievan Rus, many members of the Rurikid dynasty were killed in battle. Nevertheless, with the approval of their new overlords, surviving princes continued to rule the lands of Rus. By the mid-fourteenth century, however, the dynasty lost possession of Kiev and other western lands to Poland and Lithuania. But in the northeast the princes of Moscow, a branch of the dynasty descended from Vladimir Monomakh's grandson Vsevolod and his grandson Alexander Nevsky, gained control over the principality of Vladimir-Suzdal. Symbolized by Dmitry Donskoy's victory at the Battle of Kulikovo (1380), they cast off Mongol suzerainty and expanded their realm to create the state of Muscovy.

The Moscow princes also reordered internal dynastic relations. After an unsuccessful challenge to Basil II (ruled 1425–1462) by his uncle and cousins that resulted in an extended civil war (1430–1453), a vertical pattern of succession firmly replaced the traditional collateral one. Ivan III (ruled 1462–1505), selecting his second son over his grandson (the son of his eldest but deceased son), defined the heir to the Muscovite throne as the eldest surviving son of the ruling prince. Basil III (ruled 1505–1533) divorced his barren wife after a twenty-year marriage in order to remarry and produce a son rather than allow the throne to pass to his brother.

Dynastic reorganization enhanced the power and prestige of the monarchs, who formally adopted the title "tsar" in 1547. But when Fyodor, the son of Ivan IV "the Terrible," died in 1598, and left no direct heirs, the Rurikids' seven-century rule came to an end. After a fifteen-year interregnum, known as the Time of Troubles, the Romanov dynasty, related to the Rurikids through Fyodor's mother, replaced the Rurikid dynasty as the tsars of Russia.

*See also:* ALEXANDER YAROSLAVICH; BASIL I; BASIL II; BASIL III; DONSKOY, DMITRY IVANOVICH; FYODOR IVANOVICH; IVAN III; IVAN IV; OLEG; OLGA; RURIK; VLADIMIR MONOMAKH; VLADIMIR, ST; VIKINGS; YAROSLAV VLADIMIROVICH; YURY VLADIMIROVICH

**BIBLIOGRAPHY**

Dimnik, Martin. (1978). "Russian Princes and their Identities in the First Half of the Thirteenth Century." *Mediaeval Studies* 40:157–185.

Kollmann, Nancy Shields. (1990). "Collateral Succession in Kievan Rus." *Harvard Ukrainian Studies* 14(3/4): 377–387.

JANET MARTIN

# RUSSIA-BELARUS UNION

Belarus and Russia were constituent republics of the Soviet Union and became independent in 1991, with the collapse of the USSR. Both countries were founding members of the Commonwealth of Independent States (CIS). The traditionally close ties between Russia and Belarus and a relatively weak Belarusian national identity led to a drive toward reunification, which started already in the early 1990s. A preliminary agreement (which remained only on paper) on the establishment of a monetary union between Russia and Belarus was negotiated between the end of 1993 and 1994. While the two countries retained their own currencies, the integration process became high on the agenda after Alexander Lukashenko, a supporter of the "unification of all Slavic peoples," became the new president of Belarus in July 1994.

In April 1996 a "Treaty on Forming a Community" was signed by Lukashenko and Boris Yeltsin, president of the Russian Federation. The agreement promoted the coordination of the two countries' foreign and economic policies, created a Supreme Council and an Executive Committee of the community (both with little or no real powers), and led to the establishment of a Russia-Belarus parliamentary assembly. On April 2, 1997, Yeltsin and Lukashenko signed a second treaty establishing a union between Russia and Belarus and pledging further cooperation in the security and economic spheres, reiterating the final goal of creating a single currency. Yeltsin's resistance, however, prevented the two sides from defining concrete measures strengthening the integration between Russia and Belarus.

The 1996 and 1997 documents had little practical consequences. Russian reformers (some of them close to President Yeltsin) had a lukewarm attitude toward a possible confederation with an increasingly authoritarian Belarus. Another obstacle on the way of integration was the Russian authorities' concern that creating the union could encourage Russian ethnic republics to seek the same status as Belarus in the new confederation. In Russia the main advocates of integration with Belarus were chiefly found among the nationalists and communists, while the Belarusian opposition continued to regard with suspicion the creation of a Russia-Belarus Union (which for many had an old Soviet flavor).

In December 1998 Yeltsin and Lukashenko signed new treaties, including a declaration of unification where the two sides agreed to create in 1999 a union state with a single currency. However, in the following months Russia remained cautious about establishing a confederation with Belarus and opposed the creation of the post of a union president. After long negotiations a new union document was signed in December 1999. Once again, the agreement was of declaratory nature and this time set 2005 as the date for the currency union.

Since Vladimir Putin became Russian president in 2000 no other significant formal or concrete steps had been taken as of 2003 to lead the two countries toward some form of reunification. The Belarusian authoritarian regime and Soviet-style economy continued to represent serious obstacles for the integration of Belarus in a common state with Russia. In 2002 there was a crisis in the relations between the two countries, following Putin's proposals (rejected by Lukashenko) of de facto incorporating Belarus into the Russian Federation or, alternatively, of creating a form of chiefly economic integration based on the European Union model. Officially the Russia–Belarus monetary union remains scheduled to start in 2005, when Belarus is to adopt the Russian ruble as its legal currency.

See also: BELARUS AND BELARUSIANS; COMMONWEALTH OF INDEPENDENT STATES; LUKASHENKO, ALEXANDER GRIGORIEVICH

## BIBLIOGRAPHY

Drakokhrust, Yuri, and Furman, Dmitri. (2002). "Belarus and Russia: The Game of Virtual Integration." In Independent Belarus: Domestic Determinants, Regional Dynamics, and Implications for the West, eds. Margarita M. Balmaceda, James I. Clem, and Lisbeth L. Tarlow. Cambridge MA: Ukrainian Research Institute, Davis Center for Russian Studies, Harvard University.

Marples, David R. (1999). Belarus: A Denationalized Nation. Amsterdam: Harwood.

Radio Free Europe Radio Liberty. (2003). "Poland, Belarus, and Ukraine Report. Previous Issues." <www.rferl.org/pbureport/archives.html>.

Rontoyanni, Clelia. (2002). "Belarus and Russia: Ever Closer Allies?" In The EU and Belarus: Between Moscow and Brussels, ed. Ann Lewis. London: Federal Trust for Education and Research.

OMER FISHER

## RUSSIA COMPANY

In the early modern period, different branches of international trade were controlled by large groups of merchants linked in a single company with its own charter, monopoly rights, membership, directors, and regulations. The Russia Company (also known as the Muscovy Company), founded in the mid-sixteenth century, was one of many such organizations in England. It was the first company to be organized on a joint-stock basis, thus laying the foundations for one of the most important forms of economic association and investment in the West. In addition, through its discovery of a viable water route to Russia (the White Sea or Archangel route) and its establishment of direct, regular trade with Russia, the Russia Company introduced an important new element into Western international trade and relations in general. Prior to the company's arrival, Russia's relations with the West were almost nonexistent. Russia was truly at the far periphery of Europe, both physically and conceptually. The Russia Company's activities brought Russia into the Western orbit.

The Russia Company's trade revolved around several key commodities. Its main export to Russia was woolen cloth, the staple of English foreign trade for centuries. Because of its cost, the market for English cloth was largely limited to the elite segments of Russian society, beginning with the tsar's household. Metals were another important export, particularly from the perspective of Russian state interests. England, a major exporter of metals in this period, appears to have provided mine-deficient Russia with substantial quantities of iron, copper, and lead for use in weapons manufacture. These exports were supplemented by armaments of all kinds. Exports of gold and silver went primarily to the Russian treasury, largely for the purpose of minting the country's currency. Russian commodities handled by the Russia Company revolved heavily around products needed in the construction, outfitting, and refurbishing of ships (i.e., tar, hemp, flax, cordage, and timber). The key commodity for the Russia Company was cordage (ropes), which it produced on site in Russia. The English navy and shipping industry and other trading companies were important customers for Russian cordage. Besides cordage, the company also traded in fine Russian leather (*yufti*), tallow, and potash. Russian caviar, already a renowned delicacy in the sixteenth century, was shipped by the company to Italian ports and the Ottoman Empire.

According to traditionally accepted views, The Russia Company's considerable success in Russia in the second half of the sixteenth century was followed by decline to near oblivion by the beginning of the seventeenth century, largely as a result of strong Dutch competition in the Russian market. A comprehensive reexamination of company activities, however, challenges this long-held view, providing evidence of a substantial English presence and trade in Russia into the 1640s, Dutch activities notwithstanding. According to this revised view, the company's very success in an atmosphere of growing Russian merchant opposition to foreign competition accounts for the abrogation of the company's trade privileges in Russia in 1646 and its expulsion from the country in 1649, events that brought to an end a historic century of Anglo-Russian trade and relations.

*See also:* CAVIAR; FOREIGN TRADE; MERCHANTS; TRADE ROUTES

### BIBLIOGRAPHY

Baron, Samuel H. (1980). "The Muscovy Company, the Muscovite Merchants and the Problem of Reciprocity in Russian Foreign Trade." *Forschungen zur osteuropäischen Geschichte* 27:133–155.

Phipps, Geraldine M. (1983). *Sir John Merrick, English Merchant-Diplomat in Seventeenth Century Russia.* Newtonville, MA: Oriental Research Partners.

Salomon Arel, Maria. (1999). "Masters in Their Own House: The Russian Merchant Elite and Complaints against the English in the First Half of the Seventeenth Century," *Slavonic and East European Review* 77:401–47.

Willan, Thomas S. (1956). *The Early History of the Russia Company, 1553–1603.* Manchester, UK: Manchester University Press.

MARIA SALOMON AREL

## RUSSIAN ASSOCIATION OF PROLETARIAN WRITERS

Better known for its persecution of other writers than for its own literary efforts, the Russian Association of Proletarian Writers (Rossysskaya assotsiatsia proletarskikh pisatelei—RAPP) played a major role in the politicization of the arts in the Soviet Union. RAPP's members argued that Soviet literature needed to be proletarian literature (i.e., literature written for, though not necessarily by, members of the working class); all other literature was perceived as anti-Soviet. Therefore RAPP's leaders claimed that the Communist Party should assist RAPP in establishing the dominance of proletarian literature in the Soviet Union. RAPP reached the height of its power during the Cultural Revolution (1928–1932), and it is often viewed as the epitome of the radical artistic movements that characterized this tumultuous period.

The group, founded in 1922, was known variously as the Octobrists, Young-Guardists, or VAPP (the All-Union Association of Proletarian Writers) until May 1928, when it changed its name to RAPP. Its early membership, drawn mostly from the Komsomol (Communist Youth League) and Proletkult (Proletarian Culture) movement, was disappointed with the Party's retreat from the radical policies of the civil war period, and wished to bring a militant spirit to the "cultural front." They issued violent diatribes against non-proletarian writers, particularly the so-called fellow travelers, writers with a sympathetic, but ambivalent, attitude towards the Bolshevik cause.

RAPP's early petitions for party support led to the Central Committee's highly ambiguous June 1925 resolution "On the Policy of the Party in the Area of Belles Lettres," which recognized the importance of proletarian literature, but also called for tolerance of the fellow travelers. This was seen as a relative defeat for RAPP, and the group's claims were muted over the next two years. In 1927, however, RAPP's willingness to connect literary debates with ongoing party factional struggles won it the backing of the Stalinist faction of the Central Committee. This backing, which included financial subsidies, allowed RAPP to gain control over major literary journals, to gain influence within the Federation of Soviet Writers, and to expand its membership. By extending political categories of deviation to the arts, RAPP helped to create the crisis atmosphere and militant spirit that facilitated Stalin's rise to power.

RAPP now championed a poorly developed literary style dubbed "psychological realism" and continued to demand that literature be made accessible to working-class readers. Over the next four years, RAPP used its new powers to continue its campaign against any writer or critic who refused to follow its lead. Many of RAPP's targets, who included Boris Pilniak, Yevgeny Zamiatin, and Alexei Tolstoy, found it difficult to publish their

work under these conditions, and some were fired from their jobs or even arrested; Vladimir Mayakovsky's 1930 suicide was due in part to RAPP's persecution. RAPP also became a mass movement during this period, its membership growing to ten thousand, as it promised to mentor worker-writers who were expected to create the literature of the future.

Although RAPP was the best-known proletarian artistic group of the Cultural Revolution, its tactics and ideas were adopted by similar groups in fields such as music, architecture, and the plastic arts. RAPP had local branches throughout Russia and affiliated organizations in each Union Republic. There was also a sister peasant organization (the All-Russian Society of Peasant Writers, or VOKP). RAPP's most important leaders included the critic Leopold Averbakh, the playwright Vladimir Kirshon, and the novelists Alexander Fadeyev, Fyodor Panferov, and Yuri Libidiensky.

By 1931, RAPP's inability to produce the promised new cadres of working-class writers, continued persecution of many pro-Soviet authors, and claims to autonomy from the Central Committee led to its fall from favor with the party leadership. The Central Committee's April 1932 resolution "On the Restructuring of Literary-Artistic Organizations" ordered RAPP's dissolution. Its eventual replacement, the Union of Soviet Writers, was more inclusive and acknowledged its subordination to the Party. Without the complete politicization of literature spearheaded by RAPP, however, the powerful new Writers' Union was unthinkable.

*See also:* CULTURAL REVOLUTION; UNION OF SOVIET WRITERS

## BIBLIOGRAPHY

Brown, Edward J. (1953). *The Proletarian Episode in Russian Literature, 1928–1932*. New York: Columbia University Press.

Fitzpatrick, Sheila. (1978). "Cultural Revolution as Class War." In *Cultural Revolution in Russia*, ed. Sheila Fitzpatrick. Bloomington: Indiana University Press.

Kemp-Welch, A. (1991). *Stalin and the Literary Intelligentsia, 1928–1939*. London: Macmillan.

Maguire, Robert A. (1987). *Red Virgin Soil: Soviet Literature in the 1920s*, rev. ed. Ithaca, NY: Cornell University Press.

BRIAN KASSOF

## RUSSIAN FEDERAL SECURITIES COMMISSION

The Russian Federal Securities Commission was created in 1996 to oversee registration of equity shares issued by Russian private enterprises.

Although the stock market existed in Russia prior to mass privatization of state enterprises, the volume and significance of stock exchange transactions increased many times as a result the rapid privatization that began in 1992. It therefore became necessary for the Russian government to develop the institutional structure necessary for a stock market and private equity ownership to work efficiently and lawfully. Among other things, this requires a public registry of stock-share ownership. This had not been required prior to 1996, and Russian enterprises maintained their own registries, a situation that was conducive to fraud, misrepresentation, and difficulty of access. The 1996 Federal Securities Law mandated that companies place stock registries with an independent organization, and created the Russian Federal Securities Commission to resolve custody disputes and settlements in accordance with international practice.

The Federal Securities Commission was also charged with coordinating the activities of the several agencies that have overlapping jurisdictions governing the securities market, including the Central Bank, the Anti-Monopoly Committee, the Ministry of Finance, and certain Parliamentary committees. This has not been an easy task. Also, although legislation gives the commission the power to levy civil and even criminal penalties, it must rely upon the police and tax inspectors to enforce any penalties. Enforcement has remained a problem, but much progress has been made since 1996.

*See also:* PRIVATIZATION; STOCK MARKET

**BIBLIOGRAPHY**

Gregory, Paul R., and Stuart, Robert C. (2001). *Russian and Soviet Economic Performance and Structure.* New York: Madison Wesley.

Gustafson, Thane. (1999). *Capitalism Russian-Style.* New York: Cambridge University Press.

JAMES R. MILLAR

## RUSSIAN FEDERATION

The Russian Federation (formerly the RSFSR, one of the fifteen republics of the USSR) covers almost twice the area of the United States of America, or 17,075,200 square kilometers (6,591,100 square miles). It is divided into eighty-nine separate territories. The country reaches from Moscow in the west over the Urals and the vast Siberian plains to the Sea of Okhotsk in the east. The Russian Federation is bounded by Norway and Finland in the northwest; by Estonia, Latvia, Belarus, and Ukraine in the west; by Georgia and Azerbaijan in the southwest; and by Kazakhstan, Mongolia, and China along the southern land border. The Kaliningrad region is a Russian exclave on the Baltic Sea and is bordered by Lithuania and Poland.

The Russian Federation was established in 1991, when the USSR disintegrated and the former RSFSR became an independent state. A declaration of state sovereignty was adopted on June 12, 1991 (now a national holiday), and official independence from the USSR was established on August 24, 1991. The Russian Federation replaced the USSR as a permanent member of the United Nations Security Council. The term *Russia* has been applied loosely to the Russian Empire until 1917, to the Russian Soviet Federated Socialist Republic (RSFSR) from 1917 to 1991, to the Russian Federation since 1991, or even (incorrectly) to mean the whole of the former Union of Soviet Socialist Republics (USSR). The term has also been used to designate the area inhabited by the Russian people, as distinguished from other Eastern Slavs and from non-Slavic peoples.

Moscow, the ninth largest city in the world, the largest Russian city, and the capital of the Russian Federation, was founded in 1147. The city's focal point is Red Square, bound on one side by the Kremlin and its thick red fortress wall containing twenty towers. The tsars were crowned there; in fact, Ivan the Terrible's throne is situated near the entrance. The second largest city, St. Petersburg, is situated northwest of Moscow and was known as a cultural center with elegant palaces. The city is spread over forty-two islands in the delta of the Neva River.

The terrain of the Russian Federation consists of broad plains with low hills west of the Urals; vast coniferous forest and tundra in Siberia; and uplands and mountains along the southern border regions. Although the largest country in the world in terms of area, the Russian Federation is unfavorably located in relation to the major sea lanes of the world. Despite its size, much of the country lacks proper soils and climates (either too cold or too dry) for agriculture. It does, however, have enormous resources of oil and gas, as well as numerous trace metals.

Since 1991, Russia has struggled in its efforts to build a democratic political system and market economy to replace the strict social, political, and economic controls of the Communist period. The country adopted a constitution on December 12, 1993, and established a bicameral Federal Assembly (Federalnoye Sobraniye). Vladimir Vladimirovich Putin was elected to the office of president of the Federation on May 7, 2000, with 52.9 percent of the vote, as opposed to 29.2 percent for the Communist representative, Gennady Zyuganov, and 5.8 percent for the democratic centrist, Grigory Yavlinsky.

See also: GORBACHEV, MIKHAIL SERGEYEVICH; PUTIN, VLADIMIR VLADIMIROVICH; RUSSIAN SOVIET FEDERATED SOCIALIST REPUBLIC; YELTSIN, BORIS NIKOLAYEVICH

## BIBLIOGRAPHY

Brown, Archie, ed. (2001). *Gorbachev, Yeltsin, and Putin: Political Leadership in Russia's Transition.* Washington, DC: Carnegie Endowment for International Peace.

Herspring, Dale R., ed. (2003). *Putin's Russia: Past Imperfect, Future Uncertain.* Lanham, MD: Rowman & Littlefield.

Kotkin, Stephen. (2001). *Armageddon Averted: The Soviet Collapse, 1970–2000.* Oxford: Oxford University Press.

Malia, Martin. (1999). *Russia under Western Eyes: From the Bronze Horseman to the Lenin Mausoleum.* Cambridge, MA: Belnap Press.

Satter, David. (2003). *Darkness at Dawn: The Rise of the Russian Criminal State.* New Haven, CT: Yale University Press.

Shevtsova, Lilia. (2003). *Putin's Russia.* Washington, DC: Carnegie Endowment for International Peace.

Sunlop, John B. (1993). *The Rise of Russia and the Fall of the Soviet Empire.* Princeton, NJ: Princeton University Press.

JOHANNA GRANVILLE

# RUSSIAN GEOGRAPHICAL SOCIETY

The Russian Geographical Society is one of the world's oldest geographical societies, dating to 1845 ("Imperial Russian Geographical Society"). The name reappeared in 1917 after the October Revolution, only to be replaced by the "State Geographical Society" (1926–1938). After 1938, the organization became identified with the USSR until 1991, when it became the Russian Geographical Society again.

In 1917 the Geographical Society was composed of eleven subdivisions and 1,000 members. By 1971, membership had soared to 19,000 individuals, who sent delegates to an All-Soviet Geographical Congress held every five years. Between congresses, the affairs of the society were administered by a scientific council, selected by the delegates at the congress, and its presidium led by a president. Past presidents include Yuri Shokalsky, Nikolai Vavilov, Lev Berg, Yevgeny Pavlovsky, and Stanislav Kalesnik. Sergei Lavrov serves currently. By 2003, membership had again declined to one thousand.

In 1970 the Geographical Society, based in Leningrad, supervised fourteen geographical societies in the constituent republics, fifteen affiliates in the Russian Socialist Federal Soviet Republic (RSFSR), and approximately one hundred subbranches. Between 1947 and 1991, the society authorized discussion of more than sixty thousand scientific papers, the convening of a wide array of scientific conferences, and All-Union Congresses in Leningrad, Moscow, Kiev, Tbilisi, and several other Soviet cities. The Geographical Society also provided practical expertise and consultation to the Soviet government on issues pertaining to geography and regional development, and organized or sponsored twenty to fifty scientific expeditions every year. Society members were urged to popularize the results of their research at public meetings. More than fifty of the affiliates published their own journals, the most famous of which is the Moscow affiliate's *Problems of Geography* (*Voprosy geografii*, first published in 1946).

As of 2003, the Moscow affiliate alone could claim a mere 200 to 300 employees, who existed on paper only, coming to the offices in the affiliate's twenty-story skyscraper simply to retrieve their biweekly $35 salary. Former members provided consulting to the Russian government, while the more ambitious went into business.

See also: GEOGRAPHY; IMPERIAL RUSSIAN GEOGRAPHY SOCIETY

**BIBLIOGRAPHY**

Harris, Chauncy D. (1962). *Soviet Geography: Accomplishments and Tasks.* New York: American Geographical Society.

VICTOR L. MOTE

## RUSSIAN JUSTICE

The chief code of law in Kievan Rus, the Pravda Russkaya, or "Rus Justice," survives in about one hundred copies that may be grouped into three basic versions: Short, Expanded, and Abbreviated. The so-called Short version, usually thought to be the oldest, is attested in only two fifteenth-century copies and several from much later. Essentially a list of compensations to be paid for physical wrongs, the first section is sometimes linked with Grand Prince Yaroslav (1019–1054), whose name appears in the heading, but nowhere in the text. The second section attributes to several of Yaroslav's successors a codification of law, providing fees for the homicide of the prince's servitors as well as compensation for various property and criminal offenses. Separate articles establish provisions for the prince's "bloodwite" (wergild) collector, as well as a tithe for the church from the prince's fees. A final article somewhat incongruously establishes payments for bridge builders.

The Expanded version is much more detailed and survives in many more manuscripts; the oldest copies date from the thirteenth and fourteenth centuries, but numerous other copies originated in the fifteenth and sixteenth centuries. Whereas the Short version included no more than forty-three articles, the Expanded version includes at least 121 articles and betrays a much more consciously rational form of organization, highlighted in many copies with special headings. The first articles repeat many of the measures of the Short Pravda, but overall the Expanded version establishes a much more detailed inventory of offenses and their resolution. Separate groups of articles examine slavery, commercial transactions, and loans, as well as inheritance disputes.

The Abbreviated version, which survives in only a handful of copies, none older than the seventeenth century, seems to have been the result of a conscious reworking of the Expanded version, adapted to the circumstances of early modern Russia. Several traces of the Short Pravda remain, but the scarcity of copies along with the fact that Muscovite Rus generated its own legal codes has persuaded most scholars that this Abbreviated version had little practical importance.

The emphasis of the law in both the Short and Expanded versions is to entrust the process of conflict resolution mainly to the persons directly involved. The first article of the Short version, in fact, authorized blood vengeance by relatives of homicide victims and provided for monetary compensation only in the absence of kin. According to the second article of the Expanded version, the sons of Yaroslav outlawed vengeance justice when they met to revise the law sometime in the 1070s, after which homicides were redeemable by payment of compensation to the victim's kin, along with a fine payable to the prince. In general, compensation alone appears as a remedy in the Short Pravda, but both fines and compensation figure in the Expanded Pravda—an indication, some have argued, of a growing political apparatus that controlled litigation in later medieval Rus.

Both the Short and Expanded versions make scant reference to judicial process, however, and describe instead a self-help process that indicates the minimal role played by judicial personnel. In cases of theft, for example, the codes describe a process of confrontation, according to which the victim who recognized his stolen property was to announce his loss, and seek the help of the current owner in finding out from whom he had acquired it, and so on, all the way back to the original thief. The Expanded version articulates an identical process for slave theft, using the slave as a witness in tracing the transactions that separated the original thief from the present slaveowner.

The Pravda provides considerable information on the economy of Kievan Rus. Few articles examine farming, despite the obvious importance of agriculture to the economy. The code does establish, however, compensation for livestock either lost or stolen, and also protects some farming implements. By contrast, the Expanded version dwells at length on trading and commercial transactions, suggesting to some scholars that this law served a primarily urban and commercial society. The prominence of slavery in the law indicates that the economy and society of Kievan Rus depended upon various forms of involuntary labor, much of it probably provided by war captives. Inasmuch as the code mainly considers men rather than women, some students of Kievan society have questioned the status of women in Kievan Rus. One controversial provision seems to provide a penalty for killing a woman that is only half as large as the penalty that attached to the homicide of a man.

See also: KIEVAN RUS; NOVGOROD JUDICIAL CHARTER; PSKOV JUDICIAL CHARTER

**BIBLIOGRAPHY**

Kaiser, Daniel H. (1980). *The Growth of the Law in Medieval Russia.* Princeton, NJ: Princeton University Press.

Kaiser, Daniel H. (1991). "The Economy of Kievan Rus': Evidence from the Pravda Rus'skaia." In *Ukrainian Economic History: Interpretive Essays,* ed. I. S. Koropeckyj. Cambridge, MA: Harvard University Press.

Kaiser, Daniel H., ed., tr. (1992). *The Laws of Rus': Tenth to Fifteenth Centuries.* Salt Lake City, UT: Charles Schlacks, Jr.

Shchapov, Yaroslav N. (1993). *State and Church in Early Russia, Tenth–Thirteenth Centuries,* tr. Vic Shneierson. New Rochelle, NY: A. D. Caratzas.

Vernadsky, George. (1969). *Medieval Russian Laws.* New York: New York: Norton.

DANIEL H. KAISER

# RUSSIAN NATIONAL UNITY PARTY

The Russian National Unity Party (Russkoe natsionalnoe edinstvo) emerged in the fall of 1990 and subsequently became one of the most active of the small fascist-style parties that sprang up in Russia in the first post-Soviet decade. Founded by disaffected members of Pamyat, the party was led by Alexander Barkashov, a former electrical worker and Pamyat activist. The party espoused an ultra-nationalist, anti-semitic ideology. Its program, as set forth in Barkashov's *Azbuka russkogo nationalista* (*ABC of Russian Nationalism*), advocated the establishment of a "Greater Russia" encompassing Russia, Ukraine, and Belarus. The rule of ethnic Russians would be assured through a national dictatorship that would preside over a council dominated by ethnic Russians representing labor, management, the intelligentsia, and other groups. Non-slavic peoples would be confined to their "historic homelands" and the state would protect the genetic purity of the Russian nation through the prohibition of mixed marriages. The party advocated a foreign policy that would confront the United States, which was depicted as controlled by Jewish capital, and would be dedicated to ensuring Russia's world supremacy.

Russian National Unity operated as a paramilitary organization, rather than an orthodox party. Members were organized into detachments, underwent military training, and wore uniforms. The Party claimed that its symbol, the left swastika, had been worn by medieval Russian knights and conferred mystical powers on party members. Though Party membership probably never exceeded ten thousand, local organizations were particularly active in Moscow and several other regions. In some cities sympathetic local officials allowed party detachments to operate as informal *druzhiniki* (volunteer social monitors), a practice often accompanied by acts of violence and intimidation against ethnic minorities. In the few instances in which the party put forth candidates in elections, they were soundly defeated. After 1999 the party suffered a decline, the result of increased criticism of its program and tactics and feuding among the leadership. The party's electoral bloc, called Spas, was denied registration in the 1999 Duma elections, and court orders banned local organizations in Moscow and other key regions because of their advocacy of racial hatred and their use of Nazi symbols.

See also: PAMYAT

**BIBLIOGRAPHY**

Jackson, William D. (1999). "Fascism, Vigilantism, and the State: The Russian National Unity Movement." *Problems of Post-Communism* 46:34–42.

Shenfield, Stephen D. (2000). *Russian Fascism: Traditions Tendencies Movements.* London: M. E. Sharpe.

WILLIAM D. JACKSON

# RUSSIAN ORTHODOX CHURCH

In 988 Grand Prince Vladimir of Kiev adopted Eastern Orthodoxy from Byzantium and inaugurated a gradual Christianization of his realm. First affected were elites, with churches and observance limited to cities; several centuries elapsed before the church could penetrate the hinterland. Although the devastating Mongol conquest of 1237–1240 temporarily interrupted this process, the Mongols' religious tolerance (and tax exemptions) enabled the church to resume the building of parishes and monasteries. Simultaneously, the church emerged as an important political force, symbolizing Slavic unity amidst inter-princely conflict; the relocation of the metropolitan to Moscow played a key role in the triumph of Muscovy. There it was instrumental in formulating a new political culture based on the "Third Rome" theory, with Muscovy—after the fall of Constantinople in 1453—claiming leadership over Eastern Orthodoxy. Church councils codified the new Russian Orthodoxy, defended ecclesiastical ownership of lands and peasants, and achieved formal autocephalous status for the church (with its own patriarch) in 1589.

That triumph turned to schism (raskol). The conflict erupted in the 1650s when reformist clergy attempted to modify liturgical texts and ritual practices. At issue was the model for such changes: Reformers advocated Greek models, but opponents deemed the Orthodoxy of the Third Rome inviolable and any change tantamount to apostasy. The result was a split between the official church, supported by the state, and an underground of disaffected clergy and laity, pejoratively labeled "schismatics" by the official church but self-described as "Old Believers."

The eighteenth century brought still more profound change. Driven by the needs of war and inspired by Western models, Peter the Great seized ecclesiastical resources, restricted the church's role in secular affairs, and in 1721 replaced the patriarchate with a more tractable Synod. Although Peter drew short of secularizing church property (a common device of new monarchies hungry for resources), Catherine the Great proved less inhibited: In 1764 she sequestered church lands and peasants and allocated a small budget (ravaged, over time, by inflation). These clouds had a silver lining: The church now concentrated on its strictly religious mission, founded seminaries to train clergy, and tackled the daunting task of catechizing the mass of pious but uncomprehending believers.

Despite such gains, nineteenth-century observers discerned serious problems and shortcomings in the church. One was competition from dissenters (Old Believers, sectarians, and disbelievers) and, in borderland areas, from established faiths such as Catholicism and Lutheranism. A further cause of concern was ecclesiastical administration—in particular, its stifling centralization, the monocratic rule of bishops, and the increasingly intrusive role of the chief procurator (lay overseer of the Synod). Dismaying too was the performance of

parish clergy, a hereditary caste that proved lacking in personal commitment, suitable material support, and professional training. The parish itself, the nuclear institution of the church, appeared increasingly moribund, chiefly because the atrophy of parishioners' rights undermined their interest and active involvement. Another highly contentious issue was marriage and divorce: Having retained total control over this sphere, the church severely restricted marital dissolution, a policy that aroused growing discontent among elites, urban groups, and the peasantry.

The church did endeavor to address these issues. Before mid-century, it constructed an elaborate network of seminaries, secured subsidies for clergy in the poorest parishes, and expanded its internal mission. Far more systematic attempts came during the Great Reforms of the 1860s, including measures to abolish the hereditary caste, professionalize seminary training, restructure the parish (investing power in parish councils), and improve ecclesiastical administration and courts. But the reforms misfired and stalled, even before the "counter-reforms" of the 1880s. The revolution of 1905 triggered a new phase of desperate reformism, but it all came to naught, largely because of a skeptical, conservative state. Thus, by 1914, despite the immense size of the institution (54,923 churches; 953 monasteries; 94,629 in monastic orders and 117,915 in the parish clergy), the church suffered from a host of long-festering and debilitating problems.

The revolutions of 1917 promised relief, but ended in disaster. The reform expectations culminated in the Church Council of 1917–1918; the first since the seventeenth century, it reestablished the patriarchate (to ensure the church's autonomy) and tackled the long list of overdue reforms. But it had to operate under extremely adverse conditions, especially after October 1917: The new Bolshevik regime abolished the church's juridical status, banned clergy from education, and nationalized all church assets. The civil war of 1917–1922 brought antireligious campaigns (including the exhumation of saints' relics to expose "clerical fraud"), the closure of many ecclesiastical (especially educational, monastic, and administrative) institutions, and the arrest and execution of clergy. By 1921 the church as an institution had virtually disappeared; it existed only as individual parish churches registered by committees of laity.

Worse was to come. Even the New Economic Policy brought no respite. In 1922 the Bolsheviks ordered the confiscation of church valuables, ostensibly to feed famine victims, but actually to precipitate a schism between the "reactionary" patriarchal wing and pro-Soviet "renovationists." But that strategy failed abysmally, and, alarmed by signs of religious revival, in 1929 the Stalinist regime declared open war on the church. By 1939 all but 1,744 churches (of the 28,560 in 1928) were closed; vast numbers of believer-activists, not just clergy, were arrested and many executed in the Great Terror. Although the exigencies of World War II forced some concessions (including election of a new patriarch in 1943 and an increase in churches, although mainly in Ukraine), the postwar regime gradually returned to its antireligious policies. The post-Stalinist "thaw" of Nikita Khrushchev brought no relief; on the contrary, his antireligious campaign reduced the number of churches from 13,414 (1958) to 7,773 (1964). The subsequent Brezhnev regime eschewed such traumatic campaigns, but used its powers of repression to cause a steady decline in the institutions of the Russian Orthodox Church.

During the mid-1980s the church experienced recovery. The reformist Mikhail Gorbachev cautiously restored ties to the church and permitted it to reopen parishes, monasteries, and seminaries. The breakup of the USSR in 1991 removed the last barriers. Since 1991 the church has greatly expanded the number of parishes, monasteries, and seminaries (e.g., parishes increasing from 6,794 in 1986 to over 22,000 in 2002, including 9,000 in Ukraine). The church also assumed a prominent role in public life, guardedly under President Boris Yeltsin, at least until he signed the "Law on Freedom of Conscience and Religious Organizations" in 1997, privileging the traditional confessions and imposing limits on the activity of newer, foreign religious movements (i.e., Pentacostals). The links between the Russian Orthodox Church and the state became still more pronounced under President Vladimir Putin. Although the church faced stiff competition from other faiths (especially the proselytizing sects), it rebuilt its institutional structure and carved out a salient role in Russian post-communist life and culture.

See also: BYZANTIUM, INFLUENCE OF; HOLY SYNOD; METROPOLITAN; OLD BELIEVERS; ORTHODOXY; PATRIARCHATE; RELIGION; SAINTS

**BIBLIOGRAPHY**

Curtiss, John S. (1953). *The Russian Church and Soviet State, 1917–1950*. Boston: Little, Brown.

Ellis, Jane. (1988). *The Russian Orthodox Church: A Contemporary History*. London: Routledge.

Ware, Kallistos. (1993). *The Orthodox Church*. New York: Penguin Books.

GREGORY L. FREEZE

## RUSSIANS

The earliest origins of Russian culture are in dispute. Some believe that the ancestors of the modern Russians were seventh- or ninth-century migrants from the Vistula River valley (now Poland). Other archaeological evidence suggests that Slavic pastoralists may have spread across the central plains of Eurasia as much as a thousand years earlier, coexisting alongside northern Finnic and Lithuanian tribes. Whatever their prehistory, people sharing the same language, beliefs, social practices, and religion have occupied what is now Russia for at least a millennium. By the tenth century C.E., Eastern Slavic society was culturally distinct and highly developed in terms of agriculture, technology, commerce, and governance. Prince Vladimir I brought Byzantine Christianity to Kiev in 988 and sponsored the baptism of the peoples of Rus, a gradual process that blended Slavic pre-Christian practices with Eastern Orthodoxy.

The Russian Empire grew steadily from the eighteenth to the twentieth century through colonization of Siberia, Central Asia, and the Caucasus. The Soviet era brought further territorial expansion. Population density also grew throughout the millennium. By 1991, the year of the end of the Soviet Union, the population of the Russian Federation was 146,393,000. Ethnic Russians comprised 81 percent of this number, with more than one hundred other ethnic nationalities, many of them culturally Russified, making up the rest. There is a recognizably Russian culture among the population of the Russian Federation and strong cultural continuity among the Russians living in the newly independent republics of Central Asia, the Baltic region, and the Caucasus.

Russia's cultural history is multifaceted, encompassing both the distinct patterns of the rural peasantry and the intricate social rituals of the aristocracy, the mercantile caste, the bureaucracy, and other groups. Russia's thousand-year history of class stratification, imperial growth and contraction, political consolidation and disintegration, repression and relaxation, messianism and self-examination, and socioeconomic and cultural interconnections with other nations has had far-reaching effects on every aspect of Russian national culture.

For many centuries, the question of whether Russian culture was more "eastern" or "western" was a burning issue. Situated at the crossroads of major civilizations and empires—Scandinavian, Byzantine, Persian, Chinese, Ottoman, Austro-Hungarian, British—the peoples of Russia have profoundly influenced and been influenced by them all in terms of trade, technology, language, religion, politics, and the arts.

Since at least the time of Peter the Great, Russian writers, artists, politicians, and philosophers, as well as ordinary people in everyday discourse, have engaged in intensive cultural self-examination. Ethnic Russians have struggled to redefine their national identity in the wake of the Soviet collapse and the turmoil that accompanied the end of communism.

The northern climate has influenced cultural, social, and political institutions, settlement patterns, household configurations, village politics, agricultural systems, and technologies. Defiance of the natural limitations of this harsh environment is seen throughout Russian history and plays a significant role in local identity.

**COUNTRY AND CITY**

In 1917 the population of Russia was more than 80 percent rural. The disruptions of the Soviet period—civil war, rural collectivization, world war—brought a massive migration to the cities. By 1996, 73 percent of the population was urban. Although there are still tens of thousands of small villages, many are simply disappearing as older people die and the younger generation departs. But despite the demise of rural communities, much of the urban population retains strong material and psychological ties to the countryside. Many own modest dachas within an hour or two of their city apartments and spend their weekends and summers gardening, hiking, hunting, gathering mushrooms and berries, and swimming in lakes and rivers. Some people maintain ties to their natal villages or those of their parents or grandparents and travel there to mark significant family events.

In the years since the collapse of the Soviet Union, a tiny minority has accrued enough wealth to build private homes and estates on the outskirts of the cities, but most people live in small apartments in apartment blocks. Space in flats can be tight, so a single room may serve as living room, bedroom, and dining room. Domestic furnishing is fairly consistent, for reasons of both cultural style and limited purchasing power. The range of consumer décor choices has become enormous in the largest cities but elsewhere only slightly better than it was during the Soviet period, when state stores offered little design variation. Architectural and domestic styles are changing gradually with growing consumer opportunities and increased attention to global fashions.

At home, people spend much time in the kitchen, eating and drinking tea (or something stronger), talking, reading, watching television, cooking, or working on crafts. When guests come, people sit at the table for the entire gathering. Public spaces around apartment blocks are often decayed and dirty, so the threshold to a family's apartment marks a transition to private, clean space. Everyone removes shoes just inside the doorway to prevent dirt being brought inside, and slippers are worn at home.

Urban parks are an important space of everyday life. People spend leisure time strolling or sitting on benches to talk, smoke, play chess, or read. Smaller urban parks may center on a statue of a writer or political leader, and these squares are popular meeting places. Public plazas in urban centers have played a role in political and social life for centuries. The most famous of all, Moscow's Red Square, is a historical site of government ritual, revolutionary protest, and rebellion. The central sites where parades, concerts, and state funerals are held also provide a place for festivals, family outings, and commemorations.

**GENDER RELATIONS, FAMILY, AND KINSHIP**

Russian society has always been structured around gendered divisions of labor. Prerevolutionary rural communities were patrilocal; newly married women moved in with their husband's family and were fully subservient to his parents until they had borne sons. The details of household management were codified in texts such as the *Domostroi* that addressed even intimate practices of family life and patriarchal authority, influencing both the peasantry and the aristocracy. Around the turn of the twentieth century, rural and urban women of all classes experienced the loosening of gender norms,

A Russian mother and her children, dressed in their finest winter clothes, take a sled to the nearest village to watch television.
© STAFFAN WIDSTRAND/CORBIS

and many women pushed the boundaries of their social options.

After the 1917 revolution, communist ideology promoted the liberation of women and families from oppressive norms and structures. Women engaged in what had been male-only work in agriculture, construction, and manufacturing. During the Soviet period, they played increasingly significant roles in medicine, engineering, the sciences, and other fields. By the 1980s, one-third of the deputies in the Supreme Soviet were female, and women accounted for more than 50 percent of the students in higher education. But though "liberated" to work in the public sphere, women often retained the burden of household labor. Moreover, their equal employment status was not fully reflected in the workplace, where gender discrimination was common.

Some of the hard-earned status of women eroded after 1991. Unemployment increased in the 1990s, and women were frequently the first dis-

charged. Managerial jobs in the new commercial sectors were largely held by men, and a traditionalist view of work and family reasserted itself throughout society. The devaluation of women's labor contributions has been devastating for women who need to work. Some women became entrepreneurs, but they faced stiff gender prejudice in starting businesses. The percentage of women holding political office has declined, and women's participation in high levels of industry, the sciences, the arts, and the government has shrunk. Some young women turn to prostitution, or work in bars and nightclubs, which may seem to be a way to escape poverty.

Despite Soviet indoctrination, traditional gender ideologies never vanished: Men are not supposed to be able to cook, clean, or perform child care, whereas women are seen as driving cars, supervising others, and engaging in politics poorly. Women are held in high regard as mothers, nurturers, and bearers of culture. Although feminists have challenged these dichotomous gender norms, and few families can afford to divide labor along strict gender lines, such ideas are widespread. Students receive equal education, but some school activities and expectations are divided by gender.

Romantic love is the standard motivation for marriage, and cultural tradition idealizes the passion of lovers, often in a tragic form. People meet partners at school or university, at work, or at clubs or music venues. Premarital sex is generally tolerated. With little variation over the decades, twenty-three has been the average age at marriage. Almost half of all marriages end in divorce, with economic hardship and alcohol abuse being contributing factors. Ethnic intermarriage became fairly common in Soviet times.

The nuclear family is the fundamental domestic unit, and married couples crave apartments of their own. Since the housing shortage and the high price of new apartments make this difficult, family units are often multigenerational. Many couples with children live with a widowed parent, often a grandmother, who provides child care and cooking. A grandparent's monthly pension may be a crucial part of family income.

Kinship is reckoned bilaterally (counting both parents' sides), but naming is patrilineal. Until the mid-nineteenth century, kin terms for more than sixty relations were in use; since then the number of terms has greatly decreased. Even across distances, people maintain strong relations with their siblings, grandparents, aunts and uncles, cousins, and nieces and nephews, and many are close with even more distant relatives. Among the social factors that support such ties are the low level of geographic mobility, the importance of networks of mutual aid, and regular visits to relatives in ancestral villages for summer rest and gardening.

Childbirth practices reflect traditional ideas. Women stay in the hospital for at least a week after a birth, during which time fathers are allowed to see mother and baby only briefly. Infants used to be swaddled at birth and continue to be bundled tightly, especially when venturing outside. Many customary beliefs about medical or supernatural dangers surround pregnancy, birthing, and new babies.

Academic standards are high, and students are well trained in world history, foreign languages, music, mathematics, and science. Although the figures have gradually dropped since the Soviet years, more than 90 percent of the population completes secondary education, and around 12 percent go on for higher education. The literacy rate is one of the world's highest. Post-secondary education confers social prestige and is more and more essential for economic success.

### RELIGIOUS BELIEFS AND PRACTICES

Most Russians identify themselves as Orthodox Christians. Not all are active church members, but observance of major holidays is increasing. The state has returned thousands of churches, icons, and religious objects appropriated during the Soviet period to local religious communities. Orthodox practice hinges on the emotive experience of liturgy and the veneration of icons, and the faithful light candles, pray, and bow before sacred images of the Virgin Mary and the saints. Rural houses feature a special corner where the family's icon hangs, and many apartments have an icon shelf. Religious practices were proscribed during the Soviet era but continued anyway.

Pre-Christian practices and beliefs have persisted over a millennium of Orthodoxy. Traditional beliefs about forest and house spirits, the evil eye, and metaphysical healing are found everywhere—and are especially strong in rural areas. Certain prohibitions stem from them; for example, evil intentions are attracted by bragging about good fortune or health, and can be cured only by metaphysical intervention of some kind.

Folk medicine is highly developed. Herbal remedies are used for everyday maladies. Professional practitioners advertise their services for treating serious illnesses and life problems. Homeopathy, the application of leeches, mineral baths, light therapy, and other treatments are popular. Physicians may also prescribe herbal teas, tinctures, and plasters.

Proper treatment and remembrance of the dead is important. The dead are prevented from staying among the living by covering mirrors with black cloth, laying out the body in ways that help usher out the spirit, and accompanying the deceased from home to church and from church to cemetery in elaborate processions. In the church or hall where the body is displayed, mourners circle the open coffin counterclockwise and kiss the body or put flowers on it. After burial, mourners gather to share vodka and food while remembering the deceased with stories and anecdotes. The soul remains on earth for forty days, when a second gathering is held to bid it farewell as it departs for heaven. The anniversary of a death is memorialized every year;

some people travel long distances to visit the graves of their loved ones.

## CALENDRICAL RITUAL

Holidays fill the calendar. Some are Orthodox or pre-Christian, some mark historical events, some are secular, and a few, like Valentine's Day, are post-Soviet imports. March 8, International Women's Day, is a legal holiday. Men bring flowers to the women in their lives and congratulate female friends, coworkers, and relatives. May Day, commemorating international labor solidarity, heralds the coming of spring. Victory Day on May 9 celebrates the Soviet capture of Berlin and the end of World War II in Europe. This holiday is sacred to older people, who gather to remember family, friends, and comrades lost in the war. Russia Day, June 12, marks independence from the Soviet Union in 1991 with parades and fireworks. October Revolution Day, November 7, is celebrated mostly by communists nostalgic for Soviet power. New Year's Eve is the most lavish secular holiday. Grandfather Frost and the Snow Maiden leave gifts under a decorated New Year's Tree, and people gather for song, feasting, vodka, and champagne. The party may last all night. The observance of Christmas and Easter and other Orthodox holidays has grown since the end of Soviet religious repression.

## FOOD

Bead and potatoes are the basic everyday foods. Cabbage, carrots, and beets are staple vegetables; onions and garlic are used liberally. Russians generally love meat. Sausage, salami, pork, beef, mutton, chicken, and dried or salted fish are widely available and inexpensive.

Breakfast is a quick snack of coffee or tea with bread and sausage or cheese. Lunch is a hot meal, with soup, potatoes, macaroni, rice or buckwheat kasha, ground meat cutlets, and peas or grated cabbage (or, for business people, a quick meal in one of the increasing number of fast-food cafés). A later supper may consist of boiled potatoes, soured cabbage, and bread or simply bread and sausage or cheese. There is a huge array of cakes, pies, and chocolates.

Russian cuisine features many dairy products, such as *tvorog*, a local version of cottage cheese, and many hard cheeses and fermented milk products. These items can be purchased from large shops or farmers' markets or made at home. In provincial towns, fresh milk is sold from trucks, although bottles and cartons of pasteurized milk are available everywhere. Russians are great tea drinkers.

Fruits are widely cultivated in home gardens. Fruits and berries are made into preserves, compotes, cordials, and concentrates for the winter months. Mushroom picking is an art, and many people salt, dry, or pickle them. Cabbage, cucumbers, garlic, and tomatoes are salted or pickled. The chronic shortages of the Soviet era led many people to produce food for themselves. The impoverishment of the post-socialist era means that a significant portion of the population continues to depend on their own produce. Some estimates hold that 80 percent of the vegetables consumed in Russia are grown in small family plots.

Coffee has grown in popularity and is often served thick and strong. Although wine, beer, cognac, and champagne are popular, vodka reigns among alcoholic beverages.

Ceremonial occasions highlight food customs. Communal feasting marks birthdays, weddings, anniversaries, the achievement of a goal, important purchases, and major holidays. Tables are laden with salads, appetizers, sausage and cheese, and pickled foods, followed by meat and potatoes, and meat or cabbage pies. Vodka and wine are drunk throughout the meal, which may continue for many hours. Toasting is elaborate and can be sentimental, humorous, poetic, ribald, or reverential. Vodka is always drunk straight, accompanied by a pickled or salty food.

A growing number of people observe Lenten fasts during which they consume no meat, butter, eggs, or vodka. Easter provides an opportunity for a fast-breaking celebration with special foods.

## EVERYDAY ETIQUETTE

Language rules play a significant part in good manners. When addressing elders, except for parents and grandparents, persons of higher status, strangers, and acquaintances, people use the second-person plural pronoun. The informal second-person singular is used only among friends, within the family, and among close coworkers of equal status. Addressing someone formally entails using the person's full name and patronymic. Misuse of the informal mode is insulting.

Table rituals are also important. Hosts and hostesses try to show unfailing generosity, and guests must accept hospitality with a willingness to be served, pampered, and stuffed full of food and drink.

Sitting on the floor or putting one's shoes on a table is prohibited. Proper femininity requires that clothes be immaculately clean and pressed, grooming fastidious, and comportment elegant and reserved. By contrast, in crowds, on lines, and on public transport, active shoving and pushing are the norm. In Soviet times, demure, nonflashy dress was valued, but this norm has changed with the explosion of fashion and the growth of subcultural identity.

The word *uncultured* is used by older people against family or strangers as a reprimand for inappropriate behavior. The public use of this reprimand diminished as the social status of elders fell after the collapse of the Soviet Union, and as aggressive behavior in the cities became a mark of the coolness of youth.

## CULTURAL SYMBOLS AND ARTS

The cupolas of Moscow's St. Basil's Cathedral are a popular visual symbol of Russia both within the country and abroad. Photographs of St. Basil's and many other churches and cathedrals adorn homes, offices, and media images.

Bread symbolizes central aspects of the national self-image. It is the mark of hospitality, as in the ritual of *khleb-sol* ("bread and salt"), welcoming visitors with a round loaf with a salt cellar on top. In broader terms, bread is the symbol of life. Other foods are also cultural symbols: black caviar, which signifies luxury; mushrooms and berries, the gifts of forest and dacha; pancakes served before Lent; the potato, symbol of survival in hard times, and vodka, symbolizing camaraderie and mischief-making.

Forest plants, animals, and objects are also important symbols. Birches conjure up the romance of the countryside; wolf, bear, and fox, are ubiquitous in folktales and modern cartoons; the peasant cottage signifies the intimate world of the past. Inside the cottage are other cultural symbols: the huge clay stove, the samovar, and the Orthodox icon in its corner. Although most Russians live in urban apartments, images of traditional rural life are still meaningful.

Conversation is rich with metaphors and proverbs, summarizing a complex view of shared identity. Russians think of the soul (*dusha*) as an internal spiritual conjunction of heart, mind, and culture. Friendship depends on a meeting of souls, accomplished through shared suffering or joy—or by feasting and drinking. Soul is said to be one of the metaphysical mechanisms that unite Russians into a people (*narod*). Stemming from the ancient Slavic for "kin" and "birth," and meaning "citizens of a nation," "ethnic group," or "crowd," *narod* refers to the composite identity of the people through history and is often invoked by politicians. People speak in terms of belonging by "blood"; a person is thought of as having Russian blood, Jewish blood, Armenian blood, or some other ethnic blood, and culture is supposedly transmitted through the blood.

Cultural symbols abound in folk art. Animal, bird, plant, solar, and goddess motifs, and a palette of reds and golden yellows with traces of black and green prevail in painted wooden objects and embroidered textiles. Soviet state studios kept many folk media alive, and the postsocialist period has seen independent craftspersons return to traditional mythological motifs. Folk art objects are popular and are found in homes everywhere.

The end of Soviet power meant an explosive opening of Russia to the world, with all of the changes for better and worse that come with globalization. Popular culture in Russia has become characterized by the vibrant and fertile mixing of local and international styles in music, art, literature, and film. Obsessions with mafia criminals, the new wealthy (so-called New Russians), *biznismeny*, and modern technology fill the media. Yet alongside this, indigenous artistic genres, shared symbols and values, and social practices hold their own and continue to shape the world of meaning and identity.

*See also:* FEMINISM; FOLKLORE; MARRIAGE AND FAMILY LIFE; NATIONALISM IN THE ARTS; NATIONALITIES POLICY, SOVIET; NATIONALITIES POLICY, TSARIST; NATION AND NATIONALITY; ORTHODOXY; PEASANTRY; SLAVOPHILES

## BIBLIOGRAPHY

Balzer, Marjorie Mandelstam. (1992). *Russian Traditional Culture: Religion, Gender, and Customary Law.* Armonk, NY: M. E. Sharpe.

Billington, James H. (1970). *The Icon and the Axe: An Interpretive History of Russian Culture.* New York: Vintage Books.

Boutenko, Irene A., and Razlogov, Kirill E., eds. (1997). *Recent Social Trends in Russia, 1960–1995.* Montreal: McGill–Queen's University Press.

Boym, Svetlana. (1994). *Common Places: Mythologies of Everyday Life in Russia.* Cambridge, MA: Harvard University Press.

Dunn, Stephen P., and Dunn, Ethel. (1988). *The Peasants of Central Russia.* Prospect Heights, IL: Waveland Press.

Hilton, Alison. (1995). *Russian Folk Art.* Bloomington: Indiana University Press.

Hubbs, Joanna. (1988). *Mother Russia: The Feminine Myth in Russian Culture.* Bloomington: Indiana University Press.

Ivanits, Linda. (1989). *Russian Folk Belief.* Armonk, NY: M. E. Sharpe.

Kingston-Mann, Esther, and Mixter, Timothy, eds. (1991). *Peasant Economy, Culture and Politics of European Russia, 1800–1921.* Princeton, NJ: Princeton University Press.

Laitin, David D. (1998). *Identity in Formation: The Russian-Speaking Populations in the Near Abroad.* Ithaca, NY: Cornell University Press.

Ledeneva, Alena V. (1998). *Russia's Economy of Favours: Blat, Networking, and Informal Exchange.* Cambridge, UK: Cambridge University Press.

Millar, James R., and Wolchik, Sharon L., eds. (1994). *The Social Legacy of Communism.* Washington, DC: Woodrow Wilson Center Press.

Pesmen, Dale. (2000). *Russia and Soul: An Exploration.* Ithaca, NY: Cornell University Press.

Pilkington, Hilary. (1998). *Migration, Displacement, and Identity in Post-Soviet Russia.* London: Routledge.

Ries, Nancy. (1997). *Russian Talk: Culture and Conversation During Perestroika.* Ithaca, NY: Cornell University Press.

Rzhevsky, Nicholas, ed. (1998). *The Cambridge Companion to Modern Russian Culture.* Cambridge, UK: Cambridge University Press.

Shalin, Dmitri N., ed. (1996). *Russian Culture at the Crossroads: Paradoxes of Post-Communist Consciousness.* Boulder, CO: Westview Press.

Sokolov, Yuri M. (1971). *Russian Folklore,* tr. Catherine Ruth Smith. Detroit: Folklore Associates.

NANCY RIES

# RUSSIAN SOVIET FEDERATED SOCIALIST REPUBLIC

The Russian Soviet Federated Socialist Republic, or RSFSR, formed on November 7, 1917, was one of the four original republics in the Union of Soviet Socialist Republics (USSR) when the latter was founded by treaty in December 1922. The RSFSR's establishment was later confirmed in the 1924 constitution. The other three were Ukraine, Belorussia (now called Belarus), and Transcaucasia (divided in 1940 into Azerbaijan, Armenia, and Georgia). Even after ten more republics were added, for a total of fifteen republics, the RSFSR remained the largest, with more than half the population and three-quarters of the USSR's territory (6,591,000 square miles). Moscow was the capital of both the RSFSR and the USSR as a whole. Situated in Eastern Europe and North Asia, the RSFSR was surrounded on the east, north, and northwest by the Pacific, Arctic, and Atlantic Oceans. It had frontiers in the northwest with Norway and Finland, in the west with Poland and the three Baltic republics (Latvia, Lithuania, and Estonia), and in the south with China and Outer Mongolia and the Soviet republics of Kazakhstan, Azerbaijan, Georgia, and Ukraine. In the new Soviet Union, which geographically replaced the old Russian Empire, the name Russia was not officially used. Lenin and other Bolshevik authorities intended to blend the national and the international to recognize each nationality by granting autonomy to national groups, while binding these groups together in a higher union and allowing new groups to enter regardless of historic frontiers. In 1922 the expectation of world revolution was still alive. Thus, the founding of the USSR—and the RSFSR within it—was a decisive step toward uniting the workers of all countries into one World Soviet Socialist Republic.

Although Lenin supported national self-determination as a force to undermine the tsarist empire, he adopted federalism rather late, as a response to Ukrainian and Georgian attempts to establish truly independent republics. The Red Army crushed these attempts in 1920–1921, but such use of brute force and the specter of Great Russian chauvinism troubled Lenin. He and others pressed for the federalization not only of the sovereign republics within the USSR, but also the federalization of the RSFSR. By 1960 the RSFSR consisted of fifteen "autonomous soviet socialist republics" (ASSRs), six territories (*krai*), forty-nine regions (*oblast*), six autonomous oblasts, and ten national districts (*okrug*). The federal structure undoubtedly gave some dignity, self-respect, and sense of equal cooperation to many of the numerous nationalities.

In the late 1980s, partly due to the perestroika, glasnost, and new thinking (*novomyshlenie*) policies of the incumbent general secretary, Mikhail Gorbachev, the Soviet republics—including and especially the RSFSR—began to challenge the legislative authority of the Soviet Communist Party and the "Moscow center." By October 1990, fourteen republics had passed declarations of either independence or sovereignty over USSR laws. The RSFSR's declaration of sovereignty and the rising popularity of Boris Yeltsin (elected chairman of the Supreme Soviet of the RSFSR in May 1990 and then president of the RSFSR in June 1991) were key factors in prompting Gorbachev to attempt to replace the original 1922 union treaty with a new document giving the republics more power. This in turn prompted hardliners in the Kremlin to stage a coup in August 1991. When it failed, Yeltsin's power and influence eclipsed Gorbachev's. Yeltsin convened with leaders of Belarus, Ukraine, and Kazakhstan in Alma Ata in December 1991 to declare the nullification of the 1922 union treaty and announce the official extinction of the Soviet Union. Gorbachev publicly confirmed the latter on December 25, 1991. The RSFSR is now called the Russian Federation.

*See also:* RUSSIAN FEDERATION; UNION OF SOVIET SOCIALIST REPUBLICS

**BIBLIOGRAPHY**

Fitzsimmons, Thomas, ed. (1974). *RSFSR, Russian Soviet Federated Socialist Republic.* Westport, CT: Greenwood Publishing Group.

Gilbert, Martin. (1993). *Atlas of Russian History,* 2nd ed. New York: Oxford University Press.

Hosking, Geoffrey. (1993). *The First Socialist Society: A History of the Soviet Union from Within,* 2nd ed. Cambridge, MA: Harvard University Press.

Sakwa, Richard. (2002). *Russian Politics and Society,* 3rd ed. New York: Routledge.

JOHANNA GRANVILLE

# RUSSIAN STATE LIBRARY

The Russian State Library is the largest library in Russia; the second largest library in the world after the Library of Congress, with holdings of more than forty-two million volumes. It is also a major scientific research center for library studies, bibliography, and book studies.

Founded in the center of Moscow in 1862 as the Moscow Public Museum and Rumyantsev Museum, the Russian State Library had its origins in the library of Count Nikolai Rumyantsev (1754–1826), whose outstanding collection of books, manuscripts, and cartographic materials, including 710 manuscripts and 28,500 books, was donated to the Russian state to form the Rumyantsev Museum in St. Petersburg in 1831. The library was administered by the Imperial Public Library from 1845 to 1861, when it was transferred to Moscow. The new library grew rapidly by means of its status as a legal depository of all publications issued in the Russian empire, a privilege granted until 1862 to only three libraries: the Imperial Public Library, the Library of the Russian Academy of Sciences, and the Helsinki University Library. It also benefited from collections donated by some of Russian's most prominent public figures, scholars, scientists, and writers, and by their families.

In the prerevolutionary period, the library received more than three hundred private book collections, including those of statesman Avraam Norov; bibliographer and bibliophile Sergei Poltoratsky; philosopher Pyotr Chaadayev; writer Prince Vladimir Odoyevsky, who served as deputy director of the Imperial Public Library and director of the Rumyantsev Museum from 1846 until it moved to Moscow; and Empress Alexandra Fyodorovna, wife of Tsar Nicholas II. The library also acquired book and manuscript collections of writers Gavriil Derzhavin, Vasily Zhukovsky, Alexander Pushkin, Alexander Veltman, Fyodor Tyutchev, Nikolai Gogol, Mikhail Lermontov, Afanasy Fet, Alexander Herzen, Nikolai Nekrasov, Alexander Ostrovsky, Ivan Turgenev, Leo Tolstoy, Anton Chekhov, Vasily Rozanov, Valery Bryusov, Alexander Blok, Mikhail Bulgakov, Kornei Chukovsky, Isaac Babel, and Sergei Yesenin; literary scholars Alexander Pypin, Izmail Sreznevsky, Alexei Sobolevsky, Boris Tomashevsky, Pavel Sakulin, and Nikolai Gudzy; historians Vasily Klyuchevsky, Nikolai Karamzin, Mikhail Pogodin, and Sergei Soloviev; and librarians and bibliographers Vasily Sobolshchikov, Vladimir Mezhov, and Nikolai Lisovsky, among others. Within fifty years of its founding, it had become one of the preeminent cultural and educational institutions of Russia, combing the roles of public library, treasury of manuscripts and decorative art, and archeological and ethnographic museum.

With the nationalization of libraries and cultural institutions after the October 1917 Revolution and the move of the capital from St. Petersburg to Moscow in 1918, it became the main library of the country. Its name, which had changed in 1869 to Moscow Public and Rumyantsev Museum and in 1913 to Imperial Moscow and Rumyantsev Museum, changed again in 1917 to State Rumyantsev Museum. In 1921 the library was reorganized to become separate from the museum: It was assigned the function of a state repository, and granted the status of national library. In 1924 its name was changed to V. I. Lenin All-Russian Public Library, in 1925 to V. I. Lenin State Library of the USSR, in accordance with its new status as the national library of the USSR, and in 1992, with the dissolution of the USSR, to Russian State Library.

The Manuscript Division holds works dating from the earliest years of Slavonic script. These include the Arkhangelsk Gospel of 1092, the Mariinskoe Gospel of the eleventh century, and the Khitrovo Gospel of the late fourteenth to early fifteenth century. It possesses a valuable collection of West European manuscripts, dating as early as the twelfth century, as well as Greek, Arabic, Persian, Turkish, Indian, Chinese, and Japanese manuscripts. The library has holdings estimated at 80 percent of all known books printed in Cyrillic script from the fifteenth to the eighteenth century, including examples of early Russian printing associated with printer Ivan Fyodorov and typographer Pyotr Mstislavets, and a vast collection of eighteenth-century books printed in the civil script developed for secular works. Highlights include first and lifetime editions of Renaissance thinkers and scientists, including Nicholas Copernicus, Galileo, Giordano Bruno, René Descartes, Johannes Kepler, and Sir Thomas More. The library prides itself on its rare editions of outstanding Russian and foreign representatives of culture and science, including Dmitry Mendeleyev, Nikolai Lobachevsky, Ivan Pavlov, Konstantin Tsiolkovsky, Isaac Newton, Charles Darwin, Louis Pasteur, Albert Einstein, William Shakespeare, Miguel de Cervantes Saavedra, Voltaire, Johann Wolfgang von Goethe, George Gordon Byron, Heinrich Heine, Honoré de Balzac, Victor Hugo, Charles Dickens, Émile Zola, and Bernard Shaw.

The library was originally housed in the former residence of retired military officer Pyotr Pashkov, in a building known as Pashkov House, built by architect Vasily Bazhenov from 1784 to 1786 in the Russian classical style. The building had a reading room for twenty people and was expanded over many decades to accommodate readers and collections. In 1958 construction was completed on a new library building adjacent to the original building, with reading rooms for more than 2,000 readers. In addition, a branch opened in 1975 in Khimki on the outskirts of Moscow to house newspapers and dissertations. While focused on collection, preservation, and service relating to Russia's cultural heritage, the library's mission reflects its status as one of the world's finest repositories of the creative and intellectual output of humankind.

*See also:* NATIONAL LIBRARY OF RUSSIA

**BIBLIOGRAPHY**

Davis, Robert H., Jr., and Kasinec, Edward. (2001). "Russian State Library, Moscow." In *International Dictionary of Library Histories*, vol. 2, ed. David H. Stam. Chicago: Fitzroy Dearborn.

*The State Lenin Library of the USSR, 1862–1987*. (1987). Moscow: State Library of the USSR.

JANICE T. PILCH

## RUSSIA'S DEMOCRATIC CHOICE

Russia's Democratic Choice (Demokratichesky Vybor Rossii, or DVR) was a party with a liberal-democratic orientation, in favor of deeper market restructuring combined with minimal government involvement and feasible social programs. It was formed in the spring of 1994 out of the Duma fraction of the reformist pro-government bloc that was known as "Russia's Choice." The voters' list of the latter, led by Vice-Premier Yegor Gaidar, defender of rights Sergei Kovalev, and Minister of Social Security Ella Pamfilova, received 8.3 million votes (15.5%, second place), and forty Duma seats. Moreover, twenty-four candidates were elected in single-mandate districts, allowing them to form the largest fraction, amounting to seventy-six delegates. The political ambitions of numerous "Russia's Choice" leaders, disagreement over the Chechnya war, and the party's and fraction's loss of status and power led to the loss of many members, and at the end of the term only fifty-two delegates remained.

Russia's Democratic Choice entered the 1995 elections with an array of smaller, democratically oriented parties, in the bloc "Russia's Democratic Choice-United Democrats." Of the first three names on the list, Gaidar and Kovalev remained, but the actress Lidia Fedoseyeva Shushkina replaced Ella Pamfilova, who had established her own nominal bloc. The 1993 campaign slogan "Freedom, property, lawfulness" was exchanged for "Peace, welfare, justice." However, without administrative resources, and with the splintering of the democratic electorate among several electoral associations, the bloc collapsed, winning only 2.7 million votes (3.9%). Nine delegates from single-mandate districts constituted an unregistered delegate group, working with Yabloko. The DVR governmental positions were temporarily weakened, but with the arrival of Anatoly Chubais, first as leader of Boris Yeltsin's election campaign in 1996, then in the presidential administration and government, they were strengthened again. The Institute of Transitional Economy, founded by Yegor Gaidar after his exit from government in 1992 and closely aligned with the government's economic branch, played an integral role in DVR policy formation and training. In the 1999 elections, the party enjoyed success as part of the bloc "Union of Right Forces," (SPS), which Gaidar co-chaired. In May 2001, on the threshold of new elections, the SPS became a party with its own membership, at which point the DVR dissolved, along with other "forces of the right."

*See also:* CHUBAIS, ANATOLY BORISOVICH; GAIDAR, YEGOR TIMUROVICH; KOVALEV, SERGEI ADAMOVICH; UNION OF RIGHT FORCES; YABLOKO; YELTSIN, BORIS NIKOLEYEVICH

## BIBLIOGRAPHY

McFaul, Michael. (2001). *Russia's Unfinished Revolution: Political Change from Gorbachev to Putin.* Ithaca: Cornell University Press.

McFaul, Michael, and Markov, Sergei. (1993). *The Troubled Birth of Russian Democracy: Parties, Personalities, and Programs.* Stanford, CA: Hoover Institution Press.

McFaul, Michael and Petrov, Nikolai, eds. (1995). *Previewing Russia's 1995 Parliamentary Elections.* Washington, DC: Carnegie Endowment for International Peace.

McFaul, Michael; Petrov, Nikolai; and Ryabov, Andrei, eds. (1999). *Primer on Russia's 1999 Duma Elections.* Washington, DC: Carnegie Endowment for International Peace.

Reddaway, Peter, and Glinski, Dmitri. (2001). *The Tragedy of Russia's Reforms: Market Bolshevism against Democracy.* Washington, DC: U. S. Institute of Peace Press.

NIKOLAI PETROV

# RUSSIFICATION

The term *Russification* refers to policies designed to spread Russian culture and language among non-Russians. These programs date from the late eighteenth century, but gained importance from the 1860s. Recent historiography has discredited earlier accounts that posited a consistent plan by the tsarist government to assimilate non-Russians. Still, St. Petersburg certainly viewed Russian as the empire's predominant language, considering it natural for non-Russians to learn Russian as a means of inter-ethnic communication. While the USSR officially rejected Russification, in fact the Soviet government was vastly more successful in spreading the Russian language than its tsarist predecessors. In the post-Soviet era, nationalities such as the Tatars and Chechens often complain bitterly that the pressure of Russification has not diminished since 1992.

## TYPES OF RUSSIFICATION

An American historian, Edward C. Thaden, proposed a useful distinction between three types of Russification: unplanned, administrative, and cultural. By unplanned Russification, Thaden meant natural processes of cultural assimilation by which certain individuals or groups took on the Russian language, and often the Russian Orthodox religion, as well. Administrative Russification refers to official policies such as those requiring the use of Russian throughout all branches of the government, and is often difficult to distinguish from centralization. Cultural Russification, finally, is the effort to assimilate entire populations, replacing their original culture with Russian. Cultural Russification was uncommon in the imperial period, though rather more frequent under the Soviets. Both unplanned and administrative Russification, however, played an important role in Russian nationality policy.

## RUSSIFICATION UNDER THE TSARS

Unplanned Russification on an individual basis began early in the Muscovite period. As Muscovite power increased, in particular after the conquest of the Tatar capital of Kazan in 1552, the prestige of Russian culture grew and, with it, its attractiveness to non-Russians. Moscow encouraged its new subjects to adopt Russian Orthodoxy, but these efforts were neither particularly energetic nor consistent. Only in the mid-eighteenth century was a concerted program attempted, aimed at converting animists and Muslims in the Volga region. Under this program, many Tatars and nearly all Mordvins, Chuvash, and Votyaks converted.

Catherine the Great pressed forward with administrative Russification, particularly in the lands gained for Russia in the Polish partitions and by her wars against the Turks. Catherine did not, however, envision Russifying the population of this territory culturally. She aimed rather at rationalizing the administration of these newly acquired lands, tying them more closely to St. Petersburg. Even here her successes were rather modest.

Policies resembling cultural Russification appear for the first time during the reign of Tsar Nicholas I. Of key importance here is the concept of official nationality. Nicholas's Minister of Education, Sergei Uvarov, formulated this ideology, easily encapsulated in the phrase "orthodoxy, autocracy, and nationality." Uvarov aimed to create a modern Russian nation, united in its loyalty to the tsar, sharing the moral fundament of Russian Orthodoxy, and speaking the Russian language. Official nationalism would appear to be a blatant case of cultural Russification, aimed at the total assimilation of non-Russian cultures. Actually, Uvarov was primarily concerned with encouraging dynastic patriotism and morality: "Nationality" was, after all, the third and last element of his tripartite formula. Uvarov did hope that, over time, the tsar's German, Asian, and Baltic subjects would adopt Russian culture, but he did little on a practical level to affect such a change.

Two of the most problematic ethnic groups for Imperial Russia were the Poles and Jews. From 1815 to 1830, the Poles enjoyed a considerable degree of autonomy in the Kingdom of Poland. After the Polish insurrection of 1831, this autonomy was considerably reduced, but only after a second uprising, in 1863, did St. Petersburg adopt policies of cultural Russification. Though Polish was not entirely banned from education, imported Russian teachers set the tone. In any case, private education in Polish was forbidden. Despite all prohibitions, Polish culture continued to flourish during these decades, though Russian policies contributed to the high illiteracy rate among Poles.

For official Russia, Jews appeared to be both religiously and culturally alien. Various programs throughout the nineteenth century aimed to modernize the Jewish community, in other words

to make Jews more like educated Russians. These measures had little impact, partly because Jews widely regarded them as mere fronts for religious conversion. Only toward the end of the century did there arise a significant and rapidly growing group of Russian Jews. Indeed, the adoption of Russian culture by these Jews may be seen as one of Russification's few successes.

Few Russians considered Ukrainians and Belarusians to be separate national groups before the twentieth century. These two East Slavic groups, mainly Orthodox in religion, spoke languages that were generally seen as mere dialects of Russian. When Ukrainian nationalism gained strength from the 1860s, St. Petersburg responded with a prohibition on publishing in the Ukrainian language. Schools in Ukrainian and Belarusian areas taught in Russian, which the pupils could not always understand. Only after 1905 did Belarusians and Ukrainians gain the right to use their languages in publications and education.

During the nineteenth century, the Russian Empire acquired enormous lands in Central Asia. Administrative Russification was practiced here, and some schools for indigenous children were set up. Interest in the Russian language spread among the younger generation of educated Muslims, especially Tatars, toward the end of the century. On the whole, however, St. Petersburg lacked the funds and interest to target these groups for intensive cultural integration.

### RUSSIFICATION UNDER THE SOVIETS

Officially, the Bolsheviks, led by Vladimir I. Ulyanov (Lenin), explicitly repudiated all forms of national chauvinism, including Russification. In practice, the situation was more complicated. Lenin's insistence on a highly centralized party had already led to clashes with Jewish socialists (the Bund). The Bolsheviks supported national self-determination and condemned repressive policies toward non-Russians. Yet, as Marxists, they were primarily interested in creating a proletarian socialist culture. They were therefore quick to denounce bourgeois nationalism. After 1917, despite various programs to encourage the development of national (that is, non-Russian) cultures, party centralization meant that anyone wishing to reach the top of the Soviet hierarchy needed to be fluent in Russian and adopt many aspects of Russian-Soviet culture. One example of this is the Russian–style patronymics and surnames adopted by communist activists in Muslim republics of Central Asia.

Upon seizing power in late 1917, the Bolsheviks quickly issued a "Declaration to the Peoples of Russia," pledging an end to any national or religious discrimination, guaranteeing free cultural development, and even endorsing national self-determination. The actions of the Bolsheviks in the ensuing civil war years, however, made clear that while cultural development could be accepted and even encouraged, political autonomy, much less secession, would not be tolerated. The civil war brought Ukraine, the Caucasus, and Belarus back under Moscow's control. The Soviet Constitution of 1924 set down an ostensibly federal, but in fact highly centralized, state structure. The USSR, as its name implied, consisted of individual Soviet Socialist Republics (Russian, Ukrainian, Belarusian; later Kazakh, Georgian, and so on), all of which officially had the right to secede from the Union. This possibility remained a dead letter until the late 1980s when the Baltic republics, seized by Stalin in the early 1940s, dared to make real use of this hitherto only theoretical right.

During the Soviet period administrative Russification was nearly total; all official documents from stamps to passports to postal forms were printed in Russian or, in union republics, in Russian and the republic language, say, Latvian. Communications within the enormous bureaucracy took place in Russian, and even a Central Asian factory director or Armenian professor needed to know Russian fluently. The material and prestige value of Russian within the USSR meant that a considerable amount of unplanned Russification or simple cultural assimilation took place. Mixed marriages between Russians and members of other nationalities, for instance, most often produced Russian-speaking offspring. Many smaller nationalities, in particular within the Russian Republic (RSFSR), witnessed considerable rates of Russification, prompting national leaders in the post-Soviet period, for example in Tatarstan, to complain of the widespread de-nationalization of their people during Soviet rule.

Culturally, matters were more complicated. While non-Russian republics did have their own schools using local languages, everyone from Tallinn to Vladivostok studied Russian in school from an early age. Radio and television programs appeared in various languages but, to give only one example, even Estonian television broadcast the Russian-language Moscow news program "Vremia" every evening. Publications appeared in dozens and even hundreds of so-called Soviet languages, and

students could study even at the university level in their union republic's language. However, all dissertations at the *kandidat* (roughly, Ph.D.) or *doktor* level were written in Russian, even by students in Vilnius, Baku, or Kiev. In the Belarusian and Ukrainian republics, even obtaining an elementary education in the local language was not always simple, and parents who insisted too much ran the risk of being branded as nationalist or anti-Soviet.

The legacy of Soviet Russification in the twenty-first century remains strong but highly differentiated. When Central Asian or Belarusian leaders speak at international fora, it is nearly always in Russian. Arguably, Russian will remain the *lingua franca* in that region for some time. In the Baltic region, however, one hears little Russian (except by native speakers) and the bilingual street signs of the Soviet era have entirely vanished. For the future, Russification will remain a problem for the Russian Federation, where 20 percent of the total population is not ethnically Russian. Some of these national groups, in particular Tatars and Chechens, seem particularly resistant to further measures of Russification. For its part, the Russian Federation has officially disavowed any desire to Russify its citizens; the future will tell just how seriously one should take this official stance.

*See also:* NATIONALISM IN THE SOVIET UNION; NATIONALISM IN THE TSARIST EMPIRE; NATIONALITIES POLICIES, SOVIET; NATIONALITIES POLICIES, TSARIST; SLAVOPHILES

## BIBLIOGRAPHY

Carrère d'Encausse, Hélène. (1979). *Decline of an Empire: The Soviet Socialist Republics in Revolt*, tr. Martin Sokolinsky and Henry A. La Farge. New York: Newsweek Books.

Haltzel, Michael H., et al. (1981). *Russification in the Baltic Provinces and Finland, 1855–1914*. Princeton, NJ: Princeton University Press.

Hosking, Geoffrey. (1997). *Russia: People and Empire*. Cambridge, MA: Harvard University Press.

Kappeler, Andreas. (2001). *The Russian Empire: A Multiethnic History*, tr. Alfred Clayton. New York: Pearson Education.

Martin, Terry. (2001). *The Affirmative Action Empire: Nations and Nationalism in the Soviet Union, 1923–1939*. Ithaca, NY: Cornell University Press.

Pipes, Richard. (1964). *The Formation of the Soviet Union: Communism and Nationalism 1917–1923*. Cambridge, MA: Harvard University Press.

Riasanovsky, Nicholas. (1967). *Nicholas I and Official Nationality in Russia, 1825–1855.* Berkeley: University of California Press.

Slezkine, Yuri. (1994). *Arctic Mirrors: Russia and the Small Peoples of the North.* Ithaca, NY: Cornell University Press.

Weeks, Theodore R. (1996). *Nation and State in Late Imperial Russia: Nationalism and Russification on the Western Frontier, 1863–1914.* DeKalb, IL: Northern Illinois University Press.

THEODORE R. WEEKS

# RUSSO-JAPANESE WAR

After brokering the end of the Sino-Japanese War (1894–1895) with the Treaty of Shimonoseki, Russia placed itself on a collision course with Japan over the issue of spheres of influence in Manchuria. Relations between the two countries further deteriorated in 1898, when Russia occupied the Chinese fortress of Port Arthur (now Lu-shun), and again in 1903, when Russian economic interest focused on Korea. Japan's response to Russia's aggressive eastern policy became apparent on February 8, 1904 when Admiral Heihachiro Togo launched a surprise attack on Port Arthur. Having won control of the sea, the Japanese began landing land troops at Chemulpo (now Inchon), as far north as possible on the Korean Peninsula to avoid the bad roads. Nonetheless, the weather did not cooperate, and it was six weeks before General Tamemoto Kuroki's First Army was ready to march around the northern tip of the Bay of Korea and invade the Liao Tung Peninsula.

Russia, meanwhile, had entered the war unprepared for conflict in Asia. Its military planners had given priority to the empire's European frontiers and had not dedicated sufficient resources to the defense of its Asian interests. While the Japanese considered mainland northeastern Asia vital to their national security, the Russians viewed the region merely as a colonial interest for potential economic development and wealth. No one understood Russia's predicament as clearly as War Minister Alexei N. Kuropatkin, who, upon the outbreak of war, resigned his ministerial portfolio, assumed command of the Russian army, and proceeded to Manchuria, where he arrived in March 1904. Since his forces were being transferred from one end of the empire to the other on the single-track and still incomplete Trans-Siberian Railroad, Kuropatkin set up defenses that he hoped would give Russia at least three months to build up its military presence in the Far East.

Kuropatkin began concentrating troops between Harbin and Liao Yang, but the Japanese thwarted his plan by beginning operations in the middle of March. The Japanese movements unnerved the commander of Port Arthur, General A. M. Stoessel, who immediately appealed to Nicholas II's personally appointed viceroy for the Far East, Admiral E. I. Alexiev, for help. Alexiev ordered Kuropatkin to attack the Japanese, but the commander-in-chief, holding that he was answerable only to the tsar, refused. Thinking that Port Arthur had supplies enough to withstand a long siege, Kuropatkin had no intention of deviating from his plan. Before this dispute could be resolved, the Japanese forced Kuropatkin's hand by defeating the Russians in the hotly contested Battle of Nanshan in April.

With Port Arthur's supply lines cut after Nanshan, Kuropatkin no longer had the luxury of waiting until an overwhelming force was assembled. The major battles of the war followed: Va Fan Gou (May), Liao Yang (August), and the river Sha Ho (October), effectively concluding with Mukden in February 1905. The Russians were soundly defeated in each of these battles by an enemy that first out-thought and then outmaneuvered them. Having concentrated three armies under the overall command of Marshal Iwao Oyama, the Japanese were able to fight the war on their own terms. Ironically, by the Battle of Mukden, Kuropatkin had finally achieved numerical superiority just as the Japanese reached the end of their material and human resources, but he, his staff, and the Russian intelligence services never became aware of this advantage and were intimidated by the Japanese army's maneuverability. Further aggravating the Russian predicament was the inexplicable capitulation of Port Arthur on January 2, 1905. The situation was best described by the numerous military observers representing most of the world's nations, who noted how unmotivated Russia's army seemed in comparison to the patriotic Japanese soldiers with their strong sense of national mission.

A final event that captured the attention of the world was the saga of Russia's Baltic Fleet. By the autumn of 1904, Russia's Pacific Fleet lay in ruins, and to regain control of the sea, Nicholas II ordered the Baltic fleet to the Far East. Under the command of Admiral Z. P. Rozhestvensky, the Baltic Fleet sortied on October 15, 1904. Its round-the-world

**Allegory on Russo-Japanese peace treaty, concluded in Portsmouth, NH.** © THE ART ARCHIVE/DOMENICA DEL CORRIERE/DAGLI ORTI (A)

voyage attracted the interest of the international press, which reported its attack on British fishing vessels on the Dogger Bank (the Russians mistakenly imagined that they were Japanese warships), its search to find places to refuel and refit ships that had not been designed for such an arduous journey; and its rendezvous with reinforcements at Madagascar. By the time the fleet arrived in Asia, Togo was lying in wait and had little difficulty defeating it in the Battle of the Tsushima Straits on May 27, 1905, which dashed Russia's last hopes.

The Russo-Japanese War was the first global conflict of the modern era and the first war in which an emerging Asian nation defeated a European great power. The Japanese victory inflamed Asian nationalism and contributed to the struggle against colonialism throughout the region. The military debacle exposed the weakness of the tsarist regime and is usually considered the prime cause of the Revolution of 1905. After the complete defeat of Russia's land and naval forces, the tsar sued for peace. U.S. president Theodore Roosevelt brokered the Treaty of Portsmouth (August 23, 1905), but the Japanese believed that they had lost the peace and did not trust Western diplomacy again until after World War II. Finally, from the technical standpoint, the Russo-Japanese War was a precursor to World War I. Both sides mobilized mass armies and used trenches, machine guns, and rapid-fire artillery—weapons that help define the early twentieth century battlefield.

*See also:* BALTIC FLEET; JAPAN, RELATIONS WITH; KOREA, RELATIONS WITH; KUROPATKIN, ALEXEI NIKOLAYEVICH; MILITARY, IMPERIAL ERA; PORT ARTHUR, SEIGE OF; PORTSMOUTH, TREATY OF; REVOLUTION OF 1905; TSUSHIMA, BATTLE OF

**BIBLIOGRAPHY**
Committee of Imperial Defence, Historical Section. (1910–1920). *Official History, Naval and Military, of the Russo Japanese War.* 3 vols. London: Committee of Imperial Defence.

Connaughton, Richard M. (1988). *The War of the Rising Sun and Tumbling Bear: A Military History of the Russo-Japanese War, 1904–05.* London: Routledge.

Corbett, Julian S. (1994). *Maritime Operations in the Russo-Japanese War, 1904–05.* 2 vols. Annapolis, MD: Naval Institute Press.

German General Staff, Historical Section (1909). *The Russo-Japanese War,* tr. Karl von Donat. 9 vols. London: H. Rees.

Kinai, M., ed. (1907). *The Russo-Japanese War: Official Reports.* 2 vols. Tokyo: Shimashido.

United States, War Department, General Staff. (1907). *Reports of Military Observers Attached to the Armies in Manchuria during the Russo-Japanese War.* 5 parts. Washington, DC, Government Printing Office.

Walder, David. (1973). *The Short Victorious War: The Russo-Japanese Conflict, 1904–1905.* New York: Harper & Row.

Westwood, J. N. (1986). *Russia against Japan, 1904–05: A New Look at the Russo-Japanese War.* Albany: State University of New York Press.

JOHN W. STEINBERG

# RUSSO-PERSIAN WARS

Disputes over territories along the southwestern coast of the Caspian Sea and in the eastern Transcaucasus led to war between Russia and Persia from 1804 to 1813 and again from 1826 to 1828. The military conflict between the two empires was nothing new, but it entered a more decisive stage with the dawning of the nineteenth century. At the root of the first Russo-Persian War was the desire of Shah Fath Ali to secure his northwestern territories in the name of the Qajar dynasty. At the time, Persia's claims to Karabakh, Shirvan, Talesh, and Shakki seemed precarious in the wake of Russia's annexation in 1801 of the former kingdom of Georgia, also claimed by Persia. Meanwhile, Russia consolidated this acquisition and resumed its military penetration of border territories constituting parts of modern Azerbaijan and Armenia, with the objective of extending its imperial frontiers to the Aras and Kura rivers.

War broke out when Prince Paul Tsitsianov marched to Echmiadzin at the head of a column of Russian, Georgian, and Armenian troops. The outnumbered Russian army was unable to overcome the town's stubborn defense and several weeks later also unsuccessfully besieged Yerevan. Throughout the war, the Russians generally had the strategic initiative but lacked the strength to crush the Persian resistance. Able to commit only about ten thousand troops, a fraction of their total force in the Caucasus, the Russian commanders relied on superior tactics and weapons to overcome a numerical disadvantage of as much as five to one. Overlapping wars with Napoleonic France, Turkey (1806–1812), and Sweden (1808–1809), as well as sporadic tribal uprisings in the Caucasus, distracted the tsar's attention. Yet state-supported, centralized military organization provided Russian columns with considerable combat power. In contrast, the Persian forces were largely irregular cavalry raised and organized on a tribal basis. Abbas Mirza, heir to the throne, sought French and British instructors to modernize his army, and resorted to a guerrilla strategy that delayed the Persian defeat.

In 1810, the Persians proclaimed a holy war, but this had little effect on the eventual outcome. The Russian victories at Aslandaz in 1812 and Lankarin in 1813 sealed the verdict in Russia's favor. Under the Treaty of Golestan, Russia obtained most of the disputed territories, including Dagestan and northern Azerbaijan, and reduced the local khans to the status of vassals.

Another war between Russia and Persia broke out in 1826 following the death of Alexander I and the subsequent Decembrist revolt. Sensing opportunity, the Persians invaded in July at the instigation of Abbas Mirza, and even won some early victories against the outnumbered forces of General Alexei Yermolov, whose appeals to St. Petersburg for reinforcements went unfulfilled. With only twelve regular battalions, the Russians effectively delayed the Persian advance. A contingent of about eighteen hundred, for instance, held the strategic fortress at Shusha against a greatly superior force. On September 12, a Persian army under the personal command of Abbas Mirza was defeated at Yelizabetpol. In the spring of 1827, the Russian command passed to General Ivan Paskevich. He captured Yerevan at the end of September and crossed the Aras River to seize Tabriz. In November, Abbas Mirza reluctantly submitted. Under the Treaty of Torkamanchay (February 1828), Persia ceded Yerevan and all the territory up to the Aras River and paid a twenty million ruble indemnity.

*See also:* CAUCASUS; GEORGIA AND GEORGIANS; IRAN, RELATIONS WITH; MILITARY, IMPERIAL ERA

**BIBLIOGRAPHY**

Atkin, Muriel. (1980). *Russia and Iran, 1780–1828.* Minneapolis: University of Minnesota Press.

Curtiss, John S. (1965). *The Russian Army under Nicholas I, 1825–1855.* Durham, NC: Duke University Press.

Kazemzadeh, Firuz. (1974). "Russian Penetration of the Caucasus." In *Russian Imperialism: From Ivan the Great to the Revolution,* ed. Taras Hunczak. New Brunswick, NJ: Rutgers University Press.

ROBERT F. BAUMANN

## RUSSO-TURKISH WARS

Between Peter the Great's outright accession in 1689 and the end of Romanov dynastic rule in 1917, Russia fought eight wars (1695–1696, 1711, 1735–1739, 1768–1774, 1787–1792, 1806–1812, 1828–1829, and 1877–1878) either singly or with allies against the Ottomans. In addition, Turkey joined anti-Russian coalitions during the Crimean War (1854–1856) and World War I (1914–1918). Although these conflicts often bore religious overtones, the fighting was primarily about power and possessions. Early on, Russian incursions into Poland, the Baltics, the Crimea, and the southern steppe threatened useful Ottoman allies. By the second half of the eighteenth century, however, the issue between St. Petersburg and Constantinople had become one of titanic struggle for hegemony over the northern Black Sea and its northern and northwestern littoral. In the nineteenth century, the issue came to involve Russian aspirations for influence in the Balkans and the Middle East, access to the Mediterranean through the Turkish Straits, and hegemony over the Black Sea's Caucasian and Transcaucasian littoral. As the rivalry became increasingly one-sided in Russia's favor, St. Petersburg generally advocated maintenance of an enfeebled Turkey that would resist outside interference and influences while supporting Russia's interests.

Russia scored its most important successes in the Black Sea basin during Catherine II's First (1769–1774) and Second (1787–1792) Turkish Wars. In particular, three of her commanders, Peter Alexandrovich Rumyantsev, Alexander Vasilevich Suvorov, and Grigory Alexandrovich Potemkin, introduced into the fight a winning combination of resolve, assets, tactical mastery, logistics, colonists, and military-administrative support. Subsequently, with Imperial Russian attention and assets diverted elsewhere, and with the increasing interference of the European powers on Turkey's behalf, St. Petersburg proved unable to repeat Catherine's successes. Outside interference was no more evident than in the aftermath of the Russo-Turkish War of 1877–1878, when considerable Russian gains in the Balkans were virtually erased in June–July 1878 by the Congress of Berlin.

*See also:* MILITARY, IMPERIAL ERA; TURKEY, RELATIONS WITH

**BIBLIOGRAPHY**

Aksan, Virginia H. (2002). "Ottoman Military Matters." *Journal of Early Modern History* 6 (1):52–62.

Kagan, Frederick W., and Higham, Robin, eds. (2002). *The Military History of Tsarist Russia.* New York: Palgrave.

Menning, Bruce W. (1984). "Russian Military Innovation in the Second Half of the Eighteenth Century." *War & Society* 2 (1):23–41.

BRUCE W. MENNING

## RUTSKOI, ALEXANDER VLADIMIROVICH

(b. 1947), vice president of the Russian Federation, governor of Kursk Oblast, general-major of aviation, Hero of the Soviet Union.

Alexander Rutskoi was born on September 16, 1947 in Kmelnitsky, Ukraine, to a professional military family. He graduated from a pilot training school in 1966 and joined the Soviet Air Forces. In the 1980s he served in Afghanistan as deputy commander, commander of the air regiment, and deputy commander of aviation for the Fortieth Army. He was shot down twice; the second time, his Su-25 crashed in Pakistan, where he was interned and then repatriated. In late 1988 he received the award Hero of the Soviet Union. In 1988 and 1989 he attended the Voroshilov Military Academy of the General Staff. In 1990 he was elected to the Supreme Soviet of the RSFSR (Russian Federation) and to the Central Committee of the newly organized Communist Party of the RSFSR. He displayed a strong Russian nationalist bias and in 1991 helped to found Communists for Democracy and supported Boris Yeltsin.

Yeltsin named Rutskoi as his vice presidential running mate in his successful campaign for the presidency of Russia. During the August Coup (against Gorbachev), Rutskoi organized the defense of the Russian White House. Yeltsin promoted him to the rank of general-major and entrusted him with a number of delicate issues, such as border issue negotiations with Ukraine and Kazakhstan and Chechen independence. When Yeltsin embarked upon radical economic reforms, Rutskoi publicly expressed his doubts concerning the direction of

Vice President Alexander Rutskoi tries to calm the crowd as his 1993 parliamentary rebellion begins to collapse. © MALCOLM LINTON/LIAISON. GETTY IMAGES

Yeltsin's policy. Yeltsin moved to effectively isolate his vice president. As a consequence of these developments, Rutskoi drifted toward the parliamentary opposition led by parliament speaker Ruslan Khasbulatov. This struggle between president and parliament came to a violent head in September and October 1993. Yeltsin crushed the revolt with armed forces and arrested its leadership. Rutskoi was arrested and removed from the office of vice president, and the position of vice president was abolished.

In 1994 the Russian parliament granted amnesty to Rutskoi and other rebels of 1993. Rutskoi went on to organize a Russian nationalist party, Power (Derzhava) which competed in the 1995 parliamentary elections and joined the Red-Brown opposition to Yeltsin in the summer 1996 presidential elections. A leading figure of the anti-Yeltsin nationalist opposition, Rutskoi ran for and won the post of governor of Kursk Oblast in October 1996 and served in that office to 2000. He stood for reelection but was disqualified by the Central Elections Commission, which ordered his name stricken from the ballot for election campaign law violations and abuses as governor. Rumors interpreted the government's actions as a direct response to Rutskoi's criticism of the president during the Kursk disaster.

See also: AFGHANISTAN, RELATIONS WITH; AUGUST 1991 PUTSCH; KURSK SUBMARINE DISASTER; OCTOBER 1993 EVENTS; YELTSIN, BORIS NIKOLAYEVICH

**BIBLIOGRAPHY**

Aron, Leon. (2000). *Yeltsin: A Revolutionary Life*. New York: Thomas Dunne Books.

Chugaev, Sergei. "Khasbulatov & Co." *Bulletin of the Atomic Scientists* (January/February 1993).

JACOB W. KIPP

## RYBKIN, IVAN PETROVICH

(b. 1946), chair of the State Duma in 1994 and 1995, secretary of the Security Council from 1996 to 1998, and leader of the Socialist Party of Russia.

Ivan Rybkin was born on October 20, 1946, in the Voronezh countryside. He graduated from the Volgograd Agricultural Institute in 1968, completed graduate school there, and worked as a teacher until 1983. With the beginning of pere-

stroika, he launched an ambitious political career and became the second secretary of the Volgograd Oblast committee of the Communist Party of the Soviet Union. In 1990, he was selected as a people's delegate to the RSFSR, where he headed the Communists of Russia fraction. In 1993 and 1994 he was vice-chair of the Executive Committee of the Communist Party of the Russian Federation (KPRF), but in April 1994 he left the KPRF. As of the fall of 1993, he was a member of the Agrarian Party, on whose list he was elected to the Duma. In this capacity he proved a pragmatic politician. He lost the support of the leftists (in 1995 he was excluded from the Agrarian Party), but gained the support of the Kremlin.

In the summer of 1995, the Kremlin brought forth an initiative to create two centrist blocs for the elections: a right-centrist bloc headed by Premier Viktor Stepanovich Chernomyrdin, and a left-centrist bloc. This latter subsequently came to be called the "Ivan Rybkin bloc," which gained 1.1 percent of the electoral votes. The bloc was dissolved, but Rybkin was nonetheless elected to the Duma by single-mandate district in his homeland, Voronezh Oblast. Before the second round of presidential elections, Boris Yeltsin created the Political Advisory Council to the President of the Russian Federation, which included representatives of parties and public associations that had not made it into the Duma. Rybkin, who had recently registered the Socialist Party, was appointed chair of the council. A few months later, Rybkin replaced Alexander Lebed as secretary of the Security Council, in which capacity he worked until 1998, focusing mainly on Chechnya. His deputy was for some time Boris Berezovsky, with whom Rybkin maintains close relations.

In 2001–2002, with the discussion and adoption of the law on political parties, which required the presence of branch offices in at least half the regions of the country, the processes of integration strengthened considerably. From mid-2001 onward, Rybkin participated in talks concerning the creation of a United Social-Democratic Party of Russia, along with Mikhail Gorbachev and other well-known politicians. The unification process was difficult, due not so much to divergence of views as to a clash of ambitions. In the fall of 2001, when the process seemed complete, Rybkin's Socialist Party even disbanded, in anticipation of joining forces with the new party, but the merger broke at the last minute. It was effected only in March 2002, and on a visibly more modest scale.

On the basis of the Socialist Party, Alexei Podberezkin's Spiritual Heritage movement, and dozens of small organizations with socialist tendencies, the Socialist United Party of Russia was finally created. Rybkin became its chair. The honeymoon period was short, however, and within a few weeks, Rybkin resigned as chair and the Socialist Party of Russia left the coalition. In April 2003, at a congress of the Socialist United Party of Russia, he was officially removed from the position of chair and excluded from the party. His alleged offenses included an open letter to Putin, which called for ending the Chechnya war and beginning negotiations with Aslan Maskhadov; collaboration with the SPS; and unsanctioned contacts with Berezovsky.

*See also:* CHECHNYA AND CHECHENS; PUTIN, VLADIMIR VLADIMIROVICH

**BIBLIOGRAPHY**

McFaul, Michael. (2001). *Russia's Unfinished Revolution: Political Change from Gorbachev to Putin.* Ithaca: Cornell University Press.

McFaul, Michael, and Markov, Sergei. (1993). *The Troubled Birth of Russian Democracy: Parties, Personalities, and Programs.* Stanford, CA: Hoover Institution Press.

McFaul, Michael; Petrov, Nikolai; and Ryabov, Andrei, eds. (1999). *Primer on Russia's 1999 Duma Elections.* Washington, DC: Carnegie Endowment for International Peace.

Reddaway, Peter, and Glinski, Dmitri. (2001). *The Tragedy of Russia's Reforms: Market Bolshevism against Democracy.* Washington, DC: U.S. Institute of Peace Press.

NIKOLAI PETROV

## RYKOV, ALEXEI IVANOVICH

(1881–1938), Russian revolutionary and Soviet politician, one of the leaders of the Right opposition.

Born in Saratov province, the son of a tradesman, Alexei Rykov joined the Social Democratic Party in 1898 and supported the Bolsheviks after their split with the Mensheviks. He played an active part in the 1905 revolution. In 1907, however, he began to work for reconciliation between the two wings of the party. In exile in Paris for two years, he returned to Russia in 1911 but was soon arrested and exiled to Siberia.

Returning to Moscow after the revolution of February 1917, Rykov became a member of the Moscow and Petrograd soviets and participated in the October revolution. He became commissar for internal affairs in the first Bolshevik government, but resigned because of his support for a coalition government. In April 1918, however, he accepted the post of chairperson of the Supreme Council of the National Economy, and in February 1921 he became deputy chairman of Sovnarkom. After Lenin's death in January 1924 he became chairman. He was also a member of the Politburo from 1922 until 1930.

Rykov was a leading supporter of the New Economic Policy, and allied with Stalin in his struggle with Leon Davidovich Trotsky, Grigory Yevseyevich Zinoviev, and Lev Borisovich Kamenev, which lasted from 1926 to 1928. When Stalin lashed out against the Right Opposition, of which Rykov was one of the leaders, he was defeated, discredited, and ultimately dismissed from his senior positions by 1930. Rykov was arrested in February 1937. With Nikolai Alexandrovich Bukharin and Genrikh Grigorevich Yagoda, Rykov was one of the leading defendants at the third show trial, and was executed in March 1938.

*See also:* BOLSHEVISM; FEBRUARY REVOLUTION; MENSHEVIKS; NEW ECONOMIC POLICY; OCTOBER REVOLUTION; POLITBURO; RIGHT OPPOSITION; SOCIAL DEMOCRATIC WORKERS PARTY; SOVNARKOM

DEREK WATSON

## RYLEYEV, KONDRATY FYODOROVICH

(1795–1826), a poet who played a leading role in organizing the mutiny of the military units in St. Petersburg that occurred on December 14, 1825 (the so-called Decembrist Uprising).

Born into the family of an army officer, Kondraty Fyodorovich Ryleyev also became an officer and served in units stationed in West Europe after the defeat of Napoleon's armies. He saw the general backwardness of Russian society sharply contrasted with the capitalist countries of Western Europe. Upon returning to St. Petersburg, Ryleyev became active in a variety of social and political circles. In 1823 he joined the secret Northern Society. Situated in St. Petersburg and headed by Nikita Muraviev and Sergei Trubetskoi, it consisted of moderate reformists who leaned toward establishment of a constitutional monarchy, modeled after the English version. By contrast, the Southern Society, created by Pavel Pestel in Tulchin, gathered together more radical members of the movement, and demanded complete eradication of the extant tsarist autocracy and the establishment of a democratic republic based upon on universal suffrage.

With the exception of his earliest works, Ryleyev's poems are romantic in style. Their themes reflect patriotic sentiments and concern with the course of Russian history. His verses ushered in ideas about the duty to sacrifice one's artistic calling in service to the downtrodden masses well before Nikolay Nekrasov preached them in his own poetry. Tragically, Ryleyev was not able fully to develop his poetic talents, and his celebrity is mainly due to the martyrdom he underwent in the cause of freedom. He was one of the five rebels who were executed, along with Pestel, Kakhovskoi, Muraviev-Apostol, and Bestuzhev-Riumin, for their roles in the Decembrist Uprising. His sarcastic wit has also become legend. Apparently, just as Ryleyev was about to be hanged, the rope broke and he fell to the ground. Bruised and battered, he got up, and said, "In Russia they do not know how to do anything properly, not even how to make a rope." An accident of this sort usually resulted in a pardon, so a messenger was sent to Tsar Nicholas to know his pleasure. The tsar asked, "What did he say?" "Sire, he said that in Russia they do not even know how to make a rope properly." "Well, let the contrary be proved," said Nicholas.

*See also:* DECEMBRIST MOVEMENT AND REBELLION

**BIBLIOGRAPHY**

Obolonskii, A. V., and Ostrom, Vincent. (2003). *The Drama of Russian Political History: System Against Individuality.* College Station: Texas A&M University Press.

JOHANNA GRANVILLE

# RYUTIN, MARTEMYAN

(1890–1937), leader of an anti–Stalin opposition group that emerged within the Russian Communist Party in the 1930s.

Martemyan Ryutin was born on February 26, 1890, the son of a Siberian peasant from the Irkutsk province. He joined the Bolshevik party in 1914. During the civil war, he fought against Alexander Vasilievich Kolchak's forces in Siberia, and in the early 1920s he held party posts in Irkutsk and Dagestan. In 1925, Ryutin became party secretary in the Krasnaya Presnia district of Moscow, and in 1927 he was elected a non-voting member of the party Central Committee. In the following year he incurred Stalin's wrath for his conciliatory attitude towards Bukharin and his followers.

Experience of the collectivization drive convinced Ryutin of the ruinous nature of Stalin's economic policies, and the criticisms he voiced led, at the end of 1930, to his expulsion from the party and a brief spell of imprisonment. In 1932, Ryutin and some associates circulated a manifesto, "To All Members of the Russian Communist Party," which condemned the Stalin regime and demanded Stalin's removal from power. Ryutin also composed a more detailed analysis of Stalin's dictatorship and economic policies in the essay "Stalin and the Crisis of the Proletarian Dictatorship" (first published in 1990). He was arrested, along with his group, in September 1932. Although Stalin wanted the death penalty, the Politburo, at the insistence of Sergei Mironovich Kirov, rejected the demand, and Ryutin was sentenced to ten years imprisonment. Ryutin, however, was re-arrested in 1936 on a trumped-up charge of terrorism, and was executed on January 10, 1937.

*See also:* KIROV, SERGEI MIRONOVICH; KOLCHAK, ALEXANDER VASILIEVICH; PURGES, THE GREAT; STALIN, JOSEF VISSARIONOVICH

**BIBLIOGRAPHY**

Conquest, Robert. (1990). *The Great Terror: A Reassessment.* New York: Oxford University Press.

Getty, J. Arch, and Naumov, Oleg V. (1999). *The Road to Terror : Stalin and the Self–Destruction of the Bolsheviks, 1932-1939: Annals of Communism.* New Haven, CT: Yale University Press.

Medvedev, Roy Aleksandrovich, and Shriver, George. (1989). *Let History Judge: The Origins and Consequences of Stalinism.* New York: Columbia University Press.

Tucker, Robert C. (1990). *Stalin in Power: The Revolution from Above, 1928-1941.* New York: Norton.

JAMES WHITE

# RYZHKOV, NIKOLAI IVANOVICH

(b. 1929), USSR prime minister under Gorbachev and a leading figure in economic reform.

Born in Donetsk Oblast, Nikolai Ryzhkov joined the Party in 1956 and graduated from the Ural Polytechnical Institute in Sverdlovsk in 1959. He spent his early career as an engineer at the Or-dzhonikidze Heavy Machine-Building Institute and was named director in 1970. Following his successes in the Urals, Ryzhkov became involved in all-union economic matters.

Ryzhkov served as a deputy in the USSR Council of the Union (1974–1979) and a deputy in the USSR Council of Nationalities (1974–1984). Ryzhkov was first deputy chair of the USSR Ministry of Heavy and Transport Machine-Building (1975–1979) and later first deputy chair of the USSR State Planning Commission (Gosplan) (1979–1982). He became a full member of the CPSU Central Committee in 1981, chairing the Diplomatic Department (1982–1985) and later the USSR Council of Ministers (September 1985–December 1990), making him the de facto Soviet prime minister. Ryzhkov was the chief administrator of the Soviet economy in the last half of the 1980s. He became a full Politburo member in April 1985 and chaired the Central Committee Commission that assisted victims of the 1988 Armenian earthquake.

As the economy stalled, protests grew, and the Kremlin debated the Five-Hundred-Day Plan, Ryzhkov suffered a heart attack on December 25, 1990. He subsequently resigned, and Gorbachev replaced him with Valentin Pavlov.

Ryzhkov unsuccessfully ran against Boris Yeltsin for the Russian presidency in June 1991. He then assumed a variety of corporate positions, including chairman of the board of Tveruniversal Bank (1994–1995), chairman of the board of Prokhorovskoye Pole, and head of the Moscow Intellectual Business Club. He won a seat in the Russian State Duma in 1995 and 1999 as head of "Power to the People," a bloc aligned with the Communist Party of the Russian Federation.

See also: CENTRAL COMMITTEE; GORBACHEV, MIKHAIL SERGEYEVICH; GOSPLAN; PERESTROIKA; POLITBURO; PRIME MINISTER

**BIBLIOGRAPHY**

Goldman, Marshall. (1992). *What went Wrong with Perestroika*. New York: Norton.

ANN E. ROBERTSON

Russian Empire in Europe and Asia, 1795. © Map Collection, Yale University Library.